THE
LEGAL
ENVIRONMENT
OF BUSINESS

TEXT AND CASES

Twelfth Edition

Frank B. Cross

Herbert D. Kelleher
Centennial Professor in Business Law
University of Texas at Austin

Roger LeRoy Miller

Institute for University Studies
Arlington, Texas

Australia • Brazil • Canada • Mexico • Singapore • United Kingdom • United States

The Legal Environment of Business:
Text and Cases, Twelfth Edition
Frank B. Cross
Roger LeRoy Miller

SVP, Product: Cheryl Costantini

VP, Product: Thais Alencar

Portfolio Product Director: Joe Sabatino

Portfolio Product Manager: Effie Tsakmaklis

Learning Designer: Mara Vuillaume

Content Manager: Amanda White

Digital Project Manager: Mark Hopkinson

VP, Product Marketing: Jason Sakos

Associate Director, Product Marketing: Mary Reynolds

Associate Product Marketing Manager: Melanie Kessler

Content Acquisition Analyst: Rida Syed

Production Service: Straive

Designer: Gaby McCracken

Interior image Source: Lisa-Blue/ iStockphoto: justice scales: imagedb.com/ Shutterstock

For product information and technology assistance, contact us at
Cengage Customer & Sales Support, 1-800-354-9706
or support.cengage.com.

For permission to use material from this text or product,
submit all requests online at **www.copyright.com.**

Library of Congress Control Number: 202394177

Hard Cover Edition:
ISBN: 978-0-357-98570-0

Loose-leaf Edition:
ISBN: 978-0-357-98571-7

Cengage
5191 Natorp Boulevard
Mason, OH 45040
USA

Cengage is a leading provider of customized learning solutions. Our employees reside in nearly 40 different countries and serve digital learners in 165 countries around the world. Find your local representative at **www.cengage.com.**

To learn more about Cengage platforms and services, register or access your online learning solution, or purchase materials for your course, visit **www.cengage.com.**

Printed in the United States of America
Print Number: 01   Print Year: 2024

Brief Contents

Appendices

Contents

Concept Summaries

Exhibits

Preface

The study of the legal environment of business has universal applicability. A student entering any field of business must have at least a passing understanding of legal environment to function in the real world. *The Legal Environment of Business,* Twelfth Edition, provides the information that students need in an interesting and contemporary way.

Additionally, students preparing for a career in accounting, government and political science, economics, and even medicine can use much of the information they learn in a legal environment course. In fact, all individuals throughout their lifetimes can benefit from knowledge of intellectual property, contracts, employment discrimination, environmental law, and other legal environment topics. Consequently, we have fashioned this text as a useful "tool for living" for all of your students.

The Twelfth Edition of this best-selling text is more modern, exciting, and visually appealing than ever before. We have added a new feature, new cases, concept summaries, and exhibits. The text also contains hundreds of highlighted and numbered *Cases in Point* and *Examples,* as well as more than twenty new case problems. Special pedagogical elements within the text focus on legal, ethical, global, and corporate issues while addressing core curriculum requirements.

Highlights of the Twelfth Edition

Instructors have come to rely on the coverage, accuracy, and applicability of *The Legal Environment of Business.* To make sure that our text engages your students, solidifies their understanding of legal concepts, and provides the best teaching tools available, we offer the following.

Updated Text Information

Many changes have occurred in the legal environment landscape since the last edition of this text. Here are some new sections that provide authoritative and contemporary topics for your students:

- **New information** on the **Legalization of Marijuana** (Chapter 2)
- **New information** on the current view of **social responsibility of corporations** (Chapter 3)

- **New Information** on where a corporation is subject to **jurisdiction** (Chapter 4)
- **New section** on **"Shadow-Docket" cases** (Chapter 4)
- **New Section** on the **trend away from arbitration clauses in contracts** (Chapter 4)
- **New Information** on the **cloud-based nature of online alternative dispute resolution** (Chapter 4)
- **New Section** on defenses to **Intentional Infliction of Emotional Distress (IIED)** (Chapter 6)
- **Additional Information** on state **appropriation statutes** (Chapter 6)
- **Updated information** on the **duration of patents** issued after 2015 (Chapter 8)
- **New Information** on **BitTorrent** (Chapter 9)
- **New Section** on **Reasonable Expectation of Privacy** (Chapter 9)
- **New Section** on **Stolen Credit Card Numbers** and **Card Testing** (Chapter 10)
- **New Section** on **Ransomware** (Chapter 10)
- **New Section** on **Minors' Rights in Digital Assets** (Chapter 12)
- **New Section** on **Shipment and Destination Contracts** (Chapter 14)
- **Updating** of all dollar amounts for **bankruptcies** (Chapter 15)
- **New Section** on **Subchapter 5 Bankruptcy** (Chapter 15)
- **New Section** on **Small Business Administration (SBA) microloans** (Chapter 16)
- **New Information** on **Crowdfunding Regulations** (Chapter 18)
- **New Section** on **Employee Status and Overtime** (Chapter 19)
- **New Section** on **COVID-19 layoffs and violations of the WARN Act** (Chapter 20)
- **New Section** on **Discrimination Based on Genetic Information** (Chapter 21)
- **New Section** on **sanctuary jurisdictions** (Chapter 22)
- **New Section** on **the Holding of the *Auer* Case** (Chapter 23)
- **New Section** on the **Telephone Consumer Protection Act** and the **TRACED Act** (Chapter 24)

- **New Section** on **Limiting Consumer Confusion** (Chapter 24)
- **New Section** on **mobile sources of air pollution** (Chapter 25)
- **New Section** on **Sustainability Issues** (Chapter 25)
- **New Section** on **Energy Creation** (Chapter 25)
- **New Section** on **Waste Management** (Chapter 25)
- **New Section** on **Destruction of Species and Ecosystems** (Chapter 25)
- **New Section** on **Environmental, Social, and Governance [ESG]** (Chapter 25)
- **New Section** on **Economic Development** (Chapter 26)
- **New Section** on **Are Cryptocurrencies Subject to the *Howey* Test?** (Chapter 28)
- **New Section** on **the State Regulation of Crowdfunding** (Chapter 28)
- **New Section** on **Important Regulation A Rule Changes** (Chapter 28)
- **New Section** on **Direct Listings and Direct Public Offerings** (Chapter 28)
- **New Section** on **Special Purpose Acquisition Companies [SPACs]** (Chapter 28)
- **New Section** on the **Personal-Benefits Test** (Chapter 28)
- **New Explanation** of **Selling Short** (Chapter 28)
- **New Section** on **Social Media** (Chapter 28)

The IDDR Approach: An Emphasis on Ethics

The ability of businesspersons to reason through ethical issues is now more important than ever. For the Twelfth Edition of *the Legal Environment of Business,* we have continued to use a special framework for helping students (and businesspersons) make ethical decisions. We present **the IDDR Approach** in Chapter 3 (Ethics in Business). This systematic approach provides students with a clear step-by-step process to analyze the legal and ethical implications of decisions that arise in everyday business operations.

The IDDR Approach uses four logical steps:
- **Step 1: Inquiry**
- **Step 2: Discussion**
- **Step 3: Decision**
- **Step 4: Review**

Students can remember the first letter of each step easily by using the phrase: "I Desire to Do Right."

A Question of Ethics Throughout Text

After Chapter 3, to reinforce the application of the IDDR Approach, students are asked to use its various steps when answering each chapter's *A Question of Ethics*.

A Variety of Exciting Features

The Twelfth Edition of *the Legal Environment of Business* is filled with numerous features specifically designed to cover current legal environment topics of high interest.

Each feature is related to a topic discussed in the text and ends with *Critical Thinking Questions.* Suggested answers to all the *Critical Thinking Questions* are included in the **Solution and Answer Guide** for this text.

The Twelfth Edition includes the following entirely new feature.

1. **Cybersecurity and the Law.** Most businesses will face cybersecurity issues at least once, if not on multiple occasions. The law has something to say about these issues, as you will see in the following discussions:

- Encryption of Apple's iPhones (Chapter 2)
- The Internet of Things (Chapter 7)
- Counter-Strike: Global Offensive (Chapter 10)
- Safe Satellites (Chapter 11)
- Arby's Restaurant Group, Inc. (Chapter 13)
- Brinker International, Inc. (Chapter 16)
- The CLOUD Act (Chapter 19)

In addition, we have retained most features from previous editions.

2. *Ethics Today.* These features focus on the ethical aspects of a topic discussed in the text to emphasize that ethics is an integral part of a business law course. Examples of new features in this category include the following:

- Falling Back on Precedent (Chapter 1)
- Should the Law Require Discovery About Third-Party Litigation Financing? (Chapter 5)
- Can Someone Be Found Liable for a Tort if That Person Has Ruined the Plaintiff's Marriage? (Chapter 6)
- What Are the Privacy Implications of Facial Recognition Technology? (Chapter 9)
- Forced Online Classes and Breach of Contract Lawsuits (Chapter 13)
- Should Proxy Advisory Firms Be More Heavily Regulated by the SEC? (Chapter 18)
- Should Corporations Regulate Pronoun Use in the Workplace? (Chapter 21)
- Should Eminent Domain Be Used to Take Private Land for Recreational Uses? (Chapter 26)
- Does Corporate America Need Gender Quotas for Boards of Directors? (Chapter 28)

3. *Digital Update.* These features examine cutting-edge cyberlaw topics. Here are the new or revised features in this category:

- Revenge Porn: An Invasion of Privacy? (Chapter 6)
- Should Bitcoin and Other Cryptocurrencies Be Made Illegal? (Chapter 10)
- Big Tech's Monopoly Problem (Chapter 27)

4. *Managerial Strategy.* These features emphasize the management aspects of business law and the legal environment. New and revised topics include the following:

- When Is a Warning Legally Unassailable? (Chapter 7)
- Trademarks and Service Marks (Chapter 8)

Entire Chapter on Internet Law, Social Media, and Privacy

The Twelfth Edition again includes a complete chapter (Chapter 9) on *Internet Law, Social Media, and Privacy.* Social media have entered the mainstream and have become a part of everyday life for many businesspersons. In this special chapter, we give particular emphasis to the legal environment issues surrounding the internet, social media, and privacy. We also recognize this trend throughout the text by incorporating the internet and social media as they relate to the topics under discussion.

Highlighted and Numbered *Examples* and *Case in Point* Illustrations

Many instructors use cases and examples to illustrate how the law applies to business. Students understand legal concepts better in the context of their real-world application. Therefore, for this edition of *the Legal Environment of Business,* we have expanded the number of highlighted numbered *Examples* and *Cases in Point* in every chapter.

Examples illustrate how the law applies in a specific situation. *Cases in Point* present the facts and issues of an actual case and then describe the court's decision and rationale. These two features are uniquely designed and consecutively numbered throughout each chapter for easy reference. The *Examples* and *Cases in Point* are integrated throughout the text to help students better understand how courts apply legal principles in the real world.

You will find dozens of new *Examples* in the Twelfth Edition. You will find almost as many new *Cases in Point.* Moreover, almost all retained *Cases in Point* include additional citations to cases in 2020, 2021, 2022, and 2023.

Task-Based Simulations: A Unit-Ending Feature

A *Task-Based Simulation* feature concludes each of the five units in the Twelfth Edition. This feature presents a hypothetical business situation and then asks a series of questions about how the law applies to various actions taken by the firm. To answer the questions, the students must apply the laws discussed throughout the unit.

New Cases and Case Problems

For the Twelfth Edition, we have added numerous new cases and case problems, most from 2020, 2021, 2022, and 2023. The new cases and case problems have been carefully selected to illustrate important points of the legal environment and to be of high interest to students and instructors. We have made it a point to find recent cases that enhance learning and are relatively easy to understand.

1. *Spotlight Cases* **and** *Classic Cases.* Certain cases and case problems that are exceptionally good teaching cases are labeled as *Spotlight Cases* and *Spotlight Case Problems.* Examples include *Spotlight on Amazon, Spotlight on Beer Labels, Spotlight on Gucci, Spotlight on Nike,* and *Spotlight on the Seattle Mariners.* Instructors will find these *Spotlight Cases* useful to illustrate the legal concepts under discussion, and students will enjoy studying the cases because they involve interesting and memorable facts. Other cases have been chosen as *Classic Cases* because they establish a legal precedent in a particular area of law.

2. *Critical Thinking Section.* Each case concludes with a *Critical Thinking* section, which normally includes two questions. The questions may address *Legal Environment, E-Commerce, Economic, Environmental, Ethical, Global, Political,* or *Technological* issues, or they may ask *What If the Facts Were Different?* Each *Classic Case* ends with an *Impact of This Case on Today's Law* discussion and a *Critical Thinking* question.

3. *Longer Excerpts for Case Analysis.* We have also included one longer case excerpt in most chapter—labeled *Case Analysis*—followed by three *Legal Reasoning Questions.* The questions are designed to guide students' analysis of the case and build their legal reasoning skills. These *Case Analysis* cases may be used for case-briefing assignments.

Suggested answers to all case-ending questions and case problems are included in the **Solution and Answer Guide** for this text.

Business Case Problem With Sample Answer

In response to those instructors who would like students to have sample answers available for some of the questions and case problems, we include a *Business Case Problem With Sample Answer* in each chapter. The *Business Case Problem With Sample Answer* is based on an actual case, and students can find a sample answer at the end of the text. Suggested answers to the *Business Case Problems With Sample Answers* are provided in Appendix C and in the **Solution and Answer Guide** for this text.

Exhibits and Concept Summaries

We have spent considerable effort developing and designing all of the exhibits and concept summaries in this text to achieve better clarity and more visual appeal.

Practice and Review

In the Twelfth Edition, we offer a *Practice and Review* feature at the end of every chapter to help solidify students' understanding of the chapter materials. Each *Practice and Review* feature presents a hypothetical scenario and then asks a series of questions that require students to identify the issues and apply the legal concepts discussed in the chapter.

These features are designed to help students review the chapter topics in a simple and interesting way and to see how the legal environment principles discussed in the chapter affect the world in which they live. An instructor can use these features as the basis for in-class discussion or encourage students to use them for self-study prior to completing homework assignments. Suggested answers to the questions posed in the *Practice and Review* features can be found in the **Solution and Answer Guide** for this text.

Issue Spotters

At the conclusion of each chapter, we have included a special section with two *Issue Spotters* related to the chapter's topics. These questions facilitate student learning and review of the chapter materials. Suggested answers to the *Issue Spotters* in every chapter are provided in Appendix B and in the **Solution and Answer Guide** for this text.

Time-Limited Group Assignment

For instructors who want their students to engage in group projects, each chapter of the Twelfth Edition includes a special *Time-Limited Group Assignment*. Each activity begins by describing a business scenario and then poses several questions pertaining to the scenario. Each question is to be answered by a different group of students based on the information in the chapter. These projects may be used in class to spur discussion or as homework assignments. Suggested answers to the *Time-Limited Group Assignments* are included in the **Solution and Answer Guide** for this text.

Teaching Materials

The Legal Environment of Business, Twelfth Edition, provides a comprehensive supplements package designed to make the tasks of teaching and learning more enjoyable and efficient. The following supplements are available for instructors.

MindTap

MindTap for the Legal Environment of Business, Twelfth Edition, today's most innovative online learning platform, powers your students from memorization to mastery. *MindTap* gives you complete control of your course to provide engaging content, challenge every individual, and build student confidence.

MindTap introduces students to core concepts from the beginning of your course using a simplified learning path that progresses from understanding to application. Universal learning path features include:

- **"Why Does [Topic] Matter to Me?" Activities.** Immediately engage students with "Why Does [Topic] Matter to Me?" activities. These activities connect the upcoming chapter to an authentic, real-world scenario designed to pique engagement and emphasize relevance. Use these activities to ensure students read material *before* class and to trigger lively in-class discussion.
- **Chapter-Level eTextbook.** Foster student engagement from day one with a dynamic eTextbook that brings the value, concepts, and applications of the printed text to life. Students open an active-learning experience as each chapter provides opportunities to interact with content using the approach that's best for the individual learner.

- **"Learn It" Activities.** "Learn It" activities offer small sections of instruction that highlight the most important concepts in each chapter. Each "Learn It" activity reinforces the text's instruction and approaches concepts in a different way to promote student choice and autonomy with personalized learning. You can assign "Learn It" activities to ensure students have read and understand key concepts before class.
- **Application-Driven Chapter Assignments.** Assign carefully designed, practically focused chapter homework to ensure your students know how to apply what they have learned.
- **Practice Quizzes.** Use carefully curated practice quizzes to assess student performance and immediately identify class-wide learning needs.

To learn about MindTap visit: https://www.cengage.com/mindtap

Cengage Infuse

Cengage Infuse is embedded in the eTextbook, simple auto-graded comprehension checks, and end-of-chapter quizzes right in your LMS—no need to learn a new technology. As an instructor, you can customize the content and personalize student feedback, or use it as is to complement your existing course materials. From course setup to course management and tracking student progress, you and your students never have to leave your LMS to access high-quality, pre-organized publisher content.

Each chapter contains two Concept Check activities and one End-of-Chapter Quiz. Concept Checks are brief formative assessments that check students' understanding of major concepts. End-of-Chapter Quizzes are summative assessments of students' overall understanding of key chapter concepts. All activities are customizable and auto-graded in your LMS.

To learn more about Cengage Infuse visit: https://www.cengage.com/cengage-infuse

Cengage Instructor Center

Additional instructor resources for this product are available online. Instructor assets include an Instructor's Manual, Educator's Guide, PowerPoint® slides, and a test bank powered by Cognero®. Sign up or sign in at www.cengage.com to search for and access this product and its online resources.

The Cengage Instructor Center is an all-in-one resource for class preparation, presentation, and testing. The instructor resources available for download include:

- **Instructor's Manual.** Includes key terms with definitions, a chapter outline, activities, and discussion questions that may be conducted in an on-ground, hybrid, or online modality.
- **Solution and Answer Guide.** Provides answers to all questions presented in the text, including any critical thinking questions within chapter features and any end-of-chapter review questions and activities.
- **Test Bank.** A comprehensive test bank, offered in Blackboard, Moodle, Desire2Learn, and Canvas formats, contains learning-objective–specific true-false, multiple-choice, and essay questions for each chapter. Import the test bank into your LMS to edit and manage questions and to create tests.
- **PowerPoint Slides.** Presentations are closely tied to the Instructor Manual, providing ample opportunities for generating classroom discussion and interaction. They offer ready-to-use, visual outlines of each chapter that may be easily customized for your lectures.

Cengage Testing Powered by Cognero

Cognero is a flexible online system that allows you to author, edit, and manage test bank content from multiple Cengage solutions; create multiple-test versions in an instant; and deliver tests from your LMS, your classroom, or wherever you want.

Acknowledgments for Previous Editions

Since we began this project many years ago, a sizable number of legal environment of business professors and others have helped us in revising the book, including the following:

Peter W. Allan
Victor Valley College, California

William Dennis Ames
Indiana University of Pennsylvania

Thomas M. Apke
California State University, Fullerton

Linda Axelrod
Metropolitan State University, Minnesota

Jane Bennett
Orange Coast College, California

Robert C. Bird
University of Connecticut

Dean Bredeson
University of Texas at Austin

Sam Cassidy
University of Denver, Colorado

Thomas D. Cavenagh
North Central College, Illinois

Angela Cerino
Villanova University, Pennsylvania

Corey Ciocchetti
University of Denver, Colorado

David Cooper
Fullerton College, California

Steven R. Donley
Cypress College, California

Paul F. Dwyer
Siena College, New York

Nena Ellison
Florida Atlantic University

Joan Gabel
Florida State University

Gamewell Gant
Idaho State University

Jacqueline Hagerott
Franklin University, Ohio

Arlene M. Hibschweiler
State University of New York at Fredonia

Barbara W. Kincaid
Southern Methodist University, Texas

Marty P. Ludlum
Oklahoma City Community College

Diane May
Winona State University, Minnesota

Marty Salley McGee
South Carolina State University

Robert Mitchum
Arkansas State University Beebe

Melanie Morris
Raritan Valley Community College, New Jersey

Kathleen A. Phillips
University of Houston, Texas

David Redle
University of Akron, Ohio

Larry A. Strate
University of Nevada, Las Vegas

Dawn Swink
Minnesota State University

Brian Terry
Johnson and Wales University, Rhode Island

John Theis
Colorado Mesa University

William H. Volz
Wayne State University, Michigan

Michael G. Walsh
Villanova University, Pennsylvania

Glynda White
College of Southern Nevada

LeVon E. Wilson
Western Carolina University, North Carolina

John A. Wrieden
Florida International University

Eric D. Yordy
Northern Arizona University

Mary-Kathryn Zachary
State University of West Georgia

Appreciation for Those Who Worked on the Twelfth Edition

As in all past editions, I owe a debt of extreme gratitude to the numerous individuals who worked directly with me or for my publisher, Cengage. In particular, I wish to thank Effie Tsakmaklis, Associate Portfolio Product Manager; Joe Sabatino, Portfolio Product Director; and Amanda White, Senior Content Manager. I also thank Mara Vuillaume, Learning Designer; Mark Hopkinson, Digital Project Manager; Emily Klingberg, Product Assistant; Gaby McCracken, Visual Designer; and Rida Syed, Content Acquisition Analyst. I am indebted as well to the staff at Straive, especially Ann Borman, my project manager, for accurately generating pages for this text and making it possible for me to meet my ambitious schedule for print and digital products.

I was fortunate enough to have the copyediting of Beverly Peavler and the proofreading of Sheila Joyce. I am grateful for the many efforts of Suzanne Jasin, who helped to ensure an error-free text.

Through the years, I have enjoyed an ongoing correspondence with many of you who have found points on which you wish to comment. I continue to welcome all comments and promise to respond promptly. By incorporating your ideas, I can continue to write a business law text that is best for you and best for your students.

R.L.M.

In memoriam of Frank Cross,
Your research qualities were second to none.
Your concern and kindness toward your
students and colleagues were always heartfelt.
You will be missed.

To Ian Gowrie-Smith,
Having you as a friend for years
has enriched my life.

R.L.M.

The Foundations

LEGAL ENVIRONMENT
CROSS · MILLER

Chapter 1

Law and Legal Reasoning

One of the most important functions of law in any society is to provide stability, predictability, and continuity so that people can know how to order their affairs. If any society is to survive, its citizens must be able to determine what is legally right and legally wrong. They must know what sanctions will be imposed on them if they commit wrongful acts. If they suffer harm as a result of others' wrongful acts, they must know how they can seek compensation. By setting forth the rights, obligations, and privileges of citizens, the law enables individuals to go about their business with confidence and a certain degree of predictability.

Although law has various definitions, they all are based on the general observation that **law** consists of enforceable rules governing relationships among individuals and between individuals *and their society*. In some societies, these enforceable rules consist of unwritten principles of behavior. In other societies, they are set forth in ancient or contemporary law codes. In the United States, our rules consist of written laws and court decisions created by modern legislative and judicial bodies. Regardless of how such rules are created, they all have one feature in common: They establish rights, duties, and privileges that are consistent with the values and beliefs of their society or its ruling group.

In this introductory chapter, we look at how business law and the legal environment affect business decisions. For instance, suppose that Mototron, Inc., plans to introduce a driverless car equipped with lidar, a radar system that relies on lasers, and with artificially intelligent cameras. Even if its technicians put the vehicles through two million miles of testing on closed courses and deem them low-risk cars, Mototron cannot simply start selling rides to consumers. The company must first test the cars on public roads, which requires permission from state governments. It must also establish safety rules with federal regulators and negotiate sustainable insurance rates. At each step, Mototron will have to adjust its bottom line to take account of the legal costs of introducing cutting-edge but potentially dangerous technology into the American marketplace.

1–1 Business Activities and the Legal Environment

Laws and government regulations affect almost all business activities—from hiring and firing decisions to workplace safety, the manufacturing and marketing of products, business financing, and more. To make good business decisions, a basic knowledge of the laws and regulations governing these activities is beneficial—if not essential.

Realize also that in today's business world, knowing what conduct can lead to legal **liability** is not enough. Businesspersons must develop critical thinking and legal reasoning skills so that they can evaluate how various laws might apply to a given situation and determine the best course of action.

Our goal in this text is not only to teach you about specific laws, but also to teach you how to think about the law and the legal environment and to develop your critical-thinking and legal-reasoning skills. The laws may change, but the ability to analyze and evaluate the legal (and ethical) ramifications of situations as they arise is an invaluable and lasting skill.

1–1a Many Different Laws May Affect a Single Business Decision

As you will note, each chapter in this text covers specific areas of the law and shows how the legal rules in each area affect business activities. Although compartmentalizing the law in this fashion promotes conceptual clarity, it does not indicate the extent to which a number of different laws may apply to just one decision. Exhibit 1–1 illustrates the various areas of the law that may influence business decision making.

■ **Example 1.1** Soon after it launched, YouTube faced a potentially catastrophic $1 billion copyright infringement lawsuit. Entertainment conglomerate Viacom

Exhibit 1–1 Areas of the Law That Can Affect Business Decision Making

claimed that the video-hosting platform was not taking sufficient steps to remove unlicensed use of Viacom's content on its site. A federal judge ensured YouTube's survival by ruling that the company was in compliance with federal copyright law as long as it responded reasonably to "takedown" requests from Viacom and other content providers. Not surprisingly, with five hundred hours of video uploaded to its site each minute, YouTube has remained under constant legal pressure ever since. Liberal and conservative groups have sued the company for discriminating against their political viewpoints. It has faced regulatory scrutiny for, among other things, failing to protect users from sexual and racist harassment and hosting misleading election-related video content. At one point, the Federal Trade Commission fined the company $170 million for collecting personal information from children without their parents' consent. ■

1–1b Ethics and Business Decision Making

Merely knowing the areas of law that may affect a business decision is not sufficient in today's business world. Today, business decision makers need to consider not just whether a decision is legal, but also whether it is ethical.

Ethics generally is defined as the principles governing what constitutes right or wrong behavior. Often, as in several of the claims against YouTube discussed before, disputes arise in business because parties feel that they have been treated unfairly. Thus, the underlying reason for bringing some lawsuits is a breach of ethical duties (such as when a partner or employee attempts to secretly take advantage of a business opportunity).

Throughout this text, you will learn about the relationship between the law and ethics, as well as about some of the types of ethical questions that arise in business. In other words, you will learn about legal issues in business that do not have purely legal reasoning aspects. Rather, many legal conflicts involve ethical issues that often cannot be ignored. We have included Ethical Questions for each unit, as well as within many of the cases presented in this text. Ethics Today features, which focus on ethical considerations in today's business climate, appear in selected chapters, including this chapter. A Question of Ethics case problem is included at the end of every chapter to introduce you to the ethical aspects of specific cases involving real-life situations.

1–2 Sources of American Law

American law has numerous sources. Often, these sources of law are classified as either primary or secondary.

Primary sources of law, or sources that establish the law, include the following:

1. The U.S. Constitution and the constitutions of the various states.
2. Statutory law—including laws passed by Congress, state legislatures, or local governing bodies.
3. Regulations created by administrative agencies, such as the Federal Trade Commission.
4. Case law and common law doctrines.

Next, we describe each of these important sources of law.

Secondary sources of law are books and articles that summarize and clarify the primary sources of law. Examples include legal encyclopedias, treatises, articles in law reviews, and compilations of law, such as the *Restatements of the Law* (which will be discussed later). Courts often refer to secondary sources of law for guidance in interpreting and applying the primary sources of law discussed here.

1–2a Constitutional Law

The federal government and the states have separate written constitutions that set forth the general organization, powers, and limits of their respective governments. **Constitutional law** is the law as expressed in these constitutions.

According to Article VI of the U.S. Constitution, the Constitution is the supreme law of the land. As such, it is the basis of all law in the United States. A law in violation of the Constitution, if challenged, will be declared unconstitutional and will not be enforced, no matter what its source.

The Tenth Amendment to the U.S. Constitution reserves to the states all powers not granted to the federal government. Each state in the union has its own constitution. Unless it conflicts with the U.S. Constitution or a federal law, a state constitution is supreme within the state's borders.

1–2b Statutory Law

Laws enacted by legislative bodies at any level of government, such as statutes passed by Congress or by state legislatures, make up the body of law known as **statutory law.** When a legislature passes a statute, that statute ultimately is included in the federal code of laws or the relevant state code of laws.

Statutory law also includes local **ordinances**— regulations passed by municipal or county governing units to deal with matters not covered by federal or state law. Ordinances commonly have to do with city or county land use (zoning ordinances), building and safety codes, and other matters affecting the local community.

A federal statute, of course, applies to all states. A state statute, in contrast, applies only within the state's borders. State laws thus may vary from state to state. No federal statute may violate the U.S. Constitution, and no state statute or local ordinance may violate the U.S. Constitution or the relevant state constitution.

Statutory Conflicts Tension may sometimes arise between federal, state, and local laws. ■ **Example 1.2** Tension among levels of government is evident in the national debate over so-called sanctuary cities—cities that limit their cooperation with federal immigration authorities. Normally, law enforcement officials are supposed to alert federal immigration authorities when they come into contact with undocumented immigrants, so that the immigrants can be detained for possible deportation. But a number of cities across the United States have adopted either local ordinances or explicit policies that do not follow this procedure. Police in these cities often do not ask or report the immigration status of individuals with whom they come into contact. Other places refuse to detain undocumented immigrants who are accused of low-level offenses. ■

Uniform Laws During the 1800s, the differences among state laws frequently created difficulties for businesspersons conducting trade and commerce among the states. To counter these problems, a group of legal scholars and lawyers formed the National Conference of Commissioners on Uniform State Laws, or NCCUSL (www.uniformlaws.org), in 1892. The NCCUSL still exists today. Its object is to draft **uniform laws** (model statutes) for the states to consider adopting.

Each state has the option of adopting or rejecting a uniform law. Only if a state legislature adopts a uniform law does that law become part of the statutory law of that state. Note that a state legislature may adopt all or part of a uniform law as it is written, or the legislature may rewrite the law however the legislature wishes. Hence, even though many states may have adopted a uniform law, those states' laws may not be entirely "uniform."

The earliest uniform law, the Uniform Negotiable Instruments Law, was completed by 1896 and adopted in every state by the 1920s (although not all states used exactly the same wording). Over the following decades, other acts were drawn up in a similar manner. In all, more than two hundred uniform acts have been issued by the NCCUSL since its inception. The most ambitious uniform act of all, however, was the Uniform Commercial Code.

The Uniform Commercial Code One of the most important uniform acts is the Uniform Commercial Code (UCC), which was created through the joint efforts of the NCCUSL and the American Law Institute.[1] The UCC was first issued in 1952 and has been adopted in all fifty states,[2] the District of Columbia, and the Virgin Islands.

The UCC facilitates commerce among the states by providing a uniform, yet flexible, set of rules governing commercial transactions. Because of its importance in the area of commercial law, we cite the UCC frequently in this text.

---

1. This institute was formed in the 1920s and consists of practicing attorneys, legal scholars, and judges.
2. Louisiana has not adopted Articles 2 and 2A (covering contracts for the sale and lease of goods), however.

1–2c Administrative Law

Another important source of American law is **administrative law,** which consists of the rules, orders, and decisions of administrative agencies. An **administrative agency** is a federal, state, or local government agency established to perform a specific function. Administrative law and procedures constitute a dominant element in the regulatory environment of business.

Rules issued by various administrative agencies now affect almost every aspect of a business's operations. Regulations govern a business's capital structure and financing, its hiring and firing procedures, its relations with employees and unions, and the way it manufactures and markets its products. Regulations enacted to protect the environment also often play a significant role in business operations.

Federal Agencies At the national level, the cabinet departments of the executive branch include numerous **executive agencies.** The U.S. Food and Drug Administration, for instance, is an agency within the U.S. Department of Health and Human Services. Executive agencies are subject to the authority of the president, who has the power to appoint and remove their officers.

There are also major **independent regulatory agencies** at the federal level, such as the Federal Trade Commission, the Securities and Exchange Commission, and the Federal Communications Commission. The president's power is less pronounced in regard to independent agencies, whose officers serve for fixed terms and cannot be removed without just cause.

State and Local Agencies There are administrative agencies at the state and local levels as well. Commonly, a state agency (such as a state pollution-control agency) is created as a parallel to a federal agency (such as the Environmental Protection Agency). Just as federal statutes take precedence over conflicting state statutes, federal agency regulations take precedence over conflicting state regulations.

1–2d Case Law and Common Law Doctrines

The rules of law announced in court decisions constitute another basic source of American law. These rules include interpretations of constitutional provisions, of statutes enacted by legislatures, and of regulations created by administrative agencies.

Today, this body of judge-made law is referred to as **case law.** Case law—the doctrines and principles announced in cases—governs all areas not covered by statutory law or administrative law and is part of our common law tradition. We look at the origins and characteristics of the common law tradition in some detail in the pages that follow.

See Concept Summary 1.1 for a review of the sources of American law.

Concept Summary 1.1

Sources of American Law

Constitutional Law	• Law as expressed in the U.S. Constitution or state constitutions. • The U.S. Constitution is the supreme law of the land. • State constitutions are supreme within state borders to the extent that they do not conflict with the U.S. Constitution.
Statutory Law	• Statutes (including uniform laws) and ordinances enacted by federal, state, and local legislatures. • Federal statutes may not violate the U.S. Constitution. • State statutes and local ordinances may not violate the U.S. Constitution or the relevant state constitution.
Administrative Law	• The rules, orders, and decisions of federal, state, and local administrative agencies.
Case Law and Common Law Doctrines	• Judge-made law, including interpretations of constitutional provisions, of statutes enacted by legislatures, and of regulations created by administrative agencies.

1–3 The Common Law Tradition

Because of our colonial heritage, much of American law is based on the English legal system. Knowledge of this tradition is crucial to understanding our legal system today because judges in the United States still apply common law principles when deciding cases.

1–3a Early English Courts

After the Normans conquered England in 1066, William the Conqueror and his successors began the process of unifying the country under their rule. One of the means they utilized to do this was the establishment of the king's courts, or *curiae regis*.

Before the Norman Conquest, disputes had been settled according to the local legal customs and traditions in various regions of the country. The king's courts sought to establish a uniform set of customs for the country as a whole. What evolved in these courts was the beginning of the **common law**—a body of general rules that applied throughout the entire English realm. Eventually, the common law tradition became part of the heritage of all nations that were once British colonies, including the United States.

Courts of Law and Remedies at Law The early English king's courts could grant only very limited kinds of **remedies** (the legal means to enforce a right or to redress a wrong). If one person wronged another in some way, the king's courts could award as compensation one or more of the following: (1) land, (2) items of value, or (3) money.

The courts that awarded this compensation became known as **courts of law,** and the three remedies were called **remedies at law.** (Today, the remedy at law normally takes the form of monetary **damages**—an amount given to a party whose legal interests have been injured.) This system made the procedure for settling disputes more uniform. When a complaining party wanted a remedy other than economic compensation, however, the courts of law could do nothing, so "no remedy, no right."

Courts of Equity When individuals could not obtain an adequate remedy in a court of law, they petitioned the king for relief. Most of these petitions were decided by an adviser to the king, called a *chancellor,* who had the power to grant new and unique remedies. Eventually, formal chancery courts, or **courts of equity,** were established. *Equity* is a branch of law—founded on notions of justice and fair dealing—that seeks to supply a remedy when no adequate remedy at law is available.

Remedies in Equity The remedies granted by the equity courts became known as **remedies in equity,** or equitable remedies. These remedies include specific performance, injunction, and rescission. Specific performance involves ordering a party to perform an agreement as promised. An injunction is an order to a party to cease engaging in a specific activity or to undo some wrong or injury. Rescission is the cancellation of a contractual obligation. We will discuss these and other equitable remedies in more detail in later chapters.

As a general rule, today's courts, like the early English courts, will not grant equitable remedies unless the remedy at law—monetary damages—is inadequate. ■ **Example 1.3** Yesenia forms a contract (a legally binding agreement) to purchase a parcel of land that she thinks will be perfect for her future home. The seller **breaches** (fails to fulfill) this agreement. Yesenia could sue the seller for the return of any deposits or down payment she might have made on the land, but this is not the remedy she really wants. What Yesenia wants is to have a court order the seller to perform the contract. In other words, Yesenia will seek the equitable remedy of specific performance because monetary damages are inadequate in this situation. ■

Equitable Maxims In fashioning appropriate remedies, judges often were (and continue to be) guided by so-called **equitable maxims**—propositions or general statements of equitable rules. Exhibit 1–2 lists some important equitable maxims.

The last maxim listed in the exhibit—"Equity aids the vigilant, not those who rest on their rights"—merits special attention. It has become known as the equitable doctrine of **laches** (a term derived from the Latin *laxus*, meaning "lax" or "negligent"), and it can be used as a defense. A **defense** is an argument raised by the **defendant** (the party being sued) indicating why the **plaintiff** (the suing party) should not obtain the remedy sought. (Note that in equity proceedings, the party bringing a lawsuit is called the **petitioner,** and the party being sued is referred to as the **respondent.**)

The doctrine of laches arose to encourage people to bring lawsuits while the evidence was fresh. What constitutes a reasonable time, of course, varies according to the circumstances of the case. Time periods for different types of cases are now usually fixed by **statutes of limitations.** After the time allowed under a statute of limitations has expired, no action (lawsuit) can be brought, no matter how strong the case was originally.

Exhibit 1–2 Equitable Maxims

1. **Whoever seeks equity must do equity.** (Anyone who wishes to be treated fairly must treat others fairly.)
2. **Where there is equal equity, the law must prevail.** (The law will determine the outcome of a controversy in which the merits of both sides are equal.)
3. **One seeking the aid of an equity court must come to the court with clean hands.** (The plaintiff must have acted fairly and honestly.)
4. **Equity will not suffer a wrong to be without a remedy.** (Equitable relief will be awarded when there is a right to relief and there is no adequate remedy at law.)
5. **Equity regards substance rather than form.** (Equity is more concerned with fairness and justice than with legal technicalities.)
6. **Equity aids the vigilant, not those who rest on their rights.** (Equity will not help those who neglect their rights for an unreasonable period of time.)

1–3b Legal and Equitable Remedies Today

The establishment of courts of equity in medieval England resulted in two distinct court systems: courts of law and courts of equity. The courts had different sets of judges and granted different types of remedies. During the nineteenth century, however, most states in the United States adopted rules of procedure that resulted in the combining of courts of law and equity. A party now may request both legal and equitable remedies in the same action, and the trial court judge may grant either or both forms of relief.

The distinction between legal and equitable remedies remains relevant to students of business law and the legal environment, however, because these remedies differ. To seek the proper remedy for a wrong, you must know what remedies are available. Additionally, certain vestiges of the procedures used when there were separate courts of law and equity still exist. For instance, a party has the right to demand a jury trial in an action at law, but not in an action in equity. Exhibit 1–3 summarizes the procedural differences (applicable in most states) between an action at law and an action in equity.

1–3c The Doctrine of *Stare Decisis*

One of the unique features of the common law is that it is judge-made law. The body of principles and doctrines that form the common law emerged over time as judges decided legal controversies.

Case Precedents and Case Reporters When possible, judges attempted to be consistent and to base their decisions on the principles suggested by earlier cases. They sought to decide similar cases in a similar way, and they considered new cases with care because they knew that their decisions would make new law. Each interpretation became part of the law on the subject and thus served as a legal **precedent.** A precedent is a decision that furnishes an example or authority for deciding subsequent cases involving identical or similar legal principles or facts.

In the early years of the common law, there was no single place or publication where court opinions, or written decisions, could be found. By the fourteenth century, portions of the most important decisions from each year were being gathered together and recorded in *Year Books*, which became useful references for lawyers and judges. In the sixteenth century, the *Year Books* were discontinued, and other forms of case publication became available. Today, cases are published, or "reported," in volumes called **reporters,** or reports—and are also posted online. We describe today's case reporting system in detail later in this chapter.

Stare Decisis and the Common Law Tradition

The practice of deciding new cases with reference to former decisions, or precedents, became a cornerstone of the English and American judicial systems. The practice

Exhibit 1–3 Procedural Differences Between an Action at Law and an Action in Equity

Procedure	Action at Law	Action in Equity
Initiation of lawsuit	By filing a complaint	By filing a petition
Decision	By jury or judge	By judge (no jury)
Result	Judgment	Decree
Remedy	Monetary damages or property	Injunction, specific performance, or rescission

formed a doctrine known as **stare decisis**,[3] a Latin phrase meaning "to stand on decided cases."

Under the doctrine of *stare decisis*, judges are obligated to follow the precedents established within their jurisdictions. The term *jurisdiction* refers to a geographic area in which a court or courts have the power to apply the law. Once a court has set forth a principle of law as being applicable to a certain set of facts, that court must apply the principle in future cases involving similar facts. Courts of lower rank (within the same jurisdiction) must do likewise. Thus, *stare decisis* has two aspects:

1. A court should not overturn its own precedents unless there is a compelling reason to do so.
2. Decisions made by a higher court are binding on lower courts.

Controlling Precedents Precedents that must be followed within a jurisdiction are called *controlling precedents*. Controlling precedents are a type of binding authority. A **binding authority** is any source of law that a court must follow when deciding a case. Binding authorities include constitutions, statutes, and regulations that govern the issue being decided, as well as court decisions that are controlling precedents within the jurisdiction. United States Supreme Court case decisions, no matter how old, remain controlling until they are overruled by a subsequent decision of the Supreme Court or changed by further legislation or a constitutional amendment.

Stare Decisis and Legal Stability The doctrine of *stare decisis* helps the courts to be more efficient because, if other courts have analyzed a similar case, their legal reasoning and opinions can serve as guides. *Stare decisis* also makes the law more stable and predictable. If the law on a subject is well settled, someone bringing a case can usually rely on the court to rule based on what the law has been in the past. See this chapter's Ethics Today feature for a discussion of how courts often defer to case precedent, even when it is implied rather than overtly stated.

Although courts are obligated to follow precedents, sometimes a court will depart from the rule of precedent if it decides that the precedent should no longer be followed. If a court decides that a ruling precedent is simply incorrect or that technological or social changes have rendered the precedent inapplicable, the court might rule contrary to the precedent. Cases that overturn precedent often receive a great deal of publicity.

■ **Case in Point 1.4** The United States Supreme Court expressly overturned precedent in the case of *Brown v. Board of Education of Topeka*.[4] The Court concluded that separate educational facilities for whites and blacks, which it had previously upheld as constitutional,[5] were inherently unequal. The Supreme Court's departure from precedent in this case received a tremendous amount of publicity as people began to realize the ramifications of this change in the law. ■

Note that a lower court will sometimes avoid applying a precedent set by a higher court in its jurisdiction by distinguishing the two cases based on their facts. When this happens, the lower court's ruling stands unless it is appealed to a higher court and that court overturns the decision.

When There Is No Precedent Occasionally, courts must decide cases for which no precedents exist, called *cases of first impression*. For instance, as you will read throughout this text, the internet and certain other technologies have presented many new and challenging issues for the courts to decide.

In deciding cases of first impression, courts often look at **persuasive authorities**—legal authorities that a court may consult for guidance but that are not binding on the court. A court may consider precedents from other jurisdictions, for instance, although those precedents are not binding. A court may also consider legal principles and policies underlying previous court decisions or existing statutes. Additionally, a court might look at issues of fairness, social values and customs, and public policy (governmental policy based on widely held societal values). Today, federal courts can also look at unpublished opinions (those not intended for publication in a printed legal reporter) as sources of persuasive authority.[6]

1–3d *Stare Decisis* and Legal Reasoning

In deciding what law applies to a given dispute and then applying that law to the facts or circumstances of the case, judges rely on the process of **legal reasoning.** Through the use of legal reasoning, judges harmonize their decisions with those that have been made before, as the doctrine of *stare decisis* requires.

Students of business law and the legal environment also engage in legal reasoning. For instance, you may be asked to provide answers for some of the case problems

---

3. Pronounced *stahr*-ee dih-*si*-sis.

4. 347 U.S. 483, 74 S.Ct. 686, 98 L.Ed. 873 (1954).
5. See *Plessy v. Ferguson*, 163 U.S. 537, 16 S.Ct. 1138, 41 L.Ed. 256 (1896).
6. See Rule 32.1 of the Federal Rules of Appellate Procedure.

Ethics Today

Falling Back on Precedent

Most people know that Americans are guaranteed a fair trial, particularly in criminal cases. After all, someone accused of committing a crime faces a powerful set of government-paid persons who help the state try to win a conviction. Hence, the Sixth Amendment to the U.S. Constitution, which outlines the rights of the accused during criminal prosecutions, states that: "The accused shall enjoy the right to a speedy and public trial, by an impartial jury of the State. . . ."

Unanimous Decisions Required

In criminal trials, the standard has almost always been that the accused be convicted on the basis of a unanimous jury. In other words, all members of the jury must agree to a guilty verdict. This requirement in most states has been a method to ensure that a defendant is not convicted unless the prosecution (the State) has proved its case beyond a reasonable doubt.

Otherwise stated, in most states and in federal courts, a single juror's vote to acquit is sufficient to prevent a conviction.

Louisiana and Oregon Begged to Differ

Two states, Louisiana and Oregon, have convicted those accused of crimes based on 10-to-2 verdicts. When Evangelisto Ramos was convicted of murder in a Louisiana court because of a 10–2 jury vote, he appealed his decision all the way to the Supreme Court.

That Court ruled in Ramos's favor.[a] In doing so, it reversed a prior appeals court ruling against Ramos.

Both Ethical and Fair

Most courts in the United States and England have required unanimous decisions for decades, even centuries. This history formed a strong precedent on which the Supreme Court relied in the *Ramos* case. ". . . the Sixth Amendment term 'trial by an impartial jury' carries with it some meaning about the content and requirements of a jury trial. One such requirement is that a jury must reach a unanimous verdict in order to convict. Juror unanimity emerged as a vital common law right in fourteenth-century England, appeared in the early American state constitutions, and provided the backdrop against which the Sixth Amendment was drafted and ratified." In its written decision, the Court considered that a person accused of a criminal act cannot be found guilty without a unanimous jury decision. This ruling has been considered both ethical and fair by most commentators.

Critical Thinking Should convicted criminals in Louisiana and Oregon be able to obtain retrials if they have been convicted in a 10–2 vote of a jury? Why or why not?

a. *Ramos v. Louisiana*, 590 U.S. __ (2020), 140 S.Ct. 1390, 206 L.Ed.2d 583.

---

that appear at the end of every chapter in this text. Each problem describes the facts of a particular dispute and the legal question at issue. If you are assigned a case problem, you will be asked to determine how a court would answer that question, and why. In other words, you will need to give legal reasons for whatever conclusion you reach. We look next at the basic steps involved in legal reasoning and then describe some forms of reasoning commonly used by the courts in making their decisions.

Basic Steps in Legal Reasoning At times, the legal arguments set forth in court opinions are relatively simple and brief. At other times, the arguments are complex and lengthy. Regardless of the length of a legal argument, however, the basic steps of the legal reasoning process remain the same. These steps, which you can also follow when analyzing cases and case problems, form what is commonly referred to as the IRAC method of legal reasoning. IRAC is an acronym formed from the first letters of the words Issue, Rule, Application, and Conclusion. To apply the IRAC method, you ask the following questions:

1. **Issue—What are the key facts and issues?** Suppose that a plaintiff comes before the court claiming assault (words or acts that wrongfully and intentionally make another person fearful of immediate physical harm). The plaintiff claims that the defendant threatened her while she was sleeping. Although the plaintiff was unaware that she was being threatened, her roommate heard the defendant make the threat. The legal issue is whether the defendant's action constitutes the tort of assault, given that the plaintiff was unaware of that action at the time it occurred. (A tort is a wrongful act. As you will see later, torts fall under the governance of civil law rather than criminal law.)

2. **Rule—What rule of law applies to the case?** A rule of law may be a rule stated by the courts in previous decisions, a state or federal statute, or a state or federal

administrative agency regulation. In our hypothetical case, the plaintiff **alleges** (claims) that the defendant committed a tort. Therefore, the applicable law is the common law of torts—specifically, tort law governing assault. Case precedents involving similar facts and issues thus would be relevant. Often, more than one rule of law will be applicable to a case.

3. **Application—How does the rule of law apply to the particular facts and circumstances of this case?** This step is often the most difficult because each case presents a unique set of facts, circumstances, and parties. Although cases may be similar, no two cases are ever identical in all respects. Normally, judges (and lawyers and law students) try to find **cases on point**—previously decided cases that are as similar as possible to the one under consideration.

4. **Conclusion—What conclusion should be drawn?** This step normally presents few problems. Usually, the conclusion is evident if the previous three steps have been followed carefully.

There Is No One "Right" Answer Many people believe that there is one "right" answer to every legal question. In most legal controversies, however, there is no single correct result. Good arguments can usually be made to support either side of a legal controversy. Quite often, a case does not involve a "good" person suing a "bad" person. In many cases, both parties have acted in good faith in some measure or in bad faith to some degree. Additionally, individual judges have their own personal beliefs and philosophies. These personal factors shape the legal reasoning process. In short, the outcome of a particular lawsuit before a court cannot be predicted with certainty.

1–3e The Common Law Today

Today, the common law derived from judicial decisions continues to be applied throughout the United States. Common law doctrines and principles, however, govern only areas *not* covered by statutory or administrative law. In a dispute concerning a particular employment practice, for instance, if a statute regulates that practice, the statute will apply rather than the common law doctrine that applied before the statute was enacted. The common law tradition and its application are reviewed in Concept Summary 1.2.

Courts Interpret Statutes Even in areas governed by statutory law, judge-made law continues to be important because there is a significant interplay between statutory law and the common law. For instance, many

Concept Summary 1.2

The Common Law Tradition

Origins of Common Law	The American legal system is based on the common law tradition, which originated in medieval England.
Legal and Equitable Remedies	Remedies at law (land, items of value, or money) and remedies in equity (including specific performance, injunction, and rescission of a contractual obligation) originated in the early English courts of law and courts of equity, respectively.
Case Precedents and the Doctrine of *Stare Decisis*	In the king's courts, judges attempted to make their decisions consistent with previous decisions, called *precedents*. This practice gave rise to the doctrine of *stare decisis*. This doctrine, which became a cornerstone of the common law tradition, obligates judges to abide by precedents established in their jurisdictions.
Common Law Today	The common law governs all areas not covered by statutory law or administrative laws. Courts interpret statutes and regulations.

statutes essentially codify existing common law rules. Moreover, regulations issued by various administrative agencies usually are based, at least in part, on common law principles. Additionally, the courts, in interpreting statutory law, often rely on the common law as a guide to what the legislators intended. Frequently, the applicability of a newly enacted statute does not become clear until a body of case law develops to clarify how, when, and to whom the statute applies.

Clearly, a judge's function is not to make the laws—that is the function of the legislative branch of government—but to interpret and apply them. From a practical point of view, however, the courts play a significant role in defining the laws enacted by legislative bodies, which tend to be expressed in general terms. Judges thus have some flexibility in interpreting and applying the law. It is because of this flexibility that different courts can, and often do, arrive at different conclusions in cases that involve nearly identical issues, facts, and applicable laws.

Restatements of the Law Clarify and Illustrate the Common Law The American Law Institute (ALI) has published compilations of the common law called *Restatements of the Law*, which generally summarize the common law rules followed by most states. There are *Restatements of the Law* in the areas of contracts, torts, agency, trusts, property, restitution, security, judgments, and conflict of laws. The *Restatements,* like other secondary sources of law, do not in themselves have the force of law, but they are an important source of legal analysis and opinion. Hence, judges often rely on them in making decisions.

Many of the *Restatements* are now in their second, third, or fourth editions. We refer to the *Restatements* frequently in subsequent chapters of this text, indicating in parentheses the edition to which we are referring. For instance, we refer to the third edition of the *Restatement of the Law of Contracts* as simply the *Restatement (Third) of Contracts.*

1–4 Schools of Legal Thought

How judges apply the law to specific cases, including disputes relating to the business world, depends in part on their philosophical approaches to law. Thus, the study of law, or **jurisprudence,** involves learning about different schools of legal thought and how the approaches to law characteristic of each school can affect judicial decision making.

1–4a The Natural Law School

An age-old question about the nature of law has to do with the finality of a nation's laws. What if a particular law is deemed to be a "bad" law by a substantial number of the nation's citizens? Must they obey that law? According to the **natural law** theory, a higher, or universal, law exists that applies to all human beings. Each written law should reflect the principles inherent in natural law. If it does not, then it loses its legitimacy and need not be obeyed.

The natural law tradition is one of the oldest and most significant schools of jurisprudence. It dates back to the days of the Greek philosopher Aristotle (384–322 B.C.E.), who distinguished between natural law and the laws governing a particular nation. According to Aristotle, natural law applies universally to all humankind.

The notion that people have "natural rights" stems from the natural law tradition. Those who claim that a foreign government is depriving certain citizens of their human rights, for instance, are implicitly appealing to a higher law that has universal applicability.

1–4b The Positivist School

Positive law, or national law, is the written law of a given society at a particular time. In contrast to natural law, it applies only to the citizens of that nation or society. Those who adhere to **legal positivism** believe that there can be no higher law than a nation's positive law.

According to the positivist school, there are no "natural rights." Rather, human rights exist solely because of laws. If the laws are not enforced, anarchy will result. Thus, whether a law is "bad" or "good" is irrelevant. The law is the law and must be obeyed until it is changed—in an orderly manner through a legitimate lawmaking process. A judge who takes this view will probably be more inclined to defer to an existing law than would a judge who adheres to the natural law tradition.

1–4c The Historical School

The **historical school** of legal thought emphasizes the evolutionary process of law by concentrating on the origin and history of the legal system. This school looks to the past to discover what the principles of contemporary law should be. The legal doctrines that have withstood the passage of time—those that have worked in the past—are deemed best suited for shaping present laws. Hence, law derives its legitimacy and authority from adhering to the standards that historical development has shown to be workable. Followers of the historical school are more likely than those of other schools to strictly follow decisions made in past cases.

1–4d Legal Realism

In the 1920s and 1930s, a number of jurists and scholars, known as "legal realists," rebelled against the historical approach to law. **Legal realism** is based on the idea that law is just one of many institutions in society and that it is shaped by social forces and needs. Because the law is a human enterprise, this school reasons that judges should take social and economic realities into account when deciding cases. Legal realists also believe that the law can never be applied with total uniformity. Given that judges are human beings with unique personalities, value systems, and intellects, different judges will obviously bring different reasoning processes to the same case.

Legal realism strongly influenced the growth of what is sometimes called the **sociological school,** which views law as a tool for promoting justice in society. In the 1960s, for instance, the justices of the United States Supreme Court helped advance the civil rights movement by upholding long-neglected laws calling for equal treatment for all Americans, including African Americans and other minorities. Generally, jurists who adhere to this philosophy of law are more likely to depart from past decisions than are jurists who adhere to other schools of legal thought.

Concept Summary 1.3 reviews the schools of jurisprudential thought.

1–5 Classifications of Law

The law may be broken down according to several classification systems. One system, for instance, divides law into substantive law and procedural law. **Substantive law** consists of all laws that define, describe, regulate, and create legal rights and obligations. **Procedural law** consists of all laws that outline the methods of enforcing the rights established by substantive law.

Note that many statutes contain both substantive and procedural provisions. ■ **Example 1.5** A state law that provides employees with the right to workers' compensation benefits for on-the-job injuries is a substantive law because it creates legal rights. Procedural law establishes the method by which an employee must notify the employer about an on-the-job injury, prove the injury, and periodically submit additional proof to continue receiving workers' compensation benefits. ■

Other classification systems divide law into federal law and state law, private law (dealing with relationships between private entities) and public law (addressing the relationship between persons and their governments), and national law and international law. Here we look at still another classification system, which divides law into civil law and criminal law. We also explain what is meant by the term *cyberlaw.*

Concept Summary 1.3

Schools of Jurisprudential Thought

Natural Law School	One of the oldest and most significant schools of legal thought. Those who believe in natural law hold that there is a universal law applicable to all human beings.
Positivist School	A school of legal thought centered on the assumption that there is no law higher than the laws created by the government.
Historical School	A school of legal thought that stresses the evolutionary nature of law and looks to doctrines that have withstood the passage of time for guidance in shaping present laws.
Legal Realism	A school of legal thought that advocates a less abstract and more realistic and pragmatic approach to the law. Legal realism takes into account customary practices and the circumstances surrounding the particular transaction.

1–5a Civil Law and Criminal Law

Civil law spells out the rights and duties that exist between persons and between persons and their governments, as well as the relief available when a person's rights are violated. Typically, in a civil case, a private party sues another private party who has failed to comply with a duty. (Note that the government can also sue a party for a civil law violation.) Much of the law that we discuss in this text is civil law, including contract law and tort law.

Criminal law, in contrast, is concerned with wrongs committed against the public as a whole. Criminal acts are defined and prohibited by local, state, or federal government statutes. Criminal defendants are thus prosecuted by public officials, such as a district attorney (D.A.), on behalf of the state, not by their victims or other private parties. Some statutes, such as those protecting the environment or investors, have both civil and criminal provisions.

1–5b Cyberlaw

The use of the internet to conduct business has led to new types of legal issues. In response, courts have had to adapt traditional laws to unique situations. Additionally, legislatures at both the federal and the state levels have created laws to deal specifically with such issues.

Frequently, people use the term **cyberlaw** to refer to the emerging body of law that governs transactions conducted via the internet. Cyberlaw is not really a classification of law, though, nor is it a new type of law. Rather, it is an informal term used to refer to both new laws and modifications of traditional laws that relate to the online environment. Throughout this book, you will read how the law in a given area is evolving to govern specific legal issues that arise in the online context.

1–6 How to Find Primary Sources of Law

This text includes numerous references, or citations, to primary sources of law—federal and state statutes, the U.S. Constitution and state constitutions, regulations issued by administrative agencies, and court cases. A **citation** identifies the publication in which a legal authority—such as a statute or a court decision or other source—can be found. In this section, we explain how you can use citations to find primary sources of law. In addition to being published in sets of books, as described next, most federal and state laws and case decisions are available online.

1–6a Finding Statutory and Administrative Law

When Congress passes laws, they are collected in a publication titled *United States Statutes at Large.* When state legislatures pass laws, they are collected in similar state publications. Most frequently, however, laws are referred to in their codified form—that is, the form in which they appear in the federal and state codes. In these codes, laws are compiled by subject.

United States Code The *United States Code* (U.S.C.) arranges all existing federal laws by broad subject. Each of the fifty-two subjects is given a title and a title number. For instance, laws relating to commerce and trade are collected in Title 15, "Commerce and Trade." Each title is subdivided by sections. A citation to the U.S.C. includes both title and section numbers. Thus, a reference to "15 U.S.C. Section 1" means that the statute can be found in Section 1 of Title 15. ("Section" may be designated by the symbol §, and "Sections," by §§.)

In addition to the print publication, the federal government provides a searchable online database at www.gpo.gov. It includes the *United States Code,* the U.S. Constitution, and many other federal resources.

Commercial publications of federal laws and regulations are also available. For instance, Thomson Reuters publishes the *United States Code Annotated* (U.S.C.A.). The U.S.C.A. contains the official text of the U.S.C., plus notes (annotations) on court decisions that interpret and apply specific sections of the statutes. The U.S.C.A. also includes additional research aids, such as cross-references to related statutes, historical notes, and library references. A citation to the U.S.C.A. is similar to a citation to the U.S.C.: "15 U.S.C.A. Section 1."

State Codes State codes follow the U.S.C. pattern of arranging law by subject. They may be called codes, revisions, compilations, consolidations, general statutes, or statutes, depending on the preferences of the states.

In some codes, subjects are designated by number. In others, they are designated by name. ■ **Example 1.6** "13 Pennsylvania Consolidated Statutes Section 1101" means that the statute can be found in Title 13, Section 1101, of the Pennsylvania code. "California Commercial Code Section 1101" means that the statute can be found under the subject heading "Commercial Code" of the California code in Section 1101. Abbreviations are often used. For example, "13 Pennsylvania Consolidated Statutes Section 1101" is abbreviated "13 Pa. C.S. § 1101," and

"California Commercial Code Section 1101" is abbreviated "Cal. Com. Code § 1101." ■

Administrative Rules   Rules and regulations adopted by federal administrative agencies are initially published in the *Federal Register,* a daily publication of the U.S. government. Later, they are incorporated into the *Code of Federal Regulations* (C.F.R.). The C.F.R. is available online on the government database (www.gpo.gov).

Like the U.S.C., the C.F.R. is divided into titles. Rules within each title are assigned section numbers. A full citation to the C.F.R. includes title and section numbers.   ■ **Example 1.7**   A reference to "17 C.F.R. Section 230.504" means that the rule can be found in Section 230.504 of Title 17. ■

1–6b Finding Case Law

Before discussing the case reporting system, we need to look briefly at the court system. There are two types of courts in the United States, federal courts and state courts. Both systems consist of several levels, or tiers, of courts. Trial courts, in which evidence is presented and testimony given, are on the bottom tier. Decisions from a trial court can be appealed to a higher court, which commonly is an intermediate court of appeals, or appellate court. Decisions from these intermediate courts of appeals may be appealed to an even higher court, such as a state supreme court or the United States Supreme Court.

State Court Decisions   Most state trial court decisions are not published in books (except in New York and a few other states, which publish selected trial court opinions). Decisions from state trial courts are typically filed in the office of the clerk of the court, where the decisions are available for public inspection. (Increasingly, they can be found online as well.)

Written decisions of the appellate, or reviewing, courts, however, are published and distributed (in print and online). Many of the state court cases presented in this textbook are from state appellate courts. The reported appellate decisions are published in volumes called "reports" or "reporters," which are numbered consecutively. State appellate court decisions are found in the state reporters of that particular state. Official reports are published by the state, whereas unofficial reports are published by nongovernment entities.

Regional Reporters.   State court opinions appear in regional units of the West's National Reporter System,

published by Thomson Reuters. Most lawyers and libraries have these reporters because they report cases more quickly and are distributed more widely than the state-published reporters. In fact, many states have eliminated their own reporters in favor of the National Reporter System.

The National Reporter System divides the states into the following geographic areas: Atlantic (A., A.2d, or A.3d), North Eastern (N.E., N.E.2d, or N.E.3d), North Western (N.W. or N.W.2d), Pacific (P., P.2d, or P.3d), South Eastern (S.E. or S.E.2d), South Western (S.W., S.W.2d, or S.W.3d), and Southern (So., So.2d, or So.3d). (The 2d and 3d in the preceding abbreviations refer to Second Series and Third Series, respectively.) The states included in each of these regional divisions are indicated in Exhibit 1–4, which illustrates the National Reporter System.

Case Citations.   After appellate decisions have been published, they are normally referred to (cited) by the name of the case and the volume, name, and page number of the reporter(s) in which the opinion can be found. The citation first lists the state's official reporter (if different from the National Reporter System), then the National Reporter, and then any other selected reporter. (Citing a reporter by volume number, name, and page number, in that order, is common to all citations. The year that the decision was issued is often included at the end in parentheses.) When more than one reporter is cited for the same case, each reference is called a *parallel citation.*

Note that some states have adopted a "public domain citation system" that uses a somewhat different format for the citation. For instance, in Wisconsin, a Wisconsin Supreme Court decision might be designated "2023 WI 1," meaning that the case was decided in the year 2023 by the Wisconsin Supreme Court and was the first decision issued by that court during that year. Parallel citations to the *Wisconsin Reports* and the *North Western Reporter* are still included after the public domain citation.
■ **Example 1.8**   Consider the following case citation: *Badawi v. Albin,* 311 Neb. 603, 973 N.W.2d 714 (2022). We see that the opinion in this case can be found in Volume 311 of the *Nebraska Reports* on page 603. The parallel citation is to Volume 973 of the *North Western Reporter, Second Series,* on page 714. ■

When we present opinions in this text (starting in Chapter 2), in addition to the reporter, we give the name of the court hearing the case and the year of the court's decision. Sample citations to state court decisions are explained in Exhibit 1–5.

Exhibit 1–4 National Reporter System—Regional/Federal

Regional Reporters	Coverage Beginning	Coverage
Atlantic Reporter (A., A.2d, or A.3d)	1885	Connecticut, Delaware, District of Columbia, Maine, Maryland, New Hampshire, New Jersey, Pennsylvania, Rhode Island, and Vermont.
North Eastern Reporter (N.E., N.E.2d, or N.E.3d)	1885	Illinois, Indiana, Massachusetts, New York, and Ohio.
North Western Reporter (N.W. or N.W.2d)	1879	Iowa, Michigan, Minnesota, Nebraska, North Dakota, South Dakota, and Wisconsin.
Pacific Reporter (P., P.2d, or P.3d)	1883	Alaska, Arizona, California, Colorado, Hawaii, Idaho, Kansas, Montana, Nevada, New Mexico, Oklahoma, Oregon, Utah, Washington, and Wyoming.
South Eastern Reporter (S.E. or S.E.2d)	1887	Georgia, North Carolina, South Carolina, Virginia, and West Virginia.
South Western Reporter (S.W., S.W.2d, or S.W.3d)	1886	Arkansas, Kentucky, Missouri, Tennessee, and Texas.
Southern Reporter (So., So.2d, or So.3d)	1887	Alabama, Florida, Louisiana, and Mississippi.

Federal Reporters		
Federal Reporter (F., F.2d, F.3d, or F.4th)	1880	U.S. Circuit Courts from 1880 to 1912; U.S. Commerce Court from 1911 to 1913; U.S. District Courts from 1880 to 1932; U.S. Court of Claims (now called U.S. Court of Federal Claims) from 1929 to 1932 and since 1960; U.S. Courts of Appeals since 1891; U.S. Court of Customs and Patent Appeals since 1929; U.S. Emergency Court of Appeals since 1943.
Federal Supplement (F.Supp., F.Supp.2d, or F.Supp.3d)	1932	U.S. Court of Claims from 1932 to 1960; U.S. District Courts since 1932; U.S. Customs Court since 1956.
Federal Rules Decisions (F.R.D.)	1939	U.S. District Courts involving the Federal Rules of Civil Procedure since 1939 and Federal Rules of Criminal Procedure since 1946.
Supreme Court Reporter (S.Ct.)	1882	United States Supreme Court since the October term of 1882.
Bankruptcy Reporter (Bankr.)	1980	Bankruptcy decisions of U.S. Bankruptcy Courts, U.S. District Courts, U.S. Courts of Appeals, and the United States Supreme Court.
Military Justice Reporter (M.J.)	1978	U.S. Court of Military Appeals and Courts of Military Review for the Army, Navy, Air Force, and Coast Guard.

NATIONAL REPORTER SYSTEM MAP

Exhibit 1–5 How to Read Citations

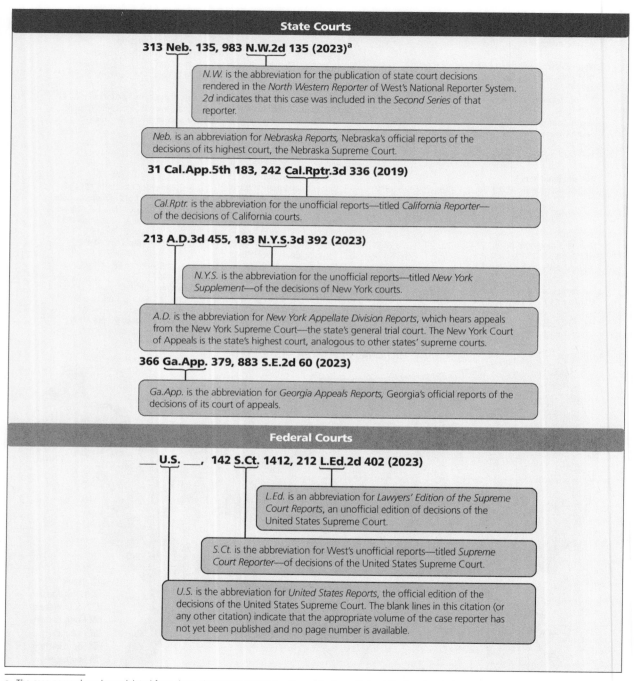

State Courts

313 Neb. 135, 983 N.W.2d 135 (2023)ᵃ

N.W. is the abbreviation for the publication of state court decisions rendered in the *North Western Reporter* of West's National Reporter System. *2d* indicates that this case was included in the *Second Series* of that reporter.

Neb. is an abbreviation for *Nebraska Reports,* Nebraska's official reports of the decisions of its highest court, the Nebraska Supreme Court.

31 Cal.App.5th 183, 242 Cal.Rptr.3d 336 (2019)

Cal.Rptr. is the abbreviation for the unofficial reports—titled *California Reporter*—of the decisions of California courts.

213 A.D.3d 455, 183 N.Y.S.3d 392 (2023)

N.Y.S. is the abbreviation for the unofficial reports—titled *New York Supplement*—of the decisions of New York courts.

A.D. is the abbreviation for *New York Appellate Division Reports*, which hears appeals from the New York Supreme Court—the state's general trial court. The New York Court of Appeals is the state's highest court, analogous to other states' supreme courts.

366 Ga.App. 379, 883 S.E.2d 60 (2023)

Ga.App. is the abbreviation for *Georgia Appeals Reports,* Georgia's official reports of the decisions of its court of appeals.

Federal Courts

___ U.S. ___, 142 S.Ct. 1412, 212 L.Ed.2d 402 (2023)

L.Ed. is an abbreviation for *Lawyers' Edition of the Supreme Court Reports*, an unofficial edition of decisions of the United States Supreme Court.

S.Ct. is the abbreviation for West's unofficial reports—titled *Supreme Court Reporter*—of decisions of the United States Supreme Court.

U.S. is the abbreviation for *United States Reports*, the official edition of the decisions of the United States Supreme Court. The blank lines in this citation (or any other citation) indicate that the appropriate volume of the case reporter has not yet been published and no page number is available.

---

a. The case names have been deleted from these citations to emphasize the publications. It should be kept in mind, however, that the name of a case is as important as the specific page numbers in the volumes in which it is found. If a citation is incorrect, the correct citation may be found in a publication's index of case names. In addition to providing a check on errors in citations, the date of a case is important because the value of a recent case as an authority is likely to be greater than that of older cases from the same court.

Exhibit 1–5 How to Read Citations—Continued

Federal Courts (Continued)

61 F.4th 426 (4th Cir. 2023)

> *4th Cir.* is an abbreviation denoting that this case was decided in the U.S. Court of Appeals for the Fourth Circuit.

324 F.Supp.3d 1172 (D.Nev. 2018)

> *D.Nev.* is an abbreviation indicating that the U.S. District Court for the District of Nevada decided this case.

Westlaw® Citations[b]

2019 WL 491862

> *WL* is an abbreviation for Westlaw. The number 2019 is the year of the document that can be found with this citation in the Westlaw database. The number 491862 is a number assigned to a specific document. A higher number indicates that a document was added to the Westlaw database later in the year.

Statutory and Other Citations

18 U.S.C. Section 1961(1)(A)

> *U.S.C.* denotes *United States Code*, the codification of *United States Statutes at Large*. The number 18 refers to the statute's U.S.C. title number and 1961 to its section number within that title. The number 1 in parentheses refers to a subsection within the section, and the letter A in parentheses to a subsection within the subsection.

UCC 2–206(1)(b)

> *UCC* is an abbreviation for *Uniform Commercial Code*. The first number 2 is a reference to an article of the UCC, and 206 to a section within that article. The number 1 in parentheses refers to a subsection within the section, and the letter b in parentheses to a subsection within the subsection.

Restatement (Third) of Torts, Section 6

> *Restatement (Third) of Torts* refers to the third edition of the American Law Institute's *Restatement of the Law of Torts*. The number 6 refers to a specific section.

17 C.F.R. Section 230.505

> *C.F.R.* is an abbreviation for *Code of Federal Regulations*, a compilation of federal administrative regulations. The number 17 designates the regulation's title number, and 230.505 designates a specific section within that title.

---

b. Many court decisions that are not yet published or that are not intended for publication can be accessed through Westlaw, an online legal database.

Federal Court Decisions Federal district (trial) court decisions are published unofficially in the *Federal Supplement* (F.Supp., F.Supp.2d, or F.Supp.3d), and opinions from the circuit courts of appeals (reviewing courts) are reported unofficially in the *Federal Reporter* (F., F.2d, or F.3d). Cases concerning federal bankruptcy law are published unofficially in the *Bankruptcy Reporter* (Bankr. or B.R.).

The official edition of the United States Supreme Court decisions is the *United States Reports* (U.S.), which is published by the federal government. Unofficial editions of Supreme Court cases include the *Supreme Court Reporter* (S.Ct.) and the *Lawyers' Edition of the Supreme Court Reports* (L.Ed. or L.Ed.2d). Sample citations for federal court decisions are also listed and explained in Exhibit 1–5.

Unpublished Opinions Many court opinions that are not yet published or that are not intended for publication can be accessed through Thomson Reuters Westlaw® (abbreviated in citations as "WL"), an online legal database. When no citation to a published reporter is available for cases cited in this text, we give the WL citation (such as 2023 WL 139279, which means it was case number 139279 decided in the year 2023). In addition, federal appellate court decisions that are designated as unpublished may appear in the *Federal Appendix* (Fed.Appx.) of the National Reporter System.

Sometimes, both in this text and in other legal sources, you will see blank lines left in a citation. This occurs when the decision will be published, but the particular volume number and page number are not yet available.

Old Case Law On a few occasions, this text cites opinions from old, classic cases dating to the nineteenth century or earlier. Some of these are from the English courts. The citations to these cases may not conform to the descriptions just presented because the reporters in which they were originally published were often known by the names of the persons who compiled the reporters.

1–7 How to Read and Understand Case Law

The decisions made by the courts establish the boundaries of the law as it applies to almost all business relationships. It thus is essential that businesspersons know how to read and understand case law.

The cases that we present in this text have been condensed from the full text of the courts' opinions and are presented in a special format. In approximately two-thirds of the cases (including the cases designated as "Classic" and "Spotlight"), we have summarized the background and facts, as well as the court's decision and remedy, in our own words. In those cases, we have included only selected excerpts from the court's opinion ("In the Language of the Court"). In the remaining one-third of the cases (labeled "Case Analysis"), we have provided a longer excerpt from the court's opinion without summarizing the background and facts or decision and remedy.

The following sections provide useful insights into how to read and understand case law.

1–7a Case Titles and Terminology

The title of a case, such as *Adams v. Jones*, indicates the names of the parties to the lawsuit. The *v.* in the case title stands for *versus,* which means "against." In the trial court, Adams was the plaintiff—the person who filed the suit. Jones was the defendant.

If the case is appealed, however, the appellate court will sometimes place the name of the party appealing the decision first, so the case may be called *Jones v. Adams* if Jones appealed. Because some appellate courts retain the trial court order of names, it is often impossible to distinguish the plaintiff from the defendant in the title of a reported appellate court decision. You must carefully read the facts of each case to identify the parties.

The following terms, phrases, and abbreviations are frequently encountered in court opinions and legal publications.

Parties to Lawsuits The party initiating a lawsuit is referred to as the *plaintiff* or *petitioner*, depending on the nature of the action. The party against whom a lawsuit is brought is the *defendant* or *respondent*. Lawsuits frequently involve more than one plaintiff and/or defendant.

When a case is appealed from the original court or jurisdiction to another court or jurisdiction, the party appealing the case is called the **appellant.** The **appellee** is the party against whom the appeal is taken. (In some appellate courts, the party appealing a case is referred to as the *petitioner*, and the party against whom the suit is brought or appealed is called the *respondent*.)

Judges and Justices The terms *judge* and *justice* are usually synonymous and represent two designations given to judges in various courts. All members of the United

States Supreme Court, for instance, are referred to as justices. *Justice* is the formal title often given to judges of appellate courts, although this is not always true. In New York, a justice is a judge of the trial court (called the Supreme Court), and a member of the Court of Appeals (the state's highest court) is called a judge.

The term *justice* is commonly abbreviated to J., and *justices,* to JJ. A United States Supreme Court case might refer to Justice Sotomayor as Sotomayor, J., or to Chief Justice Roberts as Roberts, C.J.

Decisions and Opinions Most decisions reached by reviewing, or appellate, courts are explained in written **opinions.** The opinion contains the court's reasons for its decision, the rules of law that apply, and the judgment. You may encounter several types of opinions as you read appellate cases, including the following:

- When all the judges (or justices) agree, a unanimous opinion is written for the entire court.
- When there is not unanimous agreement, a **majority opinion** is generally written. It outlines the views of the majority of the judges deciding the case.
- A judge who agrees (concurs) with the majority opinion as to the result but not as to the legal reasoning often writes a **concurring opinion.** In these opinions, judges set out the reasoning that they consider correct.
- A **dissenting opinion** presents the views of one or more judges who disagree with the majority view.
- Sometimes, no single position is fully supported by a majority of the judges deciding a case. In this situation, we may have a **plurality opinion.** This is the opinion that has the support of the largest number of judges, but the group in agreement is less than a majority.
- Finally, a court occasionally issues a ***per curiam* opinion** (*per curiam* is Latin for "of the court"), which does not indicate which judge wrote the opinion.

1–7b Sample Court Case

To illustrate the various elements contained in a court opinion, we present an annotated court opinion in Exhibit 1–6. The opinion is from an actual case, *Doe v. Knox County Board of Education,* decided in 2023.

Editorial Practice You will note that triple asterisks (* * *) and quadruple asterisks (* * * *) frequently appear in the opinion. The triple asterisks indicate that we have deleted a few words or sentences from the opinion for the sake of readability or brevity. Quadruple asterisks mean that an entire paragraph (or more) has been omitted.

Additionally, when the opinion cites another case or legal source, the citation to the case or source has been omitted, again for the sake of readability and brevity. These editorial practices are continued in the other court opinions presented in this book. In addition, whenever a court opinion includes a term or phrase that may not be readily understandable, a bracketed definition or paraphrase has been added.

Briefing Cases Knowing how to read and understand court opinions and the legal reasoning used by the courts is an essential step in undertaking accurate legal research. A further step is "briefing," or summarizing, the case.

Legal researchers routinely brief cases by reducing the texts of the opinions to their essential elements. Generally, when you brief a case, you first summarize the background and facts of the case, as the authors have done for most of the cases presented in this text. You then indicate the issue (or issues) before the court. An important element in the case brief is, of course, the court's decision on the issue and the legal reasoning used by the court in reaching that decision.

Detailed instructions on how on to brief a case are given in Appendix A, which also includes a briefed version of the sample court case presented in Exhibit 1–6.

Exhibit 1–6 A Sample Court Case

The name contains the citation—the name of the case, the name of the court that heard the case, the reporters in which the court's opinion can be found, and the year of the decision.	**DOE v. KNOX COUNTY BOARD OF EDUCATION** United States Court of Appeals, Sixth Circuit 56 F.4th 1076 (2023)
This line provides the name of the judge (or justice) who authored the court's opinion.	Eric E. *MURPHY*, Circuit Judge * * * *
The court divides the opinion into sections, each headed by an explanatory heading. The first section summarizes the facts of the case.	**BACKGROUND** * * * *
Jane Doe (for females) and *John Doe* (for males) are placeholder names that courts use to conceal the real identity of an individual for privacy purposes.	**Jane Doe,** who lives with her parents near Knoxville, Tennessee, has a condition known as "misophonia" [which is] "a disorder of decreased tolerance to specific sounds or their associated stimuli." According to Doe, the normal sounds of eating food or chewing gum cause her to suffer "great fear and anxiety." These common noises trigger a "fight or flight" sensation, forcing Doe to escape from areas in which she hears them. They also exacerbate her recurring migraines. * * * *
A fact is *alleged* if it has been claimed but not yet proven as part of the legal proceedings.	[D]oe decided to attend L&N STEM Academy. This high school's policy **allegedly** allows each teacher to decide whether students may eat food and chew gum on a class-by-class basis. Some teachers, like Doe's ninth-grade math teacher, prohibit food and gum, so she has flourished in this class. * * * But other teachers, like Doe's ninth-grade history teacher, allegedly allow "rampant" eating and chewing. The high school also allows students to eat throughout an 80-minute elective ("Genius Hour") that Doe would like to take. L&N's permissive policies have forced Doe to avoid this elective and to leave her regular classes about 50% of the time, rendering her "physically and emotionally exhausted" at day's end.
A *ground* is the basis for a conviction or belief that supports a legal argument or action.	Doe's parents repeatedly asked Doe's teachers to ban eating and chewing during her classes. But some teachers allegedly have refused on the **ground** that L&N's

Exhibit 1–6 A Sample Court Case—Continued

An *accommodation* is an often-voluntary agreement that benefits a person or organization.	official policy permits this conduct. Doe's parents thus turned to the school's administrators, asking them for this **accommodation** about halfway through her ninth-grade year. * * * The administrators denied the request.

[Doe's parents brought a lawsuit on their daughter's] behalf against Knox County. They alleged that the county's refusal to grant Doe the requested accommodation—a classroom ban on eating and chewing for all students except those with medical needs—violated the **Americans with Disabilities Act [ADA].** * * * They requested a **permanent injunction** that would require L&N to implement the accommodation for Doe.

The *Americans with Disabilities Act (ADA)* is a federal law that prohibits disability-based discrimination and requires public entities to accommodate those with disabilities.

An *injunction* is a court order commanding a person or entity to do something or prohibit a person or entity from doing something. A *permanent injunction* is typically intended to stay in place permanently following a lawsuit's resolution.

A *motion* is a request made to a judge to take some specific action that favors the requesting party. A *motion for a preliminary injunction* is a request that one of the parties of the lawsuit be ordered to do something or refrain from doing something until the lawsuit's conclusion.

Along with their complaint, Doe's parents filed a **motion for a preliminary injunction**. During the injunction briefing, Knox County explained its rationale for refusing to ban eating and chewing in Doe's classrooms. * * * Because L&N operates more like a college, it has gathering spaces that can hold only 70 to 90 students and lacks a designated "cafeteria." L&N also has only two scheduled lunch periods during the school day because of the nature of its curriculum. If students could eat only at specified times, the school would have to change its "entire schedule[.]" * * * The school thus allows teachers to permit snacking during class.

* * * *

According to L&N's principal, Doe's teachers have all requested that her peers limit eating in class. But Doe responds that her case has now attracted unwanted local attention. * * * According to her father, this attention has caused some cruel students to target Doe by making noises that trigger her condition.

* * * *

A *motion to dismiss* requests that legal proceedings be discontinued because one of the parties has stated a claim that is legally faulty or insufficient.

Procedural grounds refer to the rules of procedure that must be followed by the parties and the courts in the American legal system.

To *appeal* is to request an appellate court to review the decision of a lower court.

[After the district court granted the Board of Education's **motion to dismiss** the case on **procedural grounds**, Doe's parents **appealed** to the U.S. Court of Appeals for the Sixth Circuit.]

Continues

Exhibit 1–6 A Sample Court Case—Continued

The second major section of the opinion responds to the party's appeal.	**DISCUSSION** Doe's parents * * * ask us to grant her a preliminary injunction requiring Knox County to implement her requested eating and chewing ban under the ADA. * * * To evaluate this request, we must ask, among other questions, whether Doe's parents have shown that they will likely succeed on their claims. They argue that they will likely
Under the ADA, a *reasonable accommodation* is a modification or adjustment to a business, educational, or other systemic environment that enables a person with disabilities to have the same opportunities as those without disabilities within that environment.	succeed because the ADA [requires] schools to make **"reasonable accommodations"** for the disabled, and they describe their requested eating and chewing ban as "reasonable."
In the context of the ADA, *discrimination* refers to unequal treatment of persons with disabilities in areas such as employment, transportation, public accommodations, and access to government programs and services.	* * * [The ADA] provides: "[N]o qualified individual with a disability shall, by reason of such disability, be excluded from participation in or be denied the benefits of the services, programs, or activities of a public entity, or be subjected to **discrimination**
A *neutral policy* would be a policy that does not favor one group over or another or, in this case, impacts all students equally.	by any such entity." Doe's parents do not argue that Knox County's **neutral policy** of giving teachers the power to allow students to eat in class engages in intentional "discrimination" against Doe. * * * So [they] must show that a switch from a policy allowing food in the classroom to a policy prohibiting food qualifies as a moderate (rather than a significant) change in the relevant policy. And they must confront the suggestion from L&N's principal that this change could require the college-like school to alter its "entire schedule" because it does not have a designated cafeteria. * * * *
In the third major section of the opinion, the court states its decision.	**CONCLUSION**
An appellate court *remands* a case when it orders the lower court to rehear the case or take some other action on the appellate court's instructions.	[W]e deny the request of Doe's parents that we grant a preliminary injunction on appeal and **remand** for the district court to consider the merits [of Doe's parents' lawsuit].

Practice and Review: Law and Legal Reasoning

Suppose that the California legislature passes a law that severely restricts carbon dioxide emissions from automobiles in that state. A group of automobile manufacturers files suit against the state of California to prevent the enforcement of the law. The automakers claim that a federal law already sets fuel economy standards nationwide and that fuel economy standards are essentially the same as carbon dioxide emission standards. According to the automobile manufacturers, it is unfair to allow California to impose more stringent regulations than those set by the federal law. Using the information presented in the chapter, answer the following questions.

1. Who are the parties (the plaintiffs and the defendant) in this lawsuit?
2. Are the plaintiffs seeking a legal remedy or an equitable remedy?
3. What is the primary source of the law that is at issue here?
4. Where would you look to find the relevant California and federal laws?

Debate This . . . Under the doctrine of *stare decisis,* courts are obligated to follow the precedents established in their jurisdiction unless there is a compelling reason not to. Should U.S. courts continue to adhere to this common law principle, given that our government now regulates so many areas by statute?

Terms and Concepts

administrative agency 5
administrative law 5
alleges 10
appellant 18
appellee 18
binding authority 8
breaches 6
case law 5
cases on point 10
citation 13
civil law 13
common law 6
concurring opinion 19
constitutional law 4
courts of equity 6
courts of law 6
criminal law 13
cyberlaw 13
damages 6

defendant 6
defense 6
dissenting opinion 19
equitable maxims 6
executive agencies 5
historical school 11
independent regulatory
  agencies 5
jurisprudence 11
laches 6
law 2
legal positivism 11
legal realism 12
legal reasoning 8
liability 2
majority opinion 19
natural law 11
opinions 19
ordinances 4

persuasive authorities 8
per curiam opinion 19
petitioner 6
plaintiff 6
plurality opinion 19
precedent 7
procedural law 12
remedies 6
remedies at law 6
remedies in equity 6
reporters 7
respondent 6
sociological school 12
stare decisis 8
statutes of limitations 6
statutory law 4
substantive law 12
uniform laws 4

Issue Spotters

1. Under what circumstances might a judge rely on case law to determine the intent and purpose of a statute? (See *Sources of American Law.*)

2. After World War II, several Nazis were convicted of "crimes against humanity" by an international court. Assuming that these convicted war criminals had not disobeyed any law of their country and had merely been following their government's orders, what law had they violated? Explain. (See *Schools of Legal Thought.*)

• **Check your answers to the Issue Spotters against the answers provided in Appendix B at the end of this text.**

Business Scenarios and Case Problems

1–1. Binding Versus Persuasive Authority. A county court in Illinois is deciding a case involving an issue that has never been addressed before in that state's courts. The Iowa Supreme Court, however, recently decided a case involving a very similar fact pattern. Is the Illinois court obligated to follow the Iowa Supreme Court's decision on the issue? If the United States Supreme Court had decided a similar case, would that decision be binding on the Illinois court? Explain. (See *The Common Law Tradition*.)

1–2. Sources of Law. This chapter discussed a number of sources of American law. Which source of law takes priority in the following situations, and why? (See *Sources of American Law*.)

(a) A federal statute conflicts with the U.S. Constitution.

(b) A federal statute conflicts with a state constitutional provision.

(c) A state statute conflicts with the common law of that state.

(d) A state constitutional amendment conflicts with the U.S. Constitution.

1–3. *Stare Decisis*. In this chapter, we stated that the doctrine of *stare decisis* "became a cornerstone of the English and American judicial systems." What does *stare decisis* mean, and why has this doctrine been so fundamental to the development of our legal tradition? (See *The Common Law Tradition*.)

1–4. Spotlight on AOL—Common Law. AOL, LLC, mistakenly made public the personal information of 650,000 of its members. The members filed a suit, alleging violations of California law. AOL asked the court to dismiss the suit on the basis of a "forum-selection clause" in its member agreement that designates Virginia courts as the place where member disputes will be tried. Under a decision of the United States Supreme Court, a forum-selection clause is unenforceable "if enforcement would contravene a strong public policy of the forum in which suit is brought." California courts have declared in other cases that the AOL clause contravenes a strong public policy. If the court applies the doctrine of *stare decisis*, will it dismiss the suit? Explain. [*Doe 1 v. AOL LLC*, 552 F.3d 1077 (9th Cir. 2009)] (See *The Common Law Tradition*.)

1–5. Business Case Problem with Sample Answer—Reading Citations. Assume that you want to read the entire court opinion in the case of *Dolly Investments, LLC v. MMG Sioux City, LLC*, 984 N.W.2d 168, 2023 WL 115159 (2023). Refer to the subsection entitled "Finding Case Law" in this chapter, and then explain specifically where you would find the court's opinion. (See *How to Find Primary Sources of Law*.)

● **For a sample answer to Problem 1–5, go to Appendix B at the end of this text.**

1–6. A Question of Ethics—The Doctrine of Precedent. Sandra White operated a travel agency. To obtain lower airline fares for her nonmilitary clients, she booked military-rate travel by forwarding fake military identification cards to the airlines. The government charged White with identity theft, which requires the "use" of another's identification. The trial court had two cases that represented precedents.

In the first case, David Miller obtained a loan to buy land by representing that certain investors had approved the loan when, in fact, they had not. Miller's conviction for identity theft was overturned because he had merely said that the investors had done something when they had not. According to the court, this was not the "use" of another's identification.

In the second case, Kathy Medlock, an ambulance service operator, had transported patients when there was no medical necessity to do so. To obtain payment, Medlock had forged a physician's signature. The court concluded that this was "use" of another person's identity. [*United States v. White*, 846 F.3d 170 (6th Cir. 2017)] (See *Sources of American Law*.)

(a) Which precedent—the *Miller* case or the *Medlock* case—is similar to White's situation, and why?

(b) In the two cases cited by the court, were there any ethical differences in the actions of the parties? Explain your answer.

Time-Limited Group Assignment

1–7. Court Opinions. Read through the subsection in this chapter entitled "Decisions and Opinions." (See *How to Read and Understand Case Law*.)

(a) One group will explain the difference between a concurring opinion and a majority opinion.

(b) Another group will outline the difference between a concurring opinion and a dissenting opinion.

(c) A third group will explain why judges and justices might write concurring and dissenting opinions, given that these opinions will not affect the outcome of the case at hand, which has already been decided by majority vote.

Chapter 2

Business and the Constitution

Laws that govern business have their origin in the lawmaking authority granted by the U.S. Constitution, which is the supreme law in this country. Neither Congress nor any state may pass a law that is in conflict with the Constitution.

Disputes over constitutional rights frequently come before the courts. Suppose Rebecca visits the Boutique Bakery in Eugene, Oregon, to order a wedding cake for her upcoming marriage to Sheryl. Albert, who owns the bakery, refuses to take the order because of religious objections to same-sex marriage. Rebecca then sues Albert in state court for violating an Oregon law that prohibits discrimination against customers based on their sexual orientation.

Albert counters that compelling him to bake the cake would violate his First Amendment right to freely exercise his religious beliefs. He also argues that the state cannot force him to express a message in favor of same-sex marriage, with which he disagrees. How should the court balance Rebecca's right to be free from discrimination against Albert's rights to freedom of religion and expression? In this chapter, we will examine the impact of the Constitution on America's business landscape, as well as the courts' role in resolving the conflicts that inevitably arise when constitutional rights are at stake.

2–1 The Constitutional Powers of Government

Following the Revolutionary War (1775–83), the states adopted the Articles of Confederation. The Articles created a confederal form of government in which the states had the authority to govern themselves and the national government could exercise only limited powers. Problems soon arose because the nation was facing an economic crisis and state laws interfered with the free flow of commerce. A national convention was called, and the delegates drafted the U.S. Constitution. This document, after its ratification by the states in 1789, became the basis for an entirely new form of government.

2–1a A Federal Form of Government

The new government created by the U.S. Constitution reflected a series of compromises made by the convention delegates on various issues. Some delegates wanted sovereign power to remain with the states. Others wanted the national government alone to exercise sovereign power. The end result was a compromise—a **federal form of government** in which the national government and the states share sovereign power.

Federal Powers The Constitution sets forth specific powers that can be exercised by the national (federal) government. It further provides that the national government has the implied power to undertake actions necessary to carry out its expressly designated powers (or enumerated powers). All other powers are expressly "reserved" to the states or to the people under the Tenth Amendment to the U.S. Constitution.

Regulatory Powers of the States As part of their inherent **sovereignty** (power to govern themselves), state governments have the authority to regulate certain affairs within their borders. As mentioned, this authority stems, in part, from the Tenth Amendment, which reserves all powers not delegated to the national government to the states or to the people.

State regulatory powers are often referred to as **police powers.** The term encompasses more than just the enforcement of criminal laws. Police powers also give state governments broad rights to regulate private activities to protect or promote the public order, health, safety, morals, and general welfare. Fire and building codes, antidiscrimination laws, parking regulations, zoning restrictions, licensing requirements, and thousands of other state statutes have been enacted pursuant to states' police powers. Local governments, such as cities, also exercise police powers.[1] Generally, state laws enacted pursuant to a state's police powers carry a strong presumption of validity.

2–1b Relations Among the States

The U.S. Constitution also includes provisions concerning relations among the states in our federal system. Particularly important are the "privileges and immunities clause" and the "full faith and credit clause."

The Privileges and Immunities Clause Article IV, Section 2, of the Constitution provides that the "Citizens of each State shall be entitled to all Privileges and Immunities of Citizens in the several States." This clause is often referred to as the interstate **privileges and immunities clause.** It prevents a state from imposing unreasonable burdens on citizens of another state—particularly with regard to means of livelihood or doing business.

When a citizen of one state engages in basic and essential activities in another state (the "foreign state"), the foreign state must have a substantial reason for treating the nonresident differently than it treats its own residents. Basic activities include transferring property, seeking employment, and accessing the court system. The foreign state must also establish that its reason for the discrimination is substantially related to the state's ultimate purpose in adopting the legislation or regulating the activity.[2]

The Full Faith and Credit Clause Article IV, Section 1, of the U.S. Constitution provides that "Full Faith and Credit shall be given in each State to the public Acts, Records, and judicial Proceedings of every other State." This clause, which is referred to as the **full faith and credit clause,** applies only to civil matters. It ensures that rights established under deeds, wills, contracts, and similar instruments in one state will be honored by other states. It also ensures that any judicial decision with respect to such property rights will be honored and enforced in all states.

The full faith and credit clause has contributed to the unity of American citizens because it protects their legal rights as they move about from state to state. It also

protects the rights of those to whom they owe obligations, such as persons who have been awarded monetary damages by courts. The ability to enforce such rights is extremely important for the conduct of business in a country with a very mobile citizenry.

2–1c The Separation of Powers

To make it more difficult for the national government to use its power arbitrarily, the Constitution provided for three branches of government. The legislative branch makes the laws, the executive branch enforces the laws, and the judicial branch interprets the laws. Each branch performs a separate function, and no branch may exercise the authority of another branch.

Additionally, a system of **checks and balances** allows each branch to limit the actions of the other two branches, thus preventing any one branch from exercising too much power. Some examples of these checks and balances include the following:

1. The legislative branch (Congress) can enact a law, but the executive branch (the president) has the constitutional authority to veto that law.
2. The executive branch is responsible for foreign affairs, but treaties with foreign governments require the advice and consent of the Senate.
3. Congress determines the jurisdiction of the federal courts, and the president appoints federal judges, with the advice and consent of the Senate. The judicial branch has the power to hold actions of the other two branches unconstitutional.[3]

2–1d The Commerce Clause

To prevent states from establishing laws and regulations that would interfere with trade and commerce among the states, the Constitution expressly delegated to the national government the power to regulate interstate commerce. Article I, Section 8, of the U.S. Constitution explicitly permits Congress "[t]o regulate Commerce with foreign Nations, and among the several States, and with the Indian Tribes." This clause, referred to as the **commerce clause,** has had a greater impact on business than any other provision in the Constitution. The commerce clause provides the basis for the national government's extensive regulation of state and even local affairs.

Initially, the courts interpreted the commerce clause to apply only to commerce between the states (interstate

---

1. Local governments derive their authority to regulate their communities from the state, because they are creatures of the state. In other words, they cannot come into existence unless authorized by the state to do so.
2. This test was first announced in *Supreme Court of New Hampshire v. Piper,* 470 U.S. 274, 105 S.Ct. 1272, 84 L.Ed.2d 205 (1985). For another example, see *Lee v. Miner,* 369 F.Supp.2d 527 (D.Del. 2005).

3. The power of judicial review was established by the United States Supreme Court in *Marbury v. Madison,* 5 U.S. (1 Cranch) 137, 2 L.Ed. 60 (1803).

commerce) and not commerce within the states (intra-state commerce). That changed in 1824, however, when the United States Supreme Court decided the landmark case of *Gibbons v. Ogden.*[4] The Court held that commerce within the states could also be regulated by the national government as long as the commerce substantially affected commerce involving more than one state.

The Expansion of National Powers Under the Commerce Clause As the nation grew and faced new kinds of problems, the commerce clause became a vehicle for the additional expansion of the national government's regulatory powers. Even activities that seemed purely local

in nature came under the regulatory reach of the national government if those activities were deemed to substantially affect interstate commerce. ■ **Case in Point 2.1** In a classic case from 1942, the Supreme Court held that wheat production by an individual farmer intended wholly for consumption on his own farm was subject to federal regulation. The Court reasoned that the home consumption of wheat reduced the market demand for wheat and thus could have a substantial effect on interstate commerce.[5] ■

The following Classic Case involved a challenge to the scope of the national government's constitutional authority to regulate local activities.

---

4. 22 U.S. (9 Wheat.) 1, 6 L.Ed. 23 (1824).

5. *Wickard v. Filburn,* 317 U.S. 111, 63 S.Ct. 82, 87 L.Ed. 122 (1942).

Classic Case 2.1

Heart of Atlanta Motel v. United States

Supreme Court of the United States, 379 U.S. 241, 85 S.Ct. 348, 13 L.Ed.2d 258 (1964).

Background and Facts In the 1950s, the United States Supreme Court ruled that racial segregation imposed by the states in school systems and other public facilities violated the Constitution. Privately owned facilities were not affected until Congress passed the Civil Rights Act in 1964, which prohibited racial discrimination in "establishments affecting interstate commerce."

The owner of the Heart of Atlanta Motel, in violation of the Civil Rights Act, refused to rent rooms to African Americans. The motel owner brought an action in a federal district court to have the Civil Rights Act declared unconstitutional on the ground that Congress had exceeded its constitutional authority to regulate commerce by enacting the statute.

The owner argued that his motel was not engaged in interstate commerce but was "of a purely local character." The motel, however, was accessible to state and interstate highways. The owner advertised nationally, maintained billboards throughout the state, and accepted convention trade from outside the state (75 percent of the guests were residents of other states).

The district court ruled that the act did not violate the Constitution and enjoined (prohibited) the owner from discriminating on the basis of race. The motel owner appealed. The case ultimately went to the United States Supreme Court.

In the Language of the Court

Mr. Justice CLARK delivered the opinion of the Court.

* * * *

While the Act as adopted carried no congressional findings, the record of its passage through each house is replete with evidence of the burdens that discrimination by race or color places upon interstate commerce * * * . This testimony included the fact that our people have become increasingly mobile with millions of all races traveling from State to State; that Negroes in particular have been the subject of discrimination in transient accommodations, having to travel great distances to secure the same; that often they have been unable to obtain accommodations and have had to call upon friends to put them up overnight. * * * These exclusionary practices were found to be nationwide, the Under Secretary of Commerce testifying that there is "no question that this discrimination in the North still exists to a large

Case 2.1 Continues

Case 2.1 Continued   degree" and in the West and Midwest as well * * * . This testimony indicated a qualitative as well as quantitative effect on interstate travel by Negroes. The former was the obvious impairment of the Negro traveler's pleasure and convenience that resulted when he continually was uncertain of finding lodging. As for the latter, there was evidence that this uncertainty stemming from racial discrimination had the effect of discouraging travel on the part of a substantial portion of the Negro community * * * . We shall not burden this opinion with further details since the voluminous testimony presents overwhelming evidence that discrimination by hotels and motels impedes interstate travel.

* * * *

It is said that the operation of the motel here is of a purely local character. But, assuming this to be true, "if it is interstate commerce that feels the pinch, it does not matter how local the operation that applies the squeeze." * * * Thus the power of Congress to promote interstate commerce also includes the power to regulate the local incidents thereof, including local activities in both the States of origin and destination, which might have a substantial and harmful effect upon that commerce.

Decision and Remedy The United States Supreme Court upheld the constitutionality of the Civil Rights Act of 1964. The power of Congress to regulate interstate commerce permitted the enactment of legislation that could halt local discriminatory practices.

Critical Thinking
- **What If the Facts Were Different?** If this case had involved a small, private retail business that did not advertise nationally, would the result have been the same? Why or why not?
- **Impact of This Case on Today's Law** If the United States Supreme Court had invalidated the Civil Rights Act of 1964, the legal landscape of the United States would be much different today. The act prohibits discrimination based on race, color, national origin, religion, gender, or sexual orientation in all "public accommodations," including hotels and restaurants.

  The act also prohibits discrimination in employment based on these criteria. Although state laws now prohibit many of these forms of discrimination as well, the protections available vary from state to state—and it is not certain whether such laws would have been passed had the outcome in this case been different.

The Commerce Clause Today Currently, at least theoretically, the power over commerce authorizes the national government to regulate almost every commercial enterprise in the United States. The breadth of the commerce clause permits the national government to legislate in areas in which Congress has not explicitly been granted power. Only occasionally has the Supreme Court curbed the national government's regulatory authority under the commerce clause.

The Supreme Court has, for instance, allowed the federal government to regulate noncommercial activities relating to medical marijuana that take place wholly within a state's borders. ■ **Case in Point 2.2** More than 30 states, including California, have adopted laws that legalize marijuana for medical purposes. A significant number of states also now permit the recreational use of marijuana. Marijuana possession, however, is illegal under the federal Controlled Substances Act (CSA).[6] After the federal government seized the marijuana that two

seriously ill California women were using on the advice of their physicians, the women filed a lawsuit. They argued that it was unconstitutional for the federal statute to prohibit them from using marijuana for medical purposes that were legal within the state.

The Supreme Court, though, held that Congress has the authority to prohibit the intrastate possession and noncommercial cultivation of marijuana as part of a larger regulatory scheme (the CSA).[7] That is to say, the federal government may still prosecute individuals for possession of marijuana even if they reside in a state where the use of marijuana is legal under state law. ■

The "Dormant" Commerce Clause The Supreme Court has interpreted the commerce clause to mean that the national government has the exclusive authority to regulate commerce that substantially affects trade and

6. 21 U.S.C. Sections 801 *et seq.*

7. *Gonzales v. Raich*, 545 U.S. 1, 125 S.Ct. 2195, 162 L.Ed.2d 1 (2005). See also *United States v. Bilodeau et al.*, 24 F.4th 705 (1st Cir. 2022).

commerce among the states. This express grant of authority to the national government is often referred to as the "positive" aspect of the commerce clause. But this positive aspect also implies a negative aspect—that the states do not have the authority to regulate interstate commerce. This negative aspect of the commerce clause is often referred to as the "dormant" (implied) commerce clause.

The dormant commerce clause comes into play when state regulations affect interstate commerce. In these situations, the courts weigh the state's interest in regulating a certain matter against the burden that the state's regulation places on interstate commerce. Because courts balance the interests involved, predicting the outcome in a particular case can be difficult. State laws that alter conditions of competition to favor in-state interests over out-of-state competitors in a market are usually invalidated, however.

■ **Case in Point 2.3** Tennessee law imposed a two-year residency requirement on any business entity that wanted to acquire a state liquor license. As a result, Total Wine, a large retail liquor chain, was blocked from opening a store in Nashville. Defending this action in court, Tennessee officials claimed that the residency requirement was justified under the Twenty-First Amendment, which gives states the responsibility of regulating alcohol for public benefit. The United States Supreme Court disagreed, finding that the law was primarily designed to shield state businesses from out-of-state competition. Without any realistic connection to health and safety measures, the Court ruled, the residency requirement did not "advance a legitimate local purpose" and therefore violated the dormant commerce clause.[8] ■

2–1e The Supremacy Clause and Federal Preemption

Article VI of the U.S. Constitution, commonly referred to as the **supremacy clause,** provides that the Constitution, laws, and treaties of the United States are "the supreme Law of the Land." When there is a direct conflict between a federal law and a state law, the state law is rendered invalid. Because some powers are concurrent (shared by the federal government and the states), however, it is necessary to determine which law governs in a particular circumstance.

Preemption When Congress chooses to act exclusively in a concurrent area, **preemption** occurs. In this circumstance, a valid federal statute or regulation will take precedence over a conflicting state or local law or regulation on the same general subject.

Congressional Intent Often, it is not clear whether Congress, in passing a law, intended to preempt an entire subject area. In these situations, the courts determine whether Congress intended to exercise exclusive power.

No single factor is decisive as to whether a court will find preemption. Generally, though, congressional intent to preempt will be found if a federal law regulating an activity is so pervasive, comprehensive, or detailed that the states have little or no room to regulate in that area. In addition, when a federal statute creates an agency to enforce the law, matters that may come within the agency's jurisdiction will likely preempt state laws.

■ **Case in Point 2.4** Workers at a meat-packing factory in Texas sued Tyson Foods, alleging that unsafe working conditions at the company's factory caused them to contract COVID-19. The workers filed, among other things, a negligence claim and a claim that the company had violated the Texas governor's stay-at-home order. The question before the court was whether these two claims were preempted by federal law. The first claim, arguing negligence on the part of Tyson Foods, was indeed preempted by the federal Meat Inspection Act. The second claim was preempted by the Defense Procedure Act because the president had issued an executive order instructing the secretary of agriculture to "take all appropriate action . . . to ensure that meat and poultry processors continue operations. . . ." The court granted Tyson Foods' motion to dismiss.[9] ■

2–1f The Taxing and Spending Powers

Article I, Section 8, of the U.S. Constitution provides that Congress has the "Power to lay and collect Taxes, Duties, Imposts, and Excises." Section 8 further requires uniformity in taxation among the states, and thus Congress may not tax some states while exempting others.

In the distant past, if Congress attempted to regulate indirectly, by taxation, an area over which it had no authority, the courts would invalidate the tax. Today, however, if a tax measure is reasonable, it generally is held to be within the national taxing power. Moreover, the expansive interpretation of the commerce clause almost always provides a basis for sustaining a federal tax.

Article I, Section 8, also gives Congress its spending power—the power "to pay the Debts and provide for the common Defence and general Welfare of the

8. *Tennessee Wine and Spirits Retailers Associations v. Thomas,* 588 U.S. ___, 139 S.Ct. 2440, 204 L.Ed.2d 801 (2019).

9. *Johnson, et al. v. Tyson Foods, Inc.,* 580 F.Supp. 3d 382 (N.D. TX 2022).

United States." Through the use of its spending power, Congress can require states to comply with specified conditions of particular federal programs before the state is qualified to receive federal funds. The spending power necessarily involves policy choices, with which taxpayers (and politicians) may disagree.

2–2 Business and the Bill of Rights

The importance of a written declaration of the rights of individuals caused the first Congress of the United States to submit twelve amendments to the U.S. Constitution to the states for approval. Ten of these amendments, known as the **Bill of Rights,** were adopted in 1791 and embody a series of protections for the individual against various types of interference by the federal government.[10]

The protections guaranteed by these ten amendments are summarized in Exhibit 2–1. Some of these

10. Another of these proposed amendments was ratified more than two hundred years later (in 1992) and became the Twenty-seventh Amendment to the Constitution.

constitutional protections apply to business entities as well as individuals. For instance, corporations exist as separate legal entities, or "legal persons," and enjoy many of the same rights and privileges as "natural persons" do.

2–2a Limits on Federal and State Governmental Actions

As originally intended, the Bill of Rights limited only the powers of the national government. Over time, however, the United States Supreme Court "incorporated" most of these rights into the protections against state actions afforded by the Fourteenth Amendment to the Constitution.

The Fourteenth Amendment The Fourteenth Amendment, passed in 1868 after the Civil War, provides, in part, that "[n]o State shall . . . deprive any person of life, liberty, or property, without due process of law." Starting in 1925, the Supreme Court began to define various rights and liberties guaranteed in the U.S. Constitution as constituting "due process of law," which was required of state governments under that amendment.

Today, most of the rights and liberties set forth in the Bill of Rights apply to state governments as well as the

Exhibit 2–1 Protections Guaranteed by the Bill of Rights

First Amendment:	Guarantees the freedoms of religion, speech, and the press and the rights to assemble peaceably and to petition the government.
Second Amendment:	States that the right of the people to keep and bear arms shall not be infringed.
Third Amendment:	Prohibits, in peacetime, the lodging of soldiers in any house without the owner's consent.
Fourth Amendment:	Prohibits unreasonable searches and seizures of persons or property.
Fifth Amendment:	Guarantees the rights to indictment (formal accusation) by a grand jury, to due process of law, and to fair payment when private property is taken for public use. The Fifth Amendment also prohibits compulsory self-incrimination and double jeopardy (trial for the same crime twice).
Sixth Amendment:	Guarantees the accused in a criminal case the right to a speedy and public trial by an impartial jury and with counsel. Accused persons have the right to cross-examine witnesses against them and to solicit testimony from witnesses in their favor.
Seventh Amendment:	Guarantees the right to a trial by jury in a civil case involving at least twenty dollars.
Eighth Amendment:	Prohibits excessive bail and fines, as well as cruel and unusual punishment.
Ninth Amendment:	Establishes that the people have rights in addition to those specified in the Constitution.
Tenth Amendment:	Establishes that those powers neither delegated to the federal government nor denied to the states are reserved to the states and to the people.

national government. In other words, neither the federal government nor state governments can deprive persons of those rights and liberties.

Judicial Interpretation The rights secured by the Bill of Rights are not absolute. Many of the rights guaranteed by the first ten amendments are set forth in very general terms. The Second Amendment, for instance, states that people have a right to keep and bear arms, but it does not describe the extent of this right. As the Supreme Court has noted, this right does not mean that people can "keep and carry any weapon whatsoever in any manner whatsoever and for whatever purpose."[11] Legislatures can prohibit the carrying of concealed weapons or certain types of weapons, such as machine guns.

Ultimately, the United States Supreme Court, as the final interpreter of the Constitution, gives meaning to these rights and determines their boundaries. Changing public views on controversial topics, such as gun rights, privacy, and the rights of LGBTQ+ residents, can affect the way the Supreme Court decides a case.

2–2b Freedom of Speech

A democratic form of government cannot survive unless people can freely voice their political opinions and criticize government actions or policies. Freedom of speech, particularly political speech, is thus a prized right, and traditionally the courts have protected this right to the fullest extent possible.

Symbolic speech—gestures, movements, articles of clothing, and other forms of expressive conduct—is also given substantial protection by the courts. The Supreme Court has held that the burning of the American flag as part of a peaceful protest is a constitutionally protected form of expression.[12] Similarly, wearing a T-shirt with a photo of a presidential candidate is constitutionally protected. ■ **Example 2.5** As a form of expression, Nate has gang signs tattooed on his torso, arms, neck, and legs. If a reasonable person would interpret this conduct as conveying a message, then it might be a protected form of symbolic speech. ■

Reasonable Restrictions A balance must be struck between a government's obligation to protect its citizens and those citizens' exercise of their rights.

Expression—oral, written, or symbolized by conduct—is therefore subject to reasonable restrictions. Reasonableness is analyzed on a case-by-case basis.

(See this chapter's Digital Update feature for a discussion of how the United States Supreme Court balanced the government's obligation against the rights of a convicted sex offender.)

Content-Neutral Laws. Laws that regulate the time, manner, and place, but not the content, of speech receive less scrutiny by the courts than do laws that restrict the content of expression. If a restriction imposed by the government is content neutral, then a court may allow it. To be content neutral, the restriction must be aimed at combatting some societal problem, such as crime or drug abuse, and not be aimed at suppressing the expressive conduct or its message.

Courts have often protected nude dancing as a form of symbolic expression but typically allow content-neutral laws that ban all public nudity. ■ **Case in Point 2.6** Ria Ora was charged with dancing nude at an annual "anti-Christmas" protest in Harvard Square in Cambridge, Massachusetts, under a statute banning public displays of open and gross lewdness. Ora argued that the statute was overbroad and unconstitutional, and a trial court agreed. On appeal, however, a state appellate court upheld the statute as constitutional in situations in which there was an unsuspecting or unwilling audience.[13] ■

Laws That Restrict the Content of Speech. Any law that regulates the content of expression must serve a compelling state interest and must be narrowly written to achieve that interest. Under the **compelling government interest** test, the government's interest is balanced against the individual's constitutional right to free expression. For the statute to be valid, there must be a compelling government interest that can be furthered only by the law in question.

■ **Case in Point 2.7** The Consolidated Edison Company placed documents celebrating nuclear power in its billing envelopes. The New York Public Service Commission responded by barring all utilities from discussing public policy in communications with customers. The majority of the *Court* could not find any compelling reason for New York to restrict Consolidated Edison's free speech in this manner. The Court reasoned that the possibility that content may offend some customers does not

---

11. *District of Columbia v. Heller*, 554 U.S. 570, 128 S.Ct. 2783, 171 L.Ed.2d 637 (2008).

12. *Texas v. Johnson*, 491 U.S. 397, 109 S.Ct. 2533, 105 L.Ed.2d 342 (1989).

13. *Commonwealth of Massachusetts v. Ora*, 451 Mass. 125, 883 N.E.2d 1217 (2008). See also *Commonwealth v. Durot*, 99 Mass.App.Ct. 1103, 159 N.W.3d 1082 (2020).

Digital Update   Does Everyone Have a Constitutional Right to Use Social Media?

Social media have become the predominant means by which many Americans communicate, obtain news updates, and discover what is "trending." At least one state, though, legislated a ban on the use of social media by convicted sex offenders. One of them chose to challenge the law.

North Carolina and the Use of Social Media

North Carolina's legislature passed the "Protect Children from Sexual Predators Act" in an attempt to prevent predators from finding potential victims on the internet. Part of that act was codified as North Carolina General Statute 14-202.5. About a thousand sex offenders had been prosecuted for violating this law.

A Long Road Through the Courts

When convicted sex offender Lester Packingham, Jr., wrote a Facebook post about a traffic ticket, a police officer saw the post and reported it, and Packingham was convicted of violating a criminal statute. He fought his conviction, and on appeal, it was overturned. The state then appealed, and the North Carolina Supreme Court ruled in the state's favor.[a]

Packingham appealed to the United States Supreme Court, where he prevailed. The Court pointed out that prohibiting sex offenders from accessing all social media violates their First Amendment rights to free speech. Further, this prohibition "bars access to what for many are the principal sources of knowing current events, checking ads for employment, speaking and listening in a modern public square, and otherwise exploring the vast realms of human thought and knowledge."[b]

Critical Thinking The Court said in its opinion that "specific criminal acts are not protected speech even if speech is the means for their commission." What use of social media and the internet might therefore still be unlawful (and not protected free speech) for registered sex offenders?

---

a. *State of North Carolina v. Packingham*, 368 N.C. 380, 777 S.E.2d 738 (2015).

b. *Packingham v. State of North Carolina*, 582 U.S. 98, 137 S.Ct. 1730, 198 L.Ed.2d 273 (2017). See also *Williams v. Zmuda*, 2022 WL 683343 (D. KS 2022).

---

justify its prohibition. This is particularly true, the Court noted, given how easy it is for customers to throw any offending documents in the trash.[14] ∎

Corporate Political Speech Political speech by corporations also falls within the protection of the First Amendment. Many years ago, the United States Supreme Court struck down as unconstitutional a Massachusetts statute that prohibited corporations from making political contributions or expenditures that individuals were permitted to make.[15] As described in Case in Point 2.7, the Court has also held that a law forbidding a corporation from including inserts with its bills to

express its views on controversial issues violates the First Amendment.[16]

Corporate political speech continues to receive significant protection under the First Amendment. ∎ **Case in Point 2.8** In *Citizens United v. Federal Election Commission*,[17] the Supreme Court issued a landmark decision that overturned a twenty-year-old precedent on campaign financing. The case involved Citizens United, a nonprofit corporation.

Citizens United had produced a film called *Hillary: The Movie* that was critical of Hillary Clinton, who was seeking the Democratic nomination for the presidency. Campaign-finance law restricted Citizens United from broadcasting the movie. The Court ruled that these

---

14. *Consolidated Edison Co. v. Public Service Commission*, 447 U.S. 530, 100 S.Ct. 2326, 65 L.Ed.2d 319 (1980). See also *Brewer v. City of Albuquerque*, 18 F.4th 1205 (10th Cir. 2021).

15. *First National Bank of Boston v. Bellotti*, 435 U.S. 765, 98 S.Ct. 1407, 55 L.Ed.2d 707 (1978).

16. *Consolidated Edison Co. v. Public Service Commission*, 447 U.S. 530, 100 S.Ct. 2326, 65 L.Ed.2d 319 (1980).

17. 558 U.S. 310, 130 S.Ct. 876, 175 L.Ed.2d 753 (2010).

restrictions were unconstitutional and that the First Amendment prevents limits from being placed on independent political expenditures by corporations. ∎

Commercial Speech The courts also give substantial protection to commercial speech, which consists of communications—primarily advertising and marketing—made by business firms that involve only their commercial interests. The protection given to commercial speech under the First Amendment is less extensive than that afforded to noncommercial speech, however.

A state may restrict certain kinds of advertising, for instance, in the interest of preventing consumers from being misled. States also have a legitimate interest in roadside beautification and therefore may impose restraints on billboard advertising.

Generally, a restriction on commercial speech will be considered valid as long as it meets three criteria:

1. It must seek to implement a substantial government interest.
2. It must directly advance that interest.
3. It must go no further than necessary to accomplish its objective.

At issue in the following case was whether a government agency had unconstitutionally restricted commercial speech when it prohibited the inclusion of a certain illustration on beer labels.

Spotlight on Beer Labels

Case 2.2 Bad Frog Brewery, Inc. v. New York State Liquor Authority

United States Court of Appeals, Second Circuit, 134 F.3d 87 (1998).

Background and Facts Bad Frog Brewery, Inc., makes and sells alcoholic beverages. Some of the beverages feature labels that display a drawing of a frog making the gesture generally known as "giving the finger." Bad Frog's authorized New York distributor, Renaissance Beer Company, applied to the New York State Liquor Authority (NYSLA) for brand label approval, as required by state law before the beer could be sold in New York.

The NYSLA denied the application, in part, because "the label could appear in grocery and convenience stores, with obvious exposure on the shelf to children of tender age." Bad Frog filed a suit in a federal district court against the NYSLA, asking for, among other things, an injunction against the denial of the application. The court granted summary judgment in favor of the NYSLA. Bad Frog appealed to the U.S. Court of Appeals for the Second Circuit.

In the Language of the Court
Jon O. NEWMAN, Circuit Judge:
    * * * *
    * * * To support its asserted power to ban Bad Frog's labels [NYSLA advances] * * * the State's interest in "protecting children from vulgar and profane advertising" * * * .
    [This interest is] substantial * * * . States have a compelling interest in protecting the physical and psychological wellbeing of minors * * * .
    * * * *
    * * * NYSLA endeavors to advance the state interest in preventing exposure of children to vulgar displays by taking only the limited step of barring such displays from the labels of alcoholic beverages. In view of the wide currency of vulgar displays throughout contemporary society, including comic books targeted directly at children, barring such displays from labels for alcoholic beverages cannot realistically be expected to reduce children's exposure to such displays to any significant degree.
    * * * If New York decides to make a substantial effort to insulate children from vulgar displays in some significant sphere of activity, at least with respect to materials likely to be seen by children, NYSLA's label prohibition might well be found to make a justifiable contribution to the material advancement of such an effort, but its currently isolated response to the perceived problem, applicable only to labels on a product that children cannot purchase, does not suffice. * * * A state must

Case 2.2 Continues

Case 2.2 Continued demonstrate that its commercial speech limitation is part of a substantial effort to advance a valid state interest, not merely the removal of a few grains of offensive sand from a beach of vulgarity.

* * * *

* * * Even if we were to assume that the state materially advances its asserted interest by shielding children from viewing the Bad Frog labels, it is plainly excessive to prohibit the labels from all use, including placement on bottles displayed in bars and taverns where parental supervision of children is to be expected. Moreover, to whatever extent NYSLA is concerned that children will be harmfully exposed to the Bad Frog labels when wandering without parental supervision around grocery and convenience stores where beer is sold, that concern could be less intrusively dealt with by placing restrictions on the permissible locations where the appellant's products may be displayed within such stores.

Decision and Remedy The U.S. Court of Appeals for the Second Circuit reversed the judgment of the district court and remanded the case for the entry of a judgment in favor of Bad Frog. The NYSLA's ban on the use of the labels lacked a "reasonable fit" with the state's interest in shielding minors from vulgarity. In addition, the NYSLA had not adequately considered alternatives to the ban.

Critical Thinking

- **What If the Facts Were Different?** If Bad Frog had sought to use the offensive label to market toys instead of beer, would the court's ruling likely have been the same? Why or why not?
- **Legal Environment** Whose interests are advanced by the banning of certain types of advertising?

Unprotected Speech The United States Supreme Court has made it clear that certain types of speech will not be protected under the First Amendment. Unprotected speech includes fighting words, or words that are likely to incite others to respond violently. It also includes speech that harms the good reputation of another, or defamatory speech. In addition, speech that violates criminal laws is not constitutionally protected. Speech that violates criminal laws includes threatening speech and certain types of obscene speech, such as that involving child pornography.

Threatening Speech. In the case of threatening speech, the speaker must have posed a "true threat"—that is, must have meant to communicate a serious intent to commit an unlawful, violent act against a particular person or group. ■ **Case in Point 2.9** While awaiting trial on various firearm and drug charges, James Knox appeared in a YouTube music video called "F*** the Police." In the video, Knox identified two Pittsburgh law enforcement officers involved in his arrest and rapped that he was going to "jam this rusty knife" into one of the officer's "guts" and "chop his feet." Knox was eventually convicted of making terrorist threats. On appeal, he argued that his video was a piece of artistic expression protected by the First Amendment.

The Pennsylvania Supreme Court rejected this defense. Knox's lyrics, the court found, went well beyond a general animosity towards the police. Besides referring to the two law enforcement officers by name, Knox claimed to know when they would go off duty. He also pledged to murder one of the officer's confidential informants and bragged

about making fake 911 calls and killing any police officer who responded. According to the court, this level of specificity differentiated Knox's words from "mere" violent lyrics, which would have been protected speech, and "true threats," which were not.[18] ■

Obscene Speech. The First Amendment, as interpreted by the Supreme Court, does not protect obscene speech. Numerous state and federal statutes make it a crime to disseminate and possess obscene materials, including child pornography. Objectively defining obscene speech has proved difficult, however. It is even more difficult to prohibit the dissemination of obscenity and pornography online.

Most of Congress's attempts to pass legislation protecting minors from pornographic materials on the internet have been struck down on First Amendment grounds when challenged in court. One exception is a law that requires public schools and libraries to install **filtering software** on computers to keep children from accessing adult content.[19] Such software is designed to prevent persons from viewing certain websites based on a site's internet address or its **meta tags,** or key words. The Supreme Court held that the act does not unconstitutionally burden free speech because it is flexible and libraries can disable the filters for any patrons who ask.[20]

---

18. *Commonwealth of Pennsylvania v. Knox*, 847 Pa. 593, 190 A.3d 1146 (2018).
19. Children's Internet Protection Act (CIPA), 17 U.S.C. Sections 1701–1741.
20. *United States v. American Library Association*, 539 U.S. 194, 123 S.Ct. 2297, 156 L.Ed.2d 221 (2003). See also *State of Washington v. Smith*, 13 Wash.App.2d 1107 (2020).

2–2c Freedom of Religion

The First Amendment states that the government may neither establish any religion nor prohibit the free exercise of religious practices. The first part of this constitutional provision is referred to as the **establishment clause,** and the second part is known as the **free exercise clause**. Government action, both federal and state, must be consistent with this constitutional mandate.

The Establishment Clause The establishment clause prohibits the government from establishing a state-sponsored religion, as well as from passing laws that promote (aid or endorse) religion or show a preference for one religion over another. Although the establishment clause involves the separation of church and state, it does not require a complete separation.

Applicable Standard. Establishment clause cases often involve such issues as the legality of allowing or requiring school prayers, using state-issued vouchers to pay tuition at religious schools, and teaching creation theories versus evolution. Federal or state laws that do not promote or place a significant burden on religion are constitutional even if they have some impact on religion. For a government law or policy to be constitutional, it must not have the primary effect of promoting or inhibiting religion.

Religious Displays. Religious displays on public property have often been challenged as violating the establishment clause. The United States Supreme Court has ruled on a number of such cases, often focusing on the proximity of the religious display to nonreligious symbols or on the balance of symbols from different religions. The Supreme Court eventually decided that public displays having historical, as well as religious, significance do not necessarily violate the establishment clause.

■ **Case in Point 2.10** Mount Soledad is a prominent hill near San Diego. There has been a forty-foot cross on top of Mount Soledad since 1913. In the 1990s, a war memorial with six walls listing the names of veterans was constructed next to the cross. The site was privately owned until 2006, when Congress authorized the property's transfer to the federal government "to preserve a historically significant war memorial."

Steve Trunk and the Jewish War Veterans filed lawsuits claiming that the cross violated the establishment clause because it endorsed the Christian religion. A federal appellate court agreed, finding that the primary effect of the memorial as a whole sent a strong message of endorsement of Christianity and exclusion of non-Christian veterans. The court noted that although not all cross displays at war memorials violate the establishment clause, the cross in this case physically dominated the site. Additionally, it was originally dedicated to religious purposes, had a long history of religious use, and was the only portion visible to drivers on the freeway below.[21] ■

The Free Exercise Clause The free exercise clause guarantees that people can hold any religious beliefs they want or can hold no religious beliefs. The constitutional guarantee of personal freedom restricts only the actions of the government, however, and not those of individuals or private businesses. We examine the application of the free exercise clause of the Constitution in the following case.

---

21. *Trunk v. City of San Diego*, 629 F.3d 1099 (9th Cir. 2011). See also *Catholic Healthcare International, Inc., et al. v Genoa Charter Township, Michigan, et al.*, 2021 WL 5277096 (6th Cir. 2021).

Case 2.3

Jones v. Slade

United States Court of Appeals, Ninth Circuit, 23 F. 4th 1124 (2022)

Background and Facts Edward Lee Jones, Jr., was incarcerated at the Arizona State Prison Complex. He ordered some music CDs and two Nation of Islam texts. All the items that he ordered, including the texts, were confiscated as contraband pursuant to Arizona Department of Corrections (ADC) Order 914, which regulates the content of incoming mail. Jones sued the Arizona Department of Corrections for violating his free speech rights and for substantially burdening his religious exercise in violation of the free exercise clause of the First Amendment to the U.S. Constitution. The defendants filed a motion for summary judgment in a U.S. district court, which granted it. Jones appealed to a U.S. court of appeals.

Case 2.3 Continues

Case 2.3 Continued

In the Language of the Court

Jay S. Bybee, Circuit Judge:

* * * *

The Arizona Department of Corrections regulates the content of incoming mail pursuant to Department Order 914 (DO 914) * * * . [This order's] stated purpose is "maintaining the safety, security and orderly operations of the institutions." Under the policy, staff at each ADC facility will "open, inspect and read incoming mail to prevent criminal activity and prevent inmates from receiving contraband or any other material that may be detrimental to the safe and orderly operations of the institution." Publications—which include CDs, books, and magazines—are subject to additional procedures. * * * ADC staff inspect the content of each CD or publication that enters ADC facilities "[i]n order to assist with rehabilitation and treatment objectives, reduce sexual harassment and prevent a hostile environment for inmates, staff and volunteers." * * * DO 914.07, titled "Unauthorized Content," sets forth twenty broad categories * * *. It also has a catch-all provision for any publication deemed "detrimental to the safe, secure, and orderly operation of the institution." * * * DO 914.07 prohibits inmates from receiving publications containing the following:

> * * * *
>
> * * * "Content that is oriented toward and/or promotes racism and/or religious oppression and the superiority of one race/religion/political group over another, and/or the degradation of one race/religion/political group by another."
>
> * * * "Any publication or part of a publication that, although not specifically set forth herein, may otherwise be detrimental to the safe, secure, and orderly operation of the institution."
>
> * * * *

The following facts are largely undisputed. * * * [Jones] is a member of the Nation of Islam and a follower of the teachings of Elijah Muhammad, who Jones considers to be the last prophet of Allah. Jones believes that Elijah Muhammad's writings are essential religious texts that provide him with religious instruction, including teachings of how to pray. Jones considers Elijah Muhammad's writings central to his belief system and that reading Muhammad's texts is one way he may practice and express his religion.

* * * *

Jones had * * * ordered two books by Elijah Muhammad: *Message to the Blackman in America* (1965) and *The Fall of America* (1973). Both were excluded under DO 914.07 * * * for promoting racism or the superiority of one group. ADC staff excluded the books without review because each text had been previously excluded by an ADC facility. Jones sought second-level review of the text exclusions, but OPR informed Jones that the exclusions of *Messages to the Blackman* and *The Fall of America* had been upheld previously and that those second-level decisions would remain final.

* * * Jones lodged a * * * civil rights complaint [against several ADC employees] in district court * * *, alleging * * * violations of the Free Speech and Free Exercise Clause of the First Amendment and Due Process Clause of the Fourteenth Amendment * * *. Jones sought injunctive and monetary relief, including punitive damages * * *.

The district court granted summary judgment in favor of the Defendants on all claims.

* * * *

[With] respect to Jones's * * * free-exercise claims, * * * the [district] court held that the exclusion of the two religious texts did not substantially burden Jones's religious practice. * * *

* * * *

The Free Exercise Clause of the First Amendment, made applicable to the States through the Fourteenth Amendment, provides that "Congress shall make no law respecting an establishment of religion, or prohibiting the free exercise thereof. . . ." * * * . The right to free exercise is to be "jealously guarded." * * * But free exercise is necessarily limited by the fact of incarceration and "may be curtailed in order to achieve legitimate correctional goals or to maintain prison security." * * * To merit protection under the Free Exercise Clause, Jones's belief must be "sincerely held" and religious in nature. * * * Once a claimant demonstrates that the challenged regulation impinges on his sincerely held religious exercise, the burden shifts to the government to show that the regulation is "reasonably related to legitimate penological interests." * * *

The district court concluded that * * * Jones "failed to demonstrate that Defendants have substantially burdened the practice of his religion by excluding his two requested books." [The appellate court, however, found that the district court's analysis did] not hold up under the Free Exercise Clause. The Free Exercise Clause does not require plaintiffs to prove the centrality or consistency of their religious practice: "It is not within the judicial ken [knowledge or understanding] to question the centrality of particular beliefs or practices to a faith." * * * [I]t was impermissible for the district court to focus on whether reading Elijah Muhammad's texts is required to observe Ramadan [an Islamic holy month], rather than whether Jones sincerely believes reading these texts during Ramadan is consistent with his faith. * * *

Decision and Remedy The district court's judgment granting the defendants' motion for summary judgment was reversed. The appeals court remanded this case for further proceedings consistent with its opinion. The court concluded that there is a "material question as to whether the Arizona Department of Corrections' exclusion of Jones's religious texts pursuant to [internal regulations] infringes on his right to engage in his sincerely held religious belief, [and therefore] summary judgment was inappropriate."

Critical Thinking

- **Legal Environment** Because the plaintiff in this case was in prison, did he nonetheless have all the free exercise rights that those not incarcerated have?
- **What If the Facts Were Different?** Suppose that Jones had never declared to any prison authorities that he was religious in any way whatsoever. Do you think he would have succeeded in his request to dismiss the district court's summary judgment against him? Why or why not?

Restrictions Must Be Necessary. The government must have a compelling state interest for restricting the free exercise of religion, and the restriction must be the only way to further that interest. ■ **Case in Point 2.11** The Affordable Care Act (ACA) requires employer-sponsored health plans to provide contraceptives and pregnancy "preventive services" to employees. A company that objects to this rule for religious reasons can "opt out" by filing notice with the federal government. For Steven Hotze, the owner of Braidwood Management, the very act of filling out this paperwork went against the principles of his religious faith. To keep from having to do so, he and several other plaintiffs brought a lawsuit against the government claiming that their free exercise of religion was being violated.

A federal court in Texas agreed and issued an injunction against the ACA's contraception orders. The court found that as long as a corporate entity or business owner sincerely believes that filling out paperwork makes them complicit in providing contraceptives, that belief can be considered religious. Therefore, to require them to complete the paperwork is a substantial burden on their free exercise rights. As a result of this decision, the government would have to find another, less restrictive, way to ensure employee access to contraceptives.[22] ■

Restrictions Must Not Be a Substantial Burden. To comply with the free exercise clause, a government action must not place a substantial burden on religious practices. A burden is substantial if it pressures individuals to modify their behavior and to violate their beliefs.

Public Welfare Exception. When religious *practices* work against public policy and the public welfare, the government can act. For instance, the government can require that a child receive certain types of vaccinations or medical treatment if the child's life is in danger—regardless of the child's or parent's religious beliefs. When public safety is an issue, an individual's religious beliefs often have to give way to the government's interest in protecting the public.

2–2d Searches and Seizures

The Fourth Amendment protects the "right of the people to be secure in their persons, houses, papers, and effects." Before searching or seizing private property, law enforcement officers must usually obtain a **search warrant**—an order from a judge or other public official authorizing the search or seizure. Because of the strong government interest in protecting the public, however, a warrant normally is not required for seizures of spoiled or contaminated food. Nor are warrants required for searches of businesses in such highly regulated industries as liquor, guns, and strip mining.

---

22. *Deotte v. Azar*, 332 F.R.D. 173, 104 Fed.R.Serv.3d 566 (N.D. Tex. 2019).

To obtain a search warrant, law enforcement officers must convince a judge that they have reasonable grounds, or **probable cause,** to believe a search will reveal evidence of a specific illegality. To establish probable cause, the officers must have trustworthy evidence that would convince a reasonable person that the proposed search or seizure is more likely justified than not.

■ **Case in Point 2.12** Citlalli Flores was driving across the border into the United States from Tijuana, Mexico, when a border protection officer became suspicious because she was acting nervous and looking around inside her car. On further inspection, the officer found thirty-six pounds of marijuana hidden in the car's quarter panels. Flores claimed that she had not known about the marijuana.

Flores was arrested for importing marijuana into the United States. She then made two jail-recorded phone calls in which she asked her cousin to delete whatever he felt needed to be removed from Flores's Facebook page. The government got a warrant to search Flores's Facebook messages, where they found references to her "carrying" or "bringing" marijuana into the United States that day. Flores's Facebook posts were later used as evidence against her at trial, and she was convicted.

On appeal, the court held that the phone calls had given the officers probable cause to support a warrant to search Flores's social networking site for incriminating statements. Her conviction was affirmed.[23] ■

2–2e Self-Incrimination

The Fifth Amendment guarantees that no person "shall be compelled in any criminal case to be a witness against himself." Thus, in any court proceeding, an accused person cannot be forced to give testimony that might subject them to any criminal prosecution. The guarantee applies to both federal and state proceedings because the due process clause of the Fourteenth Amendment (discussed shortly) extends the protection to state courts.

The Fifth Amendment's guarantee against self-incrimination extends only to natural persons. Neither corporations nor partnerships receive Fifth Amendment protection. When a partnership is required to produce business records, it must therefore do so even if the information provided incriminates the individual partners of the firm. In contrast, sole proprietors and sole practitioners (those who individually own their businesses) cannot be compelled to produce their business records. These individuals have full protection against self-incrimination because there is no separate business entity.

23. *United States v. Flores*, 802 F.3d 1028 (9th Cir. 2015). See also *United States v. Turner*, 2022 WL 195083 (D. NV 2022).

2–3 Due Process and Equal Protection

Other constitutional guarantees of great significance to Americans are mandated by the due process clauses of the Fifth and Fourteenth Amendments and the equal protection clause of the Fourteenth Amendment.

2–3a Due Process

Both the Fifth and Fourteenth Amendments provide that no person shall be deprived "of life, liberty, or property, without due process of law." The **due process clause** of these constitutional amendments has two aspects—procedural and substantive. Note that the due process clause applies to "legal persons" (that is, corporations), as well as to individuals.

Procedural Due Process Procedural due process requires that any government decision to take life, liberty, or property must be made equitably. In other words, the government must give a person proper notice and an opportunity to be heard. Fair procedures must be used in determining whether a person will be subjected to punishment or to the imposition of some burden.

Fair procedure has been interpreted as requiring that the person have at least an opportunity to object to a proposed action before an impartial, neutral decision maker (who need not be a judge). ■ **Example 2.13** Doyle Burns, a nursing student in Kansas, poses for a photograph standing next to a mound of marijuana. Although she quickly deletes the photo from her library, it ends up on Facebook. When the director of nursing sees the photo, Burns is expelled. She sues for reinstatement and wins. The school violated Burns's due process rights by expelling her from the nursing program for taking a photo without giving her an opportunity to present her side to school authorities. ■

Substantive Due Process Substantive due process focuses on the content of legislation rather than the fairness of procedures. Substantive due process limits what the government may do in its legislative and executive capacities. Legislation must be fair and reasonable in content and must further a legitimate governmental objective.

If a law or other governmental action limits a fundamental right, the state must have a legitimate and compelling interest to justify its action. Fundamental rights include interstate travel, voting, marriage and family, and all First Amendment rights. Thus, for instance, a state must have a substantial reason for taking any action that infringes on a person's free speech rights.

In situations not involving fundamental rights, a law or action does not violate substantive due process if it rationally relates to any legitimate government purpose. It is almost impossible for a law or action to fail this test.

2–3b Equal Protection

Under the Fourteenth Amendment, a state may not "deny to any person within its jurisdiction the equal protection of the laws." The United States Supreme Court has interpreted the due process clause of the Fifth Amendment to make the **equal protection clause** applicable to the federal government as well. Equal protection means that the government cannot enact laws that treat similarly situated individuals differently.

Equal protection, like substantive due process, relates to the substance of a law or other governmental action. When a law or action limits the liberty of all persons, it may violate substantive due process. When a law or action limits the liberty of some persons but not others, it may violate the equal protection clause. ■ **Example 2.14** If a law prohibits all advertising on the sides of trucks, it raises a substantive due process question. If the law makes an exception to allow truck owners to advertise their own businesses, it raises an equal protection issue. ■

In an equal protection inquiry, when a law or action distinguishes between or among individuals, the basis for the distinction—that is, the classification—is examined. Depending on the classification, the courts apply different levels of scrutiny, or "tests," to determine whether the law or action violates the equal protection clause. The courts use one of three standards: strict scrutiny, intermediate scrutiny, or the "rational basis" test.

Strict Scrutiny If a law or action prohibits or inhibits some persons from exercising a fundamental right, the law or action will be subject to "strict scrutiny" by the courts. Under this standard, the classification must be necessary to promote a compelling state interest.

Compelling state interests include remedying past unconstitutional or illegal discrimination but do not include correcting the general effects of "society's discrimination." ■ **Example 2.15** For a city to give preference to minority applicants in awarding construction contracts, it normally must identify past unconstitutional or illegal discrimination against minority-owned construction firms. Because the policy is based on suspect traits (race and national origin), it will violate the equal protection clause unless it is necessary to promote a compelling

state interest. ■ Generally, few laws or actions survive strict-scrutiny analysis by the courts.

Intermediate Scrutiny Another standard, that of intermediate scrutiny, is applied in cases involving discrimination based on gender or legitimacy (children born out of wedlock). Laws using these classifications must be substantially related to important government objectives. ■ **Example 2.16** A state law prohibits the sale of low-alcohol beer (less than 0.5% alcohol by volume) to any male under the age of 18 and to any female under the age of twenty-one. Suppose that a retail liquor chain challenges this law, claiming that it unfairly exposes the chain to sanctions and loss of liquor license. Because the law does not seem to further any important government objective, the law would not survive intermediate scrutiny by a court. ■

The state also has an important objective in establishing time limits (called *statutes of limitation*) for how long after an event a particular type of action can be brought. Nevertheless, the limitation period must be substantially related to the important objective of preventing fraudulent or outdated claims. ■ **Example 2.17** A federal law requires employees to file gender discrimination complaints within 180 days of the employer's discriminatory conduct. A court will likely reject a complaint that relies on evidence of discrimination that occurred outside this 180-day period, even if that discrimination directly caused low wages within the proper time frame. If this result is unfair, it will be up to the U.S. Congress, not the courts, to amend the statute of limitations. ■

The "Rational Basis" Test In matters of economic or social welfare, a classification will be considered valid if there is any conceivable *rational basis* on which the classification might relate to a legitimate government interest. It is almost impossible for a law or action to fail the rational basis test.

■ **Case in Point 2.18** A Chicago ordinance prohibits food trucks from parking within 200 feet of the entrance of any "brick and mortar" establishment that serves food, including convenience stores with hot dog rollers. Violators of the ordinance face a fine of up to $2,000 for each day that the truck is parked within the restricted area. The owner of the Cupcakes for Courage food truck filed suit against the city, alleging that, contrary to the state constitution, the ordinance unfairly favored restaurants over "mobile food vehicles."

Applying the rational basis test, the Illinois Supreme Court rejected this claim. The court ruled that Chicago's ordinance was rationally related to the legitimate government interest of protecting the city's restaurants. To a greater degree than food trucks, the court found, restaurants contribute to Chicago's economic well-being by paying property taxes and encouraging neighborhood retail activity.[24] ■

2–4 Privacy Rights

The U.S. Constitution does not explicitly mention a general right to privacy. In a 1928 Supreme Court case, *Olmstead v. United States*,[25] Justice Louis Brandeis stated in his dissent that the right to privacy is "the most comprehensive of rights and the right most valued by civilized [people]." The majority of the justices at that time, however, did not agree with Brandeis.

It was not until the 1960s that the Supreme Court endorsed the view that the Constitution protects individual privacy rights. In a landmark 1965 case, *Griswold v. Connecticut*,[26] the Supreme Court held that a constitutional right to privacy was implied by the First, Third, Fourth, Fifth, and Ninth Amendments.

Today, privacy rights receive protection under various federal statutes as well as the U.S. Constitution. State constitutions and statutes also secure individuals' privacy rights, often to a significant degree. Privacy rights are protected to an extent under tort law, consumer law, and employment law as well. This chapter's Cybersecurity and the Law feature explores the challenges of a corporate strategy that emphasizes privacy rights in an industry marked by cyber insecurity.

---

24. *LMP Services, Inc. v. City of Chicago*, 2019 IL 123123, 160 N.E.3d 822 (2019).
25. 277 U.S. 438, 48 S.Ct. 564, 72 L.Ed. 944 (1928).

26. 381 U.S. 479, 85 S.Ct. 1678, 14 L.Ed.2d 510 (1965).

Cybersecurity and the Law   Apple Inc.

"We design Apple products to protect your privacy and give you control over your information," reads a statement on the company's website. "It is not always easy." The difficulty comes from a tension that today's technology companies cannot avoid—the tension between the individual's desire for privacy and society's desire for security.

The Encryption Debate

Each iPhone produced by Apple is encrypted so that it can be unlocked only with a password. This encryption is so strong that even Apple's technicians cannot access an iPhone without the owner's consent. This level of privacy causes problems when law enforcement needs evidence from a smartphone whose owner will not, or cannot, provide the password.

For example, Mohammed Alshamrani was killed by sheriffs' deputies after fatally shooting three people at a naval base in Pensacola, Florida. The Federal Bureau of Investigation (FBI) wanted access to Alshamrani's two iPhones to determine whether he had been in contact with other potential domestic terrorists. Apple refused to help "break into" Alshamrani's devices. Similarly, the company has declined to build "backdoor" access into iPhones, for fear any entry point will eventually be breached by hackers.

This position angers those who believe that "companies shouldn't be allowed to shield criminals and terrorists from lawful efforts to solve crimes and protect our citizens." Indeed, the U.S. Constitution does permit the government to infringe on an individual's privacy to investigate a probable crime. Nevertheless, Apple's stance has earned the company a reputation for consumer advocacy. "It's brilliant marketing," says one observer. "They're so concerned with your privacy that they're willing to wave the finger at the FBI."

Insecurities

Despite its air of invincibility, the iPhone is not hackproof. Several years before the Pensacola shooting, the FBI paid hackers to break into an iPhone owned by Syed Farook. (In tandem with his wife, Farook had fatally shot fourteen people in a terrorist attack in Southern California before being killed by law enforcement officers.) At least two software security companies, Cellebrite and Grayshift, have managed to bypass encryption codes on older iPhone models. On one occasion, Apple used federal copyright law to force Twitter to remove a tweet that contained a coded "key" that would unlock the company's encryption secrets. With each new iPhone, Apple closes these loopholes. Nonetheless, some in the security industry believe that it is fighting a losing battle against the twin privacy threats of individual hackers and government surveillance.

Critical Thinking Tim Cook, Apple's chief operating officer, has suggested that the United States Congress should pass a law limiting the ability of Apple and other tech companies to keep consumer data private. Why would a business executive make such a request?

2–4a Federal Privacy Legislation

In the last several decades, Congress has enacted a number of statutes that protect the privacy of individuals in various areas of concern. Most of these statutes deal with personal information collected by governments or private businesses.

In the 1960s, Americans were sufficiently alarmed by the accumulation of personal information in government files that they pressured Congress to pass laws permitting individuals to access their files. Congress responded by passing the Freedom of Information Act (FOIA), which allows persons to request copies of any information on them contained in federal government files. Congress later enacted the Privacy Act, which also gives persons the right to access such information.

In the 1990s, responding to the growing need to protect the privacy of individuals' health records—particularly computerized records—Congress passed the Health Insurance Portability and Accountability Act (HIPAA).[27] This act defines and limits the circumstances in which an individual's "protected health information" may be used or disclosed by healthcare providers, healthcare plans, and others. These and other major federal laws protecting privacy rights are listed and briefly described in Exhibit 2–2.

2–4b The USA Patriot Act

The USA Patriot Act was passed by Congress in the wake of the terrorist attacks of September 11, 2001, and then reauthorized twice.[28] The Patriot Act has given government officials increased authority to monitor internet activities (such as e-mail and website visits) and to gain access to personal financial information and student information. Law enforcement officials can track the telephone and e-mail communications of one party to find out the identity of the other party or parties. Privacy advocates argue that this law adversely affects the constitutional rights of all Americans, and it has been widely criticized in the media.

---

27. HIPAA was enacted as Pub. L. No. 104-191 (1996) and is codified in 29 U.S.C.A. Sections 1181 *et seq.*

28. The Uniting and Strengthening America by Providing Appropriate Tools Required to Intercept and Obstruct Terrorism Act of 2001, also known as the USA Patriot Act, was enacted as Pub. L. No. 107-56 (2001) and last amended and reauthorized in 2015.

Exhibit 2–2   Federal Legislation Relating to Privacy

Freedom of Information Act (1966)	Provides that individuals have a right to obtain access to information about them collected in government files.
Privacy Act (1974)	Protects the privacy of individuals about whom the federal government has information. Regulates agencies' use and disclosure of data, and gives individuals access to and a means to correct inaccuracies.
Electronic Communications Privacy Act (1986)	Prohibits the interception of information communicated by electronic means.
Health Insurance Portability and Accountability Act (1996)	Requires healthcare providers and healthcare plans to inform patients of their privacy rights and of how their personal medical information may be used. States that medical records may not be used for purposes unrelated to health care or disclosed without permission.
Financial Services Modernization Act (Gramm-Leach-Bliley Act) (1999)	Prohibits the disclosure of nonpublic personal information about a consumer to an unaffiliated third party unless strict disclosure and opt-out requirements are met.

Practice and Review: Business and the Constitution

A state legislature enacted a statute that required any motorcycle operator or passenger on the state's highways to wear a protective helmet. Jim Alderman, a licensed motorcycle operator, sued the state to block enforcement of the law. Alderman asserted that the statute violated the equal protection clause because it placed requirements on motorcyclists that were not imposed on other motorists. Using the information presented in the chapter, answer the following questions.

1. Why does this statute raise equal protection issues instead of substantive due process concerns?
2. What are the three levels of scrutiny that the courts use in determining whether a law violates the equal protection clause?
3. Which standard of scrutiny, or test, would apply to this situation? Why?
4. Applying this standard, is the helmet statute constitutional? Why or why not?

Debate This . . . Legislation aimed at "protecting people from themselves" concerns the individual as well as the public in general. Protective helmet laws are just one example of such legislation. Should individuals be allowed to engage in unsafe activities if they choose to do so?

Terms and Concepts

Bill of Rights 30
checks and balances 26
commerce clause 26
compelling government interest 31
due process clause 38
equal protection clause 39
establishment clause 35

federal form of government 25
filtering software 34
free exercise clause 35
full faith and credit clause 26
meta tags 34
police powers 25
preemption 29

privileges and immunities
  clause 26
probable cause 38
search warrant 37
sovereignty 25
supremacy clause 29
symbolic speech 31

Issue Spotters

1. South Dakota wants its citizens to conserve energy. To help reduce consumer consumption of electricity, the state passes a law that bans all advertising by power utilities within the state. What argument could the power utilities use as a defense to the enforcement of this state law? (See *Business and the Bill of Rights*.)

2. Suppose that a state imposes a higher tax on out-of-state companies doing business in the state than it imposes on in-state companies. Is this a violation of equal protection if the only reason for the tax is to protect the local firms from out-of-state competition? Explain. (See *The Constitutional Powers of Government*.)

• **Check your answers to the Issue Spotters against the answers provided in Appendix B at the end of this text.**

Business Scenarios and Case Problems

2–1. Commerce Clause. A Georgia state law requires the use of contoured rear-fender mudguards on trucks and trailers operating within Georgia state lines. The statute further makes it illegal for trucks and trailers to use straight mudguards. In approximately thirty-five other states, straight mudguards are legal. Moreover, in Florida, straight mudguards are explicitly required by law. There is some evidence suggesting that contoured mudguards might be a little safer than straight mudguards. Discuss whether this Georgia statute violates any constitutional provisions. (See *The Constitutional Powers of Government*.)

2–2. Equal Protection. With the objectives of preventing crime, maintaining property values, and preserving the quality of urban life, New York City enacted an ordinance to regulate the locations of adult entertainment establishments. The ordinance expressly applied to female, but not male, entertainment. Adele Buzzetti owned the Cozy Cabin, a New York City cabaret that featured female dancers. Buzzetti and an anonymous dancer filed a suit in a federal district court against the city, asking the court to block the enforcement of the ordinance. The plaintiffs argued, in part, that the ordinance violated the equal protection clause. Under the equal protection clause, what standard applies to the court's consideration of this ordinance? Under this test, how should the court rule? Why? (See *Due Process and Equal Protection.*)

2–3. Business Case Problem with Sample Answer— Freedom of Speech. Mark Wooden sent an e-mail to an alderwoman for the city of St. Louis. Attached was a nineteen-minute audio file that compared her to the biblical character Jezebel. The audio said she was a "bitch in the Sixth Ward," spending too much time with the rich and powerful and too little time with the poor. In a menacing, maniacal tone, Wooden said that he was "dusting off a sawed-off shotgun," called himself a "domestic terrorist," and referred to the assassination of President John Kennedy, the murder of federal judge John Roll, and the shooting of Representative Gabrielle Giffords. Feeling threatened, the alderwoman called the police. Wooden was convicted of harassment under a state criminal statute. Was this conviction unconstitutional under the First Amendment? Discuss. [*State of Missouri v. Wooden,* 388 S.W.3d 522 (Mo. 2013)] (See *Business and the Bill of Rights.*)

• For a sample answer to Problem 2–3, go to Appendix C at the end of this text.

2–4. Equal Protection. Abbott Laboratories licensed SmithKline Beecham Corp. to market an Abbott human immunodeficiency virus (HIV) drug in conjunction with one of SmithKline's drugs. Abbott then increased the price of its drug fourfold, forcing SmithKline to increase its prices and thereby driving business to Abbott's own combination drug. SmithKline filed a suit in a federal district court against Abbott. During jury selection, Abbott struck the only self-identified gay person among the potential jurors. Could the equal protection clause be applied to prohibit discrimination based on sexual orientation in jury selection? Discuss. [*SmithKline Beecham Corp. v. Abbott Laboratories,* 740 F.3d 471 (9th Cir. 2014)] (See *Due Process and Equal Protection.*)

2–5. Procedural Due Process. Robert Brown applied for admission to the University of Kansas School of Law. Brown answered "no" to questions on the application asking if he had a criminal history and acknowledged that a false answer constituted "cause for . . . dismissal." In fact, Brown had criminal convictions for domestic battery and driving under the influence. He was accepted for admission to the school. When school officials discovered his history, however, he was notified of their intent to dismiss him and given an opportunity

to respond in writing. He demanded a hearing. The officials refused to grant Brown a hearing and then expelled him. Did the school's actions deny Brown due process? Discuss. [*Brown v. University of Kansas,* 599 Fed.Appx. 833 (10th Cir. 2015)] (See *Due Process and Equal Protection.*)

2–6. The Commerce Clause. Regency Transportation, Inc., operates a freight business throughout the eastern United States. Regency maintains its corporate headquarters, four warehouses, and a maintenance facility and terminal location for repairing and storing vehicles in Massachusetts. All of the vehicles in Regency's fleet were bought in other states. Massachusetts imposes a use tax on all taxpayers subject to its jurisdiction, including those that do business in interstate commerce, as Regency does. When Massachusetts imposed the tax on the purchase price of each tractor and trailer in Regency's fleet, the trucking firm challenged the assessment as discriminatory under the commerce clause. What is the chief consideration under the commerce clause when a state law affects interstate commerce? Is Massachusetts's use tax valid? Explain. [*Regency Transportation, Inc. v. Commissioner of Revenue,* 473 Mass. 459, 42 N.E.3d 1133 (2016)] (See *The Constitutional Powers of Government.*)

2–7. Freedom of Speech. Wandering Dago, Inc. (WD), operates a food truck in Albany, New York. WD brands itself and the food it sells with language generally viewed as ethnic slurs. Owners Andrea Loguidice and Brandon Snooks, however, view the branding as giving a "nod to their Italian heritage" and "weakening the derogatory force of the slur." Twice, WD applied to participate as a vendor in a summer lunch program in a state-owned plaza. Both times, the New York State Office of General Services (OGS) denied the application because of WD's branding. WD filed a suit in a federal district court against RoAnn Destito, the commissioner of OGS, contending that the agency had violated WD's right to free speech. What principles apply to the government's regulation of the content of speech? How do those principles apply in WD's case? Explain. [*Wandering Dago, Inc. v. Destito,* 879 F.3d 20 (2d Cir. 2018)] (See *Business and the Bill of Rights.*)

2–8. Commercial Speech. The Texas legislature enacted provisions under the insurance code regulating "public insurance adjusting." Public insurance adjusters are often hired by an insured to help resolve and settle insurance claims. The regulations require that a public insurance adjuster must be licensed in order to adjust insurance claims on an insured's behalf. Further, any person or entity defined as a contractor is prohibited from adjusting insurance claims for properties at which the contractor is, or will be, providing contracting services. In other words, acting as a public insurance adjuster and as a contractor on the same claim is considered a conflict of interest. Stonewater Roofing, Ltd. Co., is a professional roofing company that repairs and replaces roofs in Texas but is not licensed as a public insurance adjustor. On its website, Stonewater states that it is "highly experienced with the insurance claims process." It calls itself a "trusted roofing and insurance specialist." Stonewater filed a lawsuit against the Texas

Department of Insurance that challenged the prohibitions as impermissible regulations of commercial speech and alleged that the provisions were unconstitutionally vague. The Texas Department of Insurance asked the trial court to dismiss the lawsuit, which it did. Should the Court of Appeals of Texas confirm the trial court's decision? [*Stonewater Roofing, Ltd. Co., v. Texas Department of Insurance*, 641 S.W.3d 794, 2022 WL 309437 (2022)] (See *Freedom of Speech*.)

2–9. A Question of Ethics—Free Speech. Michael Mayfield, the president of Mendo Mill and Lumber Co., in California, received a "notice of a legal claim" from Edward Starski. The "claim" alleged that a stack of lumber had fallen on a customer as a result of a Mendo employee's "incompetence." The "notice" presented a settlement offer on the customer's behalf in exchange for a release of liability for Mendo. In a follow-up phone conversation with Mayfield, Starski said that he was an attorney—which, in fact, he was not. Starski was arrested and charged with violating a state criminal statute that prohibited the unauthorized practice of law. [*People v. Starski*, 7 Cal.App.5th 215, 212 Cal.Rptr.3d 622 (1 Dist. Div. 2 2017)] (See *Business and the Bill of Rights*.)

(a) Starski argued that "creating an illusion" that he was an attorney was protected by the First Amendment. Is Starski correct? Explain.

(b) Identify, discuss, and resolve the conflict between the right to free speech and the government's regulation of the practice of law.

Time-Limited Group Assignment

2–10. Free Speech and Equal Protection. For many years, New York City has had to deal with the vandalism and defacement of public property caused by unauthorized graffiti. In an effort to stop the damage, the city banned the sale of aerosol spray-paint cans and broad-tipped indelible markers to persons under 21 years of age. The new rules also prohibited people from possessing these items on property other than their own. Within a year, five people under age 21 were cited for violations of these regulations, and 871 individuals were arrested for actually making graffiti.

Lindsey Vincenty and other artists wished to create graffiti on legal surfaces, such as canvas, wood, and clothing. Unable to buy supplies in the city or to carry them into the city from elsewhere, Vincenty and others filed a lawsuit on behalf of themselves and other young artists against Michael Bloomberg, the city's mayor, and others. The plaintiffs claimed that, among other things, the new rules violated their right to freedom of speech.

(a) One group will argue in favor of the plaintiffs and provide several reasons why the court should hold that the city's new rules violate the plaintiffs' freedom of speech. (See *Business and the Bill of Rights*.)

(b) Another group will develop a counterargument that outlines the reasons why the new rules do not violate free speech rights. (See *Business and the Bill of Rights*.)

(c) A third group will argue that the city's ban violates the equal protection clause because it applies only to persons under age twenty-one. (See *Due Process and Equal Protection*.)

Chapter 3

Ethics in Business

One of the most complex issues businesspersons and corporations face is ethics. Ethics is not as well defined as the law, and yet it can have substantial impacts on a firm's finances and reputation, especially when the firm is involved in a well-publicized scandal. Some scandals arise from activities that are legal but are ethically questionable. Other scandals arise from conduct that is both illegal and unethical.

Suppose that Annisa dropped out of Yale University to start a company in Silicon Valley (centered around Palo Alto, California) that developed and sold finger-prick blood tests. Annisa raised millions from investors by claiming that her new technology would revolutionize blood testing by providing a full range of laboratory tests from a few drops of blood. The kits were marketed as a better alternative to traditional, more expensive lab tests ordered by physicians. They were sold at drugstores for a few dollars each and touted as a way for consumers to test their blood type and monitor their cholesterol, iron, and many other conditions. Within several years, Annisa and her company were making millions. But then complaints started rolling in that the test kits did not really work as advertised and that the results were not accurate (because more blood was needed for accuracy). Numerous consumers, drugstores, and government agencies sued the company for fraudulent and misleading marketing practices. Annisa's profitable startup now faces an uncertain future.

The goal of business ethics is not to stifle innovation. There is nothing unethical about a company selling an idea or technology that is still being developed. In fact, that is exactly what many successful start-ups do—take a promising idea and develop it into a reality. But businesspersons also need to consider what will happen if new technologies or products end up not working or causing unintended consequences. Should they go ahead with production and sales? What are the ethical problems with putting a product on the market that does not perform as advertised or is unsafe? To be sure, there is not always one clear answer to an ethical question. What is clear is that rushing to production and not thinking through the ethical ramifications of decisions can be disastrous for a business.

3–1 Ethics and the Role of Business

At the most basic level, the study of **ethics** is the study of what constitutes right or wrong behavior. It is a branch of philosophy focusing on morality and the way moral principles are derived and implemented. Ethics has to do with the fairness, justness, rightness, or wrongness of an action.

The study of **business ethics** typically looks at the decisions businesses make or have to make and whether those decisions are right or wrong. It has to do with how businesspersons apply moral and ethical principles in making their decisions. Those who study business ethics also evaluate what duties and responsibilities exist or should exist for businesses.

In this book, we cover ethical issues in Ethics Today features that appear in selected chapters. We also provide an ethics-based case problem, called A Question of Ethics, at the end of every chapter. Finally, we include an Application and Ethics feature at the end of each unit to expand on the concepts of business ethics discussed in that unit.

3–1a The Relationship of Law and Ethics

The government has institutionalized some ethical rights and duties through the passage of laws and regulations. Many laws are designed to prevent fraudulent (misleading, deceptive) conduct in various contexts, including contracts, health care, financial reporting, mortgages, and sales. ■ **Example 3.1** The Fraud Reduction and Data Analytics Act was passed by Congress to identify and assess fraud risks in federal government agencies. The purpose of the law is to prevent, detect, and respond to fraud (including improper payments) in federal programs. ■

Sometimes, major legislation is passed after well-publicized ethical transgressions by industries or companies result in harm to the public. ■ **Example 3.2** After alleged ethical lapses on Wall Street contributed to a financial crisis, Congress passed the Dodd-Frank Wall Street Reform and Consumer Protection Act.[1] Dodd-Frank made sweeping changes to the United States' financial regulatory environment in an attempt to promote financial stability and protect consumers from abusive financial services practices.

Similarly, Congress enacted the Sarbanes-Oxley Act[2] (SOX) after Enron, a major energy company, engaged in risky financial maneuvers that resulted in the loss of billions of dollars to shareholders. SOX was designed to help reduce corporate fraud and unethical management decisions by setting up accountability measures for publicly traded companies. Company heads must verify that they have read quarterly and annual reports and vouch for their accuracy. SOX also requires companies to set up confidential systems so that employees and others can "raise red flags" about suspected illegal or unethical auditing and accounting practices.[3] ■

Gray Areas in the Law Laws cannot codify all ethical requirements. For a number of reasons, laws may sometimes be difficult to interpret and apply. When legislatures draft laws, they typically use broad language so that the provisions will apply in a variety of circumstances. It can be hard to determine how such broad provisions apply to specific situations. In addition, laws intended to address one situation may apply to other situations as well. And the legislative body that passes a law may not give clear guidance on the purpose of the law or the definition of terms in the law.

Other issues arise because laws are created through the political process. They therefore often involve compromises among competing interests and industries. As a result, a law's provisions may be ambiguous, may be weaker than intended by the original drafters, or may lack a means of enforcement. In short, the law is not always clear, and these "gray areas" in the law make it difficult to predict with certainty how a court will apply a given law to a particular action.

The Moral Minimum Compliance with the law is sometimes called the **moral minimum.** If people and entities merely comply with the law, they are acting at the lowest ethical level that society will tolerate.

Failure to meet the moral minimum can have significant consequences, especially in the context of litigation. A businessperson or an employee who fails to respond to the requirements in a lawsuit will find that the courts generally do not favor such actions, or lack thereof. ■ **Case in Point 3.3** Michele Womack brought an employment discrimination action against Wal-Mart. Prior to trial, Wal-Mart's attorneys requested various documents from Womack. She did not comply. She also failed to appear to answer questions from Wal-Mart's attorneys. Womack was unresponsive to emails, telephone calls, and a letter. Ultimately, a federal court in Pennsylvania ruled in Wal-Mart's favor and dismissed the case. The court found that Womack was solely responsible for failing to cooperate in pretrial actions.[4] ■

Although the moral minimum is important, the study of ethics goes well beyond these legal requirements to evaluate what is right for society. Businesspersons must remember that an action that is legal is not necessarily ethical. For instance, a company can legally refuse to negotiate liability claims for injuries allegedly caused by a faulty product. But if the company's refusal is meant to increase the injured party's legal costs and force the party to drop a legitimate claim, the company is not acting ethically.

Private Company Codes of Ethics Most companies attempt to link ethics and law through the creation of internal codes of ethics. Company codes are not laws. Instead, they are rules that the company sets forth and that it can enforce (by terminating an employee who does not follow them, for instance). Codes of conduct typically outline the company's policies on particular issues and indicate how employees are expected to act.

■ **Example 3.4** The Intel Code of Conduct is very specific. "We believe in doing the right things right everywhere we do business." The chip-manufacturing company goes on to state that it "values human dignity, individual differences, diversity of thought, and the quality of ideas, innovation, and solutions that result." It specifically prohibits dishonesty, illegal activity, retaliation, conflicts of interest, and misuse of assets. ■

---

1. Pub. L. No. 111–203, 124 Stat. 1376, July 21, 2010, 12 U.S.C. Sections 5301 *et seq.*
2. 15 U.S.C. Sections 7201 *et seq.*
3. In one such system, employees can click on an on-screen icon that anonymously links them with NAVEX Global to report suspicious accounting practices, sexual harassment, and other possibly unethical behavior.

---

4. *Womack v. Wal-Mart Stores East, L.P.,* 2021 WL 2897285 (W.D. PA 2021).

Industry Ethical Codes Numerous industries have also developed codes of ethics. The American Institute of Certified Public Accountants (AICPA) has a comprehensive Code of Professional Conduct for the ethical practicing of accounting. The American Bar Association (ABA) has model rules of professional conduct for attorneys, and the American Nurses Association (ANA) has a code of ethics that applies to nurses. These codes can give guidance to decision makers facing ethical questions. Violation of a code may result in the discipline of an employee or sanctions against a company from the industry organization. Remember, though, that these internal codes are not laws, so their effectiveness is determined by the commitment of the industry or company leadership to enforcing the codes.

■ **Case in Point 3.5** Soccer is the most popular sport on the planet. It is governed by a world soccer organization (officially referred to as FIFA). Country member associations are grouped into six continual confederations. Each geographic confederation has its own code of ethics modeled on FIFA's code of ethics. Basically, all officials must act "with absolute loyalty." They cannot accept improper personal or economic benefits. Nonetheless, numerous soccer organization officials accepted millions of dollars in bribes from sports media and marketing companies. Some of these officials were tried and convicted in the United States even though their unethical and illegal activities occurred elsewhere. Numerous officials were convicted of conspiring to commit wire fraud and money laundering, all arising out of payments and bribes to officials. When the officials involved appealed their convictions, a federal appellate court ruled that because they had a relationship with both the world and the regional soccer federations, they had a fiduciary duty [one of trust] not to accept bribes or kickbacks. This duty was explicitly laid out by the two soccer associations' codes of conduct.[5] ■

The National Association of Realtors has also promulgated a code of ethics. Its standard of care was utilized in the following case.

---

5. *U.S. v. Napout*, 963 F3d 163 (2d Cir. 2020).

Case 3.1

Greif v. Sanin
Court of Appeal, Fourth Dist., Div. 2., 74 Cal.App.5th 412 (2022).

Background and Facts Earl Greif sold ten acres of vacant land in Rancho Mirage, California, to Yardley Protective Limited Partnership. Earl signed the purchase agreement. A few days later, he decided that he had sold the vacant land for less than its fair market value. He attempted to rescind the sale. The Yardley partnership sued to enforce the purchase agreement. Greif filed cross-complaints against Yardley as well as Yardley's real estate brokers, including Sanin. A trial court entered judgment in favor of Yardley, and Greif appealed.

In the Language of the Court
CODRINGTON, J.

This is a case of seller's remorse.
* * * *

Greif appeals the judgment of dismissal of Greif's Cross-complaint against the buyer's broker, Sanin, after the trial court granted Sanin's motion [to dismiss the cross-complaint, which alleged negligence]. The trial court concluded as a matter of law that Sanin did not owe the seller any duty that Greif alleged was breached. We agree.
* * * *

* * * The parties negotiated the purchase price for the Property, which ranged from $3,399,000 to $3,380,000 to $3,350,000. Ultimately the parties agreed on the purchase price of $3,330,000. * * *
* * * *

When presenting the Purchase Agreement to Earl, Eddie [Sanin] pointed out to Earl the purchase price, which was conspicuously stated on the first page of the Purchase Agreement. * * *

Case 3.1 Continues

Case 3.1 Continued

Shortly after Earl signed the Purchase Agreement * * * Earl realized that the purchase price stated in the Purchase Agreement was $330,000.
* * * *

[Later,] Earl, with the assistance of legal counsel, rescinded the Purchase Agreement by executing escrow cancellation instructions and offered to compensate Yardley by paying interest on the amount Yardley had deposited in escrow. Yardley refused to execute the proposed escrow cancellation instructions.

In the cross-claim for negligence, Greif alleged that Sanin owed Earl a duty to be honest and truthful during the Property transaction under [California] Business & Professions Code sections 10152, and 10176, subdivisions (a)–(c), and (i).

Greif further alleged Sanin breached a duty owed to Earl by Sanin "having presumed knowledge of the fair market value of the subject Property at the time of preparing and presenting the Purchase Agreement to Greif, and Sanin's failure to raise the gross discrepancy between the true value of the Property and the purchase price stated in the Purchase Agreement." Greif alleges Sanin's acts constituted a breach of duty owed to Earl and dishonest dealing. As a direct and proximate result, Greif allegedly was damaged in a sum in excess of $250,000, which damages include those sustained due to Greif's inability to develop the Property or sell it for its true FMV [fair market value]. Yardley allegedly was jointly and severally liable for Sanin's acts and omissions.
* * * *

Under common law, generally any person who performs professional services owes a duty of care to all persons within the area of foreseeable risk. The standard of care imposed on a real estate broker thus is higher than that applicable to a layperson. The broker is subject to a duty of skill, care, and diligence commensurate with the professional standards that the real estate industry has held out to the public and that the public reasonably can expect. * * *

The standard of care of a real estate broker can be measured by the Code of Ethics of the National Association of Realtors when the broker is a "realtor" (a member of the National Association or local Board of Realtors). * * * "The Code of Ethics of the National Association of Realtors provides that it imposes `obligations that may be higher than those mandated by law, (and) in any instance where the Code of Ethics and the law conflict, the obligations of the law must take precedence (preamble)'; *while the obligation of absolute fidelity to the client's interests is primary, this does not relieve the Realtor of an obligation to treat fairly all persons to the transaction* (Article 7)."
* * * *

Under the common law, "'[t]here is little question that a real estate broker owes a duty of care to third persons in the transaction, where the broker does not have privity with, or fiduciary duties to, such third person.'" Despite the absence of privity of contract, a real estate agent is clearly under a duty to exercise reasonable care to protect those persons whom the agent is attempting to induce into entering a real estate transaction for the purpose of earning a commission.

The parties agree a buyer's broker owes a duty of care to the seller, even when the broker is the exclusive broker of the buyer. There is thus no question that Sanin owed a duty of care to the seller, Greif, not to impose a foreseeable risk on the seller unreasonably. The issue here is whether Sanin owed Earl a duty to tell him the purchase price was less than the FMV. We conclude that at the time of execution of the Purchase Agreement there was no such duty.
* * * *

Even though Greif * * * cites evidence refuting these findings, we affirm the trial court's findings because there was substantial evidence supporting them. "In assessing whether any substantial evidence exists, we view the record in the light most favorable to respondents, giving them the benefit of every reasonable inference and resolving all conflicts in their favor." It is not our role to reweigh the evidence, redetermine the credibility of the witnesses, or resolve conflicts in the testimony, and we will not disturb the judgment if there is evidence to support it.
* * * *

Decision and Remedy The California Court of Appeal affirmed the trial court's judgment. Greif had to respect the purchase agreement for the ten acres of vacant land. The court in part considered that Greif's complaint simply represented a situation of seller's remorse.

Case 3.1 Continued

Critical Thinking

- **What If the Facts Were Different?** Suppose that Greif had been a young real estate investor who bought and sold commercial property on a regular basis. Would this lawsuit have dragged on for over ten years? Why or why not?

3–1b The Role of Business in Society

Over the last two hundred years, public perception has moved toward expecting corporations to participate in society as corporate citizens. Originally, though, the only perceived duty of a corporation was to generate profits for its owners. Although many people today may view this idea as greedy or ruthless, the rationale for the profit-maximization theory is still considered valid by many.

Business as a Pure Profit Maximizer In theory, if all firms strictly adhere to the goal of maximizing profits, resources flow to where they are most highly valued by society. Corporations can focus on their strengths. Other entities that are better suited to deal with social problems and perform charitable acts can specialize in those activities. The government, through taxes and other financial allocations, can shift resources to those other entities to perform public services. Thus, profit maximization can lead to the most efficient allocation of scarce resources.

Even when profit maximization is the goal, companies benefit by ethical behavior. For instance, customer satisfaction with a company is key to its profitability. Repeat customers lead to long-term profits. When customers are happy, word gets around, and it generates more business for the firm. Unsatisfied customers go elsewhere for the goods or services that the firm provides. When a business behaves badly, customers quickly report this online by posting bad reviews on such sites as Angi, Yelp, Trustpilot, and Capterra. Bad reviews obviously hurt a business's profits, while good reviews lead to higher profits.

Business as a Corporate Citizen Over the years, many people became dissatisfied with profit-maximization theory. Investors and others began to look beyond profits and dividends and to consider the **triple bottom line**—a corporation's profits, its impact on people, and its impact on the planet. Magazines and websites began to rank companies based on their environmental impacts and their ethical decisions. Corporations came to be viewed as "citizens" that were expected to participate in bettering communities and society.

A Four-Part Analysis Whether one believes in profit-maximization theory or corporate citizenship, ethics is important in business decision making. When making decisions, a business should evaluate each of the following:

1. The legal implications of each decision.
2. The public relations impact.
3. The safety risks for consumers and employees.
4. The financial implications.

This four-part analysis will assist the firm in making decisions that not only maximize profits but also reflect good corporate citizenship.

3–1c Ethical Issues in Business

Ethical issues can arise in numerous aspects of doing business. A fundamental ethical issue for business is developing integrity and trust. Businesspersons should exhibit integrity in their dealings with other people in the company, other businesses, clients, and the community. Companies that are honest and treat others fairly earn trust.

Businesses should also ensure that the workplace respects diversity and enforces equal opportunity employment and civil rights laws. In addition, businesses must comply with a host of federal and state laws and regulations, including those pertaining to the environment, financial reporting, and safety standards. Compliance with these rules can involve ethical issues. See this chapter's Digital Update feature for a discussion of an ethical issue that has arisen from employees' work-related use of digital technology after work hours.

The most difficult aspect of ethics that businesses face is in decision making. Businesspersons must learn to recognize ethical issues, obtain the pertinent facts, evaluate the alternatives, and then make a decision. Decision makers should also test and reflect on the outcomes of their decisions. We focus here on this aspect of ethics.

Digital Update · Should Employees Have a "Right of Disconnecting"?

Almost all jobs today involve digital technology, whether it be e-mails, text messaging, internet access, or smartphone use. Most employees, when interviewed, say that digital technology increases their productivity and flexibility. The downside is what some call an "electronic leash"—employees are constantly connected and therefore end up working when they are not "at work." Over one-third of full-time workers, for example, say that they frequently check e-mails, text messages, and services such as Yammer and Slack outside normal working hours.

Do Workers Have the Right to Disconnect?

Because the boundaries between being "at work" and being "at leisure" can be so hazy, some labor unions in other countries have attempted to pass rules that allow employees to disconnect from all work-related digital communication during nonworking hours. For example, a French labor union representing high-tech workers signed an agreement with a large business association recognizing a "right of disconnecting."

In Germany, Volkswagen and BMW no longer forward e-mail to staff from company servers after the end of the working day. Other German firms have declared that workers are not expected to check e-mail on weekends and holidays. The government is considering legislating such restrictions nationwide.

What Is Work?

Today's modern digital connectivity raises issues about the definition of *work*. Employees at several major companies, including Black & Decker, T-Mobile, and Verizon, have sued for unpaid overtime related to smartphone use. In another case, a police sergeant sued the city of Chicago, claiming that he should have been paid overtime for hours spent using his personal digital assistant (PDA). The police department had issued PDAs to officers and required them to respond to work-related communications even while off duty. The court agreed that some of the officers' off-duty PDA activities were compensable. Nevertheless, it ruled in favor of the city because the officers had failed to follow proper procedures for filing overtime claims.[a]

Critical Thinking From an ethical point of view, is there any difference between calling subordinates during off hours for work-related questions and sending them e-mails or text messages?

a. *Allen v. City of Chicago*, 865 F.3d 936 (7th Cir. 2017).

3–1d The Importance of Ethical Leadership

In ethics, as in other areas, employees take their cues from management. Talking about ethical business decision making is meaningless if management does not set standards. Furthermore, to be effective, managers must apply the same standards to themselves as they do to the company's employees. This duty starts with top management.

Attitude of Top Management One of the most important ways to create and maintain an ethical workplace is for top management to demonstrate its commitment to ethical decision making. A manager who is not totally committed to an ethical workplace will rarely succeed in creating one. More than anything else, top management's behavior sets the ethical tone of a firm.

Managers have found that discharging even one employee for ethical reasons has a tremendous impact as a deterrent to unethical behavior in the workplace. This is true even if the company has a written code of ethics. If management does not enforce the company code, the code essentially does not exist.

Unrealistic Goals for Employees Certain types of behavior on the part of managers and owners contribute to unethical behavior among employees. Managers who set unrealistic production or sales goals increase the probability that employees will act unethically. If a sales quota can be met only through high-pressure, unethical sales tactics, employees will try to act "in the best interest of the company" and behave unethically. A manager who looks the other way when such behavior occurs also sets an example—one indicating that ethical transgressions will be accepted.

Note that even when large companies have policies against sales incentives, individual branches may still promote them. ■ **Example 3.6** The financial firm Morgan Stanley Smith Barney, LLC, has an internal policy barring sales contests. Nevertheless, Morgan Stanley branches in Massachusetts and Rhode Island held a sales contest in which brokers were given cash incentives of up to $5,000 for selling securities-based loans, or SBLs (loans that allow clients to borrow against their investments). Thirty financial advisers participated in the sales contest for almost a year until Morgan Stanley's compliance office noticed and halted the practice. One regional branch reportedly tripled its loans as a result of the contest. The state of Massachusetts ultimately sued Morgan Stanley, claiming that the practice violated state securities rules. ■

Fostering of Unethical Conduct Business owners and managers sometimes take more active roles in fostering unethical and illegal conduct, with negative consequences for their businesses. ■ **Case in Point 3.7** Rachel Maddox purchased a home on a hillside in Nashville. After heavy rains, Maddox noticed cracks in the basement. Also, if a tennis ball was placed on the floor, it would roll toward the front of the house. Maddox contacted Olshan Foundation Repair and Waterproofing Co., which sent Kevin Hayman to inspect her property. Hayman—described as a "certified structural technician" on work orders—suggested $27,000 of repairs. Maddox agreed, in part because of Olshan's promise of a lifetime warranty.

Several years later, further rain caused new cracks in the foundation of the house, which had again begun to tilt. After several unsuccessful attempts to correct these problems, Olshan employees stopped coming to the property or returning Maddox's calls. An independent engineer told Maddox that Olshan's "repairs" had made the house's foundation issues worse. Eventually, a local building inspector noted that the house appeared to be "sliding off the hill" and was unsafe for inhabitation. Maddox sued Olshan for fraud. At trial, a company executive admitted that Hayman's "certification" was based on a three-week course administered by the company. The court awarded Maddox $187,000 for the fair market value of her home, plus $15,000 in punitive damages because of Olshan's egregiously unethical behavior. This judgment was affirmed on appeal.[6] ■

3–2 Ethical Principles and Philosophies

How do business decision makers decide whether a given action is the "right" one for their firms? What ethical standards should be applied? Broadly speaking, **ethical reasoning**—the application of morals and ethics to a situation—applies to businesses just as it does to individuals. As businesses make decisions, they must analyze their alternatives in a variety of ways, one of which is the ethical implications of each alternative.

Generally, the study of ethics identifies two major categories—duty-based ethics and outcome-based ethics. **Duty-based ethics** is rooted in the idea that every person has certain duties to others, including both humans and the planet. **Outcome-based ethics** focuses on the impacts of a decision on society or on key stakeholders.

3–2a Duty-Based Ethics

Duty-based ethics focuses on the obligations of the corporation. It deals with standards for behavior that traditionally were derived from revealed truths, religious authorities, or philosophical reasoning. These standards involve concepts of right and wrong, duties owed, and rights to be protected. Corporations today often describe these values or duties in their mission statements or strategic plans. Some companies base their statements on a nonreligious rationale, while others derive their values from religious doctrine.

Religious Ethical Principles Nearly every religion has principles or beliefs about how one should treat others. In the Judeo-Christian tradition, the Ten Commandments of the Old Testament establish these fundamental rules for moral action. The principles of the Muslim faith are set out in the Qur'an, and Hindus find their principles in the four Vedas.

Religious rules generally are absolute with respect to the behavior of their adherents. ■ **Example 3.8** The commandment "Thou shalt not steal" is an absolute mandate for a person who believes that the Ten Commandments reflect revealed truth. Even a benevolent motive for stealing (such as Robin Hood's) cannot justify the act because the act itself is inherently immoral and thus wrong. ■

For businesses, religious principles can be a unifying force for employees or a rallying point to increase employee motivation. They can also present problems, however, because different owners, suppliers, employees, and customers may have different religious backgrounds. Engaging in an action based on religious principles, especially when those principles address socially or politically controversial topics, can lead to negative publicity and even to protests or boycotts.

Principles of Rights Another view of duty-based ethics focuses on basic rights. The principle that human beings have certain fundamental rights (to life, freedom, and the pursuit of happiness, for example) is deeply embedded in Western culture.

Those who adhere to this **principle of rights,** or "rights theory," believe that a key factor in determining whether a business decision is ethical is how that decision

---

6. *Maddox v. Olshan Foundation Repair and Waterproofing Co. of Nashville, L.P.*, 2019 WL 4464816 (Tenn.Ct.App. at Nashville 2019).

affects the rights of others. These others include the firm's owners, its employees, the consumers of its products or services, its suppliers, the community in which it does business, and society as a whole.

Conflicting Rights. A potential dilemma for those who support rights theory is that they may disagree on which rights are most important. When considering all those affected by a business decision to downsize a firm, for example, how much weight should be given to employees relative to shareholders? Which employees should be laid off first—those with the highest salaries or those who have less seniority? How should the firm weigh the rights of customers relative to the community, or employees relative to society as a whole?

Resolving Conflicts. In general, rights theorists believe that whichever right is stronger in a particular circumstance takes precedence. ■ **Example 3.9** Murray Chemical Corporation has to decide whether to keep a chemical plant in Utah open, thereby saving the jobs of a hundred and fifty workers, or shut it down. Closing the plant will avoid contaminating a river with pollutants that might endanger the health of tens of thousands of people. In this situation, a rights theorist can easily choose which group to favor because the value of the right to health and well-being is obviously stronger than a right to work. Not all choices are so clear-cut, however. ■

Kantian Ethical Principles Duty-based ethical standards may also be derived solely from philosophical reasoning. The German philosopher Immanuel Kant (1724–1804) identified some general guiding principles for moral behavior based on what he thought to be the fundamental nature of human beings. Kant believed that human beings are qualitatively different from other physical objects and are endowed with moral integrity and the capacity to reason and conduct their affairs rationally.

People Are Not a Means to an End. Based on this view of human beings, Kant said that when people are treated merely as a means to an end, they are being treated as the equivalent of objects and are being denied their basic humanity. For instance, a manager who treats subordinates as mere profit-making tools is not treating them with the respect they deserve as human beings. Such a manager is less likely to retain motivated and loyal employees than a manager who respects employees.

Categorical Imperative. When a business makes unethical decisions, it often rationalizes its action by saying that the company is "just one small part" of the problem or that its

decision has had "only a small impact." A central theme in Kantian ethics is that individuals should evaluate their actions in light of the consequences that would follow if everyone in society acted in the same way. This **categorical imperative** can be applied to any action.

■ **Example 3.10** CHS Fertilizer is deciding whether to invest in expensive equipment that will decrease profits but will also reduce pollution from its factories. If CHS has adopted Kant's categorical imperative, the decision makers will consider the consequences if every company invested in the equipment (or if no company did so). If the result would make the world a better place (less polluted), CHS's decision would be clear. ■

3–2b Outcome-Based Ethics: Utilitarianism

In contrast to duty-based ethics, outcome-based ethics focuses on the consequences of an action, not on the nature of the action itself or on any set of preestablished moral values or religious beliefs. Outcome-based ethics looks at the impacts of a decision in an attempt to maximize benefits and minimize harms.

The premier philosophical theory for outcome-based decision making is **utilitarianism,** a philosophical theory developed by Jeremy Bentham (1748–1832) and modified by John Stuart Mill (1806–1873)—both British philosophers. "The greatest good for the greatest number" is a paraphrase of the major premise of the utilitarian approach to ethics.

Cost-Benefit Analysis Under a utilitarian model of ethics, an action is morally correct, or "right," when, among the people it affects, it produces the greatest amount of good for the greatest number or creates the least amount of harm for the fewest people. When an action affects the majority adversely, it is morally wrong. Applying the utilitarian theory thus requires the following steps:

1. A determination of which individuals will be affected by the action in question.
2. A **cost-benefit analysis,** which involves an assessment of the negative and positive effects of alternative actions on these individuals.
3. A choice among alternative actions that will produce maximum societal utility (the greatest positive net benefits for the greatest number of individuals).

For instance, assume that expanding a factory would provide hundreds of jobs but generate pollution that could endanger the lives of thousands of people. A utilitarian analysis would find that not endangering the lives of thousands creates greater good than providing jobs for hundreds.

Problems with the Utilitarian Approach There are problems with a strict utilitarian analysis. In some situations, an action that produces the greatest good for the most people may not seem to be the most ethical. ■ **Example 3.11** Phazim Company is producing a drug that will cure a disease in 99 percent of patients, but the other 1 percent will experience agonizing side effects and a horrible, painful death. A quick utilitarian analysis would suggest that the drug should be produced and marketed because the majority of patients will benefit. Many people, however, have significant concerns about manufacturing a drug that might cause extreme harm to some. ■

3–2c Corporate Social Responsibility

In pairing duty-based concepts with outcome-based concepts, strategists and theorists developed the idea of the corporate citizen. **Corporate social responsibility (CSR)** combines a commitment to good citizenship with a commitment to making ethical decisions, improving society, and minimizing environmental impact.

CSR is a relatively new concept in the history of business, but is a concept that becomes more important every year. Although CSR is not imposed on corporations by law, it does involve a commitment to self-regulation in a way that attends to the text and intent of the law as well as to ethical norms and global standards. A survey of U.S. executives undertaken by the Boston College Center for Corporate Citizenship found that more than 70 percent of those polled agreed that corporate citizenship must be treated as a priority. More than 60 percent said that good corporate citizenship added to their companies' profits.

CSR can be a successful strategy for companies, but corporate decision makers must not lose track of the two descriptors in the title: *corporate* and *social*. The company must link the responsibility of citizenship with the strategy and key principles of the business. Incorporating both the social and the corporate components of CSR and making ethical decisions can help companies grow and prosper.

CSR is most successful when a company undertakes activities that are significant and related to its business operations. Some types of activities that businesses are engaging in today include the following:

1. Environmental efforts.
2. Ethical labor practices.
3. Charitable donations.
4. Volunteer work.

The Corporate Aspects of CSR Arguably, any socially responsible activity may benefit a corporation.

A corporation may see an increase in goodwill from the local community for creating a park, for instance. A corporation that is viewed as a good citizen may see an increase in sales.

At times, the benefit may not be immediate. Constructing a new plant that meets high energy and environmental standards may cost more initially. Nevertheless, over the life of the building, the savings in maintenance and utilities may more than make up for the extra cost of construction.

Surveys of college students about to enter the job market confirm that young people are looking for socially responsible employers. Socially responsible activities may thus cost a corporation now, but may lead to more committed employees. Corporations that engage in meaningful social activities retain workers longer, particularly younger ones. ■ **Example 3.12** Google's focus on social responsibility attracts many young workers. Google has worked to reduce its carbon footprint and to make its products and services better for the environment. The company promotes green commuting, recycling, and reducing energy consumption at its data centers. ■

The Social Aspects of CSR Because business controls so much of the wealth and power in this country, business has a responsibility to use that wealth and power in socially beneficial ways. Thus, the social aspects of CSR require corporations to demonstrate that they are promoting goals that society deems worthwhile and are moving toward solutions to social problems. Companies may be judged on how much they donate to social causes, as well as how they conduct their operations with respect to employment discrimination, human rights, environmental concerns, and similar issues.

Some corporations publish annual social responsibility reports, which may also be called *sustainability* or *citizenship reports*. ■ **Example 3.13** The multinational technology company Cisco Systems, Inc., issues corporate responsibility reports to demonstrate its focus on people, society, and the planet. In a recent report, Cisco outlined its commitment to developing its employees' skills, ethical conduct, and charitable donations (including matching employee contributions and giving employees time off for volunteer work). Cisco also reported on the global impact of its business in the areas of human rights, labor, privacy and data security, and responsible manufacturing. The report indicated that Cisco had completed more than a hundred energy-efficient projects and was on track to meet its goals of reducing emissions from its worldwide operations by 40 percent. ■

One Current View of the Social Responsibility of Corporations. As pointed out before, the standard view of the "right" corporate behavior in the past was simply that corporations should make the most profits for their shareholders. Today, there is a more expansive view of this subject. Consider the questioning at a recent Stanford Institute for Economic Policy Research Summit. The moderator asked the CEO of Microsoft, Satya Nadella, what was the responsibility of the corporation. Nadella answered: "The social purpose of a company is to find profitable solutions to the challenges of people and planet. Driving broad economic growth is perhaps the biggest thing that a company can do. In order to have the pie distributed evenly, the pie should first grow."

Stakeholders and CSR Another view of CSR stresses that corporations have a duty not just to shareholders, but also to other groups affected by corporate decision making, called **stakeholders.** The rationale for this "stakeholder view" is that, in some circumstances, one or more of these groups may have a greater stake in company decisions than the shareholders do.

A corporation's stakeholders include its employees, customers, creditors, suppliers, and the community in which it operates. Advocacy groups, such as environmental groups and animal rights groups, may also be stakeholders. Under the stakeholder approach, a corporation considers the impact of its decision on these stakeholders, which helps it to avoid making a decision that may appear unethical and may result in negative publicity.

The most difficult aspect of the stakeholder analysis is determining which group's interests should receive greater weight if the interests conflict. For instance, companies that are struggling financially sometimes lay off workers to reduce labor costs. But some corporations have found ways to avoid slashing their workforces and to prioritize their employees' interests. Companies finding alternatives to layoffs include Dell (extended unpaid holidays), Cisco (four-day end-of-year shutdowns), Motorola (salary cuts), and Honda (voluntary unpaid vacation time). These alternatives benefit not only the employees who get to keep their jobs, but also the community as a whole. Working people can afford to go out to local restaurants and shops and use local service providers. Thus, other businesses in the community benefit.

3–3 Sources of Ethical Issues in Business Decisions

A key to avoiding unethical conduct is to recognize how certain situations may lead individuals to act unethically. In this section, we first consider some specific areas in

which ethical decisions may often arise. We then discuss some additional problems in making ethical business decisions.

3–3a Short-Term Profit Maximization

Some businesspersons commit ethical violations because they are too focused on one issue or one needed result, such as increasing profits or outperforming the competition.

In attempting to maximize profits, corporate executives and employees have to distinguish between short-run and long-run profit maximization. In the short run, a company may increase its profits by continuing to sell a product even though it knows that the product is defective. In the long run, though, because of lawsuits, large settlements, and bad publicity, such unethical conduct will cause profits to suffer. An overemphasis on short-run profit maximization is perhaps the most common reason that ethical problems occur in business.

■ **Case in Point 3.14** Volkswagen's corporate executives were accused of cheating on the pollution emissions tests of millions of vehicles that were sold in the United States. Volkswagen (VW) eventually admitted that it had installed "defeat device" software in its diesel models. The software detected when the car was being tested and changed its performance to improve the test outcome. As a result, the diesel cars showed low emissions—a feature that made the cars more attractive to today's consumers and satisfied pollution-reduction regulations.

Ultimately, Volkswagen agreed to plead guilty to criminal charges and pay $2.8 billion in fines. The company also agreed to pay $1.5 billion to the Environmental Protection Agency to settle the federal investigation into its "clean diesel" emissions fraud. Overall, the scandal cost VW nearly $15 billion (in fines and to compensate consumers or buy back their vehicles). Six top executives at VW were charged with criminal wire fraud, conspiracy, and violations of the Clean Air Act. In the end, the company's focus on maximizing profits in the short run (due to increased sales) led to unethical conduct that hurt profits in the long run.[7] ■

In the following case, a drug manufacturer was accused of fabricating "average wholesale prices" for its drugs to maximize its profits and receive overpayments from Medicaid.

---

7. *In re Volkswagen "Clean Diesel" Marketing, Sales Practices, and Product Liability Litigation,* 229 F.Supp.3d 1052 and 2017 WL 66281 (N.D.Cal. 2017). See also 895 F.3d 597 (2018) and 894 F.3d 1030 (2018).

Watson Laboratories, Inc. v. State of Mississippi

Supreme Court of Mississippi, 241 So.3d 573 (2018).

Background and Facts Watson Laboratories, Inc., makes generic drugs, which are provided by pharmacies to Medicaid patients. In the state of Mississippi, a claim is submitted for the cost of the drug to Mississippi Medicaid. The claim is paid according to a percentage of the drug's average wholesale price (AWP). Like other drug makers, Watson published its products' AWPs. But for more than a dozen years, Watson set each AWP to meet the requirements to obtain a generic designation for the drug, without regard to the actual price.

When Mississippi Medicaid learned that the actual prices were much lower than the published AWPs, the state filed a lawsuit in a Mississippi state court against Watson, alleging fraud. The court concluded that Watson had caused the state to overpay for the drugs and ordered the payment of more than $30 million in penalties, damages, and interest. Watson appealed.

In the Language of the Court

CHAMBERLIN, Justice, for the court:

* * * *

* * * The elements of an intentional * * * fraudulent representation are:

(1) a representation, (2) its falsity, (3) its materiality, (4) the speaker's knowledge of its falsity or ignorance of its truth, (5) his intent that it should be acted on by the hearer and in the manner reasonably contemplated, (6) the hearer's ignorance of its falsity, (7) his reliance on its truth, (8) his right to rely thereon, and (9) his consequent and proximate injury.

* * * *

* * * The numbers [published] by Watson * * * were not "suggested wholesale prices" or "list prices." They were fabricated numbers tied to nothing more than a ceiling amount it was necessary to stay under in order to obtain a generic designation.

* * * Thus, Watson did make a false representation.

* * * *

* * * Watson knew that Mississippi Medicaid would rely on its false statements and benefitted from this reliance. It is evident that Watson intended to deceive Mississippi Medicaid.

* * * *

Mississippi Medicaid had every right to rely on AWP [average wholesale price] as a "starting point" or "benchmark" for determining appropriate reimbursement rates. They were held out as a "suggested wholesale price."

* * * *

Evidence in the record is sufficient to show the overpayment for the drugs in question. The extent of the damages, through just and reasonable inference, has been supported by the evidence.

* * * *

In sum, * * * Watson defrauded the State. For years, Watson intentionally published its AWPs * * * with the knowledge and intent that Mississippi Medicaid would rely on the figures for its reimbursement formulas. * * * Mississippi Medicaid did not know that the AWPs had no relation to the actual prices paid for the drugs. As such, Mississippi Medicaid continued to reasonably rely on the AWPs * * * . All the while, Watson * * * exploited Mississippi Medicaid's lack of knowledge at the expense of the taxpayers of the State of Mississippi.

Decision and Remedy The Supreme Court of Mississippi affirmed the lower court's order. Watson falsely represented its AWPs. Furthermore, "Watson knew that Mississippi Medicaid would rely on its false statements and benefitted from this reliance."

Case 3.2 Continues

Case 3.2 Continued **Critical Thinking**

- **Economic** What marketing tool did Watson gain by inflating its AWPs?
- **What If the Facts Were Different?** Watson argued that AWP was a specialized term in the pharmaceutical industry that meant "suggested price." Suppose that the court had accepted this argument. What might have been the effect of this decision?

3–3b Social Media

Advancements in technology have created various new ethical issues for companies. Here, we focus on those involving social media. Most people think of social media—Facebook, TikTok, Instagram, Snapchat, YouTube, Reddit, Tumblr, Twitter, Pinterest, WhatsApp, LinkedIn, and the like—as simply ways to communicate rapidly. But everyone knows that they can quickly encounter ethical and legal disputes for posting statements that others interpret as harassing, inappropriate, insulting, or racist. Businesses often face ethical issues with respect to these social media platforms.

The Use of Social Media to Make Hiring Decisions In the past, to learn about a prospective employee, an employer would ask the candidate's former employers for references. Today, employers are likely to also conduct internet searches to discover what job candidates have posted on their Facebook pages, blogs, and tweets.

On the one hand, job candidates may be judged by what they post on social media. On the other hand, though, they may be judged because they do not participate in social media. Given that the vast majority of younger people use social media, some employers have decided that the failure to do so raises a red flag. In either case, many people believe that judging job candidates based on what they do outside the work environment is unethical.

The Use of Social Media to Discuss Work-Related Issues Because so many Americans use social media daily, they often discuss work-related issues there. Numerous companies have strict guidelines about what is appropriate and inappropriate for employees to say when posting on their own or others' social media accounts. A number of companies have fired employees for such activities as criticizing other employees or managers through social media outlets. Until recently, such disciplinary measures were considered ethical and legal.

The Responsibility of Employers. A ruling by the National Labor Relations Board (NLRB—the federal agency that investigates unfair labor practices) has changed the legality of such actions. ■ **Example 3.15** At one time,

Costco's social media policy specified that its employees should not make statements that would damage the company, harm another person's reputation, or violate the company's policies. Employees who violated these rules were subject to discipline and could be fired.

The NLRB ruled that Costco's social media policy violated federal labor law, which protects employees' right to engage in "concerted activities." Employees can freely associate with each other and have conversations about common workplace issues without employer interference. This right extends to social media posts. Therefore, an employer cannot broadly prohibit its employees from criticizing the company or co-workers, supervisors, or managers via social media. ■

The Responsibility of Employees. While most of the discussion in this chapter concerns the ethics of business management, employee ethics is also an important issue. For instance, is it ethical for employees to make negative posts in social media about other employees or, more commonly, about managers? After all, negative comments about managers reflect badly on those managers, who often are reluctant to respond via social media to such criticism. Disgruntled employees may exaggerate the negative qualities of managers whom they do not like.

Some may consider the decision by the National Labor Relations Board outlined in Example 3.15 to be too lenient toward employees and too stringent toward management. There is likely to be an ongoing debate about how to balance employees' right to free expression against employers' right to prevent the spreading of inaccurate negative statements online.

3–3c Awareness

Regardless of the context in which a decision is called for, sometimes businesspersons are not even aware that the decision has ethical implications. Perhaps they are focused on something else, for instance, or perhaps they do not take the time to think through their actions.

■ **Case in Point 3.16** Japanese airbag maker Takata Corporation manufactured some airbags that used an ammonium nitrate–based propellant without a chemical drying agent. It was later discovered that these airbags tended to deploy explosively, especially in higher temperatures, higher humidity, and older vehicles. When the airbags deployed, metal inflator cartridges inside them sometimes ruptured, sending metal shards into the passenger cabin.

The defective airbags caused a number of deaths and injuries in the United States, and the federal government ordered recalls of the devices in nearly 42 million vehicles nationwide. Takata executives did not intend to hurt consumers and may not even have considered the ethics of their decision. Takata, however, continued to produce airbags with this defect for years. A class-action lawsuit was filed against the company, which later sought bankruptcy protection.[8] ∎

3–3d Rationalization

Sometimes, businesspersons make decisions that benefit them or their company knowing that the decisions are ethically questionable. Afterward, they rationalize their bad behavior. For instance, an employee might rationalize that it is acceptable to take company property for personal use or to lie to a client just this one time, because the employee normally does not act in this way. An executive might rationalize that unethical conduct directed against a certain competitor is acceptable because that company deserves it. Individuals might rationalize that their conduct is not unethical because it is simply a part of doing business.

One suggestion that is useful in counteracting rationalization is for businesspersons to first decide the right thing to do on an ethical level before making a business decision. Then they can figure out how to mitigate the costs of doing the right thing. This works much better to prevent unethical conduct than making decisions based solely on a financial or business basis and then trying to make that result seem ethical (by rationalizing).

3–3e Uncertainty

One common denominator identified by businesspersons who have faced ethical problems is the feeling of uncertainty. They may be uncertain as to what they should do, what they should have done, or (as mentioned) whether there was even an ethical issue or ethical breach involved. Such uncertainty is practically unavoidable, but it should be treated as an indicator of a potential ethical problem.

When employees or executives express uncertainty about a particular decision, it is therefore best to treat the situation as involving an ethical issue. Decision makers should try to identify what the ethical dilemma is and why the individual or group is feeling uneasy. They should also take the time to think through the decision completely and discuss various options. They might want to consider whether the company would be pleased if the decision was reported to its clients or to the public. Building a process that supports and assists those facing ethical dilemmas can be key to avoiding unethical business practices (and any corresponding negative publicity).

3–4 Making Ethical Business Decisions

Even if officers, directors, and others in a company want to make ethical decisions, it is not always clear what is ethical in a given situation. Sometimes, there is no "good" answer to the questions that arise. Therefore, it is important to have tools to help in the decision-making process and a framework for organizing those tools.

Several frameworks exist to help businesspersons make ethical decisions. Some frameworks focus more on legal than ethical implications. This approach tends to be primarily outcome-based and, as such, may not be appropriate for a company that is values driven or committed to corporate social responsibility (or has a consumer or investor base that is focused on CSR). Other models, such as the Business Process Pragmatism™ procedure developed by ethics consultant Leonard H. Bucklin, set out a series of steps to follow. In this text, we present a modified version of this system that we call IDDR. ("I Desire to Do Right" is a useful mnemonic device for remembering the name.)

3–4a A Systematic Approach IDDR ("I Desire to Do Right")

Using the IDDR approach involves organizing the issues and approaching them systematically. This process can help eliminate various alternatives and identify the strengths and weaknesses of the remaining alternatives. Often, the best approach is for a group (rather than an individual) to carry out the process. Thus, if individual employees are facing ethical issues, they should talk with their supervisors, and then they should perform the following steps together.

---

8. *In re Takata Airbag Products Liability Litigation*, 84 F.Supp.3d 1371 (2015). See also *In re American Medical Collection Agency, Inc.*, 410 F. Supp.3d 1350 (2019).

Step 1: Inquiry The first step in making an ethical decision is to understand the problem. If an employee feels uneasy about a particular decision, decision makers should pay attention and ask questions. People generally know when something does not "feel" right, and this is often a good indicator that there may be an ethical problem. The decision makers must identify the ethical problem and all the parties involved—the stakeholders. It is important that they *not* frame the issue in a way that gives them the answer they might prefer. After gathering the relevant facts, the decision makers can also consider which ethical theories can help them analyze the problem thoroughly. Making a list of the ethical principles that will guide the decision may be helpful at this point.

Step 2: Discussion Once the ethical problem or problems have been clarified, a list of possible actions can be compiled. In discussing these alternatives, the decision makers should take time to think through each alternative completely and analyze its potential impact on various groups of stakeholders. They must evaluate the strengths and weaknesses of each option, along with its ethical and legal consequences. It is helpful to discuss with management the ultimate goals for the decision. At this point, too, the decision makers need to consider what they should do (what is the most ethical option) before considering what they can or will do.

Step 3: Decision With all the relevant facts collected and the alternatives thoroughly analyzed and discussed, it's time to make a decision. Those participating in the decision-making process now work together to craft a consensus decision or plan of action for the company. Once the decision has been made, the decision makers should use the analysis from the discussion step to articulate the reasons they arrived at the decision. This results in documentation that can be shared with stakeholders to explain why the course of action is an ethical solution to the problem.

Step 4: Review After the decision has been made and implemented, it is important for the decision makers to review the outcome to determine whether the solution was effective. Did the action solve the ethical problem? Were the stakeholders satisfied with the result? Could anything have been handled better? The results of this evaluation can be used in making future decisions. Successful decision makers learn from their mistakes and continue to improve.

3–4b Applying the IDDR Approach— A Sample Scenario

To really understand the IDDR approach, it is helpful to work through the process by analyzing an ethical problem. Here, as a sample, we present a scenario that is based on a real story but contains fictional elements as well. The conversations and analyses included in the scenario are fictional. Because any discussions that may have taken place in the real situation took place behind closed doors, we cannot know if any ethical analysis occurred.

■ **Example 3.17** Assume that you are an intern working on a social media campaign for Duane Reade, a New York pharmacy chain. As part of your internship, you follow several celebrity social media gossip platforms and do regular internet searches looking for any picture or mention of the stores. In the course of these searches, you find a picture of Katherine Heigl leaving a Duane Reade store carrying bags imprinted with the company logo. (Katherine Heigl is a recognizable actress from television's *Grey's Anatomy* and several major movies.) You can easily copy the picture to the company's Twitter account and add a caption about her shopping at one of the stores. Having customers or potential customers see this well-known person carrying Duane Reade bags and leaving the store could increase store visits and sales.

The question is this: Is it appropriate to use Heigl's photo without her permission as part of an advertising campaign? Use the IDDR approach to analyze what you should do. Assume that you, your supervisor, and a few other members of the marketing department engage in this analysis. ■

Step 1: Inquiry To begin, clarify the nature of the problem. You want to use a picture of Heigl from a celebrity social media gossip platform to potentially increase profits for the company. The problem could be phrased in this way: "Is it ethical to use a picture of a famous person to try to improve sales without contacting that person or the photographer first?" Note that the way you frame the question will affect how you answer it. For example, if the question was phrased, "Should we steal this picture?" the answer would be obvious. Remember not to frame the issue in a way that gives you the answer you might want.

You also need to identify the stakeholders. Here, the stakeholders include Heigl, the photographer who took the picture, Heigl's fans, and the potential customers of Duane Reade. Other stakeholders include your boss (who will get credit if sales increase due to the marketing campaign), Duane Reade stockholders, and store employees (who might see an increase in customers).

When gathering the facts, determine whether there are any legal issues. Given these facts, there may be state and federal laws that would guide a decision. For instance, reproducing a photograph without the owner's permission might violate federal copyright laws. In addition, most states have laws (sometimes called "right to publicity" laws) that protect a person's name, voice, or likeness (image or picture) from being used for advertising without the person's consent.

You can also consider which ethical theories can help you analyze the problem. The ethical theories may include religious values, rights theory, the categorical imperative, and utilitarianism. Ask yourself whether it is right, or

ethical, to use Heigl's name or face without her permission as part of an advertising campaign.

Step 2: Discussion Several actions could be taken in this sample situation. Each action should be thoroughly analyzed using the various ethical approaches identified by the decision makers. The ultimate goals for the decision are to increase sales and do the least amount of harm to the business and its reputation without compromising the values of the business. In this step, it is best for decision makers to brainstorm and find as many options as possible. Here, though, we analyze only three alternatives. Exhibit 3–1 shows how these alternatives could be analyzed.

Exhibit 3–1 An Analysis of Ethical Approaches to the Sample Dilemma

Alternative	Legal Implications	Religious Values	Categorical Imperative	Rights Theory	Utilitarianism
1. Use the Picture Without Permission	How does this alternative comply with copyright law? Are there any exceptions to copyright law that would allow this use?	Is this stealing? If so, it violates religious principles. Is it stealing to use a picture taken on a public street?	If everyone did this, then the images and names of famous people would often be used to promote products. Is this a good thing or not?	Using the picture may negatively impact the social media site or Heigl's ability to make money using her image. It also may violate some right to privacy.	If we use the picture, we may see an increase in sales and an improvement in reputation. We may, however, be sued for using the image without permission.
2. Contact the Social Media Site and/or Heigl for Permission	Are there any laws that would make this alternative illegal? Are there any precautions we should take when asking for permission to avoid any appearance of threat or intimidation?	This alternative clearly is not stealing and thus would align with religious principles.	If everyone asked for permission, then such material would not be used without permission. This would seem to make the world a better place.	Getting permission would not seem to violate anyone's rights. In fact, giving someone the opportunity to decide might enhance that person's rights.	If we contact the parties for permission, we may be able to use the image, make more money, and improve our reputation. But the parties might refuse to give permission or demand payment, which would cost the company money.
3. Do Not Use the Picture	There are no legal implications to not using the picture.	This alternative clearly is not stealing and thus would align with religious principles.	If companies never used public, candid images of famous people, then all advertising would be staged. This might not make the world a better place.	Not using the picture may damage the stockholders' right to maximum income or the company's right to advertise as it sees fit.	If we do not use the picture, we avoid potential lawsuits. Alternatively, we won't have the potential increase in sales associated with the use of the famous face.

It is important to note that different ethical perspectives will be more or less helpful in different situations. In the sample scenario, a strong argument can be made that Heigl's rights to privacy and to control her image are very important. Under other circumstances, however, the right to privacy might be outweighed by some other right, such as another person's right to safety. Using multiple theories will help ensure that the decision makers can work through the analytical process and find a result.

Step 3: Decision After a discussion concerning Heigl's rights to privacy and to compensation for the use of her image, you and your fellow decision makers come to a consensus. Given the potential for increased income, you decide to use the picture. It will be posted on the company's Twitter account with a caption that reads, "Love a quick #DuaneReade run? Even @KatieHeigl can't resist shopping #NYC's favorite drugstore."

Make sure to articulate the reasons you arrived at the decision to serve as documentation explaining why the plan of action was ethical. In this meeting, the persuasive evidence was the projection for increased revenue balanced by the minimal harm to Heigl. Because the picture was taken on a public street, the people in the room did not feel that it involved a violation of any privacy right. The company would not have paid Heigl to do an advertisement. Also, because only people who followed Duane Reade on Twitter could view the tweet, the group felt the likelihood of any damage to Heigl was small. Those in the group felt that the worst that could happen would be that Heigl would ask them to remove the picture.

Step 4: Review You and the other decision makers at Duane Reade need to review the effectiveness of your decision. Assume that after the picture and caption are posted on Twitter, Heigl sees it and sues Duane Reade for "no less than $6 million." She argues that the company violated her rights by falsely claiming that she had endorsed its stores and that it misappropriated her name and likeness for a profit. The case is settled out of court, with Duane Reade paying an undisclosed amount to a foundation that Heigl created.

Here, the decision did not solve the ethical problem and, in fact, led to liability. You and the other decision makers need to determine what you could have done better. Perhaps the company should change its practices and obtain legal counsel for the marketing department—or at least hire a legal consultant when ethical issues arise. Perhaps it should establish an internal process for getting permission to use pictures from social media or other sources. In any event, the company likely should change some of its policies and practices related to social media marketing.

The decision-making process is not easy or precise. It may entail repeating steps as decision makers recognize new alternatives or as unforeseen stakeholders appear. Sometimes, the analysis will lead to a clear decision, and other times it will not. Even if it does not, though, the process will allow decision makers to enter the public phase of the decision (action) with a better idea of what consequences to expect.

For more on the IDDR approach to ethical decision making, see the Ethics Today feature.

3–5 Business Ethics on a Global Level

Just as individual religions have different moral codes, individual countries and regions have different ethical expectations and priorities. Some of these differences are based on religious values, whereas others are cultural in nature. Such differences can make it even more difficult to determine what is ethical in a particular situation.

3–5a World Religions, Cultural Norms, and Ethics

Global businesses need to be conscious of the impact of different religious principles and cultural norms on ethics. For instance, in certain countries the consumption of alcohol is forbidden for religious reasons. It would be considered unethical for a U.S. business to produce alcohol in those countries and employ local workers to assist in alcohol production.

In some other countries, women may not be treated as equals because of cultural norms or religion. In contrast, discrimination against employees on the basis of sex (or sexual orientation, race, national origin, age, or disability) is prohibited in the United States. The varying roles of women across different cultures can give rise to ethical issues regarding how women working for a U.S. company should dress or behave in certain regions of the world. Should female executives have to cover their heads? Should they avoid involvement in certain business transactions? How will various stakeholders react to whatever decisions companies make in these situations? Decision makers in charge of global business operations should keep these kinds of ethical issues in mind.

Ethics Today — Applying the IDDR Framework

Pfizer, Inc., developed a new antibiotic called Trovan (trovafloxacinmesylate). Tests in animals showed that Trovan had some life-threatening side effects, including joint disease, abnormal cartilage growth, liver damage, and a degenerative bone condition. Pfizer was seeking approval from the Food and Drug Administration (FDA) to market Trovan for use in the United States when an epidemic of bacterial meningitis swept across Nigeria.

Pfizer sent three U.S. physicians to test Trovan on children who were patients in Nigeria's Infectious Disease Hospital. Pfizer's representatives obtained all necessary approvals from the Nigerian government and had Nigerian nurses explain the details of the study to parents and inform them that participation was voluntary. They did not, however, alert the parents or patients about the serious risks involved, or tell them about an effective conventional treatment that Doctors Without Borders was providing at the same site.

The results of the study showed that Trovan had a success rate of 94.4 percent in treating the children's condition. Nevertheless, eleven children died in the experiment, and others were left blind, deaf, paralyzed, or brain damaged. Rabi Abdullahi and other Nigerian children filed a suit in a U.S. federal court against Pfizer, alleging a violation of a customary international law norm prohibiting involuntary medical experimentation on humans.

Analysis

Pfizer could have applied the IDDR approach to review the ethical conflicts in a test of Trovan.

(1) In the inquiry step, decision makers ask questions to understand the ethical dilemma, identify the stakeholders, gather relevant facts, and articulate the ethical principles at issue. (2) In the discussion step, the decision makers further explore potential actions and their effects. (3) The next step is to come to a consensus decision as to what to do. This consensus should withstand moral scrutiny and fulfill corporate, community, and individual values. (4) The last step is to review the outcome to determine whether it was effective and what the company could do better. In this instance, fully informing the patients and their parents about the risks of the treatment would have been a better course of action.

Result and Reasoning

It seems unlikely that a proposed Trovan test on children, based on the facts described here, would have survived an IDDR analysis, under either a duty-based or an outcome-based ethical standard. It also would appear that Pfizer was rushing to test and market Trovan as soon as possible. This focus on short-run profit maximization took precedence over any ethical considerations. It is often easier to see ethical lapses in retrospect than it is to identify potential ethical problems in advance, however.

Critical Thinking What might Pfizer have done differently to avert the consequences?

3–5b Avoiding Corruption

Another ethical problem in global business dealings has to do with corruption in foreign governments. Under the Foreign Corrupt Practices Act,[9] U.S. businesses are prohibited from making payments to (bribing) foreign officials to secure beneficial contracts, with certain exceptions. If such payments are lawful within the foreign country, then they are permitted. It is also acceptable to pay small amounts to minor officials to facilitate or speed up the performance of administrative services (such as approval of construction). Payments to private foreign companies or other third parties are also permissible.

Corruption is widespread in some nations, however, and it can be the norm in dealing with both government and private businesses in certain locations. Global companies must take special care when doing business in countries where corruption is common. Decision makers should discuss potential ethical problems with employees in advance and again when situations arise. The company's goal should be to ensure that it supports management and employees in doing the right thing and following the firm's anticorruption policies.

3–5c Monitoring the Employment Practices of Foreign Suppliers

Many businesses contract with companies in developing nations to produce goods, such as shoes and clothing, because the wage rates in those nations are significantly lower

---

9. 15 U.S.C. Sections 78dd-1 *et seq*. This act will be discussed in more detail in the context of criminal law.

than those in the United States. But what if one of those contractors hires women and children at below-minimum-wage rates or requires its employees to work long hours in a workplace full of health hazards? What if the company's supervisors routinely engage in workplace conduct that is offensive to women? What if factories located abroad routinely violate U.S. labor and environmental standards?

Wages and Working Conditions Allegations that a business allows its suppliers to engage in unethical practices hurt the firm's reputation. ■ **Example 3.18** Noi Supalai, a garment worker in Thailand, came forward with reports about how harshly she and other workers had been treated at Eagle Speed factory, which produced apparel for Nike Corporation. Because the workers did not produce all of the required "Just Do the Right Thing" line of products by a set deadline, Nike fined the factory and barred it from paying its workers. The factory then forced some two thousand employees to work sixteen-hour days or longer, and to take turns going home to shower. Workers eventually formed a union and named Supalai as president, but they were unsuccessful in obtaining better working conditions. A meeting was set up between Supalai and a Nike representative, but Nike did not even show up. Supalai later learned that Nike had chosen to use other suppliers. ■

Corporate Watch Groups Given today's global communications network, few companies can assume that their actions in other nations will go unnoticed by "corporate watch" groups that discover and publicize unethical corporate behavior. As a result, U.S. businesses today usually take steps to avoid such adverse publicity—either by refusing to deal with certain suppliers or by arranging to monitor their suppliers' workplaces to make sure that employees are not being mistreated.

■ **Example 3.19** A Chinese factory supplied parts for certain Apple products. After Apple discovered that the factory had violated labor and environmental standards, it began evaluating the practices at all the companies in its supply chain. Apple's audits revealed numerous violations, such as withholding worker pay as a disciplinary measure, falsifying pay records, and forcing workers to use unsafe machines. Apple terminated its relationship with one foreign supplier and turned over its findings to the Fair Labor Association, a nonprofit organization that promotes adherence to national and international labor laws, for further inquiry. ■

Practice and Review: Ethics in Business

James Stilton is the chief executive officer (CEO) of RightLiving, Inc., a company that buys life insurance policies at a discount from terminally ill persons and sells the policies to investors. RightLiving pays the terminally ill patients a percentage of the future death benefit (usually 65 percent) and then sells the policies to investors for 85 percent of the value of the future benefit. The patients receive the cash to use for medical and other expenses. The investors are "guaranteed" a positive return on their investment, and RightLiving profits on the difference between the purchase and sale prices.

Stilton is aware that some sick patients might obtain insurance policies through fraud (by not revealing the illness on the insurance application). Insurance companies that discover this will cancel the policy and refuse to pay. Stilton believes that most of the policies he has purchased are legitimate, but he knows that some probably are not. Using the information presented in this chapter, answer the following questions.

1. Would a person who adheres to the principle of rights consider it ethical for Stilton not to disclose the potential risk of cancellation to investors? Why or why not?
2. Using Immanuel Kant's categorical imperative, are the actions of RightLiving, Inc., ethical? Why or why not?
3. Under utilitarianism, are Stilton's actions ethical? Why or why not? If most of the policies are, in fact, legitimate, does this make a difference in your analysis?
4. Using the IDDR approach, discuss the decision process Stilton should use in deciding whether to disclose the risk of fraudulent policies to potential investors.

Debate This . . .   Executives in large corporations are ultimately rewarded if their companies do well, particularly as evidenced by rising stock prices. Consequently, should we let those who run corporations decide what level of negative side effects of their goods or services is "acceptable"?

Terms and Concepts

business ethics 45
categorical imperative 52
corporate social responsibility
  (CSR) 53
cost-benefit analysis 52

duty-based ethics 51
ethical reasoning 51
ethics 45
moral minimum 46
outcome-based ethics 51

principle of rights 51
stakeholders 54
triple bottom line 49
utilitarianism 52

Issue Spotters

1. Acme Corporation decides to respond to what it sees as a moral obligation to correct for past discrimination by adjusting pay differences among its employees. Does this raise an ethical conflict between Acme and its employees? Between Acme and its shareholders? Explain your answers. (See *Ethical Principles and Philosophies*.)

2. Delta Tools, Inc., markets a product that under some circumstances is capable of seriously injuring consumers. Does Delta have an ethical duty to remove this product from the market, even if the injuries result only from misuse? Why or why not? (See *Making Ethical Business Decisions*.)

• **Check your answers to the Issue Spotters against the answers provided in Appendix B at the end of this text.**

Business Scenarios and Case Problems

3–1. Business Ethics. Jason Trevor owns a commercial bakery in Blakely, Georgia, that produces a variety of goods sold in grocery stores. Trevor is required by law to perform internal tests on food produced at his plant to check for contamination. On three occasions, the tests of food products containing peanut butter were positive for salmonella contamination. Trevor was not required to report the results to U.S. Food and Drug Administration officials, however, so he did not. Instead, Trevor instructed his employees to simply repeat the tests until the results were negative. Meanwhile, the products that had originally tested positive for salmonella were eventually shipped out to retailers.

Five people who ate Trevor's baked goods that year became seriously ill, and one person died from a salmonella infection. Even though Trevor's conduct was legal, was it unethical for him to sell goods that had once tested positive for salmonella? Why or why not? (See *Ethics and the Role of Business*.)

3–2. Ethical Conduct. Internet giant Zoidle, a U.S. company, generated sales of £2.5 billion in the United Kingdom (UK) in one year (roughly $3.5 billion in U.S. dollars). The UK corporate tax rate is usually between 20 percent and 24 percent, but Zoidle paid only 3 percent (£6 million). At a press conference, company officials touted how the company took advantage of tax loopholes and sheltered profits to avoid paying the full corporate income tax. They justified their practices as ethical, declaring that it would be verging on illegal to tell shareholders that the company paid more taxes than it should.

Zoidle receives significant benefits for doing business in the UK, including large sales tax exemptions and some property tax breaks. The UK relies on the corporate income tax to provide services to the underserviced and to help run the agency that regulates corporations. Is it ethical for Zoidle to avoid paying taxes? Why or why not? (See *Ethics and the Role of Business*.)

3–3. Business Ethics. Mark Ramun worked as a manager for Allied Erecting and Dismantling Co., where he had a tense relationship with his father, who was Allied's president. After more than ten years, Mark left Allied, taking 15,000 pages of Allied's documents on DVDs and CDs, which constituted trade secrets. Later, he joined Genesis Equipment & Manufacturing, Inc., a competitor. Genesis soon developed a piece of equipment that incorporated elements of Allied equipment. How might business ethics have been violated in these circumstances? Discuss. [*Allied Erecting and Dismantling Co. v. Genesis Equipment & Manufacturing, Inc.,* 511 Fed.Appx. 398 (6th Cir. 2013)] (See *Making Ethical Business Decisions*.)

3–4. Ethical Principles. Stephen Glass made himself infamous as a dishonest journalist by fabricating material for more than forty articles for *The New Republic* magazine and other publications. He also fabricated supporting materials to delude *The New Republic*'s fact checkers. At the time, he was a law student at Georgetown University. Once suspicions were aroused, Glass tried to avoid detection. Later, Glass applied for admission to the California bar. The California Supreme Court denied his application, citing "numerous instances of dishonesty and disingenuousness" during his "rehabilitation" following the exposure of his misdeeds. How do these circumstances underscore the importance of ethics? Discuss. [*In re Glass,* 58 Cal.4th 500, 316 P.3d 1199 (2014)] (See *Ethical Principles and Philosophies*.)

3–5. Business Case Problem with Sample Answer— Business Ethics. Operating out of an apartment in Secane, Pennsylvania, Hratch Ilanjian convinced Vicken Setrakian, the president of Kenset Corp., that he was an international business-man who could help Kenset turn around its business in the Middle East. At Ilanjian's insistence, Setrakian provided confidential business documents. Claiming that they had an agreement, Ilanjian demanded full, immediate payment and threatened to disclose the confidential information to a Kenset supplier if payment was not forthcoming. Kenset denied that they had a contract and filed a suit in a federal district court against Ilanjian, seeking return of the documents. During discovery, Ilanjian was uncooperative. Who behaved unethically in these circumstances? Explain. [*Kenset Corp. v. Ilanjian,* 600 Fed.Appx. 827 (3rd Cir. 2015)] (See *Making Ethical Business Decisions.*)

• For a sample answer to Problem 3–5, go to Appendix C at the end of this text.

3–6. Spotlight on Bed Bath & Beyond—Ethics and the Role of Business. Bed Bath & Beyond Inc., sold a ceramic pot, called the "FireBurners" Pot, with a stainless steel fuel reservoir at its center and a bottle of gelled fuel called "FireGel." A red sticker on the fire pot warned, "DON'T REFILL UNTIL FLAME IS OUT & CUP IS COOL." "CARE AND USE INSTRUCTIONS" with the product cautioned, in a "WARNINGS" section, "Do not add fuel when lit and never pour gel on an open fire or hot surface." The label on the back of the fuel gel bottle instructed, "NEVER add fuel to a burning fire," and under a bold "WARNING" stated, "DANGER, FLAMMABLE LIQUID & VAPOR." M.H., a minor, was injured when a fire pot in one of the products—bought from Bed Bath & Beyond—was refueled with the gel and an explosion occurred. Safer alternatives for the design of the fire pot existed, but its manufacturer chose not to use them. In these circumstances, is Bed Bath & Beyond ethically responsible for the injury to M.H.? Discuss. [*M.H. v. Bed, Bath & Beyond, Inc.,* 156 A.D.3d 33, 64 N.Y.S.3d 205 (1 Dept. 2017)] (See *Ethics and the Role of Business.*)

3–7. Ethical Leadership. Mark Clapp and Albert DiBrito worked for the Public Safety Department (PSD) in St. Joseph, Michigan. Clapp was the director, and DiBrito was the deputy director. They were under the supervision of the city manager. One day, Clapp told Tom Vaught, a PSD employee, that the previous city manager had hired DiBrito only because DiBrito had been investigating the city manager for possible wrongdoing. Clapp said that DiBrito had dropped his investigation in exchange for the deputy director position. DiBrito learned of Clapp's statement and filed a formal complaint against him on another matter with Richard Lewis, the current city manager. The investigation that followed revealed management problems within the PSD. A consultant hired by the city concluded that Clapp's remarks about DiBrito had been "inappropriate statements for a commanding officer to make regarding a second in charge." However, the consultant also identified issues regarding DiBrito's "honesty, inappropriate statements to subordinates regarding a commanding officer, favoritism, and retaliation." How do a manager's attitudes and actions affect a workplace? What steps do you think Lewis could take to prevent future ethical misconduct? [*DiBrito v. City of St. Joseph,* 675 Fed.Appx. 593 (6th Cir. 2017)] (See *Ethics and the Role of Business.*)

3–8. Codes of Ethics. All professional organizations have their own codes of ethics. Many of them relate to the unlicensed practice of the relevant profession. Licensed veterinarians must follow the Rules of Professional Conduct for Veterinarians. Maria McElwee was a licensed chiropractor in Pennsylvania who had taken additional courses in animal chiropractic. She was not a licensed veterinarian and had never worked under the guidance of a licensed veterinarian. The Pennsylvania State Board of Veterinary Medicine filed suit against McElwee because, they contended, she was practicing veterinary medicine without having first become a licensed veterinarian. At that time, she was the owner of a practice called Critter Chiropractic, which exclusively treated animals. On her website, she offered care that "promotes healing and function within your animal's body." McElwee had completed the Options for Animals College of Animal Chiropractic Program, which does not confer a degree but considers itself a "continuing education of post-graduate education program that certifies a certificate of completion." The Pennsylvania Department of State issued an order concluding that the procedures performed by McElwee constituted the unlicensed practice of veterinary medicine. McElwee appealed. She argued that the order would deprive Pennsylvania consumers of choice in chiropractic care for their animals and would cause them economic harm. Should McElwee prevail on appeal? Why or why not? [*McElwee v. Bureau of Professional and Occupational Affairs, State Board of Veterinary Medicine,* 271 A.3d 40, 2022 WL 150852 (2022)] (See *Ethics and the Role of Business.*)

3–9. A Question of Ethics—Applying the IDDR Framework. Priscilla Dickman worked as a medical technologist at the University of Connecticut Health Center for twenty-eight years. Early in her career at the Health Center, Dickman sustained a back injury while at work. The condition eventually worsened, causing her significant back pain and disability. Her physician ordered restrictions on her work duties for several years. Then Dickman's supervisor received complaints that Dickman was getting personal phone calls and was frequently absent from her work area. Based on e-mails and other documents found on her work computer, it appeared that she had been running two side businesses (selling jewelry and providing travel agent services) while at work. The state investigated, and she was convicted of a civil ethics violation for engaging in "personal business for financial gain on state time utilizing state resources." Separate investigations resulted in criminal convictions for forgery and the filing of an unrelated fraudulent insurance claim.

Dickman "retired" from her job (after she obtained approval for disability retirement) and filed a claim with the state of Connecticut against the health center. She alleged that her former employer had initiated the investigations to harass her and force her to quit. She claimed that the Health Center was unlawfully retaliating against her for being disabled and being put on workplace restrictions. [*Dickman v. University of Connecticut Health Center,* 162 Conn.App. 441, 132 A.3d 739 (2016)] (See *Making Ethical Business Decisions.*)

(a) Assume that you are Dickman's supervisor and have been informed that she is frequently away from her desk and often makes personal phone calls. The first step of using the IDDR method is *inquiry*, so you start asking questions. Several people tell you that Dickman has offered to sell them jewelry. Others say she has offered to make travel arrangements for them. You have not spoken to Dickman directly about the complaints and are not sure if you should. You also know that the Health Center would need more evidence of wrongdoing to justify firing Dickman but are uncertain as to whether you can search her computer. Should you report your findings to management? Is there any ethical problem involved in investigating and possibly firing a long-term employee? Is it fair to terminate an employee who is under disability restrictions? How would you frame the ethical dilemma that the Health Center faced in this case, and who are the stakeholders? What ethical theories would you use to guide your decision?

(b) Now suppose that you are Dickman. You have been a medical technologist for a long time but now experience severe back pain while at your desk at the Health Center. You find that you have less pain if you get up and move around during the day, rather than just sitting. That is why you are often away from your desk. You know that you will not be able to do this job much longer, and that is why you recently started a jewelry business and began providing travel services. Sure, you have made a few personal phone calls related to those businesses while at the Health Center, but other employees make personal calls, and they have not been fired. You feel that the Health Center's investigation was intended to force you to quit because you are disabled and cannot perform the tasks that you used to perform. Using the inquiry portion of the IDDR method, how might you frame the ethical issue you face, and who are the stakeholders? What ethical principles can help you analyze the problem thoroughly?

Time-Limited Group Assignment

3–10. Corporate Social Responsibility. Methamphetamine (meth) is an addictive drug made chiefly in small toxic labs (STLs) in homes, tents, barns, and hotel rooms. The manufacturing process is dangerous, often resulting in explosions, burns, and toxic fumes. Government entities spend time and resources to find and destroy STLs, imprison meth dealers and users, treat addicts, and provide services for affected families.

Meth cannot be made without ingredients that are also used in cold and allergy medications. Arkansas has one of the highest numbers of STLs in the United States. To recoup the costs of fighting the meth epidemic, twenty counties in Arkansas filed a suit against Pfizer, Inc., which makes cold and allergy medications. They argued that it was Pfizer's ethical responsibility to either stop using the ingredients in their cold and allergy medications that can be used to make meth or to compensate the government for the amount it spends closing down meth labs. (See *Ethics and the Role of Business, Ethical Principles and Philosophies,* and *Making Ethical Business Decisions.*)

(a) The first group will outline Pfizer's ethical responsibility under the corporate social responsibility doctrine. To whom does Pfizer owe duties?

(b) The second group will formulate an argument on behalf of Pfizer that the company has not breached any of its ethical responsibilities.

(c) The third group will assume that they work for Pfizer and that the company is trying to determine the best course of action to prevent its medications from being used to make meth. The group will apply the IDDR approach and explain the steps in the reasoning used.

(d) The fourth group will adopt a utilitarian point of view and perform a cost-benefit analysis to determine what the company should do. Specifically, should the company pay compensation to the state, or should it stop using certain ingredients in its medications?

Chapter 4

Courts and Alternative Dispute Resolution

The United States has fifty-two court systems—one for each of the fifty states, one for the District of Columbia, and a federal system. Keep in mind that the federal courts are not superior to the state courts. They are simply an independent system of courts, which derives its authority from Article III, Section 2, of the U.S. Constitution. By the power given to it under the U.S. Constitution, Congress has extended the federal court system to U.S. territories such as Guam, Puerto Rico, and the Virgin Islands.[1]

Although an understanding of our nation's court systems is beneficial for anyone, it is particularly crucial

in the business world—almost every businessperson will face a lawsuit at some time. Anyone involved in business should thus be familiar with the basic requirements that must be met to bring a lawsuit before a particular court, as well as the various methods of dispute resolution available outside the courts.

Assume that QuickDoor, a food delivery service, is entangled in a labor dispute with 5,000 workers who feel they are owed back pay. If any individual worker were to go to court and win, the award would be about $2,000—not enough to interest most labor lawyers. So the workers would like to combine their grievances into a single, multi-million-dollar class-action lawsuit. QuickDoor's employment contract, however, prohibits

such lawsuits. Instead, it requires an alternative dispute resolution method called *arbitration* to settle any labor disagreements between the workers and the company.

This means that QuickDoor might have to engage in 5,000 separate arbitration hearings, costing the company about $12 million, an amount greater than the cost of the underlying dispute. Which would be most fair? Requiring QuickDoor and its workers to engage in thousands of alternative dispute resolution hearings? Or allowing a single class-action lawsuit, despite the contracts? In this chapter, we will discuss how such corporate legal disagreements are resolved, along with the benefits and drawbacks of the various forms of resolution.

---

1. In Guam and the Virgin Islands, territorial courts serve as both federal courts and state courts. In Puerto Rico, they serve only as federal courts.

4–1 The Judiciary's Role in American Government

The body of American law includes the federal and state constitutions, statutes passed by legislative bodies, administrative law, and the case decisions and legal principles that form the common law. These laws would be meaningless, however, without the courts to interpret and apply them. The essential role of the judiciary—the courts—in the American governmental system is to interpret the laws and apply them to specific situations.

4–1a Judicial Review

As the branch of government entrusted with interpreting the laws, the judiciary can decide, among other things, whether the laws or actions of the other two branches are

constitutional. The process for making such a determination is known as **judicial review.** The power of judicial review enables the judicial branch to act as a check on the other two branches of government, in line with the system of checks and balances established by the U.S. Constitution.

4–1b The Origins of Judicial Review in the United States

The power of judicial review is not mentioned in the U.S. Constitution (although many constitutional scholars believe that the founders intended the judiciary to have this power). The United States Supreme Court explicitly established this power in 1803 in the case of *Marbury v. Madison.*[2] In that decision, the Court stated, "It

---

2. 5 U.S. (1 Cranch) 137, 2 L.Ed. 60 (1803).

is emphatically the province [authority] and duty of the Judicial Department to say what the law is . . . . If two laws conflict with each other, the courts must decide on the operation of each. . . . [I]f both [a] law and the Constitution apply to a particular case, . . . the Court must determine which of these conflicting rules governs the case. This is of the very essence of judicial duty." Since the *Marbury v. Madison* decision, the power of judicial review has remained unchallenged. Today, this power is exercised by both federal and state courts. (Indeed, many other constitutional democracies, including Canada, France, and Germany, have adopted some form of judicial review.)

4–2 Basic Judicial Requirements

Before a lawsuit can be brought before a court, certain requirements must be met. These requirements relate to jurisdiction, venue, and standing to sue. We examine each of these important concepts here.

4–2a Jurisdiction

In Latin, *juris* means "law," and *diction* means "to speak." Thus, "the power to speak the law" is the literal meaning of the term **jurisdiction.** Before any court can hear a case, it must have jurisdiction over the person (or company) against whom the suit is brought (the defendant) or over the property involved in the suit. The court must also have jurisdiction over the subject matter of the dispute.

Jurisdiction Over Persons or Property Generally, a particular court can exercise *in personam* **jurisdiction** (personal jurisdiction) over any person or business that resides in a certain geographic area. A state trial court, for instance, normally has jurisdictional authority over residents (including businesses) of a particular area of the state, such as a county or district. A state's highest court (often called the *state supreme court*[3]) has jurisdictional authority over all residents within the state.

A court can also exercise jurisdiction over property that is located within its boundaries. This kind of jurisdiction is known as *in rem* **jurisdiction,** or "jurisdiction over the thing." ■ **Example 4.1** A dispute arises over the ownership of a boat in dry dock in Fort Lauderdale, Florida. The boat is owned by an Ohio resident, over whom a Florida court normally cannot exercise personal jurisdiction. The

other party to the dispute is a resident of Nebraska. In this situation, a lawsuit concerning the boat could be brought in a Florida state court on the basis of the court's *in rem* jurisdiction. ■

Long Arm Statutes and Minimum Contacts. Under the authority of a state **long arm statute,** a court can exercise personal jurisdiction over certain out-of-state defendants based on activities that took place within the state. Before a court can exercise jurisdiction, though, it must be demonstrated that the defendant had sufficient contacts, or *minimum contacts*, with the state to justify the jurisdiction.[4] Generally, the minimum-contacts requirement means that the defendant must have sufficient connection to the state for the judge to conclude that it is fair for the state to exercise power over the defendant.

If an out-of-state defendant caused an automobile accident within the state or sold defective goods within the state, for instance, a court will usually find that minimum contacts exist to exercise jurisdiction over that defendant. ■ **Case in Point 4.2** An Xbox game system caught fire in Bonnie Broquet's home in Texas and caused substantial personal injuries. Broquet filed a lawsuit in a Texas court against Ji-Haw Industrial Company, a non-resident company that made the Xbox components. Broquet alleged that Ji-Haw's components were defective and had caused the fire. Ji-Haw argued that the Texas court lacked jurisdiction over it, but a state appellate court held that the Texas long arm statute authorized the exercise of jurisdiction over the out-of-state defendant.[5] ■

Corporate Contacts. A corporation normally is subject to personal jurisdiction in the state in which it is incorporated, has its principal office, and/or is doing business. Courts apply the minimum-contacts test to determine if they can exercise jurisdiction over out-of-state corporations.

In the past, corporations were usually subject to jurisdiction in any state in which they were doing business, such as advertising or selling products. The United States Supreme Court decided that this situation made questions of jurisdiction too unpredictable. After all, many corporations do business in multiple states. The Court concluded that it was unfair to expose them to costly legal proceedings in numerous different locations. Today, a

---

3. As will be discussed shortly, a state's highest court is often referred to as the state supreme court, but there are exceptions. For instance, in New York the supreme court is a trial court.

4. The minimum-contacts standard was first established in *International Shoe Co. v. State of Washington*, 326 U.S. 310, 66 S.Ct. 154, 90 L.Ed. 95 (1945).

5. *Ji-Haw Industrial Co. v. Broquet*, 2008 WL 441822 (Tex.App.—San Antonio 2008). See also *Gomez v. Wilson*, 2022 WL 200003 (Sup. Ct.N.J., App. Div. 2022).

corporation is subject to jurisdiction only in states where it does such substantial and continuous business that it is considered "at home" in those states.[6]

Jurisdiction Over Subject Matter Jurisdiction over subject matter is a limitation on the types of cases a court can hear. In both the federal and the state court systems, there are courts of general (unlimited) jurisdiction and courts of limited jurisdiction. An example of a court of general jurisdiction is a state trial court or a federal district court. An example of a state court of limited jurisdiction is a probate court. **Probate courts** are state courts that handle only matters relating to the transfer of a person's assets and obligations after that person's death, including matters relating to the custody and guardianship of children.[7] An example of a federal court of limited subject-matter jurisdiction is a bankruptcy court. **Bankruptcy courts** handle only bankruptcy proceedings, which are governed by federal bankruptcy law.

A court's jurisdiction over subject matter is usually defined in the statute or constitution creating the court. In both the federal and the state court systems, a court's subject-matter jurisdiction can be limited by any of the following:

1. The subject of the lawsuit.
2. The sum in controversy.
3. Whether the case involves a felony (a more serious type of crime) or a misdemeanor (a less serious type of crime).
4. Whether the proceeding is a trial or an appeal.

Original and Appellate Jurisdiction The distinction between courts of original jurisdiction and courts of appellate jurisdiction normally lies in whether the case is being heard for the first time. Courts having original jurisdiction are courts of the first instance, or trial courts. These are courts in which lawsuits begin, trials take place, and evidence is presented. In the federal court system, the district courts are trial courts. In the various state court systems, the trial courts are known by various names, as will be discussed shortly.

The key point here is that any court having original jurisdiction normally serves as a trial court. Courts having appellate jurisdiction act as reviewing, or appellate, courts. In general, a case can be brought before an appellate court

only on appeal from an order or a judgment of a trial court or other lower court.

Jurisdiction of the Federal Courts Because the federal government is a government of limited powers, the jurisdiction of the federal courts is limited. Federal courts have subject-matter jurisdiction in two situations: when a federal question is involved and when there is diversity of citizenship.

Federal Questions. Article III of the U.S. Constitution establishes the boundaries of federal judicial power. Section 2 of Article III states that "the judicial Power shall extend to all Cases, in Law and Equity, arising under this Constitution, the Laws of the United States, and Treaties made, or which shall be made, under their Authority."

In effect, this clause means that whenever a plaintiff's cause of action is based, at least in part, on the U.S. Constitution, a treaty, or a federal law, a **federal question** arises. Any lawsuit involving a federal question, such as a person's rights under the U.S. Constitution, can originate in a federal court. Note that in a case based on a federal question, a federal court will apply federal law.

Diversity of Citizenship. Federal district courts can also exercise original jurisdiction over cases involving **diversity of citizenship.** The most common type of diversity jurisdiction[8] requires both of the following:

1. The plaintiff and defendant must be residents of different states.
2. The dollar amount in controversy must exceed $75,000.

For purposes of diversity jurisdiction, a corporation is a citizen of both the state in which it is incorporated and the state in which its principal place of business is located.

A case involving diversity of citizenship can be filed in the appropriate federal district court. If the case starts in a state court, it can sometimes be transferred, or "removed," to a federal court. The party seeking to move the case to federal court bears the burden of demonstrating that the *ground* for diversity exist.

■ **Case in Point 4.3** Elijah Ratcliff was involved in a civil lawsuit with Greyhound Bus Lines over a luggage theft on one of the company's buses. Greyhound is headquartered in Dallas, Texas. Ratcliff sought to have the civil trial removed to a federal court in New York. To do so, he needed to convince the federal court that he was a

---

6. *Daimler AG v. Bauman,* 571 U.S. 117, 134 S.Ct. 746, 187 L.Ed.2d 624 (2014). See also *Frank v. P.N.K. (Lake Charles) LLC,* 947 F.3d 331 (5th Cir. 2020).
7. See, for example, *Whitener as Trustees of Charles Cleveland Whitener, III Marital Trust v. Origin Bank,* 2023 WL 1169025 (Ct.App. TX, Houston 14th Dist. 2023).

8. Diversity jurisdiction also exists in cases between (1) a foreign country and citizens of a state or of different states and (2) citizens of a state and citizens or subjects of a foreign country. Cases based on these types of diversity jurisdiction occur infrequently.

resident of New York, therefore meeting the requirements of diversity of jurisdiction.

The facts were not in his favor. First, he had filed a complaint against Greyhound in Texas. His mailing address was in Texas. The luggage was stolen on a return trip he took to Texas from New York. He indicated that voter registration forms and tax returns would prove his New York residency but did not produce either. A U.S. district court concluded that Ratcliff was principally based in Texas and dismissed his case for lack of diversity jurisdiction. A federal appeals court affirmed.[9] ∎

As already noted, a federal court will apply federal law in cases involving federal questions. In a case based on diversity of citizenship, in contrast, a federal court will apply the relevant state law, which is often the law of the state in which the court sits.

Exclusive Versus Concurrent Jurisdiction
When both federal and state courts have the power to hear a case, as is true in lawsuits involving diversity of citizenship, **concurrent jurisdiction** exists. When cases can be tried only in federal courts or only in state courts, **exclusive jurisdiction** exists.

Federal courts have exclusive jurisdiction in cases involving federal crimes, bankruptcy, most patent and copyright claims, suits against the United States, and some areas of admiralty law (which governs matters involving disputes on navigable waters). State courts

also have exclusive jurisdiction over certain subjects—for instance, divorce and adoption.

When concurrent jurisdiction exists, a party may choose to bring a suit in either a federal court or a state court. Many factors can affect a party's decision to litigate in a federal versus a state court. Examples include the availability of different remedies, the distance to the respective courthouses, or the experience or reputation of a particular judge. For instance, a plaintiff might choose to litigate in a state court if the court has a reputation for awarding substantial amounts of damages or if the judge is perceived as being pro-plaintiff. The concepts of exclusive and concurrent jurisdiction are illustrated in Exhibit 4–1.

Jurisdiction in Cyberspace
The internet's capacity to bypass political and geographic boundaries undercuts the traditional basis on which courts assert personal jurisdiction. As discussed, for a court to compel a defendant to come before it, the defendant must have a sufficient connection—that is, minimum contacts—with the state. When a defendant's only contacts with the state are through a website, however, it can be difficult to determine whether these contacts are sufficient for a court to exercise jurisdiction.

The "Sliding-Scale" Standard.
The courts have developed a "sliding-scale" standard to determine when they can exercise personal jurisdiction over an out-of-state defendant based on the defendant's web activities. The sliding-scale standard identifies three types of internet

9. *Ratcliff v. Greyhound Bus Lines,* 792 Fed.Appx. 121 (2nd Cir. 2020).

Exhibit 4–1 Exclusive and Concurrent Jurisdiction

business contacts and outlines the following rules for jurisdiction:

1. When the defendant conducts substantial business over the internet (such as contracts and sales), jurisdiction is proper.

2. When there is some interactivity through a website, jurisdiction may be proper, depending on the circumstances. It is up to the courts to decide how much online interactivity is enough to satisfy the minimum-contacts requirement. ■ **Case in Point 4.4** Dr. Arthur Delahoussaye, a Louisiana resident, bought a special racing bicycle on eBay from Frederick Boelter, who lived in Wisconsin. Later, while Delahoussaye was riding the bike, the front wheel disconnected, pushing the forks of the bicycle into the ground and propelling him over the handlebars and onto the pavement. Delahoussaye suffered serious injuries. He sued Boelter in a Louisiana court, alleging that Boelter had negligently removed the retention devices designed to prevent the detachment of the front wheel.

The Louisiana court ruled that the state did not have jurisdiction over Boelter, and a state appellate court affirmed. Boelter did not have any prior relationship with Delahoussaye, did not initiate communications with Delahoussaye, and discussed the transaction with Delahoussaye only over the internet. Payment was made through an intermediary, PayPal, and Boelter shipped the bicycle to Louisiana. The sale of a single bicycle to Delahoussaye on eBay was not enough to give Louisiana state jurisdiction over Boelter, so the plaintiff's case was dismissed.[10] ■

3. When a defendant merely engages in passive advertising on the web, jurisdiction is never proper.[11]

International Jurisdictional Issues. Because the internet is international in scope, it obviously raises international jurisdictional issues. The world's courts seem to be developing a standard that echoes the requirement of minimum contacts applied by the U.S. courts.

Most courts are indicating that minimum contacts—doing business within the jurisdiction, for instance—are enough to compel a defendant to appear. The effect of this standard is that a business firm has to comply with the laws in any jurisdiction in which it targets customers for its products. This situation is complicated by the fact that many countries' laws on particular issues—free speech, for instance—are very different from U.S. laws.

The following case illustrates how federal courts apply a sliding-scale standard to determine if they can exercise jurisdiction over a foreign defendant whose only contact with the United States is through a website.

---

10. *Delahoussaye v. Boelter*, 199 So.3d 633 (La.App. 2016).
11. For a leading case on this issue, see *Zippo Manufacturing Co. v. Zippo Dot Com, Inc.*, 952 F.Supp. 1119 (W.D.Pa. 1997).

Spotlight on Gucci

Case 4.1 Gucci America, Inc. v. Wang Huoqing

United States District Court, Northern District of California, 2011 WL 30972 (2011).

Background and Facts Gucci America, Inc., a New York corporation headquartered in New York City, is part of Gucci Group, a global fashion firm with offices in China, France, Great Britain, Italy, and Japan. In connection with its products, Gucci uses twenty-one federally registered trademarks. Gucci also operates a number of boutiques, some of which are located in California.

Wang Huoqing, a resident of the People's Republic of China, operates numerous websites. When Gucci discovered that Wang Huoqing's websites offered for sale counterfeit goods—products bearing Gucci's trademarks but not genuine Gucci articles—it hired a private investigator in San Jose, California, to buy goods from the websites. The investigator purchased a wallet that was labeled Gucci but was counterfeit.

Gucci filed a trademark infringement lawsuit against Wang Huoqing in a federal district court in California seeking damages and an injunction to prevent further infringement. Wang Huoqing was notified of the lawsuit via e-mail but did not appear in court. Gucci asked the court to enter a default judgment—that is, a judgment entered when the defendant fails to appear. First, however, the court had to determine whether it had personal jurisdiction over Wang Huoqing based on the internet sales.

Case 4.1 Continues

Case 4.1 Continued

In the Language of the Court

Joseph C. SPERO, United States Magistrate Judge.

* * * *

* * * Under California's long-arm statute, federal courts in California may exercise jurisdiction to the extent permitted by the Due Process Clause of the Constitution. The Due Process Clause allows federal courts to exercise jurisdiction where * * * the defendant has had sufficient minimum contacts with the forum to subject [them] to the specific jurisdiction of the court. The courts apply a three-part test to determine whether specific jurisdiction exists:

(1) The nonresident defendant must do some act or consummate some transaction with the forum or perform some act by which [they] purposefully avail [themselves] of the privilege of conducting activities in the forum, thereby invoking the benefits and protections of its laws; (2) the claim must be one which arises out of or results from the defendant's forum-related activities; and (3) exercise of jurisdiction must be reasonable.

* * * *

In order to satisfy the first prong of the test for specific jurisdiction, a defendant must have either purposefully availed itself of the privilege of conducting business activities within the forum or purposefully directed activities toward the forum. Purposeful availment typically consists of action taking place in the forum that invokes the benefits and protections of the laws of the forum, such as executing or performing a contract within the forum. To show purposeful availment, a plaintiff must show that the defendant "engage[d] in some form of affirmative conduct allowing or promoting the transaction of business within the forum state." [Emphasis added.]

"In the internet context, the Ninth Circuit utilizes a sliding scale analysis under which 'passive' websites do not create sufficient contacts to establish purposeful availment, whereas interactive websites may create sufficient contacts, depending on how interactive the website is." * * * "Personal jurisdiction is appropriate where an entity is conducting business over the internet and has offered for sale and sold its products to forum [California] residents."

Here, the allegations and evidence presented by Plaintiffs in support of the Motion are sufficient to show purposeful availment on the part of Defendant Wang Huoqing. Plaintiffs have alleged that Defendant operates "fully interactive internet websites operating under the Subject Domain Names" and have presented evidence in the form of copies of web pages showing that the websites are, in fact, interactive. * * * Additionally, Plaintiffs allege Defendant is conducting counterfeiting and infringing activities within this Judicial District and has advertised and sold his counterfeit goods in the State of California. * * * Plaintiffs have also presented evidence of one actual sale within this district, made by investigator Robert Holmes from the website bag2do.cn. * * * Finally, Plaintiffs have presented evidence that Defendant Wang Huoqing owns or controls the twenty-eight websites listed in the Motion for Default Judgment. * * * Such commercial activity in the forum amounts to purposeful availment of the privilege of conducting activities within the forum, thus invoking the benefits and protections of its laws. Accordingly, the Court concludes that Defendant's contacts with California are sufficient to show purposeful availment.

Decision and Remedy The U.S. District Court for the Northern District of California held that it had personal jurisdiction over the foreign defendant, Wang Huoqing. The court entered a default judgment against Wang Huoqing and granted Gucci an injunction.

Critical Thinking

- **What If the Facts Were Different?** Suppose that Gucci had not presented evidence that Wang Huoqing had made one actual sale through his website to a resident of the court's district (the private investigator). Would the court still have found that it had personal jurisdiction over Wang Huoqing? Why or why not?
- **Legal Environment** Is it relevant to the analysis of jurisdiction that Gucci America's principal place of business is in New York rather than California? Explain.

Jurisdiction Summarized In summary, jurisdiction has to do with whether a court has authority to hear a case involving specific persons, property, or subject matter. To review the various types of jurisdiction discussed in this section, see Concept Summary 4.1.

4–2b Venue

Venue[12] is concerned with the most appropriate location for a trial. For instance, two state courts (or two federal courts) may have the authority to exercise jurisdiction

over a case. Nonetheless, it may be more appropriate or convenient to hear the case in one court than in the other.

The concept of venue reflects the policy that a court trying a case should be in the geographic neighborhood (usually the county) where the incident occurred or where the parties reside. Venue in a civil case typically is where the defendant resides or does business, whereas venue in a criminal case normally is where the crime occurred.

In some cases, pretrial publicity or other factors may require a change of venue to another community, especially in criminal cases in which the defendant's right to a fair and impartial jury has been impaired. Note, though, that

---

12. Pronounced *ven*-yoo.

Concept Summary 4.1

Jurisdiction

Personal	Exists when a defendant: • Is located in the court's territorial boundaries. • Qualifies under state long arm statutes. • Is a corporation doing business within the state. • Advertises, sells, or places goods into commerce within the state.
Property	Exists when the property that is subject to a lawsuit is located within the court's territorial boundaries.
Subject Matter	Limits the court's jurisdictional authority to particular types of cases. • *General jurisdiction*—Exists when a court can hear cases involving a broad array of issues. • *Limited jurisdiction*—Exists when a court is limited to a specific subject matter, such as probate or divorce.
Original	Exists with courts that have the authority to hear a case for the first time (trial courts, district courts).
Appellate	Exists with courts of appeal and review. Generally, appellate courts do not have original jurisdiction.
Federal	A federal court can exercise jurisdiction: • When the plaintiff's cause of action involves a federal question (is based at least in part on the U.S. Constitution, a treaty, or a federal law). • In cases between citizens of different states (or cases involving U.S. citizens and foreign countries or their citizens) when the amount in controversy exceeds $75,000 (diversity-of-citizenship jurisdiction).
Concurrent	Exists when both federal and state courts have authority to hear the same case.
Exclusive	Exists when only state courts or only federal courts have authority to hear a case.
Cyberspace	The courts have developed a sliding-scale standard to use in determining when jurisdiction over a website owner or operator in another state is proper.

venue has lost some significance in today's world because of the internet and 24/7 news reporting. Courts now rarely grant requests for a change of venue. Because everyone has instant access to the same information about a purported crime, courts reason that no community is more or less informed or prejudiced for or against a defendant.

4–2c Standing to Sue

Before a party can bring a lawsuit to court, that party must have **standing to sue,** or a sufficient stake in a matter to justify seeking relief through the court system. Standing means that the party that filed the action in court has a legally protected interest at stake in the litigation. At times, a person can have standing to sue on behalf of another person, such as a minor (child).

Standing can be broken down into three elements:

1. **Harm.** The party bringing the action must have suffered harm—an invasion of a legally protected interest—or must face imminent harm. The controversy must be real and substantial rather than hypothetical.
2. **Causation.** There must be a causal connection between the conduct complained of and the injury.
3. **Remedy.** It must be likely, as opposed to merely speculative, that a favorable court decision will remedy the injury suffered.

In the following case, the question of standing arose concerning a local environmentalist who regularly visited an area of wetlands for recreational purposes.

Case Analysis 4.2

The Glynn Environmental Coalition, Inc., Center for a Sustainable Coast, Inc., Jane Fraser v. Sea Island Acquisition, LLC

United States Court of Appeals, Eleventh Circuit, 26 F.4th 1235 (2022)

In the Language of the Court
PRYOR, William, Chief Judge

This appeal concerns whether a local environmentalist who regularly visits an area of wetlands to recreate and enjoy their natural beauty has standing to complain about the filling of a wetland with outside materials because it has diminished her aesthetic interest in that wetland. Because these allegations suffice to establish an injury in fact, we vacate the order of dismissal and remand for further proceedings.

At this stage, we accept as true the following allegations of the complaint. Sea Island Acquisition, LLC, owns a 0.49-acre parcel of land near Dunbar Creek in Glynn County, Georgia, next to the parking lot for its nearby hotel. The parcel is considered a wetland under the Clean Water Act. When Sea Island sought to fill that parcel with outside materials, the Act required Sea Island to obtain a certification from the State of Georgia and a permit from the United States Army Corps of Engineers.

* * * *

Nationwide Permit 39, a general permit, was issued in 2012. It allowed the filling of wetlands "for the construction . . . of commercial and institutional building foundations and . . . attendant features . . . necessary for the use and maintenance of the structures" on the wetlands. * * * In 2012, the Georgia Environmental Protection Division issued a conditional certification for all projects that were allowed by Permit 39.

On January 10, 2013, Sea Island submitted a pre-construction notification to the Corps for its plan to fill its wetland for the purpose of constructing a commercial building. The notification represented that Sea Island intended to fill 0.49 acres of what might be a wetland under the Act. Sea Island also sought a jurisdictional determination by the Corps of whether the parcel was a wetland. Sea Island proposed building "[r]etaining walls . . . to reduce [the] overall footprint of the project in the wetlands," as well as

purchasing 3.48 wetland "mitigation credits" to offset the loss of wetlands.
* * * *

Although Sea Island had represented to the Corps that it intended to construct or expand a "commercial and institutional building foundation . . . and [an] attendant feature," * * * "Sea Island intentionally and maliciously misrepresented" that intent. "Sea Island never intended to comply" with Permit 39 or the Georgia Conditional Permit and "only applied for [Permit 39] to save time and money." Instead, it intended to "landscape over" the wetland, which is near "its hotel, the Inn at Sea Island." "Sea Island filled" the wetland with "fill material . . . between February 20, 2013, and March 27, 2013," but it still has not erected nor has any intention to erect any buildings or structures on the wetland.
* * * *

The Glynn Environmental Coalition, Inc., the Center for a Sustainable Coast, Inc., and Jane Fraser sued Sea Island. The organizations are Georgia non-profit

Case 4.2 Continues

Case 4.2 Continued

corporations. Some of their members, including Fraser, reside in Glynn County near the wetland. The organizations provide their members with information concerning environmental developments in the area.

The environmentalists alleged that Sea Island did not comply with the Act's permitting process because it filled the wetland for the purpose of landscaping and not constructing a commercial structure, it did not comply with the Georgia conditional certification, the authorization under Permit 39 had expired without compliance, and the authorization was null and void because Sea Island "intentionally and maliciously misled the Corps." The environmentalists sought a declaratory judgment, an injunction "compelling Sea Island to restore" the wetland, civil penalties, and attorney's fees.

Fraser is a "resident of Glynn County" who "ha[s] lived in the area . . . for over twenty years" and is a member of both Glynn Environmental and Sustainable Coast. Fraser moved to the area "in large part due to the area's unique ecology, including its native habitat, wildlife[,] and vegetation." She "regularly recreate[s] in and enjoy[s] the aesthetics of the wetlands and marshes" in the general Dunbar Creek area. Before the fill of the wetland, Fraser "derived aesthetic pleasure" from the wetland, which she described as a "pleasing natural resource," and from "other similar wetland habitats in Glynn County by viewing the area in its *natural* habitat." (Emphasis added.) After the fill, the wetland was "replaced by *unnatural* grassed areas" and an "unnatural lawn" that is "less aesthetically pleasing." (Emphasis added.) The fill of the wetland was the partial cause of a "noticeable deterioration of the natural aesthetic beauty, water quality, and habitat of the . . . area," and Sea Island's actions "diminished" Fraser's "aesthetic and recreational value" in the wetland and "its downstream tributaries." Fraser also alleges that she "observe[s] Dunbar Creek on a daily basis" as she drives over Dunbar Creek and that she has "noticed

a significant difference in the water clarity in Dunbar Creek."

Sea Island moved to dismiss the environmentalists' amended complaint for lack of standing and for failure to state a claim upon which relief could be granted. * * * Sea Island argued that the environmentalists' allegations did not establish that any of the parties had suffered an injury in fact and that the organizations could not establish associational standing. And it contended that, assuming the allegations established a legally cognizable injury, the complaint did not establish causation or redressability. Sea Island also contested the legal sufficiency of each of the environmentalists' claims. The environmentalists responded that they had suffered environmental, aesthetic, recreational, and procedural injuries, and that the organizations had associational standing through the standing of Fraser. The environmentalists also argued that they had adequately alleged causation and redressability, and they defended their complaint on the merits.

The district court dismissed the complaint for lack of standing on the ground that the environmentalists failed to allege an injury in fact. * * *
* * * *

Article III standing requires a plaintiff to have "suffered an injury in fact, . . . that is fairly traceable to the challenged conduct of the defendant, and . . . that is likely to be redressed by a favorable judicial decision." * * * *

An injury in fact must be "concrete, particularized, and actual or imminent." * * * An injury that is "conjectural or hypothetical" is constitutionally insufficient. * * *
* * * *

An individual suffers an aesthetic injury when she "use[s] the affected area" and is a person "for whom the aesthetic . . . value of the area will be lessened by the challenged activity." * * *
* * * *

Fraser "plausibly and clearly allege[d] a concrete injury" to her aesthetic interest. Fraser gains aesthetic pleasure from viewing wetlands in their natural

habitat. She regularly recreates in the area and sees the wetland. After the wetland was replaced with sodding, she derived less pleasure from the wetland because the habitat and vegetation were unnatural. These alleged injuries are sufficient at the pleading stage because Fraser need only allege "that [s]he uses" the "area affected" and that h[er] aesthetic . . . interests . . . have been harmed." * * *
* * * *

Federal courts enjoy the power to protect an interest that is "shared by the many rather than the few." And "[t]he fact that an injury may be suffered by a large number of people does not . . . make that injury a nonjusticiable generalized grievance." An injury can be "widely shared" and remain actionable so long as "the impact on [the] plaintiff is [not] plainly undifferentiated and common to *all* members of the public." Not every citizen will drive by the wetland that Sea Island filled, nor will every citizen be bothered by not seeing the wetland in its natural state.

Even if Sea Island is correct that the environmentalists have no recreational interest in the filled wetland itself because they have no ability to recreate on Sea Island's private property, that argument does not apply to Fraser's alleged aesthetic interests in the filled wetland. A person can suffer an injury from the unsightly nature of private property under well-settled tort law, even if he cannot always prevail on his underlying claim. * * *
* * * *

Fraser adequately alleged that she suffered an injury to her aesthetic interests in the wetland because she has viewed the wetland, derived aesthetic pleasure from its natural habitat and vegetation, and now derives less pleasure from the unnatural grasses and lawn placed on the wetland. Those allegations are sufficient to establish an injury in fact at this stage, and the district court erred in concluding otherwise.

We VACATE the order of dismissal and REMAND for further proceedings.

Case 4.2 Continues

Case 4.2 Continued

Legal Reasoning Question

1. What argument did Sea Island Acquisition, LLC, use in its motion to dismiss the environmentalists' complaint?

2. Why is the requirement of standing to sue so important in our legal system?

3. Does the standing to sue requirement obligate a plaintiff to have suffered concrete, physically observable injuries? Why or why not?

4–3 The State and Federal Court Systems

Each state has its own court system. Additionally, there is a system of federal courts. The right-hand side of Exhibit 4–2 illustrates the basic organizational framework characteristic of the court systems in many states. The exhibit also shows how the federal court system is structured. We turn now to an examination of these court systems, beginning with the state courts.

4–3a The State Court Systems

No two state court systems are exactly the same. Typically, though, a state court system includes several levels, or tiers, of courts, as shown in Exhibit 4–2. State courts may include (1) trial courts of limited jurisdiction, (2) trial courts of general jurisdiction, (3) appellate courts (intermediate appellate courts), and (4) the state's highest court (often called the state supreme court).

Generally, any person who is a party to a lawsuit has the opportunity to plead the case before a trial court and then, if they lose, before at least one level of appellate court. If the case involves a federal statute or a federal constitutional issue, the decision of the state supreme court may be further appealed to the United States Supreme Court.

The states use various methods to select judges for their courts. Usually, voters elect judges, but in some states, judges are appointed. For instance, in Iowa, the governor appoints judges, and then the general population decides whether to confirm their appointment in the next general election. The states usually specify the number of years that judges will serve.

Trial Courts Trial courts are exactly what their name implies—courts in which trials are held and testimony is taken. State trial courts have either general or limited jurisdiction, as defined earlier.

General Jurisdiction. Trial courts that have general jurisdiction as to subject matter may be called county,

Exhibit 4–2 The State and Federal Court Systems

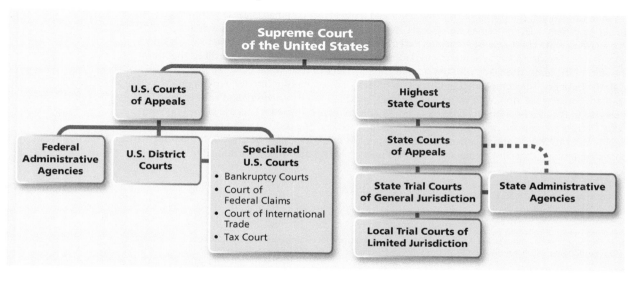

district, superior, or circuit courts.[13] State trial courts of general jurisdiction have jurisdiction over a wide variety of subjects, including both civil disputes and criminal prosecutions. In some states, trial courts of general jurisdiction may hear appeals from courts of limited jurisdiction.

Limited Jurisdiction. Courts of limited jurisdiction as to subject matter are generally inferior trial courts or minor judiciary courts. Limited jurisdiction courts might include local municipal courts (which could include separate traffic courts and drug courts) and domestic relations courts (which handle divorce and child-custody disputes).

Small claims courts are inferior trial courts that hear only civil cases involving claims of less than a certain amount, such as $5,000 (the amount varies from state to state). Procedures in small claims courts are generally informal, and lawyers are not required (in a few states, lawyers are not even allowed). Decisions of small claims courts and municipal courts may sometimes be appealed to a state trial court of general jurisdiction.

Appellate, or Reviewing, Courts Every state has at least one court of appeals (appellate court, or reviewing

---

13. The name in Ohio and Pennsylvania is Court of Common Pleas. The name in New York is Supreme Court, Trial Division.

court), which may be an intermediate appellate court or the state's highest court. About three-fourths of the states have intermediate appellate courts.

Generally, courts of appeals do not conduct new trials, in which evidence is submitted to the court and witnesses are examined. Rather, an appellate court panel of three or more judges reviews the record of the case on appeal, which includes a transcript of the trial proceedings. The appellate court hears arguments from attorneys and determines whether the trial court committed an error.

Reviewing courts focus on questions of law, not questions of fact. A **question of fact** deals with what really happened in regard to the dispute being tried—such as whether a party actually burned a flag. A **question of law** concerns the application or interpretation of the law—such as whether flag burning is a form of speech protected by the First Amendment to the U.S. Constitution. Only a judge, not a jury, can rule on questions of law.

Appellate courts normally defer (give significant weight) to the trial court's findings on questions of fact because the trial court judge and jury were in a better position to evaluate testimony. The trial court judge and jury can directly observe witnesses' gestures, demeanor, and other nonverbal behavior during the trial. An appellate court cannot. Questions of fact were at the center of the following case.

Case 4.3

Oxford Tower Apartments, LP v. Frenchie's Hair Boutique

Superior Court of Pennsylvania, 226 A.3d 626 (2020).

Background and Facts Frenchie's Hair Boutique sells hair extensions, clothing, and accessories. Rolande Christophe, the owner of Frenchie's, entered a three-year commercial lease with Oxford Tower Apartments, LP, for a small storefront. Less than two years later, Oxford filed a suit in a Pennsylvania state court against Frenchie's and Christophe, alleging breach of contract and seeking unpaid rent. The defendants counterclaimed for damages. At the trial, Christophe testified that from the start of the lease, problems with the store, including a lack of heat in the building, interfered with her business. She complained to Oxford, to no avail. Fifteen months into the term, a pipe erupted, flooding the store with water and sewage. Frenchie's lost its inventory and was required to clear out so that the flooring could be replaced. Unable to reopen the store because of the lingering odor, Christophe stopped paying rent and gave Oxford the key. The court granted possession of the premises to Oxford and awarded damages for the loss of the inventory to Christophe. Oxford appealed, arguing that Christophe and Frenchie's were still obligated to pay the unpaid rent.

In the Words of the Court

Memorandum by BENDER, P.J.E. [President Judge Emeritus[a]]

* * * *

---

a. In the Pennsylvania court system, a president judge is the executive and administrative head of the court. *Emeritus* indicates that the judge has retired from this position but retains the title of the office as an honor.

Case 4.3 Continues

Case 4.3 Continued

* * * Our appellate role * * * is to determine whether the findings of the trial court are supported by competent evidence * * *. We will reverse the trial court only if its findings of fact are not supported by competent evidence in the record.

* * * The trial court, as the finder of fact, is free to believe all, part or none of the evidence presented. Issues of credibility and conflicts in evidence are for the trial court to resolve; this Court is not permitted to reexamine the weight and credibility determination or substitute our judgment for that of the fact finder.

* * * *

Here, Appellees presented testimony regarding numerous ongoing problems that hindered their ability to conduct business and that remained unremedied by Appellant, despite Appellees' frequent complaints. Appellant argues that * * * Appellees never surrendered the premises. However, the record clearly contradicts Appellant's claim. Ms. Christophe * * * was unable to [reopen her store] due to "the foul odor of waste emanating from the floor." As a result, Ms. Christophe * * * surrendered the key to Appellant.

Appellant * * * asks this Court to reassess the credibility of the witnesses. However, it is well settled that we cannot substitute our judgment for that of the trier of fact. The trial court was free to believe certain witnesses and to disbelieve the testimony of other witnesses, as the trier of fact has the unique opportunity to see and hear subtleties of answer and movements of witnesses and parties not viewable from the cold record. The trial court concluded that the evidence presented supported a finding in favor of Appellees. We deem the trial court's determination to be well-supported by the record.

Decision and Remedy A state intermediate appellate court affirmed the lower court's order. Oxford retained possession of the premises, and Christophe and Frenchie's obtained damages for the cost of the lost inventory.

Critical Thinking

- **Economic** Should an appellate court's review of the monetary size of the damages awarded at trial be subject to the principle that limits appellate review of other evidence? Why or why not?
- **Legal** A judge or a jury can decide a question of fact, but only a judge can rule on a question of law. Why?

Highest State Courts The highest appellate court in a state is usually called the supreme court but may be designated by some other name. For instance, in both New York and Maryland, the highest state court is called the Court of Appeals. The highest state court in Maine and Massachusetts is the Supreme Judicial Court. In West Virginia, it is the Supreme Court of Appeals.

The decisions of each state's highest court on all questions of state law are final. Only when issues of federal law are involved can the United States Supreme Court overrule a decision made by a state's highest court. ■ **Example 4.5** A city enacts an ordinance that prohibits citizens from engaging in door-to-door advocacy without first registering with the mayor's office and receiving a permit. A religious group sues the city, arguing that the law violates the freedoms of speech and religion guaranteed by the First Amendment. If the state supreme court upholds the law, the group could appeal the decision to the United States Supreme Court, because a constitutional (federal) issue is involved. ■

4–3b The Federal Court System

The federal court system is basically a three-tiered model consisting of (1) U.S. district courts (trial courts of general jurisdiction) and various courts of limited jurisdiction, (2) U.S. courts of appeals (intermediate courts of appeals), and (3) the United States Supreme Court.

Unlike state court judges, who are usually elected, federal court judges—including the justices of the Supreme Court—are appointed by the president of the United States, subject to confirmation by the U.S. Senate. Federal judges receive lifetime appointments under Article III of the U.S. Constitution, which states that federal judges "hold their offices during good Behaviour." In the entire history of the United States, only a handful of federal judges have been removed from office through impeachment proceedings.

Certain federal court officers are not chosen in the way just described. This chapter's *Managerial Strategy* feature describes how U.S. magistrate judges are selected.

Managerial Strategy

Should You Consent to Have Your Business Case Decided by a U.S. Magistrate Judge?

You have a strong case in a contract dispute with one of your business's suppliers. The supplier is located in another state. Your attorney did everything necessary to obtain your "day in court." The court in question is a federal district court. But you have just found out that your case may not be heard for several years—or even longer. Your attorney tells you that the case can be heard in just a few months if you consent to place it in the hands of a U.S. magistrate judge.[a] Should you consent?

A Short History of U.S. Magistrate Judges

Congress authorized the creation of a new federal judicial officer, the U.S. magistrate, in 1968 to help reduce delays in the U.S. district courts.[b] These junior federal officers were to conduct a wide range of judicial proceedings as set out by statute and as assigned by the district judges under whom they served. In 1979, Congress gave U.S. magistrates consent jurisdiction, which authorizes them to conduct all civil trials as long as the parties consent.[c] Currently, each year magistrate judges dispose of over a million civil and criminal district court matters, which include motions and hearings.

The Selection and Quality of Magistrate Judges

As mentioned, federal district judges are nominated by the president, confirmed by the Senate, and appointed for life. In contrast, U.S. magistrate judges are selected by federal district court judges based on

the recommendations of a merit screening committee. They serve an eight-year term (which can be renewed).

By statute, magistrate judges must be chosen through a merit selection process. Applicants are interviewed by a screening committee of lawyers and others from the district in which the position will be filled.[d] Political party affiliation plays no part in the process.

A variety of experienced attorneys, administrative law judges, state court judges, and others apply for magistrate judge positions. A typical opening receives about a hundred applicants. The merit selection panel selects the five most qualified, who are then voted on by federal district court judges.

Because the selection process for a magistrate judge is not the same as for a district judge, some critics have expressed concerns about the quality of magistrate judges. Some groups, such as People for the American Way, are not in favor of allowing magistrate judges the power to decide cases. These critics believe that because of their limited terms, they are not completely immune from outside pressure.

Business Questions

1. If you were facing an especially complex legal dispute—one involving many facets and several different types of law—would you consent to allowing a U.S. magistrate judge to decide the case? Why or why not?
2. If you had to decide whether to allow a U.S. magistrate judge to hear your case, what information might you ask your attorney to provide concerning that individual?

a. 28 U.S.C. Sec 636(c); see also *Burton v. Schamp*, 25 F.4th 198 (3d Cir. 2022).
b. Federal Magistrates Act, 82 Stat. 1107, October 17, 1968.
c. U.S.C. Section 636(c)(1).
d. 28 U.S.C. Section 631(b)(5).

U.S. District Courts At the federal level, the equivalent of a state trial court of general jurisdiction is the district court. U.S. district courts have original jurisdiction in matters involving a federal question and concurrent jurisdiction with state courts when diversity jurisdiction exists. Federal cases typically originate in district courts. There are other federal courts with original, but special (or limited), jurisdiction, such as the federal bankruptcy courts and tax courts.

Every state has at least one federal district court. The number of judicial districts can vary over time,

primarily owing to population changes and corresponding changes in caseloads. Today, there are ninety-four federal judicial districts. Exhibit 4–3 shows the boundaries of both the U.S. district courts and the U.S. courts of appeals.

U.S. Courts of Appeals In the federal court system, there are thirteen U.S. courts of appeals—referred to as U.S. circuit courts of appeals. Twelve of these courts (including the Court of Appeals for the D.C. Circuit) hear appeals from the federal district courts located within

Exhibit 4–3 Geographic Boundaries of the U.S. Courts of Appeals and U.S. District Courts

Source: Administrative Office of the United States Courts.

their respective judicial circuits (shown in Exhibit 4–3).[14] The Court of Appeals for the Thirteenth Circuit, called the Federal Circuit, has national appellate jurisdiction over certain types of cases, including those involving patent law and those in which the U.S. government is a defendant.

The decisions of a circuit court of appeals are binding on all courts within the circuit court's jurisdiction. These decisions are final in most cases, but appeal to the United States Supreme Court is possible.

The United States Supreme Court The highest level of the three-tiered federal court system is the United States Supreme Court. According to the U.S. Constitution, there is only one national Supreme Court. All other courts in the federal system are considered "inferior." Congress is empowered to create inferior courts as it deems necessary. The inferior courts that Congress

has created include the second tier in our model—the U.S. circuit courts of appeals—as well as the district courts and the various federal courts of limited, or specialized, jurisdiction.

The United States Supreme Court consists of nine justices. Although the Supreme Court has original, or trial, jurisdiction in rare instances (set forth in Article III, Sections 1 and 2), most of its work is as an appeals court. The Supreme Court can review any case decided by any of the federal courts of appeals. It also has appellate authority over cases involving federal questions that have been decided in the state courts. The Supreme Court is the final authority on the Constitution and federal law.

Appeals to the Supreme Court. To bring a case before the Supreme Court, a party requests the Court to issue a writ of *certiorari*.[15] A **writ of *certiorari*** is an order issued by the Supreme Court to a lower court requiring the latter to send it the record of the case for review. The Court will

---

14. Historically, judges were required to "ride the circuit" and hear appeals in different courts around the country, which is how the name "circuit court" came about.

15. Pronounced sur-shee-uh-*rah*-ree.

not issue a writ unless at least four of the nine justices approve of it. This is called the **rule of four.**

Whether the Court will issue a writ of *certiorari* is entirely within its discretion, and most petitions for writs are denied. (Although thousands of cases are filed with the Supreme Court each year, it hears, on average, fewer than eighty of these cases.)[16] A denial of the request to issue a writ of *certiorari* is not a decision on the merits of the case, nor does it indicate agreement with the lower court's opinion. Also, denial of the writ has no value as a precedent. Denial simply means that the lower court's decision remains the law in that jurisdiction.

Petitions Granted by the Court. Typically, the Court grants petitions when cases raise important constitutional questions or when the lower courts have issued conflicting decisions on a significant issue. The justices, however, never explain their reasons for hearing certain cases and

---

16. From the mid-1950s through the early 1990s, the Supreme Court reviewed more cases per year than it has since then. In the Court's 1982–1983 term, for example, the Court issued written opinions in 151 cases. In contrast, during the last twenty years, on average, the Court has issued written opinions in only about 75 cases per year.

not others, so it is difficult to predict which type of case the Court might select.

Supreme Court "Shadow-Docket" Cases An increasing number of Court decisions are made without hearings and almost always without any comments by any of the nine justices. These decisions, officially called the "orders list," are unofficially called the *shadow docket*. The shadow docket includes so-called emergency appeals from parties that believe they will be unrecoverably harmed without a rapid response. Many requests are from condemned criminals attempting to stay their executions. There is usually only a week between an application and a decision.

Critics of the shadow docket believe that these decisions lack accountability and transparency. Justices can affirm or deny a request for a shadow-docket hearing and can keep their votes secret if they wish (which they usually do). These critics argue that the justices should at least offer a brief explanation whenever a shadow-docket decision makes a change in the status quo.

Concept Summary 4.2 reviews the courts in the federal and state court systems.

Concept Summary 4.2

Types of Courts

Trial Courts	Trial courts are courts of original jurisdiction in which actions are initiated. • *State courts* —Courts of general jurisdiction can hear any case that has not been specifically designated for another court. Courts of limited jurisdiction include, among others, domestic relations courts, probate courts, municipal courts, and small claims courts. • *Federal courts* —The federal district court is the equivalent of the state trial court. Federal courts of limited jurisdiction include the bankruptcy courts and others shown in Exhibit 4–2.
Intermediate Appellate Courts	Courts of appeals are reviewing courts. Generally, appellate courts do not have original jurisdiction. • About three-fourths of the states have intermediate appellate courts. • In the federal court system, the U.S. circuit courts of appeals are the intermediate appellate courts.
Supreme Courts	• The highest state court is that state's supreme court, although it may be called by some other name. • Appeal from state supreme courts to the United States Supreme Court is possible only if a federal question is involved. • The United States Supreme Court is the highest court in the federal court system and the final authority on the Constitution and federal law.

4–4 Alternative Dispute Resolution

Litigation—the process of resolving a dispute through the court system—is expensive and time consuming. Litigating even the simplest complaint is costly, and because of the backlog of cases pending in many courts, several years may pass before a case is actually tried. For these and other reasons, more and more businesspersons are turning to **alternative dispute resolution (ADR)** as a means of settling their disputes.

The great advantage of ADR is its flexibility. Methods of ADR range from the parties sitting down together and attempting to work out their differences to multinational corporations agreeing to resolve a dispute through a formal hearing before a panel of experts. Normally, the parties themselves can control how they will attempt to settle their dispute. They can decide what procedures will be used, whether a neutral third party will be present or make a decision, and whether that decision will be legally binding or nonbinding. ADR also offers more privacy than court proceedings and allows disputes to be resolved relatively quickly.

Today, more than 90 percent of civil lawsuits are settled before trial using some form of ADR. Indeed, most states either require or encourage parties to undertake ADR prior to trial. Many federal courts have instituted ADR programs as well. Several forms of ADR have been developed.

4–4a Negotiation

The simplest form of ADR is **negotiation,** a process in which the parties attempt to settle their dispute informally, with or without attorneys to represent them. Attorneys frequently advise their clients to negotiate a settlement voluntarily before they proceed to trial. Parties may even try to negotiate a settlement during a trial or after the trial but before an appeal. Negotiation usually involves just the parties themselves and (typically) their attorneys.

4–4b Mediation

In **mediation,** a neutral third party acts as a mediator and works with both sides in the dispute to facilitate a resolution. The mediator, who need not be a lawyer, usually charges a fee for the mediation services (which can be split between the parties). States that require parties to undergo ADR before trial often offer mediation as one of the ADR options or (as in Florida) the only option.

During mediation, the mediator normally talks with the parties separately as well as jointly, emphasizes their points of agreement, and helps them to evaluate their options. Although mediators may propose solutions (called mediator's proposals), they do not make decisions resolving the matter.

One of the biggest advantages of mediation is that it is less adversarial than litigation. In mediation, the mediator takes an active role and attempts to bring the parties together so that they can come to a mutually satisfactory resolution. The mediation process tends to reduce the antagonism between the disputants, allowing them to resume their former relationship while minimizing hostility. For this reason, mediation is often the preferred form of ADR for disputes between business partners, employers and employees, or other parties involved in long-term relationships.

4–4c Arbitration

A more formal method of ADR is **arbitration,** in which an arbitrator (a neutral third party or a panel of experts) hears a dispute and imposes a resolution on the parties. Arbitration differs from other forms of ADR in that the third party hearing the dispute makes a decision for the parties. Exhibit 4–4 outlines the basic differences among the three traditional forms of ADR.

Usually, the parties in arbitration agree that the third party's decision will be *legally binding*, although the parties can also agree to *nonbinding* arbitration. In nonbinding arbitration, the parties can go forward with a lawsuit if they do not agree with the arbitrator's decision. Arbitration that is mandated by the courts often is not binding on the parties.

In some respects, formal arbitration resembles a trial, although usually the procedural rules are much less restrictive than those governing litigation. In a typical arbitration, the parties present opening arguments and ask for specific remedies. Both sides present evidence and may call and examine witnesses. The arbitrator then renders a decision.

The Arbitrator's Decision The arbitrator's decision is called an **award.** It is usually the final word on the matter. Although the parties may appeal an arbitrator's decision, a court's review of the decision will be much more restricted in scope than an appellate court's review of a trial court's decision. The general view is that because the parties were free to frame the issues and set the powers of the arbitrator at the outset, they cannot complain about the results. A court will set aside an award only in the event of one of the following:

1. The arbitrator's conduct or "bad faith" substantially prejudiced the rights of one of the parties.
2. The award violates an established public policy.
3. The arbitrator exceeded the powers allowed in the situation—that is, arbitrated issues that the parties did not agree to submit to arbitration.

Exhibit 4–4 Basic Differences in the Traditional Forms of ADR

	Negotiation	Mediation	Arbitration
		Type of ADR	
Description	Parties meet informally with or without their attorneys and attempt to agree on a resolution. This is the simplest and least expensive method of ADR.	A neutral third party meets with the parties and emphasizes points of agreement to bring them toward resolution of their dispute, reducing hostility between the parties.	The parties present their arguments and evidence before an arbitrator at a formal hearing. The arbitrator renders a decision to resolve the parties' dispute.
Neutral Third Party Present?	No	Yes	Yes
Who Decides the Resolution?	The parties themselves reach a resolution.	The parties, but the mediator may suggest or propose a resolution.	The arbitrator imposes a resolution on the parties that may be either binding or nonbinding.

Arbitration Clauses Almost any commercial matter can be submitted to arbitration. Frequently, parties include an **arbitration clause** in a contract specifying that any dispute arising under the contract will be resolved through arbitration rather than through the court system. Parties can also agree to arbitrate a dispute *after* it arises.

Arbitration Statutes Most states have statutes (often based, in part, on the Uniform Arbitration Act) under which arbitration clauses will be enforced. Some state statutes compel arbitration of certain types of disputes, such as those involving public employees.

At the federal level, the Federal Arbitration Act (FAA), enacted in 1925, enforces arbitration clauses in contracts involving maritime activity and interstate commerce. The courts have defined "interstate commerce" broadly, and so arbitration agreements involving transactions only slightly connected to the flow of interstate commerce may fall under the FAA. The FAA established a national policy favoring arbitration that the United States Supreme Court has continued to reinforce.[17]

■ **Case in Point 4.6** Cable subscribers sued Cox Communications, Inc., in federal court. They claimed that Cox violated antitrust law by tying premium cable service to the rental of set-top cable boxes. Cox filed a motion to compel arbitration based on an agreement it had sent to its subscribers. A district court granted the motion to compel, and the subscribers appealed. A federal appellate court affirmed, based on the Federal Arbitration Act. The subscribers' antitrust claims fell within the scope of the arbitration agreement.[18] ■

The Issue of Arbitrability The terms of an arbitration agreement can limit the types of disputes that the parties agree to arbitrate. Disputes can arise, however, when the parties do not specify limits or when the parties disagree on whether a particular matter is covered by their arbitration agreement.

When one party files a lawsuit to compel arbitration, it is up to the court to resolve the issue of arbitrability. That is, the court must decide whether the matter is one that must be resolved through arbitration. If the court finds

17. See, for example, *AT&T Mobility, LLC v. Concepcion*, 563 U.S. 333, 131 S.Ct. 1740, 179 L.Ed.2d 742 (2010). See also *Aronow v. Superior Court of San Francisco County*, 2022 WL 896183, 291 Cal. Rptr.3d 784 (App.Ct.Cal., 1st Dist., Div. 4 [2022]).

18. *In re Cox Enterprises, Inc. Set-top Cable Television Box Antitrust Litigation*, 835 F.3d 1195 (10th Cir. 2016). See also *Forby v. One Technologies, L.P.*, 13 F.4th 460 (5th Cir. 2021).

that the subject matter in controversy is covered by the agreement to arbitrate, then it may compel arbitration.

Usually, a court will allow a claim to be arbitrated if the court finds that the relevant statute (the state arbitration statute or the FAA) does not exclude such claims. No party, however, will be ordered to submit a particular dispute to arbitration unless the court is convinced that the party has consented to do so. Additionally, the courts will not compel arbitration if it is clear that the arbitration rules and procedures are inherently unfair to one of the parties.

Mandatory Arbitration in the Employment Context

A significant question for businesspersons has concerned mandatory arbitration clauses in employment contracts. Many employees claim they are at a disadvantage when they are forced, as a condition of being hired, to agree to arbitrate all disputes and thus waive their rights under statutes designed to protect employees.

The United States Supreme Court, however, has held that mandatory arbitration clauses in employment contracts are generally enforceable. ■ **Case in Point 4.7** In a landmark decision, *Gilmer v. Interstate Johnson Lane Corp.*,[19] the Supreme Court held that a claim brought under a federal statute prohibiting age discrimination could be subject to arbitration. The Court concluded that the employee had waived his right to sue when he agreed, as part of a required application to be a securities representative, to arbitrate "any dispute, claim, or controversy" relating to his employment. ■

Moving Away From Arbitration Clauses

The tide in favor of arbitration may be receding. In 2021, Amazon removed its mandatory arbitration clause and class action waiver in its online terms of service agreement. Any customer who has a grievance can now pursue the dispute in a federal district court.

4–4d Other Types of ADR

The three forms of ADR just discussed are the oldest and traditionally the most commonly used forms. In addition, a variety of newer types of ADR have emerged, including those described here.

1. In **early neutral case evaluation,** the parties select a neutral third party (generally an expert in the subject matter of the dispute) and explain their respective positions to that person. The case evaluator assesses the strengths and weaknesses of each party's claims.

2. In a **mini-trial,** each party's attorney briefly argues the party's case before the other party and a panel of representatives from each side who have the authority to settle the dispute. Typically, a neutral third party (usually an expert in the area being disputed) acts as an adviser. If the parties fail to reach an agreement, the adviser renders an opinion as to how a court would likely decide the issue.

3. Numerous federal courts hold **summary jury trials,** in which the parties present their arguments and evidence and the jury renders a verdict. The jury's verdict is not binding, but it does act as a guide to both sides in reaching an agreement during the mandatory negotiations that immediately follow the trial.

4. Other alternatives being employed by the courts include summary proceedings, which dispense with some formal court procedures, and the appointment of special masters to assist judges in deciding complex issues.

4–4e Providers of ADR Services

ADR services are provided by both government agencies and private organizations. A major provider of ADR services is the American Arbitration Association (AAA), which handles thousands of claims a year in its numerous offices worldwide. (Its international branch is the ICDR—International Centre for Dispute Resolution.) Most of the largest U.S. law firms are members of this nonprofit association.

Cases brought before the AAA are heard by an expert or a panel of experts in the area relating to the dispute and are usually settled quickly. Generally, about half of the panel members are lawyers. To cover its costs, the AAA charges a fee, paid by the party filing the claim. In addition, each party to the dispute pays a specified amount for each hearing day, as well as a special additional fee in cases involving personal injuries or property loss.

Hundreds of for-profit firms around the country also provide dispute-resolution services. Typically, these firms hire retired judges to conduct arbitration hearings or otherwise assist parties in settling their disputes. The judges follow procedures similar to those of the federal courts and use similar rules. Usually, each party to the dispute pays a filing fee and a designated fee for a hearing session or conference.

---

19. 500 U.S. 20, 111 S.Ct. 1647, 114 L.Ed.2d 26 (1991).

4–4f Online Dispute Resolution

An increasing number of companies and organizations are offering dispute-resolution services using the internet. The settlement of disputes in these forums is known as **online dispute resolution (ODR).** The disputes resolved have most commonly involved rights to domain names (website addresses) or the quality of goods sold via the internet, including goods sold through internet auction sites.

Rules being developed in online forums may ultimately become a code of conduct for everyone who does business in cyberspace. Most online forums do not automatically apply the law of any specific jurisdiction. Instead, results are often based on general, universal legal principles. As with most offline methods of dispute resolution, any party may appeal to a court at any time.

ODR may be best for resolving small to medium-sized business liability claims, which may not be worth the expense of litigation or traditional ADR methods. In addition, some cities use ODR as a means of resolving claims against them. ■ **Example 4.8** New York City uses Cybersettle.com to resolve auto accident, sidewalk, and other personal-injury claims made against the city. Parties with complaints submit their demands, and the city submits its offers confidentially online. If an offer exceeds a demand, the claimant keeps half the difference as a bonus, plus the original claim. ■

Today, online dispute resolution is usually cloud based. For instance, the company Arbitration Resolution Services, Inc., is entirely cloud based. It claims that parties that use its services can save as much as 80 percent of the cost of traditional litigation in as little as 20 percent of the time.

4–5 International Dispute Resolution

Businesspersons who engage in international business transactions normally take special precautions to protect themselves in the event that a party in another country with whom they are dealing breaches an agreement. Often, parties to international contracts include special clauses in their contracts providing for how disputes arising under the contracts will be resolved. Sometimes, international treaties (formal agreements among several nations) even require parties to arbitrate any disputes.

4–5a Forum-Selection and Choice-of-Law Clauses

Parties to international transactions often include forum-selection and choice-of-law clauses in their contracts. These clauses designate the jurisdiction (court or country) where any dispute arising under the contract will be litigated and which nation's law will be applied.

When an international contract does not include such clauses, any legal proceedings arising under the contract will be more complex. For instance, litigation may take place in two or more countries, with each country applying its own national law to the particular transactions.

Furthermore, even if a plaintiff wins a favorable judgment in a lawsuit litigated in the plaintiff's country, the defendant's country could refuse to enforce the court's judgment. The judgment may be enforced in the defendant's country for reasons of courtesy. The United States, for instance, will generally enforce a foreign court's decision if it is consistent with U.S. national law and policy. Other nations, however, may not be as accommodating as the United States, and the plaintiff may be left empty-handed.

4–5b Arbitration Clauses

International contracts also often include arbitration clauses that require a neutral third party to decide any contract disputes. Many of the institutions that offer arbitration, such as the International Chamber of Commerce and the Singapore International Arbitration Centre, have formulated model clauses for parties to use. In international arbitration proceedings, the third party may be a neutral entity, a panel of individuals representing both parties' interests, or some other group or organization.

The United Nations Convention on the Recognition and Enforcement of Foreign Arbitral Awards[20] has been implemented in more than 146 countries, including the United States. This convention assists in the enforcement of arbitration clauses, as do provisions in specific treaties among nations. The American Arbitration Association provides arbitration services for international as well as domestic disputes.

---

20. June 10, 1958, 21 U.S.T. 2517, T.I.A.S. No. 6997 (the "New York Convention").

Practice and Review: Courts and Alternative Dispute Resolution

Stan Garner resides in Illinois and promotes boxing matches for SuperSports, Inc., an Illinois corporation. Garner created the concept of "Ages" promotion—a three-fight series of boxing matches pitting an older fighter (George Foreman) against a younger fighter. The concept had titles for each of the three fights, including "Battle of the Ages." Garner contacted Foreman and his manager, who both reside in Texas, to sell the idea, and they arranged a meeting in Las Vegas, Nevada. During negotiations, Foreman's manager signed a nondisclosure agreement prohibiting him from disclosing Garner's promotional concepts unless the parties signed a contract. Nevertheless, after negotiations fell through, Foreman used Garner's "Battle of the Ages" concept to promote a subsequent fight. Garner filed a suit against Foreman and his manager in a federal district court located in Illinois, alleging breach of contract. Using the information presented in the chapter, answer the following questions.

1. On what basis might the federal district court in Illinois exercise jurisdiction in this case?
2. Does the federal district court have original or appellate jurisdiction?
3. Suppose that Garner had filed his action in an Illinois state court. Could an Illinois state court have exercised personal jurisdiction over Foreman or his manager? Why or why not?
4. Now suppose that Garner had filed his action in a Nevada state court. Would that court have had personal jurisdiction over Foreman or his manager? Explain.

Debate This . . . In this age of the internet, when people communicate via e-mail, texts, tweets, Facebook, and WhatsApp, is the concept of jurisdiction losing its meaning?

Terms and Concepts

alternative dispute resolution (ADR) 81
arbitration 81
arbitration clause 82
award 81
bankruptcy courts 68
concurrent jurisdiction 69
diversity of citizenship 68
early neutral case evaluation 83
exclusive jurisdiction 69

federal question 68
in personam jurisdiction 67
in rem jurisdiction 67
judicial review 66
jurisdiction 67
litigation 81
long arm statute 67
mediation 81
mini-trial 83
negotiation 81

online dispute resolution (ODR) 84
probate courts 68
question of fact 76
question of law 76
rule of four 80
small claims courts 76
standing to sue 73
summary jury trials 83
venue 72
writ of *certiorari* 79

Issue Spotters

1. Fatma uses her smartphone to purchase a video security system for her architectural firm from Tipton, Inc., a company located in a different state. The system arrives a month after the projected delivery date, is of poor quality, and does not function as advertised. Fatma files a suit against Tipton in a state court. Does the court in Fatma's state have jurisdiction over Tipton? What factors will the court consider in determining jurisdiction? (See *Basic Judicial Requirements*.)

2. The state in which Fatma resides requires that her dispute with Tipton be submitted to mediation or nonbinding arbitration. If the dispute is not resolved, or if either party disagrees with the decision of the mediator or arbitrator, will a court hear the case? Explain. (See *Alternative Dispute Resolution*.)

• **Check your answers to the Issue Spotters against the answers provided in Appendix B at the end of this text.**

Business Scenarios and Case Problems

4–1. Standing. Jack and Maggie Turton bought a house in Jefferson County, Idaho, located directly across the street from a gravel pit. A few years later, the county converted the pit to a landfill. The landfill accepted many kinds of trash that cause harm to the environment, including major appliances, animal carcasses, containers with hazardous content warnings, leaking car batteries, and waste oil. The Turtons complained to the county, but the county did nothing. The Turtons then filed a lawsuit against the county alleging violations of federal environmental laws pertaining to groundwater contamination and other pollution. Do the Turtons have standing to sue? Why or why not? (See *Basic Judicial Requirements*.)

4–2. Arbitration. PRM Energy Systems owned patents licensed to Primenergy to use in the United States. Their contract stated that "all disputes" would be settled by arbitration. Kobe Steel of Japan was interested in using the technology represented by PRM's patents. Primenergy agreed to let Kobe use the technology in Japan without telling PRM. When PRM learned about the secret deal, the firm filed a suit against Primenergy for fraud and theft. Does this dispute go to arbitration or to trial? Why? [*PRM Energy Systems v. Primenergy*, 592 F.3d 830 (8th Cir. 2010)] (See *Alternative Dispute Resolution*.)

4–3. Spotlight on the National Football League—Arbitration. Bruce Matthews played football for the Tennessee Titans. As part of his contract, he agreed to submit any dispute to arbitration. He also agreed that Tennessee law would determine all matters related to workers' compensation. After Matthews retired, he filed a workers' compensation claim in California. The arbitrator ruled that Matthews could pursue his claim in California but only under Tennessee law. Should this award be set aside? Explain. [*National Football League Players Association v. National Football League Management Council*, 2011 WL 1137334 (S.D.Cal. 2011)] (See *Alternative Dispute Resolution*.)

4–4. Minimum Contacts. Seal Polymer Industries sold two freight containers of latex gloves to Med-Express, Inc., a company based in North Carolina. When Med-Express failed to pay the $104,000 owed for the gloves, Seal Polymer sued in an Illinois court and obtained a judgment against Med-Express. Med-Express argued that it did not have minimum contacts with Illinois because it was incorporated under North Carolina law and had its principal place of business in North Carolina. Therefore, the Illinois judgment based on personal jurisdiction was invalid. Was this argument alone sufficient to prevent the Illinois judgment from being collected against Med-Express in North Carolina? Why or why not? [*Seal Polymer Industries v. Med-Express, Inc.*, 218 N.C.App. 447, 725 S.E.2d 5 (2012)] (See *Basic Judicial Requirements*.)

4–5. Arbitration. Horton Automatics and the Industrial Division of the Communications Workers of America, the union that represented Horton's workers, negotiated a collective bargaining agreement. If an employee's discharge for a workplace-rule violation was submitted to arbitration, the agreement limited the arbitrator to determining whether the rule was reasonable and whether the employee had violated it. When Horton discharged employee Ruben de la Garza, the union appealed to arbitration. The arbitrator found that de la Garza had violated a reasonable safety rule, but "was not totally convinced" that Horton should have treated the violation more seriously than other rule violations. The arbitrator ordered de la Garza reinstated. Can a court set aside this order? Explain. [*Horton Automatics v. The Industrial Division of the Communications Workers of America, AFL-CIO*, 506 Fed.Appx. 253 (5th Cir. 2013)] (See *Alternative Dispute Resolution*.)

4–6. Business Case Problem with Sample Answer—Corporate Contacts. LG Electronics, Inc., a South Korean company, and nineteen other foreign companies participated in the global market for cathode ray tube (CRT) products. CRTs were integrated as components in consumer goods, including television sets, and were sold for many years in high volume in the United States, including the state of Washington. The state filed a suit in a Washington state court against LG and the others, alleging a conspiracy to raise prices and set production levels in the market for CRTs in violation of a state consumer protection statute. The defendants filed a motion to dismiss the suit for lack of personal jurisdiction. Should this motion be granted? Explain. [*State of Washington v. LG Electronics, Inc.*, 185 Wash.App. 394, 341 P.3d 346 (Div. 1 2015)] (See *Basic Judicial Requirements*.)

- **For a sample answer to Problem 4–6, go to Appendix C at the end of this text.**

4–7. Appellate, or Reviewing, Courts. Angelica Westbrook was employed as a collector for Franklin Collection Service, Inc. During a collection call, Westbrook told a debtor that a $15 processing fee was an "interest" charge. This violated company policy. Westbrook was fired. She filed a claim for unemployment benefits, which the Mississippi Department of Employment Security (MDES) approved. Franklin objected. At an MDES hearing, a Franklin supervisor testified that she had heard Westbrook make the false statement, although she admitted that there had been no similar incidents with Westbrook. Westbrook denied making the statement, but added that if she had said it, she did not remember it. The agency found that Franklin's reason for terminating Westbrook did not amount to the misconduct required to disqualify her for benefits and upheld the approval. Franklin appealed to a state intermediate appellate court. Is the court likely to uphold the agency's findings of fact? Explain. [*Franklin Collection Service, Inc. v. Mississippi Department of Employment Security*, 184 So.3d 330 (Miss.App. 2016)] (See *The State and Federal Court Systems*.)

4–8. Standing to Sue. Debra Laufer is disabled within the meaning of the Americans with Disabilities Act (ADA). She is an advocate for disabled people's rights and a self-proclaimed "tester" who monitors whether places of public accommodation and their websites comply with the ADA. In a lawsuit against a hotel, Laufer claimed that she suffered a "concrete" injury after she viewed the hotel's website, which omitted accessibility-related information required by federal regulations. She said that she experienced "frustration and humiliation" because she was unable to obtain the information she needed. The defendant owner of the hotel, Arpan LLC, argued that she lacked standing to sue. The district court held that Laufer had not suffered a "concrete" injury. On appeal, should the reviewing court accept the trial court's ruling? Why or why not? [*Laufer v. Arpan, LLC*, 29 F.4th 1268 (11th Cir. 2022)] (See *Basic Judicial Requirements*.)

4–9. A Question of Ethics—The IDDR Approach and Arbitration. John McAdams is a tenured professor of political science at Marquette University. McAdams posted a comment on his blog criticizing Cheryl Abbate, a philosophy instructor, for her interchange with a student in her Theory of Ethics class. Lynn Turner, also a member of the faculty, expressed a negative opinion of McAdams's comment in a letter to the Marquette Tribune. Meanwhile, on Abbate's complaint, the university convened the Faculty Hearing Committee (FHC)—which consists entirely of faculty members, including Turner—to consider the case. Acting on the FHC's recommendation, Marquette suspended McAdams for a semester without pay and ordered him to apologize to Abbate. He refused and filed a suit in a Wisconsin state court against Marquette. [*McAdams v. Marquette University*, 383 Wis.2d 358, 914 N.W.2d 708 (2018)] (See *Alternative Dispute Resolution*.)

(a) Apply the IDDR approach to consider the ethics of Marquette's convening of the FHC in McAdams's case.

(b) From a legal perspective, was the university's disciplinary procedure the functional equivalent of arbitration, limiting McAdams's right to litigate his claim in court? Explain.

Time-Limited Group Assignment

4–10. Access to Courts. Assume that a statute in your state requires that all civil lawsuits involving damages of less than $50,000 be arbitrated. Such a case can be tried in court only if a party is dissatisfied with the arbitrator's decision. The statute also provides that if a trial does not result in an improvement of more than 10 percent in the position of the party who demanded the trial, that party must pay the entire cost of the arbitration proceeding. (See *Alternative Dispute Resolution*.)

(a) One group will argue that the state statute violates litigants' rights of access to the courts and trial by jury.

(b) Another group will argue that the statute does not violate litigants' right of access to the courts.

(c) A third group will evaluate how the determination on right of access would be changed if the statute was part of a pilot program that affected only a few judicial districts in the state.

Chapter 5

Court Procedures

American and English courts follow the adversarial system of justice. Although parties are allowed to represent themselves in court (called *pro se* representation), most parties do not, because they lack the legal expertise and knowledge of court procedures that lawyers possess. Typically, the parties to lawsuits hire attorneys to represent them. Lawyers act as their clients' advocates. Each lawyer presents the client's version of the facts in such a way as to convince the judge (or the judge and jury, in a jury trial) that this version is correct. Most of the judicial procedures that you will read about are rooted in the adversarial framework of the American legal system.

5–1 Procedural Rules

The parties to a lawsuit must comply with the procedural rules of the court in which the lawsuit is filed. Although people often think that substantive law determines the outcome of a case, procedural law can have a significant impact on a person's ability to pursue a legal claim. Procedural rules provide a framework for every dispute and specify what must be done at each stage of the litigation process.

Procedural rules are complex, and they vary from court to court and from state to state. There is a set of federal rules of procedure as well as various sets of rules for state courts. Additionally, the applicable procedures will depend on whether the case is a civil or criminal proceeding. All civil trials held in federal district courts are governed by the **Federal Rules of Civil Procedure (FRCP).**[1]

5–1a Stages of Litigation

Broadly speaking, the litigation process has three phases: pretrial, trial, and posttrial. Each phase involves specific procedures, as discussed throughout this chapter. Although civil lawsuits may vary greatly in terms of complexity, cost, and detail, they typically progress through the stages charted in Exhibit 5–1.

To illustrate the procedures involved in a civil lawsuit, we will use a simple hypothetical case. The case arose from an automobile accident, which occurred when a car driven by Antonio Carvello, a resident of New Jersey, collided with a car driven by Jill Kirby, a resident of New York. The accident took place at an intersection in New York City. Kirby suffered personal injuries, which caused her to incur medical and hospital expenses as well as lost wages for four months. In all, she calculated that the cost to her of the accident was $500,000.[2] Carvello and Kirby have been unable to agree on a settlement, and Kirby now must decide whether to sue Carvello for the $500,000 compensation she feels she deserves.

5–1b Hire an Attorney

As mentioned, rules of procedure often affect the outcome of a dispute—a fact that highlights the importance of obtaining the advice of counsel. The first step taken by almost anyone contemplating a lawsuit is to seek the guidance of a licensed attorney.

In the hypothetical Kirby–Carvello case, assume that Kirby consults with a lawyer. The attorney will advise her regarding what she can expect in a lawsuit, her probability of success at trial, and the procedures that will be involved. If more than one court would have jurisdiction over the matter, the attorney will also discuss the advantages and disadvantages of filing in a particular court. In addition, the attorney will indicate how long it will take

---

1. The United States Supreme Court has authority to establish these rules, as spelled out in 28 U.S.C. Sections 2071–2077. Generally, though, the federal judiciary appoints committees that make recommendations to the Supreme Court. The Court then publishes any proposed changes in the rules and allows for public comment before finalizing the rules.

2. For simplicity, we are ignoring damages for pain and suffering and for permanent disabilities, which plaintiffs in personal-injury cases often seek.

Exhibit 5–1   Stages in a Typical Lawsuit

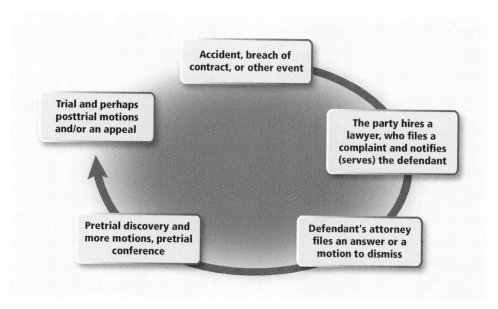

to resolve the dispute through litigation in a particular court and provide an estimate of the costs involved.

The attorney will also inform Kirby of the legal fees that she will have to pay in her attempt to collect damages from the defendant, Carvello. Attorneys base their fees on such factors as the difficulty of the matter at issue, the attorney's experience and skill, and the amount of time involved. In the United States, legal fees range from $200 to $800 per hour or even higher. The client normally must also pay various expenses related to the case (called "out-of-pocket" costs), such as court filing fees, travel expenses, and the costs of expert witnesses and investigators.

Types of Attorneys' Fees For a particular legal matter, an attorney may charge one type of fee or a combination of several types.

1. **Fixed fees** may be charged for the performance of such services as drafting a simple will.
2. **Hourly fees** may be charged for matters that will involve an indeterminate period of time. The amount of time required to bring a case to trial, for instance, probably cannot be precisely estimated in advance.
3. **Contingency fees** are fixed as a percentage (usually 33 percent) of a client's recovery in certain types of lawsuits, such as a personal-injury lawsuit.[3] If the

lawsuit is unsuccessful, the attorney receives no fee, but the client will have to reimburse the attorney for all out-of-pocket costs incurred.

Because Kirby's claim involves a personal injury, her lawyer will likely take the case on a contingency-fee basis. In some cases, winning parties may be able to recover at least some portion of their attorneys' fees from the losing party.

Settlement Considerations Once an attorney has been retained, the attorney is required to pursue a resolution of the matter on the client's behalf. Nevertheless, the amount of resources an attorney will spend on a given case is affected by the time and funds the client wishes to devote to the process.

If the client is willing to pay for a lengthy trial and one or more appeals, the attorney may pursue those actions. Often, however, after learning of the substantial costs that litigation entails, a client may decide to pursue a settlement of the claim. Attempts to settle the case may be ongoing throughout the litigation process.

Another important consideration in deciding whether to pursue litigation is the defendant's ability to pay the damages sought. Even if Kirby is awarded damages, it may be difficult to enforce the court's judgment if the amount exceeds the limits of Carvello's automobile insurance policy. (We will discuss the problems involved in enforcing a judgment later in this chapter.)

---

3. Contingency-fee arrangements are typically prohibited in criminal cases, divorce cases, and cases involving the distribution of assets after death.

5–2 Pretrial Procedures

The pretrial litigation process involves the filing of the pleadings, the gathering of evidence (called discovery), and possibly other procedures, such as a pretrial conference and jury selection.

5–2a The Pleadings

The complaint and answer (and other legal documents discussed below) are known as the **pleadings.** The pleadings inform each party of the other's claims, reveal the facts, and specify the issues (disputed questions) involved in the case. Because the rules of procedure vary depending on the jurisdiction of the court, the style and form of the pleadings may be different from those shown in this chapter.

The Plaintiff's Complaint Kirby's action against Carvello commences when her lawyer files a **complaint**[4] with the clerk of the appropriate court. Complaints can be lengthy or brief, depending on the complexity of the case and the rules of the jurisdiction. The complaint contains statements or allegations concerning the following:

1. **Jurisdiction.** Facts showing that the particular court has subject-matter and personal jurisdiction.
2. **Legal theory.** The facts establishing the plaintiff's claim and basis for relief.
3. **Remedy.** The remedy (such as the amount of damages) that the plaintiff is seeking.

Exhibit 5–2 illustrates how a complaint in the Kirby–Carvello case might appear. The complaint asserts facts indicating that the federal district court has subject-matter jurisdiction because of diversity of citizenship. It then gives a brief statement of the facts of the accident and alleges that Carvello negligently drove his vehicle through a red light, striking Kirby's car. The complaint alleges that Carvello's actions caused Kirby serious personal injury and property damage. The complaint goes on to state that Kirby is seeking $500,000 in damages. (In some state civil actions, the plaintiff need not specify the amount of damages sought.)

Service of Process. Before the court can exercise personal jurisdiction over the defendant (Carvello)—in effect, before the lawsuit can begin—the court must have proof that the defendant was notified of the lawsuit. Formally notifying the defendant of a lawsuit is called **service of process.**

The plaintiff must deliver, or serve, a copy of the complaint and a **summons** (a notice requiring the defendant to appear in court and answer the complaint) to the defendant. The summons notifies Carvello that he must file an answer to the complaint within a specified time period (twenty days in federal courts) or suffer a default judgment against him. A **default judgment** in Kirby's favor would mean that she would be awarded the damages alleged in her complaint because Carvello failed to respond to the allegations.

Method of Service. How service of process occurs depends on the rules of the court or jurisdiction in which the lawsuit is brought. Under the Federal Rules of Civil Procedure, anyone who is at least eighteen years of age and is not a party to the lawsuit can serve process in federal court cases. In state courts, the process server is often a county sheriff or an employee of an independent company that provides process service in the local area.

Usually, the server hands the summons and complaint to the defendant personally or leaves it at the defendant's residence or place of business. In cases involving corporate defendants, the summons and complaint may be served on an officer or on a registered agent (representative) of the corporation. The name of a corporation's registered agent can usually be obtained from the secretary of state's office in the state where the company incorporated its business. When the defendant cannot be reached, special rules provide for alternative means of service, such as publishing a notice in the local newspaper.

In some situations, courts allow service of process via e-mail, as long as it is reasonably calculated to provide notice and an opportunity to respond. ■ **Case in Point 5.1** A county in New York filed a petition to remove a minor child, J.T., from his mother's care due to neglect. The child's father had been deported to Jordan, and the county sought to terminate the father's parental rights. Although the father's exact whereabouts were unknown, the county caseworker had been in contact with him via e-mail. The court allowed the father to be served via e-mail because it was reasonably calculated to inform him of the proceedings and allow him an opportunity to respond.[5] ■

Waiver of Formal Service of Process. In many instances, defendants are already aware that lawsuits are being filed

---

4. Sometimes, the document filed with the court is called a *petition* or a *declaration* instead of a complaint.

5. *In re J.T.*, 53 Misc.3d 888, 37 N.Y.S.3d 846 (2016). See also *Searles v. Archangel*, 60 Cal.App.5th 43 (App.Ct.Cal. 2nd Dist., Div. 7 2021).

Exhibit 5–2 A Typical Complaint

```
                    IN THE UNITED STATES DISTRICT COURT
                   FOR THE SOUTHERN DISTRICT OF NEW YORK


                                              CIVIL NO. 9-1047
    JILL KIRBY

                        Plaintiff,

    v.                                        COMPLAINT

    ANTONIO CARVELLO

                        Defendant.


     The plaintiff brings this cause of action against the defendant, alleging as
follows:

1. This action is between the plaintiff, who is a resident of the State of
   New York, and the defendant, who is a resident of the State of New Jersey.
   There is diversity of citizenship between the parties.
2. The amount in controversy, exclusive of interest and costs, exceeds the
   sum of $75,000.
3. On September 10th, 2025, the plaintiff, Jill Kirby, was exercising good
   driving habits and reasonable care in driving her car through the
   intersection of Boardwalk and Pennsylvania Avenue, New York City, New York,
   when the defendant, Antonio Carvello, negligently drove his vehicle through
   a red light at the intersection and collided with the plaintiff's vehicle.
4. As a result of the collision, the plaintiff suffered severe physical injury,
   which prevented her from working, and property damage to her car.

     WHEREFORE, the plaintiff demands judgment against the defendant for the sum
of $500,000 plus interest at the maximum legal rate and the costs of this action.


                                    By  Joseph Roe
                                        Joseph Roe
                                        Attorney for Plaintiff
                                        100 Main Street
    1/3/26                              New York, New York
```

and are willing to waive (give up) their rights to be served personally. The Federal Rules of Civil Procedure (FRCP) and many states' rules allow defendants to waive formal service of process, provided that certain procedures are followed.

In the Kirby case, for instance, Kirby's attorney could mail to defendant Carvello a copy of the complaint, along with "Waiver of Service of Summons" forms for Carvello to sign. If Carvello signs and returns the forms within thirty days, formal service of process is waived.

Moreover, under the FRCP, defendants who agree to waive formal service of process receive additional time to respond to the complaint (sixty days, instead of twenty days). Some states provide similar incentives to encourage defendants to waive formal service of process and thereby reduce associated costs and foster cooperation between the parties.

The Defendant's Response Typically, the defendant's response to the complaint takes the form of an **answer.**

In an answer, the defendant either admits or denies each of the allegations in the plaintiff's complaint and may also set forth defenses to those allegations.

Under the federal rules, any allegations that are not denied by the defendant will be deemed by the court to have been admitted. If Carvello admits to all of Kirby's allegations in his answer, a judgment will be entered for Kirby. If Carvello denies Kirby's allegations, the matter will proceed further.

Affirmative Defenses. Carvello can also admit the truth of Kirby's complaint but raise new facts to show that he should not be held liable for Kirby's damages. This is called raising an **affirmative defense.** Defendants in both civil and criminal cases can raise affirmative defenses.

For instance, Carvello could assert Kirby's own negligence as a defense by alleging that Kirby was driving negligently at the time of the accident. In some states, a plaintiff's contributory negligence operates as a complete defense. In most states, however, the plaintiff's own negligence constitutes only a partial defense.

Counterclaims. Carvello could also deny Kirby's allegations and set forth his own claim that the accident occurred as a result of Kirby's negligence and that she therefore should pay for the damage to his car. This is appropriately called a **counterclaim.** If Carvello files a counterclaim, Kirby will have to submit an answer to the counterclaim.

5–2b Dismissals and Judgments Before Trial

Many actions for which pleadings have been filed never come to trial. The parties may, for instance, negotiate a settlement of the dispute at any stage of the litigation process. There are also numerous procedural avenues for disposing of a case without a trial. Many of them involve one or the other party's attempts to get the case dismissed through the use of various motions.

A **motion** is a procedural request submitted to the court by an attorney on behalf of the attorney's client. When a motion is filed with the court, the filing party must also provide the opposing party with a notice of motion. The notice of motion informs the opposing party that the motion has been filed. **Pretrial motions** include the motion to dismiss, the motion for judgment on the pleadings, and the motion for summary judgment, as well as the other motions listed in Exhibit 5–3.

Motion to Dismiss Either party can file a **motion to dismiss** asking the court to dismiss the case for the reasons stated in the motion. Normally, though, it is the defendant who requests dismissal.

Exhibit 5–3 Pretrial Motions

Motion to Dismiss	A motion (normally filed by the defendant) that asks the court to dismiss the case for a specified reason, such as lack of personal jurisdiction or failure to state a claim
Motion to Strike	A defendant's motion asking the court to strike (delete or remove) certain paragraphs from the complaint to better clarify the issues in dispute
Motion to Make More Definite or Certain	A motion by the defendant when the complaint is vague that asks the court to compel the plaintiff to clarify the cause of action
Motion for Judgment on the Pleadings	A motion by either party asking the court to enter judgment in their favor based on the pleadings because there are no facts in dispute
Motion to Compel Discovery	A motion asking the court to force the nonmoving party to comply with a discovery request
Motion for Summary Judgment	A motion asking the court to enter a judgment in one party's favor without a trial

A defendant can file a motion to dismiss if the plaintiff's complaint fails to state a claim for which relief (a remedy) can be granted. Such a motion asserts that even if the facts alleged in the complaint are true, they do not give rise to any legal claim against the defendant. For instance, if the allegations in Kirby's complaint do not constitute negligence on Carvello's part, Carvello can move to dismiss the case for failure to state a claim. Defendant Carvello could also file a motion to dismiss on the grounds that he was not properly served, that the court lacked jurisdiction, or that the venue was improper.

If the judge grants the motion to dismiss, the plaintiff generally is given time to file an amended complaint. If the judge denies the motion, the suit will go forward, and the defendant must then file an answer. Note that if Carvello wishes to discontinue the suit because, for instance, an out-of-court settlement has been reached, he can likewise move for dismissal. The court can also dismiss a case on its own motion.

In the following case, a condominium association sued a service company in the business of repairing building exteriors. A trial court had granted a motion to dismiss. The association appealed. In reviewing the case, the appellate court engaged in *de novo* review—that is, it reviewed the issue anew, as if the lower court had not ruled on the issue.

Case Analysis 5.1

West Bay Plaza Condominium Association, Inc. v. Sika Corporation

District Court of Appeal of Florida, 3rd Dist., 338 So.3d 32 (2022).

In the Language of the Court
GORDO, J.
West Bay Plaza Condominium Association, Inc. appeals a trial court order granting a motion to dismiss a count of its complaint due to improper venue. We have jurisdiction. Because the trial court did not err in enforcing the mandatory forum selection clause and finding venue was proper in New Jersey, we affirm.

Factual and Procedural Background
West Bay Plaza Condominium Association, Inc. governs and manages a condominium property located in Miami Beach, Florida. In late 2013 and early 2014, West Bay entered into contracts with Built Right Installers International Corporation, R.J. Miranda Consultants, Inc. and UCI Engineering, Inc., to effectuate exterior repairs to its property. In 2014, Westchester Fire Insurance Company provided West Bay a performance bond. As the repair progressed, disputes arose between the parties regarding the quality of the work, delays, and other construction issues.

In 2016, Sika Corporation, a New Jersey corporation, executed a five-year Standard Limited Warranty for West Bay for three sealant products used to repair the garage.

In February 2019, West Bay filed a complaint against Built Right, R.J. Miranda, UCI Engineering and Westchester Fire for breach of contract and professional negligence. A month later, West Bay filed an amended complaint adding Sika as a party and raised a single cause of action that alleged Sika breached the warranty because its products failed to provide a watertight barrier. Sika filed a motion to dismiss alleging Florida was an improper venue because the warranty contained a mandatory forum selection clause requiring all actions stemming from the agreement be brought in New Jersey. West Bay responded, arguing it was not bound by the forum selection clause because it was a non-signatory and even if it was, compelling reasons existed to decline enforcement of the clause in this case. On August 5, 2021, the trial court held a hearing on the motion and granted Sika's motion to dismiss, finding the parties were bound to litigate in the chosen forum, New Jersey. This appeal followed.

Legal Analysis
"The interpretation of a contractual forum selection clause is a question of law, such that our standard of review is de novo." "[A]n order granting a motion to dismiss [also] presents a pure question of law and is subject to de novo review."

"Florida law presumes that the forum selection clauses in contracts are valid and enforceable, and a party seeking to avoid enforcement of such a clause must establish that enforcement would be unjust or unreasonable." "A party seeking to avoid enforcement of a mandatory forum selection clause bears a heavy burden of establishing that the enforcement is unjust or unreasonable and must demonstrate that the contractually designated forum essentially amounts to 'no forum at all,' thereby depriving the party of its day in court."

"'[A] forum selection clause is mandatory where the plain language used by the parties indicates "exclusivity."'" Here, it is undisputed

Case 5.1 Continues

Case 5.1 Continued

by the parties that the forum selection clause at issue is mandatory.

West Bay argues, however, that because it is a non-signatory to the warranty it should not be bound by the mandatory forum selection clause. "[T]his Court has previously held that the mandatory nature of a forum selection clause 'equally applies to the non-signatory defendants due to the fact that the claims arise directly from the agreement, as well as due to the nature of the commercial relationship of the parties as it relates to the agreement itself.'" Further, where the "resolution of the plaintiffs' claims requires reference to" the agreement with the forum selection clause and the claims brought specifically reference that agreement, there is "a significant relationship and clear nexus" between the agreement and the claims and the forum selection clause

therefore applies. * * * In its complaint, West Bay solely raises a claim of breach of express warranty against Sika. Thus, because resolution of West Bay's claim requires reference to the warranty and there is a significant relationship and clear nexus between the claim and the warranty, the forum selection clause applies.

West Bay next argues that compelling reasons exist to decline enforcement of the forum selection clause because the clause creates multiple lawsuits, increased judicial labor, increased expenses to all parties and could create inconsistent results. In this case, there are no crossclaims involved or complex litigation questions. The sole cause of action against Sika is the breach of warranty claim that is completely unrelated to the other contracts and to the causes

of actions raised against the other defendants. Sika's only involvement was supplying the sealant used in the garage. "[F]orum selection clauses should be enforced in the absence of a showing that enforcement would be unreasonable or unjust." "Parties have the right to control their litigation destinies by bargaining for the ability to litigate in a specific forum." Here, West Bay seeks to raise a claim against Sika pursuant to a warranty whose terms explicitly selected New Jersey as a forum without demonstrating that enforcement of this clause would be unreasonable or unjust. We find requiring West Bay to pursue its claim for breach of warranty in New Jersey does not essentially amount "to 'no forum at all,' thereby depriving [West Bay] of its day in court."

Affirmed.

Legal Reasoning Questions

1. Compare and contrast a motion to dismiss with other pretrial motions. Identify their chief differences.

2. Why did West Bay Plaza Condominium Association initially sue Sika Corporation?

3. What is the effect of granting a motion to dismiss?

Motion for Judgment on the Pleadings At the close of the pleadings, either party may make a **motion for judgment on the pleadings.** This motion asks the court to decide the issue solely on the pleadings without proceeding to trial.

The judge will grant the motion only when there is no dispute over the facts of the case and the sole issue to be resolved is a question of law. For example, in the Kirby–Carvello case, if Carvello had admitted to all of Kirby's allegations in his answer and had raised no affirmative defenses, Kirby could file a motion for judgment on the pleadings.

In deciding a motion for judgment on the pleadings, the judge may consider only the evidence contained in

the pleadings. In contrast, in a motion for summary judgment, discussed next, the court may consider evidence outside the pleadings.

Motion for Summary Judgment Like a motion for judgment on the pleadings, a **motion for summary judgment** asks the court to grant a judgment without a trial. The motion can be made by either party before or during the trial. As with a motion for judgment on the pleadings, a court will grant a motion for summary judgment only if no facts are in dispute and the only question is how the law applies to the facts.

As mentioned, however, a motion for summary judgment differs from a motion for judgment on the pleadings in that the party filing the summary judgment motion can submit evidence obtained at any point before the trial that refutes the other party's factual claim. The evidence may consist of **affidavits** (sworn statements by parties or witnesses) or copies of documents, such as contracts, e-mails, and letters obtained during discovery (discussed next). Of course, the evidence must be admissible evidence—that is, evidence that the court would allow to be presented during the trial.

In the following case, an appellate court examined the trial court's record to determine whether the trial court's granting of summary judgment for the defendants was appropriate.

Case 5.2

L.F. v. Lake Washington School District #141
United States Court of Appeals, Ninth Circuit, 947 Fed.3d 621 (2020).

Background and Facts L.F. believed that his daughters suffered from behavioral disorders that adversely affected their educational performance. He had a number of disagreements with the Lake Washington School District staff regarding the best ways to address these issues. The school district claimed that he had engaged in a pattern of abusive communications with school staff. The school district imposed a "Communication Plan" for L.F. This plan involved limiting him to an in-person meeting with two school district administrators once every two weeks. He sued, claiming that the Communication Plan violated his First Amendment rights. A federal trial court granted summary judgment to the school district. L.F. appealed.

In the Language of the Court
Gregory A. PRESNELL, District Judge.
    * * * *

For its part, the [school] district contends that * * * L.F. engaged in a pattern of "sending incessant emails to staff accusing them of wrongdoing; making presumptuous demands; leveling demeaning insults; . . . and in face-to-face interactions, acting in an aggressive, hostile, and intimidating manner." [The school] district employees complained that L.F.'s extraordinarily time-consuming communications made District staff feel threatened and intimidated.
    * * * *

[Under the Communication Plan imposed by the District,] L.F.'s substantive communications with the District about his daughters' education would be limited to bi-weekly, in-person meetings with [administrators]. L.F. was advised not to "email or attempt to communicate (in any form) with any District employees" aside from the bi-weekly meetings, "as they will not respond to [his] emails or attempts to communicate."
    * * * *

[L.F. eventually filed suit against the district, claiming in part that the Communication Plan violated his First Amendment rights.] The parties filed cross-motions for summary judgment. [T]he district court granted the District's motion * * * [and also] found that the Communication Plan did not violate the First Amendment because it was a reasonable, viewpoint-neutral restriction in a non-public forum.
    * * * *

L.F. contends that the district court erred by failing to apply the proper standard at summary judgement and by concluding that the Communication Plan did not burden his speech.
    * * * *

In any event, the district was within its rights to impose such a limitation. Members of the public do not have a constitutional right to force the government to listen to their views. And the First Amendment does not compel the government to respond to speech directed toward it. * * *

Case 5.2 Continues

Case 5.2 Continued

[B]ecause government entities, such as the District, do not have to listen to parents' views, it is not a constitutional violation to require that parents, if they wish to be heard, communicate only with particular staff members or to do so only at a specified time and place. And because the government is under no constitutional obligation to respond to such views, there is no violation where a government entity, such as the District, ignores (or threatens to ignore) communications from outside the specified channels.

Decision and Remedy The U.S. Court of Appeals for the Ninth Circuit agreed with the trial court's granting of summary judgment for the school district. The appeals court agreed with the trial court that the Communication Plan was a reasonable effort to manage the parent's relentless and unproductive communications with the school district's staff.

Critical Thinking

- **Legal Environment** Should motions for summary judgment and other pretrial motions be abolished so that all lawsuits proceed to trial? Why or why not?
- **What If the Facts Were Different?** Suppose that L.F. communicated appropriately with school administrators and simply wanted to add one more in-person session a month. What would have been the result? Why?

5–2c Discovery

Before a trial begins, the parties can use a number of procedural devices to obtain information and gather evidence about the case. Kirby, for example, will want to know how fast Carvello was driving. She will also want to learn whether he had been drinking any alcoholic beverages, was under the influence of medication, and was wearing corrective lenses if required by law to do so while driving.

The process of obtaining information from the opposing party or from witnesses prior to trial is known as **discovery.** Discovery includes gaining access to witnesses, documents, records, and other types of evidence. In federal courts, the parties are required to make initial disclosures of relevant evidence to the opposing party. A court can impose sanctions on a party who fails to respond to discovery requests.

Discovery prevents surprises at trial by giving both parties access to evidence that might otherwise be hidden. This allows the litigants to learn as much as they can about what to expect at a trial before they reach the courtroom. Discovery also serves to narrow the issues so that trial time is spent on the main questions in the case.

Discovery Rules The FRCP and similar state rules set forth the guidelines for discovery activity. Generally, discovery is allowed regarding any matter that is relevant to the claim or defense of any party. Discovery rules also attempt to protect witnesses and parties from undue harassment, and to prevent privileged or confidential material from being disclosed. Only information that is relevant to the case at hand—or likely to lead to the discovery of relevant information—is discoverable.

If a discovery request involves privileged or confidential business information, a court can deny the request and can limit the scope of discovery in a number of ways. For instance, a court can require the party to submit the materials to the judge in a sealed envelope so that the judge can decide if they should be disclosed to the opposing party.

Because third parties sometimes finance litigation, an ethical issue about the discovery process may arise. The Ethics Today feature examines this issue.

Depositions Discovery can involve the use of depositions. A **deposition** is sworn testimony by a party to the lawsuit or by any witness, recorded by an authorized court official. The person deposed gives testimony and answers questions asked by the attorneys from both sides. The questions and answers are recorded, sworn to, and signed. These answers, of course, will help the attorneys prepare their cases.

Depositions also give attorneys the opportunity to ask immediate follow-up questions and to evaluate how their witnesses will conduct themselves at trial. In addition, depositions can be employed in court to **impeach** (challenge the credibility of) parties or witnesses who change their testimony at the trial. Finally, a deposition can be used as testimony if the witness is not available at trial.

Interrogatories Discovery can also involve **interrogatories**—written questions for which written answers are prepared and then signed under oath. The main difference between interrogatories and written depositions is that interrogatories are directed to a party to the lawsuit (the plaintiff or the defendant), not to a witness. The party usually has thirty days to prepare answers.

Ethics Today

Should the law require discovery about third-party litigation financing?

Given the popularity of gambling in our society, it should come as no surprise that there is betting on lawsuits. Most of this "action" is placed by financing firms known as third-party litigators. For instance, a third party might provide Plaintiff X with $300,000 to bring an age discrimination suit against Company Z. If Plaintiff X prevails, the third-party litigant would get back its $300,000 plus a percentage of the settlement. If Plaintiff X fails, the third-part litigant loses its $300,000 "bet."

Proponents of this multi-billion-dollar global enterprise insist that it provides individual plaintiffs and law firms with the funds they need to bring valid lawsuits. The U.S. Chamber of Commerce, among other critics, worries that plaintiffs with deep-pocketed third-party backers will force business defendants to settle frivolous lawsuits rather than pay the costs of litigating them. In addition, there is the ethical question

of control. With a large financial stake in a trial's outcome, the third-party litigant might try to dictate legal strategy or influence the settlement amount. For American civil courts to function properly, these decisions must rest solely with plaintiffs and their legal representatives.

Usually, plaintiffs are not obliged by law to disclose third-party litigants during discovery. Several states have passed laws requiring such disclosure, thus allowing courts and juries to determine for themselves the impact of outside funding on the legal proceedings. In the face of strong opposition from the third-party litigation industry, attempts to pass similar federal legislation have yet to succeed.

Critical Thinking Under what circumstances would third-party litigants not be interested in financing a lawsuit?

The party's attorney often drafts the answers to interrogatories in a manner calculated to give away as little information as possible. Whereas depositions elicit candid answers not prepared in advance, interrogatories are designed to obtain accurate information about specific topics, such as how many contracts were signed and when. The scope of interrogatories is also broader because parties are obligated to answer questions, even if that means disclosing information from their records and files. As with discovery requests, a court can impose sanctions on a party who fails to answer interrogatories.

■ **Case in Point 5.2** Ronald J. Hass (doing business as Valley Corp. and R. J. Hass Corp.) was a contractor who built a home for Ty and Karen Levine. Probuilders Specialty Insurance Co. provided commercial liability insurance for the contractor. Later, when the Levines sued Hass and his company for shoddy and incomplete work, Hass blamed the subcontractors. Probuilders provided Hass with legal representation, but the Levines won a judgment for more than $2 million. Then Probuilders sued Hass and his company, claiming that he had made misrepresentations to them regarding the facts of the case and seeking to avoid paying the judgment. Hass filed a counterclaim against Probuilders.

During discovery, Hass refused to respond fully to interrogatories and other discovery requests, and refused to give a deposition. Probuilders filed a motion to compel, and the court ordered Hass to respond to the discovery

requests. Although Probuilders sent letters specifying what was needed, Hass continued to be evasive. The court imposed sanctions on Hass more than once. Ultimately, the court found that Hass had acted willfully and in bad faith, and recommended that his answers and counterclaim against Probuilders be dismissed.[6] ■

Requests for Admissions One party can serve the other party with a written request for an admission of the truth of matters relating to the trial. Any fact admitted under such a request is conclusively established as true for the trial. For instance, Kirby can ask Carvello to admit that his driver's license was suspended at the time of the accident. A request for admission shortens the trial because the parties will not have to spend time proving facts on which they already agree.

Requests for Documents, Objects, and Entry Upon Land Parties can gain access to documents and other items not in their possession in order to inspect and examine them. Carvello, for example, can gain permission to inspect and copy Kirby's car repair bills. Likewise, a party can gain "entry upon land" to inspect the premises.

---

6. *Probuilders Specialty Insurance Co. v. Valley Corp.*, 2012 WL 6045753 (N.D.Cal. 2012). See also *Brooks v. Whitaker*, 2022 WL 741684, 2022 VI SUPER 27U (Sup.Ct.V.I., Div. St. Thomas 2022).

Requests for Examinations When the physical or mental condition of one party is in question, the opposing party can ask the court to order a physical or mental examination by an independent examiner. If the court agrees to make the order, the opposing party can obtain the results of the examination. Note that the court will make such an order only when the need for the information outweighs the right to privacy of the person to be examined.

Electronic Discovery Any relevant material, including information stored electronically, can be the object of a discovery request. The federal rules and most state rules (as well as court decisions) specifically allow individuals to obtain discovery of electronic "data compilations." Electronic evidence, or **e-evidence,** consists of all computer-generated or electronically recorded information, such as e-mail, voice mail, tweets, blogs, social media posts, spreadsheets, documents, and other data stored electronically.

E-evidence can reveal significant facts that are not discoverable by other means. Computers, smartphones, cameras, and other devices automatically record certain file information on their hard drives—such as who created the file and when, and who accessed, modified, or transmitted it. This information is called **metadata,** which can be thought of as "data about data." Metadata can be obtained only from the file in its electronic format—not from printed-out versions.

■ **Example 5.3** John McAfee, the programmer responsible for creating McAfee antivirus software, was wanted for questioning in the murder of his neighbor in Belize. McAfee left Belize and was on the run from police, but he allowed a journalist to come with him and photograph him. When the journalist posted photos of McAfee online, some metadata were attached to a photo.

The police used the metadata to pinpoint the latitude and longitude of the image and subsequently arrested McAfee in Guatemala. ■

E-Discovery Procedures. The Federal Rules of Civil Procedure deal specifically with the preservation, retrieval, and production of electronic data. Although traditional interrogatories and depositions are still used to find out whether e-evidence exists, a party usually must hire an expert to retrieve the evidence in its electronic format. The expert uses software to reconstruct e-mail, text, and other exchanges to establish who knew what and when they knew it. The expert can even recover computer files that the user thought had been deleted.

Advantages and Disadvantages. Electronic discovery has significant advantages over paper discovery. Electronic versions of documents, e-mail, and text messages can provide useful—and often quite damaging—information about how a particular matter progressed over several weeks or months. E-discovery can uncover the proverbial smoking gun that will win the lawsuit. But it is also time consuming and expensive, especially when lawsuits involve large firms with multiple offices. Many companies have found it challenging to fulfill their duty to preserve electronic evidence from a vast number of sources. Failure to do so, however, can lead to sanctions and even force companies to agree to settlements that are not in their best interests.

A failure to provide e-evidence in response to a discovery request does not always arise from an unintentional failure to preserve documents and e-mail. The following case involved a litigant that delayed a response to gain time to intentionally alter and destroy data. At issue were the sanctions imposed for this spoliation. (Spoliation of evidence occurs when a document or information that is required for discovery is destroyed or altered significantly.)

Case 5.3

Klipsch Group, Inc. v. ePRO E-Commerce Limited

United States Court of Appeals, Second Circuit, 880 F.3d 620 (2018).

Background and Facts Klipsch Group, Inc., makes sound equipment, including headphones. Klipsch filed a suit in a federal district court against ePRO E-Commerce Limited, a Chinese corporation. Klipsch alleged that ePRO had sold $5 million in counterfeit Klipsch products. ePRO claimed that the sales of relevant products amounted to less than $8,000 worldwide. In response to discovery requests, ePRO failed to timely disclose the majority of the requested documents in its possession. In addition, ePRO restricted Klipsch's access to ePRO's e-data. The court directed ePRO to hold the relevant data to preserve evidence, but the defendant failed to do so. This led to the deletion of thousands of documents and significant quantities of data. To determine what data had been blocked or lost, and what might and might not be recovered, Klipsch spent $2.7 million on a forensic examination.

Case 5.3 Continues

Case 5.3 Continued

The federal district court concluded that ePRO had willingly engaged in spoliation of e-evidence. For this misconduct, the court imposed sanctions, including an order to pay Klipsch the entire $2.7 million for its restorative discovery efforts. ePRO appealed, contending that the sanctions were "disproportionate."

In the Language of the Court

Gerard E. LYNCH, Circuit Judge:

* * * *

ePRO argues that the monetary sanctions imposed against it are so out of proportion to the value of the evidence uncovered by Klipsch's efforts or to the likely ultimate value of the case as to be impermissibly punitive and a violation of due process. That position, although superficially sympathetic given the amount of the sanction, overlooks the fact that ePRO caused Klipsch to accrue those costs by failing to comply with its discovery obligations. Such compliance is not optional or negotiable; rather, the integrity of our civil litigation process requires that the parties before us, although adversarial to one another, carry out their duties to maintain and disclose the relevant information in their possession in good faith.

The extremely broad discovery permitted by the Federal Rules depends on the parties' voluntary participation. The system functions because, in the vast majority of cases, we can rely on each side to preserve evidence and to disclose relevant information when asked (and sometimes even before then) without being forced to proceed at the point of a court order. The courts are ill-equipped to address parties that do not voluntarily comply: we do not have our own investigatory powers, and even if we did, the spoliation of evidence would frequently be extremely difficult for any outsider to detect.

Moreover, noncompliance vastly increases the cost of litigation * * * . Accordingly, we have held that discovery sanctions are proper * * * , because an alternative rule would encourage dilatory [delaying] tactics, and compliance with discovery orders would come only when the backs of counsel and the litigants were against the wall.

When we apply those principles to the case at hand, it is clear that the district court did not abuse its discretion by imposing monetary sanctions calculated to make Klipsch whole for the extra cost and efforts it reasonably undertook in response to ePRO's recalcitrance.

* * * *

In sum, we see nothing in ePRO's proportionality arguments compelling us to conclude that the district court abused its discretion by awarding full compensation for efforts that were * * * a reasonable response to ePRO's own evasive conduct. The proportionality that matters here is that the amount of the sanctions was plainly proportionate—indeed, it was exactly equivalent—to the costs ePRO inflicted on Klipsch in its reasonable efforts to remedy ePRO's misconduct.

Decision and Remedy The U.S. Court of Appeals for the Second Circuit affirmed the sanctions. "The district court's award properly reflects the additional costs ePRO imposed on its opponent by refusing to comply with its discovery obligations."

Critical Thinking

- **Economic** Should the cost of corrective discovery efforts be imposed on an uncooperative party if those efforts turn up nothing of real value to the case? Explain.
- **Legal Environment** Should it be inferred from a business's failure to keep backup copies of its database that the business must therefore have destroyed the data? Discuss.

5–2d Pretrial Conference

After discovery has taken place and before the trial begins, the attorneys may meet with the trial judge in a pretrial conference, or hearing. Usually, the conference consists of an informal discussion between the judge and the opposing attorneys after discovery has taken place. The purpose is to explore the possibility of a settlement without trial and, if this is not possible, to identify the matters in dispute and to plan the course of the trial. In particular, the parties may attempt to establish ground rules to restrict the number of expert witnesses or discuss the admissibility or costs of certain types of evidence.

5–2e The Right to a Jury Trial

The Seventh Amendment to the U.S. Constitution guarantees the right to a jury trial for cases at law in federal courts when the amount in controversy exceeds $20. Most states have similar guarantees in their own constitutions (although the threshold dollar amount is higher than $20).

The right to a trial by jury need not be exercised, and many cases are tried without a jury. In most states and in federal courts, one of the parties must request a jury, or the judge presumes the parties waive this right. If there is no jury, the judge determines the truth of the facts alleged in the case.

5–2f Jury Selection

Before a jury trial commences, a panel of jurors must be selected. Although some types of trials require twelve-person juries, most civil matters can be heard by six-person juries. The jury selection process is known as *voir dire*.[7] In most jurisdictions, attorneys for the plaintiff and

___
7. Pronounced *vwahr deehr*. These verbs, based on Old French, mean "to speak the truth." In legal language, the phrase refers to the process of questioning jurors to learn about their backgrounds, attitudes, and similar attributes.

the defendant ask prospective jurors oral questions to determine whether they are biased or have any connection with a party to the action or with a prospective witness. In some jurisdictions, the judge may do all or part of the questioning based on written questions submitted by counsel for the parties.

During *voir dire*, a party may challenge a certain number of prospective jurors peremptorily—that is, ask that an individual not be sworn in as a juror without providing any reason. Alternatively, a party may challenge a prospective juror for cause—that is, provide a reason why an individual should not be sworn in as a juror. If the judge grants the challenge, the individual is asked to step down. A prospective juror, however, may not be excluded by the use of discriminatory challenges, such as those based on racial criteria or gender.

See Concept Summary 5.1 for a review of pretrial procedures.

Concept Summary 5.1

Pretrial Procedures

The Pleadings	• *The plaintiff's complaint*—The plaintiff's statement of the cause of action and the parties involved, filed with the court by the plaintiff's attorney. After the filing, the defendant is notified of the suit through service of process. • *The defendant's response*—The defendant's response to the plaintiff's complaint may take the form of an answer, in which the defendant admits or denies the plaintiff's allegations. The defendant may also raise an affirmative defense and/or assert a counterclaim.
Pretrial Motions	• *Motion to dismiss*—See Exhibit 5–3. • *Motion for judgment on the pleadings*—May be made by either party and will be granted only if no facts are in dispute and only questions of law are at issue. • *Motion for summary judgment*—See Exhibit 5–3.
Discovery	The process of gathering evidence concerning the case, which may involve the following: • *Depositions* (sworn testimony by either party or any witness). • *Interrogatories* (in which parties to the action write answers to questions with the aid of their attorneys). • Requests for admissions, documents, examinations, or other information relating to the case. • Requests for electronically recorded information, such as e-mail, text messages, voice mail, and other data.
Pretrial Conference	A pretrial hearing, at the request of either party or the court, to identify the matters in dispute after discovery has taken place and to explore the possibility of settling the dispute without a trial. If no settlement is possible, the parties plan the course of the trial.
Jury Selection	In a jury trial, the selection of members of the jury from a pool of prospective jurors. During a process known as *voir dire*, the attorneys for both sides may challenge prospective jurors either for cause or peremptorily (for no cause).

5–3 The Trial

Various rules and procedures govern the trial phase of the litigation process. There are rules governing what kind of evidence will or will not be admitted during the trial, as well as specific procedures that the participants in the lawsuit must follow. For instance, a trial judge may instruct jurors not to communicate with anyone about the case or order reporters not to use social media to comment on the case while in the courtroom.

5–3a Opening Statements

At the beginning of the trial, both attorneys are allowed to make **opening statements** setting forth the facts that they expect to prove during the trial. The opening statement provides an opportunity for each lawyer to give a brief version of the facts and the supporting evidence that will be used during the trial. Then the plaintiff's case is presented. In our hypothetical case, Kirby's lawyer would introduce evidence (relevant documents, exhibits, and the testimony of witnesses) to support Kirby's position.

5–3b Rules of Evidence

Whether evidence will be admitted in court is determined by the **rules of evidence.** These are a series of rules that the courts have created to ensure that any evidence presented during a trial is fair and reliable. The Federal Rules of Evidence govern the admissibility of evidence in federal courts.

Evidence Must Be Relevant to the Issues Evidence will not be admitted in court unless it is relevant to the matter in question. **Relevant evidence** is evidence that tends to prove or disprove a fact in question or to establish the degree of probability of a fact or action. For instance, evidence that the defendant was at a dentist's appointment when the victim was shot would be relevant, because it would tend to prove that the defendant was not the shooter.

Hearsay Evidence Is Not Admissible Generally, hearsay is not admissible as evidence. **Hearsay** is testimony someone gives in court about a statement made by someone else who was not under oath at the time. Literally, it is what someone heard someone else say. If witnesses in the Kirby–Carvello case testified in court concerning what they heard another observer say about the accident, for instance, that testimony would be hearsay. Admitting hearsay into evidence carries many risks because, even though it may be relevant, there is no way to test its reliability.

5–3c Examination of Witnesses and Potential Motions

Because Kirby is the plaintiff, she has the burden of proving that her allegations are true. Her attorney begins the presentation of Kirby's case by calling the first witness for the plaintiff and examining, or questioning, the witness. (For both attorneys, the types of questions and the manner of asking them are governed by the rules of evidence.) This questioning is called **direct examination.**

After Kirby's attorney is finished, the witness is subject to **cross-examination** by Carvello's attorney. Then Kirby's attorney has another opportunity to question the witness in redirect examination, and Carvello's attorney may follow the redirect examination with a recross-examination. When both attorneys have finished with the first witness, Kirby's attorney calls the succeeding witnesses in the plaintiff's case. Each witness is subject to examination by the attorneys in the manner just described.

Expert Witnesses As part of their cases, both the plaintiff and the defendant may present testimony from one or more expert witnesses, such as forensic scientists, physicians, and psychologists. An expert witness is a person who, by virtue of education, training, skill, or experience, has scientific, technical, or other specialized knowledge in a particular area beyond that of an average person. In Kirby's case, her attorney might hire an accident reconstruction specialist to establish Carvello's negligence or a physician to testify to the extent of Kirby's injuries.

Normally, witnesses can testify only about the facts of a case—that is, what they personally observed. When witnesses are qualified as experts in a particular field, however, they can offer their opinions and conclusions about the evidence in that field. Because numerous experts are available for hire and expert testimony is powerful and effective with juries, there is tremendous potential for abuse. Therefore, judges act as gatekeepers to ensure that the experts are qualified. If a party believes that the opponent's expert witness is not a qualified expert in the relevant field, that party can make a motion to prevent the witness from testifying.[8]

---

8. See Edward J. Imwinkelried, *The Methods of Attacking Scientific Evidence*, 5th ed. (2014).

■ **Case in Point 5.4** Yvette Downey bought a children's bedroom set from Bob's Discount Furniture Holdings, Inc. She later discovered that it was infested with bed bugs, which had spread throughout her home. Downey spoke with Edward Gordinier, a licensed and experienced exterminator, who identified the bedroom set as the source of the problem. Although Bob's retrieved the bedroom set and refunded the purchase price, it refused to pay for the costs of extermination or any other damages. Downey sued.

Before the trial, Downey's attorney named Gordinier as a witness but did not submit a written report describing his anticipated testimony or specifying his qualifications. The defendants filed a motion to prevent his testimony. The district court refused to allow Gordinier to testify, but that decision was reversed on appeal. The appellate court concluded that Gordinier was not the type of expert who regularly was hired by plaintiffs to testify in court, in which case a report would have been required. Gordinier was simply an expert on bugs, and he was allowed to give his opinion on the infestation.[9] ■

Possible Motion and Judgment At the conclusion of the plaintiff's case, the defendant's attorney may ask the judge to direct a verdict for the defendant on the ground that no evidence has been presented to support the plaintiff's claim. This is called a **motion for a judgment as a matter of law** (or a **motion for a directed verdict** in state courts). In considering the motion, the judge looks at the evidence in the light most favorable to the plaintiff and grants the motion only if there is insufficient evidence to raise an issue of fact. (Motions for directed verdicts at this stage of a trial are seldom granted.)

Defendant's Evidence The defendant's attorney then presents the evidence and witnesses for the defendant's case. Witnesses are called and examined by the defendant's attorney. The plaintiff's attorney has the right to cross-examine them, and there may be a redirect examination and possibly a recross-examination.

At the end of the defendant's case, either attorney can move for a directed verdict. Again, the test is whether the jury can, through any reasonable interpretation of the evidence, find for the party against whom the motion has been made. After the defendant's attorney has finished introducing evidence, the plaintiff's attorney can present a **rebuttal** by offering additional evidence that refutes the defendant's case. The defendant's attorney can, in turn, refute that evidence in a **rejoinder.**

5–3d Closing Arguments, Jury Instructions, and Verdict

After both sides have rested their cases, each attorney presents a **closing argument.** In the closing argument, each attorney summarizes the facts and evidence presented during the trial and indicates why the facts and evidence support the client's claim. In addition to generally urging a verdict in favor of the client, the closing argument typically reveals the shortcomings of the points made by the opposing party during the trial.

Jury Instructions Attorneys usually present closing arguments whether or not the trial was heard by a jury. If it was a jury trial, the attorneys will have met with the judge before the closing arguments to determine how the jury will be instructed on the law. The attorneys can refer to these instructions in their closing arguments. After closing arguments are completed, the judge instructs the jury in the law that applies to the case (these instructions are often called *charges*). The jury then retires to the jury room to deliberate a verdict.

Juries are instructed on the standard of proof they must apply to the case. In most civil cases, the standard of proof is a preponderance of the evidence.[10] In other words, the plaintiff (Kirby in our hypothetical case) need only show that her factual claim is more likely to be true than the defendant's. In a criminal trial, the prosecution has a higher standard of proof to meet—it must prove its case beyond a reasonable doubt.

Verdict Once the jury has reached a decision, it issues a **verdict** in favor of one party. The verdict specifies the jury's factual findings. In some cases, the jury also decides on the amount of the award (the compensation to be paid to the prevailing party). After the announcement of the verdict, which marks the end of the trial itself, the jurors are dismissed.

See Concept Summary 5.2 for a review of trial procedures.

---

9. *Downey v. Bob's Discount Furniture Holdings, Inc.*, 633 F.3d 1 (1st Cir. 2011). See also *Macisaac v. State Farm Fire and Casualty Company*, 2021 WL 3934474 (E.D. Tenn., N. Div. 2021).

10. Note that some civil claims must be proved by "clear and convincing evidence," meaning that the evidence must show that the truth of the party's claim is highly probable. This standard is often applied in situations that present a particular danger of deception, such as allegations of fraud.

Concept Summary 5.2

Trial Procedure

Opening Statements	• Each party's attorney is allowed to present an opening statement indicating what the attorney will attempt to prove during the course of the trial.
Examination of Witnesses	• Plaintiff's introduction and direct examination of witnesses, cross-examination by defendant's attorney, possible redirect examination by plaintiff's attorney, and possible recross-examination by defendant's attorney.
	• Both the plaintiff and the defendant may present testimony from one or more expert witnesses.
	• At the close of the plaintiff's case, the defendant may make a motion for a directed verdict (or for judgment as a matter of law). If granted by the court, this motion will end the trial before the defendant presents witnesses.
	• Defendant's introduction and direct examination of witnesses, cross-examination by plaintiff's attorney, possible redirect examination by defendant's attorney, and possible recross-examination by plaintiff's attorney.
	• Possible rebuttal of defendant's argument by plaintiff's attorney, who presents more evidence.
	• Possible rejoinder by defendant's attorney to meet that evidence.
Closing Arguments, Jury Instructions, and Verdict	• Each party's attorney argues in favor of a verdict for that attorney's client.
	• The judge instructs (or charges) the jury as to how the law applies to the issue, and the jury retires to deliberate.
	• When the jury renders its verdict, the trial comes to an end.

5–4 Posttrial Motions

After the jury has rendered its verdict, either party may make a posttrial motion. The prevailing party usually requests that the court enter a judgment in accordance with the verdict. The nonprevailing party frequently files one of the motions discussed next.

5–4a Motion for a New Trial

At the end of the trial, the losing party may make a motion to set aside the adverse verdict and any judgment and to hold a new trial. After looking at all the evidence, judges will grant the **motion for a new trial** only if they believe that the jury was in error and that it is not appropriate to grant judgment for the other side.

Usually, a new trial is granted only when the jury verdict is obviously the result of a misapplication of the law or a misunderstanding of the evidence presented at trial. A new trial can also be granted on the grounds of newly discovered evidence, misconduct by the participants during the trial (such as when a juror has made prejudicial and inflammatory remarks), or an error by the judge.

5–4b Motion for Judgment *N.O.V.*

If Kirby wins and if Carvello's attorney has previously moved for a judgment as a matter of law, then Carvello's attorney can make a second motion for a judgment as a matter of law (the terminology used in federal courts).

In many state courts, if the defendant's attorney moved earlier for a directed verdict, the attorney may now make a **motion for judgment *n.o.v.***—from the Latin *non obstante veredicto*, meaning "notwithstanding the verdict." Such a motion will be granted only if the jury's verdict was unreasonable and erroneous.

If the judge grants the motion, then the jury's verdict will be set aside, and a judgment will be entered in favor of the opposing party (Carvello). If the motion is denied, Carvello may then appeal the case. Kirby may also appeal the case, even though she won at trial. She might appeal, for example, if she received a smaller monetary award than she had sought.

5–5 The Appeal

Either party may appeal not only the jury's verdict but also the judge's ruling on any pretrial or posttrial motion. Many of the appellate court cases that appear in this text involve appeals of motions for summary judgment or other motions that were denied by trial court judges.

Note that a party must have legitimate grounds to file an appeal (some legal error) and that few trial court decisions are reversed on appeal. Moreover, the expenses associated with an appeal can be considerable.

5–5a Filing the Appeal

If Carvello decides to appeal the verdict in Kirby's favor, then his attorney must file a notice of appeal with the clerk of the trial court within a prescribed period of time. Carvello then becomes the appellant or petitioner. The clerk of the trial court sends to the reviewing court (usually an intermediate court of appeals) the record on appeal. The record contains all the pleadings, motions, and other documents filed with the court and a complete written transcript of the proceedings, including testimony, arguments, jury instructions, and judicial rulings.

Carvello's attorney will file an appellate **brief** with the reviewing court. The brief is a formal legal document outlining the facts and issues of the case, the judge's rulings or jury's findings that should be reversed or modified, the applicable law, and arguments on Carvello's behalf (citing applicable statutes and relevant cases as precedents). The attorney for the appellee (Kirby, in our hypothetical case) usually files an answering brief. Carvello's attorney can file a reply, although it is not required. The reviewing court then considers the case.

5–5b Appellate Review

A court of appeals does not hear any evidence. Rather, it reviews the record for errors of law. Its decision concerning a case is based on the record on appeal and the briefs and arguments. The attorneys present oral arguments, after which the case is taken under advisement.

The court then issues a written opinion. In general, appellate courts do not reverse findings of fact unless the findings are unsupported or contradicted by the evidence.

An appellate court has the following options after reviewing a case:

1. The court can affirm the trial court's decision. (Most decisions are affirmed.)
2. The court can reverse the trial court's judgment if it concludes that the trial court erred or that the jury did not receive proper instructions.
3. The appellate court can remand (send back) the case to the trial court for further proceedings consistent with its opinion on the matter.
4. The court might also affirm or reverse a decision in part. For example, the court might affirm the jury's finding that Carvello was negligent but remand the case for further proceedings on another issue (such as the extent of Kirby's damages).
5. An appellate court can also modify a lower court's decision. If the appellate court decides that the jury awarded an excessive amount in damages, for example, the court might reduce the award to a more appropriate, or fairer, amount.

5–5c Higher Appellate Courts

If the reviewing court is an intermediate appellate court, the losing party may decide to appeal the decision to the state's highest court, usually called its *supreme court*. Although the losing party has a right to ask (petition) a higher court to review the case, the party does not have a right to have the case heard by the higher appellate court. Appellate courts normally have discretionary power and can accept or reject an appeal. Like the United States Supreme Court, state supreme courts generally deny most petitions for appeal.

If the petition for review is granted, new briefs must be filed before the state supreme court, and the attorneys may be allowed or requested to present oral arguments. Like the intermediate appellate courts, the state supreme court can reverse or affirm the lower appellate court's decision or remand the case. At this point, the case typically has reached its end (unless a federal question is at issue and one of the parties has legitimate grounds to seek review by a federal appellate court).

Concept Summary 5.3 reviews the options that the parties may pursue after the trial.

Concept Summary 5.3

Posttrial Options

Posttrial Motions	• *Motion for a new trial*—If the judge believes that the jury was in error but is not convinced that the losing party should have won, the motion normally is granted. It can also be granted on the basis of newly discovered evidence, misconduct by the participants during the trial, or error by the judge.
	• *Motion for judgment* n.o.v. ("*notwithstanding the verdict*")—The party making the motion must have filed a motion for a directed verdict at the close of the presentation of evidence during the trial. The motion will be granted if the judge is convinced that the jury was in error.
The Appeal	Either party can appeal the trial court's judgment to an appropriate court of appeals.
	• *Filing the appeal*—The appealing party must file a notice of appeal with the clerk of the trial court, who forwards the record on appeal to the appellate court. Attorneys file appellate briefs.
	• *Appellate review*—The appellate court does not hear evidence but bases its opinion, which it issues in writing, on the record on appeal and the attorneys' briefs and oral arguments. The court may affirm or reverse all (or part) of the trial court's judgment and/or remand the case for further proceedings consistent with its opinion. Most decisions are affirmed on appeal.
	• *Further review*—In some cases, further review may be sought from a higher appellate court, such as a state supreme court. If a federal question is involved, the case may ultimately be appealed to the United States Supreme Court.

5–6 Enforcing the Judgment

The uncertainties of the litigation process are compounded by the lack of guarantees that any judgment will be enforceable. Even if the jury awards Kirby the full amount of damages requested ($500,000), for instance, Carvello's auto insurance coverage might have lapsed. If so, the company would not pay any of the damages. Alternatively, Carvello's insurance policy might be limited to $250,000, meaning that Carvello personally would have to pay the remaining $250,000.

5–6a Requesting Court Assistance in Collecting the Judgment

If the defendant does not have the funds available to pay the judgment, the plaintiff can go back to the court and request that the court issue a writ of execution. A **writ of execution** is an order directing the sheriff to seize and sell the defendant's nonexempt assets, or property (certain assets are exempted by law from such actions). The proceeds of the sale are then used to pay the damages owed, and any excess proceeds are returned to the defendant. Alternatively, the nonexempt property itself could be transferred to the plaintiff in lieu of an outright payment. (Creditors' remedies, discussed elsewhere in this text, may also be available.)

5–6b Availability of Assets

The problem of collecting a judgment is less pronounced when a party is seeking to satisfy a judgment against a defendant with substantial assets that can be easily located, such as a major corporation. Usually, one of the factors considered by plaintiffs and their attorneys before a lawsuit is initiated is whether the defendant has sufficient assets to cover the amount of damages sought. In addition, during the discovery process, attorneys routinely seek information about the location of the defendant's assets that might potentially be used to satisfy a judgment.

Practice and Review: Court Procedures

Ronald Metzgar placed his fifteen-month-old son, Matthew, awake and healthy, in his playpen. Ronald left the room for five minutes and on his return found Matthew lifeless. A toy block had lodged in the boy's throat, causing him to choke to death. Ronald called 911, but efforts to revive Matthew were to no avail. There was no warning of a choking hazard on the box containing the block. Matthew's parents hired an attorney and sued Playskool, Inc., the manufacturer of the block, alleging that the manufacturer had been negligent in failing to warn of the block's hazard. Playskool filed a motion for summary judgment, arguing that the danger of a young child's choking on a small block was obvious. Using the information presented in the chapter, answer the following questions.

1. Suppose that the attorney the Metzgars hired agreed to represent them on a contingency-fee basis. What does that mean?
2. How would the Metzgars' attorney likely have served process (the summons and complaint) on Playskool, Inc.?
3. Should Playskool's request for summary judgment be granted? Why or why not?
4. Suppose that the judge denied Playskool's motion and the case proceeded to trial. After hearing all the evidence, the jury found in favor of the defendant. What options do the plaintiffs have at this point if they are not satisfied with the verdict?

Debate This . . . Some consumer advocates argue that attorneys' high contingency fees—sometimes reaching 40 percent—unfairly deprive winning plaintiffs of too much of their awards. Should the government cap contingency fees at, say, 20 percent of the award? Why or why not?

Terms and Concepts

affidavits 95
affirmative defense 92
answer 91
brief 104
closing argument 102
complaint 90
counterclaim 92
cross-examination 101
default judgment 90
deposition 96
direct examination 101
discovery 96
e-evidence 98
Federal Rules of Civil Procedure
   (FRCP) 88

hearsay 101
impeach 96
interrogatories 96
metadata 98
motion 92
motion for a directed verdict 102
motion for a judgment as a matter
   of law 102
motion for a new trial 103
motion for judgment *n.o.v.* 103
motion for judgment on the
   pleadings 94
motion for summary judgment 94
motion to dismiss 92
opening statements 101

pleadings 90
pretrial motions 92
rebuttal 102
rejoinder 102
relevant evidence 101
rules of evidence 101
service of process 90
summons 90
verdict 102
voir dire 100
writ of execution 105

Issue Spotters

1. At the trial, after Saskia calls her witnesses, offers her evidence, and otherwise presents her side of the case, Tom has at least two choices between courses of actions. Tom can call his first witness. What else might he do? (See *The Trial.*)
2. After the trial, the judge issues a judgment that includes a grant of relief for Saskia, but the relief is less than

Saskia wanted. Neither Saskia nor Tom is satisfied with this result. Who can appeal to a higher court? (See *The Appeal.*)

• **Check your answers to the Issue Spotters against the answers provided in Appendix B at the end of this text.**

Business Scenarios and Case Problems

5–1. Discovery Rules. In the past, the rules of discovery were very restrictive, and trials often turned on elements of surprise. For instance, a plaintiff would not necessarily know until the trial what the defendant's defense was going to be. In the last several decades, however, new rules of discovery have substantially changed this situation. Now each attorney can access practically all of the evidence that the other side intends to present at trial, with the exception of certain information—namely, the opposing attorney's work product. Work product is not a precise concept. Basically, it includes all of the attorney's thoughts on the case. Can you see any reason why such information should not be made available to the opposing attorney? Discuss fully. (See *Pretrial Procedures*.)

5–2. Motions. When and for what purpose is each of the following motions made? Which of them would be appropriate if a defendant claimed that the only issue between the parties was a question of law and that the law was favorable to the defendant's position? (See *Pretrial Procedures*.)

(a) A motion for judgment on the pleadings.

(b) A motion for a directed verdict.

(c) A motion for summary judgment.

(d) A motion for judgment *n.o.v.*

5–3. Motion for a New Trial. Washoe Medical Center, Inc., admitted Shirley Swisher for the treatment of a fractured pelvis. During her stay, Swisher suffered a fatal fall from her hospital bed. Gerald Parodi, the administrator of her estate, and others filed an action against Washoe seeking damages for the alleged lack of care in treating Swisher. During *voir dire*, when the plaintiffs' attorney returned a few minutes late from a break, the trial judge led the prospective jurors in a standing ovation. The judge joked with one of the prospective jurors, whom he had known in college, about his fitness to serve as a judge and personally endorsed another prospective juror's business. After the trial, the jury returned a verdict in favor of Washoe. The plaintiffs moved for a new trial, but the judge denied the motion. The plaintiffs then appealed, arguing that the tone set by the judge during *voir dire* prejudiced their right to a fair trial. Should the appellate court agree? Why or why not? (See *Posttrial Motions*.)

5–4. Discovery. Advance Technology Consultants, Inc. (ATC), contracted with RoadTrac, LLC, to provide software and client software systems for the products of global positioning satellite (GPS) technology being developed by RoadTrac. RoadTrac agreed to provide ATC with hardware with which ATC's software would interface. Problems soon arose, however. ATC claimed that RoadTrac's hardware was defective, making it difficult to develop the software. RoadTrac contended that its hardware was fully functional and that ATC had simply failed to provide supporting software.

ATC told RoadTrac that it considered their contract terminated. RoadTrac filed a suit in a Georgia state court against ATC alleging breach of contract. During discovery, RoadTrac requested ATC's customer lists and marketing procedures. ATC objected to providing this information because

RoadTrac and ATC had become competitors in the GPS industry. Should a party to a lawsuit have to hand over its confidential business secrets as part of a discovery request? Why or why not? What limitations might a court consider imposing before requiring ATC to produce this material? (See *Pretrial Procedures*.)

5–5. Business Case Problem with Sample Answer—Discovery. Jessica Lester died from injuries suffered in an auto accident caused by the driver of a truck owned by Allied Concrete Co. Jessica's widower, Isaiah, filed a suit against Allied for damages. The defendant requested copies of all of Isaiah's Facebook photos and other postings. Before responding, Isaiah "cleaned up" his Facebook page. Allied suspected that some items had been deleted, including a photo of Isaiah holding a beer can while wearing a T-shirt that declared "I [heart] hotmoms." Can this material be recovered? If so, how? What effect might Isaiah's "postings" have on the result in this case? Discuss. [*Allied Concrete Co. v. Lester,* 285 Va. 295, 736 S.E.2d 699 (2013)] (See *Pretrial Procedures*.)

- For a sample answer to Problem 5–5, go to Appendix C at the end of this text.

5–6. Motion for Summary Judgment. Rebecca Nichols drove a truck for Tri-National Logistics, Inc. (TNI). On a delivery trip, Nichols's fellow driver, James Paris, made unwelcome sexual advances. Paris continued to make advances during a subsequent mandatory layover. Nichols reported this behavior to their employer. TNI nevertheless left her with Paris in Pharr, Texas, for another seven days with no alternative form of transportation before sending a driver to pick her up. She filed a suit in a federal district court against TNI, alleging discrimination on the basis of sex in violation of Title VII of the Civil Rights Act. Disputed facts included whether Nichols subjectively felt abused by Paris and whether their employer was aware of his conduct and failed to take appropriate action. Could TNI successfully file a motion for summary judgment at this point? Explain. [*Nichols v. Tri-National Logistics, Inc.,* 809 F.3d 981 (8th Cir. 2016)] (See *Pretrial Procedures*.)

5–7. Service of Process. Bentley Bay Retail, LLC, filed a suit in a Florida state court against Soho Bay Restaurant, LLC, and against its corporate officers, Luiz and Karine Queiroz, in their individual capacities. Bentley Bay claimed that the Queirozes had breached their personal guaranty for Soho Bay's debt to Bentley Bay. The plaintiff filed notices with the court to depose the Queirozes, who resided in Brazil. The Queirozes argued that they could not be deposed in Brazil. The court ordered them to appear in Florida to provide depositions in their corporate capacity. Witnesses appearing in court outside the jurisdiction of their residence are immune from service of process while in court. On the Queirozes' appearance in Florida, can they be served with process in their individual capacities? Explain. [*Queiroz v. Bentley Bay Retail, LLC,* 43 Fla.L.Weekly D85, 237 So.3d 1108 (3 Dist. 2018)] (See *Pretrial Procedures*.)

5–8. Service of Process. Cincinnati Insurance Company (CIC) was involved in a lawsuit with Eric Hall. CIC twice requested certified-mail service on Hall at a residential address. On both occasions, electronic return receipts indicated that the summons and complaint were successfully "delivered" on specified dates and "left with individual." Someone signed for service of process. CIC moved for default judgment against Hall, citing his failure to appear or otherwise defend. A trial court dismissed the lawsuit against Hall for lack of service of process. Should the Court of Appeals of Ohio affirm the trial court's order? Why or why not? [*Cincinnati Insurance Co. v. Eric Hall, et al.,* 2022-Ohio-1112, 2022 WL 985977 (Ct. App.Ohio, 2nd Dist. 2022)] (See *Pretrial Procedures.*)

5–9. A Question of Ethics—The IDDR Approach and Complaints. John Verble worked as a financial advisor for Morgan Stanley Smith Barney, LLC. After nearly seven years, Verble was fired. He filed a suit in a federal district court against his ex-employer. In his complaint, Verble alleged that he had learned of illegal activity by Morgan Stanley and its clients. He claimed that he had reported the activity to the Federal Bureau of Investigation, and that he was fired in retaliation. His complaint contained no additional facts. [*Verble* v. *Morgan Stanley Smith Barney LLC,* 676 Fed.Appx. 421 (6th Cir. 2017)] (See *Pretrial Procedures.*)

(a) To avoid a dismissal of his suit, does Verble have a legal obligation to support his claims with more facts? Explain.

(b) Does Verble owe an ethical duty to back up his claims with more facts? Use the IDDR approach to express your answer.

Time-Limited Group Assignment

5–10. Court Procedures. Bento Cuisine is a lunch-cart business. It occupies a street corner in Texarkana, a city that straddles the border of Arkansas and Texas. Across the street—and across the state line, which runs down the middle of the street—is Rico's Tacos. The two businesses compete for customers. Recently, Bento has begun to suspect that Rico's is engaging in competitive behavior that is illegal. Bento's manager has overheard several of Rico's employees discussing these competitive tactics while on a break at a nearby Starbucks. Bento files a lawsuit against Rico's in a federal court based on diversity jurisdiction. (See *Pretrial Procedures.*)

(a) The first group will discuss whether Rico's could file a motion claiming that the federal court lacks jurisdiction over this dispute.

(b) The second group will assume that the case goes to trial. Bento's manager believes that Bento's has both the law and the facts on its side. Nevertheless, at the end of the trial, the jury decides against Bento, and the judge issues a ruling in favor of Rico's. If Bento is unwilling to accept this result, what are its options?

(c) As discussed in this chapter, hearsay is literally what a witness claims to have heard another person say. A third group will decide whether Bento's manager can testify about what he heard some of Rico's employees say to one another while at a coffee shop. This group will also discuss what makes the admissibility of hearsay evidence potentially unethical.

Unit One: Task-Based Simulation

Gabrielle owns and operates an antique furniture store in Eugene, Oregon. Initially, Gabrielle's customers were from Eugene and nearby towns in Oregon. Today, through her website, she also sells furniture to buyers around the country.

1. **Jurisdiction.** Gabrielle contracts with a furniture manufacturer in Maine to purchase five replicas of an early American dresser from the "federal period" for a price of $1,000 each. The manufacturer promises her that they will be delivered to her store in Oregon by March 1. Gabrielle has already contracted with three customers to sell them dressers, promising delivery close to March 1. The dressers are never delivered, despite the manufacturer's continuing promises that they will be shipped "soon." Where can Gabrielle file a lawsuit against the manufacturer?

2. **Service of Process.** One of Gabrielle's customers, Pierre, in Kansas, ordered an antique hutch via Gabrielle's website. After Pierre receives the hutch, he calls Gabrielle to complain that she misrepresented the hutch's quality on her website. Gabrielle contends that she did not make any misrepresentations and that Pierre has no claim. Pierre sues Gabrielle in a Kansas state court, alleging that Gabrielle is a liar and that she caused him emotional suffering during their conversations about the hutch. How can Pierre serve the summons and complaint on Gabrielle to notify her of the lawsuit?

3. **Arbitration.** Rather than litigate, Pierre and Gabrielle decide to arbitrate their dispute. The arbitrator subsequently determines that Gabrielle misrepresented the quality of the hutch on her website and enters an award of damages in favor of Pierre. If Gabrielle doesn't agree with the arbitrator's award, can she subsequently challenge it in court?

The Public and International Environment

Chapter 6

Tort Law

Part of doing business today—and, indeed, part of everyday life—is the risk of being involved in a lawsuit. The list of circumstances in which business-persons can be sued is long and varied. A customer who is injured by a security guard at a business establishment, for instance, may sue the business owner, claiming that the security guard's conduct was intentionally wrongful. A person who slips and falls at a retail store may sue the company for negligence.

Any time that one party's allegedly wrongful conduct causes injury to another, an action may arise under the law of *torts* (the word *tort* is French for "wrong"). Through tort law, society compensates those who have suffered injuries as a result of the wrongful conduct of others. Many of the lawsuits brought by or against business firms are based on various tort theories.

Consider this example: The Apogee Health Center provides plant-based supplements and pharmaceuticals. It has just developed a cannabidiol (CBD) derived from hops rather than hemp or cannabis. (Because hemp and cannabis are heavily regulated, while hops plants are not, Apogee Health's CBD is potentially extremely valuable.) In a review on its website, PotTalk—which also produces and sells CBD products—claims that it is scientifically impossible to produce a hops-derived CBD and condemns Apogee Health for "defrauding uninformed members of the alternative care community seeking pain relief." If PotTalk's accusation is false, has it committed a tort? As you will learn in this chapter, the tort of trade libel is one of many that can lead to liability for businesses. In this situation, Apogee Health could sue PotTalk for intentionally interfering with its prospective economic advantage.

6–1 The Basis of Tort Law

Two notions serve as the basis of all **torts:** wrongs and compensation. Tort law is designed to compensate those who have suffered a loss or injury due to another person's wrongful act. In a tort action, one person or group brings a lawsuit against another person or group to obtain compensation (monetary damages) or other relief for the harm suffered.

6–1a The Purpose of Tort Law

Generally, the purpose of tort law is to provide remedies for the violation of various protected interests. Society recognizes an interest in personal physical safety. Thus, tort law provides remedies for acts that cause physical injury or that interfere with physical security and freedom of movement. Society also recognizes an interest in protecting property, and tort law provides remedies for acts that cause destruction of or damage to property.

6–1b Damages Available in Tort Actions

Plaintiffs seek various remedies, or damages, in tort actions. Note that in legal usage the term "damage" refers to harm or injury to persons or property, while the term "**damages**" refers to monetary compensation for such harm or injury.

Compensatory Damages A plaintiff is awarded **compensatory damages** to compensate or reimburse the plaintiff for actual losses. Thus, the goal is to make plaintiffs whole and put them in the same position that they would have been in had the tort not occurred. Compensatory damages awards are often broken down into special damages and general damages.

Special damages compensate the plaintiff for quantifiable monetary losses, such as medical expenses and lost wages and benefits (now and in the future). Special damages might also be awarded to compensate for extra costs, the loss of irreplaceable items, and the costs of repairing or replacing damaged property.

General damages compensate individuals (not companies) for the nonmonetary aspects of the harm suffered, such as pain and suffering. A court might award general damages for physical or emotional pain and suffering, loss of companionship, loss of consortium (losing the emotional and physical benefits of a spousal relationship), disfigurement, loss of reputation, or loss or impairment of mental or physical capacity.

Punitive Damages Occasionally, the courts also award **punitive damages** in tort cases to punish the wrongdoer and deter others from similar wrongdoing. Punitive damages are appropriate only when the defendant's conduct was particularly egregious (outrageous) or reprehensible (shameful).

■ **Case in Point 6.1** Gibson's Bakery is a fifth-generation family business in Oberlin, Ohio, where Oberlin College is located. An underaged African American Oberlin College student attempted to purchase a bottle of wine at the bakery using a fake identification card. The store clerk rejected the fake ID and also noticed that the student had concealed two bottles of wine in his jacket. The salesclerk, a son of the owner, attempted to take a photo of the student, but the student slapped the phone away, striking the clerk's face. The clerk followed him into the street and held him, awaiting arrival of the police. A scuffle ensued with friends of the shoplifter. The police arrested the students, charging them with assault and the shoplifter with robbery. When rumors about the incident reached members of the student body, many of them believed that the students had been racially profiled by the young bakery clerk. Protests in front of the bakery occurred. Then Oberlin College suspended its purchasing agreement with the bakery for the school's dining halls. The bakery sued Oberlin College for tortuous interference with a business relationship. At trial, the bakery prevailed and was awarded total damages of $25 million. The award was upheld on appeal.[1] ■

Usually, punitive damages are available in *intentional* tort actions and only rarely in negligence lawsuits (negligence actions will be discussed later in this chapter). They may be awarded, however, in suits involving gross negligence. Gross negligence can be defined as an intentional failure to perform a manifest duty in reckless disregard of the consequences of such a failure for the life or property of another.

Courts exercise great restraint in granting punitive damages to plaintiffs in tort actions because punitive damages are subject to limitations under the due process clause of the U.S. Constitution. The United States Supreme Court has held that to the extent that an award of punitive damages is grossly excessive, it furthers no legitimate purpose and violates due process requirements.[2] Consequently, an appellate court will sometimes reduce the amount of punitive damages awarded to a plaintiff on the ground that it is excessive.

Legislative Caps on Damages State laws may limit the amount of damages—both punitive and general—that can be awarded to the plaintiff. More than half of the states have placed caps ranging from $250,000 to $750,000 on noneconomic general damages (such as for pain and suffering), especially in medical malpractice suits. More than thirty states have limited punitive damages, with some imposing outright bans.

6–1c Classification of Torts

There are two broad classifications of torts: intentional torts and unintentional torts (torts involving negligence). The classification of a particular tort depends largely on how the tort occurs (intentionally or negligently) and the surrounding circumstances. Intentional torts result from the intentional violation of person or property (fault plus intent). Negligence results from the breach of a duty to act reasonably (fault without intent).

6–1d Defenses

Even if a plaintiff proves all the elements of a tort, the defendant can raise a number of legally recognized defenses (reasons why the plaintiff should not obtain damages). A successful defense releases the defendant from partial or full liability for the tortious act.

The defenses available may vary depending on the specific tort involved. A common defense to intentional torts against persons, for instance, is consent. When a person consents to the act that causes the damage, there is generally no liability. The most widely used defense in negligence actions is comparative negligence.

In addition, most states have a statute of limitations that establishes the time limit (often two years from the

1. *Gibson Bros., Inc., et al. v. Oberlin College, et al.,* 187 N.E.3d 629, 2022-Ohio-1079 (Ct.App.OH 9th Dist. 2022).

2. *State Farm Mutual Automobile Insurance Co. v. Campbell*, 538 U.S. 408, 123 S.Ct. 1513, 155 L.Ed.2d 585 (2003).

date of discovering the harm) within which a particular type of lawsuit can be filed. After that time period has run, the plaintiff can no longer file a claim.

6–2 Intentional Torts Against Persons

An **intentional tort,** as the term implies, requires intent. The **tortfeasor** (the one committing the tort) must intend to commit an act, the consequences of which interfere with another's personal or business interests in a way not permitted by law. An evil or harmful motive is not required—in fact, the person committing the action may even have a beneficial motive for doing what turns out to be a tortious act.

In tort law, intent means only that the person intended the consequences of the act or knew with substantial certainty that specific consequences would result from the act. The law generally assumes that individuals intend the normal consequences of their actions. Thus, forcefully pushing another—even if done in jest—is an intentional tort (if injury results), because the object of a strong push can ordinarily be expected to fall down.

In addition, intent can be transferred when a defendant intends to harm one individual, but unintentionally harms a second person. This is called **transferred intent.** ■ **Example 6.2** Alex swings a bat intending to hit Blake but misses and hits Carson instead. Carson can sue Alex for the tort of battery (discussed shortly) because Alex's intent to harm Blake can be transferred to Carson. ■

6–2a Assault

An **assault** is any intentional and unexcused threat of immediate harmful or offensive contact—words or acts that create a reasonably believable threat. An assault can occur even if there is no actual contact with the plaintiff, provided that the defendant's conduct creates a reasonable apprehension of imminent harm in the plaintiff. Tort law aims to protect individuals from having to expect harmful or offensive contact.

6–2b Battery

If the act that created the apprehension is completed and results in harm to the plaintiff, it is a **battery**—an unexcused and harmful or offensive physical contact intentionally performed. ■ **Example 6.3** Fadely threatens Kasa with a gun and then shoots her. The pointing of the gun at Kasa is an assault. The firing of the gun (if the bullet hits Kasa) is a battery. ■

The contact can be harmful, or it can be merely offensive. Physical injury need not occur. The contact can involve any part of the body or anything attached to it—for instance, a hat, a purse, or a jacket. The contact can be made by the defendant or by some force set in motion by the defendant, such as a rock thrown by the defendant. Whether the contact is offensive is determined by the reasonable person standard.[3]

If the plaintiff shows that there was contact, and the jury (or judge, if there is no jury) agrees that the contact was offensive, then the plaintiff has a right to compensation. A plaintiff may be compensated for the emotional harm or loss of reputation resulting from a battery, as well as for physical harm. A defendant may assert self-defense or defense of others in an attempt to justify the conduct.

6–2c False Imprisonment

False imprisonment is the intentional confinement or restraint of another person's activities without justification. False imprisonment interferes with the freedom to move without restraint. The confinement can be accomplished through the use of physical barriers, physical restraint, or threats of physical force. Moral pressure does not constitute false imprisonment. It is essential that the person being restrained does not wish to be restrained. (The plaintiff's consent to the restraint bars any liability.)

Businesspersons often face suits for false imprisonment after they have attempted to confine a suspected shoplifter for questioning. Under the "privilege to detain" granted to merchants in most states, a merchant can use reasonable force to detain or delay persons suspected of shoplifting and hold them for the police. Although laws pertaining to this privilege vary from state to state, generally any detention must be conducted in a reasonable manner and for only a reasonable length of time. Undue force or unreasonable detention can lead to liability for the business.

■ **Case in Point 6.4** Justin Mills was playing blackjack at the Maryland Live! Casino when two casino employees approached him, grabbed his arm, and led him into a back hallway. The employees accused Mills of counting cards (a card-playing strategy that is not illegal in Maryland) and demanded his identification. They detained Mills and told him that they would not release him unless he produced his ID so that the casino could ban him from the premises.

Mills gave the employees his passport and was eventually allowed to leave, but he secretly recorded the

---

3. The reasonable person standard is an "objective" test of how a reasonable person would have acted under the same circumstances. See "The Duty of Care and Its Breach" later in this chapter.

interaction using the smartphone in his pocket. Mills later filed a lawsuit alleging, in part, false imprisonment. A federal district court granted Mills a summary judgment on the false imprisonment claim because the casino personnel had no legal justification for detaining him.[4] ■ In addition to private businesses, cities and counties may also face lawsuits for false imprisonment if they detain individuals without reason.

---

4. *Mills v. PPE Casino Resorts Maryland, LLC,* 2017 WL 2930460 (D.Md. 2017). See also *Huynh v. Walmart Inc.,* 30 F.4th 448 (5th Cir. 2022).

6–2d Intentional Infliction of Emotional Distress (IIED)

The tort of intentional infliction of emotional distress (IIED) involves an intentional act that amounts to extreme and outrageous conduct resulting in severe emotional distress to another. To be **actionable** (capable of serving as the ground for a lawsuit), the act must be extreme and outrageous to the point that it exceeds the bounds of decency accepted by society. The following case involved a group of plaintiffs who worked for Banana Republic. They claimed that they had suffered serious emotional trauma when they were video-recorded at work while using a private employee restroom.

I. K. v. Banana Republic, LLC, et al.
Court of Appeals of Oregon, 317 Or.App. 249, 505 P.3d 1078 (2022).

In the Language of the Court
LANDAU, S.J. [Senior Judge]
In these consolidated cases, plaintiffs allege that they suffered serious emotional trauma from having been video recorded at work while using a private employee restroom. The recording was done by a fellow employee whom plaintiffs allege their employer and one of its managers should have known would do such things had they not been negligent in their hiring and retention practices. The trial courts in both cases dismissed the complaints * * * for failure to state a claim. The courts reasoned that, under Oregon law, there can be no recovery for negligent infliction of emotional distress in the absence of physical impact or the violation of a legally protected right independent of the interest in being free from another's negligence, and here the complaints pleaded neither physical impact nor the violation of a cognizable legally protected right.
* * * *

I. Facts
* * * *
Defendant Johnny Tuck Chee Chan was a licensed pharmacist who worked at a Kaiser Permanente pharmacy. During his employment there, he secretly video recorded other employees using the store's restroom. In November 2017, Kaiser discovered Chan's secret recording and fired him. Police commenced an investigation of Chan, as did the Oregon Board of Pharmacy.

In the meantime, in May 2018, defendant Banana Republic's general manager, Teri Turner, hired Chan to work as a sales associate at its Cascade Station store. Chan once again secretly placed a camera in the store's employee restroom and recorded employees in a state of undress while using the restroom.

In November 2018, after a year-long investigation, police arrested Chan in connection with his recording of more than 50 people at the Kaiser pharmacy restroom. A few weeks later, Chan was charged with recording 27 Banana Republic employees as well.

Plaintiff I. K., an 18-year-old Banana Republic employee working at the Cascade Station store, was among those whom Chan secretly recorded. When she learned that Chan had secretly recorded her using the restroom, she experienced significant mental and emotional pain and suffering. Plaintiff C. K., another Banana Republic employee, learned that she, too, had been recorded while using the restroom and experienced significant mental and emotional pain and suffering.

In addition to suing Chan, I. K. initiated an action for negligence against Banana Republic and Turner. She alleged that defendants were negligent in hiring and retaining Chan because they should have known that he had been fired from Kaiser for secretly recording employees using the restroom. C. K. initiated a separate action against defendants for negligent hiring and retention on the same grounds, also alleging that she suffered significant mental and emotional pain and suffering.

In both cases, defendants moved to dismiss the negligent hiring and retention claims * * * for failure to state a claim. They argued that Oregon law does not recognize a claim for negligent infliction of emotional distress in the absence of allegations of physical impact or an applicable exception to the physical impact requirement. In neither complaint, they argued, is there an allegation of physical impact. Moreover, defendants argued, no exception to the physical impact rule applies. * * *
* * * *

Case 6.1 Continues

Case 6.1 Continued

II. Analysis

In reviewing the trial courts' decision to dismiss plaintiffs' claims, our task is to determine whether, viewing the allegations of the complaint in the light most favorable to plaintiffs, they have failed to state a claim as a matter of law.

Under Oregon law, a plaintiff who has suffered emotional distress as a result of a defendant's negligence ordinarily may not recover damages for such emotional harm in the absence of some sort of physical impact. There is an exception to that general rule when the defendant violated a "legally protected interest" independent of the plaintiff's interest in being free from negligent conduct. If a plaintiff establishes a negligence claim based on the violation of such an independent legally protected interest, "then, generally speaking, the pain for which recovery is allowed includes virtually any form of conscious suffering, both emotional and physical" that foreseeably resulted from the violation.

* * * *

The analysis of a claim for negligent infliction of emotional distress thus proceeds in three steps: First, we must determine whether the complaint alleges the violation of a legally protected interest. Second, we must determine whether such interest is of sufficient importance as a matter of public policy to merit protection from emotional impact. And third, we must determine whether the complaint alleges that the emotional distress was the foreseeable result of the violation of the legally protected interest.

A. The Existence of a Legally Protected Interest

* * * *

Whether an individual * * * has a legally protected interest in being free from the negligently caused emotional trauma of being video recorded while using a private restroom is an issue of first impression under the law of this state. [W]e conclude that, as a matter

of common law, plaintiffs have such a legally protected interest in being free from the emotional distress of being secretly video recorded while using a private employee restroom.

It is well established that the common law recognizes the existence of a right to privacy, as well as the right to recover damages for infliction of emotional distress based on at least some violations of that right. * * *

* * * *

Defendants argue that, in the context of determining whether a claim may be maintained for negligent infliction of emotional distress, what is relevant is the duty of the defendant, not the nature of the underlying interest that a plaintiff may possess. * * * If an employer provides a supposedly private restroom for employees and the employer knows or has reason to know that another employee has in the past placed a video recording device in such private restrooms, the employer may be liable for negligently failing to take steps to protect the employees' right to privacy and prevent the emotional distress that is likely to result from a violation of that right.

* * * *

Defendants also argue that, because the case law to date recognizes only a claim for *intentional* infliction of emotional distress resulting from a violation of the right to privacy, we cannot venture beyond those precedents. Again, we are not persuaded. No appellate decision from the courts of this state suggests—much less holds—that a negligent violation of the right to privacy may *not* support a claim for emotional distress damages. * * *

B. The Societal Importance of the Legally Protected Interest

Not just any legally protected interest warrants protection against emotional distress. The interest must be of "sufficient importance as a matter of public policy." * * * There appears to be no clear-cut test for determining whether a given interest is of "sufficient

importance." Primarily, it appears that courts compare the interest at issue with those that the courts have found to be of sufficient importance in other cases.

* * * *

In our view, the interest in avoiding the emotional trauma from being secretly video recorded in a state of undress while using a private employee restroom is at least as societally important as being free from the distress of being awakened in the night with unwanted telephone calls, or learning of a spouse's disinterment, or worrying about the damage to property caused by flooding.

* * * *

C. Foreseeability

To recover in this case, plaintiffs must establish not only the existence of an important legally protected interest but also that defendants "negligently cause[d] foreseeable, serious emotional distress." Here, plaintiffs allege that their emotional distress from having been secretly video recorded while using the employee restroom was a foreseeable result of defendants' negligent hiring and retention. Defendants respond that plaintiffs' complaint fails as a matter of law because it was not reasonably foreseeable that Chan would violate plaintiffs' right to privacy and cause their emotional distress. * * *

* * * *

In this case, plaintiffs allege that defendants knew or should have known that Chan had been fired from Kaiser for secretly recording employees using the restroom. Accepting that allegation, as we are required to do, we cannot say that it is unforeseeable as a matter of law that Chan would engage in the same behavior in his new employment.

In short, we conclude that plaintiffs alleged all the necessary elements of a claim for negligent infliction of emotional distress. The trial courts erred in reaching a contrary conclusion and in granting defendants' motions to dismiss.

Reversed and remanded.

Case 6.1 Continues

Case 6.1 Continued

Legal Reasoning Questions

1. What was the trial court's main reason for dismissing the lawsuit against the defendant?

2. What was the three-step procedure that the appeals court used to analyze the plaintiff's claim for negligent infliction of emotional distress?

3. How did the defendants argue against the plaintiffs' complaint that the infliction of emotional distress could have been reasonably foreseeable?

Outrageous Conduct Courts in most jurisdictions are wary of emotional distress claims and confine them to situations involving truly outrageous behavior. Generally, repeated annoyances (such as those experienced by a person who is being stalked), coupled with threats, are enough. Acts that cause indignity or annoyance alone usually are not sufficient.

■ **Example 6.5** A father attacks a man who has had consensual intimate relations with the father's nineteen-year-old daughter. The father handcuffs the man to a steel pole and threatens to kill him unless he leaves town immediately. The father's conduct may be sufficiently extreme and outrageous to be actionable as an intentional infliction of emotional distress. ■

Defenses to IIED In many instances, as noted throughout this textbook, courts will accept the legal fiction of corporate personhood to provide companies with the same rights before the law as individuals. It seems, however, that this fiction does not extend to IIED claims. ■ **Case in Point 6.6** Towerview Construction and Osprey Cove Real Estate worked out an agreement in which the real estate company loaned the construction company the funds to develop four residential lots. Once the lots were sold, Towerview would repay its loan. Eventually, Towerview came to believe that Osprey Cove was fraudulently taking steps to block the sale of the lots and filed suit for, among other claims, IIED. Affirming the ruling of a trial court, the Georgia Court of Appeals dismissed the claim. Both courts agreed that corporations cannot recover for IIED because they lack the ability to experience emotions.[5] ■

Other defenses to IIED are more straightforward. If the plaintiff gives consent to the outrageous conduct that leads to an IIED claim, the lawsuit is unlikely to proceed. Context also matters. Outrageous conduct that is normal under the circumstances is usually not actionable. Neither is outrageous speech when it is directed against a public figure. In most instances, such speech enjoys First Amendment protection. (The courts do examine IIED cases involving alienation of affections, as seen in the Ethics Today feature.)

---

5. *Osprey Cove Real Estate, LLC v. Towerview Construction, LLC*, 808 S.E.2d 425, 343 Ga.App. 436 (2017).

Ethics Today

Can someone be found liable for a tort if that person has ruined the plaintiff's marriage?

Many American courts once held that a wife was the property of her husband. A remnant of this principle exists in the tort law of six states: Hawaii, Mississippi, New Mexico, North Carolina, South Dakota, and Utah. In these jurisdictions, spouses of any gender can bring a lawsuit for "alienation of affections," a variation on the tort of intentional infliction of emotional distress.

Examples of defendants who were found liable for this sort of unethical behavior include a wealthy businessperson who allegedly "stole" the wife of a plumber and a female secretary who supposedly ruined a "fairy tale marriage." Although it may seem almost absurd that courts would involve themselves in such seemingly personal affairs, the consequences can be very serious. A Mississippi jury awarded the plumber $750,000, and a North Carolina appeals court upheld a $1 million payment to the harmed spouse in the "fairy tale marriage."

Case law highlights several defenses to alienation of affections. The defendant can show that there was no affection left to alienate in the failing marriage. Alternatively, the defendant can prove, through text messages, phone calls, and "hook-up" locations, that the alienating conduct took place in a different state, where such behavior is assumed to be beyond the reach of tort law.

Critical Thinking There are fifty states, but only six still have alienation of affections tort laws on their books. Why so few states?

6–2e Defamation

The freedom of speech guaranteed by the First Amendment is not absolute. The courts are required to balance the vital guarantee of free speech against other pervasive and strong social interests, including society's interest in preventing and redressing attacks on reputation.

Defamation of character involves wrongfully hurting a person's good reputation. The law imposes a general duty on all persons to refrain from making false, defamatory statements of fact about others. Breaching this duty in writing or other permanent form (such as a digital recording) involves the tort of **libel.** Breaching this duty orally involves the tort of **slander.** The tort of defamation also arises when a false statement of fact is made about a person's product, business, or legal ownership rights to property.

Establishing defamation involves proving the following elements:

1. The defendant made a false statement of fact.
2. The statement was understood as being about the plaintiff and tended to harm the plaintiff's reputation.
3. The statement was published to at least one person other than the plaintiff.
4. If the plaintiff is a public figure, that person must also prove *actual malice,* discussed later in the chapter.

Statement-of-Fact Requirement Often at issue in defamation lawsuits (including online defamation) is whether the defendant made a statement of fact or a statement of opinion. Statements of opinion normally are not actionable, because they are protected under the First Amendment.

In other words, making a negative statement about another person is not defamation unless the statement is false and represents something as a fact rather than a personal opinion. ■ **Example 6.7** The statement "Erel cheats on his taxes," if false, can lead to liability for defamation. The statement "Erel is a jerk" cannot constitute defamation because it is clearly an opinion. ■

The Publication Requirement The basis of the tort of defamation is the publication of a statement or statements that hold an individual up to contempt, ridicule, or hatred. Publication here means that the defamatory statements are communicated (either intentionally or accidentally) to persons other than the defamed party.

The courts have generally held that even dictating a letter to a secretary constitutes publication (although the publication may be privileged, a concept that will be explained shortly). Moreover, if a third party merely overhears defamatory statements by chance, the courts usually hold that this also constitutes publication. Defamatory statements made via the internet are actionable as well. Note also that any individual who repeats or republishes defamatory statements normally is liable even if that person reveals the source of the statements.

■ **Case in Point 6.8** "2 Tha Limit MC" is a motorcycle club in Kentucky. Amos Scaife, Tanesha Perkins, and Lisa Mask organized it. Scaife had a falling out with the other members, who voted to remove him from office. In the document filed with the state, Scaife accused Perkins and Mask of criminal conduct. The defendants counterclaimed, seeking damages for defamation based on the documents officially filed with the state. A trial court ruled against Scaife, and an intermediate appellate court affirmed the trial court's judgment. Once the official document that included the defamatory statement was filed with the state government, it became part of the public record. This publication made Scaife liable for defamation.[6] ■

Damages for Libel Once a defendant's liability for libel is established, general damages are presumed as a matter of law. General damages are designed to compensate the plaintiff for nonspecific harms such as disgrace or dishonor in the eyes of the community, humiliation, injured reputation, and emotional distress—harms that are difficult to measure. In other words, to recover damages, plaintiffs need not prove that they were harmed in any specific way as a result of libelous statements.

Damages for Slander In contrast to cases alleging libel, in a case alleging slander, the plaintiff must prove special damages to establish the defendant's liability. The plaintiff must show that the slanderous statement caused actual economic or monetary losses.

Unless this initial hurdle of proving special damages is overcome, a plaintiff alleging slander normally cannot go forward with the suit and recover any damages. This requirement is imposed in slander cases because oral statements have a temporary quality. In contrast, a libelous (written) statement has the quality of permanence and can be circulated widely, especially through tweets and blogs. Also, libel usually results from some degree of deliberation by the author.

Slander *Per Se* Exceptions to the burden of proving special damages in cases alleging slander are made for certain types of slanderous statements. If a false statement constitutes "slander *per se,*" it is actionable with no proof of

---

6. *Scaife v. Perkins,* __ S.W.3d __, 2020 WL 864171 (App.Ct.KY 2020).

special damages required. In most states, the following four types of declarations are considered to be slander *per se:*

1. A statement that another has a "loathsome" disease (such as a sexually transmitted disease).
2. A statement that another has committed improprieties while engaging in a profession or trade.
3. A statement that another has committed or has been imprisoned for a serious crime.
4. A statement that a person is unchaste or has engaged in serious sexual misconduct. (This usually applies only to unmarried persons and sometimes only to women.)

Defenses to Defamation Truth is normally an absolute defense against a defamation charge. In other words, if a defendant in a defamation case can prove that the allegedly defamatory statements of fact were true, normally no tort has been committed.

■ **Case in Point 6.9** David McKee, a neurologist, went to examine a patient who had been transferred from the intensive care unit (ICU) to a private room. In the room were family members of the patient, including his son. The patient's son later made the following post on a "rate your doctor" website: "[Dr. McKee] seemed upset that my father had been moved [into a private room]. Never having met my father or his family, Dr. McKee said 'When you weren't in ICU, I had to spend time finding out if you transferred or died.' When we gaped at him, he said 'Well, 44 percent of hemorrhagic strokes die within 30 days. I guess this is the better option.'"

McKee filed suit against the son for defamation but lost. The court found that all the statements made by the son were essentially true, and truth is a complete defense to a defamation action.[7] ■

In other words, true statements are not actionable no matter how disparaging. Even the presence of minor inaccuracies of expression or detail does not render basically true statements false.

Other defenses to defamation may exist if the speech is privileged or if it concerns a public figure. We discuss these defenses next. Note that the majority of defamation actions are filed in state courts, and state laws differ somewhat in the defenses they allow.

Privileged Communications. In some circumstances, a person who enjoys **privilege,** or immunity, will not be liable for defamatory statements. Privileged communications are of two types: absolute and qualified.[8] Only in judicial proceedings and certain government proceedings is *absolute*

privilege granted. Thus, statements made by attorneys and judges in the courtroom during a trial are absolutely privileged, as are statements made by government officials during legislative debate.

In other situations, a person will not be liable for defamatory statements because of *qualified,* or *conditional, privilege.* An employer's statements in written evaluations of employees, for instance, are protected by qualified privilege. Generally, if the statements are made in good faith and the publication is limited to those who have a legitimate interest in the communication, the statements fall within the area of qualified privilege.

■ **Example 6.10** Jorge has worked at Google for five years and is being considered for a management position. His supervisor, Chiya, writes a memo about Jorge's performance to those evaluating him for the position. The memo contains certain negative statements, which Chiya honestly believes are true. If Chiya limits the disclosure of the memo to company representatives, her statements will likely be protected by qualified privilege. ■

Public Figures. Politicians, entertainers, professional athletes, and others in the public eye are considered **public figures.** Public figures are regarded as "fair game." False and defamatory statements about public figures that are published in the media will not constitute defamation unless the statements are made with **actual malice.**[9] To be made with actual malice, a statement must be made with either knowledge of its falsity or a reckless disregard of the truth.

Statements made about public figures, especially when they are communicated via a public medium, usually relate to matters of general interest. They are made about people who substantially affect all of us. Furthermore, public figures generally have some access to a public medium for answering belittling falsehoods about themselves. For these reasons, public figures have a greater burden of proof in defamation cases—to show actual malice—than do private individuals.

■ **Case in Point 6.11** John Tiegen is a former U.S. Marine who defended the United States consulate in Benghazi, Libya, from a well-publicized terrorist attack. On leaving the military, Tiegen became a public speaker and a brand ambassador for several companies. Frederic Slice posted comments about Tiegen on websites operated by these companies, stating that the ex-Marine was a "liar" and had committed perjury by lying to Congress about Benghazi. Tiegen, admitting that he was a public figure, sued Slice for libel. A Texas appeals court dismissed the case because Tiegen could not show that Slice acted with actual malice. Whether or not

---

7. *McKee v. Laurion*, 825 N.W.2d 725 (Minn. 2013). See also *Smith v. City of Crosby*, __ N.W. __, 2022 WL 152015 (App.Ct. Minn. 2022).
8. Note that the term "privileged communication" in this context is not the same as privileged communication between professionals, such as attorneys, and their clients.
9. See the landmark case *New York Times Co. v. Sullivan*, 376 U.S. 254, 84 S.Ct. 710, 11 L.Ed.2d 686 (1964).

Slice's comments were true, Tiegen had produced no evidence that Slice knew the statements were false and acted with reckless disregard for the truth.[10] ∎

6–2f Invasion of Privacy

A person has a right to solitude and freedom from prying public eyes—in other words, to privacy. The courts have held that certain amendments to the U.S. Constitution

10. *Tiegen v. Slice,* 2020 WL 728426 (Tex.App.—Dallas, 2020).

imply a right to privacy. Some state constitutions explicitly provide for privacy rights, as do a number of federal and state statutes.

Tort law also safeguards these rights through the tort of invasion of privacy. Generally, to sue successfully for an invasion of privacy, a person must have a reasonable expectation of privacy, and the invasion must be highly offensive. (See this chapter's Digital Update feature for a discussion of how invasion of privacy claims can arise when someone posts pictures or videos taken with digital devices.)

Digital Update

Revenge Porn and Invasion of Privacy

Nearly every digital device today takes photos and videos at virtually no cost. Software allows the recording of conversations via Skype. Many couples immortalize their "private moments" using such digital devices. One partner may take a racy selfie and send it as an attachment to a text message or via Instagram to the other partner, for instance.

Occasionally, after a relationship ends, one partner seeks digital revenge. The result, called "revenge porn," involves the online distribution of sexually explicit images of a nonconsenting individual with the intent to humiliate that person.

State Statutes

Thirty-five states have enacted statutes that make revenge porn a crime. But each state's law is different. (In some states, it is a misdemeanor with less serious consequences, and in other states, it is a felony with more serious penalties.) In addition, most of these criminal statutes do not provide victims with a right to obtain damages. Therefore, victims have sued in civil courts on the basis of (1) invasion of privacy, (2) public disclosure of private facts, and (3) intentional infliction of emotional distress.

A Case Example

Conner Katz, unbeknownst to his girlfriend, captured a cellphone video of her performing a sexual act with him at his college fraternity house. Katz sent the video to another person via Snapchat, knowing that his girlfriend had not consented to the distribution of this image. The recipient told Katz's girlfriend about the video, and she confronted Katz via text message. Katz admitted sending the video and was apologetic, "stating he knew that it was wrong to send the video and should not have sent it without her knowledge." His girlfriend's attorney reported the incident to the local police department.

Katz was charged under a state law that criminalizes the non-consensual distribution of an intimate image ("revenge porn"). At trial, he argued that, among other things, the statute was unconstitutional and a violation

of free speech. The trial court agreed that that the statute was unconstitutional. and dismissed the case. An appellate court reversed and remanded the case for further proceedings. "Faced with the widespread and growing problem of nonconsensual pornography, the legislature acted within its authority to safeguard the health and safety of its citizens from this unique and serious crime. The State properly charged Katz with violating the statute."[a]

Revenge Porn on Social Media

Perpetrators also use social media sites, such as Facebook, Twitter, Instagram, and Reddit, to disseminate revenge porn. Even though Facebook and other companies have explicit policies against pornography and will take content down once it is reported, users often hide it within restricted or closed groups. For instance, the Senate Armed Services Committee held hearings on a private Facebook group called Marines United, which circulated nude photos of women (including fellow marines, ex-girlfriends, and strangers) without their consent. The group was closed down after one member reported it to the Marine Corps. At least one member was court-martialed.

More Than Just Pictures and Videos

Another type of online invasion of privacy occurs when the perpetrator provides detailed information about the victim without the victim's permission. The information posted online may include the victim's name, Facebook page, address, and phone number, as well as the victim's photos and videos. (This is called *doxxing*.) Many of the hosting websites have been shut down, but others are still active.

Critical Thinking In the Katz case, would the appellate court have ruled the same had the girlfriend originally agreed to allow Katz to send the video to a close friend, but later changed her mind?

a. *State v. Katz,* 179 N.E.3d 431 (S.Ct. Ind. 2022).

Invasion of Privacy Under the Common Law The following four acts qualify as invasions of privacy under the common law:

1. **Intrusion into an individual's affairs or seclusion.** Invading someone's home or searching someone's briefcase or laptop without authorization is an invasion of privacy. This tort has been held to extend to eavesdropping by wiretap, unauthorized scanning of a bank account, compulsory blood testing, and window peeping. ■ **Example 6.12** Sharon, a Walgreens' pharmacist, shares Luanna's prescription history with Moussa, who is married to Sharon and used to date Luanna. If Luanna sues, she will likely win an invasion of privacy lawsuit against Sharon and her employer, Walgreens. ■

2. **False light.** Publication of information that places a person in a false light is also an invasion of privacy. For instance, writing a story that attributes to a person ideas and opinions not held by that person is an invasion of privacy. (Publishing such a story could involve the tort of defamation as well.) ■ **Example 6.13** An Iowa newspaper prints an article saying that nineteen-year-old Yassine Alam is part of the terrorist organization Islamic State of Iraq and Syria (ISIS). Next to the article is a photo of Yassine's brother, Salaheddin. Salaheddin can sue the paper for putting him in a false light by using his photo. Also, if the report is not true, and Yassine is not involved with ISIS, Yassine can sue the paper for defamation. ■

3. **Public disclosure of private facts.** This type of invasion of privacy occurs when a person publicly discloses private facts about an individual that an ordinary person would find objectionable or embarrassing. A newspaper account of a private citizen's financial affairs could be an actionable invasion of privacy. This is so even if the information revealed is true, because it should not be a matter of public concern.

4. **Appropriation of identity.** Using a person's name, picture, likeness, or other identifiable characteristic for commercial purposes without permission is also an invasion of privacy. Individuals' right to privacy normally includes the right to the exclusive use of their identity. ■ **Example 6.14** An advertising agency asks a singer with a distinctive voice and stage presence to take part in a marketing campaign for a new automobile. The singer rejects the offer. If the agency then uses someone who imitates the singer's voice and dance moves in the ad, it will be actionable as an appropriation of identity. ■

Appropriation Statutes Most states today have codified the common law tort of appropriation of identity in statutes that establish the distinct tort of appropriation, or right of publicity. For instance, the Illinois Right of Publicity Act (IRPA) defines a person's identity as "an attribute of an individual that serves to identify that individual to an ordinary, reasonable viewer or listener."[11] Under this law, a person's identity cannot be used for commercial purposes without consent.

■ **Case in Point 6.15** The online marketplace Groupon, Inc., used an "Instagram Widget" to link publicly available photos from social networking services to member businesses. All Instagram users identify themselves with a username. Christine Dancel took a photo of herself at Philly G's restaurant and posted it on Instagram. Because of the Widget, the photo and her username—"meowchristine"—automatically appeared on Philly G's Groupon page.

Dancel sued under the IRPA, claiming that she had not given consent to Groupon. She argued that a "reasonable viewer" would know that usernames are designed to identify individuals, just like actual names. The district court disagreed, holding that, in fact, many usernames, including "meowchristine," are too obscure to establish identity. A federal appellate court affirmed, noting that while some usernames might clearly identify an individual, it would place too great a burden on courts to determine if each one did under Illinois law.[12] ■

6–2g Fraudulent Misrepresentation

A misrepresentation leads another to believe in a condition that is different from the condition that actually exists. Although persons sometimes make misrepresentations accidentally because they are unaware of the existing facts, the tort of **fraudulent misrepresentation (fraud),** involves intentional deceit for personal gain. The tort includes several elements:

1. A misrepresentation of material facts or conditions with knowledge that they are false or with reckless disregard for the truth.
2. An intent to induce another party to rely on the misrepresentation.
3. A justifiable reliance on the misrepresentation by the deceived party.
4. Damages suffered as a result of that reliance.
5. A causal connection between the misrepresentation and the injury suffered.

For fraud to occur, more than mere **puffery,** or seller's talk, must be involved. Fraud exists only when persons represent as facts something they know is untrue. For instance, it is fraud to claim that the roof of a building does not leak when one knows that it does. Facts are

---

11. 765 I.L.C.S. 1075/5, 30.
12. *Dancel v. Groupon, Inc.,* 940 F.3d 381 (7th Cir., 2019).

objectively ascertainable, whereas seller's talk (such as "I am the best accountant in town") is not, because the use of the word "best" is subjective.

■ **Case in Point 6.16** Joseph Guido bought nine rental houses in Stillwater, New York. The houses shared a waste disposal system that was not functioning. Guido hired someone to design and install a new system. When town officials later discovered sewage on the property, Guido had the system partially replaced. He then represented to prospective buyers of the property, including Danny Revell, that the "Septic system [was] totally new—each field totally replaced." In response to a questionnaire from the buyers' bank, Guido denied any knowledge of environmental problems.

A month after the sale of the houses, the septic system failed and required substantial repairs. The buyers sued Guido for fraud. A jury found in favor of the plaintiffs and awarded damages. A state intermediate appellate court affirmed the judgment on appeal. Guido knew that the septic system was not totally new and that sewage had been released on the property (an environmental problem). He had misrepresented these facts to the buyers. The buyers' reliance on Guido's statements was justifiable because a visual inspection of the property did not reveal any problems.[13] ■

Statement of Fact Versus Opinion Normally, the tort of fraudulent misrepresentation occurs only when there is reliance on a statement of fact. Sometimes, however, reliance on a statement of opinion may involve the tort of fraudulent misrepresentation if the individual making the statement of opinion has superior knowledge of the subject matter. For instance, when a lawyer makes a statement of opinion about the law in a state in which the lawyer is licensed to practice, a court might treat it as a statement of fact.

Negligent Misrepresentation Sometimes, a tort action can arise from misrepresentations that are made negligently rather than intentionally. The key difference between intentional and negligent misrepresentation is whether the person making the misrepresentation had actual knowledge of its falsity. Negligent misrepresentation requires only that the person making the statement or omission did not have a reasonable basis for believing its truthfulness.

Liability for negligent misrepresentation usually arises when the defendant who made the misrepresentation owed a duty of care to the plaintiff to supply correct information. (We discuss the duty of care in more detail later in the chapter.) Statements or omissions made by attorneys and accountants to their clients, for instance, can lead to liability for negligent misrepresentation.

6–2h Abusive or Frivolous Litigation

Tort law recognizes that people have a right not to be sued without a legally just and proper reason, and therefore it protects individuals from the misuse of litigation. Torts related to abusive litigation include malicious prosecution and abuse of process. If a party initiates a lawsuit out of malice and without a legitimate legal reason, and ends up losing the suit, that party can be sued for malicious prosecution. Abuse of process can apply to any person using a legal process against another in an improper manner or to accomplish a purpose for which the process was not designed.

The key difference between the torts of abuse of process and malicious prosecution is the level of proof. Unlike malicious prosecution, abuse of process is not limited to prior litigation and does not require the plaintiff to prove malice. It can be based on the wrongful use of subpoenas, court orders to attach or seize real property, or other types of formal legal process.

Concept Summary 6.1 reviews intentional torts against persons.

6–2i Business Torts

The torts known as business torts generally involve wrongful interference with another's business rights. Public policy favors free competition, and these torts protect against tortious interference with legitimate businesses. Business torts involving wrongful interference generally fall into two categories: interference with a contractual relationship and interference with a business relationship.

Wrongful Interference With a Contractual Relationship Three elements are necessary for wrongful interference with a contractual relationship to occur:

1. A valid, enforceable contract must exist between two parties.
2. A third party must know that this contract exists.
3. This third party must intentionally induce a party to the contract to breach the contract.

■ **Case in Point 6.17** A landmark case in this area involved an opera singer, Joanna Wagner, who was under contract to sing for a man named Lumley for a specified period of years. A man named Gye, who knew of this

---

13. *Revell v. Guido*, 124 A.D.3d 1006, 2 N.Y.S.3d 252 (3d Dept. 2015). See also *Olson v. Major League Baseball*, 29 F.4th 59 (2nd Cir. 2022).

Concept Summary 6.1

Intentional Torts Against Persons

Assault and Battery	Any unexcused and intentional act that causes another person to be apprehensive of immediate harm is an assault. An assault resulting in physical contact is a battery.
False Imprisonment	An intentional confinement or restraint of another person's movement without justification.
Intentional Infliction of Emotional Distress	An intentional act that amounts to extreme and outrageous conduct resulting in severe emotional distress to another.
Defamation (Libel or Slander)	A false statement of fact, not made under privilege, that is communicated to a third person and that causes damage to a person's reputation. For public figures, the plaintiff must also prove that the statement was made with actual malice.
Invasion of Privacy	Publishing or otherwise making known or using information relating to a person's private life and affairs, with which the public has no legitimate concern, without that person's permission or approval.
Fraudulent Misrepresentation (Fraud)	A false representation made by one party, through misstatement of facts or through conduct, with the intention of deceiving another and on which the other reasonably relies to their detriment.
Abusive or Frivolous Litigation	The filing of a lawsuit without legitimate grounds and with malice. Alternatively, the use of a legal process in an improper manner.

contract, nonetheless "enticed" Wagner to refuse to carry out the agreement, and Wagner began to sing for Gye. Gye's action constituted a tort because it interfered with the contractual relationship between Wagner and Lumley. (Wagner's refusal to carry out the agreement also entitled Lumley to sue Wagner for breach of contract.)[14] ∎

The body of tort law relating to wrongful interference with a contractual relationship has increased greatly in recent years. In principle, any lawful contract can be the basis for an action of this type. The contract could be between a firm and its employees or a firm and its customers. Sometimes, a competitor of a firm lures away one of the firm's key employees. In this situation, the original employer can recover damages from the competitor only if it can be shown that the competitor knew of the contract's existence and intentionally induced the breach.

Wrongful Interference With a Business Relationship Businesspersons devise countless schemes to attract customers. They are prohibited, however, from

unreasonably interfering with another's business in their attempts to gain a greater share of the market.

There is a difference between competitive practices and predatory behavior—actions undertaken with the intention of unlawfully driving competitors completely out of the market. Attempting to attract customers in general is a legitimate business practice, whereas specifically targeting the customers of a competitor is more likely to be predatory. A plaintiff claiming predatory behavior must show that the defendant used predatory methods to intentionally harm an established business relationship or gain a prospective economic advantage.

∎ **Example 6.18** A shopping mall contains two athletic shoe stores: Joe's and Ultimate Sport. Joe's cannot station an employee at the entrance of Ultimate Sport's to divert customers to Joe's by telling them that Joe's will beat Ultimate Sport's prices. This type of activity constitutes the tort of wrongful interference with a business relationship, which is commonly considered to be an unfair trade practice. If this activity were permitted, Joe's would reap the benefits of Ultimate Sport's advertising. ∎

---

14. *Lumley v. Gye*, 118 Eng.Rep. 749 (1853).

Defenses to Wrongful Interference A person will not be liable for the tort of wrongful interference with a contractual or business relationship if it can be shown that the interference was justified or permissible. Bona fide competitive behavior—such as marketing and advertising strategies—is a permissible interference even if it results in the breaking of a contract.

■ **Example 6.19** Taylor Meats advertises so effectively that it induces Sam's Restaurant to break its contract with Burke's Meat Company. In that situation, Burke's Meat Company will be unable to recover against Taylor Meats on a wrongful interference theory. The public policy that favors free competition through advertising outweighs any possible instability that such competitive activity might cause in contractual relations. ■

6–3 Intentional Torts Against Property

Intentional torts against property include trespass to land, trespass to personal property, conversion, and disparagement of property. These torts are wrongful actions that interfere with individuals' legally recognized rights with regard to their property.

The law distinguishes real property from personal property. Real property is land and things permanently attached to the land, such as a house. Personal property consists of all other items, including cash and securities (such as stocks and bonds).

6–3a Trespass to Land

A **trespass to land** occurs when a person, without permission, does any of the following:

1. Enters onto, above, or below the surface of land that is owned by another.
2. Causes anything to enter onto land owned by another.
3. Remains on land owned by another or permits anything to remain on it.

Actual harm to the land is not an essential element of this tort, because the tort is designed to protect the right of an owner to exclusive possession.

Common types of trespass to land include walking or driving on another's land, shooting a gun over another's land, and throwing rocks at a building that belongs to someone else. Another common form of trespass involves constructing a building so that part of it extends onto an adjoining landowner's property.

Establishing Trespass Before a person can be a trespasser, the real property owner (or another person in actual and exclusive possession of the property, such as a renter) must establish that person as a trespasser. For instance, "posted" trespass signs expressly establish as a trespasser a person who ignores these signs and enters onto the property. Any person who enters onto another's property to commit an illegal act (such as a thief entering a lumberyard at night to steal lumber) is impliedly a trespasser, with or without posted signs.

Liability for Harm At common law, a trespasser is liable for any damage caused to the property and generally cannot hold the owner liable for injuries that the trespasser sustains on the premises. This common law rule is being modified in many jurisdictions, however, in favor of a reasonable duty of care rule that varies depending on the status of the parties.

For instance, a landowner may have a duty to post a notice that guard dogs patrol the property. Also, if young children are attracted to the property by some object, such as a swimming pool or a sand pile, and are injured, the landowner may be held liable (under the attractive nuisance doctrine). Still, an owner can normally use reasonable force to remove a trespasser from the premises or detain the trespasser for a reasonable time without liability for damages.

Defenses Against Trespass to Land One defense to a claim of trespass is to show that the trespass was warranted, such as when a trespasser enters a building to assist someone in danger. Another defense exists when the trespasser possesses a license to come onto the land.

A **licensee** is one who is invited (or allowed to enter) onto the property of another for the licensee's benefit. A person who enters another's property to read an electric meter, for instance, is a licensee. Another type of licensee is someone who is camping on another person's land with the owner's permission but without paying for the privilege.

Note that licenses to enter onto another's property are revocable by the property owner. If a property owner asks a meter reader to leave and the meter reader refuses to do so, the meter reader at that point becomes a trespasser.

6–3b Trespass to Personal Property

Whenever any individual wrongfully takes or harms the personal property of another or otherwise interferes with the lawful owner's possession and enjoyment of personal property, **trespass to personal property** occurs. This tort may also be called *trespass to chattels* or *trespass to personalty*.[15] In this context, harm means not only destruction of the property, but also anything that diminishes its value, condition, or quality.

---

15. Pronounced *per*-sun-ul-tee.

Trespass to personal property involves intentional meddling with a possessory interest (one arising from possession), including barring an owner's access to personal property. ■ **Example 6.20** Kelly takes Ali's business law book as a practical joke and hides it so that Ali is unable to find it for several days before the final examination. Here, Kelly has engaged in a trespass to personal property (and also conversion, the tort discussed next). ■

If it can be shown that trespass to personal property was warranted, then a complete defense exists. Most states, for instance, allow automobile repair shops to hold a customer's car (under what is called an *artisan's lien*) when the customer refuses to pay for repairs already completed.

6–3c Conversion

Any act that deprives an owner of personal property or of the use of that property without the owner's permission and without just cause can constitute **conversion.** Even the taking of electronic records and data may form the basis of a conversion claim. Often, when conversion occurs, a trespass to personal property also occurs. The original taking of the personal property from the owner was a trespass. Wrongfully retaining the property is conversion.

Failure to Return Goods Conversion is the civil side of crimes related to theft, but it is not limited to theft. Even when the rightful owner consented to the initial taking of the property, so no theft or trespass occurred, a failure to return the property may still be conversion. ■ **Example 6.21** Chen borrows Mark's iPad mini to use while traveling home from school for the holidays. When Chen returns to school, Mark asks for his iPad back, but Chen says that he gave it to his little brother for Christmas. In this situation, Mark can sue Chen for conversion, and Chen will have to either return the iPad or pay damages equal to its replacement value. ■

Intention Conversion can occur even when persons mistakenly believed that they were entitled to the goods. In other words, good intentions are not a defense against conversion. Persons who buy stolen goods, for instance, may be sued for conversion even if they did not know the goods were stolen. If the true owner of the goods sues the buyer, the buyer must either return the property to the owner or pay the owner the full value of the property.

Conversion can also occur when the proceeds from an insurance claim are not tendered to the rightful recipient. ■ **Case in Point 6.22** Grocery Delivery E-Services USA had an agreement with Mariner Seafood, LLC, under which Mariner would supply Grocery Delivery with salmon. Flynn, the manager, president, and sole principal of Mariner, agreed to carry product recall insurance and to name Grocery Delivery as an additional insured under the policy. Mariner informed Grocery Delivery of a listeria contamination of its products, causing Grocery Delivery to recall 32,000 units and to sustain over $500,000 in losses. The insurance company paid Mariner on the claim, but Mariner (Flynn) never paid Grocery Delivery. Grocery Delivery sued Flynn for conversion. The trial court denied Flynn's motion to dismiss. On appeal, the appellate court affirmed. Mariner, through Flynn, had converted the insurance payment to its own use.[16] ■

6–3d Disparagement of Property

Disparagement of property occurs when economically injurious falsehoods are made about another's product or property rather than about another's reputation (as in the tort of defamation). Disparagement of property is a general term for torts that can be more specifically referred to as *slander of quality* or *slander of title*.

Slander of Quality The publication of false information about another's product, alleging that it is not what its seller claims, constitutes the tort of **slander of quality,** or **trade libel.** To establish trade libel, the plaintiff must prove that the improper publication caused a third person to refrain from dealing with the plaintiff and that the plaintiff sustained economic damages (such as lost profits) as a result.

An improper publication may be both a slander of quality and a defamation of character. For instance, a statement that disparages the quality of a product may also, by implication, disparage the character of a person who would sell such a product.

Slander of Title When a publication falsely denies or casts doubt on another's legal ownership of property, resulting in financial loss to the property's owner, the tort of **slander of title** occurs. Usually, this is an intentional tort in which someone knowingly publishes an untrue statement about another's ownership of certain property with the intent of discouraging a third person from dealing with the person slandered. For instance, it would be difficult for a car dealer to attract customers after competitors published a notice that the dealer's stock consisted of stolen automobiles.

See Concept Summary 6.2 for a review of intentional torts against property.

---

16. *Grocery Delivery E-Services USA, Inc. v. Flynn*, 201 A.D.3d 585, 160 N.Y.S.3d 249 (2022).

Concept Summary 6.2

Intentional Torts Against Property

Trespass to Land	The invasion of another's real property without consent or privilege. Once a person is expressly or impliedly established as a trespasser, the property owner has specific rights, which may include the right to detain or remove the trespasser.
Trespass to Personal Property	The intentional interference with an owner's right to use, possess, or enjoy the owner's personal property without the owner's consent.
Conversion	The wrongful possession or use of another person's personal property without just cause.
Disparagement of Property	Any economically injurious falsehood that is made about another's product or property; an inclusive term for the torts of slander of quality and slander of title.

6–4 Unintentional Torts— Negligence

The tort of **negligence** occurs when someone suffers injury because of another's failure to live up to a required duty of care. In contrast to intentional torts, in torts involving negligence, the tortfeasor neither wishes to bring about the consequences of the act nor believes that they will occur. The person's conduct merely creates a risk of such consequences. If no risk is created, there is no negligence.

Moreover, the risk must be foreseeable. In other words, it must be such that a reasonable person engaging in the same activity would anticipate the risk and guard against it. In determining what is reasonable conduct, courts consider the nature of the possible harm.

Many of the actions giving rise to the intentional torts discussed earlier in the chapter constitute negligence if the element of intent is missing (or cannot be proved). ■ **Example 6.23** Juan walks up to Maya and intentionally shoves her. Maya falls and breaks her arm as a result. In this situation, Juan is liable for the intentional tort of battery. If Juan carelessly bumps into Maya, however, and she falls and breaks her arm as a result, Juan's action constitutes negligence. In either situation, Juan has committed a tort. ■

To succeed in a negligence action, the plaintiff must prove each of the following:

1. **Duty.** The defendant owed a duty of care to the plaintiff.
2. **Breach.** The defendant breached that duty.
3. **Causation.** The defendant's breach caused the plaintiff's injury.
4. **Damages.** The plaintiff suffered a legally recognizable injury.

6–4a The Duty of Care and Its Breach

Central to the tort of negligence is the concept of a **duty of care.** The basic principle underlying the duty of care is that people are free to act as they please so long as their actions do not infringe on the interests of others. When someone fails to comply with the duty to exercise reasonable care, a potentially tortious act may have been committed.

Failure to live up to a standard of care may be an act (accidentally setting fire to a building) or an omission (neglecting to put out a campfire). It may be a careless act or a carefully performed but nevertheless dangerous act that results in injury. In determining whether the duty of care has been breached, courts consider several factors:

1. The nature of the act (whether it is outrageous or commonplace).
2. The manner in which the act was performed (cautiously versus heedlessly).
3. The nature of the injury (whether it is serious or slight).

Creating even a very slight risk of a dangerous explosion might be unreasonable, whereas creating a distinct possibility of someone's burning their fingers on a stove might be reasonable.

The question in the following case was whether a fraternity's local chapter and its officers owed a duty of care to their pledges.

Bogenberger v. Pi Kappa Alpha Corporation, Inc.

Supreme Court of Illinois, 2018 IL 120951, 104 N.E.3d 1110 (2018).

Background and Facts David Bogenberger attended a pledge event at the Pi Kappa Alpha fraternity house at Northern Illinois University (NIU). The NIU chapter officers planned an evening of hazing, during which the pledges were required to consume vodka provided by the members. By the end of the night, David's blood alcohol level was more than five times the legal limit. He lost consciousness. The chapter officers failed to seek medical attention. David died during the night. His father, Gary, filed a complaint in an Illinois state court against the NIU chapter and its officers, on a theory of negligence. The plaintiff alleged that the defendants required the pledges, including David, to participate in the pledge event and to consume excessive and dangerous amounts of alcohol in violation of the state's hazing statute. The court dismissed the complaint. A state intermediate appellate court reversed the dismissal. The defendants appealed to the Illinois Supreme Court.

In the Language of the Court

Justice FREEMAN delivered the judgment of the court, with opinion.

* * * *

* * * Every person owes a duty of ordinary care to all others to guard against injuries which naturally flow as a reasonably probable and foreseeable consequence of an act * * * . Where an individual's course of action creates a foreseeable risk of injury, the individual has a duty to protect others from such injury.

* * * *

To determine whether the NIU Chapter and officers owed a duty to the pledges, we look to the reasonable foreseeability of the injury, the likelihood of the injury, the magnitude of the burden of guarding against the injury, and the consequences of placing that burden on the defendant. In deciding reasonable foreseeability, an injury is not reasonably foreseeable where it results from freakish, bizarre, or fantastic circumstances. Regarding the first two factors, we cannot say that * * * an injury resulting from hazing is freakish, bizarre, or occurs under fantastic circumstances. The existence of hazing statutes across the country, including the [national Pi Kappa Alpha organization's] written policy against hazing as well as Illinois's hazing statute, indicates that injury due to hazing is reasonably foreseeable. We also find that injuries resulting from hazing events, especially those involving the consumption of large amounts of alcohol, are likely to occur. When pledges are required to consume large quantities of alcohol in short periods of time, their risk of injury is great—not only physical injury due to their inebriated condition but injury or death resulting from alcohol poisoning.

Regarding the last two factors, we find that the magnitude of the burden of guarding against injury is small and the consequences of placing that burden on the NIU Chapter and officers are reasonable. To require the NIU Chapter and officers to guard against hazing injuries is infinitesimal. Hazing is not only against the law in Illinois, it is against the university's rules as well as the Pi Kappa Alpha fraternity's rules. There can be no real burden to require the NIU Chapter and officers to comply with the law and the university's and fraternity's rules. And it seems quite reasonable to place that burden on the very people who are in charge of planning and carrying out the pledge event. We find that the NIU Chapter and the officers owed a duty to the pledges, including David, and plaintiff has sufficiently alleged a claim for negligence against them.

Decision and Remedy The Illinois Supreme Court affirmed the intermediate appellate court's reversal of the trial court's dismissal. The plaintiff's "complaint * * * may proceed against the NIU Chapter [and] its officers."

Critical Thinking

- **Legal Environment** The NIU chapter invited nonmember sorority women to participate in the hazing event by filling the pledges' cups with vodka and directing them to drink it. Did these women owe a duty of care to the pledges? Discuss.
- **What If the Facts Were Different?** Suppose that the pledges' attendance at the hazing event had been optional, and the NIU chapter had furnished alcohol, but not required its consumption. Would the result have been different? Explain.

The Reasonable Person Standard Tort law measures duty by the **reasonable person standard.** In determining whether a duty of care has been breached, the courts ask how a reasonable person would have acted in the same circumstances. The reasonable person standard is said to be objective. It is not necessarily how a particular person would act. It is society's judgment of how an ordinarily prudent person should act. If the so-called reasonable person existed, that person would be careful, conscientious, even-tempered, and honest.

The degree of care to be exercised varies, depending on the defendant's occupation or profession, the defendant's relationship with the plaintiff, and other factors. Generally, whether an action constitutes a breach of the duty of care is determined on a case-by-case basis. The outcome depends on how the judge (or jury) decides that a reasonable person in the position of the defendant would have acted in the particular circumstances of the case.

Note that the courts frequently use the reasonable person standard in other areas of law as well as in negligence cases. Indeed, the principle that individuals are required to exercise a reasonable standard of care in their activities is a pervasive concept in business law.

The Duty of Landowners Landowners are expected to exercise reasonable care to protect individuals coming onto their property from harm. In some jurisdictions, landowners may even have a duty to protect trespassers against certain risks. Landowners who rent or lease premises to tenants are expected to exercise reasonable care to ensure that the tenants and their guests are not harmed in common areas, such as stairways, entryways, and laundry rooms.

The Duty to Warn Business Invitees of Risks. Retailers and other business operators who explicitly or implicitly invite persons to come onto their premises have a duty to exercise reasonable care to protect these **business invitees.** The duty normally requires storeowners to warn business invitees of foreseeable risks, such as construction zones or wet floors, about which the owners knew or *should have known*.

■ **Example 6.24** Liz enters Kwan's neighborhood market, slips on a wet floor, and sustains injuries as a result. If there was no sign or other warning that the floor was wet at the time Liz slipped, the owner, Kwan, would be liable for damages. A court would hold that Kwan was negligent because he failed to exercise a reasonable degree of care to protect customers against foreseeable risks about which he knew or should have known. That a patron might slip on the wet floor and be injured was a foreseeable risk, and Kwan should have taken care to avoid this risk or warn the customer of it. ■

A business owner also has a duty to discover and remove any hidden dangers that might injure a customer or other invitee. Hidden dangers might include uneven surfaces or defects in the pavement of a parking lot or a walkway, or merchandise that has fallen off shelves in a store.

Obvious Risks Provide an Exception. Some risks are so obvious that an owner need not warn of them. For instance, a business owner does not need to warn customers to open a door before attempting to walk through it. Other risks, however, even though they may seem obvious to a business owner, may not be so in the eyes of another, such as a child. In addition, even if a risk is obvious, a business owner is not necessarily excused from the duty to protect customers from foreseeable harm from that risk.

The Duty of Professionals Persons who possess superior knowledge, skill, or training are held to a higher standard of care than others. Professionals—including physicians, dentists, architects, engineers, accountants, and lawyers, among others—are required to have a standard minimum level of special knowledge and ability. In determining what constitutes reasonable care in the case of professionals, the law takes their training and expertise into account. Thus, an accountant's conduct is judged not by the reasonable person standard, but by the reasonable accountant standard.

If professionals violate their duty of care toward clients, the clients may bring a suit against the professionals, alleging **malpractice,** which is essentially professional negligence. For instance, a patient might sue a physician for medical malpractice. A client might sue an attorney for legal malpractice.

6–4b Causation

Another element necessary to a negligence action is causation. If a person breaches a duty of care and someone suffers injury, the person's act must have caused the harm for it to constitute the tort of negligence.

Courts Ask Two Questions In deciding whether the requirement of causation is met, the court must address two questions:

1. **Is there causation in fact?** Did the injury occur because of the defendant's act, or would it have occurred anyway? If the injury would not have occurred without the defendant's act, then there is causation in fact.

   Causation in fact usually can be determined by use of the "but for" test: "but for" the wrongful act, the injury would not have occurred. This test seeks to determine whether there was a cause-and-effect relationship between the act and the injury suffered. In theory, causation in fact is limitless. One could claim, for example, that "but for" the creation of the world, a particular injury would not have occurred. Thus, as a practical matter, the law has to establish limits, and it does so through the concept of proximate cause.

2. **Was the act the proximate, or legal, cause of the injury?** **Proximate cause,** or legal cause, exists when the connection between an act and an injury is strong enough to justify imposing liability. Proximate cause asks whether the injuries sustained were foreseeable or were too remotely connected to the incident to trigger liability. Judges use proximate cause to limit the scope of the defendant's liability to a subset of the total number of potential plaintiffs that might have been harmed by the defendant's actions.

   ■ **Example 6.25** Ackerman carelessly leaves a campfire burning. The fire not only burns down the forest but also sets off an explosion in a nearby chemical plant that spills chemicals into a river, killing all the fish for twenty miles downstream and ruining the economy of a tourist resort. Should Ackerman be liable to the resort owners? To the tourists whose vacations were ruined? These are questions of proximate cause that a court must decide. ■

Both of these causation questions must be answered in the affirmative for liability in tort to arise. If there is causation in fact but a court decides that the defendant's action is not the proximate cause of the plaintiff's injury, the causation requirement has not been met. Therefore, the defendant normally will not be liable to the plaintiff.

Foreseeability Questions of proximate cause are linked to the concept of foreseeability because it would be unfair to impose liability on a defendant unless the defendant's actions created a foreseeable risk of injury. Generally, if the victim or the consequences of a harm done were unforeseeable, there is no proximate cause.

Probably the most cited case on the concept of foreseeability and proximate cause is the *Palsgraf* case, which established foreseeability as the test for proximate cause. ■ **Case in Point 6.26** Helen Palsgraf was waiting for a train on a station platform. A man carrying a package was rushing to catch a train that was moving away from a platform across the tracks from Palsgraf. As the man attempted to jump aboard the moving train, he seemed unsteady and about to fall. A railroad guard on the car reached forward to grab him, and another guard on the platform pushed him from behind to help him board the train.

In the process, the man's package, which (unknown to the railroad guards) contained fireworks, fell on the railroad tracks and exploded. There was nothing about the package to indicate its contents. The repercussions of the explosion caused weighing scales at the other end of the train platform to fall on Palsgraf, causing injuries for which she sued the railroad company. At the trial, the jury found that the railroad guards had been negligent in their conduct. The railroad company appealed. New York's highest state court held that the railroad company was not liable to Palsgraf. The railroad had not been negligent toward her, because injury to her was not foreseeable.[17] ■

6–4c The Injury Requirement and Damages

For tort liability to arise, the plaintiff must have suffered a legally recognizable injury. To recover damages, the plaintiff must have suffered some loss, harm, wrong, or invasion of a protected interest. Essentially, the purpose of tort law is to compensate for legally recognized harms and injuries resulting from wrongful acts. If no harm or injury results from a given negligent action, there is nothing to compensate, and no tort exists.

For instance, if you carelessly bump into a passerby, who stumbles and falls as a result, you may be liable in tort if the passerby is injured in the fall. If the person is unharmed, however, there normally can be no lawsuit for damages, because no injury was suffered.

Compensatory damages are the norm in negligence cases. A court will award punitive damages only if the defendant's conduct was grossly negligent, reflecting an intentional failure to perform a duty with reckless disregard of the consequences to others.

6–4d Good Samaritan Statutes

Most states now have what are called **Good Samaritan statutes.**[18] Under these statutes, someone who is aided voluntarily by another cannot turn around and sue the "Good Samaritan" for negligence. These laws were passed largely to protect physicians and medical personnel who volunteer their services in emergency situations to those in need, such as individuals hurt in car accidents.

---

17. *Palsgraf v. Long Island Railroad Co.*, 248 N.Y. 339, 162 N.E. 99 (1928).
18. These laws derive their name from the Good Samaritan story in the Bible. In the story, a traveler who had been robbed and beaten lay along the roadside, ignored by those passing by. Eventually, a man from the region of Samaria (the "Good Samaritan") stopped to render assistance to the injured person.

6–4e Dram Shop Acts

Many states have also passed **dram shop acts,**[19] under which a bar's owner or a bartender may be held liable for injuries caused by a person who became intoxicated while drinking at the bar. The owner or bartender may also be held responsible for continuing to serve a person who was already intoxicated.

Some states' statutes also impose liability on *social hosts* (persons hosting parties) for injuries caused by guests who became intoxicated at the hosts' homes. Under these statutes, it is unnecessary to prove that the social host was negligent. ■ **Example 6.27** Jane hosts a Super Bowl party at which Azra, a minor, sneaks alcoholic drinks. Jane is potentially liable for damages resulting from Azra's drunk driving after the party. ■

6–5 Defenses to Negligence

Defendants often defend against negligence claims by asserting that the plaintiffs have failed to prove the existence of one or more of the required elements for

---

19. A dram is a small unit of liquid, and distilled spirits were historically sold in drams. Thus, a dram shop was a place where liquor was sold in drams.

negligence. Additionally, there are three basic affirmative defenses in negligence cases (defenses that a defendant can use to avoid liability even if the facts are as the plaintiff states): assumption of risk, superseding cause, and contributory and comparative negligence.

6–5a Assumption of Risk

A plaintiff who voluntarily enters into a risky situation, knowing the risk involved, will not be allowed to recover. This is the defense of **assumption of risk,** which requires two elements:

1. Knowledge of the risk.
2. Voluntary assumption of the risk.

The defense of assumption of risk is frequently asserted when the plaintiff was injured during a recreational activity that involves known risk, such as skiing or skydiving.

Assumption of risk can apply not only to participants in sporting events, but also to spectators and bystanders who are injured while attending those events. In the following Spotlight Case, the issue was whether a spectator at a baseball game voluntarily assumed the risk of being hit by an errant ball thrown while the players were warming up before the game.

Spotlight on the Seattle Mariners

Case 6.3 Taylor v. Baseball Club of Seattle, LP
Court of Appeals of Washington, 132 Wash.App. 32, 130 P.3d 835 (2006).

Background and Facts Delinda Taylor went to a Seattle Mariners baseball game at Safeco Field with her boyfriend and her two minor sons. Their seats were four rows up from the field along the right field foul line. They arrived more than an hour before the game so that they could see the players warm up and get their autographs. When she walked in, Taylor saw that a Mariners pitcher, Freddy Garcia, was throwing a ball back and forth with José Mesa right in front of their seats.

As Taylor stood in front of her seat, she looked away from the field, and a ball thrown by Mesa got past Garcia and struck her in the face, causing serious injuries. Taylor sued the Mariners for the allegedly negligent warm-up throw. The Mariners filed a motion for summary judgment in which they argued that Taylor, a longtime Mariners fan, was familiar with baseball and the inherent risk of balls entering the stands. Thus, the motion asserted, Taylor had assumed the risk of her injury. The trial court granted the motion and dismissed Taylor's case. Taylor appealed.

In the Language of the Court
DWYER, J. [Judge]
* * * *

* * * For many decades, courts have required baseball stadiums to screen some seats—generally those behind home plate—to provide protection to spectators who choose it.

A sport spectator's assumption of risk and a defendant sports team's duty of care are accordingly discerned under the doctrine of primary assumption of risk. * * * "Implied primary assumption of risk arises where a plaintiff has impliedly consented (often in advance of any negligence by defendant) to relieve defendant of a duty to plaintiff regarding specific *known* and appreciated risks."

* * * *

Under this implied primary assumption of risk, defendant must show that plaintiff had full subjective understanding of the specific risk, both its nature and presence, and that he or she voluntarily chose to encounter the risk.

* * * It is undisputed that the warm-up is part of the sport, that spectators such as Taylor purposely attend that portion of the event, and that the Mariners permit ticket-holders to view the warm-up.

* * * We find the fact that Taylor was injured during warm-up is not legally significant because that portion of the event is necessarily incident to the game.

* * * *

Here, there is no evidence that the circumstances leading to Taylor's injury constituted an unusual danger. It is undisputed that it is the normal, every-day practice at all levels of baseball for pitchers to warm up in the manner that led to this incident. The risk of injuries such as Taylor's are within the normal comprehension of a spectator who is familiar with the game. Indeed, the possibility of an errant ball entering the stands is part of the game's attraction for many spectators.

* * * The record contains substantial evidence regarding Taylor's familiarity with the game. She attended many of her sons' baseball games, she witnessed balls entering the stands, she had watched Mariners' games both at the Kingdome and on television, and she knew that there was no screen protecting her seats, which were close to the field. In fact, as she walked to her seat, she saw the players warming up and was excited about being in an unscreened area where her party might get autographs from the players and catch balls.

Decision and Remedy The state intermediate appellate court affirmed the lower court's judgment. As a spectator who chose to sit in an unprotected area of seats, Taylor voluntarily undertook the risk associated with being hit by an errant baseball thrown during the warm-up before the game.

Critical Thinking

- **What If the Facts Were Different?** Would the result in this case have been different if it had been Taylor's minor son, rather than Taylor herself, who had been struck by the ball? Should courts apply the doctrine of assumption of risk to children? Discuss.
- **Legal Environment** What is the basis underlying the defense of assumption of risk? How does that basis support the court's decision in this case?

6–5b Superseding Cause

An unforeseeable intervening event may break the causal connection between a wrongful act and an injury to another. If so, the intervening event acts as a **superseding cause**—that is, it relieves the defendant of liability for injuries caused by the intervening event.

■ **Example 6.28** While riding his bicycle, Derrick negligently runs into Mila, who is walking on the sidewalk. As a result of the impact, Mila falls and fractures her hip. While she is waiting for help to arrive, a small aircraft crashes nearby and explodes, and some of the fiery debris hits her, causing her to sustain severe burns. Derrick will be liable for the damages related to Mila's fractured hip, because the risk of injuring her with his bicycle was foreseeable. Normally, though, Derrick will not be liable for the burns caused by the plane crash, because he could not have foreseen the risk that a plane would crash nearby and injure Mila. ■

6–5c Contributory Negligence

All individuals are expected to exercise a reasonable degree of care in looking out for themselves. In the past, under the common law doctrine of **contributory negligence,** a plaintiff who was also negligent (who failed to exercise a reasonable degree of care) could not recover anything from the defendant. Under this rule, no matter how insignificant the plaintiff's negligence was relative to the defendant's negligence, the plaintiff would be precluded from recovering any damages. Today, only a few jurisdictions still follow this doctrine.

6–5d Comparative Negligence

In most states, the doctrine of contributory negligence has been replaced by a **comparative negligence** standard. Under this standard, both the plaintiff's and the defendant's negligence are computed, and the liability for damages is distributed accordingly.

Some jurisdictions have adopted a "pure" form of comparative negligence that allows plaintiffs to recover, even if the extent of their fault was greater than that of the defendants. Under pure comparative negligence, if the plaintiff was 80 percent at fault and the defendant 20 percent at fault, the plaintiff can recover 20 percent of the damages.

Many states' comparative negligence statutes, however, contain a "50 percent" rule that prevents plaintiffs from recovering any damages if they were more than 50 percent at fault. Under this rule, plaintiffs who were 35 percent at fault can recover 65 percent of their damages, but plaintiffs who were 65 percent at fault can recover nothing.

Practice and Review: Tort Law

Astrid went to Ragged Mountain Ski Resort in New Hampshire with a friend. Astrid went snow tubing down a run designed exclusively for snow tubers. There were no Ragged Mountain employees present in the snow-tube area to instruct Astrid on the proper use of a snow tube. On her fourth run down the trail, Astrid crossed over the center line between snow-tube lanes, collided with another snow tuber, and was injured. Astrid filed a negligence action against Ragged Mountain seeking compensation for the injuries that she sustained. Two years earlier, the New Hampshire state legislature had enacted a statute that prohibited a person who participates in the sport of skiing from suing a ski-area operator for injuries caused by the risks inherent in skiing. Using the information presented in the chapter, answer the following questions.

1. What defense will Ragged Mountain probably assert?
2. The central question in this case is whether the state statute establishing that skiers assume the risks inherent in the sport bars Astrid's suit. What would your decision be on this issue? Why?
3. Suppose that the court concludes that the statute applies only to skiing and not to snow tubing. Will Astrid's lawsuit be successful? Explain.
4. Now suppose that the jury concludes that Astrid was partly at fault for the accident. Under what theory might her damages be reduced in proportion to the degree to which her actions contributed to the accident and her resulting injuries?

Debate This . . .   Each time a state legislature enacts a law that applies the assumption of risk doctrine to a particular sport, participants in that sport suffer.

Terms and Concepts

actionable 113	dram shop acts 128	puffery 119
actual malice 117	duty of care 124	punitive damages 111
assault 112	fraudulent misrepresentation	reasonable person standard 126
assumption of risk 128	(fraud) 119	slander 116
battery 112	general damages 111	slander of quality 123
business invitees 126	Good Samaritan statutes 127	slander of title 123
causation in fact 126	intentional tort 112	special damages 110
comparative negligence 130	libel 116	superseding cause 129
compensatory damages 110	licensee 122	torts 110
contributory negligence 129	malpractice 126	tortfeasor 112
conversion 123	negligence 124	trade libel 123
damages 110	privilege 117	transferred intent 112
defamation 116	proximate cause 127	trespass to land 122
disparagement of property 123	public figures 117	trespass to personal property 122

Issue Spotters

1. Jana leaves her truck's motor running while she enters a Kwik-Pik Store. The truck's transmission engages, and the vehicle crashes into a gas pump, starting a fire that spreads to a warehouse on the next block. The warehouse collapses, causing its billboard to fall and injure Raphael, a bystander. Can Raphael recover from Jana? Why or why not? (See *Unintentional Torts—Negligence*.)

2. A water pipe bursts, flooding a Metal Fabrication Company utility room and tripping the circuit breakers on a panel in the room. Metal Fabrication contacts Nouri, a licensed electrician with five years' experience, to check the damage and turn the breakers back on. Without testing for short circuits, which Nouri knows that he should do, he tries to switch on a breaker. He is electrocuted, and his wife sues Metal Fabrication for damages, alleging negligence. What might the firm successfully claim in defense? (See *Defenses to Negligence*.)

- **Check your answers to the Issue Spotters against the answers provided in Appendix B at the end of this text.**

Business Scenarios and Case Problems

6–1. Defamation. Rugga is an employee of the Dun Construction Corp. While delivering materials to a construction site, he carelessly backs Dun's truck into a passenger vehicle driven by Green. This is Rugga's second accident in six months. When the company owner, Dun, learns of this latest accident, a heated discussion ensues, and Dun fires Rugga. Dun is so angry that he immediately writes a letter to the union of which Rugga is a member and to all other construction companies in the community, stating that Rugga is the "worst driver in the city" and that "anyone who hires him is asking for legal liability." Rugga files a suit against Dun, alleging libel on the basis of the statements made in the letters. Discuss the results. (See *Intentional Torts Against Persons*.)

6–2. Intentional Infliction of Emotional Distress. While living in her home country of Tanzania, Sophia Kiwanuka signed an employment contract with Anne Margareth Bakilana, a Tanzanian living in Washington, D.C. Kiwanuka traveled to the United States to work as a babysitter and maid in Bakilana's house. When Kiwanuka arrived, Bakilana confiscated her passport, held her in isolation, and forced her to work long hours under threat of having her deported. Kiwanuka worked seven days a week without breaks and was subjected to regular verbal and psychological abuse by Bakilana. Kiwanuka filed a complaint against Bakilana for intentional infliction of emotional distress, among other claims. Bakilana argued that Kiwanuka's complaint should be dismissed because the allegations were insufficient to show outrageous intentional conduct that resulted in severe emotional distress. If you were the judge, in whose favor would you rule? Why? [*Kiwanuka v. Bakilana*, 844 F.Supp.2d 107 (D.D.C. 2012)] (See *Intentional Torts Against Persons*.)

6–3. Business Case Problem With Sample Answer— Negligence. At the Weatherford Hotel in Flagstaff, Arizona, in Room 59, a balcony extends across thirty inches of the room's only window, leaving a twelve-inch gap with a three-story drop to the concrete below. A sign prohibits smoking in the room but invites guests to "step out onto the balcony" to smoke. Toni Lucario was a guest in Room 59 when she climbed out of the window and fell to her death. Patrick McMurtry, her estate's personal representative, filed a suit against the Weatherford. Did the hotel breach a duty of care to Lucario? What might the Weatherford assert in its defense? Explain. [*McMurtry v. Weatherford Hotel, Inc.*, 231 Ariz. 244, 293 P.3d 520 (2013)] (See *Unintentional Torts—Negligence*.)

- **For a sample answer to Problem 6–3, go to Appendix C at the end of this text.**

6–4. Negligence. Ronald Rawls and Zabian Bailey were in an auto accident in Bridgeport, Connecticut. Bailey rear-ended Rawls at a stoplight. Evidence showed it was more likely than not that Bailey failed to apply his brakes in time to avoid the collision, failed to turn his vehicle to avoid the collision, failed to keep his vehicle under control, and was inattentive to his surroundings. Rawls filed a suit in a Connecticut state court against his insurance company, Progressive Northern Insurance Co., to obtain benefits under an underinsured motorist clause, alleging that Bailey had been negligent. Could Rawls collect? Discuss. [*Rawls v. Progressive Northern Insurance Co.*, 310 Conn. 768, 83 A.3d 576 (2014)] (See *Unintentional Torts—Negligence*.)

6–5. Negligence. Charles Robison, an employee of West Star Transportation, Inc., was ordered to cover an unevenly loaded flatbed trailer with a 150-pound tarpaulin (a waterproof cloth). The load included uncrated equipment and pallet crates of different heights, about thirteen feet off the ground at its highest point. While standing on the load, manipulating the tarpaulin without safety equipment or assistance, Robison fell and sustained a traumatic head injury. He filed a suit against West Star to recover for his injury. Was West Star "negligent in failing to provide a reasonably safe place to work," as Robison claimed? Explain. [*West Star Transportation, Inc. v. Robison*, 457 S.W.3d 178 (Tex.App.—Amarillo 2015)] (See *Unintentional Torts—Negligence*.)

6–6. Negligence. DSC Industrial Supply and Road Rider Supply are located in North Kitsap Business Park in Seattle, Washington. Both firms are owned by Paul and Suzanne Marshall. The Marshalls had outstanding commercial loans from Frontier Bank. The bank dispatched one of its employees, Suzette Gould, to North Kitsap to "spread Christmas cheer" to the Marshalls as an expression of appreciation for their business. Approaching the entry to Road Rider, Gould tripped over a concrete "wheel stop" and fell, suffering a broken arm and a dislocated elbow. The stop was not clearly visible, it had not been painted a contrasting color, and it was not marked with a sign. Gould had not been aware of the stop before she tripped over it. Is North Kitsap liable to Gould for negligence? Explain. [*Gould v. North Kitsap Business Park Management, LLC,* 192 Wash.App. 1021 (2016)] (See *Unintentional Torts—Negligence.*)

6–7. Defamation. Jonathan Martin, an offensive lineman with the Miami Dolphins, abruptly quit the team and checked himself into a hospital seeking psychological treatment. Later, he explained that he left because of persistent taunting from other Dolphins players. The National Football League hired attorney Theodore Wells to investigate Martin's allegations of bullying. After receiving Wells's report, the Dolphins fired their offensive line coach, James Turner. Turner was a prominent person on the Dolphins team, and during his career he chose to thrust himself further into the public arena. He was the subject of articles discussing his coaching philosophy, and the focus of one season of HBO's "Hard Knocks," showcasing his coaching style. Turner filed a suit in a federal district court against Wells, alleging defamation. He charged that Wells failed to properly analyze certain information. Is Turner likely to succeed on his claim? Explain. [*Turner v. Wells*, 879 F.3d 1254 (11th Cir. 2018)] (See *Intentional Torts Against Persons.*)

6–8. Proximate Cause. Steve Pritchard boasted to his wife and perhaps to others that he had set fires in the past to collect insurance payments. Pritchard arranged for his wife and children to be out of their residence on a certain morning. He set fire to the house, which he admitted. Both he and his wife were charged with malicious destruction of property by fire. Under federal law, that act allows punishment for arson causing death. The death occurred while firefighters were putting out the flames of the Pritchard residence. Firefighter Charles Sparks suffered a heart attack while putting out the fire. Could a jury find Pritchard guilty of causing Sparks's

death? [*U.S. v. Pritchard*, 964 F.3d 513 (2020)] (See *Unintentional Torts—Negligence.*)

6–9. Defamation. James Terry, a UPS sales director in Arizona, met with sales managers after returning from vacation. According to some of the sales managers, he acted strangely at the meeting. His speech was slurred. He was incoherent and asked the same question over and over, losing his train of thought. Three coworkers filed "reasonable cause/fitness-for-duty medical evaluation" forms providing details about Terry's behavior. UPS directed him to provide a urine sample, and he tested positive for amphetamine and marijuana. At the time, even medical marijuana in Arizona was a criminal offense. He was dismissed. Terry sued, alleging defamation. The trial court granted summary judgment to UPS on Terry's claim. He appealed. How should the appellate court rule? [*Terry v. United Parcel Service, Inc.*, 253 Ariz. 55, 508 P.3d 1137 (App.Ct.Ariz., Div.1 2022)] (See *Intentional Torts Against Persons.*)

6–10. A Question of Ethics—The IDDR Approach and Wrongful Interference. Julie Whitchurch was an employee of Vizant Technologies, LLC. After she was fired, she created a website falsely accusing Vizant of fraud and mismanagement to discourage others from doing business with the company. Vizant filed a suit in a federal district court against her, alleging wrongful interference with a business relationship. The court concluded that Whitchurch's online criticism of Vizant adversely affected its employees and operations, forced it to accept reduced compensation to obtain business, and deterred outside investment. The court ordered Whitchurch to stop her online efforts to discourage others from doing business with Vizant. [*Vizant Technologies, LLC v. Whitchurch*, 675 Fed. Appx. 201 (3d Cir. 2017)] (See *Intentional Torts Against Persons.*)

(a) How does the motivation for Whitchurch's conduct differ from other cases that involve wrongful interference? What does this suggest about the ethics in this situation? Discuss.

(b) Using the IDDR approach, analyze and evaluate Vizant's decision to file a suit against Whitchurch.

Time-Limited Group Assignment

6–11. Negligence. Patel and Gloria Bowden hosted a cookout at their home in South Carolina, inviting mostly business acquaintances. Jacey Parks, who was nineteen years old, attended the party. Alcoholic beverages were available to all of the guests, even those who, like Parks, were between the ages of eighteen and twenty-one. Parks consumed alcohol at the party and left with other guests. One of these guests detained Parks at the guest's home to give Parks time to "sober up." Parks then drove himself from this guest's home and was killed in a one-car accident. At the time of death, he had a blood alcohol content of 0.291 percent, which exceeded the state's limit for driving a motor vehicle. Gabriella, Parks's

mother, filed a suit in a South Carolina state court against the Bowdens and others, alleging that they were negligent. (See Unintentional Torts—Negligence.)

(a) The first group will present arguments in favor of holding the social hosts liable in this situation.

(b) The second group will formulate arguments against holding the social hosts liable based on principles in this chapter.

(c) The third group will determine the reasons why some courts do not treat social hosts the same as parents who serve alcoholic beverages to their underage children.

Chapter 7

Strict Liability and Product Liability

In this chapter, we look at a category of tort called **strict liability,** or *liability without fault.* Under the doctrine of strict liability, a person who engages in certain activities can be held responsible for any harm that results to others, even if the person used the utmost care.

We then look at an area of tort law of particular importance to businesspersons—product liability. The manufacturers and sellers of products may incur **product liability** when product defects cause injury or property damage to consumers, users, or bystanders.

Suppose Minsun Yang is riding a Polaris all-terrain vehicle (ATV) that bursts into flames. Under product liability laws, he could sue Polaris. Indeed, Polaris is facing numerous product liability lawsuits from plaintiffs who were harmed when one of the company's ATVs caught fire. Despite claiming that riders contributed to their burns and other injuries by misusing its products, Polaris recalled over 100,000 ATVs because of fire hazards.

Although multimillion-dollar product liability claims often involve big automakers, pharmaceutical companies, or tobacco companies, many businesses face potential liability. In fact, even small retailers may be sued when products they sell turn out to be defective. Product liability lawsuits also reach across international borders, as when a manufacturer or supplier of a defective product is located outside the United States.

7–1 Strict Liability

The modern concept of strict liability traces its origins, in part, to an English case decided in 1868. ■ **Case in Point 7.1** In the coal-mining area of Lancashire, England, the Rylands, who were mill owners, had constructed a reservoir on their land. Water from the reservoir broke through a filled-in shaft of an abandoned coal mine nearby and flooded the connecting passageways in an active coal mine owned by Fletcher.

Fletcher sued the Rylands, and the court held that the Rylands were liable, even though the circumstances did not fit within existing tort liability theories. The court held that a "person who for his own purposes brings on his land and collects and keeps there anything likely to do mischief if it escapes . . . is *prima facie*[1] answerable for all the damage which is the natural consequence of its escape."[2] ■

British courts liberally applied the doctrine that emerged from the case. Initially, though, few U.S. courts accepted the doctrine, presumably because the courts were worried about

its effect on the expansion of American business. Today, however, the doctrine of strict liability is the norm rather than the exception.

7–1a Abnormally Dangerous Activities

Strict liability for damages proximately caused by an abnormally dangerous, or ultrahazardous, activity is one application of strict liability. Courts apply the doctrine of strict liability in these situations because of the extreme risk of the activity. Abnormally dangerous activities are those that involve a high risk of serious harm to persons or property that cannot be completely guarded against by the exercise of reasonable care.

An activity such as blasting or storing explosives qualifies as abnormally dangerous, for instance. Even if blasting with dynamite is performed with all reasonable care, there is still a risk of injury. Considering the potential for harm, it seems reasonable to ask the person engaged in the activity to pay for injuries caused by that activity. Although there is no fault, there is still responsibility because of the dangerous nature of the undertaking.

Similarly, persons who keep wild animals are strictly liable for any harm inflicted by the animals. The basis for applying strict liability is that wild animals, should they

---

1. *Prima facie* is Latin for "at first sight." Legally, it refers to a fact that is presumed to be true unless contradicted by evidence.
2. *Rylands v. Fletcher*, 3 L.R.–E & I App. [Law Reports, English & Irish Appeal Cases] (H.L. [House of Lords] 1868).

escape from confinement, pose a serious risk of harm to people in the vicinity. Even an owner of domestic animals (such as dogs or horses) may be strictly liable for harm caused by those animals if the owner knew, or should have known, that the animals were dangerous or had a propensity to harm others.

7–1b Application of Strict Liability to Product Liability

A significant application of strict liability is in the area of product liability—liability of manufacturers and sellers for harmful or defective products. Liability here is a matter of social policy and is based on two factors:

1. The manufacturer can better bear the cost of injury because it can spread the cost throughout society by increasing the prices of its goods.
2. The manufacturer is making a profit from its activities and therefore should bear the cost of injury as an operating expense.

We discuss product liability in detail next. Strict liability is also applied in certain types of bailments (a bailment exists when goods are transferred temporarily into the care of another).

7–2 Product Liability

Those who make, sell, or lease goods can be held liable for physical harm or property damage caused by those goods to a consumer, user, or bystander. This is called *product liability*. Product liability may be based on the theories of negligence, misrepresentation, strict liability, and warranties. Multiple theories of liability can be, and often are, asserted in the same case. We look here at product liability based on negligence and on misrepresentation.

7–2a Based on Negligence

Negligence is the failure to exercise the degree of care that a reasonable, prudent person would have exercised under the circumstances. If a manufacturer fails to exercise "due care" to make a product safe, a person who is injured by the product may sue the manufacturer for negligence.

Due Care Must Be Exercised Manufacturers must use due care in all of the following areas:

1. Designing the product.
2. Selecting the materials.
3. Using the appropriate production process.

4. Assembling and testing the product.
5. Placing adequate warnings on the label to inform the user of dangers of which an ordinary person might not be aware.
6. Inspecting and testing any purchased components used in the product.

Privity of Contract Not Required A product liability action based on negligence does not require privity of contract between the injured plaintiff and the defendant-manufacturer. **Privity of contract** refers to the relationship that exists between the parties to a contract. Privity is the reason that normally only the parties to a contract can enforce that contract.

In the context of product liability law, though, privity is not required. Individuals who are injured by a defective product may bring negligence suits even though they were not the ones who actually purchased the products—and thus are not in privity. A manufacturer, seller, or lessor is liable for failure to exercise due care to any person who sustains an injury proximately caused by a negligently made (defective) product.

A 1916 landmark decision established this exception to the privity requirement. ■ **Case in Point 7.2** Donald MacPherson suffered injuries while riding in a Buick automobile that suddenly collapsed because one of the wheels was made of defective wood. The spokes crumbled into fragments, throwing MacPherson out of the vehicle and injuring him.

MacPherson had purchased the car from a Buick dealer, but he brought a lawsuit against the manufacturer, Buick Motor Company, alleging negligence. Buick itself had not made the wheel but had bought it from another manufacturer. There was evidence, though, that the defects could have been discovered by a reasonable inspection by Buick and that no such inspection had taken place. The primary issue was whether Buick owed a duty of care to anyone except the immediate purchaser of the car—that is, the Buick dealer. Although Buick itself had not manufactured the wheel, New York's highest state court held that Buick had a duty to inspect the wheels and that Buick "was responsible for the finished product." Therefore, Buick was liable to MacPherson for the injuries he sustained.[3] ■

"Cause in Fact" and Proximate Cause In a product liability suit based on negligence, as in any action alleging that the defendant was negligent, the plaintiff must show that the defendant's conduct was the "cause

---

3. *MacPherson v. Buick Motor Co.*, 217 N.Y. 382, 111 N.E. 1050 (1916).

in fact" of an injury. "Cause in fact" requires showing that "but for" the defendant's action, the injury would not have occurred.

It must also be determined that the defendant's act was the proximate cause of the injury. This determination focuses on the foreseeability of the consequences of the act. For proximate cause to become a relevant issue, however, a plaintiff first must establish cause in fact.

At issue in the following case was whether the proximate cause of the injury to a product's user was the manufacturer's inadequate warning or the purchaser's failure to follow the manufacturer's maintenance instructions.

Case 7.1

Primal Vantage Co. v. O'Bryan

Court of Appeals of Kentucky, __ S.W.3d __, Prod.Liab.Rep. (CCH) P 20,758, 2019 WL 6044870 (2019).

Background and Facts Dennis Martin owned a ladder stand made by Primal Vantage Company. The stand consisted of a platform fifteen feet above the ground with an attached ladder. Five polypropylene straps secured the stand to a tree. On a hunting trip on Martin's property, Kevin O'Bryan climbed the ladder of the stand. The stand had been affixed to the tree for five years without inspection or maintenance, and two of the straps had deteriorated and broken. When O'Bryan reached the platform, the remaining straps broke, and the stand collapsed. Seriously injured, paralyzed from the waist down, and suffering unremitting pain, O'Bryan filed a suit in a Kentucky state court against Primal Vantage, alleging product liability. A jury awarded O'Bryan damages on a finding that the warnings accompanying the stand were inadequate. The court ordered the damages to be paid to O'Bryan. Primal Vantage appealed.

In the Words of the Court

CLAYTON, Chief Judge:

* * * *

Primal Vantage argues that it was entitled to a directed verdict * * * . The warning label affixed to the ladder stand informed users that they must inspect the ladder stand, must not use it if parts were damaged or missing, and must always use a safety harness. Primal Vantage contends that any alleged inadequacy of these warnings could not be a proximate cause of the accident because Kevin * * * by [his] own admission never read them. The real cause of Kevin's injuries, it argues, was Martin's failure to inspect and maintain the ladderstand in accordance with the manufacturer's instructions.

* * * A directed verdict is appropriate where there is no evidence of probative [tending to prove] value to support an opposite result.

* * * *

The failure to warn adequately implicates not merely the content of the warning but also its placement and visibility on the product. The warning on the Primal Vantage ladder stand was affixed to the back of the ladder. Kevin testified that if the stand had a visible warning, he would have read it and would never have climbed up the stand * * * . Kevin's testimony * * * constitutes sufficiently probative evidence to overcome a motion for a directed verdict.

The argument that Martin's conduct in failing to inspect and maintain the ladder stand was a superseding cause relieving Primal Vantage of liability is resolved by [the principle] that, except in extraordinary circumstances, the negligence of an intervening party does not relieve the manufacturer of the duty to warn adequately. * * * The manufacturer has a duty to warn the ultimate user of any dangers in its product (other than those that are open or obvious). This duty is non-delegable * * * . If the injury was the result of the manufacturer's breach, the liability for the injury will lie with the manufacturer. A purchaser such as Martin who has notice of the dangerous condition may be concurrently liable to the ultimate user for failure to provide adequate warning, for failure to remedy the defect or on some other basis, but the purchaser's failure to act is not an intervening cause except in extraordinary circumstances. An example of an extraordinary circumstance occurs when the manufacturer claims the purchaser was notified of the defect and assumed responsibility for correcting it. No showing of such extraordinary circumstances has been made in this case.

Case 7.1 Continues

Case 7.1 Continued   **Decision and Remedy** A state intermediate appellate court affirmed the lower court's order. "Primal Vantage in the exercise of ordinary care should have been aware that the stand was unreasonably dangerous and failed to provide an adequate warning."

Critical Thinking

- **Legal Environment** Should the jury have found that O'Bryan was also at fault? How might this finding have affected the award of damages? Explain.
- **Economic** During *voir dire*, a potential juror asked whether they would be told how much Primal Vantage's insurance company would pay if O'Bryan were awarded damages. How should the court have responded? Why?

7–2b Misrepresentation

When a user or consumer is injured as a result of a manufacturer's or seller's fraudulent misrepresentation, the basis of liability may be the tort of fraud. In this situation, the misrepresentation must have been made knowingly or with reckless disregard for the facts. The intentional mislabeling of packaged cosmetics, for instance, or the intentional concealment of a product's defects constitute fraudulent misrepresentation.

In addition, the misrepresentation must be of a material fact, and the seller must have intended to induce the buyer's reliance on the misrepresentation. Misrepresentation on a label or advertisement is enough to show an intent to induce the reliance of anyone who may use the product. Finally, the buyer must have relied on the misrepresentation.

7–3 Strict Product Liability

We turn now to the application of strict liability in the area of product liability. Recall that, under the doctrine of strict liability, people may be liable for the results of their acts regardless of their intentions or their exercise of reasonable care. In addition, liability does not depend on privity of contract. In the 1960s, courts applied the doctrine of strict liability in several landmark cases involving manufactured goods, and it has since become a common method of holding manufacturers liable.

7–3a Strict Product Liability and Public Policy

The law imposes strict product liability as a matter of public policy, which may be expressed in a statute or in the common law. This public policy rests on a threefold assumption:

1. Consumers should be protected against unsafe products.

2. Manufacturers and distributors should not escape liability for faulty products simply because they are not in privity of contract with the ultimate user of those products.
3. Manufacturers and distributors can better bear the costs associated with injuries caused by their products, because they can ultimately pass the costs on to all consumers in the form of higher prices.

California was the first state to impose strict product liability in tort on manufacturers. ■ **Case in Point 7.3** William Greenman was injured when his Shopsmith combination power tool threw off a piece of wood that struck him in the head. He sued the manufacturer, claiming that he had followed the manufacturer's instructions and that the product must be defective. In a landmark decision, *Greenman v. Yuba Power Products, Inc.*,[4] the California Supreme Court set out the reason for applying tort law rather than contract law (including laws governing warranties) in cases involving consumers who were injured by defective products.

According to the *Greenman* court, the "purpose of such liability is to insure that the costs of injuries resulting from defective products are borne by the manufacturers . . . rather than by the injured persons who are powerless to protect themselves." ■ Today, the majority of states recognize strict product liability, although some state courts limit its application to situations involving personal injuries (rather than property damage).

7–3b The Requirements for Strict Product Liability

After the *Restatement (Second) of Torts* was issued in 1964, Section 402A became a widely accepted statement of how the doctrine of strict liability should be applied to sellers of goods (including manufacturers, processors, assemblers, packagers, bottlers, wholesalers, distributors, retailers, and lessors). The bases for an action in strict liability

---

4. 59 Cal.2d 57, 377 P.2d 897, 27 Cal.Rptr. 697 (1962).

that are set forth in Section 402A can be summarized as a set of six requirements.

1. The product must be in a defective condition when the defendant sells it.
2. The defendant must normally be engaged in the business of selling (or otherwise distributing) that product.
3. The product must be unreasonably dangerous to the user or consumer because of its defective condition (in most states).
4. The plaintiff must incur physical harm to self or property by use or consumption of the product.
5. The defective condition must be the proximate cause of the injury or damage.
6. The goods must not have been substantially changed from the time the product was sold to the time the injury was sustained.

Depending on the jurisdiction, if these requirements are met, a manufacturer's liability to an injured party can be almost unlimited.

Proving a Defective Condition Under these requirements, in any action against a manufacturer, seller, or lessor, the plaintiff need not show why or in what manner the product became defective. The plaintiff does, however, have to prove that the product was defective at the time it left the hands of the seller or lessor. The plaintiff must also show that this defective condition made the product "unreasonably dangerous" to the user or consumer.

Unless evidence can be presented to support the conclusion that the product was defective when it was sold or leased, the plaintiff will not succeed. If the product was delivered in a safe condition and subsequent mishandling made it harmful to the user, the seller or lessor normally is not strictly liable.

Unreasonably Dangerous Products The *Restatement* recognizes that many products cannot be made entirely safe for all uses. Thus, sellers or lessors are liable only for products that are unreasonably dangerous. A court could consider a product so defective as to be an **unreasonably dangerous product** in either of the following situations:

1. The product was dangerous beyond the expectation of the ordinary consumer.
2. A less dangerous alternative was economically feasible for the manufacturer, but the manufacturer failed to produce it.

A product may be unreasonably dangerous due to a flaw in its manufacturing, design, or warning. As discussed in this chapter's Cybersecurity and the Law feature, the law is still unsettled when it comes to a manufacturer's strict liability for a flaw in the product's online security system.

Cybersecurity and the Law   The Internet of Things

The Internet of Things (IoT) refers to devices such as window shades, refrigerators, and health monitors that are connected to the internet. Each IoT device contains software that, like software in any computer system, is vulnerable to outside attack, or hacking. The inevitable harm caused by IoT hacking is likely to impact American business in the form of strict product liability lawsuits.

Unreasonably Dangerous?

If a defective oven catches fire, under strict product liability the manufacturer will most likely be held liable for any harm that results. But what if a cybercriminal gains control of a smart oven, causing it to catch fire and injure its owner? Does an ineffective IoT security system make a product "unreasonably dangerous" to the consumer, leaving the manufacturer strictly liable? What if the problem was a glitch in the smart oven's software? Is software a "product" for the purposes of strict product liability?

As with any new legal issue caused by advancing technology, the answers to these questions will come from a combination of case law and legislation. California was the first state to regulate the IoT by requiring manufacturers of internet-connected devices to equip them with "reasonable security features."[a] Ultimately, state courts will determine to what extent this law exposes manufacturers to strict product liability. It should not take long for the issue to arise, in California and elsewhere. Approximately 25 billion IoT products are in use, with billions more poised to enter workplaces, homes, and automobiles in the near future.

Critical Thinking Security engineers discovered that faulty coding in the Chrysler Jeep's entertainment software made the car vulnerable to cyber attacks that could, ultimately, allow a hacker to gain control of the vehicle. The United States Supreme Court has allowed a breach of warranty lawsuit against Chrysler by Jeep owners who contend that they would not have purchased the cars had they known about the security defect. Why might the outcome of this case be important for strict product liability law?

a. Cal. Civ. Code Section 1798.91.04(a).

7–3c Product Defects

The *Restatement (Third) of Torts: Products Liability* defines three types of product defects that have traditionally been recognized in product liability law—manufacturing defects, design defects, and inadequate warnings.

Manufacturing Defects According to Section 2(a) of the *Restatement (Third) of Torts,* a product "contains a manufacturing defect when the product departs from its intended design even though all possible care was exercised in the preparation and marketing of the product." Basically, a manufacturing defect is a departure from a product unit's design specifications that results in products that are physically flawed, damaged, or incorrectly assembled. A glass bottle that is made too thin and explodes in a consumer's face is an example of a product with a manufacturing defect.

Quality Control. Usually, manufacturing defects occur when a manufacturer fails to assemble, test, or check the quality of a product adequately. Liability is imposed on the manufacturer (and on the wholesaler and retailer) regardless of whether the manufacturer's quality control efforts were "reasonable." The idea behind holding defendants strictly liable for manufacturing defects is to encourage greater investment in product safety and stringent quality control standards.

Expert Testimony. Cases involving allegations of a manufacturing defect are often decided based on the opinions and testimony of experts. ■ **Case in Point 7.4** Preston Cavner was seriously injured when the Cessna U206F plane he was piloting crashed shortly after takeoff. Cavner's wife, son, and a babysitter were also injured in the accident, and another son was killed. He filed a lawsuit against the manufacturer of the plane's engine, Continental Motors, Inc. (CMI), based on a manufacturing defect.

At trial, experts testified that there were "burrs," or sharp metal edges, in the Cessna's engine cylinders, a violation of CMI's design specifications. These burrs broke off and lodged in the engine's valves, leading to a loss of power and the resulting crash. A jury concluded that this manufacturing defect made the airplane unreasonably dangerous and awarded Cavner and the other injured parties more than $20 million in damages.[5] ■

Design Defects Unlike a product with a manufacturing defect, a product with a design defect is made in conformity with the manufacturer's design specifications. Nevertheless, the product results in injury to the user because the design itself was faulty. A product "is defective in design when the foreseeable risks of harm posed by the product could have been reduced or avoided by the adoption of a reasonable alternative design by the seller or other distributor, or a predecessor in the commercial chain of distribution, and the omission of the alternative design renders the product not reasonably safe."[6]

Test for Design Defects. To successfully assert a design defect, a plaintiff has to show that:

1. A reasonable alternative design was available.
2. As a result of the defendant's failure to adopt the alternative design, the product was not reasonably safe.

In other words, a manufacturer or other defendant is liable only when the harm was reasonably preventable.

Factors to Be Considered. According to the *Restatement,* a court can consider a broad range of factors in deciding claims of design defects. These include the magnitude and probability of the foreseeable risks, as well as the relative advantages and disadvantages of the product as it was designed and as it could have been designed.

Risk-Utility Analysis. Most courts engage in a risk-utility analysis to determine whether the risk of harm from the product as designed outweighs its utility to the user and to the public. ■ **Case in Point 7.5** Benjamin Riley, the county sheriff, was driving his Ford F-150 pickup truck near Ehrhardt, South Carolina, when it collided with another vehicle. The impact caused Riley's truck to leave the road and roll over. The driver's door of the truck opened in the collision, and Riley was ejected and killed.

Riley's widow, Laura, as the representative of his estate, filed a product liability suit against Ford Motor Company. She alleged that the design of the door-latch system of the truck allowed the door to open in the collision. A state court awarded the estate $900,000 in damages.

Ford appealed, but the court found that a reasonable alternative design was available for the door-latch system. Evidence showed that Ford was aware of the safety problems presented by the then-current system (a rod-linkage system). After conducting a risk-utility analysis of a different system (a cable-linkage system), Ford had concluded that the alternative system was feasible and perhaps superior. The state's highest court affirmed the damages award.[7] ■

5. *Cavner v. Continental Motors, Inc.*, 8 Wash.App.2d 1001, 2019 WL 1254015 (2019).

6. *Restatement (Third) of Torts: Products Liability*, Section 2(b).

7. *Riley v. Ford Motor Co.*, 414 S.C. 185, 777 S.E.2d 824 (2015). See also *Jolly v. General Electric Company*, 869 S.E.2d 819 (App.Ct.S.C. 2021).

Consumer-Expectation Test. Some courts apply the consumer-expectation test to determine whether a product's design was defective. Under this test, a product is unreasonably dangerous when it fails to perform in the manner that would reasonably be expected by an ordinary consumer.

■ **Case in Point 7.6** A representative from Wilson Sporting Goods Company gave Edwin Hickox an umpire's mask that was designed to be safer than other such masks. The mask had a newly designed throat guard that angled forward instead of extending straight down. Hickox was wearing the mask while working as an umpire at a game when he was struck by a ball and injured. He suffered a concussion and damage to his inner ear, which caused permanent hearing loss.

Hickox and his wife sued Wilson for product liability based on a defective design and won. Wilson appealed. The reviewing court affirmed the jury's verdict. The design was defective because "an ordinary consumer would have expected the mask to perform more safely than it did." The evidence presented to the jury had shown that Wilson's mask was more dangerous than comparable masks sold at the time.[8] ■

Inadequate Warnings A product may also be deemed defective because of inadequate instructions or warnings. A product will be considered defective "when the foreseeable risks of harm posed by the product could have been reduced or avoided by the provision of reasonable instructions or warnings by the seller or other distributor . . . and the omission of the instructions or warnings renders the product not reasonably safe."[9] Generally, a seller must also warn consumers of harm that can result from the foreseeable misuse of its product.

Note that the plaintiff must show that the inadequate warning was the proximate cause of the injuries sustained. In the following case, a drug manufacturer argued that an injured plaintiff had failed to prove that an inadequate warning was the cause of his injuries.

---

8. *Wilson Sporting Goods Co. v. Hickox*, 59 A.3d 1267 (D.C.App. 2013).
9. *Restatement (Third) of Torts: Products Liability*, Section 2(c).

Case 7.2

Stange v. Janssen Pharmaceuticals, Inc.
Superior Court of Pennsylvania, 2018 PA Super 4, 179 A.3d 45 (2018).

Background and Facts Timothy Stange was twelve years old when his doctor prescribed Risperdal, an antipsychotic drug, to treat his Tourette's syndrome. Stange subsequently developed female breasts, a condition known as gynecomastia. Surgery successfully removed Stange's breasts, but left him with permanent scars and pain. Risperdal is made by Janssen Pharmaceuticals, Inc. Janssen knew that gynecomastia was a frequent adverse event in children and adolescents who took Risperdal. But its label significantly downplayed the risk, stating, for example, that the disorder's occurrence was "rare."

Stange filed a suit in a Pennsylvania state court against Janssen, alleging that the maker had negligently failed to adequately warn of the risk of gynecomastia associated with Risperdal use. The court entered a judgment in favor of the plaintiff for more than $500,000. Janssen appealed to a state intermediate appellate court.

In the Language of the Court
Opinion by FORD ELLIOTT, P.J.E. [Presiding Judge Emeritus]
* * * *

* * * Janssen argues that Stange failed to prove proximate cause, *i.e.*, that an inadequate warning was the cause of Stange's injuries. * * * Janssen argues that it was entitled to [a judgment notwithstanding the verdict (JNOV) because] Stange failed to prove that additional risk information would have changed Dr. Kovnar's prescribing decision.

To support his claim of negligence, Stange must establish that Janssen breached its duty to warn, and that the breach caused his injuries.

A plaintiff who has established both a duty and a failure to warn must also establish causation by showing that, if properly warned, he or she would have altered behavior and avoided injury. * * * Absent proof that a more complete or explicit warning would have prevented Stange's use of Risperdal, he cannot establish that Janssen's alleged failure to warn was the proximate cause of his injuries.

Case 7.2 Continues

Case 7.2 Continued   In cases involving the failure to warn of risks associated with prescription drugs, * * * a manufacturer will be held liable only where it fails to exercise reasonable care to inform a physician of the facts which make the drug likely to be dangerous. The manufacturer has the duty to disclose risks to the physician, as opposed to the patient, because it is the duty of the prescribing physician to be fully aware of (1) the characteristics of the drug he is prescribing, (2) the amount of the drug which can be safely administered, and (3) the different medications the patient is taking. It is also the duty of the prescribing physician to advise the patient of any dangers or side effects associated with the use of the drug as well as how and when to take the drug.

* * * There was substantial evidence that Janssen intentionally downplayed the risk of gynecomastia for adolescent boys using Risperdal. * * * The * * * label * * * reported that gynecomastia occurred in less than 1% of adult patients and less than 5% of pediatric patients treated with Risperdal. Both of these warnings were inaccurate based on the scientific evidence that the Defendants possessed [which] indicated that gynecomastia was a frequent adverse event, not "rare." * * * These warnings were not accurate, strong, or clear. Instead, the warnings, to the extent they warned at all, were inaccurate and misleading about the risks of gynecomastia.

Furthermore, Dr. Kovnar, Stange's pediatric neurologist, testified that * * * he would not have prescribed Risperdal to Stange had he been aware of the increased risk.

* * * The trial court did not err in refusing to grant JNOV.

Decision and Remedy   The appellate court affirmed the judgment in favor of Stange. "Due to Janssen's inadequate labeling and failure to warn, Dr. Kovnar was unaware of the specific heightened risks associated with the use of Risperdal." Otherwise, he would have prescribed a different drug for Stange.

Critical Thinking
- **Economic**   Why did Janssen downplay the risks of Risperdal in the warnings to physicians? Discuss.
- **What If the Facts Were Different?**   Suppose that instead of suffering harm through a prescription drug's legitimate use, the plaintiff had been injured by a drug's illegal abuse. Would the result have been different? Explain.

Content of Warnings.   Important factors for a court to consider include the risks of a product, the "content and comprehensibility" and "intensity of expression" of warnings and instructions, and the "characteristics of expected user groups."[10] Courts apply a "reasonableness" test to determine if the warnings adequately alert consumers to the product's risks. For instance, children will likely respond readily to bright, bold, simple warning labels, whereas educated adults might need more detailed information. For more on tips on making sure a product's warnings are adequate, see this chapter's Managerial Strategy feature.

■ **Case in Point 7.7**   Jeffrey Johnson went to an emergency room for an episode of atrial fibrillation, a heart rhythm disorder. Dr. David Hahn used a defibrillator manufactured by Medtronic, Inc., to deliver electric shocks to Johnson's heart. The defibrillator had synchronous and asynchronous modes, and it reverted to the asynchronous mode after each use. Hahn intended to deliver synchronized shocks, which would have required him to select the synchronous mode for each shock. But Hahn did not read the device's instructions, which Medtronic had provided both in a manual and on the device itself. As a result, the physician delivered one synchronized shock, followed by twelve asynchronous shocks that endangered Johnson's life.

Johnson and his wife filed a product liability suit against Medtronic, asserting that Medtronic had provided inadequate warnings about the defibrillator and that the device had a design defect. A Missouri appellate court held that the Johnsons could not pursue a claim based on the inadequacy of Medtronic's warnings, but they could pursue a claim alleging a design defect. The court reasoned that, in some cases, "a manufacturer may be held liable where it chooses to warn of the danger . . . rather than preclude the danger by design."[11] ■

---

10. *Restatement (Third) of Torts: Products Liability*, Section 2, Comment h.

11. *Johnson v. Medtronic, Inc.*, 365 S.W.3d 226 (Mo.App. 2012). See also *Miravalle v. One World Technologies, Inc.*, 2021 WL 5801860 (E.D.MS 2021).

Obvious Risks. There is no duty to warn about risks that are obvious or commonly known. Warnings about such risks do not add to the safety of a product and could even detract from it by making other warnings seem less significant. As will be discussed later in the chapter, the obviousness of a risk and a user's decision to proceed in the face of that risk may be a defense in a product liability suit based on an inadequate warning.

Managerial Strategy   When Is a Warning Legally Unassailable?

A company can sell a perfectly manufactured and designed product, yet still face product liability lawsuits for failure to provide appropriate warnings. According to the *Restatement (Third) of Torts,* a product may be deemed defective because of inadequate instructions or warnings when the foreseeable risks of harm posed by the product could have been reduced by reasonable warnings offered by the seller or other distributor.

Manufacturers and distributors have a duty to warn users of any hidden dangers of their products. Additionally, they have a duty to instruct users about how to use the product to avoid any dangers. Warnings generally must be clear and specific. They must also be conspicuous.

When No Warning Is Required

Not all products have to provide warnings. People are expected to know that knives can cut fingers, for instance, so a seller need not place a bright orange label on each knife sold reminding consumers of this danger. Most household products are generally safe when used as intended.

In a New Jersey case, an appeals court reviewed a product liability case against the manufacturer of a Razor A–type kick scooter. A ten-year-old boy was injured when he fell and struck his face on the scooter's handlebars. The padded end caps on the handlebars had deteriorated, and the boy's mother had thrown them away, exposing the metal ends.

The boy and his mother sued, claiming that the manufacturer was required to provide a warning to prevent injuries of this type. The appellate court noted, however, that the plaintiffs were not able to claim that the Razor A was defective. "Lacking evidence that Razor A's end-cap design was defective, plaintiffs cannot show that Razor A had a duty to warn of such a defect, and therefore cannot make out their failure to warn claim."[a]

In an Indiana case, an employee of a concrete contractor was injured at a construction site when his head was struck by a sixteen-foot-long two-by-four board that had dislodged from a concrete formwork system. The employee sued the construction manage and the manufacturer of the formwork system for failure to warn.

The court decided that the danger that lumber used in this formwork system could eject and strike a person was open and obvious. Therefore, neither the construction manager nor the manufacturer of the system was liable for failing to warn the employee.[b]

Medical Warnings

In a case involving a surgical procedure, a woman suffered severe damage to her pelvis that turned out to be permanent. Her lawsuit against the manufacturer of the mesh implant that caused the damage included a failure-to-warn claim. At trial, her physician testified that, if the manufacturer's Instructions for Use had informed him about the significant possibility of permanent damage, he would have chosen a different treatment plan. A federal appeals court upheld the jury's $20 million award, holding that the manufacturer's short, generic warning of risk did not provide enough information to either the plaintiff or her physician.[c]

The appeals court noted that, if the mesh implant manufacturer had provided ample warning, it might have been protected by the learned intermediary doctrine. Under this legal theory, a properly informed physician bears the responsibility to explain the risks of any drug or medical procedure to the patient. Opioid manufacturers have turned to the learned intermediary doctrine as a defense against product liability lawsuits stemming from the many thousands of fatal overdoses linked to their product. At least one court has rejected this approach, however, holding that an opioid manufacturer's aggressive marketing strategies negated any defense that proper label warnings would have provided.[d]

Business Questions

1. To protect themselves, manufacturers have been forced to include lengthy safety warnings for their products. What might be the downside of such warnings?

2. Does a manufacturer have to create safety warnings for every product? Why or why not?

---

a. *Vann v. Toys R Us,* 2014 WL 3537937 (N.J.Sup. A.D. 2014).

b. *Gleaves v. Messer Construction Co.,* 77 N.E.3d 1244 (Ind.App. 2017).

c. *Kaiser v. Johnson & Johnson,* 947 F.3d 996 (7th Cir. 2020).

d. *Commonwealth v. Purdue Pharma, L.P. et al.,* 36 Mass.L.Rptr. 56, 2019 WL 5495866 (2019).

■ **Example 7.8** Sixteen-year-old Lana White attempts to do a back flip on a trampoline and fails. She is paralyzed as a result. There are nine warning labels affixed to the trampoline, an instruction manual with safety warnings, and a placard at the entrance advising users not to do flips. If White sues the manufacturer for inadequate warnings in this situation, she is likely to lose. The warning labels are probably sufficient to make the risks obvious and insulate the manufacturer from liability for her injuries. ■

Risks that may seem obvious to some users, though, will not be obvious to all users, especially when the users are likely to be children. A young child may not be able to read or understand warning labels or comprehend the risk of certain activities. To avoid liability, the manufacturer would have to prove that the warnings it provided were adequate to make the risk of injury obvious to a young child.[12]

State Laws and Constitutionality. An action alleging that a product is defective due to an inadequate label can be based on state law, but that law must not violate the U.S. Constitution. ■ **Case in Point 7.9** California once enacted a law imposing restrictions and a labeling requirement on the sale or rental of "violent video games" to minors. Although the video game industry had adopted a voluntary rating system for games, the legislators deemed those labels inadequate.

The Video Software Dealers Association and the Entertainment Software Association immediately filed a suit in federal court to invalidate the law, and the law was struck down. The state appealed to the United States Supreme Court. The Court found that the definition of a violent video game in California's law was unconstitutionally vague and violated the First Amendment's guarantee of freedom of speech.[13] ■

7–3d Market-Share Liability

Ordinarily, in all product liability claims, plaintiffs must prove that the defective product that caused their injuries was the product of a specific defendant. In a few situations, however, courts have dropped this requirement when plaintiffs could not prove which of many distributors of a harmful product supplied the particular product

that caused the injuries. Under a theory of **market-share liability,** a court can hold each manufacturer responsible for a percentage of the plaintiff's damages that is equal to the percentage of its market share.

■ **Case in Point 7.10** Suffolk County Water Authority (SCWA) is a municipal water supplier in New York. SCWA discovered the presence of a toxic chemical—perchloroethylene (PCE), which is used by dry cleaners and others—in its local water. SCWA filed a product liability lawsuit against Dow Chemical Corporation and other companies that manufactured and distributed PCE. Dow filed a motion to dismiss the case for failure to state a claim, because SCWA could not identify each defendant whose allegedly defective product caused the water contamination. A state trial court refused to dismiss the action, holding that SCWA's allegations were sufficient to invoke market-share liability.[14] ■

Many jurisdictions do not recognize the market-share theory of liability because they believe that it deviates too significantly from traditional legal principles. Jurisdictions that do recognize market-share liability apply it only when it is difficult to determine which company made a particular product.

7–3e Other Applications of Strict Product Liability

Almost all courts extend the strict liability of manufacturers and other sellers to injured bystanders. Thus, if a defective forklift that will not go into reverse injures a passerby, that individual can sue the manufacturer for product liability (and possibly also sue the forklift operator for negligence).

Strict product liability also applies to suppliers of component parts. ■ **Example 7.11** Toyota buys brake pads from a subcontractor and puts them in Camrys without changing their composition. If those pads are defective, both the supplier of the brake pads and Toyota will be held strictly liable for the injuries caused by the defects. ■

7–4 Defenses to Product Liability

Defendants in product liability suits can raise a number of defenses. One defense, of course, is to show that there is no basis for the plaintiff's claim. Thus, for instance, in an action based on negligence, if a defendant can show that the plaintiff has *not* met the requirements for such an

12. See, for example, *Bunch v. Hoffinger Industries, Inc.,* 123 Cal. App.4th 1278, 20 Cal.Rptr.3d 780 (2004). See also *Tran v. Nguyen,* 2018 WL 525321 (Sup.Ct. NJ, App. Div. 2018).

13. *Video Software Dealers Association v. Schwarzenegger,* 556 F.3d 950 (9th Cir. 2009); *Brown v. Entertainment Merchants Association,* 564 U.S. 786, 131 S.Ct. 2729, 180 L.Ed.2d 708 (2011); *California Chamber of Commerce v. Becerra,* 529 F.Supp.3d 1099 (E.D.CA 2022).

14. *Suffolk County Water Authority v. Dow Chemical Co.,* 44 Misc.3d 569, 987 N.Y.S.2d 819 (2014).

action (such as causation), then generally the defendant will not be liable.

Similarly, in a case involving strict product liability, a defendant can claim that the plaintiff failed to meet one of the requirements. For instance, if the defendant shows that the goods were altered after they were sold, normally the defendant will not be held liable.

7–4a Preemption

A defense that has been successfully raised by defendants in recent years is preemption—that government regulations preempt claims for product liability. An injured party may not be able to sue the manufacturer of defective products that are subject to comprehensive federal regulatory schemes.

■ **Case in Point 7.12** Medical devices are subject to extensive government regulation and undergo a rigorous premarket approval process. The United States Supreme Court decided in *Riegel v. Medtronic, Inc.,*[15] that a man who was injured by an approved medical device (a balloon catheter) could not sue its maker for product liability. The Court reasoned that Congress had created a comprehensive scheme of federal safety oversight for medical devices. The U.S. Food and Drug Administration is required to review the design, labeling, and manufacturing of medical devices before they are marketed to make sure that they are safe and effective. Because premarket approval is a "rigorous process," it preempts all common law claims challenging the safety or effectiveness of a medical device that has been approved. ■

Since the *Medtronic* decision, some courts have extended the preemption defense to other product liability actions. Other courts have been unwilling to deny an injured party relief simply because the federal government was supposed to ensure a product's safety.[16] Even the United States Supreme Court refused to extend the preemption defense to preclude a drug maker's liability in one subsequent case.[17]

7–4b Assumption of Risk

Assumption of risk can sometimes be used as a defense in a product liability action. To establish assumption of risk, the defendant must show the following:

1. The plaintiff knew and appreciated the risk created by the product defect.
2. The plaintiff voluntarily assumed the risk—by express agreement or by words or conduct—even though it was unreasonable to do so.

Some states do not allow the defense of assumption of risk in strict product liability claims, however. ■ **Case in Point 7.13** When Savannah Boles became a customer of Executive Tans, she signed a contract. One part of the contract stated that signers used the company's tanning booths at their own risk. It also released the manufacturer and others from liability for any injuries.

Later, Boles's fingers were partially amputated when they came into contact with a tanning booth's fan. Boles sued the manufacturer for strict product liability. The Colorado Supreme Court held that assumption of risk was not applicable because strict product liability is driven by public-policy considerations. The theory focuses on the nature of the product rather than the conduct of either the manufacturer or the person injured.[18] ■

The following case involves a high school student who suffered traumatic brain injury after playing in a junior varsity football game.

---

15. 552 U.S. 312, 128 S.Ct. 999, 169 L.Ed.2d 892 (2008). For another case in which the Court found preemption, see *Bruesewitz v. Wyeth, LLC,* 562 U.S. 223, 131 S.Ct. 1068, 179 L.Ed.2d 1 (2011). See also *Booth v. Bowser,* 597 F.Supp.3d 1 (D.D.C. 2022).

16. See, for example, *Fortner v. Bristol-Myers Squibb Co.,* 2017 WL 3193928 (S.D.N.Y. 2017).
17. *Wyeth v. Levine,* 555 U.S. 555, 129 S.Ct. 1187, 173 L.Ed.2d 51 (2009). See also *In re Fosamax,* 593 F.Supp.3d 96, 2022 (D.NJ 2022).
18. *Boles v. Sun Ergoline, Inc.,* 223 P.3d 724 (Col.Sup.Ct. 2010). See, in contrast, *Redden v. Clear Creek Skiing Corporation,* 490 P.3d 1063 (CO Ct.App., Div. 1 2020).

Case Analysis 7.3

Nicholas Brown v. El Dorado Union High School District

Court of Appeals of California, 3rd District, El Dorado, 76 Cal.App.5th 1003, 292 Cal.Rpt.3d 72 (App.Ct. 3d Dist. CA 2022).

Summary of the Appeal

HULL, J.

Plaintiff Nicholas Brown (Nick), through his mother and guardian *ad litem* Laurie Brown (Laurie), brought a personal injury action against defendant El Dorado Union High School District (the District) after Nick suffered a traumatic brain injury during a football game.

After the District brought a summary judgment motion, the trial court

Case 7.3 Continues

Case 7.3 Continued

granted summary judgment in favor of the District on two grounds. First, the trial court found the case was barred by the affirmative defense of an express assumption of risk due to a release and waiver Nick and his father, Read Brown (Read), signed prior to the football season. Second, the court found the action was barred by the principle of the primary assumption of risk.

Nick now appeals * * *.

Facts and History of the Proceedings

NICK BROWN

In August 2015, Nick was a sophomore at Union Mine High School and played on the junior varsity football team. Union Mine is a high school within the District.

Release and Related Documents

According to Jay Aliff, the Athletic Director for Union Mine High School, prior to the 2015–2016 academic year, every student who wished to participate in extracurricular athletics was to receive an athletic handbook from their coach or Aliff's office. According to a cover letter included in the handbook, "[t]he following information in this Extracurricular Athletic Handbook must be read, reviewed, and agreed upon by your student athlete."

Included with that handbook was an "El Dorado Union High School District Release of Liability and Assumption of Risk Agreement [for] Athletics & Cheer/ Stunt." Prior to the start of the 2015–2016 football season, Nick and his father signed this form. The release states, "my son . . . may participate in the school-related activities designated above." Someone checked the boxes for baseball and football on the release Read and Nick signed.

The release provides that if Nick "is hurt, injured, or even dies, I/we (i.e., the student, his/her parent/s, guardian/s, heir/s . . .) will not make a claim against or sue the El Dorado Union High School District (hereinafter EDUHSD), its trustees, officers, employees, and agents, or expect them to be responsible or pay for any damages."

* * * *

Read's signature on the release was sufficient to bind Nick to its terms. * * *

Also included with the handbook was a Parent Concussion/Head Injury Information Sheet that described the protocol for removing a student athlete from and then returning the student to practice and/or competition when the student athlete was suspected of sustaining a head injury. The form indicates concussion injuries "can lead to . . . severe brain swelling . . . with devastating and even fatal consequences." Read and Nick signed this form, and dated it the same date as the release.

According to Aliff, the packet with the forms and handbook also included a sheet entitled "Parent Concussion/Head Injury Symptoms & Signs." The form stated concussions could be caused "by a bump, blow, or jolt to the head, or by a blow to another part of the body with the force transmitted to the head."

In his deposition, Nick recalled receiving the handbook at least twice, including once the summer before his sophomore year. Laurie testified she saw a handbook at the beginning of each school year when Nick and his elder brother played sports. She acknowledged her sons would give her the handbook along with forms that needed to be signed, including the one about concussions.

* * * *

Coach Training & Testimony Regarding Lessons Learned

California law reflects an intention that school districts emphasize the importance of training school coaches in "a basic understanding of the signs and symptoms of concussions . . . and the appropriate response to concussions. . . ." (Ed. Code, § 35179.1, subd. (c)(6).) The CIF Bylaws require member schools to "[e]nsure that all coaches, paid and unpaid, will have completed a coaching education program that emphasizes . . . [t]raining: certification in CPR first aid, that includes training in signs and symptoms of concussions. . . ."

Nick's coaches completed concussion training.

On the motion, Nick submitted a copy of what appear to be slides or educational materials used in the training. Both parties cite to these materials to support their statements regarding what coaches learned in training. The introduction to the training indicates "medical researchers have discovered young athletes, especially kids and teens, often don't recognize their own limitations; especially when they have a concussion." "It's your responsibility, as a coach, to help recognize and make the call to pull an athlete off the field, ice, or court if you think that player might have a concussion." * * *

* * * *

During his deposition, Matthew Cathey, head coach of the junior varsity football team, testified that, based on his training, when players were on the field and when he spoke with them he would want to look at the "[e]xpression in their face. . . . The blank look. Speech, I talk to them, they're talking to me, talking back to me. Awareness, where they're at, what's going on. Speed of play. If they're still explosive, still charging the way I'd expect them or have seen them; the way they execute." * * *

* * * *

Game Day Events

Nick suffered the brain injury that is the basis for this suit on August 28, 2015, when the Union Mine junior varsity football team played a non-league game at Union Mine High School. Though the parties did not identify all of the positions Nick played, according to Cathey, Nick played quarterback for some plays during the game. Andrew Middleton, the offensive line coach, believes Nick played some plays as a receiver and running back, and played kickoff on special teams.

* * * *

Nick played every play of the game until sometime in the fourth quarter when he chose to leave the playing field. Based on game footage, Nick's last play appears to have been the 97th out of 100 plays in the game. During the play, Nick was tackled

Case 7.3 Continues

Case 7.3 Continued

by another player, but it does not appear he took a direct blow to the head or that the tackle was particularly forceful. During prior plays, it appears possible Nick took a bump to the head, but none of his tackles or falls appear particularly forceful. Though there is no continuous footage between the plays in evidence, Nick does not appear unbalanced or uncoordinated in any of the game play video. No one approached Nick or performed a close evaluation of him when he sat down after taking himself out of the game.

Five to ten minutes after Nick took himself out of the game, the game ended. During his deposition, Cathey testified that as the players were lining up for a handshake with the other team, he heard a kid slur the word "coach." He turned, and Nick had fallen towards him. Aveni approached Nick to examine him. According to Aveni, Nick was partially conscious and confused. He was perspiring and given "the weather that day," Aveni believed that the heat was an obvious possible cause of Nick's condition. Aveni initially planned to evaluate Nick for heat exhaustion. Aveni poured water over Nick's body and tried to cool him down over his scalp, but he quickly realized Nick could not answer questions. Aveni testified he noticed there "was some cognitive dysfunction. And that the unintentional clonus or movement of his hand, to me, meant immediately that there was something neurologic happening." Aveni announced to the coach and others that there was a neurological issue.

* * * *

Discussion

I

* * * *

II

Nick's Claims Are Barred Because the Browns Expressly Assumed the Risk That He Would Be Injured

The District argues, and the trial court agreed, that the release Nick and his father signed bars Nick's action against the

District due to their express assumption of risk. We agree. The release is a valid express release of liability and assumption of risk that covers both Nick's injury and the actions of the District employees, and Nick cannot establish that the District or its employees acted with gross negligence.

* * * *

B. Express Waivers of Negligence Claims in Recreational Activities Are Permissible

When an individual signs an express waiver of liability, he "promises not to exercise the right to sue for harm caused in the future by the wrongful behavior of a potential defendant, eliminating a remedy for wrongdoing." Similarly, in signing an express assumption of risk, "the potential plaintiff agrees not to expect the potential defendant to act carefully, thus eliminating the potential defendant's duty of care, and acknowledging the possibility of negligent wrongdoing. Both agreements permit behavior that normally would be actionable as tortious, although an express assumption of risk goes further, more clearly authorizing this behavior."

"'In its most basic sense, assumption of risk means that the plaintiff, in advance, has given his *express* consent to relieve the defendant of an obligation of conduct toward him, and to take his chances of injury from a known risk arising from what the defendant is to do or leave undone. . . . *The result is that the defendant is relieved of legal duty to the plaintiff; and being under no duty, he cannot be charged with negligence.*'"

* * * *

C. The Release the Browns Signed Covered Negligent Acts by the District and Its Employees and Nick's Injury

1. The Release Covered Negligent Acts by the District

The release covered negligent acts by the district and its employees.

* * * *

In signing the release, Nick and Read unequivocally agreed to assume the risk of injuries caused by the negligent acts of the District employees in coaching and supervising Nick while he played football and in treating him for those injuries. Additionally, they agreed to release the District and any of its employees from any liability associated with their possible negligence in coaching Nick and/or treating him for injuries.

Nick argues that the release here did not cover the District and his coaches' actions or inactions because "[i]t does not reference the potential for harm by coaches. It mentions nothing about a lack of monitoring, lack of assessment by qualified medical staff, or lack of emergency transport. . . . The terms are so general as to be meaningless; it applies to any school activity whether it be golf or cheerleading."

This misses the mark and mischaracterizes the facts. * * *

The signed release covered all allegedly negligent acts by coaches, and any other employee or volunteer, while they were engaged in "coach[ing], train[ing], instruct[ing], or supervis[ing]" in football. It also applied to negligent acts by coaches, and any other employees or volunteers, involved in diagnosing and/or treating Nick for potential injuries suffered while he was engaged in playing football. If the acts or inactions of district employees at issue here were at worst negligent—if they did not rise to the level of gross negligence—the Browns assumed the risk of those actions and released the District from any liability arising therefrom.

2. The Release Covered Nick's Injury

Nick suggests that he and his parents lacked the knowledge of the risk he would suffer a serious brain injury, and, therefore, the release did not exempt the District from liability associated with that injury. This argument is likewise not persuasive.

* * * *

Case 7.3 Continues

Case 7.3 Continued

Here, the Browns, "acknowledge[d] and willingly assume[d] *all risks and hazards of potential injury,* paralysis, *and death* in the school-related activity/ies," in which Nick participated. ([I]talics added.) One of Nick's own experts declared that, "[w]ell before 2015 it was common knowledge that tackle football causes severe traumatic brain injuries and permanent brain damage."

* * * *

Disposition

The judgment is affirmed.

Legal Reasoning Questions

1. At trial, did Nicholas Brown prevail?
2. What is a release?
3. In the end, did the appellate court rule that Nicholas Brown and his parents had assumed the risk of Nick playing football?

7–4c Product Misuse

Similar to the defense of voluntary assumption of risk is that of **product misuse,** which occurs when a product is used for a purpose for which it was not intended. The courts have severely limited this defense, and it is now recognized as a defense only when the particular use was not foreseeable. If the misuse is reasonably foreseeable, the seller must take measures to guard against it.

■ **Case in Point 7.14** Steven Iliades was injured when he climbed into a press machine without placing it in manual mode, as he had been trained to do. Instead, he relied on a "light curtain," which stops the press when its beam is interrupted by the wave of a hand or arm. Because his body was stuck, Iliades could not engage the light curtain.

A trial court dismissed Iliades' product liability lawsuit against the press machine's manufacturer, on the grounds that it was not reasonably foreseeable that an employee would disregard safety precautions to such an extreme degree. The Michigan Supreme Court eventually ordered a new trial, with instructions that the lower court focus not only on Iliades's misuse of the press machine, but also on whether such misuse, no matter how egregious, was reasonably foreseeable by the manufacturer.[19] ■

7–4d Comparative Negligence (Fault)

Comparative negligence, or fault, can also affect strict liability claims. Today, courts in many jurisdictions consider the negligent or intentional actions of both the plaintiff and the defendant when apportioning liability and damages. A defendant may be able to limit some of its liability if it can show that the plaintiff's misuse of the product contributed to the resulting injuries.

When proved, comparative negligence differs from other defenses in that it does not completely absolve the defendant of liability. It can, however, reduce the total amount of damages that will be awarded to the plaintiff. Note that some jurisdictions allow only intentional conduct to affect a plaintiff's recovery, whereas other states allow ordinary negligence to be used as a defense to product liability.

7–4e Commonly Known Dangers

The dangers associated with certain products (such as matches and sharp knives) are so commonly known that, as mentioned, manufacturers need not warn users of those dangers. If a defendant succeeds in convincing the court that a plaintiff's injury resulted from a commonly known danger, the defendant will not be liable.

■ **Case in Point 7.15** In a classic example, Marguerite Jamieson was injured when an elastic exercise rope slipped off her foot and struck her in the eye, causing a detachment of the retina. Jamieson claimed that the manufacturer should be liable because it had failed to warn users that the exerciser might slip off a foot in such a manner.

The court stated that to hold the manufacturer liable in these circumstances "would go beyond the reasonable dictates of justice in fixing the liabilities of manufacturers." After all, stated the court, "almost every physical object can be inherently dangerous or potentially dangerous in a sense. . . . A manufacturer cannot manufacture a knife that will not cut or a hammer that will not mash a thumb or a stove that will not burn a finger. The law does not require [manufacturers] to warn of such common dangers."[20] ■

7–4f Knowledgeable User

A related defense is the knowledgeable user defense. If a particular danger (such as electrical shock) is or should be commonly known by particular users of a product (such

19. *Iliades v. Dieffenbacher North America, Inc.,* 915 N.W.2d 338, 501 Mich. 326 (2018).

20. *Jamieson v. Woodward & Lothrop,* 247 F.2d 23 (D.C.Cir. 1957).

as electricians), the manufacturer need not warn these users of the danger.

■ **Case in Point 7.16** The parents of teenagers who had become overweight and developed health problems filed a product liability suit against McDonald's. The plaintiffs claimed that the fast-food chain had failed to warn customers of the adverse health effects of eating its food. The court rejected this claim, however, based on the knowledgeable user defense.

The court found that it is well known that the food at McDonald's contains high levels of cholesterol, fat, salt, and sugar and is therefore unhealthful. The court stated: "If consumers know (or reasonably should know) the potential ill health effects of eating at McDonald's, they cannot blame McDonald's if they, nonetheless, choose to satiate their appetite with a surfeit [excess] of supersized McDonald's products."[21] ■

21. *Pelman v. McDonald's Corp.*, 237 F.Supp.2d 512 (S.D.N.Y. 2003). See also *Brodie v. Green Spot Foods, LLC,* 503 F.Supp.3d 1 (S.D.NY 2020).

7–4g Statutes of Limitations and Repose

Statutes of limitations restrict the time within which an action may be brought. The statute of limitations for product liability cases varies according to state law. Usually, the injured party must bring a product liability claim within two to four years. Often, the running of the prescribed period is **tolled** (that is, suspended) until the party suffering an injury has discovered it or should have discovered it.

To ensure that sellers and manufacturers will not be left vulnerable to lawsuits indefinitely, many states have passed **statutes of repose,** which place outer time limits on product liability actions. For instance, a statute of repose may require that claims be brought within twelve years from the date of sale or manufacture of the defective product. If the plaintiff does not bring an action before the prescribed period expires, the seller cannot be held liable.

Concept Summary 7.1 reviews the possible defenses in product liability actions.

Concept Summary 7.1

Defenses to Product Liability

Preemption	The product is subject to comprehensive federal safety regulations.
Assumption of Risk	The user or consumer knew the risk and voluntarily assumed it.
Product Misuse	The consumer misused the product in an unforeseeable way.
Comparative Negligence	The court apportions liability if the defendant was also negligent.
Commonly Known Dangers	The product is commonly known to be dangerous.
Knowledgeable User	The particular danger is commonly known by particular users of the product.
Statutory Time Periods	The statute of limitations or statute of repose period has expired.

Practice and Review: Strict Liability and Product Liability

Shalene Kolchek bought a Great Lakes Spa from Val Porter, a dealer who was selling spas at the state fair. Kolchek signed an installment contract. Porter then handed her the manufacturer's paperwork and arranged for the spa to be delivered and installed for her. Three months later, Kolchek left her six-year-old daughter, Litisha, alone in the spa. While exploring the spa's hydromassage jets, Litisha stuck her index finger into one of the jet holes and was unable to remove her finger from the jet.

Litisha yanked hard, injuring her finger, then panicked and screamed for help. Kolchek was unable to remove Litisha's finger, and the local police and rescue team were called to assist. After a three-hour operation that included draining the spa, sawing out a section of the spa's plastic molding, and slicing the jet casing, Litisha's finger was freed. Following this procedure, the spa was no longer functional. Litisha was taken to the local emergency room, where she was told that a bone in her finger was broken in two places. Using the information presented in the chapter, answer the following questions.

1. Under which theories of product liability can Kolchek sue Porter to recover for Litisha's injuries?
2. Would privity of contract be required for Kolchek to succeed in a product liability action against Great Lakes? Explain.
3. For an action in strict product liability against Great Lakes, what six requirements must Kolchek meet?
4. What defenses to product liability might Porter or Great Lakes be able to assert?

Debate This . . . All liability suits against tobacco companies for lung cancer should be thrown out of court now and forever.

Terms and Concepts

market-share liability 142	product misuse 146	tolled 147
privity of contract 134	statutes of repose 147	unreasonably dangerous
product liability 133	strict liability 133	product 137

Issue Spotters

1. Rim Corporation makes tire rims that it sells to Superior Vehicles, Inc., which installs them on cars. One set of rims is defective, which an inspection would reveal. Superior does not inspect the rims. The car with the defective rims is sold to Town Auto Sales, which sells the car to Uri. Soon, the car is in an accident caused by the defective rims, and Uri is injured. Is Superior Vehicles liable? Explain your answer. (See *Strict Product Liability*.)

2. Bensing Company manufactures generic drugs for the treatment of heart disease. A federal law requires generic drug makers to use labels that are identical to the labels on brand-name versions of the drugs. Tamina purchased Bensing's generic drugs in Ohio and wants to sue Bensing for defective labeling based on its failure to comply with Ohio state common law (rather than the federal labeling requirements). What defense might Bensing assert to avoid liability under state law? (See *Defenses to Product Liability*.)

• **Check your answers to the Issue Spotters against the answers provided in Appendix B at the end of this text.**

Business Scenarios and Case Problems

7–1. Strict Liability. Ronnell and Marion were injured when part of a fireworks display went astray and exploded near them. They sued Pyrodyne Corp., the pyrotechnic company that was hired to set up and discharge the fireworks. Ronnell and Marion alleged, among other things, that the company should be strictly liable for damages caused by the fireworks display. Will the court agree with Ronnell and Marion? What factors will the court consider in making its decision? Discuss fully. (See *Strict Liability*.)

7–2. Product Liability. Laken, an experienced hunter, bought a paintball gun. Laken practiced with the gun and knew how to screw in the carbon dioxide cartridge, pump the gun, and use its safety and trigger. Although Laken was aware that he could purchase protective eyewear, he chose not to buy it. Laken had taken gun safety courses and understood that it was "common sense" not to shoot anyone in the face. Laken's friend, Camila, also owned a paintball gun and was similarly familiar with the gun's use and its risks.

Laken, Camila, and their friends played a game that involved shooting paintballs at cars whose occupants also had the guns. One night, while Laken and Camila were cruising with their guns, Camila shot at Laken's car, but hit Laken in the eye. Laken filed a product liability lawsuit against the manufacturer of Camila's paintball gun to recover for the injury. Laken claimed that the gun was defectively designed. During the trial, Camila testified that her gun "never malfunctioned." In whose favor should the court rule? Why? (See *Product Liability.*)

7–3. Product Misuse. Five-year-old Cheyenne Stark was riding in the backseat of her parents' Ford Taurus. Cheyenne was not sitting in a booster seat. Instead, she was using a seatbelt designed by Ford, but was wearing the shoulder belt behind her back. The car was involved in a collision. As a result, Cheyenne suffered a spinal cord injury and was paralyzed from the waist down. The family filed a suit against Ford Motor Co., alleging that the seatbelt was defectively designed. Could Ford successfully claim that Cheyenne had misused the seatbelt? Why or why not? [*Stark v. Ford Motor Co.,* 365 N.C. 468, 723 S.E.2d 753 (2012)] (See *Defenses to Product Liability.*)

7–4. Business Case Problem with Sample Answer— Product Liability. While driving on Interstate 40 in North Carolina, Carroll Jett became distracted by a texting system in the cab of his tractor-trailer truck. He smashed into several vehicles that were slowed or stopped in front of him, injuring Barbara and Michael Durkee and others. The injured motorists filed a suit in a federal district court against Geologic Solutions, Inc., the maker of the texting system, alleging product liability. Was the accident caused by Jett's inattention or the texting device? Should a manufacturer be required to design a product that is incapable of distracting a driver? Discuss. [*Durkee v. Geologic Solutions, Inc.,* 502 Fed.Appx. 326 (4th Cir. 2013)] (See *Product Liability.*)

- For a sample answer to Problem 7–4, go to Appendix C at the end of this text.

7–5. Strict Product Liability. Duval Ford, LLC, sold a new Ford F-250 pickup truck to David Sweat. Before taking delivery, Sweat ordered a lift kit to be installed on the truck by a Duval subcontractor. Sweat also replaced the tires and modified the suspension system to increase the towing capacity. Later, through Burkins Chevrolet, Sweat sold

the truck to Shaun Lesnick. Sweat had had no problems with the truck's steering or suspension, but Lesnick did. He had the steering repaired and made additional changes, including installing a steering stabilizer and replacing the tires. Two months later, Lesnick was driving the truck when the steering and suspension suddenly failed, and the truck flipped over, causing Lesnick severe injuries. Could Lesnick successfully claim that Duval and Burkins had failed to warn him of the risk of a lifted truck? Explain. [*Lesnick v. Duval Ford, LLC,* 41 Fla.L.Weekly D281, 185 So.3d 577 (1 Dist. 2016)] (See *Strict Product Liability.*)

7–6. Spotlight on Pfizer, Inc.—Defenses to Product Liability. Prescription drugs in the United States must be approved by the Food and Drug Administration (FDA) before they can be sold. A drug maker whose product is approved through the FDA's "abbreviated new drug application" (ANDA) process cannot later change the label without FDA approval. Pfizer, Inc., makes and sells Depo-T, a testosterone replacement drug classified as an ANDA-approved drug. Rodney Guilbeau filed a claim in a federal district court against Pfizer, alleging that he had suffered a "cardiovascular event" after taking Depo-T. He sought recovery based on a state-law product liability theory, arguing that Pfizer had failed to warn patients adequately about the risks. He claimed that after the drug's approval, its maker had become aware of a higher incidence of heart attacks, strokes, and other cardiovascular events among those who took it but had not added a warning to its label. What is Pfizer's best defense to this claim? Explain. [*Guilbeau v. Pfizer, Inc.,* 880 F.3d 304 (7th Cir. 2018)] (See *Defenses to Product Liability.*)

7–7. Product Misuse. Snapchat is a mobile app often called Snap by its users. It developed a feature called Speed Filter, which can record the speed of a train, plane, or automobile on a smartphone. Crystal McGee crashed her car into the back of Wentworth Maynard's car while driving 107 miles per hour. McGee told her three passengers right before the crash that she was "just trying to get the car to 100 miles per hour to post it on Snapchat" using Snapchat's Speed Filter. Wentworth Maynard suffered severe injuries. His wife, Karen Maynard, sued McGee and Snapchat, alleging that the company had negligently designed Snapchat Speed Filter. The Maynards alleged that Snapchat had designed its product to "encourage" dangerous behaviors that could be "reasonably foreseen." Snapchat answered the complaint by attaching copies of its Terms of Use and a pop-up warning, both of which stated that the app user agreed not to use Snapchat for any illegal or unauthorized purpose. The warning clearly stated "please, DO NOT Snap and drive." The trial court dismissed the case. An intermediate court reversed, but on remand, the trial court again dismissed the case by stating that Snapchat did not have a duty that would support a negligence claim. An intermediate court affirmed. The Supreme Court of Georgia heard the case. One of its main questions was whether the manufacturer (Snapchat) used reasonable care to reduce foreseeable risk of harm when selecting from alternative designs for its product. Should Snapchat be liable even if Crystal McGee misused the product? Should Snapchat have anticipated this misuse and changed its design accordingly? [*Maynard et al. v. Snapchat, Inc.,* 313 Ga. 533, 870 S.E.2d 379 (S.Ct.GA 2022)] (See *Defenses to Product Liability.*)

7–8. A Question of Ethics—The IDDR Approach and Product Liability. While replacing screws in a gutter, John Baugh fell off a ladder and landed headfirst on his concrete driveway. He sustained a severe brain injury, which permanently limited his ability to perform routine physical and intellectual functions. He filed a suit in a federal district court against Cuprum S.A. de C.V., the company that designed and made the ladder, alleging a design defect under product liability theories. Baugh weighed nearly 200 pounds, which was the stated weight limit on this ladder. Kevin Smith, a mechanical engineer, testified on Baugh's behalf that the gusset (bracket) on the ladder's right front side was too short to support Baugh's

weight. This caused the ladder's leg to fail and Baugh to fall. In Smith's opinion, a longer gusset would have prevented the accident. Cuprum argued that the accident occurred because Baugh climbed too high on the ladder and stood on its fourth step and pail shelf, neither of which were intended for the purpose. No other person witnessed Baugh using the ladder prior to his fall, however, so there was no evidence to support Cuprum's argument. [*Baugh v. Cuprum S.A. de C.V.,* 845 F.3d 838 (7th Cir. 2017)] (See *Strict Product Liability.*)

(a) What is a manufacturer's legal and ethical duty when designing and making products for consumers? Did Cuprum meet this standard? Discuss.

(b) Did the mechanical engineer's testimony establish that a reasonable alternative design was available for Cuprum's ladder? Explain.

Time-Limited Group Assignment

7–9. Product Liability. Bret D'Auguste was an experienced skier when he rented equipment to ski at Hunter Mountain Ski Bowl in New York. When D'Auguste entered an extremely difficult trail, he noticed immediately that the surface consisted of ice with almost no snow. He tried to exit the steeply declining trail by making a sharp right turn, but in the attempt, his left ski snapped off. D'Auguste lost his balance, fell, and slid down the mountain, striking his face and head against a fence along the trail. According to a report by a rental shop employee, one of the bindings on D'Auguste's skis had a "cracked heel housing." D'Auguste filed a lawsuit against the bindings' manufacturer on a theory of strict product liability. The manufacturer filed a motion for summary judgment. (See *Product Liability.*)

(a) The first group will take the position of the manufacturer and develop an argument for why the court should *grant* the summary judgment motion and dismiss the strict product liability claim.

(b) The second group will take the position of D'Auguste and formulate a basis for why the court should *deny* the motion and allow the strict product liability claim.

(c) The third group will evaluate whether D'Auguste assumed the risk of this type of injury.

(d) The fourth group will analyze whether the manufacturer could claim that D'Auguste's negligence (under the comparative negligence doctrine) contributed to his injury.

Chapter 8

Intellectual Property Rights

Intellectual property is any property that results from intellectual, creative processes—the products of an individual's mind. Although it is an abstract term for an abstract concept, intellectual property is nonetheless familiar to almost everyone. The apps for your iPhone, iPad, or Samsung Galaxy, the streaming series you watch, and the music you listen to are all forms of intellectual property.

More than two hundred years ago, the framers of the U.S. Constitution recognized the importance of protecting creative works in Article I, Section 8. Statutory protection of these rights began in the 1940s and continues to evolve to meet the needs of modern society.

Suppose that JD Beverage Company makes and sells a line of flavored vodkas called "Hot Lips Vodka." The name Hot Lips Vodka, along with an image of puckered lips, appears on the label of each bottle. The color of the lips logo depends on the vodka's flavor—red for chili pepper, green for apple, and so on. JD Beverage has registered trademarks for the name Hot Lips Vodka and the puckered lips logo, and the company heavily markets the vodka using hot lips as a theme. Sales of Hot Lips Vodka are at an all-time high.

Now another alcoholic beverage company begins to distribute a line of flavored vodkas called "Kiss Vodka." Like the Hot Lips label, the new vodka's label features the product's name and a puckered lips logo, and the company uses the lips in its marketing. JD Beverage believes that Kiss Vodka's use of the lips logo is diminishing the value of its Hot Lips brand and cutting into its sales. What can JD Beverage do? The answer lies in intellectual property law.

8–1 Trademarks and Related Property

A **trademark** is a distinctive mark, motto, device, or implement that a manufacturer stamps, prints, or otherwise affixes to the goods it produces so that they can be identified on the market and their origins made known. In other words, a trademark is a source indicator. At common law, the person who used a symbol or mark to identify a business or product was protected in the use of that trademark. Clearly, by using another's trademark, a business could lead consumers to believe that its goods were made by the other business. The law seeks to avoid this kind of confusion. (For information on how companies use trademarks and service marks, see this chapter's Managerial Strategy feature.)

Managerial Strategy — Trademarks and Service Marks

Trademarks and service marks consist of much more than well-known brand names, such as Apple and Amazon. (A service mark, as discussed later, is essentially a trademark used to identify services, such as banking or health care services, rather than products.) If you become a marketing manager, you will be involved in creating trademarks or service marks for your firm, protecting the firm's existing marks, and ensuring that you do not infringe on anyone else's marks. You will need to be aware that parts of a brand name or other forms of product identification may qualify for trademark protection. Some examples include:

1. **Catchy phrases**—Certain brands have established phrases that are associated with the brands, such as Nike's "Just Do It!" Take care to avoid using another brand's catchy phrase in your own program. Note, too, that not all phrases can become part of a trademark or service mark. When

Continues

a phrase is extremely common, the courts normally will not grant it trademark or service mark protection.

2. **Abbreviations**—The public sometimes abbreviates a well-known trademark. For instance, Budweiser beer is known as Bud and Coca-Cola as Coke.

3. **Shapes**—The shape of a brand name, a service mark, or a container can take on exclusivity if the shape clearly aids in product or service identification. Avoid using a similar shape for competing products.

4. **Ornamental colors**—Sometimes, color combinations can become part of a service mark or trademark. For example, FedEx established its unique identity with the use of bright orange and purple. The courts have protected this color combination.

5. **Ornamental designs**—Symbols and designs associated with a particular mark are normally protected, so do not attempt to copy them. For instance, Levi's places a small tag on the left side of the rear pocket of its jeans.

6. **Sounds**—Sounds can also be protected. For example, the familiar roar of the Metro-Goldwyn-Mayer (MGM) lion is protected.

When to Protect Trademarks and Service Marks

Once your company has established trademarks or service marks, it must decide how aggressively to protect those marks. If it fails to protect them, it faces the possibility that the marks will become generic. Aspirin, cellophane, thermos, dry ice, shredded wheat, and many other familiar terms were once legally protected trademarks.

Protecting exclusive rights to a mark can be expensive, however, and a company must determine how much it is worth to protect its rights. Major expenditures to protect a small company's trademarks or service marks might not be cost-effective.

Business Questions

1. The U.S. Patent and Trademark Office requires that a registered trademark or service mark be put into commercial use within six months. Extensions can be granted, but the mark must be put into commercial use within three years after the application has been approved. Why do you think the federal government established this requirement?

2. Should trademark protection apply to similarities between noncompeting products? Why or why not?

In the following classic case, the defendants argued that the Coca-Cola trademark was entitled to no protection under the law because the term did not accurately represent the product.

Classic Case 8.1

The Coca-Cola Co. v. The Koke Co. of America

Supreme Court of the United States, 254 U.S. 143, 41 S.Ct. 113, 65 L.Ed. 189 (1920).

Background and Facts John Pemberton, an Atlanta pharmacist, invented a caramel-colored, carbonated soft drink in 1886. His bookkeeper, Frank Robinson, named the beverage Coca-Cola after two of the ingredients, coca leaves and kola nuts. Asa Candler bought the Coca-Cola Company in 1891, and within seven years, he had made the soft drink available throughout the United States, as well as in parts of Canada and Mexico. Candler continued to sell Coke aggressively and to open up new markets, reaching Europe before 1910. In doing so, however, he attracted numerous competitors, some of which tried to capitalize directly on the Coke name.

The Coca-Cola Company sought to enjoin (prevent) the Koke Company of America and other beverage companies from, among other things, using the word *Koke* for their products. The Koke Company of America and other beverage companies contended that the Coca-Cola trademark was a fraudulent representation and that Coca-Cola was therefore not entitled to any help from the courts. The Koke Company and the other defendants alleged that the Coca-Cola Company, by its use of the Coca-Cola name, represented that the beverage contained cocaine (from coca leaves), which it no longer did. The trial court granted the injunction against the Koke Company, but the appellate court reversed the lower court's ruling. Coca-Cola then appealed to the United States Supreme Court.

In the Language of the Court

Mr. Justice HOLMES delivered the opinion of the Court.
     * * * *

     * * * Before 1900 the beginning of [Coca-Cola's] good will was more or less helped by the presence of cocaine, a drug that, like alcohol or caffeine or opium, may be described as a deadly poison or as a valuable [pharmaceutical item, depending on the speaker's purposes]. The amount seems to have been very small,[a] but it may have been enough to begin a bad habit and after the Food and Drug Act of June 30, 1906, if not earlier, long before this suit was brought, it was eliminated from the plaintiff's compound.

     * * * Since 1900 the sales have increased at a very great rate corresponding to a like increase in advertising. The name now characterizes a beverage to be had at almost any soda fountain. It means a single thing coming from a single source, and well known to the community. It hardly would be too much to say that the drink characterizes the name as much as the name the drink. In other words, Coca-Cola probably means to most persons the plaintiff's familiar product to be had everywhere rather than a compound of particular substances. * * * Before this suit was brought the plaintiff had advertised to the public that it must not expect and would not find cocaine, and had eliminated everything tending to suggest cocaine effects except the name and the picture of [coca] leaves and nuts, which probably conveyed little or nothing to most who saw it. It appears to us that it would be going too far to deny the plaintiff relief against a palpable [readily evident] fraud because possibly here and there an ignorant person might call for the drink with the hope for incipient cocaine intoxication. The plaintiff's position must be judged by the facts as they were when the suit was begun, not by the facts of a different condition and an earlier time.

Decision and Remedy The district court's injunction was allowed to stand. The competing beverage companies were enjoined from calling their products Koke.

Critical Thinking

- **What If the Facts Were Different?** Suppose that Coca-Cola had been trying to make the public believe that its product contained cocaine. Would the result in this case likely have been different? Why or why not?
- **Impact of This Case on Today's Law** In this early case, the United States Supreme Court made it clear that trademarks and trade names (and nicknames for those marks and names, such as the nickname "Coke" for "Coca-Cola") that are in common use receive protection under the common law. This holding is historically significant because it is the predecessor to the federal statute later passed to protect trademark rights—the Lanham Act of 1946. In many ways, this act represented a codification of common law principles governing trademarks.

a. In reality, until 1903 the amount of active cocaine in each bottle of Coke was equivalent to one "line" of cocaine.

8–1a Statutory Protection of Trademarks

Statutory protection of trademarks and related property is provided at the federal level by the Lanham Act of 1946.[1] The Lanham Act was enacted, in part, to protect manufacturers from losing business to rival companies that used confusingly similar trademarks. The act incorporates the common law of trademarks and provides remedies for owners of trademarks who wish to enforce their claims in federal court. Many states also have trademark statutes.

Trademark Dilution In 1995, Congress amended the Lanham Act by passing the Federal Trademark Dilution Act,[2] which allowed trademark owners to bring suits in federal court for trademark **dilution**. In 2006, Congress further amended the law on trademark dilution by passing the Trademark Dilution Revision Act (TDRA).[3]

1. 15 U.S.C. Sections 1051–1128.

2. 15 U.S.C. Section 1125.
3. Pub. L. No. 103-312, 120 Stat. 1730 (2006).

Under the TDRA, to state a claim for trademark dilution, a plaintiff must prove the following:

1. The plaintiff owns a famous mark that is distinctive.
2. The defendant has begun using a mark in commerce that allegedly is diluting the famous mark.
3. The similarity between the defendant's mark and the famous mark gives rise to an association between the marks.
4. The association is likely to impair the distinctiveness of the famous mark or harm its reputation.

Trademark dilution laws protect "distinctive" or "famous" trademarks (such as Rolls Royce, McDonald's, Starbucks, and Apple) from certain unauthorized uses. Such a mark is protected even when it is used on noncompeting goods or is unlikely to cause confusion. More than half of the states have also enacted trademark dilution laws.

Marks Need Not Be Identical Note that a famous mark may be diluted by the use of an identical mark or by the use of a similar mark.[4] A similar mark is more likely to lessen the value of a famous mark when the companies using the marks provide related goods or compete against each other in the same market.

■ **Case in Point 8.1** Samantha Lundberg opened a coffee shop under the name "Sambuck's Coffee" in Astoria, Oregon, even though she knew that "Starbucks" was one of the largest coffee chains in the nation. Starbucks Corporation filed a dilution lawsuit, and a federal court ruled that use of the "Sambuck's" mark constituted trademark dilution. Not only was there a "high degree" of similarity between the marks, but also both companies provided coffee-related services and marketed their services through stand-alone retail stores. Therefore, the use of the similar mark (Sambuck's) reduced the value of the famous mark (Starbucks).[5] ■

8-1b Trademark Registration

Trademarks may be registered with the state or with the federal government. To register for protection under federal trademark law, a person must file an application with the U.S. Patent and Trademark Office in Washington, D.C. Under current law, a mark can be registered (1) if it is currently in commerce or (2) if the applicant intends to put it into commerce within six months.

4. *See Moseley v. V Secret Catalogue, Inc.*, 537 U.S. 418, 123 S.Ct. 1115, 155 L.Ed.2d 1 (2003). See also *United States Trademark Holdings, Inc. v. Disney Enterprises, Inc.*, 2022 WL 558247 (Fed.Cir. 2022).
5. *Starbucks Corp. v. Lundberg*, 2005 WL 3183858 (D.Or. 2005). See also *Starbucks Corporation v. Heller*, __ F.Supp.3d __, 2014 WL 6685662 (C.D. CA 2014).

In special circumstances, the six-month period can be extended by thirty months. Thus, the applicant would have a total of three years from the date of notice of trademark approval to make use of the mark and file the required use statement. Registration is postponed until the mark is actually used. During this waiting period, any applicant can legally protect a trademark against a third party who previously has neither used the mark nor filed an application for it.

Registration is renewable between the fifth and sixth years after the initial registration and every ten years thereafter (every twenty years for trademarks registered before 1990).

8-1c Trademark Infringement

Registration of a trademark with the U.S. Patent and Trademark Office gives notice on a nationwide basis that the trademark belongs exclusively to the registrant. The registrant is also allowed to use the symbol ® to indicate that the mark has been registered. Whenever that trademark is copied to a substantial degree or used in its entirety by another, intentionally or unintentionally, the trademark has been infringed (used without authorization).

When a trademark has been infringed, the owner of the mark has a cause of action against the infringer. To succeed in a trademark infringement action, the owner must show that the defendant's use of the mark created a likelihood of confusion about the origin of the defendant's goods or services. The owner need not prove that the infringer acted intentionally or that the trademark was registered (although registration does provide proof of the date of inception of the trademark's use).

The most commonly granted remedy for trademark infringement is an injunction to prevent further infringement. Under the Lanham Act, a trademark owner that successfully proves infringement can recover actual damages, plus the profits that the infringer wrongfully received from the unauthorized use of the mark. A court can also order the destruction of any goods bearing the unauthorized trademark. In some situations, the trademark owner may also be able to recover attorneys' fees.

8-1d Distinctiveness of the Mark

A trademark must be sufficiently distinctive to enable consumers to identify the manufacturer of the goods easily and to distinguish between those goods and competing products.

Strong Marks Fanciful, arbitrary, or suggestive trademarks are generally considered to be the most distinctive (strongest) trademarks. These marks receive automatic protection because they serve to identify a particular product's source, as opposed to describing the product itself.

Fanciful and Arbitrary Trademarks. Fanciful trademarks use invented words, such as "Xerox" for one manufacturer's copiers and "Google" for a search engine. Arbitrary trademarks use common words in an uncommon way that is not descriptive of the product, such as "Dutch Boy" as a name for paint.

Even a single letter used in a particular style can be an arbitrary trademark. ■ **Case in Point 8.2** Sports entertainment company ESPN sued Quiksilver, Inc., a maker of youth-oriented clothing, alleging trademark infringement. ESPN claimed that Quiksilver's clothing used the stylized "X" mark that ESPN uses in connection with the X Games ("extreme" sports competitions).

Quiksilver filed counterclaims for trademark infringement and dilution, arguing that it had a long history of using the stylized X on its products. ESPN asked the court to dismiss Quiksilver's counterclaims, but the court refused, holding that the X on Quiksilver's clothing is clearly an arbitrary mark. The court found that the two Xs are "similar enough that a consumer might well confuse them." Therefore, Quiksilver could continue its claim for trademark infringement.[6] ■

Suggestive Trademarks. Suggestive trademarks indicate something about a product's nature, quality, or characteristics, without describing the product directly. These marks require imagination on the part of the consumer to identify the characteristic. "Dairy Queen," for instance, suggests an association between its products and milk, but it does not directly describe ice cream. A suggestive mark can be transformed into a strong mark if it achieves a high degree of marketplace recognition, such as through substantial advertising.

Secondary Meaning Descriptive terms, geographic terms, and personal names are not inherently distinctive and do not receive protection under the law until they acquire a secondary meaning. A secondary meaning may arise when customers begin to associate a specific term or phrase (such as Calvin Klein) with specific trademarked items (designer clothing and goods) made by a particular company. Whether a secondary meaning becomes attached to a name usually depends on how extensively

the product is advertised, the market for the product, the number of sales, and other factors.

Once a secondary meaning is attached to a term or name, the trademark is considered distinctive and is protected. Even a color can qualify for trademark protection, as did the color schemes used by some state university sports teams, including The Ohio State University and Louisiana State University.[7]

■ **Case in Point 8.3** Federal Express Corporation (FedEx) provides transportation and delivery services worldwide using the logo FedEx in a specific color combination. FedEx sued a competitor, JetEx Management Services, Inc., for using the same color combination and a similar name and logo. JetEx also mimicked FedEx's trademarked slogan ("The World on Time" for FedEx and "Keeping the World on Time" for JetEx). FedEx alleged trademark infringement and dilution, among other claims. A federal district court in New York granted a permanent injunction to block JetEx from using the infringing mark in FedEx colors. When JetEx (now called JetEx Air Express) continued to use the infringing mark on its vehicles, FedEx went back to court to enforce the injunction and was awarded attorneys' fees and costs.[8] ■

Generic Terms Generic terms that refer to an entire class of products, such as "bicycle" and "computer", receive no protection, even if they acquire secondary meanings. A particularly thorny problem arises when a trademark acquires generic use. For instance, aspirin and thermos were originally the names of trademarked products, but today the words are used generically. Other trademarks that have acquired generic use are escalator, trampoline, raisin bran, dry ice, lanolin, linoleum, nylon, and cornflakes.

A trademark does not become generic simply because it is commonly used, however. ■ **Case in Point 8.4** David Elliot and Chris Gillespie sought to register numerous domain names (internet addresses), including "google-disney.com" and "googlenewstvs.com." They were unable to register the names because all of them used the word "google," a trademark of Google, Inc.

Elliot and Gillespie brought an action in federal court to have the Google trademark cancelled because it had become a generic term. They argued that because most people now use "google" as a verb ("to google") when

---

6. *ESPN, Inc. v. Quiksilver, Inc.*, 586 F.Supp.2d 219 (S.D.N.Y. 2008). See also *E. Rémy Martin & Co. v. Sire Spirits LLC*, 2022 WL 94882 (S.D. NY 2022).

7. *Board of Supervisors of Louisiana State University v. Smack Apparel Co.*, 438 F.Supp.2d 653 (E.D.La. 2006). See also *Abraham v. Alpha Chi Omega*, 781 F.Supp.2d 396 (N.D.Tex. 2011).

8. *Federal Express Corp. v. JetEx Air Express, Inc.*, 2017 WL 816479 (E.D.N.Y. 2017). See also *American Automobile Association v. AAA Logistics, Inc.*, 2019 WL 1349283 (W.D.NY 2019).

referring to searching the internet with any search engine (not just Google), the term should no longer be protected. The court held that even if people do use the word "google" as a verb, it is still a protected trademark if consumers associate the noun with one company. The court concluded that "the primary significance of the word "google" to a majority of the public who utilize internet search engines is a designation of the Google search engine."[9] ∎

---

9. *Elliot v. Google, Inc.*, 45 F.Supp.3d 1156 (D.Ariz. 2014). See also *Beyond Blond Productions, LLC v. Heldman*, 2022 WL 803392 (C.D.CA 2022).

8–1e Service, Certification, and Collective Marks

A **service mark** is essentially a trademark that is used to distinguish the services (rather than the products) of one person or company from those of another. For instance, each airline has a particular mark or symbol associated with its name. Titles and character names used in radio and television are frequently registered as service marks. The following case concerns an internet domain name and whether part of it can be viewed as a service mark.

Case Analysis 8.2

In Re Vox Populi Registry LTD
United States Court of Appeals, Federal Circuit, 25 F.4th 1348 (2022).

In the Language of the Court
DYK, CIRCUIT JUDGE.
* * * *

Background

Vox is the domain registry operator for the .SUCKS generic top-level domain (gTLD) for Internet websites. [Generic domain names include .com, .net., and .org.] A registry operator "maintains the master database of all domain names registered in each top-level domain, and also generates the 'zone file,' which allows computers to route Internet traffic to and from top-level domains anywhere in the world." * * *

Vox filed two trademark applications relevant to this case. U.S. Trademark Application Serial No. 86/700,941 ("the '941 application") sought registration on the Principal Register of the standard character mark .SUCKS in Class 42 (computer and scientific services) for "[d]omain registry operator services related to the gTLD in the mark" and in Class 45 (personal and legal services) for "[d]omain name registration services featuring the gTLD in the mark" as well as "registration of domain names for identification of users on a global computer network featuring the gTLD in the mark."

The '215 application sought to register the stylized form of .SUCKS in Class 42 for "domain registry operator

services related to the gTLD in the mark." The examining attorney refused both trademark applications "on the ground that, when used in connection with the identified services, each fails to function as a mark." With respect to the '215 application, the examining attorney determined that Vox's "submitted evidence does not establish that the mark functions as a source identifier." Vox appealed these refusals to the Board.

In affirming the refusal of the '941 application, the Board concluded that the standard character mark .SUCKS "will not be perceived as a source identifier" and instead "will be perceived merely as one of many gTLDs that are used in domain names." Turning to the '215 application, the Board incorporated the reasoning with respect to the '941 application, finding "[f]or the reasons given, * * * and based on the record before us, we do not find the literal element of this mark, .SUCKS, would be perceived as source-identifying." The Board further concluded that "the stylized lettering or design element in the mark does not create a separate commercial impression and is not sufficiently distinctive to 'carry' the overall mark into registrability."

Vox appeals the Board's decision only with respect to the '215 application involving the stylized form of .SUCKS,

which appears as a "'retro,' pixelated font that resembles how letters were displayed on early LED screens." * * *

Discussion

I

Under the Lanham Act, "[n]o [service mark] by which the [services] of the applicant may be distinguished from the [services] of others shall be refused registration on the principal register on account of its nature" subject to certain exceptions. One of these exceptions is that a service mark must function to "identify and distinguish the services of one person . . . from the services of others and to indicate the source of the services." A mark that is, for example, generic or descriptive, fails to function as a source identifier, though descriptive marks can be registered if they have acquired secondary meaning in the perception of consumers.

The question whether a proposed mark is a source identifier typically arises before us in the context of whether the proposed mark is descriptive * * * Our predecessor court recognized that the source identifier and descriptiveness inquiries are "complementary and opposite sides of the same coin to the extent that a mark . . . is 'merely descriptive' of the goods." * * *
* * * *

II

Vox does not appeal the rejection of the standard character mark .SUCKS in the '941 application. Nonetheless, Vox spends much of its opening brief arguing that "even if. . . we disregard the distinctive design elements in the [stylized form of .SUCKS], . . . the evidence of record establishes that the mark still functions as a service mark and is entitled to registration." * * * We conclude that the Board did not err in finding the standard character mark not registrable, and we need not reach the question whether Vox's claim with respect to the standard character mark is barred by the doctrine of administrative preclusion.

Substantial evidence supports the Board's finding that "consumers will view [the standard character mark .SUCKS] as only a non-source identifying part of a domain name, rather than as a mark." * * *

Vox relies on a declaration by its COO [chief operating officer] stating that Vox "has spent substantial sums in the advertising and promotion of its services under the .SUCKS brand (irrespective of design format)," and referencing sample advertising and marketing materials using the stylized form of .SUCKS in the context of trade shows. The declaration states that "[a]s evidence of its successful branding, [Vox] has experienced double-digit growth in domain registrations year-over-year since the domain debuted in 2015." Advertising and sales volumes, while relevant, are not by themselves dispositive of how consumers perceive a mark. The Board found that "[a]lthough this type of evidence helps show [Vox's] intention to present the [stylized form of .SUCKS] in manners that are customary for service marks, this does not mean that consumers will perceive it as such," and additionally determined that "the evidence showing that consumers will perceive .SUCKS as merely a gTLD outweighs [Vox's] attempts to depict it as a source identifier."
* * * *

We cannot conclude that the Board's weighing of the evidence was unreasonable. Where the Board has reasonably weighed the evidence, it is not the role of this court to reweigh evidence to reach a different conclusion, and we do not do so here.
* * * *

Conclusion

The Board's decision affirming the refusal of the '215 application is affirmed.

Affirmed

Legal Reasoning Questions

1. What is the difference between a trademark and a service mark?

2. What was the plaintiff trying to accomplish in this lawsuit?

3. The trademark application was refused because ".SUCKS" would not be perceived as a source identifier. What does that mean?

Other marks protected by law include certification marks and collective marks. A **certification mark** is used by one or more persons, other than the owner, to certify the region, materials, mode of manufacture, quality, or other characteristic of specific goods or services. Certification marks include "Good Housekeeping Seal of Approval" and "UL Tested."

When used by members of a cooperative, association, or other organization, a certification mark is referred to as a **collective mark.** ■ **Example 8.5** Collective marks appear at the ends of motion picture credits to indicate the various associations and organizations that participated in the making of the films. The union marks found on the tags of certain products are also collective marks. ■

8–1f Trade Dress

The term **trade dress** refers to the image and overall appearance of a product. Trade dress is a broad concept that can include either all or part of the total image or overall impression created by a product or its packaging.

■ **Example 8.6** The distinctive decor, menu, layout, and style of service of a particular restaurant may be regarded as trade dress. Trade dress can also include the layout and appearance of a catalogue, the use of a lighthouse as part of the design of a golf hole, the fish shape of a cracker, or the G-shaped design of a Gucci watch. ■

Basically, trade dress is subject to the same protection as trademarks. In cases involving trade dress infringement, as in trademark infringement cases, a major consideration is whether consumers are likely to be confused by the allegedly infringing use.

■ **Example 8.7** Converse makes Chuck Taylor All-Star shoes. Nike, Inc., owns Converse. Nike sued thirty-one companies, including Ralph Lauren, for manufacturing shoes very similar to All-Stars. The knockoffs used the same white rubber soles, rubber caps on the toes, canvas tops, and conspicuous stitching as the All-Star shoes. Nike claimed the similarity was likely to confuse consumers. Ralph Lauren ultimately agreed to settle its dispute with Nike by destroying all remaining shoes in its line and paying Nike an undisclosed sum. ■

8–1g Counterfeit Goods

Counterfeit goods copy or otherwise imitate trademarked goods, but they are not the genuine trademarked goods. The importation of goods that bear counterfeit (fake) trademarks poses a growing problem for U.S. businesses, consumers, and law enforcement. In addition to the negative financial effects on legitimate businesses, certain counterfeit goods, such as pharmaceuticals and nutritional supplements, can present serious public health risks.

The Stop Counterfeiting in Manufactured Goods Act The Stop Counterfeiting in Manufactured Goods Act[10] (SCMGA) was enacted to combat counterfeit goods. The act makes it a crime to traffic intentionally in or attempt to traffic in counterfeit goods or services, or to knowingly use a counterfeit mark on or in connection with goods or services.

Before this act, the law did not prohibit the creation or shipment of counterfeit labels that were not attached to any product. Therefore, counterfeiters would make labels and packaging bearing another's trademark, ship the labels to another location, and then affix them to an inferior product to deceive buyers. The SCMGA closed this loophole by making it a crime to knowingly traffic in counterfeit labels, stickers, packaging, and the like, regardless of whether the items are attached to any goods.

Penalties for Counterfeiting Persons found guilty of violating the SCMGA may be fined up to $2 million or imprisoned for up to ten years (or more if they are repeat offenders). If a court finds that the statute was violated, it must order the defendant to forfeit the counterfeit products (which are then destroyed), as well as any property used in the commission of the crime. The defendant must also pay restitution to the trademark holder or victim in an amount equal to the victim's actual loss.

■ **Case in Point 8.8** Charles Anthony Jones pleaded guilty to trafficking in counterfeit prescription male erectile dysfunction drugs. The court sentenced Jones to thirty-seven months in prison and ordered him to pay $633,019 in restitution. Jones appealed, arguing that the amount awarded was more than the pharmaceutical companies' actual losses. The court agreed. The pharmaceutical companies were entitled only to their lost net profits rather than the retail price of the genuine drugs.[11] ■

8–1h Trade Names

Trademarks apply to products. A **trade name** indicates part or all of a business's name, whether the business is a sole proprietorship, a partnership, or a corporation. Generally, a trade name is directly related to a business and its goodwill.

A trade name may be protected as a trademark if the trade name is also the name of the company's trademarked product—for instance, Coca-Cola. Unless it is also used as a trademark or service mark, a trade name cannot be registered with the federal government. Trade names are protected under the common law, but only if they are unusual or fancifully used. The word "Safeway," for instance, was sufficiently fanciful to obtain protection as a trade name for a grocery chain.

■ **Case in Point 8.9** RVC Floor Décor has sold carpets and other floor coverings in New York State since 1974. It has identified itself with the trade name Floor Décor in all signage and advertising. Floor and Décor Outlets of America was founded in 2000 in Atlanta, Georgia, and has used the trade name Floor and Décor since 2003. It sells hard-surface flooring. When Floor and Décor Outlets moved into the New York metropolitan area, it spent more than $3.5 million in advertising. RVC sued Outlets for trademark infringement in New York. It sought summary judgment on a claim that its trade name had obtained secondary meaning in the minds of the public. At trial, the court rejected RVC's request for summary judgment. Whether its trade name had acquired secondary meaning could only be determined during a full trial.[12] ■

8–1i Licensing

One way to avoid litigation and still make use of another's trademark or other form of intellectual property is to obtain a license to do so. A **license** in this context is an agreement, or contract, permitting the use of a trademark, copyright, patent, or trade secret for certain purposes. The party that owns the intellectual property rights and issues the license is the licensor, and the party obtaining the license is the licensee. The licensee generally pays fees, or **royalties**, for the privilege of using the intellectual property.

A license grants only the rights expressly described in the license agreement. A licensor might, for example, allow the licensee to use the trademark as part of its company or domain name, but not otherwise use the mark with any products or services. Disputes frequently arise over licensing agreements, particularly when the license involves internet uses.

---

10. Pub. L. No. 109-181 (2006), which amended 18 U.S.C. Sections 2318–2320.
11. *United States v. Jones*, 616 Fed.Appx. 726 (5th Cir. 2015). See, in contrast, *United States v. Kim*, 988 F.3d 803 (5th Cir. 2021).
12. *RVC Floor Décor, Ltd. v. Floor and Décor Outlets of America, Inc.*, 2021 WL 4134796 (E.D. NY 2021).

8–2 Patents

A **patent** is a grant from the government that gives inventors the exclusive right to make, use, or sell their invention for a period of twenty years. Patents for designs, as opposed to those for inventions, were issued for a fourteen-year period before May 13, 2015. All design patents issued after that date are protected for fifteen years.

For many years, U.S. patent law differed from the laws of many other countries because the first person to invent a product obtained the patent rights rather than the first person to file for a patent. It was often difficult to prove who invented an item first, however, which prompted Congress to change the system in 2011 by passing the America Invents Act.[13] Now, the first person to file an application for a patent on a product or process will receive patent protection. In addition, the new law established a nine-month limit for challenging a patent on any ground.

The period of patent protection begins on the date the patent application is filed, rather than when the patent is issued, which may sometimes be years later. After the patent period ends, the product or process enters the public domain, and anyone can make, sell, or use the invention without paying the patent holder.

8–2a Searchable Patent Databases

A significant development relating to patents is the availability online of the world's patent databases. The website of the U.S. Patent and Trademark Office (www.uspto.gov) provides searchable databases covering U.S. patents granted since 1976. The website of the European Patent Office (www.epo.org) provides online access to 130 million patent documents in more than seventy nations through a searchable network of databases.

Businesses use these searchable databases in many ways. Companies may conduct patent searches to list or inventory their patents, which are valuable assets. Patent searches may also be conducted to study trends and patterns in a specific technology or to gather information about competitors in the industry.

8–2b What Is Patentable?

Under federal law, "[w]hoever invents or discovers any new and useful process, machine, manufacture, or composition of matter, or any new and useful improvement thereof, may obtain a patent therefor, subject to the conditions and requirements of this title."[14] Thus, to be patentable, the applicant must prove that the invention, discovery, process, or design is novel, useful, and not obvious in light of current technology.

In sum, almost anything is patentable, except the laws of nature, natural phenomena, and abstract ideas (including algorithms[15]). Even artistic methods and works of art, certain business processes, and the structures of storylines are patentable, provided that they are novel and not obvious.[16]

Plants that are reproduced asexually (by means other than from seed), such as hybrid or genetically engineered plants, are patentable in the United States, as are genetically engineered (or cloned) microorganisms and animals. ■ **Case in Point 8.10** Monsanto, Inc., sells its patented genetically modified (GM) seeds to farmers to help them achieve higher yields from crops using fewer pesticides. It requires farmers who buy GM seeds to sign licensing agreements promising to plant the seeds for only one crop and to pay a technology fee for each acre planted. To ensure compliance, Monsanto has many full-time employees whose job is to investigate and prosecute farmers who use the GM seeds illegally. Monsanto has filed hundreds of lawsuits against farmers in the United States and has been awarded millions of dollars in damages (not including out-of-court settlement amounts).[17] ■

8–2c Patent Infringement

If a firm makes, uses, or sells another's patented design, product, or process without the patent owner's permission, that firm commits the tort of patent infringement. Patent infringement may occur even though the patent owner has not put the patented product into commerce. Patent infringement may also occur even though not all features or parts of a product are copied. (To infringe the patent on a process, however, all steps or their equivalent must be copied.)

---

13. The full title of this law is the Leahy-Smith America Invents Act, Pub. L. No. 112-29 (2011), which amended 35 U.S.C. Sections 1, 41, and 321 of the Patent Act.

14. 35 U.S.C. Section 101.

15. An algorithm is a step-by-step procedure, formula, or set of instructions for accomplishing a specific task. An example is the set of rules used by a search engine to rank the listings contained within its index in response to a query.

16. For a United States Supreme Court case discussing the obviousness requirement, see *KSR International Co. v. Teleflex, Inc.*, 550 U.S. 398, 127 S.Ct. 1727, 167 L.Ed.2d 705 (2007).

17. See, for instance, *Monsanto Co. v. Bowman*, 657 F.3d 1341 (Fed. Cir. 2011); and *Monsanto Co. v. Scruggs*, 345 Fed.Appx. 552 (Fed. Cir. 2009).

Patent Infringement Lawsuits and High-Tech Companies Obviously, companies that specialize in developing new technology stand to lose significant profits if someone "makes, uses, or sells" devices that incorporate their patented inventions. Because these firms are the holders of numerous patents, they are frequently involved in patent infringement lawsuits (as well as other types of intellectual property disputes).

■ **Case in Point 8.11** Apple sued Samsung in federal court alleging that Samsung's Galaxy smartphones and tablets that used Google's HTC Android operating system infringed on Apple's patents. Apple has design patents that cover its devices' graphical user interface (the display of icons on the home screen), shell, and screen and button design. Apple has also patented the way information is displayed on iPhones and other devices, the way windows pop open, and the way information is scaled and rotated.

A jury found that Samsung had willfully infringed five of Apple's patents and awarded damages. The parties appealed. A judge later reduced the amount of damages awarded on the patent claims, but litigation continued. In 2015, a federal appellate court held that elements of the physical design of these two manufacturers' mobile devices and their on-screen icons were not protected under the Lanham Act. The United States Supreme Court reversed and remanded. The Court explained that the Patent Act provision governing damages for design patent infringement encompasses both a product sold to a consumer and a component of that product. Therefore, components of the infringing smartphones could be considered relevant to damages, even though the consumers could not purchase those components separately from the smartphones.[18] ■

Patent Infringement and Foreign Sales Many companies that make and sell electronics and computer software and hardware are based in foreign nations (for instance, Samsung Electronics Company is a South Korean firm). Foreign firms can apply for and obtain U.S. patent protection on items that they sell within the United States. Similarly, U.S. firms can obtain protection in foreign nations where they sell goods.

In the United States, the Supreme Court has narrowly construed patent infringement as it applies to exported software, however. As a general rule, under U.S. law, no patent infringement occurs when the product in question is made and sold in another country. ■ **Case in Point 8.12**

AT&T Corporation holds a patent on a device used to digitally encode, compress, and process recorded speech. AT&T brought an infringement case against Microsoft Corporation, which admitted that its Windows operating system incorporated software code that infringed on AT&T's patent.

The United States Supreme Court held that Microsoft was liable only for infringement in the United States and not for the Windows-based computers produced in foreign locations. The Court reasoned that Microsoft had not "supplied" the software for the computers but had only electronically transmitted a master copy, which the foreign manufacturers copied and loaded onto the computers.[19] ■

8–2d Remedies for Patent Infringement

If a patent is infringed, the patent holder may sue for relief in federal court. The patent holder can seek an injunction against the infringer and can also request damages for royalties and lost profits. In some cases, the court may grant the winning party reimbursement for attorneys' fees and costs. If the court determines that the infringement was willful, the court can triple the amount of damages awarded (treble damages).

In the past, permanent injunctions were routinely granted to prevent future infringement. Today, however, according to the United States Supreme Court, a patent holder must prove that it has suffered irreparable injury and that the public interest would not be disserved by a permanent injunction.[20] Thus, courts have discretion to decide what is equitable in the circumstances and to consider what is in the public interest rather than just the interests of the parties.

■ **Case in Point 8.13** Cordance Corporation developed some of the technology and software that automates internet communications. Cordance sued Amazon.com, Inc., for patent infringement, claiming that Amazon's one-click purchasing interface infringed on one of Cordance's patents. After a jury found Amazon guilty of infringement, Cordance requested the court to issue a permanent injunction against Amazon's infringement or, alternatively, to order Amazon to pay Cordance an ongoing royalty.

The court refused to issue a permanent injunction because Cordance had not proved that it would otherwise suffer irreparable harm. Cordance and Amazon were not

---

18. *Apple, Inc. v. Samsung Electronics Co., Ltd.*, 678 Fed.Appx. 1012 (Fed. Cir. 2017); *Samsung Electronics Co., Ltd. v. Apple, Inc.*, 580 U.S. 53, 196 L.Ed.2d 363 (2016).

19. *Microsoft Corp. v. AT & T Corp.*, 550 U.S. 437, 127 S.Ct. 1746, 167 L.Ed.2d 737 (2007).

20. *eBay, Inc. v. MercExchange, LLC*, 547 U.S. 388, 126 S.Ct. 1837, 164 L.Ed.2d 641 (2006).

direct competitors in the relevant market. Cordance had never sold or licensed the technology infringed by Amazon's one-click purchasing interface and had presented no market data or evidence to show how the infringement negatively affected Cordance. The court also refused to impose an ongoing royalty on Amazon.[21] ∎

8–3 Copyrights

A **copyright** is an intangible property right granted by federal statute to the author or originator of a literary or artistic production of a specified type. The Copyright Act of 1976,[22] as amended, governs copyrights. Works created after January 1, 1978, are automatically given statutory copyright protection for the life of the author plus 70 years. For copyrights owned by publishing houses, the copyright expires 95 years from the date of publication or 120 years from the date of creation, whichever comes first. For works by more than one author, the copyright expires 70 years after the death of the last surviving author.[23]

When copyright protection ends, works enter into the public domain. Intellectual property that has entered into the public domain belong to everyone and is not protected by copyright or patent laws.

∎ **Case in Point 8.14** The popular character Sherlock Holmes originated in stories written by Arthur Conan Doyle and published from 1887 through 1927. Over the years, elements of the characters and stories created by Doyle have appeared in books, movies, and television series, including *Elementary* on CBS and *Sherlock* on BBC.

Before 2013, those who wished to use the copyrighted Sherlock material had to pay a licensing fee to Doyle's estate. Then, in 2013, the editors of a book of Holmes-related stories filed a lawsuit in federal court claiming that the basic Sherlock Holmes story elements introduced before 1923 should no longer be protected. The court agreed and ruled that these elements have entered the public domain—that is, the copyright has expired, and they can be used without permission.[24] ∎

8–3a Registration

Copyrights can be registered with the U.S. Copyright Office (www.copyright.gov) in Washington, D.C. Registration is not required, however. A copyright owner no longer needs to place the symbol © or the term Copr. or Copyright on the work to have the work protected against infringement. Chances are that if somebody created it, somebody owns it.

Generally, copyright owners are protected against the following:

1. Reproduction of the work.
2. Development of derivative works.
3. Distribution of the work.
4. Public display of the work.

8–3b What Is Protected Expression?

Works that are copyrightable include books, records, films, artworks, architectural plans, menus, music videos, product packaging, and computer software. To be protected, a work must be "fixed in a durable medium" from which it can be perceived, reproduced, or communicated. As noted, protection is automatic, and registration is not required.

Section 102 of the Copyright Act explicitly states that it protects original works that fall into one of the following categories:

1. Literary works (including newspaper and magazine articles, computer and training manuals, catalogues, brochures, and print advertisements).
2. Musical works and accompanying words (including advertising jingles).
3. Dramatic works and accompanying music.
4. Pantomimes and choreographic works (including ballets and other forms of dance).
5. Pictorial, graphic, and sculptural works (including cartoons, maps, posters, statues, and even stuffed animals).
6. Motion pictures and other audiovisual works (including multimedia works).
7. Sound recordings.
8. Architectural works.

21. *Cordance Corp. v. Amazon.com, Inc.*, 730 F.Supp.2d 333 (D.Del. 2010). See also *Integra Lifesciences Corp. v. Hyperbranch Medical Technology, Inc.*, 2016 WL 4770244 (D. DE 2016). See, in contrast, *Sionyx LLC v. Hamamatsu Photonics K.K.*, 981 F.3d 1339 (App.Fed.Cir. 2020).

22. 17 U.S.C. Sections 101 *et seq.*

23. These time periods reflect the extensions of the length of copyright protection enacted by Congress in the Copyright Term Extension Act of 1998, 17 U.S.C. Section 302. The United States Supreme Court upheld the constitutionality of the act in 2003. *See Eldred v. Ashcroft*, 537 U.S. 186, 123 S.Ct. 769, 154 L.Ed.2d 683 (2003).

24. *Klinger v. Conan Doyle Estate, Ltd.*, 988 F.Supp.2d 879 (N.D.Ill. 2013).

Section 102 Exclusions Generally, anything that is not an original expression will not qualify for copyright protection. Facts widely known to the public are not copyrightable. Page numbers are not copyrightable because they follow a sequence known to everyone. Mathematical calculations are not copyrightable.

Furthermore, it is not possible to copyright an idea. Section 102 of the Copyright Act specifically excludes copyright protection for any "idea, procedure, process, system, method of operation, concept, principle, or discovery, regardless of the form in which it is described, explained, illustrated, or embodied." Thus, anyone can freely use the underlying ideas or principles embodied in a work.

What is copyrightable is the particular way in which an idea is expressed. Whenever an idea and an expression are inseparable, the expression cannot be copyrighted. An idea and its expression, then, must be separable to be copyrightable. Thus, for the design of a useful item to be copyrightable, the way it looks must be separate from its utilitarian (functional) purpose.

Compilations of Facts Unlike ideas, compilations of facts are copyrightable. Under Section 103 of the Copyright Act, a compilation is "a work formed by the collection and assembling of preexisting materials or data that are selected, coordinated, or arranged in such a way that the resulting work as a whole constitutes an original work of authorship."

The key requirement in the copyrightability of a compilation is originality. If the facts are selected, coordinated, or arranged in an original way, they can qualify for copyright protection. ■ **Case in Point 8.15** EC Design's LifePlanner is an elaborate spiral-bound daily planner, augmented by inspirational sayings, lists of goals, and plenty of space for personal entries. Craft Smith's Recollections Planner is a less expensive but still elaborate spiral-bound daily planner,

augmented by inspirational sayings, lists of goals, and plenty of space for personal entries.

A federal court dismissed EC's copyright infringement lawsuit against Craft Smith over the similarities between these two items for several reasons. First, the U.S. Copyright Office had rejected EC's attempt to register the LifePlanner layout because a layout is a "template of expression," not an original form of authorship. Second, as a compilation of materials gathered from other sources, the LifePlanner does not qualify as a protectable literary work. Third, the LifePlanner's utilitarian purpose—to help plan and organize one's life—is not separate enough from the way it looks to earn protection under the law.[25] ■

8–3c Copyright Infringement

Whenever the form or expression of an idea is copied, an infringement of copyright has occurred. The reproduction does not have to be exactly the same as the original, nor does it have to reproduce the original in its entirety. If a substantial part of the original is reproduced, the copyright has been infringed.

Note that when a copyright owner grants to another a license to use the work, the owner waives the right to sue that party (the licensee) for copyright infringement. In an action for copyright infringement, copying can be inferred when a plaintiff establishes that the defendant had access to the copyrighted work and that substantial similarities exist between it and the alleged copy. In the following case, involving two toy makers, the parties agreed that the plaintiff owned a valid copyright in certain toys and that the defendant had access to those products. The dispute was over the similarities between the respective products.

---

25. *Craft Smith, LLC v. EC Design, LLC*, 388 F.Supp.3d 1385 (D. Utah 2019).

LEGO A/S v. ZURU Inc.

United States Court of Appeals, Federal Circuit, 799 Fed.Appx. 823 (2020).

Background and Facts LEGO A/S is an industry leader in designing and making toys, including construction toy building elements, figures, and sets. ZURU Inc. similarly designs, makes, and sells toys. When ZURU debuted its ZURU Action Figures in Walmart stores and on the Walmart website, LEGO filed a suit in a federal district court against ZURU, alleging infringement of LEGO's copyrights covering the sculpture of its Minifigures, an iconic construction toy. LEGO posited that the Action Figures were substantially similar in overall look and feel to the Minifigures. The court agreed, and granted LEGO a preliminary injunction. ZURU appealed, arguing that "a general sense of similarity is not sufficient" to support an injunction on the basis of copyright infringement. ZURU asked the court to "note specific differences in shape, expression, and proportions" between the toys.

In the Words of the Court

CLEVENGER, Circuit Judge.

* * * *

[ZURU argues] that the district court made clearly erroneous factual findings because the ZURU Action Figure designs are allegedly different and distinct from the LEGO product designs. Specifically, ZURU argues that * * * the district court improperly relied on a vague concept of a similar feel between LEGO Minifigures and the * * * ZURU Action Figures, without discussing any specific similarities in the artistic expression. * * * Such an analysis is fundamentally at odds with * * * the * * * test for substantial similarity.

* * * The standard test for substantial similarity between two items is whether an ordinary observer, unless he set out to detect the disparities, would be disposed to overlook them, and regard the aesthetic appeal as the same. If an average lay observer would recognize the alleged copy as having been appropriated from the copyrighted work, then the two products are substantially similar. The fact-finder must examine the works for their total concept and feel.

Consideration of the total concept and feel of a work * * * is especially appropriate in an infringement action involving children's works, because children's works are often less complex than those aimed at an adult audience. * * * The district court found that the total concept and feel of the ZURU Action Figures is substantially similar to that of LEGO's Minifigures. Where, as here, ZURU only identifies alleged disparities between the two products and has failed to demonstrate instead that the total concept and feel of the two works is different, we see no reason to disagree with the district court's finding on substantial similarity.

Decision and Remedy The U.S. Court of Appeals for the Federal Circuit affirmed the lower court's findings and its entry of an injunction in LEGO's favor. The injunction restrained ZURU from manufacturing, selling, offering for sale, displaying, and importing products that allegedly infringe LEGO's copyrights.

Critical Thinking

- **Legal Environment** Accompanying LEGO's registration of its copyright are images depicting "Basic Minifigures." Rather than these images, the district court compared ZURU's Action Figures to actual LEGO Minifigures, which differ in facial expression and jacket color. Was this, as ZURU alleged, an improper comparison? Why or why not?

- **Ethical** On the eve of the trial, ZURU promised to recall its Action Figures from Walmart's stores in an effort to defeat LEGO's request for an injunction. Could this promise be considered ethical? Explain.

Remedies for Copyright Infringement Those who infringe copyrights may be liable for damages or criminal penalties. These range from actual damages or statutory damages, imposed at the court's discretion, to criminal proceedings for willful violations.

Actual damages are based on the harm caused to the copyright holder by the infringement, while statutory damages, not to exceed $150,000, are provided for under the Copyright Act. Criminal proceedings may result in fines and/or imprisonment. A court can also issue a permanent injunction against a defendant when the court deems it necessary to prevent future copyright infringement.

■ **Case in Point 8.16** Rusty Carroll operated an online term paper business, R2C2, Inc., that offered up to 300,000 research papers for sale at nine websites. Individuals whose work was posted on these websites without their permission filed a lawsuit against Carroll for copyright infringement. Because Carroll had repeatedly failed to comply with court orders regarding discovery, the court found that the copyright infringement was likely to continue unless an injunction was issued. The court therefore issued a permanent injunction prohibiting Carroll and R2C2 from selling any term paper without sworn documentary evidence that the paper's author had given permission.[26] ■

---

26. *Weidner v. Carroll*, 2010 WL 310310 (S.D.Ill. 2010).

The "Fair Use" Exception An exception to liability for copyright infringement is made under the "fair use" doctrine. In certain circumstances, a person or organization can reproduce copyrighted material without paying royalties. Section 107 of the Copyright Act provides as follows:

> [T]he fair use of a copyrighted work, including such use by reproduction in copies or phonorecords or by any other means specified by [Section 106 of the Copyright Act], for purposes such as criticism, comment, news reporting, teaching (including multiple copies for classroom use), scholarship, or research, is not an infringement of copyright. In determining whether the use made of a work in any particular case is a fair use the factors to be considered shall include—
>
> (1) the purpose and character of the use, including whether such use is of a commercial nature or is for nonprofit educational purposes;
> (2) the nature of the copyrighted work;
> (3) the amount and substantiality of the portion used in relation to the copyrighted work as a whole; and
> (4) the effect of the use upon the potential market for or value of the copyrighted work.

What Is Fair Use? Because these guidelines are very broad, the courts determine whether a particular use is fair on a case-by-case basis. Thus, anyone who reproduces copyrighted material may be committing a violation. In determining whether a use is fair, courts have often considered the fourth factor to be the most important.

■ **Case in Point 8.17** The "Jimmy Smith Rap" is a copyrighted rap recording asserting the supremacy of jazz over other types of music. "Poundcake," released many years later, was a hip-hop song in which Aubrey Graham and Shawn Carter (professionally known as Drake and Jay-Z, respectively) rap about the greatness and authenticity of their work. At the beginning of the seven-minute-long "Poundcake" recording is a sampling of thirty-five seconds of the "Jimmy Smith Rap."

The release of "Poundcake" had no effect on the demand for the "Jimmy Smith Rap," for which there was no active market at the time. Jimmy Smith's estate nevertheless sued Graham and others for copyright infringement. A district court held that the purpose and character of the use supported the fair use defense, and a federal court of appeals agreed.[27] ■

The First Sale Doctrine Section 109(a) of the Copyright Act provides that the owner of a particular item that is copyrighted can, without the authority of the copyright owner, sell or otherwise dispose of it. This rule is known as the first sale doctrine.

Under this doctrine, once a copyright owner sells or gives away a particular copy of a work, the copyright owner no longer has the right to control the distribution of that copy. Thus, for instance, a person who buys a copyrighted book can sell it to someone else.

■ **Case in Point 8.18** Supap Kirtsaeng, a citizen of Thailand, was a graduate student at the University of Southern California. He enlisted friends and family in Thailand to buy copies of textbooks there and ship them to him in the United States. Kirtsaeng resold the textbooks on eBay, where he eventually made about $100,000.

John Wiley & Sons, Inc., had printed eight of those textbooks in Asia. Wiley sued Kirtsaeng in federal district court for copyright infringement. Kirtsaeng argued that Section 109(a) of the Copyright Act allows the first purchaser-owner of a book to sell it without the copyright owner's permission. The trial court held in favor of Wiley, and that decision was affirmed on appeal. Kirtsaeng then appealed to the United States Supreme Court, which ruled in Kirtsaeng's favor. The first sale doctrine applies even to goods purchased abroad and resold in the United States.[28] ■

8–3d Copyright Protection for Software

The Computer Software Copyright Act amended the Copyright Act to include computer programs in the list of creative works protected by federal copyright law.[29] Generally, copyright protection extends to those parts of a computer program that can be read by humans, such as the "high-level" language of a source code. Protection also extends to the binary-language object code, which is readable only by the computer, and to such elements as the overall structure, sequence, and organization of a program.

Not all aspects of software are protected. Courts typically have not extended copyright protection to the "look and feel"—the general appearance, command structure, video images, menus, windows, and other screen displays—of computer programs. (Note, however, that copying the "look and feel" of another's product may be a violation of trade dress or trademark laws.) Sometimes it can be difficult for courts to decide which particular aspects of software are protected.

---

27. *Estate of Jimmy Smith v. Graham*, 799 F.Appx. 36 (2nd Cir. 2020).

28. *Kirtsaeng v. John Wiley & Sons, Inc.*, 568 U.S. 519, 133 S.Ct. 1351, 185 L.Ed.2d 392 (2013). See also *Bluetooth Sig Inc. v. FCA US LLC*, 30 F.4th 870 (9th Cir. 2022).

29. Pub. L. No. 96-517 (1980), amending 17 U.S.C. Sections 101, 117.

■ **Case in Point 8.19** Oracle America, Inc., is a software company that owns numerous application programming interfaces, or API, packages. Oracle grants licenses to others to use these API packages to write applications in the Java programming language. Java is open and free for anyone to use, but using it requires an interface. When Google began using some of Oracle's API packages to run Java on its Android mobile devices, Oracle sued for copyright infringement. Google argued that the software packages were command structure and, as such, not protected under copyright law. Ultimately, a federal appellate court concluded that the API packages were source code and were entitled to copyright protection.[30] ■

8–4 Trade Secrets

The law of trade secrets protects some business processes and information that are not, or cannot be, patented, copyrighted, or trademarked. A **trade secret** is basically information of commercial value, such as customer lists, plans, and research and development. Trade secrets may also include pricing information, marketing methods, production techniques, and generally anything that makes an individual company unique and that would have value to a competitor.

Unlike copyright and trademark protection, protection of trade secrets extends to both ideas and their expression. For this reason, and because there are no registration or filing requirements for trade secrets, trade secret protection may be well suited for software.

Of course, a company's trade secrets must be disclosed to some persons, particularly to key employees. Businesses generally attempt to protect their trade secrets by having all employees who use a protected process or information agree in their contracts, or in confidentiality agreements, never to divulge it.

8–4a State and Federal Law on Trade Secrets

Under Section 757 of the *Restatement of Torts,* those who disclose or use another's trade secret, without authorization, are liable to that other party if either of the following is true:

1. They discovered the secret by improper means.

2. Their disclosure or use constitutes a breach of a duty owed to the other party.

Stealing confidential business data by industrial espionage, such as by tapping into a competitor's computer, is a theft of trade secrets without any contractual violation and is actionable in itself.

Trade secrets have long been protected under the common law. Today, nearly every state has enacted trade secret laws based on the Uniform Trade Secrets Act.[31] Additionally, the Economic Espionage Act[32] makes the theft of trade secrets a federal crime.

8–4b Trade Secrets in Cyberspace

Computer technology is undercutting many business firms' ability to protect their confidential information, including trade secrets. For example, a dishonest employee could e-mail trade secrets in a company's computer to a competitor or a future employer. If e-mail is not an option, the employee might walk out with the information on a flash drive.

Misusing a company's social media account is yet another way in which employees may appropriate trade secrets. ■ **Case in Point 8.20** Charles Furstenau was a manager at Radiant Global Logistics, a company that helps customers with shipping needs. Disgruntled with Radiant, Furstenau decided to join a competitor, BTX Logistics. Before doing so, he apparently forwarded e-mails containing information on revenues, profit margins, preferred shippers, and financial projections from his Radiant account to his personal account. Learning this, Radiant sued Furstenau and BTX for misappropriation of trade secrets. A federal district court prohibited Furstenau from contacting clients he had worked with at Radiant for six months and indefinitely barred BTX from using the information in the e-mails to its advantage. A federal appeals court affirmed, with the caveat that Furstenau's "general knowledge" of the logistics trade, as apart from the specific data in the e-mails, did not constitute a trade secret.[33] ■

Exhibit 8–1 outlines trade secrets and other forms of intellectual property discussed in this chapter.

30. *Oracle America, Inc. v. Google Inc.*, 750 F.3d 1339 (Fed.Cir. 2014). See, in contrast, *Turret Labs USA, Inc. v. Cargosprint, LLC*, 2022 WL 701161 (2nd Cir. 2022).

31. The Uniform Trade Secrets Act, as drafted by the National Conference of Commissioners on Uniform State Laws (NCCUSL), can be found at uniformlaws.org.
32. 18 U.S.C. Sections 1831–1839.
33. *Radiant Global Logistics v. Furstenau*, 951 F.3d 393 (6th Cir. 2020).

Exhibit 8–1 Forms of Intellectual Property

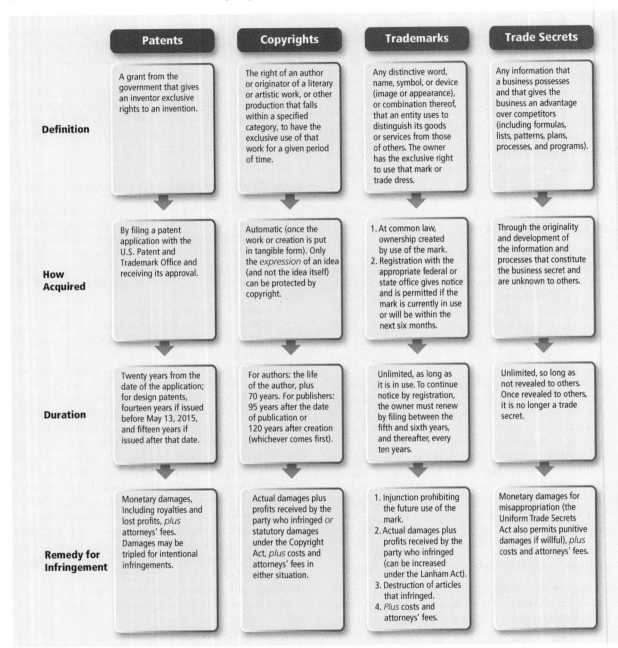

	Patents	Copyrights	Trademarks	Trade Secrets
Definition	A grant from the government that gives an inventor exclusive rights to an invention.	The right of an author or originator of a literary or artistic work, or other production that falls within a specified category, to have the exclusive use of that work for a given period of time.	Any distinctive word, name, symbol, or device (image or appearance), or combination thereof, that an entity uses to distinguish its goods or services from those of others. The owner has the exclusive right to use that mark or trade dress.	Any information that a business possesses and that gives the business an advantage over competitors (including formulas, lists, patterns, plans, processes, and programs).
How Acquired	By filing a patent application with the U.S. Patent and Trademark Office and receiving its approval.	Automatic (once the work or creation is put in tangible form). Only the *expression* of an idea (and not the idea itself) can be protected by copyright.	1. At common law, ownership created by use of the mark. 2. Registration with the appropriate federal or state office gives notice and is permitted if the mark is currently in use or will be within the next six months.	Through the originality and development of the information and processes that constitute the business secret and are unknown to others.
Duration	Twenty years from the date of the application; for design patents, fourteen years if issued before May 13, 2015, and fifteen years if issued after that date.	For authors: the life of the author, plus 70 years. For publishers: 95 years after the date of publication or 120 years after creation (whichever comes first).	Unlimited, as long as it is in use. To continue notice by registration, the owner must renew by filing between the fifth and sixth years, and thereafter, every ten years.	Unlimited, so long as not revealed to others. Once revealed to others, it is no longer a trade secret.
Remedy for Infringement	Monetary damages, Including royalties and lost profits, *plus* attorneys' fees. Damages may be tripled for intentional infringements.	Actual damages plus profits received by the party who infringed *or* statutory damages under the Copyright Act, *plus* costs and attorneys' fees in either situation.	1. Injunction prohibiting the future use of the mark. 2. Actual damages plus profits received by the party who infringed (can be increased under the Lanham Act). 3. Destruction of articles that infringed. 4. *Plus* costs and attorneys' fees.	Monetary damages for misappropriation (the Uniform Trade Secrets Act also permits punitive damages if willful), *plus* costs and attorneys' fees.

8–5 International Protection for Intellectual Property

For many years, the United States has been a party to various international agreements relating to intellectual property rights. For instance, the Paris Convention of 1883, to which almost 180 countries are signatory, allows parties in one country to file for patent and trademark protection in any of the other member countries. Other international agreements in this area include the Berne Convention, the Trade-Related Aspects of Intellectual Property Rights (known as the TRIPS agreement), the Madrid Protocol, and the Anti-Counterfeiting Trade Agreement.

8–5a The Berne Convention

Under the Berne Convention, if a U.S. citizen writes a book, every country that has signed the convention must recognize the U.S. author's copyright in the book. Also, if a citizen of a country that has not signed the convention first publishes a book in one of the 176 countries that have signed, all other countries that have signed the convention must recognize that author's copyright. Copyright notice is not needed to gain protection under the Berne Convention for works published after March 1, 1989.

In 2011, the European Union altered its copyright rules under the Berne Convention to extend the period of royalty protection for musicians from fifty years to seventy years. This decision aids major record labels as well as performers and musicians who previously faced losing royalties from sales of their older recordings. The profits of musicians and record companies have been shrinking for years because of the sharp decline in sales of compact discs and the rise in illegal downloads.

8–5b The TRIPS Agreement

The Berne Convention and other international agreements have given some protection to intellectual property on a worldwide level. None of them, however, has been as significant and far reaching in scope as the TRIPS agreement. Representatives from more than 100 nations signed the TRIPS agreement in 1994.

Establishes Standards and Procedures The TRIPS agreement established, for the first time, standards for the international protection of intellectual property rights, including patents, trademarks, and copyrights. Each member country of the World Trade Organization must include in its domestic laws broad intellectual property rights and effective remedies (including civil and criminal penalties) for violations of those rights.

Each member nation must also ensure that legal procedures are available for parties who wish to bring actions for infringement of intellectual property rights. Additionally, a related document established a mechanism for settling disputes among member nations.

Prohibits Discrimination Generally, the TRIPS agreement forbids member nations from discriminating against foreign owners of intellectual property rights in the administration, regulation, or adjudication of those rights. In other words, a member nation cannot give its own nationals (citizens) favorable treatment without offering the same treatment to nationals of all other member countries. ■ **Example 8.21** A U.S. software manufacturer brings a suit for the infringement of intellectual property rights under Germany's national laws. Because Germany is a member of the TRIPS agreement, the U.S. manufacturer is entitled to receive the same treatment as a German manufacturer. ■

8–5c The Madrid Protocol

In the past, one of the difficulties in protecting U.S. trademarks internationally was the time and expense required to apply for trademark registration in foreign nations. The filing fees and procedures for trademark registration vary significantly among individual countries. The Madrid Protocol is an international treaty designed to reduce the costs of international trademark protection. It has been signed by more than a hundred countries, including the United States. Under its provisions, a U.S. company wishing to register its trademark abroad can submit a single application and designate other member countries in which the company would like to register its mark.

8–5d The Anti-Counterfeiting Trade Agreement

In 2011, Australia, Canada, Japan, Korea, Morocco, New Zealand, Singapore, and the United States signed the Anti-Counterfeiting Trade Agreement (ACTA), an international treaty to combat global counterfeiting and piracy. Other nations have since signed the agreement.

Goals and Provisions The goals of the treaty are to increase international cooperation, facilitate the best law enforcement practices, and provide a legal framework to combat counterfeiting. ACTA applies not only to counterfeit physical goods, such as medications, but also to pirated copyrighted works being distributed via the internet. The idea is to create a new standard of enforcement for intellectual property rights that goes beyond the TRIPS agreement and encourages international cooperation and information sharing among signatory countries.

Border Searches Under ACTA, member nations are required to establish border measures that allow officials, on their own initiative, to search commercial shipments of imports and exports for counterfeit goods. The treaty neither requires nor prohibits random border searches of electronic devices, such as laptops, tablet devices, and smartphones, for infringing content.

If border authorities reasonably believe that any goods in transit are counterfeit, the treaty allows them to keep the suspect goods unless the owner proves that the items are authentic and noninfringing. The treaty allows member nations, in accordance with their own laws, to order online service providers to furnish information about suspected trademark and copyright infringers, including their identities.

Practice and Review: Intellectual Property Rights

Two computer science majors, Trent and Xavier, have an idea for a new video game, which they propose to call Hallowed. They form a business and begin developing their idea. Several months later, Trent and Xavier run into a problem with their design and consult a friend, Brad, who is an expert in designing computer source codes. After the software is completed but before Hallowed is marketed, a video game called Halo 2 is released for the Xbox and Playstation systems. Halo 2 uses source codes similar to those of Hallowed and imitates Hallowed's overall look and feel, although not all the features are alike. Using the information presented in the chapter, answer the following questions.

1. Would the name Hallowed receive protection as a trademark or as trade dress? Explain.
2. If Trent and Xavier had obtained a patent on Hallowed, would the release of Halo 2 have infringed on their patent? Why or why not?
3. Based only on the facts described above, could Trent and Xavier sue the makers of Halo 2 for copyright infringement? Why or why not?
4. Suppose that Trent and Xavier discover that Brad took the idea of Hallowed and sold it to the company that produced Halo 2. Which type of intellectual property issue does this raise?

Debate This . . .   Congress has amended copyright law several times so that copyright holders now have protection for many decades. Was Congress right in extending these copyright time periods?

Terms and Concepts

certification mark 157	license 158	trade name 158
collective mark 157	patent 159	trade secret 165
copyright 161	royalties 158	trademark 151
dilution 153	service mark 156	
intellectual property 151	trade dress 157	

Issue Spotters

1. Roslyn, a food buyer for Organic Cornucopia Food Company, decides to go into business for herself as Roslyn's Kitchen. She contacts Organic's suppliers, offering to buy their entire harvest for the next year. She also contacts Organic's customers, offering to sell her products at prices lower than Organic's prices. Has Roslyn violated any of the intellectual property rights discussed in this chapter? Explain. (See *Trade Secrets*.)

2. Global Products develops, patents, and markets software. World Copies, Inc., sells Global's software without the maker's permission. Is this patent infringement? If so, how might Global save the cost of suing World for infringement and at the same time profit from World's sales? (See *Patents*.)

• **Check your answers to the Issue Spotters against the answers provided in Appendix B at the end of this text.**

Business Scenarios and Case Problems

8–1. Fair Use. Professor Wise is teaching a summer seminar in business torts at State University. Several times during the course, he makes copies of relevant sections from business law texts and distributes them to his students. Wise does not realize that the daughter of one of the textbook authors is a member of his seminar. She tells her father about Wise's copying activities, which have taken place without her father's or

his publisher's permission. Her father sues Wise for copyright infringement. Wise claims protection under the fair use doctrine. Who will prevail? Explain. (See *Copyrights*.)

8–2. Patent Infringement. Rusland and Lyydia Doney invented a hard-bearing device for balancing rotors. Although they obtained a patent for their invention from the U.S. Patent and Trademark Office, it was never used as an automobile wheel balancer. Some time later, Exetron Corp. produced an automobile wheel balancer that used a hard-bearing device with a support plate similar to that of the Doneys' device. Given that the Doneys had not used their device for automobile wheel balancing, does Exetron's use of a similar device infringe on the Doneys' patent? Why or why not? (See *Patents.*)

8–3. Spotlight on Macy's—Copyright Infringement. United Fabrics International, Inc., bought a fabric design from an Italian designer and registered a copyright to it with the U.S. Copyright Office. When Macy's, Inc., began selling garments with a similar design, United filed a copyright infringement suit against Macy's. Macy's argued that United did not own a valid copyright to the design and so could not claim infringement. Does United have to prove that the copyright is valid to establish infringement? Explain. [*United Fabrics International, Inc. v. C & J Wear, Inc.,* 630 F.3d 1255 (9th Cir. 2011)] (See *Copyrights.*)

8–4. Copyright Infringement. SilverEdge Systems Software hired Catherine Conrad to perform a singing telegram. SilverEdge arranged for James Bendewald to record Conrad's performance of her copyrighted song to post on its website. Conrad agreed to wear a microphone to assist in the recording, told Bendewald what to film, and asked for an additional fee only if SilverEdge used the video for a commercial purpose. Later, the company chose to post a video of a different performer's singing telegram instead. Conrad filed a suit in a federal district court against SilverEdge and Bendewald for copyright infringement. Are the defendants liable? Explain. [*Conrad v. Bendewald,* 500 Fed.Appx. 526 (7th Cir. 2013)] (See *Copyrights.*)

8–5. Business Case Problem with Sample Answer— Patents. The U.S. Patent and Trademark Office (PTO) denied Raymond Gianelli's application for a patent for a "Rowing Machine"—an exercise machine on which a user *pulls* on handles to perform a rowing motion against a selected resistance. The PTO considered the device obvious in light of a previously patented "Chest Press Apparatus for Exercising Regions of the Upper Body"—an exercise machine on which a user *pushes* on handles to overcome a selected resistance. On what ground might this result be reversed on appeal? Discuss. [*In re Gianelli,* 739 F.3d 1375 (Fed. Cir. 2014)] (See *Patents.*)

- **For a sample answer to Problem 8–5, go to Appendix C at the end of this text.**

8–6. Patents. Rodney Klassen was employed by the U.S. Department of Agriculture (USDA). Without the USDA's authorization, Klassen gave Jim Ludy, a grape grower, plant material for two unreleased varieties of grapes. For almost two years, most of Ludy's plantings bore no usable fruit, none of the grapes were sold, and no plant material was given to any other person. The plantings were visible from publicly accessible roads, but none of the vines were labeled, and the variety could not be identified by simply viewing the vines.

Under patent law, an applicant may not obtain a patent for an invention that is in public use for more than one year before the date of the application. Could the USDA successfully apply for patents on the two varieties given to Ludy? Explain. [*Delano Farms Co. v. California Table Grape Commission,* 778 F.3d 1243 (Fed. Cir. 2015)] (See *Patents.*)

8–7. Copyright Infringement. Savant Homes, Inc., is a custom home designer and builder. Using what it called the "Anders Plan," Savant built a model house in Windsor, Colorado. This was a ranch house with two bedrooms on one side and a master suite on the other, separated by a combined family room, dining room, and kitchen. Ron and Tammie Wagner toured the Savant house. The same month, the Wagners hired builder Douglas Collins and his firm, Douglas Consulting, LLC, to build a house for them in Windsor. After it was built, Savant filed a suit in a federal district court against Collins for copyright infringement, alleging that the builder had copied the Anders Plan in the design and construction of the Wagner house. Collins showed that the Anders Plan consisted of standard elements and standard arrangements of elements. In these circumstances, has infringement occurred? Explain. [*Savant Homes, Inc. v. Collins,* 809 F.3d 1133 (10th Cir. 2016)] (See *Copyrights.*)

8–8. Patent Infringement. Finjan, Inc., owns a patent—U.S. Patent No. 7,418,731, or "the '731 patent"—for a system and method that provide computer security from malicious software embedded in websites on the internet. The system consists of a gateway that compares security profiles associated with requested files with the security policies of requesting users. The method includes scanning an incoming file to create the profile, which comprises a list of computer commands the file is programmed to perform. The '731 patent required "a list of computer commands." Blue Coat Systems, Inc., sold a competing product. Blue Coat's product scanned an incoming file for certain commands and created a new file called Cookie2 that contained a field showing whether, and how often, those commands appeared. Finjan filed a suit against Blue Coat, alleging patent infringement. Blue Coat argued that its profiles did not contain the '731 patent's required "list of computer commands." Did Blue Coat's product infringe Finjan's patent? Explain. [*Finjan, Inc. v. Blue Coat Systems, Inc.,* 879 F.3d 1299 (Fed. Cir. 2018)] (See *Patents.*)

8–9. Fair Use Defense. What happens when the *Star Trek* television and movie series merges with the 1990 children's classic *Oh, the Places You'll Go!*? This was the final book written by the late Theodor S. Geisel, better known as Dr. Seuss. The company ComicMix, LLC, created a so-called primer on Star Trek characters that significantly replicated broad swaths of the Dr. Seuss original. ComicMix entitled its version *Oh, the Places You'll Boldly Go!* The "Boldly" version borrowed liberally—graphically and otherwise—from the Dr. Seuss version and from other works by Dr. Seuss. The ComicMix version uses Captain Kirk and his spaceship *Enterprise* to tell readers that "life is an adventure but it will be tough." In its defense, ComicMix argued that its work was protected by fair use and therefore not an infringement of copyright. It believed that the work was obviously a parody. Should the fair use doctrine protect ComicMix? Why or why not? [*Dr. Seuss Enterprises, L.P. v. ComicMix, LLC*, 983 F.3d 443 (9th Cir. 2020)] (See *Copyrights*.)

8–10. A Question of Ethics—The IDDR Approach and Copyright Infringement. Usenet is an online bulletin board network. A user gains access to Usenet posts through a commercial service. One such service is Giganews, Inc. Although Giganews deletes or blocks posts that contain child pornography, it does not otherwise monitor content. Perfect 10, Inc., owns the copyrights to tens of thousands of images, many of which have been illegally posted on Usenet through Giganews. When Perfect 10 notified Giganews of posts that contained infringing images, the service took them down. Despite these efforts, illegal posting continued. Perfect 10 filed a suit in a federal district court against Giganews, alleging copyright infringement. [*Perfect 10, Inc. v. Giganews, Inc.*, 847 F.3d 657 (9th Cir. 2017)] (See *Copyrights*.)

(a) Is Giganews liable for copyright infringement? Do internet service providers have an ethical duty to do more to prevent infringement? Why or why not?

(b) Using the IDDR approach, decide whether a copyright owner has an ethical duty to protect against infringement.

Time-Limited Group Assignment

8–11. Patents. After years of research, your company develops a product that might revolutionize the green (environmentally conscious) building industry. The product is made from relatively inexpensive and widely available materials combined in a unique way that can substantially lower the heating and cooling costs of residential and commercial buildings. The company has registered the trademark it intends to use on the product and has filed a patent application with the U.S. Patent and Trademark Office. (See *Patents*.)

(a) One group will provide three reasons why this product does or does not qualify for patent protection.

(b) A second group will develop a four-step procedure for how the company can best protect its intellectual property rights (trademark, trade secret, and patent) and prevent domestic and foreign competitors from producing counterfeit goods or cheap knockoffs.

(c) A third group will list and explain three ways in which the company can utilize licensing.

Chapter 9

Internet Law, Social Media, and Privacy

The internet has changed our lives and our laws. Technology has put the world at our fingertips and now allows even the smallest business to reach customers around the globe. At the same time, the internet presents a variety of challenges for the law.

Courts are often in uncharted waters when deciding disputes that involve the internet, social media, and online privacy. Judges may have no common law precedents to rely on. Long-standing principles of justice may be inapplicable. New rules are evolving, but often not as quickly as technology.

Suppose that one day Frank Smith, a law student, learns that someone has created a Facebook account called "Frank Smithsexfiendman." The Facebook page associated with this account is showing doctored photos and videos. As if this were not bad enough, whoever set up the account has sent friend requests to many of Frank's family members and acquaintances, causing them to visit the embarrassing page. Frank reports the account to Facebook and requests that it be deleted because of the humiliating nature of its content.

Twenty-four hours later, the "Frank Smithsexfiendman" account remains active.

Frank has no idea who is behind this elaborate prank. Can he succeed in a lawsuit against Facebook for defamation or invasion of privacy? Proving torts online can be difficult, particularly when the person who may be liable is difficult or even impossible to identify. In this chapter, you will read about the rules pertaining to a number of online torts, as well as other legal challenges presented by the internet and social media.

9–1 Internet Law

A number of laws specifically address issues that arise only on the internet. Three such issues are unsolicited e-mail, domain names, and cybersquatting, as we discuss here. We also discuss how the law is dealing with problems of trademark infringement and dilution online.

9–1a Spam

Businesses and individuals alike are targets of **spam.**[1] Spam is the unsolicited "junk e-mail" that floods virtual mailboxes with advertisements, solicitations, and other messages. Considered relatively harmless in the early days of the internet, spam has become a serious problem and accounts for roughly 75 percent of all e-mails.

State Regulation of Spam In an attempt to combat spam, thirty-seven states have enacted laws that prohibit or regulate its use. Many state laws that regulate spam require the senders of e-mail ads to instruct the recipients

on how they can "opt out" of further e-mail ads from the same sources. For instance, in some states, an unsolicited e-mail must include a toll-free phone number or return e-mail address that the recipient can use to ask the sender to send no more unsolicited e-mails.

The Federal CAN-SPAM Act More than 20 years ago, Congress enacted the Controlling the Assault of Non-Solicited Pornography and Marketing (CAN-SPAM) Act.[2] The legislation applies to any "commercial electronic mail messages" that are sent to promote a commercial product or service. Significantly, the statute preempts state antispam laws except for those provisions in state laws that prohibit false and deceptive e-mailing practices.

Generally, the act permits the sending of unsolicited commercial e-mail but prohibits certain types of spamming activities. Prohibited activities include the use of a false return address and the use of false, misleading, or deceptive information when sending e-mail. The statute also prohibits the use of "dictionary attacks"—sending

---

1. The term *spam* is said to come from the lyrics of a Monty Python song that repeats the word *spam* over and over.

2. 15 U.S.C. Sections 7701 *et seq.*

messages to randomly generated e-mail addresses—and the "harvesting" of e-mail addresses from websites using specialized software.

■ **Case in Point 9.1** ZooBuh, an e-mail provider, advertises "Safe E-mail for Kids and Families." Consequently, its customers were not pleased when they started receiving daily e-mails from the dating website xdating. com. These messages contained fake profiles of nonexistent xdating.com members supposedly living near the recipient's location. Furthermore, when recipients clicked the "unsubscribe" option contained in the e-mails, they unwittingly signed up to receive additional xdating.com marketing materials.

Alleging that these e-mails violated the CAN-SPAM Act, ZooBuh filed suit against the company that provided xdating.com access to its customer list. ZooBuh asserted that the spam caused lost time, as its employees worked to block the offending e-mails, and lost profits, as frustrated customers cancelled ZooBuh's e-mail service. Finding for ZooBuh, a federal judge awarded the company $3 million in damages.[3] ■ Prosecuting prolific spammers, however, has done little to curb spam, which continues to flow at a rate of many billions of messages per day.

The U.S. Safe Web Act After the CAN-SPAM Act prohibited false and deceptive e-mails originating in the United States, spamming from servers located in other nations increased. These cross-border spammers generally were able to escape detection and legal sanctions because the Federal Trade Commission (FTC) lacked the authority to investigate foreign spamming.

Congress sought to rectify the situation by enacting the U.S. Safe Web Act (also known as the Undertaking Spam, Spyware, and Fraud Enforcement with Enforcers Beyond Borders Act).[4] The act allows the FTC to cooperate and share information with foreign agencies in investigating and prosecuting those involved in spamming, spyware, and various internet frauds and deceptions.

The Safe Web Act also provides a "safe harbor" for **internet service providers (ISPs)**—organizations that provide access to the internet. The safe harbor gives ISPs immunity from liability for supplying information to the FTC concerning possible unfair or deceptive conduct in foreign jurisdictions.

---

3. *Zoobuh, Inc. v. Savicom, Inc.,* 2019 WL 1466285 (D. UT 2019).
4. Pub. L. No. 109-455, 120 Stat. 3372 (2006), codified in various sections of 15 U.S.C. and 12 U.S.C. Section 3412.

9–1b Domain Names

As e-commerce expanded worldwide, one issue that emerged involved the rights of a trademark owner to use the mark as part of a domain name. A **domain name** is part of an internet address, such as "cengage.com."

Structure of Domain Names Every domain name ends with a top-level domain (TLD), which is the part of the name to the right of the period. The TLD often indicates the type of entity that operates the site. For instance, *com* is an abbreviation for *commercial*, and *edu* is short for *education*.

The second-level domain (SLD)—the part of the name to the left of the period—is chosen by the business entity or individual registering the domain name. Competition for SLDs among firms with similar names and products has led to numerous disputes. By using an identical or similar domain name, parties have attempted to profit from a competitor's **goodwill** (the nontangible value of a business).

Distribution System The Internet Corporation for Assigned Names and Numbers (ICANN), a nonprofit corporation, oversees the distribution of domain names and operates an online arbitration system. Due to numerous complaints, ICANN overhauled the domain name distribution system in 2012.

ICANN started selling new generic top-level domain names (gTLDs) for an initial price of $185,000 plus an annual fee of $25,000. Whereas the older TLDs were limited to only a few terms (such as com, net, and org), gTLDs can take any form. Many companies and corporations acquire gTLDs based on their brands, such as aol, bmw, canon, target, and walmart. Some companies have numerous gTLDs. Google's gTLDs, for instance, include android, bing, chrome, gmail, goog, and YouTube.

Because gTLDs have greatly increased the potential number of domain names, domain name registrars have proliferated. Registrar companies charge a fee to businesses and individuals to register new names and to renew annual registrations (often through automated software). Many of these companies also buy and sell expired domain names.

9–1c Cybersquatting

One of the goals of the new gTLD system was to address the problem of *cybersquatting*. **Cybersquatting** occurs when a person registers a domain name that is the same as, or confusingly similar to, the trademark of another and then offers to sell the domain name back to the trademark owner.

■ **Case in Point 9.2** Apple, Inc., has repeatedly sued cybersquatters that registered domain names similar to the names of its products, such as ipods.com. Apple won a judgment in litigation at the World Intellectual Property Organization against a company that was squatting on the domain name iPhone6s.com.[5] ■

Anticybersquatting Legislation

Because cybersquatting has led to so much litigation, Congress enacted the Anticybersquatting Consumer Protection Act (ACPA),[6] which amended the Lanham Act—the federal law protecting trademarks. The ACPA makes cybersquatting illegal when both of the following are true:

1. The domain name is identical or confusingly similar to the trademark of another.
2. The one registering, trafficking in, or using the domain name has a "bad faith intent" to profit from that trademark.

■ **Case in Point 9.3** CrossFit, Inc., is a Delaware corporation that provides personal fitness services and products. CrossFit is well known in the fitness industry and licenses affiliates to operate individual CrossFit-branded programs. CrossFit granted a license to Andres Del Cueto Davalos to operate a location in Mexico and allowed him to use the domain name "CrossFitAlfa." Davalos later registered the domain name CrossFitBeta without CrossFit's permission and then used both domain names to redirect website visitors to a third website, www.woodbox.com. Davalos was attempting to siphon off CrossFit customers to another business that he co-owned, Woodbox Training Centers, which operated in twenty-five locations across Mexico. CrossFit sued under the ACPA. Because of Davalos's bad faith intent, the court awarded CrossFit the maximum amount of statutory damages available ($100,000 for each domain name), plus costs and attorneys' fees.[7] ■

Frequent Changes in Domain Name Ownership Facilitates Cybersquatting

Despite the ACPA, cybersquatting continues to present a problem for businesses. All domain name registrars are supposed to relay information about their transactions to ICANN and other companies that keep a master list of domain names, but this does not always occur. The speed at which domain names change hands and the difficulty in tracking mass automated registrations have created an environment in which cybersquatting can flourish.

Typosquatting

Typosquatting is registering a name that is a misspelling of a popular brand, such as "googl. com" or "appple.com." Because many internet users are not perfect typists, Web pages using these misspelled names receive a lot of traffic. More traffic generally means increased profit (advertisers often pay websites based on the number of unique visits, or hits).

■ **Case in Point 9.4** Counter Balance Enterprises, Ltd., registered and used domain names that misspelled Facebook, such as "facebookbk.com" and "facemonk.com." Facebook, Inc., filed suit in a California federal court under the ACPA against Counter Balance (and ten other defendants, including Banana Ads, LLC) for typosquatting. The defendants failed to appear, and the court entered a default judgment in favor of Facebook. The court permanently enjoined the defendants from using the infringing domain names and awarded Facebook a total of $2.8 million in damages (ranging from $5,000 to $1.3 million per individual defendant).[8] ■

Typosquatting may sometimes fall beyond the reach of the ACPA. If the misspelling is significant, the trademark owner may have difficulty proving that the name is identical or confusingly similar to the trademark of another, as the ACPA requires.

Typosquatting adds costs for businesses seeking to protect their domain name rights. Companies must attempt to register not only legitimate variations of their domain names but also potential misspellings. Large corporations may have to register thousands of domain names across the globe just to protect their basic brands and trademarks.

Applicability and Sanctions of the ACPA

The ACPA applies to all domain name registrations of trademarks. Successful plaintiffs in suits brought under the act can collect actual damages and profits, or they can elect to receive statutory damages ranging from $1,000 to $100,000.

Although some companies have successfully sued under the ACPA, there are roadblocks to pursuing such lawsuits. Some domain name registrars offer privacy

5. WIPO Case No. D2012-0951.
6. 15 U.S.C. Section 8131.
7. *CrossFit, Inc. v. Davalos,* 2017 WL 733213 (N.D.Cal. 2017). See also *Boigris v. EWC P&T, LLC,* 7 F.4th 1079 (11th Cir. 2021).

8. *Facebook, Inc. v. Banana Ads, LLC,* 2013 WL 1873289 (N.D.Cal. 2013). See also *Spectrum Association Management of Texas, L.L.C. v. Lifetime HOA Management L.L.C.,* 5 F.4th 560 (5th Cir. 2021).

services that hide the true owners of websites, making it difficult for trademark owners to identify cybersquatters. Thus, before bringing a suit, a trademark owner must ask the court for a subpoena to discover the identity of the owner of the infringing website. Because of the high costs of court proceedings, discovery, and even arbitration, many disputes concerning cybersquatting are settled out of court.

To facilitate dispute resolution, ICANN offers two dispute resolution forums: the Uniform Domain-Name Dispute Resolution Policy (UDRP) and the Uniform Rapid Suspension (URS) system. More disputes are resolved through the UDRP, which allows common law trademark claims and has fewer procedural requirements. The URS system can be used only by registered trademark holders with clear-cut infringement claims.

9–1d Meta Tags

Meta tags are key words that give internet browsers specific information about a webpage. Meta tags can be used to increase the likelihood that a site will be included in search engine results, even if the site has nothing to do with the key words. In effect, one site can appropriate the key words of other sites with more frequent hits so that the appropriating site will appear in the same search engine results as the more popular sites.

Using another's trademark in a meta tag without the owner's permission normally constitutes trademark infringement. Some uses of another's trademark as a meta tag may be permissible, however, if the use is reasonably necessary and does not suggest that the owner authorized or sponsored the use.

■ **Case in Point 9.5** Farzad and Lisa Tabari are auto brokers—the personal shoppers of the automotive world. They contact authorized dealers, solicit bids, and arrange for customers to buy from the dealer offering the best combination of location, availability, and price. The Tabaris offered this service at the websites buy-a-lexus.com and buyorleaselexus.com.

Toyota Motor Sales U.S.A., Inc., the exclusive distributor of Lexus vehicles and the owner of the Lexus mark, objected to the Tabaris' practices. The Tabaris removed Toyota's photographs and logo from their site and added a disclaimer in large type at the top, but they refused to give up their domain names. Toyota sued for infringement. The court forced the Tabaris to stop using any "domain name, service mark, trademark, trade name, meta tag or other commercial indication of origin that includes the mark LEXUS."[9] ■

9–1e Trademark Dilution in the Online World

Trademark *dilution* occurs when a trademark is used, without authorization, in a way that diminishes the distinctive quality of the mark. Unlike trademark infringement, a claim of dilution does not require proof that consumers are likely to be confused by a connection between the unauthorized use and the mark. For this reason, the products involved need not be similar, as the following *Spotlight Case* illustrates.

---

9. *Toyota Motor Sales, U.S.A., Inc. v. Tabari*, 610 F.3d 1171 (9th Cir. 2010).

Spotlight on Internet Porn

Case 9.1 Hasbro, Inc. v. Internet Entertainment Group, Ltd.

United States District Court, Western District Washington, 1996 WL 84853 (1996).

Background and Facts In 1949, Hasbro, Inc.—then known as the Milton Bradley Company—published its first version of Candy Land, a children's board game. Hasbro is the owner of the trademark "Candy Land," which has been registered with the U.S. Patent and Trademark Office since 1951. Over the years, Hasbro has produced several versions of the game, including Candy Land puzzles, a travel version, a computer game, and a handheld electronic version. In the mid-1990s, Brian Cartmell and his employer, the Internet Entertainment Group, Ltd., used the term *candyland.com* as a domain name for a sexually explicit internet site. Anyone who performed an online search using the word *candyland* was directed to this adult website. Hasbro filed a trademark dilution claim in a federal court, seeking a permanent injunction to prevent the defendants from using the Candy Land trademark.

In the Language of the Court

DWYER, U.S. District Judge
* * * *

2. Hasbro has demonstrated a probability of proving that defendants Internet Entertainment Group, Ltd., Brian Cartmell and Internet Entertainment Group, Inc. (collectively referred to as "defendants") have been diluting the value of Hasbro's CANDY LAND mark by using the name CANDYLAND to identify a sexually explicit Internet site, and by using the name string "candyland.com" as an Internet domain name which, when typed into an Internet-connected computer, provides Internet users with access to that site.
* * * *

4. Hasbro has shown that defendants' use of the CANDY LAND name and the domain name candyland.com in connection with their Internet site is causing irreparable injury to Hasbro.

5. The probable harm to Hasbro from defendants' conduct outweighs any inconvenience that defendants will experience if they are required to stop using the CANDYLAND name.
* * * *

THEREFORE, IT IS HEREBY ORDERED that Hasbro's motion for preliminary injunction is granted.

Decision and Remedy The federal district court granted Hasbro an injunction against the defendants, agreeing that the domain name *candyland* was "causing irreparable injury to Hasbro." The judge ordered the defendants to immediately remove all content from the candyland.com website and to stop using the Candy Land trademark.

Critical Thinking

- **Economic** How can companies protect themselves from others who create websites that have similar domain names, and what limits each company's ability to be fully protected?
- **What If the Facts Were Different?** Suppose that the site using candyland.com had not been sexually explicit but had sold candy. Would the result have been the same? Explain.

9–1f Licensing

A company may permit another party to use a trademark (or other intellectual property) under a license. A licensor might grant a license allowing its trademark to be used as part of a domain name, for instance.

Another type of license involves the use of a product such as software. This sort of licensing is ubiquitous in the online world. When you download an application on your smartphone, tablet, or other mobile device, for instance, you are typically entering into a license agreement. You are obtaining only a license to use that app and not ownership rights in it. Apps published on Google Play, for instance, may use its licensing service to prompt users to agree to a license at the time of installation and use.

Licensing agreements frequently include restrictions that prohibit licensees from sharing the file and using it to create similar software applications. The license may also limit the use of the application to a specific device or give permission to the user for a certain period.

9–2 Copyrights in Digital Information

Copyright law is probably the most important form of intellectual property protection on the internet. This is because much of the material on the internet (including software and database information) is copyrighted, and in order for that material to be transferred online, it must be "copied." Generally, whenever a party downloads software or music into a computer's random-access memory, or RAM, without authorization, a copyright is infringed.

Initially, criminal penalties for copyright violations could be imposed only if unauthorized copies were exchanged for financial gain. Then, Congress amended the law and extended criminal liability for the piracy of copyrighted materials to persons who exchange unauthorized copies of copyrighted works without realizing a profit.

9–2a Digital Millennium Copyright Act

In 1998, Congress enacted the Digital Millennium Copyright Act (DMCA).[10] The DMCA gave significant protection to owners of copyrights in digital information. Among other things, the act established civil and criminal penalties for anyone who circumvents (bypasses) encryption software or other technological antipiracy protection. Also prohibited are the manufacture, import, sale, and distribution of devices or services for circumvention.

Allows Fair Use The DMCA provides for exceptions to fit the needs of libraries, scientists, universities, and others. In general, the law does not restrict the "fair use" of circumvention methods for educational and other noncommercial purposes. For instance, circumvention is allowed to test computer security, to conduct encryption research, to protect personal privacy, and to enable parents to monitor their children's use of the internet.

The fair use doctrine has been applied in other situations as well. ■ **Case in Point 9.6** Stephanie Lenz posted a short video on YouTube of her toddler son dancing with the Prince song "Let's Go Crazy" playing in the background. Universal Music Group (UMG) sent YouTube a take-down notice that stated the video violated copyright law under the DMCA. YouTube removed the "dancing baby" video and notified Lenz of the allegations of copyright infringement, warning her that repeated incidents of infringement could lead it to delete her account.

Lenz filed a lawsuit against UMG claiming that accusing her of infringement constituted a material misrepresentation (fraud) because UMG knew that Lenz's video was a fair use of the song. The district court held that UMG should have considered the fair use doctrine before sending the take-down notice. UMG appealed, and the U.S. Court of Appeals for the Ninth Circuit affirmed. Lenz was allowed to pursue nominal damages from UMG for sending the notice without considering whether her use was fair.[11] ■

Limits Liability of Internet Service Providers The DMCA also limits the liability of internet service providers (ISPs). Under the act, an ISP is not liable for copyright infringement by its customer unless the ISP is aware of the subscriber's violation. An ISP may be held liable only if it fails to take action to shut down the subscriber after learning of the violation. A copyright holder must act promptly, however, by pursuing a claim in court, or the subscriber has the right to be restored to online access.

9–2b File-Sharing Technology

Soon after the internet became popular, a few enterprising programmers created software to compress large data files, particularly those associated with music. The best-known compression and decompression system is MP3, which enables music fans to download songs or entire CDs onto their computers or onto portable listening devices, such as smartphones and tablets. The MP3 system also made it possible for music fans to access other fans' files by engaging in file-sharing via the internet.

Methods of File-Sharing File-sharing is accomplished through **peer-to-peer (P2P) networking** The concept is simple. Rather than going through a central web server, P2P networking uses numerous computers that are connected to one another, often via the internet. Individuals on the same network can access files stored on one another's computers through a **distributed network.** Parts of the network may be distributed all over the country or the world, which offers an unlimited number of uses.

A better method of sharing files via the internet is **cloud computing,** which is essentially a subscription-based or pay-per-use service that extends a computer's software or storage capabilities. Cloud computing can deliver a single application through a browser to multiple users. Alternatively, cloud computing might provide data storage and virtual servers that can be accessed on demand. Amazon, Alibaba, Facebook, Google, Microsoft, and Oracle are using and developing more cloud-computing services.

BitTorrent has become the most popular method of P2P file sharing. Its popularity is based on the speed with which it can send multiple large, high-quality files without using a great deal of bandwidth. There is nothing inherently illegal about using BitTorrent. When BitTorrent is used to share recorded music files, however, copyright issues arise.

Pirated Movies and Television File-sharing also creates problems for the motion picture and television industries, which lose significant amounts of revenue annually as a result of piracy. Numerous websites offer software that facilitates the illegal copying of movies and television programs. Popcorn Time, for instance, is a BitTorrent site that offers streaming services that enable users to watch pirated movies and television shows without downloading them.

---

10. 17 U.S.C. Sections 512, 1201–1205, 1301–1332; and 28 U.S.C. Section 4001.
11. *Lenz v. Universal Music Group,* 815 F.3d 1145 (9th Cir. 2016). See also *In re DMCA Section 512(h) Subpoena to YouTube (Google, Inc.),* 581 F.Supp.3d 509 (2022).

■ **Case in Point 9.7** UN4 Productions, Inc., creates and distributes a series of martial arts films called *Boyka Undisputed*. When the company determined that an unauthorized copy of *Boyka Undisputed 4* was being shared on BitTorrent, it tried to determine who was responsible for initially uploading the film. Failing in these efforts, UN4 subpoenaed a number of ISPs, requesting the "digital footprints" of anyone who had illegally downloaded *Boyka Undisputed 4* on BitTorrent.

This strategy identified five individuals whom UN4 successfully sued for infringement of its copyrighted material. Because the defendants did not profit from these "minor" infringements, a federal judge determined that UN4 was only entitled to $750 in damages from each. The judge also ordered the defendants to destroy their downloaded files of the film.[12] ■

9–3 Social Media

Social media provide a means by which people can create and exchange ideas and comments via the internet. Facebook, WhatsApp, Instagram, and YouTube are the biggest social media sites. Additional social media platforms include TikTok, Pinterest, Telegram, and Twitter, along with many others used by hundreds of millions of people worldwide.

9–3a Legal Issues

The emergence of Facebook and other social networking sites has created a number of legal and ethical issues for businesses. For instance, a firm's rights in valuable intellectual property may be infringed if users post trademarked images or copyrighted materials on these sites without permission. The content of social media may play a role in various parts of the legal process, as discussed next. Employers' social media policies may also be at issue.

Impact on Litigation Social media posts are routinely included in discovery in litigation because they can provide damaging information that establishes a person's intent or what that person knew at a particular time. Like e-mail, posts on social networks can be the smoking gun that leads to liability.

Tweets and other social media posts can also be used to reduce damages awards. ■ **Example 9.8** Jill Daniels sued for injuries she sustained in a car accident, claiming that her injuries made it impossible for her to continue working as a hairstylist. The jury initially determined that her damages were $237,000, but when the jurors saw tweets and photographs of Daniels partying in New Orleans and vacationing on the beach, they reduced the final award to $142,000. ■

Impact on Settlement Agreements Social media posts have been used to invalidate settlement agreements that contain confidentiality clauses. ■ **Case in Point 9.9** Patrick Snay was the headmaster of Gulliver Preparatory School in Florida. When Gulliver did not renew Snay's employment contract, Snay sued the school for age discrimination. During mediation, Snay agreed to settle the case for $80,000 and signed a confidentiality clause that required him and his wife not to disclose the "terms and existence" of the agreement. Nevertheless, Snay and his wife told their daughter, Dana, that the dispute had been settled and that they were happy with the results.

Dana, a college student, had recently graduated from Gulliver and, according to Snay, had suffered retaliation at the school. Dana posted a Facebook comment that said "Mama and Papa Snay won the case against Gulliver. Gulliver is now officially paying for my vacation to Europe this summer. SUCK IT." The comment went out to 1,200 of Dana's Facebook friends, many of whom were Gulliver students, and school officials soon learned of it. The school immediately notified Snay that he had breached the confidentiality clause and refused to pay the settlement amount. Ultimately, a state intermediate appellate court held that Snay had breached the confidentiality clause and therefore could not enforce the settlement agreement.[13] ■

Criminal Investigations Law enforcement uses social media to detect and prosecute criminals. A surprising number of criminals boast about their illegal activities on social media. ■ **Example 9.10** Paige Thompson, a former software engineer for Amazon, tweeted that "I've basically strapped myself with a bomb vest." Thompson was referring, metaphorically, to the punishment she was likely to receive for breaking into a server used by credit-card company Capital One and compromising the financial data of more than 100 million people. The tweet resulted in her arrest and criminal charges that carried a maximum punishment of five years in prison and a $250,000 fine. ■

---

12. *UN4 Productions, Inc. v. Primozich*, 372 F.Supp. 1129 (W.D. Wash. 2019).

13. *Gulliver Schools, Inc. v. Snay*, 137 So.3d 1045 (Fla.App. 2014). See also *Kirk v. Ratner*, 74 Cal.App.5th 1052 (Ct. of App. 2nd Dist. Div. 7 CA 2022).

Some police departments authorize officers to go undercover on social media sites. ■ **Example 9.11** As part of Operation Crew Cut, New York Police Department (NYPD) officers routinely pretend to be young women in order to "friend" suspects on Facebook. Using these fake identities, officers can avoid the social media site's privacy settings and gain valuable information about illegal activities. ■

Administrative Agency Investigations Federal regulators also use social media posts in their investigations into illegal activities. ■ **Example 9.12** Reed Hastings, a co-founder of Netflix, stated on Facebook that Netflix subscribers had watched a billion hours of video the previous month. As a result, Netflix's stock price rose, which prompted a federal agency investigation. Under securities laws, such a statement may be material information to investors. Thus, it must be disclosed to all investors, not just a select group, such as those who had access to Hastings's Facebook post.

The agency ultimately concluded that it could not hold Hastings responsible for any wrongdoing because the agency's policy on social media use was not clear. The agency then issued new guidelines that allow companies to disclose material information through social media if investors have been notified in advance. ■

In addition, administrative law judges can base their decisions on the contents of social media posts. ■ **Case in Point 9.13** Jennifer O'Brien was a tenured teacher at a public school in New Jersey when she posted two messages on her Facebook page: "I'm not a teacher—I'm a warden for future criminals!" and "They had a scared straight program in school—why couldn't I bring first graders?" Not surprisingly, outraged parents protested. The deputy superintendent of schools filed a complaint against O'Brien with the state's commissioner of education, charging her with conduct unbecoming a teacher.

After a hearing, an administrative law judge ordered that O'Brien be removed from her teaching position. O'Brien appealed to a state court, claiming that her Facebook postings were protected by the First Amendment and could not be used by the school district to discipline or discharge her. The court found that O'Brien had failed to establish that her Facebook postings were protected speech and that the seriousness of O'Brien's conduct warranted removal from her position.[14] ■

Employers' Social Media Policies Many large corporations have established specific guidelines on using social media in the workplace. Employees who use social media in a way that violates their employer's stated policies may be disciplined or fired from their jobs. Courts and administrative agencies usually uphold an employer's right to terminate a person based on violation of a social media policy.

■ **Case in Point 9.14** Virginia Rodriquez had worked for Wal-Mart Stores, Inc., for almost twenty years and had been promoted to management. Then she was disciplined for violating the company's policies by having a fellow employee use Rodriquez's password to alter the price of an item that she purchased. Under Wal-Mart's rules, another violation within a year would mean termination.

Nine months later, on Facebook, Rodriquez publicly chastised employees under her supervision for calling in sick to go to a party. The posting violated Wal-Mart's "Social Media Policy," which was "to avoid public comment that adversely affects employees." Wal-Mart terminated Rodriquez. She filed a lawsuit, alleging discrimination, but the court issued a summary judgment in Wal-Mart's favor.[15] ■

9–3b The Electronic Communications Privacy Act

The Electronic Communications Privacy Act (ECPA)[16] amended federal wiretapping law to cover electronic forms of communications. Although Congress enacted the ECPA many years before social media networks existed, the act nevertheless applies to communications through social media.

The ECPA prohibits the intentional interception of any wire, oral, or electronic communication. It also prohibits the intentional disclosure or use of the information obtained through the interception.

Exclusions for Employers Excluded from the ECPA's coverage are electronic communications through devices that an employer provides for an employee to use "in the ordinary course of its business." Consequently, if a company provides an employee with a cell phone, laptop, or tablet for ordinary business use, the company is not prohibited from intercepting business communications made on it. This "business-extension exception" permits employers

---

14. *In re O'Brien*, 2013 WL 132508 (N.J.Super.Ct.App.Div. 2013). See also *O'Laughlin v. Palm Beach County*, 30 F.4th 1045 (11th Cir. 2022).

15. *Rodriquez v. Wal-Mart Stores, Inc.*, 2013 WL 102674 (N.D.Tex. 2013). See also *Allen v. East Orange Board of Education*, 2022 WL 332910 (S.Ct.NJ, App.Div. 2022).

16. 18 U.S.C. Sections 2510–2521.

to monitor employees' electronic communications made in the ordinary course of business. It does not, however, permit employers to monitor employees' personal communications.

Another exception to the ECPA allows an employer to avoid liability under the act if the employees consent to having their electronic communications monitored by the employer.

Stored Communications Part of the ECPA is known as the Stored Communications Act (SCA).[17] The SCA prohibits intentional and unauthorized access to stored electronic communications and sets forth criminal and civil sanctions for violators. A person can violate the SCA by intentionally accessing a stored electronic communication. The SCA also prevents "providers" of communication services (such as cell phone companies and social media networks) from divulging private communications to certain entities and individuals.

■ **Case in Point 9.15** As part of an investigation into disability fraud, the New York County District Attorney's Office sought from Facebook the data and stored communications of 381 retired police officers and firefighters. The government suspected that these individuals had faked illness after 9/11 in order to obtain disability.

Facebook challenged the warrants in court, arguing that they were unconstitutional because they were overly broad. The court ruled against Facebook and ordered it to comply. It also ordered the company not to notify the users that it was disclosing their data to government investigators. Facebook complied but appealed the decision. The reviewing court held that only the individuals, not Facebook, could challenge the warrants as violations of privacy. Thus, the government was allowed to seize all of Facebook's digital data pertaining to these users.[18] ■

9–3c Protection of Social Media Passwords

Employees and applicants for jobs or colleges have sometimes been asked to divulge their social media passwords. An employer or school may look at an individual's Facebook or other account to see if it includes controversial postings such as racially discriminatory remarks or photos of drug parties. Such postings can have a negative

effect on a person's prospects even if they were made years earlier or are taken out of context.

A majority of the states have enacted legislation to protect individuals from having to disclose their social media passwords. Each state's law is slightly different. Some states, such as Michigan, prohibit employers from taking adverse action against an employee or job applicant based on what the person has posted online. Michigan's law also applies to e-mail and cloud storage accounts.

Legislation will not completely prevent employers and others from taking actions against persons based on their social network postings, though. Management and human resources personnel are unlikely to admit that they looked at someone's Facebook page and that it influenced their decision. They may not even have to admit to looking at the Facebook page if they use private browsing, which enables people to keep their Web browsing activities confidential. How, then, would rejected job applicants be able to prove that they were rejected because the employer accessed social media postings?

9–3d Company-wide Social Media Networks

Many companies, including Dell, Inc., and Nikon Instruments, form their own internal social media networks. Software companies offer a variety of systems, including Workplace from Facebook, Microsoft's SharePoint, Microsoft's Yammer, and Happeo Workplace. Posts on these internal networks, or *intranets,* are quite different from the typical posts on Facebook, LinkedIn, and Twitter. Employees use these intranets to exchange messages about topics related to their work, such as deals that are closing, new products, production flaws, how a team is solving a problem, and the details of customer orders. Thus, the tone is businesslike.

Protection of Trade Secrets An important advantage to using an internal system for employee communications is that the company can better protect its trade secrets. The company usually decides which employees can see particular intranet files and which employees will belong to each specific "social" group within the company. Companies providing internal social media networks often keep the resulting data on their own servers in secure clouds.

Other Advantages Internal social media systems also offer additional benefits. They provide real-time information about important issues, such as production glitches. Additionally, posts can include tips on how to

---

17. 18 U.S.C. Sections 2701–2711.
18. *In re 381 Search Warrants Directed to Facebook, Inc.,* 29 N.Y.3d 231, 78 N.E.3d 141, 55 N.Y.S.3d 696 (2017). See also *In re Search of Information Associated with One Account Stored at Premises Controlled by Facebook, Inc.,* 2021 WL 2302800 (D. DC 2021).

best sell new products or deal with difficult customers, as well as information about competitors' products and services.

9–4 Online Defamation

Cyber torts are torts that arise from online conduct. One of the most prevalent cyber torts is online defamation. Defamation involves wrongfully hurting a person's reputation by communicating false statements about that person to others. Because the internet enables individuals to communicate with large numbers of people simultaneously (via a blog or tweet, for instance), online defamation has become a problem in today's legal environment.

■ **Example 9.16** Ross Hansen set up several websites asserting that, among other things, California real estate developer Bradley Cohen was a scam artist with a history of serious crimes, including fraud and racketeering. As proof, the websites contained links to articles about a different Brad Cohen, a convicted criminal from Pennsylvania. When the real estate developer sued for defamation, Hansen admitted that the online allegations were false and had been designed to "inflict lots of pain" on Cohen, with whom he was engaged in a legal dispute. A federal jury in Nevada reacted to this admission by finding Hansen liable and awarding Cohen $38.3 million in damages. ■

9–4a Identifying the Author of Online Defamation

An initial issue raised by online defamation is simply discovering who is committing it. In the real world, identifying the author of a defamatory remark generally is an easy matter. It is more difficult if a business firm discovers that defamatory statements about its policies and products are being posted in an online forum, because the postings are anonymous. Therefore, a threshold barrier to anyone who seeks to bring an action for online defamation is discovering the identity of the person who posted the defamatory message.

An internet service provider (ISP) can disclose personal information about its customers only when ordered to do so by a court. Consequently, businesses and individuals are increasingly bringing lawsuits against "John Does." (John Doe, Jane Doe, and the like are fictitious names used in lawsuits when the identity of a party is not known or when parties wish to conceal their names for privacy reasons.) Then, using the authority of the courts, the plaintiffs can obtain from the ISPs the identity of the persons responsible for the defamatory website.

9–4b Liability of Internet Service Providers

Recall that under tort law those who repeat or otherwise republish a defamatory statement are normally subject to liability. Thus, newspapers, magazines, and television and radio stations are subject to liability for defamatory content that they publish or broadcast, even though the content was prepared or created by others. Applying this rule to cyberspace, however, raises an important issue: Should ISPs be regarded as publishers and therefore be held liable for defamatory messages that are posted by their users?

General Rule The Communications Decency Act (CDA) states that "[n]o provider or user of an interactive computer service shall be treated as the publisher or speaker of any information provided by another information content provider."[19] Thus, under the CDA, ISPs usually are treated differently from publishers in print and other media and are not liable for publishing defamatory statements that come from a third party.

Exceptions Although the courts generally have construed the CDA as providing a broad shield to protect ISPs from liability for third party content, some courts have started establishing limits to this immunity. ■ **Case in Point 9.17** Roommate.com, LLC, operated an online roommate-matching website that helped individuals find roommates based on their descriptions of themselves and their roommate preferences. Users responded to a series of online questions, choosing from answers in drop-down and select-a-box menus.

Some of the questions asked users to disclose their sex, family status, and sexual orientation—which is not permitted under the federal Fair Housing Act. When a nonprofit housing organization sued Roommate.com, the company claimed it was immune from liability under the CDA. A federal appellate court disagreed and ruled that Roommate.com was not immune from liability. By creating the website and the questionnaire and answer choices, Roommate.com prompted users to express discriminatory preferences and matched users based on these preferences in violation of federal law.[20] ■

In the following case, a line internet service provider, which provides access to the internet over cable TV lines, removed several videos posted by a commercial client. At issue was whether the Communications Decency Act prohibited such removals.

---

19. 47 U.S.C. Section 230.

20. *Fair Housing Council of San Fernando Valley v. Roommate.com, LLC*, 666 F.3d 1216 (9th Cir. 2012). See also *Taking Offense v. State*, 66 Cal.App.5th 696 (Ct.App., 3rd Dist. CA 2021).

Word of God Fellowship, Inc., Doing Business as Daystar Television Network v. Vimeo, Inc. et al.

Supreme Court, Appellate Division, First Department, New York, 205 A.D.3d 23, 166 N.Y.S.3d 3 (2022).

In the Language of the Court
SINGH, J.
This appeal concerns whether a video-hosting service may be held liable for its decision to remove videos that it determines violate its terms of service. Defendant Vimeo, Inc., prohibits users from posting videos that make false or misleading claims about vaccine safety. It removed five videos, posted by a commercial user, because the videos claimed that childhood vaccination leads to autism. The user sued, claiming that Vimeo had breached the parties' contract. The motion court held that liability was precluded by section 230 of the Communications Decency Act. * * * Section 230 prevents lawsuits against Internet service providers for their good-faith decisions to remove content that they consider objectionable. If service providers had to justify those decisions in court, or if plaintiffs could circumvent immunity through unsupported accusations of bad faith, section 230 would be a dead letter. * * *

Facts
Plaintiff Daystar Television Network states that it is "an evangelical Christian-based television network." It alleges that Vimeo "is a video hosting, sharing and services platform," and that defendant VHX Corporation is a wholly-owned subsidiary of Vimeo. Daystar streamed videos to its website and contracted with defendants to host those videos. Specifically, in October 2019, Daystar purchased a two-year subscription to defendants' enterprise service, which defendants called their OTT (over-the-top) service. This subscription enabled Daystar to upload up to 2000 hours of video, per year, to be hosted by Vimeo and VHX. Daystar would take full advantage of this capacity, uploading

over 3000 videos with an average length of an hour. In September 2020, it even purchased additional bandwidth.

The terms of the October 2019 purchase order incorporated Vimeo's Enterprise Terms. The Enterprise Terms, in turn, incorporated the online terms applicable to the OTT subscription service. Both the Enterprise Terms and the incorporated online terms authorized Vimeo to remove videos that failed to comply with its Acceptable Use Policy. Among potential violations of this Policy was "any content" that "[m]akes false or misleading claims about vaccination safety." Vimeo had publicly announced the introduction of these terms in a blog post on June 26, 2019.

Among the thousands of videos that Daystar uploaded to defendants' platform were six claiming a causal link between vaccines and childhood autism. On July 17, 2020, Vimeo wrote to Daystar that these videos violated Vimeo's Acceptable Use Policy. Daystar alleges that, on July 24, 2020, Vimeo removed five of the videos. Daystar does not allege that defendants terminated services to Daystar prior to expiration of the two-year subscription term, or that Vimeo took down any of Daystar's (several thousand) other videos.

Discussion
Daystar filed suit in New York County alleging breach of contract and unjust enrichment. Supreme Court dismissed the complaint as barred by Vimeo's immunity under 47 USC § 230(c)(2), the Communications Decency Act. We find that Supreme Court correctly dismissed this lawsuit.

With specified exceptions, section 230(c)(2) prohibits holding an interactive computer service provider

liable for "any action voluntarily taken in good faith to restrict access to or availability of material that the provider . . . considers to be obscene, lewd, lascivious, filthy, excessively violent, harassing, or otherwise objectionable." Courts have construed section 230 as authorizing broad immunity * * * . When a complaint makes evident that this immunity applies, the court may dismiss that complaint * * * .

Section 230(c)(2) Applies to This Suit
Daystar asserts that section 230(c)(2) does not apply to breach of contract claims. Its sole basis for this argument, however, is broad dictum in a decision that has since been withdrawn. * * * Moreover, even if there were an exception for contractual obligations to host specific content, such an exception would not apply when a contract unambiguously authorizes one party to remove the type of content at issue.

Neither is the statute limited to material explicitly associated with the service provider. Section 230 immunizes "*any* action . . . to restrict access to or availability of material" by "any information service, system, or access software provider that provides or enables computer access by multiple users to a computer server" * * * [emphasis added]. This unambiguous statutory language extends to removal of all material that a provider hosts, including material that is displayed on another party's website.

The Videos Were "Otherwise Objectionable" Under Section 230
Daystar argues that section 230(c)(2) does not cover the removed videos, because "otherwise objectionable"

Case 9.2 Continues

Case 9.2 Continued

material must resemble the other categories of material listed in section 230(c)(2). Given the differences between these categories, however, the broad final term need not have anything in common with the narrower—but varied—earlier terms * * *.

* * * *

Daystar alleges that its videos do not make "false or misleading" claims, as prohibited by Vimeo's Acceptable Use Policy. Accordingly, it argues that the videos were not "objectionable" and that Vimeo did not have the contractual right to remove those videos. This argument is unavailing, because whether content is objectionable is a subjective determination that is reserved to the service provider * * *.

Accepting as true the facts as alleged in the complaint, and according Daystar the benefit of every possible favorable inference, the face of the complaint shows that Vimeo's removal of material it considered to be "otherwise objectionable" and in violation of its Acceptable Use Policy is protected by the CDA.

Daystar Has Not Pleaded Bad Faith

Daystar argues that, even if the videos could be considered "otherwise objectionable," section 230 does not apply because defendants acted in bad faith. Daystar alleges that defendants solicited its business, that the objectionable videos were posted on Daystar's website at the time, and that defendants represented that Daystar was an ideal long term partner with content that was a good fit for their platform. At the time, Daystar hosted more than 3000 hours of content. Nevertheless, because these six videos were "not a secret," Daystar alleges that defendants "knew that Daystar's content included vaccine programming."

Even accepting Daystar's allegations as true, however, these facts do not support a finding of bad faith on the part of defendants. Daystar does not allege, for example, defendants indicated that the vaccination content specifically was a good fit or that the Acceptable Use Policy did not apply to Daystar. Nor does it allege that Vimeo's stated grounds to remove the videos were a pretext for some illicit reason * * *.

* * * *

Conclusion

Because section 230 applies, Daystar's claims for breach of contract and unjust enrichment should be dismissed, whether or not Daystar has stated a cause of action. Vimeo's right to remove the objectionable videos is determined entirely by the terms of the agreement between Daystar and Vimeo. Because a contract governs this dispute, Daystar cannot maintain a cause of action for unjust enrichment.

After due consideration, we reject Daystar's remaining arguments.

Legal Reasoning Questions

1. What is the importance of Section 230 of the Communications Decency Act?

2. Why was Section 230 important in this case?

3. How did the defendant's existing Acceptable Use Policy impact the appellate court's decision?

9–5 Other Actions Involving Online Posts

Online conduct can give rise to a wide variety of legal actions. E-mails, tweets, posts, and every sort of online communication can form the basis for almost any type of tort. For instance, in addition to defamation, suits relating to online conduct may involve allegations of wrongful interference or infliction of emotional distress. Statutes can also provide grounds for causes of action involving online conduct.

9–6 Privacy

Facebook, Google, and Yahoo have all been accused of violating users' privacy rights. The right to privacy is guaranteed implicitly by the Supreme Court's interpretation of the Bill of Rights and explicitly by some state constitutions. To maintain a suit for the invasion of privacy, though, a person must have a reasonable expectation of privacy in the relevant situation.

9-6a Reasonable Expectation of Privacy

People clearly have a reasonable expectation of privacy when they enter their personal banking or credit-card information online. They also have a reasonable expectation that online companies will follow their own privacy policies. But it is probably not reasonable to expect privacy in statements made on Twitter—or photos posted on Twitter, Flickr, or Instagram, for that matter.

The collection and use of links included in the messages of Facebook users prompted some users to file a suit against the platform for violation of privacy. Facebook confirmed that it collects the "content and other information" that users provide when they "message or communicate with others" and that it may use that information. At issue in the following case was the remedy.

Campbell v. Facebook, Inc.

United States Court of Appeals, Ninth Circuit, 951 F.3d 1106 (2020).

Background and Facts Facebook, Inc. operates a social media platform with over a billion active users, including seven of ten adults in the United States. One function allows a user to send a message that the platform describes as private because only the sender and the recipient can view the contents. Matthew Campbell, Anna St. John, and other users filed a suit in a federal district court against Facebook, alleging that the company routinely captured, read, and used links contained in the messages without the users' consent, in violation of federal privacy law. The plaintiffs claimed that Facebook used the data to facilitate targeted advertising. After four mediation sessions, the parties reached a settlement. In the agreement, Facebook promised to add a disclosure to the "Help Center" page on its platform for a year revealing that "we use tools to identify and store links shared in messages." The court concluded that the plaintiffs were not likely to prevail if the case proceeded, and approved the settlement. St. John appealed, arguing that the settlement was not fair because the plaintiffs received only "worthless" relief.

FRIEDLAND, Circuit Judge:
  * * * *

   [St. John's] argument * * * is premised on a view of the settlement's value that we decline to adopt. * * * The settlement requires Facebook to display [certain] language on its Help Center page for a year. In light of the nature of the claims here, a year-long requirement to make such a disclosure has value: it provides information to users about Facebook's message monitoring practices, making it less likely that users will unwittingly divulge private information to Facebook or third parties in the course of using Facebook's messaging platform.

   Further, * * * the relief * * * cannot be assessed in a vacuum. Rather, the settlement's benefits must be considered by comparison to what the [plaintiffs] actually gave up by settling.

   Here, the [plaintiffs] did not need to receive much for the settlement to be fair because [they] gave up very little. * * * [Under the Electronic Communications Privacy Act (ECPA), the federal statute on which their claim was based], they would have had to show that Facebook's reading of messages sent on Facebook amounted to an unlawful "interception" or wiretap. This would include proving that Facebook had improperly read Plaintiffs' messages while the messages were in "transit" as opposed to in "storage," an issue on which even Plaintiffs acknowledged "uncertainty in the law." Plaintiffs also would have had to contend with Facebook's potential argument that users had consented to the challenged practices—a defense that similarly could have precluded liability * * * . In addition, Plaintiffs would have had to overcome Facebook's potential argument that the challenged activity occurred in "the ordinary course of its business" and therefore could not be the basis for liability under [the ECPA].

   * * * The numerous challenges that Plaintiffs faced provided the parties and the district court ample support to conclude that Plaintiffs were ultimately likely to have lost this entire case.

Decision and Remedy The U.S. Court of Appeals for the Ninth Circuit affirmed the decision of the lower court. Given the unlikelihood of success if the plaintiffs had pursued their claim, "it was not unreasonable that the settlement gave [them] something of modest value."

Critical Thinking
- **Legal Environment** Is a violation of an individual's right to privacy, without more, enough to sustain a legal cause, or should additional harm be required to maintain an action? Explain.
- **Economic** Should Facebook pay platform users for its use of their private data? Discuss.

9–6b Data Collection and Cookies

Whenever a consumer purchases items online from a retailer, such as Amazon.com or Best Buy, the retailer collects information about the consumer. **Cookies** are invisible files that computers create to track a user's web-browsing activities. Cookies provide detailed information to marketers about an individual's online behavior and preferences, which is then used to personalize online services.

Over time, a retailer can amass considerable data about a person's shopping habits. Does collecting this information violate a consumer's right to privacy? Should retailers be able to pass on the data they have collected to their affiliates? Should they be able to use the information to predict what a consumer might want and then create online "coupons" customized to fit the person's buying history?

■ **Case in Point 9.18** Any device connected to the internet is capable of transmitting a multitude of information about not only the device, but also its use. Utilizing integrated software, smart TVs allow consumers to access the internet and on-demand services, including Hulu, Netflix, and Pandora. Apparently, for three years, Vizio, Inc., which installs such software on smart TVs, was secretly tracking what viewers were watching on approximately 16 million of these devices. This information was then sold to advertisers, allowing them to specifically target advertising to Vizio smart TVs and to any computers, tablets, or smartphones connected to the same network.

Several purchasers of Vizio smart TVs filed a class-action data privacy lawsuit against the company for, at a minimum, violating the Video Privacy Protection Act. Initially, Vizio insisted that by allowing advertisers to make "better-informed decisions," its actions actually benefited consumers. Eventually, however, the company reached a settlement that dispersed $11 million among more than 500,000 Vizio smart TV owners.[21] ■

9–6c Internet Companies' Privacy Policies

The Federal Trade Commission (FTC) investigates consumer complaints of privacy violations. The FTC has forced many companies, including Google, Facebook, and Twitter, to enter consent decrees that give the FTC broad power to review their privacy and data practices. It can then sue companies that violate the terms of the decrees.

As you have seen in this chapter, Facebook has had to deal with complaints about its privacy policy and has changed its policy several times to satisfy its critics and to ward off potential government investigations. Other companies, including mobile app developers, have also changed their privacy policies to provide more information to consumers. For the most part, companies—rather than courts or legislatures—have defined the privacy rights of online users. This situation, however, appears to be changing, as you will learn in this chapter's Ethics Today feature.

---
21. *In re Vizio, Inc. Consumer Privacy Litigation,* 2019 WL 3818854 (C.D. CA 2019).

Ethics Today   What are the privacy implications of facial recognition technology?

Using biometrics—the measurement and analysis of an individual's unique physical characteristics—facial recognition software can identify someone from a photo or video. The program can then compare this information with biometrical details stored in a database to create a match. This technology has potential benefits, particularly in the arenas of national security and artificial intelligence. It also has one significant potential drawback: the loss of privacy. The idea of closed-circuit cameras scanning city streets or artificial intelligence applications scouring social media to pick out faces fills many with dread. "The right to participate in society anonymously is something we cannot lose," says one privacy advocate.

Nationwide, more than sixty university administrations have promised not to link facial recognition technology with their campus security cameras. Promoters of the Coachella Arts and Music Festival and other large-scale events have made similar vows.

For their part, companies such as Amazon and Microsoft that stand to profit from selling facial recognition technology or using it in advertising agree that some form of regulation is required. Both have supported various versions of federal legislation that would allow online businesses to identify and store online images if the subjects of those images are notified and give consent.

Several states already have similar protections in place. Legislation passed many years ago in Illinois, for instance, requires companies to obtain written permission before collecting a person's facial scan, fingerprints, or other biometrics.[a] Facebook ran afoul of this law with its Tag Suggestions photo-labeling service, which uses facial recognition software to connect faces with names on its social media platforms. The company paid $550 million to settle a class action lawsuit filed by Illinois residents who claimed that Tag Suggestions violated their right to privacy.[b]

Critical Thinking Billions of users of Facebook and other social media platforms voluntarily reveal, sometimes in excruciating detail, information and photos about their personal lives. Why would these same social media users worry about facial identification by social media companies?

---
a. The Illinois Biometric Information Privacy Act, 740 ILCS 14.
b. *Patel v. Facebook, Inc.,* 932 F.3d 1264 (9th Cir. 2019). See also *Zellmer v. Facebook, Inc.,* 2022 WL 976981 (N.D. CA 2022).

Practice and Review: Internet Law, Social Media, and Privacy

While he was in high school, Joel Gibb downloaded numerous songs to his smartphone from an unlicensed file-sharing service. He used portions of the copyrighted songs when he recorded his own band and posted videos on YouTube and Facebook. Gibb also used BitTorrent to download several movies from the internet. Now he has applied to Boston University. The admissions office has requested access to his Facebook password, and he has complied. Using the information presented in the chapter, answer the following questions.

1. What laws, if any, did Gibb violate by downloading the music and videos from the internet?
2. Was Gibb's use of portions of copyrighted songs in his own music illegal? Explain.
3. Can individuals legally post copyrighted content on their Facebook pages? Why or why not?
4. Did Boston University violate any laws when it asked Joel to provide his Facebook password? Explain.

Debate This . . .   Internet service providers should be subject to the same defamation laws as newspapers, magazines, and television and radio stations.

Terms and Concepts

cloud computing 176	distributed network 176	peer-to-peer (P2P) networking 176
cookies 183	domain name 172	social media 177
cybersquatting 172	goodwill 172	spam 171
cyber torts 180	internet service providers (ISPs) 172	typosquatting 173

Issue Spotters

1. Karl self-publishes a cookbook titled *Hole Foods*, in which he sets out recipes for donuts, Bundt cakes, tortellini, and other foods with holes. To publicize the book, Karl designs the website holefoods.com. Karl appropriates the key words of other cooking and cookbook sites with more frequent hits so that holefoods.com will appear in the same search engine results as the more popular sites. Has Karl done anything wrong? Explain. (See *Internet Law*.)

2. Eagle Corporation began marketing software under the mark "Eagle." Ten years later, Eagle.com, Inc., a different company selling different products, begins to use "eagle" as part of its URL and registers it as a domain name. Can Eagle Corporation stop this use of "eagle"? If so, what must the company show? (See *Internet Law*.)

- **Check your answers to the Issue Spotters against the answers provided in Appendix B at the end of this text.**

Business Scenarios and Case Problems

9–1. Internet Service Providers. CyberConnect, Inc., is an internet service provider (ISP). Pepper is a CyberConnect subscriber. Market Reach, Inc., is an online advertising company. Using sophisticated software, Market Reach directs its ads to those users most likely to be interested in a particular product. When Pepper receives one of the ads, she objects to the content. Further, she claims that CyberConnect should pay damages for "publishing" the ad. Is the ISP regarded as a publisher and therefore liable for the content of Market Reach's ad? Why or why not? (See *Online Defamation*.)

9–2. Privacy. SeeYou, Inc., is an online social network. SeeYou's members develop personalized profiles to interact and share information—photos, videos, stories, activity updates, and other items—with other members. Members post the information that they want to share and decide with whom they want to share it. SeeYou launched a program to allow members to share what they do elsewhere online. For instance, if a member rents a movie through Netflix, SeeYou will broadcast that information to everyone in the member's online network. How can SeeYou avoid complaints that this program violates its members' privacy? (See *Privacy*.)

9–3. File-Sharing. Dartmouth College professor M. Eric Johnson, in collaboration with Tiversa, Inc., a company that monitors peer-to-peer networks to provide security services, wrote an article titled "Data Hemorrhages in the Health-Care Sector." In preparing the article, Johnson and Tiversa searched the networks for data that could be used to commit medical or financial identity theft. They found a document that contained the Social Security numbers, insurance information, and treatment codes for patients of LabMD, Inc. Tiversa notified LabMD of the find in order to solicit its business. Instead of hiring Tiversa, however, LabMD filed a suit in a federal district court against the company, alleging trespass, conversion, and violations of federal statutes. What do these facts indicate about the security of private information? Explain. How should the court rule? [*LabMD, Inc. v. Tiversa, Inc.,* 509 Fed.Appx. 842 (11th Cir. 2013)] (See *Copyrights in Digital Information*.)

9–4. Business Case Problem with Sample Answer— Social Media. Mohammad Omar Aly Hassan and nine others were indicted in a federal district court on charges of conspiring to advance violent jihad (holy war against enemies of Islam) and other offenses related to terrorism. The evidence at Hassan's trial included postings he had made on Facebook concerning his adherence to violent jihadist ideology. Convicted, Hassan appealed, contending that the Facebook items had not been properly authenticated (established as his own comments). How might the government show the connection between postings on Facebook and those who post them? Discuss. [*United States v. Hassan,* 742 F.3d 104 (4th Cir. 2014)] (See *Social Media*.)

- **For a sample answer to Problem 9–4, go to Appendix C at the end of this text.**

9–5. Social Media. Kenneth Wheeler was angry at certain police officers in Grand Junction, Colorado, because of a driving-under-the-influence arrest that he viewed as unjust. While in Italy, Wheeler posted a statement to his Facebook page urging his "religious followers" to "kill cops, drown them in the blood of their children, hunt them down and kill their entire bloodlines" and provided names. Later, Wheeler added a post to "commit a massacre in the Stepping Stones preschool and day care, just walk in and kill everybody." Could a reasonable person conclude that Wheeler's posts were true threats? How might law enforcement officers use Wheeler's posts? Explain. [*United States v. Wheeler,* 776 F.3d 736 (10th Cir. 2015)] (See *Social Media*.)

9–6. Social Media. Irvin Smith was charged in a Georgia state court with burglary and theft. Before the trial, during the selection of the jury, the state prosecutor asked the prospective jurors whether they knew Smith. No one responded affirmatively. Jurors were chosen and sworn in, without objection. After the trial, during deliberations, the jurors indicated to the court that they were deadlocked. The court charged them to try again. Meanwhile, the prosecutor learned that "Juror 4" appeared as a friend on the defendant's Facebook page and filed a motion to dismiss her. The court replaced Juror 4 with an alternate. Was this an appropriate action, or was it an "abuse of discretion"? Should the court have admitted evidence that Facebook friends do not always actually know each other? Discuss. [*Smith v. State of Georgia,* 335 Ga.App. 497, 782 S.E.2d 305 (2016)] (See *Social Media*.)

9–7. Internet Law. Jason Smathers, an employee of America Online (AOL), misappropriated an AOL customer list with 92 million screen names. He sold the list for $28,000 to Sean Dunaway, who sold it to Braden Bournival. Bournival used it to send AOL customers more than 3 billion unsolicited, deceptive e-mail ads. AOL estimated its cost of processing the ads to be

at least $300,000. Convicted of conspiring to relay deceptive e-mail in violation of federal law, Smathers was ordered to pay AOL restitution of $84,000 (treble the amount for which he had sold the AOL customer list). Smathers appealed, seeking to reduce the amount. He cited a judgment in a civil suit for a different offense against Bournival and others for which AOL had collected $95,000. Smathers also argued that his obligation should be reduced by restitution payments made by Dunaway. Which federal law did Smathers violate? Should the amount of his restitution be reduced? Explain. [*United States v. Smathers,* 879 F.3d 453 (2d. Cir. 2018)] (See *Internet Law*.)

9–8. Social Media. A school district had a long-standing business relationship with Riley's American Heritage Farms, a company that provides field-trip venues for public school children. The principal shareholder of the company, James Patrick Riley, had personal social media accounts, including one on Twitter. Riley posted negative tweets about Senators Elizabeth Warren and Kirsten Gillibrand, and also tweeted about gender issues. None of Riley's tweets appeared on any of Riley's Farms' social media accounts or website. None of the tweets referenced Riley's Farms, the school district, or school field trips in general.

In an e-mail to her child's teacher, a parent indicated that she did not feel comfortable "patronizing an establishment whose owner might be inclined to direct bigoted opinions toward [her] child or other vulnerable children in the group." As a result of parental complaints about the tweets, the school district broke off its business relationship with Riley's Farms. The company and its principal shareholder then sued the district. A federal trial court granted summary judgment for school officials. Was summary judgment appropriate in this case? Why or why not? [*Riley's American Heritage Farms v. Elsasser,* 29 F.4th 484 (9th Cir. 2022)] (See *Social Media*.)

9–9. A Question of Ethics—The IDDR Approach and Social Media. One August morning, around 6:30 a.m., a fire occurred at Ray and Christine Nixon's home in West Monroe, Louisiana, while the Nixons were inside the home. The Nixons told Detective Gary Gilley of the Ouachita Parish Sheriff's Department that they believed the fire had been deliberately set by Matthew Alexander, a former employee of Ray's company. Ray gave Alexander's phone number to Gilley, who contacted the number's service provider, Verizon Wireless Services, L.L.C. Gilley said that he was investigating a house fire and that he wanted to know where the number's subscriber had been that day. He did not present a warrant, but he did certify that Verizon's response would be considered an "emergency disclosure." [*Alexander v. Verizon Wireless Services, L.L.C.,* 875 F.3d 243 (5th Cir. 2017)] (See *Social Media*.)

(a) Using the Inquiry and Discussion steps in the IDDR approach, identify the ethical dilemma that Verizon faced in this situation and actions that the company might have taken to resolve that issue.

(b) Suppose that Verizon gave Gilley the requested information and that later Alexander filed a suit against the provider, alleging a violation of the Stored Communications Act. Could Verizon successfully plead "good faith" in its defense?

Time-Limited Group Assignment

9–10. File-Sharing. James, Chang, and Sixta are roommates. They are music fans and frequently listen to the same artists and songs. They regularly exchange MP3 music files that contain songs from their favorite artists. (See *Copyrights in Digital Information*.)

(a) One group of students will decide whether the fact that the roommates are transferring files among themselves for no monetary benefit precludes them from being subject to copyright law.

(b) A second group will consider the situation in which each roommate bought music on CDs, downloaded it to their computers, and then gave the CDs to the other roommates to do the same. Does this violate copyright law? Is it the same as file-sharing digital music? Explain.

(c) A third group will consider streaming music services. If one roommate subscribes to a streaming service and the other roommates use the service for free, would this violate copyright law? Why or why not?

Chapter 10

Criminal Law and Cyber Crime

Criminal law is an important part of the legal environment of business. Society imposes a variety of sanctions to protect businesses from harm so that they can compete and flourish. These sanctions include damages for various types of tortious conduct, damages for breach of contract, and various equitable remedies. Additional sanctions are imposed under criminal law.

Many statutes regulating business provide for criminal as well as civil sanctions. For instance, federal statutes that protect the environment often include criminal sanctions. Large companies that violate environmental laws may face criminal penalties that include millions of dollars in fines.

10–1 Civil Law and Criminal Law

Civil law pertains to the duties that exist between persons or between persons and their governments. Criminal law, in contrast, has to do with crime. A **crime** can be defined as a wrong against society set forth in a statute and punishable by a fine and/or imprisonment—or, in some cases, death.

10–1a Key Differences Between Civil Law and Criminal Law

Criminal law differs in a number of ways from civil law. Exhibit 10–1 summarizes these and other important differences between civil law and criminal law.

Prosecuted by the State In civil cases, those who have suffered harm bring lawsuits against those who caused the harm. In contrast, because crimes are offenses against society, they are prosecuted by a public official, such as a district attorney (D.A.) or an attorney general (A.G.), not by the victims. Once a crime has been reported, the D.A.'s office decides whether to file criminal charges and to what extent to pursue the prosecution or carry out additional investigation.

Burden of Proof In a civil case, plaintiffs usually must prove their case by a preponderance of the evidence. Under this standard, a plaintiff must convince the court that based on the evidence presented by both parties, it is more likely than not that the plaintiff's allegation is true.

In a criminal case, in contrast, the government must prove its case **beyond a reasonable doubt.** If the jury views the evidence in the case as reasonably permitting either a guilty or a not guilty verdict, then the jury's verdict must be not guilty. In other words, the government (prosecutor) must prove beyond a reasonable doubt that

Exhibit 10–1 Key Differences Between Civil Law and Criminal Law

Issue	Civil Law	Criminal Law
Party who brings suit	The person who suffered harm.	The state.
Wrongful act	Causing harm to a person or to a person's property.	Violating a statute that prohibits some type of activity.
Burden of proof	Preponderance of the evidence.	Beyond a reasonable doubt.
Verdict	Three-fourths majority (typically).	Unanimous (almost always).
Remedy	Damages to compensate for the harm or a decree to achieve an equitable result.	Punishment (fine, imprisonment, or death).

the defendant has committed every essential element of the offense charged.

Note also that in a criminal case, the jury's verdict must be unanimous—agreed to by all members of the jury—to convict the defendant.[1] (In a civil trial by jury, in contrast, typically only three-fourths of the jurors need to agree.)

Criminal Sanctions The sanctions imposed on criminal wrongdoers are normally harsher than those applied in civil cases. Remember that the purpose of tort law is to enable a person harmed by a wrongful act to obtain compensation from the wrongdoer, rather than to punish the wrongdoer. In contrast, criminal sanctions are designed to punish those who commit crimes and to deter others from committing similar acts in the future.

Criminal sanctions include fines as well as the much stiffer penalty of the loss of liberty by incarceration in a jail or prison. Most criminal sanctions also involve probation and sometimes require performance of community service, completion of an educational or treatment program, or payment of restitution. The harshest criminal sanction is, of course, the death penalty.

10–1b Civil Liability for Criminal Acts

Some torts, such as assault and battery, provide a basis for a criminal prosecution as well as a civil action in tort. ■ **Example 10.1** Chudy is walking down the street, minding his own business, when a person attacks him. In the ensuing struggle, the attacker stabs Chudy several times, seriously injuring him. A police officer restrains and arrests the assailant. In this situation, the attacker may be subject both to criminal prosecution by the state and to a tort lawsuit brought by Chudy to obtain compensation for his injuries. ■

Exhibit 10–2 illustrates how the same wrongful act can result in both a civil (tort) action and a criminal action against the wrongdoer.

---

1. At one time, two states, Louisiana and Oregon, allowed jury verdicts that were not unanimous. See *Ramos v. Louisiana*, 590 U.S. __, 140 S.Ct. 1390, 206 L.Ed.2d 583 (2020).

Exhibit 10–2 Civil (Tort) Lawsuit and Criminal Prosecution for the Same Act

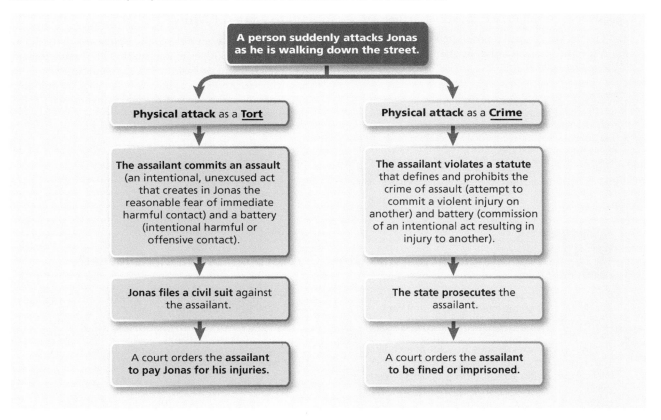

A person suddenly attacks Jonas as he is walking down the street.

Physical attack as a <u>Tort</u>

The assailant commits an assault (an intentional, unexcused act that creates in Jonas the reasonable fear of immediate harmful contact) and a battery (intentional harmful or offensive contact).

Jonas files a civil suit against the assailant.

A court orders the **assailant to pay Jonas for his injuries.**

Physical attack as a <u>Crime</u>

The assailant violates a statute that defines and prohibits the crime of assault (attempt to commit a violent injury on another) and battery (commission of an intentional act resulting in injury to another).

The state prosecutes the assailant.

A court orders the **assailant to be fined or imprisoned.**

10–1c Classification of Crimes

Depending on their degree of seriousness, crimes are classified as felonies or misdemeanors. **Felonies** are serious crimes punishable by death or by imprisonment for more than one year.[2] Many states also define different degrees of felony offenses and vary the punishment according to the degree.[3] For instance, most jurisdictions punish a burglary that involves forced entry into a home at night more harshly than a burglary that involves breaking into a non-residential building during the day.

Misdemeanors are less serious crimes, punishable by a fine or by confinement for up to a year. **Petty offenses** are minor violations, such as jaywalking or violations of building codes, considered to be a subset of misdemeanors. Even for petty offenses, however, a guilty party can be put in jail for a few days, fined, or both, depending on state or local law. Whether a crime is a felony or a misdemeanor can determine in which court the case is tried and, in some states, whether the defendant has a right to a jury trial.

10–2 Criminal Liability

The following two elements normally must exist simultaneously for a person to be convicted of a crime:

1. The performance of a prohibited act *(actus reus)*.
2. A specified state of mind, or intent, on the part of the actor *(mens rea)*.

---

2. Federal law and most state laws use this definition, but there is some variation among states as to the length of imprisonment associated with a felony conviction.
3. The American Law Institute issued the Model Penal Code in 1962 to help states standardize their penal laws. Note, however, that the Model Penal Code is not a uniform code, and each state has developed its own set of laws governing criminal acts. Thus, types of crimes and prescribed punishments may differ from one jurisdiction to another.

10–2a The Criminal Act

Every criminal statute prohibits certain behavior. Most crimes require an act of commission—that is, a person must do something in order to be accused of a crime. In criminal law, a prohibited act is referred to as the **actus reus**,[4] or guilty act. In some instances, an act of omission can be a crime, but only when a person has a legal duty to perform the omitted act, such as filing a tax return.

The guilty act requirement is based on one of the premises of criminal law—that a person should be punished for harm done to society. For a crime to exist, the guilty act must thus cause some harm to a person or to property. Thinking about killing someone or about stealing a car may be morally wrong, but the thoughts do no harm until they are translated into action.

Of course, a person can be punished for *attempting* murder or robbery, but normally only if that person has taken substantial steps toward the criminal objective. Additionally, the person must have specifically intended to commit the crime to be convicted of an attempt. (Are online cryptocurrencies causing so much harm that they should be made illegal? See this chapter's Digital Update feature for a discussion.)

10–2b State of Mind

Mens rea,[5] or wrongful mental state, also is typically required to establish criminal liability. The required mental state, or intent, is indicated in the applicable statute or law. Murder, for instance, involves the guilty act of killing another human being, and the guilty mental state is the desire, or intent, to take another's life. For theft, the guilty act is the taking of another person's property. The mental state involves both the awareness that the property

---

4. Pronounced *ak*-tuhs *ray*-uhs.
5. Pronounced *mehns ray*-uh.

Bitcoin and all other cryptocurrencies illegal. The major problem government officials claim is that cryptocurrencies are tailor-made for criminal activity. Anyone can use Bitcoin without providing a name or identity, and it is difficult to trace online purchases made using this form of trade.

Consequently, Bitcoin is the currency of choice on the *dark web,* a part of the internet that can only be accessed through special methods designed to obscure the identity of providers and users. An estimated $500 million in Bitcoin is spent on dark web markets each month. Law enforcement officials believe that the dark web is an important source of distribution for synthetic opioids, which cause of thousands of deaths in the United States each year. In Park City, Utah, two thirteen-year-old boys overdosed on a synthetic opioid known as Pinky that they purchased using Bitcoin on the dark web.

Stateless Currency

There is little evidence that a federal law banning Bitcoin and other cryptocurrencies, if passed, would have much effect. Buyers and sellers using Bitcoin are almost always able to remain anonymous. Furthermore, it can be difficult for law enforcement to determine the source not only of cryptocurrency-related crime, but of any criminal activity that takes place online. As one expert puts it, "You can't prevent people from holding ones and zeros on a device in their pocket."

Critical Thinking Despite Bitcoin's oversized presence on the dark web, only about 1 percent of all transactions using the cryptocurrency involve an illegal exchange of goods. How does this fact impact arguments in favor of banning Bitcoin?

belongs to another and the desire to deprive the owner of it. A court can also find that the required mental state is present when the defendant acts recklessly or is criminally negligent.

A criminal conspiracy exists when two or more people agree to commit an unlawful act, and then take some action toward its completion. The required mental state involves both the intent to agree and the intent to commit the underlying crime. In the following case, the issue was whether the evidence was sufficient to prove that the defendant had "knowingly and voluntarily" participated in a conspiracy to commit healthcare fraud.

Case 10.1

United States v. Crabtree

United States Court of Appeals, Eleventh Circuit, 878 F.3d 1274 (2018).

Background and Facts Health Care Solutions Network, Inc. (HCSN), operated mental health centers to provide psychiatric therapy. HCSN organized its business around procuring, retaining, and readmitting patients to maximize billing potential, without respect to their health needs. It ensured that patient files complied with strict Medicare requirements by editing intake information, fabricating treatment plans, and falsifying therapy and treatment notes. The scheme spanned seven years and amounted to more than $63 million in fraudulent claims.

At one of HCSN's facilities, Doris Crabtree was responsible for patient therapy notes. The notes were systematically altered and falsified to support Medicare claims. Convicted in a federal district court of conspiracy to commit healthcare fraud, Crabtree appealed to the U.S. Court of Appeals for the Eleventh Circuit. She argued that she had only been negligent and careless.

In the Language of the Court
WILSON, Circuit Judge
* * * *

* * * According to Crabtree, * * * the evidence against [her] was primarily circumstantial and * * * did not show that [she] knowingly and voluntarily joined a conspiracy to defraud Medicare.
* * * *

* * * The very nature of conspiracy frequently requires that the existence of an agreement be proved by inferences from the conduct of the alleged participants or from circumstantial evidence of a scheme. The government need only prove that the defendant knew of the essential nature of the conspiracy, and we

Case 10.1 Continues

Case 10.1 Continued   will affirm a conspiracy conviction when the circumstances surrounding a person's presence at the scene of conspiratorial activity are so obvious that knowledge of its character can fairly be attributed to [her]. The government can show that a defendant voluntarily joined a conspiracy through proof of surrounding circumstances such as acts committed by the defendant which furthered the purpose of the conspiracy.

* * * *

The government put forth considerable evidence that Crabtree [was] directly aware of the essential nature of the conspiracy and that the circumstances at HCSN were so obvious that knowledge of the fraud's character can fairly be attributed to [her]. Multiple former employees testified that Crabtree * * * complied with their requests to doctor patient notes so that they would pass Medicare review. * * * Numerous witnesses spoke of the overwhelming evidence that patients were unqualified for * * * treatment [at HCSN]: that it was obvious, and widely observed, that patients at HCSN suffered from Alzheimer's, dementia, autism, and forms of mental retardation that rendered treatment ineffective; that this was evidenced, for example, by patients * * * who were unable to engage in group therapy sessions; and that Crabtree [was] involved in multiple conversations about the unsuitability of [the] patients for * * * treatment [at HCSN]. One former employee put it simply: "everybody was aware of the fraud."

Likewise, a reasonable jury could have found that Crabtree * * * voluntarily joined the conspiracy, given the substantial evidence of [her] role in furthering the fraud. The government put forth evidence that Crabtree * * * complied with requests to alter and fabricate notes for billing and Medicare auditing purposes; * * * and that [she] misrepresented the therapy that patients received when, for example, they * * * were * * * absent but notes indicated that they participated fully.

Decision and Remedy   The federal appellate court affirmed Crabtree's conviction. The court concluded that Crabtree "had knowledge of the conspiracy at HCSN" and that she had "voluntarily joined the conspiracy, given the substantial evidence of [her] role in furthering the fraud."

Critical Thinking

- **Legal Environment**   Could Crabtree have successfully avoided her conviction by arguing that her only "crime" was naively trusting her co-workers? Why or why not?
- **Ethical**   It seems reasonable to assume that one of the purposes of any business is to maximize billing potential. When does conduct to accomplish that purpose become unethical?

Recklessness   Defendants are criminally reckless if they consciously disregard a substantial and unjustifiable risk. ■ **Example 10.2**   A claustrophobic patient at the Vanderbilt University Medical Center in Nashville, Tennessee, was about to undergo a full body scan, which requires lying inside a large tube-like machine for about thirty minutes. A nurse, meaning to inject the patient with the anti-anxiety drug Versed, mistakenly injected her with vecuronium, a powerful narcotic used to keep patients from moving during surgery.

The mistake occurred, apparently, because both drugs start with "ve." After the patient died, state law enforcement officials charged the nurse with reckless homicide. When medical professionals do not read the label of a drug they are about to inject into a patient, they have arguably created a substantial and unjustifiable risk of severe harm or death. ■

Criminal Negligence   Criminal negligence involves the mental state in which the defendant takes an unjustified, substantial, and foreseeable risk that results in harm.

Defendants can be negligent even if they were not actually aware of the risk but should have been aware of it.[6]

A homicide is classified as involuntary manslaughter when it results from an act of criminal negligence and there is no intent to kill. ■ **Example 10.3**   Demolition contractor Griffith Campbell was convicted of involuntary manslaughter after he caused a brick wall to collapse onto a Salvation Army store. Not only did Campbell remove support beams and joists to sell for salvage, making the wall unstable, but he also negligently conducted the demolition during business hours, leading to the deaths of six people in the thrift shop. ■

Federal Crimes.   The federal criminal code lists more than four thousand criminal offenses, many of which do not require a specific mental state. In addition, many of these rules do not require intent.

■ **Example 10.4**   Eddie Leroy Anderson, a retired logger and former science teacher, went digging for

---

6. Model Penal Code Section 2.02(2)(d).

arrowheads with his son near a campground in Idaho. They did not realize that they were on federal land and that it is a felony to remove artifacts from federal land without a permit. Although the crime carries a penalty of as much as two years in prison, the father and son pleaded guilty, and each received a sentence of probation and a $1,500 fine. ■

Strict liability crimes are particularly common in environmental laws, laws aimed at combatting illegal drugs, and other laws affecting public health, safety, and welfare. Under federal law, for instance, tenants can be evicted from public housing if one of their relatives or a guest used illegal drugs inside the dwelling—regardless of whether the tenant knew about the drug activity.

State Crimes. Many states have also enacted laws that punish behavior as criminal without the need to show criminal intent. ■ **Example 10.5** In several states, a vendor who sells alcohol to someone under the age of twenty-one has committed a crime. Under these laws, vendors can be convicted of the crime regardless of their intent or their knowledge of the customer's actual age. ■

10–2c Corporate Criminal Liability

A corporation is a legal entity created under the laws of a state. At one time, it was thought that a corporation could not incur criminal liability because, although a corporation is a legal person, it can act only through its agents (corporate directors, officers, and employees). Therefore, the corporate entity itself could not "intend" to commit a crime. Over time, this view has changed. Obviously, corporations cannot be imprisoned, but they can be fined or denied certain legal privileges (such as necessary licenses).

Liability of the Corporate Entity Today, corporations normally are liable for the crimes committed by their agents and employees within the course and scope of their employment.[7] For liability to be imposed, the prosecutor generally must show that the corporation could have prevented the act or that a supervisor authorized or had knowledge of the act. In addition, corporations can be criminally liable for failing to perform specific duties imposed by law (such as duties under environmental laws or securities laws).

■ **Case in Point 10.6** A prostitution ring, the Gold Club, was operating out of some motels in West Virginia. A motel manager, who was also a corporate officer, gave discounted rates to Gold Club prostitutes, and they paid him in cash. The corporation received a portion of the funds generated by the Gold Club's illegal operations. A jury found that the corporation was criminally liable because a supervisor within the corporation—the motel manager—had knowledge of the prostitution activities and the corporation had allowed it to continue.[8] ■

Liability of Corporate Officers and Directors

Corporate directors and officers are personally liable for the crimes they commit, regardless of whether the crimes were committed for their private benefit or on the corporation's behalf. Additionally, corporate directors and officers may be held liable for the actions of employees under their supervision. Under the responsible corporate officer doctrine, a court may impose criminal liability on a corporate officer who participated in, directed, or merely knew about a given criminal violation.

■ **Case in Point 10.7** Austin DeCoster owned and controlled Quality Egg, LLC, an egg production and processing company with facilities across Iowa. His son Peter DeCoster was the chief operating officer. Due to unsanitary conditions in some of its facilities, Quality shipped and sold eggs that contained salmonella bacteria, which sickened thousands of people across the United States.

The federal government prosecuted the DeCosters under the responsible corporate officer doctrine based, in part, on Quality's failure to comply with regulations affecting egg production facilities. The DeCosters ultimately pleaded guilty to violating three criminal statutes. But when they were ordered to serve three months in jail, the DeCosters challenged the sentence as unconstitutional. The court held that the sentence of incarceration was appropriate because the evidence suggested that the defendants knew about the unsanitary conditions in their processing plants.[9] ■

10–3 Types of Crimes

Federal, state, and local laws provide for the classification and punishment of hundreds of thousands of different criminal acts. Generally, though, criminal acts fall into five broad categories: violent crime (crimes against persons), property crime, public order crime, white-collar

---

7. See Model Penal Code Section 2.07.

8. As a result of the convictions, the motel manager was sentenced to fifteen months in prison, and the corporation was ordered to forfeit the motel property. *United States v. Singh,* 518 F.3d 236 (4th Cir. 2008). See also *United States v. Arthur,* 2022 WL 294292 (D.MD So.Div. 2022).

9. *United States v. Quality Egg, LLC,* 99 F.Supp.3d 920 (N.D. Iowa 2015).

crime, and organized crime. In addition, when crimes are committed in cyberspace rather than in the physical world, we often refer to them as *cyber crimes*.

10–3a Violent Crime

Certain crimes are called *violent crimes*, or *crimes against persons*, because they cause others to suffer harm or death. Murder is a violent crime. So is sexual assault, or rape. **Robbery**—defined as the taking of money, personal property, or any other article of value from a person by means of force or fear—is also a violent crime. Typically, states have more severe penalties for aggravated robbery—robbery with the use of a deadly weapon.

Assault and battery, which are torts, are also classified as violent crimes. ■ **Example 10.8** Restaurateur Mario Batali was criminally charged with indecent assault and battery arising from an incident at a Boston restaurant. While taking a selfie with an admirer, he allegedly kissed and fondled her and, when she tried to escape his grasp, aggressively touched her face. ■

Each violent crime is further classified by degree, depending on the circumstances surrounding the criminal act. These circumstances include the intent of the person committing the crime and whether a weapon was used. For crimes other than murder, the level of pain and suffering experienced by the victim is also a factor.

10–3b Property Crime

The most common type of criminal activity is property crime, in which the goal of the offender is some form of economic gain or the damaging of property. Robbery is a form of property crime, as well as a violent crime, because the offender seeks to gain the property of another.

Burglary Traditionally, **burglary** was defined as breaking and entering the dwelling of another at night with the intent to commit a felony. This definition was aimed at protecting an individual's home and its occupants.

Most state statutes have eliminated some of the requirements found in the common law definition. The time of day at which the breaking and entering occurs, for instance, is usually immaterial. State statutes frequently omit the element of breaking, and some states do not require that the building be a dwelling. When a deadly weapon is used in a burglary, the perpetrator can be charged with aggravated burglary and punished more severely.

Larceny Under the common law, the crime of **larceny** involved the unlawful taking and carrying away of someone else's personal property with the intent to permanently deprive the owner of possession. Put simply,

larceny is stealing, or theft. Whereas robbery involves force or fear, larceny does not. Therefore, picking pockets is larceny, not robbery. Similarly, an employee taking company products and supplies home for personal use without permission is committing larceny.

Obtaining Goods by False Pretenses Obtaining goods by means of false pretenses is a form of theft that involves trickery or fraud, such as using someone else's credit card number without permission. Statutes dealing with such illegal activities vary widely from state to state. They often apply not only to property, but also to services and cash.

■ **Case in Point 10.9** Corey Fleck sold some cattle that were subject to debts he owed to others. In connection with the sale, Fleck was issued a check naming him and those who had an interest in the cattle as payees. The check was cashed, and the funds deposited in Fleck's bank account. The bank then learned that all the endorsements of the other people who had interests in the cattle were fraudulent. The bank withdrew the money from Fleck's account. Subsequently, the other people who had interests in the cattle received their funds.

The state of North Dakota charged Fleck with one count of theft of property by deception, and a jury convicted him. On appeal, he claimed that he had not knowingly obtained property by deception. The appellate court upheld the conviction.[10] ■

Theft Sometimes, state statutes consolidate the crime of obtaining goods by false pretenses with other property offenses, such as larceny and embezzlement (discussed shortly), into a single crime called simply "theft." Under such a statute, it is not necessary for a defendant to be charged specifically with larceny or obtaining goods by false pretenses. Petty theft is the theft of a small quantity of cash or low-value goods. Grand theft is the theft of a larger amount of cash or higher-value property.

Receiving Stolen Goods It is a crime to receive goods that a person knows or should have known were stolen or illegally obtained. To be convicted, the recipient of such goods need not know the true identity of the owner or the thief and need not have paid for the goods. All that is necessary is that the recipient knows or should know that the goods are stolen, which implies an intent to deprive the true owner of those goods.

Arson The willful and malicious burning of a building (or, in some states, a vehicle or other item of personal property) is the crime of **arson.** At common law, arson

---

10. *State v. Fleck,* 971 N.W.2d 387 (Sup.Ct. ND 2022).

applied only to burning down another person's house. The law was designed to protect human life. Today, arson statutes have been extended to cover the destruction of any building, regardless of ownership, by fire or explosion.

Every state has a special statute that covers the act of burning a building for the purpose of collecting insurance. (Of course, the insurer need not pay the claim when insurance fraud is proved.)

Forgery The fraudulent making or altering of any writing (including an electronic record) in a way that changes the legal rights and liabilities of another is **forgery.** ■ **Example 10.10** Without authorization, Minsun signs Bennett's name on the back of a check made out to Bennett and attempts to cash it. Minsun is committing forgery. ■ Forgery also includes changing trademarks, falsifying public records, counterfeiting, and altering a legal document.

10–3c Public Order Crime

Historically, societies have always outlawed activities that are considered contrary to public values and morals. Today, the most common public order crimes include public drunkenness, prostitution, gambling, and illegal drug use. These crimes are sometimes referred to as *victimless crimes* because they normally harm only the offender. From a broader perspective, however, they are deemed detrimental to society as a whole because they may create an environment that gives rise to property and violent crimes.

■ **Example 10.11** A man is stumbling through a mall parking lot, screaming obscenities. A sheriff's deputy arrives on the scene and—noting that the man is slurring his speech, has droopy, bloodshot eyes, and smells of alcohol—arrests him for public intoxication. Under state law, this public order crime is a misdemeanor punishable by a fine of no more than $500. ■

10–3d White-Collar Crime

Crimes occurring in the business context are popularly referred to as *white-collar crimes*, although this is not an official legal term. Ordinarily, **white-collar crime** involves an illegal act or series of acts committed by an individual or business entity using some nonviolent means to obtain a personal or business advantage.

White-collar crime usually takes place in the course of a legitimate business activity. Corporate crimes fall into this category. Certain property crimes, such as larceny and forgery, may also be white-collar crimes if they occur within the business context. The crimes discussed next normally occur only in the business context.

Embezzlement When a person who is entrusted with another person's property fraudulently appropriates it, **embezzlement** occurs. Embezzlement is not larceny, because the wrongdoer does not physically take the property from another's possession, and it is not robbery, because no force or fear is used.

Typically, embezzlement is carried out by an employee who steals funds a small amount at a time over a long period. In a number of businesses, corporate officers or accountants have fraudulently converted funds for their own benefit and then "fixed" the books to cover up their crimes.

Embezzlement occurs whether the embezzler takes the funds directly from the victim or from a third person. If financial officers of a large corporation pocket checks from third parties that were given them to deposit into the corporate account, they are embezzling.

The intent to return embezzled property—or its actual return—is not a defense to the crime of embezzlement, as the following Spotlight Case illustrates.

Spotlight on White-Collar Crime

Case 10.2 People v. Sisuphan

Court of Appeal of California, First District, 181 Cal.App.4th 800, 104 Cal.Rptr.3d 654 (2010).

Background and Facts Lou Sisuphan was the director of finance at a Toyota dealership. His responsibilities included managing the financing contracts for vehicle sales and working with lenders to obtain payments. Sisuphan complained repeatedly to management about the performance and attitude of one of the finance managers, Ian McClelland. The general manager, Michael Christian, would not terminate McClelland "because he brought a lot of money into the dealership."

Case 10.2 Continues

Case 10.2 Continued

One day, McClelland accepted $22,600 in cash and two checks totaling $7,275.51 from a customer in payment for a car. McClelland placed the cash, the checks, and a copy of the receipt in a large envelope. As he tried to drop the envelope into the safe through a mechanism at its top, the envelope became stuck. While McClelland went for assistance, Sisuphan wiggled the envelope free and kept it. On McClelland's return, Sisuphan told him that the envelope had dropped into the safe. When the payment turned up missing, Christian told all the managers he would not bring criminal charges if the payment was returned within twenty-four hours.

After the twenty-four-hour period had lapsed, Sisuphan told Christian that he had taken the envelope, and he returned the cash and checks to Christian. Sisuphan claimed that he had no intention of stealing the payment but had taken it to get McClelland fired. Christian fired Sisuphan the next day, and the district attorney later charged Sisuphan with embezzlement.

After a jury trial, Sisuphan was found guilty. Sisuphan appealed, arguing that the trial court had erred by excluding evidence that he had returned the payment. The trial court had concluded that the evidence was not relevant because return of the property is not a defense to embezzlement.

In the Language of the Court

JENKINS, J. [Judge]

* * * *

Fraudulent intent is an essential element of embezzlement. Although restoration of the property is not a defense, evidence of repayment may be relevant to the extent it shows that a defendant's intent at the time of the taking was not fraudulent. Such evidence is admissible "only when [a] defendant shows a relevant and probative [confirming] link in his subsequent actions from which it might be inferred his original intent was innocent." The question before us, therefore, is whether evidence that Sisuphan returned the money reasonably tends to prove he lacked the requisite intent at the time of the taking.

Section 508 [of the California Penal Code], which sets out the offense of which Sisuphan was convicted, provides: "Every clerk, agent, or servant of any person who fraudulently appropriates to his own use, or secretes with a fraudulent intent to appropriate to his own use, any property of another which has come into his control or care by virtue of his employment * * * is guilty of embezzlement." Sisuphan denies he ever intended "to use the [money] to financially better himself, even temporarily" and contends the evidence he sought to introduce showed "he returned the [money] without having appropriated it to his own use in any way." He argues that this evidence negates fraudulent intent because it supports his claim that he took the money to get McClelland fired and acted "to help his company by drawing attention to the inadequacy and incompetency of an employee." We reject these contentions.

In determining whether Sisuphan's intent was fraudulent at the time of the taking, the issue is not whether he intended to spend the money, but whether he intended to use it for a purpose other than that for which the dealership entrusted it to him. The offense of embezzlement contemplates a principal's entrustment of property to an agent for certain purposes and the agent's breach of that trust by acting outside his authority in his use of the property. * * * Sisuphan's undisputed purpose—to get McClelland fired—was beyond the scope of his responsibility and therefore outside the trust afforded him by the dealership. Accordingly, even if the proffered evidence shows he took the money for this purpose, it does not tend to prove he lacked fraudulent intent, and the trial court properly excluded this evidence.

Decision and Remedy The California appellate court affirmed the trial court's decision. The fact that Sisuphan had returned the payment was irrelevant. He was guilty of embezzlement.

Critical Thinking

- **Legal Environment** Why was Sisuphan convicted of embezzlement instead of larceny? What is the difference between these two crimes?
- **Ethical** Given that Sisuphan returned the cash and checks, was it fair of the dealership's general manager to terminate Sisuphan's employment? Why or why not?

Mail and Wire Fraud Among the most potent weapons against white-collar criminals are the federal laws that prohibit mail fraud[11] and wire fraud.[12] These laws make it a federal crime to devise any scheme that uses U.S. mail, commercial carriers (FedEx, UPS), or wire (telegraph, telephone, television, the internet, e-mail, or text) with the intent to defraud the public. These laws are often applied when persons send out advertisements, e-mails, or text messages with the intent to obtain cash or property by false pretenses.

■ **Case in Point 10.12** Donovan Davis and several associates launched Capital Blu Management to trade in the foreign currency marketplace. Over the course of several days, Capital Blu engaged in a disastrous series of trades, losing almost $3 million. Davis feared that if these losses were reported to investors, they would abandon the company and his reputation in the financial community would suffer. So Capital Blu sent out a monthly report via mail and e-mail falsely reporting a 1.6 percent gain.

This monthly pattern of transmitting fraudulent reports continued until regulators shut Capital Blu down a year later. In a ruling upheld on appeal, a federal trial court found Davis responsible for $10 million in investor losses and convicted him on six counts of mail fraud and one count of wire fraud.[13] ■

The maximum penalty under these statutes is substantial. Persons convicted of mail, wire, and internet fraud may be imprisoned for up to twenty years and/or fined. If the violation affects a financial institution or involves fraud in connection with emergency disaster-relief funds, the violator may be fined up to $1 million, imprisoned for up to thirty years, or both.

Bribery The crime of bribery involves offering to give something of value to a person in an attempt to influence that person in a way that serves a private interest. Three types of bribery are considered crimes: bribery of public officials, commercial bribery, and bribery of foreign officials.

The bribe itself can be anything the recipient considers to be valuable, but the defendant must have intended it as a bribe. Realize that the crime of bribery occurs when the bribe is offered—it is not required that the bribe be accepted. Accepting a bribe is a separate crime.

Commercial bribery involves corrupt dealings between private persons or businesses. Typically, people make commercial bribes to obtain proprietary information, cover up an inferior product, or secure new business. Industrial espionage sometimes involves commercial bribes. ■ **Example 10.13** Augusto works at the firm of Jacoby & Meyers. He offers to pay Laurel, an employee in a competing firm, to give him that firm's trade secrets and pricing schedules. Augusto has committed commercial bribery. ■ So-called kickbacks, or payoffs for special favors or services, are a form of commercial bribery in some situations.

The Foreign Corrupt Practices Act In many foreign countries, government officials make the decisions on most major construction and manufacturing contracts because of extensive government regulation and control over trade and industry. Side payments to government officials in exchange for favorable business contracts are not unusual in such countries. The Foreign Corrupt Practices Act[14] (FCPA) prohibits U.S. businesspersons from bribing foreign officials to secure beneficial contracts. Firms that violate the FCPA can be fined up to $2 million. Individuals can be fined up to $100,000 and imprisoned for up to five years.

Prohibition Against the Bribery of Foreign Officials. The first part of the FCPA applies to all U.S. companies and their directors, officers, shareholders, employees, and agents. This part of the act prohibits the bribery of most officials of foreign governments if the purpose of the payment is to motivate the officials to act in their official capacity to provide business opportunities.

The FCPA does not prohibit payments made to minor officials whose duties are ministerial. A ministerial action is a routine activity, such as the processing of paperwork, that involves little or no discretion. These payments are often referred to as "grease," or facilitating payments. They are meant to accelerate the performance of administrative services that might otherwise be carried out at a slow pace. Thus, for instance, if a firm makes a payment to a minor official to speed up an import licensing process, the firm has not violated the FCPA.

Generally, the act permits payments to foreign officials if such payments are lawful within the foreign country. Payments to private foreign companies or other third parties are permissible—unless the U.S. firm knows that the payments will be passed on to a foreign government in violation of the FCPA.

Accounting Requirements. In the past, bribes were often concealed in corporate financial records. Thus, the second part of the FCPA is directed toward accountants. All companies must keep detailed records that "accurately and fairly" reflect their financial activities. Their accounting systems must provide "reasonable assurance" that all transactions entered into by the companies are

---

11. The Mail Fraud Act, 18 U.S.C. Sections 1341–1342.
12. 18 U.S.C. Section 1343.
13. *United States v. Davis,* 789 Fed.Appx. 105 (11th Cir. 2019).
14. 15 U.S.C., Sections 78dd-1, *et seq.*

accounted for and legal. These requirements assist in detecting illegal bribes. The FCPA prohibits any person from making false statements to accountants or false entries in any record or account.

Bankruptcy Fraud Federal bankruptcy law allows individuals and businesses to be relieved of oppressive debt through bankruptcy proceedings. Numerous white-collar crimes may be committed during the many phases of a bankruptcy action. A creditor may file a false claim against the debtor, which is a crime. Also, a debtor may fraudulently transfer assets to favored parties before or after the bankruptcy is filed. For instance, a company-owned automobile may be "sold" at a bargain price to a trusted friend or relative. Closely related to the crime of fraudulent transfer of property is the crime of fraudulent concealment of property, such as the hiding of gold coins.

Insider Trading An individual who obtains "inside information" about the plans of a publicly listed corporation can often make stock-trading profits by purchasing or selling corporate securities based on this information. Insider trading is a violation of securities law. Basically, a person who possesses inside information and has a duty not to disclose it to outsiders may not trade on that information. A person may not profit from the purchase or sale of securities based on inside information until the information is made available to the public.

Theft of Trade Secrets and Other Intellectual Property The Economic Espionage Act[15] makes the theft of trade secrets a federal crime. The act also makes it a federal crime to buy or possess another person's trade secrets, knowing that the trade secrets were stolen or otherwise acquired without the owner's authorization.

Violations of the Economic Espionage Act can result in steep penalties: imprisonment for up to ten years and a fine of up to $500,000. A corporation or other organization can be fined up to $5 million. Additionally, any property acquired as a result of the violation, such as airplanes and automobiles, is subject to criminal forfeiture, or seizure by the government. Similarly, any property used in the commission of the violation is subject to forfeiture.

10–3e Organized Crime

White-collar crime takes place within the confines of the legitimate business world. Organized crime, in contrast, operates illegitimately by, among other things, providing illegal goods and services. Traditionally, organized crime has been involved in gambling, prostitution, illegal narcotics, counterfeiting, and loan sharking (lending funds at higher-than-legal interest rates), along with more recent ventures into credit card scams and numerous cyber crimes.

Money Laundering The profits from organized crime and illegal activities amount to billions of dollars a year. Under federal law, banks, savings and loan associations, and other financial institutions are required to report currency transactions involving more than $10,000. Consequently, those who engage in illegal activities face difficulties in depositing their cash profits from illegal transactions.

As an alternative to storing the cash from illegal transactions in a safe-deposit box, wrongdoers and racketeers often launder "dirty" money through legitimate businesses to make it "clean." **Money laundering** is engaging in financial transactions to conceal the identity, source, or destination of illegally gained funds.

■ **Example 10.14** Leo, a successful drug dealer, becomes a partner with a restaurateur. Little by little, the restaurant shows increasing profits. As a partner in the restaurant, Leo is able to report the "profits" of the restaurant as legitimate income on which he pays federal and state taxes. He can then spend those funds without worrying that his lifestyle may exceed the level possible with his reported income. ■

Racketeering To curb the entry of organized crime into the legitimate business world, Congress enacted the Racketeer Influenced and Corrupt Organizations Act (RICO).[16] The statute makes it a federal crime to:

1. Use income obtained from racketeering activity to purchase any interest in an enterprise.
2. Acquire or maintain an interest in an enterprise through racketeering activity.
3. Conduct or participate in the affairs of an enterprise through racketeering activity.
4. Conspire to do any of the preceding activities.

Broad Application of RICO. The broad language of RICO has allowed it to be applied in cases that have little or nothing to do with organized crime. RICO incorporates by reference twenty-six separate types of federal crimes and nine types of state felonies.[17] If a person commits two of these offenses, they are guilty of "racketeering activity."

---

15. 18 U.S.C. Sections 1831–1839.

16. 18 U.S.C. Sections 1961–1968.
17. See 18 U.S.C. Section 1961(1)(A). The crimes listed in this section include murder, kidnapping, gambling, arson, robbery, bribery, extortion, money laundering, securities fraud, counterfeiting, dealing in obscene matter, dealing in controlled substances (illegal drugs), and a number of others.

Under the criminal provisions of RICO, any individual found guilty is subject to a fine of up to $25,000 per violation, imprisonment for up to twenty years, or both. Additionally, any assets (property or cash) that were acquired as a result of the illegal activity or that were "involved in" or an "instrumentality of" the activity are subject to government forfeiture.

Civil Liability. In the event of a RICO violation, the government can seek not only criminal penalties but also civil penalties. The government can, for instance, seek the divestiture of a defendant's interest in a business or the dissolution of the business. (Divestiture refers to forfeiture of the defendant's interest and its subsequent sale.)

Moreover, in some cases, the statute allows private individuals to sue violators and potentially recover three times their actual losses (treble damages), plus attorneys' fees, for business injuries caused by a RICO violation. This is perhaps the most controversial aspect of RICO and one that continues to cause debate in the nation's federal courts. The prospect of receiving treble damages in civil RICO lawsuits has given plaintiffs a financial incentive to pursue businesses and employers for violations.

See Concept Summary 10.1 for a review of the different types of crimes.

10–4 Defenses to Criminal Liability

Persons charged with crimes may be relieved of criminal liability if they can show that their criminal actions were justified under the circumstances. In certain situations, the law may also allow persons to be excused from criminal liability because they lack the required mental state. We look at several defenses to criminal liability here.

Note that procedural violations (such as obtaining evidence without a valid search warrant) may also operate as defenses. Evidence obtained in violation of a defendant's constitutional rights may not be admitted in court. If the evidence is suppressed, then there may be no basis for prosecuting the defendant.

10–4a Justifiable Use of Force

Probably the best-known defense to criminal liability is **self-defense.** Other situations, however, also justify the use of force: the defense of one's dwelling, the defense of other property, and the prevention of a crime. In all these situations, it is important to distinguish between deadly and nondeadly force. Deadly force is likely to result in death or serious bodily harm. Nondeadly force is force that reasonably appears necessary to prevent the imminent use of criminal force.

Concept Summary 10.1

Types of Crimes

Violent Crime	Crimes that cause others to suffer harm or death, such as murder, assault and battery, and robbery.
Property Crime	Crimes in which the goal of the offender is some form of economic gain or the damaging of property. Property crime includes theft-related offenses such as burglary, larceny, and forgery.
Public Order Crime	Crimes that are contrary to public values and morals, such as public drunkenness and prostitution.
White-Collar Crime	An illegal act or series of acts committed by an individual or business entity using some nonviolent means to obtain a personal or business advantage. These crimes are usually committed in the course of a legitimate occupation. Examples include embezzlement, bribery, and fraud.
Organized Crime	Crime conducted by groups operating illegitimately to provide illegal goods and services, such as narcotics. Organized crime may also include money laundering and racketeering.

Generally speaking, people can use the amount of nondeadly force that seems necessary to protect themselves, their dwellings, or other property, or to prevent the commission of a crime. Deadly force can be used in self-defense only when the defender reasonably believes that imminent death or grievous bodily harm will otherwise result. In addition, normally the attacker must be using unlawful force, and the defender must not have initiated or provoked the attack.

Many states are expanding the situations in which the use of deadly force can be justified. Florida, for instance, allows the use of deadly force to prevent the commission of a "forcible felony," including robbery, carjacking, and sexual battery.

10-4b Necessity

Sometimes, criminal defendants can be relieved of liability by showing **necessity**—that a criminal act was necessary to prevent an even greater harm. ■ **Example 10.15** Bella is a convicted felon and, as such, is legally prohibited from possessing a firearm. While she is in a convenience store, a man draws a gun, points it at the cashier, and demands all the cash in the register. Afraid that the man will start shooting, Bella grabs the gun and holds onto it until police arrive. In this situation, if Bella is charged with possession of a firearm, she can assert the defense of necessity. ■

10-4c Insanity

A person who suffers from a mental illness may be incapable of the state of mind required to commit a crime. Thus, insanity may be a defense to a criminal charge. Note that an insanity defense does not enable a person to avoid imprisonment. It simply means that a defendant who successfully proves insanity will be placed in a mental institution.

■ **Example 10.16** Medina Espinosa of Beaver Dam, Wisconsin, was charged with first degree murder for shooting his ex-wife fifteen times. Ten days earlier, Espinosa apparently had been accidentally exposed to harmful chemicals at the Kraft Heinz factory where he worked. According to Espinosa's attorney, these chemicals caused neurological damage that left Espinosa unable to form the intent necessary to held responsible for his ex-wife's murder. Consequently, he pleaded not guilty by reason of insanity. ■

10-4d Mistake

Everyone has heard the saying "Ignorance of the law is no excuse." Ordinarily, ignorance of the law or a mistaken idea about what the law requires is not a valid defense. A mistake of fact, however, as opposed to a mistake of law, can normally excuse criminal responsibility if it negates the mental state necessary to commit a crime. ■ **Example 10.17** Malik mistakenly walks off with Alexandra's briefcase. If Malik genuinely thought that the case was his, there is no theft. Theft requires knowledge that the property belongs to another. (If Malik's act causes Alexandra to incur damages, however, she may sue him in a civil tort action for trespass to personal property or conversion.) ■

10-4e Duress

Duress exists when the wrongful threat of one person induces another person to perform an act that person would not otherwise have performed. In such a situation, duress is said to negate the mental state necessary to commit a crime because the defendant was forced or compelled to commit the act.

Duress can be used as a defense to most crimes except murder. Both the definition of duress and the types of crimes that it can excuse vary among the states, however. Generally, to successfully assert duress as a defense, defendants must reasonably have believed that they were in immediate danger, and the jury (or judge) must conclude that this belief was reasonable.

10-4f Entrapment

Entrapment is a defense designed to prevent police officers or other government agents from enticing persons to commit crimes in order to later prosecute them for those crimes. In the typical entrapment case, an undercover agent suggests that a crime be committed and somehow pressures or induces an individual to commit it. The agent then arrests the individual for the crime.

For entrapment to be considered a defense, both the suggestion and the inducement must take place. The defense is not intended to prevent law enforcement agents from setting a trap for an unwary criminal. Rather, its purpose is to prevent them from pushing the individual into a criminal act. The crucial issue is whether the person who committed a crime was predisposed to commit the illegal act or did so only because the agent induced it.

10-4g Statute of Limitations

With some exceptions, such as the crime of murder, statutes of limitations apply to crimes just as they do to civil wrongs. In other words, the government must initiate criminal prosecution within a certain number of years. If a criminal action is brought after the statutory period has expired, the accused person can raise the statute of limitations as a defense.

The running of the period in a statute of limitations may be tolled—that is, suspended or stopped temporarily—if the defendant is a minor or is not in the jurisdiction. When the defendant reaches the age of majority or returns to the jurisdiction, the statutory period begins to run again.

10–4h Immunity

Accused persons are understandably reluctant to give information if it will be used to prosecute them, and they cannot be forced to do so. The privilege against **self-incrimination** is guaranteed by a clause in the Fifth Amendment to the U.S. Constitution. The clause reads "nor shall [any person] be compelled in any criminal case to be a witness against himself."

When the state wishes to obtain information from a person accused of a crime, the state can grant immunity from prosecution. Alternatively, the state can agree to prosecute the accused for a less serious offense in exchange for the information. Once immunity is given, the person has an absolute privilege against self-incrimination and therefore can no longer refuse to testify on Fifth Amendment grounds.

Often, a grant of immunity from prosecution for a serious crime is part of the **plea bargaining** between the defending and prosecuting attorneys. The defendant may be convicted of a lesser offense, while the state uses the defendant's testimony to prosecute accomplices for serious crimes carrying heavy penalties.

10–5 Criminal Procedures

Criminal law brings the force of the state, with all of its resources, to bear against the individual. Criminal procedures are designed to protect the constitutional rights of individuals and to prevent the arbitrary use of power on the part of the government.

The U.S. Constitution provides specific safeguards for those accused of crimes. The United States Supreme Court has ruled that most of these safeguards apply not only in federal court but also in state courts by virtue of the due process clause of the Fourteenth Amendment. These protections include the following:

1. The Fourth Amendment protection from unreasonable searches and seizures.
2. The Fourth Amendment requirement that no warrant for a search or an arrest be issued without probable cause.
3. The Fifth Amendment requirement that no one be deprived of "life, liberty, or property without due process of law."
4. The Fifth Amendment prohibition against **double jeopardy** (trying someone twice for the same criminal offense).[18]

5. The Fifth Amendment requirement that persons cannot be required to be witnesses against (incriminate) themselves.
6. The Sixth Amendment guarantees of a speedy trial, a trial by jury, a public trial, the right to confront witnesses, and the right to a lawyer at various stages in some proceedings.
7. The Eighth Amendment prohibitions against excessive bail and fines and against cruel and unusual punishment.

10–5a Fourth Amendment Protections

The Fourth Amendment protects the "right of the people to be secure in their persons, houses, papers, and effects." Before searching or seizing private property, normally law enforcement officers must obtain a **search warrant**—an order from a judge or other public official authorizing the search or seizure.

Advances in technology allow the authorities to track phone calls and vehicle movements with greater ease and precision. The use of such technology can constitute a search within the meaning of the Fourth Amendment. ■ **Case in Point 10.18** Antoine Jones owned and operated a nightclub in the District of Columbia. Government agents suspected that he was also trafficking in narcotics. As part of their investigation, agents obtained a warrant to attach a global positioning system (GPS) device to Jones's wife's car, which Jones regularly used. The warrant authorized installation in the District of Columbia within ten days, but agents installed the device on the eleventh day in Maryland.

The agents then tracked the vehicle's movement for about a month, eventually arresting Jones for possession of and intent to distribute cocaine. Jones was convicted. He appealed, arguing that the government did not have a valid warrant for the GPS tracking. The United States Supreme Court held that the attachment of a GPS tracking device to a suspect's vehicle does constitute a Fourth Amendment search. The Court did not rule on whether the search in this case was unreasonable, however, and allowed Jones's conviction to stand.[19] ■

Probable Cause To obtain a search warrant, law enforcement officers must convince a judge that they have reasonable grounds, or **probable cause,** to believe a search will reveal a specific illegality. Probable cause requires the officers to have trustworthy evidence that would convince

---

18. The prohibition against double jeopardy does not preclude the crime victim from bringing a *civil* suit against that same person to recover damages, however. Additionally, a state's prosecution of a crime will not prevent a separate federal prosecution of the same crime, and vice versa.

19. *United States v. Jones,* 565 U.S. 400, 132 S.Ct. 945, 181 L.Ed.2d 911 (2012). See, in contrast, *U.S. v. Alakom-Zed Crayne Pobre,* 2022 WL 1136891 (D.MD 2022).

a reasonable person that the proposed search or seizure is more likely justified than not.

Scope of Warrant The Fourth Amendment prohibits general warrants. It requires a specific description of what is to be searched or seized. General searches through a person's belongings are impermissible. The search cannot extend beyond what is described in the warrant.

Reasonable Expectation of Privacy The Fourth Amendment protects only against searches that violate a person's reasonable expectation of privacy. A reasonable expectation of privacy exists if (1) the individual expects privacy and (2) the person's expectation is one that society as a whole would consider legitimate.

10–5b The Exclusionary Rule

Under what is known as the **exclusionary rule,** any evidence obtained in violation of the constitutional rights spelled out in the Fourth, Fifth, and Sixth Amendments generally is not admissible at trial. All evidence derived from the illegally obtained evidence is known as the "fruit of the poisonous tree," and it normally must also be excluded from the trial proceedings. For instance, if a confession is obtained after an illegal arrest, the arrest is the "poisonous tree," and the confession, if "tainted" by the arrest, is the "fruit."

The purpose of the exclusionary rule is to deter police from conducting warrantless searches and engaging in other misconduct. The rule can sometimes lead to injustice, however. If evidence of a defendant's guilt was obtained improperly (without a valid search warrant, for instance), it normally cannot be used against the defendant in court.

10–5c The *Miranda* Rule

In *Miranda v. Arizona,*[20] a landmark case decided in 1966, the United States Supreme Court established the rule that individuals who are arrested must be informed of certain constitutional rights. Suspects must be informed of their Fifth Amendment right to remain silent and their Sixth Amendment right to counsel. If the arresting officers fail to inform a criminal suspect of these constitutional rights, any statements the suspect makes normally will not be admissible in court.

Although the Supreme Court's decision in the *Miranda* case was controversial, it has survived several attempts by Congress to overrule it. Over time, however, the Supreme Court has made a number of exceptions to the *Miranda* ruling.

10–5d Criminal Process

A criminal prosecution differs significantly from a civil case in several respects. These differences reflect the desire to safeguard the rights of the individual against the state. Exhibit 10–3 summarizes the major steps in processing a criminal case, several of which we discuss here.

Arrest Before a warrant for arrest can be issued, there must be probable cause to believe that the individual in question has committed a crime. Note that probable cause involves a substantial likelihood that the person has committed a crime, not just a possibility. Arrests can be made without a warrant if there is no time to obtain one, but the action of the arresting officer is still judged by the standard of probable cause.

Indictment or Information Individuals must be formally charged with having committed specific crimes before they can be brought to trial. If issued by a grand jury, such a charge is called an **indictment.**[21] A **grand jury** does not determine the guilt or innocence of an accused party. Rather, its function is to hear the state's evidence and to determine whether a reasonable basis (probable cause) exists for believing that a crime has been committed and that a trial ought to be held. For less serious crimes, an individual may be formally charged with a crime by an **information,** or criminal complaint, issued by a government prosecutor.

Trial At a criminal trial, the accused person does not have to prove anything. The entire burden of proof is on the prosecutor (the state). The prosecution must show that, based on all the evidence, the defendant's guilt is established beyond a reasonable doubt. If there is reasonable doubt, then the verdict must be "not guilty." Returning a verdict of "not guilty" is not the same as stating that the defendant is innocent. It merely means that not enough evidence was properly presented to the court to prove guilt beyond a reasonable doubt.

At the conclusion of the trial, a convicted defendant will be sentenced by the court. The U.S. Sentencing Commission performs the task of standardizing sentences for federal crimes. The commission's guidelines establish a range of possible penalties, but judges are allowed to depart from the guidelines if circumstances warrant. Sentencing guidelines also provide for enhanced punishment for white-collar crimes, violations of the Sarbanes-Oxley Act, and violations of securities laws.

20. 384 U.S. 436, 86 S.Ct. 1602, 16 L.Ed.2d 694 (1966).

21. Pronounced in-*dyte*-ment.

Exhibit 10–3 Major Procedural Steps in a Criminal Case

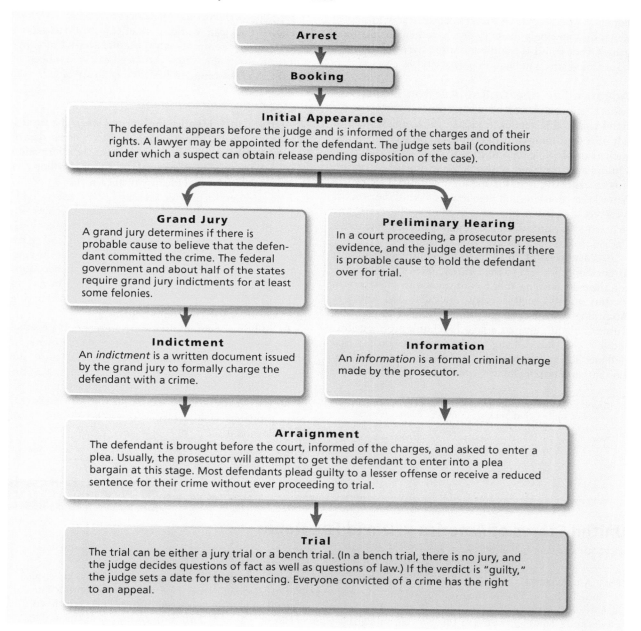

10–6 Cyber Crime

The U.S. Department of Justice broadly defines **computer crime** as any violation of criminal law that involves knowledge of computer technology for its perpetration, investigation, or prosecution. Many computer crimes fall under the broad label of **cyber crime,** which describes criminal activity occurring via a computer in the virtual community of the internet.

Most cyber crimes are simply existing crimes, such as fraud and theft, in which the internet is the instrument of wrongdoing. Here, we look at several types of activities that constitute cyber crimes against persons or property.

10–6a Cyber Fraud

Fraud, as discussed in an earlier chapter, is any misrepresentation knowingly made to deceive others for personal gain. **Cyber fraud** is fraud committed over the internet. Cyber fraud affects millions of people worldwide every day.

Advance Fee and Online Auction Fraud Two widely reported forms of cyber crime are advance fee fraud and online auction fraud. In the simplest form of advance fee fraud, consumers order and pay for items, such as automobiles or antiques, that are never delivered. Online auction fraud is also straightforward. A person lists an expensive item for auction, on either a legitimate or a fake auction site, and then refuses to send the product after receiving payment. Or, as a variation, the wrongdoer may send the purchaser an item that is worth less than the one offered in the auction.

■ **Case in Point 10.19** A group of Romanians were arrested and brought to the United States to face charges for allegedly stealing millions of dollars from American victims on sites such as eBay, Craigslist, and Amazon. According to the federal government, one of the suspects, Ionut Ciobanu, created a fake Facebook profile calling himself "Sgt. Judith Lane" of the U.S. Air Force, a ruse designed to reassure potential purchasers about the non-existent automobiles he was selling online.[22] ■

22. *United States v. Andrei-Catlin Stoica, et al.* and *United States v. Ologeanu, et al.*, __ Fed.Annx. __ (E.D. KY C. Div. Lexington 2020). Here, a federal grand jury in Lexington, Kentucky, handed down a 24-count indictment against 15 foreign nationals.

10–6b Cyber Theft

In cyberspace, thieves are not subject to the physical limitations of the "real" world. A thief can steal data stored in a networked computer with internet access from anywhere on the globe. Only the speed of the connection and the thief's equipment limit the quantity of data that can be stolen.

Identity Theft **Identity theft** occurs when the wrongdoer steals a form of identification—such as a name, date of birth, or Social Security number—and uses the information to access the victim's financial resources. Millions of Americans are victims of identity theft each year.

The internet has provided relatively easy access to private data, because frequent web surfers surrender a wealth of information about themselves. Websites use "cookies" to collect data on those who visit their sites and make purchases. Often, sites store information such as the consumers' names, e-mail addresses, social media accounts, and credit card numbers. Identity thieves may be able to steal this information by fooling a website into thinking that they are the true account holders.

In addition, people often enter important personal information, such as their birthdays, hometowns, or employers, on social media sites. Identity thieves can use such information to convince a third party to reveal someone's Social Security or bank account number.

Identity theft has occurred frequently within government programs such as Medicaid. That is the subject of the following case.

Case Analysis 10.3

United States of America v. David Fox Dubin

United States Court of Appeals, 5th Circuit, 27 F.4th 1021 (2022).

PRISCILLA R. OWEN, C.J.

Much ink has been spilled about "identity theft" in dissenting opinions in today's case. However, the text of 18 U.S.C. [Section] 1028A(a)(1) does not contain the words "identity theft" or even "theft." The text of the statute instead imposes a sentencing enhancement for the commission of enumerated federal felonies when the criminal "knowingly . . . uses, without lawful authority, a means of identification of another person." Our focus must be on the actual text of the statute and not the meaning or scope of "identity theft."

David Dubin was convicted under 18 U.S.C. [Section] 1347(a) of "defraud[ing] a[] health care benefit program" or "obtain[ing], by means of false or fraudulent pretenses [or] representations . . . money . . . owned by, or under the custody or control of, a[] health care benefit program" (in this case Medicaid), "in connection with the delivery of or payment for health care benefits, items, or services." He was also convicted under 18 U.S.C. [Section] 1349 of conspiracy to commit a [Section] 1347(a) offense. The en banc court has held that these felony convictions stand.

The principal issue that has divided our court is the proper construction of [Section] 1028A(a)(1), which sets forth a sentencing enhancement. That section provides "[w]hoever, during and in relation to any felony violation enumerated in subsection (c), knowingly transfers, possesses, or uses, without lawful authority, a means of identification of another person" shall receive an additional two years of imprisonment. The health care fraud and conspiracy offenses of which Dubin was convicted are felony violations enumerated in subsection (c)(5) of [Section] 1028A.

The resolution of this issue turns on the meaning of the phrase "uses, without lawful authority, a means of identification of another person" in [Section]1028A(a)(1). At Dubin's trial, the jury found that he did "use[], without lawful authority, a means of identification of another person" in committing the offenses set forth in [Section] 1347(a) and [Section] 1349. That sentencing enhancement conviction must be affirmed based on a straightforward reading of [Section] 1028A(a)(1) and the evidence before the jury. Relevant here is Dubin's fraudulent billing pertaining to Patient L, who was a minor and whose initials are AS. Dubin had the "lawful authority" to use Medicaid Patient L's identifying information to obtain lawful reimbursements from the government for covered services, but Dubin also "use[d]" Patient L's identifying information "during and in relation to" the felonies of Medicaid fraud and conspiracy to commit Medicaid fraud. That "use" was "without lawful authority."

* * * *

* * * In health care benefit fraud cases that use real people's identifying information to perpetrate the fraud, the criminal enterprise depends entirely upon access to and unlawful use of "a means of identification of another person." There is a direct causal link between the "use[], without lawful authority, [of] a means of identification of another person" and the offense, regardless of whether the offense was overbilling for services provided or billing when no services at all were provided. Those engaged in health care fraud like that committed by Dubin actively seek, then mine, sources of "a means of identification of another person" because those "means of identification of another person" are what they use to perpetrate the fraud. Health care fraud like that committed by Dubin costs taxpayers billions of dollars each year.

* * * *

There is certainly nothing "breathtaking" about punishing a criminal who, for example, commits fraud by overbilling $100,000 for medical services the same as a criminal who bills $100,000 for medical services that were not provided. Both have committed the *same crime* * * *.

I

It should be beyond debate that Dubin "used" Patient L's identifying information "during and in relation to" the offenses for which he was convicted. He could not have effectuated the health care fraud or the conspiracy to commit health care fraud without using Patient L's identifying information.

The focus should be on whether he "use[d]" the identifying information "without lawful authority." The authority to use Patient L's identifying information came from both Patient L (or someone authorized to act on the minor patient's behalf) and the Medicaid program itself. But neither Patient L nor Medicaid authorized Dubin to use that information or Patient L's name to commit health care fraud. * * *

Dubin, a managing partner at a psychological services company, directed that company to overbill for mental health evaluations at an emergency shelter for children. Dubin falsified information in at least four respects. First, he billed at a rate set for a licensed psychologist, even though a clinician without that credential saw Patient L (AS), and the billing rates for the actual provider could only be billed under Medicaid regulations at a much lower rate. Second, Dubin instructed employees to bill the maximum number of hours (eight) permitted by Medicaid regulations for certain services, even if the actual number of hours they spent performing the services was less. Third, Dubin billed for an evaluation that his company only partially performed. Patient L underwent psychological

testing but did not receive a clinical interview. Nor did the shelter receive any report describing the patient's condition or any recommended treatment, which was necessary in order to bill for the evaluation. The fact that an evaluation occurred was useless to the shelter, and to Patient L, unless the provider furnished a report of the outcome of the evaluation. Fourth, Dubin falsified the date that services were provided since, had he used the correct date, the services would have been ineligible for reimbursement because they were performed within a twelve-month period for which maximum benefits had already been paid. Medicaid covers one psychological evaluation each year. After Dubin learned that Patient L (AS) had already been evaluated within a one-year period, Dubin billed Medicaid using a falsified treatment date.

Dubin challenges his [Section] 1028A(a)(1) conviction on the ground that he did not "use" Patient L's identity within the meaning of the statute. He contends that his overbilling concerned only "how and when" Patient L was evaluated, since Patient L did receive some services. * * *

* * * *

Dubin's conviction must be affirmed based on the text of [Section] 1028A(a)(1). Nor is [Section] 1028A(a)(1)'s scope "breathtaking" when applied to health care fraud like that committed by Dubin. Neither Medicaid beneficiaries nor taxpayers who are the actual victims of Medicaid fraud would find it shocking or unreasonable to impose an additional sentence of two years of imprisonment when health care providers use unique Medicaid identifying numbers and Medicaid patients' names to submit fraudulent claims that result in billions of dollars of losses to the health care system each year.

* * * *

Legal Reasoning Questions

1. How was identity theft a relevant concept in this case?

2. What is the difference between effectuating health care fraud and conspiracy to commit health care fraud?

3. Why did the defendant Dubin falsify the date when services were provided?

Stolen Credit Card Numbers. More than half of identity thefts involve the misappropriation of credit card accounts. In most situations, the legitimate holders of credit cards are not held responsible for the costs of purchases made with a stolen number. The loss is borne by the businesses and banks.

■ **Example 10.20** The Northeast convenience store chain Wawa announced that a security breach in its computer system had allowed cyberthieves to obtain some of the company's stored credit card payment data. Two months later, someone going by the name of Joker Stash started posting these data for sale on the dark web, asking about $17 apiece for the credit card numbers of about 30 million Wawa customers. ■

Card Testing Online markets are particularly attractive for credit card thieves because they can engage in a practice called "card testing." This involves using a stolen credit card number, or thousands of stolen credit card numbers, to make very small online purchases, perhaps no larger than two dollars. If the fraudulent transaction is successful, the criminal will raise the amount of the purchases until the issuing financial institution or the real owner notices. This chapter's Cybersecurity and the Law feature explores another tactic designed to "cash in" stolen credit card numbers online.

Password Theft The more personal information cyber criminals obtain, the easier it is for them to find a victim's online username at a particular website. Once the online username has been compromised, it is easier to steal the victim's password, which is often the last line of defense to financial information.

Numerous software programs aid identity thieves in illegally obtaining passwords. A technique called keystroke logging, for instance, relies on software that embeds itself in a victim's computer and records every keystroke made on that computer. Usernames and passwords are then recorded and sold to the highest bidder. Internet users should also be wary of any links contained in e-mails sent from unknown sources. These links can sometimes be used to illegally obtain personal information.

Phishing A form of identity theft known as **phishing** has added a different wrinkle to the practice. In a phishing attack, the perpetrator "fishes" for financial data and

---

Cybersecurity and the Law   Counter Strike: Global Offensive

The online video game Counter Strike: Global Offensive (CS:GO) involves two teams whose goal is to eliminate the other while carrying out objectives such as planting a bomb or protecting hostages. CS:GO gamers, of which there are approximately 18 million, also try to gain "loot boxes" that allow them to upgrade their characters or weapons. Initially, the only way to open the loot box was to purchase a "container key" from Valve Corporation, which sells and operates CS:GO. Eventually, however, it became possible to trade loot boxes and container keys for "real" money on various internet marketplaces.

The problem with this system became clear when Valve suspended all trading of container keys between players. Such activity, the company announced, had become "fraud sourced." In other words, the trading of container keys was being used to launder income from credit card fraud. Valve's actions highlight the opportunities presented to cyber criminals by online gaming markets. Cybercriminals can use their illicit earnings or stolen credit card numbers to buy virtual items and then sell those items—often at a discounted price—to other gamers in exchange for "real" money.

The Displacement Effect

According to "the displacement effect," as some parts of an economy become more highly regulated, tainted funds move to the less regulated parts of the economy. Under federal banking laws, only "convertible virtual currency" (CVC) is subject to regulation designed to combat money laundering. To fall under the definition of CVC, the virtual currency must have a value in real currency or act as a substitute for real currency.[a] This definition does not cover CS:GO's container keys. Consequently, such online video games will continue to attract the wrong type of player.

Critical Thinking One suggestion for alleviating the problem of "fraud-sourced" money is to require proof of identity from anyone who wants to trade virtual items on online gaming platforms. Do you think this strategy would be successful? Why or why not?

a. 31 U.S.C. Section 5330.

passwords from consumers by posing as a legitimate business, such as a bank or credit card company. The "phisher" uses an e-mail, text message, or social media post to ask the recipient to update or confirm vital information. Often, the request includes a threat that an account or some other service will be discontinued if the information is not provided. Once the unsuspecting individual enters the information, the phisher can sell it or use it to masquerade as that person or drain the person's bank or credit account.

■ **Example 10.21** Customers of FedEx received an official-looking text informing them that they needed to set up delivery preferences for a package. The text included a link to do so. If clicked, the link took potential victims to a purported Amazon.com website promising them a "reward" if they filled out a customer satisfaction survey. To claim the reward, they needed to provide their home address and a credit card number for shipping and handling. The FedEx texts and Amazon websites, of course, were fake. People who did provide their personal data, besides being susceptible to identify theft, were unwittingly signing up to pay $98.95 a month for additional nonexistent "rewards" in the future. ■

10–6c Hacking

A **hacker** is someone who uses one computer to break into another. The danger posed by hackers is significantly increased by **botnets,** or networks of computers that have been appropriated by hackers without the knowledge of their owners. A hacker may secretly install a program on thousands, even millions, of personal computer "robots," or "bots." The program, in turn, allows the hacker to forward transmissions to an even larger number of systems.

Malware Botnets are only one form of **malware,** a term that refers to any program that is harmful to a computer or, by extension, a computer user. Malware can be programmed to perform a number of functions, such as prompting host computers to continually "crash" and reboot or otherwise infecting the systems.

Another type of malware is a **worm**—a software program that can reproduce itself as it spreads from one computer to the next. The Conflicker worm, for instance, spread to more than a million computers around the world within a three-week period. A **virus,** yet another form of malware, is also able to reproduce itself but must be attached to an "infested" host file to travel from one computer network to another.

Service-Based Hacking Many companies offer "software as a service." Instead of buying software to

install on a computer, a user connects to web-based software. Users can then write e-mails, edit spreadsheets, and perform other tasks using their web browsers.

Cyber criminals have adapted this method to provide "crimeware as a service." Would-be thieves no longer must be computer hackers to create a botnet or steal banking information and credit card numbers. They can rent the online services of cyber criminals to do the work for a small price. Fake security software (also known as scareware) is a common example.

Cyberterrorism Cyberterrorists, as well as hackers, may target businesses. The goals of a hacking operation might include a wholesale theft of data, such as a merchant's customer files, or the monitoring of a computer to discover a business firm's plans and transactions. A cyberterrorist might also want to insert false codes or data. For instance, the processing control system of a food manufacturer could be changed to alter the levels of ingredients so that consumers of the food would become ill.

A few years ago, cyberterrorists from a Russian-linked cyber-crime group called DarkSide were able to shut down Colonial Pipeline, a major oil-product pipeline company, which caused gasoline shortages in the U.S. Northeast and elsewhere. A cyberterrorist attack on a major financial institution, such as the New York Stock Exchange or a large bank, could leave securities or money markets in flux. Such an attack could seriously affect U.S. citizens, business operations, and national security.

Ransomware Cybercriminals have increased **ransomware** attacks throughout the United States and elsewhere. In these attacks, companies are locked out of their computer databases, even if the data are stored on a remote cloud server. While most of the attacks have targeted private businesses, attacks have also been aimed at hospitals and government water treatment plants. Typically, ransomware criminals encrypt a victim's data and then demand a ransom payment, sometimes in the millions, to return access. Most ransomware criminals operate out of Russia, which has refused to help the United States to reduce these activities. U.S. businesses and government entities are estimated to lose about $20 to $30 billion a year to ransomware criminals.

10–6d Prosecuting Cyber Crime

Cyber crime raises new issues in the investigation of crimes and the prosecution of offenders. Determining the "location" of a cyber crime and identifying a criminal in cyberspace present significant challenges for law enforcement.

Jurisdiction and Identification Challenges A threshold issue is, of course, jurisdiction. States and nations have jurisdiction, or authority, over crimes committed within their boundaries. But geographic boundaries simply do not apply in cyberspace. A person who commits an act against a business in California, where the act is a cyber crime, might never have set foot in California. Instead, the perpetrator might reside in another state or, more often, another nation, where the act may not be a crime. Indeed, many cyber crimes emanate from Russia and China.

Identifying the wrongdoer can also be difficult. Cyber criminals do not leave physical traces, such as fingerprints or DNA samples, as evidence of their crimes. Even electronic "footprints" can be hard to find and follow. For instance, cyber criminals may employ software to mask their IP addresses (codes that identify individual computers) and the IP addresses of those with whom they communicate. Law enforcement must hire computer forensic experts to bypass the software and track down the criminal. For these reasons, laws written to protect physical property are often difficult to apply in cyberspace.

The Computer Fraud and Abuse Act One of the most significant federal statutes specifically addressing cyber crime is the Counterfeit Access Device and Computer Fraud and Abuse Act.[23] This act is commonly known as the Computer Fraud and Abuse Act (CFAA).

Among other things, the CFAA provides that a person who accesses any computer (including a tablet or smartphone) online, without authority, to obtain classified, restricted, or protected data (or attempts to do so) is subject to criminal prosecution. Such data may include financial and credit records, medical records, legal files, military and national security files, and other confidential information. The data can be located in government or private computers. The crime has two elements: accessing a computer without authority and taking data.

The theft is a felony if it is committed for a commercial purpose or for private financial gain, or if the value of the stolen data exceeds $5,000. Penalties include fines and imprisonment for up to twenty years. A person who violates the CFAA can also be sued in a civil action for damages.

---

23. 18 U.S.C. Section 1030.

Practice and Review: Criminal Law and Cyber Crime

Edward Hanousek worked for Pacific & Arctic Railway and Navigation Company (P&A) as a roadmaster of the White Pass & Yukon Railroad in Alaska. Hanousek was responsible "for every detail of the safe and efficient maintenance and construction of track, structures and marine facilities of the entire railroad," including special projects. One project was a rock quarry, known as "6-mile," above the Skagway River. Next to the quarry, and just beneath the surface, ran a high-pressure oil pipeline owned by Pacific & Arctic Pipeline, Inc., P&A's sister company. When the quarry's backhoe operator punctured the pipeline, an estimated 1,000 to 5,000 gallons of oil were discharged into the river. Hanousek was charged with negligently discharging a harmful quantity of oil into a navigable water of the United States in violation of the criminal provisions of the Clean Water Act (CWA). Using the information presented in the chapter, answer the following questions.

1. Did Hanousek have the required mental state (*mens rea*) to be convicted of a crime? Why or why not?
2. Which theory discussed in the chapter would enable a court to hold Hanousek criminally liable for violating the statute if he participated in, directed, or merely knew about the specific violation?
3. Could the backhoe operator who punctured the pipeline also be charged with a crime in this situation? Explain.
4. Suppose that at trial, Hanousek argued that he should not be convicted because he was not aware of the requirements of the CWA. Would this defense be successful? Why or why not?

Debate This . . .   Because of the huge increase in new criminal laws, particularly by the federal government, Americans may be breaking the law regularly without knowing it. Should Congress rescind many of the more than four thousand federal crimes now on the books?

Terms and Concepts

actus reus 190
arson 194
beyond a reasonable doubt 188
botnets 207
burglary 194
computer crime 203
crime 188
cyber crime 203
cyber fraud 204
double jeopardy 201
duress 200
embezzlement 195
entrapment 200

exclusionary rule 202
felonies 190
forgery 195
grand jury 202
hacker 207
identity theft 204
indictment 202
information 202
larceny 194
malware 207
mens rea 190
misdemeanors 190
money laundering 198

necessity 200
petty offenses 190
phishing 206
plea bargaining 201
probable cause 201
ransomware 207
robbery 194
search warrant 201
self-defense 199
self-incrimination 201
virus 207
white-collar crime 195
worm 207

Issue Spotters

1. Issa takes her roommate's credit card without permission, intending to charge expenses that she incurs on a vacation. Her first stop is a gas station, where she uses the card to pay for gas. With respect to the gas station, has she committed a crime? If so, what is it? (See *Types of Crimes.*)

2. Without permission, Jaxon downloads consumer credit files from a computer belonging to Consumer Credit Agency. He then sells the data to Dawn. Has Jaxon committed a crime? If so, what is it? (See *Cyber Crime.*)

• Check your answers to the Issue Spotters against the answers provided in Appendix B at the end of this text.

Business Scenarios and Case Problems

10–1. Types of Cyber Crimes. The following situations are similar, but each represents a variation of a particular crime. Identify the crime involved in each of the following situations. (See *Cyber Crime.*)

(a) Chen, posing fraudulently as being from Centell, the provider of Emily's security software, sends a text message to Emily, stating that the company has observed suspicious activity in her account and on her network. The text asks Emily to call Chen immediately to provide a new credit card number and password to update her security software and reopen the account.

(b) Claiming falsely to be Big Buy Retail Finance Company, Conner sends an e-mail to Dino, asking him to confirm or update his personal security information to prevent his Big Buy account from being discontinued.

10–2. Cyber Scam. Kayla, a student at Learnwell University, owes $20,000 in unpaid tuition. If Kayla does not pay the tuition, Learnwell will not allow her to graduate. To obtain the funds to pay the debt, she sends e-mails to people who she does not personally know asking for financial help to send Milo, her disabled child, to a special school. In reality, Kayla has no children. Is this a crime? If so, which one? (See *Cyber Crime.*)

10–3. Business Case Problem with Sample Answer—White-Collar Crime. Matthew Simpson and others created and operated a series of corporate entities to defraud telecommunications companies, creditors, credit reporting agencies,

and others. Through these entities, Simpson and his confederates used routing codes and spoofing services to make long-distance calls appear to be local. They stole other firms' network capacity and diverted payments to themselves. They leased goods and services without paying for them. To hide their association with their corporate entities and with each other, they used false identities, addresses, and credit histories, and issued false bills, invoices, financial statements, and credit references. Did these acts constitute mail and wire fraud? Discuss. [*United States v. Simpson,* 741 F.3d 539 (5th Cir. 2014)] (See *Types of Crimes.*)

• For a sample answer to Problem 10–3, go to Appendix C at the end of this text.

10–4. Defenses to Criminal Liability. George Castro told Ambrosio Medrano that a bribe to a certain corrupt Los Angeles County official would buy a contract with the county hospitals. To share in the deal, Medrano recruited Gustavo Buenrostro. In turn, Buenrostro contacted his friend James Barta, the owner of Sav-Rx, which provides prescription benefit management services. Barta was asked to pay a "finder's fee" to Castro. He did not pay, even after frequent e-mails and calls with deadlines and ultimatums delivered over a period of months. Eventually, Barta wrote Castro a Sav-Rx check for $6,500, saying that it was to help his friend Buenrostro. Castro was an FBI agent, and the county official and contract were fictional. Barta was charged with conspiracy to commit bribery. At trial, the government conceded that Barta was not predisposed to commit the crime. Could he be absolved of the charge on a defense of entrapment? Explain. [*United States v. Barta*, 776 F.3d 931 (7th Cir. 2015)] (See *Defenses to Criminal Liability*.)

10–5. Criminal Process. Gary Peters fraudulently told an undocumented immigrant that Peters could help him obtain lawful status. Peters said that he knew immigration officials and asked for money to aid in the process. The victim paid Peters at least $25,000 in wire transfers and checks. Peters had others call the victim, falsely represent that they were agents with the U.S. Department of Homeland Security, and induce continued payments. He threatened to contact authorities to detain or deport the victim and his wife. Peters was charged with wire fraud and convicted in a federal district court. Peters's attorney argued that his client's criminal history was partially due to "difficult personal times" caused by divorce, illness, and job loss. Despite this claim, Peters was sentenced to forty-eight months imprisonment, which exceeded the federal sentencing guidelines but was less than the statutory maximum of twenty years. Was this sentence too harsh? Was it too lenient? Discuss. [*United States v. Peters*, 597 Fed.Appx. 1033 (11th Cir. 2015)] (See *Criminal Procedures*.)

10–6. Criminal Procedures. Federal officers obtained a warrant to arrest Kateena Norman on charges of credit card fraud and identity theft. Evidence of the crime included videos, photos, and a fingerprint on a fraudulent check. A previous search of Norman's house had uncovered credit cards, new merchandise, and identifying information for other persons. An internet account registered to the address had been used to apply for fraudulent credit cards, and a fraudulently obtained rental car was parked on the property. As the officers arrested Norman outside her house, they saw another woman and a caged pit bull inside. They believed that Norman's boyfriend, who had a criminal record and was also suspected of identity theft, could be there as well. In less than a minute, the officers searched only those areas within the house in which a person could hide. Would it be reasonable to admit evidence revealed in this "protective sweep" during Norman's trial on the arrest charges? Discuss. [*United States v. Norman*, 638 Fed.Appx. 934 (11th Cir. 2016)] (See *Criminal Procedures*.)

10–7. State of Mind: *Mens rea*. Prestige Energy Products LLC met with representatives of Courtesy Dodge and offered to install new lighting in the showroom. Courtesy Dodge paid Prestige Energy 75 percent of the contract price before the work began. The check was deposited into Prestige Energy's bank account. After a few months, the lighting project stalled. Apparently there had been a "falling out" between Michael Lewis and Bradley Brussow, who were operating Prestige Energy Products. Lewis told Courtesy Dodge that his company, Prestige NRGY Products, would handle the rest of the work. After the work was completed, Courtesy Dodge issued a final check for $23,826.26 to Prestige NRGY and gave the check to Lewis. Lewis never presented the check to Prestige Energy. When Brussow finally asked Courtesy Dodge why it had not been paid, Courtesy Dodge indicated it had already issued the final check to Prestige NRGY. Subsequently, Michael Lewis was charged with embezzlement and using a computer to commit a crime. He was convicted. On appeal, he claimed that he had not been allowed to present a proper defense to show that he did not have criminal intent. He further argued that what was at issue was a simple contract dispute, rather than a criminal action. How should the appellate court rule? [*State of Michigan v. Michael Charles Lewis*, 2022 WL 726798 (Ct.App. MI 2022)] (See *Criminal Liability*.)

10–8. A Question of Ethics—The IDDR Approach and Identity Theft. Heesham Broussard obtained counterfeit money instruments. To distribute them, he used account information and numbers on compromised FedEx accounts procured from hackers. Text messages from Broussard indicated that he had participated previously in a similar scam and that he knew the packages would be delivered only if the FedEx accounts were "good." For his use of the accounts, Broussard was charged with identity theft. In defense, he argued that the government could not prove he knew the misappropriated accounts belonged to real persons or businesses. [*United States v. Broussard*, 675 Fed.Appx. 454 (5th Cir. 2017)] (See *Cyber Crime*.)

(a) Does the evidence support Broussard's assertion? From an ethical perspective, does it matter whether he knew that the accounts belonged to real customers? Why or why not?

(b) Assuming that FedEx knew its customers' account information had been compromised, use the IDDR approach to consider whether the company had an ethical obligation to take steps to protect those customers from theft.

Time-Limited Group Assignment

10–9. Cyber Crime. Cyber crime costs consumers billions of dollars per year, and it costs businesses, including banks and other credit card issuers, even more. Nonetheless, when cyber criminals are caught and convicted, they are rarely ordered to pay restitution or sentenced to long prison terms. (See *Cyber Crime*.)

(a) One group should formulate an argument that stiffer sentences would reduce the amount of cyber crime.

(b) A second group should determine how businesspersons might best protect themselves from cyber crime and avoid the associated costs.

(c) A third group should decide how and when a court should order cyber criminals to pay restitution to their victims. Should victims whose computers have been infected with worms or viruses be entitled to restitution, or only victims of theft who have experienced financial loss? What should the measure of restitution be? Should large companies that are victims of cyber crime be entitled to the same restitution as individuals?

Unit Two: Task-Based Simulation

CompTac, Inc., which is headquartered in San Francisco, California, is one of the leading software manufacturers in the United States. The company invests millions of dollars to research and develop new software applications and computer games, which are sold worldwide. It also has a large service department and takes great pains to offer its customers excellent support services.

1. **Negligence.** A customer at one of CompTac's retail stores stumbles over a crate in the parking lot and breaks her leg. Just moments earlier, the crate had fallen off a CompTac truck that was delivering goods from a CompTac warehouse to the store. The customer sues CompTac, alleging negligence. Will she succeed in her suit? Why or why not?

2. **Wrongful Interference.** Roban Electronics, a software manufacturer and one of CompTac's major competitors, has been trying to convince one of CompTac's key employees, Jim Baxter, to come to work for Roban. Roban knows that Baxter has a written employment contract with CompTac, which Baxter would breach if he left CompTac before the contract expired. Baxter goes to work for Roban, and the departure of a key employee causes CompTac to suffer substantial losses due to delays in completing new software. Can CompTac sue Roban to recoup some of these losses? If so, on what ground?

3. **Cyber Crime.** One of CompTac's employees in its accounting division, Alan Green, has a gambling problem. To repay a gambling debt of $10,000, Green decides to "borrow" from CompTac to cover the debt. Using his knowledge of Comp-Tac account numbers, Green electronically transfers $10,000 from a CompTac account into his personal checking account. A week later, he is luckier at gambling and uses the same electronic procedures to transfer funds from his personal checking account back to the CompTac account. Has Green committed any crimes? If so, what are they?

4. **Intellectual Property.** CompTac wants to sell one of its best-selling software programs to An Phat Company, a firm located in Ho Chi Minh City, Vietnam. CompTac is concerned, however, that after an initial purchase, An Phat will duplicate the software without permission (in violation of U.S. copyright laws) and sell the illegal software to other firms in Vietnam. How can CompTac protect its software from being pirated by An Phat Company?

5. **Privacy and Social Media.** CompTac seeks to hire fourteen new employees. Its human resources (HR) department asks all candidates during their interview to disclose their social media passwords so that the company can access their social media accounts. Is it legal for employers to ask prospective employees for their social media passwords? Explain. If CompTac does not ask for passwords, can it legally look at a person's online posts when evaluating whether to hire or fire the person?

Chapter 11

International and Space Law

Commerce has always crossed national borders. But technology has fueled dramatic growth in world trade and the emergence of a global business community. Exchanges of goods, services, and intellectual property on a global level are now routine. Therefore, students of business law and the legal environment should be familiar with the laws pertaining to international business transactions.

Laws affecting the international legal environment of business include both international law and national law.

International law can be defined as a body of law—formed as a result of international customs, treaties, and organizations—that governs relations among or between nations. International law may be created when individual nations agree to comply with certain standards (such as by signing a treaty). It may also be created when industries or nations establish international standards for private transactions that cross national borders (such as a law that prohibits importation of genetically modified organisms).

National law is the law of a particular nation, such as Brazil, Germany, Japan, or the United States. In some ways, national laws that involve property rights, border searches, regulations, and taxes effectively become international law when they are applied at a nation's borders.

An emerging area of global importance is space law, which governs humans' activities in outer space. Space law also has both international and national components.

11–1 International Law

The major difference between international law and national law is that government authorities can enforce national law. What government, however, can enforce international law?

By definition, a nation is a sovereign entity—which means that there is no higher authority to which that nation must submit. If a nation violates an international law and persuasive tactics fail, other countries or international organizations have no recourse except to take coercive actions. Coercive actions might include economic sanctions, severance of diplomatic relations, boycotts, and, as a last resort, war against the violating nation.

■ **Example 11.1** North Korea has repeatedly conducted nuclear weapon and ballistic missile tests in violation of international law. In response, the United States and the European Union have imposed numerous economic sanctions against North Korea, including an embargo on imports of oil and exports of coal. ■

In essence, international law attempts to reconcile each country's need to be the final authority over its own affairs with the desire of nations to benefit economically from

trade and harmonious relations with one another. Sovereign nations can, and do, voluntarily agree to be governed in certain respects by international law, usually for the purpose of facilitating international trade and commerce. As a result, a body of international law has evolved.

11–1a Sources of International Law

Basically, there are three sources of international law: international customs, treaties and international agreements, and international organizations. We look at each of these sources here.

International Customs One important source of international law consists of the international customs that have evolved among nations in their relations with one another. Article 38(1) of the Statute of the International Court of Justice refers to an international custom as "evidence of a general practice accepted as law." The legal principles and doctrines that you will read about shortly are rooted in international customs and traditions that have evolved over time in the international arena.

Treaties and International Agreements Treaties and other explicit agreements between or among foreign nations provide another important source of international law. A **treaty** is an agreement or contract between two or more nations that has been authorized and ratified by the supreme power of each nation. Under Article II, Section 2, of the U.S. Constitution, the president has the power "by and with the Advice and Consent of the Senate, to make Treaties, provided two-thirds of the Senators present concur."

A bilateral agreement, as the term implies, is an agreement formed by two nations to govern their commercial exchanges or other relations with one another. A multilateral agreement is formed by several nations. For instance, regional trade associations such as the Andean Community, the Association of Southeast Asian Nations, and the European Union are the result of multilateral trade agreements.

International Organizations The term **international organization** generally refers to an organization composed mainly of officials of member nations and usually established by treaty. The United States is a member of more than one hundred multilateral and bilateral organizations, including at least twenty through the United Nations.

Adopt Resolutions. International organizations adopt resolutions, declarations, and other types of standards that often require nations to behave in a particular manner. The General Assembly of the United Nations, for instance, has adopted numerous nonbinding resolutions and declarations that embody principles of international law. Disputes with respect to these resolutions and declarations may be brought before the International Court of Justice. That court, however, normally has authority to settle legal disputes only when nations voluntarily submit to its jurisdiction.

Create Uniform Rules. The United Nations Commission on International Trade Law has made considerable progress in establishing uniformity in international law as it relates to trade and commerce. One of the commission's most significant creations to date is the 1980 Convention on Contracts for the International Sale of Goods (CISG).

The CISG is similar to Article 2 of the Uniform Commercial Code in that it is designed to settle disputes between parties to sales contracts. It spells out the duties of international buyers and sellers that will apply if the parties have not agreed otherwise in their contracts. The CISG governs only sales contracts between trading partners in nations that have ratified the CISG.

11–1b Common Law and Civil Law Systems

Companies operating in foreign nations are subject not only to international agreements but also to the laws of the nations in which they operate. In addition, international disputes are often resolved through the court systems of individual nations. Therefore, businesspersons should have some familiarity with these nations' legal systems.

Generally, legal systems around the globe are divided into common law and civil law systems. Exhibit 11–1 lists some of the nations that use civil law systems and some that use common law systems.

Common Law Systems Recall that in a common law system, such as the United States, the courts independently develop the rules governing certain areas of law, such as torts and contracts. These common law rules apply to all areas not covered by statutory law. Although the common law doctrine of *stare decisis* normally obligates judges to follow precedential decisions in their jurisdictions, courts may modify or even overturn precedents when deemed necessary.

Civil Law Systems In contrast to common law countries, most European nations, as well as nations in Latin America, Africa, and Asia, base their legal systems on Roman civil law, or code law. The term "civil law," as used here, refers not to civil as opposed to criminal law but to codified law—an ordered grouping of legal principles enacted into law by a legislature or other governing body.

In a **civil law system,** the primary source of law is a statutory code. Courts interpret the code and apply the rules to individual cases, but courts may not depart from the code and develop their own laws. Judicial precedents are not binding, as they are in a common law system. In theory, the law code sets forth all of the principles needed for the legal system. Trial procedures also differ in civil law systems. Unlike judges in common law systems, judges in civil systems often actively question witnesses.

Islamic Legal Systems A third, less prevalent, legal system is common in Islamic countries, where the law is often influenced by *sharia,* the religious law of Islam. *Sharia* is a comprehensive code of principles that governs both the public and the private lives of persons of the Islamic faith. *Sharia* directs many aspects of day-to-day

Exhibit 11–1 The Legal Systems of Selected Nations

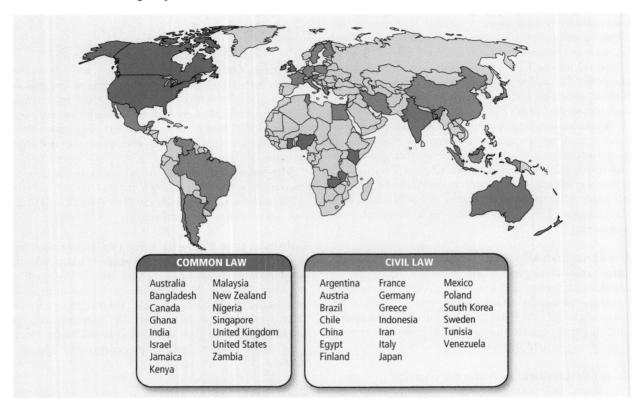

COMMON LAW		CIVIL LAW		
Australia	Malaysia	Argentina	France	Mexico
Bangladesh	New Zealand	Austria	Germany	Poland
Canada	Nigeria	Brazil	Greece	South Korea
Ghana	Singapore	Chile	Indonesia	Sweden
India	United Kingdom	China	Iran	Tunisia
Israel	United States	Egypt	Italy	Venezuela
Jamaica	Zambia	Finland	Japan	
Kenya				

life, including politics, economics, banking, business law, contract law, and social issues.

Although *sharia* affects the legal codes of many Islamic countries, the extent of its impact, as well as its interpretation, vary widely. In some Middle Eastern nations, aspects of *sharia* have been codified and are enforced by national judicial systems.

11–1c International Principles and Doctrines

Over time, a number of legal principles and doctrines have evolved in the international context. These principles and doctrines are employed by the courts of various nations to resolve or reduce conflicts that involve a foreign element. The three important legal principles discussed next are based primarily on courtesy and respect, and are applied in the interests of maintaining harmonious relations among nations.

The Principle of Comity The principle of **comity** basically refers to legal reciprocity. One nation will defer and give effect to the executive, legislative, and judicial acts of another country, as long as the acts are consistent with the law and public policy of the accommodating nation. For instance, a U.S. court ordinarily will recognize and enforce a default judgment from an Australian court because the legal procedures in Australia are compatible with those in the United States. Nearly all nations recognize the validity of marriage decrees (at least, those between a man and a woman) issued in another country.

■ **Case in Point 11.2** MD Helicopters, Inc., based in Arizona, failed to deliver eight helicopters to the Netherlands' National Police Services Agency. The National Police successfully sued MD for breach of contract in court proceedings in the Netherlands. The Netherlands government, representing its police force, then brought suit in Arizona to compel MD to pay the prescribed damages. The Netherlands based its claim on an Arizona statute that recognizes foreign-country judgments if the relevant laws of that country are "similar" to those of Arizona.

MD countered that no Netherlands law addressed the issues relating to its dispute with the National Police. Rather, only court decisions did so. A state appeals court rejected this argument, finding that a party seeking damages would follow essentially the same legal procedures in the Netherlands as it would in Arizona. Therefore, the court ordered MD to pay the National Police nearly $15 million, as determined by the Dutch court.[1] ■

The Act of State Doctrine The **act of state doctrine** is another important international doctrine. It provides that the judicial branch of one country will not examine the validity of public acts committed by a recognized foreign government within that government's own territory.

■ **Case in Point 11.3** Spectrum Stores, Inc., a gasoline retailer in the United States, filed a lawsuit in a U.S. court against Citgo Petroleum Corporation, which is owned by the government of Venezuela. Spectrum alleged that Citgo had conspired with other oil companies in Venezuela and Saudi Arabia to limit production of crude oil and thereby fix the prices of petroleum products sold in the United States. Because Citgo is owned by a foreign government, the U.S. court dismissed the case under the act of state doctrine. A government controls the natural resources, such as oil reserves, within its territory. A U.S. court will not rule on the validity of a foreign government's acts within its own territory.[2] ■

When a Foreign Government Takes Private Property. The act of state doctrine can have important consequences for individuals and firms doing business with, and investing in, other countries. This doctrine is frequently employed in cases involving expropriation or confiscation.

Expropriation occurs when a government seizes a privately owned business or privately owned goods for a proper public purpose and awards just compensation. When a government seizes private property for an illegal purpose and without just compensation, the taking is referred to as a **confiscation.** The line between these two forms of taking is sometimes blurred because of differing interpretations of what is illegal and what constitutes just compensation.

■ **Example 11.4** Flaherty, Inc., a U.S. company, owns a mine in Brazil. The government of Brazil seizes the mine for public use and claims that the profits Flaherty has already realized from the mine constitute just compensation. Flaherty disagrees, but the act of state doctrine may prevent the company's recovery in a U.S. court. ■

Note that in a case alleging that a foreign government has wrongfully taken the plaintiff's property, the defendant government has the burden of proving that the taking was an expropriation, not a confiscation.

Doctrine May Immunize a Foreign Government's Actions. When applicable, both the act of state doctrine and the doctrine of sovereign immunity, which we discuss next, tend to shield foreign nations from the jurisdiction of U.S. courts. As a result, firms or individuals that own property overseas generally have little legal protection against government actions in the countries where they operate.

The Doctrine of Sovereign Immunity When certain conditions are satisfied, the doctrine of **sovereign immunity** exempts foreign nations from the jurisdiction of the U.S. courts. In 1976, Congress codified this rule in the Foreign Sovereign Immunities Act (FSIA).[3]

■ **Case in Point 11.5** A federal district court held that the United States had jurisdiction over an art theft claim against Germany that dated back to the Nazi regime. The plaintiffs, including Alan Philipp, were descendants of Jewish art dealers in Frankfurt who had owned the Welfenschatz collection of medieval art. The plaintiffs argued that the art dealers had been terrorized by the Nazis and forced to sell the collection in 1935 for much less than its market price. (Adolf Hitler had allegedly discussed in letters how Nazis should take action to "save the Welfenschatz.") Germany claimed immunity under the FSIA, but the federal judge disagreed. The court was convinced by the plaintiffs that Germany was not entitled to sovereign immunity in this case.[4] ■

The FSIA exclusively governs the circumstances in which an action may be brought in the United States against a foreign nation, including attempts to attach a foreign nation's property. Because the law is jurisdictional in nature, a plaintiff generally has the burden of showing that a defendant is not entitled to sovereign immunity.

1. *State of Netherlands v. MD Helicopters, Inc.*, 462 P.3d 1038 (Ariz. Ct. App., Div. 1 2020).
2. *Spectrum Stores, Inc. v. Citgo Petroleum Corp.*, 632 F.3d 938 (5th Cir. 2011). See also *In re Terrorist Attacks on September 11, 2001*, 2021 WL 5331720 (S.D. NY 2021).
3. 28 U.S.C. Sections 1602–1611.
4. *Philipp v. Federal Republic of Germany*, 248 F.Supp.3d 59 (D.D.C. 2017). See also *Philipp v. Stiftung Preussischer Kulturbesitz*, 2021 WL 3144958 (D.D.C. 2021).

When a Foreign State Will Not Be Immune. Section 1605 of the FSIA sets forth the major exceptions to the jurisdictional immunity of a foreign state. A foreign state is not immune from the jurisdiction of U.S. courts in the following situations:

1. When the foreign state has waived its immunity either explicitly or by implication.
2. When the foreign state has engaged in commercial activity within the United States or in commercial activity outside the United States that has "a direct effect in the United States."
3. When the foreign state has committed a tort in the United States or has violated certain international laws.
4. When a foreign state that has been designated "a state sponsor of terrorism" is sued under the FSIA for "personal injury or death that was caused by an act of torture" or a related act of terrorism.

The following case involved the discovery of several shipwrecks off the coast of Florida, including one ship that had belonged to the Royal Navy of France about five hundred years ago. At issue was the applicability of the commercial activity exception to the doctrine of sovereign immunity.

Case Analysis 11.1

Global Marine Exploration, Inc. v. Republic of France
United States Court of Appeals, Eleventh Circuit, 33 F.4th 1312 (2022).

In the Language of the Court
LAGOA, C.J.

This case arises out of the discovery of several shipwrecks found off the coast of Cape Canaveral, Florida, including *La Trinité*, the flagship of the 1565 fleet of the Royal Navy of France, which was captained by Jean Ribault. In 1565, Ribault was dispatched by the French Admiral Gaspard II de Coligny to reinforce the French Huguenot settlement of Fort Caroline located on the St. Johns River near what is now Jacksonville, Florida. The Spanish, however, also laid claim to what they called La Florida, and Pedro Menéndez de Avilés had founded the Spanish settlement of St. Augustine near the French Fort Caroline. King Phillip II of Spain ordered Menéndez de Avilés to destroy the French settlement. Following a skirmish at the mouth of the St. Johns River with Spanish ships, Ribault left in pursuit of the Spanish flagship, the *San Pelayo*. Ribault encountered a hurricane which destroyed his fleet and drove Ribault and his surviving crew members ashore. That same hurricane allowed Menéndez de Avilés to succeed in capturing Fort Caroline after an overland expedition from St. Augustine. After Fort Caroline was destroyed, no further French settlements were established in Florida.

Global Marine Exploration, Inc. ("GME"), conducts marine salvage activities and discovers historic shipwreck sites in Florida's coastal waters. GME entered into authorization agreements with the Florida Department of State, Division of Historical Resources ("FDOS"), to conduct salvage activities in Florida coastal waters off Cape Canaveral. * * * GME discovered several shipwreck sites and informed FDOS of its discovery. Soon after, however, GME learned that FDOS was in contact with the Republic of France to recover the shipwreck sites, assuming that one of the sites was *La Trinité*. GME subsequently filed an * * * action against the "Unidentified, Wrecked and (for Finders-Right Purposes) Abandoned Sailing Vessel" in federal court. FDOS and France became parties to that action, and the Middle District of Florida concluded that the identity of the [property] was *La Trinité* and that *La Trinité* is France's sovereign property. GME did not appeal * * *.

Following [this trial, referred to as *GME I*], GME sued France, alleging [various] claims * * *. France moved to dismiss GME's * * * complaint under Federal Rule of Civil Procedure 12(b)(1), arguing that the district court lacked subject matter jurisdiction under

the Foreign Sovereign Immunities Act ("FSIA") and that the commercial activity exception to the FSIA was inapplicable. The district court agreed with France, finding that the FSIA's commercial activity exception did not apply, and dismissed GME's claims. GME now appeals the district court's dismissal, contending that France engaged in commercial activity such that the FSIA's commercial activity exception applies.

For the reasons discussed below, and with the benefit of oral argument, we conclude that the FSIA's commercial activity exception applies. Accordingly, we reverse the district court's Rule 12(b)(1) dismissal and remand for further proceedings.

I. Factual and Procedural Background
* * * Florida granted GME a fixed-term "cultural resource recovery easement for salvage exploration and operational purposes" on Florida-owned submerged lands, as well as permits for GME to use those submerged lands and navigable waters for construction work. GME then "undertook prolonged and expensive research, survey, reporting, and identification of shipwrecked sites," including artifacts, "with reasonable

investment-backed expectation[s] and program assurances that its salvage activity" would be fully compensated in line with the value of the discovered sites. In doing so, "GME expended millions of dollars and enormous time and effort."

* * * *

At some point, GME learned that FDOS was "collaborating and negotiating" with France to recover the shipwreck sites discovered by GME without its involvement. * * * Concerned by this development, GME filed [the *GME I*] action * * * and FDOS and France became parties to that action.

* * * Ultimately, the *GME I* district court granted France's motion to dismiss the action for lack of subject matter jurisdiction because it concluded that the [property] at issue was *La Trinité,* which was France's sovereign property.

[Following the *GME I* trial], France and FDOS entered into a "Declaration of Intention Between the State of Florida and the Republic of France On the shipwrecks of Jean Ribault's fleet" (the "Declaration of Intent"). The Declaration of Intent stated that, as a result of the district court's decision in *GME I,* France was authorized "to begin recovery operations" of *La Trinité* and that the signatories would cooperate "concerning research on, and protection and preservation of" *La Trinité.* * * *

[Later,] GME sued France, alleging that "France is sending missions to Florida to oversee the project and provide scientific expertise" under the Declaration of Intent and that "work is on-going." GME also asserted that France was performing commercial activity in Florida through France's agreement with FDOS and others, "and by activities undertaken or to be undertaken, in relation to GME's discovered shipwreck sites for which GME claims rights and interest."

* * * *

France moved to dismiss GME's amended complaint * * *, arguing that the district court lacked subject matter jurisdiction under the FSIA

and that GME failed to show that the commercial activity exception to the FSIA applied. In particular, France contended that the core conduct at issue was its "intergovernmental cooperation for the historic preservation of [its] military vessel," which was manifestly a governmental function. * * *

The district court granted France's motion to dismiss. The district court explained that the commercial activity exception had three components: whether "(1) the action is based upon (2) a commercial activity (3) carried on in the United States by a foreign state." The district court concluded that the action at issue was "France's intergovernmental declaration with Florida—and its overall relationship with Florida regarding the shipwreck sites," which "lack[ed] . . . a commercial nature" because France was not involved in "the type of actions by which a private party engages in trade and traffic or commerce." While noting that private actors sometimes engage in marine exploration and shipwreck recovery and preservation efforts, the district court reasoned "that alone did not make France's activities commercial." The district court explained that "the nature of France's activity is the recovery and disposition of its own sovereign military property" and that its choice to recover or preserve the property was not like "entering a market and behaving as a private person would." The district court noted that the Declaration of Intent, signed by government actors, showed that France and FDOS were working together to protect and preserve *La Trinité* and that, as such, France had not entered the market or engaged in trade or commerce.

The district court therefore concluded it lacked subject matter jurisdiction under the FSIA.

This timely appeal ensued.

* * * *

III. Analysis

On appeal, GME argues that the district court erred in dismissing its amended complaint for two reasons. First, GME asserts that the district court erroneously determined that the FSIA's commercial

activity exception to foreign sovereign immunity did not apply to France's activities in the case. Second, GME contends that its action against France was "based upon" France's commercial activities such that subject matter jurisdiction existed under the FSIA. We address these arguments in turn.

A. Whether France's activities are "commercial activities" under the FSIA

The FSIA "supplies the ground rules for 'obtaining jurisdiction over a foreign state in the courts of this country.'" The FSIA "creates a baseline of immunity from suit," and "unless a specified exception applies, a federal court lacks subject-matter jurisdiction over a claim against a foreign state,"

One such exception is the "commercial activity" exception contained in the first clause of 28 U.S.C. [Section] 1605(a)(2). The exception provides that "[a] foreign state shall not be immune from the jurisdiction of courts of the United States or of the States in any case . . . in which the action is based upon a commercial activity carried on in the United States by the foreign state." * * * Title 28 U.S.C. [Section] 1603(d) defines "commercial activity" as "either a regular course of commercial conduct or a particular commercial transaction or act," and states that "[t]he commercial character of an activity shall be determined by reference to the nature of the course of conduct or particular transaction or act, rather than by reference to its purpose."

While the definition in [Section] 1603(d) "leaves the critical term 'commercial' largely undefined," the Supreme Court has explained that "when a foreign government acts, not as regulator of a market, but in the manner of a private player within it, the foreign sovereign's actions are 'commercial' within the meaning of the FSIA." Additionally, because the FSIA "provides that the commercial character of an act is to be determined by reference to its 'nature' rather than its

Case 11.1 Continues

'purpose,' the question is not whether the foreign government is acting with a profit motive or instead with the aim of fulfilling uniquely sovereign objectives." Instead, we must determine "whether the particular actions that the foreign state performs (whatever the motive behind them) are the *type* of actions by which a private party engages in 'trade and traffic or commerce.'" * * *

    * * * *

    GME contends that the district court erred in finding that France's activities—a "marine archeological recovery project for recovery of six historical shipwreck sites in Florida"— did not constitute "commercial activity" under the FSIA. GME argues that the "what" of France's activity—effecting archaeological salvage recovery of historic shipwreck sites—and the

"means" employed for the activity—e.g., negotiating agreements with Florida and others; directing, coordinating, and participating in recovery efforts; securing private and grant source fundings; and conserving and arranging for the exhibition of artifacts—are commercial in nature. GME notes that similar types of activity are performed in commerce by private entities, including GME itself, "with which [FDOS] proposed to 'partner' for the same project." And GME asserts that the district court improperly looked to the "governmental direction or purpose" of France's activities, which is irrelevant to the question of an activity's commercial nature.

    We agree with GME and conclude that the nature of France's activities here are commercial under the FSIA.

As set forth by the Declaration of Intent, France, in cooperation with FDOS, planned to engage in a marine archaeological recovery project of the shipwreck sites off the coast of Cape Canaveral. * * *

    * * * *

    We therefore conclude that France's activities here are commercial activities under the FSIA.

    * * * *

IV. Conclusion

For these reasons, we reverse the district court's order dismissing GME's amended complaint for lack of subject matter jurisdiction and remand for further proceedings.

    REVERSED and REMANDED.

Legal Reasoning Questions

1. What was the main argument that Global Marine Exploration (GME) provided to support this lawsuit?

2. France argued that GME failed to show that the commercial activity exception to the FSIA applied. What was France's principal argument?

3. Was the trial court convinced by GME's arguments?

Application of the Act. When courts apply the FSIA, questions frequently arise as to whether an entity is a "foreign state" and what constitutes a "commercial activity." Under Section 1603 of the FSIA, a foreign state includes both a political subdivision of a foreign state and an instrumentality of a foreign state. An instrumentality includes any department or agency of any branch of a government.

    Section 1603 broadly defines a commercial activity as a regular course of commercial conduct, a transaction, or an act that is carried out by a foreign state within the United States. Section 1603, however, does not describe the particulars of what constitutes a commercial activity. Thus, the courts are left to decide whether a particular activity is governmental or commercial in nature.

    See Exhibit 11–2 for a graphic illustration of the three principles of international law just discussed.

11–2 Doing Business Internationally

A U.S. domestic firm can engage in international business transactions in a number of ways. The simplest way is for U.S. firms to **export** their goods and services to foreign markets. Alternatively, a U.S. firm can establish foreign production facilities to be closer to the foreign market or markets in which its products are sold. The advantages may include lower labor costs, fewer government regulations, and lower taxes and trade barriers. A domestic firm can also obtain revenues by licensing its technology to an existing foreign company or by selling franchises to overseas entities. (In some situations, domestic companies have profited by marketing goods, such as beer, as "imported" when they are not, as discussed in this chapter's Ethics Today feature.)

Exhibit 11–2 Examples of International Principles and Doctrines

The Principle of Comity	The Act of State Doctrine	The Doctrine of Sovereign Immunity
Nations will defer to and give effect to the laws and judicial decrees of other nations when those laws are consistent with their own.	U.S. courts will avoid passing judgment on the validity of public acts committed by a recognized foreign government within its own territory.	Foreign nations are immune from U.S. jurisdiction under the Foreign Sovereign Immunities Act when certain circumstances are satisfied. Some major exceptions apply, however.
Example: A U.S. court will most likely uphold the validity of a contract created in England, because England's legal procedures are compatible with those of the United States.	*Example:* A U.S. gas company files a lawsuit against a Saudi Arabian petroleum company, claiming a price-fixing conspiracy. A U.S. court will dismiss the case under the act of state doctrine because Saudi Arabia controls its own natural resources.	*Example:* A German governmental agency engages in commercial activity in New York. If a party in New York files a lawsuit against the agency, the foreign state is not immune from U.S. jurisdiction.

Ethics Today

Is It Ethical (and Legal) to Brew "Imported" Beer Brands Domestically?

Imported beer represents about 20 percent of total beer purchases in the United States. While imported beer generally costs more than domestic beer, those who purchase and consume it believe that its superior taste justifies the higher price.

When Imported Beer Really Isn't Imported

Many consumers are unaware that some beers marketed as imports are made in the United States. For instance, many people think of Beck's beer as German, but for a number of years, Beck's has been brewed in St. Louis, Missouri. Foster's beer ads feature Australian countryside scenes and Australian accents, yet Foster's is brewed in Fort Worth, Texas. Killian's Irish Red is not brewed in Ireland. It is brewed in Colorado. Kirin sells itself as Japanese, but it is not made in Asia. It is brewed in Virginia and Southern California. The Japanese beer Sapporo that is sold in the United States is actually brewed in Canada. Bass Ale and Cerveza Patagonia are also brewed in the United States.

A Violation of Country-of-Origin Labeling

A number of lawsuits have been filed against the owners of imported beer brands brewed in the United States. Many of them have been class actions brought

under state consumer protection laws involving country-of-origin labeling violations. One such suit was filed against Anheuser-Busch Companies, LLC, for mislabeling the origin of Beck's beer. The plaintiffs argued that labels such as "Brewed under the German Purity Law of 1516" and "Originated in Bremen, Germany" were misleading because the beer was brewed in the United States. The defendants argued that text on each bottle stated that the beer was a "Product of U.S.A." The case was ultimately settled out of court. Under the settlement, purchasers of Beck's beer could apply for up to $50 in refunds.[a]

Country-of-Origin Labeling Lawsuits Can Go Either Way

Plaintiffs who allege mislabeling do not always win their cases, of course. For instance, Antonia Bowring filed a class-action lawsuit against Sapporo, U.S.A., Inc., claiming that the company had misled customers by labeling and marketing the beer as imported. A federal district court in New York dismissed the case for failure to state a cause of action. The beer label clearly

---

a. *Marty v. Anheuser-Busch Companies, LLC,* 43 F.Supp.3d 1333 (S.D. Fla. 2014); and 2016 WL 397593 (S.D.Fla. 2016).

indicates that the beer is "Imported by Sapporo U.S.A. Inc., New York, NY" and "Brewed and canned [or bottled] by Sapporo Brewing Company, Guelph, Ontario, Canada."[b]

In a similar case, a New York resident filed a class-action claim for false advertising and violation of state consumer protection laws against Miller Brewing Company because Foster's beer is not made in Australia. A federal district court ruled that the plaintiff failed to state a cause of action because the labels on Foster's beer clearly stated it was brewed in the U.S.

b. *Bowring v. Sapporo U.S.A., Inc.,* 234 F.Supp.3d 386 (E.D.N.Y. 2017). See also *Culver v. Unilever United States, Inc.,* 2021 WL 2943937 (C.D. CA 2021).

"under the supervision of Foster's Australia, Ltd." The court dismissed the case, finding that no reasonable consumer could have been deceived.[c]

Critical Thinking Imported beer is not the only product whose labeling may be misleading. For instance, although BMW is a German brand, most BMW X3s and X5s purchased in the United States are manufactured in South Carolina. Are there any legal or ethical issues involved?

c. *Nelson v. MillerCoors, LLC,* 246 F.Supp.3d 666 (E.D.N.Y. 2017). See also *Wargo v. Hillshire Brands Company,* 599 F.Supp.3d 164, UCC Rep.Serv.2d 793 (S.D. NY 2022).

11–2a Exporting

Exporting can take two forms: direct exporting and indirect exporting. Companies that export indirectly can make use of agency relationships or distributorships.

Direct Versus Indirect Exporting In direct exporting, a U.S. company signs a sales contract with a foreign purchaser that provides for the conditions of shipment and payment for the goods.

If sufficient business develops in a foreign country, a U.S. company may establish a specialized marketing organization there by appointing a foreign agent or a foreign distributor. This is called *indirect exporting.*

Agency Relationships Versus Distributorships When a U.S. firm engaged in indirect exporting wishes to limit its involvement in an international market, it will typically establish an agency relationship with a foreign firm. The foreign firm then acts as the U.S. firm's agent and can enter contracts in the foreign location on behalf of the principal (the U.S. company).

When a foreign country represents a substantial market, a U.S. firm may wish to appoint a distributor located in that country. The U.S. firm and the distributor enter into a **distribution agreement.** This is a contract setting out the terms and conditions of the distributorship, such as price, currency of payment, guarantee of supply availability, and method of payment. Disputes concerning distribution agreements may involve jurisdictional or other issues, as well as contract law.

11–2b Manufacturing Abroad

An alternative to direct or indirect exporting is the establishment of foreign manufacturing facilities. Typically, U.S. firms establish manufacturing plants abroad when they believe that by doing so, they will reduce costs. Costs for labor, shipping, and raw materials may be lower in foreign nations, which can enable the business to compete more effectively in foreign markets.

Foreign firms have done the same in the United States. Sony, Honda, and other Japanese manufacturers, for instance, have established U.S. plants to avoid import duties that the U.S. Congress may impose on Japanese products entering this country.

There are several ways in which an American firm can manufacture in other countries. They include licensing and franchising, as well as investing in a wholly owned subsidiary or a joint venture.

Licensing A U.S. firm may license a foreign manufacturing company to use its copyrighted, patented, or trademarked intellectual property or trade secrets. Basically, licensing allows the foreign firm to use an established brand name for a fee. A licensing agreement with a foreign-based firm is much the same as any other licensing agreement. Its terms require a payment of royalties on some basis—such as so many cents per unit produced or a certain percentage of profits from units sold in a particular geographic territory.

■ **Example 11.6** The Coca-Cola Bottling Company licenses firms worldwide to use (and keep confidential) its secret formula for the syrup in its soft drink. In return,

A choice-of-law clause designates the applicable law. Both are useful additions to international contracts.

11–5 U.S. Laws in a Global Context

The globalization of business raises questions about the extraterritorial application of a nation's laws—that is, the effect of the country's laws outside its boundaries. To what extent do U.S. domestic laws apply to other nations' businesses? To what extent do U.S. domestic laws apply to U.S. firms doing business abroad? Here, we discuss the extraterritorial application of certain U.S. laws, including antitrust laws, tort laws, and laws prohibiting employment discrimination.

11–5a U.S. Antitrust Laws

U.S. antitrust laws have a wide application. They may subject firms in foreign nations to their provisions, as well as protect foreign consumers and competitors from violations committed by U.S. citizens. Section 1 of the Sherman Act—the most important U.S. antitrust law—provides for the extraterritorial effect of the U.S. antitrust laws.

Any conspiracy that has a substantial effect on U.S. commerce is within the reach of the Sherman Act. The law applies even if the violation occurs outside the United States, and foreign governments as well as businesses can be sued for violations. Before U.S. courts will exercise jurisdiction and apply antitrust laws, however, it must be shown that the alleged violation had a substantial effect on U.S. commerce.

■ **Example 11.9** An investigation by the U.S. government revealed that a Tokyo-based auto-parts supplier, Furukawa Electric Company, and its executives had conspired with competitors in an international price-fixing agreement. The agreement lasted more than ten years and resulted in automobile manufacturers' paying noncompetitive, higher prices for parts in cars sold to U.S. consumers. Because the conspiracy had a substantial effect on U.S. commerce, the United States had jurisdiction to prosecute the case. Furukawa agreed to plead guilty and pay a $200 million fine. The Furukawa executives from Japan also agreed to serve up to eighteen months in a U.S. prison and to cooperate fully with the ongoing investigation. ■

11–5b International Tort Claims

The international application of tort liability is growing in significance and controversy. An increasing number of U.S. plaintiffs are suing foreign (or U.S.) entities for torts that these entities have allegedly committed overseas. Often, these cases involve human rights violations by foreign governments.

The Alien Tort Statute (ATS)[9] allows foreign citizens to bring civil suits in U.S. courts for injuries caused by violations of the law of nations or a treaty of the United States. As a result, foreign plaintiffs increasingly used this act to bring actions against companies operating in nations such as Colombia, Ecuador, Egypt, Guatemala, India, Indonesia, Nigeria, and Saudi Arabia. Critics argued that such suits extended the application of the ATS too far. The United States Supreme Court apparently agreed when it held that foreign corporations could no longer be defendants in suits brought under the ATS.[10]

In the following Spotlight Case, the United States Supreme Court considered the parameters of the ATS. The question was whether the statute allows U.S. courts to exercise jurisdiction over a cause of action based on conduct that occurred outside the United States.

---

9. 28 U.S.C. Section 1350.
10. *Jesner v. Arab Bank, PLC*, 584 U.S. ___, 138 S.Ct. 1396, 200 L.Ed.2d 612 (2018). See also *Mwani v. Al-Qaeda*, 2022 WL 1165911 (D.D.C. 2022).

Spotlight on International Torts

Case 11.3 Daimler AG[a] v. Bauman

Supreme Court of the United States, 571 U.S. 117, 134 S.Ct. 746, 187 L.Ed.2d 624 (2014).

Background and Facts Barbara Bauman and twenty-one other residents of Argentina filed a suit in a federal district court in California against Daimler AG, a German company. They alleged that Mercedes-Benz (MB) Argentina, a subsidiary of Daimler, had collaborated with state security forces to

---

a. The initials *A.G.* stand for *aktiengesellschaft*, which is similar to the U.S. corporate form of business in Austria, Germany, and Switzerland.

Case 11.3 Continues

Case 11.3 Continued   kidnap, detain, torture, and kill certain MB Argentina workers. These workers included the plaintiffs and some of their relatives. Their claims were asserted under the Alien Tort Statute.

Personal jurisdiction was based on the California contacts of Mercedes-Benz USA (MBUSA), a Daimler subsidiary incorporated in Delaware with its principal place of business in New Jersey. MBUSA distributes Daimler-made vehicles to dealerships throughout the United States, including California. The district court dismissed the suit for lack of jurisdiction. The U.S. Court of Appeals for the Ninth Circuit reversed this ruling. Daimler appealed to the United States Supreme Court.

In the Language of the Court

Justice GINSBURG delivered the opinion of the Court.

* * * *

Even if we were to assume that MBUSA is at home in California, and further to assume MBUSA's contacts are imputable [attributable] to Daimler, there would still be no basis to subject Daimler to general jurisdiction in California, for Daimler's slim contacts with the State hardly render it at home there.

* * * Only a limited set of affiliations with a forum will render a defendant amenable to all-purpose jurisdiction there. For an individual, the paradigm forum [the typical forum] for the exercise of general jurisdiction is the individual's domicile; for a corporation, it is an equivalent place, one in which the corporation is fairly regarded as at home. With respect to a corporation, the place of incorporation and principal place of business are paradigm * * * bases for general jurisdiction. Those affiliations have the virtue of being unique—that is, each ordinarily indicates only one place—as well as easily ascertainable. These bases afford plaintiffs recourse to at least one clear and certain forum in which a corporate defendant may be sued on any and all claims.

[This does not mean] that a corporation may be subject to general jurisdiction *only* in a forum where it is incorporated or has its principal place of business * * *. [But] plaintiffs would have us look beyond the exemplar bases identified [above] and approve the exercise of general jurisdiction in every State in which a corporation engages in a substantial, continuous, and systematic course of business. That formulation, we hold, is unacceptably grasping.

* * * The inquiry * * * is not whether a foreign corporation's in-forum contacts can be said to be in some sense continuous and systematic; it is whether that corporation's affiliations with the State are so continuous and systematic as to render it essentially at home in the forum State.

Here, neither Daimler nor MBUSA is incorporated in California, nor does either entity have its principal place of business there. If Daimler's California activities sufficed to allow adjudication of this Argentina-rooted case in California, the same global reach would presumably be available in every other State in which MBUSA's sales are sizable. Such exorbitant exercises of all-purpose jurisdiction would scarcely permit out-of-state defendants to structure their primary conduct with some minimum assurance as to where that conduct will and will not render them liable to suit.

It was therefore [an] error for the Ninth Circuit to conclude that Daimler, even with MBUSA's contacts attributed to it, was at home in California, and hence subject to suit there on claims by foreign plaintiffs having nothing to do with anything that occurred or had its principal impact in California.

Decision and Remedy The United States Supreme Court reversed the decision of the lower court. A federal district court in California could not exercise jurisdiction over Daimler in this case, given the absence of any California connection to the atrocities, perpetrators, or victims described in the complaint.

Critical Thinking

- **Legal Environment** What are the consequences for Daimler of the decision in this case?
- **Global** If the Court had adopted the plaintiffs' argument, how might U.S. citizens have been affected?

11–5c Antidiscrimination Laws

Federal laws in the United States prohibit discrimination on the basis of race, color, national origin, religion, gender, age, and disability. These laws, as they affect employment relationships, generally apply extraterritorially.

Thus, U.S. employees working abroad for U.S. employers are protected under the Age Discrimination in Employment Act. Similarly, the Americans with Disabilities Act, which requires employers to accommodate the needs of workers with disabilities, applies to U.S. nationals working abroad for U.S. firms.

In addition, the major U.S. law regulating employment discrimination—Title VII of the Civil Rights Act—applies extraterritorially to all U.S. employees working for U.S. employers abroad. Generally, U.S. employers must abide by U.S. discrimination laws unless to do so would violate the laws of the country where their workplaces are located. This "foreign laws exception" allows employers to avoid being subjected to conflicting laws.

11–6 Space Law

Space law consists of the international and national laws that govern activities in outer space. For the first fifty years of space exploration, national governments conducted most of those activities. Thus, space law was directed primarily at governments and government activities. More recently, private companies have undertaken many space-related activities and opened outer space to the rest of us. Space law, accordingly, faces new challenges.

11–6a International Space Law

International space law consists of international treaties—primarily negotiated by the United Nations (U.N.)—and U.N. resolutions. These sources recognize fundamentally that activities conducted in outer space and the benefits derived from those activities should improve the welfare of all nations and all humanity.

The major space law treaties were concluded by the U.N. Committee on the Peaceful Uses of Outer Space (COPUOS). COPUOS also administers the treaties and advises the international community on space policy matters.

Exploration and Exploitation The foundation of international space law is the U.N. Treaty on Principles Governing the Activities of States in the Exploration and Use of Outer Space, including the Moon and Other Celestial Bodies.[11] This treaty—generally referred to as the Outer Space Treaty—established the framework for later international agreements and U.N. resolutions.

The Outer Space Treaty expresses general principles that have been expanded and applied in subsequent treaties. In Article I and Article II, outer space is declared to be free for the exploration and use of all nations. The moon, the planets, asteroids, and other celestial bodies are not subject to the appropriation of any single nation.[12] In addition, space objects are to be used exclusively for peaceful purposes. No weapons of mass destruction are permitted in outer space under Article IV.[13]

According to Article VI, each nation is responsible for its activities in outer space, whether they are conducted by the government or by a private entity. In fact, the activities of private entities require authorization and supervision by a government. Article VIII provides that each nation retains jurisdiction and control over its space objects and the personnel on them. Article VII imposes on each nation liability for damage caused by its space objects. Finally, Article IX requires that space exploration be conducted so as to avoid "harmful contamination."[14]

Astronauts and Space Objects The Outer Space Treaty was followed by several other agreements:

- The Agreement on the Rescue of Astronauts, the Return of Astronauts and the Return of Objects Launched into Outer Space (the Rescue Agreement).[15]
- The Convention on International Liability for Damage Caused by Space Objects (the Liability Convention).[16]
- The Convention on Registration of Objects Launched into Outer Space (the Registration Convention).[17]

---

11. 18 U.S.T. 2410, T.I.A.S. 6347, 610 U.N.T.S. 205.
12. After the treaty entered into force, the United States and Russia conducted joint space activities.
13. Establishing military bases, testing weapons, and conducting military maneuvers are prohibited.
14. Other articles promote further international cooperation in the exploration and use of space.
15. 19 U.S.T. 7570, T.I.A.S. 6599, 672 U.N.T.S. 119.
16. 24 U.S.T. 2389, T.I.A.S. 7762, 961 U.N.T.S. 187.
17. 28 U.S.T. 695, T.I.A.S. 8480, 1023 U.N.T.S. 15.

The Rescue Agreement expands on Articles V and VIII of the Outer Space Treaty. It provides that each nation will undertake to rescue and assist astronauts in distress and return them to their "launching State." All nations are to assist in recovering space objects that return to earth outside the territory of the launching state.

The Liability Convention elaborates on Article VII of the Outer Space Treaty. This agreement provides that a launching state is absolutely liable for personal injury and property damage caused by its space objects on the surface of the earth or to aircraft in flight. Liability for injury or damage in space is subject to a determination of fault. The convention also prescribes procedures for the settlement of claims for damages.

The Registration Convention provides for the mandatory registration of objects launched into outer space. Each launching state is to maintain a registry of the objects that it launches into space. The intent is to assist in the objects' identification. (See this chapter's Cybersecurity and the Law feature for insights into a problem that was given little consideration at the time these international agreements were made.)

11–6b U.S. Space Law

In the United States, each government agency that operates or authorizes spacecraft is responsible for complying with U.S. law and international treaties. Federal law, state law, and more than half a century of common practices in space-related industries also affect government and private space activities.

Commercial Spaceflight The Federal Aviation Administration (FAA) regulates private spaceports and the launch and reentry of private spacecraft under the Commercial Space Launch Act, which dates back to 1986.

The FAA has established licensing and safety criteria for private spacecraft. Some states, including Florida, New Mexico, Texas, and Virginia, limit the liability of space tourism providers under state tort law. But state legislatures and, ultimately, courts will need to consider other issues in this context, including insurance requirements and the enforceability of liability waivers.

In 2015, Congress enacted landmark legislation called the U.S. Commercial Space Launch Competitiveness

---

Cybersecurity and the Law   Safe Satellites

By the early 2020s, more than 8,000 human-made satellites orbited the Earth. By the end of the decade, a single aerospace manufacturer—Space X—plans to have launched up to 42,000 satellites. Other companies, including Amazon, Facebook, and Bharti Global, have similar plans. The potential benefits of this vast array include high-speed 5G internet access to every corner of the planet, improved global navigation systems, and an enhanced ability to monitor meteorological conditions.

This space traffic also poses potential problems, such as high-speed collisions, dead satellites that threaten other spacecraft, and disruption of the work of astronomers. To no one's surprise, the specter of hacking also looms large in the satellite industry's future.

Hacking in Space

According to computer security experts, satellites are particularly susceptible to being hacked. Until recently, satellite engineers have not emphasized cybersecurity in their design and construction plans. To reduce costs, satellite builders often patch together these devices with less expensive computer components using open-source

technology, giving hackers numerous vulnerabilities to exploit. Additionally, numerous satellites already in orbit were launched many years ago, before cybersecurity was a concern. Controlling these defenseless satellites might be as easy as setting up a ground antenna and waiting for one to pass overhead.

Hacking in Space—The Consequences

Hackers could shut down a targeted satellite. Or they could jam the satellite's signals, wreaking havoc on communications and other critical infrastructure systems. Steerable satellites could be hijacked to "attack" other objects, in space or closer to Earth. Currently, no governmental body in the United States has created any cybersecurity guidelines for satellite operations. In this vacuum, it is not clear who would be legally responsible for a security breach in a satellite, nor is there sufficient relevant case law to help American courts determine civil liability for any harm done by a hacked, rogue satellite.

Critical Thinking Why is international law better suited for satellite regulation than national law?

Act.[18] The act, aimed at encouraging commercial space-flight companies, streamlines regulatory processes and promotes safety standards. In addition, it provides that if a U.S. citizen or company retrieves minerals or other resources from an asteroid or other space location, that person or company owns them.

Exports of Space Technology

Under U.S. regulations, all spacecraft are classified as "defense articles." The defense classification restricts the transfer of space technology and related information to any foreign person or nation under the U.S. Department of State's International Traffic in Arms Regulations.[19] This restriction makes it difficult for U.S. space companies to compete in global space markets.

---

18. Pub. L. No. 114-90, 129 Stat. 704, November 25, 2015.
19. 22 C.F.R. Sections 120.1 *et seq.*

Property Rights to Space Resources

Article II of the Outer Space Treaty bans the national appropriation of territory in space. If the United States cannot appropriate territory in space, then it cannot give U.S. citizens title to property associated with this territory. Under U.S. law, the government must have sovereignty over territory before it can confer title to associated property to its citizens.

Article VIII, however, provides that a state party to the treaty retains jurisdiction over objects on its space registry that are launched into space. In addition, Article IX prohibits interference with space activities. In effect, these provisions confer the protections associated with property rights on private space activities.

The U.S. Commercial Space Launch Competitiveness Act changed the law somewhat by granting private citizens property rights over asteroid resources that they obtain from space. The act specifically recognizes that the United States is not attempting to assert sovereignty or exclusive right or jurisdiction over any celestial body.

Practice and Review: International and Space Law

Robco, Inc., was a Florida arms dealer. The armed forces of Honduras contracted to purchase weapons from Robco over a six-year period. After the government was replaced and a democracy installed, the Honduran government sought to reduce the size of its military, and its relationship with Robco deteriorated. Honduras refused to honor the contract and purchase the inventory of arms, which Robco could sell only at a much lower price. Robco filed a suit in a federal district court in the United States to recover damages for this breach of contract by the government of Honduras. Using the information presented in the chapter, answer the following questions.

1. Should the Foreign Sovereign Immunities Act (FSIA) preclude this lawsuit? Why or why not?
2. Does the act of state doctrine bar Robco from seeking to enforce the contract? Explain.
3. Suppose that prior to this lawsuit, the new government of Honduras enacted a law making it illegal to purchase weapons from foreign arms dealers. What doctrine of deference might lead a U.S. court to dismiss Robco's case in that situation?
4. Now suppose that the U.S. court hears the case and awards damages to Robco. The government of Honduras, however, has no assets in the United States that can be used to satisfy the judgment. Under which doctrine might Robco be able to collect the damages by asking another nation's court to enforce the U.S. judgment?

Debate This . . . The U.S. federal courts are accepting too many lawsuits initiated by foreigners that concern matters not relevant to this country.

Terms and Concepts

act of state doctrine 215
civil law system 213
comity 214
confiscation 215
distribution agreement 220
dumping 222
export 218

expropriation 215
international law 212
international organization 213
national law 212
normal trade relations (NTR) status 223
quotas 221

sovereign immunity 215
space law 227
tariffs 222
treaty 213

Issue Spotters

1. Café Rojo, Ltd., an Ecuadoran firm, agrees to sell coffee beans to Dark Roast Coffee Company, a U.S. firm. Dark Roast accepts the beans but refuses to pay. Café Rojo sues Dark Roast in an Ecuadoran court and is awarded damages, but Dark Roast's assets are in the United States. Under what circumstances would a U.S. court enforce the judgment of the Ecuadoran court? (See *International Law*.)

2. Gems International, Ltd., is a foreign firm that has a 12 percent share of the U.S. market for diamonds. To capture a larger share, Gems offers its products at a below-cost discount to U.S. buyers (and inflates the prices in its own country to make up the difference). How can this attempt to undersell U.S. businesses be defeated? (See *Regulation of Specific Business Activities*.)

• Check your answers to the Issue Spotters against the answers provided in Appendix B at the end of this text.

Business Scenarios and Case Problems

11-1. Doing Business Internationally. Macrotech, Inc., develops an innovative computer chip and obtains a patent on it. The firm markets the chip under the trademarked brand name "Flash." Macrotech wants to sell the chip to Nitron, Ltd., in Pacifica, a foreign country. Macrotech is concerned, however, that after an initial purchase, Nitron will duplicate the chip, pirate it, and sell the pirated version to computer manufacturers in Pacifica. To avoid this possibility, Macrotech could establish its own manufacturing facility in Pacifica, but it does not want to do this. How can Macrotech, without establishing a manufacturing facility in Pacifica, protect Flash from being pirated by Nitron? (See *Doing Business Internationally*.)

11-2. Dumping. The U.S. pineapple industry alleged that producers of canned pineapple from the Philippines were selling their canned pineapple in the United States for less than its fair market value (dumping). In addition to canned pineapple, the Philippine producers exported other products, such as pineapple juice and juice concentrate. These products used separate parts of the same fresh pineapple used for the canned pineapple. All these products shared raw material costs with the canned fruit, according to the producers' own financial records. To determine fair value and antidumping duties, the pineapple industry argued that a court should calculate the Philippine producers' cost of production and allocate a portion of the shared fruit costs to the canned fruit. The result of this allocation showed that more than 90 percent of the canned fruit sales were below the cost of production. Is this a reasonable approach to determining the production costs and fair market value of canned pineapple in the United States? Why or why not? (See *Regulation of Specific Business Activities*.)

11-3. Sovereign Immunity. Taconic Plastics, Ltd., is a manufacturer incorporated in Ireland with its principal place of business in New York. Taconic enters into a contract with a German firm, Werner Voss Architects and Engineers, acting as an agent for the government of Saudi Arabia. The contract calls for Taconic to supply special material for tents designed to shelter religious pilgrims visiting holy sites in Saudi Arabia. Most of the material is made in, and shipped from, New York. The German company does not pay Taconic and files for bankruptcy. Taconic files a suit in a U.S. court against the government of Saudi Arabia, seeking to collect $3 million. The defendant files a motion to dismiss the suit based on the doctrine of sovereign immunity. Under what circumstances does this doctrine apply? What are its exceptions? Should this suit be dismissed? Explain. (See *International Law*.)

11-4. Business Case Problem With Sample Answer— Import Controls. The Wind Tower Trade Coalition is an association of domestic manufacturers of utility-scale wind towers. The coalition filed a suit in the U.S. Court of International Trade against the U.S. Department of Commerce. It challenged the Commerce Department's decision to impose only prospective antidumping duties, rather than retrospective (retroactive) duties, on imports of utility-scale wind towers from China and Vietnam. The department had found that the domestic industry had not suffered any "material injury" or "threat of material injury" from such imports. It had further found that the industry would be protected by a prospective assessment. Can an antidumping duty be assessed retrospectively? If so, should it be assessed here? Discuss. [*Wind Tower Trade Coalition v. United States,* 741 F.3d 89 (Fed. Cir. 2014)] (See *Regulation of Specific Business Activities.*)

- For a sample answer to Problem 11–4, go to Appendix C at the end of this text.

11-5. The Principle of Comity. Holocaust survivors and the heirs of Holocaust victims filed a suit in a U.S. federal district court against the Hungarian national railway, the Hungarian national bank, and several private Hungarian banks. The plaintiffs alleged that the defendants had participated in expropriating the property of Hungarian Jews who were victims of the Holocaust. The claims arose from events in Hungary seventy years earlier. The plaintiffs, however, had not exhausted remedies available through Hungarian courts. Indeed, they had not even attempted to seek remedies in Hungarian courts, and they did not provide a legally compelling reason for their failure to do so. The defendants asked the court to dismiss the suit. Does the principle of comity support the defendants' request? Explain. [*Fischer v. Magyar Államvasutak Zrt.,* 777 F.3d 847 (7th Cir. 2015)] (See *International Law.*)

11-6. International Law. For fifty years, the Soviet Union made and sold Stolichnaya vodka. At the time, VVO-SPI, a Soviet state enterprise, licensed the Stolichnaya trademark in the United States. When the Soviet Union collapsed, VVO-SPI was purportedly privatized and fell under the control of Spirits International B.V. (SPI). In 2000, a Russian court held that VVO-SPI had not been validly privatized under Russian law. Thus, ownership of the Stolichnaya mark remained with the Soviet Union's successor, the Russian Federation. The Russian Federation assigned the mark to Federal Treasury Enterprise Sojuzplodoimport (FTE). FTE then filed a suit in a U.S. federal district court against SPI, asserting unlawful misappropriation and commercial exploitation of the mark in violation of the Lanham Act. Is the validity of the assignment of the mark to FTE a question to be determined by the court? Why or why not? [*Federal Treasury Enterprise Sojuzplodoimport v. Spirits International B.V.,* 809 F.3d 737 (2d Cir. 2016)] (See *International Law.*)

11-7. Import Controls. Goods exported to a foreign country for repair or alteration can qualify for tariff-free or reduced-tariff treatment when they re-enter the United States. But the goods do not qualify for favorable import-duty treatment if, in the foreign country, they are transformed into commercially different goods. Daimler-Chrysler Sprinter vans are marketed in the United States as cargo vans. Pleasure-Way Industries, Inc., bought 144 Sprinter vans and exported them to Canada for conversion into motor homes. This included the installation of fully plumbed and furnished kitchens, bathrooms, and sleeping quarters. After the conversion, Pleasure-Way sought to import the vehicles back into the United States to market the motor homes under new model names as upscale leisure vehicles at prices double or triple the price for Sprinter vans. Do the converted vans qualify for favorable import-tariff treatment? Discuss. [*Pleasure-Way Industries, Inc. v. United States*, 878 F.3d 1348 (Fed. Cir. 2018)] (See *Regulation of Specific Business Activities.*)

11-8. Sovereign Immunity. Rasha Mohammad was employed as an administrative assistant by the State of Kuwait's consulate in Los Angeles. She filed suit alleging that she had been constructively terminated due to discrimination based on her religion, gender, and natural origin. The consulate moved to dismiss the action based on sovereign immunity. The district court denied the motion, finding it had jurisdiction under the commercial activity exception to the Foreign Sovereign Immunities Act (FSIA). Rasha Mohammad was not a diplomat, civil servant, or military officer. She was a Syrian national living in California as a legal permanent resident, and eventually a U.S. citizen. Should the appellate court accept the trial court's decision? Why or why not? [*Mohammad v. General Consulate of State of Kuwait in Los Angeles*, 28 F.4th 980 [9th Cir. (2022)] (See *International Law.*)

11-9. A Question of Ethics—The IDDR Approach and Foreign Jurisdiction. Incorporated under Venezuelan law, a subsidiary of U.S.-based Helmerich & Payne International Drilling Company supplied oil-drilling rigs to entities that were part of the government of Venezuela. The government fell behind in payment on contracts for the use of the rigs. When the overdue amounts topped $100 million, the government nationalized the rigs and took possession. Helmerich filed a suit in a U.S. federal district court against Venezuela, claiming expropriation of property in violation of international law. Helmerich asserted that the U.S. court had jurisdiction under the Foreign Sovereign Immunities Act (FSIA). [*Bolivarian Republic of Venezuela v. Helmerich & Payne International Drilling Co.,* 581 U.S. 170, 137 S.Ct. 1312, 197 L.Ed.2d 663 (2017)] (See *International Law.*)

(a) Venezuela argued that the FSIA did not apply because Helmerich did not have rights in the rigs, which were the subsidiary's property. Does that fact make Helmerich's claim frivolous and unethical? Explain.

(b) Using the IDDR approach, determine whether a company is ethically obligated to become familiar with the political situation before doing business in another country.

Time-Limited Group Assignment

11-10. Expanding Abroad. Assume that you are manufacturing iPad accessories and that your business is becoming more successful. You are now considering expanding operations into another country. (See *Doing Business Internationally*.)

(a) One group will explore the costs and benefits of advertising on the internet.

(b) Another group will consider whether to take in a partner from a foreign nation and will explain the benefits and risks of having a foreign partner.

(c) A third group will discuss what problems may arise if a business chooses to manufacture in a foreign location.

Unit Two: Task-Based Simulation

CompTac, Inc., which is headquartered in San Francisco, California, is one of the leading software manufacturers in the United States. The company invests millions of dollars to research and develop new software applications and computer games, which are sold worldwide. It also has a large service department and takes great pains to offer its customers excellent support services.

1. **Negligence.** A customer at one of CompTac's retail stores stumbles over a crate in the parking lot and breaks her leg. Just moments earlier, the crate had fallen off a CompTac truck that was delivering goods from a CompTac warehouse to the store. The customer sues CompTac, alleging negligence. Will she succeed in her suit? Why or why not?

2. **Wrongful Interference.** Roban Electronics, a software manufacturer and one of CompTac's major competitors, has been trying to convince one of CompTac's key employees, Jim Baxter, to come to work for Roban. Roban knows that Baxter has a written employment contract with CompTac, which Baxter would breach if he left CompTac before the contract expired. Baxter goes to work for Roban, and the departure of a key employee causes Comp-Tac to suffer substantial losses due to delays in completing new software. Can CompTac sue Roban to recoup some of these losses? If so, on what ground?

3. **Cyber Crime.** One of CompTac's employees in its accounting division, Alan Green, has a gambling problem. To repay a gambling debt of $10,000, Green decides to "borrow" from CompTac to cover the debt. Using his knowledge of CompTac account numbers, Green electronically transfers $10,000 from a CompTac account into his personal checking account. A week later, he is luckier at gambling and uses the same electronic procedures to transfer funds from his personal checking account back to the CompTac account. Has Green committed any crimes? If so, what are they?

4. **Intellectual Property.** CompTac wants to sell one of its best-selling software programs to An Phat Company, a firm located in Ho Chi Minh City, Vietnam. CompTac is concerned, however, that after an initial purchase, An Phat will duplicate the software without permission (in violation of U.S. copyright laws) and sell the illegal software to other firms in Vietnam. How can CompTac protect its software from being pirated by An Phat Company?

5. **Privacy and Social Media.** CompTac seeks to hire fourteen new employees. Its human resources (HR) department asks all candidates during their interview to disclose their social media passwords so that the company can access their social media accounts. Is it legal for employers to ask prospective employees for their social media passwords? Explain. If CompTac does not ask for passwords, can it legally look at a person's online posts when evaluating whether to hire or fire the person?

6. **International Law.** To offer goods at low prices, CompTac software reduces its costs by obtaining products made, distributed, and shipped by companies located in other countries. Because of developments affecting the global economy, the prices that CompTac's sources charge the U.S. retailer are increasing. CompTac wants to take steps to reduce those expenses. Also, as the economies in other nations grow, CompTac is interested in expanding its retail operations into those markets. What are CompTac's options for attaining these goals? What are the characteristics of each of these choices?

The Commercial Environment

Chapter 12

Formation of Traditional and E-Contracts

No aspect of modern life is entirely free of contractual relationships. You acquire rights and obligations, for instance, when you borrow funds, buy or lease a house, obtain insurance, and purchase goods or services. Contract law is designed to provide stability and predictability, as well as certainty, in the marketplace.

Contract law deals with, among other things, the formation and keeping of promises. A **promise** is a declaration by a person (the *promisor*) to do or not to do a certain act. As a result, the person to whom the promise is made (the *promisee*) has a right to expect or demand that something either will or will not happen in the future.

Like other types of law, contract law reflects our social values, interests, and expectations at a given point in time. It shows, for instance, to what extent our society allows people to make promises or commitments that are legally binding. It distinguishes between promises that create only *moral* obligations (such as a promise to take a friend to lunch) and promises that are legally binding (such as a promise to pay for items ordered online).

Contract law also demonstrates which excuses our society accepts for breaking certain types of promises. In addition, it indicates which promises are considered to be contrary to public policy—against the interests of society as a whole—and therefore legally invalid. When the person making a promise is a child, for instance, a question will arise as to whether the promise should be enforced. Resolving such questions is the essence of contract law.

12–1 An Overview of Contract Law

Before we look at the numerous rules that courts use to determine whether a particular promise will be enforced, it is necessary to understand some fundamental concepts of contract law. In this section, we describe the sources and general function of contract law and introduce the objective theory of contracts.

12–1a Sources of Contract Law

The common law governs all contracts except when it has been modified or replaced by statutory law, such as the Uniform Commercial Code (UCC), or by administrative agency regulations. Contracts relating to services, real estate, employment, and insurance, for instance, generally are governed by the common law of contracts.

Contracts for the sale and lease of goods, however, are governed by the UCC—to the extent that the UCC has modified general contract law. In the discussion of general contract law that follows, we indicate in footnotes the areas in which the UCC has significantly altered common law contract principles.

12–1b The Definition of a Contract

A **contract** is "a promise or a set of promises for the breach of which the law gives a remedy, or the performance of which the law in some way recognizes as a duty."[1] Put simply, a contract is an agreement that can be enforced in court. It is formed by two or more parties who agree to perform or to refrain from performing some act now or in the future.

Generally, contract disputes arise when there is a promise of future performance. If the contractual promise is not fulfilled, the party who made it is subject to the sanctions of a court. That party may be required to pay damages for failing to perform the contractual promise. In a few instances, the party may be required to perform the promised act.

12–1c The Objective Theory of Contracts

In determining whether a contract has been formed, the element of intent is of prime importance. In contract

---

1. *Restatement (Second) of Contracts,* Section 1.

law, intent is determined by what is called the **objective theory of contracts,** not by the personal or subjective intent or belief of a party.

The theory is that a party's intention to enter into a legally binding agreement, or contract, is judged by outward, objective facts. The facts are as interpreted by a reasonable person, rather than by the party's own secret, subjective intentions. Objective facts may include:

1. What the party said when entering into the contract.
2. How the party acted or appeared (intent may be manifested by conduct as well as by oral or written words).
3. The circumstances surrounding the transaction.

■ **Case in Point 12.1** The Leaf Clean Energy Company, an investment firm, invested $30 million in notes issued by Invenergy Wind, a wind energy developer. The investment contract prohibited Invenergy from conducting a "Material Partial Sale" of its assets without Leaf's consent. If such a sale occurred, then Invenergy was required to pay Leaf a penalty. After Invenergy concluded a $1.8 billion "Material Partial Sale" without Leaf's consent, the investment company sued to recoup its penalty under the contract, which was about $126 million.

A lower court agreed that Invenergy breached the contract but awarded Leaf only one dollar in damages. The court reasoned that it would be unfair for Leaf to gain such a large amount when it had not suffered any actual harm. Applying the objective theory of contracts, the Delaware Supreme Court reversed and ordered Invenergy the pay Leaf the $126 million. The appellate court scolded the lower court for ignoring the "clear and unambiguous" terms of the contract, which were designed to prevent Invenergy from making any major financial decisions without Leaf's consent.[2] ■

12–1d Requirements of a Valid Contract

The following list briefly describes the four requirements that must be met before a valid contract exists. If any of these elements is lacking, no contract will have been formed. Each requirement will be explained more fully in subsequent chapters.

1. **Agreement.** An agreement to form a contract includes an offer and an acceptance. One party must offer to enter into a legal agreement, and another party must accept the terms of the offer.
2. **Consideration.** Any promises made by the parties to the contract must be supported by legally sufficient and bargained-for consideration (something of value received or promised, such as money, to convince a person to make a deal).
3. **Contractual capacity.** Both parties entering into the contract must have the contractual capacity to do so. The law must recognize them as possessing characteristics that qualify them as competent parties.
4. **Legality.** The contract's purpose must be to accomplish some goal that is legal and not against public policy.

12–1e Types of Contracts

There are many types of contracts. They are categorized based on legal distinctions as to their formation, performance, and enforceability.

Bilateral Versus Unilateral Contracts Every contract involves at least two parties. The **offeror** is the party making the offer. The **offeree** is the party to whom the offer is made. Whether the contract is classified as *bilateral* or *unilateral* depends on what the offeree must do to accept the offer and bind the offeror to a contract.

If the offeree can accept simply by promising to perform, the contract is a **bilateral contract**. Hence, a bilateral contract is a "promise for a promise." No performance, such as payment of funds or delivery of goods, need take place for a bilateral contract to be formed. The contract comes into existence at the moment the promises are exchanged.

If the offer is phrased so that the offeree can accept only by completing the contract performance, the contract is a **unilateral contract**. Hence, a unilateral contract is a "promise for an act." In other words, a unilateral contract is formed not at the moment when promises are exchanged but at the moment when the contract is performed.

■ **Example 12.2** Reese says to Celia, "If you drive my car from New York to Los Angeles, I'll give you $1,000." Only on Celia's completion of the act—bringing the car to Los Angeles—does she fully accept Reese's offer to pay $1,000. If she chooses not to accept the offer to drive the car to Los Angeles, there are no legal consequences. ■

Formal Versus Informal Contracts Formal **contracts** are contracts that require a special form or method of creation (formation) to be enforceable.[3]

---

2. *Leaf Invenergy Company v. Invenergy Renewables, LLC,* 210 A.3d 688 (S.Ct. Del. 2019).

3. See *Restatement (Second) of Contracts,* Section 6, which explains that formal contracts include (1) contracts under seal, (2) recognizances, (3) negotiable instruments, and (4) letters of credit.

One example is negotiable instruments, which include checks, drafts, promissory notes, bills of exchange, and certificates of deposit. Negotiable instruments are formal contracts because, under the Uniform Commercial Code (UCC), a special form and language are required to create them. *Letters of credit*, which are frequently used in international sales contracts, are another type of formal contract.

Informal contracts (also called *simple contracts*) include all other contracts. No special form is required (except for certain types of contracts that must be in writing), as the contracts are usually based on their substance rather than their form. Typically, businesspersons put their contracts in writing (including electronic records) to ensure that there is some proof of a contract's existence should disputes arise.

Express Versus Implied Contracts Contracts may also be categorized as *express* or *implied*. In an **express contract,** the terms of the agreement are fully and explicitly stated in words, oral or written. A signed lease for an apartment or a house is an express written contract. If one classmate calls another on the phone and agrees to buy her textbooks from last semester for $200, an express oral contract has been made.

A contract that is implied from the conduct of the parties is called an **implied contract** (or sometimes an *implied-in-fact* contract). This type of contract differs from an express contract in that the conduct of the parties, rather than their words, creates and defines the terms of the contract.

Requirements for Implied Contracts. For an implied contract to arise, certain requirements must be met. Normally, if the following conditions exist, a court will hold that an implied contract was formed:

1. The plaintiff furnished some service or property.
2. The plaintiff expected to be paid for that service or property, and the defendant knew or should have known that payment was expected.
3. The defendant had a chance to reject the services or property and did not.

■ **Example 12.3** Ketill, a small-business owner, needs an accountant to complete his tax return. He drops by a local accountant's office, explains his situation to the accountant, and learns what fees she charges. The next day, he returns and gives the receptionist all of the necessary documents to complete his return. Then he walks out without saying anything further to the accountant. In this situation, Ketill has entered into an implied contract to pay the accountant the usual fees for her services. The contract is implied because of Ketill's conduct and hers. She expects to be paid for completing the tax return, and by bringing in the records she will need to do the job, Ketill has implied an intent to pay her. ■

Mixed Contracts with Express and Implied Terms. Note that a contract may be a mixture of an express contract and an implied contract. In other words, a contract may contain some express terms and some implied terms. During the construction of a home, for instance, the homeowner often asks the builder to make changes in the original specifications.

■ **Case in Point 12.4** Lamar Hopkins hired Uhrhahn Construction & Design, Inc., for several projects in building his home. For each project, the parties signed a written contract that was based on a cost estimate and specifications and that required changes to the agreement to be in writing. While the work was in progress, however, Hopkins repeatedly asked Uhrhahn to deviate from the contract specifications, which Uhrhahn did. None of these requests was made in writing.

One day, Hopkins asked Uhrhahn to use Durisol blocks instead of the cinder blocks specified in the original contract, indicating that the cost would be the same. Uhrhahn used the Durisol blocks but demanded extra payment when it became clear that the Durisol blocks were more complicated to install. Although Hopkins had paid for the other deviations from the contract that he had orally requested, he refused to pay Uhrhahn for the substitution of the Durisol blocks. Uhrhahn sued for breach of contract. The court found that Hopkins, through his conduct, had waived the provision requiring written contract modification and had created an implied contract to pay the extra cost of installing the Durisol blocks.[4] ■

Executed Versus Executory Contract Contracts are also classified according to the degree to which they have been performed. A contract that has been fully performed on both sides is called an

---
4. *Uhrhahn Construction & Design, Inc. v. Hopkins,* 179 P.3d 808 (Utah App. 2008). See, in contrast, *Harris v. County of Orange,* 17 F.4th 849 (9th Cir. 2021).

executed contract. A contract that has not been fully performed by the parties is called an **executory contract.** If one party has fully performed but the other has not, the contract is said to be executed on the one side and executory on the other, but the contract is still classified as executory.

■ **Example 12.5** Jackson, Inc., agreed to buy ten tons of coal from the Northern Coal Company. Northern delivered the coal to Jackson's steel mill, where it is being burned. At this point, the contract is executed on the part of Northern and executory on Jackson's part. After Jackson pays Northern, the contract will be executed on both sides. ■

Enforceable Versus Unenforceable Contracts

A **valid contract** has the elements necessary to entitle at least one of the parties to enforce it in court. Those elements, as mentioned earlier, consist of (1) an agreement (offer and acceptance), (2) supported by legally sufficient consideration, (3) made by parties who have the legal capacity to enter into the contract, (4) for a legal purpose. An **unenforceable contract** is one that cannot be enforced because of certain legal defenses against it. It is not unenforceable because a party failed to satisfy a legal requirement of the contract. Rather, it is a valid contract rendered unenforceable by some statute or law. For instance, certain contracts must be in writing, and if they are not, they will not be enforceable except in certain exceptional circumstances.

Voidable Contracts. A **voidable contract** is a valid contract but one that can be avoided at the option of one or both of the parties. The party having the option can elect either to avoid any duty to perform or to ratify (make valid) the contract. If the contract is avoided, both parties are released from it. If it is ratified, both parties must fully perform their respective legal obligations.

Void Contracts. A **void contract** is no contract at all. The terms "void" and "contract" are contradictory. None of the parties have any legal obligations if a contract is void. A contract can be void because one of the parties was determined by a court to be mentally incompetent, for instance, or because the purpose of the contract was illegal.

To review the various types of contracts, see Concept Summary 12.1.

Concept Summary 12.1

Types of Contracts

Formation	• *Bilateral*—A promise for a promise. • *Unilateral*—A promise for an act; acceptance is the completed performance of the act. • *Formal*—Requires a special form for creation. • *Informal*—Requires no special form for creation. • *Express*—Formed by words (oral, written, or a combination). • *Implied*—Formed by the conduct of the parties.
Performance	• *Executed*—A fully performed contract. • *Executory*—A contract not fully performed.
Enforceability	• *Valid*—The contract has the necessary contractual elements: agreement (offer and acceptance), consideration, legal capacity of the parties, and legal purpose. • *Voidable*—One party has the option of avoiding or enforcing the contractual obligation. • *Unenforceable*—A contract exists, but it cannot be enforced because of a legal defense. • *Void*—No contract exists, or there is a contract without legal obligations.

12–2 Agreement

An essential element for contract formation is **agreement**—the parties must agree on the terms of the contract and manifest to each other their *mutual assent* (agreement) to the same bargain. Ordinarily, agreement is evidenced by two events: an *offer* and an *acceptance*. One party offers a certain bargain to another party, who then accepts that bargain. Once an agreement is reached, if the other elements of a contract (consideration, capacity, and legality) are present, a valid contract is formed.

12–2a Requirements of the Offer

An **offer** is a promise or commitment to do or refrain from doing some specified action in the future. The party making an offer is called the *offeror*, and the party to whom the offer is made is called the *offeree*. Under the common law, three elements are necessary for an offer to be effective:

1. The offeror must have a serious intention to become bound by the offer.

2. The terms of the offer must be reasonably certain, or definite, so that the parties and the court can ascertain the terms of the contract.

3. The offer must be communicated to the offeree.

Once an effective offer has been made, the offeree's acceptance of that offer creates a legally binding contract (providing the other essential elements for a valid and enforceable contract are present).

Intention The first requirement for an effective offer is a serious intent on the part of the offeror. Serious intent is not determined by the subjective intentions, beliefs, and assumptions of the offeror. Rather, it is determined by what a reasonable person in the offeree's position would conclude that the offeror's words and actions meant.

Offers made in obvious anger, jest, or undue excitement do not meet the serious-and-objective-intent test. A reasonable person would realize that such offers were not made seriously. Because these offers are not effective, an offeree's acceptance does not create an agreement.

In the classic case presented next, the court considered whether an offer made "after a few drinks" met the serious-and-objective-intent requirement.

Classic Case 12.1

Lucy v. Zehmer

Supreme Court of Appeals of Virginia, 196 Va. 493, 84 S.E.2d 516 (1954).

Background and Facts W. O. Lucy, the plaintiff, filed a suit against A. H. and Ida Zehmer, the defendants, to compel the Zehmers to transfer title of their property, known as the Ferguson Farm, to the Lucys (W. O. and his wife) for $50,000, as the Zehmers had allegedly agreed to do. Lucy had known A. H. Zehmer for fifteen or twenty years and for the last eight years or so had been anxious to buy the Ferguson Farm from him. One night, Lucy stopped to visit the Zehmers in the combination restaurant, filling station, and motor court they operated. While there, Lucy tried to buy the Ferguson Farm once again. This time he tried a new approach. According to the trial court transcript, Lucy said to Zehmer, "I bet you wouldn't take $50,000 for that place." Zehmer replied, "Yes, I would too; you wouldn't give fifty." Throughout the evening, the conversation returned to the sale of the Ferguson Farm for $50,000. All the while, the men continued to drink whiskey and engage in light conversation.

Eventually, Lucy enticed Zehmer to write up an agreement to the effect that the Zehmers would sell the Ferguson Farm to Lucy for $50,000. Later, Lucy sued Zehmer to compel him to go through with the sale. Zehmer argued that he had been drunk and that the offer had been made in jest and hence was unenforceable. The trial court agreed with Zehmer, and Lucy appealed.

In the Language of the Court
BUCHANAN, J. [Justice] delivered the opinion of the court.
* * * *

In his testimony, Zehmer claimed that he "was high as a Georgia pine," and that the transaction "was just a bunch of two doggoned drunks bluffing to see who could talk the biggest and say the most." That claim is inconsistent with his attempt to testify in great detail as to what was said and what was done.

Case 12.1 Continues

Case 12.1 Continued * * * *

The appearance of the contract, the fact that it was under discussion for forty minutes or more before it was signed; Lucy's objection to the first draft because it was written in the singular, and he wanted Mrs. Zehmer to sign it also; the rewriting to meet that objection and the signing by Mrs. Zehmer; the discussion of what was to be included in the sale, the provision for the examination of the title, the completeness of the instrument that was executed, the taking possession of it by Lucy with no request or suggestion by either of the defendants that he give it back, are facts which furnish persuasive evidence that the execution of the contract was a serious business transaction rather than a casual, jesting matter as defendants now contend.

* * * *

In the field of contracts, as generally elsewhere, we must look to the outward expression of a person as manifesting his intention rather than to his secret and unexpressed intention. The law imputes to a person an intention corresponding to the reasonable meaning of his words and acts.

* * * *

Whether the writing signed by the defendants and now sought to be enforced by the complainants was the result of a serious offer by Lucy and a serious acceptance by the defendants, or was a serious offer by Lucy and an acceptance in secret jest by the defendants, in either event it constituted a binding contract of sale between the parties.

Decision and Remedy The Supreme Court of Appeals of Virginia determined that the writing was an enforceable contract and reversed the ruling of the lower court. The Zehmers were required by court order to follow through with the sale of the Ferguson Farm to Lucy.

Critical Thinking

- **What If the Facts Were Different?** Suppose that the day after Lucy signed the purchase agreement, he decided that he did not want the farm after all, and Zehmer sued Lucy to perform the contract. Would this change in the facts alter the court's decision that Lucy and Zehmer had created an enforceable contract? Why or why not?
- **Impact of This Case on Today's Law** This is a classic case in contract law because it illustrates so clearly the objective theory of contracts with respect to determining whether a serious offer was intended. Today, the courts continue to apply the objective theory of contracts and routinely cite *Lucy v. Zehmer* as a significant precedent in this area.

Situations in Which Intent May Be Lacking The concept of intention can be further clarified by looking at statements that are not offers and situations in which the parties' intent to be bound might be questionable.

1. **Expressions of opinion.** An expression of opinion is not an offer. It does not indicate an intention to enter into a binding agreement.
2. **Statements of future intent.** A statement of an intention to do something in the future (such as "I plan to sell my Verizon stock") is not an offer.
3. **Preliminary negotiations.** A request or invitation to negotiate is not an offer. It only expresses a willingness to discuss the possibility of entering into a contract. Statements such as "Will you sell your farm?" or "I wouldn't sell my car for less than $18,000" are examples.
4. **Invitations to bid.** When a government entity or private firm needs to have construction work done,

contractors are invited to submit bids. The invitation to submit bids is not an offer. The bids that contractors submit are offers, however, and the government entity or private firm can bind the contractor by accepting the bid.
5. **Advertisements and price lists.** In general, representations made in advertisements and price lists are treated not as offers to contract but as invitations to negotiate.[5]
6. **Live and online auctions.** In a live auction, a seller "offers" goods for sale through an auctioneer, but this is not an offer to form a contract. Rather, it is an invitation asking bidders to submit offers. In the context of an auction, a bidder is the offeror, and the auctioneer is the offeree. The offer is accepted when the auctioneer strikes the hammer.

---

5. *Restatement (Second) of Contracts,* Section 26, Comment b.

The most familiar type of auction today takes place online through websites like eBay and eBid. "Offers" to sell an item on these sites generally are treated as invitations to negotiate. Unlike live auctions, online auctions are automated. Buyers can enter incremental bids on an item (without approving each price increase) up to a specified amount or without a limit.

Agreements to Agree. Traditionally, agreements to agree—that is, agreements to agree to the material terms of a contract at some future date—were not considered to be binding contracts. The modern view, however, is that agreements to agree may be enforceable agreements (contracts) if it is clear that the parties intended to be bound by the agreements. In other words, under the modern view the emphasis is on the parties' intent rather than on form.

■ **Case in Point 12.6** After a person was injured and nearly drowned on a water ride at one of its amusement parks, Six Flags, Inc., filed a lawsuit against the manufacturer that had designed the ride. The defendant manufacturer claimed that the parties did not have a binding contract but had only engaged in preliminary negotiations that were never formalized in a construction contract.

The court, however, held that the evidence was sufficient to show an intent to be bound. The evidence included a faxed document specifying the details of the water ride, along with the parties' subsequent actions (having begun construction and written notes on the faxed document). The manufacturer was required to provide insurance for the water ride at Six Flags. In addition, its insurer was required to defend Six Flags in the personal-injury lawsuit that arose out of the incident.[6] ■

Preliminary Agreements. Increasingly, the courts are holding that a preliminary agreement constitutes a binding contract if the parties have agreed on all essential terms and no disputed issues remain to be resolved. In contrast, if the parties agree on certain major terms but leave other terms open for further negotiation, a preliminary agreement is normally not binding. The parties are bound only in the sense that they have committed themselves to negotiate the undecided terms in good faith in an effort to reach a final agreement.

Definiteness of Terms The second requirement for an effective offer involves the definiteness of its terms.

An offer must have reasonably definite terms so that a court can determine if a breach has occurred and give an appropriate remedy.[7] The specific terms required depend, of course, on the type of contract. Generally, a contract must include the following terms, either expressed in the contract or capable of being reasonably inferred from it:

1. The identification of the parties.
2. The identification of the object or subject matter of the contract (also the quantity, when appropriate), including the work to be performed, with specific identification of such items as goods, services, and land.
3. The consideration to be paid.
4. The time of payment, delivery, or performance.

An offer may invite an acceptance to be worded in such specific terms that the contract is made definite. ■ **Example 12.7** Nintendo of America, Inc., contacts your local game store and offers to sell "from one to twenty-five Nintendo Switch gaming systems for $220 each. State number desired in acceptance." You agree to buy twenty systems. Because the quantity is specified in the acceptance, the terms are definite, and the contract is enforceable. ■

When the parties have clearly manifested their intent to form a contract, courts sometimes are willing to supply a missing term in a contract, especially a sales contract.[8] But a court will not rewrite a contract if the parties' expression of intent is too vague or uncertain to be given any precise meaning.

Communication The third requirement for an effective offer is communication—the offer must be communicated to the offeree. Ordinarily, one cannot agree to a bargain without knowing that it exists. ■ **Case in Point 12.8** Adwoa Gyabaah was hit by a bus owned by Rivlab Transportation Corporation. Gyabaah filed a suit in a New York state court against the bus company. Rivlab's insurer offered to tender the company's policy limit of $1 million in full settlement of Gyabaah's claims. On the advice of her attorney, Jeffrey Aronsky, Gyabaah signed a release (a contract forfeiting the right to pursue a legal claim) to obtain the settlement funds.

The release, however, was not sent to Rivlab or its insurer, National Casualty. Moreover, Gyabaah claimed that she had not decided whether to settle. Two months

6. *Six Flags, Inc. v. Steadfast Insurance Co.,* 474 F.Supp.2d 201 (D.Mass. 2007). See also *Maxum Indemnity Co. v. Thermax, Inc.,* 2020 WL 9743907 (D.Mass. 2020).

7. *Restatement (Second) of Contracts,* Section 33.

8. See UCC 2–204. Article 2 of the UCC modifies general contract law by requiring less specificity, or definiteness of terms, in sales and lease contracts.

later, Gyabaah changed lawyers and changed her mind about signing the release. Her former attorney, Aronsky, filed a motion to enforce the release so that he could obtain his fees from the settlement funds. The court denied the motion, and Aronsky appealed. The reviewing court held that there was no binding settlement agreement. The release was never delivered to Rivlab or its insurer, nor was acceptance of the settlement offer otherwise communicated to them.[9] ■

12–2b Termination of the Offer

The communication of an effective offer to an offeree gives the offeree the power to transform the offer into a binding legal obligation (a contract) by an acceptance. This power of acceptance does not continue forever, though. It can be terminated either by action of the parties or by operation of law.

Termination by Action of the Offeror The offeror's act of revoking, or withdrawing, an offer is known as **revocation**. Unless an offer is irrevocable, the offeror usually can revoke the offer, as long as the revocation is communicated to the offeree before the offeree accepts. Revocation may be accomplished by either of the following:

1. Express repudiation of the offer (such as "I withdraw my previous offer of October 17").
2. Performance of acts that are inconsistent with the existence of the offer and are made known to the offeree (for instance, selling the offered property to another person in the offeree's presence).

In most states, a revocation becomes effective when the offeree or the offeree's agent (a person acting on behalf of the offeree) actually receives it. Therefore, a revocation sent via FedEx April 1 and delivered at the offeree's residence or place of business on April 3 becomes effective on April 3.

Although most offers are revocable, some can be made irrevocable—that is, they cannot be revoked. One form of irrevocable offer is an **option contract**. An option contract is created when an offeror promises to hold an offer open for a specified period of time in return for a payment (consideration) given by the offeree. An option contract takes away the offeror's power to revoke the offer for the period of time specified in the option.

Option contracts are frequently used in conjunction with the sale or lease of real estate. ■ **Example 12.9** Antonio agrees to lease a house from Jackson, the property owner. The lease contract includes a clause stating that Antonio is paying an additional $25,000 for an option to purchase the property within a specified period of time. If Antonio decides not to purchase the house after the specified period has lapsed, he loses the $25,000, and Jackson is free to sell the property to another buyer. ■

Termination by Action of the Offeree If the offeree rejects the offer—by words or by conduct—the offer is terminated. Any subsequent attempt by the offeree to accept will be construed as a new offer, giving the original offeror (now the offeree) the power of acceptance.

Like a revocation, a rejection of an offer is effective only when it is actually received by the offeror or the offeror's agent. ■ **Example 12.10** Goldfinch Farms offers to sell specialty Maitake mushrooms to a Japanese buyer, Kinoko Foods. If Kinoko rejects the offer by sending a letter via U.S. mail, the rejection will not be effective (and the offer will not be terminated) until Goldfinch receives the letter. ■

Inquiries About an Offer. Merely inquiring about the "firmness" of an offer does not constitute rejection. ■ **Example 12.11** Damba offers to buy Francie's digital pen for $100. Francie responds, "Is that your best offer?" A reasonable person would conclude that Francie has not rejected the offer but has merely made an inquiry. Francie could still accept and bind Damba to the $100 price. ■

Counteroffer. A **counteroffer** is a rejection of the original offer and the simultaneous making of a new offer. ■ **Example 12.12** Burke, a beet farmer, offers to sell her product to Lang, the owner of the Lang's Roadside Veggie Stand, for $1.70 a pound. Lang responds, "Your price is too high. I'll offer to pay $1.30 a pound for your beets." Lang's response is a counteroffer because it rejects Burke's offer to sell her beets at $1.70 a pound and creates a new offer by Lang to purchase the beets at $1.30 a pound. ■

At common law, the **mirror image rule** requires the offeree's acceptance to match the offeror's offer exactly—to mirror the offer. Any change in, or addition to, the terms of the original offer automatically terminates that offer and substitutes the counteroffer. The counteroffer, of course, need not be accepted, but if the original offeror

9. *Gyabaah v. Rivlab Transportation Corp.*, 102 A.D.3d 451, 958 N.Y.S.2d 109 (2013). See also *HNA Sweden Hospitality Management AB v. Equities First Holdings, LCC*, 2021 WL 1907603 (S.D.IN 2021).

does accept the terms of the counteroffer, a valid contract is created.[10]

Termination by Operation of Law The power of the offeree to transform the offer into a binding legal obligation can be terminated by operation of law through the occurrence of any of the following events:

1. Lapse of time.
2. Destruction of the specific subject matter of the offer.
3. Death or incompetence of the offeror or the offeree.
4. Supervening illegality of the proposed contract.

Lapse of Time. An offer terminates automatically by law when the period of time specified in the offer has passed. If the offer states that it will be left open until a particular date, then the offer will terminate at midnight on that day. If the offer states that it will be open for a number of days, this time period normally begins to run when the offeree receives the offer (not when it is formed or sent).

If the offer does not specify a time for acceptance, the offer terminates at the end of a reasonable period of time. What constitutes a reasonable period of time depends on the subject matter of the contract, business and market conditions, and other relevant circumstances. An offer to sell farm produce, for instance, will terminate sooner than an offer to sell farm equipment. Farm produce is perishable and is also subject to greater fluctuations in market value.

Destruction, Death, or Incompetence. An offer is automatically terminated if the specific subject matter of the offer (such as a car or a house) is destroyed before the offer is accepted.[11] Notice of the destruction is not required for the offer to terminate.

Supervening Illegality. A statute or court decision that makes an offer illegal automatically terminates the offer.[12] ■ **Example 12.13** Lee offers to lend Malina $10,000 at an annual interest rate of 15 percent. Before Malina can accept the offer, a law is enacted that prohibits interest rates higher than 8 percent. Lee's offer is automatically terminated. (If the statute is enacted after Malina accepts the offer, a valid contract is formed, but the contract may still be unenforceable.) ■

Concept Summary 12.2 reviews the ways in which an offer can be terminated.

---

10. The mirror image rule has been greatly modified in regard to sales contracts. Section 2–207 of the UCC provides that a contract is formed if the offeree makes a definite expression of acceptance (such as signing a form in the appropriate location), even though the terms of the acceptance modify or add to the terms of the original offer.

11. *Restatement (Second) of Contracts,* Section 36.
12. *Restatement (Second) of Contracts,* Section 36.

Concept Summary 12.2

Methods by Which an Offer Can Be Terminated

By Action of the Parties	• Revocation • Rejection • Counteroffer
By Operation of Law	• Lapse of time • Destruction of the subject matter • Death or incompetence of the offeror or offeree • Supervening illegality

12–2c Acceptance

Acceptance is a voluntary act by the offeree that shows assent (agreement) to the terms of an offer. The offeree's act may consist of words or conduct. The acceptance must be unequivocal and must be communicated to the offeror. Generally, only the person to whom the offer is made or that person's agent can accept the offer and create a binding contract.

Unequivocal Acceptance To exercise the power of acceptance effectively, the offeree must accept unequivocally. This is the mirror image rule previously mentioned. An acceptance may be unequivocal even though the offeree expresses dissatisfaction with the contract. For instance, "I accept the offer, but can you give me a better price?" or "I accept, but please send a written contract" is an effective acceptance. (Notice how important each word is!)

An acceptance cannot impose new conditions or change the terms of the original offer. If it does, the acceptance may be considered a counteroffer, which is a rejection of the original offer. For instance, the statement "I accept the offer but only if I can pay on ninety days' credit" is a counteroffer and not an unequivocal acceptance.

Note that even when the additional terms are construed as a counteroffer, the other party can accept the terms by words or by conduct. ■ **Case in Point 12.14** Lagrange Development is a nonprofit corporation in Ohio that acquires and rehabilitates real property. Sonja Brown presented Lagrange with a written offer to buy a particular house for $79,900. Lagrange's executive director, Terry Glazer, penciled in modifications to the offer—an increased purchase price of $84,200 and a later date for acceptance. Glazer initialed the changes and signed the document.

Brown initialed the date change but not the price increase, and did not sign the revised document. Nevertheless, Brown went through with the sale and received ownership of the property. When a dispute later arose as to the purchase price, a court found that Glazer's modification of the terms had constituted a counteroffer, which Brown had accepted by performance. Therefore, the contract was enforceable for the modified price of $84,200.[13] ■

Silence as Acceptance Ordinarily, silence cannot constitute acceptance, even if the offeror states, "By your silence and inaction, you will be deemed to have accepted this offer." An offeree should not be obligated to act affirmatively to reject an offer when no consideration (nothing of value) has passed to the offeree to impose such a duty.

In some instances, however, the offeree does have a duty to speak, and silence or inaction will operate as an acceptance. Silence can constitute an acceptance when the offeree has had prior dealings with the offeror. ■ **Example 12.15** Marabel's restaurant routinely receives shipments of produce from a certain supplier. That supplier notifies Marabel's that it is raising its prices because its crops were damaged by a late freeze. If the restaurant does not respond in any way, the silence may operate as an acceptance, and the supplier will be justified in continuing regular shipments. ■

Communication of Acceptance Whether the offeror must be notified of the acceptance depends on the nature of the contract. In a unilateral contract, the full performance of some act is called for. Acceptance is usually evident, and notification is therefore unnecessary (unless the law requires it or the offeror asks for it). In a bilateral contract, in contrast, communication of acceptance is necessary, because acceptance is in the form of a promise. The bilateral contract is formed when the promise is made rather than when the act is performed.

Mode and Timeliness of Acceptance In bilateral contracts, acceptance must be timely. The general rule is that acceptance in a bilateral contract is timely if it is made before the offer is terminated. Problems may arise, though, when the parties involved are not dealing face to face. In such situations, the offeree should use an authorized mode of communication.

The Mailbox Rule. Acceptance takes effect, thus completing formation of the contract, at the time the offeree sends or delivers the communication via the mode expressly or impliedly authorized by the offeror. This is the so-called **mailbox rule**, also called the *deposited acceptance rule*, which the majority of courts follow. Under this rule, if the authorized mode of communication is the mail, then an acceptance becomes valid when it is dispatched (placed in the control of the U.S. Postal Service)—not when it is received by the offeror. (Note, however, that if the offer stipulates when acceptance will be effective, then the offer will not be effective until the time specified.)

The mailbox rule does not apply to instantaneous forms of communication, such as when the parties are dealing face to face, by telephone, by fax, and (usually) by e-mail or text messaging. Under the Uniform Electronic Transactions Act, e-mail is considered sent when it either leaves the control of the sender or is received by the recipient. This rule takes the place of the mailbox rule when the parties have agreed to conduct transactions electronically and allows an e-mail acceptance to become effective when sent.

---

13. *Brown v. Lagrange Development Corp.*, 2015-Ohio-133, 2015 WL 223877 (Ohio App. 2015). See also *Nieberding v. Barrante*, 2021-Ohio-2593, 2021 WL 3204858 (Ohio App. 8th Dist., 2021).

Authorized Means of Acceptance. A means of communicating acceptance can be expressly authorized by the offeror or impliedly authorized by the facts and circumstances of the situation. An acceptance sent by means not expressly or impliedly authorized normally is not effective until it is received by the offeror.

When an offeror specifies how acceptance should be made (for instance, by overnight delivery), express authorization is said to exist. The contract is not formed unless the offeree uses that specified mode of acceptance. Moreover, both offeror and offeree are bound in contract the moment this means of acceptance is employed.

If the offeror does not expressly authorize a certain mode of acceptance, then acceptance can be made by any reasonable means. Courts look at the prevailing business usages and the surrounding circumstances to determine whether the mode of acceptance used was reasonable.

Usually, the offeror's choice of a particular means in making the offer implies that the offeree can use the same or a faster means for acceptance. Thus, if the offer is made via Priority U.S. mail, it would be reasonable to accept the offer via Priority mail or by a faster method, such as overnight delivery.

Substitute Method of Acceptance. Sometimes, the offeror authorizes a particular method of acceptance, but the offeree accepts by a different means. In that situation, the acceptance may still be effective if the substituted method serves the same purpose as the authorized means.

Acceptance by a substitute method is not effective on dispatch, however. No contract will be formed until the acceptance is received by the offeror. ■ **Example 12.16** Bennion's offer specifies acceptance via FedEx overnight delivery, but the offeree accepts instead by overnight delivery from UPS. The substitute method of acceptance will still be effective, but not until the offeror (Bennion) receives it from UPS. ■

12–3 E-Contracts

Numerous contracts are formed online. Electronic contracts, or **e-contracts,** must meet the same basic requirements (agreement, consideration, contractual capacity, and legality) as paper contracts. Disputes concerning e-contracts, however, tend to center on contract terms and whether the parties voluntarily agreed to those terms.

Online contracts may be formed not only for the sale of goods and services but also for licensing. The "sale" of software generally involves a *license*, or a right to use the software, rather than the passage of title (ownership rights) from the seller to the buyer. When you download an app on your smartphone, you select "I agree" several times to indicate that you agree to the terms and conditions under which you will use the software.

As you read through the following subsections, you will see that we typically refer to the *offeror* and the *offeree* as a seller and a buyer. Keep in mind, though, that in many online transactions these parties would be more accurately described as a *licensor* and a *licensee*.

12–3a Online Offers

Sellers doing business via the internet can protect themselves against contract disputes and legal liability by creating offers that clearly spell out the terms that will govern their transactions if the offers are accepted. All important terms should be conspicuous and easy to view.

The seller's website should include a hypertext link to a page containing the full contract so that potential buyers are made aware of the terms to which they are assenting. The contract generally must be displayed online in a readable format, such as a twelve-point typeface. All provisions should be reasonably clear.

Provisions to Include An important point to keep in mind is that the offeror (the seller) controls the offer and thus the resulting contract. Sellers should therefore anticipate the terms they want to include in a contract and provide for those terms in the offer. In some instances, a standardized contract form may suffice.

At a minimum, an online offer should include the following provisions:

1. **Acceptance of terms.** A clause that clearly indicates what constitutes the buyer's agreement to the terms of the offer, such as a box containing the words "I accept" that the buyer can click.
2. **Payment.** A provision specifying how payment for the goods (including any applicable taxes) must be made.
3. **Return policy.** A statement of the seller's refund and return policies.
4. **Disclaimer.** Disclaimers of liability for certain uses of the goods. For instance, an online seller of business forms may add a disclaimer stating that the seller does not accept responsibility for the buyer's reliance on the forms rather than on an attorney's advice.
5. **Limitation on remedies.** A provision specifying the remedies available to the buyer if the goods are found to be defective or if the contract is otherwise breached. Any limitation of remedies should be clearly spelled out.

6. **Privacy policy.** A statement indicating how the seller will use the information gathered about the buyer.
7. **Dispute resolution.** Provisions relating to dispute settlement, which we examine more closely in the following section.

Dispute-Settlement Provisions Online offers frequently include provisions relating to dispute settlement. For instance, an offer might include an arbitration clause specifying that any dispute arising under the contract will be arbitrated in a designated forum. The parties might also select the forum and the law that will govern any disputes.

Forum-Selection Clause. Many online contracts contain a **forum-selection clause** indicating the forum, or location (such as a court or jurisdiction), in which contract disputes will be resolved. Significant jurisdictional issues may arise when parties are at a great distance, as they often are when they form contracts via the internet. A forum-selection clause will help to avert future jurisdictional problems and also help to ensure that the seller will not be required to appear in court in a distant state.

■ **Case in Point 12.17** Rebecca Bextel developed a business plan to sell online greeting cards for the benefit of charitable organizations. She hired Tekstir to develop the website for her venture, called Ecocards. Several months later, Bextel filed suit against Tekstir in a Wyoming state court, claiming the company had failed to meet its contractual obligations. Tekstir argued that the contract with Bextel included a forum-selection clause requiring any disputes to be litigated in Orange County, California. The Supreme Court of Wyoming held that the forum-selection clause was enforceable and granted Tekstir's motion to dismiss.[14] ■

12–3b Online Acceptances

The *Restatement (Second) of Contracts,* which is a compilation of common law contract principles, states that parties may agree to a contract "by written or spoken words or by other acts or by failure to act."[15] The Uniform Commercial Code (UCC), which governs sales contracts, has a similar provision. Section 2–204 of the UCC states that any contract for the sale of goods "may be made in any manner sufficient to show agreement, including conduct by both parties which recognizes the existence of such a contract." The courts have used these provisions in determining what constitutes an online acceptance.

Click-On Agreements The courts have concluded that the act of clicking on a box labeled "I accept" or "I agree" can indicate acceptance of an online offer. The agreement resulting from such an acceptance is often called a **click-on agreement** (sometimes referred to as a *click-on license* or *click-wrap agreement*).

Generally, the law does not require that the parties read all of the terms in a contract for it to be effective. Therefore, clicking on a box that states "I agree" to certain terms can be enough. The terms may be contained on a website through which the buyer is obtaining goods or services. They may also appear on a screen when software is downloaded from the internet.

■ **Case in Point 12.18** Any person who agrees to work as an Uber driver must enter into a services agreement and driver addendum contract with Uber Technologies, Inc. The contracts include an arbitration provision. New drivers must click the "Yes, I agree" button to use the Uber app and to start picking up passengers.

A group of Chinese-speaking Uber drivers filed a breach of contract suit against the company. Uber responded with a motion to compel arbitration, which a federal district court granted. The plaintiffs had downloaded the Chinese version of the Uber app and could read the arbitration provision in their native language. Each had clicked on the button and agreed to arbitrate any disputes (whether or not they had actually read the clause). Thus, the arbitration clause was enforceable, and the lawsuit was dismissed.[16] ■

Shrink-Wrap Agreements With a **shrink-wrap agreement** (or shrink-wrap license), the terms are expressed inside the box in which the goods are packaged. (The term "shrink-wrap" refers to the plastic that covers the box.) Usually, parties who open the boxes are told that they agree to the terms by keeping whatever is in the box. Similarly, when purchasers open software packages, they agree to abide by the terms of the limited license agreement included with the software.

In most instances, a shrink-wrap agreement is not between a retailer and a buyer, but is between the manufacturer of the hardware or software and the ultimate buyer-user of the product. The terms generally concern warranties, remedies, and other issues associated with the use of the product.

---

14. *Ecocards v. Tekstir, Inc.,* 2020 WY 38, 459 P.3d 1111 (2020).
15. *Restatement (Second) of Contracts,* Section 19.
16. *Kai Peng v. Uber Technologies, Inc.,* 237 F.Supp.3d 36 (E.D.N.Y. 2017).

Shrink-Wrap Agreements and Enforceable Contract Terms. In some cases, the courts have enforced the terms of shrink-wrap agreements in the same way as the terms of other contracts. These courts have reasoned that by including the terms with the product, the seller proposed a contract. The buyer could accept this contract by using the product after having an opportunity to read the terms. Thus, a buyer's failure to object to terms contained within a shrink-wrapped software package may constitute an acceptance of the terms by conduct. ◼

Shrink-Wrap Terms That May Not Be Enforced. Sometimes, the courts have refused to enforce certain terms included in shrink-wrap agreements because the buyer did not expressly consent to them. An important factor is when the parties formed their contract.

If a buyer orders a product over the telephone, for instance, and is not informed of an arbitration clause or a forum-selection clause at that time, the buyer clearly has not expressly agreed to these terms. If the buyer discovers the clauses after the parties have entered into a contract, a court may conclude that those terms were proposals for additional terms and were not part of the contract.

◼ **Case in Point 12.19** David Noble purchased a Samsung Smartwatch from an AT&T store after seeing ads saying that its battery life was twenty-four to forty-eight hours with typical use. But Noble's Smartwatch battery lasted only about four hours, so he returned the Smartwatch and received a new one. The second Smartwatch suffered from the same battery problem. Noble again went to the AT&T store and, this time, was directed to ship the Smartwatch to Samsung. Samsung sent Noble a third Smartwatch with equally poor battery life. Noble then filed a suit against Samsung in a federal district court. Samsung filed a motion to compel arbitration, which the district court denied. Samsung appealed.

Inside each of the Smartwatch boxes that Noble received was a tiny booklet titled "Health and Safety and Warranty Guide" that included a standard limited warranty. On page ninety-seven of the guide, a boldfaced question read, "What is the procedure for resolving disputes?" Under that was a statement saying that any disputes would be resolved exclusively through binding arbitration. The court held that this language "tucked away in a brochure" was not sufficient to show that Noble had agreed to arbitration. Because consumers were not given reasonable notice of the arbitration clause (on the outside of the guide or somewhere obvious in the packaging), it was unenforceable.[17] ◼

Browse-Wrap Terms. Like the terms of a click-on agreement, **browse-wrap terms** can appear in a transaction conducted over the internet. Unlike the terms in a click-on agreement, however, browse-wrap terms do not require the buyer or user to assent to the terms before, say, downloading or using certain software.

◼ **Case in Point 12.20** RVShare is an online rental platform through which users can arrange to rent recreational vehicles from owners. Tal Becker used the platform and completed the online booking process. In doing so, he agreed to the required terms of service, which included an arbitration clause. Users are informed of the existence of the arbitration clause on the first page of the terms of service. Based on subsequent problems, Becker brought claims of fraud against RVShare. RVShare countered that Becker had agreed to arbitration.

For a browse-wrap agreement, Florida law requires proper notice and the opportunity for users to review the agreement. Such agreements have been enforced when the hyperlink to terms and conditions is conspicuous. A trial court found that the hyperlink in this case was sufficient under this standard. The plaintiff was obligated to arbitrate his dispute.[18] ◼

12–4 Consideration

Under the common law, a primary basis for the enforcement of promises is consideration. **Consideration** usually is defined as the value given in return for a promise (in a bilateral contract) or in return for a performance (in a unilateral contract). It is the inducement, price, or motive that causes a party to enter into an agreement.

As long as consideration is present, the courts generally do not interfere with contracts based on the amount of consideration paid. It is up to the contracting parties to determine how much their bargain is worth. Often, consideration is broken down into two parts: (1) something of legally sufficient value must be given in exchange for the promise, and (2) there must be a bargained-for exchange.

12–4a Legally Sufficient Value

To be legally sufficient, consideration must be something of value in the eyes of the law. The "something of legally sufficient value" may consist of the following:

1. A promise to do something that one has no prior legal duty to do.

---

17. *Noble v. Samsung Electronics Company, Inc.,* 682 Fed.Appx. 113 (3d Cir. 2017).

18. *Scott v. RVShare LLC,* 2022 WL 866259 (M.D.TN 2022).

2. The performance of an action that one is otherwise not obligated to undertake.
3. The refraining from an action that one has a legal right to undertake (called a **forbearance**).

Consideration in bilateral contracts normally consists of a promise in return for a promise. In a contract for the sale of goods, for instance, the seller promises to ship specific goods to the buyer, and the buyer promises to pay for those goods. Each of these promises constitutes consideration for the contract.

In contrast, unilateral contracts involve a promise in return for a performance (an action). ■ **Example 12.21** Anita says to her neighbor, "When you finish painting the garage, I will pay you $800." Anita's neighbor paints the garage. The act of painting the garage is the consideration that creates Anita's contractual obligation to pay her neighbor $800.

12–4b Bargained-for Exchange

The second element of consideration is that it must provide the basis for the bargain struck between the contracting parties. That is, the item of value must be given or promised by the promisor (offeror) in return for the promisee's promise, performance, or promise of performance.

This element of bargained-for exchange distinguishes contracts from gifts. ■ **Case in Point 12.22** Rachel Thomas was admitted to a hospital emergency room with pregnancy-related complications. The attending physician, Dr. Archer, recommended that she be transported by medevac (helicopter) to a different facility. The woman and her husband informed the physician that they needed their insurer's preauthorization for that course of action. Otherwise, they could be personally liable for the costs. Dr. Archer allegedly promised to call the insurer and, if it would not approve the medevac, have the hospital bear the costs itself. But the physician failed to contact the insurer until much later, and the insurer declined coverage.

The couple sued the hospital, claiming breach of contract by Dr. Archer. The court ruled in favor of the hospital, and the case was appealed to the Alaska Supreme Court. That court held that the physician's alleged promise about insurance and payment did not give rise to an enforceable contract. There was no evidence that the hospital sought any consideration from the Thomases for the physician's alleged promise. Thus, there was no "bargained-for" consideration. The court affirmed the dismissal of the Thomases' contract claim (but remanded the case on the issue of promissory estoppel, a concept that will be discussed shortly).[19]

12–4c Agreements That Lack Consideration

Sometimes, one of the parties (or both parties) to an agreement may think that consideration has been exchanged when in fact it has not. Here, we look at some situations in which the parties' promises or actions do not qualify as contractual consideration.

Preexisting Duty Under most circumstances, a promise to do what one already has a legal duty to do does not constitute legally sufficient consideration. The preexisting legal duty may be imposed by law or may arise out of a previous contract. A sheriff, for instance, has a duty to investigate crime and to arrest criminals. Hence, a sheriff cannot collect a reward for providing information leading to the capture of a criminal.

Likewise, if a party is already bound by contract to perform a certain duty, that duty cannot serve as consideration for a second contract. ■ **Example 12.23** Ellery Contractors begins construction on a seven-story office building and after three months demands an extra $75,000 on its contract. If the extra $75,000 is not paid, the contractor will stop working. The owner of the land, finding no one else to complete the construction, agrees to pay the extra $75,000. The agreement is unenforceable because it is not supported by legally sufficient consideration. Ellery Contractors had a preexisting contractual duty to complete the building. ■

Unforeseen Difficulties The rule regarding preexisting duty is meant to prevent extortion and the so-called holdup game. Nonetheless, if, during performance of a contract, extraordinary difficulties arise that were totally unforeseen at the time the contract was formed, a court may allow an exception to the rule. The key is whether the court finds that the modification is fair and equitable in view of circumstances not anticipated by the parties when the contract was made.[20]

Suppose that in Example 12.23, Ellery Contractors had asked for the extra $75,000 because it encountered a rock formation that no one knew existed. If the landowner agrees to pay the extra $75,000 to excavate the rock and the court finds that it is fair to do so, Ellery Contractors can enforce the agreement. If rock formations are common in the area, however, the court may determine that the contractor should have known of the risk. In that situation, the court may choose to apply the preexisting duty rule and prevent Ellery Contractors from obtaining the extra $75,000.

---

19. *Thomas v. Archer*, 384 P.3d 791 (Alaska 2016). See also *Bakhshi v. Vaarlaer*, 2021-Ohio-13 (2nd App. Dist. 2021).

20. *Restatement (Second) of Contracts*, Section 73.

Rescission and New Contract The law recognizes that two parties can mutually agree to rescind, or cancel, their contract, at least to the extent that it is executory (still to be carried out). **Rescission**[21] is the unmaking of a contract so as to return the parties to the positions they occupied before the contract was made.

Sometimes, parties rescind a contract and make a new contract at the same time. When this occurs, it is often difficult to determine whether there was consideration for the new contract, or whether the parties had a preexisting duty under the previous contract. If a court finds there was a preexisting duty, then the new contract will be invalid because there was no consideration.

12–4d Past Consideration

Promises made in return for actions or events that have already taken place are unenforceable. These promises lack consideration in that the element of bargained-for exchange is missing. In short, you can bargain for something to take place now or in the future but not for something that has already taken place. Therefore, **past consideration** is no consideration.

■ **Case in Point 12.24** Jamil Blackmon became friends with Allen Iverson when Iverson was a high school student who showed tremendous promise as an athlete. One evening, Blackmon suggested that Iverson use "The Answer" as a nickname in the summer league basketball tournaments. Blackmon said that Iverson would be "The Answer" to all of the National Basketball Association's woes. Later that night, Iverson said that he would give Blackmon 25 percent of any proceeds from the merchandising of products that used "The Answer" as a logo or a slogan. Because Iverson's promise was made in return for past consideration, it was unenforceable. In effect, Iverson stated his intention to give Blackmon a gift.[22] ■

In a variety of situations, an employer will often ask an employee to sign a noncompete agreement, also called a *covenant not to compete*. Under such an agreement, the employee agrees not to compete with the employer for a certain period of time after the employment relationship ends. When a current employee is required to sign a noncompete agreement, that employee's current employment is not sufficient consideration for the agreement, because the individual is already employed. To be valid, the agreement requires new consideration.

12–4e Illusory Promises

If the terms of the contract express such uncertainty of performance that the promisor has not definitely promised to do anything, the promise is said to be illusory—without consideration and unenforceable. A promise is illusory when it fails to bind the promisor.

■ **Example 12.25** The president of Tuscan Corporation says to her employees, "If profits continue to be high, everyone will get a 10 percent bonus at the end of the year—if management agrees." This is an illusory promise, or no promise at all, because performance depends solely on the discretion of management. There is no bargained-for consideration. The statement indicates only that management may or may not do something in the future. Therefore, even though the employees work hard and profits remain high, the company is not obligated to pay the bonus now or later. ■

12–4f Settlement of Claims

Businesspersons and others often enter into contracts to settle legal claims. It is important to understand the nature of consideration given in these kinds of settlement agreements, or contracts. A claim may be settled through an accord and satisfaction, a release, or a covenant not to sue.

Accord and Satisfaction In an **accord and satisfaction**, a debtor offers to pay, and a creditor accepts, a lesser amount than the creditor originally claimed was owed. The accord is the agreement. In the accord, one party undertakes to give or perform, and the other to accept, in satisfaction of a claim, something other than that on which the parties originally agreed. Satisfaction is the performance (usually payment) that takes place after the accord is executed.

A basic rule is that there can be no satisfaction unless there is first an accord. In addition, for accord and satisfaction to occur, the amount of the debt must be in dispute.

Liquidated Debts If a debt is liquidated, accord and satisfaction cannot take place. A **liquidated debt** is one whose amount has been ascertained, fixed, agreed on, settled, or exactly determined.

■ **Example 12.26** Barbara Kwan signs an installment loan contract with her bank. In the contract, Kwan agrees to pay a set rate of interest on a specified amount of borrowed funds at monthly intervals for two years. Because both parties know the precise amount of the total obligation, it is a liquidated debt. ■

In the majority of states, a creditor's acceptance of a sum less than the entire amount of a liquidated debt is

21. Pronounced reh-*sih*-zhen.
22. *Blackmon v. Iverson,* 324 F.Supp.2d 602 (E.D.Pa. 2003). See also *Rubin v. Hughes,* 507 P.3d 119, 408 Mont. 219, 2022 MT 74 (S.Ct. MT 2022).

not satisfaction, and the balance of the debt is still legally owed. The reason for this rule is that the debtor has given no consideration to satisfy the obligation of paying the balance to the creditor. The debtor had a preexisting legal obligation to pay the entire debt. (Of course, even with liquidated debts, creditors often do negotiate debt settlement agreements with debtors for a lesser amount than was originally owed. Creditors sometimes even forgive, or write off, a liquidated debt as uncollectible.)

Unliquidated Debts An **unliquidated debt** is the opposite of a liquidated debt. The amount of the debt is not settled, fixed, agreed on, ascertained, or determined, and reasonable persons may differ over the amount owed. In these circumstances, acceptance of a lesser sum operates as satisfaction, or discharge, of the debt because there is valid consideration. The parties give up a legal right to contest the amount in dispute.

Release A **release** is a contract in which one party forfeits the right to pursue a legal claim against the other party. It bars any further recovery beyond the terms stated in the release.

A release will generally be binding if it meets the following requirements:

1. The agreement is made in good faith (honestly).
2. The release contract is in a signed writing (required in many states).
3. The contract is accompanied by consideration.

Clearly, individuals are better off knowing the extent of their injuries or damages before signing a release. ■ **Example 12.27** Lupe's car is damaged in an automobile accident caused by Dexter's negligence. Dexter offers to give her $3,000 if she will release him from further liability resulting from the accident. Lupe agrees and signs the release.

If Lupe later discovers that it will cost $4,200 to repair her car, she normally cannot recover the additional amount from Dexter. Lupe is limited to the $3,000 specified in the release. Lupe and Dexter voluntarily agreed to the terms in the release, which was in a signed writing, and sufficient consideration was present. The consideration was the legal right Lupe forfeited to sue to recover damages, should they be more than $3,000, in exchange for Dexter's promise to give her $3,000. ■

12–4g Covenant Not to Sue

Unlike a release, a **covenant not to sue** does not always bar further recovery. The parties simply substitute a contractual obligation for some other type of legal action based on a valid claim. Suppose that, in Example 12.27, Lupe agrees with Dexter not to sue for damages in a tort action if he will pay for the damage to her car. If Dexter fails to pay for the repairs, Lupe can bring an action against him for breach of contract.

As the following case illustrates, a covenant not to sue can form the basis for a dismissal of the claims of either party to the covenant.

Spotlight on Nike

Case 12.2 Already, LLC v. Nike, Inc.

Supreme Court of the United States, 568 U.S. 85, 133 S.Ct. 721, 184 L.Ed.2d 553 (2013).

Background and Facts Nike, Inc., designs, makes, and sells athletic footwear, including a line of shoes known as "Air Force 1." Already, LLC, also designs and markets athletic footwear, including the "Sugar" and "Soulja Boy" lines. Nike filed a suit in a federal district court against Already, alleging that Soulja Boys and Sugars infringed the Air Force 1 trademark. Already filed a counterclaim, contending that the Air Force 1 trademark was invalid.

While the suit was pending, Nike issued a covenant not to sue. Nike promised not to raise any trademark claims against Already or any affiliated entity based on Already's existing footwear designs or any future Already designs that constituted a "colorable imitation" of Already's current products. Nike then filed a motion to dismiss its own claims and to dismiss Already's counterclaim. Already opposed the dismissal of its counterclaim, but the court granted Nike's motion. The U.S. Court of Appeals for the Second Circuit affirmed. Already appealed to the United States Supreme Court.

Case 12.2 Continues

Case 12.2 Continued

In the Language of the Court
Chief Justice ROBERTS delivered the opinion of the Court.

* * * *

* * * A defendant cannot automatically moot a case simply by ending its unlawful conduct once sued. [A matter is moot if it involves no actual controversy for the court to decide, and federal courts will dismiss moot cases.] Otherwise, a defendant could engage in unlawful conduct, stop when sued to have the case declared moot, then pick up where he left off, repeating this cycle until he achieves all his unlawful ends. Given this concern, * * * a defendant claiming that its voluntary compliance moots a case bears the formidable burden of showing that it is absolutely clear the allegedly wrongful behavior could not reasonably be expected to recur. [This is the voluntary cessation test.]

* * * *

We begin our analysis with the terms of the covenant:

[Nike] unconditionally and irrevocably covenants to refrain from making *any* claim(s) or demand(s) * * * against Already or *any* of its * * * related business entities * * * [including] distributors * * * and employees of such entities and *all* customers * * * on account of any possible cause of action based on or involving trademark infringement * * * relating to the NIKE Mark based on the appearance of *any* of Already's current and/or previous footwear product designs, and *any* colorable imitations thereof, regardless of whether that footwear is produced * * * or otherwise used in commerce.

The breadth of this covenant suffices to meet the burden imposed by the voluntary cessation test.

In addition, Nike originally argued that the Sugars and Soulja Boys infringed its trademark; in other words, Nike believed those shoes were "colorable imitations" of the Air Force 1s. Nike's covenant now allows Already to produce all of its existing footwear designs—including the Sugar and Soulja Boy—and any "colorable imitation" of those designs. * * * It is hard to imagine a scenario that would potentially infringe Nike's trademark and yet not fall under the covenant. Nike, having taken the position in court that there is no prospect of such a shoe, would be hard pressed to assert the contrary down the road. If such a shoe exists, the parties have not pointed to it, there is no evidence that Already has dreamt of it, and we cannot conceive of it. It sits, as far as we can tell, on a shelf between Dorothy's ruby slippers and Perseus's winged sandals.

* * * *

* * * Given the covenant's broad language, and given that Already has asserted no concrete plans to engage in conduct not covered by the covenant, we can conclude the case is moot because the challenged conduct cannot reasonably be expected to recur.

Decision and Remedy The United States Supreme Court affirmed the judgment of the lower court. Under the covenant not to sue, Nike could not file a claim for trademark infringement against Already, and Already could not assert that Nike's trademark was invalid.

Critical Thinking
- **Economic** Why would any party agree to a covenant not to sue?
- **Legal Environment** Which types of contracts are similar to covenants not to sue? Explain.

12–4h Promissory Estoppel

Sometimes, individuals rely on promises to their detriment, and their reliance may form a basis for a court to infer contract rights and duties. Under the doctrine of **promissory estoppel** (also called *detrimental reliance*), a person who has reasonably and substantially relied on the promise of another may be able to obtain some measure of recovery.

Promissory estoppel is applied in a wide variety of contexts in which a promise is otherwise unenforceable,

such as when a promise is made without consideration. Under this doctrine, a court may enforce an otherwise unenforceable promise to avoid the injustice that would otherwise result. For the promissory estoppel doctrine to be applied, the following elements are required:

1. There must be a clear and definite promise.
2. The promisor should have expected that the promisee would rely on the promise.
3. The promisee reasonably relied on the promise by acting or refraining from some act.

4. The promisee's reliance was definite and resulted in substantial detriment.

5. Enforcement of the promise is necessary to avoid injustice.

If these requirements are met, a promise may be enforced even though it is not supported by consideration. In essence, the promisor will be **estopped** (prevented) from asserting the lack of consideration as a defense.

Promissory estoppel is similar in some ways to the doctrine of quasi contract. In both situations, a court, acting in the interests of equity, imposes contract obligations on the parties to prevent unfairness even though no actual contract exists. The difference is that with quasi contract, no promise was made at all. In contrast, with promissory estoppel, an unenforceable promise was made and relied on but not performed.

12–5 Contractual Capacity

In addition to agreement and consideration, for a contract to be deemed valid, the parties to the contract must have **contractual capacity**—the legal ability to enter into a contractual relationship. Courts generally presume the existence of contractual capacity, but in some situations, as when a person is young or mentally incompetent, capacity may be lacking or questionable.

12–5a Minors

Today, in almost all states, the *age of majority* (when a person is no longer a minor) for contractual purposes is eighteen years.[23] In addition, some states provide for the termination of minority on marriage.

Minority status may also be terminated by a minor's *emancipation*, which occurs when a child's parent or legal guardian relinquishes the legal right to exercise control over the child. Normally, minors who leave home to support themselves are considered emancipated. Several jurisdictions permit minors themselves to petition a court for emancipation.

The general rule is that a minor can enter into any contract that an adult can, except contracts prohibited by law for minors (such as contracts to purchase tobacco or alcoholic beverages). A contract entered into by a minor, however, is voidable at the option of that minor, subject to certain exceptions. To exercise the option to avoid a contract, a minor need only manifest (clearly show) an intention not to be bound by it. The minor "avoids" the contract by disaffirming it.

The legal avoidance, or setting aside, of a contractual obligation is referred to as **disaffirmance**. To disaffirm, minors must express their intent, through words or conduct, not to be bound to the contract.

■ **Case in Point 12.28** Fifteen-year-old Morgan Kelly was a cadet in her high school's Navy Junior Reserve Officer Training Corps. As part of the program, she visited a U.S. Marine Corps training facility. To enter the camp, she was required to sign a waiver that exempted the Marines from all liability for any injuries arising from her visit. Such a waiver is a type of exculpatory clause.

While participating in activities on the camp's confidence-building course, Kelly fell from the "Slide for Life" and suffered serious injuries. She filed a suit to recover her medical costs. The Marines asserted that she had signed their waiver of liability. Kelly claimed that she had disaffirmed the waiver when she filed suit. The court ruled in Kelly's favor. Liability waivers are generally enforceable contracts, but a minor can avoid a contract by disaffirming it.[24] ■

Note that adults who enter into contracts with minors cannot avoid their contractual duties on the ground that the minors can do so. Unless the minor exercises the option to disaffirm the contract, the adult party normally is bound by it. On disaffirming a contract, a minor normally can recover any property transferred to the adult as consideration, even if the property is in the possession of a third party.

Minors' Rights in Digital Assets. Minors own many digital assets, including e-mail accounts, social media accounts, digital photos, and, to a lesser extent, text messages. In addition, they own virtual assets associated with online games and other forms of digital media.

What happens to these assets when a minor dies? Under current law in most states, minors have no right to decide what happens to their digital property at death. In most states, minors have the right to contract with online businesses, to marry, and to seek and gain employment, but they are currently denied a basic right of property ownership—the right to pass their digital property to their heirs in the manner that they wish. More generally, minors do not have the right of succession—they are

---

23. The age of majority may still be twenty-one for other purposes, such as the purchase and consumption of alcoholic beverages.

24. *Kelly v. United States,* 809 F.Supp.2d 429 (E.D.N.C. 2011). See *Lukken v. Fleischer,* 962 N.W.2d 71 (S.Ct. IA 2021).

legally incapable of deciding how any of their property is distributed at death.

12–5b Intoxication

Intoxication is a condition in which a person's normal capacity to act or think is inhibited by alcohol or some other drug. A contract entered into by an intoxicated person can be either voidable or valid (and thus enforceable). If the person was sufficiently intoxicated to lack mental capacity, then the agreement may be voidable even if the intoxication was purely voluntary. If, despite intoxication, the person understood the legal consequences of the agreement, the contract will be enforceable.

Courts look at objective indications of intoxicated persons' condition to determine if they possessed or lacked the required capacity. It is difficult to prove that their judgment was so severely impaired that they could not comprehend the legal consequences of entering into a contract. Therefore, courts rarely permit contracts to be avoided due to intoxication.

Disaffirmance If a contract is voidable because one party was intoxicated, that person has the option of disaffirming it while intoxicated and for a reasonable time after becoming sober. The person claiming intoxication typically must be able to return all consideration received unless the contract involved necessaries. Contracts for necessaries are voidable, but the intoxicated person is liable in quasi contract for the reasonable value of the consideration received.

Ratification An intoxicated person, after becoming sober, may ratify a contract expressly or impliedly, just as a minor may do on reaching majority. Implied ratification occurs when a person enters into a contract while intoxicated and fails to disaffirm the contract within a reasonable time after becoming sober. Acts or conduct inconsistent with an intent to disaffirm—such as the continued use of property purchased under a voidable contract—will also normally ratify the contract.

12–5c Mental Incompetence

Contracts made by mentally incompetent persons can be void, voidable, or valid. We look here at the circumstances that determine when each of these classifications applies. If a court has previously determined that a person is mentally incompetent, any contract made by that person is void—no contract exists. On determining that someone

is mentally incompetent, the court appoints a guardian to represent the individual. Only the guardian can enter into binding legal obligations on behalf of the mentally incompetent person.

If a court has not previously judged a person to be mentally incompetent but the person was incompetent at the time the contract was formed, the contract may be voidable. The contract is voidable if the person was unaware of entering into the contract or lacked the mental capacity to comprehend its nature, purpose, and consequences. In such situations, the contract is voidable (or can be ratified) at the option of the mentally incompetent person but not at the option of the other party.

■ **Case in Point 12.29** Annabelle Duffie was mildly mentally disabled and, at age seventy, started suffering from dementia. For her entire life, she had lived with her brother, Jerome. When Jerome died, he left Annabelle his property, including 180 acres of timberland near Hope, Arkansas, valued at more than $400,000. Less than three months later, Annabelle signed a deed granting her interest in the tract to Charles and Joanne Black. The Blacks agreed to pay Annabelle $150,000 in monthly payments of $1,000.

Later, Annabelle's nephew, Jack, was appointed to be her legal guardian. On her behalf, Jack filed a lawsuit in an Arkansas state court against the Blacks, seeking to void the land deal because of Annabelle's lack of mental competence. The court ordered the Blacks to return the property to Annabelle. They appealed. A state intermediate appellate court affirmed. The evidence showed that Annabelle had been mentally disabled her entire life. She lacked the cognitive ability to make the complex financial decisions involved in selling property. Therefore, the contract was voidable.[25] ■

When the Contract Will Be Valid A contract entered into by a mentally incompetent person (not previously declared incompetent by a court) may be valid if the person had capacity at the time the contract was formed. Some people who are incompetent due to age or illness have lucid intervals—periods during which their intelligence, judgment, and will are temporarily restored. During such intervals, they will be considered to have legal capacity to enter into contracts.

25. *Black v. Duffie*, 2016 Ark.App. 584, 508 S.W.3d 40 (2016). See also *Moye-Lyons v. North Carolina Department of Public Instruction*, 872 S.E.2d 537, 2022-NCCOA-260 (Ct.App. NC 2022).

12–6 Legality

For a contract to be valid and enforceable, it must be formed for a legal purpose. A contract to do something that is prohibited by federal or state statutory law is illegal and, as such, void from the outset and thus unenforceable. Additionally, a contract to commit a tortious act (such as an agreement to engage in defamation or fraud) is contrary to public policy and therefore illegal and unenforceable.

12–6a Contracts Contrary to Statute

Statutes often set forth rules specifying what may be included in contracts and what is prohibited. We now examine several ways in which contracts may be contrary to statute and thus illegal.

Contracts to Commit a Crime Any contract to commit a crime is in violation of a statute. Thus, a contract to sell illegal drugs in violation of criminal laws is unenforceable, as is a contract to hide a corporation's violation of securities laws or environmental regulations.

Sometimes, the object or performance of a contract is rendered illegal by a statute after the parties entered into the contract. In that situation, the contract is considered to be discharged (terminated) by law.

Usury Almost every state has a statute that sets the maximum rate of interest that can be charged for different types of transactions, including ordinary loans. A lender who makes a loan at an interest rate above the lawful maximum commits **usury**.

Although usurious contracts are illegal, most states simply limit the interest that the lender may collect on the contract to the lawful maximum interest rate in that state. In a few states, the lender can recover the principal amount of the loan but no interest. In addition, states can make exceptions to facilitate business transactions. For instance, many states exempt corporate loans from the usury laws, and nearly all states allow higher-interest-rate loans for borrowers who could not otherwise obtain loans.

Gambling Gambling is the creation of risk for the purpose of assuming it. Any scheme that involves the distribution of property by chance among persons who have paid valuable consideration for the opportunity (chance) to receive the property is gambling.

Traditionally, the states deemed gambling contracts illegal and thus void. Today, many states allow (and regulate) certain forms of gambling, such as horse racing, video poker machines, and charity-sponsored bingo. In addition, nearly all states allow state-operated lotteries, as well as gambling on Native American reservations. Even in states that permit certain types of gambling, though, courts often find that gambling contracts are illegal.

Licensing Statutes All states require members of certain professions—including physicians, lawyers, real estate brokers, accountants, architects, electricians, and stockbrokers—to have licenses. Some licenses are obtained only after extensive schooling and examinations, which indicate to the public that a special skill has been acquired. Others require only that the applicant be of good moral character and pay a fee.

Whether a contract with an unlicensed person is legal and enforceable depends on the purpose of the licensing statute. If the statute's purpose is to protect the public from unauthorized practitioners (such as unlicensed attorneys and electricians), then a contract involving an unlicensed practitioner is generally illegal and unenforceable. If the statute's purpose is merely to raise government revenues, however, a court may enforce the contract and fine the unlicensed person.

12–6b Contracts Contrary to Public Policy

Although contracts involve private parties, some are not enforceable because of the negative impact they would have on society. These contracts are said to be contrary to public policy. Examples include a contract to commit an immoral act, such as selling a child, and a contract that prohibits marriage. Business contracts that may be against public policy include contracts in restraint of trade and unconscionable contracts or clauses.

Contracts in Restraint of Trade The United States has a strong public policy favoring competition in the economy. Thus, contracts in restraint of trade (anticompetitive agreements) generally are unenforceable because they are contrary to public policy. Typically, such contracts also violate one or more federal or state antitrust statutes.

An exception is recognized when the restraint is reasonable and is contained in an ancillary (secondary or subordinate) clause in a contract. Such restraints often are included in contracts for the sale of an ongoing business and for employment contracts.

Covenants Not to Compete and the Sale of an Ongoing Business. Many contracts involve a type of restraint called a **covenant not to compete**, or a *restrictive covenant* (promise). A covenant not to compete may be created when a merchant who sells a store agrees not to open a new store in a certain geographic area surrounding the old business. Such an agreement enables the seller to sell, and the purchaser to buy, the goodwill and reputation of an ongoing business without having to worry that the seller will open a competing business a block away. Provided the restrictive covenant is reasonable and is an ancillary part of the sale of an ongoing business, it is enforceable.

Covenants Not to Compete in Employment Contracts.
Sometimes, agreements not to compete (also referred to as *noncompete agreements*) are included in employment contracts. People in middle- or upper-level management positions commonly agree not to work for competitors or not to start competing businesses for a specified period of time after termination of employment.

Noncompete agreements are legal in most states so long as the specified period of time (of restraint) is not excessive in duration and the geographic restriction is reasonable. What constitutes a reasonable time period may be shorter in the online environment than in conventional employment contracts. Because the geographical restrictions apply worldwide, the time restrictions may be shorter.

Companies sometimes also use these covenants as the starting point for lawsuits against competitors. ■ **Case Example 12.30** Dana Clement was an administrator with Compassus, a hospice care provider in Houston. She left, taking a number of colleagues with her, to form a new branch of Crossroads Hospice in the same city. Compassus brought a number of claims, including conspiracy, against Crossroads, relying primarily on a covenant in its contract with Clement that forbade her from soliciting Compassus workers for employment elsewhere. A Texas appellate court dismissed the lawsuit, ruling that Crossroads could not be held responsible for Clement's actions. In large part, the court based its decision on the fact that Crossroads was unaware of the covenant when it hired Clement and the other ex-Compassus employees.[26] ■

Enforcement Issues.
The laws governing the enforceability of covenants not to compete vary significantly from state to state. California prohibits the enforcement of covenants not to compete altogether. In some states, including Texas, such a covenant will not be enforced unless the employee has received some benefit in return for signing the noncompete agreement. This is true even if the covenant is reasonable as to time and area. If the employee receives no benefit, the covenant will be deemed void.

Occasionally, depending on the jurisdiction, courts will reform covenants not to compete. If a covenant is found to be unreasonable in time or geographic area, the court may convert the terms into reasonable ones and then enforce the reformed covenant. Such court actions present a problem, though, in that the judge implicitly becomes a party to the contract. Consequently, courts usually resort to contract **reformation** only when necessary to prevent undue burdens or hardships.

Unconscionable Contracts or Clauses A court ordinarily does not look at the fairness or equity of a contract (or inquire into the adequacy of consideration). Persons are assumed to be reasonably intelligent, and the courts will not come to their aid just because they have made unwise or foolish bargains.

In certain circumstances, however, bargains are so oppressive that the courts relieve innocent parties of part or all of their duties. Such bargains are deemed **unconscionable**[27] because they are so unscrupulous or grossly unfair as to be "void of conscience." The Uniform Commercial Code (UCC) incorporates the concept of unconscionability in its provisions regarding the sale and lease of goods.

Procedural unconscionability often involves inconspicuous print, unintelligible language ("legalese"), or one party's lack of an opportunity to read the contract or ask questions about its meaning. This type of unconscionability typically arises when a party's lack of knowledge or understanding of the contract terms deprived the party of any meaningful choice.

Procedural unconscionability can also occur when there is such disparity in bargaining power between the two parties that the weaker party's consent is not voluntary. This type of situation often involves an *adhesion contract*, which is a contract written exclusively by one party and presented to the other on a take-it-or-leave-it basis. In other words, the party to whom the contract is presented (usually a buyer or borrower) has no opportunity to negotiate its terms.

■ **Case in Point 12.31** Lianna Saribekyan placed diamonds, gold, and other collectibles in a safety deposit box at the Bank of America's (BANA's) Universal City, California, branch. A few months later, this branch was slated for closure. Without informing Saribekyan, bank employees drilled open her deposit box and placed its contents, unsecured, in storage for several days. Millions of dollars' worth of the items went missing, including

26. *Crossroads Hospice, Inc. v. FC Compassus, LLC,* 606 S.W.3d 294 (Ct.App.TX, 1st Dist.—Houston 2020).

27. Pronounced un-*kon*-shun-uh-bul.

four bags of diamonds inventoried by BANA as "beads" and a container full of gold that had been replaced with pennies.

The trial court found BANA liable but limited its payout to $2,460 because the bank's Safety Deposit Rules and Regulations capped damages for negligence at ten times the safety deposit box's annual rent. A California appellate court reversed, identifying a contract of adhesion. To support this conclusion, the court noted that the limitation of liability provision was "buried" in the small print of a five-page supplement to the original agreement, an addendum that Saribekyan was never shown. Furthermore, the court found BANA's negligence so grievous that to limit damages in such a way would "shock the conscience."[28] ■

Substantive Unconscionability. Substantive unconscionability occurs when contracts, or portions of contracts, are oppressive or overly harsh. Courts generally focus on provisions that deprive one party of the benefits of the agreement or leave that party without a remedy for nonperformance by the other.

Substantive unconscionability can arise in a wide variety of business contexts. For instance, a contract clause that gives the business entity unconstrained access to the courts but requires the other party to arbitrate any dispute with the firm may be unconscionable.

Exculpatory Clauses Often closely related to the concept of unconscionability are **exculpatory clauses,** which release a party from liability in the event of

monetary or physical injury no matter who is at fault. Indeed, courts sometimes refuse to enforce such clauses on the ground that they are unconscionable.

Often Violate Public Policy. Most courts view exculpatory clauses with disfavor. Exculpatory clauses found in rental agreements for commercial property are frequently held to be contrary to public policy, and such clauses are almost always unenforceable in residential property leases. Courts also usually hold that exculpatory clauses are against public policy in the employment context. Thus, employers frequently cannot enforce exculpatory clauses in contracts with employees or independent contractors to avoid liability for work-related injuries.

When Courts Will Enforce Exculpatory Clauses Courts do enforce exculpatory clauses if they are reasonable, do not violate public policy, and do not protect parties from liability for intentional misconduct. The language used must not be ambiguous, and the parties must have been in relatively equal bargaining positions.

Businesses such as health clubs, racetracks, amusement parks, skiing facilities, horse-rental operations, golf-cart concessions, and skydiving organizations frequently use exculpatory clauses to limit their liability for patrons' injuries. Because these services are not essential, the companies offering them have no relative advantage in bargaining strength, and anyone contracting for their services does so voluntarily. Courts also may enforce reasonable exculpatory clauses in loan documents, real estate contracts, and trust agreements.

In the following case, the question before the court was whether an exculpatory clause in a gym membership contract was valid.

28. *Saribekyan v. Bank of America, NA,* 2020 WL 38676 (2nd Dist., Div. 3 CA 2020).

Milshteyn v. Fitness International, LLC.

Superior Court of Pennsylvania, 271 A.3d. 498 (2022).

In the Language of the Court
PANELLA, P.J.
* * * *

The Milshteyns were members of an L.A. Fitness facility in Philadelphia, Pennsylvania. Relevantly, when they joined the facility in 2011, the Milshteyns executed a Membership Agreement.

On June 11, 2017, the Milshteyns were in the pool area of the L.A. Fitness at the time of a power outage. Peter slipped while descending the stairs from the pool to the locker room in the dark. As a result of his fall, Peter sustained a fracture to his right elbow.

The Milshteyns filed a complaint on May 16, 2019, which included

Peter's claim for premises liability * * *. The complaint alleged that L.A. Fitness employees were negligent in, *inter alia* [among other things], creating the dangerous condition of "low or no lighting," failing to inspect or repair the area where Peter fell, and failing to warn Peter of the defective condition. * * *

Case 12.3 Continues

Case 12.3 Continued

On November 2, 2020, Defendants filed a motion for summary judgment, again asserting, *inter alia,* that the Milshteyns' Membership Agreement precluded their claims.

* * * *

* * * The Milshteyns also argued that the Membership Agreement constitutes a contract of adhesion, which is unconscionable, and therefore unenforceable. * * *

The trial court conducted a hearing on Defendants' motion for summary judgment on January 12, 2021. By an order dated January 13, 2021, the trial court granted Defendants' motion for summary judgment. Specifically, regarding Fitness & Sports Clubs, the trial court concluded that the release contained in the Membership Agreement foreclosed the Milshteyns' claims; the Milshteyns did not establish that the Membership Agreement was a contract of adhesion; * * * .

* * * *

The Milshteyns first claim that the trial court erred in determining that the Membership Agreement is not a contract of adhesion. The Milshteyns argue that the waiver of liability provision in the Membership Agreement "overwhelmingly and unreasonably favors" Defendants by shielding Defendants from liability. According to the Milshteyns, Peter was incapable of negotiating the terms of the Membership Agreement and could not reject the waiver of liability provision without rejecting the entire transaction.

Exculpatory provisions in contracts are generally enforceable if they are clear and meet three other conditions:

It is generally accepted that an exculpatory clause is valid where three conditions are met. First, the clause must not contravene public policy. Secondly, the contract must be between persons relating entirely to their own private affairs and thirdly, each party must be a free bargaining agent to the agreement so that the contract is not one of adhesion. ...[O]nce an exculpatory clause is determined to be valid, it will, nevertheless, still be unenforceable unless the language of the parties is clear that a person is being relieved of liability for his own acts of negligence. In interpreting such clauses we listed as guiding standards that: 1) the contract language must be construed strictly, since exculpatory language is not favored by the law; 2) the contract must state the intention of the parties with the greatest particularity, beyond doubt by express stipulation, and no inference from words of general import can establish the intent of the parties; 3) the language of the contract must be construed, in cases of ambiguity, against the party seeking immunity from liability; and 4) the burden of establishing the immunity is upon the party invoking protection under the clause.

In [another relevant case], this Court addressed the same exculpatory provision in an L.A. Fitness Membership Agreement and concluded that the provision was enforceable. [The plaintiff in that case] was a member of an L.A. Fitness facility, and his Membership Agreement contained a "release and waiver of liability and indemnity" nearly identical to the provision in the contract signed by Peter. [This plaintiff] filed a negligence action after he slipped and fell on the wet floor of a locker room in the facility. The facility filed a motion for summary judgment based, in part, on the terms of the waiver provision.

The trial court entered judgment in favor of the facility.

On appeal, this Court concluded that the trial court had properly granted summary judgment in favor of the facility based on the waiver provision. First, this Court concluded that the relevant provision was not against public policy, as "[the plaintiff] was engaged in a voluntary athletic or recreational activity: going to the gym." * * * Additionally, this Court rejected [the plaintiff's] contention that the Membership Agreement was a contract of adhesion, explaining that "an exculpatory agreement involving use of a commercial facility for voluntary athletic or recreational activities is not considered a contract of adhesion because the signer is under no compulsion, economic or otherwise, to participate, much less to sign the exculpatory agreement, because it does not relate to essential services. . . ."

Here, the trial court, relying on [this similar case], concluded that the Membership Agreement was not unconscionable or a contract of adhesion. The record confirms that the Milshteyns executed the Membership Agreement for the purpose of participating in a voluntary athletic activity, and they were under no compulsion to complete an agreement for this non-essential service. * * * Additionally, in signing the Membership Agreement, Peter acknowledged that he had read and understood the agreement, including the exculpatory provision. * * *

* * * *

Based upon the foregoing, we affirm the trial court's order granting summary judgment in favor of Defendants.

Order affirmed.

Judgment Entered.

Legal Reasoning Questions

1. What was the reason for the original complaint against Fitness International, LLC?

2. The plaintiffs argued that the fitness club's membership agreement was a contract of adhesion. What does that mean?

3. Why did the trial court agree that the waiver of liability in the Membership Agreement was an acceptable exculpatory clause?

Discriminatory Contracts Contracts in which a party promises to discriminate on the basis of race, color, national origin, religion, gender, sexual orientation, age, or disability are contrary to both statute and public policy. They are also unenforceable.[29] For instance, if a property owner promises in a contract not to sell the property to a member of a particular race, the contract is unenforceable. The public policy underlying these prohibitions is very strong, and the courts are quick to invalidate discriminatory contracts.

12-7 Form—The Writing Requirement

A contract that is otherwise valid may still be unenforceable if it is not in the proper form. Certain types of contracts are required to be in writing or evidenced by a memorandum or an electronic record. An agreement subject to the writing requirement does not necessarily have to be written on paper. An exchange of e-mails that evidences the parties' contract can be sufficient, provided that they are "signed," or agreed to, by the party against whom enforcement is sought. Every state has a statute that stipulates what types of contracts must be in writing. We refer to such a statute as the **Statute of Frauds.** The actual name of the Statute of Frauds is misleading because the statute does not apply to fraud. Rather, it denies enforceability to certain contracts that do not comply with its writing requirements.

The following types of contracts are generally required to be in writing or evidenced by a written memorandum or electronic record:

1. Contracts involving interests in land.
2. Contracts that cannot by their terms be performed within one year from the day after the date of formation.
3. Collateral, or secondary, contracts, such as promises to answer for the debt or duty of another and promises by the administrator or executor of an estate to pay a debt of the estate personally—that is, out of their own pocket.
4. Promises made in consideration of marriage.
5. Under the Uniform Commercial Code (UCC), contracts for the sale of goods priced at $500 or more.

12-8 Third Party Rights

Once it has been determined that a valid and legally enforceable contract exists, attention can turn to the rights and duties of the parties to the contract. A contract is a private agreement between the parties who have entered into it, and traditionally these parties alone have rights and liabilities under the contract. This principle is referred to as **privity of contract.** A *third party*—one who is not a direct party to a particular contract—normally does not have rights under that contract.

There are exceptions to the rule of privity of contract. For instance, privity of contract is not required to recover damages under product liability laws. Hence, a person injured by a defective product can still recover damages even though that person was not the buyer of the product.

There are two other exceptions. One exception allows a party to a contract to transfer the rights or duties arising from the contract to another person through an *assignment* (of rights) or a *delegation* (of duties). The other exception involves a *third party beneficiary contract*—a contract in which the parties intend to benefit a third party.

In a bilateral contract, the two parties have corresponding rights and duties. One party has a right to require the other to perform some task, and the other has a duty to perform it. The transfer of contractual rights to a third party is known as an **assignment.** The transfer of contractual duties to a third party is known as a **delegation.** An assignment or a delegation occurs after the original contract was made.

12-8a Assignments

Assignments are important because they are used in many types of business financing. Lending institutions, such as banks, frequently assign their rights to receive payments under their loan contracts to other firms, which pay for those rights. ■ **Example 12.32** Tia obtains a loan from a bank to finance an online business venture. She may later receive a notice from the bank stating that it has transferred (assigned) its rights to receive payments on the loan to another firm. When it is time to repay the loan, Tia must make the payments to that other firm. ■

The Effect of an Assignment In an assignment, the party assigning the rights to a third party is known as the **assignor,**[30] and the party receiving the rights is the

---

29. The major federal statute prohibiting discrimination is the Civil Rights Act of 1964, 42 U.S.C. Sections 2000e–2000e-17.

30. Pronounced uh-*sye*-nore.

assignee.[31] Other traditional terms used to describe the parties in assignment relationships are **obligee** (the person to whom a duty, or obligation, is owed) and **obligor** (the person who is obligated to perform the duty).

Extinguishes the Rights of the Assignor. When rights under a contract are assigned unconditionally, the rights of the assignor are extinguished. The third party (the assignee) has a right to demand performance from the other original party to the contract. The assignee takes only those rights that the assignor originally had, however.

12–8b Delegations

Just as a party can transfer rights through an assignment, a party can also transfer duties. Duties are not assigned, however—they are delegated. The party delegating the duties is the *delegator,* and the party to whom the duties are delegated is the *delegatee.* Normally, a delegation of duties does not relieve the delegator of the obligation to perform in the event that the delegatee fails to do so.

No special form is required to create a valid delegation of duties. As long as the delegator expresses an intention to make the delegation, it is effective. The delegator need not even use the word *delegate.*

Duties That Cannot Be Delegated As a general rule, any duty can be delegated. There are, however, some exceptions to this rule. Delegation is prohibited in the following circumstances:

1. When special trust has been placed in the obligor or when performance depends on the personal skill or talents of the obligor.
2. When performance by a third party will vary materially from that expected by the obligee.
3. When the contract expressly prohibits delegation.

12–8c Third Party Beneficiaries

Another exception to the doctrine of privity of contract arises when the contract is intended to benefit a third party. The original parties to a contract can agree that the contract performance should be rendered to or directly benefit a third person. When this happens, the third person becomes an intended **third party beneficiary** of the contract. As the **intended beneficiary** of the contract, the third party has legal rights and can sue the promisor directly for breach of the contract.

12–8d Who Is the Promisor?

Who, though, is the promisor? In a bilateral contract, both parties to the contract make promises that can be enforced, so the court has to determine which party made the promise that benefits the third party. That person is the promisor. In effect, allowing a third party to sue the promisor directly circumvents the "middle person" (the promisee) and thus reduces the burden on the courts. Otherwise, the third party would sue the promisee, who would then sue the promisor.

■ **Case in Point 12.33** The classic case that gave third party beneficiaries the right to bring a suit directly against a promisor was decided in 1859. The case involved three parties—Holly, Lawrence, and Fox. Holly had borrowed $300 from Lawrence. Shortly thereafter, Holly loaned $300 to Fox, who in return promised Holly that he would pay Holly's debt to Lawrence on the following day. When Lawrence failed to obtain the $300 from Fox, he sued Fox to recover the funds. The court had to decide whether Lawrence could sue Fox directly (rather than suing Holly). The court held that when "a promise [is] made for the benefit of another, he for whose benefit it is made may bring an action for its breach."[32] ■

The law distinguishes between *intended* beneficiaries and *incidental* beneficiaries. An *incidental beneficiary* is a third person who receives a benefit from a contract even though that person's benefit is not the reason the contract was made. Because the benefit is unintentional, an incidental beneficiary cannot sue to enforce the contract. Only intended beneficiaries acquire legal rights in a contract.

---

31. Pronounced uh-sye-*nee.*

32. *Lawrence v. Fox,* 20 N.Y. 268 (1859).

Practice and Review: Formation of Traditional and E-Contracts

Shane Durbin wanted to have a recording studio custom-built in his home. He sent invitations to a number of local contractors to submit bids on the project. Rory Amstel submitted the lowest bid, which was $20,000 less than any of the other bids Durbin received. Durbin called Amstel to ascertain the type and quality of the materials that were included in the bid and to find out if he could substitute a superior brand of acoustic tiles for the same bid price. Amstel said he would have to check into the price difference. The parties also discussed a possible start date for construction. Two weeks later, Durbin changed his mind and decided not to go forward with his plan to build a recording studio. Amstel filed a suit against Durbin for breach of contract. Using the information presented in the chapter, answer the following questions.

1. Did Amstel's bid meet the requirements of an offer? Explain.
2. Was there an acceptance of the offer? Why or why not?
3. How is an offer terminated? Assuming that Durbin did not inform Amstel that he was rejecting the offer, was the offer terminated at any time described here? Explain.

Debate This ... The terms and conditions in click-on agreements are so long and detailed that no one ever reads the agreements. Therefore, the act of clicking on "I agree" is not really an acceptance.

Terms and Concepts

acceptance 243
accord and satisfaction 248
agreement 238
assignee 258
assignment 257
assignor 257
bilateral contract 235
browse-wrap terms 246
click-on agreement 245
consideration 246
contract 234
contractual capacity 251
counteroffer 241
covenant not to compete 253
covenant not to sue 249
delegation 257
disaffirmance 251
e-contracts 244
estopped 251

exculpatory clause 255
executed contract 237
executory contract 237
express contract 236
forbearance 247
formal contracts 235
forum selection clause 245
implied contract 236
informal contracts 236
intended beneficiary 258
liquidated debt 248
mailbox rule 243
mirror image rule 241
objective theory of contracts 235
offer 238
offeree 235
offeror 235
option contract 241
past consideration 248

privity of contract 257
promise 234
promissory estoppel 250
reformation 254
release 249
rescission 248
revocation 241
shrink-wrap agreement 245
Statute of Frauds 257
third party beneficiary 258
unconscionable 254
unenforceable contract 237
unilateral contract 235
unliquidated debt 249
usury 253
valid contract 237
void contract 237
voidable contract 237

Issue Spotters

1. Applied Products, Inc., does business with Beltway Distributors, Inc., online. Under the Uniform Electronic Transactions Act, what determines the effect of the electronic documents evidencing the parties' deal? Is a party's "signature" necessary? Explain. (See *E-Contracts*.)

2. Before Maria starts her first year of college, Fred promises to give her $5,000 when she graduates. She goes to college, borrowing and spending far more than $5,000. At the beginning of the spring semester of her senior year, she reminds Fred of the promise. Fred sends her a note that says, "I revoke the promise." Is Fred's promise binding? Explain. (See *Consideration*.)

• **Check your answers to the Issue Spotters against the answers provided in Appendix B at the end of this text.**

Business Scenarios and Case Problems

12–1. Unilateral Contract. Rocky Mountain Races, Inc., sponsors the "Pioneer Trail Ultramarathon," with an advertised first prize of $10,000. The rules require the competitors to run one hundred miles from the floor of Blackwater Canyon to the top of Pinnacle Mountain. The rules also provide that Rocky reserves the right to change the terms of the race at any time. Monica enters the race and is declared the winner. Rocky offers her a prize of $1,000 instead of $10,000. Did Rocky and Monica have a contract? Explain. (See *An Overview of Contract Law.*)

12–2. Preexisting Duty. Tabor is a buyer of file cabinets manufactured by Martin. Martin's contract with Tabor calls for delivery of fifty file cabinets at $40 per cabinet in five equal installments. After delivery of two installments (twenty cabinets), Martin informs Tabor that because of inflation, Martin is losing money. Martin will promise to deliver the remaining thirty cabinets only if Tabor will pay $50 per cabinet. Tabor agrees in writing to do so. Discuss whether Martin can legally collect the additional $100 on delivery to Tabor of the next installment of ten cabinets. (See *Consideration.*)

12–3. Business Case Problem With Sample Answer— Requirements of the Offer. Technical Consumer Products, Inc. (TCP), makes and distributes energy-efficient lighting products. Emily Bahr was TCP's district sales manager in Minnesota, North Dakota, and South Dakota when the company announced the details of a bonus plan. A district sales manager who achieved 100 percent year-over-year sales growth and a 42 percent gross margin would earn 200 percent of their base salary as a bonus. TCP retained absolute discretion to modify the plan. Bahr's base salary was $42,500. Her final sales results for the year showed 113 percent year-over-year sales growth and a 42 percent gross margin. She anticipated a bonus of $85,945, but TCP could not afford to pay the bonuses as planned, and Bahr received only $34,229. In response to Bahr's claim for breach of contract, TCP argued that the bonus plan was too indefinite to be an offer. Is TCP correct? Explain. [*Bahr v. Technical Consumer Products, Inc.*, 601 Fed.Appx. 359 (6th Cir. 2015)] (See *Agreement.*)

• **For a sample answer to Problem 12–3, go to Appendix C at the end of this text.**

12–4. Acceptance. Altisource Portfolio Solutions, Inc., is a global corporation that provides real property owners with a variety of services, including property preservation— repairs, debris removal, and so on. Lucas Contracting, Inc., is a small trade contractor in Carrollton, Ohio. On behalf of Altisource, Berghorst Enterprises, LLC, hired Lucas to perform preservation work on certain foreclosed properties in eastern Ohio. When Berghorst did not pay for the work, Lucas filed a suit in an Ohio state court against Altisource. Before the trial, Lucas e-mailed the terms of a settlement.

The same day, Altisource e-mailed a response that did not challenge or contradict Lucas's proposal and indicated agreement to it. Two days later, however, Altisource forwarded a settlement document that contained additional terms. Which proposal most likely satisfies the element of agreement to establish a contract? Explain. [*Lucas Contracting, Inc. v. Altisource Portfolio Solutions, Inc.*, 2016-Ohio-474 (5 Dist. 2016)] (See *Agreement.*)

12–5. Agreements That Lack Consideration. Arkansas-Missouri Forest Products, LLC (Ark-Mo), sells supplies to make wood pallets. Blue Chip Manufacturing (BCM) makes pallets. Mark Garnett, an owner of Ark-Mo, and Stuart Lerner, an owner of BCM, went into business together. Garnett and Lerner agreed that Ark-Mo would have a 30-percent ownership interest in their future projects. When Lerner formed Blue Chip Recycling, LLC (BCR), to manage a pallet repair facility in California, however, he allocated only a 5-percent interest to Ark-Mo. Garnett objected. In a "Telephone Deal," Lerner then promised Garnett that Ark-Mo would receive a 30-percent interest in their future projects in the Midwest, and Garnett agreed to forgo an ownership interest in BCR. But when Blue Chip III, LLC (BC III), was formed to operate a repair facility in the Midwest, Lerner told Garnett that he "was not getting anything." Ark-Mo filed a suit in a Missouri state court against Lerner, alleging breach of contract. Was there consideration to support the Telephone Deal? Explain. [*Arkansas-Missouri Forest Products, LLC v. Lerner*, 486 S.W.3d 438 (Mo.App.E.D. 2016)] (See *Consideration.*)

12–6. Legality. Sue Ann Apolinar hired a guide through Arkansas Valley Adventures, LLC, for a rafting excursion on the Arkansas River. At the outfitter's office, Apolinar signed a release that detailed potential hazards and risks, including "overturning," "unpredictable currents," "obstacles" in the water, and "drowning." The release clearly stated that her signature discharged Arkansas Valley from liability for all claims arising in connection with the trip. On the river, while attempting to maneuver around a rapid, the raft capsized. The current swept Apolinar into a logjam where, despite efforts to save her, she drowned. Her son, Jesus Espinoza, Jr., filed a suit in a federal district court against the rafting company, alleging negligence. What are the arguments for and against enforcing the release that Apolinar signed? Discuss. [*Espinoza v. Arkansas Valley Adventures, LLC*, 809 F.3d 1150 (10th Cir. 2016)] (See *Legality.*)

12–7. Online Acceptances. Airbnb, Inc., maintains a website that lists, advertises, and takes fees or commissions for property rentals posted on the site. To offer or book accommodations on the site, a party must register and create an account. The sign-up screen states, "By clicking 'Sign Up' . . . you confirm that you accept the Terms of Service"

(TOS). The TOS, which are hyperlinked, include a mandatory arbitration provision. Francesco Plazza registered with Airbnb and created an account but did not read the TOS. Later, Plazza filed a suit in a federal district court against Airbnb, alleging that the defendant was acting as an unlicensed real estate broker and committing deceptive trade practices in violation of New York state law. Airbnb filed a motion to compel arbitration, pursuant to the TOS. Can Plazza avoid arbitration? Explain. [*Plazza v. Airbnb, Inc.*, 289 F.Supp.3d 537 (S.D.N.Y. 2018)] (See *E-Contracts*.)

12–8. Contracts Contrary to Public Policy. P.M. and C.M. (the "Ms") are married and live in Iowa. Unable to conceive their own child, they signed a contract with T.B., who, in exchange for $13,000 and medical expenses, agreed to be impregnated with embryos fertilized with P.M.'s sperm and the ova of an anonymous donor. T.B. agreed to carry the pregnancy to term, and she and her spouse, D.B., (the "Bs") promised to hand over the baby at birth to the Ms. During the pregnancy, the relations between the parties deteriorated. When the baby was born, T.B. refused to honor the agreement to give up the child. Meanwhile, genetic testing excluded T.B. and D.B. as the biological parents and established P.M. as the father. Iowa exempts "surrogacy" from a state criminal statute that prohibits selling babies. There is no other state law on point. Is the contract between the Ms and the Bs enforceable? Discuss. [*P.M. v. T.B.*, 907 N.W.2d 522 (Iowa 2018)] (See *Legality*.)

12–9. Implied Contracts. Francisco Sanchez entered into a contract with Arthur Perry. Sanchez claimed he had not been paid the full amount he was due for his labor under the contract. According to Sanchez, he had orally agreed to do the work for $18,000 and thus was still owed $13,244.32. Perry argued that Sanchez had signed a contract to do the work for less. The trial court ascertained that the document purportedly signed by Sanchez was not a valid and enforceable contract. On appeal to the Court of Appeals of Tennessee, should the appellate court uphold the trial court's ruling that Sanchez was still owed money? [*Sanchez v. Perry*, 2022 WL 1077320 (Ct.App.TN at Jackson (2022)] (See *Types of Contracts*.)

12–10. A Question of Ethics—The IDDR Approach and Minors. Sky High Sports Nashville Operations, LLC, operated a trampoline park in Nashville, Tennessee. At the park, during a dodgeball tournament, Jacob Blackwell, a minor, suffered a torn tendon and a broken tibia. His mother, Crystal, filed a suit on his behalf in a Tennessee state court against Sky High, alleging negligence and seeking $500,000 to cover medical and other expenses. Sky High asserted that the claim was barred by a waiver of liability in a contract between the parties, which the defendant asked the court to enforce. The waiver released Sky High from liability for any "negligent acts or omissions." [*Blackwell v. Sky High Sports Nashville Operations, LLC*, 523 S.W.3d 624 (Tenn.Ct.App. 2017)] (See *Contractual Capacity*.)

(a) Should Sky High offer a defense to the suit? What might Sky High argue as a reason for enforcing the waiver? Use the IDDR approach to answer these questions.

(b) Would it be unethical to allow Jacob to recover damages? Apply the IDDR approach to explain.

Time-Limited Group Assignment

12–11. Preexisting Duty. Melissa Faraj owns a lot and wants to build a house according to a particular set of plans and specifications. She solicits bids from building contractors and receives three bids: one from Carlton for $160,000, one from Feldberg for $158,000, and one from Siegel for $153,000. She accepts Siegel's bid. One month after beginning construction of the house, Siegel contacts Faraj and tells her that because of inflation and a recent price hike for materials, his costs have gone up. He says he will not finish the house unless Faraj agrees to pay an extra $13,000. Faraj reluctantly agrees to pay the additional sum. (See *Consideration*.)

(a) One group will discuss whether a contractor can ever raise the price of completing construction because of inflation and the rising cost of materials.

(b) A second group will assume that after the house is finished, Faraj refuses to pay the extra $13,000. The group will decide whether Faraj is legally required to pay this additional amount.

(c) A third group will discuss the types of extraordinary difficulties that could arise during construction that would justify a contractor's charging more than the original bid.

Chapter 13

Contract Performance, Breach, and Remedies

In a perfect world, every party who signs a contract would perform their duties completely and in a timely fashion, thereby discharging the contract. The real world is more complicated. Events often occur that affect our performance or our ability to perform contractual duties.

In addition, the duty to perform under a contract is not always *absolute*. It may instead be *conditioned* on the occurrence or nonoccurrence of a certain event. The legal environment of business requires the identification of some point at which the parties can reasonably know that their duties have ended.

When one party breaches a contract, the other party—the nonbreaching party—can choose one or more of several remedies. A *remedy* is the relief provided for an innocent party when the other party has breached the contract. It is the means employed to enforce a right or to redress an injury. Remedies may include *damages, rescission* and *restitution, specific performance,* and *reformation*.

13–1 Voluntary Consent

An otherwise valid contract may still be unenforceable if the parties have not genuinely agreed to its terms. A lack of **voluntary consent** (assent) can be used as a defense to the contract's enforceability.

Voluntary consent may be lacking because of a mistake, misrepresentation, undue influence, or duress—in other words, because there is no true "meeting of the minds." Generally, a party who demonstrates that they did not truly agree to the terms of a contract has a choice. That party can choose either to carry out the contract or to rescind (cancel) it and thus avoid the entire transaction.

13–1a Mistakes

We all make mistakes, so it is not surprising that mistakes are made when contracts are formed. In certain circumstances, contract law allows a contract to be avoided on the basis of mistake.

It is important to distinguish between *mistakes of fact* and *mistakes of value or quality*. Only a mistake of fact makes a contract voidable. Also, the mistake must involve some *material fact*—a fact that a reasonable person would consider important when determining their course of action.

Mistakes of fact occur in two forms—*bilateral* and *unilateral*. A unilateral mistake is made by only *one* of the contracting parties. A bilateral, or mutual, mistake is made by *both* of the parties. We look next at these two types of mistakes and illustrate them graphically in Exhibit 13–1.

Unilateral Mistakes of Fact A **unilateral mistake** is made by only one of the parties. In general, a unilateral mistake does not give the mistaken party any right to relief from the contract. Normally, the contract is enforceable.

■ **Example 13.1** Elena intends to sell her jet ski for $2,500. When she learns that Chin is interested in buying a used jet ski, she sends him an e-mail offering to sell the jet ski to him. When typing the e-mail, however, she mistakenly keys in the price of $1,500. Chin immediately sends Elena an e-mail reply accepting her offer. Even though Elena intended to sell her personal jet ski for $2,500, she has made a unilateral mistake and is bound by the contract to sell it to Chin for $1,500. ■

This general rule has at least two exceptions.[1] The contract may not be enforceable if:

1. The *other* party to the contract knows or should have known that a mistake of fact was made.

---

1. The *Restatement (Second) of Contracts,* Section 153, liberalizes the general rule to take into account the modern trend of allowing avoidance even though only one party has been mistaken.

Exhibit 13–1 Mistakes of Fact

2. The error was due to a substantial mathematical mistake in addition, subtraction, division, or multiplication and was made inadvertently and without gross (extreme) negligence. If, for instance, a contractor's bid was significantly low because the contractor made a mistake in addition when totaling the estimated costs, any contract resulting from the bid normally may be rescinded.

Of course, in both situations, the mistake must still involve some material fact.

Bilateral (Mutual) Mistakes of Fact
A **bilateral mistake** is a "mutual misunderstanding concerning a basic assumption on which the contract was made."[2] Note that, as with unilateral mistakes, the mistake must be about a material fact.

When both parties are mistaken about the same material fact, the contract can be rescinded by either party. ■ **Case in Point 13.2** Jason Allen was injured in a work-related automobile accident. Allen's employer had workers' compensation insurance with Accident Fund Insurance Company of America. After a series of disputes and negotiations, Allen and Accident Fund entered into a voluntary payment agreement (VPA) contract under which the insurance company consented to pay Allen $264.53 per week for 54.2 weeks.

Neither side noticed, however, that the arithmetic of the VPA was wrong. Accident Fund should have been paying Allen $264.53 per week for 131.7 weeks, not 54.2 weeks. A Michigan appellate court found that the faulty calculations

escaped the notice of both parties. To correct this bilateral mistake, the court ordered that the VPA be reformed with the correct figures, reflecting the intentions of Allen and Accident Fund at the time of their agreement.[3] ■

A word or term in a contract may be subject to more than one reasonable interpretation. If the parties to the contract attach materially different meanings to the term, a court may allow the contract to be rescinded because there has been no true "meeting of the minds."

Mistakes of Value
If a mistake concerns the future market value or quality of the object of the contract, the mistake is one of value, and the contract normally is enforceable. ■ **Example 13.3** Sung buys a violin from Bev for $250. Although the violin is very old, neither party believes that it is valuable. Later, however, an antiques dealer informs the parties that the violin is rare and worth thousands of dollars. Here, both parties were mistaken, but the mistake is a mistake of value rather than a mistake of fact. Because mistakes of value do not warrant contract rescission, Bev normally cannot rescind the contract. ■

The reason that mistakes of value do not affect the enforceability of contracts is that value is variable. Depending on the time, place, and other circumstances, the same item may be worth considerably different amounts. When parties form a contract, their agreement establishes the value of the object of their transaction—for the moment. Both parties are considered to have assumed the risk that the value will change in the future or prove to be different from what they thought. Without

---

2. *Restatement (Second) of Contracts,* Section 152.

3. *Allen v. Charlevoix Abstract & Engineering Company,* 929 N.W.2d 804, 326 Mich.App. 658 (2019).

this rule, almost any party who did not receive what they considered a fair bargain could argue mistake.

13–1b Fraudulent Misrepresentation

Although fraud is a tort, the presence of fraud also affects the authenticity of the innocent party's consent to the contract. When an innocent party is fraudulently induced to enter into a contract, the contract usually can be avoided, because that party has not voluntarily consented to its terms. The innocent party can either rescind the contract and be restored to their original position or enforce the contract and seek damages for any harms resulting from the fraud.

Generally, fraudulent misrepresentation refers only to misrepresentation that is consciously false and is intended to mislead another. The person making the fraudulent misrepresentation knows or believes that the assertion is false or knows that there is no basis (stated or implied) for the assertion. Typically, fraudulent misrepresentation consists of the following elements:

1. A misrepresentation of a material fact must occur.
2. There must be an intent to deceive.
3. The innocent party must justifiably rely on the misrepresentation.
4. To collect damages, the innocent party must have been harmed as a result of the misrepresentation.

Misrepresentation Has Occurred The first element of proving fraud is to show that misrepresentation of a material fact has occurred. This misrepresentation can occur by words or actions. For instance, the statement "This sculpture was created by Michelangelo" is a misrepresentation of fact if another artist sculpted the statue. Similarly, if a customer asks to see only paintings by Edward Hopper and the gallery owner immediately leads the customer to paintings that were not done by Hopper, the owner's actions may be a misrepresentation.

■ **Case in Point 13.4** Fraud may involve actual or implicit misrepresentation of material facts. Nigerian-born Oluchi Ijeoma Nwankwo immigrated to the United States and became a naturalized citizen. Another Nigerian, Nnamdi Kenfrancis Uzodinma, was still living in Nigeria when he contacted Oluchi via Facebook. After a courtship on Facebook, the two agreed to marry. They were married in the United States but never physically consummated the marriage.

Nnamdi ultimately became a naturalized citizen, and after that his behavior changed. He stopped depositing his paychecks in the couple's joint bank account, deleted his Facebook account, and disappeared. Oluchi filed a complaint to have the marriage annulled on the ground that Nnamdi had engaged in fraud through misrepresentation of material facts. Specifically, she claimed that he married her only to obtain U.S. citizenship. Oluchi prevailed in court.[4] ■

The following case concerns the effect of a merger clause on an allegation of fraud. A merger clause is a contract clause stating that the contract embodies the entire agreement between the parties. In other words, no separate agreements between the parties are to be considered in interpreting the contract.

---

4. *Nwankwo v. Uzodinma*, 185 N.E.3d 513, 2022-Ohio-565 (Ct.App. OH, 12th District 2022).

Case 13.1

McCullough v. Allstate Property and Casualty Insurance Co.

Alabama Court of Civil Appeals, 256 So.3d 103 (2018).

Background and Facts Allstate Property and Casualty Insurance Company issued a policy to Jerry McCullough, insuring his pickup truck. McCullough loaned the truck to an acquaintance, who returned it damaged. McCullough filed a claim on the policy. Allstate treated the claim as involving multiple different claims (each with a $250 deductible) and reported these claims to Verisk Analytics Automobile Property Loss Underwriting Service (A-PLUS).[a]

---

a. A-PLUS reports information received from insurance companies regarding claims. The reports can affect a claimant's insurance costs.

Contending that the damage had resulted from only one claim, McCullough filed a suit in a federal district court against Allstate. The insurer agreed to settle the suit for $8,000. McCullough agreed to this amount, but only if Allstate corrected the report to reflect that he was making only one insurance claim and that Allstate paid nothing on that claim. Allstate's lawyer sent McCullough an e-mail agreeing to these terms, but the promise was not included in the release and settlement agreement that the parties signed. The release had a merger clause saying that there were no other agreements, verbal or otherwise, between the parties except as set forth in the contract.

Later, McCullough learned that Allstate had reported to A-PLUS that it had paid $8,000 to him on his claim. He filed a suit in an Alabama state court against Allstate, seeking damages for fraud. Both parties filed motions for summary judgment. The court granted Allstate's motion and denied McCullough's. McCullough appealed.

In the Language of the Court
MOORE, Judge.
* * * *

On appeal, McCullough argues that the trial court erred in granting Allstate's motion for a summary judgment * * *. Allstate simply argued that McCullough's claim was barred by * * * the release. McCullough argues, though, that he should be permitted to present * * * evidence to prove that the release was procured by fraud.

The law in this state renders [a] merger clause ineffective to bar * * * evidence of fraud in the inducement or procurement of a contract. * * * Such a holding is required. To hold otherwise is to encourage deliberate fraud.

* * * Allstate was incorrect in its argument that McCullough's claim * * * was barred * * * by the language of the release. * * * Therefore, Allstate's summary-judgment motion was due to be denied.
* * * *

McCullough also argues that the trial court erred in denying his motion for * * * summary judgment on his claim.

According to McCullough, he informed Allstate, through its attorney, that he would not settle the federal lawsuit unless Allstate reported no payment on the claim. McCullough averred [declared] that Allstate's attorney * * * informed McCullough that Allstate had reported * * * that it had paid nothing on the claim. According to McCullough, that fact * * * led McCullough to settle the federal lawsuit because he believed that no reported payment on the claim would be on record; however, Allstate subsequently reported the $8,000 payment to * * * A-PLUS.

Although McCullough presented evidence of fraud, the release contained a merger clause * * *. Considering that the release did not specify that Allstate must report that nothing was paid on the claim, coupled with * * * the merger clause, we conclude that there is a genuine issue of material fact as to whether Allstate, willfully to deceive, or recklessly without knowledge, agreed to report an amount of $0 on the claim and whether McCullough reasonably relied on any representation outside those contained in the release.

Based on the foregoing, McCullough's motion for * * * summary judgment on his claim * * * was properly denied.

Decision and Remedy A state intermediate appellate court reversed the lower court's summary judgment in favor of Allstate, affirmed the court's denial of McCullough's motion for summary judgment, and remanded the case. Genuine issues of material fact precluded summary judgment on McCullough's claim for fraudulent misrepresentation.

Critical Thinking
- **Legal Environment** In most cases involving the interpretation and application of a contract, a party is not allowed to present evidence outside the "four corners" of the parties' expression of their agreement. Why not?
- **What If the Facts Were Different?** Suppose that under the law, a merger clause barred evidence of fraud in the inducement of a contract. How would this affect contract negotiations? Would the result in this case have been different? Discuss.

Misrepresentation by Conduct. Misrepresentation also occurs when a party takes specific action to conceal a fact that is material to the contract. Therefore, if a seller's actions prevent a buyer from learning of some fact that is material to the contract, the seller's behavior constitutes misrepresentation by conduct.

Statements of Opinion. Statements of opinion and representations of future facts (predictions) generally are not subject to claims of fraud. Statements such as "This land will be worth twice as much next year" and "This car will last for years and years" are statements of opinion, not fact. A fact is objective and verifiable, whereas an opinion is usually subject to debate. Contracting parties should know the difference and should not rely on statements of opinion.

Here, as in other areas of contract law, every person is expected to exercise care and judgment when entering into contracts. The law will not come to the aid of someone who simply makes an unwise bargain. Nevertheless, in certain situations, such as when a naïve purchaser relies on an opinion from an expert, the innocent party may be entitled to rescission or reformation.

Intent to Deceive The second element of fraud is knowledge on the part of the misrepresenting party that facts have been falsely represented. This element, normally called *scienter,*[5] or "guilty knowledge," signifies that there was an intent to deceive.

Scienter clearly exists if a party knows that a fact is not as stated. ■ **Example 13.5** Reyna applies for a position as a business law professor two weeks after her release from prison. On her résumé, she lies and says that she was a corporate president for fourteen years and taught business law at another college. After she is hired, her probation officer alerts the school to her criminal history. The school immediately fires her. If Reyna sues the school for breach of her employment contract, she is unlikely to succeed. Because Reyna clearly exhibited an intent to deceive the college by not disclosing her history, the school can rescind her employment contract without incurring liability. ■

Justifiable Reliance on the Misrepresentation The third element of fraud is reasonably justifiable reliance on the misrepresentation of fact. That means the deceived party must have a justifiable reason for relying on the misrepresentation. Also, the misrepresentation

must be an important factor (but not necessarily the sole factor) in inducing the deceived party to enter into the contract. Reliance is not justified if the innocent party knows the true facts or relies on obviously extravagant statements (such as, "this pickup truck will get sixty miles to the gallon").

Injury to the Innocent Party Most courts do not require a showing of injury in an action to rescind a contract. These courts hold that because rescission returns the parties to the positions they held before the contract was made, a showing of injury to the innocent party is unnecessary.

In contrast, to recover damages caused by fraud, proof of harm is universally required. The measure of damages is ordinarily equal to the property's value had it been delivered as represented, less the actual price paid for the property.

Because fraud actions necessarily involve wrongful conduct, courts may also sometimes award punitive damages, which are not ordinarily available in contract actions. The potential for punitive damage awards leads many plaintiffs to assert fraudulent misrepresentation claims in their contract disputes.

13–1c Undue Influence

Undue influence arises from relationships in which one party can greatly influence another party, thus overcoming that party's free will. A contract entered into under excessive or undue influence lacks voluntary consent and is therefore voidable.

In various types of relationships, one party may have the opportunity to dominate and unfairly influence another party. Minors and elderly people, for instance, are often under the influence of guardians (persons who are legally responsible for them). If a guardian induces a young or elderly ward (a person whom the guardian looks after) to enter into a contract that benefits the guardian, the guardian may have exerted undue influence. Undue influence can arise from a number of fiduciary relationships, such as physician–patient, parent–child, husband–wife, or guardian–ward situations.

The essential feature of undue influence is that the party being taken advantage of does not exercise free will in entering into a contract. It is not enough that a person is elderly or suffers from some physical or mental impairment. There must be clear and convincing evidence that the person did not act out of free will. Similarly, the existence of a fiduciary relationship alone is insufficient to prove undue influence.

5. Pronounced sy-*en*-ter.

13–1d Duress

Agreement to the terms of a contract is not voluntary if one of the parties is forced into the agreement. The use of threats to force a party to enter into a contract constitutes **duress.** Similarly, the use of blackmail or extortion to induce consent to a contract is duress. Duress is both a defense to the enforcement of a contract and a ground for the rescission of a contract.

To establish duress, there must be proof of a threat to do something that the threatening party has no right to do. Generally, for duress to occur, the threatened act must be wrongful or illegal. It also must render the person who is threatened incapable of exercising free will. A threat to exercise a legal right, such as the right to sue someone, ordinarily does not constitute duress.

13–2 Performance and Discharge

The most common way to **discharge,** or terminate, contractual duties is by the **performance** of those duties. For instance, a buyer and seller enter into an agreement via e-mail for the sale of a Lexus RZ for $63,000. This contract will be discharged by performance when the buyer pays $63,000 to the seller and the seller transfers possession of the Lexus to the buyer.

13–2a Conditions

In most contracts, promises of performance are not expressly conditioned or qualified. Instead, they are absolute promises. They must be performed, or the parties promising the acts will be in breach of contract.

In some situations, however, performance is conditioned. A **condition** is a qualification in a contract based on a possible future event. The occurrence or nonoccurrence of the event will trigger the performance of a legal obligation or terminate an existing legal obligation. If the condition is not satisfied, the obligations of the parties are discharged.

■ **Case in Point 13.6** A couple divorced. As part of an Agreement Incident to Divorce (AID), the father was to pay $11,500 per month for each of their two children. The AID constituted an enforceable contract. Both agreed that the wife and children would engage in an "alternative" lifestyle in which they would travel and live abroad at times for the purpose of educating the children in other cultures and languages. The wife agreed as a condition precedent to receiving the support payments that she and the children would maintain a normal, although alternative, lifestyle. The father became increasingly

concerned that the children were not enrolled in a school environment. The mother rarely enrolled the children in school, but rather taught them without any set curriculum. She referred to her teaching methods as "unschooling." Then the mother moved with their children to Victoria, British Columbia, to care for her ailing parents. The father requested that the mother return the children into his possession, and he purchased airline tickets for their return. The mother refused. The father stopped paying the agreed-upon support payments. Ultimately, a trial court found that the mother had not met the condition precedent in the AID. An appeals court affirmed the judgment of the trial court.[6] ■

13–2b Discharge by Performance

The great majority of contracts, as noted earlier, are discharged by performance. The contract comes to an end when both parties fulfill their respective duties by performing the acts they have promised.

Performance can also be accomplished by tender. **Tender** is an unconditional offer to perform by a person who is ready, willing, and able to do so. Therefore, a seller who places goods at the disposal of a buyer has tendered delivery and can demand payment. A buyer who offers to pay for goods has tendered payment and can demand delivery of the goods.

Once performance has been tendered, the party making the tender has done everything possible to carry out the terms of the contract. If the other party then refuses to perform, the party making the tender can sue for breach of contract. There are two basic types of performance—*complete performance* and *substantial performance.*

Complete Performance When a party performs exactly as agreed, the party's performance is said to be complete. Normally, conditions expressly stated in a contract must fully occur in all respects for complete performance (strict performance) of the contract to take place. Any deviation breaches the contract and discharges the other party's obligation to perform.

Most construction contracts, for instance, require the builder to meet certain specifications. If the specifications are conditions, complete performance is required to avoid material breach (material breach will be discussed shortly). If the conditions are met, the other party to the contract must then fulfill the obligation to pay the builder.

---

6. *Interest of O.K.L.,* 2022 WL 951245 (Ct.App. TX, Dallas 2022).

If the parties to the contract did not expressly make the specifications a condition, however, and the builder fails to meet the specifications, performance is not complete. What effect does such a failure have on the other party's obligation to pay? The answer is part of the doctrine of *substantial performance*.

Substantial Performance A party who in good faith performs substantially all of the terms of a contract can enforce the contract against the other party under the doctrine of substantial performance. The basic requirements for performance to qualify as substantial are as follows:

1. The party must have performed in good faith. Intentional failure to comply with the contract terms is a breach of the contract.
2. The performance must not vary greatly from the performance promised in the contract. An omission, variance, or defect in performance is considered minor if it can easily be remedied by compensation (monetary damages).
3. The performance must create substantially the same benefits as those promised in the contract.

Courts Must Decide. Courts decide whether the performance was substantial on a case-by-case basis, examining all of the facts of the particular situation. ■ **Case in Point 13.7** Magic Carpet Ride (MCR) purchased a used airplane from Rugger Investment Group. The contract required the airplane to be free from any liens, or legal claims. In fact, the airplane was burdened with a lien at the time of the sale. The two sides amended their contract, giving Rugger an additional ninety days to remove the lien or pay MCR a $90,000 penalty.

Rugger obtained the lien release, eight days too late. MCR sued for breach of contract to recover the $90,000

penalty. A California appeals court found that (1) Rugger had tried in good faith to meet the ninety-day deadline; and that (2) MCR had received all bargained-for benefits. As it would have been unfair for MCR to get the airplane and an additional $90,000, the court decided that the eight-day delay did not bar Rugger from claiming substantial performance under the terms of the amended contract.[7] ■

Effect on Duty to Perform. If one party's performance is substantial, the other party's duty to perform remains absolute. In other words, the parties must continue performing under the contract. For instance, the party that substantially performed is entitled to payment. If performance is not substantial, there is a material breach (to be discussed shortly), and the nonbreaching party is excused from further performance.

Measure of Damages. Because substantial performance is not perfect, the other party is entitled to damages to compensate for the failure to comply with the contract. The measure of the damages is the cost to bring the object of the contract into compliance with its terms, if that cost is reasonable under the circumstances.

What if the cost is unreasonable? Then the measure of damages is the difference in value between the performance rendered and the performance that would have been rendered if the contract had been performed completely.

The following case is a classic illustration that there is no exact formula for deciding when a contract has been substantially performed.

---

7. *Magic Carpet Ride LLC v. Rugger Investment Group, L.L.C.,* 41 Cal. App. 5th 357, 254 Cal.Rptr.3d 313 (Cal.App., 4th Dist., Div. 3, CA 2019).

Classic Case 13.2

Jacob & Youngs v. Kent
Court of Appeals of New York, 230 N.Y. 239, 129 N.E. 889 (1921).

Background and Facts The plaintiff, Jacob & Youngs, Inc., was a builder that had contracted with George Kent to construct a country residence for him. A specification in the building contract required that "all wrought-iron pipe must be well galvanized, lap welded pipe of the grade known as 'standard pipe' of Reading manufacture." Jacob & Youngs installed substantially similar pipe that was not of Reading manufacture. When Kent became aware of the difference, he ordered the builder to remove all of the plumbing and replace it with the Reading type. To do so would have required removing finished walls that encased the plumbing—an expensive and difficult task. The builder explained that the plumbing was of the same quality, appearance, value, and cost as Reading pipe. When Kent nevertheless refused to pay the $3,483.46 still owed for the work, Jacob & Youngs sued to compel payment. The trial court ruled in favor of Kent. The plaintiff appealed, and the appellate court reversed the trial court's decision. Kent then appealed to the Court of Appeals of New York, the state's highest court.

In the Language of the Court

CARDOZO, Justice.

* * * *

* * * The courts never say that one who makes a contract fills the measure of his duty by less than full performance. They do say, however, that an omission, both trivial and innocent, will sometimes be atoned [compensated] for by allowance of the resulting damage, and will not always be the breach of a condition * * *.

* * * Where the line is to be drawn between the important and the trivial cannot be settled by a formula. * * * We must weigh the purpose to be served, the desire to be gratified, the excuse for deviation from the letter, [and] the cruelty of enforced adherence. Then only can we tell whether literal fulfillment is to be implied by law as a condition.

* * * We think the measure of the allowance is not the cost of replacement, which would be great, but the difference in value, which would be either nominal or nothing. * * * The owner is entitled to the money which will permit him to complete, unless the cost of completion is grossly and unfairly out of proportion to the good to be attained.

Decision and Remedy New York's highest court affirmed the appellate court's decision, holding that Jacob & Youngs had substantially performed the contract.

Critical Thinking

- **Legal Environment** The New York Court of Appeals found that Jacob & Youngs had substantially performed the contract. To what, if any, remedy was Kent entitled?
- **Impact of This Case on Today's Law** At the time of the Jacob & Youngs case, some courts did not apply the doctrine of substantial performance to disputes involving breaches of contract. This landmark decision contributed to a developing trend toward equity and fairness in those circumstances. Today, an unintentional and trivial deviation from the terms of a contract will not prevent its enforcement but will permit an adjustment in the value of its performance.

Performance to the Satisfaction of Another

Contracts often state that completed work must personally satisfy one of the parties or a third person. The question then is whether this satisfaction becomes a condition precedent, requiring actual personal satisfaction or approval for discharge, or whether the performance need only satisfy a reasonable person.

When the subject matter of the contract is personal, the obligation is conditional, and performance must actually satisfy the party specified in the contract. For instance, contracts for portraits, works of art, and tailoring are considered personal because they involve matters of personal taste. Therefore, only the personal satisfaction of the party fulfills the condition. (An exception exists, of course, if a court finds that the party is expressing dissatisfaction simply to avoid payment or otherwise is not acting in good faith.)

Most other contracts need to be performed only to the satisfaction of a reasonable person unless they expressly state otherwise. When the subject matter of the contract is mechanical, courts are more likely to find that the performing party has performed satisfactorily if a reasonable person would be satisfied with what was done.

When contracts require performance to the satisfaction of a third party with superior knowledge or training in the subject matter—such as a supervising engineer—the courts are divided. A majority of courts require the work to be satisfactory to a reasonable person, but some courts require the personal satisfaction of the third party designated in the contract. (Again, the personal judgment must be made honestly, or the condition will be excused.)

Material Breach of Contract A **breach of contract** is the nonperformance of a contractual duty. The breach is material when performance is not at least substantial. As mentioned earlier, when there is a material breach, the nonbreaching party is excused from the performance of contractual duties. That party can also sue the breaching party for damages resulting from the breach.

■ **Example 13.8** When country singer Garth Brooks's mother died, he donated $500,000 to a hospital in his hometown in Oklahoma to build a new women's health center named after his mother. After several years passed and the health center was not built, Brooks demanded a refund. The hospital refused, claiming that while it had promised to honor his mother in some way, it had not promised to build a women's health center. Brooks sued for breach of contract. A jury determined that the hospital's failure to build a women's health center and name it after Brooks's mother was a material breach of the contract. The jury awarded Brooks $1 million in damages. ■

If the breach is minor (not material), the nonbreaching party's duty to perform is not entirely excused, but it can sometimes be suspended until the breach has been remedied. Once the minor breach has been cured, the nonbreaching party must resume performance of the contractual obligations.

Note that any breach entitles the nonbreaching party to sue for damages, but only a material breach discharges the nonbreaching party from the contract. The policy underlying these rules allows a contract to go forward when only minor problems occur but allows it to be terminated if major difficulties arise. Exhibit 13–2 reviews how performance can discharge a contract.

Anticipatory Repudiation Before either party to a contract has a duty to perform, one of the parties may refuse to carry out their contractual obligations. This is called **anticipatory repudiation** of the contract.

When an anticipatory repudiation occurs, it is treated as a material breach of the contract, and the nonbreaching party is permitted to bring an action for damages immediately. The nonbreaching party can file a suit even if the scheduled time for performance under the contract is still in the future. Until the nonbreaching party treats an early repudiation as a breach, however, the repudiating party can retract the anticipatory repudiation by proper notice and restore the parties to their original obligations.[8]

An anticipatory repudiation is treated as a present, material breach for two reasons. First, the nonbreaching party should not be required to remain ready and willing to perform when the other party has already repudiated

---

8. See UCC 2–611.

Exhibit 13–2   Discharge by Performance

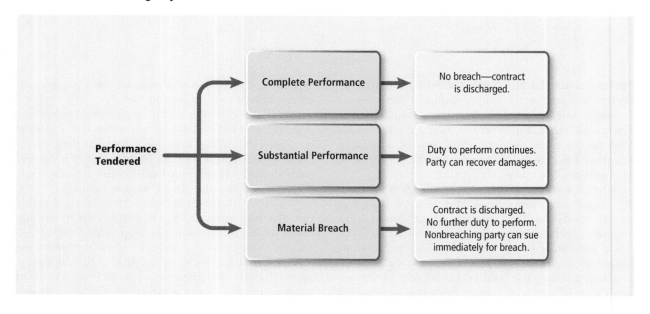

the contract. Second, the nonbreaching party should have the opportunity to seek a similar contract elsewhere and may have a duty to do so to minimize loss.[9]

Time for Performance If no time for performance is stated in a contract, a reasonable time is implied.[10] If a specific time is stated, the parties must usually perform by that time. Unless time is expressly stated to be vital, though, a delay in performance will not destroy the performing party's right to payment.

When time is expressly stated to be "of the essence," or vital, the parties normally must perform within the stated time period, because the time element becomes a condition. Even when the contract states that time is of the essence, however, a court may find that a party who fails to complain about the other party's delay has waived the breach of the time provision.

13–2c Discharge by Agreement

Any contract can be discharged by agreement of the parties. The agreement can be contained in the original contract, or the parties can form a new contract for the express purpose of discharging the original contract.

Discharge by Mutual Rescission As mentioned in previous chapters, rescission is the process by which a contract is canceled or terminated and the parties are returned to the positions they occupied prior to forming it. For **mutual rescission** to take place, the parties must make another agreement that also satisfies the legal requirements for a contract. There must be an offer, an acceptance, and consideration. Ordinarily, if the parties agree to rescind the original contract, their promises not to perform the acts stipulated in the original contract will be legal consideration for the second contract (the rescission).

Agreements to rescind most executory contracts (in which neither party has performed) are enforceable, whether the original agreement was made orally or in writing. Under the Uniform Commercial Code (UCC), however, agreements to rescind a sales contract must be in writing (or contained in an electronic record) when the contract requires a written rescission.[11] Agreements to

rescind contracts involving transfers of realty also must be evidenced by a writing or record.

When one party has fully performed, an agreement to cancel the original contract normally will not be enforceable unless there is additional consideration. Because the performing party has received no consideration for the promise to call off the original bargain, additional consideration is necessary to support a rescission contract.

Discharge by Novation A contractual obligation may also be discharged through novation. A **novation** occurs when both of the parties to a contract agree to substitute a third party for one of the original parties. The requirements of a novation are as follows:

1. A previous valid obligation.
2. An agreement by all parties to a new contract.
3. The extinguishing of the old obligation (discharge of the prior party).
4. A new contract that is valid.

■ **Example 13.9** Union Corporation contracts to sell its pharmaceutical division to British Pharmaceuticals, Ltd. Before the transfer is completed, Union, British Pharmaceuticals, and a third company, Otis Chemicals, execute a new agreement to transfer all of British Pharmaceuticals' rights and duties in the transaction to Otis Chemicals. As long as the new contract is supported by consideration, the novation will discharge the original contract (between Union and British Pharmaceuticals) and replace it with the new contract (between Union and Otis Chemicals). ■

A novation expressly or impliedly revokes and discharges a prior contract. The parties involved may expressly state in the new contract that the old contract is now discharged. If the parties do not expressly discharge the old contract, it will be impliedly discharged if the new contract's terms are inconsistent with the old contract's terms. It is this immediate discharge of the prior contract that distinguishes a novation from both an accord and satisfaction, discussed shortly, and an assignment of all rights.

Discharge by Settlement Agreement A compromise, or settlement agreement, that arises out of a genuine dispute over the obligations under an existing contract will be recognized at law. The agreement will be substituted as a new contract and will either expressly or impliedly revoke and discharge the obligations under the prior contract. In contrast to a novation, a substituted agreement does not involve a third party. Rather, the two original parties to the contract form a different agreement to substitute for the original one.

---

9. The doctrine of anticipatory repudiation first arose in the landmark case of *Hochster v. De La Tour,* 2 Ellis and Blackburn Reports 678 (1853). An English court recognized the delay and expense inherent in a rule requiring a nonbreaching party to wait until the time of performance before suing on an anticipatory repudiation.
10. See UCC 2–204.
11. UCC 2–209(2), (4).

Discharge by Accord and Satisfaction In an accord and satisfaction, the parties agree to accept performance that is different from the performance originally promised. An accord is a contract to perform some act to satisfy an existing contractual duty that is not yet discharged.[12] A satisfaction is the performance of the accord agreement. An accord and its satisfaction discharge the original contractual obligation.

Once the accord has been made, the original obligation is merely suspended until the accord agreement is fully performed (a satisfaction). If it is not performed, the obligee (the one to whom performance is owed) can file a lawsuit based on either the original obligation or the accord. ■ **Example 13.10** Fahreed has a judgment against Ling for $8,000. Later, both parties agree that the judgment can be satisfied by Ling's transfer of his automobile to Fahreed. This agreement to accept the auto in lieu of $8,000 in cash is the accord. If Ling transfers the car to Fahreed, the accord is fully performed (satisfied), and the debt is discharged. If Ling refuses to transfer the car, the accord is breached. Because the original obligation was merely suspended, Fahreed can sue Ling to enforce the original judgment for $8,000 in cash or bring an action for breach of the accord. ■

13–2d Discharge by Operation of Law

Under specified circumstances, contractual duties may be discharged by operation of law. These circumstances include material alteration of the contract, the running of the statute of limitations, bankruptcy, and the impossibility or impracticability of performance.

Material Alteration of the Contract To discourage parties from altering written contracts, the law allows an innocent party to be discharged when the other party has materially altered a written contract without consent. For instance, suppose that a party alters a material term of a contract, such as the stated quantity or price, without the knowledge or consent of the other party. In this situation, the party who was unaware of the alteration can treat the contract as discharged.

Statutes of Limitations As mentioned earlier in this text, statutes of limitations restrict the period during which a party can sue on a particular cause of action. After the applicable limitations period has passed, a suit can no longer be brought. The limitations period for bringing suits for breach of oral contracts usually is two to three years, and for written contracts, four to five years. Parties

generally have ten to twenty years to file for recovery of amounts awarded in judgments, depending on state law.

Lawsuits for breach of a contract for the sale of goods usually must be brought within four years after the cause of action has accrued.[13] A cause of action for a sales contract generally accrues when the breach occurs, even if the aggrieved party is not aware of the breach. A breach of warranty normally occurs when the seller delivers the goods to the buyer. In their original contract, the parties can agree to reduce this four-year period to not less than one year, but they cannot agree to extend it.

Bankruptcy A proceeding in bankruptcy attempts to allocate the debtor's assets to the creditors in a fair and equitable fashion. Once the assets have been allocated, the debtor receives a **discharge in bankruptcy.** A discharge in bankruptcy ordinarily prevents the creditors from enforcing most of the debtor's contracts. Partial payment of a debt after discharge in bankruptcy will not revive the debt.

Impossibility of Performance After a contract has been made, supervening events (such as a fire) may make performance impossible in an objective sense. This is known as **impossibility of performance** and can discharge a contract. The doctrine of impossibility of performance applies only when the parties could not have reasonably foreseen, at the time the contract was formed, the event that rendered performance impossible.

Objective impossibility ("It can't be done") must be distinguished from *subjective impossibility* ("I'm sorry, I simply can't do it"). An example of subjective impossibility occurs when a party cannot deliver goods on time because of freight car shortages or cannot make payment on time because the bank is closed. In effect, in each of these situations the party is saying, "It is impossible for me to perform," not "It is impossible for anyone to perform." Accordingly, such excuses do not discharge a contract, and the nonperforming party is normally held in breach of contract.

When Performance Is Impossible. Three basic types of situations may qualify as grounds for the discharge of contractual obligations based on impossibility of performance:

1. **When one of the parties to a personal contract dies or becomes incapacitated prior to performance.** ■ **Example 13.11** Frederic, a famous dancer,

---

12. *Restatement (Second) of Contracts,* Section 281.

13. Section 2–725 of the UCC contains this four-year limitation period.

contracts with Ethereal Dancing Guild to play a lead-ing role in its new ballet. Before the ballet can be per-formed, Frederic becomes ill and dies. His personal performance was essential to the completion of the contract. Thus, his death discharges the contract and his estate's liability for his nonperformance. ■

2. **When the specific subject matter of the contract is destroyed.** ■ **Example 13.12** A-1 Farm Equipment agrees to sell Gunther the green tractor on its lot and promises to have the tractor ready for Gunther to pick up on Saturday. On Friday night, however, a truck veers off the nearby highway and smashes into the tractor, destroying it beyond repair. Because the con-tract was for this specific tractor, A-1's performance is rendered impossible owing to the accident. ■

3. **When a change in law renders performance ille-gal.** ■ **Example 13.13** Hopper contracts with Play-list, Inc., to create a website through which users can post and share movies, music, and other forms of digital entertainment. Hopper begins working on the new website. Before the site is operational, however, Congress passes the No Online Piracy in Entertain-ment (NOPE) Act. The NOPE Act makes it illegal to operate a website on which copyrighted works are posted without the copyright owners' consent. In this situation, the contract is discharged by opera-tion of law. The purpose of the contract has been rendered illegal, and contract performance is objec-tively impossible. ■

Temporary Impossibility. An occurrence or event that makes performance temporarily impossible operates to

suspend performance until the impossibility ceases. ■ **Case in Point 13.14** During the earliest months of the COVID-19 public health emergency, the governor of Connecticut issued executive orders that closed or severely restricted the operation of various businesses, including bars and restaurants. Did those executive orders affect the enforceability of commercial lease agreements? Downtown Soho, LLC, leased premises for its fine dining restaurant but breached the lease agreement by failing to pay rent during the COVID emergency. A trial court entered judgment for the landlord and awarded $200,308.76 in damages. The defendants appealed. The reviewing court pointed out that there was not in fact a temporary impossibility to run the restaurant because the lease agreement did not prohibit curbside or takeout service. As a matter of law, running a restaurant became highly burdensome financially, "but not factually impossible." The appeals court did, however, reverse the trial court's judgment with respect to the award of damages—they were too high.[14] ■

Sometimes, the lapse of time and the change in cir-cumstances surrounding the contract make it substantially more burdensome for the parties to perform the promised acts. In that situation, the contract is discharged.

It can be difficult to predict how a court will—or should—rule on whether performance is impossible in a particular situation, as discussed in this chapter's Ethics Today feature.

14. *AGW Sono Partners, LLC v. Downtown Soho, LLC,* 273 A.3d 186, 343 Conn. 309 (Sup.Ct. CT 2022).

Ethics Today — When Is Impossibility of Performance a Valid Defense?

The doctrine of impossibility of performance is applied only when the parties could not have reasonably foreseen, at the time the contract was formed, the event or events that rendered performance impossible. In some cases, the courts may seem to go too far in holding that the parties should have foreseen certain events or conditions. Such a holding means that the parties cannot avoid their contractual obligations under the doctrine of impossibility of performance.

Actually, courts today are more likely to allow parties to raise this defense than courts in the past, which rarely excused parties from performance under the impossibility doctrine. Indeed, until the latter part of the nineteenth century, courts were reluctant to

discharge a contract even when performance appeared to be impossible.

Generally, the courts must balance the freedom of parties to contract (and thereby assume the risks involved) against the injustice that may result when certain contractual obligations are enforced. If the courts allowed parties to raise impossibility of performance as a defense to contractual obligations more often, freedom of contract would suffer.

Critical Thinking Why might those entering into contracts be worse off in the long run if the courts increasingly accepted impossibility of performance as a defense?

Commercial Impracticability Courts may also excuse parties from their performance when it becomes much more difficult or expensive than the parties originally contemplated at the time the contract was formed. In one classic case, for instance, a court held that a contract could be discharged because a party would otherwise have had to pay ten times more than the original estimate to excavate a certain amount of gravel.[15]

For someone to invoke the doctrine of **commercial impracticability** successfully, however, the anticipated performance must become significantly more difficult or costly. In addition, the added burden of performing must not have been foreseeable by the parties when the contract was made.

Frustration of Purpose Closely allied with the doctrine of commercial impracticability is the doctrine of **frustration of purpose.** In principle, a contract will be discharged if unforeseen supervening circumstances make it impossible to attain the purpose both parties had in mind when they made the contract. There are some differences between these doctrines, however. Commercial impracticability usually involves an event that increases the cost or difficulty of performance. In contrast, frustration of purpose typically involves an event that decreases the value of what a party receives under the contract.[16]

See Exhibit 13–3 for a summary of the ways in which a contract can be discharged.

---

15. *Mineral Park Land Co. v. Howard,* 172 Cal. 289, 156 P. 458 (1916).

16. See, for instance, *Direct Supply, Inc. v. Specialty Hospitals of America, LLC,* 935 F.Supp.2d 137 (D.C.Cir. 2013).

13–3 Damages

A breach of contract entitles the nonbreaching party to sue for monetary damages. In contract law, damages compensate the nonbreaching party for the loss of the bargain (whereas tort law damages compensate for harm suffered as a result of another's wrongful act). Often, courts say that innocent parties are to be placed in the position they would have occupied had the contract been fully performed.[17]

Realize at the outset, though, that collecting damages through a court judgment requires litigation, which can be expensive and time consuming. Also keep in mind that court judgments are often difficult to enforce, particularly if the breaching party does not have sufficient assets to pay the damages awarded. For these reasons, most parties settle their lawsuits for damages (or other remedies) prior to trial.

13–3a Types of Damages

There are four broad categories of damages:

1. Compensatory (to cover direct losses and costs).
2. Consequential (to cover indirect and foreseeable losses).
3. Punitive (to punish and deter wrongdoing).
4. Nominal (to recognize wrongdoing when no monetary loss is shown).

---

17. *Restatement (Second) of Contracts,* Section 347.

Exhibit 13–3 Contract Discharge

By Operation of Law	By Performance	By Agreement
• Material alteration • Statutes of limitations • Bankruptcy • Impossibility or impracticability of performance • Frustration of purpose	• Complete • Substantial	• Mutual rescission • Novation • Settlement agreement • Accord and satisfaction

By Failure of a Condition	By Breach
If performance is conditional, duty to perform does not become absolute until that condition occurs.	• Material breach • Anticipatory repudiation

Compensatory and punitive damages were discussed in the context of tort law. Here, we look at these types of damages, as well as consequential and nominal damages, in the context of contract law.

Compensatory Damages Damages that compensate the nonbreaching party for the loss of the bargain are known as *compensatory damages*. These damages compensate the injured party only for damages actually sustained and proved to have arisen directly from the loss of the bargain caused by the breach of contract. They simply replace what was lost because of the wrong or damage and, for this reason, are often said to "make the person whole."

■ **Case in Point 13.15** Owens Community College lost its accreditation from the National League for Nursing Accreditation Commission (NLNAC) in July. The college did not inform its nursing students of this development until after classes had started in the fall. Carianne

Baird and sixty-one other students from the program filed a breach of contract suit against Owens.

An Ohio appeals court determined that a contract existed in which the students had paid their fees in exchange for a degree from an NLNAC-accredited institution. By losing that accreditation, Owens breached the contract. The court also recognized the probability that this breach would harm the plaintiffs' career prospects. Therefore, compensatory damages could be determined by measuring the difference between a student's future earnings capacity as a graduate of an NLNAC-accredited nursing college and the student's future earnings capacity as a graduate of now-unaccredited Owens.[18] ■

This chapter's Cybersecurity and the Law feature examines contract formation and compensatory damages issues that arise when a popular fast-food chain suffers a significant data breach.

Cybersecurity and the Law — Arby's Restaurant Group, Inc.

The restaurant chain Arby's was the target of third-party hackers who breached its credit card point-of-sale machines and stole the personal information of hundreds of thousands of customers. A group of these customers sued the company. The plaintiffs claimed that despite being aware of other high-profile data breaches in the business world, Arby's failed to make meaningful improvements in the security of its point-of-sale network. The plaintiffs contended that, in any modern business transaction, there is an implied contract that, in return for a consumer's patronage, the retailer promises to take sufficient measures to protect the consumer's private information.

Arby's countered that the plaintiffs could not unilaterally impose a contractual obligation to safeguard credit card data. The company insisted that its only responsibility was to provide food in return for payment for the food. Rejecting these arguments, a

federal court in Georgia ruled that a reasonable jury could find that an implied contract existed between Arby's and the plaintiffs. When customers use a credit card, the court concluded, they intend to share their financial information only with the merchant. If the customers had known that this information was at risk of being stolen, they likely would have taken their business elsewhere.[a]

Critical Thinking Suppose a court rules that Arby's weak point-of-sale security system does constitute a breach of its contract. What might be some of the compensatory damages due to Arby's customers who had their credit card information stolen by hackers?

a. *In re Arby's Restaurant Group Litigation*, 2018 WL 2128441 (N.D. Georgia—Atlanta Div., 2018). See also *Leonard v. McMenamins, Inc.*, 2022 WL 4017674 (W.D. WA 2022).

Standard Measure. The standard measure of compensatory damages is the difference between the value of the breaching party's promised performance under the contract and the value of the actual performance. This amount is reduced by any loss that the injured party has avoided. See this chapter's Ethics Today feature for possible breach of contract issues

when colleges and universities force their students to stay off campus and to take classes online.

18. *Baird v. Owens Community College*, 2016-Ohio-537 (Ohio Ct.App.,10th Dist. 2016). See also *Iron Vine Security, LLC v. Cygnacom Solutions, Inc.*, 274 A.3d 328 (D.C.Ct.App. 2022).

Ethics Today

Forced Online Classes and Breach of Contract Lawsuits

Many colleges and universities banned in-person learning during the COVID-19 pandemic. No state or federal health agency required or even recommended such actions. (In contrast, many politicians argued in favor of "shutting down" in-person teaching at all levels.) In most instances, full tuition had to be paid even though all learning was online. It is well known in academia that online teaching costs significantly less than in-person teaching. At a minimum, one could argue that students who were not allowed in-person learning should have received a discount on their tuition and fees. Most did not.

A Breach of Contract

A university-to-student legal relationship is grounded in contract. The question remains whether the implied contract between higher education institutions and their students guarantees in-person learning.

Many breach-of-contract lawsuits were brought by students. Most were unsuccessful. Courts usually applied the doctrine of impossibility. Political recommendations (and sometimes outright bans) against in-person learning rendered the contracted-for in-person learning services impossible. Some courts even ruled that universities did not contractually promise in-person learning.

Online University Programs Marketed Differently

Given that online learning programs existed before many universities shut down in-person learning, we know that such online programs were marketed (and continue to be marketed) differently. Typically, they have cost less to students. Additionally, empirical evidence shows that online learning underperforms in comparison to in-person instruction.

Critical Thinking Why did most students who were denied in-person learning nonetheless agree to continue paying full tuition?

Expenses that are caused directly by a breach of contract—such as those incurred to obtain performance from another source—are known as **incidental damages.**

Note that the measure of compensatory damages often varies by type of contract. Certain types of contracts deserve special mention.

Sale of Goods. In a contract for the sale of goods, the usual measure of compensatory damages is an amount equal to the difference between the contract price and the market price.

Sometimes, the buyer breaches when the seller has not yet produced the goods. In that situation, compensatory damages normally equal lost profits on the sale, not the difference between the contract price and the market price.

Sale of Land. Ordinarily, because each parcel of land is unique, the remedy for a seller's breach of a contract for a sale of real estate is specific performance. That is, the buyer is awarded the bargained-for parcel of property. (*Specific performance* will be discussed more fully later in this chapter.) The majority of states follow this rule.

When the buyer is the party in breach, the measure of damages is typically the difference between the contract price and the market price of the land. The same measure is used when specific performance is not available (because the seller has sold the property to someone else, for instance).

A minority of states apply a different rule when the seller breaches the contract, and the breach is not deliberate (not intentional). These states limit the prospective buyer's damages to a refund of any down payment made plus any expenses incurred (such as fees for title searches, attorneys, and escrows). Thus, the minority rule effectively returns purchasers to the positions they occupied prior to the sale, rather than giving them the benefit of the bargain.

Construction Contracts. The measure of compensatory damages in a building or construction contract varies depending on which party breaches and when the breach occurs.

1. **Breach by owner.** The owner may breach at three different stages—before, during, or after performance. If the owner breaches before performance has begun, the contractor can recover only the profits that would have been made on the contract. (Profits equal the total contract price less the cost of materials and labor.) If the owner breaches during performance, the contractor can recover the profits plus the costs incurred in partially constructing the building. If the owner breaches after the construction has been completed, the contractor can recover the entire contract price, plus interest.

2. **Breach by contractor.** When the construction contractor breaches the contract—either by failing to

begin construction or by stopping work partway through the project—the measure of damages is the cost of completion. The cost of completion includes reasonable compensation for any delay in performance. If the contractor finishes late, the measure of damages is the loss of use.

■ **Case in Point 13.16** To remodel his home in Connecticut, Richard Viola hired J. S. Benson of J. S. Benson Woodworking & Design as his contractor. Over a period of five years, Viola paid Benson more than $500,000 to fabricate and install windows and doors, nearly $50,000 for the purchase of lumber, and $10,000 to ship and store the lumber, as well as $111,000 toward the contract price. Nevertheless, Benson failed to complete the project and would not give Viola the lumber that he had purchased despite repeated requests. Viola eventually sued Benson for breaching the contract. A state court held that Benson had breached the contract and ordered him to pay $848,000 in damages. The damages awarded included additional amounts to reimburse Viola for attorneys' fees, rental costs (because he was unable to live in the home), and property taxes.[19] ■

3. **Breach by both owner and contractor.** When the performance of both parties—the construction contractor and the owner—falls short of what their contract required, the courts attempt to strike a fair balance in awarding damages.

Consequential Damages Foreseeable damages that result from a party's breach of contract are called **consequential damages,** or special damages. They differ from compensatory damages in that they are caused by special circumstances beyond the contract itself. They flow from the consequences, or results, of a breach. For the nonbreaching party to recover consequential damages, the breaching party must have known (or had reason to know) that special circumstances would cause the nonbreaching party to suffer an additional loss.[20]

When a seller fails to deliver goods, knowing that the buyer is planning to use or resell those goods immediately, a court may award consequential damages for the loss of profits from the planned resale. ■ **Example 13.17** Javed contracts to buy a certain quantity of Quench, a specialty sports drink, from Nathan. Nathan knows that Javed has contracted with Renata to resell and ship the Quench within hours of its receipt. The beverage will then be sold to fans attending the Super Bowl. Nathan fails to deliver the Quench on time. Javed can recover the consequential damages—the loss of profits from the planned resale to Renata—caused by the nondelivery. (If Javed instead purchases Quench from another vendor and resells them to Renata, he can recover only compensatory damages for any difference between the contract price and the market price.) ■

Punitive Damages Punitive damages are very seldom awarded in lawsuits for breach of contract. Because punitive damages are designed to punish a wrongdoer and set an example to deter similar conduct in the future, they have no legitimate place in contract law. A contract is simply a civil relationship between the parties. The law may compensate one party for the loss of the bargain—no more and no less. When a person's actions cause both a breach of contract and a tort (such as fraud), however, punitive damages may be available.

Nominal Damages When no actual damage or financial loss results from a breach of contract and only a technical injury is involved, the court may award **nominal damages** to the innocent party. Awards of nominal damages are often small, such as one dollar, but they do establish that the defendant acted wrongfully. Most lawsuits for nominal damages are brought as a matter of principle under the theory that a breach has occurred and some damages must be imposed regardless of actual loss.

13–3b Liquidated Damages Versus Penalties

A **liquidated damages** provision in a contract specifies that a certain dollar amount is to be paid in the event of a future default or breach of contract. (*Liquidated* means determined, settled, or fixed.)

Liquidated damages differ from penalties. Like liquidated damages, a **penalty** specifies a certain amount to be paid in the event of a default or breach of contract. Unlike liquidated damages, it is designed to penalize the breaching party, not to make the innocent party whole.

Liquidated damages provisions usually are enforceable. In contrast, if a court finds that a provision calls for a penalty, the agreement as to the amount will not be enforced. Recovery will be limited to actual damages.

---

19. *Viola v. J.S. Benson,* 2017 WL 2817404 (Conn.Super.Ct. 2017). See also *Gravina Siding and Windows Company v. Gravina,* 516 P.3d 37, 2022 COA 50 (Co.Ct.App., Div. 1 2022).

20. This rule was first enunciated in *Hadley v. Baxendale,* 156 Eng.Rep. 145 (1854).

Enforceability To determine if a particular provision is for liquidated damages or for a penalty, a court must answer two questions:

1. When the contract was entered into, was it apparent that damages would be difficult to estimate in the event of a breach?
2. Was the amount set as damages a reasonable estimate and not excessive?

If the answers to both questions are yes, the provision normally will be enforced. If either answer is no, the provision usually will not be enforced.

In the following Spotlight Case, the court had to decide whether a clause in a contract was an enforceable liquidated damages provision or an unenforceable penalty.

Spotlight on Liquidated Damages

Case 13.3 Kent State University v. Ford

Court of Appeals of Ohio, Eleventh District, Portage County, 2015-Ohio-41, 26 N.E.3d 868 (2015).

Background and Facts Gene Ford signed a five-year contract with Kent State University in Ohio to work as the head coach for the men's basketball team. The contract provided that if Ford quit before the end of the term, he would pay liquidated damages to the school. The amount was to equal his salary ($300,000) multiplied by the number of years remaining on the contract. Laing Kennedy, Kent State's athletic director, told Ford that the contract would be renegotiated within a few years. Four years before the contract expired, however, Ford left Kent State and began to coach for Bradley University at an annual salary of $700,000. Kent State filed a suit in an Ohio state court against Ford, alleging breach of contract. The court enforced the liquidated damages clause and awarded the university $1.2 million. Ford appealed, arguing that the liquidated damages clause in his employment contract was an unenforceable penalty.

In the Language of the Court

Diane V. GRENDELL, J. [Judge]

* * * *

* * * The parties agreed on an amount of damages, stated in clear terms in Ford's * * * employment contract. * * * It is apparent that such damages were difficult, if not impossible, to determine. * * * The departure of a university's head basketball coach may result in a decrease in ticket sales, impact the ability to successfully recruit players and community support for the team, and require a search for both a new coach and additional coaching staff. Many of these damages cannot be easily measured or proven. This is especially true given the nature of how such factors may change over the course of different coaches' tenures with a sports program or team.

* * * *

* * * Kennedy's statements to Ford that the contract would be renegotiated within a few years made it clear that Kent State desired Ford to have long-term employment, which was necessary to establish the stability in the program that would benefit recruitment, retention of assistant coaching staff, and community participation and involvement. The breach of the contract impacted all of these areas.

* * * *

Regarding the alleged unreasonableness of the damages, * * * based on the record, we find that the damages were reasonable. * * * Finding a coach of a similar skill and experience level as Ford, which was gained based partially on the investment of Kent State in his development, would have an increased cost. This is evident from the fact that Ford was able to more than double his yearly salary when hired by Bradley University. The salary Ford earned at Bradley shows the loss of market value in coaching experienced by Kent State, $400,000 per year, for four years. Although this may not have been known

at the time the contract was executed, it could have been anticipated, and was presumably why Kent State wanted to renegotiate the contract * * * . There was also an asserted decrease in ticket sales, costs associated with the trips for the coaching search, and additional potential sums that may be expended.
* * * *

As discussed extensively above, there was justification for seeking liquidated damages to compensate for Kent State's losses, and, thus, there was a valid compensatory purpose for including the clause. * * * Given all of the circumstances and facts in this case, and the consideration of the factors above, we cannot find that the liquidated damages clause was a penalty.

Decision and Remedy A state intermediate appellate court affirmed the lower court's award. At the time Ford's contract was entered into, ascertaining the damages resulting from a breach was "difficult, if not impossible." The court found, "based on the record, . . . that the damages were reasonable." Thus, the clause was not a penalty—it had "a valid compensatory purpose."

Critical Thinking
- **Cultural** How does a college basketball team's record of wins and losses, and its ranking in its conference, support the court's decision in this case?

13–4 Equitable Remedies for Contract Breach

Sometimes, damages are an inadequate remedy for a breach of contract. In these situations, the nonbreaching party may ask the court for an equitable remedy. Equitable remedies include rescission and restitution, specific performance, and reformation.

13–4a Rescission and Restitution

Rescission is essentially an action to undo, or terminate, a contract—to return the contracting parties to the positions they occupied prior to the transaction.[21] When fraud, a mistake, duress, undue influence, misrepresentation, or lack of capacity to contract is present, unilateral rescission is available. Rescission may also be available by statute. The failure of one party to perform entitles the other party to rescind the contract. The rescinding party must give prompt notice to the breaching party.

Rescission of a contract based on a breach is appropriate where the breach is found to be material and willful. A party seeking rescission must also show that the contracting parties can be restored to their positions before the contract was formed.

Generally, to rescind a contract, both parties must make **restitution** to each other by returning goods, property, or funds previously conveyed.[22] If the property or goods can be returned, they must be. If the goods or property have been consumed, restitution must be made in an equivalent dollar amount.

Essentially, restitution involves the plaintiff's recapture of a benefit conferred on the defendant that has unjustly enriched that party. ■ **Example 13.18** Katie contracts with Mikhail to design a house for her. Katie pays Mikhail $9,000 and agrees to make two more payments of $9,000 (for a total of $27,000) as the design progresses. The next day, Mikhail calls Katie and tells her that he has taken a position with a large architectural firm in another state and cannot design the house. Katie decides to hire another architect that afternoon. Katie can obtain restitution of the $9,000. ■

13–4b Specific Performance

The equitable remedy of **specific performance** calls for the performance of the act promised in the contract. This remedy is attractive to a nonbreaching party because it provides the exact bargain promised in the contract. It also avoids some of the problems inherent in a suit for damages, such as collecting a judgment and arranging another contract. In addition, the actual performance may be more valuable than the monetary damages.

---

21. The rescission discussed here is unilateral rescission, in which only one party wants to undo the contract. In mutual rescission, both parties agree to undo the contract. Mutual rescission discharges the contract, whereas unilateral rescission generally is available as a remedy for breach of contract.

22. *Restatement (Second) of Contracts*, Section 370.

Normally, however, specific performance will not be granted unless the party's legal remedy (monetary damages) is inadequate.[23] For this reason, contracts for the sale of goods rarely qualify for specific performance. The legal remedy—monetary damages—is ordinarily adequate in such situations because substantially identical goods can be bought or sold in the market. Only if the goods are unique will a court grant specific performance. For instance, paintings, sculptures, or rare books or coins are so unique that monetary damages will not enable a buyer to obtain substantially identical substitutes in the market.

Sale of Land A court may grant specific performance to a buyer in an action for a breach of contract involving the sale of land. In this situation, the legal remedy of monetary damages may not compensate the buyer adequately. After all, every parcel of land is unique: The same land in the same location obviously cannot be obtained elsewhere. Only when specific performance is unavailable (such as when the seller has sold the property to someone else) will monetary damages be awarded instead.

A seller of land can also seek specific performance of the contract. ■ **Case in Point 13.19** Harmony Development agreed to sell seven acres of a planned subdivision to Jerry Davis for $1.5 million. The contract required Harmony to spend $1.85 million improving the property so that Davis could construct a health club on it. After Harmony made the improvements, Davis informed the company that the subdivision no longer "fit" with his plans and refused to complete the purchase. Harmony sued for breach of contract. The Wyoming Supreme Court granted specific performance, calling the remedy "a means of compelling [Davis] to do precisely what he should have done without being coerced by a court."[24] ■

Contracts for Personal Services Contracts for personal services require one party to work personally for another party. Courts generally refuse to grant specific performance of personal-service contracts. One reason is that to order a party to perform personal services against

that party's will amounts to a type of involuntary servitude.[25]

13–4c Reformation

Reformation is an equitable remedy used when the parties have imperfectly expressed their agreement in writing. Reformation allows a court to rewrite the contract to reflect the parties' true intentions.

Fraud or Mutual Mistake Is Present Courts order reformation most often when fraud or mutual mistake (for example, a clerical error) is present. Typically, a party seeks reformation so that some other remedy may then be pursued.

■ **Example 13.20** If Carson contracts to buy a fork-lift from Yoshie but their contract mistakenly refers to a crane, a mutual mistake has occurred. Accordingly, a court can reform the contract so that it conforms to the parties' intentions and accurately refers to the forklift being sold. ■

Written Contract Incorrectly States the Parties' Oral Agreement A court will also reform a contract when two parties enter into a binding oral contract but later make an error when they attempt to put the terms into writing. Normally, a court will allow into evidence the correct terms of the oral contract, thereby reforming the written contract.

Covenants Not to Compete Courts also may reform contracts that contain a written covenant not to compete. Such covenants are often included in contracts for the sale of ongoing businesses and in employment contracts. The agreements restrict the area and time in which one party can directly compete with the other party.

A covenant not to compete may have a valid and legitimate purpose but may impose unreasonable area or time restraints. In such instances, some courts will reform the restraints by making them reasonable and will then enforce the entire contract as reformed. Other courts will throw out the entire restrictive covenant as illegal. Thus, when businesspersons create restrictive covenants, they must make sure that the restrictions imposed are reasonable.

In the following case, two former employees of a real estate title company attempted to start a competing business.

---

23. *Restatement (Second) of Contracts,* Section 359.
24. *Davis v. Harmony Development LLC,* 2020 WY 39, 460 P.3d 230 (S.Ct.WY 2020).
25. Involuntary servitude, or slavery, is contrary to the public policy expressed in the Thirteenth Amendment to the U.S. Constitution. A court can, however, enter an order (injunction) prohibiting a person who breached a personal-service contract from engaging in similar contracts for a period of time in the future.

Combs v. Elite Title Company, Inc.

Court of Appeals of Arkansas, Division II, 646 S.W.3d 230, 2022 Ark.App. 231 (2022).

In the Language of the Court

RAYMOND R. ABRAMSON, J.

This is an * * * appeal of an amended preliminary injunction enjoining appellants Chance Combs and Preston Long from conducting a similar business as their former employer, appellee Elite Title Company ("Elite"). Appellants assert that we should * * * thereby find that the noncompete provision is unenforceable in its entirety because (1) there is no valid protectable interest of the employer since the agreement merely protects against ordinary competition; (2) the circuit court is prohibited from enforcing the agreement other than as specifically written under common-law standards; and (3) the covenant is overly broad geographically because it includes areas outside those of Elite's trade area. We disagree and affirm.

Elite is a title company that has been in business since 1994. * * * Elite is differentiated from other title companies because of its trade secrets. One of Elite's confidential trade secrets is its title plant. The title plant is a proprietary-software program owned by Elite that indexes the first deed that is filed of record in the county and goes forward to the present. It allows Elite to conduct searches quickly and efficiently. Elite maintains it is one of its largest assets with a seven-figure value.

Elite markets its title plant and the availability of those services to customers on its website. Elite does not let other title companies use its title plant. Appellant Combs admitted that the database containing the title plant could be considered a trade secret. Elite requires employees to keep information about the title plant confidential, and they must have a password to access the title plant. Elite's pricing and customers are also Elite's confidential trade secrets.

* * * *

Elite also requires employees to sign a confidentiality and noncompetition agreement when they are hired to protect Elite and its confidential trade secrets. In March 2013, Elite hired appellant Long to work as a closing coordinator, and he eventually became a closing agent. Long was Ms. Burg's stepson for many years. As part of his employment, Long entered into a confidentiality and noncompetition agreement with Elite. * * *

* * * *

In April 2015, Elite hired appellant Combs to serve as in-house legal counsel after he had graduated from law school. After failing the bar exam, Elite trained Combs in the title department and helped him obtain his title-agent license. A year later, Combs passed the bar exam and became Elite's in-house counsel in addition to being a title agent. As part of his employment, Combs entered into a confidentiality and noncompetition agreement with Elite. * * *

* * * *

Combs and Long each were head of their departments and had significant knowledge of all of Elite's trade secrets and how Elite is run. They had access to Elite's title plant and pricing. Appellants had to log in with a password to be able to access the customers' files and paperwork.

Both appellants agreed to sign and did sign the confidentiality and noncompetition agreements ("Agreements"), which prohibit employees of Elite from working for a direct competitor of Elite and/or soliciting current and former customers of Elite during their employment and for a period of two years after their employment ends. The Agreements also prohibit using or disclosing Elite's confidential information and trade secrets. * * *

* * * Elite discovered appellants were working for a competitor called Apex Title in Rogers, Arkansas. Apex Title was located only in Oklahoma, but it opened a Rogers location around October 8, 2020. Combs had a 10 percent ownership interest in the Apex Rogers location, and Long had a 30 percent ownership interest.

Long testified that he began discussions with Apex about going to work for the company in the late summer of 2020. After appellants resigned from Elite, significant Elite business was being transferred to Apex Title. * * *

Appellants admitted they violated the noncompetition agreements. Elite sought the injunction as a result of the violations of the Agreements and to protect Elite's trade secrets. After a hearing held on April 15, 2021, the circuit court found that the appellants lacked credibility—specifically, the court could not take them at their word, and the appellants' testimony conflicted with one another. * * *

The circuit court entered its preliminary injunction on May 3, 2021, * * *. The amended preliminary injunction states: "The Court finds Elite has a protectable interest in its pricing strategies, customer lists, customer relationships and its title plant. The Agreement is reasonable with regard to its two (2) year term and its geographic scope. Therefore, the Agreements are valid and enforceable." The amended preliminary injunction further states:

The risk of irreparable harm is supported by the transfer of client business from Elite to Defendants.

Case 13.4 Continues

Case 13.4 Continued

A likelihood of success on the merits is supported by the Defendants' admissions regarding their violations of the terms of the Agreements, * * *.

* * * *

* * *Appellants claim that Elite's title plant and pricing information are not protectable business interests.

However, appellants fail to cite any authority or convincing legal argument for their baseless assertion that Elite's title plant and pricing plans are not protectable interests. * * *

* * * *

"The enforceability of a covenant not to compete depends upon its reasonableness in light of the particular facts of the case." "A reasonably drawn covenant not to compete is an effective means by which a principal may protect its customers and its confidential information from appropriation and use by former agents or competitors."

* * * *

For all the reasons outlined above, we hold that the circuit court did not clearly err in finding that Elite has a protectable interest in its pricing strategies, customer lists, customer relationships, and title plant; that the Agreements are reasonable with regard to the geographic scope; and that the Agreements are valid and enforceable. The circuit court did not abuse its discretion in holding that Elite demonstrated a likelihood of success on the merits of its complaint and irreparable harm in the absence of the preliminary injunction. Thus, we affirm.

Affirmed.

Legal Reasoning Questions

1. Combs and Long, the appellants, claimed that the noncompete provision that they agreed to was unenforceable. What was their argument?
2. Why did Elite Title Company argue that its so-called title plant constituted a trade secret?
3. When did Elite Title Company require its employees to sign its confidentiality and noncompetition agreement?

Exhibit 13–4 Remedies for Breach of Contract

Exhibit 13–4 graphically summarizes the remedies that are available to the nonbreaching party.

13-5 Contract Provisions Limiting Remedies

A contract may include provisions stating that no damages can be recovered for certain types of breaches or that damages will be limited to a maximum amount. A contract may also provide that the only remedy for breach is replacement, repair, or refund of the purchase price. Finally, a contract may provide that one party can seek injunctive relief if the other party breaches the contract. Provisions stating that no damages can be recovered are called *exculpatory clauses*. Provisions that affect the availability of certain remedies are called *limitation-of-liability clauses*.

The Uniform Commercial Code (UCC) provides that in a contract for the sale of goods, remedies can be limited. We will examine the UCC provisions on limitations of remedies in a later chapter in the context of contracts for the sale or lease of goods.

Whether a limitation-of-liability clause in a contract will be enforced depends on the type of breach that is excused by the provision. Normally, a provision excluding liability for fraudulent or intentional injury will not be enforced. Likewise, a clause excluding liability for illegal acts, acts that are contrary to public policy, or violations of law will not be enforced. A clause that excludes liability for negligence may be enforced in some situations when the parties have roughly equal bargaining positions.

Practice and Review: Contract Performance, Breach, and Remedies

Val's Foods signs a contract to buy 1,500 pounds of basil from Sun Farms, a small organic herb grower, as long as an independent organization inspects the crop and certifies that it contains no pesticide or herbicide residue. Val's has a contract with several restaurant chains to supply pesto and intends to use Sun Farms' basil in the pesto to fulfill these contracts. While Sun Farms is preparing to harvest the basil, an unexpected hailstorm destroys half the crop. Sun Farms attempts to purchase additional basil from other farms, but it is late in the season, and the price is twice the normal market price. Sun Farms is too small to absorb this cost and immediately notifies Val's that it will not fulfill the contract. Using the information presented in the chapter, answer the following questions.

1. Suppose that the basil does not pass the chemical-residue inspection. Which concept discussed in the chapter might allow Val's to refuse to perform the contract in this situation?
2. Under which legal theory or theories might Sun Farms claim that its obligation under the contract has been discharged by operation of law? Discuss fully.
3. Suppose that Sun Farms contacts every basil grower in the country and buys the last remaining chemical-free basil anywhere. Nevertheless, Sun Farms is able to ship only 1,475 pounds to Val's. Would this fulfill Sun Farms' obligations to Val's? Why or why not?
4. Now suppose that Sun Farms sells its operations to Happy Valley Farms. As a part of the sale, all three parties agree that Happy Valley will provide the basil as stated under the original contract. What is this type of agreement called?

Debate This . . .   *The doctrine of commercial impracticability should be abolished.*

Terms and Concepts

anticipatory repudiation 270	frustration of purpose 274	reformation 280
bilateral mistake 263	impossibility of performance 272	restitution 279
breach of contract 270	incidental damages 276	specific performance 279
commercial impracticability 274	liquidated damages 277	tender 267
condition 267	mutual rescission 271	undue influence 266
consequential damages 277	nominal damages 277	unilateral mistake 262
discharge 267	novation 271	voluntary consent 262
discharge in bankruptcy 272	penalty 277	
duress 267	performance 267	

Issue Spotters

1. Ready Foods contracts to buy two hundred carloads of frozen pizzas from Stealth Distributors. Before Ready or Stealth starts performing, can the parties call off the deal? What if Stealth has already shipped the pizzas? Explain your answers. (See *Performance and Discharge.*)
2. Greg contracts to build a storage shed for Haney, who pays Greg in advance, but Greg completes only half the work. Haney pays Ipswich $500 to finish the shed. If Haney sues Greg, what will be the measure of recovery? (See *Damages.*)

• **Check your answers to the Issue Spotters against the answers provided in Appendix B at the end of this text.**

Business Scenarios and Case Problems

13–1. Conditions of Performance. The Caplans contract with Faithful Construction, Inc., to build a house for them for $360,000. The specifications state "all plumbing bowls and fixtures . . . to be Crane brand." The Caplans leave on vacation, and during their absence, Faithful is unable to buy and install Crane plumbing fixtures. Instead, Faithful installs Kohler brand fixtures, an equivalent in the industry. On completion of the building contract, the Caplans inspect the work, discover the substitution, and refuse to accept the house, claiming Faithful has breached the conditions set forth in the specifications. Discuss fully the Caplans' claim. (See *Performance and Discharge.*)

13–2. Undue Influence. Juan is an elderly man who lives with his nephew, Samuel. Juan is totally dependent on Samuel's support. Samuel tells Juan that unless he transfers a tract of land he owns to Samuel for a price 35 percent below its market value, Samuel will no longer support and take care of him. Juan enters into the contract. Discuss fully whether Juan can set aside this contract. (See *Voluntary Consent.*)

13–3. Material Breach. The Northeast Independent School District in Bexar County, Texas, hired STR Constructors, Ltd., to renovate a middle school. STR subcontracted the tile work in the school's kitchen to Newman Tile, Inc. (NTI). The project had already fallen behind schedule. As a result, STR allowed other workers to walk over and damage the newly installed tile before it had cured, forcing NTI to constantly redo its work. Despite NTI's requests for payment, STR remitted only half the amount due under their contract. When the school district refused to accept the kitchen, including the tile work, STR told NTI to quickly make repairs. A week later, STR terminated their contract. Did STR breach the contract with NTI? Explain. [*STR Constructors, Ltd. v. Newman Tile, Inc.*, 395 S.W.3d 383 (Tex. App.—El Paso 2013)] (See *Performance and Discharge.*)

13–4. Discharge by Operation of Law. Dr. Jake Lambert signed an employment agreement with Baptist Health Services, Inc., to provide cardiothoracic surgery services to Baptist Memorial Hospital–North Mississippi, Inc., in Oxford, Mississippi. Complaints about Lambert's behavior arose almost immediately. He was evaluated by a team of doctors and psychologists, who diagnosed him as suffering from obsessive-compulsive personality disorder and concluded that he was unfit to practice medicine. Based on this conclusion, the hospital suspended his staff privileges. Citing the suspension, Baptist Health Services claimed that Lambert had breached his employment contract. What is Lambert's best defense to this claim? Explain. [*Baptist Memorial Hospital–North Mississippi, Inc. v. Lambert*, 157 So.3d 109 (Miss.App. 2015)] (See *Performance and Discharge.*)

13–5. Business Case Problem With Sample Answer— Limitation-of-Liability Clauses. Mia Eriksson was a seventeen-year-old competitor in horseback-riding events. Her riding coach was Kristi Nunnink. Eriksson signed an agreement that released Nunnink from all liability except for damages caused by Nunnink's "direct, willful and wanton negligence." During an event at Galway Downs in Temecula, California, Eriksson's horse struck a hurdle. She fell from the horse and the horse fell on her, causing her death. Her parents, Karan and Stan Eriksson, filed a suit in a California state court against Nunnink for wrongful death. Is the limitation-of-liability agreement that Eriksson signed likely to be enforced in her parents' case? If so, how will it affect their claim? Explain. [*Eriksson v. Nunnink*, 233 Cal.App.4th 708, 183 Cal.Rptr.3d 234 (4 Dist. 2015)] (See *Contract Provisions Limiting Remedies.*)

- **For a sample answer to Problem 13–5, go to Appendix C at the end of this text.**

13–6. Damages. Robert Morris was a licensed insurance agent working for his father's independent insurance agency when he contacted Farmers Insurance Exchange in Alabama about becoming a Farmers agent. According to Farmers' company policy, Morris was an unsuitable candidate due to his relationship with his father's agency. But no Farmers representative told Morris of this policy, and none of the documents that he signed expressed it. Farmers trained Morris and appointed him its agent. About three years later, however, Farmers terminated the appointment for "a conflict of interest because his father was in the insurance business." Morris filed a suit in an Alabama state court against Farmers, claiming that he had been fraudulently induced to leave his father's agency to work for Farmers. If Morris was successful, what type of damages was he most likely awarded? What was the measure of damages? Discuss. [*Farmers Insurance Exchange v. Morris*, 228 So.3d 971 (Ala. 2016)] (See *Damages.*)

13–7. Substantial Performance. Melissa Gallegos bought a used 1996 Saturn automobile for $2,155 from Raul Quintero, doing business as JR's Motors. Their written contract focused primarily on the transfer of physical possession of the vehicle and did not mention who would pay the taxes on the sale. Gallegos paid Quintero $2,200, believing that this amount included the taxes. When she asked him for the title to the vehicle, he told her that only the state could provide the title and only after the taxes were paid. Quintero added that they had orally agreed Gallegos would pay the taxes. Without the title, Gallegos could not obtain license plates and legally operate the vehicle. More than six years later, she filed a suit in a Texas state court against Quintero, alleging breach of contract. Did Quintero substantially perform his obligation under the contract? Explain. [*Gallegos v. Quintero*, 2018 WL 655539 (Tex.App.—Corpus Christi-Edinburg 2018)] (See *Performance and Discharge.*)

13–8. Reformation. Dr. John Holm signed a two-year employment agreement with Gateway Anesthesia Associates, PLLC. During negotiations for the agreement, Gateway's president, Dr. Jon Nottingham, told Holm that on completion of the contract he would become a partner in the firm and that during the term he would be paid "like a partner." The written agreement did not reflect this promise—the contract read that Holm would be paid based on "net collections" for his services and did not state that he would become a partner. Later, Gateway told Holm that it did not intend to make him a partner. Holm filed a complaint in an Arizona state court against Gateway, alleging breach. Before the trial, Holm filed a motion to reform the contract to express what he had been told. Nottingham did not dispute Holm's account. What is the basis for the reformation of a contract? Is it appropriate in this case? Why or why not? [*Holm v. Gateway Anesthesia Associates, PLLC,* 2018 WL 770503 (Ariz.Ct.App. Div. 1 2018)] (See *Equitable Remedies for Contract Breach.*)

13–9. Discharge by Novation. Atlantic Pacific Scaffolding Equipment (AT-PAC) and Gulf South Services, Inc., (GSSI) engaged in business dealings for over a decade. GSSI eventually stopped making payments on monies owed. ATPAC sent GSSI a statement reflecting a balance owed totaling over $1.5 million. The two businesses negotiated an agreement in which GSSI would pay about $1.5 million to purchase over 100,000 pieces of leased equipment. AT-PAC filed a suit because GSSI did not follow through with that agreement. GSSI then agreed to pay AT-PAC $35,000 per month in three payments totaling $105,000. The trial court concluded that the debt GSSI owed for rentals was thereby extinguished by a novation. On appeal, AT-PAC claimed that the trial court erred in finding a novation. Did

the supposed novation satisfy all necessary elements? Should the appeals court accept the trial court's decision? [*Atlantic Pacific Equipment, Inc. v. Gulf South Services, Inc.,* 342 So.3d 898 (Ct.App. LA, 1st Cir. 2022)] (See *Discharge by Agreement.*)

13–10. A Question of Ethics—The IDDR Approach and Fraudulent Misrepresentation. Data Consulting Group contracted with Weston Medsurg Center, PLLC, a healthcare facility in Charlotte, North Carolina, to install, maintain, and manage Weston's computers and software. At about the same time, Ginger Blackwood began to work for Weston as a medical billing and coding specialist. Soon, she was submitting false time reports and converting Weston documents and data to her own purposes. At Blackwood's request, Data Consulting manager Nasko Dinev removed evidence of Blackwood's actions from her work computer. [*Weston Medsurg Center, PLLC v. Blackwood,* 795 S.E.2d 829 (N.C.Ct. App. 2017)] (See *Voluntary Consent.*)

(a) What should Weston do when it learns of these activities? With respect to this situation, identify and consider the firm's primary ethical dilemma using the IDDR approach.

(b) Suppose that despite Dinev's efforts, Weston is later able to recover the data that was removed from Blackwood's work computer. How might this affect Weston's choices? Discuss.

Time-Limited Group Assignment

13–11. Breach and Remedies. Frances Morelli agreed to sell Judith Bucklin a house in Rhode Island for $177,000. The sale was supposed to be closed by September 1. The contract included a provision that "if Seller is unable to convey good, clear, insurable, and marketable title, Buyer shall have the option to: (a) accept such title as Seller is able to convey without reduction of the Purchase Price, or (b) cancel this Agreement and receive a return of all Deposits."

An examination of the public records revealed that the house did not have marketable title. Bucklin offered Morelli additional time to resolve the problem, and the closing did not occur as scheduled. Morelli decided that "the deal was over" and offered to return the deposit. Bucklin refused and, in mid-October, decided to exercise her

option to accept the house without marketable title. She notified Morelli, who did not respond. She then filed a lawsuit against Morelli in a state court. (See *Performance and Discharge* and *Damages.*)

(a) One group will discuss whether Morelli breached the contract and will decide in whose favor the court should rule.

(b) A second group will assume that Morelli did breach the contract and will determine what the appropriate remedy is in this situation.

(c) A third group will list some possible reasons why Bucklin wanted to go through with the transaction even when faced with not receiving marketable title.

Chapter 14

Sales and Lease Contracts

When we turn to contracts for the sale and lease of goods, we move away from common law principles and into the area of statutory law. State statutory law governing sales and lease transactions is based on the Uniform Commercial Code (UCC), which has been adopted as law by all of the states.[1] Of all the attempts to produce a uniform body of laws relating to commercial transactions in the United States, none has been as successful as the UCC.

The goal of the UCC is to simplify and to streamline commercial transactions. The UCC allows parties to form sales and lease contracts, including those entered into online, without observing the same degree of formality used in forming other types of contracts.

Today, businesses often engage in sales and lease transactions on a global scale. The United Nations Convention on Contracts for the International Sale of Goods (CISG) governs international sales contracts. The CISG is a model uniform law that applies only when a nation has adopted it, just as the UCC applies only to the extent that it has been adopted by a state.

---

1. Louisiana has not adopted Articles 2 and 2A, however.

14–1 The Scope of Articles 2 (Sales) and 2A (Leases)

Article 2 of the UCC sets forth the requirements for sales contracts, as well as the duties and obligations of the parties involved in the sales contract. Article 2A covers similar issues for lease contracts. Bear in mind, however, that the parties to sales or lease contracts are free to agree to terms different from those stated in the UCC.

14–1a Article 2—The Sale of Goods

Article 2 of the UCC (as adopted by state statutes) governs **sales contracts,** or contracts for the sale of goods. To facilitate commercial transactions, Article 2 modifies some of the common law contract requirements discussed in the previous chapters.

To the extent that it has not been modified by the UCC, however, the common law of contracts also applies to sales contracts. In other words, the common law requirements for a valid contract—agreement consideration, capacity, and legality—are also applicable to sales contracts.

In general, the rule is that whenever a conflict arises between a common law contract rule and the state statutory law based on the UCC, the UCC controls. Thus, when a UCC provision addresses a certain issue, the UCC rule governs. When the UCC is silent, the common law governs. The relationship between general contract law and the law governing sales of goods is illustrated in Exhibit 14–1.

In regard to Article 2, keep two points in mind.

1. Article 2 deals with the sale of goods. It does not deal with real property (real estate), services, or intangible property such as stocks and bonds. Thus, if the subject matter of a dispute is goods, the UCC governs. If it is real estate or services, the common law applies.

2. In some situations, the rules can vary depending on whether the buyer or the seller is a merchant.

We look now at how the UCC defines a *sale, goods,* and *merchant status.*

What Is a Sale? The UCC defines a **sale** as "the passing of title [evidence of ownership rights] from the seller to the buyer for a price" [UCC 2–106(1)]. The price may be payable in cash or in other goods or services. ■ **Case in Point 14.1** Blasini, Inc., contracted to buy the business assets of the Attic Bar & Grill in Omaha, Nebraska, from Cheran Investments, LLC. Blasini obtained insurance and was making monthly payments

Exhibit 14–1   The Law Governing Contracts

This exhibit graphically illustrates the relationship between general contract law and statutory law (UCC Articles 2 and 2A) governing contracts for the sale and lease of goods. Sales contracts are not governed exclusively by Article 2 of the UCC but are also governed by general contract law whenever it is relevant and has not been modified by the UCC.

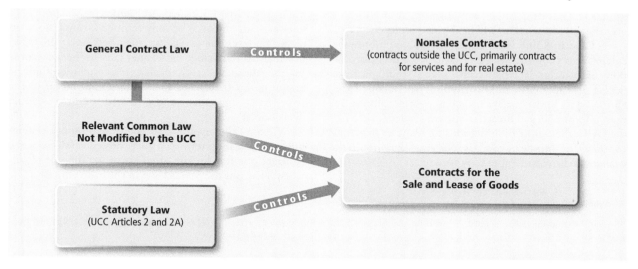

on the assets, which included furniture and equipment. A fire broke out and damaged the assets involved in the sale. Because the purchase price had not yet been fully paid, a dispute arose concerning who was entitled to the insurance proceeds for the damage.

Nautilus Insurance Company asked a Nebraska state court to resolve the matter. Ultimately, a state appellate court held that the sale of the Attic's business assets involved goods, and thus the agreement was governed by the UCC. Under UCC 2–401, title to the goods passed to Blasini at the time of contract formation, regardless of whether the entire purchase price had been paid. Therefore, Blasini was entitled to the insurance proceeds.[2] ■

What Are Goods?   To be characterized as a good, an item of property must be tangible, and it must be movable. **Tangible property** has physical existence—it can be touched or seen. **Intangible property**—such as corporate stocks and bonds, patents and copyrights, and ordinary contract rights—has only conceptual existence and thus does not come under Article 2. A movable item can be carried from place to place. Hence, real estate is excluded from Article 2.

Goods Associated With Real Estate.   Goods associated with real estate often do fall within the scope of Article 2 [UCC 2–107]. For instance, a contract for the sale of minerals, oil, or gas is a contract for the sale of goods if severance, or separation, is to be made by the seller. Similarly, a contract for the sale of growing crops or timber to be cut is a contract for the sale of goods regardless of who severs them from the land.

■ **Case in Point 14.2**   Raymond M. Gee and Adam A. Martin assisted Delta Speir Plantation LLC in obtaining a large tract of land in South Carolina. Gee and Martin alleged that they were entitled to two payments, one of which would be 20 percent of the proceeds of Delta Speir's sale of timber rights to a third party. A dispute arose over whether the timber contract was for the sale of goods. The appellate court pointed out that a contract for the sale of timber to be cut is always a contract for the sale of goods. Further, the appellate court argued that it does not matter whether "the subject matter [timber] is to be severed by the buyer or by the seller even though it forms part of the realty at the time of contracting." Thus, when Delta Speir sold the timber to the third party, a contract for the sale of goods occurred.[3] ■

2. *Nautilus Insurance Co. v. Cheran Investments, LLC,* 2016 WL 2979659 (Neb.Ct.App. 2016).

3. *Gee v. Delta Speir Plantation LLC,* 20 WL 575589 (4th Cir. 2022).

Goods and Services Combined. When contracts involve a combination of goods and services, courts generally use the **predominant-factor test** to determine whether a contract is primarily for the sale of goods or the sale of services.[4] If a court decides that a mixed contract is primarily a goods contract, any dispute, even a dispute over the services portion, will be decided under the UCC.

■ **Case in Point 14.3** Paper City, a microbrewery, entered into a contract with La Resistance, a beer distribution company, under which La Resistance would purchase beer from Paper City and distribute it to retailers. Paper City sued La Resistance for breach of contract almost five years after the alleged breach occurred. Under Article 2 of the UCC, the statute of limitations for disputes involving contracts for the sale of goods is four years. As a result, the trial court dismissed Paper City's lawsuit.

Paper City appealed, claiming that its contract with La Resistance was for services, not goods, and was therefore not covered by Article 2. Paper City argued that, under the contract and according to "industry standards," La Resistance provided services such as managing Paper City's accounts and representing Paper City at trade shows. The only financial transactions on record between the two companies, however, were those in which La Resistance paid Paper City for beer. Accordingly, a Massachusetts appeals court concluded that the sale of goods (beer) was the predominant factor in the two parties' agreement and affirmed the lower's court decision.[5] ■

When a cellular phone company sells both a cellular phone and a long-term contract for cell services, is the contract one for the sale of goods or for the sale of services? That was the major issue in the following case.

---

4. UCC 2–314(1) does stipulate that serving food or drinks is a "sale of goods" for purposes of the implied warranty of merchantability, which will be discussed in the context of warranties. The UCC also specifies that selling unborn animals or rare coins qualifies as a "sale of goods."

5. *Paper City Brewery Co., Inc. v. La Resistance, Inc.,* 124 N.E.3d 159, 95 Mass.App.Ct. 1103 (2019).

Case Analysis 14.1

Leslie Tweedie and Christina Waugh, on behalf of themselves and others similarly situated v. US Asset Management, Inc.

Supreme Court of Appeals of West Virginia, __ S.E. __, 2022 WL 1223939 (2022).

In the Language of the Court
PER CURIAM [By the court]
* * * *

This matter stems from Petitioners' previous relationships with AT&T. Both Petitioners were former AT&T customers who obtained cellular phone devices and services from AT&T. * * * Ms. Waugh entered electronically signed written contracts with AT&T for cellular phone and hotspot service. She also received cellular phone devices at the time. Following Ms. Waugh's agreement to receive cellular phone service, she received monthly billing statements from AT&T. After some time, Ms. Waugh began to question the amounts she was being charged and stopped paying AT&T. Ms. Waugh's AT&T account remained

open until AT&T charged off her past due debt in 2010. Subsequently, USAM [US Asset Management, Inc.] bought Ms. Waugh's debt from AT&T, and on January 30, 2015, USAM's debt collector mailed Ms. Waugh a collection letter seeking to collect on the debt originally owed to AT&T.

On June 15, 2007, Ms. Tweedie also opened an account with AT&T for a cellular phone device and cellular phone service. * * * Ms. Tweedie began to receive monthly billing statements and later started to question the amounts being charged. Ms. Tweedie stopped making regular payments, and AT&T charged off the debt on her account on March 13, 2009. USAM then purchased Ms. Tweedie's debt from AT&T, and on November 16, 2014, USAM's debt

collector sent Ms. Tweedie a collection letter seeking to collect on the debt on USAM's behalf.

Petitioners filed a class action complaint on November 26, 2018, in the Circuit Court of Fayette County. The complaint alleged that USAM violated the West Virginia Consumer Credit and Protection Act ("WVCCPA") when it attempted to collect sales contract debts that were more than four years after default and, therefore, time-barred by the four-year statute of limitations in the Uniform Commercial Code ("UCC"). * * * Petitioners' claims failed because: (1) the UCC statute of limitations was not applicable to the debts at issue because they were for services, not goods; (2) the time-barred debt disclosure therefore was not required; * * *.

* * * Petitioners argued that the underlying agreements were hybrid transactions for both goods and services and that the predominant purpose of the agreements was the purchase of the respective cellular devices rather than the cellular service. USAM filed a reply continuing to argue that the underlying agreements were solely for services, not goods. Alternatively, USAM contended that assuming arguendo [for the sake of argument] that the underlying agreements were hybrid agreements that contained both the sale of goods and services, the predominant purpose was for services.

* * * *

* * * The court found that "[s]ince phones were received by [the Petitioners] at the time the contract[s] w[ere] entered, the [c]ourt considers the contract[s] between [the Petitioners] and AT&T mixed or hybrid contract[s] involving both services and goods." Accordingly, the circuit court analyzed the underlying case pursuant to a predominant purpose test and concluded that the contracts entered by Petitioners with AT&T were predominantly for the purpose of obtaining cellular phone services. * * * the court determined that the letters to Petitioners did not require the time-barred debt disclosures pursuant to West Virginia Code [Section] 46A-2-128(f) because the four-year statute of limitations set forth in West Virginia Code [Section] 46-2-725 did not apply, but instead, the ten-year statute of limitations set forth in West Virginia Code [Section] 55-2-6 was applicable. Because the debt was not time-barred and the

disclosures were not required, the circuit court found that "no genuine issue of material fact * * * remain[ed], nor [was] further inquiry desirable or necessary to clarify the application of the law." The circuit court then granted USAM's motion for summary judgment and dismissed the matter with prejudice. This appeal followed.

* * * *

We agree that the evidence presented supports an award of summary judgment in favor of USAM; however, we base our decision on reasoning different than that relied on by the circuit court. Namely, we find that the evidence presented in the record demonstrates that the contracts and debts purchased by USAM upon which USAM was seeking to recover were based solely on cellular phone services, not a cellular phone device purchase or a hybrid thereof. * * *

* * * *

* * * We must examine whether the respective contracts involve only the provision of services or if the sale of goods is also involved in any capacity. First, as it relates to Ms. Waugh, the underlying record demonstrates that the contract and debt sought to be recovered were solely for services. Specifically, the record sets forth the following: (1) Ms. Waugh testified during her deposition that it was her understanding that she was paying for the service plan and not for the cellular phone devices; (2) there is nothing in the language of the service agreements signed by Ms. Waugh that indicates in

any way that the contracts encompassed the sale of a cellular phone device; and (3) there is nothing in the language of the monthly statements received by Ms. Waugh for the debt sought to be recovered that indicates the charges were for a cellular phone device— rather, the monthly statements indicate that they were for cellular phone service charges. Likewise, as it relates to Ms. Tweedie, the underlying record once again demonstrates that the contract and debt sought to be recovered were solely for services. While Ms. Tweedie did state in her deposition that she believed she purchased a Blackberry cellular phone at the time she opened her account and believed that the purchase price was supposed to be added to her bill, she was unsure of the exact purchase price and could not provide any additional details with any degree of certainty. However, like Ms. Waugh, there is nothing in the language of the monthly statements received by Ms. Tweedie for the debt sought to be recovered that indicates in any way that the charges were for a cellular phone device; rather it is clear that the charges were for cellular phone services. Accordingly, we find that there is no genuine issue of material fact and that the contracts at issue were solely for the provision of cellular phone services. * * *

For the reasons set forth herein, we affirm the circuit court's October 14, 2020, order granting summary judgment in favor of USAM.

Affirmed.

Legal Reasoning Questions

1. Is there any significance in the fact that Ms. Waugh electronically signed written contracts with AT&T? Why or why not?

2. Why would the plaintiffs want this dispute to be governed by the Uniform Commercial Code?

3. What was US Asset Management, Inc.'s main defense?

Who Is a Merchant? Article 2 governs the sale of goods in general. It applies to sales transactions between all buyers and sellers. In a limited number of instances, though, the UCC presumes that special business standards ought to be imposed because of merchants' relatively high degree of commercial expertise.[6] Such standards do not apply to the casual or inexperienced seller or buyer (consumer).

Section 2–104 sets forth three ways in which merchant status can arise:

1. A merchant is a person who deals in goods of the kind involved in the sales contract. Thus, a retailer, a wholesaler, or a manufacturer is a merchant of the goods sold in the relevant business. A merchant for one type of goods is not necessarily a merchant for another type. For instance, a sporting goods retailer is a merchant when selling tennis rackets but not when selling a used computer.
2. A merchant is a person who, by occupation, can be assumed to have knowledge and skill unique to the practices or goods involved in the transaction. This broad definition may include banks and universities as merchants.
3. A person who employs a merchant as a broker, agent, or other intermediary has the status of merchant in that transaction. Hence, if an art collector hires a broker to purchase or sell art for her, the collector is considered a merchant in the transaction.

In summary, persons are **merchants** when they, acting in a mercantile capacity, possess or use an expertise specifically related to the goods being sold. This basic distinction is not always clear-cut. For instance, state courts appear to be split on whether farmers should be considered merchants.

14–1b Article 2A—Leases

Leases of personal property (goods such as automobiles and industrial equipment) have become increasingly common. In this context, a lease is a transfer of the right to possess and use goods for a period of time in exchange for payment. Article 2A of the UCC was created to fill the need for uniform guidelines in this area.

Article 2A covers any transaction that creates a lease of goods or a sublease of goods [UCC 2A–102, 2A–103(1)(k)]. Article 2A is essentially a repetition of Article 2, except that it applies to leases of goods rather than sales of goods and thus varies to reflect differences between sales and lease transactions. (Note that Article 2A is not concerned with leases of real property, such as land or buildings.)

14–2 The Formation of Sales and Lease Contracts

In regard to the formation of sales and lease contracts, the UCC modifies the common law in several ways. We look here at how Articles 2 and 2A of the UCC modify common law contract rules. Remember, though, that parties to sales and lease contracts are basically free to establish whatever terms they wish.

The UCC comes into play when the parties either fail to provide certain terms in their contract or wish to change the effect of the UCC's terms in the contract's application. The UCC makes this very clear by its repeated use of such phrases as "unless the parties otherwise agree" and "absent a contrary agreement by the parties."

14–2a Offer

In general contract law, the moment a definite offer is met by an unqualified acceptance, a binding contract is formed. In commercial sales transactions, the verbal exchanges, correspondence, and actions of the parties may not reveal exactly when a binding contractual obligation arises. The UCC states that an agreement sufficient to constitute a contract can exist even if the moment of its making is undetermined [UCC 2–204(2), 2A–204(2)].

Open Terms Under the common law of contracts, an offer must be definite enough for the parties (and the courts) to ascertain its essential terms when it is accepted. In contrast, the UCC states that a sales or lease contract will not fail for indefiniteness even if one or more terms are left open as long as both of the following are true:

1. The parties intended to make a contract.
2. There is a reasonably certain basis for the court to grant an appropriate remedy [UCC 2–204(3), 2A–204(3)].

The UCC provides numerous open-term provisions (discussed next) that can be used to fill the gaps in a contract. Thus, if a dispute occurs, all that is necessary to

---

6. The provisions that apply only to merchants deal principally with the Statute of Frauds, firm offers, confirmatory memoranda, warranties, and contract modification. These special rules reflect expedient business practices commonly known to merchants in the commercial setting. They will be discussed later in this chapter.

prove the existence of a contract is an indication (such as a purchase order) that there is a contract. Missing terms can be proved by evidence, or a court can presume that the parties intended whatever is reasonable under the circumstances.

Keep in mind, though, that if too many terms are left open, a court may find that the parties did not intend to form a contract. Also, the quantity of goods involved usually must be expressly stated in the contract. If the quantity term is left open, the courts will have no basis for determining a remedy.[7]

Requirements Contracts. Requirements contracts are common in the business world and normally are enforceable. In a **requirements contract,** the buyer agrees to purchase and the seller agrees to sell all or up to a stated amount of what the buyer requires.

■ **Example 14.4** Newport Cannery forms a contract with Victor Tu. The cannery agrees to purchase from Tu, and Tu agrees to sell to the cannery, all of the green beans that the cannery requires during the following summer. There is implicit consideration in this contract because the buyer (the cannery) gives up the right to buy goods (green beans) from any other seller. This forfeited right creates a legal detriment—that is, consideration. ■

If, however, the buyer promises to purchase only if they wish to do so, the promise is illusory (without consideration) and unenforceable by either party. Similarly, if the buyer reserves the right to buy the goods from someone other than the seller, the promise is unenforceable (illusory) as a requirements contract.

Output Contracts. In an **output contract,** the seller agrees to sell and the buyer agrees to buy all or up to a stated amount of what the seller produces. ■ **Example 14.5** Aura Sewell has planted two acres of organic tomatoes. Bella Union, a local restaurant, agrees to buy all of the tomatoes that Aura produces that year to use at the restaurant. Again, because the seller essentially forfeits the right to sell goods to another buyer, there is implicit consideration in an output contract. ■

The UCC imposes a *good faith limitation* on requirements and output contracts. The quantity under such contracts is the amount of requirements or the amount of output that occurs during a normal production period. The actual quantity purchased or sold cannot be unreasonably disproportionate to normal or comparable prior requirements or output [UCC 2–306(1)].

Merchant's Firm Offer Under regular contract principles, an offer can be revoked at any time before acceptance. The major common law exception is an *option contract*, in which the offeree pays consideration for the offeror's irrevocable promise to keep the offer open for a stated period. The UCC creates a second exception for *firm offers* made by a merchant concerning the sale or lease of goods (regardless of whether or not the offeree is a merchant).

A **firm offer** arises when a merchant-offeror gives assurances in a signed writing that the offer will remain open. The merchant's firm offer is irrevocable without the necessity of consideration for the stated period or, if no definite period is stated, a reasonable period (neither to exceed three months) [UCC 2–205, 2A–205].

To qualify as a firm offer, the offer must be:

1. Written (or electronically recorded, such as in an e-mail).
2. Signed by the offeror.

■ **Example 14.6** Osaka, a used-car dealer, e-mails a letter to Gomez on January 1, stating, "I have a used Toyota RAV4 on the lot that I'll sell you for $22,000 any time between now and January 31." This e-mail creates a firm offer, and Osaka will be liable for breach of contract if he sells the RAV4 to another person before January 31. ■

When a firm offer is contained in a form contract prepared by the offeree, the offeror must also sign a separate assurance of the firm offer. The requirement of a separate signature ensures that the offeror will be made aware of the firm offer.

For instance, an offeree might respond to an initial offer by sending its own form contract containing a clause stating that the offer will remain open for three months. If the firm offer is buried amid copious language on the last page of the offeree's form contract, the offeror may inadvertently sign the contract without realizing that it contains a firm offer. This would defeat the purpose of the rule—which is to give effect to a merchant's deliberate intent to be bound to a firm offer.

14–2b Acceptance

Acceptance of an offer to buy, sell, or lease goods generally may be made in any reasonable manner and by any reasonable means. The UCC permits acceptance of an offer to buy goods "either by a prompt promise to ship or by the prompt or current shipment of conforming or

---

7. See *Hanson v. Maeder,* 957 N.W.2d 22, 103 UCC Rep.Serv.2d 1146 (2021).

nonconforming goods" [UCC 2–206(1)(b)]. *Conforming goods* accord with the contract's terms, whereas *nonconforming goods* do not.

The prompt shipment of nonconforming goods constitutes both an acceptance, which creates a contract, and a breach of that contract. This rule does not apply if the seller **seasonably** (within a reasonable amount of time) notifies the buyer that the nonconforming shipment is offered only as an accommodation, or as a favor. The notice of accommodation must clearly indicate to the buyer that the shipment does not constitute an acceptance and that, therefore, no contract has been formed.

■ **Example 14.7** Mendez orders one thousand blue smart fitness watches from Halderson. Halderson ships one thousand black smart fitness watches to Mendez. If Halderson notifies Mendez that it has only black watches in stock, and the black watches are being sent as an accommodation, then the shipment is an offer. A contract will be formed only if Mendez accepts the black watches.

If, however, Halderson ships black watches without notifying Mendez that the goods are being sent as an accommodation, the shipment is both an acceptance and a breach of the resulting contract. Mendez can sue Halderson for any appropriate damages. ■

Communication of Acceptance

Under the common law, because a unilateral offer invites acceptance by performance, the offeree need not notify the offeror of performance unless the offeror would not otherwise know about it. In other words, a unilateral offer can be accepted by beginning performance.

The UCC is more stringent than the common law in this regard because it requires notification. Under the UCC, if the offeror is not notified within a reasonable time that the offeree has accepted the contract by beginning performance, then the offeror can treat the offer as having lapsed before acceptance [UCC 2–206(2), 2A–206(2)].

Additional Terms

Recall that under the common law, the mirror image rule requires that the terms of the acceptance exactly match those of the offer. ■ **Example 14.8** Adderson e-mails an offer to sell twenty Samsung Galaxy tablets to Beale. If Beale accepts the offer but changes it to require more powerful tablets, then there is no contract if the mirror image rule applies. ■

To avoid such problems, the UCC dispenses with the mirror image rule. Under the UCC, a contract is formed if the offeree's response indicates a definite acceptance of the offer, even if the acceptance includes terms additional to or different from those contained in the offer [UCC 2–207(1)]. Whether the additional terms become part of the contract depends, in part, on whether the parties are nonmerchants or merchants.

Rules When One Party or Both Parties Are Nonmerchants. If one (or both) of the parties is a nonmerchant, the contract is formed according to the terms of the original offer. The contract does not include any of the additional terms in the acceptance [UCC 2–207(2)].

Rules When Both Parties Are Merchants. The UCC includes a special rule for merchants to avoid the "battle of the forms," which occurs when two merchants exchange separate standard forms containing different contract terms.

Under UCC 2–207(2), in contracts between merchants, the additional terms automatically become part of the contract unless one of the following conditions arises:

1. The original offer expressly limited acceptance to its terms.
2. The new or changed terms materially alter the contract.
3. The offeror objects to the new or changed terms within a reasonable period of time.

When determining whether an alteration is material, courts consider several factors. Generally, if the modification does not involve any unreasonable element of surprise or hardship for the offeror, a court will hold that the modification did not materially alter the contract.

Conditioned on Offeror's Assent. The offeree's response is not an acceptance if it contains additional or different terms and is expressly conditioned on the offeror's assent to those terms [UCC 2–207(1)]. This is true whether or not the parties are merchants.

■ **Example 14.9** Philips offers to sell Hundert 650 pounds of turkey thighs at a specified price and with specified delivery terms. Hundert responds, "I accept your offer for 650 pounds of turkey thighs on the condition that you agree to give me ninety days to pay for them." Hundert's response will be construed not as an acceptance but as a counteroffer, which Philips may or may not accept. ■

Additional Terms May Be Stricken. The UCC provides yet another option for dealing with conflicting terms in the parties' writings. Section 2–207(3) states that conduct by both parties that recognizes the existence of a contract is sufficient to establish a contract for sale. This is so even if the writings of the parties do not otherwise establish a contract. In this situation, "the terms of the particular contract will consist of those terms on which the writings of the parties agree, together with any supplementary terms incorporated under any other provisions of this Act." In a dispute over contract terms, this provision allows a court simply to strike from the contract those terms on which the parties do not agree.

14–2c Consideration

The common law rule that a contract requires consideration also applies to sales and lease contracts. Unlike the common law, however, the UCC does not require a contract modification to be supported by new consideration. The UCC states that an agreement modifying a contract for the sale or lease of goods "needs no consideration to

be binding" [UCC 2–209(1), 2A–208(1)]. Of course, any contract modification must be made in good faith [UCC 1–304].

In some situations, an agreement to modify a sales or lease contract without consideration must be in writing to be enforceable. For instance, if the contract itself specifies that any changes to the contract must be in a signed writing, only those changes agreed to in a signed writing are enforceable.

Sometimes, when a consumer (nonmerchant) is buying goods from a merchant-seller, the merchant supplies a form that contains a prohibition against oral modification. In those situations, the consumer must sign a separate acknowledgment of the clause for it to be enforceable [UCC 2–209(2), 2A–208(2)]. Also, any modification that makes a sales contract come under Article 2's writing requirement (its Statute of Frauds, discussed next) usually requires a writing to be enforceable.

See Concept Summary 14.1 for a review of the UCC's rules on offer, acceptance, and consideration.

Concept Summary 14.1
Offer, Acceptance, and Consideration Under the UCC

Offer	• Not all terms have to be included for a contract to be formed. • The price does not have to be included for a contract to be formed. • Particulars of performance can be left open. • An offer by a merchant in a signed writing with assurances that the offer will not be withdrawn is irrevocable without consideration (for up to three months).
Acceptance	• Acceptance may be made by any reasonable means of communication. It is effective when dispatched. • An offer can be made by a promise to ship or by the shipment of conforming goods, or by prompt shipment of nonconforming goods unless accompanied by a notice of accommodation. • Acceptance by performance requires notice within a reasonable time. Otherwise, the offer can be treated as lapsed. • A definite expression of acceptance creates a contract even if the terms of the acceptance differ from those of the offer (unless acceptance is expressly conditioned on consent to the additional or different terms).
Consideration	• A *modification* of a contract for the sale or lease of goods does not require consideration as long as it is made in good faith.

14–2d The Statute of Frauds

The UCC contains Statute of Frauds provisions covering sales and lease contracts. Under these provisions, sales contracts for goods priced at $500 or more and lease contracts requiring total payments of $1,000 or more must be in writing to be enforceable [UCC 2–201(1), 2A–201(1)]. (These low threshold amounts may eventually be raised.)

Sufficiency of the Writing A writing, including an e-mail or other electronic record, will be sufficient to satisfy the UCC's Statute of Frauds as long as it:

1. Indicates that the parties intended to form a contract.
2. Is signed by the party (or agent of the party) against whom enforcement is sought. (Remember that a typed name can qualify as a signature on an electronic record.)

The contract normally will not be enforceable beyond the quantity of goods shown in the writing, however. All other terms can be proved in court by oral testimony. For leases, the writing must reasonably identify and describe the goods leased and the lease term.

Special Rules for Contracts Between Merchants The UCC provides a special rule for merchants in sales transactions (there is no corresponding rule that applies to leases under Article 2A). Merchants can satisfy the Statute of Frauds if, after the parties have agreed orally, one of the merchants sends a signed written confirmation to the other merchant within a reasonable time.

The communication must indicate the terms of the agreement, and the merchant receiving the confirmation must have reason to know of its contents. Unless the merchant who receives the confirmation gives written notice of objection to its contents within ten days after receipt, the writing is sufficient against the receiving merchant, even though that merchant has not signed it [UCC 2–201(2)].

■ **Example 14.10** Alfonso is a merchant-buyer in Cleveland. He contracts over the telephone to purchase $6,000 worth of spare aircraft parts from Jacy, a merchant-seller in New York City. Two days later, Jacy e-mails a signed confirmation detailing the terms of the oral contract, and Alfonso subsequently receives it. Alfonso does not notify Jacy in writing that he objects to the contents of the confirmation within ten days of receipt. Therefore, Alfonso cannot raise the Statute of Frauds as a defense against the enforcement of the oral contract. ■

Exceptions The UCC defines three exceptions to the writing requirements of the Statute of Frauds. An oral contract for the sale of goods priced at $500 or more or the lease of goods involving total payments of $1,000 or more will be enforceable despite the absence of a writing in the circumstances described next [UCC 2–201(3), 2A–201(4)].

Specially Manufactured Goods. An oral contract for the sale or lease of custom-made goods will be enforceable if:

1. The goods are specially manufactured for a particular buyer or specially manufactured or obtained for a particular lessee.
2. The goods are not suitable for resale or lease to others in the ordinary course of the seller's or lessor's business.
3. The seller or lessor has substantially started to manufacture the goods or has made commitments for the manufacture or procurement of the goods.

In these situations, once the seller or lessor has taken action, the buyer or lessee cannot repudiate the agreement claiming the Statute of Frauds as a defense.

14–2e Unconscionability

An unconscionable contract is one that is so unfair and one-sided that it would be unreasonable to enforce it. The UCC allows a court to evaluate a contract or any clause in a contract, and if the court deems it to have been unconscionable at the time it was made, the court can do any of the following [UCC 2–302, 2A–108]:

1. Refuse to enforce the contract.
2. Enforce the remainder of the contract without the unconscionable part.
3. Limit the application of the unconscionable term to avoid an unconscionable result.

The following classic case illustrates an early application of the UCC's unconscionability provisions.

Jones v. Star Credit Corp.

Supreme Court of New York, Nassau County, 59 Misc.2d 189, 298 N.Y.S.2d 264 (1969).

Background and Facts   The Joneses agreed to purchase a freezer for $900 as the result of a salesperson's visit to their home. Tax and financing charges raised the total price to $1,234.80. Later, the Joneses, who had made payments totaling $619.88, brought a suit in a New York state court to have the purchase contract declared unconscionable under the UCC. At trial, the freezer was found to have a maximum retail value of approximately $300.

In the Language of the Court

Sol M. WACHTLER, Justice.

* * * *

* * * [Section 2–302 of the UCC] authorizes the court to find, as a matter of law, that a contract or a clause of a contract was "unconscionable at the time it was made," and upon so finding the court may refuse to enforce the contract, excise the objectionable clause or limit the application of the clause to avoid an unconscionable result.

* * * *

* * * The question which presents itself is whether or not, under the circumstances of this case, the sale of a freezer unit having a retail value of $300 for $900 ($1,439.69 including credit charges and $18 sales tax) is unconscionable as a matter of law.

Concededly, deciding [this case] is substantially easier than explaining it. No doubt, the mathematical disparity between $300, which presumably includes a reasonable profit margin, and $900, which is exorbitant on its face, carries the greatest weight. Credit charges alone exceed by more than $100 the retail value of the freezer. These alone may be sufficient to sustain the decision. Yet, a caveat [warning] is warranted lest we reduce the import of Section 2–302 solely to a mathematical ratio formula. It may, at times, be that; yet it may also be much more. The very limited financial resources of the purchaser, known to the sellers at the time of the sale, is entitled to weight in the balance. Indeed, the value disparity itself leads inevitably to the felt conclusion that knowing advantage was taken of the plaintiffs. In addition, the meaningfulness of choice essential to the making of a contract can be negated by a gross inequality of bargaining power.

* * * *

* * * The defendant has already been amply compensated. In accordance with the statute, the application of the payment provision should be limited to amounts already paid by the plaintiffs and the contract be reformed and amended by changing the payments called for therein to equal the amount of payment actually so paid by the plaintiffs.

Decision and Remedy   The court held that the contract was not enforceable and reformed the contract so that no further payments were required.

Critical Thinking

- **Social** Why would the seller's knowledge of the buyers' limited resources support a finding of unconscionability?
- **Impact of This Case on Today's Law** This early classic case illustrates the approach that many courts take today when deciding whether a sales contract is unconscionable—an approach that focuses on "excessive" price and unequal bargaining power. Most of the litigants who have used UCC 2–302 successfully could demonstrate both an absence of meaningful choice and contract terms that were unreasonably favorable to the other party.

14–3 Title, Risk, and Insurable Interest

Before the creation of the Uniform Commercial Code (UCC), "title"—the right of ownership—was the central concept in sales law. Title controlled all issues of rights and remedies of the parties to a sales contract. There were numerous problems with this concept, however.

Because of such problems, the UCC has separated the question of title as much as possible from the question of the rights and obligations of buyers, sellers, and third parties. In some situations, title is still relevant under the UCC, and the UCC has special rules for determining who has title. (These rules do not apply to leased goods, obviously, because title remains with the lessor, or owner, of the goods.) In most situations, however, the UCC has replaced the concept of title with three other concepts: identification, risk of loss, and insurable interest.

14–3a Identification

Before any interest in goods can pass from the seller or lessor to the buyer or lessee, the goods must be (1) in existence and (2) identified to the contract [UCC 2–105(2)]. **Identification** takes place when specific goods are designated as the subject matter of a sales or lease contract.

Title and risk of loss cannot pass to the buyer from the seller unless the goods are identified to the contract. (As mentioned, title to leased goods remains with the lessor.) Identification is significant because it gives the buyer or lessee the right to insure (or to have an insurable interest in) the goods and the right to recover from third parties who damage the goods.

The parties can agree in their contract on when identification will take place. (This type of agreement does not effectively pass title and risk of loss on future goods, such as unborn cattle, however.) If the parties do not so specify, the UCC provisions discussed here determine when identification takes place [UCC 2–501(1), 2A–217].

Existing Goods If the contract calls for the sale or lease of specific and determined goods that are already in existence, identification takes place at the time the contract is made. ■ **Example 14.11** Litco Company contracts to lease a fleet of twenty cars designated by their vehicle identification numbers (VINs). Because the cars are identified by their VINs, identification has taken place, and Litco acquires an insurable interest in the cars at the time of contracting. ■

Future Goods Any goods that are not in existence at the time of contracting are known as *future goods*. The following rules apply to identification of future goods:

1. If a sale or lease involves unborn animals to be born within twelve months after contracting, identification takes place when the animals are conceived.
2. If a sale involves crops that are to be harvested within twelve months (or in the next harvest season occurring after contracting, whichever is longer), identification takes place when the crops are planted. If the sales contract does not refer to crops by when they will be harvested, then identification takes place when the crops begin to grow.
3. In a sale or lease of any other future goods, identification occurs when the seller or lessor ships, marks, or otherwise designates the goods as those to which the contract refers. Future goods that fall into this category might include solar panels that are to be designed and manufactured after a contract is signed for their purchase.[8]

Goods That Are Part of a Larger Mass Goods that are part of a larger mass are identified when the goods are marked, shipped, or somehow designated by the seller or lessor as the particular goods to pass under the contract. ■ **Example 14.12** Shing orders 10,000 pairs of men's jeans from a lot that contains 90,000 articles of clothing for men, women, and children. Until the seller separates the 10,000 pairs of men's jeans from the other items, title and risk of loss remain with the seller. ■

A common exception to this rule involves fungible goods. **Fungible goods** are goods that are alike naturally, by agreement, or by trade usage. Typical examples include specific grades or types of wheat, petroleum, and cooking oil, which usually are stored in large containers. Owners of fungible goods typically hold title as tenants in common (owners with undivided shares of the whole), which facilitates further sales. A seller-owner can pass title and risk of loss to the buyer without actually separating the goods. The buyer replaces the seller as an owner in common [UCC 2–105(4)].

■ **Example 14.13** Alvarez, Braudel, and Carpenter are farmers. They deposit, respectively, 5,000 bushels, 3,000 bushels, and 2,000 bushels of grain of the same grade and quality in a grain elevator. The three become owners in common, with Alvarez owning 50 percent

---

8. *In re Zhejiang Topoint Photovoltaic Co., Ltd.*, 2015 WL 2260647 (D.N.J. 2015). See, in contrast, *World Class Wholesale LLC v. Star Industries, Inc.*, 101 UCC Rep.Serv.2d 421, 2020 WL 1069466 (Sup.Ct.Del. 2020).

of the 10,000 bushels, Braudel 30 percent, and Carpenter 20 percent. Alvarez contracts to sell her 5,000 bushels of grain to Treyton. Because the goods are fungible, she can pass title and risk of loss to Treyton without physically separating the 5,000 bushels. Treyton now becomes an owner in common with Braudel and Carpenter. ■

It is important to emphasize that what makes goods fungible is not simply that they are alike, but that they are of an identical grade or type.

14–3b When Title Passes

Once goods exist and are identified, the provisions of UCC 2–401 apply to the passage of title. In nearly all subsections of UCC 2–401, the words "unless otherwise explicitly agreed" appear. In other words, the buyer and the seller can reach an explicit agreement as to when title will pass.

Without an explicit agreement to the contrary, title passes to the buyer at the time and the place the seller performs by delivering the goods [UCC 2–401(2)]. For instance, if a person buys cattle at a livestock auction, title will pass to the buyer when the cattle are physically delivered (unless otherwise agreed).

■ **Case in Point 14.14** Timothy Allen contracted with Indy Route 66 Cycles, Inc., to have a motorcycle custom built for him. Indy built the motorcycle and issued a "Certificate of Origin." Later, federal law enforcement officers arrested Allen on drug charges and seized his property, including the Indy-made cycle, which officers found at the home of Allen's sister, Tena. The government alleged that the motorcycle was subject to forfeiture as the proceeds of drug trafficking.

Indy filed a claim against the government, arguing that it owned the cycle because it still possessed the "Certificate of Origin." The court applied UCC Section 2–401(2) and ruled in favor of the government. Testimony by Indy's former vice president was "inconclusive" but implied that Indy had delivered the motorcycle to Allen. Indy had given up possession of the cycle to Allen, and this was sufficient to pass title, even though Indy had kept a "Certificate of Origin."[9] ■

Shipment and Destination Contracts Unless otherwise agreed, delivery arrangements can determine when title passes from the seller to the buyer. If the contract includes no other requirements, delivery takes place at the seller's place of business—or, if the parties know that the seller keeps the goods at some other place, at the location where the seller keeps the goods. If the seller has no place of business, delivery takes place at the seller's residence [UCC 2-308]. Many contracts, however, especially when the seller and the buyer are at some distance from one another, provide for the goods to be shipped by carrier.

In a **shipment contract,** the seller is required or authorized to ship goods by carrier, such as a trucking company. The seller is required only to deliver the goods into the hands of the carrier, and title passes to the buyer at the time and place of shipment [UCC 2–401(2)(a)].

In a **destination contract,** the seller is required to deliver the goods to a particular destination, usually directly to the buyer, but sometimes to another party designated by the buyer. Title passes to the buyer when the goods are tendered at that destination [UCC 2–401(2)(b)]. Tender of delivery occurs when the seller places or holds conforming goods at the buyer's disposal (with any necessary notice), enabling the buyer to take possession [UCC 2–503(1)].

A contract that requires the seller to send the goods but does not specify a destination for delivery is understood to require only that the seller place the goods in the hands of the carrier. Therefore, generally, a contract that specifies that the seller will send the goods is assumed to be a shipment contract if nothing to the contrary is stated in the contract.

Delivery Without Movement of the Goods Sometimes, a sales contract does not call for the seller to ship or deliver the goods (such as when the buyer is to pick up the goods). In that situation, the passage of title depends on whether the seller must deliver a **document of title,** such as a bill of lading or a warehouse receipt, to the buyer. A bill of lading[10] is a receipt for goods that is signed by a carrier and serves as a contract for the transportation of the goods. A warehouse receipt is a receipt issued by a warehouser for goods stored in a warehouse.

When a Title Document Is Required. When a title document is required, title passes to the buyer when and where the document is delivered. Thus, if the goods are stored in a warehouse, title passes to the buyer when

9. *United States v. 2007 Custom Motorcycle,* 2011 WL 232331 (D.Ariz. 2011). See also *Global Hookah Distributors, Inc. v. Department of Revenue,* 2021 WL 3732047 (Or. Tax Ct., Reg. Div., Tobacco Products Tax 2021).

10. The term "bill of lading" has been used by international carriers for many years. It derives from "bill," which historically referred to a schedule of costs for services, and the verb "to lade," which means to load cargo onto a ship or other carrier.

the appropriate documents are delivered to the buyer. The goods never move. In fact, the buyer can choose to leave the goods at the same warehouse for a period of time, and the buyer's title to those goods will be unaffected.

When a Title Document Is Not Required. When no document of title is required and the goods are identified to the contract, title passes at the time and place the sales contract is made. If the goods have not been identified, title does not pass until identification occurs.

■ **Case in Point 14.15** Alaska Air Group, Inc. (AAG), and Horizon Air Industries, Inc., contracted to purchase thirty Embraer 175 (E175) regional jets from the manufacturer. Deliveries began, but Horizon was experiencing a shortage of pilots and did not have enough pilots who were qualified to fly the E175. After ten of the E175s had been delivered to Horizon, AAG and Horizon delayed further deliveries until Horizon had more qualified pilots.

The International Brotherhood of Teamsters, Airline Division, and its Airline Professionals Association (the union) filed a lawsuit against AAG and Horizon alleging labor law violations. The union claimed that AAG and Horizon had committed to acquiring no fewer than thirty of the E175s to be flown exclusively by the union's pilots. The union argued that five of the E175s intended for Horizon were subsequently "diverted" to, and acquired by, SkyWest, which violated the rights of union pilots.

The court, however, applied UCC Section 2–401 to the dispute over these five aircraft and ruled that title to goods (when no document of title is required) does not pass until identification occurs. Horizon's purchase contract did not identify the specific aircraft to be sold, such as by serial or registration numbers, and there was no clear evidence that the SkyWest E175s were ever "earmarked" for Horizon. Thus, the sale of five E175s to SkyWest did not affect Horizon's agreement to purchase thirty E175s and did not violate the rights of the union pilots. The court therefore dismissed the complaint against AAG and Horizon.[11] ■

14–3c Risk of Loss

At the various stages of a sale or lease transaction, the question may arise as to who bears the risk of loss. In other words, who suffers the financial loss if the goods are damaged, destroyed, or lost in transit? Under the UCC, risk of loss does not necessarily pass with title. When risk of loss passes from a seller or lessor to a buyer or lessee is generally determined by the contract between the parties.

Sometimes, the contract states expressly when the risk of loss passes. At other times, it does not, and a court must interpret the existing terms to determine whether the risk has passed. When no provision in the contract indicates when risk passes, the UCC provides special rules, based on delivery terms, to guide the courts.

Delivery With Movement of the Goods—Carrier Cases When the contract involves movement of the goods via a common carrier but does not specify when risk of loss passes, the courts first look for specific delivery terms in the contract. Unless the parties agree otherwise, these terms will determine which party will pay the costs of delivering the goods and who will bear the risk of loss. If the contract does not include these terms, then the courts must decide whether the contract is a shipment or a destination contract.

Shipment Contracts. In a shipment contract, the seller or lessor is required or authorized to ship goods by carrier, but is not required to deliver them to a particular destination. The risk of loss in a shipment contract passes to the buyer or lessee when the goods are delivered to the carrier [UCC 2–509(1)(a), 2A–219(2)(a)].

■ **Example 14.16** Pitman, a seller in Texas, sells five hundred cases of grapefruit to a buyer in New York, F.O.B. Houston. This term authorizes shipment by carrier and indicates that the buyer is to pay the transportation charges. Risk passes to the buyer when conforming goods are properly placed in the possession of the carrier in Houston. If the goods are damaged in transit, the loss is the buyer's. (Actually, buyers have recourse against carriers, subject to certain limitations, and they usually insure the goods from the time the goods leave the seller.) ■

Destination Contracts. In a destination contract, the risk of loss passes to the buyer or lessee when the goods are tendered to the buyer or lessee at the specified destination [UCC 2–509(1)(b), 2A–219(2)(b)]. In Example 14.16, if the contract had been a destination contract, F.O.B. New York, risk of loss during transit to New York would have been the seller's. Risk of loss would not have passed to the buyer until the carrier tendered the grapefruit to the buyer in New York.

Whether a contract is a shipment contract or a destination contract can have significant consequences for the parties. When an agreement is ambiguous as to whether it is a shipment or a destination contract, courts normally will presume that it is a shipment contract. Thus, the parties must use clear and explicit language to overcome this presumption and create a destination contract.

---

11. *International Brotherhood of Teamsters, Airline Division v. Alaska Air Group, Inc.,* 2018 WL 3328226 (W.D.Wash. 2018).

Delivery Without Movement of the Goods The UCC also addresses situations in which the contract does not require the goods to be shipped or moved. Frequently, the buyer or lessee is to pick up the goods from the seller or lessor, or the goods are to be held by a bailee. A **bailment** is a temporary delivery of personal property, without passage of title, into the care of another, called a *bailee.* Under the UCC, a bailee is a party who—by a bill of lading, warehouse receipt, or other document of title—acknowledges possession of goods and/or contracts to deliver them. For instance, a warehousing company or a trucking company may be a bailee.

Goods Held by the Seller. When the seller keeps the goods for pickup, a document of title usually is not used. If the seller is not a merchant, the risk of loss to goods held by the seller passes to the buyer on *tender of delivery* [UCC 2–509(3)]. Thus, the sellers bear the risk of loss until they make the goods available to the buyers and notify the buyers that the goods are ready to be picked up.

If the seller is a merchant, risk of loss to goods held by the seller passes to the buyer when the buyer actually takes physical possession of the goods [UCC 2–509(3)]. In other words, the merchant bears the risk of loss between the time the contract is formed and the time the buyer picks up the goods.

Goods Held by a Bailee. When a bailee is holding goods that are to be delivered under a contract without being moved, the goods are usually represented by a document of title. The title document may be written on paper or evidenced by an electronic record.

A document of title is either *negotiable* or *nonnegotiable,* depending on whether the transferee is a buyer or lessee and on how the title document is transferred. Negotiable and nonnegotiable documents may transfer different rights to the goods that the documents cover.

With a negotiable document of title, a party can transfer the rights by signing and delivering, or in some situations simply delivering, the document. The rights to the goods—free of any claims against the party that issued the document—pass with the document to the transferee. With a nonnegotiable document of title, the transferee obtains only the rights that the party transferring it had, subject to any prior claims.

When goods are held by a bailee, risk of loss passes to the buyer when one of the following occurs:

1. The buyer receives a negotiable document of title for the goods.
2. The bailee acknowledges the buyer's right to possess the goods.

3. The buyer has received a nonnegotiable document of title, and the buyer has had a reasonable time to present the document to the bailee and demand the goods. If the bailee refuses to honor the document, the risk of loss remains with the seller [UCC 2–503(4)(b), 2–509(2)].

With respect to leases, if goods held by a bailee are to be delivered without being moved, the risk of loss passes to the lessee on acknowledgment by the bailee of the lessee's right to possession of the goods [UCC 2A–219(2)(b)].

Risk of Loss When a Sales or Lease Contract Is Breached When a sales or lease contract is breached, the transfer of risk operates differently depending on which party breaches. Generally, the party in breach bears the risk of loss. When the seller or lessor breaches and the goods are so nonconforming that the buyer has the right to reject them, the risk of loss does not pass to the buyer until either:

1. The defects are **cured** (that is, the goods are repaired, replaced, or discounted in price by the seller).
2. The buyer accepts the goods in spite of their defects (thus waiving the right to reject).

When the buyer or lessee breaches, the general rule is that when a buyer or lessee breaches a contract, the risk of loss immediately shifts to the buyer or lessee. This rule has three important limitations [UCC 2–510(3), 2A–220(2)]:

1. The seller or lessor must already have identified the contract goods.
2. The buyer or lessee bears the risk for only a commercially reasonable time after the seller or lessor has learned of the breach.
3. The buyer or lessee is liable only to the extent of any deficiency in the seller's or lessor's insurance coverage.

14–3d Insurable Interest

Parties to sales and lease contracts often obtain insurance coverage to protect against damage, loss, or destruction of goods. Any party purchasing insurance, however, must have a sufficient interest in the insured item to obtain a valid policy. Insurance laws—not the UCC—determine sufficiency. The UCC is helpful, though, because it contains certain rules regarding insurable interests in goods.

A buyer or lessee has an **insurable interest** in identified goods. The moment the contract goods are identified by the seller or lessor, the buyer or lessee has a property interest in them. That interest allows the buyer or lessee to obtain the necessary insurance coverage for those goods even before the risk of loss has passed [UCC 2–501(1), 2A–218(1)].

Identification can be made at any time and in any manner agreed to by the parties. When the parties do not explicitly agree on identification in their contract, then the UCC provisions on identification discussed in this chapter apply. Thus, for instance, absent a contract provision to the contrary, a buyer obtains an insurable interest in crops at the time they are planted.

A seller has an insurable interest in goods as long as the seller retains title to the goods. Even after title passes to a buyer, a seller who has a security interest (a right to secure payment) in the goods still has an insurable interest [UCC 2–501(2)]. Thus, both the buyer and the seller can have an insurable interest in identical goods at the same time. Of course, the buyer or seller must sustain an actual loss to have the right to recover from an insurance company.

In regard to leases, the lessor retains an insurable interest in leased goods unless the lessee exercises an option to buy. In that event, the risk of loss passes to the lessee [UCC 2A–218(3)].

14–4 Performance and Breach of Sales and Lease Contracts

The performance that is required of the parties under a sales or lease contract consists of their duties and obligations under the terms of the contract. The basic obligation of the seller or lessor is to transfer and deliver conforming goods. The basic obligation of the buyer or lessee is to accept and pay for conforming goods in accordance with the contract [UCC 2–301, 2A–516(1)].

Overall performance of a sales or lease contract is controlled by the agreement between the parties. When the contract is unclear and disputes arise, the courts look to the UCC and impose standards of good faith and commercial reasonableness.

The obligations of good faith and commercial reasonableness underlie every sales and lease contract. The UCC's good faith provision, which can never be disclaimed, reads as follows: "Every contract or duty within this Act imposes an obligation of good faith in its performance or enforcement" [UCC 1–304]. "Good faith" means honesty in fact. For a merchant, it means honesty in fact and the observance of reasonable commercial standards of fair dealing in the trade [UCC 2–103(1)(b)].

In other words, merchants are held to a higher standard of performance or duty than are nonmerchants.

14–4a Obligations of the Seller or Lessor

The basic duty of the seller or lessor is to deliver the goods called for under the contract to the buyer or lessee. Goods that conform to the contract description in every way are called **conforming goods.** To fulfill the contract, the seller or lessor must either deliver or tender delivery of conforming goods to the buyer or lessee.

Tender of Delivery **Tender of delivery** occurs when the seller or lessor makes conforming goods available and gives the buyer or lessee whatever notification is reasonably necessary to enable the buyer or lessee to take delivery [UCC 2–503(1), 2A–508(1)].

Tender must occur at a reasonable hour and in a reasonable manner. For instance, a seller cannot call the buyer at 2:00 A.M. and say, "The goods are ready. I'll give you twenty minutes to get them." Unless the parties have agreed otherwise, the goods must be tendered for delivery at a reasonable hour and kept available for a reasonable time to enable the buyer to take possession [UCC 2–503(1)(a)].

Normally, all goods called for by a contract must be tendered in a single delivery unless the parties have agreed on delivery in several lots or installments (discussed shortly) [UCC 2–307, 2–612, 2A–510]. ■ **Example 14.17** An order for 1,000 Under Armour men's shirts cannot be delivered two shirts at a time. The parties may agree, however, that the shirts will be delivered in four orders of 250 each as they are produced (for summer, fall, winter, and spring inventory). Tender of delivery may then occur in this manner. ■

Place of Delivery The buyer and seller (or lessor and lessee) may agree that the goods will be delivered to a particular destination where the buyer or lessee will take possession. If the contract does not indicate where the goods will be delivered, then the place for delivery will be one of the following:

1. The seller's place of business.
2. The seller's residence, if the seller has no business location [UCC 2–308(a)].
3. The location of the goods, if both parties know at the time of contracting that the goods are located somewhere other than the seller's business [UCC 2–308(b)].

■ **Example 14.18** Li Wan and Boyd both live in San Francisco. In San Francisco, Li Wan contracts to sell Boyd five used trucks, which both parties know are located in a Chicago warehouse. If nothing more is specified in the contract, the place of delivery for the trucks is Chicago. Li Wan may tender delivery by giving Boyd either a negotiable or a nonnegotiable document of title. Alternatively, Li Wan may obtain the bailee's (warehouser's) acknowledgment that Boyd is entitled to possession. ■

Delivery via Carrier In many instances, it is clear from the surrounding circumstances or delivery terms in the contract (such as F.O.B. or F.A.S.) that the parties intended the goods to be moved by a carrier. In carrier contracts, the seller fulfills the obligation to deliver the goods through either a shipment contract or a destination contract.

Shipment Contracts. Recall that a *shipment contract* requires or authorizes the seller to ship goods by a carrier, rather than to deliver them at a particular destination [UCC 2–319, 2–509(1)(a)]. Under a shipment contract, unless otherwise agreed, the seller must do the following:

1. Place the goods into the hands of the carrier.
2. Make a contract for their transportation that is reasonable according to the nature of the goods and their value. (For instance, certain types of goods need refrigeration in transit.)
3. Obtain and promptly deliver or tender to the buyer any documents necessary to enable the buyer to obtain possession of the goods from the carrier.
4. Promptly notify the buyer that shipment has been made [UCC 2–504].

If the seller does not make a reasonable contract for transportation or notify the buyer of the shipment, the buyer can reject the goods, but only if a material loss or a significant delay results. ■ **Example 14.19** Zigi's Organic Fruits sells strawberries to Lozier under a shipment contract. If Zigi's does not arrange for refrigerated transportation and the berries spoil during transport, a material loss to Lozier will likely result. ■

Of course, the parties are free to make agreements that alter the UCC's rules and allow the buyer to reject goods for other reasons.

Destination Contracts. In a *destination contract*, the seller agrees to deliver conforming goods to the buyer at a particular destination. The goods must be tendered at a reasonable hour and held at the buyer's disposal for a reasonable length of time. The seller must also give the buyer appropriate notice and any necessary documents to enable the buyer to obtain delivery from the carrier [UCC 2–503].

The Perfect Tender Rule The seller or lessor has an obligation to ship or tender conforming goods. The buyer

or lessee is then obligated to accept and pay for the goods according to the contract terms [UCC 2–507].

Under the common law, the seller was obligated to deliver goods that conformed with the terms of the contract in every detail (unless the doctrine of substantial performance applied). This was called the **perfect tender rule.** The UCC preserves the perfect tender rule by providing that if goods or tender of delivery fails in any respect to conform to the contract, the buyer or lessee may accept the goods, reject the entire shipment, or accept part and reject part [UCC 2–601, 2A–509].

The corollary to this rule is that if the goods conform in every respect, the buyer or lessee does not have a right to reject the goods. ■ **Case in Point 14.20** U.S. Golf & Tennis Centers, Inc., agreed to buy 96,000 golf balls from Wilson Sporting Goods Company for a total price of $20,000. Wilson represented that U.S. Golf was receiving its lowest price ($5 per two-dozen unit).

Wilson shipped golf balls to U.S. Golf that conformed to the contract in quantity and quality, but it did not receive payment. U.S. Golf claimed that it had learned that Wilson had sold the product for $2 per unit to another buyer. U.S. Golf asked Wilson to reduce the contract price of the balls to $4 per unit. Wilson refused and filed a suit. The court ruled in favor of Wilson. Because it was undisputed that the shipment of golf balls conformed to the contract specifications, U.S. Golf was obligated to accept the goods and pay the agreed-on price.[12] ■

Exceptions to the Perfect Tender Rule Because of the rigidity of the perfect tender rule, several exceptions to the rule have been created. The parties may agree, for instance, that defective goods or parts will not be rejected if the seller or lessor is able to repair or replace them within a reasonable period of time. In this situation, the perfect tender rule does not apply.

Cure. The UCC does not specifically define the term "cure," but it refers to the right of the seller or lessor to repair, adjust, or replace defective or nonconforming goods [UCC 2–508, 2A–513]. The seller or lessor has a right to attempt to cure a defect when the following are true:

1. A delivery is rejected because the goods were nonconforming.
2. The time for performance has not yet expired.

---

12. *Wilson Sporting Goods Co. v. U.S. Golf and Tennis Centers, Inc.,* 2012 WL 601804 (Tenn.App. 2012). See also *AMG Vanadium LLC v. Global Advanced Metals U.S.A., Inc.,* UCC Rep.Serv.2d 162, 2020 WL 1233752 (2020).

3. The seller or lessor provides timely notice to the buyer or lessee of the intention to cure.
4. The cure can be made within the contract time for performance.

Even if the contract time for performance has expired, the seller or lessor can still cure if there were reasonable grounds to believe that the nonconforming tender would be acceptable to the buyer or lessee [UCC 2–508(2), 2A–513(2)].

The right to cure substantially restricts the right of the buyer or lessee to reject goods. To reject, the buyer or lessee must inform the seller or lessor of the particular defect. If the defect is not disclosed, the buyer or lessee cannot later assert the defect as a defense if the defect is one that the seller or lessor could have cured. Generally, buyers and lessees must act in good faith and state specific reasons for refusing to accept goods [UCC 2–605, 2A–514].

Substitution of Carriers. Sometimes, an agreed-on manner of delivery (such as the use of a particular carrier) becomes impracticable or unavailable through no fault of either party. In that situation, if a commercially reasonable substitute is available, this substitute performance is sufficient tender to the buyer and must be used [UCC 2–614(1)]. The seller or lessor is required to arrange for a substitute carrier and normally is responsible for any additional shipping costs (unless the contract states otherwise).

Commercial Impracticability. Occurrences unforeseen by either party when a contract was made may make performance commercially impracticable. When this occurs, the perfect tender rule no longer applies. The seller or lessor must, however, notify the buyer or lessee as soon as practicable that there will be a delay or nondelivery [UCC 2–615, 2A–405].

Commercial impracticability arises only when the parties, at the time the contract was made, had no reason to anticipate that the event would occur. It does not extend to problems that could have been foreseen, such as an increase in cost resulting from inflation.

■ **Case in Point 14.21** In a classic 1970s case, Maple Farms, Inc., entered into a contract to supply a school district in New York with milk for one school year. The contract price was the market price of milk in June, but by December, the price of raw milk had increased by 23 percent. Maple Farms stood to lose $7,350 on this contract (and more on similar contracts with other school districts). To avoid performing the contract, Maple Farms filed a suit and claimed that the unanticipated cost increases made performance "impracticable." A New York trial court disagreed. Because inflation and fluctuating prices could have been foreseen, they did not render performance of this contract impracticable. The court granted summary judgment in favor of the school district.[13] ■

Sometimes, the unforeseen event only partially affects the capacity of the seller or lessor to perform. Therefore, the seller or lessor can partially fulfill the contract but cannot tender total performance. In this event, the seller or lessor is required to distribute any remaining goods or deliveries fairly and reasonably among the parties to whom it is contractually obligated [UCC 2–615(b), 2A–405(b)]. The buyer or lessee must receive notice of the allocation and has the right to accept or reject it [UCC 2–615(c), 2A–405(c)].

Destruction of Identified Goods Sometimes, an unexpected event, such as a fire, totally destroys goods through no fault of either party before risk passes to the buyer or lessee. In such a situation, if the goods were identified at the time the contract was formed, the parties are excused from performance [UCC 2–613, 2A–221]. If the goods are only partially destroyed, the buyer or lessee can inspect them and either treat the contract as void or accept the damaged goods with a reduction in the contract price.

Assurance and Cooperation. If one party has reasonable grounds to believe that the other party will not perform, the first party may in writing "demand adequate assurance of due performance" from the other party. Until such assurance is received, the first party may suspend further performance without liability. What constitutes "reasonable grounds" is determined by commercial standards. If the requested assurances are not forthcoming within a reasonable time (not to exceed thirty days), the failure to respond may be treated as a repudiation of the contract [UCC 2–609, 2A–401].

Sometimes, the performance of one party depends on the cooperation of the other. When cooperation is not forthcoming, the first party can either proceed to perform the contract in any reasonable manner or suspend performance without liability and hold the uncooperative party in breach [UCC 2–311(3)].

14–4b Obligations of the Buyer or Lessee

The main obligation of the buyer or lessee under a sales or lease contract is to pay for the goods tendered. Once the seller or lessor has adequately tendered delivery, the buyer

---

13. *Maple Farms, Inc. v. City School District of Elmira, New York,* 76 Misc.2d 1080, 352 N.Y.S.2d 784 (1974).

or lessee is obligated to accept the goods and pay for them according to the terms of the contract.

Payment In the absence of any specific agreements, the buyer or lessee must make payment at the time and place the goods are received [UCC 2–310(a), 2A–516(1)]. When a sale is made on credit, the buyer is obligated to pay according to the specified credit terms (for example, 60, 90, or 120 days), not when the goods are received. The credit period usually begins on the date of shipment [UCC 2–310(d)]. Under a lease contract, a lessee must make the lease payment that was specified in the contract [UCC 2A–516(1)].

Payment can be made by any means agreed on between the parties—cash or any other method generally acceptable in the commercial world. If the seller demands cash, the seller must give the buyer reasonable time to obtain it [UCC 2–511].

Right of Inspection Unless the parties otherwise agree, or for C.O.D. (collect on delivery) transactions, the buyer or lessee has an absolute right to inspect the goods before making payment. This right allows the buyer or lessee to verify that the goods tendered or delivered conform to the contract. If the goods are not as ordered, the buyer or lessee has no duty to pay. An opportunity for inspection is therefore a condition precedent to the right of the seller or lessor to enforce payment [UCC 2–513(1), 2A–515(1)].

Inspection can take place at any reasonable place and time and in any reasonable manner. Generally, what is reasonable is determined by custom of the trade, past practices of the parties, and the like. The buyer bears the costs of inspecting the goods but can recover the costs from the seller if the goods do not conform and are rejected [UCC 2–513(2)].

Acceptance After having had a reasonable opportunity to inspect the goods, the buyer or lessee can demonstrate acceptance in any of the following ways:

1. The buyer or lessee indicates (by words or conduct) to the seller or lessor that the goods are conforming or that the goods will be retained in spite of their nonconformity [UCC 2–606(1)(a), 2A–515(1)(a)].
2. The buyer or lessee fails to reject the goods within a reasonable period of time [UCC 2–602(1), 2–606(1)(b), 2A–515(1)(b)].
3. In sales contracts, the buyer will be deemed to have accepted the goods by performing any act inconsistent with the seller's ownership. For instance, any use or resale of the goods—except for the limited purpose of testing or inspecting the goods—generally constitutes an acceptance [UCC 2–606(1)(c)].

■ **Case in Point 14.22** Hemacare Plus, Inc., ordered more than $660,000 in specialty pharmaceutical products from Cardinal Health 108, LLC. Cardinal supplied the products, which Hemacare used and did not reject or return. Hemacare did not pay the invoices for the goods delivered, however, so Cardinal filed a breach action in a federal district court. Because Hemacare had used the pharmaceutical products, the court found that it had accepted the goods. Therefore, the court granted a summary judgment to Cardinal, awarding $688,920 in damages (including interest, attorneys' fees, and costs).[14] ■

Partial Acceptance If some of the goods delivered do not conform to the contract and the seller or lessor has failed to cure, the buyer or lessee can make a partial acceptance [UCC 2–601(c), 2A–509(1)]. The same is true if the nonconformity was not reasonably discoverable before acceptance. (In the latter situation, the buyer or lessee may be able to revoke the acceptance, as will be discussed later in this chapter.)

A buyer or lessee cannot accept less than a single commercial unit, however. The UCC defines a commercial unit as a unit of goods that, by commercial usage, is viewed as a "single whole" for purposes of sale. A commercial unit cannot be divided without materially impairing the character of the unit, its market value, or its use [UCC 2–105(6), 2A–103(1)(c)]. A commercial unit can be a single article (such as a machine), a set of articles (such as a suite of furniture), a quantity (such as a bale, a gross, or a carload), or any other unit treated in the trade as a single whole.

Anticipatory Repudiation What if, before the time for contract performance, one party clearly communicates to the other the intention not to perform? Such an action is a breach of the contract by anticipatory repudiation.

When anticipatory repudiation occurs, the nonbreaching party has a choice of two responses:

1. Treat the repudiation as a final breach by pursuing a remedy.
2. Wait to see if the repudiating party will decide to honor the contract despite the avowed intention to renege [UCC 2–610, 2A–402].

In either situation, the nonbreaching party may suspend performance.

14. *Cardinal Health 108, LLC v. Hemacare Plus, Inc.,* 2017 WL 114405 (S.D.Ala. 2017). See also *Export Development Canada v. Shore Acres Plant Farm, Inc.,* 526 F.Supp.3d 1139, 104 UCC Rep.Serv.2d 476 (S.D. AL 2021).

The UCC permits the breaching party to "retract" a repudiation (subject to some limitations). This can be done by any method that clearly indicates the party's intent to perform. Once retraction is made, the rights of the repudiating party under the contract are reinstated. There can be no retraction, however, if since the time of the repudiation the other party has canceled or materially changed position or otherwise indicated that the repudiation is final [UCC 2–611, 2A–403].

14–5 Remedies of the Seller or Lessor

Note that remedies for breach under the UCC are cumulative in nature—meaning that the aggrieved party is not limited to one exclusive remedy. When the buyer or lessee is in breach, the remedies available to the seller or lessor depend on the circumstances existing at the time of the breach.

14–5a When the Goods Are in the Possession of the Seller or Lessor

If the buyer or lessee breaches the contract before the goods have been delivered, the seller or lessor has the right to pursue the following remedies:

1. Cancel (rescind) the contract.
2. Withhold delivery of the goods.
3. Resell the goods and sue to recover damages.
4. Sue to recover the purchase price or lease payments due.
5. Sue to recover damages for the buyer's nonacceptance of goods.

The Right to Cancel the Contract If the buyer or lessee breaches the contract, the seller or lessor can choose to simply cancel the contract [UCC 2–703(f), 2A–523(1)(a)]. The seller or lessor must notify the buyer or lessee of the cancellation, and at that point all remaining obligations of the seller or lessor are discharged. The buyer or lessee is not discharged from all remaining obligations, however. That party is in breach, and the seller or lessor can pursue remedies available under the UCC for breach.

The Right to Withhold Delivery In general, sellers and lessors can withhold delivery or discontinue performance of their obligations under sales or lease contracts when the buyers or lessees are in breach [UCC

2–703(a), 2A–523(1)(c)]. This is true whether a buyer or lessee has wrongfully rejected or revoked acceptance of contract goods (discussed later), failed to make a payment, or repudiated the contract. The seller or lessor can also refuse to deliver the goods to a buyer or lessee who is insolvent (unable to pay debts as they become due) unless the buyer or lessee pays in cash [UCC 2–702(1), 2A–525(1)].

The Right to Resell or Dispose of the Goods When a buyer or lessee breaches or repudiates the contract while the seller or lessor is in possession of the goods, the seller or lessor can resell or dispose of the goods. Any resale of the goods must be made in good faith and in a commercially reasonable manner. The seller must give the original buyer reasonable notice of the resale, unless the goods are perishable or will rapidly decline in value [UCC 2–706(2), (3)].

The seller can retain any profits made as a result of the sale and can hold the buyer or lessee liable for any loss [UCC 2–703(d), 2–706(1), 2A–523(1)(e), 2A–527(1)]. (Here, a loss is any deficiency between the resale price and the contract price.) In lease transactions, the lessor can lease the goods to another party and recover damages from the original lessee. Damages include any unpaid lease payments up to the time the new lease begins. The lessor can also recover any deficiency between the lease payments due under the original lease and those due under the new lease, along with incidental damages [UCC 2A–527(2)].

When the goods contracted for are unfinished at the time of the breach, the seller or lessor can do either of the following:

1. Cease manufacturing the goods and resell them for scrap or salvage value.
2. Complete the manufacture and resell or dispose of the goods, and hold the buyer or lessee liable for any deficiency.

In choosing between these two alternatives, the seller or lessor must exercise reasonable commercial judgment in order to mitigate the loss and obtain maximum value from the unfinished goods [UCC 2–704(2), 2A–524(2)].

The Right to Recover the Purchase Price or Lease Payments Due Under the UCC, an unpaid seller or lessor can bring an action to recover the purchase price or the payments due under the lease contract, plus incidental damages [UCC 2–709(1), 2A–529(1)]. If a seller or lessor is unable to resell or dispose of the goods and sues for the contract price or lease payments due, the goods must be held for the buyer or lessee unless resale becomes possible. The seller or lessor can resell the goods at any time before collecting the judgment from the buyer or lessee. If the goods are resold, the net proceeds from the sale must be credited to the buyer or lessee because of the duty to mitigate damages.

The Right to Recover Damages for the Buyer's Nonacceptance If a buyer or lessee repudiates a contract or wrongfully refuses to accept the goods, a seller or lessor can bring an action to recover the damages sustained. Ordinarily, the amount of damages equals the difference between the contract price or lease payments and the market price or lease payments at the time and place of tender of the goods, plus incidental damages [UCC 2–708(1), 2A–528(1)].

When the ordinary measure of damages is inadequate to put the seller or lessor in as good a position as the buyer's or lessee's performance would have, the UCC provides an alternative. In that situation, the proper measure of damages is the lost profits of the seller or lessor, including a reasonable allowance for overhead and other expenses [UCC 2–708(2), 2A–528(2)].

When the Goods Are in Transit When the seller or lessor has delivered the goods to a carrier or a bailee but the buyer or lessee has not yet received them, the goods are said to be in transit.

Effect of Insolvency and Breach If the seller or lessor learns that the buyer or lessee is insolvent, the seller or lessor can stop the delivery of the goods in transit, regardless of the quantity of goods shipped. A different rule applies if the buyer or lessee is in breach but is not insolvent. In this situation, the seller or lessor can stop the goods in transit only if the quantity shipped is at least a carload, a truckload, a planeload, or a larger shipment [UCC 2–705(1), 2A–526(1)].

Requirements for Stopping Delivery To stop delivery, the seller or lessor must timely notify the carrier or other bailee that the goods are to be returned or held for the seller or lessor. If the carrier has sufficient time to stop delivery, the goods must be held and delivered according to the instructions of the seller or lessor. The seller or lessor is liable to the carrier for any additional costs incurred [UCC 2–705(3), 2A–526(3)].

The seller or lessor has the right to stop delivery of the goods under UCC 2–705(2) and 2A–526(2) until the time when:

1. The buyer or lessee receives the goods.

2. The carrier or the bailee acknowledges the rights of the buyer or lessee in the goods (by reshipping or holding the goods for the buyer or lessee, for example).

3. A negotiable document of title covering the goods has been properly transferred to the buyer in a sales transaction, giving the buyer ownership rights in the goods [UCC 2–705(2)].

After reclaiming the goods, the seller or lessor can pursue the remedies allowed to sellers and lessors when the goods are in their possession.

14–5b Remedies of the Buyer or Lessee

When the seller or lessor breaches the contract, the buyer or lessee has numerous remedies available under the UCC. Like the remedies available to sellers and lessors, the remedies available to buyers and lessees depend on the circumstances at the time of the breach. Relevant factors include whether the seller has refused to deliver conforming goods or has delivered nonconforming goods.

The Right to Cancel the Contract When a seller or lessor fails to make proper delivery or repudiates the contract, the buyer or lessee can cancel, or rescind, the contract. The buyer or lessee is relieved of any further obligations under the contract but retains all rights to other remedies against the seller or lessor [UCC 2–711(1), 2A–508(1)(a)]. (The right to cancel the contract is also available to a buyer or lessee who has rightfully rejected goods or revoked acceptance, as will be discussed shortly.)

The Right to Obtain Goods Upon Insolvency If a buyer or lessee has partially or fully paid for goods that are in the possession of a seller or lessor who becomes insolvent, the buyer or lessee can obtain the goods. The seller or lessor must have become insolvent within ten days after receiving the first payment, and the goods must be identified to the contract. To exercise this right, the buyer or lessee must pay the seller or lessor any unpaid balance of the purchase price or lease payments [UCC 2–502, 2A–522].

The Right to Obtain Specific Performance A buyer or lessee can obtain specific performance if the goods are unique or the remedy at law (monetary damages) is inadequate [UCC 2–716(1), 2A–521(1)]. Ordinarily, an award of damages is sufficient to compensate the buyer or lessee for the loss of the bargain. When the contract is for the purchase of a particular work of art or a similarly unique item, however, damages may not be sufficient.

Under these circumstances, equity requires that the seller or lessor perform by delivering the particular goods identified to the contract.

The Right of Cover In certain situations, buyers and lessees can protect themselves by obtaining **cover**—that is, by buying or leasing substitute goods for those that were due under the contract. This option is available when the seller or lessor repudiates the contract or fails to deliver the goods, or when a buyer or lessee has rightfully rejected goods or revoked acceptance. In purchasing or leasing substitute goods, the buyer or lessee must act in good faith and without unreasonable delay [UCC 2–712, 2A–518].

After obtaining substitute goods, the buyer or lessee can recover the following from the seller or lessor:

1. The difference between the cost of cover and the contract price (or lease payments).
2. Incidental damages that resulted from the breach.
3. Consequential damages to compensate for indirect losses (such as lost profits) resulting from the breach that were reasonably foreseeable at the time of contract formation. The amount of consequential damages is reduced by any amount the buyer or lessee saved as a result of the breach. (For instance, the buyer might obtain cover without having to pay delivery charges that were part of the original sales contract.)

Buyers and lessees are not required to cover, and failure to do so will not bar them from using any other remedies available under the UCC. A buyer or lessee who fails to cover, however, risks collecting a lower amount of consequential damages. A court may reduce the consequential damages by the amount of the loss that could have been avoided had the buyer or lessee purchased or leased substitute goods.

The Right to Replevy Goods Buyers and lessees also have the right to replevy goods. **Replevin**[15] is an action to recover identified goods in the hands of a party who is unlawfully withholding them. Under the UCC, a buyer or lessee can replevy goods identified to the contract if the seller or lessor has repudiated or breached the contract. To maintain an action to replevy goods, buyers and lessees usually must show that they were unable to cover for the goods after making a reasonable effort [UCC 2–716(3), 2A–521(3)].

The Right to Recover Damages If a seller or lessor repudiates the contract or fails to deliver the goods, the buyer or lessee can sue for damages. For the buyer, the measure of recovery is the difference between the contract price and the market price of the goods at the time the buyer learned of the breach. For the lessee, the measure is the difference between the lease payments and the lease payments that could be obtained for the goods at the time the lessee learned of the breach. The market price or market lease payments are determined at the place where the seller or lessor was supposed to deliver the goods. The buyer or lessee can also recover incidental and consequential damages less the expenses that were saved as a result of the breach [UCC 2–713, 2A–519].

■ **Case in Point 14.23** Les Entreprises Jacques Defour & Fils, Inc., contracted to buy a thirty-thousand-gallon industrial tank from Dinsick Equipment Corporation for $70,000. Les Entreprises hired Xaak Transport, Inc., to pick up the tank, but when Xaak arrived at the pickup location, there was no tank. Les Entreprises paid Xaak $7,459 for its services and filed a suit against Dinsick. The court awarded compensatory damages of $70,000 for the tank and incidental damages of $7,459 for the transport.

To establish a breach of contract requires an enforceable contract, substantial performance by the nonbreaching party, a breach by the other party, and damages. In this case, Les Entreprises agreed to buy a tank and paid the price. Dinsick failed to tender or deliver the tank, or to refund the price. The shipping costs were a necessary part of performance, so this was a reasonable expense.[16] ■

The Right to Reject the Goods If either the goods or their tender fails to conform to the contract in any respect, the buyer or lessee can reject all of the goods or any commercial unit of the goods [UCC 2–601, 2A–509]. On rejecting the goods, the buyer or lessee may obtain cover or cancel the contract, and may seek damages just as if the seller or lessor had refused to deliver the goods.

The buyer or lessee must reject the goods within a reasonable amount of time after delivery or tender of delivery and must seasonably notify the seller or lessor [UCC 2–602(1), 2A–509(2)]. If the buyer or lessee fails to reject the goods within a reasonable amount of time, acceptance will be presumed.

When rejecting goods, the buyer or lessee must also designate defects that are ascertainable by reasonable inspection. Failure to do so precludes the buyer or lessee from using such defects to justify rejection or to establish breach if the seller or lessor could have cured the defects [UCC 2–605, 2A–514].

---

15. Pronounced ruh-*pleh*-vun, derived from the Old French word *plevir,* meaning "to pledge."

16. *Les Entreprises Jacques Defour & Fils, Inc. v. Dinsick Equipment Corp.,* 2011 WL 307501 (N.D.Ill. 2011).

Revocation of Acceptance Acceptance of the goods precludes buyers or lessees from exercising the right of rejection. It does not necessarily prevent them from pursuing other remedies, however. In certain circumstances, buyers or lessees are permitted to revoke their acceptance of the goods.

Acceptance of a lot or a commercial unit can be revoked if the nonconformity substantially impairs the value of the lot or unit and if one of the following factors is present:

1. Acceptance was based on the reasonable assumption that the nonconformity would be cured, and it has not been cured within a reasonable period of time [UCC 2–608(1)(a), 2A–517(1)(a)].
2. The failure of the buyer or lessee to discover the nonconformity was reasonably induced either by the difficulty of discovery before acceptance or by assurances made by the seller or lessor [UCC 2–608(1)(b), 2A–517(1)(b)].

The Right to Recover Damages for Accepted Goods A buyer or lessee who has accepted nonconforming goods may also keep the goods and recover damages [UCC 2–714(1), 2A–519(3)]. To do so, the buyer or lessee must notify the seller or lessor of the breach within a reasonable time after the defect was or should have been discovered. Failure to give notice of the defects (breach) to the seller or lessor normally bars the buyer or lessee from pursuing any remedy [UCC 2–607(3), 2A–516(3)]. In addition, the parties to a sales or lease contract can insert into the contract a provision requiring the buyer or lessee to give notice of any defects in the goods within a prescribed period.

When the goods delivered are not as promised, the measure of damages generally equals the difference between the value of the goods as accepted and their value if they had been delivered as warranted. An exception occurs if special circumstances show proximately caused damages of a different amount [UCC 2–714(2), 2A–519(4)]. The buyer or lessee is also entitled to incidental and consequential damages when appropriate [UCC 2–714(3), 2A–519]. With proper notice to the seller or lessor, the buyer or lessee can also deduct all or any part of the damages from the price or lease payments still due under the contract [UCC 2–717, 2A–516(1)].

Is two years after a sale of goods a reasonable time in which to discover a defect in those goods and notify the seller of a breach? That was the question in the following case.

Spotlight on Baseball Cards

Case 14.3 Fitl v. Strek

Supreme Court of Nebraska, 269 Neb. 51, 690 N.W.2d 605 (2005).

Background and Facts In 1995, James Fitl attended a sports-card show in San Francisco, California, where he met Mark Strek, doing business as Star Cards of San Francisco, an exhibitor at the show. Later, on Strek's representation that a certain 1952 Mickey Mantle Topps baseball card was in near-mint condition, Fitl bought the card from Strek for $17,750. Strek delivered it to Fitl in Omaha, Nebraska, and Fitl placed it in a safe-deposit box.

In May 1997, Fitl sent the card to Professional Sports Authenticators (PSA), a sports-card grading service. PSA told Fitl that the card was ungradable because it had been discolored and doctored. Fitl complained to Strek, who replied that Fitl should have initiated a return of the card sooner. According to Strek, "a typical grace period for the unconditional return of a card [was within] 7 days to 1 month" of its receipt. In August, Fitl sent the card to ASA Accugrade, Inc. (ASA), another grading service, for a second opinion of the value. ASA also concluded that the card had been refinished and trimmed. Fitl filed a suit in a Nebraska state court against Strek, seeking damages. The court awarded Fitl $17,750, plus his court costs. Strek appealed to the Nebraska Supreme Court.

In the Language of the Court
WRIGHT, J. [Judge]
* * * *

Strek claims that the [trial] court erred in determining that notification of the defective condition of the baseball card 2 years after the date of purchase was timely pursuant to [UCC] 2–607(3)(a).

Case 14.3 Continues

Case 14.3 Continued

* * * The [trial] court found that Fitl had notified Strek within a reasonable time after discovery of the breach. Therefore, our review is whether the [trial] court's finding as to the reasonableness of the notice was clearly erroneous.

Section 2–607(3)(a) states: "Where a tender has been accepted * * * the buyer must within a reasonable time after he discovers or should have discovered any breach notify the seller of breach or be barred from any remedy." [Under UCC 1–204(2),] "what is a reasonable time for taking any action depends on the nature, purpose and circumstances of such action."

The notice requirement set forth in Section 2–607(3)(a) serves three purposes.

* * * The most important one is to enable the seller to make efforts to cure the breach by making adjustments or replacements in order to minimize the buyer's damages and the seller's liability. A second policy is to provide the seller a reasonable opportunity to learn the facts so that he may adequately prepare for negotiation and defend himself in a suit. A third policy * * * is the same as the policy behind statutes of limitation: to provide a seller with a terminal point in time for liability.

* * * A party is justified in relying upon a representation made to the party as a positive statement of fact when an investigation would be required to ascertain its falsity. In order for Fitl to have determined that the baseball card had been altered, he would have been required to conduct an investigation. We find that he was not required to do so. Once Fitl learned that the baseball card had been altered, he gave notice to Strek.

* * * One of the most important policies behind the notice requirement * * * is to allow the seller to cure the breach by making adjustments or replacements to minimize the buyer's damages and the seller's liability. However, even if Fitl had learned immediately upon taking possession of the baseball card that it was not authentic and had notified Strek at that time, there is no evidence that Strek could have made any adjustment or taken any action that would have minimized his liability. In its altered condition, the baseball card was worthless.

* * * Earlier notification would not have helped Strek prepare for negotiation or defend himself in a suit because the damage to Fitl could not be repaired. Thus, the policies behind the notice requirement, to allow the seller to correct a defect, to prepare for negotiation and litigation, and to protect against stale claims at a time beyond which an investigation can be completed, were not unfairly prejudiced by the lack of an earlier notice to Strek. Any problem Strek may have had with the party from whom he obtained the baseball card was a separate matter from his transaction with Fitl, and an investigation into the source of the altered card would not have minimized Fitl's damages.

Decision and Remedy The state supreme court affirmed the decision of the lower court. Under the circumstances, notice of a defect in the card two years after its purchase was reasonable. The buyer had reasonably relied on the seller's representation that the card was "authentic" (which it was not), and when the defects were discovered, the buyer had given timely notice.

Critical Thinking

- **Legal Environment** What might a court award to a buyer who prevails in a dispute such as the one in this case?
- **What If the Facts Were Different?** Suppose that Fitl and Strek had included in their deal a written clause requiring Fitl to give notice of any defect in the card within "7 days to 1 month" of its receipt. Would the result have been different? Why or why not?

14–6 Warranties

Most goods are covered by some type of warranty designed to protect buyers. In sales and lease law, a warranty is an assurance or guarantee by the seller or lessor about the quality and features of the goods being sold or leased.

The Uniform Commercial Code (UCC) has numerous rules governing product warranties as they occur in sales and lease contracts. Articles 2 (on sales) and 2A (on leases) designate several types of warranties that can arise in a sales or lease contract, including warranties of title, express warranties, and implied warranties. In addition, federal law imposes certain requirements on warranties.

Because a warranty imposes a duty on the seller or lessor, a breach of warranty is a breach of the seller's or lessor's promise. Assuming that the parties have not agreed to limit or modify the remedies available, if the seller or lessor breaches a warranty, the buyer or lessee can sue to recover damages. Under some circumstances, a breach of warranty can allow the buyer or lessee to rescind (cancel) the agreement.

14–6a Warranties of Title

Under the UCC, three types of title warranties—good title, no liens, and no infringements—can automatically arise in sales and lease contracts [UCC 2–312, 2A–211]. Normally, a seller or lessor can disclaim or modify these title warranties only by including specific language in the contract. For instance, sellers may assert that they are transferring only such rights, title, and interest as they have in the goods.

In most sales, sellers warrant that they have good and valid title to the goods sold and that the transfer of the title is rightful [UCC 2–312(1)(a)]. If the buyer subsequently learns that the seller did not have valid title to the goods that were purchased, the buyer can sue the seller for breach of this warranty. (There is no warranty of good title in lease contracts because title to the goods does not pass to the lessee.)

A second warranty of title protects buyers and lessees who are unaware of any encumbrances against goods at the time the contract is made [UCC 2–312(1)(b), 2A–211(1)]. (Such encumbrances—that is, claims, charges, or liabilities—are usually called liens.[17])

This warranty protects buyers who, for instance, unknowingly purchase goods that are subject to a creditor's security interest. (A security interest in this context is an interest in the goods that secures payment or performance of an obligation.) If a creditor legally repossesses the goods from a buyer who had no actual knowledge of the security interest, the buyer can recover from the seller for breach of warranty. (In contrast, a buyer who has actual knowledge of a security interest has no recourse against a seller.)

A third type of warranty of title arises automatically when the seller or lessor is a merchant. A merchant-seller or lessor warrants that the buyer or lessee takes the goods free of infringements from any copyright, trademark, or patent claims of a third person[2] [UCC 2–312(3), 2A–211(2)]. If the buyer or lessor is subsequently sued

by a third party holding copyright, trademark, or patent rights in the goods, then this warranty is breached.

14–6b Express Warranties

A seller or lessor can create an **express warranty** by making representations concerning the quality, condition, description, or performance potential of the goods.

Statements That Create Express Warranties Under UCC 2–313 and 2A–210, express warranties arise when a seller or lessor indicates any of the following:

1. That the goods conform to any affirmation of fact or promise that the seller or lessor makes to the buyer or lessee about the goods. (An *affirmation of fact* is a declaration that something is true.) Such affirmations or promises are usually made during the bargaining process.
2. That the goods conform to any description of them.
3. That the goods conform to any sample or model of the goods shown to the buyer or lessee.

Express warranties can be found in a seller's or lessor's advertisement, brochure, or promotional materials, in addition to being made orally or in an express warranty provision in a sales or lease contract.

Basis of the Bargain To create an express warranty, a seller or lessor does not have to use formal words, such as "warrant" or "guarantee." It is only necessary that a reasonable buyer or lessee would regard the representation as being part of the basis of the bargain [UCC 2–313(2), 2A–210(2)].

The UCC does not explicitly define the phrase "basis of the bargain." Generally, it means that the buyer or lessee must have relied on the representation at the time of entering into the agreement. Therefore, a court must determine in each case whether a representation was made at such a time and in such a way that it induced the buyer or lessee to enter into the contract.

Statements of Opinion and Value Only statements of fact create express warranties. A seller or lessor who states an opinion about or recommends the goods thus does not create an express warranty [UCC 2–313(2), 2A–210(2)].

■ **Case in Point 14.24** Harry's Dairy entered a contract to purchase 3,000 tons of hay from Jeff Good. Harry's Dairy stopped accepting Good's hay because of mold. After Good sued Harry's Dairy for breach of contract, Harry's Dairy countersued, professing that Good had violated an

---

17. Pronounced *liens*.

express warranty. This claim was based on a statement that Good made to one of the dairy's representatives when asked about the impact of recent weather on the product. Good said that "the hay had not been exposed to weather that would result in damage or mold to the hay." The Idaho Supreme Court dismissed Harry's Dairy's claim, holding that no express warranty existed because Good's statement was neither an "affirmation of fact" about the possibility of mold nor a "promise" that the hay would not be moldy.[18] ■

Similarly, a seller or lessor who makes a statement about the value or worth of the goods does not create an express warranty. Thus, a statement such as "this is worth a fortune" or "anywhere else you'd pay $10,000 for it" usually does not create a warranty.

14–6c Implied Warranties

An **implied warranty** is one that the law derives by inference from the nature of the transaction or the relative situations or circumstances of the parties. Under the UCC, merchants impliedly warrant that the goods they sell or lease are merchantable and, in certain circumstances, fit for a particular purpose. In addition, an implied warranty may arise from a course of dealing or usage of trade.

Implied Warranty of Merchantability Every sale or lease of goods made by a merchant who deals in goods of the kind sold or leased automatically gives rise to an **implied warranty of merchantability** [UCC 2–314, 2A–212]. Thus, a merchant who is in the business of selling ski equipment makes an implied warranty of merchantability every time he sells a pair of skis. A neighbor selling her skis at a garage sale does not (because she is not in the business of selling goods of this type).

To be merchantable, goods must be "reasonably fit for the ordinary purposes for which such goods are used." They must be of at least average, fair, or medium-grade quality. The quality must be comparable to quality that will pass without objection in the trade or market for goods of the same description. The goods must also be adequately packaged and labeled, and they must conform to the promises or affirmations of fact made on the container or label, if any.

When goods are nonmerchantable, or defective, the buyer can sue for breach of the implied warranty of merchantability. ■ **Case in Point 14.25** Joy Pipe, USA, L.P., is in the business of selling steel couplings for use in oil field drilling operations. Joy Pipe entered into a contract with Fremak Industries (a broker) to purchase grade P-110 steel made in India by ISMT Limited. When the steel arrived, Joy Pipe machined it into couplings, which it then sold to its customers. Two companies that used these couplings in oil wells had well failures and notified Joy Pipe.

Joy Pipe then discovered that the ISMT steel it had purchased was of a much lower grade than P-110. It was the lower quality that had caused the couplings to fail. After Joy Pipe paid another company to locate and replace the nonconforming steel, it sued ISMT, in part for breach of the implied warranty of merchantability. A jury awarded Joy Pipe nearly $3 million in damages, and an appellate court affirmed the jury's award.[19] ■

It is possible for the implied warranty of merchantability to be breached even when the merchant did not know or could not have discovered that a product was defective. Of course, merchants are not absolute insurers against every perceived defect. A bar of soap, for instance, is not unmerchantable merely because a user could slip and fall by stepping on it.

Implied Warranty of Fitness for a Particular Purpose The **implied warranty of fitness for a particular purpose** arises in the sale or lease of goods when a seller or lessor (merchant or nonmerchant) knows both of the following:

1. The particular purpose for which a buyer or lessee will use the goods.
2. That the buyer or lessee is relying on the skill and judgment of the seller or lessor to select suitable goods [UCC 2–315, 2A–213].

A "particular purpose" of the buyer or lessee differs from the "ordinary purpose for which goods are used" (merchantability). Goods can be merchantable but unfit for a particular purpose.

■ **Example 14.26** Sheryl needs a gallon of paint to match the color of her living room walls—a light shade somewhere between coral and peach. She takes a sample to Sherwin-Williams and requests a gallon of paint of that color. Instead, the salesperson gives her a gallon of bright blue paint. Here, the salesperson has not breached any

18. *Good v. Harry's Dairy, LLC,* 461 P.3d 765, 166 Idaho 483, 101 UCC Rep.Serv.2d 950 (S.Ct. ID, Boise, 2020).

19. *Joy Pipe, USA, L.P. v. ISMT Limited,* 703 Fed.Appx. 253, 93 UCC Rep.Serv.2d 154 (5th Cir. 2017).

warranty of implied merchantability—the bright blue paint is of high quality and suitable for interior walls. The salesperson has breached an implied warranty of fitness for a particular purpose, though, because the paint is not the right color for Sheryl's purpose (to match her living room walls). ■

A seller or lessor need not have actual knowledge of the buyer's or lessee's particular purpose. It is sufficient if a seller or lessor "has reason to know" the purpose. For an implied warranty to be created, however, the buyer or lessee must have relied on the skill or judgment of the seller or lessor in selecting or furnishing suitable goods. Moreover, the seller or lessor must have had reason to know about the buyer's or lessee's reliance.

Warranties Implied From Prior Dealings or Trade Custom

Implied warranties can also arise (or be excluded or modified) as a result of course of dealing or usage of trade [UCC 2–314(3), 2A–212(3)]. Without evidence to the contrary, when both parties to a sales or lease contract have knowledge of a well-recognized trade custom, the courts will infer that both parties intended for that custom to apply to their contract.

■ **Example 14.27** Industry-wide custom is to lubricate a new car before it is delivered. If a dealer fails to lubricate a car, the dealer can be held liable to a buyer for damages resulting from the breach of an implied warranty. (This would also be negligence on the part of the dealer.) ■

14–6d Warranty Disclaimers and Limitations on Liability

The UCC generally permits warranties to be disclaimed or limited by specific and unambiguous language, provided that this is done in a manner that protects the buyer or lessee from surprise. Because each type of warranty is created in a different way, the manner in which a seller or lessor can disclaim warranties varies with the type of warranty.

Express Warranties

A seller or lessor can disclaim all oral express warranties by including in the contract a written disclaimer. The disclaimer must be in language that is clear and conspicuous and must be called to a buyer's or lessee's attention [UCC 2–316(1), 2A–214(1)]. This allows the seller or lessor to avoid false allegations that oral warranties were made. It also ensures that only representations made by properly authorized individuals are included in the bargain.

Note that a buyer or lessee must be made aware of any warranty disclaimers or modifications at the time the contract is formed. In other words, the seller or lessor cannot modify any warranties or disclaimers made during the bargaining process without the consent of the buyer or lessee.

Implied Warranties

Normally, unless circumstances indicate otherwise, the implied warranties of merchantability and fitness are disclaimed by an expression such as "as is" or "with all faults." Both parties must be able to clearly understand from the language used that there are no implied warranties [UCC 2–316(3)(a), 2A–214(3)(a)]. Note that some states have laws that forbid "as is" sales. Other states do not allow disclaimers of warranties of merchantability for consumer goods.

14–7 Contracts for the International Sale of Goods

International sales contracts between firms or individuals located in different countries may be governed by the 1980 United Nations Convention on Contracts for the International Sale of Goods (CISG). The CISG governs international contracts only if the countries of the parties to the contract have ratified the CISG and if the parties have not agreed that some other law will govern their contract.

The CISG has been adopted by more than eighty-four countries, including the United States, Canada, some Central and South American countries, China, most European nations, Japan, and Mexico. That means that the CISG is the uniform international sales law of countries that account for more than two-thirds of all global trade.

14–7a Applicability of the CISG

Essentially, the CISG is to international sales contracts what Article 2 of the UCC is to domestic sales contracts. In domestic transactions, the UCC applies when the parties to a contract for a sale of goods have failed to specify in writing some important term, such as price or delivery. Similarly, whenever the parties to international transactions have failed to specify in writing the precise terms of a contract, the CISG will be applied.

Unlike the UCC, *the CISG does not apply to consumer sales.* Neither the UCC nor the CISG applies to contracts for services.

14–7b A Comparison of CISG and UCC Provisions

The provisions of the CISG, although similar for the most part to those of the UCC, differ from them in some respects. Major differences exist between the CISG and the UCC in regard to the mirror image rule and irrevocable offers, for instance. If the CISG and the UCC conflict, the CISG applies (because it is a treaty of the U.S. national government and therefore is supreme).

The Mirror Image Rule Under the UCC, a definite expression of acceptance that contains additional terms can still result in the formation of a contract, unless the additional terms are conditioned on the assent of the offeror. In other words, as we have explained, the UCC does away with the mirror image rule in domestic sales contracts.

Under the CISG, however, a contract can be formed even though the acceptance contains additional terms, unless the additional terms materially alter the contract. If an additional term relates to payment, quality, quantity, price, time and place of delivery, extent of one party's liability to the other, or the settlement of disputes, the CISG considers the added term a material alteration. In effect, then, the CISG requires that the terms of the acceptance mirror those of the offer.

Irrevocable Offers UCC 2–205 provides that a merchant's firm offer is irrevocable, even without consideration, if the merchant gives assurances in a signed writing. In contrast, under the CISG, an offer can become irrevocable without a signed writing. Article 16(2) of the CISG provides that an offer will be irrevocable if:

1. The offeror states orally that the offer is irrevocable.
2. The offeree reasonably relies on the offer as being irrevocable.

In both of these situations, the offer will be irrevocable even without a writing and without consideration.

Practice and Review: Sales and Lease Contracts

Guy Holcomb owns and operates Oasis Goodtime Emporium, an adult entertainment establishment. Holcomb wanted to create an adult Internet system for Oasis that would offer customers adult-theme videos and "live" chat room programs using performers at the club. On May 10, Holcomb signed a work order authorizing Thomas Consulting Group (TCG) "to deliver a working prototype of a customer chat system, demonstrating the integration of live video and chatting in a Web browser." In exchange for creating the prototype, Holcomb agreed to pay TCG $64,697. On May 20, Holcomb signed an additional work order in the amount of $12,943 for TCG to install a customized firewall system. The work orders stated that Holcomb would make monthly installment payments to TCG, and both parties expected the work would be finished by September.

Due to unforeseen problems largely attributable to system configuration and software incompatibility, the project required more time than anticipated. By the end of the summer, the website was still not ready, and Holcomb had fallen behind in his payments to TCG. TCG threatened to cease work and file a suit for breach of contract unless the bill was paid. Rather than make further payments, Holcomb wanted to abandon the project. Using the information presented in the chapter, answer the following questions.

1. Would a court be likely to decide that the transaction between Holcomb and TCG was covered by the Uniform Commercial Code (UCC)? Why or why not?
2. Would a court be likely to consider Holcomb a merchant under the UCC? Why or why not?
3. Did the parties have a valid contract under the UCC? Were any terms left open in the contract? If so, which terms? How would a court deal with open terms?
4. Suppose that Holcomb and TCG meet in October in an attempt to resolve their problems. At that time, the parties reach an oral agreement that TCG will continue to work without demanding full payment of the past due amounts and Holcomb will pay TCG $5,000 per week. Assuming the contract falls under the UCC, is the oral agreement enforceable? Why or why not?

Debate This . . .   *The UCC should require the same degree of definiteness of terms, especially with respect to price and quantity, as contract law does.*

Terms and Concepts

Issue Spotters

1. E-Design, Inc., orders 150 computer desks. Fav-O-Rite Supplies, Inc., ships 150 printer stands. Is this an acceptance of the offer or a counteroffer? If it is an acceptance, is it a breach of the contract? Why or why not? What if Fav-O-Rite told E-Design it was sending the printer stands as "an accommodation"? (See *The Formation of Sales and Lease Contracts.*)

2. Country Fruit Stand orders eighty cases of peaches from Downey Farms. Without stating a reason, Downey delivers thirty cases instead of eighty and delivers at the wrong time. Does Country have the right to reject the shipment? Explain. (See *Performance Obligations in Sales and Lease Contracts.*)

- **Check your answers to the Issue Spotters against the answers provided in Appendix B at the end of this text.**

Business Scenarios and Case Problems

14–1. Merchant's Firm Offer. On May 1, Jennings, a car dealer, e-mails Wheeler and says, "I have a 1955 Thunderbird convertible in mint condition that I will sell you for $13,500 at any time before June 9. [Signed] Peter Jennings." By May 15, having heard nothing from Wheeler, Jennings sells the car to another. On May 29, Wheeler accepts Jennings's offer and tenders $13,500. When told Jennings has sold the car to another, Wheeler claims Jennings has breached their contract. Is Jennings in breach? Explain. (See *The Formation of Sales and Lease Contracts.*)

14–2. Additional Terms. Strike offers to sell Bailey one thousand shirts for a stated price. The offer declares that shipment will be made by Dependable truck line. Bailey replies, "I accept your offer for one thousand shirts at the price quoted. Delivery to be by Yellow Express truck line." Both Strike and Bailey are merchants. Three weeks later, Strike ships the shirts by Dependable truck line, and Bailey refuses to accept delivery. Strike sues for breach of contract. Bailey claims that there never was a contract because his reply, which included a modification of carriers, did not constitute an acceptance. Bailey further claims that even if there had been a contract, Strike would have been in breach because Strike shipped the shirts by Dependable, contrary to the contract terms. Discuss fully Bailey's claims. (See *The Formation of Sales and Lease Contracts.*)

14–3. Goods and Services Combined. Allied Shelving and Equipment, Inc., sells and installs shelving systems. National Deli, LLC, contracted with Allied to provide and install a parallel rack system (a series of large shelves) in National's warehouse. Both parties were dissatisfied with the result. National filed a suit in a Florida state court against Allied, which filed a counterclaim. Each contended that the other had materially breached the contract. The court applied common law contract principles to rule in National's favor on both claims. Allied appealed, arguing that the court should have applied the UCC. When does a court apply common law principles to a contract that involves both goods and services? In this case, why might an appellate court rule that the UCC should be applied instead? Explain. [*Allied Shelving & Equipment, Inc. v. National Deli, LLC,* 40 Fla. L.Weekly D145, 154 So.3d 482 (Dist.Ct.App. 2015)] (See *The Scope of Articles 2 (Sales) and 2A (Leases).*)

14–4. Express Warranties. Charity Bell bought a used Toyota Avalon from Awny Gobran of Gobran Auto Sales, Inc. The odometer showed that the car had been driven 147,000 miles. Bell asked whether it had been in any accidents. Gobran replied that it was in good condition. The parties signed a warranty disclaimer that the vehicle was sold "as is." Problems with the car arose the same day as the purchase. Gobran made a few ineffectual attempts to repair it before refusing to do more. Meanwhile, Bell obtained a vehicle history report from Carfax, which showed that the Avalon had been damaged in an accident and that its last reported odometer reading was 237,271.

Was the "as is" disclaimer sufficient to put Bell on notice that the odometer reading could be false and that the car might have been in an accident? Can Gobran avoid any liability that might otherwise be imposed because Bell did not obtain the Carfax report until *after* she bought the car? Discuss. [*Gobran Auto Sales, Inc. v. Bell*, 335 Ga.App. 873, 783 S.E.2d 389 (2016)] (See *Warranties*.)

14–5. Acceptance. New England Precision Grinding, Inc. (NEPG), sells precision medical parts in Massachusetts. NEPG agreed to supply Kyphon, Inc., with stylets and nozzles. NEPG contracted with Simply Surgical, LLC, to obtain the parts from Iscon Surgicals, Ltd. The contract did not mention Kyphon or require Kyphon's acceptance of the parts. Before shipping, Iscon would certify that the parts conformed to NEPG's specifications. On receiving the parts, NEPG would certify that they conformed to Kyphon's specifications. On delivery, Kyphon would also inspect the parts.

After about half a dozen transactions, NEPG's payments to Simply Surgical lagged, and the seller refused to make further deliveries. NEPG filed a suit in a Massachusetts state court against Simply Surgical, alleging breach of contract. NEPG claimed that Kyphon had rejected some of the parts, which gave NEPG the right not to pay for them. Do the UCC's rules with respect to acceptance support or undercut the parties' actions? Discuss. [*New England Precision Grinding, Inc. v. Simply Surgical, LLC*, 89 Mass.App.Ct. 176, 46 N.E.3d 590 (2016)] (See *The Formation of Sales and Lease Contracts*.)

14–6. Business Case Problem With Sample Answer— Remedies of the Buyer or Lessee. M.C. and Linda Morris own a home in Gulfport, Mississippi, that was extensively damaged in Hurricane Katrina. The Morrises contracted with Inside Outside, Inc. (IO), to rebuild their kitchen. When the new kitchen cabinets were delivered, some defects were apparent, and as installation progressed, others were revealed. IO ordered replacement parts to cure the defects. Before the parts arrived, however, the parties' relationship deteriorated, and IO offered to remove the cabinets and refund the price. The Morrises also asked to be repaid for the installation fee. IO refused but emphasized that it was willing to fulfill its contractual obligations. At this point, are the Morrises entitled to revoke their acceptance of the cabinets? Why or why not? [*Morris v. Inside Outside, Inc.*, 185 So.3d 413 (Miss.Ct.App. 2016)] (See *Remedies for Breach of Sales and Lease Contracts*.)

- **For a sample answer for Problem 14–6, go to Appendix C at the end of this text.**

14–7. Requirements Contracts. Medalist Golf, Inc., a high-end golf course builder, was working on a new golf course project in Missouri. Chris Williams, doing business as Cane Creek Sod, submitted a bid with Medalist to provide Meyer Zoysia grass sod for the project. Williams and Medalist executed a "grass supplier agreement" that specified the type and quality of grass to be used, as well as the price, and gave Medalist a right to inspect and reject the sod. The parties estimated the quantity of sod needed for the project to be twenty-one acres. Williams had approximately sixty-five acres of Meyer Zoysia grass sod growing at the time. The agreement did not specify the amount of sod that Medalist would purchase from Williams, nor did it say that Medalist would buy Williams's sod exclusively. Later, when Medalist had an expert inspect Williams's sod (before it was harvested), the expert concluded that it did not meet the quality standards required for the project. Medalist therefore rejected the sod. Williams sued for breach of contract. Was the "grass supplier agreement" enforceable as a requirements contract? Why or why not? [*Williams v. Medalist Golf, Inc.*, 910 F.3d 1041 (8th Cir. 2018)] (See *The Formation of Sales and Lease Contracts*.)

14–8. Implied Warranties. Harold Moore bought a barrel-racing horse named Clear Boggy for $100,000 for his daughter. The seller was Betty Roper, who appraises barrel-racing horses. (Barrel racing is a rodeo event in which a horse and rider attempt to complete a cloverleaf pattern around preset barrels in the fastest time.) Clear Boggy was promoted for sale as a competitive barrel-racing horse. On inquiry, Roper represented that Clear Boggy did not have any performance issues or medical problems, and that the only medications the horse had been given were hock injections, a common treatment.

Shortly after the purchase, Clear Boggy began exhibiting significant performance problems, including nervousness, unwillingness to practice, and stalling during runs. Roper then disclosed that the horse had been given shoulder injections prior to the sale and had previously stalled in competition. Moore took the horse to a veterinarian and discovered that it suffered from arthritis, impinged vertebrae, front-left-foot problems, and a right-hind-leg fracture. The vet recommended, and Moore paid for, surgery to repair the leg fracture, but Clear Boggy remained unfit for competition. Moore also discovered that the horse had been scratched from a competition prior to the sale because it was injured. Can Moore prevail in a lawsuit against Roper for breach of the implied warranty of fitness for a particular purpose? Why or why not? [*Moore v. Roper*, 2018 WL 1123868 (E.D.Okla. 2018)] (See *Warranties*.)

14–9. Statute of Frauds. SunOpta Grains and Foods, Inc., sold sunflower kernels to food manufacturer TreeHouse Foods, Inc. Later, SunOpta recalled the kernels because they were contaminated. TreeHouse then sued for breach of contract and breach of expressed and implied warranties, among other things. One issue that arose involved the placement of the signature lines in the contracts. The signature lines did not appear at the ends of the contracts but preceded certain "terms and conditions." TreeHouse argued that the signatures therefore did not apply to anything that followed the signature lines. Do the signatures to a contract have to be placed at the end of the contract to be enforceable? [*TreeHouse Foods, Inc. v. SunOpta Grains and Foods, Inc.*, 463 F.Supp.3d 801 (N.D. IL 2020)] (See *The Formation of Sales and Lease Contracts.*)

14–10. A Question of Ethics—The IDDR Approach and Buyer's Remedies. Samsung Telecommunications America, LLC, makes Galaxy phones. Daniel Norcia bought a Galaxy S4 in a Verizon store in San Francisco, California. A Verizon employee opened the box, unpacked the phone, and helped Norcia transfer his contacts to the new phone. Norcia took the phone, and its charger and headphones, and left the store. Less than a year later, he filed an action

on behalf of himself and other Galaxy S4 buyers in a federal district court against Samsung, alleging that the manufacturer misrepresented the phone's storage capacity and rigged it to operate at a higher speed when it was being tested. [*Norcia v. Samsung Telecommunications America, LLC*, 845 F.3d 1279 (9th Cir. 2017)] (See *Remedies for Breach of Sales and Lease Contracts.*)

(a) Samsung included an arbitration provision in a brochure in the Galaxy S4 box. Would it be ethical of Samsung to assert the arbitration clause?

(b) Why would corporate decision makers choose to misrepresent their product? Explain, using the *Discussion* and *Review* steps of the IDDR approach.

Time-Limited Group Assignment

14–11. Warranties. Milan purchased saffron extract, marketed as "America's Hottest New Way to a Flat Belly," online from Dr. Chen. The website stated that recently published studies showed a significant weight loss (more than 25 percent) for people who used pure saffron extract as a supplement *without diet or exercise.* Dr. Chen said that the saffron suppresses appetite by increasing levels of serotonin, which reduces emotional eating. Milan took the extract as directed without any resulting weight loss. (See *Warranties.*)

(a) The first group will determine whether Dr. Chen's website made any express warranty on the saffron extract or its effectiveness in causing weight loss.

(b) The second group will discuss whether the implied warranty of merchantability applies to the purchase of weight-loss supplements.

(c) The third group will decide if Dr. Chen's sale of saffron extract breached the implied warranty of fitness for a particular purpose.

(d) The fourth group will evaluate the possible success of a suit against a company that offers weight-loss products requiring no diet or exercise given that, according to current common knowledge, people must burn more calories than they consume to lose weight.

Chapter 15

Creditor–Debtor Relations and Bankruptcy

Many people struggle to pay their debts. Although in the old days, debtors were punished and sometimes even sent to prison for failing to pay what they owed, debtors today rarely go to jail. They have many other options, including *bankruptcy*, which is the last resort in resolving creditor–debtor problems.

The right to petition for bankruptcy relief under federal law is an essential aspect of our capitalistic society, in which we have great opportunities for financial success but may also encounter financial difficulties. For instance, many retail chains (including Radio Shack, Sears, and Toys R Us) have filed for bankruptcy in the last decade, in part due to increased online shopping and

COVID-19 shutdowns. Shopping malls throughout America are struggling to keep their anchor stores (such as Nordstrom and Macy's) open and profitable, given the prevalence of Amazon and other Internet sellers. Brick-and-mortar retailers are expected to continue filing for bankruptcy for years to come. Therefore, every businessperson should have some understanding of this topic.

15–1 Laws Assisting Creditors

Normally, creditors have no problem collecting the debts owed to them. When disputes arise over the amount owed, however, or when a debtor simply cannot or will not pay, what happens? What remedies are available to creditors when a debtor **defaults** (fails to pay as promised)? Here, we examine some basic laws that assist the creditor and debtor in resolving their dispute before the debtor resorts to bankruptcy.

The remedies we discuss next are available regardless of whether a creditor is secured or unsecured. *Secured creditors* are those whose loans are backed by *collateral*, which is specific property (such as a car or a house) pledged by a borrower to ensure repayment. The loans made by *unsecured creditors*, such as companies that provide credit cards, are not backed by collateral.

15–1a Liens

A **lien** is an encumbrance on (claim against) property to satisfy a debt or protect a claim for the payment of a debt. Liens may arise under the common law (usually by possession of the property) or under statutory law. *Mechanic's liens* are statutory liens, whereas *artisan's liens* were recognized at common law. *Judicial liens* may be used by a creditor to collect on a debt before or after a judgment is entered by a court. Liens are a very important tool for

creditors because they generally take priority over other claims against the same property.

Mechanic's Liens Sometimes, a person who has contracted for labor, services, or materials to be furnished for making improvements on real property does not immediately pay for the improvements. When that happens, the creditor can place a **mechanic's lien** on the property.

Real Property Secures the Debt. A mechanic's lien creates a special type of debtor–creditor relationship in which the real estate itself becomes security for the debt. ■ **Example 15.1** Kirk contracts to paint Tanya's house for an agreed-on price to cover labor and materials. If Tanya refuses to pay or pays only a portion of the charges after the work is completed, a mechanic's lien against the property can be created. Kirk is then a lienholder, and the real property is encumbered (burdened) with the mechanic's lien for the amount owed. ■

If the property owner fails to pay the debt, the lienholder is technically entitled to foreclose on the real estate and sell it. (As will be discussed, *foreclosure* is the process by which a creditor legally takes a debtor's property to satisfy a debt.) The sale proceeds are then used to pay the debt and the costs of the legal proceedings. The surplus, if any, is paid to the former owner.

Artisan's Liens When a debtor fails to pay for labor and materials furnished for the repair or improvement of personal property, a creditor can recover payment through an **artisan's lien.** Artisan's liens usually take priority over other creditors' claims to the same property.

Lienholder Must Retain Possession. In contrast to a mechanic's lien, an artisan's lien is possessory. That is, the lienholder ordinarily must have retained possession of the property and have expressly or impliedly agreed to provide the services on a cash, not a credit, basis. The lien remains in existence as long as the lienholder maintains possession, and the lien is terminated once possession is voluntarily surrendered, unless the surrender is only temporary.

◼ **Case in Point 15.2** Carrollton Exempted Village School District (in Ohio) hired Clean Vehicle Solutions America, LLC (CVSA, based in New York), to convert ten school buses from diesel to compressed natural gas. The contract price was $660,000. The district paid a $400,000 deposit and agreed to pay installments of $26,000 to CVSA after the delivery of each converted bus. After the first two buses were delivered, the district refused to continue the contract, claiming that the conversion made the two buses unsafe to drive.

Both parties filed breach-of-contract lawsuits. CVSA also asserted an artisan's lien over two other buses that it still had in its possession because it had started converting them to natural gas and spent $65,000 doing so. Regardless of the outcome in the parties' lawsuits, CVSA has an artisan's lien that gives it a priority claim to those two buses so long as they remain in its possession. The buses will act as security for the district's payment of at least the amount CVSA has spent converting them to natural gas.[1] ◼

Foreclosure on Personal Property. Modern statutes permit the holder of an artisan's lien to foreclose and sell the property subject to the lien to satisfy the debt. As with a mechanic's lien, the lienholder is required to give notice to the owner of the property before the foreclosure and sale. The sale proceeds are used to pay the debt and the costs of the legal proceedings, and the surplus, if any, is paid to the former owner.

Judicial Liens When a debt is past due, a creditor can bring a legal action against the debtor to collect the debt. If the action is successful, the court awards the creditor a judgment against the debtor (usually for the amount of the debt plus any interest and legal costs incurred). Frequently, however, the creditor is unable to collect the awarded amount.

To ensure that a judgment in the creditor's favor will be collectible, the creditor may request that certain property of the debtor be seized to satisfy the debt. A court's order to seize the debtor's property is known as a *writ of attachment* if it is issued before a judgment. If the order is issued after a judgment, it is referred to as a *writ of execution.*

Writ of Attachment. In the context of judicial liens, **attachment** refers to a court-ordered seizure and taking into custody of property before a judgment is obtained on a past-due debt. (Attachment has a different meaning in the context of secured transactions.) Because attachment is a prejudgment remedy, it occurs either at the time a lawsuit is filed or immediately afterward.

A creditor must comply with the specific state's statutory restrictions and requirements. The due process clause of the Fourteenth Amendment to the U.S. Constitution requires that the debtor be given notice and an opportunity to be heard. The creditor must have an enforceable right to payment of the debt under law and must follow certain procedures. Otherwise, the creditor can be liable for damages for wrongful attachment.

The typical procedure for attachment is as follows:

1. The creditor files with the court an *affidavit* (a written statement, made under oath). The affidavit states that the debtor has failed to pay and indicates the statutory grounds under which attachment is sought.
2. The creditor must post a bond to cover at least the court costs, the value of the property attached, and the value of the loss of use of that property suffered by the debtor.
3. When the court is satisfied that all the requirements have been met, it issues a **writ of attachment.** The writ directs the sheriff or other officer to seize the debtor's nonexempt property. If the creditor prevails at trial, the seized property can be sold to satisfy the judgment.

Writ of Execution. If a creditor wins a judgment against a debtor and the debtor will not or cannot pay the amount due, the creditor can request a **writ of execution** from the court. A writ of execution is an order that directs the sheriff to seize (levy) and sell any of the debtor's nonexempt real or personal property. The writ applies only to property that is within the court's geographic jurisdiction (usually the county in which the courthouse is located).

The proceeds of the sale are used to pay the judgment, accrued interest, and costs of the sale. Any excess is paid to the debtor. The debtor can pay the judgment and redeem the nonexempt property at any time before the sale takes place.

---

1. *Clean Vehicle Solutions America, LLC v. Carrollton Exempted Village School District Board of Education,* 2015 WL 5459852 (S.D.N.Y. 2015). See also *McCann v. Webb,* 2022-Ohio-2318 (Ohio Ct. App., 4th Dist. 2022).

15–1b Garnishment

An order for **garnishment** permits a creditor to collect a debt by seizing property of the debtor that is being held by a third party. As a result of a garnishment proceeding, for instance, the debtor's employer may be ordered by the court to turn over a portion of the debtor's wages to pay the debt. Many other types of property can be garnished as well, including funds in a bank account, tax refunds, pensions, and trust funds. It is only necessary that the property is not exempt from garnishment and is in the possession of a third party.

■ **Case in Point 15.3**   When Edward G. Tinsley divorced Michelle Townsend, they entered into a marital settlement contract. They agreed to sell the marital home and split the proceeds evenly. But Tinsley refused to cooperate with the sale. A court therefore appointed a trustee to sell the house for them and ordered the sheriff to evict Tinsley. Tinsley then conveyed the house to a trust established in his name. Even after the sheriff evicted Tinsley from the house and changed the locks, Tinsley managed to move back in and change the locks again.

Tinsley was arrested for trespassing and charged with contempt of court (for disobeying court orders). In the meantime, Tinsley secretly sold the home for $150,000 and deposited the proceeds into a bank account held in the name of Edward G. Tinsley Living Trust at SunTrust Bank. After learning of the sale, the court-appointed trustee obtained a writ of garnishment on all of Tinsley's and his trust's bank accounts at SunTrust Bank. Despite numerous objections from Tinsley (and a trial and appeal), SunTrust Bank eventually complied with the garnishment order and sent all the funds to the trustee.[2] ■

Procedures   Garnishment can be a prejudgment remedy, requiring a hearing before a court, but it is most often a postjudgment remedy. State law governs garnishment actions, so the specific procedures vary from state to state.

In some states, the judgment creditor needs to obtain only one order of garnishment, which will then apply continuously to the judgment debtor's wages until the entire debt is paid. In other states, the judgment creditor must go back to court for a separate order of garnishment for each pay period.

See this chapter's Ethics Today feature for a discussion of how a creditor can obtain a garnishment order even when a debtor crosses state lines in an attempt to avoid paying the debt.

2. *Tinsley v. SunTrust Bank*, 2016 WL 687545 (Special Ct.App. MD 2016). See also *Burhill Leasing Corp. v. Jeffery T. Graham*, 2022-Ohio-3757, 199 N.E.3d 642 (Ohio Ct. App. 2nd Dist. 2022).

Ethics Today — Creditors' Rights When Debtors Move to Another State

Creditors have rights when debtors default. The former often go to court and win judgments against the latter. But what can creditors do when judgment debtors simply "pack up and leave"? That is to say, when debtors engage in the ethically suspect action of crossing state lines to avoid judgments, is there recourse for creditors?

Full Faith and Credit

The Constitution of the United States provides that full faith and credit shall be given in each state to the public acts, records, and judicial proceedings of every other state.[a] Among other things, this means that judgments made in one state will be honored in other states. Fortunately for creditors, there is a long judicial history of the application of judgments to debtors who have moved to another state.[b]

The Uniform Enforcement of Foreign Judgments Act

Nearly all of the states have adopted the Uniform Enforcement of Foreign Judgments Act.[c] The act allows judgments obtained in one jurisdiction (such as a state) to be "domesticated" (recognized and enforced) in a different jurisdiction (such as another state). One goal is to prevent judgment debtors from evading payment of their obligations by relocating to another state.

In most states, domestication of a foreign judgment can be accomplished rapidly. The judgment creditor files an authenticated copy of the judgment in the "foreign" state, along with an affidavit and a notice of foreign judgment. The notice of domestication action then is provided to the debtor. A local court enters an order affirming that the foreign judgment has been domesticated.

a. U.S. Const., Art. IV, Section 1.
b. See, for example, *Aultman, Miller & Co. v. Mills*, 9 Wash. 68, 36 P. 1046 (1894).
c. Originally issued by the National Conference of Commissioners on Uniform State Laws (NCCUSL) in 1948. Revised in 1964.

The equivalent at the federal level involves registering judgments between federal courts.[d] Unlike state court domestication procedures, federal court domestication procedures do not require that notice be given to the judgment debtor.

Time Is of the Essence

Once domestication of a foreign judgment has occurred, judgment creditors must record the domestication order with the proper authorities within the jurisdiction to put others on notice. Thus, if real property is involved, a title search will show the foreign judgment against the debtor who has an ownership interest in the real property.

All states have specific lifespans (statutes of limitations) for foreign judgments. Often, a judgment debtor will attempt to counter a foreign judgment by claiming that the lifespan of the foreign judgment has lapsed. Domestications of foreign judgments can be renewed, however.

Garnishment Actions

When a judgment debtor moves to another state, one method of obtaining repayment for debts owed is through the process of garnishment. The benefit for the creditor in such cases is that judgment debtors are often surprised when their bank accounts are frozen or their regular salaries are reduced. Garnishments are typically served against a bank, which then has to freeze any accounts belonging to the debtor.

....

Critical Thinking Is it fair that property or wage garnishments may "surprise" a judgment debtor?

d. 28 U.S.C. Section 1963.

Laws Limiting the Amount of Wages Subject to Garnishment Both federal and state laws limit the amount that can be taken from a debtor's weekly take-home pay through garnishment proceedings. Federal law provides a minimal framework to protect debtors from losing all their income to pay judgment debts. State laws also provide dollar exemptions, and these amounts are often larger than those provided by federal law. Under federal law, an employer cannot dismiss an employee because the employee's wages are being garnished.

15–1c Creditors' Composition Agreements

Creditors may contract with a debtor to discharge the debtor's liquidated debts (debts that are definite, or fixed, in amount) on the debtor's payment of a sum less than that owed. These agreements are referred to as **creditors' composition agreements** (or *composition agreements*) and usually are held to be enforceable unless they are formed under duress.

In the strictest sense, the surety is primarily liable for the debt of the principal. The creditor can demand payment from the surety from the moment the debt is due. The creditor need not exhaust all legal remedies against the principal debtor before holding the surety responsible for payment.

■ **Example 15.4** Roberto Delmar wants to borrow from the bank to buy a used car. Because Roberto is still in college, the bank will not lend him the funds without a cosigner. Roberto's father, José Delmar, who has dealt with the bank before, agrees to cosign the note, thereby becoming a surety who is jointly liable for payment of the debt. When José Delmar cosigns the note, he becomes primarily liable to the bank. On the note's due date, the bank can seek payment from either Roberto or José Delmar, or both jointly. ■

Guaranty With a suretyship arrangement, the surety is primarily liable for the debtor's obligation. With a guaranty arrangement, the **guarantor**—the third person making the guaranty—is secondarily liable.

The guarantor can be required to pay the obligation only after the principal debtor defaults, and usually only after the creditor has made an attempt to collect from the debtor. The guaranty contract terms determine the extent and time of the guarantor's liability.

■ **Case in Point 15.5** Staff members at Altercare, a nursing home, told resident Connie Turner that her insurance company was covering all costs related to her stay. After Turner left Altercare, however, the nursing home sued to recover an unpaid bill of nearly $8,000. The trial court found that, because the assurances on which she had relied were untrue, Turner did not owe Altercare any repayment. Altercare then tried to recover the costs from Victoria Cox, Turner's granddaughter, who had signed several forms as guarantor of Turner's financial obligations to Altercare. An Ohio appeals court blocked this maneuver, holding that a guarantor could not be held responsible for debts that the debtor was not legally required to pay.[3] ■

Actions That Release the Surety and the Guarantor

Basically, the same actions release either a surety or a guarantor from an obligation. In general, the following rules apply to both sureties and guarantors, but for simplicity, we refer just to sureties.

1. **Material modification.** Making any material modification to the terms of the original contract without the surety's consent will discharge the surety's obligation. (The extent to which the surety is discharged depends on whether the surety was compensated and the amount of loss suffered from the modification. For instance, a father who receives no consideration for acting as a surety on his daughter's loan will be completely discharged if the loan contract is modified without his consent.)

2. **Surrender of property.** If a creditor surrenders the collateral to the debtor or impairs the collateral without the surety's consent, these acts can reduce the obligation of the surety. If the creditor's actions reduce the value of the property used as collateral, the surety is released to the extent of any loss suffered.

3. **Payment or tender of payment.** Naturally, any payment of the principal obligation by the debtor or by another person on the debtor's behalf will discharge the surety from the obligation. Even if the creditor refused to accept the payment when it was tendered, if the creditor knew about the suretyship, the obligation of the surety can be discharged.

Defenses of the Surety and the Guarantor

Generally, the surety or guarantor can also assert any of the defenses available to the principal debtor to avoid liability on the obligation to the creditor. A few exceptions do exist, however. They apply to both sureties and guarantors, but again, for simplicity, we refer just to sureties.

1. **Incapacity and bankruptcy.** Incapacity and bankruptcy are personal defenses, which can be asserted only by the person who is affected. Therefore, the surety cannot assert the principal debtor's incapacity or bankruptcy as a defense. (Sureties may assert their own incapacity or bankruptcy as a defense, of course.)

2. **Statute of limitations.** The surety cannot assert the statute of limitations as a defense. (In contrast, the principal debtor can claim the statute of limitations as a defense to payment.)

3. **Fraud.** A surety can, in some instances, assert fraud as a defense. In most states, the creditor must inform the surety, before the formation of the suretyship contract, of material facts known by the creditor that would substantially increase the surety's risk. Failure to so inform may constitute fraud and may render the suretyship obligation voidable.

Rights of the Surety and the Guarantor

A surety or guarantor who pays the debt owed to the creditor acquires certain rights, as discussed next. Again, for simplicity, the discussion refers just to sureties.

The Right of Subrogation The surety has the legal **right of subrogation.** Simply stated, this means that any right that the creditor had against the debtor now becomes the right of the surety. Included are creditor rights in bankruptcy, rights to collateral possessed by the creditor, and rights to judgments obtained by the creditor. In short, the surety now stands in the shoes of the creditor and may pursue any remedies that were available to the creditor against the debtor.

The Right of Reimbursement The surety has a **right of reimbursement** from the debtor. Basically, the surety is entitled to receive from the debtor all outlays made on behalf of the suretyship arrangement. Such outlays can include expenses incurred as well as the actual amount of the debt paid to the creditor.

The Right of Contribution Two or more sureties are called **co-sureties.** Individual co-sureties have a **right of contribution** when they pay more than their proportionate share on a debtor's default. That means the co-surety who has overpaid is entitled to recover from the other co-sureties the amount paid above the surety's obligation. Generally, a co-surety's liability either is determined by agreement or, in the absence of agreement, is set at the maximum liability under the suretyship contract.

■ **Example 15.6** Yasser and Stuart, two co-sureties, are obligated under a suretyship contract to guarantee Jules's debt. Stuart's maximum liability is $15,000, and Yasser's is $10,000. Jules owes $10,000 and is in default. Stuart pays the creditor the entire $10,000.

In the absence of an agreement to the contrary, Stuart can recover $4,000 from Yasser. The amount of the debt that Yasser agreed to cover ($10,000) is divided by the

---

3. *Altercare of Canal Winchester Post-Acute Rehabilitation Center, Inc. v. Turner,* 2019-Ohio-1011, 2019 WL 1313218 (Ohio Ct. App., 10th Dist. 2019). See also *Lakhi v. Meritra Health Care, LLC,* 2022-Ohio-3062, 2022 WL 4002922 (Ohio Ct. App., 10th Dist. 2022).

total amount that he and Stuart together agreed to cover ($25,000). The result is multiplied by the amount of the default, yielding the amount that Yasser owes—($10,000 ÷ $25,000) × $10,000 = $4,000. ∎

15–2 Mortgages

When individuals purchase real property, they typically make a **down payment** in cash and borrow the remaining funds from a financial institution. The borrowed funds are secured by a **mortgage**—a written instrument that gives the creditor a lien on the debtor's real property as security for payment of a debt. The creditor is the "mortgagee," and the debtor is the "mortgagor."

15–2a Fixed-Rate Versus Adjustable-Rate Mortgages

Lenders offer various types of mortgages to meet the needs of different borrowers, but a basic distinction is whether the interest rate is fixed or variable. A fixed-rate mortgage has a fixed, or unchanging, rate of interest, so the payments remain the same for the duration of the loan. Lenders determine the interest rate for a standard fixed-rate mortgage loan based on a variety of factors, including the borrower's credit history, credit score, income, and debts.

With an adjustable-rate mortgage (ARM), the rate of interest paid by the borrower changes periodically. Typically, the initial interest rate for an ARM is set at a relatively low fixed rate for a specified period, such as a year or three years. After that time, the interest rate adjusts periodically—often, annually. The interest rate adjustment is calculated by adding a certain number of percentage points (called the *margin*) to an index rate (one of various government interest rates).

ARMs contractually shift the risk that the interest rate will change from the lender to the borrower. Borrowers will have lower initial payments if they are willing to assume the risk of all future interest rate increases.

15–2b Mortgage Provisions

Because a mortgage involves a transfer of real property, it must be in writing to comply with the Statute of Frauds. Mortgages normally are lengthy and formal documents containing many provisions, including the following:

1. The terms of the underlying loan. These include the loan amount, the interest rate, the period of repayment, and other important financial terms, such as the margin and index rate for an ARM.

2. A prepayment penalty clause. A **prepayment penalty clause** requires the borrower to pay a penalty if the mortgage is repaid in full within a certain period. A prepayment penalty helps to protect the lender should the borrower refinance within a short time after obtaining a mortgage.

3. Provisions relating to the maintenance of the property. Because the mortgage conveys an interest in the property to the lender, the lender often requires the borrower to maintain the property to protect the lender's investment.

4. A statement obligating the borrower to maintain homeowner's insurance on the property. **Homeowner's insurance** protects the lender's interest in the event of a loss due to certain hazards, such as fire or storm damage.

5. A list of the non-loan financial obligations to be borne by the borrower. For instance, the borrower typically is required to pay all property taxes, assessments, and other claims against the property.

6. Creditor protections. When creditors extend mortgages, they are advancing a significant amount of funds for a number of years. Consequently, creditors usually require debtors to obtain **mortgage insurance** if they do not make a down payment of at least 20 percent of the purchase price.

Creditors record the mortgage with the appropriate office in the county where the property is located so that their interest in the property is officially on record.

15–2c Mortgage Foreclosure

If the homeowner defaults, or fails to make the mortgage payments, the lender has the right to foreclose on the mortgaged property. **Foreclosure** is the legal process by which the lender repossesses and auctions off the property that has secured the loan.

Foreclosure is expensive and time consuming. It generally benefits neither the borrowers, who lose their homes, nor the lenders, which face the prospect of losses on their loans. Therefore, both lenders and borrowers are motivated to avoid foreclosure proceedings if possible.

Ways to Avoid Foreclosure Possible methods of avoiding foreclosure include a forbearance, workout agreement, and short sale.

A **forbearance** is a postponement of part or all of the payments on a loan for a limited time. This option works well when the debtor can solve the problem by securing a new job, selling the property, or finding another acceptable solution.

A **workout agreement** is a contract that describes the respective rights and responsibilities of the borrower and the lender as they try to resolve the default. Usually, the lender agrees to delay seeking foreclosure. In exchange, the borrower provides additional financial information that might be used to modify the mortgage.

A lender may sometimes agree to a **short sale,** which is a sale of the property for less than the balance due on the mortgage loan. Typically, the borrower has to show some hardship, such as the loss of a job, a decline in the value of the home, a divorce, or a death in the household. The lender often has approval rights in a short sale, so the sale process may take much longer than an ordinary real estate transaction.

Foreclosure Procedure If all efforts to find another solution fail, the lender will proceed to foreclosure. The lender must strictly comply with the state statute governing foreclosures.

In the following case, a property owner defaulted on her mortgage, and the lender obtained a writ of execution for a sheriff's sale of the property. After the sale, the former owner asked the court that had issued the writ to set aside the sale, and the court refused. In doing so, did the court abuse its discretion?

Banc of California, N.A. v. Madhok

Superior Court of New Jersey, Appellate Division, __ N.J.Super. __, 2019 WL 149660 (2019).

Background and Facts Ritu Madhok borrowed $213,069 from Banc of California, N.A., to buy a house in Iselin, New Jersey. She executed a note for the amount and a mortgage to secure payment of the note. Ten months later, she stopped making payments. Banc of California filed an action in a New Jersey state court to foreclose on the mortgage. The court granted the bank's request for a sheriff's sale of the property.

The sale was postponed for three months to give Madhok an opportunity to submit a loss mitigation package—which is an application to avoid foreclosure that includes a statement of personal financial difficulties, along with pay stubs, tax returns, bank statements, and other information to support the statement. Madhok provided a partial, incomplete package the day before the sale, and the sale went ahead as scheduled. More than a month later, Madhok filed a motion to vacate the sale. The court denied the motion. She appealed, arguing that the court's denial of the motion was an abuse of discretion.

In the Language of the Court
PER CURIAM. [By the Whole Court]
* * * *

Foreclosure proceedings seek primary or principal relief which is equitable in nature. An application to open, vacate or otherwise set aside a foreclosure judgment or proceeding * * * is subject to an abuse of discretion standard. Accordingly, a trial judge's application or denial of equitable remedies should not be disturbed unless it can be shown that the trial court palpably abused its discretion, that is, that its finding was so wide off the mark that a manifest denial of justice resulted.

A motion to vacate a sheriff's sale is governed by [New Jersey] Rule [of Court] 4:65-5, which states that any objection to the sale must be served "within ten days after the sale or at any time thereafter before the delivery of the conveyance." Examples of valid grounds for objection include fraud, accident, surprise, irregularity, or impropriety in the sheriff's sale. None of these grounds are applicable here.

Under Rule 4:65-5, the trial court has discretion to set aside a sale if the defendant alleges a valid independent ground for equitable relief. * * * However, despite the court's broad discretion to employ equitable remedies, this power should be sparingly exercised and a sale [should] be vacated only when necessary to correct a plain injustice.

Here, [after the default] defendant procrastinated until the eve of the sheriff's sale to pursue loss mitigation options, coupled with the submission of an incomplete loss mitigation application. * * * Under these circumstances, we cannot find that the trial court abused its discretion in denying defendant's motion, made one month after the sheriff's sale.

Decision and Remedy A state intermediate appellate court affirmed the lower court's order denying Madhok's motion to vacate the sheriff's sale. The lower court did not abuse its discretion by refusing Madhok's request. She delayed until the day before the sale to apply for a loan modification and then provided only a partial loss mitigation application.

Critical Thinking

- **Economic** The bank was willing to process a loan modification on the debtor's loss mitigation application while simultaneously pursuing foreclosure on her property. Is this dual tracking an abusive practice? Explain.
- **What If the Facts Were Different?** Suppose that before the sale, Madhok had filed a motion for more time to file a complete loss mitigation application. Would the result have been different? Discuss.

Redemption Rights Every state allows a defaulting borrower to redeem the property before the foreclosure sale by paying the full amount of the debt, plus any interest and costs that have accrued. This **equitable right of redemption** gives the defaulting buyer a chance to regain title and possession after default.

The statutory right of redemption, in contrast, entitles the borrower to repurchase property after a judicial foreclosure. In other words, in states that provide for statutory redemption, the homeowner has a right to buy the property back from a third party who bought it at a foreclosure sale. Generally, the borrower may exercise this right for up to one year from the time the house is sold at a foreclosure

sale. The borrower may retain possession of the property after the foreclosure sale until the statutory redemption period ends. If the borrower does not exercise the right of redemption, the new buyer receives title to and possession of the property.

15–2d Suretyship and Guaranty

When a third person promises to pay a debt owed by another in the event that the debtor, or principal, does not pay, either a *suretyship* or a *guaranty* relationship is created. Exhibit 15–1 illustrates these relationships. The third person's creditworthiness becomes the security for the debt owed.

Exhibit 15–1 Suretyship and Guaranty Parties

In a suretyship or guaranty arrangement, a third party promises to be responsible for a debtor's obligations. A third party who agrees to be responsible for the debt even if the primary debtor does not default is known as a *surety*. A third party who agrees to be secondarily responsible for the debt—that is, responsible only if the primary debtor defaults—is known as a *guarantor*. Normally, a promise of guaranty (a collateral, or secondary, promise) must be in writing to be enforceable.

Principal Debtor

Creditor

Surety (Primary Liability to Creditor) or **Guarantor** (Secondary Liability to Creditor)

Normally a guaranty must be in writing to be enforceable under the Statute of Frauds, unless its main purpose is to benefit the guarantor. Traditionally, a suretyship agreement did not require a writing to be enforceable, and oral surety agreements were sufficient. Today, however, some states require a writing to enforce a suretyship.

At common law, there were significant differences in the liability of a surety and a guarantor. Today, however, the distinctions outlined here have been abolished in some states.

Suretyship A contract of strict **suretyship** is a promise made by a third person to be responsible for the debtor's obligation. It is an express contract between the **surety** (the third party) and the creditor.

15–3 Protection for Debtors

The law protects debtors as well as creditors. Consumer protection statutes protect debtors' rights, for instance, and bankruptcy laws are designed specifically to assist debtors in need of help. In addition, in most states, certain types of real and personal property are exempt from execution or attachment. State exemption statutes usually include both real and personal property.

15–3a Exempted Real Property

Probably the most familiar exemption is the **homestead exemption.** The purpose of the homestead exemption is to ensure that the debtor will retain some form of shelter.

The General Rule Each state permits the debtor to retain the value of the family home up to a specified dollar amount free from the claims of unsecured creditors or trustees in bankruptcy. (Note that federal bankruptcy law places a cap on the amount that debtors filing bankruptcy can claim as exempt under their states' homestead exemption.)

■ **Example 15.7** Vince Beere owes Chris Veltman $40,000. The debt is the subject of a lawsuit, and the court awards Veltman a judgment of $40,000 against Beere. Beere's homestead (property and house) is valued at $50,000, and the homestead exemption is $25,000. There are no outstanding mortgages or other liens on his homestead. To satisfy the judgment debt, Beere's family home is sold at public auction for $45,000. The proceeds of the sale are distributed as follows:

1. Beere is given $25,000 as his homestead exemption.
2. Veltman is paid $20,000 toward the judgment debt, leaving a $20,000 *deficiency judgment* (that is, "left-over debt"). The deficiency judgment can be satisfied

from any other nonexempt property (personal or real) that Beere may own, if permitted by state law. ■

Limitations In a few states, statutes allow the homestead exemption only if the judgment debtor has a family. If a judgment debtor does not have a family, a creditor may be entitled to collect the full amount realized from the sale of the debtor's home. In addition, the homestead exemption interacts with other areas of law and can sometimes operate to cancel out a portion of a lien on a debtor's real property.

15–3b Exempted Personal Property

Personal property that is most often exempt from satisfaction of judgment debts includes the following:

1. Household furniture up to a specified dollar amount.
2. Clothing and certain personal possessions, such as family pictures or a Bible.
3. A vehicle (or vehicles) for transportation (up to a specified dollar amount).
4. Certain classified animals, usually livestock but including pets.
5. Equipment that the debtor uses in a business or trade, such as tools or professional instruments, up to a specified dollar amount.

15–4 The Bankruptcy Code

Bankruptcy relief is provided under federal law. Although state laws may play a role in bankruptcy proceedings, particularly state property laws, the governing law is based on federal legislation.

Article I, Section 8, of the U.S. Constitution gave Congress the power to establish "uniform laws on the subject of bankruptcies throughout the United States." Federal bankruptcy legislation was first enacted in 1898 and since then has undergone several modifications, most recently in the 2005 Bankruptcy Reform Act. Federal bankruptcy laws (as amended) are called the Bankruptcy Code or, more simply, the Code.

15–4a Bankruptcy Courts

Bankruptcy proceedings are held in federal bankruptcy courts, which are under the authority of U.S. district courts. Rulings from bankruptcy courts can be appealed to the district courts.

A bankruptcy court can conduct a jury trial if the appropriate district court has authorized it and the parties to the bankruptcy consent. Bankruptcy courts follow the Federal Rules of Bankruptcy Procedure rather than the Federal Rules of Civil Procedure. Bankruptcy court judges are appointed for terms of fourteen years.

15–4b Types of Bankruptcy Relief

The Bankruptcy Code is contained in Title 11 of the *United States Code* and has eight chapters. Chapters 1, 3, and 5 of the Code contain general definitional provisions, as well as provisions governing case administration, creditors, the debtor, and the estate. These three chapters normally apply to all kinds of bankruptcies.

Four chapters of the Code set forth the most important types of relief that debtors can seek:

1. Chapter 7 provides for **liquidation** proceedings (the selling of all nonexempt assets and the distribution of the proceeds to the debtor's creditors).
2. Chapter 11 governs reorganizations.
3. Chapters 12 (for family farmers and family fishermen) and 13 (for individuals) provide for the adjustment of debts by persons with regular incomes.[4]

Note that a debtor (except for a municipality) need not be insolvent[5] to file for bankruptcy relief under the Bankruptcy Code. Anyone obligated to a creditor can declare bankruptcy.

15–4c Special Requirements for Consumer-Debtors

A **consumer-debtor** is a debtor whose debts result primarily from the purchase of goods for personal, family, or household use. The Bankruptcy Code requires that the clerk of the court give all consumer-debtors written notice of the general purpose, benefits, and costs of each chapter under which they might proceed. In addition, the clerk must provide consumer-debtors with information on the types of services available from credit counseling agencies.

15–5 Liquidation Proceedings

Liquidation under Chapter 7 of the Bankruptcy Code is probably the most familiar type of bankruptcy proceeding and is often referred to as an *ordinary*, or *straight, bankruptcy*. Put simply, a debtor in a liquidation bankruptcy turns all assets over to a **bankruptcy trustee,** a person appointed by the court to manage the debtor's funds. The trustee sells the nonexempt assets and distributes the proceeds to creditors. With certain exceptions, the debtor is then granted a **discharge** of the remaining debts and is no longer obligated to pay.

Any "person"—defined as including individuals, partnerships, and corporations[6]—may be a debtor in a liquidation proceeding. A husband and wife may file jointly for bankruptcy under a single petition. Railroads, insurance companies, banks, savings and loan associations, investment companies licensed by the Small Business Administration, and credit unions cannot be debtors in a liquidation bankruptcy. Other chapters of the Bankruptcy Code or other federal or state statutes apply to them.

A straight bankruptcy can be commenced by the filing of either a voluntary or an involuntary **petition in bankruptcy**—the document that is filed with a bankruptcy court to initiate bankruptcy proceedings. If a debtor files the petition, the bankruptcy is voluntary. If one or more creditors file a petition to force the debtor into bankruptcy, the bankruptcy is involuntary.

15–5a Voluntary Bankruptcy

To bring a voluntary petition in bankruptcy, the debtor files official forms designated for that purpose in the bankruptcy court. The law now requires that before debtors can file a petition, they must receive credit counseling from an approved nonprofit agency within the 180-day period preceding the date of filing. Debtors filing a Chapter 7 petition must include a certificate proving that they have received individual or group counseling from an approved agency within the last 180 days.

Consumer-debtors filing for liquidation bankruptcy must confirm the accuracy of the petition's contents. The debtors must also state in the petition, at the time of filing, that they understand the relief available under other chapters of the Code and have chosen to proceed under Chapter 7.

Attorneys representing consumer-debtors must file an affidavit stating that they have informed the debtors of

---

4. There are no Chapters 2, 4, 6, 8, or 10 in Title 11. Such "gaps" are not uncommon in the *United States Code*. They occur because chapter numbers (or other subdivisional unit numbers) are sometimes reserved for future use when a statute is enacted. (A gap may also appear if a law has been repealed.)

5. The inability to pay debts as they become due is known as *equitable insolvency*. Balance sheet insolvency, which exists when a debtor's liabilities exceed assets, is not the test. Thus, debtors whose cash-flow problems become severe may petition for bankruptcy voluntarily or be forced into involuntary bankruptcy even though their assets far exceed their liabilities.

6. The definition of corporation includes unincorporated companies and associations. It also covers labor unions.

the relief available under each chapter of the Bankruptcy Code. In addition, the attorneys must reasonably attempt to verify the accuracy of the consumer-debtors' petitions and schedules (described next). Failure to do so is considered perjury.

Chapter 7 Schedules

The voluntary petition must contain the following schedules:

1. A list of both secured and unsecured creditors, their addresses, and the amount of debt owed to each.
2. A statement of the financial affairs of the debtor.
3. A list of all property owned by the debtor, including property that the debtor claims is exempt.
4. A list of current income and expenses.
5. A certificate of credit counseling.
6. Proof of payments received from employers within sixty days prior to the filing of the petition.
7. A statement of the amount of monthly income, itemized to show how the amount is calculated.
8. A copy of the debtor's federal income tax return for the most recent year ending immediately before the filing of the petition.

The official forms must be completed accurately, sworn to under oath, and signed by the debtor. To conceal assets or knowingly supply false information on these schedules is a crime under the bankruptcy laws.

With the exception of tax returns, failure to file the required schedules within forty-five days after the filing of the petition will result in an automatic dismissal of the petition. (An extension may be granted, however.) The debtor has up to seven days before the date of the first creditors' meeting to provide a copy of the most recent tax returns to the trustee.

Tax Returns During Bankruptcy

In addition, a debtor may be required to file a tax return at the end of each tax year while the case is pending and to provide a copy to the court. This may be done at the request of the court or the **U.S. trustee**—a government official who performs administrative tasks that a bankruptcy judge would otherwise have to perform. Any party in interest (a party, such as a creditor, who has a valid interest in the outcome of the proceedings) may make this request as well. Debtors may also be required to file tax returns during Chapter 11 and 13 bankruptcies.

Substantial Abuse—Means Test

A bankruptcy court can dismiss a Chapter 7 petition if the use of Chapter 7 constitutes a "substantial abuse" of bankruptcy law. The revised Code provides a means test to determine a debtor's eligibility for Chapter 7. The purpose of the test is to keep upper-income people from abusing the bankruptcy process by filing for Chapter 7, as was thought to have happened in the past. The test forces more people to file for Chapter 13 bankruptcy rather than have their debts discharged under Chapter 7.

The Basic Formula. Debtors wishing to file for bankruptcy must complete the means test to determine whether they qualify for Chapter 7. A debtor's average monthly income in recent months is compared with the median income in the geographic area in which the person lives. (The U.S. Trustee Program provides these data at its website, www.justice.gov/ust.) If the debtor's income is below the median income, the debtor usually is allowed to file for Chapter 7 bankruptcy, as there is no presumption of bankruptcy abuse.

Applying the Means Test to Future Disposable Income. If the debtor's income is above the median income, then further calculations must be made to determine the debtor's future disposable income. As a basis for the calculations, it is presumed that the debtor's recent monthly income will continue for the next sixty months. Disposable income is then calculated by subtracting living expenses and secured debt payments, such as mortgage payments, from monthly income.

Living expenses are amounts allowed under formulas used by the Internal Revenue Service (IRS). The IRS allowances include modest allocations for food, clothing, housing, utilities, transportation (including a car payment), health care, and other necessities. (The U.S. Trustee Program's website also provides these amounts.) The allowances do not include expenditures for items such as cell phones and cable television service.

Can the Debtor Afford to Pay Unsecured Debts? Once future disposable income has been estimated, that amount is used to determine whether the debtor will have income that could be applied to unsecured debts. The courts may also consider bad faith or other circumstances indicating abuse on the part of the debtor.

■ **Case in Point 15.8** John and Sarah Buoy filed for Chapter 7 bankruptcy. For the past three months, John's gross monthly income had been $4,900, and Sarah's had been $6,761. They had five children. They owed secured debts of $34,321 on a Subaru Impreza and a BMW 328i, on which they intended to continue making loan payments (this is called *reaffirmation*, as will be discussed later). They owed $123,000 on a mortgage and $19,000 in student loans, and their unsecured debts were $4,900.

An auditor for the U.S. Trustee Program reviewed the Buoys' Chapter 7 schedule and concluded that the family's gross income figures were understated. Because of a mistake in math, the Buoys had miscalculated their income by approximately $800 a month (or nearly $650 after taxes). The debtors claimed that they had incurred additional expenses after filing the petition, including orthodontic braces and another car. Even with those expenses, however, the court found that they would have an additional $400 a month in future disposable income and would receive sizeable tax refunds. The court concluded that the Buoys could afford to pay their debts and dismissed the Chapter 7 petition for substantial abuse.[7] ▪

Additional Grounds for Dismissal As already noted, a court can dismiss a debtor's voluntary petition for Chapter 7 relief for substantial abuse or for failure to provide the necessary documents within the specified time.

In addition, a court might dismiss a Chapter 7 case in two other situations. First, if the debtor has been convicted of a violent crime or a drug-trafficking offense, the victim can file a motion to dismiss the voluntary petition.[8] Second, if the debtor fails to pay postpetition domestic-support obligations (which include child and spousal support), the court may dismiss the debtor's petition.

Order for Relief If the voluntary petition for bankruptcy is found to be proper, the filing of the petition will itself constitute an **order for relief.** (An order for relief is a court's grant of assistance to a petitioner.) Once a consumer-debtor's voluntary petition has been filed, the trustee and creditors must be given notice of the order for relief by mail not more than twenty days after entry of the order.

15–5b Involuntary Bankruptcy

An involuntary bankruptcy occurs when the debtor's creditors force the debtor into bankruptcy proceedings. An involuntary case cannot be filed against a charitable institution or a farmer (an individual or business that receives more than 50 percent of gross income from farming operations).

An involuntary petition should not be used as an everyday debt-collection device, and the Code provides penalties for the filing of frivolous petitions against debtors. If the court dismisses an involuntary petition, the petitioning creditors may be required to pay the costs and attorneys' fees incurred by the debtor in defending against

the petition. If the petition was filed in bad faith, damages can be awarded for injury to the debtor's reputation. Punitive damages may also be awarded.

Requirements For an involuntary action to be filed, the following requirements must be met:

1. If the debtor has twelve or more creditors, three or more of these creditors having unsecured claims totaling at least $18,600 must join in the petition.
2. If a debtor has fewer than twelve creditors, one or more creditors having a claim totaling $18,600 or more may file.[9]

Order for Relief If the debtor challenges the involuntary petition, a hearing will be held, and the bankruptcy court will enter an order for relief if it finds either of the following:

1. The debtor is not paying debts as they come due.
2. A general receiver, assignee, or custodian took possession of, or was appointed to take charge of, substantially all of the debtor's property within 120 days before the filing of the petition.

If the court grants an order for relief, the debtor will be required to supply the same information in the bankruptcy schedules as in a voluntary bankruptcy.

15–5c Automatic Stay

The moment a petition, either voluntary or involuntary, is filed, an **automatic stay,** or suspension, of all actions by creditors against the debtor or the debtor's property normally goes into effect. The automatic stay prohibits creditors from taking any act to collect, assess, or recover a claim against the debtor that arose before the filing of the petition. The stay normally continues until the bankruptcy proceeding is closed or dismissed. (In some circumstances, it is possible to petition the bankruptcy court for relief from the automatic stay, as will be discussed shortly.)

If a creditor knowingly violates the automatic stay (a willful violation), any injured party, including the debtor, is entitled to recover actual damages, costs, and attorneys' fees. Punitive damages may be awarded as well.

▪ **Case in Point 15.9** Stefanie Kuehn filed for bankruptcy. When she requested a transcript from the university at which she had obtained her master's degree, the university refused because she owed more than $6,000 in tuition. Kuehn complained to the bankruptcy court, which ruled that the university had violated the automatic stay by refusing

7. *In re Buoy*, ___ Bankr. ___, 2017 WL 3194755 (N.D. OH, W.Div. 2017). See also *In re Johns-Manville Corporation*, 2022 WL 4487889 (2nd Cir. 2022).
8. Note that the court may not dismiss a case on this ground if the debtor's bankruptcy is necessary to satisfy a claim for a domestic-support obligation.
9. 11 U.S.C. Section 303. The amounts stated in this chapter are in accordance with those computed on April 1, 2022. The dollar amounts are adjusted every three years on April 1.

to provide a transcript in an attempt to collect an unpaid tuition debt. The decision was affirmed on appeal.[10] ■

---

10. *In re Kuehn*, 563 F.3d 289 (7th Cir. 2009). See also *In re Cordova*, 635 B.R. 321 (Bkr. Ct., N.D. IL, E.Div. 2021).

The following case involved the foreclosure sale of a house whose tenant had filed for bankruptcy. The question before an appeals court was whether the automatic stay precluded the sale.

Case Analysis 15.2

In re Fogarty

United States Court of Appeals, Second Circuit, 39 F.4th 62, 71 Bankr.Ct.Dec. 179 (2022).

In the Language of the Court

CARNEY, Circuit Judge

Debtor-Appellee Eileen Fogarty held a 99% interest in 72 Grandview LLC (the "LLC"), an entity that owned a property (the "Property") that Fogarty occupied as her primary residence. In 2010, the LLC stopped making payments on the Mortgage and Note secured by the Property, leading Appellant Bayview Loan Servicing LLC ("Bayview") in 2011 to initiate a state court foreclosure action (the "Foreclosure Action") as the owner and holder of the Note and Mortgage. Seeking a state court order that would permit the sale, Bayview named both the LLC and Fogarty as defendants in the Foreclosure Action.

In January 2018, Bayview obtained a judgment in the Foreclosure Action, which in effect authorized Bayview to sell the Property under the supervision of a court-appointed referee. The sale was scheduled for April 2018. Four days before the scheduled sale, Fogarty petitioned for bankruptcy in the Eastern District of New York under Chapter 7 of the Bankruptcy Code. On the eve of the sale, her counsel notified Bayview of her petition and her position that proceeding with the sale would violate the automatic stay triggered by her petition. Bayview promptly countered that, [because] the LLC alone owned the Property and the LLC had not filed for bankruptcy, no relevant stay was in effect. It then proceeded as scheduled and the Property was sold to a third party.

Fogarty then sought sanctions against Bayview in the bankruptcy court, asserting Bayview's willful violation of the automatic stay. The bankruptcy court denied Fogarty's motion, but on appeal the district court reversed, finding that because Fogarty was a named defendant in the Foreclosure Action, the sale violated the automatic stay. It further found the violation to be willful because Bayview knew of the petition when it proceeded. It remanded to the bankruptcy court for assessment and award of actual damages and consideration of a punitive damages award. Bayview now appeals.

As a matter of first impression, we hold that two of the Bankruptcy Code's automatic stay provisions are violated by the foreclosure sale of a property when the debtor is a named party in the foreclosure proceedings, even if the debtor's direct interest in the property is only possessory. Accordingly, we conclude that Bayview willfully violated the automatic stay when it completed the foreclosure sale while knowing that Fogarty, a named defendant in the Foreclosure Action, had filed a bankruptcy petition. Bayview could and should have sought relief in advance from the bankruptcy court. * * *

* * * *

* * * [O]n the eve of the Sale, counsel for Fogarty contacted counsel for Bayview by phone, and in a confirmation email that evening conveyed his firm's opinion that " * * * the automatic stay is in effect" and that

"continuation of the [Sale] will be in violation of the stay." The email further stated that Fogarty would seek "costs, fees and sanctions for such violation of the stay" if the Sale proceeded the next day as planned. * * *

Counsel for Bayview responded the next morning, minutes before the scheduled Sale, dismissing Fogarty's warning. * * *

* * * *

Bayview proceeded with the Sale as scheduled. The Property was sold to a third party. The "Terms of Sale" document, dated April 17, in which the supervising referee set the particulars of the sale, was filed in the bankruptcy court not long after. The document named both the LLC and Fogarty as defendants in the caption. It set the date for delivery of the referee's deed as May 17.

* * * *

The Bankruptcy Code's automatic stay provisions, set forth in Section 362, "protect bankruptcy estates by restraining any formal or informal action or legal proceeding that might dissipate estate assets or interfere with the trustee's orderly administration of the estate." * * * The automatic stay is "one of the fundamental debtor protections provided by the bankruptcy laws, designed to relieve the financial pressures that drove debtors into bankruptcy." Because "the automatic stay is imposed by Congressional mandate and not by court order," no court action is needed for the stay to become effective.

A. Under the plain text of Section 362, the Sale violated the automatic stay

It is undisputed that, under Section 362, Fogarty's bankruptcy filing on April 13, 2018, triggered an automatic stay. And, as Bayview concedes, Fogarty's possessory interest as a tenant of the Property was part of her bankruptcy estate and protected by the automatic stay. "[A] mere possessory interest in real property, without any accompanying legal interest, is sufficient to trigger the protection of the automatic stay."

* * * *

Conclusion

We have considered all of Bayview's remaining arguments and find in them no basis for reversal. For the reasons set forth above, the July 1, 2020, order of the district court is AFFIRMED and the case is REMANDED for further proceedings consistent with this Opinion.

Legal Reasoning Questions

1. Could Bayview reasonably argue that it did not willfully violate the automatic stay? Why or why not?

2. When the court discusses a "possessory interest" in the property, what is it referring to?

3. How might Bayview have avoided any issue with the automatic stay provisions of the Bankruptcy Code?

The Adequate Protection Doctrine Underlying the Code's automatic-stay provision for a secured creditor is a concept known as *adequate protection*. The **adequate protection doctrine,** among other things, protects secured creditors from losing their security as a result of the automatic stay.

The bankruptcy court can provide adequate protection by requiring the debtor or trustee to make periodic cash payments or a one-time cash payment. The court can also require the debtor or trustee to provide additional collateral or replacement liens to the extent that the stay may actually cause the value of the property to decrease.

Exceptions to the Automatic Stay The Code provides several exceptions to the automatic stay. The following are not stayed:

1. Domestic-support obligations, including any debt owed to or recoverable by a spouse, a former spouse, a child of the debtor, that child's parent or guardian, or a governmental unit.
2. Proceedings against the debtor related to divorce, child custody or visitation, domestic violence, and support enforcement.
3. Investigations by a securities regulatory agency (such as an investigation into insider trading).
4. Certain statutory liens for property taxes.

Requests for Relief From the Automatic Stay A *secured creditor* or other party in interest can petition the bankruptcy court for relief from the automatic stay. If a creditor or other party requests relief from the stay, the stay will automatically terminate sixty days after the request, unless the court grants an extension[11] or the parties agree otherwise.

Secured Property The automatic stay on *secured property* terminates forty-five days after the creditors' meeting unless the debtor redeems or reaffirms certain debts. (Creditors' meetings and reaffirmation will be discussed later in this chapter.) In other words, the debtor cannot keep the secured property (such as a financed automobile), even if they continue to make payments on it, without reinstating the rights of the secured party to collect on the debt.

Bad Faith If the debtor had two or more bankruptcy petitions dismissed during the prior year, the Code presumes bad faith. In such a situation, the automatic stay does not go into effect until the court determines that the petition was filed in good faith.

In addition, the automatic stay on secured debts will terminate thirty days after the petition is filed if the debtor filed a bankruptcy petition that was dismissed within the prior year. Any party in interest can request that the court extend the stay by showing that the filing is in good faith.

15–5d Estate in Bankruptcy

On the commencement of a liquidation proceeding under Chapter 7, an estate in bankruptcy (sometimes called an *estate in property*) is created. The estate consists

---

11. The court might grant an extension, for instance, on a motion by the trustee that the property is of value to the estate.

of all the debtor's interests in property currently held, wherever located. The estate in bankruptcy includes all of the following:

1. Community property (property jointly owned by married persons in certain states).
2. Property transferred in a transaction voidable by the trustee.
3. Proceeds and profits from the property of the estate.

Certain after-acquired property to which the debtor becomes entitled within 180 days after filing may also become part of the estate. Such after-acquired property includes gifts, inheritances, property settlements (from divorce), and life insurance death proceeds.

Generally, though, the filing of a bankruptcy petition fixes a dividing line. Property acquired prior to the filing of the petition becomes property of the estate, and property acquired after the filing of the petition, except as just noted, remains the debtor's.

15–5e The Bankruptcy Trustee

Promptly after the order for relief in the liquidation proceeding has been entered, a trustee is appointed. The basic duty of the trustee is to collect the debtor's available estate and reduce it to cash for distribution, preserving the interests of both the debtor and the unsecured creditors. The trustee is held accountable for administering the debtor's estate.

To enable the trustee to accomplish this duty, the Code gives the trustee certain powers, stated in both general and specific terms. These powers must be exercised within two years of the order for relief.

Review for Substantial Abuse The trustee is required to promptly review all materials filed by the debtor to determine if there is substantial abuse. Within ten days after the first meeting of the creditors (discussed shortly), the trustee must file a statement indicating whether the case is presumed to be an abuse under the means test. The trustee must provide a copy of this statement to all creditors within five days.

When there is a presumption of abuse, the trustee must either file a motion to dismiss the petition (or convert it to a Chapter 13 petition) or file a statement explaining why a motion would not be appropriate. If the debtor owes a domestic-support obligation (such as child support), the trustee must provide written notice of the bankruptcy to the claim holder (a former spouse, for instance).

The Trustee's Powers The trustee has the power to require persons holding the debtor's property at the time

the petition is filed to deliver the property to the trustee.[12] To enable the trustee to implement this power, the Code provides that the trustee has rights equivalent to those of certain other parties, such as a creditor who has a judicial lien. This power of a trustee, which is equivalent to that of a lien creditor, is known as the *strong-arm power*.

In addition, the trustee has specific powers of avoidance. They enable the trustee to set aside (avoid) a sale or other transfer of the debtor's property and take the property back for the debtor's estate. These powers apply to voidable rights available to the debtor, preferences, and fraudulent transfers by the debtor. Each power is discussed in more detail next. A trustee can also avoid certain statutory liens.

The debtor shares most of the trustee's avoidance powers. Thus, if the trustee does not take action to enforce one of the rights just mentioned, the debtor in a liquidation bankruptcy can enforce that right.[13]

Voidable Rights A trustee steps into the shoes of the debtor. Thus, any reason that debtors can use to obtain the return of their property can be used by trustees as well. These grounds include fraud, duress, incapacity, and mutual mistake.

■ **Example 15.10** Ben sells his boat to Tara. Tara gives Ben a check, knowing that she has insufficient funds in her bank account to cover the check. Tara has committed fraud. Ben has the right to avoid that transfer and recover the boat from Tara. If Ben files for bankruptcy relief under Chapter 7, the trustee can exercise the same right to recover the boat from Tara, and the boat becomes a part of the debtor's estate. ■

Preferences A debtor is not permitted to transfer property or to make a payment that favors—or gives a **preference** to—one creditor over others. The trustee is allowed to recover payments made both voluntarily and involuntarily to one creditor in preference over another.

To have made a recoverable preferential payment, an insolvent debtor must have transferred property, for a preexisting debt, within ninety days before the filing of the bankruptcy petition. The transfer must have given the creditor more than the creditor would have received as a

---

12. Usually, the trustee takes constructive, rather than actual, possession of the debtor's property. For instance, to obtain control of a debtor's business inventory, a trustee might change the locks on the doors to the business and hire a security guard.
13. Under a Chapter 11 bankruptcy, for which no trustee other than the debtor generally exists, the debtor has the same avoidance powers as a trustee under Chapter 7. Under Chapters 12 and 13, a trustee must be appointed.

result of the bankruptcy proceedings. The Code presumes that a debtor is insolvent during the ninety-day period before filing a petition.

If a **preferred creditor** (one who has received a preferential transfer) has sold the property to an innocent third party, the trustee cannot recover the property from the innocent party. The preferred creditor, however, generally can be held liable for the value of the property.

Preferences to Insiders. Sometimes, the creditor receiving the preference is an insider. An **insider** is an individual, partner, partnership, corporation, or officer or director of a corporation (or a relative of one of these) who has a close relationship with the debtor. In this situation, the avoidance power of the trustee extends to transfers made within one year before filing. (If the transfer was fraudulent, as will be discussed shortly, the trustee can avoid transfers made within two years before filing.) The trustee must, however, prove that the debtor was insolvent when the transfer occurred and that the transfer was made to or for the benefit of an insider.

Transfers That Do Not Constitute Preferences. Not all transfers are preferences. Most courts generally assume that payment for services rendered within fifteen days before the payment is not a preference. In addition, if a creditor receives payment in the ordinary course of business from a debtor, such as payment of last month's cell phone bill, the bankruptcy trustee cannot recover the payment.

In a case when the debts are not primarily consumer debts, the Code also permits the transfer of property to a creditor up to a specified total value ($7,575 until April 1, 2025, when the limit will be increased) without the transfer constituting a preference. Payment of domestic-support debts does not constitute a preference.

Fraudulent Transfers   A trustee may avoid fraudulent transfers or obligations if they (1) were made within two years prior to the filing of the petition or (2) were made with actual intent to hinder, delay, or defraud a creditor. ■ **Case in Point 15.11** David Dearmond owned interests in several companies, including Briartowne, LLC, Hillside, LLC, and Bluffs of Sevier County, LLC. When Briartowne defaulted on a $623,499 promissory note, SmartBank filed an action against Briartowne, Dearmond, and others.

Five months later, Dearmond sold a property to his fiancée, Patricia Harper, for $90,000, after having recently bought it for $400,000. Two days after that, Dearmond created two irrevocable trust agreements and transferred all of his interest in Hillside and Bluffs of Sevier County to those trusts. The trusts named Harper as the primary beneficiary. Although SmartBank obtained a judgment against Dearmond (and the other owners of Briartowne), it was unable to collect from these assets.

A year and a half later, Dearmond filed a petition for bankruptcy. The trustee filed a motion seeking to avoid the fraudulent transfers made to benefit Harper. The court concluded that the transfers should be set aside because they were made with actual intent to hinder, delay, or defraud a creditor. The court entered a judgment for the trustee in an amount equivalent to the value of the fraudulent transfers.[14] ■

Transfers made for less than reasonably equivalent consideration are also vulnerable if the debtor thereby became insolvent or was left engaged in business with an unreasonably small amount of capital. When a fraudulent transfer is made outside the Code's two-year limit, creditors may seek alternative relief under state laws. Some state laws may allow creditors to recover transfers made up to three years before the filing of a petition.

15–5f Exemptions

An individual debtor is entitled to exempt (exclude) certain property from the bankruptcy up to a specified dollar amount that changes every three years:[15]

1. A portion of equity in the debtor's home (the homestead exemption).
2. Motor vehicles, up to a certain value (usually just one vehicle).
3. Reasonably necessary clothing, household goods and furnishings, and household appliances (the aggregate value not to exceed a certain amount).
4. Jewelry, up to a certain value.
5. Tools of the debtor's trade or profession, up to a certain value.
6. A portion of unpaid but earned wages.
7. Pensions.
8. Public benefits, including public assistance (welfare), Social Security, and unemployment compensation, accumulated in a bank account.
9. Damages awarded for personal injury up to a certain amount.

---

14. *In re Dearmond,* 2017 WL 4220396 (Bankr. E.D. TN 2017).

15. The dollar amounts stated in the Bankruptcy Code are adjusted automatically every three years on April 1 based on changes in the Consumer Price Index. The adjusted amounts are rounded to the nearest $25.

Property that is not exempt under federal law includes bank accounts, cash, family heirlooms, collections of stamps and coins, second cars, and vacation homes.

Individual states have the power to pass legislation precluding debtors from using the federal exemptions within the state. A majority of the states have done this. In those states, debtors may use only state, not federal, exemptions. In the rest of the states, debtors may choose either the exemptions provided under state law or the federal exemptions.

15–5g Creditors' Meeting

Within a reasonable time after the order for relief has been granted (not more than forty days), the trustee must call a meeting of the creditors listed in the schedules filed by the debtor. The bankruptcy judge does not attend this meeting. The debtor is required to attend (unless excused by the court) and to submit to examination under oath by the creditors and the trustee. At the meeting, the trustee ensures that the debtor is aware of the potential consequences of bankruptcy and of the possibility of filing under a different chapter of the Code.

15–5h Creditors' Claims

To be entitled to receive a portion of the debtor's estate, each creditor normally files a proof of claim with the bankruptcy court within ninety days of the creditors' meeting. A proof of claim is necessary if there is any dispute concerning the claim. The proof of claim lists the creditor's name and address, as well as the amount that the creditor asserts is owed to the creditor by the debtor.

When the debtor has no assets—called a "no-asset case"—creditors are notified of the debtor's petition for bankruptcy but are instructed not to file a claim. In no-asset cases, the unsecured creditors will receive no payment, and most, if not all, of these debts will be discharged.

15–5i Distribution of Property

The Code provides specific rules for the distribution of the debtor's property to secured and unsecured creditors. If any amount remains after the priority classes of creditors have been satisfied, it is turned over to the debtor.

Distribution to Secured Creditors The Code requires that consumer-debtors file a statement of intention with respect to secured collateral. They can choose to pay off the debt and redeem the collateral,

claim it is exempt, reaffirm the debt and continue making payments, or surrender the property to the secured party.

If the collateral is surrendered to the secured party, the secured party can either (1) accept it in full satisfaction of the debt or (2) sell it and use the proceeds to pay off the debt. Thus, the secured party has priority over unsecured parties as to the proceeds from the disposition of the collateral. Should the collateral be insufficient to cover the secured debt owed, the secured creditor becomes an unsecured creditor for the difference (deficiency).

There are limited exceptions to these rules. For instance, certain unsecured creditors can sometimes step into the shoes of secured tax creditors in Chapter 7 liquidation proceedings. In such situations, when the collateral securing the tax claims is sold, the unsecured creditors are paid first. This exception does not include holders of unsecured claims for administrative expenses incurred in Chapter 11 cases that are converted to Chapter 7 liquidations.

Distribution to Unsecured Creditors Bankruptcy law establishes an order of priority for debts owed to unsecured creditors, and they are paid in the order of their priority. Claims for domestic-support obligations, such as child support and alimony, have the highest priority among unsecured creditors, so these claims must be paid first. Each class, or group, must be fully paid before the next class is entitled to any of the remaining proceeds.

If there are insufficient proceeds to fully pay all the creditors in a class, the proceeds are distributed proportionately to the creditors in that class. Classes lower in priority receive nothing. In almost all Chapter 7 bankruptcies, the funds will be insufficient to pay all creditors.

Exhibit 15–2 illustrates the collection and distribution of property in most voluntary bankruptcies. The exhibit includes a listing of the classes of unsecured creditors.

15–5j Discharge

From the debtor's point of view, the primary purpose of liquidation is to obtain a fresh start through a discharge of debts. A discharge voids, or sets aside, any judgment on a discharged debt and prevents any action to collect it. Certain debts, however, are not dischargeable in bankruptcy. Also, certain debtors may not qualify to have all debts discharged in bankruptcy. These situations are discussed next.

Exhibit 15–2 Collection and Distribution of Property in Most Voluntary Bankruptcies

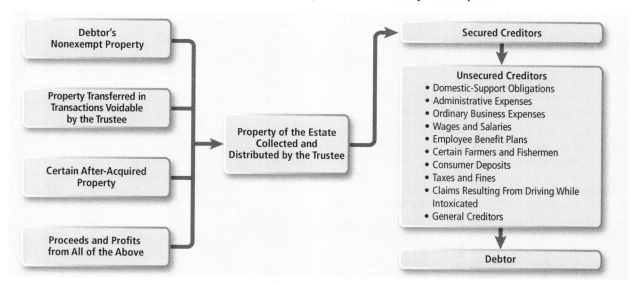

Exceptions to Discharge Claims that are not dischargeable in bankruptcy include the following:

1. Claims for back taxes accruing within two years prior to bankruptcy.
2. Claims for amounts borrowed by the debtor to pay federal taxes or any nondischargeable taxes.
3. Claims against property or funds obtained by the debtor under false pretenses or by false representations.
4. Claims by creditors who were not notified of the bankruptcy. These claims did not appear on the schedules the debtor was required to file.
5. Claims based on fraud or misuse of funds by the debtor while acting in a fiduciary capacity or claims involving the debtor's embezzlement or larceny.
6. Domestic-support obligations and property settlements as provided for in a separation agreement or divorce decree.
7. Claims for amounts due on a retirement account loan.
8. Claims based on willful or malicious conduct by the debtor toward another or the property of another. ■ **Case in Point 15.12** Anthony Mickletz owned a pizza restaurant that employed John Carmello. One night after Carmello had finished his shift, Mickletz called him back into the restaurant and accused him of stealing. An argument ensued, and Mickletz shoved Carmello, causing him to fall and injure his back.

Because Mickletz did not provide workers' compensation coverage as required by law, the state prosecuted him criminally. He was ordered to pay more than $45,000 in restitution to Carmello for his injuries. Carmello also filed a civil suit against Mickletz, which the parties agreed to settle for $175,000. Later, Mickletz filed a petition for bankruptcy. Carmello argued that these debts were nondischargeable, and the court agreed. The exception from discharge includes any debts for willful (deliberate or intentional) injury, and Mickletz's actions were deliberate.[16] ■

9. Certain government fines and penalties.
10. Student loans unless payment of the loans imposes an undue hardship on the debtor and the debtor's dependents (when paying the loan would leave the debtor unable to maintain a minimum standard of living, for instance).
11. Consumer debts of more than a specified amount ($800 in 2022) for luxury goods or services owed to a single creditor incurred within ninety days of the order for relief.
12. Cash advances totaling more than a threshold amount ($1,100 in 2022) that are extensions of open-end

---

16. *In re Mickletz,* 544 Bankr. 804 (E.D.Pa. 2016); see also *In re Dilworth,* 71 Bankr.Ct.Dec. 110 (Bkr. Ct. D. CT 2022).

consumer credit obtained by the debtor within seventy days of the order for relief.

13. Judgments against a debtor as a result of the debtor's operation of a motor vehicle while intoxicated.

14. Fees or assessments arising from property in a homeowners' association, as long as the debtor retained an interest in the property.

15. Taxes with respect to which the debtor failed to provide required or requested tax documents.

■ **Case in Point 15.13** At the time he filed for Chapter 7 bankruptcy, Terence Wolfe had not been consistently employed for twenty years. He had been fired from numerous positions for behavioral issues and had difficulty finding and holding a job. Wolfe had been diagnosed with personality disorders and ultimately was granted disability status by the U.S. government. He was living on disability payments of $1,126 per month at the time he filed for Chapter 7 bankruptcy.

Among Wolfe's debts were more than $131,000 in student loan debts. Wolfe sought to have these debts discharged because repaying them would constitute undue hardship. The court agreed and granted a discharge. According to the court, although Wolfe is intelligent, "he has been unable, for more than two decades, to maintain full-time employment for any meaningful length of time. He is living at a minimal standard of living and it is unlikely that he will ever be able to repay these loans."[17] ■

Objections to Discharge In addition to the exceptions to discharge previously discussed, a bankruptcy

court may also deny discharge based on the debtor's conduct. Grounds for denial of discharge of the debtor include the following:

1. The debtor's concealment or destruction of property with the intent to hinder, delay, or defraud a creditor.

2. The debtor's fraudulent concealment or destruction of financial records.

3. The grant of a discharge to the debtor within eight years before the petition was filed.

4. The debtor's failure to complete the required consumer education course.

5. The debtor's involvement in proceedings in which the debtor could be found guilty of a felony. (Basically, a court may not discharge any debt until the completion of felony proceedings against the debtor.)

When a discharge is denied under any of these circumstances, the debtor's assets are still distributed to the creditors. After the bankruptcy proceeding, however, the debtor remains liable for the unpaid portion of all claims.

In addition, a discharge may be revoked within one year if it is discovered that the debtor acted fraudulently or dishonestly during the bankruptcy proceeding. If that occurs, a creditor whose claim was not satisfied in the distribution of the debtor's property can proceed with a claim against the debtor.

In the following case, a married couple—two surgeons—claimed that they had only $400,000 in assets, with liabilities of over $5.6 million. They argued that they could not cover their monthly expenses. But they failed to explain a large quantity of "lost assets" and other assets transferred to their children.

---

17. *In re Wolfe*, 501 Bankr. 426 (M.D.Fla. 2011). See also *In re Wheat*, 2022 WL 243221 (Bankr. Ct., M.D. AL 2022).

Case 15.3

In re Dykes

United States Court of Appeals, Eighth Circuit, 954 F.3d 1157, 68 Bankr.Ct.Dec. 148, Bankr. L. Rep. P 85,510 (2020).

Background and Facts Daryll and Sharon Dykes filed a petition for Chapter 7 relief in a federal bankruptcy court, reporting just under $400,000 in assets, over $5.6 million in liabilities, and a monthly income insufficient to cover expenses.

Both Daryll and Sharon were surgeons, at one time earning more than $1 million per year and living in a $3 million home. They had lost the home to foreclosure, and their household goods had later been auctioned by a storage facility when the couple did not pay the storage fees.

In the schedules filed with the bankruptcy petition, the Dykeses did not explain or make an accounting for "hundreds of thousands of dollars" in purportedly lost property, nor did they disclose "substantial" transfers of their assets to their children. Creditors filing claims in the proceeding included the mortgagee who had foreclosed on their home, the homebuilder, and a jeweler.

Before the Dykeses' assets were fully gathered and the estate administered, the bankruptcy court denied a discharge. A Bankruptcy Appellate Panel (BAP) upheld the denial because of the debtors' undocumented purchases and returns of hundreds of thousands of dollars in watches and jewelry.

The Dykeses appealed to the U.S. Court of Appeals for the Eighth Circuit.

In the Language of the Court

LOKEN, Circuit Judge.

* * * *

[The Bankruptcy Code] authorizes denial of discharge if "the debtor has concealed, destroyed, mutilated, falsified, or failed to keep or preserve any recorded information, including books, documents, records, and papers, from which the debtor's financial condition or business transactions might be ascertained, unless such act or failure to act was justified under all of the circumstances of the case." This provision makes the privilege of discharge dependent on a true presentation of the debtor's financial affairs.

* * * *

We agree with the BAP that the * * * Debtors' failure to keep adequate records left the bankruptcy court without a way to determine the exact transactions between the Debtors and the jeweler.

Mr. Dykes's return of twenty-seven valuable watches and [a diamond] ring to [the jeweler] was * * * a sudden and large dissipation of assets. * * * Mr. Dykes * * * was a sophisticated collector of highly valuable watches and jewelry, and his purchase and return transactions had a significant impact on Debtors' financial condition. The transactions also impacted the legitimacy of the jeweler's bankruptcy claim * * * . The only record of the returns was a receipt that utterly failed to substantiate the financial effect of the transaction.

* * * *

We agree with the BAP * * * that Debtors failed to justify their failure to keep adequate records. At the time Mr. Dykes returned the watches * * * , Debtors were considering bankruptcy, and creditors were circling. * * * In these circumstances, a reasonable person would insist on documenting the impact of this transaction on his financial condition.

Decision and Remedy   The U.S. Court of Appeals for the Eighth Circuit agreed with the BAP and affirmed the bankruptcy court's judgment. The Dykeses were denied a discharge in bankruptcy.

Critical Thinking

- **Legal Environment**   In determining whether a debtor's failure to keep adequate records was justified, the Bankruptcy Code requires a determination based on all the circumstances of the case. What factors might a court weigh in making this determination? Discuss.

- **Economic**   How might the Dykeses have established, or at least indicated, the fair market value of the watches and jewelry at the time of their return in order to avoid the result in this case? Explain.

15–5k   Reaffirmation of Debt

An agreement to pay a debt dischargeable in bankruptcy is called a **reaffirmation agreement.** A debtor may wish to pay a debt—such as a debt owed to a family member, physician, bank, or some other creditor—even though the debt could be discharged in bankruptcy. Also, as noted previously, a debtor cannot retain secured property while continuing to pay without entering into a reaffirmation agreement.

Procedures   To be enforceable, reaffirmation agreements must be made before the debtor is granted a discharge. The agreement must be signed and filed with the court. Court approval is required unless the debtor is represented by an attorney during the negotiation of the reaffirmation and submits the proper documents and certifications. Even when the debtor is represented by an attorney, court approval may be required if it appears that the reaffirmation will result in undue hardship to the debtor.

When court approval is required, a separate hearing will take place. The court will approve the reaffirmation only if it finds that the agreement will not result in undue hardship to the debtor and that the reaffirmation is consistent with the debtor's best interests.

Required Disclosures To discourage creditors from engaging in abusive reaffirmation practices, the law provides specific language for disclosures that must be given to debtors entering into reaffirmation agreements. Among other things, these disclosures explain that the debtor is not required to reaffirm any debt. They also inform the debtor that liens on secured property, such as mortgages and cars, will remain in effect even if the debt is not reaffirmed.

The reaffirmation agreement must disclose the amount of the debt reaffirmed, the rate of interest, the date payments begin, and the right to rescind. The disclosures also caution the debtor: "Only agree to reaffirm a debt if it is in your best interest. Be sure you can afford the payments you agree to make."

The original disclosure documents must be signed by the debtor, certified by the debtor's attorney, and filed with the court at the same time as the reaffirmation agreement. A reaffirmation agreement that is not accompanied by the original signed disclosures will not be effective.

■ **Case in Point 15.14** Teresa Chandler took out a loan with Peoples Bank to be paid in forty-eight installments. After making thirteen timely payments, she missed one on July 7. On July 30, she filed for Chapter 7 bankruptcy. On August 8, she made her fourteenth payment, which Peoples Bank applied to the missed July 7 payment. She and Peoples Bank then signed a standard reaffirmation agreement, which was filed with a Kentucky bankruptcy court on September 11. Because of the missed payment, every payment that Chandler made under the reaffirmation agreement was considered one month late, leading to "harassment," extra fees, and penalties.

Chandler filed a complaint alleging that Peoples Bank had violated the reaffirmation agreement. An appeals court determined that Chandler mistakenly believed the missed July 7 payment to have been forgiven by her declaration of bankruptcy. When a reaffirmation agreement does not specifically differ from the original agreement, the original agreement controls. Therefore, she still owed Peoples Bank a total of forty-eight payments, not forty-seven. Furthermore, the court noted, as the reaffirmation agreement went into effect on September 11, the bank could not have violated it by any action linked to a payment made on August 8.[18] ■

---

18. *Chandler v. Peoples Bank & Trust Company of Hazard,* 769 Fed. Appx. 242 (6th Cir. 2019).

15–6 Reorganizations

The type of bankruptcy proceeding most commonly used by corporate debtors is the Chapter 11 reorganization. In a reorganization, the creditors and the debtor formulate a plan under which the debtor pays a portion of the debts and is discharged of the remainder. The debtor is allowed to continue in business. Although this type of bankruptcy generally involves a corporate reorganization, any debtor (except a stockbroker or a commodities broker) who is eligible for Chapter 7 relief is eligible for relief under Chapter 11. Railroads are also eligible.

Congress has established a "fast-track" Chapter 11 procedure for small-business debtors whose liabilities do not exceed a specified amount (about $3 million) and who do not own or manage real estate. The fast track enables a debtor to avoid the appointment of a creditors' committee and also shortens the filing periods and relaxes certain other requirements. Because the process is shorter and simpler, it is less costly.

The same principles that govern the filing of a liquidation (Chapter 7) petition apply to reorganization (Chapter 11) proceedings. The case may be brought either voluntarily or involuntarily. The automatic-stay provision and its exceptions (such as substantial abuse), as well as the adequate protection doctrine, apply in reorganizations.

15–6a Best Interests of the Creditors

Once a Chapter 11 petition has been filed, a bankruptcy court can dismiss or suspend proceedings at any time if dismissal or suspension would better serve the interests of the creditors. Before taking such an action, the court must give notice and conduct a hearing. The Code also allows a court, after notice and a hearing, to dismiss a case under reorganization "for cause" when there is no reasonable likelihood of rehabilitation. Similarly, a court can dismiss when there is an inability to effect a plan or an unreasonable delay by the debtor that may harm the interests of creditors. A debtor whose petition is dismissed for these reasons can file a subsequent Chapter 11 petition in the future.

15–6b Debtor in Possession

On entry of the order for relief, the debtor generally continues to operate the business as a **debtor in possession (DIP).** The court, however, may appoint a trustee (often referred to as a *receiver*) to operate the debtor's business. The court will choose this action if gross mismanagement of the business is shown or if appointing a trustee is in the best interests of the estate.

A family fisherman is one whose gross income is at least 50 percent dependent on commercial fishing operations[23] and whose debts are at least 80 percent related to commercial fishing. The total debt for a family fisherman must not exceed a certain amount (about $2.3 million in 2022). As with family farmers, a partnership or close corporation can also qualify.

Filing the Petition   The procedure for filing a family-farmer or family-fisherman bankruptcy plan is similar to the procedure for filing a repayment plan under Chapter 13. The debtor must file a plan not later than ninety days after the order for relief has been entered. The filing of the petition acts as an automatic stay against creditors' and co-obligors' actions against the estate.

A farmer or fisherman who has already filed a reorganization or repayment plan may convert it to a Chapter 12 plan. The debtor may also convert a Chapter 12 plan to a liquidation plan.

Content and Confirmation of the Plan   The content of a plan under Chapter 12 is basically the same as that of a Chapter 13 repayment plan. Generally, the plan must be confirmed or denied within forty-five days of filing.

The plan must provide for payment of secured debts at the value of the collateral. If the secured debt exceeds the value of the collateral, the remaining debt is unsecured.

For unsecured debtors, the plan must be confirmed in either of the following circumstances: (1) the value of the property to be distributed under the plan equals the amount of the claim, or (2) the plan provides that all of the debtor's disposable income to be received in a three-year period (or longer, by court approval) will be applied to making payments. Disposable income is all income received less amounts needed to support the farmer or fisherman and family and to continue the farming or commercial fishing operation. Completion of payments under the plan discharges all debts provided for by the plan.

---

23. Commercial fishing operations include catching, harvesting, or raising fish, shrimp, lobsters, urchins, seaweed, shellfish, or other aquatic species or products.

Practice and Review: Creditor–Debtor Relations and Bankruptcy

Three months ago, Janet Hart's husband of twenty years died of cancer. Although he had medical insurance, he left Janet with outstanding medical bills of more than $50,000. Janet has two teenage daughters to support. She has worked at the local library for the past ten years, earning $1,500 per month. Since her husband's death, she has also received $1,500 in Social Security benefits and $1,100 in life insurance proceeds every month, for a total monthly income of $4,100. After making the mortgage payment of $1,500 and paying the amounts due on other debts, Janet has barely enough left to buy groceries for her family. She decides to file for Chapter 7 bankruptcy, hoping for a fresh start. Using the information presented in the chapter, answer the following questions.

1. What must Janet do before filing a petition for relief under Chapter 7?
2. How much time does Janet have after filing the bankruptcy petition to submit the required schedules? What happens if Janet does not meet the deadline?
3. Assume that Janet files a petition under Chapter 7. Further assume that the median family income in the geographic area in which Janet lives is $49,300. What steps would a court take to determine whether Janet's petition is presumed to be "substantial abuse" using the means test?
4. Suppose that the court determines that no *presumption* of substantial abuse applies in Janet's case. Nevertheless, the court finds that Janet does have the ability to pay at least a portion of the medical bills out of her disposable income. What would the court likely order in that situation?

Debate This ...   *Rather than being allowed to file Chapter 7 bankruptcy petitions, individuals and couples should always be forced to make an effort to pay off their debts through Chapter 13.*

Terms and Concepts

adequate protection doctrine 329
artisan's lien 317
attachment 317
automatic stay 327
bankruptcy trustee 325
consumer-debtor 325
co-surety 320
cram-down provision 337
creditors' composition
  agreement 319
debtor in possession (DIP) 336
default 316
discharge 325
down payment 321

forbearance 321
foreclosure 321
garnishment 318
guarantor 319
homeowner's insurance 321
homestead exemption 324
insider 331
lien 316
liquidation 325
mechanic's lien 316
mortgage 321
mortgage insurance 321
order for relief 327
petition in bankruptcy 325

preference 330
preferred creditor 331
prepayment penalty clause 321
reaffirmation agreement 335
right of contribution 320
right of reimbursement 320
right of subrogation 320
short sale 322
surety 324
suretyship 324
U.S. trustee 326
workout agreement 322
writ of attachment 317
writ of execution 317

Issue Spotters

1. Alyssa owes Don $5,000 and refuses to pay. Don obtains a garnishment order and serves it on Alyssa's employer. If the employer complies with the order and Alyssa stays on the job, is one order enough to garnish Alyssa's wages for each pay period until the debt is paid? Explain. (See *Laws Assisting Creditors*.)

2. After graduating from college, Tina works briefly as a salesperson before filing for bankruptcy. Tina's petition states that her only debts are student loans, taxes accruing within the last year, and a claim against her based on her misuse of customers' funds during her employment. Are these debts dischargeable in bankruptcy? Explain. (See *Liquidation Proceedings*.)

• **Check your answers to the Issue Spotters against the answers provided in Appendix B at the end of this text.**

Business Scenarios and Case Problems

15–1. Liens. Nabil is the owner of a relatively old home valued at $105,000. The home's electrical system is failing, and the wiring needs to be replaced. Nabil contracts with Kandhari Electrical to replace the electrical system. Kandhari performs the repairs, and on June 1 submits a bill of $10,000 to Nabil. Because of financial difficulties, Nabil does not pay the bill. Nabil's only asset is his home, but his state's homestead exemption is $60,000. Discuss fully Kandhari's remedies in this situation. (See *Laws Assisting Creditors*.)

15–2. Voluntary Versus Involuntary Bankruptcy. Burke has been a rancher all her life, raising cattle and crops. Her ranch is valued at $500,000, almost all of which is exempt under state law. Burke has eight creditors and a total indebtedness of $70,000. Two of her largest creditors are Oman ($30,000 owed) and Sneed ($25,000 owed). The other six creditors have claims of less than $5,000 each. A drought has ruined all of Burke's crops and forced her to sell many of her

cattle at a loss. She cannot pay off her creditors. (See *Liquidation Proceedings*.)

(a) Under the Bankruptcy Code, can Burke, with a $500,000 ranch, voluntarily petition herself into bankruptcy? Explain.

(b) Could either Oman or Sneed force Burke into involuntary bankruptcy? Explain.

15–3. Business Case Problem With Sample Answer—Discharge in Bankruptcy. Like many students, Barbara Hann financed her education partially through loans. These loans included three federally insured Stafford Loans of $7,500 each ($22,500 in total). Hann believed that she had repaid the loans, but when she filed a Chapter 13 petition, Educational Credit Management Corp. (ECMC) filed an unsecured proof of claim based on the loans. Hann objected. At a hearing at which ECMC failed to appear, Hann submitted correspondence from the lender that indicated the loans had been paid. The court entered an order sustaining Hann's objection. Despite the order, can ECMC resume its effort to collect on Hann's loans? Explain. [*In re Hann*, 711 F.3d 235 (1st Cir. 2013)] (See *Liquidation Proceedings*.)

• **For a sample answer to Problem 15–3, go to Appendix C at the end of this text.**

15–4. Discharge. Michael and Dianne Shankle divorced. An Arkansas state court ordered Michael to pay Dianne alimony and child support, as well as half of the $184,000 in their investment accounts. Instead, Michael withdrew more than half of the investment funds and spent them. Over the next several years, the court repeatedly held Michael in contempt for failing to pay Dianne. Six years later, Michael filed for Chapter 7 bankruptcy, including in the petition's schedule the debt to Dianne of unpaid alimony, child support, and investment funds. Is Michael entitled to a discharge of this debt, or does it qualify as an exception? Explain. [*In re Shankle*, 554 Fed.Appx. 264 (5th Cir. 2014)] (See *Liquidation Proceedings*.)

15–5. Discharge Under Chapter 13. James Thomas and Jennifer Clark married and had two children. They bought a home in Ironton, Ohio, with a loan secured by a mortgage. Later, they took out a second mortgage. On their divorce, the court gave Clark custody of the children and required Clark to pay the first mortgage. The divorce decree also required Thomas and Clark to make equal payments on the second mortgage and provided that Clark would receive all proceeds on the sale of the home. Thomas failed to make any payments, and Clark sold the home. At that point, she learned that Auto Now had a lien on the home because Thomas had not made payments on his car. Clark used all the sale proceeds to pay off the lien and the mortgages. When Thomas filed a petition for a Chapter 13 bankruptcy in a federal bankruptcy court, Clark filed a proof of claim for the mortgage and lien debts. Clark claimed that Thomas should not be able to discharge these debts because they were part of his domestic-support obligations. Are these debts dischargeable? Explain. [*In re Thomas*, 591 Fed.Appx. 443 (6th Cir. 2015)] (See *Bankruptcy Relief Under Chapter 12 and Chapter 13*.)

15–6. Liquidation Proceedings. Jeffrey Krueger and Michael Torres, shareholders of Cru Energy, Inc., were embroiled in litigation in a Texas state court. Both claimed to act on Cru's behalf, and each charged the other with attempting to obtain control of Cru through fraud and other misconduct. Temporarily prohibited from participating in Cru's business, Krueger formed Kru, a company with the same business plan and many of the same shareholders as Cru. Meanwhile, to delay the state court proceedings, Krueger filed a petition for a Chapter 7 liquidation in a federal bankruptcy court. He did not reveal his interest in Kru to the bankruptcy court. Ownership of Krueger's Cru shares passed to the bankruptcy trustee, but Krueger ignored this. He called a meeting of Cru's shareholders—except

Torres—and voted those shares to remove Torres from the board and elect himself chairman, president, chief executive officer, and treasurer. The Cru board then dismissed all of Cru's claims against Krueger in his suit with Torres. Are there sufficient grounds for the bankruptcy court to dismiss Krueger's bankruptcy petition? Discuss. [*In re Krueger*, 812 F.3d 365 (5th Cir. 2016)] (See *Liquidation Proceedings*.)

15–7. Garnishment. Grand Harbour Condominium Owners Association, Inc., obtained a judgment in an Ohio state court against Gene and Nancy Grogg for $45,458. To satisfy the judgment, Grand Harbour filed a notice of garnishment with the court, seeking funds held by the Groggs in various banks. The Groggs disputed Grand Harbour's right to garnish the funds. They claimed that the funds were exempt Social Security and pension proceeds, but they offered no proof of this claim. The banks responded by depositing $23,911 with the court. These funds were delivered to Grand Harbour. Later, the Groggs filed a petition for bankruptcy in a federal bankruptcy court and were granted a discharge of debts. The Groggs then filed a "motion to return funds to debtors" but provided no evidence that their debt to Grand Harbour had been included in the bankruptcy discharge. What is Grand Harbour's best argument in response to the Groggs' motion? [*Grand Harbour Condominium Owners Association, Inc. v. Grogg*, 2016-Ohio-1386 (Ohio Ct.App. 2016)] (See *Laws Assisting Creditors*.)

15–8. The Reorganization Plan. Under the "plain language" of the Bankruptcy Code, at least one class of creditors must accept a Chapter 11 plan for it to be confirmed. Transwest Resort Properties, Inc., and four related companies filed a petition for bankruptcy under Chapter 11. The five debtors filed a joint reorganization plan. Several classes of their creditors approved the plan. Grasslawn Lodging, LLC, filed a claim based on its loan to two of the companies and objected to the plan. Grasslawn further asserted that the Code's confirmation requirement applied on a "per debtor," not a "per plan," basis, and because Grasslawn was the only class member for two of the debtors, the plan in this case did not meet the test. Can the court order a "cram-down"? Why or why not? [*In the Matter of Transwest Resort Properties, Inc.*, 881 F.3d 724 (9th Cir. 2018)] (See *Reorganizations*.)

15–9. Garnishment. Gwendolyn Berry pleaded guilty to stealing funds from her employer. At sentencing, she was ordered to pay restitution of more than $2 million. To enforce this judgment, the government garnished 50 percent of two investment retirement accounts (IRAs) belonging to Gwendolyn's husband, Michael. A federal appeals court upheld this garnishment, holding that in Texas, where the Berrys were residents, a spouse has one-half interest in another spouse's solely managed community property, including IRAs. Therefore, half of Michael's IRA was part of Gwendolyn's garnishable property. Attempting to reduce the amount of the court order, the Berrys cited a federal law that limits restitution-related garnishments to 25 percent of "weekly earnings." If Michael liquidated his IRA, they argued, that would be the same as getting "earnings," and thus the law applied to the case. Should an appellate court accept this argument? [*United States v. Berry*, 951 F.3d 632 (5th Cir. 2020)] (See *Laws Assisting Creditors*.)

15–10. A Question of Ethics—The IDDR Approach and Reorganization. Jevic Transportation Corporation filed a petition in a federal bankruptcy court for a Chapter 11 reorganization. A group of former Jevic truck drivers, including Casimir Czyzewski, filed a suit and won a judgment against the firm for unpaid wages. This judgment entitled the workers to payment from Jevic's estate ahead of its unsecured creditors. Later, some of Jevic's unsecured creditors filed a suit against some of its other unsecured creditors. The plaintiffs won a

judgment on the ground that the firm's payments to the defendants constituted fraudulent transfers and preferences. These parties then negotiated, without the truck drivers' consent, a settlement agreement that called for the workers to receive nothing on their claims while the creditors were to be paid proportionately. [*Czyzewski v. Jevic Holding Corp.*, __ U.S. __, 137 S.Ct. 973, 197 L.Ed.2d 398 (2017)] (See *Reorganizations*.)

(a) Was it ethical of the truck drivers to obtain a judgment entitling them to payment ahead of the unsecured creditors? Why or why not?

(b) Was it ethical of the unsecured creditors to agree that the workers would receive nothing on their claims? Use the IDDR approach to decide.

Time-Limited Group Assignment

15–11. Student Loan Debt. Cathy Coleman took out loans to complete her college education. After graduation, Coleman was irregularly employed as a teacher before filing a petition in a federal bankruptcy court under Chapter 13. The court confirmed a five-year plan under which Coleman was required to commit all of her disposable income to paying the student loans. Less than a year later, when Coleman was laid off, she still owed more than $100,000 to Educational Credit Management Corporation. Coleman asked the court to discharge the debt on the ground that it would be an undue hardship for her to pay it. (See *Liquidation Proceedings*.)

(a) The first group will determine when a debtor normally is entitled to a discharge under Chapter 13.

(b) The second group will discuss whether student loans are dischargeable and when "undue hardship" is a legitimate ground for an exception to the general rule.

(c) The third group will outline the goals of bankruptcy law and make an argument, based on these facts and principles, in support of Coleman's request.

Unit Three: Task-Based Simulation

Alberto Corelli offers to pay $2,500 to purchase a painting titled *Moonrise* from Tara Shelley, an artist whose works have been causing a stir in the art world. Shelley accepts Corelli's offer. Assuming that the contract has met all of the requirements for a valid contract, answer the following questions.

1. **Minors.** Corelli is a minor when he purchases the painting. Is the contract void? Is it voidable? What is the difference between these two conditions? A month after his eighteenth birthday, Corelli decides that he would rather have the $2,500 than the painting. He informs Shelley that he is disaffirming the contract and requests that Shelley return the $2,500 to him. When she refuses to do so, Corelli brings a court action to recover the $2,500. What will the court likely decide in this situation? Why?

2. **Capacity.** Both parties are adults, and the contract, which is in writing, states that Corelli will pay Shelley the $2,500 the following day. In the meantime, Shelley allows Corelli to take the painting home with him. The next day, Corelli's son returns the painting to Shelley, stating that he is canceling the contract. He explains that lately his father has been behaving strangely, that he seems to be mentally incompetent at times, and that he clearly was not acting rationally when he bought the painting, which he could not afford. Is the contract enforceable? Discuss fully.

3. **Agreement in E-Contracts.** Both parties are adults. Shelley, on her website, offers to sell the painting for $2,500. Corelli accepts the offer by clicking on an "I accept" box on the computer screen displaying the offer. Among other terms, the online offer includes a

forum-selection clause stating that any disputes under the contract are to be resolved by a court in California, the state in which Shelley lives. After Corelli receives the painting, he notices a smear of paint across the lower corner that was not visible in the digitized image that appeared on Shelley's website. Corelli calls Shelley, tells her about the smear, and says that he wants to cancel the contract and return the painting.

When Shelley refuses to cooperate, Corelli sues her in a Texas state court, seeking to rescind the contract. Shelley claims that any suit against her must be filed in a California court in accordance with the forum-selection clause. Corelli maintains that the forum-selection clause is unconscionable and should not be enforced. What factors will the court consider in deciding this case? What will the court likely decide? Would it matter whether Corelli read the terms of the online offer before clicking on "I accept"?

4. **Impossibility of Performance.** Both parties are adults, and the contract is in writing. The contract calls for Shelley to deliver the painting to Corelli's gallery in two weeks. Corelli has already arranged to sell the painting to a third party for $4,000 (a $1,500 profit), but it must be available for the third party in two weeks, or the sale will not go through. Shelley knows this but does not deliver the painting at the time promised. Corelli sues Shelley for $1,500 in damages. Shelley claims that performance was impossible because her mother became seriously ill and required Shelley's care. Who will win this lawsuit, and why?

The Business and Employment Environment

Chapter 16

Small Businesses and Franchises

A goal of many business students is to become an **entrepreneur,** one who initiates and assumes the financial risk of a new business enterprise and undertakes to provide or control its management. Many of today's biggest corporations, such as Apple, Alphabet (Google), and Amazon, were originally very small companies started by entrepreneurs. Jeff Bezos, founder of Amazon, and Steve Jobs, founder of Apple, started their companies in their garages.

One of the first decisions an entrepreneur must make is which form of business organization will be most appropriate for the new endeavor. In selecting an organizational form, the entrepreneur will consider a number of factors. These include (1) ease of creation, (2) the liability of the owners, (3) tax considerations, and (4) the ability to raise capital. Keep these factors in mind as you read this unit and learn about the various forms of business organization. Remember, too, in considering these business forms that the primary motive of an entrepreneur is to make profits.

Traditionally, entrepreneurs have used three major business forms—the sole proprietorship, the partnership, and the corporation. In this chapter, we examine sole proprietorships and also look at franchises. Although the franchise is not, strictly speaking, a business organizational form, it is widely used today by entrepreneurs.

16–1 General Considerations for Small Businesses

Most small businesses begin as sole proprietorships. Once the business is under way, the sole proprietorship form may become too limited. The owner and any additional investors may then want to establish a more formal organization, such as a limited partnership (LP), a limited liability partnership (LLP), a limited liability company (LLC), or a corporation. These forms of business limit the owner's personal liability, or legal responsibility, for business debts and obligations. Each business form has its own advantages and disadvantages, but legal limited liability generally is necessary for those who wish to raise outside capital.

16–1a Requirements for All Business Forms

Any business, whatever its form, has to meet a variety of legal requirements, which typically relate to the following:

1. Business name registration.
2. Occupational licensing.
3. State tax registration (for instance, to obtain permits for collecting and remitting sales taxes).
4. Health and environmental permits.
5. Zoning and building codes.
6. Import/export regulations.

If the business has employees, the owner must also comply with a host of laws governing the workplace.

16–1b Protecting Intellectual Property

Protecting rights in intellectual property is a central concern for many small businesses. For instance, software companies and app developers depend on their copyrights and patents to protect their investments in the research and development required to create new programs. Without copyright or patent protection, a competitor or a customer could simply copy the software or app.

Trademarks Choosing a trademark or service mark and making sure that it is protected under trademark law can be crucial to the success of a new business venture. Indeed, a factor to consider in choosing a name for a business entity is whether the business name will be used as a trademark. The general rule is that a trademark cannot be the same as another's mark or so similar that confusion might result.

For the most protection, trademarks should be registered with the U.S. Patent and Trademark Office (PTO).

If a mark is federally registered, the owner may use the symbol ® with the mark. This well-known symbol puts others on notice of the registration and helps to prevent trademark infringement. An owner who has not registered can use the symbol ™. Registration with the PTO should be renewed five years after the initial registration and at ten-year intervals thereafter.

Trade Secrets Much of the value of a small business may lie in its trade secrets, such as information about product development, production processes and techniques, and customer lists. Preserving the secrecy of the information is necessary for legal protection.

As a practical matter, trade secrets must be divulged to key employees. Thus, any business runs the risk that those employees might disclose the secrets to competitors—or even set up competing businesses themselves.

To protect their trade secrets, companies may require employees who have access to trade secrets to agree in their employment contracts never to divulge those secrets. A small business may also choose to include a covenant not to compete in an employment contract. A noncompete clause will help to protect against the possibility that a key employee will go to work for a competitor or set up a competing business.

16–1c Obtaining Loans

Raising capital is critical to the growth of most small businesses. In the early days of a business, the sole proprietor may be able to contribute sufficient capital, but as the business becomes successful, more funds may be needed. The owner may want to raise capital from external sources to expand the business. One way to do this is to borrow funds.

Obtaining a bank loan is beneficial for small businesses because it allows the owner to retain full ownership and control of the business. Note, though, that the bank may place some restrictions on future business decisions as a condition of granting the loan. In addition, bank loans may not be available for some businesses. Banks are usually reluctant to lend significant sums to businesses that are not yet established. Even if a bank is willing to make such a loan, the bank may require personal guaranty contracts from the owner, putting the owner's personal assets at risk.

Loans with desirable terms may be available to small businesses from the U.S. Small Business Administration (SBA). The SBA offers small loans, called *microloans*, of up to $50,000 (the average is about $13,000). These loans are available through certain nonprofit, community-based organizations that have experience in lending.

Be aware that the SBA requires business owners to put some of their own funds at risk in the business.

In addition, many states offer small-business grants to individuals starting a business.

16–2 Sole Proprietorships

In the earliest stages, as mentioned, a small business may operate as a **sole proprietorship,** which is the simplest form of business. In this form, the owner is the business. Thus, anyone who does business without creating a separate business organization has a sole proprietorship. The law considers all new, single-owner businesses to be sole proprietorships unless the owner affirmatively adopts some other form.

More than two-thirds of all U.S. businesses are sole proprietorships. Sole proprietors can own and manage any type of business from an informal home-office or web-based undertaking to a large restaurant or construction firm. Most sole proprietorships are small enterprises, however. About 99 percent of the sole proprietorships in the United States have revenues of less than $1 million per year.

16–2a Advantages of the Sole Proprietorship

A major advantage of the sole proprietorship is that the proprietor owns the entire business and receives all of the profits (because of assuming all of the risk). In addition, starting a sole proprietorship is easier and less costly than starting any other kind of business because few legal formalities are required. Generally, no documents need to be filed with the government to start a sole proprietorship.[1]

Taxes A sole proprietor pays only personal income taxes (including Social Security and Medicare taxes) on the business's profits. The profits are reported as personal income on the proprietor's personal income tax return. In other words, the business itself need not file an income tax return. Sole proprietors are allowed to establish retirement accounts that are tax-exempt until the funds are withdrawn.

In the following case, a sole proprietor sold his cabinet and furniture business to another sole proprietor and later filed a claim to recover for a breach of contract from one of the business's customers. Considering that the seller no longer owned the business, on what basis did he have standing to pursue the claim?

---

1. Small sole proprietorships may, however, need to comply with zoning requirements, obtain appropriate licenses from the state, and the like.

Port Orchard Airport, Inc. v. Wagner

Court of Appeals of Washington, Division 2, 12 Wash.App.2d 1029, 2020 WL 901452 (2020).

Background and Facts Shannon Wagner was the owner of Northwest Cabinets & Furniture, a sole proprietorship, in Port Orchard, Washington, when he sold the business and its assets to Claire Misenar. Those assets included the business's books and records, computers and software, fixtures and furniture, phone system, phone number, trade name and all other intellectual property, domain name, social media accounts, and inventory. Wagner continued to work for the business, and within two years, Wagner and Misenar were married.

Later, Wagner filed a breach of contract claim in a Washington state court against Port Orchard Airport, Inc. for work performed by Northwest Cabinets & Furniture after Wagner had sold the business and married Misenar. A jury awarded damages, but the court found that Wagner was not the owner of the business, concluded that he lacked standing to assert the claim, and granted Port Orchard's motion to dismiss. Wagner appealed.

In the Language of the Court

SUTTON, J. [Judge]

* * * *

Wagner had a community property interest in the business, and therefore, he had standing to assert [the claim] against Port Orchard Airport.

* * * *

Every action shall be prosecuted in the name of the real party in interest. A party has standing to pursue an action when he or she is within the protected zone of interests and has suffered an injury in fact. The party must have a real interest in the subject matter, that is, a present, substantial interest, as distinguished from a mere expectancy, or future, contingent interest.

The trial court's standing decision was largely based on its conclusion that the business was Misenar's separate property. We disagree. When an individual does business as a sole proprietorship, the individual and the sole proprietorship are legally indistinguishable. An individual does not create a separate legal entity by doing business as a sole proprietor.

A community property interest may be a sufficiently real interest to confer standing. In Washington, all property acquired during marriage is presumptively community property.

The findings of fact establish that Wagner sold his business to Misenar. Although Misenar purchased the business, she purchased only the assets of the business. The business itself is inseparable from Misenar because it is a sole proprietorship. Because the sole proprietorship is indistinguishable from Misenar and is community property, we hold that the trial court erred by dismissing Wagner's [claim] for lack of standing.

Decision and Remedy A state intermediate appellate court reversed the trial court's order dismissing Wagner's claim and remanded the case with instructions to the trial court to reinstate the jury verdict in Wagner's favor.

Critical Thinking

- **Legal Environment** The trial court ruled that Wagner could have been an agent for "the business." Why, in the view of the appellate court, did this ruling make no sense?
- **What If the Facts Were Different?** Suppose that instead of Wagner, Misenar had pursued the claim in the case against Port Orchard. Would the result have been different? Discuss.

Flexibility A sole proprietorship offers more flexibility than does a partnership or a corporation. The sole proprietor is free to make any decision concerning the business—including what kind of business to pursue, whom to hire, and when to take a vacation. The sole proprietor can sell or transfer all or part of the business to another party at any time without seeking approval from anyone else. In contrast, approval is typically required from partners in a partnership and from shareholders in a corporation.

16–2b Disadvantages of the Sole Proprietorship

The major disadvantage of the sole proprietorship is that the proprietor alone bears the burden of any losses or liabilities incurred by the business enterprise. In other words, the sole proprietor has unlimited liability for all obligations that arise in doing business. Any lawsuit against the business or its employees can lead to unlimited personal liability for the owner of a sole proprietorship.

Personal Assets at Risk Creditors can pursue the owner's personal assets to satisfy any business debts. Although sole proprietors may obtain insurance to protect the business, liability can easily exceed policy limits. This unlimited liability is a major factor to be considered in choosing a business form.

■ **Example 16.1** Sheila Fowler operates a golf shop near a world-class golf course as a sole proprietorship. One of Fowler's employees fails to secure a display of golf clubs. They fall on Dean Maheesh, a professional golfer, and seriously injure him. If Maheesh sues Fowler's shop and wins, Fowler's personal liability could easily exceed the limits of her insurance policy. Fowler could lose not only her business, but also her house, car, and any other personal assets that can be attached to pay the judgment. ■

This chapter's Digital Update feature further demonstrates how difficult it is for a sole proprietor to escape liability for acts taken on behalf of the business entity, no matter what it is named.

Digital Update

"Doing Business As" a Sole Proprietor

Suppose Jane Smith wants to start a face-mask manufacturing business as a sole proprietor. Jane finds the name "Jane Smith's Face Masks" uninspiring. She would rather call her new venture, "Masks All Mighty." Because the business name is different from her name, in many states Jane will be required to file a "Doing Business As" (DBA), which provides notice to the public of the true owner of the enterprise.

Simple, Inexpensive, and Separate

Even if it were not legally required, many sole proprietors would file for DBAs, known in some jurisdictions as Fictitious Business Names (FBNs). For the most part, DBAs are simple and inexpensive to create. As in the case of Jane Smith, they allow the sole proprietor to match the name to the product or service provided in a marketing-friendly way. DBAs also provide privacy and a degree of separation for sole proprietors who might not want their personal names easily connected to the business.

Regulations for DBAs vary from state to state. In most instances, the sole proprietor must go online and check a state database to ensure that the new trade name is not already being used. In many, though not all, states, the entire DBA process can be completed on the internet, with costs as low as $45 and approval waiting times as short as one week.

The DBA Effect

The fact that the name of the business owner and the business name are different does not change the basic rule that, with a sole proprietorship, the owner is the business. A federal court felt the need to drive this legal point home to David Ruiz after a restaurant that Ruiz owned as a sole proprietor showed a televised boxing match without paying a licensing fee. When the licensor sued, Ruiz said that he had leased the restaurant, Cotija Mex Grill, to Enrique Hernandez before the night of the match. Therefore, Ruiz claimed, he was not responsible for the incident.

"It is unclear," said the court, "how Ruiz could lease Cotija to Hernandez when Cotija, as a sole proprietorship, is legally indistinct from Ruiz." Because Ruiz and the restaurant, with its DBA, were a single legal entity, the court ruled, Ruiz could be held liable for Cotija Mex Grill's wrongdoing.[a]

....

Critical Thinking After filing a DBA or FBN, the sole proprietor must publish the statement in a newspaper to notify the public. For the most part, online DBA

notification is not an option. Should it be? Explain your answer.

_____

a. *G & G Closed Circuit Events, LLC v. Gonzalez Ruiz*, 379 F.Supp.3d 1061 (S.D. Cal. 2019). See also *G & G Closed Circuit Events, LLC v. Infante*, 2022 WL 411847 (E.D. CA 2022).

Lack of Continuity and Limited Ability to Raise Capital The sole proprietorship also has the disadvantage of lacking continuity after the death of the proprietor. When the owner dies, so does the business—it is automatically dissolved.

Another disadvantage is that in raising capital, proprietors are limited to their personal funds and any loans that they can obtain for the business. Lenders may be unwilling to make loans to sole proprietorships, particularly start-ups, because sole proprietors risk unlimited personal liability and may not be able to pay.

16–3 Franchises

Instead of setting up a sole proprietorship to market their own products or services, many entrepreneurs opt to purchase a franchise. A **franchise** is an arrangement in which the owner of intellectual property—such as a trademark, a trade name, or a copyright—licenses others to use it in the selling of goods or services. A **franchisee** (a purchaser of a franchise) is generally legally independent of the **franchisor** (the seller of the franchise). At the same time, the franchisee is economically dependent on the franchisor's integrated business system. In other words, a franchisee can operate as an independent businessperson but still obtain the advantages of a regional or national organization.

Today, franchising companies and their franchisees account for a significant portion of all retail sales in this country. Well-known franchises include McDonald's, 7-Eleven, Dunkin', Taco Bell, and Holiday Inn. Franchising has also become a popular way for businesses to expand their operations internationally without violating the legal restrictions that many nations impose on foreign ownership of businesses.

16–3a Types of Franchises

Many different kinds of businesses sell franchises, and numerous types of franchises are available. Generally, though, franchises fall into one of three classifications:

distributorships, chain-style business operations, and manufacturing arrangements.

Distributorship In a distributorship, a manufacturer (the franchisor) licenses a dealer (the franchisee) to sell its product. Often, a distributorship covers an exclusive territory. Automobile dealerships and beer distributorships are common examples.

■ **Example 16.2** Black Bear Beer Company distributes its brands of beer through a network of authorized wholesale distributors, each with an assigned territory. Marik signs a distributorship contract for the area from Gainesville to Ocala, Florida. If the contract states that Marik is the exclusive distributor in that area, then no other franchisee may distribute Black Bear beer in that region. ■

Chain-Style Business Operation In a *chain-style business operation*, a franchise operates under a franchisor's trade name and is identified as a member of a select group of dealers that engage in the franchisor's business. The franchisee is generally required to follow standardized or prescribed methods of operation. Often, the franchisor insists that the franchisee maintain certain standards of performance.

In addition, the franchisee may be required to obtain materials and supplies exclusively from the franchisor. Chipotle Mexican Grill and most other fast-food chains are examples of this type of franchise. Chain-style franchises are also common in service-related businesses, including real estate brokerage firms, such as Century 21, and tax-preparing services, such as H&R Block, Inc.

Manufacturing Arrangement In a *manufacturing, or processing-plant, arrangement*, the franchisor transmits to the franchisee the essential ingredients or formula to make a particular product. The franchisee then markets the product either at wholesale or at retail in accordance with the franchisor's standards. Examples of this type of franchise include Pepsi-Cola and other soft-drink bottling companies.

16–3b Laws Governing Franchising

Because a franchise relationship is primarily a contractual relationship, it is governed by contract law. If the franchise exists primarily for the sale of products manufactured by the franchisor, the law governing sales contracts as expressed in Article 2 of the Uniform Commercial Code applies.

Additionally, the federal government and most states have enacted laws governing certain aspects of franchising. Generally, these laws are designed to protect prospective franchisees from dishonest franchisors and to prevent franchisors from terminating franchises without good cause.

Federal Regulation of Franchises The federal government regulates franchising through laws that apply to specific industries and through the Franchise Rule, created by the Federal Trade Commission (FTC).

Industry-Specific Standards. Congress has enacted laws that protect franchisees in certain industries, such as automobile dealerships and service stations. These laws protect the franchisee from unreasonable demands and bad faith terminations of the franchise by the franchisor.

In the automobile industry, a manufacturer-franchisor cannot make unreasonable demands of dealer-franchisees or set unrealistically high sales quotas. If a manufacturer-franchisor terminates a franchise because of a dealer-franchisee's failure to comply with unreasonable demands, the manufacturer may be liable for damages.[2]

Similarly, federal law prescribes the conditions under which a franchisor of service stations can terminate the franchise.[3] In addition, federal antitrust laws sometimes apply in specified circumstances to prohibit certain types of anticompetitive agreements.

The Franchise Rule. The FTC's Franchise Rule requires franchisors to disclose certain material facts that a prospective franchisee needs in order to make an informed decision concerning the purchase of a franchise.[4] Those who violate the Franchise Rule are subject to substantial civil penalties, and the FTC can sue on behalf of injured parties to recover damages.

---

2. Automobile Dealers' Franchise Act, also known as the Automobile Dealers' Day in Court Act, 15 U.S.C. Sections 1221 *et seq.*
3. Petroleum Marketing Practices Act (PMPA), 15 U.S.C. Sections 2801 *et seq.*
4. 16 C.F.R. Section 436.1.

Exhibit 16–1   The FTC's Franchise Rule Requirements

Requirement	Explanation
Written (or Electronic) Disclosures	The franchisor must make numerous disclosures, such as the range of goods and services included and the value and estimated profitability of the franchise. Disclosures can be delivered on paper or electronically. Prospective franchisees must be able to download or save any electronic disclosure documents.
Reasonable Basis for Any Representations	To prevent deception, all representations made to a prospective franchisee must have a reasonable basis at the time they are made.
Projected Earnings Figures	If a franchisor provides projected earnings figures, the franchisor must indicate whether the figures are based on actual data or hypothetical examples. The Franchise Rule does not require franchisors to provide potential earnings figures, however.
Actual Data	If a franchisor makes sales or earnings projections based on actual data for a specific franchise location, the franchisor must disclose the number and percentage of its existing franchises that have achieved this result.
Explanation of Terms	Franchisors are required to explain termination, cancellation, and renewal provisions of the franchise contract to potential franchisees before the agreement is signed.

The rule requires the franchisor to make numerous written disclosures to prospective franchisees (see Exhibit 16–1). All representations made to a prospective franchisee must have a reasonable basis. For instance, if a franchisor provides projected earnings figures, the franchisor must indicate whether the figures are based on actual data or hypothetical examples. If a franchisor makes sales or earnings projections based on actual data for a specific franchise location, the franchisor must disclose the number and percentage of its existing franchises that have achieved this result.

State Regulation of Franchising State legislation varies but often is aimed at protecting franchisees from unfair practices and bad faith terminations by franchisors.

A number of states have laws similar to the federal rules that require franchisors to provide presale disclosures to prospective franchisees. Many state laws require that a disclosure document (known as the Franchise Disclosure Document, or FDD) be registered or filed with a state official. State laws may also require that a franchisor submit advertising aimed at prospective franchisees to the state for approval.

To protect franchisees, a state law might require the disclosure of information such as the actual costs of operation, recurring expenses, and profits earned, along with evidence substantiating these figures. State laws related to deceptive trade practices may also apply and prohibit certain types of actions by franchisors.

16–3c The Franchise Contract

The franchise relationship is defined by the contract between the franchisor and the franchisee. The franchise contract specifies the terms and conditions of the franchise and spells out the rights and duties of the franchisor and the franchisee. If either party fails to perform its contractual duties, that party may be subject to a lawsuit for breach of contract. Furthermore, if a franchisee is induced to enter into a franchise contract by the franchisor's fraudulent misrepresentation, the franchisor may be liable for damages. Generally, statutes and the case law governing franchising tend to emphasize the importance of good faith and fair dealing in franchise relationships.

Because each type of franchise relationship has its own characteristics, franchise contracts tend to differ. Nonetheless, certain major issues typically are addressed in a franchise contract. We look at some of them next.

Payment for the Franchise The franchisee ordinarily pays an initial fee or lump-sum price for the franchise license (the privilege of being granted a franchise). This fee is separate from the various products that the franchisee purchases from or through the franchisor. The franchise agreement may also require the franchisee to pay a percentage of the franchisor's advertising costs and certain administrative expenses.

In some industries, the franchisor relies heavily on the initial sale of the franchise for realizing a profit. In other industries, the continued dealing between the parties brings profit to both. Generally, the franchisor receives a stated percentage of the annual (or monthly) sales or volume of business done by the franchisee.

Business Premises The franchise agreement may specify whether the premises for the business must be leased or purchased outright. Sometimes, a building must be constructed to meet the terms of the agreement. The agreement will specify whether the franchisor or the franchisee is responsible for supplying equipment and furnishings for the premises.

Location of the Franchise Typically, the franchisor determines the territory to be served. Some franchise contracts give the franchisee exclusive rights, or "territorial rights," to a certain geographic area. Other franchise contracts, while defining the territory allotted to a particular franchise, either specifically state that the franchise is nonexclusive or are silent on the issue of territorial rights.

Many franchise disputes arise over territorial rights, and the implied covenant of good faith and fair dealing often comes into play in this area of franchising. If the contract does not grant exclusive territorial rights to the franchisee and the franchisor allows a competing franchise to be established nearby, the franchisee may suffer significant lost profits. In this situation, a court may hold that the franchisor breached an implied covenant of good faith and fair dealing.

Business Organization The franchisor may require that the business use a particular organizational form and capital structure. The franchise agreement may also set out standards such as sales quotas and record-keeping requirements. Additionally, a franchisor may retain stringent control over the training of personnel involved in the operation and over administrative aspects of the business.

Quality Control by the Franchisor The day-to-day operation of the franchise business normally is left up to the franchisee. Nonetheless, the franchise agreement may specify that the franchisor will provide some degree of supervision and control so that it can protect the franchise's name and reputation.

Means of Control. When the franchise prepares a product, such as food, or provides a service, such as motel accommodations, the contract often states that the franchisor will establish certain standards for the facility. Typically, the contract will state that the franchisor is permitted to make periodic inspections to ensure that the standards are being maintained.

As a means of controlling quality, franchise agreements also typically limit the franchisee's ability to sell the franchise to another party. ■ **Example 16.3** Mark Keller, Inc., an authorized Jaguar franchise, contracts to sell its dealership to Henrique Autos West. A Jaguar franchise generally cannot be sold without Jaguar Cars' (Tata Motors) permission. Prospective franchisees must meet Jaguar's

customer satisfaction standards. If Henrique Autos fails to meet those standards, Jaguar can refuse to allow the sale and can terminate the franchise. ■

Degree of Control. As a general rule, the validity of a provision permitting the franchisor to establish and enforce certain quality standards is unquestioned. The franchisor has a legitimate interest in maintaining the quality of the product or service to protect its name and reputation.

If a franchisor exercises too much control over the operations of its franchisees, however, the franchisor risks potential liability. A franchisor may occasionally be held liable—under the doctrine of *respondeat superior*—for the tortious acts of the franchisees' employees. (This chapter's Cybersecurity and the Law feature looks at the issue of control in the context of online security breaches.)

Cybersecurity and the Law — Brinker International, Inc.

The news that Brinker International, Inc., was the defendant in a cybersecurity class-action lawsuit did not attract much attention outside the business world.[a] The reason: Brinker, a franchisor, has only a fraction as much name recognition as its main franchise, Chili's Grill & Bar. But when the payment systems at a number of Chili's restaurants were hacked, Brinker was the entity sued, underscoring a growing dilemma for franchisors in the era of large-scale data breaches.

Attacking the Franchise

Because of the massive number of credit card transactions they process, franchises are a common target of hackers. In case after case, involving franchises such as Dairy Queen, UPS, Wendy's, and Goodwill, hackers have used malware to infiltrate the merchant's point-of-sale (POS) system. Even though the franchisee usually has actual control over the POS terminals that have been hacked, the focus in the wake of a data breach is almost always on the franchisor.

In some instances, the Franchise Disclosure Document (FDD) contains specific provisions that detail the responsibilities and obligations of both franchisors and franchisees with regard to data

protection. Many FDDs are vague when it comes to cybersecurity, however, leaving the impression that the franchisor, which generally has control over the franchisee's information technology (IT) systems, must provide security for those systems. Furthermore, as far as plaintiffs' attorneys are concerned, the "deep pockets" of the franchisor hold more promise for a large settlement than the relatively limited resources of any individual franchisee. So after a franchisee suffers a data breach, the blame and potential liability almost always end up with the franchisor, as was the case with Brinker.

Critical Thinking Suppose a franchisor has two choices when it comes to cybersecurity in its FDD. The franchisor can either (a) assume control and responsibility for a franchisee's privacy security system, or (b) avoid this control and responsibility, leaving POS security in the hands of the franchisee. Which is the better choice? Why?

---

a. See *In re Brinker Data Incident Litigation*, 2020 WL 691848 (M.D. FL 2020). See also *Allgood v. PaperlessPay Corporation*, 2022 WL 846070 (M.D. FL 2022).

■ **Example 16.4** The National Labor Relations Board (NLRB) received 180 employee complaints that certain McDonald's restaurants had engaged in unfair labor practices. Employees alleged that the restaurants had fired or penalized workers for participating in protests over wages and working conditions. Investigators found that at least some of the complaints had merit. The NLRB ruled that McDonald's USA, LLC, could be held jointly liable along with several of its franchisees for labor and wage violations. The NLRB reasoned that McDonald's exerts sufficient control over its franchisees to be found liable for the franchisees' employment law violations. ■

Pricing Arrangements Franchises provide the franchisor with an outlet for the firm's goods and services. Depending on the nature of the business, the franchisor may require the franchisee to purchase certain supplies from the franchisor at an established price. A franchisor cannot, however, set the prices at which the franchisee will resell the goods. Such price setting may be a violation of state or federal antitrust laws, or

both. A franchisor can suggest retail prices but cannot mandate them.

16–3c Franchise Termination

The duration of the franchise is a matter to be determined between the parties. Sometimes, a franchise relationship starts with a short trial period, such as a year, so that the franchisee and the franchisor can determine whether they want to stay in business with one another. At other times, the duration of the franchise contract correlates with the term of the lease for the business premises, and both are renewable at the end of that period.

Grounds for Termination Set by the Franchise Contract Usually, the franchise agreement specifies that termination must be "for cause" and then defines the grounds for termination. Cause might include, for instance, the death or disability of the franchisee, insolvency of the franchisee, breach of the franchise agreement, or failure to meet specified sales quotas.

In the following case, a franchisee contended that the franchisor did not have good cause for termination.

Case 16.2

S&P Brake Supply, Inc. v. Daimler Trucks North America, LLC

Montana Supreme Court, 2018 MT 25, 390 Mont. 243, 411 P.3d 1264 (2018).

Background and Facts S&P Brake Supply, Inc., was the sole authorized dealer for Western Star Trucks in Yellowstone County, Montana. S&P operated its franchise under an agreement with Daimler Trucks North America, LLC. The agreement required that S&P sell a certain number of trucks in its area of responsibility (Yellowstone County). Over a three-year period, S&P sold only two trucks. Daimler advised its franchisee to use more effective marketing strategies and to hire more sales staff, among other things.

The next year, primarily because of S&P's failure to meet its sales goals, Daimler notified S&P that the franchise was being terminated. S&P objected, but the Montana Department of Justice, Motor Vehicle Division, ruled in Daimler's favor, and a state court upheld the department's decision. S&P appealed to the Montana Supreme Court.

In the Language of the Court
Justice Jim RICE delivered the Opinion of the Court.
* * * *

S&P argues * * * the [lower] court erred in its assessment of the [Montana Department of Justice, Motor Vehicle Division's] determination.
* * * *

S&P argues that an analysis of its sales performance [should have been] restricted to evidence related to Yellowstone County. Daimler established that S&P had failed to meet new truck sales objectives * * *,

Case 16.2 Continues

Case 16.2 Continued which are set for all Western Star dealers using an algorithm that considers market factors and the population of a dealer's area of responsibility [AOR]. * * * Daimler offered its analysis of S&P's "dealer market share," which compared how many trucks S&P sold in its AOR to how many Western Star trucks were annually registered in Yellowstone County, to measure how well S&P was reaching and serving local customers. Of the seven Western Star trucks registered in Yellowstone County [during the last four years of S&P's franchise,] only two had been sold by S&P, an indicator to Daimler that S&P was not well serving its market, as the majority of customers were purchasing their Western Star trucks elsewhere. This evidence was premised upon S&P's performance in Yellowstone County.

Daimler also argued S&P's "dealer market share" was low compared to Western Star's "regional market share," a factor which is compiled from national truck registration data to compare S&P's sales performance in its AOR with Western Star's regional performance. While this assessment included evidence from outside the Yellowstone County franchise location, the [lower] court properly noted that limiting the evidence to only Yellowstone County would not allow a comparison to other dealers where there is only one dealer in a county, reasoning that "when only one franchisee exists in a market, expanded data must be considered. Otherwise, a lone franchisee could never be terminated."

* * * The Department found, "The bottom line is that S&P's sales were deficient no matter which way one analyzed the data," and this determination was supported by substantial evidence.

Decision and Remedy The Montana Supreme Court affirmed the judgment of the lower court. The court concluded, "The evidence focused on S&P's performance in Yellowstone County and was properly considered." Thus, Daimler had the grounds to terminate S&P's franchise.

Critical Thinking

- **Legal Environment** Considering that S&P was the only Western Star truck dealer in Yellowstone County, did discontinuing the franchise injure the public interest? Explain.
- **Economic** The department concluded that S&P's failure to use more effective marketing strategies and to hire more sales staff breached the franchise agreement. S&P argued that these were not material breaches because the agreement's fundamental purpose was to sell trucks. Is S&P correct? Discuss.

Notice Requirements. Most franchise contracts provide that notice of termination must be given. If no set time for termination is specified, then a reasonable time, with notice, is implied. A franchisee must be given reasonable time to wind up the business—that is, to do the accounting and return the copyright or trademark or any other property of the franchisor.

Opportunity to Cure a Breach. A franchise agreement may allow the franchisee to attempt to cure an ordinary, curable breach within a certain time after notice so as to postpone, or even avoid, termination. Even when a contract contains a notice-and-cure provision, however, a franchisee's breach of the duty of honesty and fidelity may be enough to allow the franchisor to terminate the franchise.

■ **Case in Point 16.5** Milind and Minaxi Upadhyaya entered into a franchise contract with 7-Eleven, Inc., to operate a store in Pennsylvania. The contract included a notice-and-cure provision. Under 7-Eleven's usual contract, franchisees lease the store and equipment, and receive a license to use 7-Eleven's trademarks and other intellectual property. 7-Eleven receives a percentage of the store's gross profit (net sales less the cost of goods sold).

A 7-Eleven manager noticed a high rate of certain questionable transactions at the Upadhyayas' store and began investigating. The investigation continued for nearly two years and revealed that the store had been misreporting its sales so as to conceal sales proceeds from 7-Eleven. Evidence indicated that nearly one-third of the store's sales transactions had not been properly recorded. 7-Eleven sent a "non-curable" notice of material breach and termination of the franchise to the Upadhyayas. The franchisees argued that they had not been given an opportunity to cure the breach. The court found there was sufficient evidence of fraud to warrant immediate termination without an opportunity to cure.[5] ■

---

5. *7-Eleven, Inc. v. Upadhyaya*, 926 F.Supp.2d 614 (E.D.Penn. 2013).

Wrongful Termination Because a franchisor's termination of a franchise often has adverse consequences for the franchisee, much franchise litigation involves claims of wrongful termination. Generally, the termination provisions of contracts are more favorable to the franchisor than to the franchisee. This means that the franchisee, who normally invests substantial time and financial resources in making the franchise operation successful, may receive little or nothing for the business on termination. The franchisor owns the trademark and hence the business.

It is in this area that statutory and case law become important. The federal and state laws discussed earlier attempt, among other things, to protect franchisees from the arbitrary or unfair termination of their franchises by the franchisors.

The Importance of Good Faith and Fair Dealing
Generally, both statutory law and case law emphasize the importance of good faith and fair dealing in terminating a franchise relationship. In determining whether a franchisor has acted in good faith when terminating a franchise agreement, the courts usually try to balance the rights of both parties.

If a court perceives that a franchisor has arbitrarily or unfairly terminated a franchise, the franchisee will be provided with a remedy for wrongful termination. A court will be less likely to consider a termination wrongful if the franchisor's decision was made in the normal course of business and reasonable notice was given.

16–4 Partnerships

A **partnership** arises from an agreement, express or implied, between two or more persons to carry on a business for a profit. Partners are co-owners of the business and have joint control over its operation and the right to share in its profits.

16–4a Basic Partnership Concepts

Partnerships are governed both by common law concepts—in particular, those relating to agency—and by statutory law. As in so many other areas of business law, the National Conference of Commissioners on Uniform State Laws has drafted uniform laws for partnerships, and these have been widely adopted by the states.

Agency Concepts and Partnership Law When two or more persons agree to do business as partners, they enter into a special relationship with one another. To an extent, their relationship is similar to an agency relationship because each partner is deemed to be the agent of the other partners and of the partnership. Thus, agency concepts apply—specifically, the imputation of knowledge of, and responsibility for, acts carried out within the scope of the partnership relationship. In their relationships with one another, partners, like agents, are bound by fiduciary ties.

In one important way, however, partnership law differs from agency law. The partners in a partnership agree to commit funds or other assets, labor, and skills to the business with the understanding that profits and losses will be shared. Thus, each partner has an ownership interest in the firm. In a nonpartnership agency relationship, the agent usually does not have an ownership interest in the business and is not obligated to bear a portion of ordinary business losses.

The Uniform Partnership Act The Uniform Partnership Act (UPA) governs the operation of partnerships in the absence of express agreement and has done much to reduce controversies in the law relating to partnerships. A majority of the states have enacted the amended version of the UPA.

Definition of a Partnership The UPA defines a **partnership** as "an association of two or more persons to carry on as co-owners a business for profit" [UPA 101(6)]. Note that the UPA's definition of "person" includes corporations, so a corporation can be a partner in a partnership [UPA 101(10)]. The intent to associate is a key element of a partnership, and one cannot join a partnership unless all other partners consent [UPA 401(i)].

Essential Elements of a Partnership Questions may sometimes arise as to whether a business enterprise is a legal partnership, especially when there is no formal, written partnership agreement. To determine whether a partnership exists, courts usually look for three essential elements, which are implicit in the UPA's definition:

1. A sharing of profits or losses.
2. A joint ownership of the business.
3. An equal right to be involved in the management of the business.

If the evidence in a particular case is insufficient to establish all three factors, the UPA provides a set of guidelines to be used.

The Sharing of Profits and Losses. The sharing of both profits and losses from a business creates a presumption that a partnership exists. ■ **Case in Point 16.6** David Tubb, representing Superior Shooting Systems, Inc., entered into an agreement with Aspect International, Inc., to create a business that would make and sell ammunition to the public. Their contract stated that both companies would participate in the business and split the profits equally, but it did not say explicitly that they would share the losses. It also did not specify what type of entity the business would be.

A dispute arose between the two companies, and the matter ended up in court. A Texas appellate court held that the two corporations had created a partnership even though there was no express agreement to share in losses. Because they had agreed to share control and ownership of the business and to split the profits equally, they would also have to share the losses equally.[6] ■

A court will not presume that a partnership exists if shared profits were received as payment of any of the following [UPA 202(c)(3)]:

1. A debt by installments or interest on a loan.
2. Wages of an employee or payment for the services of an independent contractor.
3. Rent to a landlord.
4. An annuity to a surviving spouse or representative of a deceased partner.
5. A sale of the **goodwill** (the valuable reputation of a business viewed as an intangible asset) of a business or property.

■ **Example 16.7** A debtor, Snopel, owes a creditor, Natasha, $5,000 on an unsecured debt. They agree that Snopel will pay 10 percent of his monthly business profits to Natasha until the loan with interest has been repaid. Although Snopel and Natasha are sharing profits from the business, they are not presumed to be partners. ■

Joint Property Ownership. Joint ownership of property does not in and of itself create a partnership [UPA 202(c)(1) and (2)]. The parties' intentions are key. ■ **Example 16.8** Chiang and Burke jointly own farmland and lease it to a farmer for a share of the profits from the farming operation in lieu of fixed rental payments. This arrangement normally would not make Chiang, Burke, and the farmer partners. ■

Entity Versus Aggregate At common law, a partnership was treated only as an aggregate of individuals and never as a separate legal entity. Thus, at common law

a lawsuit could never be brought by or against the firm in its own name. Each individual partner had to sue or be sued.

Today, in contrast, a majority of the states follow the UPA and treat a partnership as an entity for most purposes. For instance, a partnership usually can sue or be sued, collect judgments, and have all accounting performed in the name of the partnership entity [UPA 201, 307(a)].

As an entity, a partnership may hold the title to real or personal property in its name rather than in the names of the individual partners. Additionally, federal procedural laws permit the partnership to be treated as an entity in suits in federal courts and bankruptcy proceedings.

Tax Treatment of Partnerships Modern law does treat a partnership as an aggregate of the individual partners rather than a separate legal entity in one situation—for federal income tax purposes. The partnership is a pass-through entity and not a taxpaying entity. A **pass-through entity** is a business entity that has no tax liability. The entity's income is passed through to the owners, who pay income taxes on it.

Thus, the income or losses the partnership incurs are "passed through" the entity framework and attributed to the partners on their individual tax returns. The partnership itself pays no taxes and is responsible only for filing an **information return** with the Internal Revenue Service.

A partner's profit from the partnership (whether distributed or not) is taxed as individual income to the individual partner. Similarly, partners can deduct a share of the partnership's losses on their individual tax returns (in proportion to their partnership interests).

16–4b Formation and Operation

A partnership is a voluntary association of individuals. As such, it is formed by the agreement of the partners. As a general rule, agreements to form a partnership can be oral, written, or implied by conduct. Some partnership agreements, however, such as one authorizing partners to transfer interests in real property, must be in writing to be legally enforceable.

A partnership agreement, also known as **articles of partnership,** can include almost any terms that the parties wish, unless they are illegal or contrary to public policy or statute [UPA 103].

The rights and duties of partners are governed largely by the specific terms of their partnership agreement. In the absence of provisions to the contrary in the partnership agreement, the law imposes certain rights and duties, as discussed in the following subsections. The character

6. *Tubb v. Aspect International, Inc.,* 2017 WL 192919 (Tex. App.—Tyler 2017). See also *Johnson and Henderson Partnership v. Henderson,* 321 Or.App. 134, 516 P.3d 726 (2022).

and nature of the partnership business generally influence the application of these rights and duties.

Duration of the Partnership The partnership agreement can specify the duration of the partnership by stating that it will continue until a designated date or until the completion of a particular project. A partnership of this type is called a *partnership for a term*. Generally, withdrawing from a partnership for a term prematurely (before the expiration date) constitutes a breach of the agreement, and the responsible partner can be held liable for any resulting losses [UPA 602(b)(2)]. If no fixed duration is specified, the partnership is a partnership at will. A partnership at will can be dissolved at any time without liability.

Partnership by Estoppel When a third person has reasonably and detrimentally relied on the representation that a nonpartner was part of a partnership, a court may conclude that a **partnership by estoppel** exists.

Liability Imposed. A partnership by estoppel may arise when a person who is not a partner gives the impression of being a partner and makes representations that third parties rely on. In this situation, a court may impose liability—but not partnership rights—on the alleged partner.

■ **Case in Point 16.9** Sanitation District No. 1 (SD1) contracted with DCI Properties to upgrade the sewage systems of several counties in Northern Kentucky. DCI contracted with Coppage Construction Company to provide the labor, goods, and services for the construction project. After a series of disputes, DCI terminated its contract with Coppage. In a lawsuit against SD1, Coppage alleged that it had extended credit, consisting of goods and services, to DCI based on its belief that DCI and SD1 were partners.

The trial court dismissed the claim, holding that SD1 and DC1 were not partners and therefore SD1 could not be liable to Coppage for any damages resulting from DCI's actions. A state appeals court reversed, noting that SD1 had assured Coppage that it was backing the project financially and that, on one occasion, SD1—not DCI— had made a payment to Coppage. Even if there was no legal partnership between DCI and SD1, the court ruled, Coppage should be given the chance to argue that there was an "apparent" partnership under the doctrine of partnership by estoppel.[7] ■

Rights of Partners The rights of partners in a partnership relate to the following areas: management, interest in the partnership, compensation, inspection of books, accounting, and property.

Management Rights. In a general partnership, all partners have equal rights in managing the partnership [UPA 401(f)]. Unless the partners agree otherwise, each partner has one vote in management matters regardless of the proportional size of the partner's interest in the firm. In a large partnership, partners often agree to delegate daily management responsibilities to a management committee made up of one or more of the partners.

A majority vote controls decisions on ordinary matters connected with partnership business, unless otherwise specified in the agreement. Decisions that significantly change the nature of the partnership or that are outside the ordinary course of the partnership business, however, require the unanimous consent of the partners [UPA 301(2), 401(i), 401(j)]. For instance, unanimous consent is generally required for a partnership to admit new partners, to amend the partnership agreement, or to enter a new line of business.

Interest in the Partnership. Each partner is entitled to the proportion of business profits and losses that is specified in the partnership agreement. If the agreement does not apportion profits (indicate how the profits will be shared), the UPA provides that profits will be shared equally. If the agreement does not apportion losses, losses will be shared in the same ratio as profits [UPA 401(b)].

■ **Example 16.10** The partnership agreement between Rick and Bogdan provides for capital contributions of $60,000 from Rick and $40,000 from Bogdan. If the agreement is silent as to how Rick and Bogdan will share profits or losses, they will share both profits and losses equally.

In contrast, if the agreement provides for profits to be shared in the same ratio as capital contributions, 60 percent of the profits will go to Rick, and 40 percent will go to Bogdan. Unless the agreement provides otherwise, losses will be shared in the same ratio as profits. ■

Compensation. Devoting time, skill, and energy to partnership business is a partner's duty and generally is not a compensable service. Rather, as mentioned, a partner's income from the partnership takes the form of a distribution of profits. Partners can, of course, agree otherwise. For instance, the managing partner of a law firm often receives a salary—in addition to a share of profits—for performing special administrative or managerial duties.

---

7. *Coppage Construction Company, Inc. v. Sanitation District No. 1*, 2019 WL 6795706 (KY App. 2019).

Inspection of the Books Partnership books and records must be kept accessible to all partners. Each partner has the right to receive full and complete information concerning the conduct of all aspects of partnership business [UPA 403]. Partners have a duty to provide the information to the firm, which has a duty to preserve it and to keep accurate records.

The partnership books must be kept at the firm's principal business office (unless the partners agree otherwise). Every partner is entitled to inspect all books and records on demand and can make copies of the materials. The personal representative of a deceased partner's estate has the same right of access to partnership books and records that the decedent would have had [UPA 403].

Accounting of Partnership Assets or Profits An accounting of partnership assets or profits is required to determine the value of each partner's share in the partnership. An accounting can be performed voluntarily, or it can be compelled by court order. Under UPA 405(b), a partner has the right to bring an action for an accounting during the term of the partnership, as well as on the partnership's dissolution.

Property Rights Property acquired by a partnership is the property of the partnership and not of the partners individually [UPA 203]. Partnership property includes all property that was originally contributed to the partnership and anything later purchased by the partnership or in the partnership's name (except in rare circumstances) [UPA 204].

A partner may use or possess partnership property only on behalf of the partnership [UPA 401(g)]. A partner is not a co-owner of partnership property and has no right to sell, mortgage, or transfer partnership property to another [UPA 501].

Because partnership property is owned by the partnership and not by the individual partners, the property cannot be used to satisfy the personal debts of individual partners. A partner's creditor, however, can petition a court for a **charging order** to attach the partner's interest in the partnership to satisfy the partner's obligation [UPA 502]. A partner's interest in the partnership includes a proportionate share of any profits that are distributed. A partner can also assign the partner's right to receive a share of the partnership profits to another to satisfy a debt.

16–4c Duties and Liabilities of Partners

The duties and liabilities of partners are derived from agency law. Each partner is an agent of every other partner and acts as both a principal and an agent in any business transaction within the scope of the partnership agreement.

Each partner is also a general agent of the partnership in carrying out the usual business of the firm "or business of the kind carried on by the partnership" [UPA 301(1)]. Thus, every act of a partner concerning partnership business and "business of the kind" and every contract signed in the partnership's name bind the firm.

Fiduciary Duties The fiduciary duties that a partner owes to the partnership and to the other partners are the duty of care and the duty of loyalty [UPA 404(a)]. Under the UPA, a partner's duty of care is limited to refraining from "grossly negligent or reckless conduct, intentional misconduct, or a knowing violation of law" [UPA 404(c)]. A partner is not liable to the partnership for simple negligence or honest errors in judgment in conducting partnership business.

The duty of loyalty requires a partner to account to the partnership for "any property, profit, or benefit" derived by the partner in the conduct of the partnership's business or from the use of its property. A partner must also refrain from competing with the partnership in business or dealing with the firm as an adverse party [UPA 404(b)].

The duty of loyalty can be breached by self-dealing, misusing partnership property, disclosing trade secrets, or usurping a partnership business opportunity. The following case is a classic example.

Classic Case 16.3

Meinhard v. Salmon

Court of Appeals of New York, 249 N.Y. 458, 164 N.E. 545 (1928).

Background and Facts Walter Salmon negotiated a twenty-year lease for the Hotel Bristol in New York City. To pay for the conversion of the building into shops and offices, Salmon entered into an agreement with Morton Meinhard to assume half of the cost. They agreed to share the profits and losses from the joint venture. (A joint venture is similar to a partnership but typically is created for a single project.) Salmon was to have the sole power to manage the building, however.

Less than four months before the end of the lease term, the building's owner, Elbridge Gerry, approached Salmon about a project to raze the converted structure, clear five adjacent lots, and construct a single building across the whole property. Salmon agreed and signed a new lease in the name of his own business, Midpoint Realty Company, without telling Meinhard. When Meinhard learned of the deal, he filed a suit in a New York state court against Salmon, seeking his share of the profits from the lease that Salmon had signed in breach of his fiduciary duties. The court ruled in Meinhard's favor, and Salmon appealed.

In the Language of the Court

CARDOZO, C.J. [Chief Justice]
    * * * *

Joint adventurers, like copartners, owe to one another, while the enterprise continues, the duty of the finest loyalty. Many forms of conduct permissible in a work-a-day world for those acting at arm's length are forbidden to those bound by fiduciary ties. * * * Not honesty alone, but the punctilio [strictness in observance of details] of an honor the most sensitive, is then the standard of behavior. As to this there has developed a tradition that is unbending and inveterate [entrenched]. Uncompromising rigidity has been the attitude of courts * * * when petitioned to undermine the rule of undivided loyalty.

* * * The trouble about [Salmon's] conduct is that he excluded his coadventurer from any chance to compete, from any chance to enjoy the opportunity for benefit.

* * * The very fact that Salmon was in control with exclusive powers of direction charged him the more obviously with the duty of disclosure, [because] only through disclosure could opportunity be equalized.

* * * Authority is, of course, abundant that one partner may not appropriate to his own use a renewal of a lease, though its term is to begin at the expiration of the partnership. The lease at hand with its many changes is not strictly a renewal. Even so, the standard of loyalty for those in trust relations is without the fixed divisions of a graduated scale. * * * A man obtaining [an] * * * opportunity * * * by the position he occupies as a partner is bound by his obligation to his copartners in such dealings not to separate his interest from theirs, but, if he acquires any benefit, to communicate it to them. Certain it is also that there may be no abuse of special opportunities growing out of a special trust as manager or agent.

* * * Very likely [Salmon] assumed in all good faith that with the approaching end of the venture he might ignore his coadventurer and take the extension for himself. He had given to the enterprise time and labor as well as money. He had made it a success. Meinhard, who had given money, but neither time nor labor, had already been richly paid. * * * [But] Salmon had put himself in a position in which thought of self was to be renounced, however hard the abnegation [self-denial]. He was much more than a coadventurer. He was a managing coadventurer. For him and for those like him the rule of undivided loyalty is relentless and supreme.

Decision and Remedy The Court of Appeals of New York held that Salmon had breached his fiduciary duty by failing to inform Meinhard of the business opportunity and secretly taking advantage of it himself. The court granted Meinhard an interest "measured by the value of half of the entire lease."

Critical Thinking

• **What If the Facts Were Different?** Suppose that Salmon had disclosed Gerry's proposal to Meinhard, who had said that he was not interested. Would the result in this case have been different? Explain.

• **Impact of This Case on Today's Law** This classic case involved a joint venture, not a partnership. At the time, a member of a joint venture had only the duty to refrain from actively subverting the rights of the other members. The decision in this case imposed the highest standard of loyalty on joint-venture members. The duty is now the same in both joint ventures and partnerships. Courts today frequently quote the eloquent language used in this opinion when describing the standard of loyalty that applies to partnerships.

A partner's fiduciary duties may not be waived or eliminated in the partnership agreement. In fulfilling them, each partner must act consistently with the obligation of good faith and fair dealing [UPA 103(b), 404(d)]. The agreement can specify acts that the partners agree will violate a fiduciary duty.

Note that a partner may pursue personal interests without automatically violating these duties [UPA 404(e)]. The key is whether the partner has disclosed the interest to the other partners. ■ **Example 16.11** Jayne Trell, a partner at Jacoby & Meyers, owns a shopping mall. Trell may vote against a partnership proposal to open a competing mall, provided that she fully discloses her interest in the existing shopping mall to the other partners at the firm. ■

Authority of Partners

Authority of Partners The UPA affirms general principles of agency law that pertain to a partner's authority to bind a partnership in contract. If a partner acts within the scope of that authority, the partnership is legally bound to honor the partner's commitments to third parties.

A partner may also subject the partnership to tort liability under agency principles. When a partner is carrying on partnership business with third parties in the usual way, apparent authority exists, and both the partner and the firm share liability. The partnership will not be liable, however, if the third parties know that the partner has no such authority.

Limitations on Authority. A partnership may limit a partner's capacity to act as the firm's agent or transfer property on its behalf by filing a "statement of partnership authority" in a designated state office [UPA 105, 303]. Such limits on a partner's authority normally are effective only with respect to third parties who are notified of the limitation. (An exception is made in real estate transactions when the statement of authority has been recorded with the appropriate state office.)

The Scope of Implied Powers. The agency concepts relating to apparent authority, actual authority, and ratification apply to partnerships. The extent of implied authority generally is broader for partners than for ordinary agents, however.

In an ordinary partnership, the partners can exercise all implied powers reasonably necessary and customary to carry on the partnership's specific business. Some customarily implied powers include the authority to make warranties on goods in the sales business and the power to enter into contracts consistent with the firm's regular course of business.

Liability of Partners One significant disadvantage associated with a general partnership is that the partners are personally liable for the debts of the partnership. In most states, the liability is essentially unlimited, because the acts of one partner in the ordinary course of business subject the other partners to personal liability [UPA 305]. Note that normally the partnership's assets must be exhausted before creditors can reach the partners' individual assets.

Joint Liability. Each partner in a partnership generally is jointly liable for the partnership's obligations. **Joint liability** means that a third party must sue all of the partners as a group, but each partner can be held liable for the full amount. If, for instance, a third party sues one partner on a partnership contract, that partner has the right to demand that the other partners be sued as well. In fact, if all of the partners are not named as defendants in a lawsuit, then the assets of the partnership cannot be used to satisfy any judgment in that case.

Joint and Several Liability. In the majority of the states, under UPA 306(a), partners are both jointly and severally (separately, or individually) liable for all partnership obligations. **Joint and several liability** means that a third party has the option of suing all of the partners together (jointly) or one or more of the partners separately (severally). All partners in a partnership can be held liable even if a particular partner did not participate in, know about, or ratify the conduct that gave rise to the lawsuit.

A judgment against one partner severally does not extinguish the others' liability. (Similarly, a release of one partner does not discharge the partners' several liability.) Those not sued in the first action normally may be sued subsequently, unless the court in the first action held that the partnership was in no way liable. A plaintiff who is successful in a suit against a partner or partners may collect on the judgment only against the assets of those partners named as defendants.

Indemnification. With joint and several liability, a partner who commits a tort can be required to indemnify (reimburse) the partnership for any damages it pays. Indemnification will typically be granted unless the tort was committed in the ordinary course of the partnership's business.

■ **Example 16.12** Nicole Martin, a partner at Patti's Café, is working in the café's kitchen one day when her young son suffers serious injuries to his hands from a dough press. Her son, through his father, files a negligence lawsuit against the partnership. Even if the suit is successful and the partnership pays damages to Martin's son, the firm, Patti's Café, is not entitled to indemnification. Martin would not be required to indemnify the partnership because her negligence occurred in the ordinary course of the partnership's business (making food for customers). ■

Liability of Incoming Partners. A partner newly admitted to an existing partnership is not personally liable for any partnership obligations incurred before the person became a partner [UPA 306(b)]. The new partner's liability to the partnership's existing creditors is limited to that partner's capital contribution to the firm.

■ **Example 16.13** Smartclub, an existing partnership with four members, admits a new partner, Alex Jaff. He contributes $100,000 to the partnership. Smartclub has debts amounting to $600,000 at the time Jaff joins the firm. Although Jaff's capital contribution of $100,000 can be used to satisfy Smartclub's obligations, Jaff is not personally liable for partnership debts incurred before he became a partner. If, however, the partnership incurs additional debts after Jaff becomes a partner, he will be personally liable for those amounts, along with all the other partners. ■

16–4d Dissociation and Termination

Dissociation occurs when a partner leaves the partnership. Dissociation normally terminates the partner's actual authority to act for the partnership and to participate in running its business.

Once dissociation occurs, the partnership may continue to do business without the dissociated partner. In that case, the partnership purchases the dissociated partner's interest in the business. If the partners no longer wish to (or are unable to) continue the business, the partnership may be terminated (dissolved).

Events That Cause Dissociation Under UPA 601, a partner can be dissociated from a partnership in any of the following ways:

1. By the partner's voluntarily giving notice of an "express will to withdraw." (When a partner gives notice of intent to withdraw, the remaining partners must decide whether to continue the partnership business. If they decide not to continue, the voluntary dissociation of a partner will dissolve the firm [UPA 801(1)].)
2. By the occurrence of an event specified in the partnership agreement.
3. By a unanimous vote of the other partners under certain circumstances, such as the partner's transfer

of substantially all of the partner's interest in the partnership.
4. By order of a court or arbitrator if the partner has engaged in wrongful conduct that affects the partnership business. The court can order dissociation if a partner breached the partnership agreement or violated a duty owed to the partnership or to the other partners. Dissociation may also be ordered if the partner engaged in conduct that makes it "not reasonably practicable to carry on the business in partnership with the partner" [UPA 601(5)].
5. By the partner's declaring bankruptcy, assigning transferable interest in the partnership for the benefit of creditors, or becoming physically or mentally incapacitated, or by the partner's death.

Wrongful Dissociation A partner has the power to dissociate from a partnership at any time but may not have the right to do so. If the partner lacks the right to dissociate, then the dissociation is considered wrongful under the law [UPA 602]. When a partner's dissociation breaches a partnership agreement, for instance, it is wrongful.

■ **Example 16.14** Jenkins & Whalen's partnership agreement states that it is a breach of the agreement for any partner to assign partnership property to a creditor without the consent of the other partners. If Kenzie, a partner, makes such an assignment, she has not only breached the agreement but has also wrongfully dissociated from the partnership. ■

A partner who wrongfully dissociates is liable to the partnership and to the other partners for damages caused by the dissociation. This liability is in addition to any other obligation of the partner to the partnership or to the other partners.

Effects of Dissociation Dissociation (rightful or wrongful) affects the rights and duties of the dissociated partner and requires that the partnership purchase the partner's interest. It also alters the liability of the partners to third parties.

A partner's right to participate in the management and conduct of the partnership business terminates on the partner's dissociation [UPA 603]. The partner's duty of loyalty also ends. A partner's duty of care continues only with respect to events that occurred before dissociation, unless the partner participates in winding up the partnership's business (discussed shortly).

■ **Example 16.15** Mida is a partner at the accounting firm Bubb & Flint. If she leaves the partnership, she can immediately compete with the firm for new clients. She must exercise care in completing ongoing client transactions that involved the partnership, however. She must also account to Bubb & Flint for any fees received from the former clients based on those transactions. ■

Buyouts. After dissociation, the dissociated partner's interest in the partnership must be purchased according to the rules in UPA 701. The **buyout price** is based on the amount that would have been distributed to the partner if the partnership had been wound up on the date of dissociation. Offset against the price are amounts owed by the partner to the partnership, including damages for wrongful dissociation, if applicable.

Liability to Third Parties. For two years after a partner dissociates from a continuing partnership, the partnership may be bound by the acts of the dissociated partner based on apparent authority [UPA 702]. In other words, if a third party reasonably believed at the time of a transaction that the dissociated partner was still a partner, the partnership may be liable. Similarly, a dissociated partner may be liable for partnership obligations entered into during the two-year period following dissociation [UPA 703].

To avoid this possible liability, a partnership should notify its creditors, customers, and clients of a partner's dissociation. In addition, either the partnership or the dissociated partner can file a statement of dissociation in the appropriate state office to limit the dissociated partner's authority to ninety days after the filing [UPA 704]. Filing this statement helps to minimize the firm's potential liability for the former partner, and vice versa.

Partnership Termination The same events that cause dissociation can result in the end of the partnership if the remaining partners no longer wish to (or are unable to) continue the partnership business. The termination of a partnership is referred to as **dissolution,** which essentially means the commencement of the winding up process. **Winding up** is the job of collecting, liquidating, and distributing the partnership assets.

Dissolution. Dissolution of a partnership generally can be brought about by acts of the partners, by operation of law, or by judicial decree [UPA 801]. Any partnership (including one for a fixed term) can be dissolved by the partners' agreement. If the partnership agreement states that it will dissolve on a certain event, such as a partner's death or bankruptcy, then the occurrence of that event will dissolve the partnership. A partnership for a fixed term or a particular undertaking is dissolved by operation of law at the expiration of the term or on the completion of the undertaking.

■ **Case in Point 16.16** Will Sukenik and Irvin Fine formed PDC Office Park as general partners. Under the partnership agreement, on the death of one partner, the other had thirty days to elect to continue the partnership. Fine died, but Sukenik failed to take this step. A third party that owned a limited interest in PDC convinced a trial court that the partnership had to be dissolved and its assets liquidated. Although Sukenik tried numerous delaying tactics to block this dissolution, including a breach of contract suit against the third party, a state appeals court ruled that the terms of the partnership were clear and must be respected.[8] ■

Winding Up and Distribution of Assets. After dissolution, the partnership continues for the limited purpose of winding up the business. The partners cannot create new obligations on behalf of the partnership. They have authority only to complete transactions begun but not finished at the time of dissolution and to wind up the business of the partnership [UPA 803, 804(1)].

Winding up includes collecting and preserving partnership assets, discharging liabilities (paying debts), and accounting to the partners for the value of their individual interests in the partnership. Partners continue to have fiduciary duties to one another and to the firm during this process.

UPA 401(h) provides that a partner is entitled to compensation for services in winding up partnership affairs above and apart from the partner's share in the partnership profits. A partner may also receive reimbursement for expenses incurred in the process.

Both creditors of the partnership and creditors of the individual partners can make claims on the partnership's assets. In general, partnership creditors share proportionately with the partners' individual creditors in the partners' assets, which include their interests in the partnership.

A partnership's assets are distributed according to the following priorities [UPA 807]:

1. Payment of debts, including those owed to partner and nonpartner creditors.
2. Return of capital contributions and distribution of profits to partners.

If the partnership's liabilities are greater than its assets, the partners bear the losses in the same proportion in which they shared the profits unless they have agreed otherwise.

---

8. *810 Properties, LLP, et al. v. Will Sukenik, et al.,* 2020-Ohio-1623, 153 N.E.3d 990 (OH App. 2020).

Partnership Buy-Sell Agreements. Before entering into a partnership, partners may agree on how the assets will be valued and divided in the event that the partnership dissolves. Such an agreement may eliminate costly negotiations or litigation later.

The agreement may provide for one or more partners to buy out the other or others, should the situation warrant. This is called a **buy-sell agreement,** or simply a buy-out agreement. Alternatively, the agreement may specify that one or more partners will determine the value of the interest being sold and that the other or others will decide whether to buy or sell.

As stated earlier, under UPA 701, if a partner's dissociation does not result in a dissolution of the partnership, a buyout of the partner's interest is mandatory. The UPA contains an extensive set of buyout rules that apply when the partners do not have a buyout agreement. Basically, a withdrawing partner receives the same amount as if the business were winding up.

Practice and Review: Small Businesses and Franchises

Carlos Del Rey decided to open a Mexican fast-food restaurant and signed a franchise contract with a national chain called La Grande Enchilada. The contract required the franchisee to strictly follow the franchisor's operating manual and stated that failure to do so would be grounds for terminating the franchise contract. The manual set forth detailed operating procedures and safety standards, and provided that a La Grande Enchilada representative would inspect the restaurant monthly to ensure compliance.

Nine months after Del Rey began operating his restaurant, a spark from the grill ignited an oily towel in the kitchen. No one was injured, but by the time firefighters were able to put out the fire, the kitchen had sustained extensive damage. The cook told the fire department that the towel was "about two feet from the grill" when it caught fire. This was in compliance with the franchisor's manual that required towels be placed at least one foot from the grills. Nevertheless, the next day La Grande Enchilada notified Del Rey that his franchise would terminate in thirty days for failure to follow the prescribed safety procedures. Using the information presented in the chapter, answer the following questions.

1. What type of franchise was Del Rey's La Grande Enchilada restaurant?
2. If Del Rey operated the restaurant as a sole proprietorship, who bore the loss for the damaged kitchen? Explain.
3. Assume that Del Rey filed a lawsuit against La Grande Enchilada, claiming that his franchise was wrongfully terminated. What is the main factor that a court would consider in determining whether the franchise was wrongfully terminated?
4. Would a court be likely to rule that La Grande Enchilada had good cause to terminate Del Rey's franchise in this situation? Why or why not?

Debate This . . . *A partnership should automatically end when one partner dissociates from the firm.*

Terms and Concepts

Issue Spotters

1. Darnell and Eliana are partners in D&E Designs, an architectural firm. When Darnell dies, his widow claims that as Darnell's heir, she is entitled to take his place as Eliana's partner or to receive a share of the firm's assets. Is she right? Why or why not? (See *Partnerships*.)

2. Anchor Bottling Company and U.S. Beverages, Inc. (USB), enter into a franchise agreement that states the franchise may be terminated at any time "for cause." Anchor fails to meet USB's specified sales quota. Does this constitute "cause" for termination? Why or why not? (See *Franchises*.)

- **Check your answers to the Issue Spotters against the answers provided in Appendix B at the end of this text.**

Business Scenarios and Case Problems

16–1. Franchising. Maria, Pablo, and Vicky are recent college graduates who would like to go into business for themselves. They are considering purchasing a franchise. If they enter into a franchising arrangement, they would have the support of a large company that could answer any questions they might have. Also, a firm that has been in business for many years would be experienced in dealing with some of the problems that novice businesspersons might encounter. These and other attributes of franchises can lessen some of the risks of the marketplace. What other aspects of franchising—positive and negative—should Maria, Pablo, and Vicky consider before committing themselves to a particular franchise? (See *Franchises*.)

16–2. Partnership Formation. Daniel is the owner of a chain of shoe stores. He hires Rubya to be the manager of a new store, which is to open in Grand Rapids, Michigan. Daniel, by written contract, agrees to pay Rubya a monthly salary and 20 percent of the profits. Without Daniel's knowledge, Rubya represents himself to Classen as Daniel's partner and shows Classen the agreement to share profits. Classen extends credit to Rubya. Rubya defaults. Discuss whether Classen can hold Daniel liable as a partner. (See *Partnerships*.)

16–3. Control of a Franchise. National Foods, Inc., sells franchises to its fast-food restaurants, known as Chicky-D's. Under the franchise agreement, franchisees agree to hire and train employees strictly according to Chicky-D's standards. Chicky-D's regional supervisors are required to approve all job candidates before they are hired and all general policies affecting those employees. Chicky-D's reserves the right to terminate a franchise for violating the franchisor's rules. In practice, however, Chicky-D's regional supervisors routinely approve new employees and individual franchisees' policies. After several incidents of racist comments and conduct by Tim, a recently hired assistant manager at a Chicky-D's, Sharon, a counterperson at the restaurant, resigns. Sharon files a suit in a federal district court against National. National files a motion for summary judgment, arguing that it is not liable for harassment by franchise employees. Will the court grant National's motion? Why or why not? (See *Franchises*.)

16–4. Winding Up. Dan and Lori Cole operated a Curves franchise exercise facility in Angola, Indiana, as a partnership. The firm leased commercial space from Flying Cat, LLC, for a renewable three-year term and renewed the lease for a second three-year term. But two years after the renewal, the Coles divorced. By the end of the second term, Flying Cat was owed more than $21,000 on the lease. Without telling the landlord about the divorce, Lori signed another extension. More rent went unpaid. Flying Cat obtained a judgment in an Indiana state court against the partnership for almost $50,000. Can Dan be held liable? Why or why not? [*Curves for Women Angola v. Flying Cat*, LLC, 983 N.E.2d 629 (Ind.App. 2013)] (See *Partnerships*.)

16–5. Spotlight on Liberty Tax Service—Quality Control. JTH Tax, Inc., doing business as Liberty Tax Service, provides tax preparation and related loan services through company-owned and franchised stores. Liberty's agreement with its franchisees reserved the right to control their ads. In operations manuals, Liberty provided step-by-step instructions, directions, and limitations regarding the franchisees' ads and retained the right to unilaterally modify the steps at any time. The California attorney general filed a suit in a California state court against Liberty, alleging that its franchisees had used misleading or deceptive ads regarding refund anticipation loans and e-refund checks. Can Liberty be held liable? Discuss. [*People v. JTH Tax, Inc.*, 212 Cal. App.4th 1219, 151 Cal.Rptr.3d 728 (1 Dist. 2013)] (See *Franchises*.)

16–6. Quality Control. The franchise agreement of Domino's Pizza, LLC, sets out operational standards, including safety requirements, for a franchisee to follow but provides that the franchisee is an independent contractor. Each franchisee is free to use its own means and methods. For example, Domino's does not know whether a franchisee's delivery drivers are complying with vehicle safety requirements. MAC Pizza Management, Inc., operates a Domino's franchise. A vehicle driven by Joshua Balka, a MAC delivery driver, hydroplaned due to a bald tire and wet pavement. It struck the vehicle of Devavaram and

Ruth Christopher, killing Ruth and injuring Devavaram. Is Domino's liable for negligence? Explain. [*Domino's Pizza, LLC v. Reddy*, 2015 WL 1247349 (Tex.App.—Beaumont 2015)] (See *Franchises*.)

16–7. Business Case Problem With Sample Answer—Franchise Termination. Executive Home Care Franchising, LLC, sells in-home health-care franchises. Clint, Massare, and Greer Marshall entered into a franchise agreement with Executive Home Care. The agreement provided that the franchisees' failure to comply with the agreement's terms would likely cause irreparable harm to the franchisor, entitling it to an injunction. About two years later, the Marshalls gave up their franchise. They returned thirteen boxes of documents, stationery, operating manuals, marketing materials, and other items—everything in their possession that featured Executive Home Care trademarks. They quit operating out of the franchised location. They transferred the phone number back to the franchisor and informed their clients that they were no longer associated with Executive Home Care. They continued to engage in the home health-care business, however, under the name "Well-Being Home Care Corp." Is Executive Home Care entitled to an injunction against the Marshalls and their new company? Discuss. [*Executive Home Care Franchising, LLC v. Marshall Health Corp.*, 642 Fed. Appx. 181 (3d Cir. 2016)] (See *Franchises*.)

- **For a sample answer to Problem 16–7, go to Appendix C at the end of this text.**

16–8. Dissociation and Dissolution. Marc Malfitano and seven others formed Poughkeepsie Galleria as a partnership to own and manage a shopping mall in New York. The partnership agreement stated that "all decisions to be made by the Partners shall be made by the casting of votes" with "no less than fifty-one percent" of the partners "required to approve any matter." The agreement also provided that the partnership would dissolve on "the election of the Partners" or "the happening of any event which makes it unlawful for the business . . . to be carried on." Later, Malfitano decided to dissociate from the firm and wrote to the other partners, "I hereby elect to dissolve the Partnership." Did Malfitano have the power and the right to dissociate from Poughkeepsie Galleria? Could he unilaterally dissolve the partnership? Can the other partners continue the business? Which, if any, of these actions violate the partnership agreement? Discuss. [*Congel v. Malfitano*, 31 N.Y.3d 272, 76 N.Y.S.3d 873, 101 N.E.3d 341 (2018)] (See *Partnerships*.)

16–9. Breach of Franchise Agreement. After giving up his Taco Bell franchise, Roy Upshaw opened new restaurants called Taco Hut. He later renamed the restaurants Taco Casa and began franchising them in the mid-1980s. He was unable to obtain a federally registered trademark for Taco Casa, however, because someone else owned the mark. Andrew Wilson, on behalf of Lacado, L.L.C., negotiated with Upshaw to obtain Taco Casa franchises. Upshaw assured Wilson that Upshaw owned the Taco Casa trademark. Eventually, Wilson signed three 20-year franchise agreements with Taco Casa. Wilson later discovered that Upshaw did not own the Taco Casa trademark. Wilson (through Lacado, L.L.C.) filed suit against Upshaw and others, raising a claim for breach of the franchise agreement. A jury found the franchisor had breached the franchise agreement and had committed fraud. Upshaw appealed. How should the Court of Appeals of Texas rule? [*Upshaw and R&S Upshaw Franchising, L.L.C. v. Lacado, L.L.C.*, 650 S.W.3d 61 (TX App., Fort Worth, 2021). (See *Franchises*.)

16–10. A Question of Ethics—The IDDR Approach and Sole Proprietorships. Tom George was the sole owner of Turbine Component Super Market, LLC (TCSM), when its existence was terminated by the state of Texas. A TCSM creditor, Turbine Resources Unlimited, filed and won a suit in a Texas state court against George for breach of contract. The plaintiff sought to collect the amount of the judgment through a sale of George's property. Instead of turning his assets over to the court, however, George tried to hide them by reforming TCSM. Without telling the court, he paid an unrelated debt with $100,000 of TCSM's funds. George claimed that the funds were a loan and that he was merely an employee of TCSM. [*Mitchell v. Turbine Resources Unlimited, Inc.*, 523 S.W.3d 189 (Tex.App.—Houston 2017)] (See *Sole Proprietorships*.)

(a) Is it more likely that the court will recognize TCSM as an LLC or a sole proprietorship? Why?

(b) Using the *Discussion* step of the IDDR approach, consider whether the owner of a business has an ethical obligation to represent the character and purpose of the organization truthfully.

Time-Limited Group Assignment

16–11. Liability of Partners. At least six months before the Summer Olympic Games in Atlanta, Georgia, Stafford Fontenot and four others agreed to sell Cajun food at the games and began making preparations. On May 19, the group (calling themselves "Prairie Cajun Seafood Catering of Louisiana") applied for a business license from the county health department. Later, Ted Norris sold a mobile kitchen to them for $40,000. They gave Norris an $8,000 check drawn on the "Prairie Cajun Seafood Catering of Louisiana" account and

two promissory notes, one for $12,000 and the other for $20,000. The notes, which were dated June 12, listed only Fontenot "d/b/a Prairie Cajun Seafood" as the maker (*d/b/a* is an abbreviation for "doing business as").

On July 31, Fontenot and his friends signed a partnership agreement, which listed specific percentages of profits and losses. They drove the mobile kitchen to Atlanta, but business was disastrous. When the notes were not paid, Norris filed a suit in a Louisiana state court against Fontenot, seeking payment. (See *Partnerships*.)

(a) The first group will discuss the elements of a partnership and determine whether a partnership exists among Fontenot and the others.

(b) The second group will determine who can be held liable on the notes and why.

(c) The third group will discuss the concept of "d/b/a," or "doing business as." Does a person who uses this designation when signing checks or promissory notes avoid liability on the checks or notes?

Chapter 17

Limited Liability Business Forms

Our government allows entrepreneurs to choose from a variety of business organizational forms. In selecting among them, businesspersons are motivated to choose organizational forms that limit their liability. Limited liability may allow them to take more business risk, which is associated with the potential for higher profits.

An increasingly common form of business organization is the limited liability company (LLC). LLCs have become the organizational form of choice among many small businesses. Other limited liability business forms include the *limited liability partnership (LLP)* and the *limited liability limited partnership (LLLP)*.

17–1 The Limited Liability Company

A **limited liability company (LLC)** is a hybrid that combines the limited liability aspects of a corporation and the tax advantages of a partnership. The LLC has been available for only a few decades, but it has become the preferred structure for many small businesses.

LLCs are governed by state statutes, which vary from state to state. In an attempt to create more uniformity, the National Conference of Commissioners on Uniform State Laws issued the Uniform Limited Liability Company Act (ULLCA), most recently revised in 2006. About 40 percent of the states have adopted the act.

Although the law governing LLCs remains far from uniform, some provisions are common to most state statutes. We base our discussion of LLCs on these common elements.

17–1a The Nature of the LLC

LLCs share many characteristics with corporations. Like corporations, LLCs must be formed and operated in compliance with state law. Like the shareholders of a corporation, the owners of an LLC, who are called **members,** enjoy limited liability [ULLCA 303].

Limited Liability of Members Members of LLCs are shielded from personal liability in most situations. In other words, the liability of members normally is limited to the amount of their investment.

An exception arises when a member has significantly contributed to an LLC's tortious conduct. ■ **Case in Point 17.1**

JGR Technologies, LLC, provided various internet-related services for the Missouri Radio Ozarks Network (ORN). Following a fee dispute between the two companies, Luke Baugh, a JGR employee, "seized" several internet domain names owned by ORN that were associated with its radio stations, including kuku.com. Baugh then sold kuku.com to a foreign buyer for $50,000.

The trial court found Baugh and three JGR members liable for the tort of conversion, which occurs when someone intentionally interferes with another's personal property. The JGR members appealed on the grounds that they were shielded by law from liability for Baugh's acts on behalf of the LLC. A state appeals court noted that a great deal of evidence had been presented at trial showing the extent to which the three LLC members "participated in or directed" Baugh's tortious conduct. Consequently, the appeals court affirmed the trial court's decision. The members could be held personally liable for such conduct. They, along with Baugh, owed ORN $50,000 in damages plus interest.[1] ■

When Liability May Be Imposed The members of an LLC, like the shareholders in a corporation, can lose their limited personal liability in certain circumstances. For instance, when an individual guarantees payment of a business loan to the LLC, that individual is personally liable for the business's obligation. In addition, if an LLC member fails to comply with certain formalities, such as by commingling personal and business funds, a court can impose personal liability.

---

1. *Missouri Ozarks Radio, Network, Inc. v. Baugh*, 598 S.W.3d 154 (Mo. Ct. App. 2020).

Under various principles of corporate law, courts may hold the owners of a business liable for its debts. On rare occasions, for instance, courts ignore the corporate structure ("pierce the corporate veil") to expose the shareholders to personal liability when it is required to achieve justice.

Similarly, courts will sometimes pierce the veil of an LLC to hold its members personally liable. Note, however, that courts have reserved piercing the veil of an LLC for circumstances that are clearly extraordinary. There must normally be some flagrant disregard of the LLC formalities, as well as fraud or malfeasance on the part of the LLC member.

■ **Case in Point 17.2** Tom and Shannon Brown purchased a new home in Hattiesburg, Mississippi, from Ray Richard and Nick Welch. Richard had hired Waldron Properties, LLC (WP), to build the home. Several years later, cracks began to develop in the walls of the Browns' home as a result of defects in the construction of the foundation. The Browns sued Murray Waldron, the sole member of WP, for breach of warranty under the state's New Home Warranty Act (NHWA). Because the required NHWA notice they had received when they bought the home was signed by Waldron personally, they claimed that Waldron was personally liable.

The trial court found that WP, not Waldron individually, was the builder of the Browns' home. The Browns appealed. They contended that even if WP was the builder, the court should pierce the veil of the LLC and hold Waldron personally liable. The state appellate court disagreed and affirmed the lower court's ruling. The Browns had not entered into a contract with either Waldron or WP. There was not sufficient evidence that Waldron had disregarded LLC formalities or had engaged in fraud or other misconduct to justify piercing the LLC's veil to hold him personally liable.[2] ■

Other Similarities to Corporations Another similarity between corporations and LLCs is that LLCs are legal entities apart from their owners. As a legal person, the LLC can sue or be sued, enter into contracts, and hold title to property [ULLCA 201]. The terminology used to describe LLCs formed in other states or nations is also similar to that used in corporate law. For instance, an LLC or corporation formed in one state but doing business in another state is referred to in the second state as a "foreign" LLC or corporation.

2. *Brown v. Waldron*, 186 So.3d 955 (Miss.App. 2016). See also *Lancaster v. Miller*, 319 So.3d 1174 (Miss.App. 2021).

17–1b The Formation of the LLC

LLCs are creatures of statute and thus must follow state statutory requirements.

Articles of Organization To form an LLC, **articles of organization** must be filed with a central state agency—usually the secretary of state's office [ULLCA 202]. Typically, the articles must include the name of the business, its principal address, the name and address of a registered agent, the members' names, and how the LLC will be managed [ULLCA 203]. The business's name must include the words Limited Liability Company or the initials LLC [ULLCA 105(a)]. Although a majority of the states permit one-member LLCs, some states require at least two members.

Preformation Contracts Businesspersons sometimes enter into contracts on behalf of a business organization that is not yet formed. Persons who are forming a corporation, for instance, may enter into contracts during the process of incorporation but before the corporation becomes a legal entity. These contracts are referred to as "preincorporation contracts." The individual promoters who sign the contracts are bound to their terms. Once the corporation is formed and adopts the preincorporation contracts (by means of a novation, which substitutes a new contract for the old contract), it can enforce the contract terms.

In dealing with the preorganization contracts of LLCs, courts may apply the well-established principles of corporate law relating to preincorporation contracts. That is, when the promoters of an LLC enter into preformation contracts, the LLC, once formed, can adopt the contracts by a novation and then enforce them.

■ **Example 17.3** Park, LLC, enters into an agreement to sell a hotel to View Associates, Ltd. View Associates then assigns the rights to the purchase of this hotel to another company called Devel, LLC. At the time of the rights assignment, Devel does not yet exist. It is legally created two months later. Park, LLC, subsequently refuses to sell the hotel to Devel. Devel then sues for breach of the purchase agreement. Most likely, a court will rule in favor of Devel, LLC, even though it did not exist when the agreement was executed. Once the legal entity comes into existence, it should be able to enforce any preorganization contract made on its behalf. ■

17–1c Jurisdictional Requirements

As we have seen, LLCs and corporations share several characteristics, but a significant difference between these organizational forms involves federal jurisdictional requirements. Under the federal jurisdiction statute, a corporation is deemed to be a citizen of the state where it is incorporated and maintains its principal place of business. The statute does not mention the state citizenship of partnerships, LLCs, and other unincorporated associations. The courts, however, have tended to regard these entities as citizens of every state of which their members are citizens.

The state citizenship of an LLC may come into play when a party sues the LLC based on diversity of citizenship. Remember that when parties to a lawsuit are from different states and the amount in controversy exceeds $75,000, a federal court can exercise diversity jurisdiction. Total diversity of citizenship must exist, however.

■ **Example 17.4**   Jen Fong, a citizen of New York, wishes to bring a suit against Skycel, an LLC formed under the laws of Connecticut. One of Skycel's members also lives in New York. Fong will not be able to bring a suit against Skycel in federal court on the basis of diversity jurisdiction because the defendant LLC is also a citizen of New York. The same would be true if Fong was bringing a suit against multiple defendants and one of the defendants lived in New York. ■

17–1d Advantages of the LLC

The LLC offers many advantages to businesspersons, which is why this form of business organization has become increasingly popular.

Limited Liability   A key advantage of the LLC is the limited liability of its members. The LLC as an entity can be held liable for any loss or injury caused by the wrongful acts or omissions of its members. As we have seen, however, members themselves generally are not personally liable.

In the following case, the court had to decide whether an LLC's member and manager could be held personally liable for the firm's failure to meet its obligations to a creditor.

Case 17.1

Nesset, Inc. v. Jones

Court of Appeals of Iowa, 947 N.W.2d 664 (2020).

Background and Facts   Larry Nesset, the owner of Nesset, Inc., doing business as Weber Paint and Glass, subcontracted to complete various remodeling projects for the renovation of the hundred-year-old Sokol building in Cedar Rapids, Iowa, owned by Green Development, LLC. After Green Development's general contractor, Miles Wilson, left the project, Nesset began to deal directly with the LLC's owner, Charles Jones. They did not enter into a written contract.

Some of Nesset's invoices to Green Development were not paid. In text messages, Jones affirmed his intent to pay the past due bills but failed to do so. Eventually, Nesset filed a petition in an Iowa state court against Jones and his LLC to collect on the debt, alleging breach of contract. Jones answered that Weber Paint could only have had a contractual relationship with Green Development, not with him personally. Nesset argued that Jones's promises to pay were not written on LLC letterhead and did not include his title in the LLC.

The trial court issued a judgment in Nesset's favor, holding Jones personally liable for $17,708.33, plus interest and attorney's fees. Jones appealed.

In the Language of the Court

TABOR, Presiding Judge.

* * * *

* * * By its nature, a limited liability company is an entity distinct from its members. And critically, a member or manager is not liable for the debts, obligations, or other liabilities of a limited liability company, whether arising in contract, tort, or otherwise solely because of acting as a member or manager. Only under exceptional circumstances will a court pierce the veil of an LLC and hold a member or manager individually liable.

Case 17.1 Continues

Case 17.1 Continued

When deciding whether piercing an LLC's veil is appropriate, we look for these circumstances: (1) it is undercapitalized, (2) it is without separate books, (3) its finances are not separated from individual finances, (4) it pays an individual's obligations, (5) it is used to promote fraud or illegality, or (6) it is merely a sham.

* * * *

* * * The burden [is on Nesset], as plaintiff, to show exceptional circumstances exist to warrant imposing personal liability on Jones, as a member of the LLC that owns the Sokol building. And [Nesset] did not show such extraordinary circumstances existed. At trial, Nesset acknowledged Jones acted as the owner's representative when he took over the general contracting duties from Wilson. When Jones made partial payments to Weber Paint, he did so on the Green Development account. [Nesset] offered no evidence the LLC was undercapitalized, lacked separate books or finances, was promoting any fraud or illegality, or was a sham.

At most, [Nesset] asserts Jones's promises to pay were not made solely in his representative capacity as a member or manager of the LLC * * * . This assertion does not justify a court in veil piercing. Nothing about the casual nature of Jones's text messages undermines the financial soundness or legitimacy of his LLC structure.

Decision and Remedy A state intermediate appellate court reversed the trial court's ruling on the question of Jones's personal liability for his LLC's debt. "The record does not support the [trial] court's conclusion that Jones is individually liable."

Critical Thinking

- **Legal Environment** Besides the "exceptional circumstances" noted by the court in the Nesset case, in what situations might an LLC's member or manager be personally liable for the liability of the company? Explain.
- **Economic** Why does the law allow—and even encourage—limits on the liability of a business organization's owners and managers for the firm's actions? Discuss.

Flexibility in Taxation Another advantage of the LLC is its flexibility in regard to taxation. An LLC that has two or more members can choose to be taxed as either a partnership or a corporation. A corporate entity normally must pay income taxes on its profits, and the shareholders must then pay personal income taxes on any of those profits that are distributed as dividends. An LLC that wants to distribute profits to its members almost always prefers to be taxed as a partnership to avoid the "double taxation" that is characteristic of the corporate entity.

Unless an LLC indicates that it wishes to be taxed as a corporation, the Internal Revenue Service (IRS) automatically taxes it as a partnership. This means that the LLC, as an entity, pays no taxes. Rather, as in a partnership, profits are "passed through" the LLC to the members, who then personally pay taxes on the profits. If an LLC's members want to reinvest profits in the business rather than distribute the profits to members, however, they may prefer to be taxed as a corporation. Corporate income tax rates may be lower than personal tax rates.

Part of the attractiveness of the LLC is this flexibility with respect to taxation.

An LLC that has only one member cannot be taxed as a partnership. For federal income tax purposes, one-member LLCs are automatically taxed as sole proprietorships unless they indicate that they wish to be taxed as corporations. With respect to state taxes, most states follow the IRS rules.

Management and Foreign Investors Another advantage of the LLC for businesspersons is the flexibility it offers in terms of business operations and management, as will be discussed shortly. Foreign investors are allowed to become LLC members, so organizing as an LLC can enable a business to attract investors from other countries. (Many nations—including France, Germany, Ireland, Japan, the United Kingdom, and countries in Latin America—have business forms that provide for limited liability in much the same way as LLCs do.)

17–1e Disadvantages of the LLC

The main disadvantage of the LLC is that state LLC statutes are not uniform. Therefore, businesses that operate in more than one state may not receive consistent treatment in these states.

Generally, most states apply to a foreign LLC (an LLC formed in another state) the law of the state where the LLC was formed. Difficulties can arise, though, when one state's court must interpret and apply another state's laws.

17–2 LLC Management and Operation

The members of an LLC have considerable flexibility in managing and operating the business. Here, we discuss management options, fiduciary duties owed, and the operating agreement and general operating procedures of LLCs.

17–2a Management of an LLC

Basically, LLC members have two options for managing the firm, as shown in Exhibit 17–1. The firm can be either a "member-managed" LLC or a "manager-managed" LLC.

Exhibit 17–1 Management of an LLC

Most state LLC statutes and the ULLCA provide that unless the articles of organization specify otherwise, an LLC is assumed to be member managed [ULLCA 203(a)(6)].

In a member-managed LLC, all of the members participate in management, and decisions are made by majority vote [ULLCA 404(a)]. In a manager-managed LLC, the members designate a group of persons to manage the firm. The management group may consist of only members, both members and nonmembers, or only nonmembers.

17–2b Fiduciary Duties

Under the ULLCA, managers in a manager-managed LLC owe fiduciary duties (the duty of loyalty and the duty of care) to the LLC and its members [ULLCA 409(a), 409(h)]. (This same rule applies in corporate law—corporate directors and officers owe fiduciary duties to the corporation and its shareholders.) Because not all states have adopted the ULLCA, some state statutes provide that managers owe fiduciary duties only to the LLC and not to the LLC's members.

To whom the fiduciary duties are owed can affect the outcome of litigation. ■ **Example 17.5** Abeeku and his children, Bodua and Xhosa, form an LLC along with Lezanne. The LLC is called Abeeku Plumbing, LLC. Xhosa and Lezanne are managers. Eventually, Bodua quits the firm. Two years later, Abeeku "fires" Xhosa and Lezanne. He denies them access to the LLC's books and offices, but continues to operate the business.

Xhosa and Lezanne file suit in state court against Abeeku, claiming breach of fiduciary duty. If the state has adopted the ULLCA, a court will find that Abeeku did not have authority under the terms of the LLC's operating agreement to fire two managers. Therefore, the "firing" will become part of Xhosa and Lezanne's breach-of-fiduciary-duty claim. ■

17–2c The LLC Operating Agreement

The members of an LLC can decide how to operate the various aspects of the business by forming an **operating agreement** [ULLCA 103(a)]. In many states, an operating agreement is not required for an LLC to exist, and if there is one, it need not be in writing. Generally, though, LLC members should protect their interests by creating a written operating agreement.

Operating agreements typically contain provisions relating to the following areas:

1. Management and how future managers will be chosen or removed. (Although most LLC statutes are silent on this issue, the ULLCA provides that members

may choose and remove managers by majority vote
[ULLCA 404(b)(3)].)
2. How profits will be divided.
3. How membership interests may be transferred.
4. Whether the dissociation of a member, such as by
   death or departure, will trigger dissolution of the
   LLC, and how a buyout price will be calculated in
   the event of a member's dissociation.
5. Whether formal members' meetings will be held.
6. How voting rights will be apportioned. (If the agreement does not cover voting, LLC statutes in most
   states provide that voting rights are apportioned
   according to capital contributions. Some states provide that, in the absence of an agreement to the contrary, each member has one vote.)

The provisions commonly included in operating
agreements are also shown in Exhibit 17–2.

If a dispute arises and there is no agreement covering
the topic under dispute, the state LLC statute will govern
the outcome. For instance, most LLC statutes provide
that if the members have not specified how profits will be
divided, they will be divided equally among the members.
When an issue is not covered by an operating agreement
or by an LLC statute, the courts often apply principles of
partnership law.

Sometimes, as in the following case, an operating agreement and the state's LLC statutes are applied
together to determine the outcome of a dispute between
the members of an LLC.

Exhibit 17–2 Provisions Commonly Included in an LLC Operating Agreement

Management	Sets forth who will manage the LLC and how future managers will be chosen or removed. (The ULLCA provides that members may choose and remove managers by majority vote.)
Profits	Establishes how profits will be divided among members.
Membership	Specifies how membership interests may be transferred.
Dissociation and Dissolution	Clarifies which events cause the dissociation of a member—such as by death or retirement—and trigger the LLC's dissolution. Provides a method of calculating a buyout price for a member's dissociation.
Member Meetings	Determines whether or not formal members' meetings will be held.
Voting Rights	Details how voting rights will be apportioned, such as according to each member's capital contribution or by allowing one vote for each member.

Schaefer v. Orth

Court of Appeals of Wisconsin, 2018 WI App 35, 382 Wis.2d 271, 915 N.W.2d 730 (2018).

Background and Facts Jason Schaefer and Randy Orth created Grilled Cheese, LLC, to own and operate a "Tom and Chee" franchise, a casual restaurant specializing in grilled cheese sandwiches and soups. The operating agreement provided that Schaefer would be responsible for the restaurant's day-to-day operations, for which the LLC would pay him a monthly salary and bonuses. Orth would be responsible for the LLC's business and financial decisions and would not receive any compensation.

The restaurant reported a profit only in its first full month of operations. Five months later, when Schaefer was not paid his salary and bonuses, he quit. Later, Orth closed the restaurant and worked to wind up the business. Both parties lost the entire amounts they had invested in the LLC. Schaefer filed a suit in a Wisconsin state court against Orth, claiming Orth had breached their contract by failing to pay Schaefer's salary. The court directed a verdict in Orth's favor. Schaefer appealed.

In the Language of the Court
PER CURIAM [By the Whole Court].
* * * *

* * * The [lower] court granted Orth's motion for a directed verdict because it determined there was no credible evidence to support a conclusion that Orth was personally liable to Schaefer for the unpaid wages and bonuses to which Schaefer was entitled under the operating agreement.

At trial, both Orth and Schaefer testified it was the LLC's responsibility to pay Schaefer the wages and bonuses set forth in the operating agreement, and Orth was not personally required to pay Schaefer those amounts.

The operating agreement's unambiguous language confirms that the LLC, not Orth, was responsible for paying Schaefer's wages and bonuses. The section of the agreement pertaining to "Distributions" specifically lists Schaefer's wages and bonuses as distributions to be paid to Schaefer before other distributions to the LLC's members. The agreement specifies that distributions are made from *the LLC's* available funds. The section of the agreement pertaining to "Profits" similarly states that, in the case of any profit resulting from the LLC's operations, "the LLC shall, as the first priority, allocate Profit to Schaefer to the extent, if any, that (A) all service compensation accruing in his favor through the date of the relevant allocation, exceeds (B) all prior allocations under this Clause." The agreement defines the term profit as *the LLC's* profit.

The language cited above plainly demonstrates that the LLC was responsible for paying Schaefer's wages and bonuses. Wisconsin's LLC statutes provide that "the debts, obligations and liabilities of a limited liability company, whether arising in contract, tort or otherwise, shall be solely the debts, obligations and liabilities of the limited liability company." With certain exceptions not applicable here, "a member or manager of a limited liability company is not personally liable for any debt, obligation or liability of the limited liability company, except that a member or manager may become personally liable by his or her acts or conduct other than as a member or manager." There is no evidence Orth was acting outside his capacity as a member or manager of the LLC when he failed to pay Schaefer's wages and bonuses. As a result, Orth is not personally liable to Schaefer for the payment of those amounts.

Decision and Remedy A state intermediate appellate court affirmed the lower court's judgment. "The evidence presented at trial does not permit a legal conclusion that Orth was personally liable to Schaefer for" his unpaid salary and bonuses.

Critical Thinking

- **Economic** The operating agreement stated that an "aggrieved party may pursue all redress permitted by law," including attorneys' fees. Under this provision, is Schaefer entitled to an award of attorneys' fees even though the trial court granted Orth's motion for a directed verdict? Discuss.

- **Legal Environment** Could Schaefer have sued the LLC to recover his unpaid salary and bonuses? Explain.

17–3 Dissociation and Dissolution of an LLC

Recall that in a partnership, dissociation occurs when a partner ceases to be associated in the carrying on of the partnership business. The same concept applies to LLCs. And like a partner in a partnership, a member of an LLC has the power to dissociate at any time but may not have the right to dissociate.

Under the ULLCA, the events that trigger a member's dissociation from an LLC are similar to the events causing a partner to be dissociated under the Uniform Partnership Act (UPA). These include voluntary withdrawal, expulsion by other members, court order, incompetence, bankruptcy, and death. Generally, if a member dies or otherwise dissociates from an LLC, the other members may continue to carry on the LLC business unless the operating agreement provides otherwise.

17–3a Effects of Dissociation

When members dissociate from an LLC, they lose the right to participate in management and the right to act as agents for the LLC. The members' duty of loyalty to the LLC also terminates, and the duty of care continues only with respect to events that occurred before dissociation.

Generally, dissociated members also have a right to have their interest in the LLC bought out by the other members. The LLC's operating agreement may contain provisions establishing a buyout price. If it does not, the interest is usually purchased at fair value. In states that have adopted the ULLCA, the LLC must purchase the interest at fair value within 120 days after the dissociation.

If the member's dissociation violates the LLC's operating agreement, it is considered legally wrongful, and the dissociated member can be held liable for damages caused by the dissociation. ■ **Example 17.6** Giorgi and Sadat are members in an LLC. Giorgi manages the accounts,

and Sadat, who has many connections in the community and is a skilled investor, brings in the business. If Sadat wrongfully dissociates from the LLC, the LLC's business will suffer, and Giorgi can hold Sadat liable for the loss of business resulting from her withdrawal. ■

17–3b Dissolution

Regardless of whether a member's dissociation is wrongful or rightful, normally the dissociated member has no right to force the LLC to dissolve. The remaining members can opt either to continue or to dissolve the business.

Members can also stipulate in their operating agreement that certain events will cause dissolution, or they can agree that they have the power to dissolve the LLC by vote. As with partnerships, a court can order an LLC to be dissolved in certain circumstances. For instance, a court might order dissolution when the members have engaged in illegal or oppressive conduct, or when it is no longer feasible to carry on the business.

■ **Case in Point 17.7** Charles Timmons was a member of Lake City Golf Club, a limited liability company operated by another member, Claude Saint Marie. Timmons became disenchanted with Saint Marie's management of the club's finances and filed suit against Lake City. The settlement agreement from this action granted Timmons $1,750,000, to be paid by Lake City in installments. When Lake City was unable to make these payments, Timmons sued again. This time, an arbitrator decided that, given its precarious financial situation, Lake City must be judicially dissolved. A trial court eventually found that Timmons was owed about $1,850,000 of the proceeds from this dissolution, an amount upheld on appeal.[3] ■

A judge's exercise of discretion to order the dissolution of an LLC was disputed in the following case.

3. *Timmons v. Lakes City Golf, LLC,* 293 So.3d 596 (Fla. Dist. Ct. App., 1st Dist. 2020).

Case Analysis 17.3

Reese v. Newman

District of Columbia Court of Appeals, 131 A.3d 880 (2016).

In the Language of the Court
KING, Senior Judge:

* * * Allison Reese and * * * Nicole Newman were co-owners of ANR Construction Management, LLC * * *.

Following disputes over management of the company, Newman notified Reese in writing that she intended to * * * dissolve and wind-up the LLC. Reese did not want to dissolve the LLC

but preferred that Newman simply be dissociated so that Reese could continue the business herself. Newman filed an action [against Reese] for judicial dissolution in [a District of Columbia court]. Reese filed a counterclaim for Newman's dissociation * * * . Following a jury trial, the jury * * * found grounds for both judicial dissolution and forced dissociation of Newman; the court, thereafter, ordered judicial dissolution of the LLC. * * * Reese appeals.

* * * *

Reese argues that the trial court erred when it purported to use discretion in choosing between dissolution of the LLC, as proposed by Newman, and forcing dissociation of Newman from the LLC, as proposed by Reese. Reese argues that the [District of Columbia (D.C.)] statute [governing dissociation from an LLC] does not allow for any discretion by the court, and that, in fact, the statute mandates that the court order dissociation of Newman based on the jury's findings.

In matters of statutory interpretation, we review the trial court's decision *de novo*. Our analysis starts with the plain language of the statute, as the general rule of statutory interpretation is that the intent of the lawmaker is to be found in the language that he has used. To that end, the words of the statute should be construed according to their ordinary sense and with the meaning commonly attributed to them.

Reese argues that the court was required to dissociate Newman from the LLC under [D.C. Code] Section 29–806.02(5) which reads:

A person shall be dissociated as a member from a limited liability company when:

* * * *

(5) On application by the company, the person is expelled as a member by judicial order because the person has:

(A) Engaged, or is engaging, in wrongful conduct that has adversely and materially affected, or will adversely and materially affect, the company's activities and affairs;

(B) Willfully or persistently committed, or is willfully and persistently committing, a material breach of the operating agreement or the person's duties or obligations under Section 29–804.09; or

(C) Engaged, or is engaging, in conduct relating to the company's activities which makes it not reasonably practicable to carry on the activities with the person as a member.

Reese's interpretation of the statute is that, upon application to the court by a company, a judge shall dissociate a member of an LLC, when that member commits any one of the actions described in subsections (5)(A)–(C).

* * * While the introductory language of Section 29–806.02 does use the word "shall"—that command is in no way directed at the trial judge. It reads, "a person shall be dissociated * * * when," and then goes on to recite fifteen separate circumstances describing different occasions when a person shall be dissociated from an LLC. That is to say, when one of the events described in subparagraphs (1) through (15) occurs, the member shall be dissociated. Subparagraph (5), however, is merely one instance for which a person shall be dissociated; that is, when and if a judge has ordered a member expelled because she finds that any conditions under (5)(A)–(C) have been established. In other words, the command in the introductory language is not directed at the trial judge, it is directed at all the circumstances set forth in subparagraphs (1) through (15) * * * . There is nothing in the language of Section 29–806.02(5) that strips a judge of her discretion because it does not require the judge to expel the member if any of the enumerated conditions are established. In short, Section 29–806.02(5) means: when a judge has used her discretion to expel a member of an LLC by judicial order, under any of the enumerated circumstances in (5)(A)–(C), that member shall be dissociated.

* * * Although Reese argues that the language of the "dissociation" section of the District's code should be read as forcing the hand of a trial judge who finds grounds for dissociation, Reese attempts to read the "dissolution" section differently.

Reese differentiates the sections by pointing to the dissolution section's

express authorization to order a remedy other than dissolution in Section 29–807.01(b) which provides: "in a proceeding brought under subsection (a)(5) of this section, the * * * Court may order a remedy other than dissolution." While we are satisfied that judicial dissolution of an LLC is discretionary under this statute, Reese's attempt to buttress [reinforce] her argument that Section 29–806.02(5) is compulsory by pointing to this express provision in the dissolution section and the absence of a similar express provision in the dissociation section is unavailing. First, * * * the only "shall" in the dissociation section is in the introductory language, and the same "shall" can be found in the same place, in the dissolution section: "a limited liability company is dissolved, and its activities and affairs *shall be wound up,* upon the occurrence of any of the following." If that language does not make the rest of the section mandatory in the dissolution section, and we are persuaded that it does not, it cannot be said that the "shall" in the introduction of the dissociation section does the opposite.

* * * *

In sum, we hold that Section 29–806.02(5) can only be interpreted to mean: when a judge finds that any of the events in (5)(A)–(C) have taken place, she may (*i.e.,* has discretion to) expel by judicial order a member of an LLC, and when a judge has done so the member shall be dissociated. Moreover, when both grounds for dissociation of a member and dissolution of the LLC exist, the trial judge has discretion to choose either alternative.

Here, the jury * * * found that grounds were present for either outcome. The trial judge acknowledged that both options were on the table and then exercised her discretion in ordering that dissolution take place. We find no reason to disturb that order.

* * * *

Accordingly, the judgment in this appeal is therefore affirmed.

Case 17.3 Continues

Legal Reasoning Questions

1. What dispute gave rise to the action filed in the court in this case? How did that dispute lead to the issue on appeal?

2. What is the role of an appellate court when reviewing the exercise of discretion by a trial court?

3. Newman alleged that after she delivered her notice to dissolve ANR, Reese locked her out of the LLC's bank accounts, blocked her access to the LLC's files and e-mail, and ended her salary and health benefits. Did any of the jury's findings support these allegations? Explain.

17–3c Winding Up

When an LLC is dissolved, any members who did not wrongfully dissociate may participate in the winding up process. To wind up the business, members must collect, liquidate, and distribute the LLC's assets.

Members may preserve the assets for a reasonable time to optimize their return, and they continue to have the authority to perform reasonable acts in conjunction with winding up. In other words, the LLC will be bound by the reasonable acts of its members during the winding up process.

Once all of the LLC's assets have been sold, the proceeds are distributed. Debts to creditors are paid first (including debts owed to members who are creditors of the LLC). The members' capital contributions are returned next, and any remaining amounts are then distributed to members in equal shares or according to their operating agreement.

17–4 Limited Liability Partnerships

The **limited liability partnership (LLP)** is a hybrid form of business designed mostly for professionals who normally do business as partners in a partnership. Almost all of the states have enacted LLP statutes.

The major advantage of the LLP is that it allows a partnership to continue as a pass-through entity for tax purposes but limits the personal liability of the partners. The LLP is especially attractive for professional service firms and family businesses. All of the "Big Four" accounting firms—the four largest international accountancy and professional services firms—are organized as LLPs: Deloitte, LLP; Ernst & Young, LLP; KPMG, LLP; and PwC, LLP.

17–4a Formation of an LLP

LLPs must be formed and operated in compliance with state statutes, which may include provisions of the UPA. The appropriate form must be filed with a central state agency, usually the secretary of state's office, and the business's name must include either "Limited Liability Partnership" or "LLP" [UPA 1001, 1002]. An LLP must file an annual report with the state to remain qualified as an LLP in that state [UPA 1003].

In most states, it is relatively easy to convert a general partnership into an LLP because the firm's basic organizational structure remains the same. Additionally, all of the statutory and common law rules governing partnerships still apply, apart from those modified by the LLP statute. Normally, LLP statutes are simply amendments to a state's already existing partnership law.

17–4b Liability in an LLP

An LLP allows professionals, such as attorneys and accountants, to avoid personal liability for the malpractice of other partners. Of course, a partner in an LLP is still liable for the partner's own wrongful acts, such as negligence. Also liable is the partner who supervised the individual who committed a wrongful act. (This generally is true for all types of partners and partnerships, not just LLPs.)

■ **Example 17.8** Five lawyers operate a law firm as an LLP. One of the attorneys, Ulrich, is sued for malpractice and loses. The firm's malpractice insurance is insufficient to pay the judgment. If the firm had been organized as a general partnership, the personal assets of the other attorneys could be used to satisfy the obligation. Because the firm is organized as an LLP, however, no other partners at the firm can be held personally liable for Ulrich's malpractice, unless they acted as Ulrich's supervisors. In the absence of a supervisor, only Ulrich's personal assets can be used to satisfy the judgment. ■

Although LLP statutes vary from state to state, generally each state statute limits the liability of partners in some way. For instance, Delaware law protects each innocent partner from the "debts and obligations of the partnership arising from negligence, wrongful acts, or misconduct." The UPA more broadly exempts partners in an LLP from personal liability for any partnership obligation, "whether arising in contract, tort, or otherwise" [UPA 306(c)].

Liability Outside the State of Formation When an LLP formed in one state wants to do business in another state, it may be required to file a statement of foreign qualification in the second state [UPA 1102]. Because state LLP statutes are not uniform, a question sometimes arises as to which law applies if the LLP statutes in the two states provide different liability protection. Most states apply the law of the state in which the LLP was formed, even when the firm does business in another state, which is also the rule under UPA 1101.

Sharing Liability Among Partners When more than one partner in an LLP commits malpractice, a question arises as to how liability should be shared. Is each partner *jointly and severally liable* for the entire result, as a general partner would be in most states?

Some states provide instead for proportionate liability—that is, for separate determinations of the negligence of the partners. ■ **Example 17.9** Accountants Zach and Lyla are partners in an LLP, with Zach supervising Lyla. Lyla negligently fails to file a tax return for a client, Centaur Tools. Centaur files a suit against Zach and Lyla. Under a proportionate liability statute, Zach will be liable for no more than his portion of the responsibility for the missed tax deadline. In a state that does not allow for proportionate liability, Zach can be held liable for the entire loss. ■

17-4c Family Limited Liability Partnerships

A **family limited liability partnership (FLLP)** is a limited liability partnership in which the partners are related to each other—for example, as spouses, parents and children, siblings, or cousins. A person acting in a fiduciary capacity for persons so related can also be a partner. All of the partners must be natural persons or be acting in a fiduciary capacity for the benefit of natural persons.

Probably the most significant use of the FLLP is in agriculture. Family-owned farms sometimes find this form of business organization beneficial. The FLLP offers the same advantages as other LLPs with certain additional advantages. For instance, in Iowa, FLLPs are exempt from real estate transfer taxes when partnership real estate is transferred among partners.

17-5 Limited Partnerships

We now look at a business organizational form that limits the liability of some of its owners—the **limited partnership (LP).** Limited partnerships originated in medieval Europe and have been in existence in the United States since the early 1800s. Today, most states and the District of Columbia have adopted laws based on the Revised Uniform Limited Partnership Act (RULPA).

Limited partnerships differ from general partnerships in several ways. Exhibit 17–3 compares the characteristics of general and limited partnerships.

A limited partnership consists of at least one **general partner** and one or more **limited partners.** A general partner assumes management responsibility for the partnership and has full responsibility for the partnership and for all its debts. A limited partner contributes cash or other property and owns an interest in the firm but is not involved in management responsibilities. Limited partners are not personally liable for partnership debts beyond the amount of their investment. If limited partners take part in the management of the business, however, they may forfeit that limited liability.

■ **Case in Point 17.10** Valley View Enterprises, Inc., built Pine Lakes Golf Club and Estates in Trumbull County, Ohio, in two phases. Valley View Properties, Ltd., a limited partnership, cut out the roadways and constructed sewer, water, and stormwater lines with inlets. Joseph Ferrara was the owner and the president of Valley View Enterprises and the sole general partner of Valley View Properties.

Ferrara failed to obtain the proper permits for the development work in a timely manner and failed to comply with their requirements once they had been obtained. As a result, the state's attorney general, Michael DeWine, sued the Valley View entities and Ferrara for violating Ohio's water pollution control laws. Ultimately, a state appellate court held that Ferrara was liable because he was the sole general partner of Valley View Properties (even though he was not subject to liability as an officer of the corporation).[4] ■

17-5a Formation of an LP

In contrast to the private and informal agreement that usually suffices to form a general partnership, the formation of a limited partnership is a public and formal proceeding. The partners must strictly follow statutory requirements. Not only must a limited partnership have at least one general partner and one limited partner, but the partners must also sign a **certificate of limited partnership.**

The certificate of limited partnership must include certain information, including the name, mailing address, and capital contribution of each general and limited partner.

---

4. *DeWine v. Valley View Enterprises, Inc.,* 2015-Ohio-1222 (Ct.App. 2015). See also *ASR 2620-2630 Fountainview, LP v. ASR 2620-2630 Fountainview GP, LLC,* 282 S.W.3d 556 (TX App., Houston, 14th Dist. 2019).

Exhibit 17–3 A Comparison of General Partnerships and Limited Partnerships

	General Partnership (UPA)	Limited Partnership (RULPA)
Creation	By agreement of two or more persons to carry on a business as co-owners for profit.	By agreement of two or more persons to carry on a business as co-owners for profit. Must include one or more general partners and one or more limited partners. Filing of a certificate with the secretary of state is required.
Sharing of Profits and Losses	By agreement. In the absence of agreement, profits are shared equally by the partners, and losses are shared in the same ratio as profits.	Profits are shared as required in the certificate agreement, and losses are shared likewise, up to the amount of the limited partners' capital contributions. In the absence of a provision in the certificate agreement, profits and losses are shared on the basis of percentages of capital contributions.
Liability	Unlimited personal liability of all partners.	Unlimited personal liability of all general partners; limited partners liable only to the extent of their capital contributions.
Capital Contribution	No minimum or mandatory amount; set by agreement.	Set by agreement.
Management	By agreement. In the absence of agreement, all partners have an equal voice.	Only the general partner (or general partners). Limited partners have no voice. Limited partners who participate in management are subject to liability as general partners if a third party has reason to believe that they are general partners. Safe harbors allow a limited partner to engage in certain activities without incurring personal liability for participating in management.
Duration	Terminated by agreement of the partners, but can continue to do business even when a partner dissociates from the partnership.	Terminated by agreement in the certificate or by retirement, death, or mental incompetence of a general partner in the absence of the right of the other general partners to continue the partnership. Death of a limited partner does not terminate the partnership, unless after the death no limited partners remain.
Distribution of Assets on Liquidation— Order of Priorities	1. Payment of debts, including those owed to partner and nonpartner creditors. 2. Return of capital contributions and distribution of profit to partners.	1. Outside creditors and partner creditors. 2. Partners and former partners entitled to distributions of partnership assets. 3. Unless otherwise agreed, return of capital contributions and distribution of profit to partners.

The certificate must be filed with the designated state official—under the RULPA, the secretary of state. The certificate is usually open to public inspection.

17–5b Liabilities of Partners in an LP

General partners are personally liable to the partnership's creditors. Thus, at least one general partner is necessary in a limited partnership so that someone has personal liability. This policy can be circumvented in states that allow a corporation to be the general partner in a partnership. Because the corporation has limited

liability by virtue of corporation statutes, if a corporation is the general partner, no one in the limited partnership has personal liability.

The liability of limited partners, as mentioned, is limited to the capital that they contribute or agree to contribute to the partnership [RULPA 502]. Limited partners enjoy this limited liability only so long as they do not participate in management [RULPA 303].

A limited partner who participates in management and control of the business will be just as liable as a general partner to any creditor who transacts business with the limited partnership. Liability arises when the creditor believes, based on the limited partner's conduct, that the limited partner is a general partner [RULPA 303]. Such conduct includes acting as a general partner, knowingly allowing one's name to be used in partnership business, or contributing services to the partnership. The extent to which a limited partner can engage in management before being exposed to liability is not always clear, however.

A number of "safe harbors" protect a limited partner from liability for acting as a general partner [RULPA 303(a)]. For instance, safe harbors allow a limited partner to consult with the general partner regarding partnership business, act as a contractor or employee of the partnership, and participate in winding up the business. A limited partner who engages in only one of the safe-harbor activities normally is not exposed to personal liability for participating in the management and control of the business.

17–5c Rights and Duties in an LP

With the exception of the right to participate in management, limited partners have essentially the same rights as general partners. Limited partners have a right of access to the partnership's books and to information regarding partnership business. On dissolution of the partnership, limited partners are entitled to a return of their contributions in accordance with the partnership certificate [RULPA 201(a)(10)]. They can also assign their interests subject to the certificate [RULPA 702, 704]. In addition, they can sue an outside party on behalf of the firm if the general partners with authority to do so have refused to file suit [RULPA 1001].

17–5d Dissociation and Dissolution

A general partner has the power to voluntarily dissociate, or withdraw, from a limited partnership unless the partnership agreement specifies otherwise. Under the RULPA, a limited partner can withdraw from the partnership by giving six months' notice, unless the partnership agreement specifies a term. In reality, though, most limited partnership agreements do specify a term, which eliminates the limited partner's right to withdraw. Also, some states have passed laws prohibiting the withdrawal of limited partners.

Events That Cause Dissociation In a limited partnership, a general partner's voluntary dissociation from the firm normally will lead to dissolution unless all partners agree to continue the business. Similarly, the bankruptcy, retirement, death, or mental incompetence of a general partner will cause the dissociation of that partner and the dissolution of the limited partnership unless the other members agree to continue the firm [RULPA 801].

Bankruptcy of a limited partner, however, does not dissolve the partnership unless it causes the bankruptcy of the firm. In addition, death or an assignment of the interest (right to receive distributions) of a limited partner does not dissolve a limited partnership [RULPA 702, 704, 705]. A limited partnership can be dissolved by court decree [RULPA 802].

Distribution of Assets On dissolution, creditors' claims, including those of partners who are creditors, take first priority. After that, partners and former partners receive unpaid distributions of partnership assets. Unless otherwise agreed, they are also entitled to a return of their contributions in the proportions in which they share in distributions [RULPA 804].

Valuation of Assets Disputes commonly arise about how the partnership's assets should be valued and distributed and whether the business should be sold. ■ **Case in Point 17.11** Actor Kevin Costner was a limited partner in Midnight Star Enterprises, LP, which runs a casino, bar, and restaurant in South Dakota. There were two other limited partners, Carla and Francis Caneva, who owned a small percentage of the partnership (3.25 units each) and received salaries for managing its operations. Another company owned by Costner, Midnight Star Enterprises, Limited (MSEL), was the general partner. Costner thus controlled a majority of the partnership (93.5 units).

When communications broke down between the partners, MSEL asked a court to dissolve the partnership. MSEL's accountant determined that the firm's fair market value was $3.1 million. The Canevas presented evidence that a competitor would buy the business for $6.2 million. The Canevas wanted the court to force Costner to either buy the business for that price within ten days or sell it on the open market to the highest bidder. Ultimately, the state's highest court held in favor of Costner. A partner cannot force the sale of a limited partnership when the other partners want to continue the business. The court also accepted the $3.1 million buyout price of MSEL's accountant and ordered Costner to pay the Canevas the value of their 6.5 partnership units.[5] ■

Buy-Sell Agreements As mentioned earlier, partners can agree ahead of time on how the partnership's assets will be valued and divided if the partnership dissolves. This is true for limited partnerships as well as for general partnerships. Buy-sell agreements can help the partners avoid disputes. Nonetheless, buy-sell agreements do not eliminate all potential for litigation, especially if the terms are subject to more than one interpretation.

---

5. *In re Dissolution of Midnight Star Enterprises, LP,* 2006 SD 98, 724 N.W.2d 334 (2006). In the context of a limited liability company, see *Equity Partners HG, LLC v. Samson, Inc.,* 2019 WL 8752231 (D.S.D., W. Div. 2019).

Example 17.12 Bio Pork LLP (BP) is an Iowa limited liability partnership in the business of raising hogs. A partnership buy-sell agreement requires BP to buy a disassociating partner's interest unless the purchase would impair the firm's capital or its cash flow. In that situation, BP can postpone the purchase until the impairment situation improves but then must purchase the interest within thirty days.

Two of BP's limited partners notified BP of their disassociation, and a wave of similar notices from other limited partners followed. BP declared an impairment circumstance and refused to buy out any of the limited partners. Two limited partners filed a suit in which they ask a state court to order BP to buy out their partnership units. BP argued that it could not do so because of impairment circumstances. The court found that the language of the buy-sell agreement made the sale mandatory. The impairment circumstances only delayed the purchase. ■

17–5e Limited Liability Limited Partnerships

A **limited liability limited partnership (LLLP)** is a type of limited partnership. An LLLP differs from a limited partnership in that a general partner in an LLLP has the same liability as a limited partner in a limited partnership. In other words, the liability of all partners is limited to the amount of their investments in the firm.

A few states provide expressly for LLLPs. In states that do not provide for LLLPs but do allow for limited partnerships and limited liability partnerships, a limited partnership may still be able to register with the state as an LLLP.

Practice and Review: Limited Liability Business Forms

The city of Papagos, Arizona, had a deteriorating bridge in need of repair on a prominent public roadway. The city posted notices seeking proposals for an artistic bridge design and reconstruction. Davidson Masonry, LLC, which was owned and managed by Carl Davidson and his wife, Marilyn Rowe, decided to submit a bid to create a decorative concrete structure that incorporated artistic metalwork. They contacted Shana Lafayette, a local sculptor who specialized in large-scale metal creations, to help them design the bridge. The city selected their bridge design and awarded them the contract for a commission of $184,000.

Davidson Masonry and Lafayette then entered into an agreement to work together on the bridge project. Davidson Masonry agreed to install and pay for concrete and structural work, and Lafayette agreed to install the metalwork at her expense. They agreed that overall profits would be split, with 25 percent going to Lafayette and 75 percent going to Davidson Masonry. Lafayette designed numerous metal sculptures of trout that were incorporated into colorful decorative concrete forms designed by Rowe. Davidson performed the structural engineering. The group worked together successfully until the completion of the project. Using the information presented in the chapter, answer the following questions.

1. Would Davidson Masonry automatically be taxed as a partnership or a corporation?
2. Is Davidson Masonry member managed or manager managed?
3. Suppose that during construction, Lafayette asked Carl Davidson to rent space in a warehouse that was close to the bridge so that she could work on her sculptures near the site where they would eventually be installed. Carl Davidson signed the rental contract in his own name rather than the name of the LLC. The other members of Davidson Masonry were not aware of the rental agreement. In this situation, would a court likely hold that Davidson Masonry was liable on the contract that Carl Davidson had entered? Why or why not?
4. Now suppose that Rowe has an argument with her husband and wants to withdraw from being a member of Davidson Masonry. What is the term for such a withdrawal, and what effect would it have on the LLC?

Debate This . . .   Because LLCs are essentially just partnerships with limited liability for members, all partnership laws should apply.

Terms and Concepts

articles of organization 370
certificate of limited partnership 379

family limited liability partnership (FLLP) 379
general partner 379

limited liability company (LLC) 369
limited liability limited partnership (LLLP) 382

Issue Spotters

1. Gabriel, Harris, and Ida are members of Jeweled Watches, LLC. What are their options with respect to the management of their firm? (See *LLC Management and Operation*.)

2. Dorinda, Luis, and Elizabeth form a limited partnership. Dorinda is a general partner, and Luis and Elizabeth are limited partners. If Elizabeth is petitioned into involuntary bankruptcy, will that cause a dissolution of the limited partnership? (See *Limited Partnerships*.)

• **Check your answers to the Issue Spotters against the answers provided in Appendix B at the end of this text.**

Business Scenarios and Case Problems

17–1. Limited Liability Companies. John, Lesa, and Tabir form a limited liability company. John contributes 60 percent of the capital, and Lesa and Tabir each contribute 20 percent. Nothing is decided about how profits will be divided. John assumes that he will be entitled to 60 percent of the profits, in accordance with his contribution. Lesa and Tabir, however, assume that the profits will be divided equally. A dispute over the profits arises, and ultimately a court has to decide the issue. What law will the court apply? In most states, what will result? How could this dispute have been avoided in the first place? Discuss fully. (See *The Limited Liability Company*.)

17–2. Diversity Jurisdiction and Limited Liability Companies. Joe, a resident of New Jersey, wants to open a restaurant. He asks Kay, his friend, an experienced attorney and a New Yorker, for her business and legal advice in exchange for a 20 percent ownership interest in the restaurant. Kay helps Joe negotiate a lease for the restaurant premises and advises Joe to organize the business as a limited liability company (LLC).

Joe forms Café Olé, LLC, and with Kay's help, obtains financing. Then, the night before the restaurant opens, Joe tells Kay that he is "cutting her out of the deal." The restaurant proves to be a success. Kay wants to file a suit in a federal district court against Joe and the LLC. Can a federal court exercise jurisdiction over the parties based on diversity of citizenship? Explain. (See *The Limited Liability Company*.)

17–3. LLC Dissolution. Walter Van Houten and John King formed 1545 Ocean Avenue, LLC, with each managing 50 percent of the business. Its purpose was to renovate an existing building and construct a new commercial building. Van Houten and King quarreled over many aspects of the work on the properties. King claimed that Van Houten paid the contractors too much for the work performed. As the projects neared completion, King demanded that the LLC be dissolved and that Van Houten agree to a buyout. Because the parties could not agree on a buyout, King sued for dissolution. The trial court enjoined (prevented) further work on the projects until the dispute was settled. As the ground for dissolution, King cited the fights over management decisions. There was no claim of fraud or frustration of purpose. The trial court ordered that the LLC be dissolved, and Van Houten appealed. Should either of the owners be forced to dissolve the LLC before the completion of its purpose—that is, before the building projects are finished? Explain. [*In re 1545 Ocean Avenue, LLC*, 72 A.D.3d 121, 893 N.Y.S.2d 590 (2010)] (See *Dissociation and Dissolution of an LLC*.)

17–4. Business Case Problem With Sample Answer— LLC Operation. After Hurricane Katrina struck the Gulf Coast, James Williford, Patricia Mosser, Marquetta Smith, and Michael Floyd formed Bluewater Logistics, LLC, to bid on construction contracts. Under Mississippi law, every member of a member-managed LLC is entitled to participate in managing the business. The operating agreement provided for a "super majority" 75 percent vote to remove a member who "has either committed a felony or under any other circumstances that would jeopardize the company status" as a contractor. After Bluewater had completed more than $5 million in contracts, Smith told Williford that she, Mosser, and Floyd were exercising their "super majority" vote to fire him. No reason was provided. Williford sued Bluewater and the other members. Did Smith, Mosser, and Floyd breach the state LLC statute, their fiduciary duties, or the Bluewater operating agreement? Discuss. [*Bluewater Logistics, LLC v. Williford*, 55 So.3d 148 (Miss. 2011)] (See *LLC Management and Operation*.)

• **For a sample answer to Problem 17–4, go to Appendix C at the end of this text.**

17–5. Jurisdictional Requirements. Fadal Machining Centers, LLC, and MAG Industrial Automation Centers, LLC, sued a New Jersey–based corporation, Mid-Atlantic CNC, Inc., in federal district court. Ten percent of MAG was owned by SP MAG Holdings, a Delaware LLC. SP MAG had six members, including a Delaware limited partnership called Silver Point Capital Fund and a Delaware LLC called SPCP Group III. In turn, Silver Point and SPCP Group had a common member, Robert O'Shea, who was a New Jersey citizen. Assuming that the amount in controversy exceeds $75,000, does the district court have diversity jurisdiction? Why or why not? [*Fadal Machining Centers, LLC v. Mid-Atlantic CNC, Inc.*, 464 Fed.Appx. 672 (9th Cir. 2012)] (See *The Limited Liability Company*.)

17–6. Jurisdictional Requirements. Siloam Springs Hotel, LLC, operates a Hampton Inn in Siloam Springs, Arkansas.

Siloam bought insurance from Century Surety Company to cover the hotel. When guests suffered injuries due to a leak of carbon monoxide from the heating element of an indoor swimming pool, Siloam filed a claim with Century. Century denied coverage, which Siloam disputed. Century asked a federal district court to resolve the dispute. In asserting that the federal court had jurisdiction, Century noted that the amount in controversy exceeded $75,000 and that the parties had complete diversity of citizenship. Century is "a corporation organized under the laws of Ohio, with its principal place of business in Michigan," and Siloam is "a corporation organized under the laws of Oklahoma, with its principal place of business in Arkansas." Can the court exercise diversity jurisdiction in this case? Discuss. [*Siloam Springs Hotel, LLC v. Century Surety Co.*, 781 F.3d 1233 (10th Cir. 2015)] (See *The Limited Liability Company*.)

17–7. Limited Liability. Vision Metals, Inc., owned and operated a pipe manufacturing facility that caused groundwater contamination. The Texas Commission on Environmental Quality (TCEQ) issued a plan that obligated Vision to treat the water and monitor the treatment. Later, Vision sold the property to White Lion Holdings, LLC. Bernard Morello, the sole member of White Lion, knew of the environmental obligations accompanying the property. When White Lion failed to comply with the TCEQ plan, the agency filed a suit in a Texas state court against Morello, asserting violations of the state's environmental rules. Morello was charged with personally removing the facility's treatment plant and monitoring system. Considering the nature of an LLC, what is Morello's best argument that he is not liable? Is this argument likely to succeed? Explain. [*State of Texas v. Morello*, 61 Tex.Sup.Ct.J. 381, 547 S.W.3d 881 (2018)] (See *The Limited Liability Company*.)

17–8. Partnership Requirements. Sunil Kumar Mehta wished to acquire West Oaks Mall in Houston, Texas, but needed $10 million in funding to do so. Through his bank, he met Mohammed Ahmed, a successful local businessperson. Ahmed was not interested in lending funds to Mehta but indicated that he would consider a partnership deal. Verbally, Mehta agreed to a 65/35 split, with Mehta having the majority stake. Unbeknownst to Ahmed, Mehta convinced the seller that he and his son had sufficient funds to finance the deal themselves. Mehta secretly proceeded to seek alternative financing so that he could usurp the opportunity for himself. Then Mehta told Ahmed he no longer wanted to jointly acquire the shopping mall as partners. Ahmed sued Mehta for breach of fiduciary duty, unjust enrichment, and fraud. Ahmed alleged that a fiduciary relationship was created when he and Mehta agreed to form a partnership for the purpose of buying and developing the shopping mall. In a jury trial, Ahmed prevailed. Mehta appealed. Were the verbal discussions between the two parties sufficient to create a partnership? [*Mehta v. Ahmed*, 2022 WL3720181 (TX App., Houston (1st Dist.) 2022)] (See *Basic Partnership Concepts*.)

17–9. A Question of Ethics—The IDDR Approach and LLC Operation and Management. Q Restaurant Group Holdings, LLC, owns and operates Q-BBQ restaurants. Michael Lapidus managed the restaurants and conducted the day-to-day operations. This included bargaining with the restaurants' vendors, buying the supplies, keeping the books and records of account, and handling the company's money. Lapidus also dealt with the staff and made the hiring and firing decisions. He was expected to use his best efforts to grow the profitability of the restaurants. The LLC discovered, however, that Lapidus was misappropriating and converting company funds to his own use. He was also exposing the LLC to liability by mistreating female employees and vendors. When the members voted to terminate Lapidus, he changed the passwords on the Q-BBQ social media accounts, interfered with the employees during their work hours, and refused to return company property in his possession. [*Q Restaurant Group Holdings, LLC v. Lapidus*, 2017 IL App (2d) 170804-U (2017)] (See *LLC Management and Operation*.)

(a) What action should the LLC take against Lapidus? Consider the ethics of each of the options, using the IDDR approach.

(b) Suppose that Lapidus was in the midst of a contentious divorce, experiencing severe financial problems, and undergoing psychological distress as a consequence. Could these issues excuse his conduct at work? Discuss.

Time-Limited Group Assignment

17–10. Fiduciary Duties in LLCs. Newbury Properties Group owns, manages, and develops real property. Jerry Stoker and the Stoker Group, Inc. (the Stokers), also develop real property. Newbury entered into agreements with the Stokers concerning a large tract of property in Georgia. The parties formed Bellemare, LLC, to develop various parcels of the tract for residential purposes. The operating agreement of Bellemare indicated that "no Member shall be accountable to the LLC or to any other Member with respect to any other business or activity even if the business or activity competes with the LLC's business." Later, when Newbury contracted with other parties to develop parcels within the tract in competition with Bellemare, LLC, the Stokers sued, alleging breach of fiduciary duty. (See *LLC Management and Operation*.)

(a) The first group will discuss and outline the fiduciary duties that the members of an LLC owe to each other.

(b) The second group will determine whether the terms of an operating agreement can alter these fiduciary duties.

(c) The third group will decide in whose favor the court should rule in this situation.

Chapter 18

Corporate Formation and Financing

The *corporation* is a creature of statute. A corporation is an artificial being, existing only in law and being neither tangible nor visible. Its existence generally depends on state law, although some corporations, especially public organizations, are created under federal law. Each state has its own body of corporate law, and these laws are not entirely uniform.

The Model Business Corporation Act (MBCA) is a codification of modern corporation law that has been influential in shaping state corporation statutes. Today, the majority of state statutes are guided by the most recent version of the MBCA, often referred to as the Revised Model Business Corporation Act (RMBCA).

Keep in mind, however, that there is considerable variation among the laws of states that have used the MBCA or the RMBCA as a basis for their statutes. In addition, several states do not follow either act. Consequently, individual state corporation laws should be relied on to determine corporate law rather than the MBCA or RMBCA.

18–1 The Nature and Classification of Corporations

A **corporation** is a legal entity created and recognized by state law. This business entity can have one or more owners (called *shareholders*), and it operates under a name distinct from the names of its owners. Both individuals and other businesses can be shareholders. The corporation substitutes itself for its shareholders when conducting corporate business and incurring liability. Its authority to act and the liability for its actions, however, are separate and apart from the shareholders who own it.

A corporation is recognized under U.S. law as a person—an artificial *legal person*, as opposed to a *natural person*. As a "person," it enjoys many of the same rights and privileges under state and federal law that U.S. citizens enjoy. For instance, corporations possess the same right of access to the courts as citizens and can sue or be sued. The constitutional guarantees of due process, free speech, and freedom from unreasonable searches and seizures also apply to corporations.

18–1a Corporate Personnel

In a corporation, the responsibility for the overall management of the firm is entrusted to a *board of directors*, whose members are elected by the shareholders. The board of directors makes the policy decisions and hires corporate officers and other employees to run the daily business operations.

When an individual purchases a share of stock in a corporation, that person becomes a shareholder and an owner of the corporation. Unlike the partners in a partnership, the body of shareholders can change constantly without affecting the continued existence of the corporation. A shareholder can sue the corporation, and the corporation can sue a shareholder. Additionally, under certain circumstances, a shareholder can sue on behalf of a corporation.

18–1b The Limited Liability of Shareholders

One of the key advantages of the corporate form is the limited liability of its owners. Normally, corporate shareholders are not personally liable for the obligations of the corporation beyond the extent of their investments.

In certain limited situations, however, a court can pierce the corporate veil and impose liability on shareholders for the corporation's obligations. Additionally, creditors often will not extend credit to small companies unless the shareholders assume personal liability, as guarantors, for corporate obligations.

18–1c Corporate Earnings and Taxation

When a corporation earns profits, it can either pass them on to shareholders in the form of dividends or retain them as profits. These **retained earnings,** if invested properly, will yield higher corporate profits in the future. In theory, higher profits will cause the price of the company's stock to rise. Individual shareholders can then reap the benefits in the capital gains they receive when they sell their stock.

Corporate Taxation Whether a corporation retains its profits or passes them on to the shareholders as dividends, those profits are subject to income taxation by various levels of government. Failure to pay taxes can lead to severe consequences. The state can suspend the organization's corporate status until the taxes are paid and can even dissolve the corporation for failing to pay taxes.

Another important aspect of corporate taxation is that corporate profits can be subject to double taxation. The company pays tax on its profits. Then, if the profits are passed on to the shareholders as dividends, the shareholders must also pay income tax on them. (This is true unless the dividends represent distributions of capital, which are returns of holders' investments in the stock of the company.) The corporation normally does not receive a tax deduction for dividends it distributes. This double-taxation feature is one of the major disadvantages of the corporate form.

Holding Companies Some U.S. corporations use holding companies to reduce or defer their U.S. income taxes. At its simplest, a **holding company** (sometimes referred to as a *parent company*) is a company whose business activity consists of holding shares in another company. Typically, the holding company is established in a low-tax or no-tax offshore jurisdiction, such as the Cayman Islands, Dubai, Luxembourg, Monaco, or Panama.

Sometimes, a U.S. corporation sets up a holding company in a low-tax offshore environment and then transfers its cash, bonds, stocks, and other investments to the holding company. In general, any profits received by the holding company on these investments are taxed at the rate of the offshore jurisdiction where the company is registered. Once the profits are brought "onshore," though, they are taxed at the federal corporate income tax rate. Any payments received by the shareholders are also taxable at the full U.S. rates.

18–1d Criminal Acts

Under modern criminal law, a corporation may be held liable for the criminal acts of its agents and employees. Although corporations cannot be imprisoned, they can be fined. (Of course, corporate directors and officers can be imprisoned, and many have been.) In addition, under sentencing guidelines for crimes committed by corporate employees (white-collar crimes), corporations can face fines amounting to hundreds of millions of dollars.

18–1e Tort Liability

A corporation is liable for the torts committed by its agents or officers within the course and scope of their employment. The doctrine of *respondeat superior* applies to corporations in the same way as it does to other agency relationships.

A claim against a corporate employer based on *respondeat superior* requires a showing that the individual who committed the tort was an employee acting in the course of employment.

18–1f Classification of Corporations

Corporations can be classified in several ways. The classification of a corporation normally depends on its location, purpose, and ownership characteristics, as described in the following subsections.

Domestic, Foreign, and Alien Corporations A corporation is referred to as a **domestic corporation** by its home state (the state in which it incorporates). A corporation formed in one state but doing business in another is referred to in the second state as a **foreign corporation.** A corporation formed in another country (say, Mexico) but doing business in the United States is referred to in the United States as an **alien corporation.**

A corporation does not have an automatic right to do business in a state other than its state of incorporation. In some instances, it must obtain a certificate of authority in any state in which it plans to do business. Once the certificate has been issued, the corporation generally can exercise in that state all of the powers conferred on it by its home state. If a foreign corporation does business in a state without obtaining a certificate of authority, the state can impose substantial fines and sanctions on that corporation.

Note that most state statutes specify certain activities, such as soliciting orders via the internet, that are not considered "doing business" within the state. For instance, a foreign corporation normally does not need a certificate of authority to sell goods or services via the internet or by mail.

Given the mobility of the modern corporation, courts are often asked to determine what constitutes "doing business" in a state for jurisdictional purposes. ■ **Case in Point 18.1** South Carolina resident Bud Fidrych severely injured his thumb at the Boscolo-Milano Hotel in Milan, Italy. Fidrych subsequently filed a negligence lawsuit in federal district court in South Carolina against Marriott International, Inc., a Delaware corporation with which Boscolo-Milano was affiliated.

The district court established that Marriott did not own or operate Boscolo-Milano, nor did it own or operate any hotels in South Carolina, although it had ninety franchisees and licensees in the state. Fidrych also argued that Marriott had ties to South Carolina through its booking website, which enabled visitors to book hotels in South Carolina, and through its South Carolina certificate of authority. But these minimal contacts did not, the district court ruled, make Marriott "at home" in South Carolina for jurisdictional purposes. Therefore, Fidrych's lawsuit could not proceed. A federal appeals court agreed, concluding that, if Fidrych's suit was allowed, Marriott could theoretically, and unfairly, face legal action in every state in the union.[1] ■

1. *Fidrych v. Marriott International, Inc.*, 952 F.3d 124 (4th Cir. 2020).

Public and Private Corporations A **public corporation** is a corporation formed by the government to meet some political or governmental purpose. Cities and towns that incorporate are common examples. In addition, many federal government organizations, such as the U.S. Postal Service, the Tennessee Valley Authority, and AMTRAK, are public corporations.

The following case involved an Alabama public university that opened an office in North Carolina as a nonprofit corporation under a North Carolina state statute. Can the North Carolina entity avoid being sued in North Carolina because it has sovereign immunity as an Alabama public corporation?

Farmer v. Troy University

Supreme Court of North Carolina, 879 S.E.2d 123, 2022, 382 N.C. 366, 2022-NCSC-107 (2022).

In the Language of the Court
EARLS, Justice

I. Background

Troy University, a state institution, has its primary campus in Troy, Alabama. Although Troy University does not have a campus in North Carolina, it registered with the North Carolina Secretary of State as a nonprofit corporation on 25 September 2006 and leased an office building in Fayetteville, North Carolina, near Fort Bragg, where it conducted its business. Mr. Farmer was hired by Troy University in May 2014 as a recruiter and worked there until 9 September 2015. As part of his employment, Mr. Farmer recruited military personnel from Fort Bragg to take on-line educational courses that originated from Troy University's main campus in Troy, Alabama. Throughout his employment, he was the top recruiter in the southeastern region of the United States.

Mr. Farmer claims that while employed at Troy University, he was subjected to frequent and ongoing sexual harassment by Pamela Gainey and Karen Tillery, both of whom also worked at

the Troy University office in Fayetteville, North Carolina. * * *.

Around May 2015, Mr. Farmer filed a complaint with both Troy University's Human Resources Department and Troy University's District Director about the sexual harassment he and other males had experienced. Although Mr. Farmer had given Troy University the names of several witnesses, Troy University did not interview any witnesses before deciding that Mr. Farmer's complaint lacked merit.

Mr. Farmer further alleges that, following his May 2015 complaint, Ms. Gainey retaliated against him by increasing his work hours and making his working conditions unreasonably onerous. On 9 September 2015, Mr. Farmer was terminated from his job at Troy University. * * * As a result of this treatment, and his termination from Troy University, Mr. Farmer became homeless, could not obtain another job, and suffered serious mental health consequences.

On 24 July 2018, Mr. Farmer filed this suit against Troy University and the

individual defendants, Ms. Gainey and Ms. Tillery. Mr. Farmer asserted claims against Troy University for (1) wrongful discharge from employment in violation of public policy, and (2) negligent retention or supervision of an employee, or both. He also asserted claims against all defendants for intentional infliction of mental and emotional distress and tortious interference with contractual rights. In the alternative, Mr. Farmer also advanced a claim against all defendants alleging a violation of his rights under the North Carolina Constitution, in the event that the trial court found his other claims were barred by sovereign immunity.
* * * *

II. Sovereign Immunity
* * * *

The initial issue in this appeal is whether Mr. Farmer's state tort claims against defendants are barred in North Carolina under the doctrine of sovereign immunity by virtue of Troy University's status in Alabama as a public university. The Court of Appeals concluded that * * * no suit may be maintained because "States retain their sovereign immunity

Case 18.1 Continues

Case 18.1 Continued

from private suits brought in the courts of other States."

* * * *

III. Waiver of Sovereign Immunity

* * * [T]his Court must determine whether Troy University has explicitly waived its sovereign immunity from suit in North Carolina. As the Court of Appeals noted, any waiver of sovereign immunity must be explicit. Nonetheless, United States Supreme Court precedent does not support the Court of Appeals' conclusion that a sue-and-be-sued clause cannot constitute an explicit waiver of sovereign immunity. Specifically, we find that when Troy University registered as a nonprofit corporation here and engaged in business in North Carolina, it accepted the sue-and-be-sued clause in the North Carolina Nonprofit Corporation Act and thereby explicitly waived its sovereign immunity from suits in this state.

The North Carolina Nonprofit Corporation Act covers all nonprofit corporations in North Carolina. This act contains a sue-and-be-sued clause. Specifically, the Act provides:

> (a) Unless its articles of incorporation or this Chapter provides otherwise, every corporation has perpetual duration and succession in its corporate name and has the same powers as an individual to do all things necessary or convenient to carry out its affairs, including without limitation, power: (1) *To sue and be sued,* complain and defend in its corporate name. . . .

* * * *

The parties in this case disagree about how to characterize Troy University's activities. While Troy University asserts its purpose in North Carolina was to

continue the governmental function of higher education, Mr. Farmer argues Troy University's activities were commercial in nature because they involved marketing and selling on-line educational programs. While providing students with an education may be a governmental activity for the Alabama Government in Alabama, here Troy University was engaged in the business of recruiting students for on-line education— recruitment that occurred in North Carolina for students who remained in North Carolina. The complaint clearly alleges that while in North Carolina, Troy University engaged in marketing and recruitment. Mr. Farmer's job was to help Troy University carry out its commercial activities by recruiting military personnel in North Carolina to enroll in and pay for educational courses. Because Troy University engaged in commercial rather than governmental activity, the sue-and-be-sued clause is to be liberally construed.

In doing so, this Court concludes that when Troy University chose to do business in North Carolina, while knowing it was subject to the North Carolina Nonprofit Corporation Act and able to take advantage of the Act's sue-and-be-sued clause * * * , it explicitly waived its sovereign immunity. * * *

Troy University argues that under this Court's precedent, a sue-and-be-sued clause "is not always construed as an express waiver of sovereign immunity and is not dispositive of the immunity defense when suit is brought against an agency of the State." But this Court's [previous] holding * * * is not inconsistent with our ruling today. Simply because something is not "always . . . an express waiver of sovereign immunity", does not mean it can never be a waiver of the same. * * *

* * * *

* * * [W]e find that when Troy University obtained a certificate of authority to operate in North Carolina, it waived any sovereign immunity it had and agreed to be treated like "a domestic corporation of like character."

* * * *

* * * By requesting and receiving a certificate of authority to do business in North Carolina, renting a building here, and hiring local staff, Troy University, as an arm of the State of Alabama, consented to be treated like "a domestic corporation of like character," and to be sued in North Carolina.

* * * *

IV. Conclusion

While the United States Constitution requires States to afford one another sovereign immunity from private suits brought in other states, this privilege can be explicitly waived through a sue-and-be-sued clause. When Troy University entered North Carolina and conducted business in North Carolina, while knowing it was subject to the North Carolina Nonprofit Corporation Act and its sue-and-be-sued clause, it explicitly waived its sovereign immunity. Additionally, by requesting and receiving a certificate of authority to do business in North Carolina, Troy University consented to be treated like "a domestic corporation of like character" and therefore to be sued in North Carolina. Accordingly, concluding that the doctrine of sovereign immunity does not bar Mr. Farmer's suit against these defendants, we reverse the Court of Appeals decision and remand this case to that court for further proceedings consistent with this opinion.

REVERSED AND REMANDED.

Legal Reasoning Questions

1. What is sovereign immunity?

2. Would the outcome of this case have been different had Troy University offered only on-campus learning possibilities? Why or why not?

3. Would the outcome of this case have been different if the plaintiff had been a woman who claimed sexual harassment by several male employees? Why or why not?

claiming to be an agent of a corporation that does not in fact exist.

When justice requires, courts in some states will treat an alleged corporation as if it were an actual corporation for the purpose of determining rights and liabilities in particular circumstances. Recognition of corporate status does not extend beyond the resolution of the problem at hand.

■ **Case in Point 18.4** 55 Day Spa, Inc., signed a three-year lease to rent premises owned by Ilan Weiss, who represented himself as a managing member of TY Builders II, LLC. Three months later, 55 Day Spa informed Weiss that it would be vacating the premises. Weiss, now operating as TY Builders II, Inc., filed an action to recover damages for breach of contract. 55 Day Spa moved for the lawsuit to be dismissed, arguing that because TY Builders II, Inc., did not exist when the lease was signed, the corporation could not enforce the terms of the document.

A New York trial court found that 55 Day Spa had recognized Weiss as a valid business operation—regardless of the form—when negotiating for the use of the property. Therefore, it should not be allowed to use Weiss's lack of proper incorporation as an excuse to break the contract. A state appeals court agreed, holding that, pursuant to the doctrine of incorporation by estoppel, TY Builders II, Inc., should be "deemed to exist" for the purpose of Weiss's contract with 55 Day Spa.[7] ■

18–2e Corporate Powers

When a corporation is created, the express and implied powers necessary to achieve its purpose also come into existence.

Express Powers The express powers of a corporation are found in its articles of incorporation, in the law of the state of incorporation, and in the state and federal constitutions. Corporate bylaws and the resolutions of the corporation's board of directors also establish express powers.

The following order of priority is used if a conflict arises among the various documents involving a corporation:

1. The U.S. Constitution.
2. State constitutions.
3. State statutes.
4. The articles of incorporation.
5. Bylaws.
6. Resolutions of the board of directors.

It is important that the bylaws set forth the specific operating rules of the corporation. State corporation statutes frequently provide default rules that apply if the company's bylaws are silent on an issue.

On occasion, the U.S. government steps in to challenge what a corporation may consider one of its express powers. This chapter's Cybersecurity and the Law feature discusses steps taken by the U.S. government that threaten the ability of corporations to protect cloud-based data.

Implied Powers When a corporation is created, it acquires certain implied powers. Barring express constitutional, statutory, or other prohibitions, the corporation has the implied power to perform all acts reasonably necessary to accomplish its corporate purposes. For this reason, a corporation has the implied power to borrow and lend funds within certain limits and to extend credit to parties with whom it has contracts.

Most often, the president or chief executive officer of the corporation signs the necessary documents on behalf of the corporation. Such corporate officers have the implied power to bind the corporation in matters directly connected with the ordinary business affairs of the enterprise.

There are limits to what a corporate officer can do. For instance, a corporate officer does not have the authority to bind the corporation to an action that will greatly affect the corporate purpose or undertaking, such as the sale of substantial corporate assets.

Ultra Vires* Doctrine** The term ***ultra vires means "beyond the power." In corporate law, acts of a corporation that are beyond its express or implied powers are *ultra vires* acts. In the past, most cases dealing with *ultra vires* acts involved contracts made for unauthorized purposes. Now, because the articles of incorporation of most private corporations do not state a specific purpose, the *ultra vires* doctrine has declined in importance.

Nevertheless, cases involving *ultra vires* acts are sometimes brought against nonprofit corporations or municipal (public) corporations. ■ **Case in Point 18.5** Four men formed a nonprofit corporation to create the Armenian Genocide Museum & Memorial (AGM&M). The bylaws appointed them as trustees (similar to corporate directors) for life. One of the trustees, Gerard Cafesjian, became the chair and president of AGM&M. Eventually, the relationship among the trustees deteriorated, and Cafesjian resigned.

The corporation then brought a suit claiming that Cafesjian had engaged in numerous *ultra vires* acts, self-dealing, and mismanagement. Although the bylaws

---

7. *TY Bldrs. II, Inc. v. 55 Day Spa, Inc.,* 167 A.D.3d 679, 90 N.Y.S.3d 47 (2018).

Cybersecurity and the Law — The CLOUD Act

The case before the U.S. Supreme Court involved a battle of wills between the U.S. government and Microsoft Corporation in its role as a Cloud Service Provider (CSP). The federal government had issued a warrant to Microsoft to produce e-mails related to a criminal narcotics investigation. The e-mails were hosted in a Microsoft cloud storage location in Ireland. Microsoft refused to comply with the warrant, arguing that the reach of the U.S. government stopped at the U.S. border.[a]

Congress resolved the issue by enacting the Clarifying Lawful Overseas Use of Data Act (CLOUD Act).[b] This legislation provides the U.S. government with access to cloud-based data held by U.S. CSPs regardless of where in the world that data is physically stored. For purposes of the law, cloud-based data includes e-mails, texts, instant messages, remote or backup data storage, wireless calls, and other forms of cloud processing of business information. The U.S. Department of Justice heralded passage of the CLOUD Act as "critical" to global investigations of terrorism, cybercrime, and the sexual exploitation of children.

a. *United States v. Microsoft Corp.*, 548 U.S. __,138 S.Ct. 1186, 200 L.Ed.2d 610 (2018). See also *United States v. Maxwell*, 2022 WL 576306 (S.D. NY 2022).

b. 18 U.S.C. Section 2703.

Qualified Foreign Governments

The CLOUD Act also creates a framework for the United States to enter into treaties that would give Qualified Foreign Governments (QFGs) access to cloud data stored by the "Big Five" American CSPs—Amazon, Apple, Facebook (Meta), Google (Alphabet), and Microsoft. For U.S. businesses, the potential consequences of this provision are significant. Suppose a U.S. company called Ramway, Inc., uses Google to store its digital data in the cloud. A QFG suspects that Ramway is involved in criminal activity. Without involving U.S. courts, Google could provide the QFG with access to Ramway's digital data as part of that foreign government's criminal investigation.

In this scenario, Ramway may never even be aware of the QFG's request, or of Google's compliance with it. The CLOUD Act does not require the CSP or foreign government to disclose data requests to the targeted CSP customer. Domestically, the Big Five CSPs receive more than 175,000 requests for information linked to criminal investigations from American law enforcement agencies each year.

Critical Thinking What type of American businesses are impacted by the CLOUD Act? What steps should these businesses take in response to the CLOUD Act?

---

required an 80 percent affirmative vote of the trustees to take action, Cafesjian had taken many actions without the board's approval. He had also entered into contracts for real estate transactions in which he had a personal interest. Because Cafesjian had taken actions that exceeded his authority and had failed to follow rules set forth in the bylaws, the court ruled that the corporation could go forward with its suit.[8] ■

Remedies for *Ultra Vires* Acts Under Section 3.04 of the RMBCA, shareholders can seek an injunction from a court to prevent (or stop) the corporation from engaging in *ultra vires* acts. The attorney general in the state of incorporation can also bring an action to obtain an injunction against the *ultra vires* transactions or to seek dissolution of the corporation. The corporation or its shareholders (on behalf of the corporation) can

8. *Armenian Assembly of America, Inc. v. Cafesjian*, 692 F.Supp.2d 20 (D.C. Cir. 2010). See also *Ye v. Zhang*, 2021 WL 5862093 (S.D. TX, Houston Div. 2021).

seek damages from the officers and directors who were responsible for the *ultra vires* acts.

18–3 Piercing the Corporate Veil

Occasionally, the owners use a corporate entity to perpetrate a fraud, circumvent the law, or in some other way accomplish an illegitimate objective. In these situations, the courts will ignore the corporate structure by **piercing the corporate veil** and exposing the shareholders to personal liability [RMBCA 2.04].

Generally, courts pierce the veil when the corporate privilege is abused for personal benefit or when the corporate business is treated so carelessly that it is indistinguishable from that of a controlling shareholder. When the facts show that great injustice would result from a shareholder's use of a corporation to avoid individual responsibility, a court will look behind the corporate structure to the individual shareholders.

18–3a Factors That Lead Courts to Pierce the Corporate Veil

The following are some of the factors that frequently cause the courts to pierce the corporate veil.

1. A party is tricked or misled into dealing with the corporation rather than the individual.
2. The corporation is set up never to make a profit or always to be insolvent. Alternatively, it is too thinly capitalized—that is, it has insufficient capital at the time it is formed to meet its prospective debts or potential liabilities.
3. The corporation is formed to evade an existing legal obligation.
4. Statutory corporate formalities, such as holding required corporation meetings, are not followed.
5. Personal and corporate interests are mixed together, or **commingled,** to such an extent that the corporation has no separate identity.

The courts may use the same criteria in deciding whether to pierce the corporate veil of an LLC. ■ **Case in Point 18.6** Timothy Hunsaker was the sole member of Breawick, LLC, a construction company. Cheryl Denny hired Breawick to build a house. Denny claimed Hunsaker altered the building plans without her consent and made requests for additional payments amounting to $20,000 that were not in the contract. Hunsaker eventually quit working before the house was finished, forcing Denny to hire another company to repair the many construction flaws that he had left behind.

The trial court found that Breawick had breached the contract with Denny by charging excessive costs without her approval and failing to perform in a "workmanlike" manner. These acts were so egregious that the court was willing to pierce the corporate veil and hold Hunsaker personally liable for the amount Denny spent to finish the house. An appellate court affirmed. Hunsaker drew funds from Breawick's bank account to pay for personal expenses and took no steps to distinguish himself from the corporate entity. The appeals court therefore concluded that Breawick was Hunsaker's "alter ego" and had no separate existence of its own.[9] ■

18–3b A Potential Problem for Close Corporations

The potential for corporate assets to be used for personal benefit is especially great in a close corporation. In such a corporation, the separate status of the corporate entity and the shareholders (often family members) must be carefully preserved. Practices that invite trouble for a close corporation include the commingling of corporate and personal funds and the shareholders' continuous personal use of corporate property (for instance, vehicles).

Typically, courts are reluctant to hold shareholders in close corporations personally liable for corporate obligations unless there is some evidence of fraud or wrongdoing. ■ **Case in Point 18.7** Pip, Jimmy, and Theodore Brennan are brothers and shareholders of Brennan's, Inc., which owns and operates New Orleans's famous Brennan's Restaurant. As a close corporation, Brennan's, Inc., did not hold formal corporate meetings with agendas and minutes, but it did maintain corporate books, hold corporate bank accounts, and file corporate tax returns.

The Brennan brothers retained attorney Edward Colbert to represent them in a family matter, and the attorney's bills were sent to the restaurant and paid from the corporate account. Later, when Brennan's, Inc., sued Colbert for malpractice, Colbert argued that the court should pierce the corporate veil because the Brennan brothers did not observe corporate formalities. The court refused to do so, however, because there was no evidence of fraud, malfeasance, or other wrongdoing by the Brennan brothers. There is no requirement for small, close corporations to operate with the formality usually expected of larger corporations.[10] ■

18–3c The Alter-Ego Theory

Sometimes, courts pierce the corporate veil under the theory that the corporation was not operated as a separate entity. Rather, it was just another side (the alter ego) of the individual or group that actually controlled the corporation. This is called the *alter-ego theory.*

The alter-ego theory is applied when a corporation is so dominated and controlled by an individual (or group) that the separate identities of the person (or group) and the corporation are no longer distinct. Courts use the alter-ego theory to avoid injustice or fraud that would result if wrongdoers were allowed to hide behind the protection of limited liability.

■ **Case in Point 18.8** Steiner Electric Company (Steiner) is an Illinois corporation that sells electrical products. Steiner sold goods to Delta Equipment Company and Sackett Systems, Inc., on credit. Both Delta and Sackett were owned and controlled by a single shareholder—Leonard Maniscalco. Steiner was not fully paid for the products it sold on credit to Delta and Sackett. Eventually, Steiner sued Delta and won a default

9. *Denny v. Breawick, LLC.,* 137 N.E.3d 578, 2019-Ohio-2066 (Ohio Ct. App. 2019).

10. *Brennan's, Inc. v. Colbert,* 85 So.3d 787 (La.App.4th Cir. 2012). See also *Hickey v. Angelo,* 274 So.3d 47 (LA App. 4th Cir. 2019).

judgment, but by that time, Delta had been dissolved. Steiner then asked a state court to pierce the corporate veil and hold Maniscalco liable for the debts of the two companies, claiming the companies were merely Maniscalco's alter egos.

The court agreed and held Maniscalco liable. Delta and Sackett were inadequately capitalized, transactions were not properly documented, funds were commingled, and corporate formalities were not observed. Maniscalco had consistently treated both companies in such a manner that they were, in practice, his alter egos.[11] ∎

18–3d Corporate Financing

Part of the process of corporate formation involves financing. Corporations normally are financed by the issuance and sale of corporate securities. **Securities**—stocks and bonds—evidence an ownership interest in a corporation or a promise of repayment of debt by a corporation.

Bonds **Bonds** are *debt securities*, which represent the borrowing of funds. Bonds are issued by business firms and by governments at all levels as evidence of funds they are borrowing from investors.

Bonds normally have a designated *maturity date*—the date when the principal, or face amount, of the bond is returned to the bondholder. Bondholders also receive fixed-dollar interest payments, usually semiannually, during the period of time prior to maturity. For that reason, they are sometimes referred to as *fixed-income securities*. Because debt financing represents a legal obligation of the corporation, various features and terms of a particular bond issue are specified in a lending agreement.

Of course, not all debt is in the form of bonds. For instance, some debt is in the form of accounts payable and notes payable, which typically are short-term debts. Bonds are simply a way for the corporation to split up its long-term debt so that it can be more easily marketed.

Stocks Issuing stocks is another way for corporations to obtain financing [RMBCA 6.01]. **Stocks,** or equity securities, represent the purchase of ownership in the business firm. The two major types are common stock and preferred stock. The true ownership of a corporation is represented by **common stock.** Common stock provides an interest in the corporation with regard to (1) control, (2) earnings, and (3) net assets. A shareholder's interest is generally proportionate to the number of shares they own out of the total number of shares issued. Any person who purchases common stock acquires voting rights—one vote per share held.

An issuing firm is not obligated to return a principal amount per share to each holder of its common stock, nor does the firm have to guarantee a dividend. Indeed, some corporations never pay dividends. Holders of common stock are investors who assume a residual position in the overall financial structure of a business. They benefit when the market price of the stock increases. In terms of receiving payment for their investments, they are last in line.

Preferred stock is an equity security with preferences. Usually, this means that holders of preferred stock have priority over holders of common stock as to dividends and payment on dissolution of the corporation. The preferences must be stated in the articles of incorporation. Holders of preferred stock may or may not have the right to vote.

Like other equity securities, preferred shares have no fixed maturity date on which the firm must pay them off. Although firms occasionally buy back preferred stock, they are not legally obligated to do so.

Holders of preferred stock have assumed a more cautious position than holders of common stock. They have a stronger position than common shareholders with respect to dividends and claims on assets. For instance, they receive fixed dividends periodically. They will not, however, share in the full prosperity of the firm if it grows successfully over time, although they may benefit to some extent from changes in the market price of the shares.

Venture Capital and Private Equity Capital
Corporations traditionally obtain financing by issuing and selling stocks and bonds in the capital market. Many investors do not want to purchase stock in a business that lacks a track record, however, and banks generally are reluctant to extend loans to high-risk enterprises. Therefore, to obtain funds, many entrepreneurs seek alternative financing.

Venture Capital Start-up businesses and high-risk enterprises often obtain venture capital financing. **Venture capital** is capital provided to new businesses by professional, outside investors (*venture capitalists*, usually groups of wealthy investors and securities firms). Venture capital investments are high risk—the investors must be willing to lose all of their invested funds—but offer the potential for well-above-average returns in the future.

To obtain venture capital financing, the start-up business typically gives up a share of its ownership to the venture capitalists. In addition to funding, venture capitalists may provide managerial and technical

11. *Steiner Electric Co. v. Maniscalco,* 2016 IL App (1st) 132023, 51 N.E.3d 45 (2016). For a different outcome, see *Cortlandt Street Recovery Corp. v. TPG Capital Management, L.P.,* 76 Misc.3d 1224(A), 176 N.Y.S.3d 474, 2022 WL 14725934 (S.Ct. N.Y. County 2022).

expertise, and they nearly always are given some control over the new company's decisions. Many internet-based companies, such as Google and Amazon, were initially financed by venture capital.

Private Equity Capital Private equity firms pool funds from wealthy investors and use this **private equity capital** to invest in existing corporations. Usually, a private equity firm buys an entire corporation and then reorganizes it. Sometimes, divisions of the purchased company are sold off to pay down debt.

Ultimately, the private equity firm may sell shares in the reorganized (and perhaps more profitable) company to the public in an *initial public offering (IPO)*. Then the private equity firm can make profits by selling its shares in the company to the public.

Crowdfunding Start-up businesses can also attempt to obtain financing through *crowdfunding*. **Crowdfunding** is a cooperative activity in which people network and pool funds and other resources via the internet to assist a cause or invest in a venture. Sometimes, crowdfunding is used to raise funds for charitable purposes, such as disaster relief, but increasingly it is being used to finance budding entrepreneurs.

In 2016, Securities and Exchange Commission (SEC) rules went into effect to allow companies to offer and sell securities through crowdfunding. The rules removed a decades-old ban on public solicitation for private investments, which means that companies can advertise investment opportunities to the general public. According to the SEC, the rules are intended to help smaller companies raise capital while providing investors with additional protections.

All crowdfunding transactions under the SEC's regulation must take place through an SEC-registered intermediary, either a broker-dealer or a funding portal. A company may raise a maximum total of $5 million through crowdfunding during a twelve-month period. A set of disclosures must be provided in filings with the SEC and to potential investors. Securities purchased in a crowdfunding transaction generally cannot be resold for one year.

18–4 Corporate Directors and Officers

A corporation joins together the efforts and resources of a large number of individuals for the purpose of producing greater returns than they could have achieved individually.

These individuals—corporate directors, officers, and shareholders—all play different roles within the corporate entity.

Sometimes, actions that may benefit the corporation as a whole do not coincide with the separate interests of the individuals making up the corporation. In such situations, it is important to know the rights and duties of all participants in the corporate enterprise.

18–4a Role of Directors and Officers

The board of directors is the ultimate authority in every corporation. Directors have responsibility for all policymaking decisions necessary to the management of all corporate affairs. Additionally, the directors must act as a body in carrying out routine corporate business. The board selects and removes the corporate officers, determines the capital structure of the corporation, and declares dividends. Each director has one vote, and customarily the majority rules.

Directors are sometimes inappropriately characterized as *agents* because they act on behalf of the corporation. No individual director, however, can act as an agent to bind the corporation. As a group, directors collectively control the corporation in a way that no agent is able to control a principal. In addition, although directors occupy positions of trust and control over the corporation, they are not *trustees*, because they do not hold title to property for the use and benefit of others.

Few qualifications are required for directors. Only a handful of states impose minimum age and residency requirements. A director may be a shareholder, but that is not necessary (unless the articles of incorporation or bylaws require ownership interest).

Election of Directors Subject to statutory limitations, the number of directors is set forth in the corporation's articles or bylaws. Historically, the minimum number of directors has been three, but today many states permit fewer. Normally, the incorporators may appoint the first board of directors in the articles of incorporation. If not, then the incorporators hold a meeting after incorporation to elect the directors and complete any other business necessary (such as adopting bylaws). The initial board serves until the first annual shareholders' meeting. Subsequent directors are elected by a majority vote of the shareholders.

A director usually serves for a term of one year—from annual meeting to annual meeting. Most state statutes permit longer and staggered terms. A common practice is to elect one-third of the board members each year for a three-year term. In this way, there is greater management continuity.

A director can be removed for cause—that is, for failing to perform a required duty—either as specified in the articles or bylaws or by shareholder action. The board of directors may also have the power to remove a director for cause, subject to shareholder review. In most states, a director cannot be removed without cause unless the shareholders reserved the right to do so at the time of election.

Vacancies occur on the board if a director dies or resigns or when a new position is created through amendment of the articles or bylaws. In these situations, either the shareholders or the board itself can fill the vacant position, depending on state law or on the provisions of the bylaws. Often, for instance, an election is held and shareholders vote to fill the vacancy. Note that even when an election is authorized, a court can invalidate the results if the directors have attempted to manipulate the election in order to reduce the shareholders' influence.

Compensation of Directors In the past, corporate directors were rarely compensated. Today, directors are often paid at least nominal sums. In large corporations, they may receive more substantial compensation because of the time, work, effort, and especially risk involved.

Most states permit the corporate articles or bylaws to authorize compensation for directors. In fact, the Revised Model Business Corporation Act (RMBCA) states that unless the articles or bylaws provide otherwise, the board itself may set the directors' compensation [RMBCA 8.11]. Directors also receive indirect benefits, such as business contacts and prestige, and other rewards, such as stock options.

In many corporations, directors are also chief corporate officers (such as president or chief executive officer) and receive compensation in their managerial positions. A director who is also an officer of the corporation is referred to as an **inside director,** whereas a director who does not hold a management position is an **outside director.** Typically, a corporation's board of directors includes both inside and outside directors.

Board of Directors' Meetings The board of directors conducts business by holding formal meetings with recorded minutes. The dates of regular meetings are usually established in the articles or bylaws or by board resolution, and ordinarily no further notice is required. Special meetings can be called as well, with notice sent to all directors.

Most states allow directors to participate in board of directors' meetings from remote locations. Directors can participate via telephone or web conferencing software such as Zoom, Livestorm, WebEx, or Microsoft Connect, provided that all the directors can simultaneously hear each other during the meeting [RMBCA 8.20].

Normally, a majority of the board of directors constitutes a quorum [RMBCA 8.24]. A **quorum** is the minimum number of members of a body of officials or other group that must be present for business to be validly transacted. Some state statutes specifically allow corporations to set a quorum at less than a majority but not less than one-third of the directors.

Once a quorum is present, the directors transact business and vote on issues affecting the corporation. Each director present at the meeting has one vote. Ordinary matters generally require a simple majority vote, but certain extraordinary issues may require a greater-than-majority vote.

Committees of the Board of Directors When a board of directors has a large number of members and must deal with myriad complex business issues, meetings can become unwieldy. Therefore, the boards of large, publicly held corporations typically create committees of directors and delegate certain tasks to these committees. By focusing on specific subjects, committees can increase the efficiency of the board.

Two common types of committees are the executive committee and the audit committee. An executive committee handles interim management decisions between board meetings. It is limited to dealing with ordinary business matters and does not have the power to declare dividends, amend the bylaws, or authorize the issuance of stock. The audit committee is responsible for the selection, compensation, and oversight of the independent public accountants that audit the firm's financial records. The Sarbanes-Oxley Act requires all publicly held corporations to have an audit committee.

Rights of Directors A corporate director must have certain rights to function properly in that position, including the rights of participation, inspection, and indemnification.

Right to Participation The right to participation means that directors are entitled to participate in all board of directors' meetings and have a right to be notified of these meetings. Because the dates of regular board meetings are usually specified in the bylaws, no notice of these meetings is required. If special meetings are called, however, notice is required unless waived by the director [RMBCA 8.23].

Right of Inspection A director also has a right of inspection, which means that each director can access the corporation's books and records, facilities, and premises. Inspection rights are essential for directors to make informed decisions and to exercise the necessary supervision over corporate officers and employees. This right of inspection is almost absolute and cannot be restricted by the articles, bylaws, or any act of the board of directors.

■ **Case in Point 18.9** NavLink, Inc., a Delaware corporation, provides high-end data management for customers and governments in Saudi Arabia, Qatar, Lebanon, and the United Arab Emirates. NavLink's co-founders, George Chammas and Laurent Delifer, were directors of the company at the time in question.

Chammas and Delifer were concerned about the company's 2015 annual budget and three-year operating plan. Despite repeated requests, Chammas was never given the meeting minutes from several board meetings in 2015. Chammas and Delifer believed that the other directors were withholding information and holding secret "pre-board meetings" at which plans and decisions were being made without them. They filed a suit in a Delaware state court seeking inspection rights.

The court ordered NavLink to provide the plaintiffs with board meeting minutes and with communications from NavLink's secretary regarding the minutes. The plaintiffs were also entitled to inspect corporate documents and communications concerning NavLink's budget and three-year plan.[12] ■

Right to Indemnification When a director becomes involved in litigation by virtue of board membership, the director may have a right to indemnification (reimbursement) for the legal costs, fees, and damages incurred. Most states allow corporations to indemnify and purchase liability insurance for corporate directors [RMBCA 8.51].

Corporate Officers and Executives Corporate officers and other executive employees are hired by the board of directors. At a minimum, most corporations have a president, one or more vice presidents, a secretary, and a treasurer. In most states, an individual can hold more than one office, such as president and secretary, and can be both an officer and a director of the corporation.

In addition to carrying out the duties articulated in the bylaws, corporate and managerial officers act as agents of the corporation. Therefore, the ordinary rules of agency normally apply to their employment.

Corporate officers and other high-level managers are employees of the company, so their rights are defined by employment contracts. Nevertheless, the board of directors normally can remove a corporate officer at any time

with or without cause. If the directors remove an officer in violation of the terms of an employment contract, however, the corporation may be liable for breach of contract.

18–4b Duties and Liabilities of Directors and Officers

The duties of corporate directors and officers are similar because both groups are involved in decision making and are in positions of control. Directors and officers are considered to be fiduciaries of the corporation because their relationship with the corporation and its shareholders is one of trust and confidence. As fiduciaries, directors and officers owe ethical—and legal—duties to the corporation and to the shareholders as a group. These fiduciary duties include the duty of care and the duty of loyalty.

Duty of Care Directors and officers must exercise due care in performing their duties. The standard of due care has been variously described in judicial decisions and codified in many state corporation codes. Generally, it requires a director or officer to:

1. Act in good faith (honestly).
2. Exercise the care that an ordinarily prudent (careful) person would exercise in similar circumstances.
3. Do what the director or officer believes is in the best interests of the corporation [RMBCA 8.30(a), 8.42(a)].

If directors or officers fail to exercise due care and the corporation or its shareholders suffer harm as a result, the directors or officers can be held liable for negligence. (An exception is made if the business judgment rule applies, as discussed shortly.)

Duty to Make Informed Decisions Directors and officers are expected to be informed on corporate matters and to conduct a reasonable investigation of the situation before making a decision. They must, for instance, attend meetings and presentations, ask for information from those who have it, read reports, and review other written materials. In other words, directors and officers must investigate, study, and discuss matters and evaluate alternatives before making a decision. They cannot decide on the spur of the moment without adequate research.

Although directors and officers are expected to act in accordance with their own knowledge and training, they are also normally entitled to rely on information given to them by certain other persons. Under the laws of most states and Section 8.30(b) of the RMBCA, such persons include competent officers or employees, professionals such as attorneys and accountants, and committees of the

---

12. *Chammas v. NavLink, Inc.,* 2016 WL 767714 (Del.Ch. 2016). See also *Moraski v. Your M.D., S.C.,* 982 N.W.2d 359, 2022 WI App 56 (WI App. 2022).

board of directors. (The committee must be one on which the director does not serve, however.) The reliance must be in good faith to insulate a director from liability if the information later proves to be inaccurate or unreliable.

Duty to Exercise Reasonable Supervision Directors are also expected to exercise a reasonable amount of supervision when they delegate work to corporate officers and employees.

Dissenting Directors Directors' votes at board of directors' meetings should be entered into the minutes. Sometimes, an individual director disagrees with the majority's vote (which becomes an act of the board of directors). Unless a dissent is entered in the minutes, the director is presumed to have assented. If the directors are later held liable for mismanagement as a result of a decision, dissenting directors are rarely held individually liable to the corporation. For this reason, a director who is absent from a given meeting sometimes registers a dissent with the secretary of the board regarding actions taken at the meeting.

The Business Judgment Rule Directors and officers are expected to exercise due care and to use their best judgment in guiding corporate management, but they are not insurers of business success. Under the **business judgment rule,** a corporate director or officer will not be liable to the corporation or to its shareholders for honest mistakes of judgment and bad business decisions.

Courts give significant deference to the decisions of corporate directors and officers, and consider the reasonableness of a decision at the time it was made, without the benefit of hindsight. Thus, corporate decision makers are not subjected to second-guessing by shareholders or others in the corporation.

The business judgment rule will apply as long as the directors or officers:

1. Took reasonable steps to become informed about the matter.
2. Had a rational basis for their decisions.
3. Did not have a conflict between their personal interests and the interest of the corporation.

Duty of Loyalty Loyalty can be defined as faithfulness to one's obligations and duties. In the corporate context, the duty of loyalty requires directors and officers to subordinate their personal interests to the welfare of the corporation. For instance, directors cannot use corporate funds or confidential corporate information for personal advantage and must refrain from self-dealing.

Cases dealing with the duty of loyalty typically involve one or more of the following:

1. Competing with the corporation.
2. Usurping (taking personal advantage of) a corporate opportunity.
3. Pursuing an interest that conflicts with that of the corporation.
4. Using information that is not available to the public to make a profit trading securities (insider trading).
5. Authorizing a corporate transaction that is detrimental to minority shareholders.
6. Selling control over the corporation.

The following Classic Case illustrates the conflict that can arise between a corporate officer's personal interest and the officer's duty of loyalty.

Classic Case 18.2

Guth v. Loft, Inc.

Supreme Court of Delaware, 23 Del.Ch. 255, 5 A.2d 503 (1939).

Background and Facts In 1930, Charles Guth became the president of Loft, Inc., a candy-and-restaurant chain. Guth and his family also owned Grace Company, which made syrups for soft drinks. Coca-Cola Company supplied Loft with cola syrup. Unhappy with what he felt was Coca-Cola's high price, Guth entered into an agreement with Roy Megargel to acquire the trademark and formula for Pepsi-Cola and form Pepsi-Cola Corporation. Neither Guth nor Megargel could finance the new venture, however, and Grace Company was insolvent.

Without the knowledge of Loft's board, Guth used Loft's capital, credit, facilities, and employees to further the Pepsi enterprise. At Guth's direction, a Loft employee made the concentrate for the syrup, which was sent to Grace to add sugar and water. Loft charged Grace for the concentrate but allowed forty months' credit. Grace charged Pepsi for the syrup but also granted substantial credit. Grace sold the syrup to Pepsi's customers, including Loft, which paid on delivery or within thirty days. Loft also paid for Pepsi's advertising. Finally, with profits declining as a result of switching from Coca-Cola, Loft filed a suit in a Delaware state court against Guth, Grace, and Pepsi, seeking their Pepsi stock and an accounting. The court entered a judgment in the plaintiff's favor. The defendants appealed to the Delaware Supreme Court.

In the Language of the Court

LAYTON, Chief Justice, delivering the opinion of the court:
* * * *

Corporate officers and directors are not permitted to use their position of trust and confidence to further their private interests. * * * They stand in a fiduciary relation to the corporation and its stockholders. A public policy, existing through the years, and derived from a profound knowledge of human characteristics and motives, has established a rule that demands of a corporate officer or director, peremptorily [not open for debate] and inexorably [unavoidably], the most scrupulous observance of his duty, not only affirmatively to protect the interests of the corporation committed to his charge, but also to refrain from doing anything that would work injury to the corporation * * * . The rule that requires an undivided and unselfish loyalty to the corporation demands that there shall be no conflict between duty and self-interest.
* * * *

* * * If there is presented to a corporate officer or director a business opportunity which the corporation is financially able to undertake [that] is * * * in the line of the corporation's business and is of practical advantage to it * * * and, by embracing the opportunity, the self-interest of the officer or director will be brought into conflict with that of his corporation, the law will not permit him to seize the opportunity for himself. * * * In such circumstances, * * * the corporation may elect to claim all of the benefits of the transaction for itself, and the law will impress a trust in favor of the corporation upon the property, interests and profits so acquired.
* * * *

* * * The appellants contend that no conflict of interest between Guth and Loft resulted from his acquirement and exploitation of the Pepsi-Cola opportunity [and] that the acquisition did not place Guth in competition with Loft * * * . [In this case, however,] Guth was Loft, and Guth was Pepsi. He absolutely controlled Loft. His authority over Pepsi was supreme. As Pepsi, he created and controlled the supply of Pepsi-Cola syrup, and he determined the price and the terms. What he offered, as Pepsi, he had the power, as Loft, to accept. Upon any consideration of human characteristics and motives, he created a conflict between self-interest and duty. He made himself the judge in his own cause. * * * Moreover, a reasonable probability of injury to Loft resulted from the situation forced upon it. Guth was in the same position to impose his terms upon Loft as had been the Coca-Cola Company.

* * * The facts and circumstances demonstrate that Guth's appropriation of the Pepsi-Cola opportunity to himself placed him in a competitive position with Loft with respect to a commodity essential to it, thereby rendering his personal interests incompatible with the superior interests of his corporation; and this situation was accomplished, not openly and with his own resources, but secretly and with the money and facilities of the corporation which was committed to his protection.

Decision and Remedy The Delaware Supreme Court upheld the judgment of the lower court. The state supreme court was "convinced that the opportunity to acquire the Pepsi-Cola trademark and formula, goodwill and business belonged to [Loft], and that Guth, as its President, had no right to appropriate the opportunity to himself."

Critical Thinking

- **What If the Facts Were Different?** Suppose that Loft's board of directors had approved Pepsi-Cola's use of its personnel and equipment. Would the court's decision have been different? Discuss.
- **Impact of This Case on Today's Law** This early Delaware decision was one of the first to set forth a test for determining when a corporate officer or director has breached the duty of loyalty. The test has two basic parts: Was the opportunity reasonably related to the corporation's line of business, and was the corporation financially able to undertake the opportunity? The court also considered whether the corporation had an interest or expectancy in the opportunity. It recognized that when the corporation had "no interest or expectancy, the officer or director is entitled to treat the opportunity as his own."

Conflicts of Interest   Corporate directors often have many business affiliations, and a director may sit on the board of more than one corporation. Of course, directors are precluded from entering into or supporting businesses that operate in direct competition with corporations on whose boards they serve. Their fiduciary duty requires them to make a full disclosure of any potential conflicts of interest that might arise in any corporate transaction [RMBCA 8.60].

Sometimes, a corporation enters into a contract or engages in a transaction in which an officer or director has a personal interest. The director or officer must make a full disclosure of the nature of the conflicting interest and all facts pertinent to the transaction. A director must also abstain from voting on the proposed transaction. When these rules are followed, the transaction can proceed. Otherwise, directors would be prevented from ever having financial dealings with the corporations they serve.

■ **Example 18.10**   Ballo Corporation needs office space. Stephanie Colson, one of its five directors, owns the building adjoining the corporation's headquarters. Colson can negotiate a lease for the space to Ballo if she fully discloses her conflicting interest and any facts known to her about the proposed transaction to Ballo and the other four directors. If the lease arrangement is fair and reasonable, Colson abstains from voting on it, and the other members of the corporation's board of directors unanimously approve it, the contract is valid. ■

Liability of Directors and Officers   Directors and officers are exposed to liability on many fronts. They can be held liable for negligence in certain circumstances, as previously discussed. They may also be held liable for the crimes and torts committed by themselves or by corporate employees under their supervision.

Additionally, if shareholders perceive that the corporate directors are not acting in the best interests of the corporation, they may sue the directors on behalf of the corporation. (This is known as a *shareholder's derivative suit*, which will be discussed later in this chapter.) Directors and officers can also be held personally liable under a number of statutes, such as statutes enacted to protect consumers or the environment.

18–5 The Role of Shareholders

The acquisition of a share of stock makes a person an owner and a shareholder in a corporation. Shareholders thus own the corporation. Although they have no legal title to corporate property, such as buildings and equipment, they do have an equitable (ownership) interest in the firm.

As a general rule, shareholders have no responsibility for the daily management of the corporation, although they are ultimately responsible for choosing the board of directors, which does have such control. Ordinarily, corporate officers and other employees owe no direct duty to individual shareholders (unless some contract or special relationship exists between them in addition to the corporate relationship).

The duty of officers and directors is to act in the best interests of the corporation and its shareholder-owners as a whole. In turn, as you will read later in this chapter, controlling shareholders owe a fiduciary duty to minority shareholders.

18–5a Shareholders' Powers

Shareholders must approve fundamental changes affecting the corporation before the changes can be implemented. Hence, shareholder approval normally is required to amend the articles of incorporation or bylaws, to conduct a merger or dissolve the corporation, and to sell all or substantially all of the corporation's assets. Some of these powers are subject to prior board approval. Shareholder approval may also be requested (though it is not required) for certain other actions, such as to approve an independent auditor.

Shareholders also have the power to vote to elect or remove members of the board of directors. As described earlier, the first board of directors is either named in the articles of incorporation or chosen by the incorporators to serve until the first shareholders' meeting. From that time on, selection and retention of directors are exclusively shareholder functions.

Directors usually serve their full terms. If the shareholders judge them unsatisfactory, they are simply not reelected. Shareholders have the inherent power, however, to remove a director from office for cause (breach of duty or misconduct) by a majority vote. Some state statutes (and some articles of incorporation) permit removal of directors without cause by the vote of a majority of the shareholders entitled to vote.

18–5b Shareholders' Meetings

Shareholders' meetings must occur at least annually. In addition, special meetings can be called to deal with urgent matters. A corporation must notify its shareholders of the date, time, and place of an annual or special shareholders' meeting at least ten days, but not more than sixty days, before the meeting date [RMBCA 7.05]. (The date and time of the annual meeting can be specified in the bylaws.) Notice of a special meeting must include a statement of the purpose of the meeting, and business transacted at the meeting is limited to that purpose.

The RMBCA does not specify how the notice must be given. Most corporations do specify in their bylaws the acceptable methods of notifying shareholders about meetings. Also, some states' incorporation statutes outline the means of notice that a corporation can use in that jurisdiction. For instance, in Alaska, notice may be given in person, by mail, or by fax, e-mail, blog, or web post—as long as the shareholder has agreed to that electronic method.

Proxies It usually is not practical for owners of only a few shares of stock of publicly traded corporations to attend a shareholders' meeting. Therefore, the law allows stockholders to appoint another person as their agent to vote their shares at the meeting. The agent's formal authorization to vote the shares is called a **proxy** (from the Latin *procurare,* meaning "to manage or take care of"). Proxy materials are sent to all shareholders before shareholders' meetings.

Management often solicits proxies, but any person can solicit proxies to concentrate voting power. Proxies have been used by groups of shareholders as a device for taking over a corporation. Proxies normally are revocable (can be withdrawn), unless they are specifically designated as irrevocable and coupled with an interest. A proxy is coupled with an interest when, for instance, the person receiving the proxies from shareholders has agreed to buy their shares. Under RMBCA 7.22(c), proxies are valid for eleven months, unless the proxy agreement mandates a longer period.

Shareholder Proposals When shareholders want to change a company policy, they can put their ideas up for a shareholder vote. They do this by submitting a shareholder proposal to the board of directors and asking the board to include the proposal in the proxy materials that are sent to all shareholders before meetings.

Rules for Proxies and Shareholder Proposals The Securities and Exchange Commission (SEC) regulates the purchase and sale of securities. The SEC has special provisions relating to proxies and shareholder proposals. SEC Rule 14a-8 provides that all shareholders who own stock worth at least $1,000 are eligible to submit proposals for inclusion in corporate proxy materials. The corporation is required to include information on whatever proposals will be considered at the shareholders' meeting along with proxy materials. Only those proposals that relate to significant policy considerations, not ordinary business operations, must be included.

Under the SEC's e-proxy rules, all public companies must post their proxy materials on the internet and notify shareholders how to find that information. Although the law requires proxy materials to be posted online, public companies may also send the materials to shareholders by other means, including paper documents sent by mail.

Proxy advisory firms provide data and recommendations to help large investment groups, such as mutual funds, vote on proxy measures at shareholders' meetings. Should proxy advisory firms be regulated? That is the subject of the Ethics Today feature in this chapter.

18–5c Shareholder Voting

Shareholders exercise ownership control through the power of their votes. Corporate business matters are presented in the form of *resolutions*, which shareholders vote to approve or disapprove. Each common shareholder normally is entitled to one vote per share.

The articles of incorporation can exclude or limit voting rights, particularly for certain classes of shares. For instance, owners of preferred shares are usually denied the right to vote [RMBCA 7.21]. If a state statute requires specific voting procedures, the corporation's articles or bylaws must be consistent with the statute.

Quorum Requirements For shareholders to act during a meeting, a quorum must be present. Generally, a quorum exists when shareholders holding more than 50 percent of the outstanding shares are present. State laws often permit the articles of incorporation to set higher or lower quorum requirements, however. In some states, obtaining the unanimous written consent of shareholders is a permissible alternative to holding a shareholders' meeting [RMBCA 7.25].

Voting Requirements Once a quorum is present, voting can proceed. If a state statute requires specific voting procedures, the corporation's articles or bylaws must be consistent with the statute. A majority vote of the shares represented at the meeting usually is required to pass resolutions. At times, more than a simple majority vote is required, either by a state statute or by the corporate articles. Extraordinary corporate matters, such as a merger, consolidation, or dissolution of the corporation, require approval by a higher percentage of all corporate shares entitled to vote [RMBCA 7.27].

■ **Case in Point 18.11** Tesla, Inc.'s Board of Directors approved an incentive-laden compensation plan for Elon Musk, the electric car company's chief executive officer

Ethics Today

Should proxy advisory firms be more heavily regulated by the SEC?

Hundreds of shareholder proposals are put forward each year, making it difficult for institutional investors to stay current. As a result, these investors rely on proxy advisory firms for recommendations on how to vote at corporate annual meetings. Given that institutional investors hold close to 80 percent of American shares, proxy advisory firms have a significant influence on the success or failure of many shareholder proposals. Supporters of these firms believe that this influence acts as a positive check on "egregious management behavior" in a way that individual investors could never hope to accomplish.

At the same time, just two firms—Institutional Shareholder Services (ISS) and Glass Lewis—control about 97 percent of the proxy advisory market. Given the widespread practice of "robo-voting," in which institutional investors automatically follow the advice of proxy advisors, these two firms, by one estimate, control nearly 38 percent of all shareholder votes in the United States.

Furthermore, critics believe that proxy advisory firms generally favor shareholder proposals that advocate environmental and social agendas, regardless of the proposals' impact on corporate profits or shareholder value. In recent years, the SEC has tried to curb the influence of the proxy industry by subjecting it to antifraud regulations that punish false or misleading statements and by requiring more transparency regarding the motives behind proxy voting advice.

Critical Thinking Why do you think most large institutional investors rely on proxy advisory firms to decide how to vote on shareholder proposals?

(CEO). The board then called a special meeting of Tesla stockholders to vote on the plan. Because CEO compensation is not considered an "extraordinary" corporate matter, no special voting requirements applied. With a quorum established, 73 percent of the shares present at the meeting voted in favor of the plan. This tally represented only 47 percent of all shares, not counting those controlled by Musk and his wife.

In response to a lawsuit filed by an unhappy stockholder, a Delaware court rejected the argument that the vote was invalid because it did not represent the majority view of all disinterested stockholders. Under state law, as long as a majority of shares entitled to vote are present at a meeting, and the majority of those shares vote "yes," the result is valid. The court did, however, allow the stockholder to challenge Musk's compensation—which could be as high as $56 billion—on the grounds that it was unfairly excessive.[13] ∎

Voting Lists The corporation prepares a voting list before each shareholders' meeting. Ordinarily, only persons whose names appear on the corporation's stockholder records as owners are entitled to vote.

The voting list contains the name and address of each shareholder as shown on the corporate records on a given cutoff date, or record date. (Under RMBCA 7.07, the

bylaws or board of directors may fix a record date that is as much as seventy days before the meeting.) The voting list also includes the number of voting shares held by each owner. The list is usually kept at the corporate headquarters and must be made available for shareholder inspection [RMBCA 7.20].

Cumulative Voting Most states permit, and many require, shareholders to elect directors by cumulative voting, a voting method designed to allow minority shareholders to be represented on the board of directors. When cumulative voting is not required, the entire board can be elected by a majority of shares.

Formula. With cumulative voting, each shareholder is entitled to a total number of votes equal to the number of board members to be elected multiplied by the number of voting shares that the shareholder owns. The shareholder can cast all of these votes for one candidate or split them among several nominees for director. All candidates stand for election at the same time.

How Cumulative Voting Works. Cumulative voting can best be understood by example. ∎ **Example 18.12** A corporation has 10,000 shares issued and outstanding. The minority shareholders hold 3,000 shares, and the majority shareholders hold the other 7,000 shares. Three members of the board are to be elected. The majority shareholders' nominees are Alvarez, Beasley, and Caravel. The minority

13. *Tometta v. Musk*, 250 A.3d 793 (Del.Ch. 2019).

shareholders' nominee is Dovrik. Can Dovrik be elected to the board by the minority shareholders?

If cumulative voting is allowed, the answer is yes. The minority shareholders have 9,000 votes among them (the number of directors to be elected times the number of shares, or 3 × 3,000 = 9,000 votes). All of these votes can be cast to elect Dovrik. The majority shareholders have 21,000 votes (3 × 7,000 = 21,000 votes), but these votes must be distributed among their three nominees.

The principle of cumulative voting is that no matter how the majority shareholders cast their 21,000 votes, they will not be able to elect all three directors if the minority shareholders cast all of their 9,000 votes for Dovrik, as illustrated in Exhibit 18–1. ∎

Other Voting Techniques Before a shareholders' meeting, a group of shareholders can agree in writing to vote their shares together in a specified manner. Such agreements, called *shareholder voting agreements*, usually are held to be valid and enforceable. A shareholder can also vote by proxy, as noted earlier.

Another technique is for shareholders to enter into a voting trust. A **voting trust** is an agreement (a trust contract) under which shareholders assign the right to vote their shares to a trustee, usually for a specified period of time. The trustee is then responsible for voting the shares on behalf of all the shareholders in the trust. The shareholders retain all rights of ownership (for instance, the right to receive dividend payments) except the power to vote the shares [RMBCA 7.30].

18–5d Rights of Shareholders

Shareholders possess numerous rights in addition to the right to vote their shares, and we examine several here.

Stock Certificates In the past, corporations commonly issued **stock certificates** that evidenced ownership of a specified number of shares in the corporation. Only a few jurisdictions still require physical stock certificates, and shareholders there have the right to demand that the corporation issue certificates (or replace those that were lost or destroyed). Stock is intangible personal property, however, and the ownership right exists independently of the certificate itself.

In most states and under RMBCA 6.26, a board of directors may provide that shares of stock will be uncertificated, or "paperless"—that is, no physical stock certificates will be issued. Notice of shareholders' meetings, dividends, and operational and financial reports are distributed according to the ownership lists recorded in the corporation's books.

Preemptive Rights Sometimes, the articles of incorporation grant preemptive rights to shareholders [RMBCA 6.30]. With **preemptive rights,** a shareholder receives a preference over all other purchasers to subscribe to or purchase a prorated share of a new issue of stock. Generally, preemptive rights must be exercised within a specific time period (usually thirty days).

A shareholder who is given preemptive rights can purchase a percentage of the new shares being issued that is

Exhibit 18–1 Results of Cumulative Voting

Ballot	Majority Shareholder Votes			Minority Shareholder Votes	Directors Elected
	Alvarez	Beasley	Caravel	Dovrik	
1	10,000	10,000	1,000	9,000	Alvarez, Beasley, Dovrik
2	9,001	9,000	2,999	9,000	Alvarez, Beasley, Dovrik
3	6,000	7,000	8,000	9,000	Beasley, Caravel, Dovrik

equal to the percentage of shares the shareholder already holds in the company. This allows each shareholder to maintain proportionate control, voting power, and financial interest in the corporation. ■ **Example 18.13** Katlin is a shareholder who owns 10 percent of a company. Because she also has preemptive rights, she can buy 10 percent of any new issue (to maintain her 10 percent position). Thus, if the corporation issues 1,000 more shares, Katlin can buy 100 of the new shares. ■

Preemptive rights are most important in close corporations because each shareholder owns a relatively small number of shares but controls a substantial interest in the corporation. Without preemptive rights, it would be possible for a shareholder to lose proportionate control over the firm. Nevertheless, preemptive rights do not exist unless provided for in the articles of incorporation.

Stock Warrants **Stock warrants** are rights given by a company to buy stock at a stated price by a specified date. Usually, when preemptive rights exist and a corporation is issuing additional shares, it gives its shareholders stock warrants. Warrants are often publicly traded on securities exchanges.

Dividends As mentioned, a **dividend** is a distribution of corporate profits or income ordered by the directors and paid to the shareholders in proportion to their shares in the corporation. Dividends can be paid in cash, property, stock of the corporation that is paying the dividends, or stock of other corporations.[14]

State laws vary, but each state determines the general circumstances and legal requirements under which dividends are paid. State laws also control the sources of revenue to be used. All states allow dividends to be paid from the undistributed net profits earned by the corporation, for instance. A number of states allow dividends to be paid out of any surplus.

Illegal Dividends Dividends are illegal if they are improperly paid from an unauthorized account or if their payment causes the corporation to become insolvent (unable to pay its debts as they come due). Generally, shareholders must return illegal dividends only if they knew that the dividends were illegal when the payment was received (or if the dividends were paid when the corporation was insolvent). Whenever dividends are illegal or improper, the board of directors can be held personally liable for the amount of the payment.

---

14. On one occasion, a distillery declared and paid a dividend in bonded whiskey.

The Directors' Failure to Declare a Dividend When directors fail to declare a dividend, shareholders can ask a court to compel the directors to do so. To succeed, the shareholders must show that the directors have acted so unreasonably in withholding the dividend that their conduct is an abuse of their discretion.

Often, a corporation accumulates large cash reserves for a legitimate corporate purpose, such as expansion or research. The mere fact that the firm has sufficient earnings or surplus available to pay a dividend normally is not enough to compel the directors to declare a dividend. The courts are reluctant to interfere with corporate operations and will not compel directors to declare dividends unless abuse of discretion is clearly shown.

Inspection Rights Shareholders in a corporation enjoy both common law and statutory inspection rights. The RMBCA provides that every shareholder is entitled to examine specified corporate records, including voting lists [RMBCA 7.20, 16.02]. The shareholder may inspect in person, or an attorney, accountant, or other authorized individual can do so as the shareholder's agent. In some states, a shareholder must have held the shares for a minimum period of time immediately preceding the demand to inspect or must hold a certain percentage of outstanding shares.

A shareholder has a right to inspect and copy corporate books and records only for a *proper purpose*, and the request to inspect must be made in advance. A shareholder who is denied the right of inspection can seek a court order to compel the inspection.

■ **Case in Point 18.14** Trading Block Holdings, Inc., offers online brokerage services. On April 1, some shareholders of Trading Block, through an attorney, sent a letter asking to inspect specific items in the corporation's books and records. The letter indicated that the purpose was to determine the financial condition of the company, how it was being managed, and whether the company's financial practices were appropriate. It also stated that the shareholders wanted to know whether Trading Block's management had engaged in any self-dealing that had negatively impacted the company as a whole.

On April 30, Trading Block responded with a letter stating that the plaintiffs were on a "fishing expedition" and did not have a proper purpose for inspecting the corporate records. Eventually, the shareholders filed a motion to compel inspection in an Illinois state court. The trial court denied the plaintiffs' motion. On appeal, the reviewing court held that the plaintiffs' allegations of self-dealing by Trading Block's directors and officers constituted a proper purpose for their inspection request. The trial court's decision was reversed.[15] ■

Potential for Abuse

The power of inspection is fraught with potential abuses, and the corporation is allowed to protect itself from them. For instance, a shareholder can properly be denied access to corporate records to prevent harassment or to protect trade secrets or other confidential corporate information.[16]

In the following case, the court considered whether a corporation can deny a shareholder access to its records based on the circumstances under which the shareholder acquired the shares.

---

15. *Sunlitz Holding Co., W.L.L. v. Trading Block Holdings, Inc.*, 2014 IL App (1st) 133938, 17 N.E.3d 715 (4th Dist. 2014). In the context of an LLC, see *Benjamin v. Island Management, LLC*, 341 Conn. 189, 267 A.3d 19 (Mass. S.Ct. 2021).

16. See, for example, *United Technologies Corp. v. Treppel*, 109 A.3d 553 (Del. 2014), and then *Rivest v. Hauppauge Digital, Inc.*, 2022 WL 203202 (Ct. Chancery Del. 2022).

Transfer of Shares

Corporate stock represents an ownership right in intangible personal property. The law generally recognizes the owner's right to transfer stock to another person unless there are valid restrictions on its transferability, such as frequently occur with close corporation stock.

When shares are transferred, a new entry is made in the corporate stock book to indicate the new owner. Until the corporation is notified and the entry is complete, all rights—including voting rights, notice of shareholders' meetings, and the right to dividend distributions—remain with the current record owner.

The Shareholder's Derivative Suit

When the corporation is harmed by the actions of a third party, the directors can bring a lawsuit in the name of the corporation against that party. If the corporate directors fail to bring a lawsuit, shareholders can do so "derivatively" in what is known as a **shareholder's derivative suit.**

The right of shareholders to bring a derivative action is especially important when the wrong suffered by the

---

Case 18.3

Hammoud v. Advent Home Medical, Inc.

Court of Appeals of Michigan, 2018 WL 1072988 (2018).

Background and Facts Advent Home Medical, Inc., is a family-owned close corporation. Carlia Cichon is Advent's president. Her daughter, Amanda Hammoud, owned 400 shares of Advent stock, representing 40 percent of the total shares. Hammoud submitted a written request to Cichon to review Advent's financial records. When Advent did not respond, Hammoud filed a complaint in a Michigan state court, seeking an order to compel the corporation to permit an inspection. Advent asserted that Hammoud was not entitled to inspect because she had procured her shares through fraud, threats, and duress. Hammoud provided the court with a notarized transfer of stock certificate verifying her status as a shareholder. The court granted Hammoud's motion to compel, ordering the corporation to produce the information that Hammoud sought. Advent appealed.

In the Language of the Court

PER CURIAM. [By the Whole Court]

The Michigan Business Corporation Act (MBCA) grants shareholders certain rights to examine corporate books and records. A simple written request suffices to compel the production of some records. To review others, a shareholder must advance a proper purpose.

* * * *

* * * Hammoud sent a letter to Cichon seeking Advent's balance sheet from the end of the preceding fiscal year, "its statement of income for the fiscal year," "and, if prepared by the corporation, its statement of source and application for funds for the fiscal year." Hammoud also sought to inspect Advent's "stock ledger and list of shareholders" as well as "the corporation's accounting records, including its general ledgers, bank statements, profit and loss statements, balance sheets, tax returns and payroll records." Hammoud described that her interest was "to monitor the financial health of the corporation, especially

Case 18.3 Continues

Case 18.3 Continued

given recent communications about the corporation's financial position and financial decisions reducing benefits and payments to shareholders and employees." Hammoud additionally asserted that she needed the records "to affirm" her "ownership/shareholder share" and to ensure that Advent was "in compliance with its Articles of Incorporation, By-Laws, and Policies and Procedures."

* * * *

Advent's fraud-related defenses to Hammoud's records request are simply irrelevant. The [MBCA] is unambiguous: a "shareholder" has a right to inspect corporate books if certain prerequisites are met. Hammoud easily satisfied the definition of a shareholder; she presented documents verifying that status. Advent produced no evidence to the contrary. How or why Hammoud became a shareholder is not probative of whether she is, in fact, a shareholder. Nor does such evidence create a material issue in an action brought to enforce shareholder rights.

* * * *

* * * A shareholder who has a genuine, good faith interest in the corporation's welfare or her own as a shareholder is entitled to inspect those corporate books that bear on her concerns. Hammoud's letter satisfied that standard.

Decision and Remedy A state intermediate appellate court affirmed the lower court's order compelling Advent to produce the records that Hammoud sought to inspect. "Hammoud was a shareholder when she sent her written request [and she] supplied a proper purpose for all the records she requested."

Critical Thinking

- **Legal Environment** Cichon insisted that she had transferred shares in Advent to Hammoud only because her daughter had threatened to prevent Cichon from visiting her grandchildren. Should the court have been persuaded by this argument to deny Hammoud's motion? Explain.
- **What If the Facts Were Different?** Suppose that Hammoud had stated her purpose for an inspection of Advent's records as "speculation of mismanagement." Would the result have been different? Discuss.

---

corporation results from the actions of the corporate directors and officers. For obvious reasons, the directors and officers would probably be unwilling to take any action against themselves.

Before shareholders can bring a derivative suit, they must submit a written demand to the corporation, asking the board of directors to take appropriate action [RMBCA 7.40]. The directors then have ninety days in which to act. Only if they refuse to do so can the derivative suit go forward. In addition, a court will dismiss a derivative suit if a majority of the directors or an independent panel determines in good faith that the lawsuit is not in the best interests of the corporation [RMBCA 7.44].

When shareholders bring a derivative suit, they are not pursuing rights or benefits for themselves personally but are acting as guardians of the corporate entity. Therefore, if the suit is successful, any damages recovered normally go into the corporation's treasury, not to the shareholders personally.[17]

18–5e Duties and Liabilities of Shareholders

One of the hallmarks of the corporate form of organization is that shareholders are not personally liable for the debts of the corporation. If the corporation fails, the shareholders can lose their investments, but that generally is the limit of their liability. As discussed previously, in certain instances, a court will pierce the corporate veil (disregard the corporate entity) and hold the shareholders individually liable. But these situations are the exception, not the rule.

A shareholder can also be personally liable in certain other rare instances. One relates to illegal dividends, which were mentioned previously. Another relates to "watered stock." Finally, in certain instances, a majority shareholder who engages in oppressive conduct or attempts to exclude minority shareholders from receiving certain benefits can be held personally liable.

Watered Stock When a corporation issues shares for less than their fair market value, the shares are referred

---

17. The shareholders may be entitled to reimbursement for reasonable expenses of the derivative lawsuit, including attorneys' fees.

to as **watered stock.**[18] Usually, the shareholder who receives watered stock must pay the difference to the corporation (the shareholder is personally liable). In some states, the shareholder who receives watered stock may be liable to creditors of the corporation for unpaid corporate debts.

■ **Example 18.15** During the formation of a corporation, Gomez, one of the incorporators, transfers his property, Sunset Beach, to the corporation for 10,000 shares of stock at a par value of $100 per share for a total price of $1 million. After the property is transferred and the shares are issued, Sunset Beach is carried on the corporate books at a value of $1 million.

On appraisal, it is discovered that the market value of the property at the time of transfer was only $500,000. The shares issued to Gomez are therefore watered stock, and he is liable to the corporation for the difference between the value of the shares and the value of the property. ■

Duties of Majority Shareholders In some instances, a majority shareholder is regarded as having a fiduciary duty to the corporation and to the minority shareholders. This duty arises when a single shareholder (or a few shareholders acting in concert) owns a sufficient number of shares to exercise *de facto* control over the corporation. In these situations, the majority shareholder owes a fiduciary duty to the minority shareholders.

When a majority shareholder breaches this fiduciary duty, the minority shareholders can sue for damages. A breach of fiduciary duties by those who control a close corporation normally constitutes what is known as *oppressive conduct*. A common example of a breach of fiduciary duty occurs when the majority shareholders "freeze out" the minority shareholders and exclude them from certain benefits of participating in the firm.

■ **Example 18.16** Raja, Jordan, and Barbara form a close corporation to operate a machine shop. Raja and Jordan own 75 percent of the shares in the company, but all three are directors. After disagreements arise, Raja asks the company to purchase his shares, but his requests are refused. A few years later, Raja dies, and his wife, Ella, inherits his shares. Jordan and Barbara refuse to perform a valuation of the company, deny Ella access to corporate information, do not declare any dividends, and refuse to elect Ella as a director. In this situation, the majority shareholders have violated their fiduciary duty to Ella. ■

18–6 Major Business Forms Compared

When deciding which form of business organization to choose, businesspersons normally consider several factors, including ease of creation, the liability of the owners, tax considerations, and the ability to raise capital. Each major form of business organization offers distinct advantages and disadvantages with respect to these and other factors.

Exhibit 18–2 summarizes the essential advantages and disadvantages of each of the forms of business organization discussed in this text.

---

18. The term "watered stock" was originally used to describe cattle that were kept thirsty during a long drive and then were allowed to drink large quantities of water just before their sale. The increased weight of the "watered stock" allowed the seller to reap a higher profit.

Exhibit 18–2 Major Forms of Business Compared

	Sole Proprietorship	Partnership	Corporation
Method of Creation	Created at will by owner.	Created by agreement of the parties.	Authorized by the state under the state's corporation law.
Legal Position	Not a separate entity; owner is the business.	A general partnership is a separate legal entity in most states.	Always a legal entity separate and distinct from its owners—a legal fiction for the purposes of owning property and being a party to litigation.
Liability	Unlimited liability.	Unlimited liability.	Limited liability of shareholders—shareholders are not liable for the debts of the corporation.
Duration	Determined by owner; automatically dissolved on owner's death.	Terminated by agreement of the partners, but can continue to do business even when a partner dissociates from the partnership.	Can have perpetual existence.
Transferability of Interest	Interest can be transferred, but individual's proprietorship then ends.	Although partnership interest can be assigned, assignee does not have full rights of a partner.	Shares of stock can be transferred.
Management	Completely at owner's discretion.	Each partner has a direct and equal voice in management unless expressly agreed otherwise in the partnership agreement.	Shareholders elect directors, who set policy and appoint officers.
Taxation	Owner pays personal taxes on business income.	Each partner pays pro rata share of income taxes on net profits, whether or not they are distributed.	Double taxation—corporation pays income tax on net profits, with no deduction for dividends, and shareholders pay income tax on disbursed dividends they receive.
Organizational Fees, Annual License Fees, and Annual Reports	None or minimal.	None or minimal.	All required.
Transaction of Business in Other States	Generally no limitation.	Generally no limitation.[a]	Normally must qualify to do business and obtain certificate of authority.

a. A few states have enacted statutes requiring that foreign partnerships qualify to do business there.

	Limited Partnership	Limited Liability Company	Limited Liability Partnership
Method of Creation	Created by agreement to carry on a business for profit. At least one party must be a general partner and the other(s) limited partner(s). Certificate of limited partnership is filed.	Created by an agreement of the member-owners of the company. Articles of organization are filed. Charter must be issued by the state.	Created by agreement of the partners. A statement of qualification for the limited liability partnership is filed.
Legal Position	Treated as a legal entity.	Treated as a legal entity.	Generally, treated the same as a general partnership.
Liability	Unlimited liability of all general partners. Limited partners are liable only to the extent of capital contributions.	Member-owners' liability is limited to the amount of capital contributions or investments.	Varies, but under the Uniform Partnership Act, liability of a partner for acts committed by other partners is limited.
Duration	By agreement in certificate, or by termination of the last general partner (retirement, death, or the like) or last limited partner.	Unless a single-member LLC, can have perpetual existence (same as a corporation).	Remains in existence until cancellation or revocation.
Transferability of Interest	Interest can be assigned, but if assignee becomes a member with consent of other partners, certificate must be amended.	Member interests are freely transferable.	Interest can be assigned the same as in a general partnership.
Management	General partners have equal voice or by agreement. Limited partners may not retain limited liability if they actively participate in management.	Member-owners can fully participate in management or can designate a group of persons to manage on behalf of the members.	Same as a general partnership.
Taxation	Generally taxed as a partnership.	LLC is not taxed, and members are taxed personally on profits "passed through" the LLC.	Same as a general partnership.
Organizational Fees, Annual License Fees, and Annual Reports	Organizational fee required; usually not others.	Organizational fee required. Others vary with states.	Fees are set by each state for filing statements of qualification, statements of foreign qualification, and annual reports.
Transaction of Business in Other States	Generally no limitations.	Generally no limitations, but may vary depending on state.	Must file a statement of foreign qualification before doing business in another state.

Practice and Review: Corporations

William Sharp was the sole shareholder and manager of Chickasaw Club, Inc., an S corporation that operated a popular nightclub of the same name in Columbus, Georgia. Sharp maintained a corporate checking account but paid the club's employees, suppliers, and entertainers in cash out of the club's proceeds. Sharp owned the property on which the club was located. He rented it to the club but made mortgage payments out of the club's proceeds and often paid other personal expenses with Chickasaw corporate funds.

At 12:45 A.M. on July 31, eighteen-year-old Aubrey Lynn Pursley, who was already intoxicated, entered the Chickasaw Club. A city ordinance prohibited individuals under the age of twenty-one from entering nightclubs, but Chickasaw employees did not check Pursley's identification to verify her age. Pursley drank more alcohol at Chickasaw and was visibly intoxicated when she left the club at 3:00 A.M. with a beer in her hand. Shortly afterward, Pursley lost control of her car, struck a tree, and was killed. Joseph Dancause, Pursley's stepfather, filed a tort lawsuit in a Georgia state court against Chickasaw Club, Inc., and William Sharp, seeking damages. Using the information presented in the chapter, answer the following questions.

1. Under what theory might the court in this case make an exception to the limited liability of shareholders and hold Sharp personally liable for the damages? What factors would be relevant to the court's decision?
2. Suppose that Chickasaw's articles of incorporation failed to describe the corporation's purpose or management structure, as required by state law. Would the court be likely to rule that Sharp is personally liable to Dancause on that basis? Why or why not?
3. Suppose that the club extended credit to its regular patrons, although neither the articles of incorporation nor the corporate bylaws authorized this practice. Would the corporation likely have the power to engage in this activity? Explain.
4. How would the court classify the Chickasaw Club corporation—domestic or foreign, public or private? Why?

Debate This . . . The sole shareholder of an S corporation should not be able to avoid liability for the torts of their employees.

Terms and Concepts

alien corporation 386	foreign corporation 386	S corporation 390
articles of incorporation 391	holding company 386	securities 396
benefit corporation 390	inside director 398	shareholder agreement 389
bond 396	outside director 398	shareholder's derivative suit 407
business judgment rule 400	piercing the corporate veil 394	stock 396
bylaws 392	preemptive rights 405	stock certificate 405
close corporation 389	preferred stock 396	stock warrant 406
commingled 395	private equity capital 397	*ultra vires* 393
common stock 396	proxy 403	venture capital 396
corporation 385	public corporation 387	voting trust 405
crowdfunding 397	publicly held corporation 389	watered stock 409
dividend 406	quorum 398	
domestic corporation 386	retained earnings 386	

Issue Spotters

1. Northwest Brands, Inc., is a small business incorporated in Minnesota. Its one class of stock is owned by twelve members of a single family. Ordinarily, corporate income is taxed at the corporate and shareholder levels. Is there a way for Northwest Brands to avoid this double taxation? Explain your answer. (See *Nature and Classification*.)

2. Wonder Corporation has an opportunity to buy stock in XL, Inc. The directors decide that instead of having Wonder buying the stock, the directors will buy it. Yvon, a Wonder shareholder, learns of the purchase and wants to sue the directors on Wonder's behalf. Can she do it? Explain. (See *Shareholders*.)

- **Check your answers to the Issue Spotters against the answers provided in Appendix B at the end of this text.**

Business Scenarios and Case Problems

18–1. Preincorporation. Cummings, Okawa, and Taft are recent college graduates who want to form a corporation to manufacture and sell digital tablets. Peterson tells them he will set in motion the formation of their corporation. First, Peterson makes a contract with Owens for the purchase of a piece of land for $200,000. Owens does not know of the prospective corporate formation at the time the contract is signed. Second, Peterson makes a contract with Babcock to build a small plant on the property being purchased. Babcock's contract is conditional on the corporation's formation. Peterson secures all necessary capitalization and files the articles of incorporation. (See *Corporate Formation and Powers*.)

(a) Discuss whether the newly formed corporation, Peterson, or both are liable on the contracts with Owens and Babcock.

(b) Discuss whether the corporation is automatically liable to Babcock on formation.

18–2. Conflicts of Interest. Oxy Corp. is negotiating with Wick Construction Co. for the renovation of Oxy's corporate headquarters. Wick, the owner of Wick Construction Co., is also one of the five members of Oxy's board of directors. The contract terms are standard for this type of contract. Wick has previously informed two of the other directors of his interest in the construction company. Oxy's board approves the contract by a three-to-two vote, with Wick voting with the majority. Discuss whether this contract is binding on the corporation. (See *Corporate Directors and Officers*.)

18–3. Duty of Loyalty. Kids International Corporation produced children's wear for Walmart and other retailers. Gila Dweck was a Kids director and its chief executive officer. Because she felt that she was not paid enough, she started Success Apparel to compete with Kids. Success operated out of Kids' premises, used its employees, borrowed on its credit, took advantage of its business opportunities, and capitalized on its customer relationships. As an "administrative fee," Dweck paid Kids 1 percent of Success's total sales. Did Dweck breach any fiduciary duties? Explain. [*Dweck v. Nasser*, 2012 WL 3194069 (Del.Ch. 2012)] (See *Corporate Directors and Officers*.)

18–4. Tort Liability. Jennifer Hoffman took her cell phone to a store owned by R&K Trading, Inc., for repairs. Later, Hoffman filed a suit in a New York state court against R&K, Verizon Wireless, Inc., and others. Hoffman sought to recover damages for a variety of torts, including infliction of emotional distress and negligent hiring and supervision. She alleged that an R&K employee, Keith Press, had examined her phone in a back room, accessed private photos of her stored on her phone, and disseminated the photos to the public. Hoffman testified that "after the incident, she learned from another R&K employee that personal information and pictures had been removed from the phones of other customers." Can R&K be held liable for the torts of its employees? Explain. [*Hoffman v. Verizon Wireless, Inc.*, 125 A.D.3d 806, 5 N.Y.S.3d 123 (2 Dept. 2015)] (See *Nature and Classification*.)

18–5. Piercing the Corporate Veil. In New York City, 2406-12 Amsterdam Associates, LLC, brought an action in a New York state court against Alianza Dominicana and Alianza, LLC, to recover unpaid rent. The plaintiff asserted cause to pierce the corporate veil, alleging that Alianza Dominicana had made promises to pay its rent while discreetly forming Alianza, LLC, to avoid liability for it. According to 2406-12, Alianza, LLC, was 90 percent owned by Alianza Dominicana, had no employees, and had no function but to hold Alianza Dominicana's assets away from its creditors. The defendants filed a motion to dismiss the plaintiff's claim. Assuming that 2406-12's allegations are true, are there sufficient grounds to pierce the corporate veil of Alianza, LLC? Discuss. [*2406-12 Amsterdam Associates, LLC v. Alianza, LLC,* 136 A.D.3d 512, 25 N.Y.S.3d 167 (1 Dept. 2016)] (See *Piercing the Corporate Veil*.)

18–6. Business Case Problem With Sample Answer— Rights of Shareholders. FCR Realty, LLC, and Clifford B. Green & Sons, Inc., were co-owned by three brothers— Frederick, Clifford Jr., and Richard Green. Each brother was a shareholder of the corporation. Frederick was a controlling shareholder, as well as president. Each brother owned a one-third interest in the LLC. Clifford believed that Frederick had misused LLC and corporate funds to pay nonexistent debts and liabilities and had diverted LLC assets to the corporation. He also contended that Frederick had disbursed about $1.8 million in corporate funds to Frederick's own separate business. Clifford hired an attorney and filed an action on behalf of the two companies against Frederick for breach of fiduciary duty. Frederick argued that Clifford lacked the knowledge necessary to adequately represent the companies' interests because he did not understand financial statements. Can Clifford maintain the action against Frederick? If so, and if the suit is successful, who would recover any damages? Explain. [*FCR Realty, LLC v. Green*, 2016 WL 571449 (Conn. Super.Ct. 2016)] (See *Shareholders*.)

- **For a sample answer to Problem 18–6, go to Appendix C at the end of this text.**

18–7. Duties and Liabilities of Directors and Officers. M&M Country Store, Inc., operated a gas station and convenience store. Debra Kelly bought M&M from Mary Millett. Under the purchase agreement, Millett was to remain as the corporation's sole shareholder until the price was fully paid. A default on any payment would result in the return of M&M to Millett. During Kelly's management of M&M, taxes were not remitted, vendors were not paid, repairs were not made, and the store's gas tanks and shelves were often empty. Kelly commingled company and personal funds, kept inaccurate records, and allowed M&M's business licenses and insurance policies to lapse. After she defaulted on her payments to Millett and surrendered M&M, the company incurred significant expenses to pay outstanding bills and replenish the inventory. Can M&M recover these costs from Kelly? Explain. [*M&M Country Store, Inc. v. Kelly*, 159 A.D.3d 1102, 71 N.Y.S.3d 707 (3 Dept. 2018)] (See *Corporate Directors and Officers*.)

18–8. Certificate of Authority. Armour Pipe Line Company assigned leases to its existing oil wells in Texas to Sandel Energy, Inc. The assignment included royalties for the oil produced from the wells. Armour specified that the assignment "does not pertain to production attributable to these leases from any new wells," reserving for itself an interest in those royalties. Later, Armour—a foreign corporation in Texas—forfeited its certificate of authority to do business in the state. More than three years later, the certificate was reissued. Meanwhile, new wells were drilled on the leases. Sandel filed a suit in a Texas state court against Armour, claiming that the reservation of a royalty interest in those wells was "ineffective" because of the temporary forfeiture. When and why does a corporation need a certificate of authority? Is Armour entitled to the royalties from the new wells? Discuss. [*Armour Pipeline Co. v. Sandel Energy, Inc.*, 546 S.W.3d 455 (Tex.App.—Houston (14th Dist.) 2018)] (See *Nature and Classification*.)

18–9. Close Corporations. Bruce Rowe and Clifford Daly were business partners for several decades. They started out doing business by forming Quality Composites, Inc. (QCI), a close corporation. Daly and Rowe each owned 50 percent of QCI. Both were officers and directors of the corporation, and each had appointed one additional director. QCI owned the rights to a product known as Braze Tape, a material used to bind metal products together. QCI had purchased the rights in Braze Tape, including the manufacturing process, from Coating Applications, Inc. (CAI), a corporation owned in part by Rowe. By agreement, CAI was authorized to sell and manufacture Braze Tape. In addition, QCI was a subtenant of CAI's office premises. Rowe came to believe that Daly was

producing Braze Tape on his own, outside the company structure, and misrepresenting the quality of the product. Rowe evicted Daly and QCI from the CAI office premises. Daly, both individually and derivatively on behalf of QCI, filed suit against Rowe. The complaint asserted claims for breach of fiduciary duty and breach of contract, among other things. Rowe filed counterclaims alleging breach of fiduciary duty and other actions. The trial court found in favor of most of Daly's claims. The defendants appealed. They argued, among other things, that Daly lacked standing to pursue a direct claim for breach of fiduciary duty because he had not suffered an injury separate from the injury to QCI. How should the appeals court rule? [*Daly v. Rowe*, 199 N.E.3d 237, 2022-Ohio-3750 (2022)] (See *The Nature and Classification of Corporations*.)

18–10. A Question of Ethics—The IDDR Approach and Piercing the Corporate Veil. The University of Missouri requires employees to disclose inventions developed during their employment so that the university can choose whether to exercise the right to ownership. Galen Suppes was an associate professor at the university, and the university provided the lab he used for his work. In the lab, he developed the technology to transform glycerol, a byproduct of biodiesel production, into propylene glycol, a compound used to make antifreeze. Without informing the university, Suppes formed Renewable Alternatives (RA) to patent the invention and license the ownership rights. On learning of these actions, the university filed a suit in a Missouri state court against Suppes for breach of the duty of loyalty. The court ordered him to assign his invention to the university. On appeal, Suppes alleged that he had improperly been held liable for the actions of RA. He argued that the university had failed to make a case for piercing the corporate veil on the alter-ego theory. A state intermediate appellate court affirmed the lower court's order. "The University was not required to show that Suppes was the alter ego of RA . . . . The University brought a breach of loyalty claim directly against Suppes for Suppes's own actions." [*Curators of University of Missouri v. Suppes*, __ S.W.3d __, 2019 WL 121983 (Mo.App. W.D. 2019)] (See *Piercing the Corporate Veil*.)

(a) Apply the IDDR approach to evaluate the ethics of Suppes's decision to profit from his research without informing his employer.

(b) What might a university do to encourage innovation by its employees and avoid disputes over the ownership rights to the results? Discuss.

Time-Limited Group Assignment

18–11. Corporate Versus LLC Form of Business. The limited liability company (LLC) may be the best organizational form for most businesses. For a significant number of firms, however, the corporate form or some other form of organization may be better. (See *Nature and Classification*.)

(a) The first group will outline several reasons why a firm might be better off as a corporation than as an LLC.

(b) The second group will discuss the differences between corporations and LLCs in terms of their management structures.

Chapter 19

Agency Relationships

One of the most common, important, and pervasive legal relationships is that of **agency.** In an agency relationship involving two parties, one of the parties, called the *agent*, agrees to represent or act for the other, called the *principal*. The principal has the right to control the agent's conduct in matters entrusted to the agent.

Agency relationships are crucial in the business world. By using agents, a principal can conduct multiple business operations at the same time in different locations. Indeed, the only way that certain business entities can function is through their agents. For instance, a corporate officer is an agent who serves in a representative capacity for the corporation. The officer has the authority to bind the corporation to a contract. Only through its officers can corporations enter into contracts.

Most employees are also considered to be agents of their employers.

Today, however, the United States is experiencing a trend toward a so-called *gig economy*, which centers on short-term, independent workers who are not employees. Companies like Uber and Lyft provide evidence of this trend. This type of on-demand employment raises questions related to agency, making agency an increasingly important topic for students of business law and the legal environment to understand.

19–1 Agency Relationships

Section 1.01 of the *Restatement (Third) of Agency*[1] defines "agency" as "the fiduciary relationship that arises when one person (a 'principal') manifests assent to another person (an 'agent') that the agent shall act on the principal's behalf and subject to the principal's control, and the agent manifests or otherwise consents so to act." In other words, in a principal–agent relationship, the parties have agreed that the agent will act on behalf and instead of the principal in negotiating and transacting business with third parties.

The term **fiduciary** is at the heart of agency law. This term can be used both as a noun and as an adjective. When used as a noun, it refers to a person having a duty created by a particular undertaking to act primarily for another's benefit in matters connected with the undertaking. When used as an adjective, as in the phrase "fiduciary relationship," it means that the relationship involves trust and confidence.

Agency relationships commonly exist between employers and employees. Agency relationships may sometimes also exist between employers and independent contractors who are hired to perform special tasks or services.

19–1a Employer–Employee Relationships

Normally, all employees who deal with third parties are deemed to be agents. A salesperson in a department store, for instance, is an agent of the store's owner (the principal) and acts on the owner's behalf. Any sale of goods made by the salesperson to a customer is binding on the principal. Similarly, most representations of fact made by the salesperson with respect to the goods sold are binding on the principal.

Because employees who deal with third parties generally are deemed to be agents of their employers, agency law and employment law overlap considerably. Agency relationships, however, can exist outside an employer–employee relationship, so agency law has a broader reach than employment law. Additionally, agency law is based on the common law, whereas much employment law is statutory law.

Employment laws (state and federal) apply only to the employer–employee relationship. Statutes governing Social Security, withholding taxes, workers' compensation, unemployment compensation, workplace safety, and employment discrimination apply only in an employer–employee relationship. These laws do not apply to independent contractors.

---

1. The *Restatement (Third) of Agency* is an authoritative summary of the law of agency and is often referred to by judges in their decisions and opinions.

19–1b Employer–Independent Contractor Relationships

Independent contractors are not employees because, by definition, those who hire them have no control over the details of their work performance. Section 2 of the *Restatement (Second) of Agency* defines an **independent contractor** as follows:

> [An independent contractor is] a person who contracts with another to do something for [the other] but who is not controlled by the other nor subject to the other's right to control with respect to [the independent contractor's] physical conduct in the performance of the undertaking. [The independent contractor] may or may not be an agent.[2]

Building contractors and subcontractors are independent contractors. A property owner who hires a contractor

and subcontractors to complete a project does not control the details of the way they perform their work. Truck drivers who own their vehicles and hire out on a per-job basis are independent contractors, but truck drivers who drive company trucks on a regular basis usually are employees.

The relationship between a principal and an independent contractor may or may not involve an agency relationship. To illustrate: Homeowners who hire real estate brokers to sell their houses have contracted with independent contractors (the brokers). Each homeowner has also established an agency relationship with the broker for the specific purpose of selling the property. Similarly, insurance agents are both independent contractors and agents of the insurance company for which they sell policies. (Note that an insurance broker, in contrast, normally is an agent of the person obtaining insurance and not of the insurance company.)

In the following case, the defendants hired a general contractor to build a house for them. One of the independent contractors hired by the general contractor was injured on the job. Were the homeowners liable for that person's injuries?

---

2. The *Restatement (Third) of Agency* no longer uses the term *independent contractor*, but we retain it in this text because it is still widely used.

Case **19.1**

Anderson v. Harris
Court of Appeals of Texas (1st Dist.), 2022 WL 14980145 (2022).

Background and Facts Orea and Shonia Harris hired general contractor Patrick Knapp to build a house on their property. Knapp hired Billy Anderson to help construct the roof of the house. One day, while on the roof, Anderson slipped on a piece of wet, unsecured sheet metal and fell about 30 feet to the ground, suffering serious injuries. He sued the Harrises as owners of the premises on which he fell.

The Harrises filed a motion for summary judgment, which the trial court granted. Anderson appealed.

In the Language of the Court
Gordon Goodman, J.

Anderson * * * contends the trial court erred in granting the Harrises' * * * summary-judgment motion because he produced enough evidence to raise a fact issue on his premises-liability claim.

After adequate time for discovery, a party may move for summary judgment on the basis that there is no evidence to support one or more essential elements of the nonmovant's [Anderson's] claim. The nonmovant must respond by producing "at least a scintilla" of evidence raising a genuine issue of material fact as to each challenged element. If the nonmovant does not produce any evidence or produces "less than a scintilla of evidence," the trial court must grant the summary-judgment motion. "Less than a scintilla of evidence exists when the evidence is 'so weak as to do no more than create a mere surmise or suspicion' of a fact." * * *

* * * *

2. Applicable law

In a premises-liability case, the duty a premises owner owes to the plaintiff depends on the plaintiff's status at the time of the incident. An employee of an independent contractor working on the premises, as Anderson was here, is an invitee on the premises. A premises owner generally owes an invitee a duty to keep the premises reasonably safe from dangerous conditions. When the invitee is an independent contractor's employee, there are two types of dangerous conditions, or premises defects, that may give rise to liability.

The first type of dangerous condition is a defect that exists on the premises when the employee or independent contractor enters. For this type of dangerous condition, the premises owner "has a duty to inspect the premises and warn the independent contractor/invitee of dangerous conditions that are not open and obvious and that the owner knows or should have known exist." This type of dangerous condition includes only "concealed hazards" that already exist when the independent contractor enters the premises. * * *

The second type of dangerous condition is one that "arises as a result of the independent contractor's work activity." For this type of dangerous condition, the premises owner generally "owes no duty to the independent contractor's employees because an owner generally has no duty to ensure that an independent contractor performs its work in a safe manner." * * * To prevail on this type of dangerous-condition claim, a plaintiff must establish both the premises owner's right to control and the traditional premises-liability elements.

3. Analysis

In their * * * motion for summary judgment, the Harrises asserted there was no evidence of two elements of Anderson's premises-liability claim: (1) the Harrises' control over the independent contractor's work; and (2) the Harrises' actual or constructive knowledge of the dangerous condition that caused Anderson's injury. We conclude that in response to the * * * summary-judgment motion, Anderson did not produce enough evidence to raise a fact issue as to these two elements.
     * * * *

We conclude that Anderson did not produce enough evidence to raise a fact issue as to the Harrises' actual or constructive knowledge of the dangerous condition, so he cannot recover on a claim for either type of dangerous condition. Further, even if this case involved the second type of dangerous condition—one arising from the independent contractor's work activity—we conclude Anderson did not produce enough evidence to raise a fact issue as to the Harrises' control over the independent contractor's work activity.

a. Knowledge of dangerous condition

In their no-evidence summary-judgment motion, the Harrises claimed they did not have actual or constructive knowledge of the wet, unsecured sheet metal on the roof of the house because they did not live on the property at the time, the house was still under construction, and they were not on the property on the day Anderson fell.
     * * * *

On appeal, Anderson argues that the Harrises had constructive knowledge of the unsecured sheet metal because the independent contractor, Knapp, had knowledge of the dangerous condition, and his knowledge can be imputed to the Harrises because Knapp was their agent. * * *
     * * * *

Anderson failed to provide any evidence that either the Harrises or Knapp, if he was their agent, knew about the unsecured sheet metal. Thus, he failed to raise a genuine issue of material fact as to the knowledge element of his premises-liability claim. * * *

b. Control over work activity

Even if this case involved the type of dangerous condition that arises from an independent contractor's work activity, the Harrises would owe no duty to Anderson unless he can demonstrate they "retain[ed] the right of supervisory control over work on the premises." The parties agree there was no contract explicitly assigning the Harrises the right to control the work activity, so to demonstrate the Harrises' control, Anderson would need to show they actually controlled the work activity. Anderson did not produce evidence to raise a fact issue as to the Harrises' control over the independent contractor's work activity.
     * * * *

Case 19.1 Continues

Case 19.1 Continued

Decision and Remedy The Court of Appeals of Texas, First District, affirmed the trial court's judgment. Anderson was an independent contractor working for a general contractor. The Harrises could not be held liable for his injuries.

Critical Thinking Question

- **What If the Facts Were Different?** Suppose that Anderson prevailed. Suppose further that this type of independent contractor liability became the law of the land. How would general contractors likely react?

19–1c Determination of Employee Status

The courts are frequently asked to determine whether a particular worker is an employee or an independent contractor. How a court decides this issue can have a significant effect on the rights and liabilities of the parties.

Criteria Used by the Courts In deciding whether a worker is categorized as an employee or an independent contractor, courts often consider the following questions:

1. **How much control does the employer exercise over the details of the work?** If the employer exercises considerable control over the details of the work and the day-to-day activities of the worker, this indicates employee status. This is perhaps the most important factor weighed by the courts in determining employee status.
2. **Is the worker engaged in an occupation or business distinct from that of the employer?** If so, this points to independent-contractor, not employee, status.
3. **Is the work usually done under the employer's direction or by a specialist without supervision?** If the work is usually done under the employer's direction, this indicates employee status.
4. **Does the employer supply the tools at the place of work?** If so, this indicates employee status.
5. **For how long is the person employed?** If the person is employed for a long period of time, this indicates employee status.
6. **What is the method of payment—by time period or at the completion of the job?** Payment by time period, such as once every two weeks or once a month, indicates employee status.
7. **What degree of skill is required of the worker?** If a great degree of skill is required, this may indicate that the person is an independent contractor hired for a specialized job and not an employee.

Workers sometimes benefit from having employee status. For instance, employers are required to pay certain taxes, such as Social Security and unemployment taxes, for employees but not for independent contractors. In addition, federal statutes governing employment discrimination apply only in employer–employee relationships.

Employee Status and Overtime According to federal law, employers must pay certain employees at least one-and-one-half times their regular hourly rate for overtime, defined as those hours worked in excess of forty hours per week. Independent contractors are exempt from these overtime rules.

■ **Case in Point 19.1** Petroplex Pipe & Construction, Inc., hired Joseph Hobbs and Drake Feeney as pipe welders on various construction projects, classifying them as independent contractors. Petroplex paid Hobbs and Feeney between $70 and $80 an hour. The two men generally worked from 7 A.M. to 5 P.M., six days a week, as determined by Petroplex. The welders supplied their own trucks and equipment. They also designated themselves "self-employed" on tax returns and claimed thousands of dollars in deductions for work-related expenses.

After leaving Petroplex, Hobbs and Feeney filed suit against the company, alleging that they had been misclassified as independent contractors and deserved significant overtime pay. A federal appeals court determined that, although the issue was not clear cut, as a matter of "economic reality" Hobbs and Feeney were too dependent on Petroplex to be considered "in business for [themselves]." Petroplex assigned the welders specific tasks on different work sites, set their hours, and determined their wages. Furthermore, for the several years in question, Hobbs and Feeney worked exclusively for Petroplex. Consequently, the court found that the welders were employees and should be compensated as such.[3] ■

Criteria Used by the IRS The Internal Revenue Service (IRS) has established its own criteria for determining whether a worker is an independent contractor or an employee. The most important factor is the degree of control the business exercises over the worker.

---

3. *Hobbs v. Petroplex Pipe and Construction, Inc.*, 946 F.3d 824, 170 Lab.Cas. P 36,762 (5th Cir. 2020).

The IRS tends to closely scrutinize a firm's classification of its workers because, as mentioned, employers can avoid certain tax liabilities by hiring independent contractors instead of employees. Even when a firm has classified a worker as an independent contractor, the IRS may decide that the worker is actually an employee. If the IRS decides that an employee is misclassified, the employer will be responsible for paying any applicable Social Security, withholding, and unemployment taxes due for that employee.

Employee Status and "Works for Hire" Ordinarily, a person who creates a copyrighted work is the owner of it—unless it is a "work for hire." Under the Copyright Act, any copyrighted work created by employees within the scope of their employment at the request of the employer is a "work for hire." The employer owns the copyright to the work.

In contrast, when an employer hires an independent contractor—such as a freelance artist, writer, or software engineer—the independent contractor normally owns the copyright. An exception is made if the parties agree in writing that the work is a "work for hire" and the work falls into one of nine specific categories, including audiovisual works, collective works (such as magazines), motion pictures, textbooks, tests, and translations.

■ **Case in Point 19.2** Over the course of fifty-five years, Stanley Kauffmann contributed numerous film reviews and other articles to *The New Republic* (*TNR*) magazine. At no time was Kauffmann an employee of TNR. After Kauffmann died in 2014, forty-four of the articles he wrote for *TNR* in 1999 appeared without permission in an anthology. Kaufmann's estate sued for copyright infringement. The publisher of the anthology produced a letter, signed in 2004 by Kauffmann and *TNR*'s literary editor, stating that "all articles [Kauffmann has] written for *The New Republic* have been 'works for hire'" and therefore belonged to *TNR*.

A U.S. appeals court ruled that Kauffmann, as an independent contractor, retained ownership of the forty-four articles. The legislative intent behind the "work for hire" writing requirement was to make this area of the law more predictable by requiring tangible evidence of the parties' objectives at the time of the agreement. This intent would be frustrated, ruled the court, if parties could enter into a work-for-hire agreement years after the work in question was created.[4] ■

---

4. *Estate of Kauffmann v. Rochester Institute of Technology,* 932 F.3d 74, 2019 Copr.L.Dec. P 31,497 (2nd Cir. 2019).

19–2 Formation of the Agency Relationship

Agency relationships normally are consensual. They come about by voluntary consent and agreement between the parties. Normally, the agreement need not be in writing, and consideration is not required.

A person must have contractual capacity to be a principal. The idea is that those who cannot legally enter into contracts directly should not be allowed to do so indirectly through an agent. Any person can be an agent, however, regardless of whether that person has the capacity to contract (including minors).

An agency relationship can be created for any legal purpose. An agency relationship created for a purpose that is illegal or contrary to public policy is unenforceable. ■ **Example 19.3** Archer (as principal) contracts with Burke (as agent) to sell illegal narcotics. The agency relationship is unenforceable because selling illegal narcotics is a felony and is contrary to public policy. If Burke sells the narcotics and keeps the profits, Archer cannot sue to enforce the agency agreement. ■

An agency relationship can arise in four ways: by agreement of the parties, by ratification, by estoppel, and by operation of law.

19–2a Agency by Agreement

Most agency relationships are based on an express or implied agreement that the agent will act for the principal and that the principal agrees to have the agent so act. An agency agreement can take the form of an express written contract or be created by an oral agreement, such as when a person hires a neighbor to mow his lawn on a regular basis.

An agency agreement can also be implied by conduct. ■ **Case in Point 19.4** Gilbert Bishop was admitted to a nursing home, Laurel Creek Health Care Center, suffering from various physical ailments. He was not able to use his hands well enough to write but was otherwise mentally competent. Bishop's sister offered to sign the admission papers for him, but it was Laurel Creek's policy to have the patient's spouse sign the forms if the patient could not.

Bishop's sister then brought his wife, Anna, to the hospital to sign the paperwork, which included a mandatory arbitration clause. Later, when the family filed a lawsuit against Laurel Creek, the nursing home sought to enforce the arbitration clause. Ultimately, a Kentucky appellate court held that Bishop was bound by the contract and the arbitration clause his wife had signed. Bishop's conduct had indicated that he was giving his wife authority to act as his agent in signing the admission papers.[5] ■

19–2b Agency by Ratification

On occasion, a person who is in fact not an agent (or who is an agent acting outside the scope of agency authority) makes a contract on behalf of another (a principal). If the principal approves or affirms that contract by word or by action, an agency relationship is created by ratification. Ratification involves a question of intent, and intent can be expressed by either words or conduct.

19–2c Agency by Estoppel

Sometimes, a principal causes a third person to believe that another person is the principal's agent, and the third person reasonably relies on that belief. When this occurs, the principal is "estopped to deny" (prevented from denying) the agency relationship. The principal's actions have created the appearance of an agency that does not in fact exist, creating an agency by estoppel.

The Third Party's Reliance Must Be Reasonable The third person must prove the belief that an agency relationship existed was reasonable. Facts and circumstances must show that an ordinary, prudent person familiar with business practice and custom would have been justified in concluding that the agent had authority.

Created by the Principal's Conduct Note that the acts or declarations of a purported agent in and of themselves do not create an agency by estoppel. Rather, it is the deeds or statements of the principal that create an agency by estoppel.

■ **Case in Point 19.5** Aaron Reidel was experiencing severe back pain when he visited the emergency room at Lodi Community Hospital. The attending emergency room physician, an independent contractor, misdiagnosed Reidel's condition. Reidel filed suit against Lodi, alleging that the physician's negligence was the proximate cause of his subsequent paraplegia. Lodi argued that it was not liable because the physician was not the hospital's employee or agent. An Ohio jury disagreed, awarding Reidel $5.2 million in damages.

A state appeals court affirmed, holding that a hospital can, depending on the circumstances, be liable under the doctrine of agency by estoppel for the negligence of an independent contractor physician. Crucially, the court

noted, the public is rarely aware of the technical employment arrangements between a hospital and its staff. In this case, Reidel only chose Lodi because it was nearby at the time of his medical emergency. He reasonably expected to be treated by a physician employed by Lodi and to be able to hold Lodi responsible for any resulting negligence.[6] ■

19–2d Agency by Operation of Law

The courts may find an agency relationship in the absence of a formal agreement in other situations as well. This may occur in family relationships, such as when one spouse purchases certain basic necessaries and charges them to the other spouse's account. The courts often rule that a spouse is liable for payment for the necessaries because of either a social policy or a legal duty to supply necessaries to family members.

Agency by operation of law may also occur in emergency situations. If an agent cannot contact the principal and failure to act would cause the principal substantial loss, the agent may take steps beyond the scope of the agent's authority. For instance, a railroad engineer may contract on behalf of the employer for medical care for an injured motorist hit by the train.

19–3 Duties, Rights, and Remedies of Agents and Principals

Once the principal–agent relationship has been created, both parties have duties that govern their conduct. As discussed previously, the principal–agent relationship is *fiduciary*—based on trust. In a fiduciary relationship, each party owes the other the duty to act with the utmost good faith. In this section, we examine the various duties of agents and principals.

19–3a Agent's Duties to the Principal

Generally, the agent owes the principal five duties— performance, notification, loyalty, obedience, and accounting (see Exhibit 19–1).

Performance An implied condition in every agency contract is the agent's agreement to use reasonable diligence and skill in performing the work. When agents fail to perform their duties, liability for breach of contract may result.

5. *Laurel Creek Health Care Center v. Bishop,* 2010 WL 985299 (Ky.App. 2010).

6. *Riedel v. Akron General Health System,* 2018-Ohio-840, 97 N.E.3d 508 (2018).

Exhibit 19–1 Duties of the Agent

The degree of skill or care required of an agent is usually that expected of a reasonable person under similar circumstances. Generally, this is interpreted to mean ordinary care. Agents who have represented themselves as possessing special skills, however, are expected to exercise the degree of skill claimed. Failure to do so constitutes a breach of duty.

Not all agency relationships are based on contract. In some situations, an agent acts gratuitously—that is, without payment. Gratuitous agents cannot be liable for breach of contract because there is no contract. They are subject only to tort liability. Once gratuitous agents have begun to act in an agency capacity, they have the duty to continue to perform in that capacity. A gratuitous agent must perform in an acceptable manner and is subject to the same standards of care and duty to perform as other agents.

■ **Example 19.6** Bower's friend Verona is a real estate broker. Verona offers to sell Bower's vacation home at no charge. If Verona never attempts to sell the home, Bower has no legal cause of action to force her to do so. If Verona does attempt to sell the home to Friedman, but then performs so negligently that the sale falls through, normally Bower can sue Verona for negligence. ■

Notification Agents are required to notify the principal of all matters that come to their attention concerning the subject matter of the agency. This is the duty of notification, or the duty to inform.

■ **Example 19.7** Perez, an artist, is about to negotiate a contract to sell a series of paintings to Barber's Art Gallery for $25,000. Perez's agent learns that Barber is insolvent and will be unable to pay for the paintings. The agent has a duty to inform Perez of Barber's insolvency because it is relevant to the subject matter of the agency, which is the sale of Perez's paintings. ■

Generally, the law assumes that the principal is aware of any information acquired by the agent that is relevant to the agency—regardless of whether the agent actually passes on this information to the principal. It is a basic tenet of agency law that notice to the agent is notice to the principal.

Loyalty Loyalty is one of the most fundamental duties in a fiduciary relationship. Basically, the agent has the duty to act solely for the benefit of the principal and not in the interest of the agent or a third party. For instance, an agent cannot represent two principals in the same transaction unless both know of the dual capacity and consent to it.

The duty of loyalty also means that any information or knowledge acquired through the agency relationship is confidential. It is a breach of loyalty to disclose such information either during the agency relationship or after its termination. Typical examples of confidential information are trade secrets and customer lists compiled by the principal.

The agent's loyalty must be undivided. The agent's actions must be strictly for the benefit of the principal and must not result in any secret profit for the agent.

■ **Example 19.8** Don contracts with Zorba, a real estate agent, to negotiate the purchase of an office building. Zorba discovers that the property owner will sell the building only as a package deal with another parcel. Zorba buys the two properties, intending to resell the building to Don. Zorba has breached his fiduciary duty. As a real estate agent, Zorba has a duty to communicate all offers to Don, his principal, and not to purchase the property secretly and then resell it to Don. Zorba is required to act in Don's best interests and can become the purchaser in this situation only with Don's knowledge and approval. ■

Obedience When acting on behalf of the principal, an agent has a duty to follow all lawful and clearly stated instructions of the principal. Any deviation from such instructions is a violation of this duty.

During emergency situations, however, when the principal cannot be consulted, the agent may deviate from the instructions without violating this duty. Whenever instructions are not clearly stated, the agent can fulfill the duty of obedience by acting in good faith and in a manner reasonable under the circumstances.

Accounting Unless the agent and principal agree otherwise, the agent must keep and make available to the principal an account of all property and funds received and paid out on the principal's behalf. This includes gifts from third parties in connection with the agency. ■ **Example 19.9** Marla is a salesperson for Roadway Supplies. Knife River Construction gives Marla a new tablet as a gift for prompt deliveries of Roadway's paving materials. The tablet belongs to Roadway. ■

The agent has a duty to maintain a separate account for the principal's funds and must not intermingle these funds with the agent's personal funds. If a licensed professional (such as an attorney) violates this duty, the professional may be subject to disciplinary action by the licensing authority (such as the state bar association). Of course, the professional will also be liable to the client (the principal) for failure to account.

19–3b Principal's Duties to the Agent

The principal also has certain duties to the agent (as shown in Exhibit 19–2). These duties relate to compensation, reimbursement and indemnification, cooperation, and safe working conditions.

Compensation In general, when a principal requests certain services from an agent, the agent reasonably expects payment. For instance, when an accountant or an attorney is asked to act as an agent, an agreement to compensate the agent for this service is implied. The principal therefore has a duty to pay the agent for services rendered.

Unless the agency relationship is gratuitous and the agent does not act in exchange for payment, the principal must pay the agreed-on value for the agent's services. If no amount has been expressly agreed on, then the principal owes the agent the customary compensation for such services. The principal also has a duty to pay that compensation in a timely manner.

■ **Case in Point 19.10** Keith Miller worked as a sales representative for Paul M. Wolff Company, a subcontractor specializing in concrete-finishing services. Sales representatives at Wolff are paid a 15 percent commission on

Exhibit 19–2 Duties of the Principal

projects that meet a 35 percent gross profit threshold. The commission is paid after the projects are completed. When Miller resigned, he asked for commissions on fourteen projects for which he had secured contracts but which had not yet been completed. Wolff refused, so Miller sued.

The court found that "an agent is entitled to receive commissions on sales that result from the agent's efforts," even after the employment or agency relationship ends. Miller had met the gross profit threshold on ten of the unfinished projects, and therefore, he was entitled to more than $21,000 in commissions.[7] ■

Reimbursement and Indemnification

When an agent disburses funds at the request of the principal, the principal has a duty to reimburse the agent. The principal must also reimburse the agent (even a gratuitous agent) for any necessary expenses incurred in the course of the reasonable performance of agency duties. Agents cannot recover for expenses incurred as a result of their own misconduct or negligence.

Subject to the terms of the agency agreement, the principal has the duty to indemnify (compensate) an agent for liabilities incurred because of authorized and lawful acts and transactions. For instance, if the agent, on the principal's behalf, forms a contract with a third party, and the principal fails to perform the contract, the third party may sue the agent for damages. In this situation, the principal is obligated to compensate the agent for any costs incurred by the agent as a result of the principal's failure to perform.

---

7. *Miller v. Paul M. Wolff Co.,* 178 Wash.App. 957, 316 P.3d 1113 (2014).

Additionally, the principal must indemnify the agent for the value of benefits that the agent confers on the principal. The amount of indemnification usually is specified in the agency contract. If it is not, the courts will look to the nature of the business and the type of loss to determine the amount. Note that this rule applies to acts by gratuitous agents as well.

Cooperation

A principal has a duty to cooperate with the agent and to assist the agent in performing their duties. The principal must do nothing to prevent that performance.

For instance, when a principal grants an agent an exclusive territory, the principal creates an **exclusive agency,** in which the principal cannot compete with the agent or appoint or allow another agent to compete. A principal who does so violates the exclusive agency and is exposed to liability for the agent's lost profits.

■ **Example 19.11** Valentina (the principal) creates an exclusive agency by granting Andrew (the agent) a territory within which only Andrew may sell Valentina's organic skin care products. If Valentina starts to sell the products herself within Andrew's territory—or permits another agent to do so—Valentina has failed to cooperate with the agent. Because she has violated the exclusive agency, Valentina can be held liable for Andrew's lost sales or profits. ■

In the following case, a pair of potential homebuyers entered into an agreement with a realtor to act as the buyers' exclusive agent in locating and purchasing property. Later, the buyers executed an exclusive agency agreement with a different realtor. Neither agent knew about the other until the buyers found a home that they liked and bought it.

Case Analysis 19.2

NRT New England, LLC v. Jones

Appellate Court of Connecticut, 162 Conn.App. 840, 134 A.3d 632 (2016).

In the Language of the Court
HARPER, J. [Judge]
* * * *

The defendant [Christopher Jones] met Andrea Woolston, a licensed realtor working as an independent contractor [for NRT New England, LLC, doing business as Coldwell Banker Residential Brokerage], in October 2010. The defendant expressed to Woolston a desire to purchase a home for himself and his then fiancée, Katherine Wiltshire. One of the first things Woolston asked

the defendant was whether he was represented by another agent. The defendant responded that he was not. After a number of conversations about the defendant's needs and wishes, the parties executed an exclusive right to represent buyer agreement (agreement), which established, among other things, that Woolston was the defendant's exclusive agent for finding, negotiating, and purchasing property. Over the next several months, Woolston devoted a substantial amount of time searching for

properties for the defendant to purchase. Specifically, Woolston researched available properties at six town halls in the communities in which the defendant was interested. She showcased a number of properties personally to the defendant and Wiltshire and introduced many more to them through e-mail. Woolston and the defendant had at least twenty appointments where they viewed multiple properties. Additionally, Woolston visited many properties alone to determine if they were suitable for the

Case 19.2 Continues

Case 19.2 Continued

defendant. Altogether, Woolston spent hundreds of hours seeking a suitable home for the defendant.

The agreement was in effect from January 11, 2011 until July 11, 2011, and set forth the geographical area that the defendant was interested in and the rate of compensation for the plaintiff's services. With respect to geographical area, the parties agreed that Woolston would seek properties in Killingworth, Guilford, Essex, Old Saybrook, Deep River, Lyme, and Old Lyme [Connecticut]. With respect to compensation, the defendant agreed to pay the plaintiff a commission equal to 2.5 percent of the purchase price of the property "if the [buyer] or any person or entity acting on the [buyer's] behalf purchases, options, exchanges, leases or trades any property, through the efforts of anyone, including the [buyer]." The agreement imposed the following duties on the defendant: "The [buyer] will not deal directly with any other broker, agent or licensee during the term of this agreement. The [buyer] will notify other brokers, agents or licensees at first contact that the [buyer] is being exclusively represented by [NRT]. The [buyer] will disclose to [NRT] any past and/or current contacts for any real property or with any other real estate broker or agent."

On May 10, 2011, the defendant informed Woolston via e-mail that he and Wiltshire purchased property at 300 Vineyard Point Road in Guilford for $1,375,000. The defendant learned of this property on May 4, 2011, from Mary Jane Burt, a realtor with H. Pearce Real Estate (H. Pearce), who previously had represented Wiltshire with the sale of her house in Hamden [Connecticut]. Woolston subsequently confronted the defendant and eventually learned that he

and Wiltshire previously had executed an exclusive right to represent buyer agreement with Burt and H. Pearce. This agreement was in effect from August 1, 2010, until August 1, 2011, and contained a provision designating Burt as the exclusive agent for the defendant and Wiltshire. Thus, at the time the defendant purchased the property in Guilford, he was under contract for exclusive agency with both Woolston and Burt. The defendant never told Woolston or Burt that he had two agreements in effect at the same time. Woolston notified her superiors of what had transpired.

* * * [NRT] filed a * * * complaint [in a Connecticut state court] against the defendant [for] breach of contract * * * . After a trial * * * , the court * * * found that the plaintiff had proven * * * breach of contract * * * and damages. * * * The court awarded the plaintiff $34,375 in damages [which represented 2.5 percent of the purchase price for the Vineyard Point property] plus attorney's fees and costs. This appeal followed.

* * * *

The defendant * * * claims that the agreement was unenforceable. Specifically, he argues that the court improperly * * * found that it was inequitable to deny the plaintiff recovery.

* * * *

There is ample evidence in the record to support the court's conclusion that denying the plaintiff relief would be inequitable. Woolston testified, and the defendant himself conceded, that she rendered a significant amount of services to the defendant over several months. Specifically, Woolston researched properties at town halls for availability and encumbrances, contacted property owners, arranged personal visits, prepared

and presented literature to the defendant on available properties, and attended appointments with the defendant and Wiltshire. Woolston spent hundreds of hours working for the defendant in total.

The defendant, on the other hand, accepted Woolston's services while under contract with another agent in violation of the agreement. Indeed, the defendant acknowledged that he was untruthful with Woolston at the beginning of their relationship when he told her that he was not represented by another agent. In fact, he was scheduling appointments and viewing properties with both Woolston and Burt at approximately the same time in May 2011. For example, the defendant e-mailed Woolston on May 2, 2011, thanking her for showing him a property. Approximately one week later, the defendant e-mailed Woolston to inform her that he viewed 300 Vineyard Point Road with Burt and had "put in an all cash bid that has been accepted."

The defendant nevertheless argues that it would not be inequitable to deny recovery to the plaintiff because Woolston performed no services in connection with his purchase of 300 Vineyard Point Road. We are not persuaded. The defendant agreed to pay a commission "equal to 2.5% of the purchase price if the [buyer] or any person or entity acting on the [buyer's] behalf purchases * * * any property, through the efforts of anyone, including the [buyer], where an agreement to purchase the property was entered into during the term of this agreement." However unjust this result may seem to the defendant in hindsight, we cannot say it is inequitable because it is precisely what he agreed to.

* * * *

The judgment is affirmed.

Legal Reasoning Questions

1. What is the advantage to a principal of an exclusive agency agreement? What was the advantage to Jones of his agreement with Woolston? Discuss.

2. Why, in addition to damages, was the plaintiff awarded attorneys' fees and costs?

3. Jones's agreement with Woolston provided that on the purchase of the property, NRT "will, whenever feasible, seek compensation from the seller or the seller's agent." The court determined that it was not feasible. Why would it not be reasonable in this situation to ask the seller of the property to pay part of Woolston's commission?

Safe Working Conditions The common law requires the principal to provide safe working premises, equipment, and conditions for all agents and employees. The principal has a duty to inspect working areas and to warn agents and employees about any unsafe situations. When the agent is an employee, the employer's liability is frequently covered by state workers' compensation insurance. In addition, federal and state statutes often require the employer to meet certain safety standards.

19–3c Rights and Remedies of Agents and Principals

In general, for every duty of the principal, the agent has a corresponding right, and vice versa. When one party to the agency relationship violates their duty to the other party, the nonbreaching party is entitled to a remedy. The remedies available arise out of contract and tort law and include monetary damages, termination of the agency relationship, an injunction, and required accountings. As mentioned, the agent has the right to be compensated, to be reimbursed and indemnified, and to have a safe working environment. An agent also has the right to perform agency duties without interference by the principal. Remedies of the agent for breach of duty by the principal follow normal contract and tort remedies. An agent can also withhold further performance and demand that the principal give an accounting in certain situations.

A principal has contract remedies for an agent's breach of fiduciary duties. The principal also has tort remedies if the agent engages in misrepresentation, negligence, deceit, libel, slander, or trespass. In addition, any breach of a fiduciary duty by an agent may justify the principal's termination of the agency.

19–4 Scope of Agent's Authority

The liability of a principal to third parties with whom an agent contracts depends on whether the agent had the authority to enter into legally binding contracts on the principal's behalf. An agent's authority can be either actual (express or implied) or apparent. If an agent contracts outside the scope of this authority, the principal may still become liable by ratifying the contract.

19–4a Express Authority

Express authority is authority declared in clear, direct, and definite terms. Express authority can be given orally or in writing.

The Equal Dignity Rule In most states, the **equal dignity rule** requires that if the contract being executed is or must be in writing, then the agent's authority must also be in writing. (Recall that a writing includes an electronic record.) Failure to comply with the equal dignity rule can make a contract voidable at the option of the principal. The law regards the contract at that point as a mere offer. If the principal decides to accept the offer, the acceptance must be ratified, or affirmed, in writing.

■ **Example 19.12** Paloma (the principal) orally asks Austin (the agent) to sell a ranch that Paloma owns. Austin finds a buyer and signs a sales contract on behalf of Paloma to sell the ranch. Because a contract for an interest in real property must be in writing, the equal dignity rule applies. The buyer cannot enforce the contract unless Paloma subsequently ratifies Austin's agency status in a writing. Once the sales contract is ratified, either party can enforce rights under the contract. ■

Modern business practice allows several exceptions to the equal dignity rule:

1. An executive officer of a corporation normally can conduct ordinary business transactions without obtaining written authority from the corporation.
2. When the agent acts in the presence of the principal, the rule does not apply.
3. When the agent's act of signing is merely a formality, then the agent does not need written authority to sign. ■ **Example 19.13** Sandra Healy (the principal) negotiates a contract but is called out of town the day it is to be signed. If Healy orally authorizes Derek Santini to sign, the oral authorization is sufficient. ■

Power of Attorney Giving an agent a **power of attorney** confers express authority.[8] The power of attorney is a written document and is usually notarized. (A document is notarized when a **notary public**—a person authorized to attest to the authenticity of signatures—signs and dates the document and imprints it with a seal of authority.) Most states have statutory provisions for creating a power of attorney.

A power of attorney can be special (permitting the agent to perform specified acts only), or it can be general (permitting the agent to transact all business for the principal). Because a general power of attorney grants extensive authority to the agent, it should be

---

8. An agent who holds a power of attorney is called an *attorney-in-fact* for the principal. The holder does not have to be an attorney-at-law (and often is not).

used with great caution and usually only in exceptional circumstances. Ordinarily, a power of attorney terminates on the incapacity or death of the person giving the power.[9]

19–4b Implied Authority

An agent has the **implied authority** to do what is reasonably necessary to carry out express authority and accomplish the objectives of the agency. Authority can also be implied by custom or inferred from the position the agent occupies.

■ **Example 19.14** Tian is employed by Packard Grocery to manage one of its stores. Packard has not expressly stated that Tian has authority to contract with third persons. Nevertheless, authority to manage a business implies authority to do what is reasonably required (as is customary or can be inferred from a manager's position) to operate the business. This includes forming contracts to hire employees, buying merchandise and equipment, and advertising the products sold in the store. ■

Note, however, that agents' implied authority cannot contradict their express authority. Thus, if a principal has limited an agent's express authority, then the fact that the agent customarily would have such authority is irrelevant. ■ **Example 19.15** Juanita Alvarez is the owner of six Baja Tacos restaurants. Alvarez (the principal) strictly

forbids the restaurant managers (agents) from entering into contracts to hire additional workers. Therefore, the fact that managers customarily would have authority to hire employees is immaterial. ■

19–4c Apparent Authority

Actual authority (express or implied) arises from what the principal makes clear to the agent. Apparent authority, in contrast, arises from what the principal causes a third party to believe. An agent has **apparent authority** when the principal, by either word or action, causes a third party reasonably to believe that the agent has authority to act, even though the agent has no express or implied authority.

A Pattern of Conduct Apparent authority usually comes into existence through a principal's pattern of conduct over time. ■ **Example 19.16** Bailey is a traveling salesperson. She solicits orders for goods but does not carry them with her. She normally would not have the implied authority to collect payments from customers on behalf of the principal. Suppose that she does accept payments from Corgley Enterprises, however, and submits them to the principal's accounting department for processing. If the principal does nothing to stop Bailey from continuing this practice, a pattern develops over time, and the principal confers apparent authority on Bailey to accept payments from Corgley. ■

At issue in the following Spotlight Case was whether the manager of a horse breeding operation had the authority to bind the farm's owner in a contract guaranteeing breeding rights.

9. A durable power of attorney, however, continues to be effective despite the principal's incapacity or death. An elderly person, for instance, might grant a durable power of attorney to provide for the handling of property and investments or specific healthcare needs in case of incompetence.

Spotlight on Apparent Authority of Managers

Case 19.3 Lundberg v. Church Farm, Inc.
Appellate Court of Illinois, Second District, 151 Ill.App.3d 452, 502 N.E.2d 806 (1986).

Background and Facts Gilbert Church owned a horse breeding farm managed by Herb Bagley. Advertisements for the breeding rights to one of Church Farm's stallions, Imperial Guard, directed all inquiries to "Herb Bagley, Manager." Vern and Gail Lundberg bred Thoroughbred horses. The Lundbergs contacted Bagley and executed a preprinted contract giving them breeding rights to Imperial Guard "at Imperial Guard's location," subject to approval of the mares by Church. Bagley handwrote a statement on the contract that guaranteed the Lundbergs "six live foals in the first two years." He then signed it "Gilbert G. Church by H. Bagley."

The Lundbergs bred four mares, which resulted in one live foal. Church then moved Imperial Guard from Illinois to Oklahoma. The Lundbergs sued Church for breaching the contract by moving the horse. Church claimed that Bagley was not authorized to sign contracts for Church or to change or add terms, but only to present preprinted contracts to potential buyers. Church testified that although Bagley was his farm manager and the contact person for breeding rights, Bagley had never before modified the preprinted forms or signed Church's name on them. The jury found in favor of the Lundbergs and awarded $147,000 in damages. Church appealed.

In the Language of the Court

Justice UNVERZAGT delivered the opinion of the court.

* * * *

* * * Defendant contends that plaintiffs have failed to establish that Bagley had apparent authority to negotiate and sign the Lundberg contract for Church Farm * * *.

The party asserting an agency has the burden of proving its existence * * * but may do so by inference and circumstantial evidence. * * * Additionally, an agent may bind his principal by acts which the principal has not given him actual authority to perform, but which he appears authorized to perform. * * * An agent's apparent authority is that authority which "the principal knowingly permits the agent to assume or which he holds his agent out as possessing. It is the authority that a reasonably prudent man, exercising diligence and discretion, in view of the principal's conduct, would naturally suppose the agent to possess."

Plaintiffs produced evidence at trial that Gil Church approved the Imperial Guard advertisement listing Herb Bagley as Church Farm's manager, and directing all inquiries to him. Church also permitted Bagley to live on the farm and to handle its daily operations. Bagley was the only person available to visitors to the farm. Bagley answered Church Farm's phone calls, and there was a preprinted signature line for him on the breeding rights package.

The conclusion is inescapable that Gil Church affirmatively placed Bagley in a managerial position giving him complete control of Church Farm and its dealings with the public. We believe that this is just the sort of "holding out" of an agent by a principal that justifies a third person's reliance on the agent's authority.

We cannot accept defendant's contention that the Lundbergs were affirmatively obligated to seek out Church to ascertain the actual extent of Bagley's authority. Where an agent has apparent authority to act, the principal will be liable in spite of any undisclosed limitations the principal has placed on that authority.

Decision and Remedy   The state appellate court affirmed the lower court's judgment in favor of the Lundbergs for $147,000. Because Church had allowed circumstances to lead the Lundbergs to believe Bagley had the authority to negotiate and sign the contract, Church was bound by Bagley's actions.

Critical Thinking

- **Legal Environment**   The court held that Church had allowed the Lundbergs to believe that Bagley was his agent. What steps could Church have taken to protect himself against a finding of apparent authority?

- **Ethical**   Does a principal have an ethical responsibility to inform an unaware third party that an apparent agent does not in fact have the authority to act on the principal's behalf? Explain.

Apparent Authority and Estoppel   A court can apply the doctrine of agency by estoppel when a principal has given a third party reason to believe that an agent has authority to act. If the third party honestly relies on the principal's representations and suffers harm as a result, the principal may be estopped (prevented) from denying that the agent had authority.

19–4d Emergency Powers

When an unforeseen emergency demands action by the agent to protect or preserve the property and rights of the principal, but the agent is unable to communicate with the principal, the agent has emergency power. ■ **Example 19.17** Rob Fulsom is an engineer for Pacific Drilling Company. While Fulsom is acting within the scope of his employment, he is severely injured in an accident on an oil rig many miles from home. Acosta, the rig supervisor, directs Thompson, a physician, to give medical aid to Fulsom and to charge Pacific for the medical services.

Acosta, an agent, has no express or implied authority to bind the principal, Pacific Drilling, for Thompson's medical services. Because of the emergency situation, however, the law recognizes Acosta as having authority to act appropriately under the circumstances. ■

19–4e Ratification

Ratification occurs when the principal affirms, or accepts responsibility for, an agent's unauthorized act. When ratification occurs, the principal is bound to the agent's act, and the act is treated as if it had been authorized by the principal from the outset. Ratification can be either express or implied.

If the principal does not ratify a contract entered into by the agent, the principal is not bound, and the third party's agreement with the agent is viewed as merely an unaccepted offer. The third party can revoke it at any time, without liability, before the principal ratifies the contract. The agent, however, may be liable to the third party for misrepresenting the agent's authority.

The requirements for ratification can be summarized as follows:

1. The agent must have acted on behalf of an identified principal who subsequently ratifies the action.
2. The principal must know all of the material facts involved in the transaction. If a principal ratifies a contract without knowing all of the facts, the principal can rescind (cancel) the contract.[10]
3. The principal must affirm the agent's act in its entirety.
4. The principal must have the legal capacity to authorize the transaction at the time the agent engages in the act and at the time the principal ratifies. The third

party must also have the legal capacity to engage in the transaction.
5. The principal's affirmation (ratification) must occur before the third party withdraws from the transaction.
6. The principal must observe the same formalities when ratifying the act as would have been required to authorize it initially.

19–5 Liability for Agency Relationships

Liability for contracts formed by an agent depends on how the principal is classified and on whether the actions of the agent were authorized or unauthorized. Principals are classified as *disclosed*, *partially disclosed*, or *undisclosed*.

1. A **disclosed principal** is a principal whose identity is known by the third party at the time the contract is made by the agent.
2. A **partially disclosed principal** is a principal whose identity is not known by the third party. Nevertheless, the third party knows that the agent is or may be acting for a principal at the time the contract is made. ■ **Example 19.18** Eileen has contracted with a real estate agent to sell certain property. She wishes to keep her identity a secret, but the agent makes it clear to potential buyers of the property that he is acting in an agency capacity. In this situation, Eileen is a partially disclosed principal. ■
3. An **undisclosed principal** is a principal whose identity is totally unknown by the third party. In addition, the third party has no knowledge that the agent is acting in an agency capacity at the time the contract is made.

Authorized Acts If an agent acts within the scope of authority, normally the principal is obligated to perform the contract regardless of whether the principal was disclosed, partially disclosed, or undisclosed. Whether the agent may also be held liable under the contract, however, depends on the disclosed, partially disclosed, or undisclosed status of the principal.

Disclosed or Partially Disclosed Principal. A disclosed or partially disclosed principal is liable to a third party for a contract made by the agent. If the principal is disclosed, the agent has no contractual liability for the nonperformance of the principal or the third party. If the principal is partially disclosed, in most states the agent is also treated as a party to the contract. Thus,

---

10. Note that if the third party has changed position in reliance on the apparent contract, the principal can still rescind the contract but must reimburse the third party for any costs.

company based in Israel, contracted with a New Jersey firm, Piermont Products, LLC, to distribute its products in the United States and Canada. The parties' contract required six months' notice of termination, during which time Smart Trike was to continue paying commissions to Piermont for products that were sold. When Smart Trike terminated the agreement without providing the required notice, Piermont sued for breach of contract. The court held in favor of Piermont. Under the terms of the agreement, Piermont was entitled to receive notice of termination and commissions for Smart Trike products that it sold during the six months following the notice.[14] ■

Even in an agency at will—in which either party may terminate at any time—the principal who wishes to terminate must give the agent reasonable notice. The notice must be at least sufficient to allow the agent to recoup expenses and, in some situations, to make a normal profit.

Notice of Termination When the parties terminate an agency, it is the principal's duty to inform any third parties who know of the existence of the agency that it has been terminated. Although an agent's actual authority ends when the agency is terminated, the agent's apparent authority continues until the third party receives notice (from any source) that such authority has been terminated.

No particular form is required for notice of termination to be effective. If the principal knows that a third party has dealt with the agent, the principal is expected to notify that person directly. For third parties who have heard about the agency but have not yet dealt with the agent, constructive notice is sufficient.[15] If the agent's authority is written, however, normally it must be revoked in writing (unless the written document contains an expiration date).

19–6b Termination by Operation of Law

Certain events terminate agency authority automatically because their occurrence makes it impossible for the agent to perform or improbable that the principal would continue to want performance. We look at these events here. Note that when an agency terminates by operation of law, there is no duty to notify third persons unless the agent's authority is coupled with an interest.

1. **Death or insanity.** The general rule is that the death or insanity of either the principal or the agent automatically and immediately terminates an ordinary agency relationship.[16] Knowledge of the death or insanity is not required.
2. **Impossibility.** When the specific subject matter of an agency is destroyed or lost, the agency terminates. Similarly, when it is impossible for the agent to perform the agency lawfully because of a change in the law, the agency terminates.
3. **Changed circumstances.** Sometimes, an event occurs that has such an unusual effect on the subject matter of the agency that the agent can reasonably infer that the principal will not want the agency to continue. In such situations, the agency terminates. ■ **Example 19.26** Baird hires Joslen to sell a tract of land for $40,000. Subsequently, Joslen learns that there is oil under the land and that the land is worth $1 million. The agency and Joslen's authority to sell the land for $40,000 are terminated. ■
4. **Bankruptcy.** If either the principal or the agent petitions for bankruptcy, the agency usually is terminated. In certain circumstances, such as when the agent's financial status is irrelevant to the purpose of the agency, the agency relationship may continue. Insolvency, as distinct from bankruptcy, does not necessarily terminate the relationship. (Insolvent persons cannot pay debts as they come due or have liabilities that exceed their assets.)
5. **War.** When the principal's country and the agent's country are at war with each other, the agency is terminated. In this situation, the agency is automatically suspended or terminated because there is no way to enforce the legal rights and obligations of the parties.

14. *Smart Trike, MNF, PTE, Ltd. v. Piermont Products, LLC,* 147 A.D.3d 477, 48 N.Y.S.3d 23 (2017). For a case involving agency termination based on race, see *Cruz v. Farmers Insurance Exchange,* 42 F.4th 1205 (10th Cir. 2022).

15. Persons have constructive notice of a fact if they could have discovered the fact through proper diligence. Constructive notice may be accomplished by publishing a notice in the media or posting it at a designated public place.

16. An exception to this rule exists in the bank–customer relationship. A bank, as agent, can continue to exercise specific types of authority after the customer's death or insanity and can continue to pay checks drawn by the customer for ten days after death.

Practice and Review: Agency Relationships

Lynne Meyer, on her way to a business meeting and in a hurry, stopped at a Buy-Mart store for a new car charger for her smartphone. There was a long line at one of the checkout counters, but a cashier, Valerie Watts, opened another counter and began loading the cash drawer. Meyer told Watts that she was in a hurry and asked Watts to work faster. Instead, Watts slowed her pace. At this point, Meyer hit Watts. It is not clear whether Meyer hit Watts intentionally or, in an attempt to retrieve the car charger, hit her inadvertently.

In response, Watts grabbed Meyer by the hair and hit her repeatedly in the back of the head, while Meyer screamed for help. Management personnel separated the two women and questioned them about the incident. Watts was immediately fired for violating the store's no-fighting policy. Meyer subsequently sued Buy-Mart, alleging that the store was liable for the tort (assault and battery) committed by its employee. Using the information presented in the chapter, answer the following questions.

1. Under what doctrine discussed in this chapter might Buy-Mart be held liable for the tort committed by Watts?
2. What is the key factor in determining whether Buy-Mart is liable under this doctrine?
3. How is Buy-Mart's potential liability affected by whether Watts's behavior constituted an intentional tort or a tort of negligence?
4. Suppose that when Watts applied for the job at Buy-Mart, she disclosed in her application that she had previously been convicted of felony assault and battery. Nevertheless, Buy-Mart hired Watts as a cashier. How might this fact affect Buy-Mart's liability for Watts's actions?

Debate This ... The doctrine of respondeat superior should be modified to make agents solely liable for their tortious (wrongful) acts committed within the scope of employment.

Terms and Concepts

agency 415
apparent authority 426
disclosed principal 428
e-agent 429
equal dignity rule 425
exclusive agency 423

express authority 425
fiduciary 415
implied authority 426
independent contractor 416
notary public 425
partially disclosed principal 428

power of attorney 425
ratification 428
respondeat superior 430
undisclosed principal 428
vicarious liability 430

Issue Spotters

1. Winona contracted with XtremeCast, a broadcast media firm, to cohost an Internet-streaming sports program. Winona and XtremeCast signed a new contract for each episode. In each contract, Winona agreed to work a certain number of days for a certain salary. During each broadcast, Winona was free to improvise her performance. She had no other obligation to work for XtremeCast. Was Winona an independent contractor? (See *Agency Law*.)
2. Davis contracts with Estee to buy a certain horse on her behalf. Estee asks Davis not to reveal her identity. Davis makes a deal with Farmland Stables, the owner of the horse, and makes a down payment. Estee does not pay the rest of the price. Farmland Stables sues Davis for breach of contract. Can Davis hold Estee liable for whatever damages he has to pay? Why or why not? (See *Liability in Agency Relationships*.)

• **Check your answers to the Issue Spotters against the answers provided in Appendix B at the end of this text.**

Business Scenarios and Case Problems

19–1. *Respondeat Superior.* ABC Tire Corp. hires Arnez as a traveling salesperson and assigns him a geographic area and time schedule in which to solicit orders and service customers. Arnez is given a company car to use in covering the territory. One day, Arnez decides to take his personal car to cover part of his territory. It is 11:00 A.M., and Arnez has just finished calling on all customers in the city of Tarrytown. His next appointment is at 2:00 P.M. in the city of Austex, twenty miles down the road. Arnez starts out for Austex, but halfway there he decides to visit a former college roommate who runs a farm ten miles off the main highway. Arnez is enjoying his visit with his former roommate when he realizes that it is 1:45 P.M. and that he will be late for the appointment in Austex. Driving at a high speed down the country road to reach the main highway, Arnez crashes his car into a tractor, severely injuring Thomas, the driver of the tractor. Thomas claims that he can hold ABC Tire Corp. liable for his injuries. Discuss fully ABC's liability in this situation. (See *Liability in Agency Relationships.*)

19–2. Duty of Loyalty. Peter hires Alice as an agent to sell a piece of property he owns. The price is to be at least $30,000. Alice discovers that the fair market value of Peter's property is actually at least $45,000 and could be higher because a shopping mall is going to be built nearby. Alice forms a real estate partnership with her cousin Carl. Then she prepares for Peter's signature a contract for the sale of the property to Carl for $32,000. Peter signs the contract. Just before closing and passage of title, Peter learns about the shopping mall and the increased fair market value of his property. Peter refuses to deed the property to Carl. Carl claims that Alice, as Peter's agent, solicited a price above that agreed on when the agency was created and that the contract is therefore binding and enforceable. Discuss fully whether Peter is bound to this contract. (See *Duties, Rights, and Remedies of Agents and Principals.*)

19–3. Employee Versus Independent Contractor. Stephen Hemmerling was a driver for the Happy Cab Company. Hemmerling paid certain fixed expenses and followed various rules relating to the use of the cab, the hours that could be worked, and the solicitation of fares, among other things. Rates were set by the state. Happy Cab did not withhold taxes from Hemmerling's pay. While driving the cab, Hemmerling was injured in an accident and filed a claim for workers' compensation benefits in a state court. Such benefits are not available to independent contractors. On what basis might the court hold that Hemmerling was an employee? Explain. (See *Agency Law.*)

19–4. Business Case Problem With Sample Answer— Determining Employee Status. Nelson Ovalles worked as a cable installer for Cox Rhode Island Telecom, LLC, under an agreement with a third party, M&M Communications, Inc. The agreement stated that no employer-employee relationship existed between Cox and M&M's technicians, including Ovalles. Ovalles was required to designate his affiliation with Cox on his work van, clothing, and identification badge. Cox had minimal contact with him, however, and had limited power to control how he performed his duties. Cox supplied cable wire and similar items, but the equipment was delivered to M&M, not to Ovalles. On a workday, while Ovalles was fulfilling a work order, his van rear-ended a car driven by Barbara Cayer. Is Cox liable to Cayer? Explain. [*Cayer v. Cox Rhode Island Telecom, LLC,* 85 A.3d 1140 (R.I. 2014)] (See *Agency Law.*)

- For a sample answer to Problem 19–4, go to Appendix C at the end of this text.

19–5. Agency Relationships. Standard Oil of Connecticut, Inc., sells home heating, cooling, and security systems. Standard schedules installation and service appointments with its customers and then contracts with installers and technicians to do the work. The company requires an installer or technician to complete a project by a certain time but to otherwise "exercise independent judgment and control in the execution of any work." The installers and technicians are licensed and certified by the state. Standard does not train them, provide instruction manuals, supervise them at customers' homes, or inspect their work. The installers and technicians use their own equipment and tools, and they can choose which days they work. Standard pays a set rate per project. According to criteria used by the courts, are these installers and technicians independent contractors or employees? Why? [*Standard Oil of Connecticut, Inc. v. Administrator, Unemployment Compensation Act,* 320 Conn. 611, 134 A.3d 581 (2016)] (See *Agency Law.*)

19–6. Agent's Authority. Kindred Nursing Centers East, LLC, owns and operates Whitesburg Gardens, a long-term care and rehabilitation facility, in Huntsville, Alabama. Lorene Jones was admitted to the facility following knee-replacement surgery. Jones's daughter, Yvonne Barbour, signed the admission forms required by Whitesburg Gardens as her mother's representative in her presence. Jones did not object. The forms included an "Alternative Dispute Resolution Agreement," which provided for binding arbitration in the event of a dispute between "the Resident" (Jones) and "the Facility" (Whitesburg Gardens). Six days later, Jones was transferred to a different facility. After recovering from the surgery, she filed a suit in an Alabama state court against Kindred, alleging substandard care on a claim of negligence. Can Jones be compelled to submit her claim to arbitration? Explain. [*Kindred Nursing Centers East, LLC v. Jones,* 201 So.3d 1146 (Ala. 2016)] (See *Agent's Authority.*)

19–7. Agent's Authority. Devin Fink was the manager of Precision Tune Auto Care in Charlotte, North Carolina. Randall Stywall brought her car to the shop to have the rear shocks replaced. Fink filled out the service order with an estimate of the cost. Later, Stywall returned to pick up her car, and Fink collected payment for the work. When Stywall started to drive away, however, the car bounced as if the shocks had not been replaced. A complaint to Precision's corporate office resulted in the discovery that, in fact, the work had not been done and Fink had kept the payment. He was charged with larceny against his employer. He argued that he had not committed this crime because the victim was Stywall, not Precision. Which agency principles support the charge against Fink? Explain. [*State of North Carolina v. Fink,* 798 S.E.2d 537 (2017)] (See *Agent's Authority.*)

19–8. Agency Relationships. Jane Westmas was killed when a tree branch cut by Creekside Tree Service, Inc., fell on her. At the time, Jane was walking on a public path through the private property of Conference Point Center on the shore of Lake Geneva in Wisconsin. Conference Point had contracted with Creekside to trim and remove trees from its property, but the owner had no control of the details of Creekside's work. Jane's husband, John, and her son, Jason, filed a suit in a Wisconsin state court against Creekside, alleging that the service's negligence caused her death. Creekside contended that it was immune from the suit under a state statute providing that "no . . . agent of an owner is liable for the death of . . . a person engaging in a recreational activity on the owner's property." Could Creekside be held liable for Jane's death? Why or why not? [*Westmas v. Creekside Tree Service, Inc.*, 2018 WI 12, 379 Wis.2d 471, 907 N.W.2d 68 (2018)] (See *Agency Law.*)

19–9. Liability for Agent's Torts. Steven Henderson slipped and fell after stepping out of his car near a worksite, allegedly sustaining injuries. Henderson later sued Atmos Energy Corporation, claiming that Atmos was vicariously liable for the worksite conditions. The work had been performed by Miller Pipeline, LLC, an independent subcontractor for Atmos. Louisiana law states that a principal is not liable for the torts of an independent contractor unless the principal exercises operational control over, or expressly or impliedly authorizes, the independent contractor's actions. The contract

between Atmos and Miller contained an independent contractor provision and a termination-at-will provision. Atmos's only liability on termination was to pay Miller the unpaid balance due for work performed. Should the court rule in favor of Atmos? Why or why not? [*Henderson v. Atmos Energy Corporation*, 2022 WL 3657191 (5th Cir. 2022)] (See *Liability for Torts and Crimes.*)

19–10. A Question of Ethics—The IDDR Approach and Agency Relationships. The sale of insurance is a highly specialized field that requires considerable training, education, and skill. American Family Insurance Company sells its products through a network of insurance agents. At the start of their tenure, the agents sign an agreement stating that they are independent contractors. They work out of their own offices, set their own hours, provide the resources to run their offices, and hire and pay their own staff members. The agents file their taxes as independent contractors and deduct their expenses as self-employed business owners. American Family requires the agents to file daily activity reports, prioritize the sale of certain policies, and engage in specific sales tactics. The company approves the agents' office locations and imposes qualifications on their staff members. The agents are paid in commissions. Walid Jammal and other agents filed a suit in a federal district court against American Family, claiming that the company classified them as independent contractors to deprive them of employee benefits. [*Jammal v. American Family Insurance Co.*, 914 F.3d 449 (6th Cir. 2019)] (See *Agency Law.*)

(a) Use the IDDR approach to consider the ethics of American Family's decision not to provide its agents with employee benefits.

(b) Apply the criteria used by the courts to decide whether the agents in this case should be categorized as employees or independent contractors.

Time-Limited Group Assignment

19–11. Liability for Independent Contractor's Torts. Dean Brothers Corp. owns and operates a steel drum manufacturing plant. Lowell Wyden, the plant superintendent, hired Best Security Patrol, Inc. (BSP), a security company, to guard Dean property and "deter thieves and vandals." Some BSP security guards, as Wyden knew, carried firearms. Pete Sidell, a BSP security guard, was not certified as an armed guard but nevertheless came to work with his gun (in a briefcase).

While working at the Dean plant on October 31, Sidell fired his gun at Tyrone Gaines, in the belief that Gaines was an intruder. The bullet struck and killed Gaines. Gaines's mother filed a lawsuit claiming that her son's death was the result of BSP's negligence, for which Dean was responsible. (See *Liability in Agency Relationships.*)

(a) The first group will determine what the plaintiff's best argument is to establish that Dean is responsible for BSP's actions.

(b) The second group will discuss Dean's best defense and formulate arguments to support it.

(c) The third group will consider slightly different facts. Suppose that Dean Brothers had an express policy prohibiting all security guards from carrying firearms on its property and that Wyden had told BSP about this policy. Nevertheless, Sidell had brought his weapon to work and then fired it, killing Gaines. Could Dean be held responsible for negligence in that situation? Explain.

Chapter 20

Employment Law

Until the early 1900s, most employer–employee relationships were governed by the common law. Even today, under the common law employment-at-will doctrine, private employers have considerable freedom to hire and fire workers at will, regardless of the employees' performance.

Numerous statutes and administrative agency regulations now also govern the workplace. Thus, to a large extent, statutory law has displaced common law doctrines. In this chapter and the next, we look at the most significant laws regulating employment relationships.

Note that the distinction made under agency law between employee status and independent-contractor status is important here. The employment laws that will be discussed apply only to the employer–employee relationship. They do not apply to independent contractors.

Suppose that Josip works as an activities director for Valley Manor, a retirement community that offers several independent- and assisted-living options. As director, Josip normally spends his days at the Manor, where he hires and supervises other employees. One day, though, when another employee calls in sick, Josip accompanies residents on an excursion to a local art museum.

During the trip, Josip falls down some cement stairs and breaks his pelvis. He is taken by ambulance to a hospital, where he is told that he will need surgery and likely have a long recovery time. Does Josip qualify for workers' compensation coverage, or did this injury occur outside the scope of his employment? What about the time he will need to take off from work—is Josip entitled to take unpaid medical leave under federal law? If he takes unpaid leave, can he return to his original position afterward? These are some of the employment issues that will be discussed in this chapter.

20–1 Employment at Will

Employment relationships have traditionally been governed by the common law doctrine of **employment at will.** Under this doctrine, either party may terminate the employment relationship at any time and for any reason, unless doing so violates an employee's statutory or contractual rights.

Today, the majority of U.S. workers continue to have the legal status of "employees at will." In other words, this common law doctrine is still in widespread use, and only one state (Montana) does not apply it.

Nonetheless, federal and state statutes governing employment relationships prevent the doctrine from being applied in a number of circumstances. An employer may not fire an employee if doing so would violate a federal or state statute, such as a law prohibiting employment discrimination.

20–1a Common Law Exceptions to the Employment-at-Will Doctrine

As noted, statutory law has affected the application of the employment-at-will doctrine. In addition, the courts have carved out various exceptions to the doctrine based on contract theory, tort theory, and public policy.

Exceptions Based on Contract Theory Some courts have held that an implied employment contract exists between the employer and the employee. An employee who is fired outside the terms of the implied contract may succeed in an action for breach of contract even though no written employment contract exists.

■ **Example 20.1** BDI Enterprises' employment manual and personnel bulletin both state that, as a matter of policy, workers will be dismissed only for good cause. Julie Chin is an employee at BDI. If Chin reasonably expects BDI to follow this policy, a court may find that there is an implied contract based on the terms stated in the manual and bulletin. ■ Generally, the key consideration in determining whether an employment manual creates an implied contractual obligation is the employee's reasonable expectations.

An employer's oral promises to employees regarding discharge policy may also be considered part of an implied contract. If the employer fires a worker in a manner contrary to what was promised, a court may hold that the employer has violated the implied contract and is liable for damages.

Exceptions Based on Tort Theory In some situations, the discharge of an employee may give rise to an action for wrongful discharge (discussed shortly) under tort theories. Abusive discharge procedures may result in a lawsuit for intentional infliction of emotional distress or defamation. In addition, some courts have permitted workers to sue their employers under the tort theory of fraud. Fraud might be alleged when an employer made false promises to a prospective employee.

■ **Example 20.2** Goldfinch Consulting, Inc., induces Brianna to leave a lucrative job and move to another state by offering her "a long-term job with a thriving business." In fact, Goldfinch is not only having significant financial problems but is also planning a merger that will result in the elimination of the position offered to Brianna. If she takes the job in reliance on Goldfinch's representations and is fired shortly thereafter, Brianna may be able to bring an action against the employer for fraud. ■

Exceptions Based on Public Policy The most common exception to the employment-at-will doctrine is made on the basis that the employer's reason for firing the employee violates a fundamental public policy of the jurisdiction. Generally, the courts require that the public policy involved be expressed clearly in the statutory law governing the jurisdiction.

The public-policy exception may apply to an employee discharged for **whistleblowing**—that is, telling government authorities, upper-level managers, or the media that the employer is engaged in some unsafe or illegal activity. Normally, however, whistleblowers seek protection from retaliatory discharge under federal and state statutes, such as the Whistleblower Protection Act.[1]

■ **Case in Point 20.3** Dale Yurk was employed at Application Software Technology (AST) Corporation. He discovered that AST was planning to reuse and resell software that it had developed for the city of Detroit. Yurk

contacted his superiors—including the company's chief executive officer—and told them that he believed the resale infringed on the city's intellectual property rights. Shortly afterward, AST terminated Yurk's employment.

Yurk sued AST, alleging that the company had violated both the Whistleblower Protection Act and public policy. A federal district court held that Yurk had stated a claim under the Whistleblower Protection Act but dismissed the claim alleging that the company had violated public policy.[2] ■

20–1b Wrongful Discharge

Whenever an employer discharges an employee in violation of an employment contract or a statutory law protecting employees, the employee may bring an action for **wrongful discharge.** For instance, an employee who is terminated in retaliation for some protected activity, such as whistleblowing or participating in an employment-discrimination investigation, can sue for wrongful discharge.

Even if an employer's actions do not violate any provisions in an employment contract or statute, the employer may still be subject to liability. An employee can sue for wrongful discharge under a common law doctrine, such as a tort theory or agency. For instance, suppose that while firing an employee, an employer publicly discloses private facts about the employee's sex life. That employee could sue for wrongful discharge based on an invasion of privacy. Similarly, if salespersons are fired because they refuse to participate in falsifying consumers' credit applications as instructed by their employer, they can sue for wrongful discharge as a matter of public policy.[3]

20–2 Wages, Hours, and Layoffs

In the 1930s, Congress enacted several laws to regulate the wages and working hours of employees, including the following:

1. The Davis-Bacon Act[4] requires contractors and subcontractors working on federal government construction projects to pay "prevailing wages" to their employees.

1. 5 U.S.C. Sections 1201 *et seq.,* and 2302(b)(8) – (9).

2. *Yurk v. Application Software Technology Corp.,* 2017 WL 661014 (E.D.Mich. 2017).
3. See *Anderson v. Reeds Jewelers, Inc.,* 2017 WL 1987249 (E.D.Va. 2017). See also *Jones v. McLaren Medical Management, Inc.,* 2022 WL 5264754 (Mich. App. 2022).
4. 40 U.S.C. Sections 276a–276a-5.

2. The Walsh-Healey Act[5] applies to U.S. government contracts. It requires that a minimum wage, as well as overtime pay at 1.5 times regular pay rates, be paid to employees of manufacturers or suppliers entering into contracts with agencies of the federal government.

3. The Fair Labor Standards Act (FLSA)[6] extended wage-hour requirements to cover all employers engaged in interstate commerce or in producing goods for interstate commerce. Certain other types of businesses were included as well. The FLSA, as amended, provides the most comprehensive federal regulation of wages and hours today.

20–2a Child Labor

The FLSA prohibits oppressive child labor. Restrictions on child labor differ by age group.

Children under fourteen years of age are allowed to do only certain types of work. They can deliver newspapers, work for their parents, and be employed in entertainment and (with some exceptions) agriculture. Children aged fourteen and fifteen are allowed to work, but not in hazardous occupations. There are also restrictions on how many hours per day and per week children in these age groups can work.

Working times and hours are not restricted for persons between the ages of sixteen and eighteen, but they cannot be employed in hazardous jobs. None of these restrictions apply to persons over the age of eighteen.

20–2b Minimum Wages

The FLSA provides that a **minimum wage** must be paid to covered nonexempt employees. Most states also have minimum wages. More than half of the states have set their minimum wages above the federal minimum wage. When the state minimum wage is greater than the federal minimum wage, the employee is entitled to the higher wage. ■ **Example 20.4** Seattle, Washington, has one of the highest minimum wages in the country, at between $16.50 and $18.69 an hour. Various studies have shown that Seattle employees who worked in low-paying jobs when this minimum wage went into effect saw their take-home pay increase or stay the same while working fewer hours. At the same time, the higher minimum wage likely discouraged new hires in certain fields and caused employers to provide new hires with fewer hours of work. In other words, employers reacted to the higher labor costs in a rational manner. ■

5. 41 U.S.C. Sections 35–45.
6. 29 U.S.C. Sections 201–260.

20–2c Tipped Workers

When an employee receives tips while on the job, the FLSA gives employers a tip credit toward the minimum wage amount. The employer is required to pay only $2.13 an hour in direct wages—if that amount, plus the tips received, equals at least the federal minimum wage. If an employee's tips and direct wages do not equal the federal minimum wage, the employer must make up the difference. Note that some states have enacted laws to prevent employers from including tips in the minimum wage. In these states, tipped workers receive the regular minimum wage.

20–2d Tip-Sharing Systems

In the early 2020s, the Department of Labor issued a series of regulations concerning tips and tip sharing. When service employees are paid the full minimum wage and take no tip credit, employees who are not tipped can participate in a tip pool. This applies to, for example, cooks and dishwashers in restaurants. An employer that collects tips to create a mandatory tip pool must fully distribute the tips within the pay period. The goal of the new regulations is to reduce wage disparities among all workers who contribute to customers' experiences.

The new regulations reemphasize the fact that an employer cannot keep employees' tips under any circumstances. Also, managers and supervisors may not keep tips received by employees, including through tip pools.

20–2e Overtime Provisions and Exemptions

Under the FLSA, employees who work more than forty hours per week must be paid no less than 1.5 times their regular pay for all hours worked over forty. The FLSA overtime provisions apply only after an employee has worked more than forty hours per week. Therefore, employees who work ten hours a day, four days per week, are not entitled to overtime pay.

Certain employees are exempt from the FLSA's overtime provisions. These employees generally include executive, administrative, and professional employees, as well as outside salespersons and those who create computer code. Executive and administrative employees are those whose primary duty is management and who exercise discretion and independent judgment.

■ **Case in Point 20.5** A group of cable technicians working for HD and Associates (HDA) alleged that they did not receive overtime pay in violation of the Fair Labor Standards Act. A federal district court granted summary judgment in favor of HDA. It ruled that the technicians and HDA were not covered by federal legislation and that, even if they were, they qualified for a bona fide exemption (which was based on the fact that they were earning the equivalent of commissions and not hourly wages) and were therefore exempt from the overtime provisions. The technicians appealed. The appeals court found that the technicians were paid the same amount per repair job, no matter how much time they spent. Therefore, the faster they finished their repairs, the more work orders they were allowed to engage in. The court found that as a result, the HDA technicians were paid a bona fide commission and were therefore exempt from federal overtime requirements.[7] ■

Along with exempt employees, workers who make more than a specified amount are not eligible for overtime pay under the FLSA. An employer can voluntarily pay overtime to ineligible employees but cannot waive or reduce the overtime requirements of the FLSA.

The question in the following case was whether an auto dealer's service advisors fit within the FLSA overtime-pay exemption.

---

7. *Taylor v. HD and Associates, L.L.C.*, 45 F.4th 833 (5th Cir. 2022).

Case 20.1

Encino Motorcars, LLC v. Navarro

Supreme Court of the United States, 584 U.S. __, 138 S.Ct. 1134, 200 L.Ed.2d 433 (2018).

Background and Facts Encino Motorcars, LLC, owned a Mercedes-Benz dealership in California. Encino employed service advisors whose duties included suggesting repair and maintenance services, recording service orders, following up with customers as the services are performed, and explaining all the work performed, among other functions.

Some of Encino's service advisors, including Hector Navarro, filed a suit against Encino in a federal district court, alleging that the dealership had violated the Fair Labor Standards Act (FLSA) by failing to pay them overtime. Encino argued that the FLSA's exemption from the overtime-pay requirement applied to Navarro and its other service advisors. The court agreed and dismissed the complaint. The U.S. Court of Appeals for the Ninth Circuit reversed the dismissal. Encino appealed to the United States Supreme Court.

In the Language of the Court
Justice THOMAS delivered the opinion of the Court.
* * * *

The FLSA exempts from its overtime-pay requirement "any salesman, partsman, or mechanic primarily engaged in selling or servicing automobiles, trucks, or farm implements, if he is employed by a nonmanufacturing establishment primarily engaged in the business of selling such vehicles or implements to ultimate purchasers." The parties agree that [Encino] is a "nonmanufacturing establishment primarily engaged in the business of selling [automobiles] to ultimate purchasers." The parties also agree that a service advisor is not a "partsman" or "mechanic," and that a service advisor is not "primarily engaged * * * in selling automobiles." The question, then, is whether service advisors are "salesmen * * * primarily engaged in * * * servicing automobiles." We conclude that they are.
* * * *

A service advisor is obviously a "salesman." The term "salesman" is not defined in the statute, so we give the term its ordinary meaning. The ordinary meaning of "salesman" is someone who sells goods or services. Service advisors do precisely that. * * * Service advisors sell customers services for their vehicles.
* * * *

Service advisors are also "primarily engaged in * * * servicing automobiles." The word "servicing" in this context can mean either the action of maintaining or repairing a motor vehicle, or the action of providing a service. Service advisors satisfy both definitions. Service advisors are integral to the servicing process. * * * If you ask the average customer who services his car, the primary, and perhaps only, person he is likely to identify is his service advisor.

True, service advisors do not spend most of their time physically repairing automobiles. But the statutory language is not so constrained. All agree that partsmen, for example, are "primarily engaged in * * * servicing automobiles." But partsmen, like service advisors, do not spend most of their time under the hood. Instead, they obtain the vehicle parts * * * and provide those parts to the mechanics. In other words, the phrase "primarily engaged in * * * servicing automobiles" must include some individuals who do not physically repair automobiles themselves but who are integrally involved in the servicing process. That description applies to partsmen and service advisors alike.

Decision and Remedy The United States Supreme Court reversed the federal appellate court's decision and remanded the case. Navarro and the other service advisors were exempt from the overtime-pay requirement of the FLSA and thus not entitled to overtime pay.

Critical Thinking

- **Legal Environment** The salesmen, mechanics, and partsmen identified in the FLSA exemption work irregular hours, sometimes away from their principal work site. Service advisors typically work ordinary, fixed schedules on-site. Should the Court have considered these attributes in making its decision in the Encino case? Discuss.
- **What If the Facts Were Different?** Suppose that the FLSA exemption covered "any salesman or mechanic primarily engaged in selling or servicing automobiles" but not "any partsman." Would the result have been different? Explain.

20–2f Interaction of State and Federal Wage and Overtime Laws

State legislation may include rules that impact federal wage and overtime laws. For instance, if a state requires employers to give employees one day off per week, an employee who works that day may be entitled to overtime wages.

■ **Case in Point 20.6** Christopher Mendoza and Meagan Gordon were Nordstrom employees in California. Nordstrom had asked both Mendoza and Gordon to fill in for other employees. As a result, both had worked more than six consecutive days without receiving a day off. California state law prohibits employers from causing employees "to work more than six days in seven." The employees filed suit against Nordstrom, Inc., and the case ultimately came before the California Supreme Court.

At issue was whether the law applies on a calendar basis, with each workweek considered a fixed unit, or on a rolling basis. If the rolling basis was used, as Nordstrom argued that it should be, employees could work more than six consecutive days if on average they had one day off per seven. The state's highest court held that Nordstrom had violated California's law. Employees are entitled to one day off each workweek, not one day in seven on a rolling basis. Employees could choose to work the seventh day, but employers could not encourage or force them to do so, the court said.[8] ■

20–2g Layoffs

The Worker Adjustment and Retraining Notification (WARN) Act[9] applies to employers with at least one hundred full-time employees. The act requires these employers to provide sixty days' notice before implementing a mass layoff or closing a plant that employs more than fifty full-time workers. A mass layoff is a layoff of at least one-third of the full-time employees at a particular job site.

The WARN Act is intended to give workers advance notice so that they can start looking for new jobs while they are still employed. It is also intended to alert state agencies so that they can provide training and other resources for displaced workers. Employers thus must provide advance notice of the layoff both to the affected workers and to state and local government authorities. (An employer may notify the workers' union representative, if the workers are members of a labor union.) Even companies that anticipate filing for bankruptcy normally must provide notice under the WARN Act.

An employer that violates the WARN Act can be fined up to $500 for each day of the violation. Employees can recover back pay for each day of the violation (up to sixty days), plus reasonable attorneys' fees.

During the COVID-19 pandemic, many businesses either were forced to shut down or lost so much business that they laid off many employees. Some lawsuits were filed by employees, arguing that such layoffs were undertaken in violation of the WARN Act. Employers countered that the COVID-19 layoffs were a form of natural disaster, which constitutes an exemption to the WARN Act.

20-3 Family and Medical Leave

The Family and Medical Leave Act (FMLA)[10] allows employees to take time off work for family or medical reasons or in certain situations that arise from military

---

8. *Mendoza v. Nordstrom, Inc.,* 2 Cal.5th 1074, 216 Cal.Rptr.3d 889, 393 P.3d 375 (2017). See also *Barragan v. Home Depot U.S.A., Inc.,* 2021 WL 3634851 (S.D. CA 2021).
9. 29 U.S.C. Sections 2101 *et seq.*
10. 29 U.S.C. Sections 2601, 2611–2619, 2651–2654.

service. A majority of the states have similar legislation. The FMLA does not supersede any state or local law that provides more generous protection.

20–3a Coverage and Applicability

The FMLA requires employers that have fifty or more employees to provide unpaid leave for specified reasons. (Some employers voluntarily offer paid family leave, but this is not a requirement of the FMLA.) The FMLA expressly covers private and public (government) employees who have worked for their employers for at least a year.

An eligible employee may take up to twelve weeks of leave within a twelve-month period for any of the following reasons:

1. To care for a newborn baby within one year of birth.
2. To care for an adopted or foster child within one year of the time the child is placed with the employee.
3. To care for the employee's spouse, child, or parent who has a serious health condition.
4. If the employee suffers from a serious health condition and is unable to perform the essential functions of the job.
5. For any qualifying exigency (nonmedical emergency) arising out of the fact that the employee's spouse, son, daughter, or parent is a covered military member on active duty.[11] For instance, an employee can take leave to arrange for child care or to deal with financial or legal matters when a spouse is being deployed overseas.

In addition, an employee may take up to twenty-six weeks of military caregiver leave within a twelve-month period to care for a family member with a serious injury or illness incurred as a result of military duty.[12]

20–3b Benefits and Protections

When an employee takes FMLA leave, the employer must continue the worker's healthcare coverage on the same terms as if the employee had continued to work. On returning from FMLA leave, most employees must be restored to their original position or to a comparable position (with nearly equivalent pay and benefits, for instance). An important exception allows the employer to avoid reinstating a key employee—defined as an employee whose pay falls within the top 10 percent of the firm's workforce.

20–3c Violations

An employer that violates the FMLA can be required to provide various remedies, including the following:

1. Damages to compensate the employee for lost wages and benefits, denied compensation, and actual monetary losses (such as the cost of providing care for a family member). Compensatory damages are available up to an amount equivalent to the employee's wages for twelve weeks.
2. Job reinstatement.
3. Promotion, if a promotion has been denied.

A successful plaintiff is also entitled to court costs and attorneys' fees. In addition, if the plaintiff shows that the employer acted in bad faith, the plaintiff can receive two times the amount of damages awarded by a judge or jury. Supervisors can also be held personally liable, as employers, for violations of the act.

Employers generally are required to notify employees when an absence will be counted against FMLA leave. If an employer fails to provide such notice, and that failure to notify causes harm to the employee, the employer can be sanctioned.[13]

20–4 Health, Safety, and Income Security

Under the common law, employees who were injured on the job had to file lawsuits against their employers to obtain recovery. Today, numerous state and federal statutes protect employees from the risk of accidental injury, death, or disease resulting from their employment. In addition, the government protects employees' income through Social Security, Medicare, unemployment insurance, and the regulation of pensions and health insurance plans.

20–4a The Occupational Safety and Health Act

At the federal level, the primary legislation protecting employees' health and safety is the Occupational Safety and Health Act,[14] which is administered by the Occupational Safety and Health Administration (OSHA). The act imposes on employers a general duty to keep the workplace safe.

---

11. 29 C.F.R. Section 825.126.
12. 29 C.F.R. Section 825.200.

13. This was the United States Supreme Court's holding in *Ragsdale v. Wolverine World Wide, Inc.,* 535 U.S. 81, 122 S.Ct. 1155, 152 L.Ed.2d 167 (2002). See also *Towamencin Township v. Pennsylvania Labor Relations Board,* 2022 WL 5370672 (PA Commonwealth Ct. 2022).
14. 29 U.S.C. Sections 553, 651–678.

To this end, OSHA has established specific safety standards that employers must follow, depending on the industry. For instance, OSHA regulations require the use of safety guards on certain mechanical equipment. Regulations also set maximum levels of exposure to substances in the workplace that may be harmful to workers' health.

■ **Case in Point 20.7** James Bobo worked at the Tennessee Valley Authority (TVA) nuclear power plant for more than twenty-two years. He eventually contracted asbestos-induced lung cancer. After his death, his wife, Barbara, was diagnosed with malignant mesothelioma. She sued TVA in federal court, alleging that its negligence had resulted in her being exposed to "take-home" asbestos when she washed her husband's work clothes over the years. Although she died prior to trial, her children continued the suit.

At trial, the plaintiffs proved that TVA knew about OSHA regulations—adopted during the time of James's employment—to protect not only workers but also their families. These rules were aimed at preventing asbestos fibers from clinging to an employee's street clothes, skin, or hair and being taken off TVA property. The court held in favor of the plaintiffs and awarded $3.3 million. TVA appealed. A federal appellate court affirmed that TVA was liable for failing to follow OSHA regulations but remanded the case for a recalculation of the damages awarded.[15] ■

---

15. *Bobo v. Tennessee Valley Authority,* 855 F.3d 1294 (11th Cir. 2017). See also *Walsh v. Walmart, Inc.,* 49 F.4th 821 (2nd Cir. 2022).

Notices, Records, and Reports The Occupational Safety and Health Act requires that employers post certain notices in the workplace, maintain specific records, and submit reports. Employers with eleven or more employees are required to keep occupational injury and illness records for each employee. Each record must be made available for inspection when requested by an OSHA compliance officer.

Whenever a work-related fatality or serious injury requiring hospitalization occurs, employers must report directly to OSHA. The employer must notify OSHA within eight hours if an employee dies and submit a report within twenty-four hours for any inpatient hospitalization, amputation, or loss of an eye. A company that fails to do so will be fined. Following the incident, a complete inspection of the premises is mandatory.

Inspections OSHA compliance officers may enter and inspect the facilities of any establishment covered by the Occupational Safety and Health Act. Employees may also file complaints of violations. Under the act, an employer cannot discharge an employee who files a complaint or who, in good faith, refuses to work in a high-risk area if bodily harm or death might result.

In the following case, an employer cited for an OSHA violation tried to minimize its own fault by focusing the court's attention on the injured employee's failure to follow workplace safety rules.

Case 20.2

Packers Sanitation Services, Inc. v. Occupational Safety and Health Review Commission

United States Court of Appeals, Eleventh Circuit, 795 Fed.Appx. 814 (2020).

Background and Facts Packers Sanitation Services, Inc., provides cleaning services to a poultry processing facility in Gainesville, Georgia. At the facility is a machine known as a quill puller for removing the tail feathers of a chicken. A Packers employee hosing down the quill puller stepped too close to the machine. Its rotating augers caught the employee's glove, pulled in his hand, and amputated a fingertip.

The Occupational Safety and Health Administration investigated the accident and cited Packers for failing to appropriately guard the quill puller. Packers contested the citation, arguing that the injured employee had violated a workplace rule requiring each employee to stay at least two feet away from an active quill puller.

After a hearing, an administrative law judge (ALJ) affirmed the violation. The Occupational Safety and Health Review Commission declined to review the ALJ's decision. Packers appealed to the U.S. Court of Appeals for the Eleventh Circuit.

Case 20.2 Continues

Case 20.2 Continued

In the Language of the Court

PER CURIAM:

* * * *

* * * [Under federal regulations] Packers was required to provide one or more methods of machine guarding to protect the operator from hazards such as ingoing nip points. * * * The machine-guarding standard requires physical guarding.

The quill puller's two augurs form an ingoing nip point. * * * Due to operational necessity, it was reasonably predictable that an employee would enter the zone of danger near that nip point. The injured employee in this case was tasked with hosing down the quill puller to knock off larger pieces of debris. There was no external line or barrier marking a two-foot distance from the machine—the safe distance that Packers identified. Nor was there a hard physical barrier preventing the employee from accessing the nip point. As such, * * * it was reasonably predictable that the employee would inadvertently veer too close to the nip point.

Packers' argument that the employee would have faced no danger had he observed the two-foot rule is likewise unsuccessful. To the extent that it seeks to blame the injured employee for failing to follow that rule, Packers misses the mark. The machine-guarding standard would mean little if a company could escape responsibility merely by reminding its employees to stay a safe distance from dangerous machines. After all, common human errors such as neglect, distraction, inattention or inadvertence [carelessness], which might cause an employee to enter the zone of danger, are part of the basis for the standards in the first place.

* * * *

The only remaining issue as to the machine-guarding standard, then, is whether Packers was aware of the dangerous condition. * * * That the company was aware of the hazard [was evidenced by the fact that] supervisors walked past the quill puller regularly and could easily see that it lacked the necessary physical guards.

Decision and Remedy The U.S. Court of Appeals for the Eleventh Circuit upheld the ALJ's determination. "Sufficient evidence supported the ALJ's findings underlying its conclusion that Packers violated the machine-guarding standard."

Critical Thinking

- **Legal Environment** As a defense to the citation for an OSHA violation, Packers argued that the injured employee violated the proximity rule. Was this defense relevant to the question before the court? Discuss.

- **What If the Facts Were Different?** Suppose that in this case the employee had refused to clean the unguarded quill puller, and Packers had discharged him before the accident took place. Would the result have been different? Explain.

20–4b State Workers' Compensation Laws

State **workers' compensation laws** establish an administrative procedure for compensating workers injured on the job. Instead of suing, an injured worker files a claim with the state agency or board that administers local workers' compensation claims.

All states require employers to provide workers' compensation insurance, but the specific rules vary by state. Most states have a state fund that employers pay into for workers' compensation coverage. Usually, employers can purchase insurance from a private insurer as an alternative to paying into the state fund. Most states also allow certain employers to be self-insured—that is, employers that show an ability to pay claims do not need to buy insurance.

No state covers all employees under its workers' compensation statute. Typically, domestic workers, agricultural workers, temporary employees, and employees of common carriers (companies that provide transportation services to the public) are excluded. Minors are covered.

Requirements for Receiving Workers' Compensation In general, the only requirements to recover benefits under state workers' compensation laws are:

1. The existence of an employment relationship.
2. An accidental injury that occurred on the job or in the course of employment, regardless of fault. (An injury that occurs while an employee is commuting to or from work usually is not covered.)

■ **Example 20.8** Dynea USA, Inc., required its employees to wear steel-toed boots for safety. The boots caused employee Tony Schrader to develop a sore on his leg. The skin over Schrader's sore broke, and within a week, he was hospitalized with a methicillin-resistant staphylococcus aureus (MRSA) infection. He filed a workers' compensation claim. Dynea argued that Schrader's injury did not occur on the job because the MRSA bacteria that caused the infection were on Schrader's skin before he came to work. Nevertheless, Schrader was entitled to workers' compensation benefits. Dynea required its employees to wear the boots that caused the sore on Schrader's leg, which subsequently became infected with MRSA. Even if the bacteria were on Schrader's skin before he came to work, it was the rubbing of the boot at work that caused the sore through which the bacteria entered his body. Therefore, the injury occurred on the job, and Schrader qualified for workers' compensation. ■

Injured employees must notify their employer promptly (usually within thirty days of the accident). Generally, an employee must also file a workers' compensation claim within a certain period (sixty days to two years) from the time the injury is first noticed, rather than from the time of the accident.

Workers' Compensation Versus Litigation An employee who accepts workers' compensation benefits may not sue for injuries caused by the employer's negligence. By barring lawsuits for negligence, workers' compensation laws also prevent employers from avoiding liability by using defenses such as contributory negligence or assumption of risk. A worker may sue an employer who intentionally injures the worker, however.

20–4c Income Security

Federal and state governments participate in insurance programs designed to protect employees and their families from the financial impact of retirement, disability, death, hospitalization, and unemployment. The key federal law in this area is the Social Security Act.[16]

Social Security The Social Security Act provides for old-age (retirement), survivors', and disability insurance. The act is therefore often referred to as OASDI. Retired workers who are covered by Social Security receive monthly payments from the Social Security Administration, which administers the Social Security Act. Social Security benefits are fixed by statute but increase automatically with increases in the cost of living.

Medicare Medicare is a federal government health-insurance program administered by the Social Security Administration for people sixty-five years of age and older and for some under age sixty-five who are disabled. It originally had two parts, one pertaining to hospital costs and the other to nonhospital medical costs, such as visits to physicians' offices. It now offers additional coverage options and a prescription-drug plan. People who have Medicare hospital insurance can obtain additional federal medical insurance if they pay monthly premiums.

Tax Contributions Under the Federal Insurance Contributions Act (FICA),[17] both employers and employees contribute to Social Security and Medicare, although the contributions are determined differently. The employer withholds the employee's FICA contributions from the employee's wages and ordinarily matches the contributions.

For Social Security, the basis for the contributions is the employee's annual wage base—the maximum amount of the employee's wages that is subject to the tax. The wage threshold changes annually. The Social Security tax rate is currently 12.4 percent, but the rate changes periodically.

The Medicare tax rate is 2.9 percent. Unlike Social Security, Medicare has no cap on the amount of wages subject to the tax. So even if an employee's salary is well above the cap for Social Security, the employee will still owe Medicare tax on the total earned income.

For Social Security and Medicare together, typically the employer and the employee each pay 7.65 percent. This is equivalent to 6.2 percent (half of 12.4 percent) for Social Security plus 1.45 percent (half of 2.9 percent) for Medicare up to the maximum wage

---

16. 42 U.S.C. Sections 301–1397e.
17. 26 U.S.C. Sections 3101–3125.

base (which usually changes every year). Any earned income above that threshold is taxed only for Medicare. Self-employed persons pay both the employer's and the employee's portions of the Social Security and Medicare taxes. Additionally, under the Affordable Care Act, high-income earners are subject to an additional Medicare tax.

Private Retirement Plans The major federal statute that regulates employee retirement plans is the Employee Retirement Income Security Act (ERISA).[18] This act empowers a branch of the U.S. Department of Labor to enforce its provisions governing employers that have private pension funds for their employees. ERISA does not require an employer to establish a pension plan. When a plan exists, however, ERISA provides standards for its management.

ERISA created the Pension Benefit Guaranty Corporation (PBGC), an independent federal agency, to provide timely and uninterrupted payment of voluntary private pension benefits. The pension plans pay annual insurance premiums (at set rates adjusted for inflation) to the PBGC, which then pays benefits to participants in the event that a plan is unable to do so.

A key provision of ERISA concerns vesting. **Vesting** gives employees a legal right to receive pension benefits when they stop working. Before ERISA was enacted, some employees who had worked for companies for many years received no pension benefits when their employment terminated, because those benefits had not vested. Under ERISA, generally all employee contributions to pension plans vest immediately. Employee rights to employer contributions vest after five years of employment.

Unemployment Insurance The Federal Unemployment Tax Act (FUTA)[19] created a state-administered system that provides unemployment compensation to eligible individuals who have lost their jobs. The FUTA and state laws require employers that fall under the provisions of the act to pay unemployment taxes at regular intervals. The proceeds from these taxes are then paid out to qualified unemployed workers.

To be eligible for unemployment compensation, a worker must be willing and able to work. Normally, workers must be actively seeking employment to continue receiving benefits. Workers who have been fired for

misconduct or who have voluntarily left their jobs are not generally eligible for benefits.

■ **Example 20.9** Eleni works for Bailey Snowboards in Vermont. One day at work, Eleni receives a text from her son saying that he has been taken to the hospital. Eleni rushes to the hospital and does not return to work for several days. Bailey hires someone else for Eleni's position, and Eleni files for unemployment benefits. Eleni's claim will be denied because she left her job voluntarily and made no effort to maintain contact with her employer. ■

COBRA The Consolidated Omnibus Budget Reconciliation Act (COBRA)[20] enables employees to continue, for a limited time, their healthcare coverage after they are no longer eligible for group health-insurance plans. The workers—not the employers—pay the premiums for the continued coverage.

COBRA prohibits an employer from eliminating a worker's medical, vision, or dental insurance when the worker's employment is terminated or when a reduction in the worker's hours would affect coverage. Termination of employment may be voluntary or involuntary. Only workers fired for gross misconduct are excluded from protection. Employers, with some exceptions, must inform employees of COBRA's provisions before the termination or reduction of work hours.

A worker has sixty days from the date on which the group coverage would stop to decide whether to continue with the employer's group insurance plan. If the worker chooses to continue coverage, the employer is obligated to keep the policy active for up to eighteen months (twenty-nine months if the worker is disabled). The coverage must be the same as that provided to the worker (and the worker's family members) prior to the termination or reduction of work. An employer that does not comply with COBRA risks substantial penalties, including a tax of up to 10 percent of the annual cost of the group plan or $500,000, whichever is less.

After some workers lost their COBRA coverage because of the length of the COVID-19 pandemic, the Biden administration instituted a temporary subsidy plan called ARPA-21 COBRA premium assistance. This subsidy, which is no longer in effect, was available only to individuals eligible for COBRA.

Employer-Sponsored Group Health Plans The Health Insurance Portability and Accountability Act (HIPAA)[21] contains provisions that affect employer-sponsored group health plans. For instance, HIPAA

18. 29 U.S.C. Sections 1001 *et seq.*
19. 26 U.S.C. Sections 3301–3310.
20. 29 U.S.C. Sections 1161–1169.
21. 29 U.S.C. Sections 1181 *et seq.*

restricts the manner in which employers collect, use, and disclose the health information of employees and their families. Employers must designate privacy officials, distribute privacy notices, and train employees to ensure that employees' health information is not disclosed to unauthorized parties.

Failure to comply with HIPAA regulations can result in civil penalties of up to $100 per person per violation (with a cap of $25,000 per year). Employers are also subject to criminal prosecution for certain types of HIPAA violations. An employer can face up to $250,000 in criminal fines and imprisonment for up to ten years if convicted.

Affordable Care Act The Affordable Care Act[22] (commonly referred to as *Obamacare*) requires most employers with fifty or more full-time employees to offer health-insurance benefits. Under the act, any business offering health benefits to its employees (even if not legally required to do so) may be eligible for tax credits of up to 35 percent to offset the costs.

An employer who fails to provide health benefits as required under the statute can be fined up to $2,000 for each employee after the first thirty people. (This is known as the *50/30 rule:* Employers with fifty employees must provide insurance, and those failing to do so will be fined for each employee after the first thirty.) An employer who offers a plan that costs an employee more than 9.5 percent of the employee's income may be assessed a penalty.

20–5 Employee Privacy Rights

Concerns about the privacy rights of employees have arisen as employers have purportedly used invasive tactics to monitor and screen workers. Perhaps the greatest privacy concern in employment today involves electronic monitoring of employees' activities.

20–5a Electronic Monitoring

More than half of employers engage in some form of electronic monitoring of their employees. Many employers review employees' e-mail, as well as their social media posts and other internet messages. Employers may also make video recordings of their employees at work,

record their telephone conversations, and listen to their voice mail.

Employee Privacy Protection Employees of private (nongovernment) employers have some privacy protection under tort law and state constitutions. In addition, state and federal statutes may limit an employer's conduct in certain respects. For instance, the Electronic Communications Privacy Act prohibits employers from intercepting an employee's personal electronic communications unless they are made on devices and systems furnished by the employer.

Nonetheless, employers do have considerable leeway to monitor employees in the workplace. In addition, private employers generally are free to use filtering software to block access to certain websites, such as sites containing sexually explicit images. The First Amendment's protection of free speech prevents only government employers from restraining speech by blocking websites.

Reasonable Expectation of Privacy When determining whether an employer should be held liable for violating an employee's privacy rights, the courts generally weigh the employer's interests against the employee's reasonable expectation of privacy. Normally, if employees have been informed that their communications are being monitored, they cannot reasonably expect those interactions to be private. In addition, a court will typically hold that employees do not have a reasonable expectation of privacy when using a system (such as an intranet or internal e-mail system) provided by the employer.

If employees are not informed that certain communications are being monitored, the employer may be held liable for invading their privacy. Most employers that engage in electronic monitoring notify their employees about the monitoring. Nevertheless, a general policy may not sufficiently protect an employer monitoring forms of communications that the policy fails to mention. For instance, notifying employees that their e-mails and phone calls may be monitored does not necessarily protect an employer who monitors social media posts or text messages.

20–5b Other Types of Monitoring

In addition to monitoring their employees' online activities, employers also engage in other types of employee screening and monitoring. The practices discussed next have often been challenged as violations of employee privacy rights.

---

22. Pub. L. No. 111-148, 124 Stat. 119, March 23, 2010, codified in various sections of 42 U.S.C.

Lie-Detector Tests At one time, many employers required employees or job applicants to take polygraph examinations (lie-detector tests). Today, the Employee Polygraph Protection Act[23] generally prohibits employers from requiring employees or job applicants to take lie-detector tests or suggesting or requesting that they do so. The act also restricts employers' ability to use or ask about the results of any lie-detector test or to take any negative employment action based on the results.

Certain employers are exempt from these prohibitions. Federal, state, and local government employers, and certain security service firms, may conduct polygraph tests. In addition, companies that manufacture and distribute controlled substances may perform lie-detector tests. Other employers may use polygraph tests when investigating losses attributable to theft, including embezzlement and the theft of trade secrets.

Drug Testing In the interests of public safety and to reduce unnecessary costs, many employers, including the government, require their employees to submit to drug testing.

Public Employers. Government (public) employers are constrained in drug testing by the Fourth Amendment

to the U.S. Constitution, which prohibits unreasonable searches and seizures. Drug testing of public employees is allowed by statute for transportation workers, however. Courts normally uphold drug testing of certain employees when drug use in a particular job may threaten public safety. Also, when there is a reasonable basis for suspecting public employees of drug use, courts often find that drug testing does not violate the Fourth Amendment.

Private Employers. The Fourth Amendment does not apply to drug testing conducted by private employers. Hence, the privacy rights and drug testing of private-sector employees are governed by state law. Many states have statutes that allow drug testing by private employers but restrict when and how the testing may be performed. A collective bargaining agreement may also provide protection against drug testing (or may authorize drug testing in certain conditions).

The permissibility of testing a private employee for drugs often hinges on whether the employer's testing was reasonable. Random drug tests and even "zero-tolerance" policies (which deny a "second chance" to employees who test positive for drugs) have been held to be reasonable. It is also reasonable to require employees of private employers who are under contract with the federal government to undergo standard background investigations to disclose potential drug use.

---

23. 29 U.S.C. Sections 2001 *et seq.*

Practice and Review: Employment Law

Rick Saldona worked as a traveling salesperson for Aimer Winery. Sales constituted 90 percent of Saldona's work time. Saldona worked an average of fifty hours per week but received no overtime pay. Saldona had worked for Aimer for ten years when his new supervisor, Caesar Braxton, claimed that he had been inflating his reported sales calls and required him to submit to a polygraph test. Saldona reported Braxton to the U.S. Department of Labor, which prohibited Aimer from requiring Saldona to take a polygraph test for this purpose.

Shortly after that, Saldona's wife, Venita, fell from a ladder and sustained a head injury while employed as a full-time agricultural harvester. Saldona presented Aimer's human resources department with a letter from his wife's physician indicating that she would need daily care for several months, and Saldona took leave for three months. Aimer had sixty-three employees at that time. When Saldona returned to Aimer, he was informed that his position had been eliminated because his sales territory had been combined with an adjacent territory. Using the information presented in the chapter, answer the following questions.

1. Would Saldona have been legally entitled to receive overtime pay at a higher rate? Why or why not?
2. What is the maximum length of time Saldona would have been allowed to take leave to care for his injured spouse?
3. Under what circumstances would Aimer have been allowed to require an employee to take a polygraph test?
4. Would Aimer likely be able to avoid reinstating Saldona under the *key employee* exception? Why or why not?

Debate This ... The U.S. labor market is highly competitive, so state and federal laws that require overtime pay are unnecessary and should be abolished.

Terms and Concepts

employment at will 437
minimum wage 439

vesting 446
whistleblowing 438

workers' compensation laws 444
wrongful discharge 438

Issue Spotters

1. American Manufacturing Company (AMC) issues an employee handbook that states that employees will be discharged only for good cause. One day, Greg, an AMC supervisor, says to Larry, "I don't like your looks. You're fired." Can AMC be held liable for breach of contract? If so, why? If not, why? (See *Employment at Will*.)

2. Erin, an employee of Fine Print Shop, is injured on the job. For Erin to obtain workers' compensation, must her injury have been caused by Fine Print's negligence? Does it matter whether the action causing the injury was intentional? Explain. (See *Health, Safety, and Income Security*.)

• **Check your answers to the Issue Spotters against the answers provided in Appendix B at the end of this text.**

Business Scenarios and Case Problems

20–1. Family and Medical Leave Act. Serge worked for Service Attendant Corporation (SAC). He requested time off under the Family and Medical Leave Act (FMLA) from April 29 through May 31 to undergo treatment for alcoholism. For the month of May, he was hospitalized as part of the treatment. When he did not return to work on June 1, SAC fired him. Did SAC violate Serge's rights under the FMLA? Explain your answer. (See *Family and Medical Leave*.)

20–2. Wrongful Discharge. Denton and Carlo were employed at an appliance plant. Their job required them to perform occasional maintenance work while standing on a wire mesh twenty feet above the plant floor. Other employees had fallen through the mesh, and one of them had been killed by the fall. When their supervisor told them to perform tasks that would likely involve walking on the mesh, Denton and Carlo refused because they feared they might suffer bodily injury or death. Because they refused to do the requested work, the two employees were fired from their jobs. Was their discharge wrongful? If so, under what federal employment law? To what federal agency or department should they turn for assistance? (See *Employment at Will*.)

20–3. Spotlight on Coca Cola—Family and Medical Leave Act. Jennifer Willis worked for Coca Cola Enterprises, Inc. (CCE), in Louisiana as a senior account manager. On a Monday in May 2003, Willis called her supervisor to tell him that she was sick and would not be able to work that day. She also said that she was pregnant, but she did not say she was sick because of the pregnancy. On Tuesday, she called to ask where to report to work and was told that she could not return without a doctor's release. She said that she had a doctor's appointment on "Wednesday," which her supervisor understood to be the next day. Willis meant the following Wednesday.

For more than a week, Willis did not contact CCE. When she returned to work, she was told that she had violated CCE's "No Call/No Show" policy. Under this policy "an employee absent from work for three consecutive days

without notifying the supervisor during that period will be considered to have voluntarily resigned." She was fired.

Willis filed a suit in a federal district court against CCE under the Family and Medical Leave Act (FMLA). To be eligible for FMLA leave, an employee must inform an employer of the reason for the leave. Did Willis meet this requirement? Did CCE's response to Willis's absence violate the FMLA? Explain. [*Willis v. Coca Cola Enterprises, Inc.*, 445 F.3d 413 (5th Cir. 2006)] (See *Family and Medical Leave*.)

20–4. Exceptions to the Employment-at-Will Doctrine. Li Li worked for Packard Bioscience, and Mark Schmeizl was her supervisor. Schmeizl told Li to call Packard's competitors, pretend to be a potential customer, and request "pricing information and literature." Li refused to perform the assignment. She told Schmeizl that she thought the work was illegal and recommended that he contact Packard's legal department. Although a lawyer recommended against the practice, Schmeizl insisted that Li perform the calls. Moreover, he later wrote negative performance reviews because she was unable to get the requested information when she called competitors and identified herself as a Packard employee. Several months later, Li was terminated on Schmeizl's recommendation. Can Li bring a claim for wrongful discharge? Why or why not? [*Li Li v. Canberra Industries*, 134 Conn.App. 448, 39 A.3d 789 (2012)] (See *Employment at Will*.)

20–5. Business Case Problem With Sample Answer—Unemployment Compensation. Fior Ramirez worked as a housekeeper for Remington Lodging & Hospitality, a hotel in Atlantic Beach, Florida. After her father in the Dominican Republic suffered a stroke, she asked her employer for time off to be with him. Ramirez's manager, Katie Berkowski, refused the request. Two days later, Berkowski received a call from Ramirez to say that she was with her father. He died about a week later, and Ramirez returned to work, but Berkowski told her that she had abandoned her position. Ramirez applied for unemployment compensation. Under the applicable state statute, "an employee is disqualified from receiving benefits if he or she voluntarily left work without good cause." Does Ramirez qualify for benefits? Explain. [*Ramirez v. Reemployment Assistance Appeals Commission*, 39 Fla.L.Weekly D317, 135 So.3d 408 (1 Dist. 2014)] (See *Health, Safety, and Income Security*.)

- For a sample answer to Problem 20–5, go to Appendix C at the end of this text.

20–6. Unemployment Compensation. Jefferson Partners, LP, entered into a contract (known as a collective bargaining agreement) with the Amalgamated Transit Union. Under the contract, drivers had to either join the union or pay a fair share—85 percent—of union dues, which were used to pay for administrative costs incurred by the union. An employee who refused to pay was subject to discharge. Jefferson hired Tiffany Thompson to work as a bus driver. When told about the requirement, Thompson said that she thought it was unfair and illegal. She refused either to join the union or to pay the dues. More than two years later, she was fired on the ground that her continued refusal constituted misconduct. Is Thompson eligible for unemployment compensation? Explain. [*Thompson v. Jefferson Partners, LP*, 2016 WL 953038 (Minn.Ct.App. 2016)] (See *Health, Safety, and Income Security*.)

20–7. Family and Medical Leave. To qualify for leave under the Family and Medical Leave Act (FMLA), an employee must comply with their employer's usual and customary notice requirements, including call-in policies. Robert Stein, an employee of Atlas Industries, Inc., tore his meniscus (a knee injury) at work. Stein took medical leave to have surgery on the knee. Ten weeks into his recovery, Stein's doctor notified Atlas that Stein could return to work with light-duty restrictions in two days. Stein, however, thought he was on leave for several more weeks. Atlas company policy provided that employees who missed three workdays without notification were subject to automatic termination. Stein did not return to work or call in as Atlas expected. Four days later, he was fired. Did Stein's discharge violate the FMLA? Discuss. [*Stein v. Atlas Industries, Inc.*, 730 Fed.Appx. 313 (6th Cir. 2018)] (See *Family and Medical Leave*.)

20–8. A Question of Ethics—The IDDR Approach and Employee Privacy Rights. Scherer Design Group, LLC (SDG), provides telecommunications services. Chad Schwartz, an SDG employee, sought to obtain an ownership stake in the firm. When this proved unsuccessful, Schwartz quit to start a competing firm, Ahead Engineering, LLC, and recruited Daniel Hernandez, an SDG colleague, to join him. Hernandez used an SDG computer to transmit his employer's client information to Schwartz's firm via Facebook. One of SDG's largest clients, ExteNet, left SDG to become Schwartz's client. After Hernandez resigned, SDG used his company laptop to surreptitiously (secretively) access his Facebook account, which revealed the actions Hernandez had taken to secure SDG's client information and trade secrets. SDG filed a suit in a federal district court against Schwartz's firm and Hernandez, claiming a breach of the duty of loyalty and seeking an injunction to stop their solicitation of SDG's clients. The defendants argued that SDG's "hacking" of Hernandez's Facebook account barred the plaintiff's right to injunctive relief (under the equitable doctrine of unclean hands). [*Scherer Design Group, LLC v. Ahead Engineering, LLC*, 764 Fed.Appx. 147 (3d Cir. 2019)] (See *Employee Privacy Rights*.)

(a) Use the IDDR approach to evaluate the ethics of SDG's decision to access Hernandez's Facebook account.

(b) Should SDG's use of a company laptop to access Hernandez's Facebook account bar SDG's right to an injunction? Explain.

Time-Limited Group Assignment

20–9. Wrongful Discharge. Stefan Sorril, a health teacher at Madison Middle School and a triathlete, appeared shirtless and showed off his "ripped" body as an extra on an episode of a new reality TV show. A week after the show aired, school officials called him into the district office and asked for his resignation. Sorril later claimed that he was pressured and coerced into resigning. He said the school officials had informed him that—as a result of his appearance on the show—he would no longer be offered tenure (a senior academic's contractual right not to be terminated without just cause). Sorril subsequently sued for wrongful discharge. (See *Employment at Will*.)

(a) The first group will discuss whether Sorril was an employee at will and how that status would affect his claim.

(b) The second group will determine if Sorril can assert any of the exceptions to the employment-at-will doctrine.

(c) The third group will decide whether the school district should be held liable for wrongful discharge and explain its reasoning.

Chapter 21

Employment Discrimination

Out of the 1960s civil rights movement to end racial and other forms of discrimination grew a body of law protecting employees against discrimination in the workplace. Legislation, judicial decisions, and administrative agency actions restrict employers from discriminating against workers on the basis of race, color, religion, national origin, gender, sexual orientation, age, or disability. A class of persons defined by one or more of these criteria is known as a **protected class.**

Several federal statutes prohibit **employment discrimination** against members of protected classes. The most important is Title VII of the Civil Rights Act.[1] Title VII prohibits employment discrimination on the basis of

race, color, religion, national origin, gender, and sexual orientation. The Age Discrimination in Employment Act[2] and the Americans with Disabilities Act[3] prohibit discrimination on the basis of age and disability, respectively. The protections afforded under these laws also extend to U.S. citizens who are working abroad for U.S. firms or for companies that are controlled by U.S. firms.

Suppose that Ellie, a manager at a large accounting firm, is up for promotion. Ellie's job performance reviews have been uniformly positive, with one superior calling her an "outstanding professional" with "strong character and integrity." Furthermore, Ellie has

recently played a key role in the firm's winning a multi-million-dollar contract with a local professional sports team.

After failing to get the promotion, Ellie learns that she is not popular among some of her co-workers. Specifically, Ellie discovers a series of memos in which some of the firm's male partners complain that she is too "manly" and needs "a course at charm school." One partner writes that, to get promoted, Ellie would need to "walk, talk, and dress more femininely and wear make-up." Can Ellie sue for employment discrimination? Are the memos sufficient evidence to prove that she was not promoted because of her gender? These are the kinds of questions that will be answered in this chapter.

1. 42 U.S.C. Sections 2000e–2000e-17.

2. 29 U.S.C. Sections 621–634.

3. 42 U.S.C. Sections 12102–12118.

21–1 Title VII of the Civil Rights Act

Title VII of the Civil Rights Act prohibits job discrimination against employees, applicants, and union members on the basis of race, color, national origin, religion, gender, and sexual orientation at any stage of employment. Title VII bans discrimination in the hiring process, discipline procedures, discharge, promotion, and benefits.

Title VII applies to employers with fifteen or more employees and labor unions with fifteen or more members. It also applies to labor unions that operate hiring halls (where members go regularly to be assigned jobs), employment agencies, and state and local governing units or agencies. The United States Supreme Court has ruled that an employer with fewer than fifteen employees is not automatically shielded from a lawsuit filed under

Title VII.[4] In addition, the act prohibits discrimination in most federal government employment. When Title VII applies to the employer, any employee—including an undocumented worker—can bring an action for employment discrimination.

21–1a The Equal Employment Opportunity Commission

The Equal Employment Opportunity Commission (EEOC) monitors compliance with Title VII. An employee alleging discrimination must file a claim with the EEOC before a lawsuit can be brought against the

4. *Arbaugh v. Y&H Corp.,* 546 U.S. 500, 126 S.Ct. 1235, 163 L.Ed.2d 1097 (2006). Thousands of more recent cases have been based in part on this decision. See, for example, *Weingeist v. Pickled Punk Sublease LLC,* 2023 WL 1434267 (S.D. NY 2023).

employer. The EEOC may investigate the dispute and attempt to obtain the parties' voluntary consent to an out-of-court settlement. If a voluntary agreement cannot be reached, the EEOC may file a suit against the employer on the employee's behalf.

■ **Example 21.1** Luis, who is of Puerto Rican descent, gets a job at an Albertson's grocery store in San Diego. A training video instructs employees not to speak Spanish if there is a non-Spanish-speaking customer present. On his third day at Albertson's, Luis is reprimanded by a supervisor for speaking Spanish to a Latino customer. Later, Luis is prohibited from speaking Spanish with his co-workers during breaks. He is also harassed by some other employees for speaking Spanish at any time.

Luis files a claim with the EEOC because of this treatment. In turn, the EEOC sues Albertson's, alleging that its enforcement of an unwritten, blanket "speak-English-only" policy is a form of national origin discrimination against Hispanic and Latino employees under Title VII. ■

The EEOC does not investigate every claim of employment discrimination. Generally, it takes only "priority cases," such as cases involving retaliatory discharge (firing an employee in retaliation for submitting a claim to the EEOC) and cases involving types of discrimination that are of particular concern to the EEOC. If the EEOC decides not to investigate a claim, the EEOC issues a "right to sue" that allows the employee to bring a lawsuit against the employer.

21–1b Limitations on Class Actions

The United States Supreme Court issued an important decision that limited the rights of employees to bring discrimination claims against their employer as a group, or class. The Court held that to bring a class action, employees must prove a company-wide policy of discrimination that had a common effect on all the plaintiffs covered by the action.[5]

21–1c Intentional and Unintentional Discrimination

Title VII of the Civil Rights Act prohibits both intentional and unintentional discrimination.

Intentional Discrimination Intentional discrimination by an employer against an employee is known as **disparate-treatment discrimination.** Because intent may sometimes be difficult to prove, courts have

established certain procedures for resolving disparate-treatment cases.

A plaintiff who sues on the basis of disparate-treatment discrimination must first make out a ***prima facie* case.** *Prima facie* is Latin for "at first sight" or "on its face." Legally, it refers to a fact that is presumed to be true unless contradicted by evidence.

Establishing a *Prima Facie* Case. To establish a *prima facie* case of disparate-treatment discrimination in hiring, a plaintiff must show all of the following:

1. The plaintiff is a member of a protected class.
2. The plaintiff applied and was qualified for the job in question.
3. The plaintiff was rejected by the employer.
4. The employer continued to seek applicants for the position or filled the position with a person not in a protected class.

A plaintiff who can meet these relatively easy requirements has made out a *prima facie* case of illegal discrimination in hiring and will win in the absence of a legally acceptable employer defense.

Sometimes, current and former employees make claims of discrimination. When employees allege that the employer fired or took some other adverse employment action against them, the same basic requirements apply. To establish a *prima facie* case, the plaintiffs must show that they were fired or treated adversely for discriminatory reasons.

Burden-Shifting Procedure. Once the *prima facie* case is established, the burden shifts to the employer-defendant, who must articulate a legal reason for not hiring the plaintiff. (Again, this also applies to firing and other adverse employment actions.) If the employer did not have a legal reason for taking the adverse employment action, the plaintiff wins.

If the employer can articulate a legitimate reason for the action, the burden shifts back to the plaintiff. To prevail, the plaintiff must then show that the employer's reason is a pretext (not the true reason) and that the employer's decision was actually motivated by discriminatory intent.

Unintentional Discrimination Employers often use interviews and tests to choose from among a large number of applicants for job openings. Minimum educational requirements are also common. These practices and procedures may have an unintended discriminatory impact on a protected class. **Disparate-impact discrimination** occurs when a protected group of people is adversely affected by an employer's practices, procedures, or tests, even though they do not appear to be discriminatory.

---

5. *Wal-Mart Stores, Inc. v. Dukes,* 564 U.S. 338, 131 S.Ct. 2541, 180 L.Ed.2d 374 (2011). See a negative outcome in *Elson v. Black,* 56 F.4th 1002 (5th Cir. 2023).

In a disparate-impact discrimination case, the complaining party must first show that the employer's practices, procedures, or tests are effectively discriminatory. Once the plaintiff has made out a *prima facie* case, the burden of proof shifts to the employer to show that the practices or procedures in question were justified.

There are two ways of showing that an employer's practices, procedures, or tests are effectively discriminatory—that is, that disparate-impact discrimination exists.

Pool of Applicants. A plaintiff can prove a disparate impact by comparing the employer's workforce to the pool of qualified individuals available in the local labor market. The plaintiff must show that (1) as a result of educational or other job requirements or hiring procedures, (2) the percentage of nonwhites, women, or members of other protected classes in the employer's workforce (3) does not reflect the percentage of that group in the pool of qualified applicants. A plaintiff who can show a connection between the practice and the disparity has made out a *prima facie* case and need not provide evidence of discriminatory intent.

Rate of Hiring. A plaintiff can also prove disparate-impact discrimination by comparing the employer's selection rates of members and nonmembers of a protected class (nonwhites and whites, for instance, or women and men). When an educational or other job requirement or hiring procedure excludes members of a protected class from an employer's workforce at a substantially higher rate than nonmembers, discrimination occurs.

Under EEOC guidelines, a selection rate for a protected class that is less than four-fifths, or 80 percent, of the rate for the group with the highest rate of hiring generally is regarded as evidence of disparate impact. ■ **Example 21.2** Shady Cove District Fire Department administers an exam to applicants for the position of firefighter. At the exam session, one hundred white applicants take the test, and fifty pass and are hired—a selection rate of 50 percent. At the same exam session, sixty minority applicants take the test, but only twelve pass and are hired—a selection rate of 20 percent. Because 20 percent is less than four-fifths (80 percent) of 50 percent, the test will be considered discriminatory under EEOC guidelines. ■

21–1d Discrimination Based on Race, Color, and National Origin

Title VII prohibits employers from discriminating against employees or job applicants on the basis of race, color, or national origin. Race is interpreted broadly to apply to the ancestry or ethnic characteristics of a group of persons,

such as Native Americans. National origin refers to discrimination based on a person's birth in another country or the person's ancestry or culture.

■ **Case in Point 21.3** Larisa Thompson was born in Russia. She worked for Little America Hotel Co. for over a decade and became a gift store supervisor in the retail department. Late in that period, a co-worker was promoted to become her immediate supervisor. Thompson had a history of problems in following rules and interacting with coworkers and was frequently disciplined by her new supervisor. She was eventually terminated for a variety of reasons, including disobeying her general manager, who had been coaching her for more than a year to improve her actions and attitude. After she was fired, she filed suit against her employer, claiming that her supervisor had demonstrated anti-Russian bias. She argued that all of the supervisor's complaints about her employee activities were pretextual and that the real reason was anti-Russian hostility. A federal trial court ruled in favor of Little America's request for summary judgment. Thompson appealed. The Court of Appeals for the Tenth Circuit affirmed, holding that no reasonable juror could conclude that Little America's stated reasons for terminating Thompson were a mere pretext.[6] ■

Reverse Discrimination Title VII also protects against "reverse discrimination"—that is, discrimination against members of a majority group, such as white males. ■ **Case in Point 21.4** Montana's Department of Transportation receives federal funds for transportation projects. As a condition of receiving the funds, Montana was required to set up a program to avoid discrimination and promote awarding contracts to disadvantaged business enterprises (DBEs). DBEs are businesses owned by members of socially and economically disadvantaged groups, such as minority groups. Mountain West Holding Company, Inc., installs signs, guardrails, and concrete barriers on highways in Montana and competes against DBEs for contracts.

Mountain West sued the state in federal court for violating Title VII by giving preference to DBEs. At trial, the court pointed out that any classifications based on race are permissible "only if they are narrowly tailored measures that further compelling governmental interests." Montana thus had the burden of showing that its DBE program met this requirement. To show that the DBE program addressed actual discrimination, the state presented a study that reported disparities in state-awarded contracts and provided anecdotal evidence of a "good ol'

6. *Thompson v. Little America Hotel Co.,* 2022 WL 10832885 (10th Cir. 2022).

boys'" network within the state's contracting industry. The district court accepted this evidence and concluded that Montana had satisfied its burden. A federal appellate court reversed, though, finding that the evidence was insufficient to prove a history of discrimination that would justify the preferences given to DBEs.[7] ■

Potential Section 1981 Claims Victims of racial or ethnic discrimination may also have a cause of action under 42 U.S.C. Section 1981. This section, which was enacted in 1866 to protect the rights of freed slaves, prohibits discrimination on the basis of race or ethnicity in the formation or enforcement of contracts. Because employment is often a contractual relationship, Section 1981 can provide an alternative basis for a plaintiff's action and is potentially advantageous because there is no limit on the damages that can be awarded. (There are some caps on damages under Title VII, as will be discussed later in this chapter.)

21–1e Discrimination Based on Religion

Title VII of the Civil Rights Act also prohibits government employers, private employers, and unions from discriminating against persons because of their religion. Employers cannot treat their employees more or less favorably based on their religious beliefs or practices. In addition, they cannot require employees to participate in any religious activity or forbid them from participating in one.

Reasonable Accommodation An employer must "reasonably accommodate" the religious practices and sincerely held religious beliefs of its employees, unless to do so would cause undue hardship to the employer's business. An employee's religion might prohibit the employee from working on a certain day of the week, for instance, or at a certain type of job. Reasonable accommodation is required even if the belief is not based on the doctrines of a traditionally recognized religion, such as Christianity or Judaism, or of a denomination, such as Baptist.
■ **Example 21.5** Tomilina, who is Jewish, works as a hairdresser for Sally's Salon. Two weeks before Yom Kippur, Tomilina asks Sally if she can have a day off on the Jewish holiday, which always falls on a Saturday. Sally denies the request. Tomilina fails to show up for work on Yom Kippur, and Sally fires her. When Tomilina sues Sally for religious discrimination, Sally presents two defenses. First, reasonably accommodating Tomilina's request would have caused undue hardship, because Saturday is the salon's busiest day of the week and Sally needs all her employees serving customers. Second, Tomilina is not a religious person, and the day off was really for personal reasons. If Tomilina can show that (a) she was able to reschedule her Saturday appointments, and (b) her religious beliefs are sincere, then she will most likely prevail in her Title VII suit against Sally. ■

Undue Hardship A reasonable attempt to accommodate does not necessarily require the employer to make every change an employee requests or to make a permanent change for an employee's benefit. An employer is not required to make an accommodation that would cause the employer undue hardship.
■ **Case in Point 21.6** Leontine worked as an administrative assistant in the emergency department at Children's Hospital Boston. The hospital started requiring all employees who worked in or had access to patient-care areas to receive the influenza (flu) vaccine. When Leontine, who had taken a tetanus vaccine, refused to get the flu vaccine based on her religious beliefs, the hospital terminated her employment. Leontine filed a lawsuit alleging religious discrimination. The hospital argued that allowing Leontine to keep her patient-care position without receiving the vaccine would create an undue hardship. The court agreed and granted a summary judgment for the hospital.[8] ■

21–1f Discrimination Based on Gender

Under Title VII and other federal acts, employers are forbidden from discriminating against employees on the basis of gender. Employers are prohibited from classifying or advertising jobs as male or female unless they can prove that the gender of the applicant is essential to the job. In addition, employers cannot have separate male and female seniority lists and cannot refuse to promote employees based on their gender.

Gender Must Be a Determining Factor Generally, to succeed in a suit for gender discrimination, a plaintiff must demonstrate that gender was a determining factor in the employer's decision to hire, fire, or promote the plaintiff. Typically, this involves looking at all of the surrounding circumstances.
■ **Case in Point 21.7** Evangeline Parker received multiple promotions at Reema Consulting Services, Inc. (RCSI). In response, a jealous co-worker told other employees that Parker had received the promotions

7. *Mountain West Holding Co., Inc. v. State of Montana,* 691 Fed.Appx. 326 (9th Cir. 2017). See also *Holland v. Mercy Health,* 2022 WL 2783886 (6th Cir. 2022).

8. *Robinson v. Children's Hospital Boston,* 2016 WL 1337255 (D.Mass. 2016). See also *Aukamp-Corcoran v. Lancaster General Hospital,* 106 Empl. Prac. Dec. P 46, 940, 2022 Fair Empl.Prac.Cas. 55838 (E.D. PA 2022).

because she had sex with a superior. After this false rumor spread, Parker was informed that she had become ineligible for further advancement because of the "situation" that she had brought to the workplace.

A trial court barred Parker's gender discrimination lawsuit, finding that RCSI's actions, while reprehensible, were based on her alleged conduct (the affair with her superior), not her gender. A federal appeals court disagreed, emphasizing the continuing power of the cultural stereotype that women use sex to succeed in the business world. This same stereotype does not apply to successful men. Therefore, the court ruled, gender was a possible determining factor in RCSI's conduct toward Parker, and her lawsuit could proceed.[9] ■

The Federal Bureau of Investigation (FBI) requires that its applicants meet certain physical fitness standards. For women, the standards include the ability to complete a minimum of fourteen push-ups. Men must be able to complete at least thirty. Whether this difference constituted discrimination on the basis of gender was at issue in the following case.

---

9. *Parker v. Reema Consulting Services, Inc.*, 915 F.3d 297 (4th Cir. 2019). See a different result in *Gaines v. Baltimore Police Department*, 2022 WL 1451629 (D. MD 2022).

Case Analysis 21.1

Bauer v. Lynch
United States Court of Appeals, Fourth Circuit, 812 F.3d 340 (2016).

In the Language of the Court
KING, Circuit Judge.
* * * *

The FBI [Federal Bureau of Investigation] trains its Special Agent recruits at the FBI Academy in Quantico, Virginia. * * * All Trainees must pass a physical fitness test (the "PFT").

* * * The FBI requires every Special Agent recruit to pass the PFT twice: once to gain admission to the Academy, and a second time to graduate.
* * * *

* * * Trainees * * * need to satisfy the following standards * * * :

Event	Men	Women
Sit-ups	38	35
300-meter sprint	52.4s	64.9s
Push-ups	30	14
1.5-mile run	12m, 42s	13m, 5s

* * * *

After the attacks of September 11, 2001, * * * Jay Bauer resolved to contribute to the defense of our country by becoming a Special Agent in the FBI. [At the time,] he * * * served as an assistant professor at the University of Wisconsin–Milwaukee.

* * * Bauer took the PFT for the first time and failed. Although he achieved sixteen points on the test, Bauer completed only twenty-five push-ups * * * . The FBI allowed Bauer to retest [three months later] and he passed, that time completing thirty-two push-ups. With his fitness screening complete, the FBI invited Bauer to report to the Academy.

Week	Sit-ups	300-meter sprint (sec.)	Push-ups	1.5-mile run (min.)	Total Points
1	40 (2)	42.6 (8)	26 (0)	10:49 (4)	14
7	47 (4)	43.4 (7)	25 (0)	10:24 (5)	16
14	50 (6)	43.7 (7)	28 (0)	10:45 (4)	17
18	51 (6)	43.8 (7)	27 (0)	11:09 (4)	17
22	49 (5)	44.1 (6)	29 (0)	10:57 (4)	15

Bauer's time at the Academy largely showed great potential for a career as a Special Agent. He passed all academic tests, demonstrated proficiency in his firearms and defensive tactics training, and met all expectations for the practical applications and skills components of the Academy. Bauer's classmates also selected him as the class leader and spokesperson for the Academy graduation. Unfortunately, Bauer faced a dilemma: he was unable to pass the PFT at Quantico.

During his twenty-two weeks at the Academy, Bauer took the PFT five times. On each occasion, he would have passed but for his failure to achieve the minimum standard for push-ups. Bauer's results, and his corresponding point scores for each event, were as follows:

Following his final failure of the PFT, Bauer * * * was [allowed to] resign with the possibility of future employment with the FBI * * * . Bauer * * * immediately signed a resignation letter. Two weeks later, the FBI offered Bauer a position as an Intelligence Analyst in its Chicago Field Office. He accepted and has been employed in that position since.
* * * *

* * * Bauer filed this Title VII action in [a federal district court] against [Loretta Lynch,] the Attorney General. According to the claims in Bauer's complaint, the FBI's use of the gender-normed PFT standards contravened * * * Title VII * * * which prohibits sex discrimination by federal employers.
* * * *

Case 21.1 Continues

Case 21.1 Continued

In his summary judgment motion, Bauer maintained that the FBI's use of the gender-normed PFT standards was facially discriminatory [discriminatory on its face—that is, obviously discriminatory].

* * * *

* * * The district court agreed with Bauer, granting his motion for summary judgment.

* * * *

The Attorney General * * * filed a timely * * * appeal.

* * * *

Title VII requires that any "personnel actions affecting employees or applicants for employment" taken by federal employers "shall be made free from any discrimination based on * * * sex." * * * A plaintiff is entitled to demonstrate discrimination by showing that the employer uses a facially discriminatory employment practice. [The Supreme Court has outlined] a "simple test" for identifying facial sex discrimination: such discrimination appears "where the evidence shows treatment of a person in a manner which but for that person's sex would be different."

* * * The district court applied [this] test and concluded that, because Bauer would have been held to a lower

minimum number of push-ups had he been a woman, the gender-normed PFT standards constitute facial sex discrimination. The Attorney General maintains on appeal, however, that because the PFT assesses an overall level of physical fitness, and equally fit men and women possess innate physiological differences that lead to different performance outcomes, the PFT's gender-normed standards actually require the same level of fitness for all Trainees. In that way, the Attorney General contends, the PFT standards do not treat the sexes differently and therefore do not contravene Title VII.

* * * *

* * * The Attorney General * * * maintains that * * * some differential treatment of men and women based upon inherent physiological differences is not only lawful but also potentially required.

* * * *

Men and women simply are not physiologically the same for the purposes of physical fitness programs. * * * Physical fitness standards suitable for men may not always be suitable for women, and accommodations addressing

physiological differences between the sexes are not necessarily unlawful.

* * * The physiological differences between men and women impact their relative abilities to demonstrate the same levels of physical fitness. In other words, equally fit men and women demonstrate their fitness differently. Whether physical fitness standards discriminate based on sex, therefore, depends on whether they require men and women to demonstrate different levels of fitness.

Put succinctly, an employer does not contravene [violate] Title VII when it utilizes physical fitness standards that distinguish between the sexes on the basis of their physiological differences but impose an equal burden of compliance on both men and women, requiring the same level of physical fitness of each. Because the FBI purports to assess physical fitness by imposing the same burden on both men and women, this rule applies to Bauer's Title VII claims. Accordingly, the district court erred in failing to apply the rule in its disposition of Bauer's motion for summary judgment.

* * * *

Pursuant to the foregoing, we vacate the judgment of the district court and remand for * * * further proceedings.

Legal Reasoning Questions

1. According to the reasoning of the court in the *Bauer* case, when do different employment standards for men and women satisfy Title VII's requirement of equality?
2. In what other circumstances might the rule in this case apply?
3. If Bauer had ultimately succeeded in his claim, what might the remedy have been? What else might have resulted?

Pregnancy Discrimination The Pregnancy Discrimination Act[10] expanded Title VII's definition of gender discrimination to include discrimination based on pregnancy. Women affected by pregnancy, childbirth, or related medical conditions must be treated the same as other persons not so affected but similar in ability to work. For instance, an employer cannot discriminate against a pregnant woman by withholding benefits available to others under employee benefit programs.

Post-Pregnancy Discrimination An employer must continue to reasonably accommodate an employee's

medical conditions related to pregnancy and childbirth even after the pregnancy has ended. ■ **Case in Point 21.8** Professional Ambulance, LLC, hired Allison Mayer as an emergency medical technician (EMT) while she was still breastfeeding an infant. She was supposed to work three twelve-hour shifts a week, but Professional did not provide her with a schedule so that she could arrange child care. Mayer informed Professional that she needed to take short breaks to use a pump to express breast milk. At first, her supervisor told her to take these breaks in the restroom, but Mayer objected because the conditions were unsanitary. Then she was told to take the breaks in an office that was not private or secure, which made her uncomfortable because the male EMTs could hear her pumping.

---

10. 42 U.S.C. Section 2000e(k).

A few weeks later, Professional fired Mayer, claiming that it was because other employees had complained that she was rude and abusive. The employer refused to provide her with further explanation and replaced her with a male EMT with fewer qualifications. Mayer sued. A federal district court found that Mayer had established a *prima facie* case of discrimination on the basis of pregnancy, childbirth, or related medical conditions.[11] ■

Wage Discrimination The Equal Pay Act[12] requires equal pay for male and female employees working at the same establishment doing similar work. To determine whether the Equal Pay Act has been violated, a court looks to the primary duties of the two jobs—the job content rather than the job description controls. If a court finds that the wage differential is due to "any factor other than gender," such as a seniority or merit system, then it does not violate the Equal Pay Act.

The Lilly Ledbetter Fair Pay Act made discriminatory wages actionable under federal law regardless of when the discrimination began.[13] Previously, plaintiffs had to file a complaint within a limited time period. Today, if a plaintiff continues to work for the employer while receiving discriminatory wages, the time period for filing a complaint is practically unlimited.

---

11. *Mayer v. Professional Ambulance, LLC*, 211 F.Supp.3d 408 (D.R.I. 2016). See a different decision in *Tsepenyuk v. Fred Alger & Company, Inc.*, 2022 Fair Empl.Prac.Cas. 107,403 (S.D. NY 2022).
12. 29 U.S.C. Section 206(d).
13. Pub. L. No. 111-2, 123 Stat. 5 (January 5, 2009), amending 42 U.S.C. Section 2000e-5[e].

Discrimination Against Transgender Persons In the past, most courts held that Title VII does not protect transgender persons from discrimination. The situation has changed, however. ■ **Case in Point 21.9** Dr. Deborah Fabian applied for a position as an on-call orthopedic surgeon at the Hospital of Central Connecticut. The hospital apparently declined to hire Fabian because she disclosed her identity as a transgender woman. Fabian sued the hospital alleging violations of Title VII of the Civil Rights Act and the Connecticut Fair Employment Practices Act (CFEPA).

The hospital filed a summary judgment motion, arguing that neither Title VII nor the Connecticut statute prohibits discrimination on the basis of transgender identity. The federal district court rejected this argument, however, finding that discrimination on the basis of transgender identity is discrimination on the basis of sex for Title VII purposes. Fabian was entitled to take her case to a jury and argue violations of Title VII and the CFEPA.[14] ■

The Supreme Court on June 15, 2020, in the case *Bostock v. Clayton County*,[15] ruled that an employer who fires an individual merely for being gay, lesbian, or transgender violates Title VII. In other words, adverse employment decisions based on gender identity are necessarily a form of gender discrimination and therefore illegal.

Is a corporation required to respect the pronouns that its employees choose? This is the question in the Ethics Today feature.

---

14. *Fabian v. Hospital of Central Connecticut*, 172 F.Supp.3d 509 (D.Conn. 2016).
15. 590 U.S. __, 140 S.Ct. 1731, 207 L.Ed.2d 218 (2020).

Ethics Today Should corporations regulate pronoun use in the workplace?

A former Nike employee, Jazz Lyles, self-identifies as transmasculine and chooses to be referred to by the pronouns they/them/their. After being repeatedly "misgendered," or denied a preferred gender identity, by co-workers, Lyles left Nike and filed a $1.1 million discrimination lawsuit against the company. Could this situation have been avoided?

Along with society at large, corporate America is being asked by many transgender and gender-nonconforming individuals to use pronouns other than he/him/his or she/her/hers. When this doesn't happen, according to one employment attorney, bias takes place in the form of "disbelief, disregard, and disrespect."

Federal law is unsettled about the extent to which Title VII covers gender identity pronouns, and only about half the states have legislation specifically addressing the issue. As a result, employers are often at a loss for guidance when it comes to resolving these disputes, particularly when one employee's religious beliefs clash with another's gender identity requirements. A solution favored by many human resources experts is a workplace policy based on the concept of respect. That is, employees do not have to "embrace or value" a colleague's choice of pronoun use, but they do have to respect it.

Critical Thinking How can companies avoid issues with correct pronouns to refer to their employees?

21–1g Constructive Discharge

The majority of Title VII complaints involve unlawful discrimination in decisions to hire or fire employees. In some situations, however, employees who leave their jobs voluntarily can claim that they were "constructively discharged" by the employer. **Constructive discharge** occurs when the employer causes the employee's working conditions to be so intolerable that a reasonable person in the employee's position would feel compelled to quit.

When constructive discharge is claimed, the employee can pursue damages for loss of income, including back pay. These damages ordinarily are not available to an employee who left a job voluntarily.

Proving Constructive Discharge To prove constructive discharge, an employee must present objective proof of intolerable working conditions. The employee must also show that the employer knew or had reason to know about these conditions yet failed to correct them within a reasonable time period. In addition, courts generally require the employee to show causation—that the employer's unlawful discrimination caused the working conditions to be intolerable. Put in a different way, the employee's resignation must be a foreseeable result of the employer's discriminatory action. Courts weigh the facts on a case-by-case basis.

Employee demotion is one of the most frequently cited reasons for a finding of constructive discharge, particularly when the employee was subjected to humiliation. ■ **Example 21.10** Khalil's employer humiliates him by informing him in front of his co-workers that he is being demoted to an inferior position. Khalil's co-workers then continually insult him, harass him, and make derogatory remarks to him about his national origin (he is from Iran). The employer is aware of this discriminatory treatment but does nothing to remedy the situation, despite Khalil's repeated complaints. After several months, Khalil quits his job and files a Title VII claim. In this situation, Khalil will likely have sufficient evidence to maintain an action for constructive discharge in violation of Title VII. ■

Applies to All Title VII Discrimination Plaintiffs can use constructive discharge to establish any type of discrimination claim under Title VII, including race, color, national origin, religion, gender, and pregnancy. It is most commonly asserted in cases involving sexual harassment. Constructive discharge may also be used in cases involving discrimination based on age or disability (discussed later in this chapter).

21–1h Sexual Harassment

Title VII also protects employees against **sexual harassment** in the workplace. Sexual harassment can take two forms:

1. *Quid pro quo* harassment occurs when sexual favors are demanded in return for job opportunities, promotions, salary increases, or other benefits. *Quid pro quo* is a Latin phrase that is often translated as "something in exchange for something else."

2. Hostile-environment harassment occurs when a pattern of sexually offensive conduct runs throughout the workplace and the employer has not taken steps to prevent or discourage it. Such harassment exists when the workplace is permeated with discriminatory intimidation, ridicule, and insult, and this harassment is so severe or pervasive that it alters the conditions of employment.

Harassment by Supervisors For an employer to be held liable for a supervisor's sexual harassment, the supervisor normally must have taken a tangible employment action against the employee. A **tangible employment action** is a significant change in employment status or benefits. Such an action occurs when an employee is fired, refused a promotion, demoted, or reassigned to a position with significantly different responsibilities, for instance. Only a supervisor, or another person acting with the authority of the employer, can cause this sort of harm. A constructive discharge also qualifies as a tangible employment action.

The United States Supreme Court issued several important rulings in cases alleging sexual harassment by supervisors that established what is known as the "*Ellerth/Faragher* affirmative defense."[16] The defense has two elements:

1. The employer must have taken reasonable care to prevent and promptly correct any sexually harassing behavior (by establishing effective harassment policies and complaint procedures, for instance).

2. The plaintiff-employee must have unreasonably failed to take advantage of preventive or corrective opportunities provided by the employer to avoid harm.

An employer that can prove both elements normally will not be liable for a supervisor's harassment.

---

16. *Burlington Industries, Inc. v. Ellerth,* 524 U.S. 742, 118 S.Ct. 2257, 141 L.Ed.2d 633 (1998); and *Faragher v. City of Boca Raton,* 524 U.S. 775, 118 S.Ct. 2275, 141 L.Ed.2d 662 (1998).

Retaliation by Employers Employers sometimes retaliate against employees who complain about sexual harassment or other Title VII violations. Retaliation can take many forms. An employer might demote or fire the person, or otherwise change the terms, conditions, and benefits of employment.

Title VII prohibits retaliation, and employees can sue their employers when it occurs. In a retaliation action, an individual claims to have suffered harm as a result of making a charge, testifying, or participating in a Title VII investigation or proceeding.

Requirements for Protection. To be protected under Title VII's retaliation provisions, the plaintiff must have opposed a practice prohibited by Title VII and suffered an adverse employment action as a result of that opposition. ■ **Example 21.11** Myrta is in a tenure-track teaching position at the University of Puerto Rico School of Law. At the end of her probationary period, she requests a one-year extension for her tenure review. The dean agrees but makes a statement calling her insecure, immature, and fragile. One of her colleagues comments that she shows poor judgment and exhibits personality flaws.

After Myrta complains in writing to the chancellor, the dean of the law school denies the one-year extension request. Myrta files a retaliation lawsuit, claiming that the dean retaliated against her for complaining to the chancellor about "discriminatory" comments made in the course of her request for an extension.

A court likely will hold that Myrta did not provide a reasonable foundation for a retaliation action. Under Title VII, an employer may not retaliate against an employee because that employee opposes a practice prohibited by Title VII. In fact, though, Myrta did not allege any facts that could be construed as gender-based discrimination. To be sure, the comments she complained about were hardly flattering, but they were entirely gender-neutral. Thus, she most likely was not engaging in protected conduct when she opposed the remarks. ■

Protection May Extend to Others. Title VII's retaliation protection extends to employees who speak out about discrimination against other employees during an employer's internal investigation. For instance, Title VII may protect an employee who is fired after his wife files a gender discrimination claim against their employer.

Harassment by Co-Workers and Others When the harassment of co-workers, rather than supervisors, creates a hostile working environment, an employee may still have a cause of action against the employer. Normally, though, the employer will be held liable only if management knew or should have known about the harassment and failed to take immediate remedial action.

Occasionally, a court may also hold an employer liable for harassment by nonemployees if the employer knew about the harassment and failed to take corrective action. ■ **Example 21.12** Jordan, who owns and manages a Great Bites restaurant, knows that one of his regular customers, Dean, repeatedly harasses Kaylia, a waitress. If Jordan does nothing and permits the harassment to continue, he may be liable under Title VII even though Dean is not an employee of the restaurant. ■

In the following case, a female firefighter claimed that her male co-workers subjected her to a hostile working environment and that the fire department knew about the harassment but failed to act. The city (the defendant) responded that there was no evidence to support this claim.

Case 21.2

Franchina v. City of Providence

United States Court of Appeals, First Circuit, 881 F.3d 32 (2018).

Background and Facts Lori Franchina, a rescue lieutenant with the Providence Fire Department in Rhode Island, was assigned to work a shift with fellow firefighter Andre Ferro. During the shift, Ferro subjected her to unprofessional sexual comments and conduct. Based on Franchina's account of Ferro's actions, fire chief Curt Varone filed an intra-department complaint charging Ferro with sexual harassment. No action was taken. Other firefighters then began to treat Franchina with contempt. She was spit on and shoved and was forced to undergo verbal assaults, insubordination, and other kinds of negative treatment. She submitted forty different complaints of harassment to her superiors.

Case 21.2 Continues

Case 21.2 Continued

Franchina filed a suit in a federal district court against the city of Providence, asserting that she was subjected to a hostile work environment as a result of her gender in violation of Title VII. The city argued that Franchina presented no evidence to support her claim. A jury issued a verdict in her favor and awarded damages. The city appealed.

In the Language of the Court

THOMPSON, Circuit Judge.

Sticks and stones may break some bones, but harassment can hurt forever.

* * * *

Here, Franchina presented a plethora [a great deal] of evidence showing that the impetus [motivation] for the discrimination she sustained was based in part on her being a female. In gender discrimination cases premised on a hostile work environment, Title VII permits a plaintiff to prove unlawful discrimination by demonstrating that the workplace is permeated with discriminatory intimidation, ridicule, and insult that is sufficiently severe or pervasive to alter the conditions of the victim's employment and create an abusive working environment. Evidence of sexual remarks, innuendos, ridicule, and intimidation may be sufficient to support a jury verdict for a hostile work environment. Here, there was repeated evidence that Franchina was called a "bitch," * * *, and "Frangina" [a combination of her last name and the word "vagina"]. The use of these words is inherently gender-specific and their repeated and hostile use * * * can reasonably be considered evidence of sexual harassment. In fact, a raft of case law * * * establishes that the use of sexually degrading, gender-specific epithets, such as "slut," * * *, "whore," and "bitch" * * *, has been consistently held to constitute harassment based upon sex. This case is no different. In fact, there was more.

There was also evidence that [within the fire department] women were treated as less competent; a treatment barred by Title VII. The critical issue, Title VII's text indicates, is whether members of one sex are exposed to disadvantageous terms or conditions of employment to which members of the other sex are not exposed. There was evidence that men treated women better when they were perceived as willing to have sex with them. There was evidence that Franchina was subjected to humiliating sexual remarks and innuendos by Ferro, including asking the plaintiff if she wanted to have babies and if he could help her conceive. This type of sexually based *animus* [hostility] is a hallmark of Title VII.

In sum, the jury heard evidence of repeated hostile, gender-based epithets, ill treatment of women as workers, sexual innuendoes, and preferential treatment for women who were more likely to sleep with the men of the department. This sampling of evidence demonstrates that the accumulated effect * * * taken together constitutes a hostile work environment.

Decision and Remedy The U.S. Court of Appeals for the First Circuit affirmed the judgment. "The abuse Lori Franchina suffered at the hands of the Providence Fire Department is nothing short of abhorrent * * * . Employers should be cautioned that turning a blind eye to blatant discrimination does not generally fare well under anti-discrimination laws like Title VII."

Critical Thinking

- **Economic** Because of the constant harassment, Franchina had to be placed on injured-on-duty status. Later, diagnosed with severe post-traumatic stress disorder and unable to work again as a rescue lieutenant, she "retired." What is the appropriate measure of damages for this result? Discuss.

- **Legal Environment** What steps might an employer take to avoid the circumstances that occurred in the Franchina case?

Same-Gender Harassment In *Oncale v. Sundowner Offshore Services, Inc.,*[17] the United States Supreme Court held that Title VII protection extends to individuals who are sexually harassed by members of the same gender. Proving that the harassment in same-gender cases is

"based on sex" can be difficult, though. It is easier to establish a case of same-gender harassment when the harasser is homosexual.

Sexual-Orientation Harassment Title VII did not explicitly prohibit discrimination or harassment based on a person's sexual orientation. Nonetheless, at least one federal court ruled that sexual orientation was protected

17. 523 U.S. 75, 118 S.Ct. 998, 140 L.Ed.2d 207 (1998). See also *Arnold v. Miller,* 2023 WL 156872 (S.D. IN 2023).

In the Language of the Court

PER CURIAM:

* * * *

* * * Plaintiff's * * * testimony established that (1) answering customer service calls was "just about all" he did in his position on the ATM team; (2) he was one of four employees on the ATM team, each of whom was placed in a queue to answer calls; and (3) that Plaintiff was at times the only person available to answer calls. In the light of this evidence, * * * answering customer service calls constituted an essential function of Plaintiff's job.

* * * *

An employer is liable for unlawful discrimination under the ADA when the employer fails to make reasonable accommodations to the known physical or mental limitations of an otherwise qualified individual with a disability—unless doing so would impose an undue hardship on the employer. An accommodation is reasonable only if it enables the employee to perform the essential functions of the job. The employee bears the burden of identifying an accommodation and demonstrating that it is reasonable.

* * * *

Plaintiff has established that his request to take short breaks was a reasonable one. * * * Plaintiff could control his anger in part by taking short breaks, which would thus enable him to perform an essential function of his job. While Plaintiff worked on the NOC team, Young had allowed Plaintiff to take short breaks with positive results.

* * * Plaintiff testified * * * that when he transferred to Mason's team the accommodations provided previously by Young "all stopped." The chief accommodation Plaintiff received while working for Young was the ability to take short breaks. * * * Plaintiff was not permitted to take short breaks while working for Mason. Because an employer's failure to provide a reasonable accommodation is itself a violation of the ADA, Synovus is unentitled to summary judgment.

Decision and Remedy The U.S. Court of Appeals for the Eleventh Circuit vacated the lower court's summary judgment in Synovus's favor on Kassa's failure-to-accommodate claim and remanded the case for further proceedings.

Critical Thinking

- **Legal Environment** Could Synovus have successfully claimed that Kassa's short breaks created an undue hardship? Explain.
- **What If the Facts Were Different?** Suppose that instead of asking to take a short break whenever he had an episode, Kassa had asked if he could take customer service calls only from technicians, work nights, or work from home. Would the result have been different? Discuss.

Job Applications and Physical Exams Employers must modify their job-application and selection process so that those with disabilities can compete for jobs with those who do not have disabilities. For instance, a job announcement might be modified to allow applicants to respond by e-mail or text as well as by telephone, so that it does not discriminate against potential applicants with hearing impairments.

Employers are restricted in the kinds of questions they may ask on job-application forms and during pre-employment interviews. In addition, employers cannot require persons with disabilities to submit to preemployment physicals unless such exams are required of all other applicants. An employer can disqualify the applicant only if the medical problems discovered during a preemployment physical would make it impossible for the applicant to perform the job.

Substance Abusers Drug addiction is considered a disability under the ADA because it is a substantially limiting impairment. The act does not protect individuals who are actually using illegal drugs, however. Instead, the ADA protects only persons with former drug addictions—those who have completed or are now participating in a supervised drug-rehabilitation program. Individuals who have used drugs casually in the past also are not protected under the act. They are not considered addicts and therefore do not have a disability (addiction).

People suffering from alcoholism are also protected by the ADA. Employers cannot legally discriminate against employees simply because they suffer from alcoholism. Of course, employers can prohibit the use of alcohol in the workplace and require that employees not be under the influence of alcohol while working. Employers can also fire or refuse to hire a person who is an alcoholic if (1) the person poses a substantial risk of harm to self or others, and (2) the risk cannot be reduced by reasonable accommodation.

21–4 Discrimination Based on Military Status

The Uniformed Services Employment and Reemployment Rights Act (USERRA)[30] prohibits discrimination against persons who have served in the military. In effect, the USERRA makes military service and status a protected class and gives members of this class a right to sue an employer for violations.

21–4a Broad Application and Provisions

The USERRA covers all employers, public and private, large and small. Even an employer with only one employee is subject to its provisions.[31] The act also applies to United States employers operating in foreign countries.

Under the USERRA, military plaintiffs can sue not only the employer but also individual employees who were acting in an official capacity for the employer. In other words, these employees—supervisors, for instance—can be held personally liable for violations. Additionally, there is no statute of limitations for bringing a lawsuit. The cause of action could have arisen ten weeks or ten years before the suit was filed.

The USERRA specifies that veterans can be terminated from their employment only "for cause." The employer is obligated to give employees a list of all the behaviors that would trigger a for-cause termination.

21–4b *Prima Facie* Case of Discrimination Under the USERRA

To establish a *prima facie* case of discrimination under the USERRA, the plaintiff must establish that the employer took an adverse employment action based in part on the employee's connection with the military. The connection to the military may be through the

plaintiff's membership, service, or application for service, or it may be through providing testimony or statements concerning the military service of another.[32] If another similarly situated person who did not serve in the military or engage in a protected activity was treated more favorably than the plaintiff, the employer has violated the USERRA.

■ **Case in Point 21.18** Baldo Bello, a staff sergeant with the United States Marine Corps Reserve, was employed by the Village of Skokie as a police officer. Police officers in Skokie normally have nine regular days off (RDOs) per month and eight sick days per year. Skokie officers who are in the reserve receive two weeks of paid leave for annual training each summer, but they do not receive pay for the required weekend military training.

During his first four years as an officer at Skokie, Bello always requested RDOs to cover his weekend training. After that, he started requesting military leave for the two to four days of drills per month, in addition to his nine RDOs. Skokie at first granted Bello military leave for monthly drills but later began to deny the requests.

When Skokie officials told Bello that he needed to schedule his RDOs to cover his weekend military training, Bello filed a suit in a federal district court alleging violations of the USERRA. Skokie filed a motion for summary judgment, which the court denied. The court found that Bello was meeting his employer's legitimate expectations. Bello was therefore entitled to a trial on the issue of whether Skokie had treated his leave requests less favorably than requests from other employees.[33] ■

21–4c Plaintiffs May Be Entitled to Promotions

Under the USERRA, returning service members are to be reemployed in the jobs that they would have attained had they not been absent for military service. Reinstatement could affect their seniority, status, pay, and other rights and benefits (such as health and pension plans). In essence, this means that a returning service member who successfully sues an employer for violations of the USERRA could receive not only damages and reinstatement but also a promotion.

Concept Summary 21.1 reviews the coverage of the employment discrimination laws discussed in this chapter.

30. Pub. L. No. 103-353, codified at 38 U.S.C. Sections 4301-4335.
31. 20 C.F.R. Section 1002.34(a).
32. 38 U.S.C. Section 4311(c).
33. *Bello v. Village of Skokie,* 151 F.Supp.3d 849 (N.D.Ill. 2015). See also *Venticinque v. City of Chicago Department of Aviation,* 2022 WL 4095056 (N.D. IL, E.Div. 2022).

Concept Summary 21.1

Coverage of Employment Discrimination Laws

Title VII of the Civil Rights Act	• Prohibits discrimination based on race, color, national origin, religion, gender, sexual orientation, and pregnancy; prohibits sexual harassment. • Applies to employers with fifteen or more employees.
Age Discrimination in Employment Act	• Prohibits discrimination against persons over forty years of age. • Applies to employers with twenty or more employees.
Americans with Disabilities Act (as amended)	• Prohibits discrimination against persons with a mental or physical impairment that substantially limits a major life activity or who have a record of such an impairment, or who are regarded as having such an impairment, or who are associated with a disabled person. • Applies to employers with fifteen or more employees.
Uniformed Services Employment and Reemployment Rights Act	• Prohibits discrimination against persons who have served in the military. • Applies to all employers, even if they have only one employee.

21–5 Defenses to Employment Discrimination

The first line of defense for an employer charged with employment discrimination is to assert that the plaintiff has failed to meet the initial burden of proving that discrimination occurred. As noted, plaintiffs bringing age discrimination claims may find it difficult to meet this initial burden because they must prove that age discrimination was the reason for their employer's decision.

Once a plaintiff succeeds in proving that discrimination occurred, the burden shifts to the employer to justify the discriminatory practice. Possible justifications include that the discrimination resulted from a business necessity, a bona fide occupational qualification, or a seniority system. In some situations, as noted earlier, an effective antiharassment policy and prompt remedial action when harassment occurs may shield employers from liability for sexual harassment under Title VII.

21–5a Business Necessity

An employer may defend against a claim of disparate-impact (unintentional) discrimination by asserting that a practice that has a discriminatory effect is a **business necessity.** ■ **Example 21.19** EarthFix, Inc., an international consulting agency, requires its applicants to be fluent in at least two languages. If this requirement is shown to have a discriminatory effect, EarthFix can defend it based on business necessity. That is, the company can argue that its workers must speak more than one language to perform their jobs at the required level of competence. If EarthFix can demonstrate a definite connection between this requirement and job performance, it normally will succeed in this business necessity defense. ■

21–5b Bona Fide Occupational Qualification

Another defense applies when discrimination against a protected class is essential to a job—that is, when a particular trait is a **bona fide occupational qualification (BFOQ).** Note that race, color, and national origin can never be BFOQs.

Generally, courts have restricted the BFOQ defense to situations in which the employee's gender or religion is essential to the job. For instance, a women's clothing store might legitimately hire only female sales attendants if part of an attendant's job involves assisting clients in the store's dressing rooms.

21–5c Seniority Systems

An employer with a history of discrimination may have no members of protected classes in upper-level positions. Nevertheless, the employer may have a defense against a discrimination suit if promotions or other job benefits have been distributed according to a fair seniority system. In a **seniority system,** workers with more years of service are promoted first or laid off last.

■ **Case in Point 21.20** Charee Stanley worked as a flight attendant for ExpressJet Airlines, Inc. A practicing Muslim, Stanley, for religious reasons, requested that she be excused from preparing and serving alcohol during flights. ExpressJet refused this accommodation, which would have been at odds with a collective bargaining agreement (CBA) between the airline and its employees.

The CBA gave senior flight attendants the ability to choose work assignments, including whether to serve alcohol. Because of her short tenure with the airline, Stanley was frequently the junior attendant on a particular flight. Consequently, she was required by the CBA to serve alcohol if her senior partner declined to do so. A federal appeals court ruled that ExpressJet would violate this seniority system if it granted Stanley's accommodation request, and therefore her religious discrimination claim was preempted by the CBA.[34] ■

21–5d After-Acquired Evidence of Employee Misconduct

In some situations, employers have attempted to avoid liability for employment discrimination on the basis of "after-acquired evidence" of an employee's misconduct. After-acquired evidence refers to evidence that the employer discovers after a lawsuit has been filed.

■ **Example 21.21** Pratt Legal Services fires Karlha, who then sues Pratt for employment discrimination. During pretrial investigation, Pratt discovers that Karlha made material misrepresentations on her job application. Had Pratt known of these misrepresentations, it would have had grounds to fire Karlha. ■

After-acquired evidence of wrongdoing cannot shield an employer entirely from liability for employment discrimination. It may, however, be used to limit the amount of damages for which the employer is liable.

21–6 Affirmative Action

Federal statutes and regulations providing for equal opportunity in the workplace were designed to reduce or eliminate discriminatory practices with respect to hiring, retaining, and promoting employees. **Affirmative**

action programs go a step further and attempt to "make up" for past patterns of discrimination by giving members of protected classes preferential treatment in hiring or promotion. During the 1960s, all federal and state government agencies, private companies that contracted to do business with the federal government, and institutions that received federal funding were required to implement affirmative action policies.

Title VII of the Civil Rights Act neither requires nor prohibits affirmative action. Thus, most private companies and organizations have not been required to implement affirmative action policies, though many have done so voluntarily. Affirmative action programs have been controversial, however, particularly when they have resulted in reverse discrimination against members of a majority group, such as white males.

21–6a Equal Protection Issues

Because of their inherently discriminatory nature, affirmative action programs may violate the equal protection clause of the Fourteenth Amendment to the U.S. Constitution. Any federal, state, or local government affirmative action program that uses racial or ethnic classifications as the basis for making decisions is subject to strict scrutiny by the courts—the highest standard to meet.

Today, an affirmative action program normally is constitutional only if it attempts to remedy past discrimination and does not make use of quotas or preferences. Furthermore, once such a program has succeeded in the goal of remedying past discrimination, it must be changed or eliminated.

21–6b State Laws Prohibiting Affirmative Action Programs

Some states have enacted laws that prohibit affirmative action programs at public institutions (colleges, universities, and state agencies) within their borders. These states include California, Maryland, Michigan, New Hampshire, Oklahoma, Virginia, and Washington. The United States Supreme Court has recognized that states have the power to enact such bans.

■ **Case in Point 21.22** Michigan voters passed an initiative to amend the state's constitution to prohibit publicly funded colleges from granting preferential treatment to any group on the basis of race, sex, color, ethnicity, or national origin. The law also prohibited Michigan from considering race and gender in public hiring and contracting decisions.

---

34. *Stanley v. ExpressJet Airlines, Inc.,* 808 Fed.Appx. 351 (6th Cir. 2020).

A group that supports affirmative action programs in education sued the state's attorney general and others, claiming that the initiative deprived minority groups of equal protection and violated the U.S. Constitution. A federal appellate court agreed that the law violated the equal protection clause, but the United States Supreme Court reversed. The Court did not rule on the constitutionality of any specific affirmative action program but held that a state has the inherent power to ban affirmative action within that state.[35] ∎

---

35. *Schuette v. Coalition to Defend Affirmative Action, Integration, and Immigrant Rights,* 572 U.S. 291, 134 S.Ct. 1623, 188 L.Ed.2d 613 (2014). See also *Students for Fair Admissions, Inc. v. University of Texas at Austin,* 338 F.R.D. 364, 392 Ed. Law Rep. 849 (W.D. TX, Austin Div. 2021).

Practice and Review: Employment Discrimination

Amaani Lyle, an African American woman, was hired by Warner Brothers Television Productions to be a scriptwriters' assistant for the writers of *Friends,* a popular television series. One of her essential job duties was to type detailed notes for the scriptwriters during brainstorming sessions in which they discussed jokes, dialogue, and story lines. The writers then combed through Lyle's notes after the meetings for script material. During these meetings, the three male scriptwriters told lewd and vulgar jokes and made sexually explicit comments and gestures. They often talked about their personal sexual experiences and fantasies, and some of these conversations were then used in episodes of *Friends.*

During the meetings, Lyle never complained that she found the writers' conduct offensive. After four months, Lyle was fired because she could not type fast enough to keep up with the writers' conversations during the meetings. She filed a suit against Warner Brothers, alleging sexual harassment and claiming that her termination was based on racial discrimination. Using the information presented in the chapter, answer the following questions.

1. Would Lyle's claim of racial discrimination be for intentional (disparate-treatment) or unintentional (disparate-impact) discrimination? Explain.
2. Can Lyle establish a *prima facie* case of racial discrimination? Why or why not?
3. When Lyle was hired, she was told that typing speed was extremely important to the position. At the time, she maintained that she could type eighty words per minute, so she was not given a typing test. It later turned out that Lyle could type only fifty words per minute. What impact might typing speed have on Lyle's lawsuit?
4. Lyle's sexual-harassment claim is based on the hostile working environment created by the writers' sexually offensive conduct at meetings that she was required to attend. The writers, however, argue that their behavior was essential to the "creative process" of writing for *Friends,* a show that routinely contained sexual innuendos and adult humor. Which defense discussed in the chapter might Warner Brothers assert using this argument?

Debate This . . . Members of minority groups and women no longer need special legislation to protect them from employment discrimination.

Terms and Concepts

affirmative action 468
bona fide occupational qualification (BFOQ) 467
business necessity 467
constructive discharge 458

disparate-impact discrimination 452
disparate-treatment discrimination 452
employment discrimination 451

prima facie case 452
protected class 451
seniority system 468
sexual harassment 458
tangible employment action 458

Issue Spotters

1. Ruth is a supervisor for a Subs & Suds restaurant. Tim is a Subs & Suds employee. The owner announces that some employees will be discharged. Ruth tells Tim that if he has sex with her, he can keep his job. Is this sexual harassment? Why or why not? (See *Title VII of the Civil Rights Act*.)

2. Koko, a person with a disability, applies for a job at Lively Sales Corporation for which she is well qualified, but she is rejected. Lively continues to seek applicants and eventually fills the position with a person who does not have a disability. Could Koko succeed in a suit against Lively for discrimination? Explain. (See *Discrimination Based on Disability*.)

- Check your answers to the Issue Spotters against the answers provided in Appendix B at the end of this text.

Business Scenarios and Case Problems

21–1. Title VII Violations. Discuss fully whether either of the following actions would constitute a violation of Title VII of the Civil Rights Act, as amended. (See *Title VII of the Civil Rights Act*.)

(a) Tennington, Inc., is a consulting firm with ten employees. These employees travel on consulting jobs in seven states. Tennington has an employment record of hiring only white males.

(b) Novo Films is making a movie about Africa and needs to employ approximately one hundred extras for this picture. To hire these extras, Novo advertises in all major newspapers in Southern California. The ad states that only African Americans need apply.

21–2. Religious Discrimination. Gina Gomez, a devout Roman Catholic, worked for Sam's Department Stores, Inc., in Phoenix, Arizona. Sam's considered Gomez a productive employee because her sales exceeded $200,000 per year. At the time, the store gave its managers the discretion to grant unpaid leave to employees but prohibited vacations or leave during the holiday season—October through December. Gomez felt that she had a "calling" to go on a "pilgrimage" in October to a location in Bosnia where some persons claimed to have had visions of the Virgin Mary. The Catholic Church had not designated the site an official pilgrimage site, the visions were not expected to be stronger in October, and tours were available at other times. The store managers denied Gomez's request for leave, but she had a nonrefundable ticket and left anyway. Sam's terminated her employment, and she could not find another job. Can Gomez establish a *prima facie* case of religious discrimination? Explain. (See *Title VII of the Civil Rights Act*.)

21–3. Sexual Harassment by a Co-Worker. Billie Bradford worked for the Kentucky Department of Community Based Services (DCBS). One of Bradford's co-workers, Lisa Stander, routinely engaged in extreme sexual behavior (such as touching herself and making crude comments) in Bradford's presence. Bradford and others regularly complained about Stander's conduct to their supervisor, Angie Taylor. Rather than resolve the problem, Taylor nonchalantly told Stander to stop, encouraged Bradford to talk to Stander, and suggested that Stander was just having fun. Assuming that Bradford was subjected to a hostile work environment, could DCBS be liable? Why or why not? [*Bradford v. Department of Community Based Services*, 2012 WL 360032 (E.D. KY, N. Div, at Covington 2012)] (See *Title VII of the Civil Rights Act*.)

21–4. Discrimination Based on Disability. Cynthia Horn worked for Knight Facilities Management–GM, Inc., in Detroit, Michigan, as a janitor. When Horn developed a sensitivity to cleaning products, her physician gave her a "no exposure to cleaning solutions" restriction. Knight discussed possible accommodations with Horn. She suggested that restrooms be eliminated from her cleaning route or that she be provided with a respirator. Knight explained that she would be exposed to cleaning solutions in any situation and concluded that there was no work available within her physician's restriction. Has Knight violated the Americans with Disabilities Act by failing to provide Horn with the requested accommodations? Explain. [*Horn v. Knight Facilities Management–GM, Inc.*, 556 Fed.Appx. 452 (6th Cir. 2014)] (See *Discrimination Based on Disability*.)

21–5. Business Case Problem With Sample Answer—Sexual Harassment. Jamel Blanton was a male employee at a Pizza Hut restaurant operated by Newton Associates, Inc., in San Antonio, Texas. Blanton was subjected to sexual and racial harassment by the general manager, who was female. Newton had a clear, straightforward antidiscrimination policy and complaint procedure. The policy provided that in such a situation, an employee should complain to the harasser's supervisor. Blanton alerted a shift leader and an assistant manager about the harassment, but they were subordinate to the general manager and did not report the harassment to higher-level management. When Blanton finally complained to a manager with authority over the general manager, the employer investigated and fired the general manager within four days. Blanton filed a suit in a federal district court against Newton, seeking to impose liability on the employer for the general manager's actions. What is Newton's best defense? Discuss. [*Blanton v. Newton Associates, Inc.*, 593 Fed.Appx. 389 (5th Cir. 2015)] (See *Title VII of the Civil Rights Act*.)

- For a sample answer to Problem 21-5, go to Appendix C at the end of this text.

21–6. Discrimination Based on Disability. Dennis Wallace was a deputy sheriff for Stanislaus County, California, when he injured his left knee. After surgery, he was subject to limits on prolonged standing, walking, and running. The county assigned him to work as a bailiff. The sergeants who supervised him rated his performance above average. Less than a year later, without consulting those supervisors, the county placed him on an unpaid leave of absence, under the mistaken belief that he could not safely perform the essential functions of the job. Wallace filed an action in a California state court against the county, alleging discrimination based on disability. Under state law, discriminatory intent is shown by evidence that an actual or perceived disability was a "substantial motivating factor or reason" for an employer's adverse employment action. An employee is not required to show that the action was motivated by animosity or ill will. Could Wallace likely prove the "substantial motivating factor or reason" element? Explain. [*Wallace v. County of Stanislaus,* 245 Cal.App.4th 109, 199 Cal.Rptr.3d 462 (5th Dist. 2016)] (See *Discrimination Based on Disability.*)

21–7. Age Discrimination. Robert Bledsoe worked for the Tennessee Valley Authority (TVA) for a number of years beginning in 1985. For much of his career, he worked as an assistant unit operator at the Sequoyah Nuclear Plant. He later became a Nuclear Student Generation Plant Operating trainer. Bledsoe took medical leave in 2016, had a liver transplant, and returned to work in 2017. Following the surgery, he took medication and occasionally used a cane. His supervisor, Christopher Dahlman, began to pressure him to retire because of his health and age. When a committee of the board of directors of the TVA demoted Bledsoe, he brought an action against his employer alleging, in part, discrimination based on age. In a federal district court, the TVA was granted summary judgment. Bledsoe appealed. How should the appellate court rule? [*Bledsoe v. Tennessee Valley Authority Board of Directors,* 42 F.4th 568 (6th Cir. 2022)] (See *Discrimination Based on Age.*)

21–8. Discrimination Based on Genetic Information. Vincent Jackson was one of many unsuccessful job applicants for openings at Dollar General. He, along with the Equal Employment Opportunity Commission, contended that Dollar General violated the Americans with Disabilities Act and the Genetic Information Nondiscrimination Act when hiring general warehouse workers for its Bessemer, Alabama, facility. The company used a post-offer medical examination that screened out some applicants based on actual or perceived disabilities. Dollar General admitted in court proceedings that its agent, Middle Creek Medical Center, asked Dollar General job candidates whether their grandparents, parents, or children had had significant medical problems. Should a federal court allow the plaintiffs to go to trial on this issue? [*Equal Employment Opportunity Commission v. Dolgen Corp. L.L.C.,* 2022 WL 2959569 (M.D. AL, S. Div. 2022). (See *Discrimination Based on Disability.*)

21–9. A Question of Ethics—The IDDR Approach and Unintentional Discrimination. McLane Company is a supply-chain services company that distributes goods to retailers. McLane requires employees with physically demanding jobs to have physical evaluations, both when they start work and when they return after medical leave. After working in a physically demanding job for McLane for eight years, Damiana Ochoa took maternity leave. When she returned to work, she failed the physical evaluation and was fired. She filed a discrimination complaint with the Equal Employment Opportunity Commission (EEOC). The agency issued a subpoena—an order to appear in court—seeking the names and contact information of McLane employees who had been asked to have evaluations throughout the company's national operations. [*McLane Co. v. EEOC,* 581 U.S. 72, 137 S.Ct. 1159, 197 L.Ed.2d 500 (2017)] (See *Title VII of the Civil Rights Act.*)

(a) On what legal ground might McLane legitimately refuse to comply with the EEOC's subpoena? What practical factors could affect the choice not to comply? Discuss.

(b) Using the IDDR approach, consider whether McLane has an ethical duty to comply with the subpoena.

Time-Limited Group Assignment

21–10. Racial Discrimination. Two African American plaintiffs sued the producers of the reality television series *The Bachelor* and *The Bachelorette* for racial discrimination. The plaintiffs claimed that the shows had never featured persons of color in the lead roles. The plaintiffs also alleged that the producers did not provide people of color who auditioned for the lead roles with the same opportunities to compete as white people who auditioned. (See *Title VII of the Civil Rights Act.*)

(a) The first group will assess whether the plaintiffs can establish a *prima facie* case of disparate-treatment discrimination.

(b) The second group will consider whether the plaintiffs can establish disparate-impact discrimination.

(c) The third group will assume that the plaintiffs established a *prima facie* case and that the burden has shifted to the employer to articulate a legal reason for not hiring the plaintiffs. What legitimate reasons might the employer assert for not hiring the plaintiffs in this situation? Should the law require television producers to hire persons of color for lead roles in reality television shows? Discuss.

Chapter 22

Immigration and Labor Law

Immigration law and policy in the United States are topics of significant national debate. To a substantial degree, the immigration debate concerns the nation's employment environment. For this reason, Congress enacted legislation in the late twentieth century to prohibit employers from hiring illegal immigrants. Today, immigration law has evolved into a myriad of complex rules that employers must follow.

The origin of many of the laws pertaining to the workplace can be traced back to the Industrial Revolution of the nineteenth century. During the Industrial Revolution, fewer Americans were self-employed than ever before, and employers generally set the terms of employment. Moreover, with increasing industrialization, the size of workplaces and the number of on-the-job hazards increased. Workers came to believe that to counter the power and freedom of their employers and to protect themselves, they needed to organize into unions.

Beginning in 1932, Congress enacted a number of statutes that generally increased employees' rights. At the heart of these rights is the right to join unions and engage in collective bargaining with management to negotiate working conditions, salaries, and benefits for a group of workers. This chapter also examines strikes, lockouts, and the labor practices that are considered unfair under federal law.

22–1 Immigration Law

The United States did not have any laws restricting immigration until the late nineteenth century. Immigration law has become increasingly important in recent years. Because U.S. employers face penalties if they hire undocumented workers, it is necessary for businesspersons to understand immigration laws. The most important laws affecting immigration in the context of employment are the Immigration Reform and Control Act (IRCA)[1] and the Immigration Act.[2]

22–1a The Immigration Reform and Control Act (IRCA)

When the IRCA was enacted in 1986, it provided amnesty to certain groups of aliens living illegally in the United States at the time. It also established a system that sanctions employers that hire immigrants who lack work authorization. The IRCA makes it illegal to hire, recruit, or refer for a fee someone not authorized to work in this country. Through Immigration and Customs Enforcement officers, the federal government conducts compliance audits and engages in enforcement actions against employers who hire undocumented workers.

I-9 Employment Verification To comply with the IRCA, an employer is required to perform **I-9 verifications** for new hires, including those hired as "contractors" or "day workers" if they work under the employer's direct supervision. Form I-9, Employment Eligibility Verification, which is available from U.S. Citizenship and Immigration Services,[3] must be completed within three days of a worker's commencement of employment. The three-day period allows the employer to check the form's accuracy and to review and verify documents establishing the prospective worker's identity and eligibility for employment in the United States.

Documentation Requirements The employer must declare, under penalty of perjury, that an employee

---

1. 9 U.S.C. Section 1802.
2. This act amended various provisions of the Immigration and Nationality Act of 1952, 8 U.S.C. Sections 1101 *et seq.*

3. U.S. Citizenship and Immigration Services is a federal agency that is part of the U.S. Department of Homeland Security.

produced documents establishing the employee's identity and legal employability. A U.S. passport establishing the person's citizenship is acceptable documentation. So is a document authorizing a foreign citizen to work in the United States, such as a permanent resident card.

Most legal actions alleging violations of I-9 rules are brought against employees who provide false information or documentation. If an employee enters false information on the I-9 form or presents false documentation, the employer can fire the worker, who then may be subject to deportation. Nevertheless, employers must be honest when verifying an employee's documentation. If an employer "should have known" that the worker was unauthorized, the employer has violated the rules.

Enforcement U.S. Immigration and Customs Enforcement (ICE) is the largest investigative arm of the U.S. Department of Homeland Security. ICE has a general inspection program that conducts random compliance audits. Other audits may occur if the agency receives a written complaint alleging that an employer has committed violations. Government inspections include a review of an employer's file of I-9 forms. The government does not need a subpoena or a warrant to conduct such an inspection.

If an investigation reveals a possible violation, ICE may bring an administrative action and issue a Notice of Intent to Fine, which sets out the charges against the employer. The employer has a right to a hearing on the enforcement action if it files a request within thirty days. This hearing is conducted before an administrative law judge, and the employer has a right to counsel and to discovery. The typical defense in such actions is good faith or substantial compliance with the documentation provisions.

22–1b The Immigration Act

Often, U.S. businesses find that they cannot hire enough domestic workers with specialized skills. For this reason, U.S. immigration laws have long made provisions for businesses to hire specially qualified foreign workers.

The Immigration Act of 1990 placed caps on the number of visas (entry permits) that can be issued to immigrants each year, including employment-based visas. Employment-based visas may be classified as permanent (immigrant) or temporary (nonimmigrant). Employers who wish to hire workers with either type of visa must comply with detailed government regulations.[4]

---

4. The most relevant regulations can be found at 20 C.F.R. Section 655 (for temporary employment) and 20 C.F.R. Section 656 (for permanent employment).

I-551 Permanent Resident Card A company seeking to hire a noncitizen worker may do so if the worker is self-authorized. To be self-authorized, a worker must either be a lawful permanent resident or have a valid temporary Employment Authorization Document. A lawful permanent resident can prove this status to an employer by presenting an **I-551 Permanent Resident Card,** known as a *green card*, or a properly stamped foreign passport.

Many immigrant workers are not self-authorized, and an employer that wishes to hire them can attempt to obtain labor certification, or green cards, for them. A limited number of new green cards are issued each year. A green card can be obtained only for a person who is being hired for a permanent, full-time position. (A separate authorization system provides for the temporary entry and hiring of nonimmigrant visa workers.)

To gain authorization for hiring a foreign worker, an employer must show that no U.S. worker is qualified, willing, and able to take the job. The government has detailed regulations governing the advertising of positions as well as the certification process. Any U.S. applicants who meet the stated job qualifications must be interviewed for the position. The employer must also be able to show that the qualifications required for the job are a business necessity.

The H-1B Visa Program The most common and controversial visa program today is the H-1B visa system. To obtain an H1-B visa, the potential employee must be qualified in a "specialty occupation," meaning that the individual has highly specialized knowledge and has attained a bachelor's or higher degree or its equivalent. Individuals with H-1B visas can stay in the United States for three to six years and can work only for the sponsoring employer.

The recipients of these visas include numerous high-tech workers. A maximum of sixty-five thousand H-1B visas are set aside each year for new immigrants. That limit is typically reached within the first few weeks of the year. Consequently, technology companies often complain that Congress needs to expand the number of H-1B visas available, to encourage the best and the brightest minds to work in the United States. Critics of the H-1B visa program, however, believe that employers are sometimes using it to replace American workers with lower-paid foreign labor.

Labor Certification An employer who wishes to submit an H-1B application must first file a Labor Certification application on a form known as ETA 9035. The employer must agree to provide a wage level at least equal to the wages offered to other individuals with similar experience and qualifications. The employer must also show that the hiring will not adversely affect other workers similarly employed. The employer is required to inform U.S. workers of the intent to hire a foreign worker by posting the form. The U.S. Department of Labor reviews the applications and may reject them for omissions or inaccuracies.

22–1c State Immigration Legislation

Until 2010, federal law exclusively governed immigration and the treatment of illegal immigrants. Then Arizona enacted a law that required Arizona law enforcement officials to identify and charge immigrants in Arizona who were there illegally, potentially leading to the immigrants' deportation. Among other things, that law required immigrants to carry their papers at all times and allowed police to check a person's immigration status during any law enforcement action.

In *Arizona v. United States,* the United States Supreme Court upheld the controversial "show-me-your-papers" provision, which requires police to check the immigration status of persons stopped for other violations. All other provisions of Arizona's law were struck down as unconstitutional violations of the supremacy clause. The Supreme Court's decision does not prohibit states from enacting laws related to immigration, but it does set some limits.

Some states and cities have become so-called *sanctuary jurisdictions*—political jurisdictions that choose not to turn over undocumented individuals to federal immigration authorities. Sanctuary policies have come under growing scrutiny since the relatively large increase in the number of undocumented aliens crossing the U.S. southern border.

22–2 Labor Unions

In the 1930s, in addition to wage and hour laws, Congress enacted the first of several labor laws. These laws protect employees' rights to join labor unions, to bargain with management over the terms and conditions of employment, and to conduct strikes.

22–2a Federal Labor Laws

Federal labor laws governing union–employer relations have developed considerably since the first law was enacted in 1932. Initially, the laws were concerned with protecting the rights and interests of workers. Subsequent legislation placed some restraints on unions and granted

rights to employers. We look here at four major federal statutes regulating union–employer relations.

Norris-LaGuardia Act Congress protected peaceful strikes, picketing, and boycotts in 1932 in the Norris-LaGuardia Act.[5] The statute restricted the power of federal courts to issue injunctions against unions engaged in peaceful strikes. In effect, this act declared a national policy permitting employees to organize.

National Labor Relations Act One of the foremost statutes regulating labor is the 1935 National Labor Relations Act (NLRA).[6] This act established the rights of employees to engage in collective bargaining and to strike.

Unfair Labor Practices. The NLRA specifically defined a number of employer practices as unfair to labor:

1. Interference with the efforts of employees to form, join, or assist labor organizations or to engage in concerted activities for their mutual aid or protection.
2. An employer's domination of a labor organization or contribution of financial or other support to it.
3. Discrimination in the hiring of or the awarding of tenure to employees for reason of union affiliation.
4. Discrimination against employees for filing charges under the act or giving testimony under the act.
5. Refusal to bargain collectively with the duly designated representative of the employees.

The National Labor Relations Board. The NLRA created the National Labor Relations Board (NLRB) to oversee union elections and to prevent employers from engaging in unfair and illegal union activities and unfair labor practices.

The NLRB has the authority to investigate employees' charges of unfair labor practices and to file complaints against employers in response to these charges. When violations are found, the NLRB may issue a **cease-and-desist order** compelling the employer to stop engaging in the unfair practices. Cease-and-desist orders can be enforced by a federal appellate court if necessary. After the NLRB rules on claims of unfair labor practices, its decision may be appealed to a federal court.

■ **Case in Point 22.1** Ozburn-Hessey Logistics (OHL) had a discipline policy under which an employee could be fired for accumulating more than twelve tardiness and absence "points." After OHL replaced its push-button clocks with time-screen clocks, employee Laura Keele

---

5. 29 U.S.C. Sections 101–110, 113–115.
6. 20 U.S.C. Sections 151–169.

checked in one minute late. Keele claimed the new system confused her, causing the delay. Nonetheless, OHL assessed Keele a tardiness point, her thirteenth, and she was fired.

The NLRB filed a complaint against OHL for unfair labor practices, asserting that the upgrade in clocks should have been negotiated with Keele's union. Because it was not, her firing violated federal labor law. In a hearing, an administrative law judge determined that the difference between pushing a touch screen and pushing a plastic button was not a "significant" change in the terms of Keele's employment, and a federal appeals court agreed. Therefore, OHL's decision to switch clocks did not require collective bargaining, and Keele's firing was not an unfair labor practice.[7] ■

Good Faith Bargaining. Under the NLRA, employers and unions have a duty to bargain in good faith. Bargaining over certain subjects is mandatory, and a party's refusal to bargain over these subjects is an unfair labor practice that can be reported to the NLRB. For instance, bargaining is mandatory for subjects relating to wages or working hours.

Workers Protected by the NLRA. To be protected under the NLRA, an individual must be an employee or a job applicant. (If job applicants were not covered, the NLRA's ban on discrimination in regard to hiring would mean little.) Additionally, individuals who are hired by a union to organize a company (union organizers) are to be considered employees of the company for NLRA purposes.[8]

Even a temporary worker hired through an employment agency might qualify for protection under the NLRA. The same cannot be said for some faculty members at private universities, however. ■ **Case in Point 22.2** A group of non-tenure-track adjunct instructors at the University of Southern California (USC) voted to join a union. USC refused to negotiate with these adjuncts on the ground that, like tenured professors, they are "managers" of university policy who are barred from unionizing. In contrast, "employees" are permitted to unionize under the NLRA. A federal appeals court ruled against USC in this instance, but established guidelines that will make it more difficult for non-tenure-track adjunct faculty at private universities to claim employee status in the future.[9] ■

Labor-Management Relations Act The Labor-Management Relations Act (LMRA or Taft-Hartley Act)[10] was passed in 1947 to prohibit certain unfair union practices. For instance, the act outlawed the **closed shop**—a firm that requires union membership as a condition of employment. The act preserved the legality of the union shop, however. A **union shop** does not require union membership as a prerequisite for employment but can, and usually does, require that workers join the union after a specified time on the job.

The LMRA also prohibited unions from refusing to bargain with employers, engaging in certain types of picketing, and featherbedding (causing employers to hire more employees than they need). In addition, the act allowed individual states to pass **right-to-work laws**—laws making it illegal for union membership to be required for continued employment in any establishment. Thus, union shops are technically illegal in the twenty-seven states that have right-to-work laws.

Labor-Management Reporting and Disclosure Act The Labor-Management Reporting and Disclosure Act (LMRDA)[11] established an employee bill of rights and reporting requirements for union activities. The act also outlawed **hot-cargo agreements,** in which employers voluntarily agree with unions not to handle, use, or deal in goods of other employers produced by nonunion employees.

The LMRDA strictly regulates unions' internal business procedures, including elections. For instance, it requires unions to hold regularly scheduled elections of officers using secret ballots. Ex-convicts are prohibited from holding union office. Moreover, union officials are accountable for union property and funds. Members have the right to attend and to participate in union meetings, to nominate officers, and to vote in most union proceedings.

22–3 Union Organization

Typically, the first step in organizing a union at a particular firm is to have the workers sign authorization cards. An **authorization card** usually states that the worker desires to have a certain union, such as the United Auto Workers, represent the workforce.

If a majority of the workers sign authorization cards, the union organizers (unionizers) present the cards to the employer and ask for formal recognition of the union.

7. *Ozburn-Hessey Logistics, LLC v. NLRB,* 803 Fed.Appx. 876 (6th Cir. 2020).
8. See the United States Supreme Court's landmark decision in *NLRB v. Town & Country Electric, Inc.,* 516 U.S. 85, 116 S.Ct. 450, 133 L.Ed.2d 371 (1995).
9. *University of Southern California v. NLRB,* 918 F.3d 126, 440 U.S.App.D.C. 59 (D.D.C. 2019).
10. 29 U.S.C. Sections 141 *et seq.*
11. 29 U.S.C. Sections 401 *et seq.*

The employer is not required to recognize the union at this point, but it may do so voluntarily on a showing of majority support.

22–3a Union Elections

If the employer does not voluntarily recognize the union—or if less than a majority of the workers sign authorization cards—the union organizers can petition for an election. The organizers present the authorization cards to the NLRB with a petition to hold an election on unionization. For an election to be held, they must demonstrate that at least 30 percent of the workers to be represented support a union or an election.

Appropriate Bargaining Unit Not every group of workers can form a single union. The proposed union must represent an appropriate bargaining unit. One key requirement is a mutuality of interest among all the workers to be represented by the union. Factors considered in determining whether there is a mutuality of interest include the similarity of the jobs of the workers to be unionized and their physical location.

NLRB Rules Expedite Elections NLRB rules that took effect in 2015 significantly reduced the time between the filing of a petition and the ensuing election. As a result, the time before an election is held has changed from an average of thirty-eight days to as little as ten days after the filing. This change favors unions because it gives employers less time to respond

to organizing campaigns, which unions often spend months preparing.

The NLRB now requires that a company hold a pre-election hearing within eight days after it receives a petition for an organizing election. On the day before the hearing, the company must also submit a "statement of position" laying out every argument it intends to make against the union. Any argument that the company does not include in its position paper can be excluded from evidence at the hearing. Once the hearing is held, an election can be scheduled right away.

Voting If an election is held, the NLRB supervises the election and ensures secret voting and voter eligibility. If the proposed union receives majority support in a fair election, the NLRB certifies the union as the bargaining representative for the employees.

22–3b Union Election Campaigns

Many disputes between labor and management arise during union election campaigns. Generally, the employer has control over unionizing activities that take place on company property and during working hours. Thus, the employer may limit the campaign activities of union supporters as long as it has a legitimate business reason for doing so. The employer may also reasonably limit when and where union solicitation may occur in the workplace, provided that the employer is not discriminating against the union. (Can union organizers use company e-mail during campaigns? See this chapter's Managerial Strategy feature for a discussion of this topic.)

Managerial Strategy   Union Organizing Using a Company's E-Mail System

When union organizers start an organizing drive, there are certain restrictions on what they can do, particularly within the workplace. Both employers and employees must comply with Section 7 of the National Labor Relations Act (NLRA).

Protected Concerted Activities

Under Section 7, employees have certain rights to communicate among themselves. Section 7 states, "Employees shall have the right to self-organization, . . . and to engage in other concerted activities for the purpose of collective bargaining or other mutual aid or protection. . . ."

What about communication via e-mail? Can union organizers use a company-operated e-mail system for

organizing purposes? Companies typically provide e-mail systems so that employees can communicate with outsiders and among themselves as part of their jobs. Generally, company policies have prohibited the use of company-owned and -operated e-mail systems for other than job-related communications. Starting in the early 2000s, some union organizers challenged this prohibition.

The NLRB's Perspective Evolves

The National Labor Relations Board (NLRB) has reversed course several times on this issue, reflecting the changing politics of board members. In the mid-2010s, the NLRB ruled that, if an employer provides workers an e-mail system for work functions, then its employees should have a right under the NLRA to use that same system to discuss any work-related concerns, including union activity.[a]

About five years later, the NLRB heard a case involving a Las Vegas casino that prohibited employees from using company e-mails to discuss working conditions.[b] Upholding the casino's right to do so, the board broadly revoked the right of workers to conduct union affairs on employer-operated e-mail systems. The NLRB held that businesses have a constitutionally protected right to control or limit the use of their

a. *Purple Communications, Inc. and Communication Workers of America, AFL-CIO,* Cases 21-CA-095151, 21-RC-091531, and 21-RC-091584, March 16, 2015.
b. *Caesar's Entertainment, Inc. and NLRB,* Case 28-CA-060841, December 17, 2019.

property, which includes digital communications. The prohibition must, however, be nondiscriminatory. That is, a business cannot ban union-related e-mails while allowing communications about other subjects that are not strictly work related.

Business Questions

1. Employees meeting around the water cooler or coffee machine have always had the right to discuss work-related matters. Is an employer-provided e-mail system or social media outlet simply a digital water cooler? Why or why not?

2. If your company instituted a policy stating that employees should "think carefully about 'friending' co-workers," would that policy be lawful? Why or why not?

■ **Example 22.3** A union is seeking to organize clerks at a department store owned by Amanti Enterprises. Amanti can prohibit all union solicitation in areas of the store open to the public because the unionizing activities could interfere with the store's business. It can also restrict union-related activities to coffee breaks and lunch hours. If Amanti allows solicitation for charitable causes in the workplace, however, it may not prohibit union solicitation. ■

An employer may campaign among its workers against the union, but the NLRB carefully monitors and

regulates the tactics used by management. If the employer issues threats ("If the union wins, you'll all be fired") or engages in other unfair labor practices, the NLRB may certify the union even though the union lost the election. Alternatively, the NLRB may ask a court to order a new election.

Whether an employer violated its employees' rights under the National Labor Relations Act during a union election campaign was at issue in the following case.

Case Analysis 22.1

Exela Enterprise Solutions, Incorporated v. National Labor Relations Board
United States Court of Appeals, Fifth Circuit, 32 F.4th 436 (2022).

In the Language of the Court
CLEMENT, Judge

Exela Enterprise Solutions, Inc. ("Exela"), seeks review of a National Labor Relations Board ("NLRB" or "Board") order finding that Exela violated the National Labor Relations Act ("NLRA") by refusing to bargain with the United Steel, Paper and Forestry, Rubber, Manufacturing, Energy, Allied Industrial and Service Workers International Union, AFL-CIO-CLC ("Union"). The Board cross-petitions for enforcement.
* * *

I

Exela provides office services and facilities management at a Bristol-Myers Squibb warehouse in New Brunswick, New Jersey. On March 29, 2019, the Board conducted a representation election at Exela's New Brunswick site. Of fourteen eligible voters, eight employees voted for Union representation and six voted against it.

Exela filed timely objections to the conduct of the Union on the morning of the election and sought to set aside the results. Following a hearing, a Hearing Officer of the NLRB recommended

overruling each objection and certifying the Union as the exclusive collective-bargaining representative. A Regional Director of the NLRB adopted the findings and recommendation and certified the Union. The Board declined review.

Exela nevertheless advised that it would not engage in bargaining because it did not consider the Union to be the properly certified representative of its employees. The Union filed an unfair labor practice charge with the NLRB. The then-Acting General Counsel issued a complaint, asserting that Exela violated

Case 22.1 Continues

Case 22.1 Continued

the NLRA by refusing to bargain in good faith with the Union. In its answer, Exela reasserted that the Union had been improperly certified. * * *

The Acting General Counsel moved for summary judgment, which the Board granted, finding that Exela failed to offer new evidence or special circumstances warranting review of the certification decision. * * * The Board's order required Exela to cease and desist from unfair labor practices, to bargain with the Union upon request, to embody any understanding reached in a signed agreement, and to post appropriate notice. Exela petitioned this Court for review. The Board applied for cross-enforcement of its order certifying the Union as the exclusive collective-bargaining representative of Exela employees at the New Brunswick site.

II

* * * *

III

Now, we turn to Exela's contention that the Board improperly ruled that Exela violated Sections 8(a)(1) and (5) of the NLRA. We review representation proceedings for the limited purpose of deciding whether to enforce, modify, or set aside the Board's unfair-labor-practice order in whole or in part. The Board's enforcement order turns on the validity of its earlier decision to certify the union. In turn, the certification order will be enforced if the Board's factual findings are "supported by substantial evidence on the record considered as a whole." "Substantial evidence is that which is relevant and sufficient for a reasonable mind to accept as adequate to support a conclusion. It is more than a mere scintilla, and less than a preponderance."

We are guided by the "strong presumption" that representation elections "reflect the true desires of the employees." Therefore, the party challenging the outcome "bears the entire burden of adducing *prima facie* facts sufficient to invalidate the election." That showing requires "specific evidence of specific events from or about specific people" establishing a level of interference with employees' free choice that tended to or did materially influence the results of the election.

A

First, Exela objected that the election should be set aside because an alleged agent of the Union, Fred Johnson, spoke with Exela employees during their shifts within twenty-four hours of the election, in violation of the Board's rule * * *.

On the morning of the election, Wanda Rodriguez, an Exela employee, observed Johnson "huddling" with three eligible voters in the receiving area during their shifts. Johnson was an employee of Jones Lange LaSalle ("JLL"), a separate employer with employees also working at the New Brunswick site. As part of his job duties, he routinely picked up packages in the receiving area, which is in a large, open warehouse space. Johnson also served as Union steward for a unit of JLL employees at the New Brunswick site.

Rodriguez told her supervisor, Jo Ann Lee, that Johnson was "huddled up with some of the staff." Lee then approached Johnson and asked if he needed help. He said that he had been looking for a package and eventually left without any packages. Neither Lee nor Rodriguez overheard the content of Johnson's discussion with the Exela employees.

* * * *

Here, the record does not reflect that Johnson had any involvement with the Exela organizing campaign. And Exela presented no evidence that the Union otherwise vested Johnson with authority to organize an Exela bargaining unit. But

the record does support that Johnson was *not* an agent of the Union. Brian Callow, a Union representative, testified that he and Arturo Archila were the only people assigned to the Exela organizing campaign. And Clifford Gray, an Exela employee, corroborated this statement. The Board was justified in finding that Johnson did not have actual authority to act on behalf of the Union with respect to the Exela election.

As for apparent authority, the Regional Director concluded that no evidence supported that *the Union* created a perception that Johnson acted on its behalf with respect to the Exela bargaining unit. We agree.

* * * *

B

Exela next contends that the Board abused its discretion when it overruled Exela's objection that two representatives of the Union stood near the polling site shortly before the polls opened.

* * * *

* * * Here, the record is devoid of evidence that Callow and Archila reentered the voting area or had conversations with eligible voters, much less prolonged conversations. Exela does not claim that any voters were even present at the polling site—whether in the parking lot, voting area, or in line to vote—at the same time as the Union representatives. The Board reasonably concluded that the conduct was not objectionable * * *.

* * * *

The Board was justified in overruling Exela's election objection.

Because substantial evidence in the record supports the findings on which the Board based its certification decision, there is no basis to set aside the Board's order concluding that Exela violated Sections 8(a)(1) and (5) of the NLRA. We DENY Exela's petition for review, and GRANT the Board's cross-petition for enforcement.

Legal Reasoning Questions

1. What did the court of appeals ruling mean for Exela Enterprise Solutions?
2. In proceedings such as those in this case, does the union have to prove that the election was valid, or does the employer have to prove that it was invalid?
3. Can Exela further appeal this decision from the United States Court of Appeals, Fifth Circuit?

22–3c Collective Bargaining

If the NLRB certifies the union, the union becomes the exclusive bargaining representative of the workers. The central legal right of a union is to engage in collective bargaining on the members' behalf. **Collective bargaining** is the process by which labor and management negotiate the terms and conditions of employment. Collective bargaining allows the representatives elected by union members to speak on behalf of the members at the bargaining table. Subjects for negotiation may include workplace safety, employee discounts, health-care plans, pension funds, and apprentice and scholarship programs.

Once an employer and a union sit down at the conference table, they must negotiate in good faith and make a reasonable effort to come to an agreement. They are not obligated to reach an agreement. They must, however, approach the negotiations with the idea that an agreement is possible. Both parties may engage in hard bargaining, but the bargaining process itself must be geared to reaching a compromise—not avoiding a compromise.

Although good faith is a matter of subjective intent, a party's actions can be used to evaluate the party's good or bad faith. Exhibit 22–1 illustrates some differences between good faith and bad faith bargaining. If an employer (or a union) refuses to bargain in good faith without justification, it has committed an unfair labor practice.

22–4 Strikes and Lockouts

Even when labor and management have bargained in good faith, they may be unable to reach a final agreement. When extensive collective bargaining has been conducted and an impasse results, the union may call a strike against the employer to pressure it into making concessions.

In a **strike,** the unionized employees leave their jobs and refuse to work. The workers also typically picket the workplace, standing outside the facility with signs stating their complaints. A strike is an extreme action. Striking workers lose their rights to be paid, and management loses production and may lose customers when orders cannot be filled.

Most strikes take the form of "economic strikes," which are initiated because the union wants a better contract. ■ **Example 22.4** Teachers in Eagle Point, Oregon, engage in an economic strike after contract negotiations with the school district fail to bring an agreement on pay, working hours, and subcontracting jobs. The unionized teachers picket outside the school building. Classes are canceled for a few weeks until the district can find substitute teachers who will fill in during the strike. ■

Exhibit 22–1 Good Faith Versus Bad Faith in Collective Bargaining

Good Faith Bargaining	Bad Faith Bargaining
1. Negotiating with the belief that an agreement is possible	1. Excessive delaying tactics
2. Seriously considering the other side's positions	2. Insistence on unreasonable contract terms
3. Making reasonable proposals	3. Rejecting a proposal without offering a counterproposal
4. Being willing to compromise	4. Engaging in a campaign among workers to undermine the union
5. Sending bargainers who have the authority to enter into agreements for the company	5. Constantly shifting positions on disputed contract terms
	6. Sending bargainers who lack authority to commit the company to a contract

22–4a The Right to Strike

The right to strike is guaranteed by the NLRA, within limits. Strike activities, such as picketing, are protected by the free speech guarantee of the First Amendment to the U.S. Constitution. Persons who are not employees have a right to participate in picketing an employer. The NLRA also gives workers the right to refuse to cross a picket line of fellow workers engaged in a lawful strike. Employers are permitted to hire replacement workers to substitute for the striking workers.

22–4b Illegal Strikes

In the following situations, the conduct of the strikers may cause the strikes to be illegal:

1. **Violent strikes.** The use of violence (including the threat of violence) against management employees or substitute workers is illegal.
2. **Massed picketing.** If the strikers form a barrier and deny management or other nonunion workers access to the plant, the strike is illegal.
3. **Sit-down strikes.** Strikes in which employees simply stay in the plant without working are illegal.
4. **No-strike clause.** A strike may be illegal if it contravenes a no-strike clause that was in the previous collective bargaining agreement between the employer and the union.
5. **Secondary boycotts.** A **secondary boycott** is an illegal strike that is directed against someone other than the strikers' employer, such as companies that sell materials to the employer. ■ **Example 22.5** The unionized workers of SemiCo go out on strike. To increase their economic leverage, the workers picket the leading suppliers and customers of SemiCo in an attempt to hurt the company's business. SemiCo is considered the primary employer, and its suppliers and customers are considered secondary employers. Picketing of the suppliers or customers is a secondary boycott. ■
6. **Wildcat strikes.** A wildcat strike occurs when a small number of workers, perhaps dissatisfied with a union's representation, call their own strike. The union is the exclusive bargaining representative of a group of workers, and only the union can call a strike. Therefore, a wildcat strike, unauthorized by the certified union, is illegal.

22–4c After a Strike Ends

In a typical strike, the employer has a right to hire permanent replacements during the strike. The employer need not terminate the replacement workers when the economic strikers seek to return to work. In other words, striking workers are not guaranteed the right to return to their jobs after the strike if satisfactory replacement workers have been found.

If the employer has not hired replacement workers to fill the strikers' positions, however, then the employer must rehire the economic strikers to fill any vacancies. Employers may not discriminate against former economic strikers, and those who are rehired retain their seniority rights.

22–4d Lockouts

Lockouts are the employer's counterpart to the workers' right to strike. A **lockout** occurs when the employer shuts down to prevent employees from working. Lockouts usually are used when the employer believes that a strike is imminent or the parties have reached a stalemate in collective bargaining.

■ **Example 22.6** In December 2021, a new collective bargaining agreement was due between the Major League Baseball Players' Association and the major league team owners. The Major League Baseball Commissioner, Rob Manfred, implemented a lockout as a means of creating leverage during negotiations with the players' union. The move stopped offseason play, and as a result, unsigned players were forbidden from signing major-league contracts with teams. After months of negotiations, the lockout ended on March 10, 2022. ■

Some lockouts are illegal. An employer may not use a lockout as a tool to break the union and pressure employees into decertification, which occurs when union members vote to dissociate from the union. An employer must be able to show some economic justification for the lockout.

22–5 Unfair Labor Practices

The preceding sections have discussed unfair labor practices involved in union elections, collective bargaining, and strikes. Many unfair labor practices may occur within

Exhibit 22–2 Basic Unfair Labor Practices

It is unfair for employers to...	It is unfair for unions to...
1. Refuse to recognize a union and refuse to bargain in good faith. 2. Interfere with, restrain, or coerce employees in their efforts to form a union and bargain collectively. 3. Dominate a union. 4. Discriminate against union workers. 5. Punish employees for engaging in concerted activity.	1. Refuse to bargain in good faith. 2. Picket to coerce unionization without the support of a majority of the employees. 3. Demand the hiring of unnecessary excess workers. 4. Discriminate against nonunion workers. 5. Agree to participate in a secondary boycott. 6. Engage in an illegal strike. 7. Charge excessive membership fees.

the normal working relationship as well. The most important of these practices are discussed in the following sections and listed in Exhibit 22–2.

22–5a Employer's Unfair Labor Practices

Thousands of complaints are filed each year by employees claiming that their employer has engaged in an unfair labor practice in violation of the NLRA. Charges often arise when an employer coerces, interferes with, or refuses to recognize an employee's protected rights.

Employer's Refusal to Recognize the Union and to Negotiate As discussed, once a union has been certified, an employer must recognize and bargain in good faith with the union. Failure to do so is an unfair labor practice.

Certification places responsibility on the union as well. Because the NLRA embraces a policy of majority rule, certification of the union as the bargaining unit's representative binds all of the employees in that bargaining unit. Thus, the union must fairly represent all the members of the bargaining unit.

Certification does not mean that a union will continue indefinitely as the exclusive representative of the bargaining unit. If the union loses the support of a majority of those it represents, an employer is not obligated to continue to recognize or negotiate with the union.

As a practical matter, a newly elected representative needs time to establish itself among the workers and to begin to formulate and implement its programs.

Therefore, a union is immune from attack by employers and from repudiation by the employees for a period of one year after certification.

Employer's Interference in Union Activities The NLRA declares it to be an unfair labor practice for an employer to interfere with, restrain, or coerce employees in the exercise of their rights to form a union and bargain collectively. Unlawful employer interference may take a variety of forms.

Courts have found it an unfair labor practice for an employer to make threats that may interfere with an employee's decision to join a union. Even asking employees about their views on the union may be considered coercive. Employees responding to such questioning must be able to remain anonymous and must receive assurances against employer reprisals.

Employers also may not prohibit certain forms of union activity in the workplace. If an employee has a grievance with the company, the employer cannot prevent the union's participation in support of that employee.

If an employer has unlawfully interfered with the operation of a union, the NLRB or a reviewing court may issue a cease-and-desist order. The company typically is required to post the order on a bulletin board and renounce its past unlawful conduct.

Protected, concerted activity can take many forms. In the following case, the court had to decide whether an employee's objection to another employee's discharge was "insubordinate behavior" or a protected act.

Staffing Network Holdings, LLC v. National Labor Relations Board

United States Court of Appeals, Seventh Circuit, 815 F.3d 296 (2016).

Background and Facts   Staffing Network Holdings, LLC, provides temporary and long-term employees to a variety of employers, including ReaderLink, a company that fills book orders for other businesses. ReaderLink's workers include "pickers," who select books to fill orders and place the books in boxes. Other employees include "stockers," who bring the boxes to the pickers to fill.

One afternoon, Staffing Network's on-site manager at ReaderLink, Andy Vega, fired a stocker for his "attitude." Griselda Barrera, Olga Gutierrez, and other pickers complained that this was not fair. Vega replied that he could send them all home. Barrera told the others to "stand up against all the injustice." Vega told her to leave. She protested but left. Later, she was told not to return.

Barrera filed a claim for unemployment compensation. The state asked Staffing Network to provide the reason for her separation from work, to which Staffing Network responded that Barrera was disrupting production. Barrera also filed an unfair labor practice charge with the National Labor Relations Board (NLRB). The NLRB filed a complaint against Staffing Network for terminating Barrera. An administrative law judge (ALJ) rejected the employer's claim that Barrera's "insubordinate behavior" justified the discharge, and ordered reinstatement and payment of back wages and benefits. Staffing Network petitioned for review. The NLRB petitioned for enforcement of the ALJ's order.

In the Language of the Court

ROVNER, Circuit Judge.
* * * *

Accepting the ALJ's factual findings (which were in turn affirmed by the Board), the only * * * question is whether those facts lend substantial evidence to the Board's finding that the company wrongfully terminated Barrera * * * . *An employer violates [the National Labor Relations Act] when it threatens employees with discipline or discharge for engaging in concerted activity that is protected.* Threats of discharge, discipline, other reprisals against employees for engaging in union activity violate the Act because these acts reasonably tend to coerce employees in the exercise of their rights, regardless of whether they do, in fact, coerce. The tendency to coerce is judged from the viewpoint of the employee. [Emphasis added.]

* * * The company's response to the State's unemployment inquiry provides a veritable smoking gun on the issue of the reason for Barrera's termination. Asked to provide the reason for Barrera's involuntary separation, Staffing Network explained that after a stocker was told to speed up his work, Barrera objected and then began "talking to some of the ladies in the line disrupting the production." According to Vega's own description of events, after he told Barrera to punch out and go home "if she does not want to work," Barrera "ignored the request and continued to get the ladies in the line worked up saying this was going against the law and that they have to stand up against all the injustice we are committing. Due to this, Griselda Barrera cannot return to ReaderLink." With this response to the State, the company essentially admitted the relevant facts supporting the ALJ's conclusion. *It is well settled that a brief, on-the-job work-stoppage is a form of economic pressure entitled to protection under the Act.* That is the type of action that Vega described in his response to the State in justifying Barrera's discharge. Witness testimony also supported the finding that Staffing Network terminated Barrera because of her concerted, protected activity in protesting Vega's treatment of [the stocker] in relation to the terms and conditions of his employment and that of the pickers. Namely, Barrera and Gutierrez both testified that Vega told Barrera to leave because she and the other pickers protested Vega's unfair treatment of [the stocker]. Therefore, substantial evidence supports the Board's finding that the company violated the Act when it discharged Barrera for engaging in protected, concerted activity. [Emphasis added.]

Decision and Remedy   The U.S. Court of Appeals for the Seventh Circuit denied Staffing Network's petition for review and granted the NLRB's petition for enforcement of the ALJ's order.

"The pickers' temporary work stoppage and complaints to Vega regarding his treatment of [the fired stocker] constituted protected, concerted activity."

Critical Thinking

- **Legal Environment** The NLRB ordered Staffing Network to reinstate Barrera at ReaderLink and to pay her back wages and benefits. What other remedies might be appropriate in this case?
- **What If the Facts Were Different?** Suppose that instead of telling Barrera to leave Vega had said, "Get back to work" and had then left the area. Would the result have been different? Discuss.

Employer's Domination of a Union In the early days of unionization, employers fought back by forming employer-sponsored unions to represent employees. These "company unions" were seldom more than the puppets of management. The NLRA outlawed company unions and any other form of employer domination of workers' unions.

Under the law against employer domination, an employer can have no say in which employees belong to the union or which employees serve as union officers. Nor may supervisors or other management personnel participate in union meetings.

Company actions that support a union may be considered improper potential domination. A company cannot give union workers pay for time spent on union activities, because this is considered undue support for the union. A company may not provide financial aid to a union and may not solicit workers to join a union.

Employer's Discrimination Against Union Employees The NLRA prohibits employers from discriminating against workers because they are union officers or are otherwise associated with a union. When workers must be laid off, the company cannot consider union participation as a criterion for deciding whom to fire.

The provisions prohibiting discrimination also apply to hiring decisions. ■ **Example 22.7** Certain employees of SemiCo are represented by a union, but the company is attempting to weaken the union's strength. The company is prohibited from requiring potential new hires to guarantee that they will not join the union. ■

22–5b Union's Unfair Labor Practices

Certain union activities are declared to be unfair labor practices by the Labor-Management Relations Act. Secondary boycotts and illegal strikes, discussed earlier, are examples of such unfair labor practices.

Coercion Another significant unfair labor practice by a union is coercion or restraint to affect an employee's decision to participate in or refrain from participating in union activities. Obviously, it is unlawful for a union to threaten an employee or a family with violence for failure to join the union. The law's prohibition includes economic coercion as well. ■ **Example 22.8** A union official declares, "We have a lot of power here. You had better join the union, or you may lose your job." This threat is an unfair labor practice. ■

The NLRA provides unions with the authority to regulate their own internal affairs, which includes disciplining union members. This discipline cannot be used in an improperly coercive fashion, however. ■ **Example 22.9** Jake Kowalski is a union member who feels that the union is no longer providing proper representation for employees at his workplace. He starts a campaign to decertify the union. The union may expel Kowalski from membership, but it may not fine or otherwise discipline him. ■

Discrimination A union may not discriminate against workers because they refuse to join. In addition, the Labor-Management Relations Act also prohibits a union from using its influence to cause an employer to discriminate against workers who refuse to join the union. A union cannot force an employer to deny promotions to workers who fail to join the union.

Other Unfair Practices Other unfair labor practices by unions include demanding the hiring of unnecessary workers, participating in picketing to coerce unionization without majority employee support, and refusing to engage in good faith bargaining with employer representatives.

Unions are allowed to bargain for certain "union security clauses" in contracts. Although closed shops are illegal, a union can bargain for a provision that requires workers to contribute to the union within thirty days after they are hired. This is typically called a union shop, or agency shop, clause.

The union shop clause can compel workers to begin paying dues to the certified union but cannot require the worker to "join" the union. Dues payment can be required to prevent workers from taking the benefits of union bargaining without contributing to the union's efforts. The clause cannot require workers to contribute their efforts to the union, however, or to go out on strike.

Even a requirement of dues payment has its limits. Excessive initiation fees or dues may be illegal. Unions often use their revenues to contribute to causes or to lobby politicians. A nonunion employee subject to a union shop clause who must pay dues cannot be required to contribute to this sort of union expenditure.

In the following case, a union used picketing as part of a campaign to organize the employees of a hotel in Hawaii. The picketing did not deny management or non-union employees access to the hotel, but it did block or impede employees and others from entering or exiting the premises for brief periods of time. Was the evidence sufficient to support an order finding that the union's actions restrained or coerced employees in violation of the National Labor Relations Act?

Unite Here! Local 5 v. National Labor Relations Board

United States Court of Appeals, Ninth Circuit, 768 Fed.Appx. 627 (2019).

Background and Facts   Unite Here! Local 5 sponsored pickets at the Aston Waikiki Beach Hotel in Honolulu, Hawaii. For several months, on a regular basis, individuals numbering from twelve to two hundred marched across the hotel's entrance at its *porte cochere*—a one-way, U-shaped, covered driveway. The picketing blocked or impeded hotel employees and others from entering or exiting the hotel for a few minutes at a time. Taxis and other vehicles, including cars driven by guests, were also stopped and delayed.

Aqua-Aston Hospitality, LLC, the Aston's operator, filed charges with the National Labor Relations Board (NLRB) against Unite Here! Local 5. The filing prompted the NLRB to issue two complaints against the union. After hearings, the union was found to have violated the National Labor Relations Act (NLRA). On review, the NLRB affirmed the finding. Unite Here! Local 5 petitioned the U.S. Court of Appeals for the Ninth Circuit for a review of the NLRB's decision.

In the Language of the Court

MEMORANDUM.

* * * *

The NLRB bears primary responsibility for developing and applying national labor policy. *So long as the Board's interpretation of the [National Labor Relations] Act [NLRA] in a case is rational and consistent with the statute, its rulings are afforded considerable deference.* The NLRB's findings of fact are conclusive if they are supported by substantial evidence on the record as a whole. As to a factual finding, the court may not displace the Board's choice between two fairly conflicting views, even though the court would justifiably have made a different choice had the matter been before it *de novo.* Given the NLRB's special expertise in the field of labor relations, we defer to the reasonable derivative inferences drawn by the Board from credited evidence. [Emphasis added.]

Section 7 of the NLRA grants employees "the right to self-organization, to form, join, or assist labor organizations, to bargain collectively through representatives of their own choosing, and to engage in other concerted activities for the purpose of collective bargaining or other mutual aid or protection." It also guarantees employees "the right to refrain from any or all of such activities." Section 8(b)(1)(A) makes it "an unfair labor practice for a labor organization or its agents * * * to restrain or coerce * * * employees in the exercise of the rights guaranteed in section [7 of the Act]." Determining the existence of a restraint or coercion turns on whether the misconduct is such that, under the circumstances existing, it may reasonably tend to coerce or intimidate employees in the exercise of rights protected under the Act.

Substantial evidence supports the NLRB's finding that the Union had deliberately, repeatedly, and persistently blocked numerous vehicles driven by employees for 1–4 minutes at a time, and engaged in similar conduct by temporarily blocking numerous vehicles in the presence or view of the hotel valet and bell employees. The NLRB * * * rejected the Union's argument that its conduct was brief and merely inconvenienced vehicles and was minor or *de minimis* [too minor to be of legal consequence], and distinguished the Union's actions from cases that involved only a few affected employees during months of picketing. Short delays, occurring regularly over the course of months and affecting workers during their performance of work duties, as well as others in the presence of employees, is sufficient to reasonably find that such actions violated the NLRA. The explanations of the NLRB's legal position * * * were therefore not inadequate, irrational or arbitrary.

Decision and Remedy The U.S. Court of Appeals for the Ninth Circuit affirmed the decision of the NLRB and the findings of its administrative law judges that the union was in violation of the NLRA.

Critical Thinking
- **Economic** Why are strikers permitted to picket, but not to picket aggressively? Discuss.
- **Legal Environment** What penalty should be imposed on Unite Here! Local 5 for its misconduct? Explain.

Practice and Review: Immigration and Labor Law

In April, several employees of Javatech, Inc., a computer hardware developer with 250 employees, started organizing the Javatech Employees Union (JEU). When Javatech refused to voluntarily recognize the union, organizers petitioned the National Labor Relations Board (NLRB) for an election. In June, the NLRB conducted an election that showed that a majority of Javatech employees supported the union. JEU was certified and began bargaining with management over wages and benefits.

The following January, Javatech management offered the JEU a 1 percent annual wage increase for all employees with no other changes in employment benefits. The JEU countered by requesting a 3 percent wage increase and an employee health-insurance package. Javatech management responded that the 1 percent wage increase was the company's only offer. The JEU petitioned the NLRB for an order requesting good faith bargaining. After meeting with an NLRB representative, Javatech management still refused to consider modifying its position. JEU leaders then became embroiled in a dispute about whether the JEU should accept this offer or go on strike.

New union leaders were elected in July, and the employer refused to meet with the new JEU representatives, claiming that the union no longer had majority support from employees. In August, a group of seven Javatech engineers began feeling ill while working with a new adhesive used in creating motherboards. The seven engineers discussed going on strike without union support. Before they had reached an agreement, one of the engineers, Rosa Molina, became dizzy while working with the adhesive and walked out of the workplace. Using the information presented in the chapter, answer the following questions.

1. How many of Javatech's 250 employees must have signed authorization cards to allow the JEU to petition the NLRB for an election?
2. What must Javatech change in its collective bargaining negotiations to demonstrate that it is bargaining in good faith with the JEU, as required by labor law?
3. Could the seven engineers legally call a strike? What would such a strike be called?
4. Would Molina's safety walkout be protected under the Labor-Management Relations Act? Explain.

Debate This . . . To attract the brightest minds to work in the United States, there should be no limit on the number of H-1B visas available to immigrants with highly specialized knowledge.

Terms and Concepts

authorization card 475
cease-and-desist order 474
closed shop 475
collective bargaining 479

hot-cargo agreements 475
I-9 verifications 472
I-551 Permanent Resident Card 473
lockout 480

right-to-work laws 475
secondary boycott 480
strike 479
union shop 475

Issue Spotters

1. Aanan Gara is the head of human resources at Skytech, Inc., a firm in Silicon Valley, California. Because Skytech cannot find enough domestic workers with specialized skills, Gara wants to recruit qualified employees from other nations. What must Gara do under the Immigration Act to hire foreign employees for Skytech? (See *Immigration Law*.)

2. Onyx applies for work with Precision Design Company, which requires union membership as a condition

of employment. She also applies for work with Quality Engineering, Inc., which does not require union membership as a condition of employment but requires employees to join a union after six months on the job. Are these conditions legal? Why or why not? (See *Federal Labor Laws*.)

• **Check your answers to the Issue Spotters against the answers provided in Appendix B at the end of this text.**

Business Scenarios and Case Problems

22–1. Unfair Labor Practices. Consolidated Stores is undergoing a unionization campaign. Prior to the union election, management states that the union is unnecessary to protect workers. Management also provides bonuses and wage increases to the workers during this period. The employees reject the union. Union organizers protest that the wage increases during the election campaign unfairly prejudiced the vote. Should these wage increases be regarded as an unfair labor practice? Discuss. (See *Unfair Labor Practices*.)

22–2. Appropriate Bargaining Unit. A group of employees at the Briarwood Furniture Company's manufacturing plant were interested in joining a union. Briarwood employs four hundred unskilled workers and one hundred skilled workers in its plant. The unskilled workers operate the industrial machinery used in processing Briarwood's line of standardized plastic office furniture. The skilled workers, who work in an entirely separate part of the plant, are experienced artisans who craft Briarwood's line of expensive wood furniture products. Do you see any problems with a single union's representing all the workers at the Briarwood plant? Explain. (See *Union Organization*.)

22–3. Spotlight on Verizon—Collective Bargaining. Verizon New York, Inc. (VNY), provides telecommunications services. VNY and the Communications Workers of America (CWA) are parties to collective bargaining agreements covering installation and maintenance employees. At one time, VNY supported annual blood drives. VNY, the CWA, and charitable organizations jointly set dates, arranged appointments, and adjusted work schedules for the drives. For each drive, about a thousand employees, including managers, spent up to four hours traveling to a donor site, giving blood, recovering, and returning to their jobs. Employees received

full pay for the time. In 2001, VNY told the CWA that it would no longer allow employees to participate "on Company time," claiming that it had experienced problems meeting customer requests for service during the drives. The CWA filed a complaint with the National Labor Relations Board (NLRB), asking that VNY be ordered to bargain over the decision. Did VNY commit an unfair labor practice? Should the NLRB grant the CWA's request? Why or why not? [*Verizon New York, Inc. v. National Labor Relations Board*, 360 F.3d 206 (D.C. Cir. 2004)] (See *Union Organization*.)

22–4. Immigration Work Status. Mohammad Hashmi, a citizen of Pakistan, entered the United States on a student visa. Two years later, when he applied for a job at Compu-Credit, he completed an I-9 form and checked the box to indicate that he was "a citizen or national of the United States." Soon after submitting that form, he married a U.S. citizen. Several months later, the federal immigration services claimed that Hashmi had misrepresented himself as a U.S. citizen. Hashmi contended that he had not misrepresented himself. At an administrative hearing, he testified that when he filled out the I-9 form he believed that he was a "national of the United States" because he was legally in the country under a student visa and was going to marry a U.S. citizen. He requested that his immigration status be adjusted to account for the fact that he was employed and married to an American. The immigration judge rejected that request and found that Hashmi had made a false claim on the I-9 form. He ruled that Hashmi was "inadmissible" to the United States and that his legal status in the country could not be amended because of his marriage or employment. Hashmi appealed. Should Hashmi's visa status be changed because of his marriage and employment? Why or why not? How should the appellate court rule in this case? [*Hashmi v. Mukasey*, 533 F.3d 700 (8th Cir. 2008)] (See *Immigration Law*.)

22–5. Business Case Problem With Sample Answer—Unfair Labor Practices. The Laborers' International Union of North America, Local 578, and Shaw Stone & Webster Construction, Inc., agreed on a provision in their collective bargaining agreement that required all employees to pay dues to the union. Sebedeo Lopez went to work for Shaw Stone without paying the union dues. When the union pressed the company to fire him, Lopez agreed to pay. The union continued to demand his discharge, however, and Shaw Stone fired him. Was the union guilty of unfair labor practices? Why or why not? [*Laborers' International Union of North America, Local 578 v. National Labor Relations Board*, 594 F.3d 732 (10th Cir. 2010)] (See *Unfair Labor Practices.*)

- For a sample answer to Problem 22–5, go to Appendix C at the end of this text.

22–6. Collective Bargaining. SDBC Holdings, Inc., acquired Stella D'oro Biscuit Company, a bakery in New York City. At the time, a collective bargaining agreement existed between Stella D'oro and Local 50, Bakery, Confectionary, Tobacco Workers and Grain Millers International Union. During negotiations to renew the agreement, Stella D'oro refused to give the union a copy of the company's financial statement. Stella D'oro did allow Local 50 to examine and take notes on the financial statement and offered the union an opportunity to make its own copy. Did Stella D'oro engage in an unfair labor practice? Discuss. [*SDBC Holdings, Inc. v. National Labor Relations Board*, 711 F.3d 281 (2d Cir. 2013)] (See *Union Organization.*)

22–7. Labor Unions. Carol Garcia and Pedro Salgado were bus drivers for Latino Express, Inc., a transportation company. Garcia and Salgado began soliciting signatures from other drivers to certify the Teamsters Local Union No. 777 as the official representative of the employees. Latino Express fired Garcia and Salgado. The two drivers filed a claim with the National Labor Relations Board (NLRB), alleging that the employer had committed an unfair labor practice. Which employer practice defined by the National Labor Relations Act did the plaintiffs most likely charge Latino Express with committing? Is the employer's discharge of Garcia and Salgado likely to be construed as a legitimate act in opposition to union solicitation? If a violation is found, what can the NLRB do? Discuss. [*Ohr v. Latino Express, Inc.*, 776 F.3d 469 (7th Cir. 2015)] (See *Union Organization.*)

22–8. A Question of Ethics—The IDDR Approach and Immigration Law. Split Rail Fence Company sells and installs fencing materials in Colorado. U.S. Immigration and Customs Enforcement (ICE) sent Split Rail a list of the company's employees whose documentation did not satisfy the Form I-9 employment eligibility verification requirements. The list included long-term workers who had been involved in company activities, parties, and picnics. They had bank accounts, driver's licenses, cars, homes, and mortgages. At Split Rail's request, the employees orally verified that they were eligible to work in the United States. Unwilling to accept the oral verifications, ICE filed a complaint against Split Rail for its continued employment of the individuals. [*Split Rail Fence Co. v. United States*, 852 F.3d 1228 (10th Cir. 2017)] (See *Immigration Law.*)

(a) Using the IDDR approach, identify Split Rail's ethical dilemma. What steps might the company take to resolve it? Explain.

(b) Is penalizing employers the best approach to take in attempting to curb illegal immigration? Discuss.

Time-Limited Group Assignment

22–9. Immigration. Nicole Tipton and Sadik Seferi owned and operated a restaurant in Iowa. Acting on a tip from the local police, agents of Immigration and Customs Enforcement executed search warrants at the restaurant and at an apartment where some restaurant workers lived. The agents discovered six undocumented aliens who worked at the restaurant and lived together. When the I-9 forms for the restaurant's employees were reviewed, none were found for the six aliens. They were paid in cash while other employees were paid by check. Tipton and Seferi were charged with hiring and harboring undocumented aliens. (See *Immigration Law.*)

(a) The first group will develop an argument that Tipton and Seferi were guilty of hiring and harboring illegal aliens.

(b) The second group will assess whether Tipton and Seferi can assert a defense by claiming that they did not know that the workers were unauthorized aliens.

(c) The third group will determine the potential penalties that Tipton and Seferi could face for violating the Immigration Reform and Control Act by hiring six unauthorized workers.

Unit Four: Task-Based Simulation

Two brothers, Ray and Paul Ashford, start a business—Ashford Brothers, Inc.—manufacturing a new type of battery system for hybrid automobiles. The batteries hit the market at the perfect time and are in great demand.

1. **Agency.** Loren, one of Ashford's salespersons, anxious to make a sale, intentionally quotes a price to a customer that is $500 lower than Ashford has authorized for the product. The customer purchases the product at the quoted price. When Ashford learns of the deal, it claims that it is not legally bound to the sales contract because it has not authorized Loren to sell the product at that price. Is Ashford bound to the contract? Discuss fully.

2. **Workers' Compensation.** One day, Gina, an Ashford employee, suffers a serious burn when she accidentally spills some acid on her hand. The accident occurs because another employee, who is suspected of using illegal drugs, carelessly bumps into her. Gina's hand requires a series of skin grafts before it heals sufficiently to allow her to return to work. Gina wants to obtain compensation for her lost wages and medical expenses. Can she do that? If so, how?

3. **Drug Testing.** After Gina's injury, Ashford decides to conduct random drug tests on all of its employees.

Several employees claim that the testing violates their privacy rights, and they file a lawsuit. What factors will the court consider in deciding whether the random drug testing is legally permissible?

4. **COBRA.** Ashford provides health insurance for its two hundred employees, including Dan. For personal medical reasons, Dan takes twelve weeks' leave. During this period, can Dan continue his coverage under Ashford's health-insurance plan? After Dan returns to work, Ashford closes Dan's division and terminates the employees, including Dan. Can Dan continue his coverage under Ashford's health-insurance plan after the termination? Explain.

5. **Sexual Harassment.** Aretha, another employee at Ashford, is disgusted by the sexually offensive behavior of several male employees. She complains to her supervisor on several occasions about the behavior, but the supervisor merely laughs at her concerns. Aretha decides to bring a legal action against the company for sexual harassment. Does Aretha's complaint concern *quid pro quo* harassment or hostile-environment harassment? What federal statute protects employees from sexual harassment? What remedies are available under that statute? What procedures must Aretha follow in pursuing her legal action?

The Regulatory Environment

Chapter 23

Administrative Agencies

Government agencies established to administer the law have a great impact on the day-to-day operations of businesses. In its early years, the United States had a simple, nonindustrial economy with little regulation. As the economy has grown and become more complex, the size of government has also increased, and so has the number, size, and power of administrative agencies.

Administrative agencies make policy decisions that can profoundly influence American industries. For instance, the Federal Communications Commission (FCC) is working to facilitate the country's switch from fourth-generation (4G) to fifth-generation (5G) wireless technology. By investing billions of tax dollars in rural broadband connections and preempting local regulations on cell towers, the FCC hopes to encourage private telecommunications companies to make 5G wireless networks—with connection speeds from 10 to 100 times faster than those offered by 4G—commonplace by the end of the decade.

As the number of agencies has multiplied, so have the rules, orders, and decisions that they issue. Today, there are rules covering almost every aspect of a business's operations. These regulations make up the body of administrative law.

23–1 The Practical Significance of Administrative Law

Whereas statutory law is created by legislatures, administrative law is created by administrative agencies. When Congress (or a state legislature) enacts legislation, it typically adopts a rather general statute and leaves its implementation to an **administrative agency.** The agency then creates the detailed rules and regulations necessary to carry out the statute. The administrative agency, with its specialized personnel, has the time, resources, and expertise to make the detailed decisions required for regulation.

23–1a Administrative Agencies Exist at All Levels of Government

Administrative agencies are spread throughout the government. At the federal level, the Securities and Exchange Commission regulates a firm's capital structure and financing, as well as its financial reporting. The National Labor Relations Board oversees relations between a firm and any unions with which it may deal. The Equal Employment Opportunity Commission also regulates employer-employee relationships. The Environmental Protection Agency and the Occupational Safety and Health Administration affect the way a firm manufactures its products, and the Federal Trade Commission influences the way it markets those products.

There are administrative agencies at the state and local levels as well. Commonly, a state agency (such as a state pollution-control agency) is created as a parallel to a federal agency (such as the Environmental Protection Agency). Just as federal statutes take precedence over conflicting state statutes, so do federal agency regulations take precedence over conflicting state regulations. Because the rules of state and local agencies vary widely, we focus here exclusively on federal administrative law.

23–1b Agencies Provide a Comprehensive Regulatory Scheme

Often, administrative agencies at various levels of government work together and share the responsibility of creating and enforcing particular regulations. ■ **Example 23.1** When Congress enacted the Clean Air Act, it provided only general directions for the prevention of air pollution. The specific pollution-control requirements imposed on businesses are almost entirely the product of decisions made by the Environmental Protection Agency (EPA). Moreover, the EPA works with parallel environmental agencies at the state level to analyze existing data and determine the appropriate pollution-control standards. ■

Legislation and regulations have significant benefits—in the example of the Clean Air Act, a cleaner environment than existed in decades past. At the same time, these benefits entail considerable costs for business. The EPA has estimated the costs of compliance with the Clean Air Act at many tens of billions of dollars yearly. Although the agency has calculated that the overall benefits of its regulations often exceed their costs, the burden on business is substantial. Business therefore has a strong incentive to try to influence the regulatory environment through lobbying.

23–2 Agency Creation and Powers

Congress creates federal administrative agencies. By delegating some of its authority to make and implement laws, Congress can indirectly monitor a particular area in which it has passed legislation. Delegation enables Congress to avoid becoming bogged down in the details relating to enforcement—details that are often best left to specialists.

To create an administrative agency, Congress passes **enabling legislation,** which specifies the name, purposes, functions, and powers of the agency being created. Federal administrative agencies can exercise only those powers that Congress has delegated to them in enabling legislation. Through similar enabling acts, state legislatures create state administrative agencies.

An agency's enabling statute defines its legal authority. An agency cannot regulate beyond the powers granted by the statute, and it may be required to take some regulatory action by the terms of that statute. When regulated groups oppose a rule adopted by an agency, they often bring a lawsuit arguing that the rule was not authorized by the enabling statute and is therefore void. Conversely, a group may file a suit claiming that an agency has illegally failed to pursue regulation required by the enabling statute.

23–2a Enabling Legislation—An Example

Congress created the Federal Trade Commission (FTC) in the Federal Trade Commission Act.[1] The act prohibits unfair methods of competition and deceptive trade practices. It also describes the procedures that the FTC must follow to charge persons or organizations with violations of the act, and it provides for judicial review of agency orders. The act grants the FTC the power to do the following:

1. Create "rules and regulations for the purpose of carrying out the Act."

2. Conduct investigations of business practices.
3. Obtain reports from interstate corporations concerning their business practices.
4. Investigate possible violations of federal antitrust statutes. (The FTC shares this task with the Antitrust Division of the U.S. Department of Justice.)
5. Publish findings of its investigations.
6. Recommend new legislation.
7. Hold trial-like hearings to resolve certain trade disputes that involve FTC regulations or federal antitrust laws.

The commission that heads the FTC is composed of five members. The president, with the advice and consent of the Senate, appoints each of the FTC commissioners for a term of seven years. The president also designates one of the commissioners to be the chair.

23–2b Types of Agencies

There are two basic types of administrative agencies: executive agencies and independent regulatory agencies.

Federal executive agencies include the cabinet departments of the executive branch, which assist the president in carrying out executive functions, and the subagencies within the cabinet departments. The Occupational Safety and Health Administration, for instance, is a subagency within the U.S. Department of Labor. Executive agencies usually have a single administrator, director, or secretary who is appointed by the president to oversee the agency and can be removed by the president at any time. Exhibit 23–1 lists the cabinet departments and some of their most important subagencies.

Independent regulatory agencies, such as the Federal Trade Commission and the Securities and Exchange Commission (SEC), are outside the federal executive departments (those headed by a cabinet secretary). The president's power is less pronounced in regard to independent agencies, whose officers serve for fixed terms and cannot be removed without just cause. See Exhibit 23–2 for a list of selected independent regulatory agencies and their principal functions.

23–2c Agency Powers and the Constitution

Administrative agencies occupy an unusual niche in the U.S. governmental structure, because they exercise powers that normally are divided among the three branches of government. Agencies' powers include functions associated with the legislature (rulemaking), the executive branch (enforcement), and the courts (adjudication).

---

1. 15 U.S.C. Sections 41–58.

Exhibit 23-1 Executive Departments and Important Subagencies

Department	Selected Subagencies
State	Passport Office; Bureau of Diplomatic Security; Foreign Service; Bureau of Intelligence and Research
Treasury	Internal Revenue Service; U.S. Mint
Interior	U.S. Fish and Wildlife Service; National Park Service; Bureau of Indian Affairs; Bureau of Land Management
Justice[a]	Federal Bureau of Investigation; Drug Enforcement Administration; Bureau of Prisons; U.S. Marshals Service
Agriculture	Soil Conservation Service; Agricultural Research Service; Food Safety and Inspection Service
Commerce[b]	Bureau of the Census; Bureau of Economic Analysis; U.S. Patent and Trademark Office; National Oceanic and Atmospheric Administration
Labor[b]	Occupational Safety and Health Administration; Bureau of Labor Statistics; Employment Standards Administration; Office of Labor-Management Standards
Defense[c]	National Security Agency; Joint Chiefs of Staff; Departments of the Air Force, Navy, Army
Housing and Urban Development	Government National Mortgage Association; Office of Fair Housing and Equal Opportunity
Transportation	Federal Aviation Administration; Federal Highway Administration; National Highway Traffic Safety Administration
Energy	Office of Civilian Radioactive Waste Management; Office of Nuclear Energy; Energy Information Administration
Health and Human Services[d]	Food and Drug Administration; Centers for Medicare and Medicaid Services; Centers for Disease Control and Prevention; National Institutes of Health
Education[d]	Office of Elementary and Secondary Education; Office of Postsecondary Education; Office of Vocational and Adult Education
Veterans Affairs	Veterans Health Administration; Veterans Benefits Administration; National Cemetery Administration
Homeland Security	U.S. Citizenship and Immigration Services; Directorate of Border and Transportation Services; U.S. Coast Guard; Federal Emergency Management Agency

a. Formed from the Office of the Attorney General.
b. Formed from the Department of Commerce and Labor.
c. Formed from the Department of War and the Department of the Navy.
d. Formed from the Department of Health, Education, and Welfare.

The constitutional principle of checks and balances allows each branch of government to act as a check on the actions of the other two branches. Furthermore, the U.S. Constitution authorizes only the legislative branch to create laws. Yet administrative agencies, to which the Constitution does not specifically refer, can make **legislative rules,** or substantive rules, that are as legally binding as laws that Congress passes.

Administrative agencies also issue **interpretive rules,** which simply declare policy and do not affect legal rights or obligations. ■ **Example 23.2** The Equal Employment Opportunity Commission periodically issues interpretive rules indicating how it plans to interpret the provisions of certain statutes, such as the Americans with Disabilities Act. These informal rules provide enforcement guidelines for agency officials. ■

Exhibit 23–2 Selected Independent Regulatory Agencies

Name of Agency	Principal Duties
Federal Trade Commission (FTC)	Prevents businesses from engaging in unfair trade practices; stops the formation of monopolies in the business sector.
Securities and Exchange Commission (SEC)	Regulates the nation's stock exchanges, in which shares of stock are bought and sold; enforces the securities laws.
Federal Communications Commission (FCC)	Regulates communications by telegraph, cable, telephone, radio, satellite, Internet, and television.
National Labor Relations Board (NLRB)	Protects employees' rights to join unions and bargain collectively with employers; attempts to prevent unfair labor practices by both employers and unions.
Equal Employment Opportunity Commission (EEOC)	Works to eliminate discrimination in employment based on religion, gender, race, color, disability, national origin, or age; investigates claims of discrimination.
Environmental Protection Agency (EPA)	Undertakes programs aimed at reducing air and water pollution; works with state and local agencies to help fight environmental hazards.

The Delegation Doctrine Courts generally hold that Article I of the U.S. Constitution is the basis for all administrative law. Section 1 of that article grants all legislative powers to Congress and requires Congress to oversee the implementation of all laws. Article I, Section 8, gives Congress the power to make all laws necessary for executing its specified powers. Under what is known as the **delegation doctrine,** courts interpret these passages as granting Congress the power to establish administrative agencies and delegate to them the power to create rules for implementing those laws.

The three branches of government exercise certain controls over agency powers and functions, as discussed next, but in many ways administrative agencies function independently. For this reason, administrative agencies, which constitute the **bureaucracy,** are sometimes referred to as *the fourth branch of the U.S. government.*

Executive Controls The executive branch of government exercises control over agencies both through the president's power to appoint federal officers and through the president's veto power. The president may veto enabling legislation passed by Congress or congressional attempts to modify an existing agency's authority.

Legislative Controls Congress exercises authority over agency powers through legislation. Congress gives power to an agency through enabling legislation and can

take power away—or even abolish an agency altogether—through subsequent legislation. Legislative authority is required to fund an agency, and enabling legislation usually sets certain time and monetary limits on the funding of particular programs. Congress can always revise these limits.

In addition to its power to create and fund agencies, Congress has the authority to investigate the implementation of its laws and the agencies that it has created. Congress also has the power to "freeze" the enforcement of most federal regulations before the regulations take effect. (Another legislative check on agency actions is the Administrative Procedure Act, discussed shortly.)

Judicial Controls The judicial branch exercises control over agency powers through the courts' review of agency actions. As you will read shortly, the Administrative Procedure Act provides for judicial review of most agency decisions. Agency actions are not automatically subject to judicial review, however. The party seeking court review must first exhaust all administrative remedies under what is called the **exhaustion doctrine** before seeking court review.[2]

■ **Example 23.3** The Federal Trade Commission (FTC) claims that Sysco Industries used deceptive advertising and orders it to run new ads correcting the misstatements. Sysco contends that its ads were not deceptive.

---

2. The plaintiff must also have standing to sue the agency.

Under the exhaustion doctrine, Sysco must go through the entire FTC process before it can bring a suit against the FTC in court to challenge the order. ■

23–2d The Administrative Procedure Act

Sometimes, Congress specifies certain procedural requirements in an agency's enabling legislation. In the absence of any directives from Congress concerning a particular agency procedure, the Administrative Procedure Act (APA)[3] applies.

The Arbitrary and Capricious Test One of Congress's goals in enacting the APA was to provide for more judicial control over administrative agencies. To that end, the APA provides that courts should "hold unlawful and set aside" agency actions found to be "arbitrary, capricious, an abuse of discretion, or otherwise not in

accordance with law."[4] Under this standard, parties can challenge regulations as contrary to law or as so irrational that they are arbitrary and capricious.

There is no precise definition of what makes a rule arbitrary and capricious, but the standard includes factors such as whether the agency has done any of the following:

1. Failed to provide a rational explanation for its decision.
2. Changed its prior policy without justification.
3. Considered legally inappropriate factors.
4. Entirely failed to consider a relevant factor.
5. Rendered a decision plainly contrary to the evidence.

The following case involved a challenge to the boundaries of a wild and scenic river established by the National Park Service. The plaintiff—an owner of land that fell within the protected area—claimed that the boundaries were set arbitrarily and capriciously.

---

3. 5 U.S.C. Sections 551–706.

4. 5 U.S.C. Section 706(2)(A).

Simmons v. Smith

United States Court of Appeals, Eighth Circuit, **888** F.3d 994 (2018).

Background and Facts The Niobrara River runs through northern Nebraska before flowing into the Missouri River along the border between Nebraska and South Dakota. Pursuant to the Niobrara Scenic River Designation Act, the National Park Service (NPS)—led by Paul Hedren, the NPS superintendent of the Niobrara—established the boundaries of the Niobrara Scenic River Area (NSRA). The process involved public meetings, conversations with local landowners and other stakeholders, and scientific evidence. The statute required the agency to focus on protecting five "outstandingly remarkable values" (ORVs)—scenic, recreational, geologic, fish and wildlife, and paleontological.

Lee Simmons operated a recreational outfitter business on the Niobrara. At least twenty-five acres of his land fell within the NSRA boundaries established by the NPS. Arguing that the agency acted arbitrarily and capriciously in drawing those boundaries, Simmons filed a suit in a federal district court against Paul Smith, the agency's acting director. The court issued a judgment in Smith's favor. Simmons appealed.

In the Language of the Court
KELLY, Circuit Judge.
＊ ＊ ＊ ＊

Simmons ＊ ＊ ＊ argues that NPS acted arbitrarily and capriciously in setting the boundary on his property because it did not identify specific ORVs that existed in that area. We agree with Simmons's premise to a certain extent, but, based on the facts of this case, we reach the opposite conclusion. In crafting the boundaries, NPS *is* required to use the ORV determinations as a guide to decide which land should be included within the boundary in order to protect and enhance the ORVs. But ＊ ＊ ＊ NPS is not required to include only land with outstandingly remarkable values. ＊ ＊ ＊ NPS explained that [the placement of the] boundary ＊ ＊ ＊ sought to balance the various ORVs "as equitably as possible" ＊ ＊ ＊. Thus, as long as the boundary placement was rationally connected to the protection of ORVs, NPS was not required to identify a specific ORV on any specific piece of property. And Simmons does not allege that NPS acted contrary to its stated objective of protecting these values.

Moreover, the record amply demonstrates that multiple ORVs were identified within the boundary line in question. Specifically, Simmons's land contains a large portion of viewshed [a geographical area that includes all line-of-site property viewable from that location] that is directly downstream from Berry Bridge, which is a common launch point for recreational canoeists on the river. His land also contains a large and particularly impressive stand of ponderosa pine trees and habitats that support bald eagle foraging. Indeed, the final boundary line on Simmons's property tracks quite closely the extent of the viewshed and the ponderosa stand. Simmons does not dispute these facts. Instead, he relies on a statement by Hedren—made during a lengthy deposition—in which he said that he could not identify specific features on Simmons's property. But, read in context, that statement indicates confusion about the location of Simmons's property, not confusion about the existence of ORVs. At various other points in the deposition, Hedren clearly and specifically identified which ORVs motivated his boundary determination on this property.

In sum, we see no flaw—either generally or related specifically to Simmons's property—in the public, thorough, and comprehensive process that NPS undertook to establish the boundaries of the NSRA.

Decision and Remedy The U.S. Court of Appeals for the Eighth Circuit affirmed the judgment of the lower court. "NPS engaged in a methodical, time-consuming boundary-drawing process. It used the appropriate statutory standard to identify outstandingly remarkable values and it drew a boundary line that sought to protect those values."

Critical Thinking

- **Economic** Why would an owner of land that falls within the boundaries of a wild and scenic river challenge those boundaries?
- **What If the Facts Were Different?** Suppose that instead of establishing the boundaries of the NSRA to protect ORVs, the NPS had drawn the boundaries to set the area's size at a certain number of acres. Would the result in this case have been different? Explain.

Fair Notice The APA also includes many requirements concerning the notice that regulatory agencies must give to those affected by its regulations. For instance, an agency may change the way it applies a certain regulatory principle. Before the change can be carried out, the agency must give fair notice of what conduct will be expected in the future.

■ **Example 23.4** The Federal Communications Commission (FCC) changes its policy regarding obscene language so that even a single profanity uttered on a radio or television program violates industry regulations. Before this new policy is announced, a musician says the F-word on an awards show broadcast by Fox Television. The FCC cannot sanction Fox for the obscenity because the company did not have fair notice of the rule change. ■

23–3 The Administrative Process

All federal agencies must follow specific procedural requirements as they go about fulfilling their three basic functions: rulemaking, enforcement, and adjudication.

These three functions make up what is known as the **administrative process.** As mentioned, the APA imposes requirements that all federal agencies must follow in the absence of contrary provisions in the enabling legislation. This act is an integral part of the administrative process.

23–3a Rulemaking

The major function of an administrative agency is **rulemaking**—the formulation of new regulations, or rules. The APA defines a rule as "an agency statement of general or particular applicability and future effect designed to implement, interpret, or prescribe law and policy."[5]

Regulations are sometimes said to be legislative because, like statutes, they have a binding effect. Thus, violators of agency rules may be punished. Because agency rules have such significant legal force, the APA established procedures for agencies to follow in creating, amending, or removing rules.

---

5. 5 U.S.C. Section 551(4).

Many rules must be adopted using the APA's **notice-and-comment rulemaking,** which involves three basic steps:

1. Notice of the proposed rulemaking.
2. A comment period.
3. The final rule.

The APA recognizes some limited exceptions to its procedural requirements, but they are seldom invoked.

■ **Case in Point 23.5** The Occupational Safety and Health Act authorized the Occupational Safety and Health Administration (OSHA) to develop and issue rules governing safety in the workplace. When OSHA wants to formulate rules regarding safety in an industry, it usually has to follow the specific notice-and-comment procedures outlined by the APA. To expedite the issuance of safety regulations, however, this rulemaking process was suspended for two years after the act's passage in 1970. During that time, the federal government introduced a regulation requiring all manufacturers and suppliers working under federal contract to provide employees exposed to corrosive materials with access to quick-drenching eyewash facilities.

About twenty years later, without notice and comment, the quick-drenching provision was extended to private companies in other industries, including construction. After being cited for a "serious" violation of this rule, Kiewit Power Constructors filed a motion arguing that the regulation was invalid because OSHA had not properly subjected it to notice-and-comment rulemaking. Acknowledging that the language of the original legislation was unhelpful, a federal appeals court relied on congressional intent in deciding against Kiewit. Because the stated goal of the act was to ensure "safe and healthful working conditions" for America's workforce, the court found that OSHA's quick-drenching provision could be applied to private companies in the construction industry.[6] ■

The impetus for rulemaking may come from various sources, including Congress and the agency itself. In addition, private parties may petition an agency to begin a rulemaking (or repeal a rule). For instance, environmental groups have petitioned for stricter air-pollution controls to combat emissions that may contribute to climate change.

Notice of the Proposed Rulemaking When a federal agency decides to create a new rule, the agency publishes a notice of the proposed rulemaking proceedings in the *Federal Register*. The *Federal Register* is a daily publication of the executive branch that prints government orders, rules, and regulations.

The notice states where and when the proceedings will be held, the agency's legal authority for making the rule (usually its enabling legislation), and the terms or subject matter of the rule. The agency must also make available to the public certain other information, such as the key scientific data underlying the proposal. The proposed rule is often reported by the news media and published in the trade journals of the industries that will be affected.

Comment Period Following the publication of the notice of the proposed rulemaking proceedings, the agency must allow ample time for persons to comment in writing on the proposed rule. The purpose of this comment period is to give interested parties the opportunity to express their views on the proposed rule in an effort to influence agency policy. The comments can be made in writing or, if a hearing is held, orally. All comments become a public record that others can examine.

■ **Example 23.6** Chidozie Trucking learns that the U.S. Department of Transportation is considering a new regulation that will have a negative impact on its ability to do business and on its profits. A notice of the rulemaking is published in the *Federal Register*. Later, a public hearing is held so that proponents and opponents can offer evidence and question witnesses. At this hearing, Chidozie's owner orally expresses an opinion about the pending rule. ■

The agency need not respond to all comments, but it must respond to any significant comments that bear directly on the proposed rule. The agency responds by either modifying its final rule or explaining, in a statement accompanying the final rule, why it did not make any changes. In some circumstances, particularly when less formal procedures are used, an agency may accept comments after the comment period is closed.

The Final Rule After the agency reviews the comments, it drafts the final rule and publishes it in the *Federal Register*. The final rule can include modifications based on the public comments. If substantial changes are made, however, a new proposal and a new opportunity for comment are required. The final rule is later compiled along with the rules and regulations of other federal administrative agencies in the *Code of Federal Regulations*.

Final rules have binding legal effect unless the courts later overturn them. If an agency fails to follow proper rulemaking procedures when it issues a final rule, however, the resulting rule may not be binding.

6. *Kiewit Power Constructors Co. v. Secretary of Labor, U.S. Department of Labor,* 959 F.3d 381 (D.C. Cir. 2020). See also *In re National Nurses United,* 47 F.4th 746 (D.D.C. Cir. 2022).

■ **Example 23.7** Members of the Hemp Industries Association (HIA) manufacture and sell food products made from hemp seed and oil. These products may contain trace amounts of THC, a component of marijuana. Without following formal rulemaking procedures, the Drug Enforcement Administration (DEA) publishes rules that effectively ban the possession and sale of HIA's food products, treating them as controlled substances. A court will most likely overturn the rules because the DEA did not follow formal rulemaking procedures. ■

Informal Agency Actions Rather than take the time to conduct notice-and-comment rulemaking, agencies have increasingly used more informal methods of policymaking, such as issuing interpretive rules and guidance documents. As mentioned earlier, unlike legislative rules, interpretive rules simply declare policy and do not affect legal rights or obligations. Guidance documents advise the public on the agencies' legal and policy positions.

Informal agency actions are exempt from the APA's requirements because they do not establish legal rights. A party cannot be directly prosecuted for violating an interpretive rule or a guidance document. Nevertheless, an informal action can be important because it warns regulated entities that the agency may engage in formal rulemaking if they ignore its informal policymaking.

23–3b Enforcement

Although rulemaking is the most prominent agency activity, rule enforcement is also critical. Often, an agency enforces its own rules. After a final rule is issued, agencies conduct investigations to monitor compliance with the rule or the terms of the enabling statute.

An agency investigation of this kind might begin when the agency receives a report of a possible violation. In addition, many agency rules require compliance reporting from regulated entities, and such a report may trigger an enforcement investigation.

Inspections and Tests In conducting investigations, many agencies gather information through on-site inspections. Sometimes, inspecting an office, a factory, or some other business facility is the only way to obtain the evidence needed to prove a regulatory violation. At other times, an inspection or test is used in place of a formal hearing to show the need to correct or prevent an undesirable condition.

Administrative inspections and tests cover a wide range of activities, including safety inspections of underground coal mines, safety tests of commercial equipment and automobiles, and environmental monitoring of factory emissions. An agency may also ask a firm or individual to submit certain documents or records to the agency for examination.

Normally, business firms comply with agency requests to inspect facilities or business records because it is in any firm's interest to maintain a good relationship with regulatory bodies. In some instances, however, such as when a firm thinks an agency's request is unreasonable and disruptive, the firm may refuse to comply with the request. In such situations, an agency may resort to the use of a subpoena or a search warrant.

Subpoenas There are two basic types of subpoenas. The subpoena *ad testificandum*[7] ("to testify") is an ordinary subpoena. It is a writ, or order, compelling a witness to appear at an agency hearing. The subpoena *duces tecum*[8] ("bring it with you") compels an individual or organization to hand over books, papers, records, or documents to the agency. An administrative agency may use either type of subpoena to obtain testimony or documents.

There are limits on what an agency can demand. To determine whether an agency is abusing its discretion in pursuing information as part of an investigation, a court may consider such factors as the following.

1. **The purpose of the investigation.** An investigation must have a legitimate purpose. An agency may not issue an administrative subpoena to inspect business records if the motive is to harass or pressure the business into settling an unrelated matter, for example.
2. **The relevance of the information being sought.** Information is relevant if it reveals that the law is being violated or if it assures the agency that the law is not being violated.
3. **The specificity of the demand for testimony or documents.** A subpoena must, for instance, adequately describe the material being sought.
4. **The burden of the demand on the party from whom the information is sought.** For instance, the cost to the company of copying requested documents or providing digital information may become burdensome. (Note that a business generally is protected from revealing information such as trade secrets.)

Search Warrants The Fourth Amendment protects against unreasonable searches and seizures by requiring that in most instances a physical search for evidence must be conducted under the authority of a search warrant. An

---

7. Pronounced ad tes-te-fe-*kan*-dum.
8. Pronounced *doo*-suhs *tee*-kum.

agency's search warrant is an order directing law enforcement officials to search a specific place for a specific item and seize it for the agency.[9]

Agencies can conduct warrantless searches in several situations. Warrants are not required to conduct searches in highly regulated industries. Firms that sell firearms or liquor, for instance, are automatically subject to inspections without warrants. Sometimes, a statute permits warrantless searches of certain types of hazardous operations, such as coal mines. Also, a warrantless inspection in an emergency situation is normally considered reasonable.

23-3c Adjudication

After conducting an investigation of a suspected rule violation, an agency may initiate an administrative action against an individual or organization. Most administrative actions are resolved through negotiated settlements at their initial stages. Sometimes, though, an action ends in formal **adjudication**—the resolution of the dispute through a hearing conducted by the agency.

Negotiated Settlements Depending on the agency, negotiations may involve a simple conversation or a series of informal conferences. Whatever form the negotiations take, their purpose is to rectify the problem to the agency's satisfaction and eliminate the need for additional proceedings.

Settlement is an appealing option to firms for two reasons: to avoid appearing uncooperative and to avoid the expense involved in formal adjudication proceedings and in possible later appeals. Settlement is also an attractive option for agencies. To conserve their resources and avoid formal actions, administrative agencies devote a great deal of effort to giving advice and negotiating solutions to problems.

Formal Complaints If a settlement cannot be reached, the agency may issue a formal complaint against the suspected violator. ■ **Example 23.8** The Environmental Protection Agency (EPA) finds that Quispe Manufacturing, Inc., is polluting groundwater in violation of federal pollution laws. The EPA issues a complaint against Quispe in an effort to bring the plant into compliance with federal regulations. This complaint is a public document, and a press release may accompany it. Quispe will respond by filing an answer to the EPA's allegations. If Quispe and the EPA cannot agree on a settlement, the case will be adjudicated. ■

The Hearing Agency adjudication may involve a trial-like arbitration procedure before an **administrative law judge (ALJ)**. The Administrative Procedure Act requires that before the hearing takes place, the agency must issue a notice that includes the facts and law on which the complaint is based, the legal authority for the hearing, and its time and place. The administrative agency adjudication process is described next and illustrated graphically in Exhibit 23–3.

The Role of the Administrative Law Judge An ALJ presides over the hearing and has the power to administer oaths, take testimony, rule on questions of evidence, and make determinations of fact. Technically, the ALJ, who works for the agency prosecuting the case, is not an independent judge. Nevertheless, the law requires an ALJ to be unbiased.

Exhibit 23–3 The Formal Administrative Agency Adjudication Process

Complaint

Answer

Hearing Before Administrative Law Judge

Order of Administrative Law Judge

Appeal to Governing Board of Agency

Final Agency Order

Court Review of Agency Decision

Court Order

---

9. The United States Supreme Court held that the warrant requirement applies to the administrative process in *Marshall v. Barlow's, Inc.*, 436 U.S. 307, 98 S.Ct. 1816, 56 L.Ed.2d 305 (1978).

Certain safeguards prevent bias on the part of the ALJ and promote fairness in the proceedings. For instance, the APA requires that the ALJ be separate from an agency's investigative and prosecutorial staff. The APA also prohibits *ex parte* (private) communications between the ALJ and any party to an agency proceeding, including the agency and the company involved. Finally, provisions of the APA protect the ALJ from agency disciplinary actions unless the agency can show good cause for such an action.

Hearing Procedures Hearing procedures vary widely from agency to agency. Administrative agencies generally exercise substantial discretion over the type of procedure that will be used. Frequently, disputes are resolved through informal adjudication proceedings. ■ **Example 23.9** The Federal Trade Commission (FTC) charges Choi Foods, Inc., with deceptive advertising. Representatives of Choi Foods and the FTC, their counsel, and the ALJ meet at a table in a conference room to resolve the dispute informally. ■

A formal adjudicatory hearing, in contrast, resembles a trial in many respects. Prior to the hearing, the parties are permitted to undertake discovery, which may involve depositions, interrogatories, and requests for documents or other information. The discovery process usually is not quite as extensive as it would be in a court proceeding.

The hearing itself must comply with the procedural requirements of the APA and must also meet the constitutional standards of due process. The burden of proof in an enforcement proceeding is placed on the agency. During the hearing, the parties may give testimony, present other evidence, and cross-examine adverse witnesses.

Trials and administrative agency hearings do differ in some respects. A significant difference is that normally much more information, including hearsay (secondhand information), can be introduced as evidence during an administrative hearing.

Agency Orders Following a hearing, the ALJ renders an **initial order,** or decision, on the case. Either party can appeal the ALJ's decision to the board or commission that governs the agency. If displeased with the result, the party can appeal that decision to a federal appellate court. ■ **Example 23.10** The EPA issues a complaint against Bahadur Manufacturing, Inc., for polluting groundwater. The complaint results in a hearing before an ALJ, who rules in the EPA's favor. If Bahadur is dissatisfied with the decision, it can appeal to the EPA commission and then to a federal appellate court. ■

If no party appeals the case, the ALJ's decision becomes the **final order** of the agency. The ALJ's decision also becomes final if a party appeals and the commission and the court decline to review the case. If a party appeals and the case is reviewed, the final order comes from the commission's decision (or, if that decision is appealed, that of the reviewing court).

In the following case, a builder cited by the Occupational Safety and Health Administration for violations of federal safety regulations did not challenge the applicability of the regulations, nor did the builder challenge the agency's *prima facie* case against it. But the builder did contest the administrative law judge's (ALJ's) conclusion that the violations were willful.

Case 23.2

Edwin Taylor Corp. v. U.S. Department of Labor
United States Court of Appeals, Eleventh Circuit, 814 Fed.Appx. 498 (2020).

Background and Facts Edwin Taylor Corporation was retained to construct shells for five three-story condominiums. Paul Barros and Bronson Ostrander were superintendents of the building site, and Jay Zimmerman managed them. David Patton, one of the owners of Edwin Taylor, regularly received photos and messages regarding the work. Under this supervisory authority, Edwin Taylor employees were responsible for enforcing safety protocols and correcting potential safety violations at the site. For block and framing work, Edwin Taylor subcontracted with Adelo & Fernanda Construction Inc., which subcontracted with Francisco Sanchez Hernandez to assist with the framing.

During construction, workers built the frames higher than six feet without guardrails. One of Hernandez's workers fell twenty-two feet through an unguarded opening and died. The Occupational Safety and Health Administration (OSHA) opened an investigation. After the incident, guardrails were installed in most areas of the worksite, but an OSHA officer still found a lack of fall protection one week later.

The U.S. Department of Labor cited Edwin Taylor for willful violations of OSHA safety regulations and assessed a penalty of $126,749. Edwin Taylor contested the citation to the Occupational Safety and Health Review Commission. The Commission's administrative law judge (ALJ) affirmed the citation but reduced the penalty to $101,399.20.

Case 23.2 Continues

Case 23.2 Continued   Edwin Taylor appealed to a federal court, asserting that there was insufficient evidence for the ALJ to conclude that the builder had willfully violated the regulations.

In the Language of the Court

PER CURIAM:

* * * *

* * * In her order, the ALJ stated that "a willful violation is one committed with intentional, knowing or voluntary disregard for the requirement of the [Occupational Safety and Health] Act or with plain indifference to employee safety." Because the ALJ's definition of willful conduct aligns with our own, we uphold it here.

Having determined that the ALJ applied the proper legal standard, we next consider whether substantial evidence supports her conclusions.

* * * *

* * * In making her decision, the ALJ relied on testimony from Edwin Taylor employees showing that they knew of the fall protection regulations required for greater than six-foot fall risks, yet disregarded that risk at its worksite. [The] evidence shows that Mr. Barros, Mr. Ostrander, Mr. Zimmerman, and Mr. Patton were aware of the risk posed by working at the condominium developments without fall protection. Those Edwin Taylor supervisors knew that workers would be working on second and third stories of the condominiums and that they would be exposed to floor openings. Notwithstanding this knowledge of the fall hazard and worker exposure above six feet on the second and third levels, Edwin Taylor supervisors did nothing to prevent an accidental fall beyond cursory discussions with Mr. Sanchez about the need for fall protection. Edwin Taylor did not instruct anyone at the worksite to install guardrails. Nor did it supply guardrail equipment to the worksite crew—even though the needed equipment was at the job site.

* * * After a close review of the administrative record * * *, we agree that substantial evidence supports the [ALJ's] conclusion that Edwin Taylor committed * * * willful OSHA violations.

Decision and Remedy The U.S. Court of Appeals for the Eleventh Circuit affirmed the ALJ's classification of Edwin Taylor's violations as willful and upheld the resulting penalty.

Critical Thinking

- **Legal Environment** Could a willful violation of a safety regulation be established if an employer did not know of the rule's requirements? Explain.
- **What If the Facts Were Different?** Suppose that one of the superintendents of Edwin Taylor's build site had told Hernandez's workers to put up the railings, but they had refused. Would the result have been different? Discuss.

23–4 Judicial Deference to Agency Decisions

When asked to review agency decisions, courts historically granted deference to the agency's judgment. In other words, the courts tended to accept the agency's judgment, often citing the agency's great expertise in the subject area of the regulation. This deference seems especially appropriate when applied to an agency's analysis of factual questions, but should it also extend to an agency's interpretation of its own legal authority? In *Chevron U.S.A., Inc. v. Natural Resources Defense Council, Inc.,*[10] the United States Supreme Court held that it should. By so ruling, the Court created a standard of broadened deference to agencies on questions of legal interpretation.

23–4a The Holding of the *Chevron* Case

At issue in the *Chevron* case was whether the courts should defer to an agency's interpretation of a statute giving it authority to act. The Environmental Protection Agency (EPA) had interpreted the phrase "stationary source" in the Clean Air Act as referring to an entire manufacturing plant, and not to each facility within a plant. The agency's interpretation enabled it to adopt the so-called bubble policy, which allowed companies to offset increases in emissions in part of a plant with decreases elsewhere in the plant. This interpretation reduced pollution-control compliance costs to manufacturers. An environmental group challenged the legality of the EPA's interpretation.

The Supreme Court held that the courts should defer to an agency's interpretation of law as well as fact. The Court found that the agency's interpretation of the statute was reasonable. The Court's decision in the *Chevron* case created a new standard for courts to use when reviewing

---

10. 467 U.S. 837, 104 S.Ct. 2778, 81 L.Ed.2d 694 (1984).

agency interpretations of law. This standard involves the following two questions:

1. Did Congress directly address the issue in dispute in the statute? If so, the statutory language prevails.
2. If the statute is silent or ambiguous, is the agency's interpretation "reasonable"? If it is, a court should uphold the agency's interpretation even if the court would have interpreted the law differently.

23–4b When Courts Will Give *Chevron* Deference to Agency Interpretation

The notion that courts should defer to agencies on matters of law has been controversial. Under the holding of

the *Chevron* case, when the meaning of a particular statute's language is unclear and an agency interprets it, the court must follow the agency's interpretation as long as it is reasonable. This has led to considerable litigation to test the boundaries of the *Chevron* holding, and many agency interpretations continue to be challenged in court. Some commentators believe that conservative justices on the United States Supreme Court will ultimately overturn the deference required under the *Chevron* decision.

When the language in a statute is clear, the *Chevron* deference normally does not apply. The Court of Appeals for the District of Columbia Circuit used, in part, this principle to decide an important administrative law case that involved security concerns about China.

Case Analysis 23.3

China Telecom (Americas) Corporation v. Federal Communications Commission

United States Court of Appeals, District of Columbia Circuit, 57 F.4th 256 (2022).

In the Language of the Court
EDWARDS, Senior Circuit Judge:

Confronted with reliable claims of escalating Chinese cyber threats targeting the United States, the Federal Communications Commission ("FCC" or "Commission") revoked the authority of China Telecom (Americas) Corp. ("China Telecom") to operate domestic and international transmission lines pursuant to section 214 of the Communications Act of 1934. China Telecom now petitions for review.

After two rounds of written submissions and one round of public comments, the Commission found that China Telecom, "a U.S. subsidiary of a Chinese state-owned enterprise, is subject to exploitation, influence, and control by the Chinese government." The Commission also found that China Telecom's "ownership and control by the Chinese government raise significant national security and law enforcement risks by providing opportunities for [China Telecom], its parent entities, and the Chinese government to access, store, disrupt, and/or misroute U.S. communications, which in turn allow them to engage in espionage and other harmful activities against the United States." * * *

Before this court, China Telecom argues that the Revocation Order is arbitrary, capricious, and unsupported by substantial evidence. It dismisses as speculative the Commission's concern that China Telecom will be used as a vector of cyberwarfare against the United States and disputes the Commission's conclusion that its conduct constituted breaches of the Letter of Assurances. * * *

We find no merit in China Telecom's claims. Therefore, we deny the petition for review. In reaching this judgment, we have not found it necessary to rely on the classified record. The Commission's determinations that China Telecom poses a national security risk and breached its Letter of Assurances are supported by reasoned decision making and substantial evidence in the unclassified record. In addition, we hold that no statute, regulation, past practice, or constitutional provision required the Commission to afford China Telecom any additional procedures beyond the paper hearing it received.

I. BACKGROUND
A. Section 214 Authorizations
The Communications Act of 1934 tasks the FCC with regulating the nation's communications infrastructure. One of

the principal purposes of the statute is "national defense." In furtherance of this statutory purpose, any carrier seeking to use or operate a transmission line for interstate or foreign communications must first obtain a "section 214 authorization" from the Commission. And the Commission "may attach to the [214 authorization] such terms and conditions as in its judgment the public convenience and necessity may require."

The Commission has granted blanket authority for any carrier to construct, operate, or transmit over domestic transmission lines, "subject to the Commission's ability to revoke [that] authority when warranted to protect the public interest." If a carrier seeks to construct, operate, or transmit over international transmission lines, it must obtain specific authorization from the Commission, and the Commission may later revoke that authorization if warranted to protect the public interest.

A crucial factor considered by the Commission in granting or revoking section 214 authorizations is whether a carrier's use of domestic or international transmission lines raises any national security, law enforcement, or foreign policy concerns. * * *
* * * *

Case 23.3 Continues

Case 23.3 Continued

B. National Security Landscape

* * * *

* * * China has augmented the level of state control over the cyber practices of Chinese companies. Its 2017 Cybersecurity Law requires Chinese companies to cooperate with state agencies on cybersecurity supervision and inspection. And its 2018 Regulation on Internet Security Supervision by Public Security Organs authorizes the [Chinese] Ministry of Public Security to conduct on-site and remote inspections of Chinese telecommunication and network companies. Consistent with this increasing state control over Chinese telecommunication companies, China Telecom's parent company amended its Articles of Association, pursuant to "the Constitution of the Communist Party of China," to set up Party organizations to perform "core leadership and political functions" and advise the board of directors.

C. Proceedings Before the FCC

In April 2020—against this backdrop of tightening Chinese government control over Chinese companies and escalating Chinese cyber threats—several Executive Branch agencies, including the DOJ, DHS, and State Department, recommended that the FCC revoke China Telecom's section 214 authorizations. The Executive Branch agencies focused on "the substantial and unacceptable national security and law enforcement risks associated with China Telecom's continued access to U.S. telecommunications infrastructure pursuant to its international Section 214 authorizations."

Shortly after receiving the Executive Branch agencies' recommendation, the Commission issued a show cause order directing China Telecom to show why the Commission should not initiate revocation proceedings. In response, China Telecom filed a seventy-two-page brief with fifteen additional exhibits.

In December 2020, the Commission found sufficient cause and initiated full revocation proceedings, granting China Telecom a public comment period and another opportunity to file written submissions. In addition to its public comments, China Telecom filed another sixty-two pages of legal and factual arguments. After reviewing the record, the Commission found China Telecom's arguments unconvincing. In November 2021, the Commission revoked China Telecom's section 214 authorizations and ordered the company to discontinue by January 2022 any services that it offered pursuant to its FCC authorizations.

* * * *

II. ANALYSIS

A. Standards of Review

Because the brief filed on behalf of Respondents, the Federal Communications Commission and the United States of America, amply and accurately sets forth the Standard of Review and finds no objection from Petitioner, China Telecom, we adopt much of what has been offered by Respondents:

Under the Administrative Procedure Act, a court may not overturn agency action unless it is arbitrary, capricious, or otherwise contrary to law. Under this "deferential" standard, "[a] court simply ensures that the agency has acted within a zone of reasonableness and, in particular, has reasonably considered the relevant issues and reasonably explained the decision." Courts must "presume the validity of agency action and must affirm unless the Commission failed to consider relevant factors or made a clear error in judgment." And a reviewing court must "accept the Commission's findings of fact so long as they are supported by substantial evidence on the record as a whole."

The Commission's interpretation of statutes it administers, such as section 214, is reviewed under the principles set forth in *Chevron U.S.A., Inc. v. Nat. Res. Def. Council, Inc.,* 467 U.S. 837 (1984). Under *Chevron,* "if the statute is silent or ambiguous with respect to [a] specific issue, the question for the court is whether the agency's answer is based on a permissible construction of the statute. *Chevron* deference does not apply where the statute is clear."

Finally, as to agency procedures, the "established principle" is that "administrative agencies 'should be free to fashion their own rules of procedure and to pursue methods of inquiry capable of permitting them to discharge their multitudinous duties.'" ("The Commission may conduct its proceedings in such manner as will best conduce to the proper dispatch of business and to the ends of justice.").

B. Substantial Evidence in the Unclassified Record Supports the Revocation Order

We hold that the Commission's Revocation Order is supported by reasoned decision making and substantial evidence in the unclassified record. As noted above, in assessing China Telecom's petition for review, we have given no consideration or weight to any evidence in the classified record.

We find that the Commission's conclusion that China Telecom poses an unacceptable national security risk is supported by the record and justifies the Commission's Revocation Order. We also find the Commission's conclusion that China Telecom breached its Letter of Assurances is supported by the record and independently justifies the Commission's Revocation Order.

* * * *

III. CONCLUSION

For the reasons set forth above, we deny the petition for review.

So ordered.

Legal Reasoning Questions

1. Why was the 2017 Chinese cyber security law important in this case?

2. Why wasn't so-called *Chevron* deference an issue in this case?

3. Did the Federal Communications Commission need to examine classified materials in order to make its decision?

23–4c The Holding of the *Auer* Case

If the *Chevron* ruling applies to an administrative agency's interpretation of a statute, what deference should courts give administrative agencies when they are interpreting their own regulations? The United States Supreme Court addressed this question with its decision in *Auer v. Robbins*.[11]

The case involved a group of sergeants and lieutenants employed by the St. Louis (Missouri) Police Department who filed a lawsuit seeking overtime pay. Several lower courts rejected these demands based on the U.S. Department of Labor's determination that, under the Fair Labor Standards Act, the St. Louis police officials were exempt from overtime requirements. Relying on the principles established in the *Chevron* case, the Supreme Court affirmed, holding that judges should defer to administrative agencies' reasonable interpretation of their own regulations.

The *Auer* decision was criticized for giving administrative agencies too much power. Nonetheless, the Supreme Court effectively reaffirmed that holding in a more recent case featuring a Vietnam War veteran who had been denied disability benefits for his post-traumatic stress disorder by the Department of Veterans Affairs. In *Kisor v. Wilkie,* the Supreme Court found that an administrative agency should be granted deference in applying its own rules if (1) the rule is "genuinely ambiguous" and (2) the agency's application of the rule is, again, reasonable.[12]

23–5 Public Accountability

As a result of public concern over the powers exercised by administrative agencies, Congress passed several laws to make agencies more accountable through public scrutiny. Here, we discuss the most significant of these laws.

23–5a Freedom of Information Act

The Freedom of Information Act (FOIA)[13] requires the federal government to disclose certain records to any person or entity on written request, even if no reason is given for the request. All federal government agencies must make their records available electronically on the internet and in other electronic formats.

The FOIA exempts certain types of records, such as those pertaining to national security and those containing information that is confidential or personal. ■ **Example 23.11** Juanita, a reporter from an online health magazine, makes an FOIA request to the Centers for Disease Control and Prevention for a list of people who have contracted a highly contagious virus. The Centers for Disease Control and Prevention will not have to comply, because the requested information is confidential and personal. ■

For other records, a request that complies with the FOIA procedures need only contain a reasonable description of the information sought. An agency's failure to comply with an FOIA request can be challenged in a federal district court. The media, industry trade associations, public-interest groups, and even companies seeking information about competitors rely on these FOIA provisions to obtain information from government agencies.

23–5b Government in the Sunshine Act

The Government in the Sunshine Act,[14] or open meeting law, requires that "every portion of every meeting of an agency" be open to "public observation." The act also requires that the public be provided with adequate advance notice of scheduled meetings and agendas.

Like the FOIA, the Sunshine Act contains certain exceptions. Closed meetings are permitted in the following situations:

1. The subject of the meeting concerns accusing any person of a crime.
2. Open meetings would frustrate implementation of future agency actions.
3. The subject of the meeting involves matters relating to future litigation or rulemaking.

Courts interpret these exceptions to allow open access whenever possible.

23–5c Regulatory Flexibility Act

Concern over the effects of regulation on the efficiency of businesses, particularly smaller ones, led Congress to pass the Regulatory Flexibility Act.[15] Under this act, whenever a new regulation will have a "significant impact upon a substantial number of small entities," the agency must conduct a regulatory flexibility analysis. The analysis must

---

11. 519 U.S. 452, 117 S.Ct. 905, 137 L.Ed.2d 79 (1997).
12. 588 U.S. __, 139 S.Ct. 2400, 204 L.Ed.2d 841 (2019). See also *ASANTE, et al., v. Alex M. AZAR II,* 2023 WL 1991642 (D.D.C. 2023).
13. 5 U.S.C. Section 552.

14. 5 U.S.C. Section 552b.
15. 5 U.S.C. Sections 601–612.

measure the cost that the rule would impose on small businesses and consider less burdensome alternatives. The act also contains provisions to alert small businesses about forthcoming regulations. The act relieved small businesses of some record-keeping burdens, especially with regard to hazardous waste management.

23–5d Small Business Regulatory Enforcement Fairness Act

The Small Business Regulatory Enforcement Fairness Act[16] includes various provisions intended to ease the regulatory burden on small businesses.

---

16. 5 U.S.C. Sections 801 *et seq.*

1. Federal agencies must prepare guides that explain in plain English how small businesses can comply with federal regulations.
2. Congress may review new federal regulations for at least sixty days before they take effect, giving opponents of the rules time to present their arguments.
3. The courts may enforce the Regulatory Flexibility Act. This provision helps to ensure that federal agencies will consider ways to reduce the economic impact of new regulations on small businesses.
4. The Office of the National Ombudsman at the Small Business Administration was set up to receive comments from small businesses about their dealings with federal agencies. Based on these comments, Regional Small Business Fairness Boards rate the agencies and publicize their findings.

Practice and Review: Administrative Agencies

Assume that the Securities and Exchange Commission (SEC) has a rule that it will enforce statutory provisions prohibiting insider trading only when the insiders make monetary profits for themselves. Then the SEC makes a new rule, declaring that it will now bring enforcement actions against individuals for insider trading even if the individuals did not personally profit from the transactions. In making the new rule, the SEC does not conduct a rulemaking procedure but simply announces its decision. A stockbrokerage firm objects that the new rule was unlawfully developed without opportunity for public comment. The brokerage firm challenges the rule in an action that ultimately is reviewed by a federal appellate court. Using the information presented in the chapter, answer the following questions.

1. Is the SEC an executive agency or an independent regulatory agency? Does it matter to the outcome of this dispute? Explain.
2. Suppose that the SEC asserts that it has always had the statutory authority to pursue persons for insider trading regardless of whether they personally profited from the transactions. This is the only argument the SEC makes to justify changing its enforcement rules. Would a court be likely to find that the SEC's action was arbitrary and capricious under the Administrative Procedure Act (APA)? Why or why not?
3. Would a court be likely to give *Chevron* deference to the SEC's interpretation of the law on insider trading? Why or why not?
4. Now assume that a court finds that the new rule is merely "interpretive." What effect would this determination have on whether the SEC had to follow the APA's rulemaking procedures?

Debate This . . . Because an administrative law judge (ALJ) acts as both judge and jury, there should always be at least three ALJs in each administrative hearing.

Terms and Concepts

adjudication 498
administrative agency 490
administrative law judge (ALJ) 498
administrative process 495
bureaucracy 493

delegation doctrine 493
enabling legislation 491
exhaustion doctrine 493
final order 499
initial order 499

interpretive rules 492
legislative rules 492
notice-and-comment
  rulemaking 496
rulemaking 495

Issue Spotters

1. The U.S. Department of Transportation (DOT) sometimes hears an appeal from a party whose contract with the DOT has been canceled. An administrative law judge (ALJ) who works for the DOT hears this appeal. What safeguards promote the ALJ's fairness? (See *The Administrative Process*.)

2. Techplate Corporation learns that a federal administrative agency is considering a rule that will have a negative impact on the firm's ability to do business. Does the firm have any opportunity to express its opinion about the pending rule? Explain. (See *The Administrative Process*.)

- **Check your answers to the Issue Spotters against the answers provided in Appendix B at the end of this text.**

Business Scenarios and Case Problems

23–1. Rulemaking and Adjudication Powers. For decades, the Federal Trade Commission (FTC) resolved fair trade and advertising disputes through individual adjudications. Then the FTC began promulgating rules that defined fair and unfair trade practices. In cases involving violations of these rules, the due process rights of participants were more limited and did not include cross-examination. Although anyone charged with violating a rule would receive a full adjudication, the legitimacy of the rule itself could not be challenged in the adjudication. Furthermore, a party charged with violating a rule was almost certain to lose the adjudication. Affected parties complained to a court, arguing that their rights before the FTC were unduly limited by the new rules. What would the court examine to determine whether to uphold the new rules? (See *The Administrative Process*.)

23–2. Informal Rulemaking. Assume that the Food and Drug Administration (FDA), using proper procedures, adopts a rule describing its future investigations. This new rule covers all future circumstances in which the FDA wants to regulate food additives. Under the new rule, the FDA is not to regulate food additives without giving food companies an opportunity to cross-examine witnesses. Later, the FDA wants to regulate methylisocyanate, a food additive. The FDA undertakes an informal rulemaking procedure, without cross-examination, and regulates methylisocyanate. Producers protest, saying that the FDA promised them the opportunity for cross-examination. The FDA responds that the Administrative Procedure Act does not require such cross-examination and that it is free to withdraw the promise made in its new rule. If the producers challenge the FDA in court, on what basis would the court rule in their favor? Explain. (See *The Administrative Process*.)

23–3. Business Case Problem With Sample Answer—Agency Powers. A well-documented rise in global temperatures has coincided with a significant increase in the concentration of carbon dioxide in the atmosphere. Many scientists believe that the two trends are related, because when carbon dioxide is released into the atmosphere, it produces a greenhouse effect, trapping solar heat. Under the Clean Air Act (CAA), the Environmental Protection Agency (EPA) is authorized to regulate "any" air pollutants "emitted into . . . the ambient air" that in its "judgment cause, or contribute to, air pollution."

A group of private organizations asked the EPA to regulate carbon dioxide and other "greenhouse gas" emissions from new motor vehicles. The EPA refused, stating, among other things, that the most recent congressional amendments to the CAA did not authorize any new, binding auto emissions limits. Nineteen states, including Massachusetts, asked a district court to review the EPA's denial. Did the EPA have the authority to regulate greenhouse gas emissions from new motor vehicles? If so, was its stated reason for refusing to do so consistent with that authority? Discuss. [*Commonwealth of Massachusetts v. Environmental Protection Agency*, 549 U.S. 497, 127 S.Ct. 1438, 167 L.Ed.2d 248 (2007)] (See *Agency Creation and Powers*.)

- **For a sample answer to Problem 23–3, go to Appendix C at the end of this text.**

23–4. Arbitrary and Capricious Test. Michael Manin, an airline pilot, was twice convicted of disorderly conduct, a minor misdemeanor. To renew his flight certification with the National Transportation Safety Board (NTSB), Manin filed an application that asked him about his criminal history. He did not disclose his two convictions. When these came to light more than ten years later, Manin argued that he had not known that he was required to report convictions for minor misdemeanors. The NTSB's policy was to consider an applicant's understanding of what information a question sought before determining whether an answer was false. But without explanation, the agency departed from this policy, refused to consider Manin's argument, and revoked his certification. Was this action arbitrary or capricious? Explain. [*Manin v. National Transportation Safety Board*, 627 F.3d 1239 (D.C. Cir. 2011)] (See *Agency Creation and Powers*.)

23–5. Adjudication. Mechanics replaced a brake assembly on the landing gear of a CRJ–700 plane operated by GoJet Airlines, LLC. The mechanics installed gear pins to lock the assembly in place during the repair but failed to remove one of the pins after they had finished. On the plane's next flight, a warning light alerted the pilots that the landing gear would not retract after takeoff. There was a potential for danger, but the pilots flew the CRJ–700 safely back to the departure airport. No one was injured, and no property was damaged. The Federal Aviation Administration (FAA) cited GoJet for violating FAA regulations by "carelessly or recklessly operating an unairworthy airplane." GoJet objected to the citation. To which court can GoJet appeal for review? On what ground might that court decline to review the case? [*GoJet Airlines, LLC v. Federal Aviation Administration,* 743 F.3d 1168 (8th Cir. 2014)] (See *The Administrative Process.*)

23–6. Judicial Deference to Agency Decisions. Knox Creek Coal Corporation operates coal mines in West Virginia. The U.S. Department of Labor charged Knox's Tiller No. 1 Mine with "significant and substantial" (S&S) violations of the Federal Mine Safety and Health Act. According to the charges, inadequately sealed enclosures of electrical equipment in the mine created the potential for an explosion. The Mine Act designates a violation as S&S when it "could significantly and substantially contribute to the cause and effect of a coal or other mine safety or health hazard." Challenging the S&S determination, Knox filed a suit against the secretary of labor. The secretary argued that "could" means "merely possible"—if there is a violation, the existence of a hazard is assumed. This position was consistent with agency and judicial precedent and the Mine Act's history and purpose. Knox argued that "could" requires proof of the likelihood of a hazard. When does a court defer to an agency's interpretation of law? Do those circumstances exist in this case? Discuss. [*Knox Creek Coal Corp. v. Secretary of Labor,* 811 F.3d 148 (4th Cir. 2016)] (See *Judicial Deference to Agency Decisions.*)

23–7. The Arbitrary and Capricious Test. The Sikh Cultural Society, Inc. (SCS), petitioned the United States Citizenship and Immigration Services (USCIS) for a special immigrant religious worker visa for Birender Singh. The USCIS denied the request for several reasons. Despite certain statutory requirements, there were discrepancies or inadequate evidence as to Singh's compensation, housing, and employment history. The SCS did not provide all of the requested information. In addition, the SCS did not show that Singh had worked continuously for the previous two years. The SCS filed a suit in a federal district court against the USCIS, arguing that the denial was arbitrary and capricious. In applying the arbitrary and capricious standard, what agency actions or omissions does a court typically consider? Does the denial of Singh's visa pass the test? Explain. [*Sikh Cultural Society, Inc. v. United States Citizenship and Immigration Services,* 720 Fed.Appx. 649 (2d Cir. 2018)] (See *Agency Creation and Powers.*)

23–8. Evidence Required During an Administrative Process. Eric Marsh, an employee of New River Electrical Corporation, suffered severe burns when he picked up a live electrical wire at a job site. The Occupational Safety & Health Administration (OSHA) investigated the accident, determined that New River had committed serious violations of applicable safety regulations, and fined the company $38,802. New River appealed. An administrative law judge affirmed OSHA's decision (although he decreased the penalty to $12,934). Evidence showed that no one at New River had tested, tagged, or grounded the transformer that connected the cable that shocked Eric Marsh. There was some evidence that New River foremen had falsified some information relating to the accident. Nonetheless, in its appeal, New River argued that to establish an OSHA violation, the Secretary of Labor must prove, among other things, that the employer had actual or constructive knowledge of the relevant OSHA violation. Should the United States Court of Appeals for the Fourth Circuit support OSHA's decision? Why or why not? [*New River Electrical Corporation v. Occupational Safety & Health Review Commission,* 25 F.4th 213 (4th Cir. 2022)] (See *The Administrative Process.*)

23–9. A Question of Ethics—The IDDR Approach and the Arbitrary and Capricious Test. The Delaware River Port Authority (DRPA) solicited bids to repaint the Commodore Barry Bridge, a mile-long structure spanning the Delaware River between New Jersey and Pennsylvania. Alpha Painting & Construction Company, an experienced contractor that had previously worked for the DRPA, submitted the lowest bid. Under DRPA guidelines, a "responsible" contractor has the "capacity" and "capability" to do a certain job. A "responsive" contractor includes all required documents with its bid. Alpha's bid did not include certain required accident and insurance data. For this reason, and without checking further, the DRPA declared that Alpha was "not responsible" and awarded the contract to the second-lowest bidder. [*Alpha Painting & Construction Co. v. Delaware River Port Authority,* 853 F.3d 671 (3d Cir. 2017)] (See *Agency Creation and Powers.*)

(a) Using the Inquiry step of the IDDR approach, identify the ethical issue the DRPA faced when deciding whether to accept or reject Alpha's bid.

(b) Using the Discussion step of the IDDR approach, consider whether the DRPA's rejection of Alpha was ethical.

Time-Limited Group Assignment

23–10. Investigation. Kathleen Dodge was a flight attendant for United Continental Holdings, Inc. (UCH). After being assigned to work in Paris, France, she became pregnant. Because UCH does not allow its flight attendants to fly during their third trimester of pregnancy, Dodge was placed on involuntary leave. She applied for temporary disability benefits through the French social security system. Her request was denied because UCH does not contribute to the

French system on behalf of its U.S.-based flight attendants. Dodge filed a charge of discrimination with the U.S. Equal Employment Opportunity Commission (EEOC), alleging that UCH had discriminated against her and other Americans. The EEOC issued a subpoena, asking UCH to detail all benefits received by all UCH employees living outside the United States. UCH refused to provide the information on the ground that it was irrelevant and compliance would be unduly burdensome. The EEOC filed a suit in a federal district court against UCH. (See *The Administrative Process.*)

(a) The first group will decide whether the court should enforce the subpoena and explain why or why not.

(b) The second group will discuss whether the EEOC should be able to force a U.S. company operating overseas to provide the same disability benefits to employees located there as it does to employees in the United States.

(c) The third group will determine whether UCH should be required to contribute to the French social security system for employees who reside in France and explain why or why not.

Chapter 24

Consumer Protection

All statutes, agency rules, and common law judicial decisions that serve to protect the interests of consumers are classified as **consumer law.** Traditionally, in disputes involving consumers, it was assumed that the freedom to contract carried with it the obligation to live by the deal made. Over time, this attitude has changed considerably.

Today, countless federal and state laws attempt to protect consumers from unfair trade practices, unsafe products, discriminatory or unreasonable credit requirements, and other problems related to consumer transactions. Nearly every agency and department of the federal government has an office of consumer affairs, and most states have one or more such offices. The state attorney general's office typically assists consumers as well.

In the last several decades, there has been a renewed interest in attempting to protect consumers in their dealings with credit-card companies, financial institutions, and insurance companies. Congress has enacted credit-card regulations and financial reforms to regulate the nation's largest banks. It has also enacted healthcare reforms and revised food safety laws.

24–1 Advertising, Marketing, and Sales

Numerous federal laws have been passed to define the duties of sellers and the rights of consumers. Exhibit 24–1 shows many of the areas of consumer law that are regulated by federal statutes. We begin our discussion of this legislation by examining some of the laws and regulations relating to advertising, marketing, and sales. Although we focus on federal law, realize that state consumer protection laws in these and other areas often provide more sweeping and significant protections than do federal laws.

24–1a Deceptive Advertising

One of the most important federal consumer protection laws is the Federal Trade Commission Act.[1] The act created the Federal Trade Commission (FTC) to carry out the broadly stated goal of preventing unfair and deceptive trade practices, including deceptive advertising.

Generally, **deceptive advertising** occurs if a reasonable consumer would be misled by the advertising claim. Vague generalities and obvious exaggerations, known as "puffery," are permissible. ■ **Case in Point 24.1** Sheila Cruz and others sued Anheuser-Busch Companies, LLC, for falsely advertising "Bud Light Lime-A-Rita" beverages as "light." She argued that the word "light" was misleading because the drinks contained more calories than light beer (Bud Light). The court dismissed Cruz's case, and a federal appellate court affirmed. The Lime-A-Rita beverages were advertised as "Margaritas with a Twist," so no reasonable consumer would believe they were the same as light beer. They also contained fewer calories than traditional tequila margaritas. Thus, the court concluded that the label was not misleading.[2] ■

When an advertising claim takes on the appearance of authenticity, however, it may create problems. In the following case, a group of dog food purchasers sued a dog food manufacturer, alleging that claims on the dog food packaging were more than mere puffery.

---

1. 15 U.S.C. Sections 41–58.

2. *Cruz v. Anheuser-Busch Companies, LLC,* 682 Fed.Appx. 583 (9th Cir. 2017). See also *Crawford v. AriZona Beverages USA LLC,* 2023 WL 1100260 (S.D. IL 2023).

Renfro v. Champion Petfoods USA, Inc.

United States Court of Appeals, Tenth Circuit, 25 F.4th 1293 (2022).

In the Language of the Court

TYMKOVICH, Chief Judge.

A group of pet owners brought a class action against Champion Petfoods USA, Inc., alleging representations on Champion's packaging on its Acana and Orijen brands of dog food were false and misleading. Champion's dog food packaging contains a number of claims about the product, advertising the food as "Biologically Appropriate," "Trusted Everywhere," using "Fresh and Regional Ingredients," and containing "Ingredients We Love [From] People We Trust." The district court dismissed the claims as either unactionable puffery or overly subjective and therefore not materially misleading to a reasonable consumer.

* * * *

I. Background

Champion is a pet food producer located in Auburn, Kentucky, where it manufactures pet food that is distributed throughout the United States. It launched a food brand called Acana in the 1990s, and in 2006 another called Orijen. Champion's Orijen brand was aimed at offering a premium product to consumers that would mirror foods dogs might encounter in the wild. Champion marketed Orijen as "Biologically Appropriate" dog food that contained the "richness, freshness, and variety" of meats dogs were "evolved to eat." Champion later employed the same nutritional philosophy with its Acana brand as well.

The food packaging reflected this branding. For example, on Orijen bags, the packaging explained that "Biologically Appropriate" meant that the food would "nourish as nature intended."

The Orijen packaging also advertised it was "Trusted Everywhere" and contained "Fresh Regional Ingredients" "Grown Close to Home" that were "ethically raised by people we know and trust[.]"

On the packaging of certain dog food formulas, Champion made more specific

claims. For example, on the packaging of the Orijen Six Fish formula, Champion listed the approximate amount of each fish included by weight. Champion noted that some of the fish—such as the wild monkfish and wild Alaskan cod—were fresh or raw, while other fish included were fresh, raw, or dried. And it also noted that only eleven of the thirteen pounds in the bag were fish.

* * * *

1. Affirmative Misrepresentations

The Colorado Consumer Protection Act * * * "was enacted to provide prompt, economical, and readily available remedies against consumer fraud." For a plaintiff to recover on a claim under the Colorado Consumer Protection Act, the plaintiff must prove by a preponderance of the evidence that: (1) the defendant engaged in an unfair or deceptive trade practice; (2) the challenged practice occurred in the course of the defendant's business; (3) the deceptive trade practice significantly impacted the public as actual or potential consumers of the defendant's goods; (4) the plaintiff suffered injury in fact to a legally protected interest; and (5) the deceptive trade practice caused actual damages or losses to the plaintiff.

* * * Among the deceptive trade practices alleged by Plaintiffs are that Champion: "knowingly or recklessly ma[de] a false representation as to the characteristics, ingredients, uses, benefits, alterations, or quantities of goods [or] food[.]" * * *

* * * *

Under Colorado law, misrepresentation is defined as a "false or misleading statement that induces the recipient to act or refrain from acting[.]" But misrepresentation is only actionable when "it is made 'either with knowledge of its untruth, or recklessly and willfully made without regard to its consequences, and with an intent to mislead and

deceive the plaintiff.'" "Thus, a party may establish a deceptive trade practice by proof that a defendant knowingly made a misrepresentation that induces a party's action or inaction[.]" And in addition, the alleged "representation of a fact must be . . . material[.]"

But "[m]ere statements of opinion such as puffing or praise of goods by seller is no warranty." Instead, the term "puffery" is used to "characterize those vague generalities that no reasonable person would rely on as assertions of particular facts." These kinds of statements cannot form the basis for any claim of misrepresentation of fact. "[G]eneral statements of opinion typically constitute protected puffery, while specific representations of fact can form the basis of a deceptive trade practice claim." For example, a Colorado court concluded GM's representation that "Chevy's business is providing the right truck for your business" was not an affirmation of fact and was not actionable because it was "merely [GM]'s opinion or commendation of [its] goods." Colorado courts have continued to make clear that common-law doctrines inform the meaning and application of the CCPA.

* * * *

B. Application

Applying Colorado law, we conclude [that] none of the phrases supports claims for deceptive advertising.

1. "Trusted Everywhere" and "Ingredients We Love [From] People We Trust"

The district court correctly found that the statements "Trusted Everywhere" and "Ingredients We Love [From] People We Trust" are unactionable puffery. No reasonable consumer would have concluded these "vague generalities" were anything other than boilerplate statements of opinion.

* * * *

Case 24.1 Continues

Case 24.1 Continued

2. "Fresh and Regional"

The district court concluded that the statement "Fresh Regional Ingredients" was either not empirically verifiable or unactionable puffery.

The statement stands among other claims that the food was "the fullest expression of [Champion's] . . . fresh regional ingredients commitment," that "focus[ed] on local ingredients that are

ethically raised by people [Champion] know[s] and trust[s]." The district court found that these statements were "inherently subjective ideals" because no court or jury could decide what amount of fresh or regional ingredients "would be enough" to establish focus or commitment.

We agree with the district court that the phrase can only be understood in the context of the entire packaging of Champion's dog food. But even if we

take the claim "Fresh and Regional" on its own, it too is a "vague generality" that would not mislead a reasonable consumer who examined the entire package. * * *

* * * *

IV. Conclusion

For these reasons, we AFFIRM the district court's dismissal of Plaintiffs' complaint.

Legal Reasoning Questions

1. How could the plaintiffs in this case disprove the claims made on the dog food packaging?

2. What would have been necessary for the plaintiffs to recover on a claim under the Colorado Consumer Protection Act?

3. Under Colorado law, how must a party establish a deceptive trade practice?

Exhibit 24–1 Selected Areas of Consumer Law Regulated by Statutes

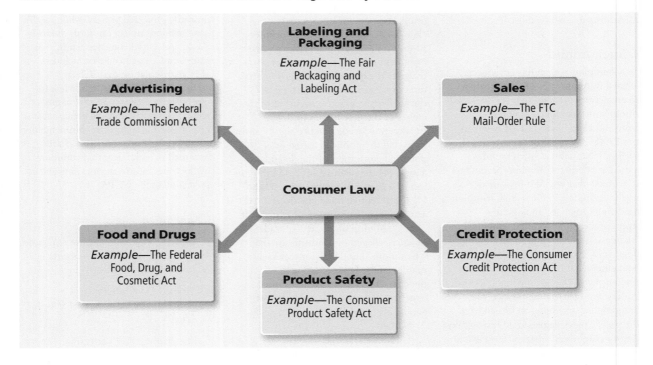

Claims That Appear to Be Based on Factual Evidence Advertising that appears to be based on factual evidence but, in fact, is not reasonably supported by evidence will be deemed deceptive. ■ **Example 24.2** HealthfulLab, Inc., advertises that its weight-loss supplement ("The Ultimate Skinny Pill") helps users lose substantial amounts of weight extremely rapidly. The ad

claims that "clinical studies prove" that people who take the pill lose "as much as fifteen to seventeen pounds per week and as much as 50 percent of all excess weight in just fourteen days, without dieting or exercising." The FTC sues HealthfulLab for deceptive advertising. During FTC proceedings, an expert hired by the FTC testifies that losing the amount of weight advertised would require a 200-pound person to run between fifty-seven and sixty-eight miles every day. The court probably will conclude that the advertisement is false and misleading, will grant the FTC summary judgment, and will issue a permanent injunction to stop HealthfulLab from running the ads. ■

Claims Based on Half-Truths Some advertisements contain "half-truths," meaning that the presented information is true but incomplete and may therefore lead consumers to a false conclusion. In addition, advertising that contains an endorsement by a celebrity may be deemed deceptive if the celebrity does not actually use the product.

Bait-and-Switch Advertising The FTC has issued rules that govern specific advertising techniques. One of the most important rules is contained in the FTC's "Guides Against Bait Advertising."[3]

Some retailers systematically advertise merchandise at low prices to get customers into their stores. But when the customers arrive, they find that the merchandise is not in stock. Salespersons then encourage them to purchase more expensive items instead. This practice, known as **bait-and-switch advertising**, is a form of deceptive advertising. The low price is the "bait" to lure the consumer into the store. The salesperson is instructed to "switch" the consumer to a different, more expensive item.

Under the FTC guidelines, bait-and-switch advertising occurs if the seller does any of the following:

1. Refuses to show the advertised item.
2. Fails to have a reasonable quantity of the item in stock.
3. Fails to promise to deliver the advertised item within a reasonable time.
4. Discourages employees from selling the advertised item.

Online Deceptive Advertising Deceptive advertising occurs in the online environment as well as offline. The FTC actively monitors online advertising. It has identified hundreds of websites that have made false or deceptive claims for products and services ranging from medical treatments to exercise equipment and weight-loss aids.

The FTC has issued guidelines to help online businesses comply with existing laws prohibiting deceptive advertising. These guidelines include the following requirement.

1. All ads—both online and offline—must be truthful and not misleading.
2. The claims made in an ad must be substantiated—that is, advertisers must have evidence to back up their claims.

---

3. 16 C.F.R. Part 238.

3. Ads cannot be unfair, which the FTC defines as "likely to cause substantial consumer injury that consumers could not reasonably avoid and that is not outweighed by the benefit to consumers or competition."
4. Ads must disclose relevant limitations and qualifying information concerning the claims advertisers are making.
5. Required disclosures must be "clear and conspicuous." For instance, because consumers may not read an entire web page, an online disclosure should be placed as close as possible to the claim being qualified. Generally, hyperlinks to disclosures are recommended only for lengthy disclosures. If a hyperlink is used, it should be obvious and should be placed as close as possible to the information it qualifies.

Federal Trade Commission Actions The FTC receives complaints from many sources, including competitors of alleged violators, consumers, trade associations, Better Business Bureaus, and government organizations and officials. When the agency receives numerous and widespread complaints about a particular problem, normally it will investigate.

Formal Complaint. If the FTC concludes that a given advertisement is unfair or deceptive, it drafts a formal complaint, which is sent to the alleged offender. The company may agree to settle the complaint without further proceedings. If not, the FTC can conduct a hearing in which the company can present its defense. The agency also can file lawsuits seeking injunctions, civil penalties, and other forms of relief in federal court.

■ **Example 24.3** The popular online dating service Match.com allows users to maintain free profiles on its website. These users cannot, however, respond to other members without paying a subscription fee. The FTC sued the corporate parent of Match.com for engaging in deceptive advertising practices designed to "trick" nonpaying members into purchasing access to the site. According to the FTC's complaint, Match.com sent millions of fake "You caught his eye" e-mails to users with free accounts, suggesting that another member was romantically interested in them. At least 500,000 users, the agency estimates, were convinced to buy paid subscriptions after being flattered by these fraudulent e-mails. ■

FTC Orders and Remedies. If the FTC succeeds in proving that an advertisement is unfair or deceptive, it usually issues a **cease-and-desist order** requiring the company to stop the challenged advertising. In some circumstances, it may also impose a sanction known as **counteradvertising.** This requires the company to advertise anew—in print, on the internet, on radio, and on television—to inform the public about the earlier misinformation. The FTC sometimes institutes a **multiple product order,** which requires a firm to stop false advertising for all of its products, not just the product involved in the original action.

Damages When Consumers Are Injured. When a company's deceptive ad involves wrongful charges to consumers, the FTC may seek other remedies, including damages. ■ **Case in Point 24.4** The FTC sued the University of Phoenix (UOP), a for-profit university, and its parent corporation over a deceptive advertising campaign (titled "Let's Get to Work") that focused on prospective students' career prospects. The campaign's social media, television, and radio advertisements made it appear that the school was working with high-profile employers such as Yahoo!, Microsoft, Twitter, and Adobe to find jobs for UOP graduates. In reality, none of these "corporate partners" had any connection with UOP.

Conceding wrongdoing, UOP agreed to settle with the FTC for $191 million. While $50 million of this amount went to the FTC as a fine, the remaining $141 million was used to pay off the debts of UOP students who had been misled by the deceptive advertisements.[4] ■

Restitution Possible. When a company's deceptive advertising leads to wrongful payments by consumers, the FTC may seek other remedies, including restitution. ■ **Case in Point 24.5** Verity International, Ltd., billed phone-line subscribers who accessed certain online pornography sites at the rate for international calls to Madagascar. When consumers complained about the charges, Verity told them that the charges were valid and had to be paid, or the consumers would face further collection actions. A federal appellate court held that this representation of "uncontestability" was deceptive and a violation of the FTC act. The court ordered Verity to pay nearly $18 million in restitution to consumers.[5] ■

False Advertising Claims Under the Lanham Act The Lanham Act[6] protects trademarks, and it also covers false advertising claims. To state a successful claim for false advertising under this act, a business must establish each of the following elements:

1. An injury to a commercial interest in reputation or sales.
2. Direct causation of the injury by false or deceptive advertising.
3. A loss of business from buyers who were deceived by the advertising.

State Laws Concerning False Advertising State consumer-fraud statutes also prohibit false, misleading, and deceptive advertising. Recovery under a state law typically requires proof of the following elements.

1. The defendant committed a deceptive or unfair act.
2. The act was committed in the course of trade or commerce.
3. The defendant intended that others rely on the deception.
4. The plaintiff suffered actual damages proximately caused by the deception.

At issue in the following case was a plaintiff's claim under Illinois's consumer fraud statute.

---

4. *Federal Trade Commission v. The University of Phoenix, Inc.,* 2:19-CV-05772 (D. Ariz. 2019).

5. *Federal Trade Commission v. Verity International, Ltd.,* 443 F.3d 48 (2d Cir. 2006).

6. 15 U.S.C. Sections 1051 *et seq.*

Case 24.2

Haywood v. Massage Envy Franchising, LLC

United States Court of Appeals, Seventh Circuit, 887 F.3d 329 (2018).

Background and Facts Massage Envy, LLC, is a franchisor based in Arizona that grants licenses to independently owned and operated entities for the use of its name, trademark, and standardized operations. Massage Envy's website advertises its services, including an "Introductory 1-hour Massage Session." At the bottom of the home page, a link to "pricing and promotional details" leads to a page with disclaimers. One disclaimer, titled "Session," explains that a "session includes massage or facial and time for consultation and dressing."

Through the website, Kathy Haywood, a resident of Illinois, scheduled an appointment. At the session, for which Haywood paid with a gift card, she received a massage that lasted no more than fifty minutes. Citing Massage Envy's online ad, Haywood filed a suit in a federal district court against the company, alleging unfair and deceptive business practices in violation of the Illinois Consumer Fraud and Deceptive Business Practices Act (ICFA). The court dismissed the claim. Haywood appealed.

In the Language of the Court

BAUER, Circuit Judge.

* * * *

To state a claim under the ICFA * * * Haywood must plausibly allege: (1) a deceptive act or promise by Massage Envy; (2) Massage Envy's intent that she rely on the deceptive act; (3) the deceptive act occurred during a course of conduct involving trade or commerce; and (4) actual damage as a result of the deceptive act. Actual damage in this context means that Haywood must have suffered actual pecuniary [financial] loss. Additionally, the deceptive act must have been the "but-for" cause of the damage.

* * * *

* * * [Haywood's] allegations fail to establish the requisite causation. * * * Here, the only reasonable conclusion is that Massage Envy's representations regarding the one-hour massage session were not the but-for cause of any alleged injury. There is no allegation in the complaint that her belief about the length of the massage caused Haywood to make the appointment. To the contrary, the only reasonable and plausible inference is that only the receipt of a gift card caused her to book a massage; the alleged deceptive representations did not influence that decision. * * * She cannot, based on these allegations, establish that Massage Envy's alleged deception was the but-for cause of her injury, and her claims fail as a result.

Decision and Remedy The U.S. Court of Appeals for the Seventh Circuit affirmed the dismissal. "The district court did not abuse its discretion in dismissing the complaint."

Critical Thinking

- **Economic** A fraud injury can be measured in two ways. As a loss of the benefit of the bargain, damages consist of the difference between the value of what was promised and the value of what was received. Under the out-of-pocket rule, the measure is the difference between the price paid and the market value of what was received. If Haywood had established her claim, which of these methods would have applied? Why?
- **What If the Facts Were Different?** Suppose that reliance was not an element of a consumer fraud claim under the ICFA. Would the result in this case have been different? Explain.

24–1b Marketing

In addition to regulating advertising practices, Congress has passed several laws to protect consumers against other marketing practices.

Telephone Solicitation The Telephone Consumer Protection Act (TCPA)[7] prohibits telephone solicitation using an automatic telephone dialing system or a prerecorded voice. The TCPA, which is enforced by the FCC, has long been considered lacking when it comes to protecting consumers against unsolicited robocalls. This term refers generally to telemarketing calls or texts generated using computerized autodialing technology. By the end of the 2010s, American were receiving between 5 and 6 billion unsolicited robocalls each month. In response, Congress passed the TRACED Act, an amendment to the TCPA that broadens the definition of prohibited robocalls and requires telephone providers to offer consumers more effective robocall-blocking options.[8] The amendments also give the FCC the ability to impose substantial fines on individuals or businesses entities—up to $20,489 for a single robocall violation and up to $153,669 for a repeat offense.

---

7. 47 U.S.C. Sections 227 *et seq.*

8. *Pallone-Thune Telephone Robocall Abuse Criminal Enforcement and Deterrence Act,* 47 U.S.C. Section 227(b).

Fraudulent Telemarketing The Telemarketing and Consumer Fraud and Abuse Prevention Act[9] directed the FTC to establish rules governing telemarketing and to bring actions against fraudulent telemarketers.

The FTC's Telemarketing Sales Rule (TSR)[10] requires a telemarketer to identify the seller's name, describe the product being sold, and disclose all material facts related to the sale (such as the total cost). The TSR makes it illegal for telemarketers to misrepresent information or facts about their goods or services. A telemarketer must also remove a consumer's name from its list of potential contacts if the customer so requests.

An amendment to the TSR established the national Do Not Call Registry. Telemarketers must refrain from calling those consumers who have placed their names on the list. The TSR applies to any offer made to consumers in the United States—even if the offer comes from a foreign firm.

■ **Example 24.6** Jason formed Instantaneous Response Systems, LLC (IRS), to sell medical alert monitoring systems to elderly people. His sales personnel call only people aged sixty-four years and older. The IRS telemarketers, using company-supplied scripts, falsely tell consumers that they are calling in response to a request for information about the company's medical alert services. Many consumers who did not even order the IRS system are billed for it. They receive follow-up letters accusing them of nonpayment. When they object, IRS employees resort to threats.

The FTC sues IRS and Jason for violating the Telemarketing Sales Rule. The FTC will normally prevail. A court likely will order Jason to pay millions in fines and will permanently enjoin Jason from marketing medical alert systems. ■

24–1c Sales

A number of statutes protect consumers by requiring the disclosure of certain terms in sales transactions and providing rules governing unsolicited merchandise. The FTC has regulatory authority in this area, as do some other federal agencies.

Many states and the FTC have **"cooling-off" laws** that permit the buyers of goods sold door-to-door to cancel their contracts within three business days. The FTC rule also requires that consumers be notified in Spanish of this right if the oral negotiations for the sale were in that language.

The contracts that fall under these cancellation rules include trade show sales contracts, contracts for home equity loans, internet purchase contracts, and home (door-to-door) sales contracts. In addition, certain states have passed laws allowing consumers to cancel contracts for dating services, gym memberships, and weight loss programs.

The FTC Mail or Telephone Order Merchandise Rule[11] protects consumers who purchase goods via mail, internet, phone, or fax. Merchants are required to ship orders within the time promised in their advertisements and to notify consumers when orders cannot be shipped on time. If the seller does not give an estimated shipping time, it must ship within thirty days. Merchants must also issue a refund within a specified period of time when a consumer cancels an order.

24–2 Labeling and Packaging Laws

A number of federal and state laws deal specifically with the information given on labels and packages. In general, labels must be accurate, and they must use words that are easily understood by an ordinary consumer. In some instances, labels must specify the raw materials used in the product, such as the percentage of cotton, nylon, or other fiber used in a garment. In other instances, the product must carry a warning, such as those required on cigarette and e-cigarette packages and advertising.[12]

24–2a Automobile Fuel Economy Labels

The Energy Policy and Conservation Act (EPCA)[13] requires automakers to attach an information label to every new car. The label must include the Environmental Protection Agency's fuel economy estimate for the vehicle. ■ **Case in Point 24.7** Gaetano Paduano bought a new Honda Civic Hybrid in California. The information label on the car included the fuel economy estimate from the Environmental Protection Agency (EPA). Honda's sales brochure added, "Just drive the Hybrid like you would a conventional car and save on fuel bills."

When Paduano discovered that the car's fuel economy was less than half of the EPA's estimate, he sued Honda for deceptive advertising under a California law. The automaker claimed that the federal law (the EPCA)

---

9. 15 U.S.C. Sections 6101–6108.
10. 16 C.F.R. Part 310.

11. 16 C.F.R. Part 435.
12. 15 U.S.C. Sections 1331–1341.
13. 49 U.S.C. Section 32908(b)(1).

preempted the state's deceptive advertising law. The court held in Paduano's favor, finding that the federal statute did not preempt a claim for deceptive advertising made under state law.[14] ■

24–2b Food Labeling

Because the quality and safety of food are so important to consumers, several statutes deal specifically with food labeling. The Fair Packaging and Labeling Act[15] requires that food product labels identify (1) the product, (2) the net quantity of the contents (and, if the number of servings is stated, the size of a serving), (3) the manufacturer, and (4) the packager or distributor. The act includes additional requirements concerning descriptions on packages, savings claims, components of nonfood products, and standards for the partial filling of packages.

Nutritional Content of Food Products Food products must bear labels detailing the nutritional content, including the number of calories and the amounts of various nutrients that the food contains. The Nutrition Labeling and Education Act[16] requires food labels to provide standard nutrition facts and regulates the use of such terms as "fresh" and "low fat."

The U.S. Food and Drug Administration (FDA) and the U.S. Department of Agriculture (USDA) are the primary agencies that issue regulations on food labeling. These rules are published in the *Federal Register* and updated annually.

Limiting Consumer Confusion FDA regulations define dairy products as coming from milk-producing animals such as cows and goats. Yet supermarkets are filled with drinks made from non-dairy sources such as almonds and cashews that are labeled "milk." A similar phenomenon exists in the meat industry, with a proliferation of plant- and soy-based products mimicking the shape and taste of animal meat. Representatives of the traditional dairy and beef industries believe that labeling these alternative food sources as "milk" and "burgers" risks confusing consumers.

A number of states and the federal government are considering legislation that would ban the use of words such as "milk" and "burger" on the labels of products that are not derived from animal sources. Critics of this regulatory trend reject the idea that consumers are unsure as to whether almond milk comes from a cow or an Impossible Burger is made with beef. Any confusion that might exist, these observers point out, can be cleared up by the nutritional content label.

■ **Case in Point 24.8** A group of California consumers brought a class action lawsuit against Blue Diamond Growers, claiming that the company mislabeled its almond beverages as "almond milk." The plaintiffs insisted that the product should be labeled "imitation milk" because its similarity to dairy milk is confusing to consumers. A federal appeals court dismissed this lawsuit, finding that a "reasonable consumer" will not be deceived into thinking that almond milk is a substitute for or an equivalent to dairy milk. As long as Blue Diamond accurately labels and advertises its almond milk, the court held, it is not "misleading" under federal or state law.[17] ■

Caloric Content of Restaurant Foods The Affordable Care Act, or Obamacare, included provisions aimed at combating the problem of obesity in the United States. All restaurant chains with twenty or more locations are now required to post the caloric content of the foods on their menus so that customers will know how many calories the foods contain.[18] Foods offered through vending machines must also be labeled so that their caloric content is visible to would-be purchasers.

In addition, restaurants must post guidelines on the number of calories that an average person requires daily so that customers can determine what portion of a day's calories a particular food will provide. The hope is that consumers, armed with this information, will consider the number of calories when they make their food choices. The federal law on menu labeling supersedes all previous state and local laws in this area.

24–3 Protection of Health and Safety

Although labeling and packaging laws promote consumer health and safety, there is a significant distinction between regulating the information dispensed about a product and regulating the actual content of the product. The classic example is tobacco products. Producers of tobacco

---

14. *Paduano v. American Honda Motor Co.,* 169 Cal.App.4th 1453, 88 Cal.Rptr.3d 90 (2009). For the opposite result, see *In re Ford Motor Co. F-150 and Ranger Truck Fuel Economy Marketing and Sales Practices Litigation,* 2022 WL 551221 (E.D. MI 2022).

15. 15 U.S.C. Sections 1451–1461.

16. 21 U.S.C. Section 343.1.

17. *Painter v. Blue Diamond Growers,* 757 Fed.Appx. 517 (9th Cir. 2018).

18. See Section 4205 of the Patient Protection and Affordable Care Act, Pub. L. No. 111-148, 124 Stat. 119 (2010).

products must use labels that warn consumers about the health hazards associated with their use, but the sale of tobacco products has not been subjected to significant restrictions. We now examine various laws that regulate the actual products made available to consumers.

24–3a The Federal Food, Drug, and Cosmetic Act

The most important federal legislation regulating food and drugs is the Federal Food, Drug, and Cosmetic Act (FDCA).[19] The act protects consumers against adulterated (contaminated) and misbranded foods and drugs. The FDCA establishes food standards, specifies safe levels of potentially hazardous food additives, and provides classifications of foods and food advertising. Most of these statutory requirements are monitored and enforced by the FDA.

Interestingly, the European Union and a number of other countries, such as Canada, have banned some foods that the FDA assumes to be safe. These foods include brominated vegetable oil (a common ingredient in sports drinks, such as Gatorade) and Olestra/Olean (a cholesterol-free fat substitute found in certain potato chips). Food products containing such substances may not be sold in the European Union. Similarly, certain food colorings found in processed foods in the United States (in M&M'S and Kraft macaroni and cheese, for instance) are not allowed in foods in some other countries.

Tainted Foods In the last twenty years or so, many people in the United States have contracted food poisoning from eating foods that were contaminated, often with salmonella or *E. coli* bacteria. In response to the problem of food contamination, Congress enacted the Food Safety Modernization Act (FSMA)[20] to provide greater government control over the U.S. food safety system. The act gives the FDA authority to directly recall any food products that it suspects are tainted, rather than relying on the producers to recall items.

The FSMA requires anyone who manufactures, processes, packs, distributes, receives, holds, or imports food products to pay a fee and register with the U.S. Department of Health and Human Services. (There are some exceptions for small farmers.) Owners and operators of such facilities are required to analyze and identify food safety hazards, implement preventive controls, monitor effectiveness, and take corrective actions. The FSMA places additional restrictions on importers of food and requires them to verify that imported foods meet U.S. safety standards.

Drugs and Medical Devices The FDA is also responsible under the FDCA for ensuring that drugs are safe and effective before they are marketed to the public. Because the FDA must ensure the safety of new medications, there is always a delay before drugs are available to the public, and this sometimes leads to controversy.

The FDA has been criticized for being slow in recognizing the addictive qualities of prescription opioids such as OxyContin and fentanyl, which have been linked to hundreds of thousands of overdose deaths. In recent years, the FDA has increased its regulatory efforts, sometimes with effective curtailment of somewhat hard-to-believe claims of pharmaceuticals.

■ **Case in Point 24.9** Pharmaceutical Manufacturing Research Services, Inc. (PMRS), sought approval from the FDA to advertise a new prescription opioid drug as being less subject to abuse and addiction than other opioids. The company claimed that its product contained a purplish dye that would "create a visual deterrent" to intravenous injection. Furthermore, the drug's label would recommend a maximum daily dose below industry standards.

The FDA denied approval on the ground that PMRS had not provided any evidence that, based on its physical and chemical properties, the drug actually carried less potential for abuse. A federal appeals court upheld the FDA's decision, finding that a proposed label heralding PMRS's product as "the safest opioid" on the market would be false or misleading.[21] ■

24–3b The Consumer Product Safety Act

The Consumer Product Safety Act created a comprehensive regulatory scheme over consumer safety matters and established the Consumer Product Safety Commission (CPSC).

The CPSC's Authority The CPSC conducts research on the safety of individual consumer products and maintains a clearinghouse on the risks associated with

19. 21 U.S.C. Sections 301–393.
20. Pub. L. No. 111-353, 124 Stat. 3885 (2011). This statute affected numerous parts of Title 21 of the U.S.C.
21. *Pharmaceutical Manufacturing Research Services, Inc. v. Food & Drug Administration,* 957 F.3d 254, 446 U.S.App.D.C. 362 (D.C. Cir. 2020).

various products. The Consumer Product Safety Act authorizes the CPSC to do the following:

1. Set safety standards for consumer products.
2. Ban the manufacture and sale of any product that the commission believes poses an "unreasonable risk" to consumers. (Products banned by the CPSC have included various types of fireworks, cribs, and toys, as well as many products containing asbestos or vinyl chloride.)
3. Remove from the market any products it believes to be imminently hazardous. The CPSC frequently works in conjunction with manufacturers to conduct voluntary recalls of defective products from stores. ■ **Example 24.10** In cooperation with the CPSC, the Scandinavian company IKEA recalled three million baby bed canopies and thirty million wall-mounted children's lamps because they posed a strangulation risk to children. ■
4. Require manufacturers to report on any products already sold or intended for sale if the products have proved to be hazardous.
5. Administer other product-safety legislation, including the Child Protection and Toy Safety Act[22] and the Federal Hazardous Substances Act.[23]

Notification Requirements The Consumer Product Safety Act requires the distributors of consumer products to notify the CPSC immediately if they receive information that a product "contains a defect which . . . creates a substantial risk to the public" or "an unreasonable risk of serious injury or death."

■ **Example 24.11** A company that sells juicers receives twenty-three letters from customers complaining that during operation the juicer suddenly exploded, sending pieces of glass and razor-sharp metal across the room. The company must immediately notify the CPSC because the alleged defect creates a substantial risk to the public. ■

24–3c Healthcare Reforms

Healthcare reforms enacted in 2010 (the Affordable Care Act, or Obamacare) made some changes in Americans' rights and benefits with regard to health care.[24] The legislation also affected certain insurance company practices.

Expanded Coverage for Children and Seniors The reforms enabled more children to obtain health-insurance coverage and allowed young adults (under age twenty-six) to remain on their parents' health insurance policies. The legislation also ended lifetime limits and most annual limits on care, and gave insured persons access to recommended preventive services (such as cancer screening and vaccinations) without cost. Some Medicare drug benefits were also changed.

Controlling Costs of Health Insurance In an attempt to control the rising costs of health insurance, certain restrictions were placed on insurance companies. Insurance companies must spend at least 85 percent of all premium dollars collected from large employers (80 percent of the premiums collected from individuals and small employers) on benefits and quality improvement. If insurance companies do not meet these goals, they must provide rebates to consumers. Additionally, states can require insurance companies to justify any premium increases to be eligible to participate in state-sponsored health-insurance exchanges.

24–4 Credit Protection

Credit protection is one of the more important aspects of consumer protection legislation. Nearly 80 percent of U.S. consumers have credit cards, and most carry a balance on these cards—a total of more than $1 trillion nationwide. The Consumer Financial Protection Bureau (CFPB) is the agency that oversees the credit practices of banks, mortgage lenders, and credit-card companies.

24–4a The Truth-in-Lending Act

A key statute regulating the credit and credit-card industries is the Truth-in-Lending Act (TILA), the name commonly given to Title I of the Consumer Credit Protection Act, as amended.[25] The TILA is basically a disclosure law. It is administered by the Federal Reserve Board and requires sellers and lenders to disclose credit terms and loan terms so that individuals can shop around for the best financing arrangements.

Application TILA requirements apply only to those who, in the ordinary course of business, lend funds, sell on credit, or arrange for the extension of credit. Thus, sales or loans made between two consumers do not come

22. 15 U.S.C. Section 1262(e).
23. 15 U.S.C. Sections 1261–1278.
24. Patient Protection and Affordable Health Care Act, Pub. L. No. 111-148, 124 Stat. 119 (2010); and the Health Care and Education Reconciliation Act, Pub. L. No. 111-152, 124 Stat. 1029 (2010).
25. 15 U.S.C. Sections 1601–1693r.

under the protection of the act. Additionally, this law protects only debtors who are natural persons (as opposed to the artificial "person" of a corporation). It does not extend to other legal entities.

Disclosure Requirements The TILA's disclosure requirements are contained in **Regulation Z,** issued by the Federal Reserve Board of Governors. If the contracting parties are subject to the TILA, the requirements of Regulation Z apply to any transaction involving an installment sales contract that calls for payment to be made in more than four installments. Transactions subject to Regulation Z typically include installment loans, retail and installment sales, car loans, home-improvement loans, and certain real estate loans if the amount of financing is less than $25,000.

Under the provisions of the TILA, all of the terms of a credit instrument must be clearly and conspicuously disclosed. A lender must disclose the annual percentage rate (APR), finance charge, amount financed, and total payments (the sum of the amount loaned, plus any fees, finance charges, and interest). If a creditor fails to follow the exact procedures required by the TILA, the creditor risks contract rescission (cancellation) under the act.

Equal Credit Opportunity The Equal Credit Opportunity Act (ECOA)[26] amended the TILA. The ECOA prohibits the denial of credit solely on the basis of race, religion, national origin, color, gender, marital status, or age. The act also prohibits credit discrimination on the basis of whether an individual receives certain forms of income, such as public-assistance benefits.

Courts tend to interpret the ECOA's protections broadly, particularly when the lending institution is perceived to have treated a credit applicant unfairly. ■ **Case in Point 24.12** Chase Bank USA rejected Jeffrey Chen's application for a credit card, citing his previous "unsatisfactory relationship with the bank" as the only reason for the denial. Chen filed suit against Chase for violating the ECOA. Chase moved for dismissal of the action because Chen could not show that he had been the victim of discrimination based on any of the factors listed above.

Investigating the legislative record of the ECOA, a federal court found that Congress intended the law not only to discourage discriminatory practices, but also to "educate" consumers such as Chen. Under this education requirement, "instead of being told only that they do not meet a particular creditor's standards," banks must provide rejected credit applicants with specific reasons for the denial. Because Chase failed to do so in this instance, the court ruled that Chen's action under the ECOA could proceed.[27] ■

Credit-Card Rules The TILA also contains provisions regarding credit cards. One provision limits the liability of a cardholder to $50 per card for unauthorized charges made before the creditor is notified that the card has been lost. If a consumer receives an unsolicited credit card in the mail that is later stolen, the company that issued the card cannot charge the consumer for any unauthorized charges.

Another provision requires credit-card companies to disclose the balance computation method that is used to determine the outstanding balance and to state when finance charges begin to accrue. Other provisions set forth procedures for resolving billing disputes with the credit-card company. These procedures are used if, for instance, a cardholder thinks that an error has occurred in billing or wishes to withhold payment for a faulty product purchased by credit card.

Amendments to Credit-Card Rules Amendments to the TILA's credit-card rules added the following protections.

1. A company may not retroactively increase the interest rates on existing card balances unless the account is sixty days delinquent.
2. A company must provide forty-five days' advance notice to consumers before changing its credit-card terms.
3. Monthly bills must be sent to cardholders twenty-one days before the due date.
4. The interest rate charged on a customer's credit-card balance may not be increased except in specific situations, such as when a promotional rate ends.
5. A company may not charge over-limit fees except in specified situations.
6. When the customer has balances at different interest rates, payments in excess of the minimum amount due must be applied first to the balance with the highest rate. (For instance, a higher interest rate is commonly charged for cash advances.)
7. A company may not compute finance charges based on the previous billing cycle (a practice known as *double-cycle billing*). Double-cycle billing hurts consumers because they are charged interest for the previous cycle even if they have paid the bill in full.

---

26. 15 U.S.C. Sections 1691–1691f.

27. *Chen v. Chase Bank USA, N.A.,* 393 F.Supp.3d 850 (N.D. CA 2019). See also *Willams v. Nationstar Mortgage, LLC,* 2023 WL 396136 (M.D. LA 2023).

24–4b The Fair Credit Reporting Act

The Fair Credit Reporting Act (FCRA)[28] protects consumers against inaccurate credit reporting and requires that lenders and other creditors report correct, relevant, and up-to-date information. The act provides that

consumer credit reporting agencies may issue credit reports to users only for specified purposes. Legitimate purposes include extending credit, issuing insurance policies, and responding to a consumer's request.

Whether a debt is legally enforceable is a central fact about that debt. The question before the court in the following case was whether a collection letter's failure to include information concerning a debt's enforceability violated the FDCPA.

---

28. 15 U.S.C. Sections 1681–1681x.

Case 24.3

Manuel v. Merchants and Professional Bureau, Inc.

United States Court of Appeals, Fifth Circuit, 956 F.3d 822 (2020).

Background and Facts Silvia Manuel owed Texas Orthopedics, Sports and Rehabilitation Associates $250. The debt was transferred to Merchants and Professional Bureau, Inc., for collection. After six years with no effort to collect, Merchants sent Manuel four collection letters. By that time, a four-year Texas statute of limitations barred any suit to collect the debt. But the collection letters did not disclose this fact, nor that a partial payment might renew the limitations period.

Manuel filed a suit in a federal district court against Merchants, claiming that without these disclosures the collection letters were false and misleading under the Fair Debt Collection Practices Act (FDCPA). The court issued a summary judgment in Manuel's favor and awarded her the maximum $1,000 statutory damages. Merchants appealed, arguing that a settlement offer or a litigation threat is the only way a debt collector can mislead a consumer regarding an old debt.

In the Language of the Court

PATRICK E. HIGGINBOTHAM, Circuit Judge:

* * * *

The question * * * is not whether the letters include a settlement offer or litigation threat but whether, read as a whole, they misrepresent the legal enforceability and character of the debt.

* * * *

Read as a whole, several aspects of the * * * letters from Merchants lead us to [conclude that the collection letters are misleading]. First, the letters do not just fail to warn that Texas has a statute of limitations or how that statute may affect the collection methods available to Merchants—the letters do not even state when the debt was incurred. If they had, they might give a consumer at least some inkling that the debt might be too old to be legally enforceable.

* * * The letters are rife with characterization of a soon-to-expire special deal or offer [and] hint at "additional collection efforts" should Manuel not pay the debt * * *. The combined effect of the letters' vague language and their silence as to the debt's time-barred nature leaves [a] consumer with the impression that the debt is enforceable, and that if payment is not levied quickly then adverse collection efforts will follow.

That consumer does not know the terms of the special offer * * * and that consumer does not know what collection efforts will follow if payment is withheld. Where the FDCPA requires clarity, * * * ambiguity itself can prove a violation. * * * Merchants' letters are examples of careful and crafted ambiguity.

* * * *

Thus, these letters seeking collection of time-barred debt, filled with ambiguous offers and threats with no indication that the debt is old, much less that the limitations period has run, misrepresent the legal enforceability of the underlying debt in violation of [the FDCPA].

Decision and Remedy The U.S. Court of Appeals for the Fifth Circuit affirmed the judgment of the lower court. Manuel was awarded the maximum $1,000 statutory damages.

Case 24.3 Continues

Case 24.3 Continued

Critical Thinking

- **Legal Environment** How might Merchants have phrased its debt collection letters to meet the standards of the FDCPA? Explain.
- **Economic** Why would a debt collector use carefully crafted, ambiguous language in an attempt to collect an old debt? Discuss.

Consumer Notification and Inaccurate Information Any time a consumer is denied credit or insurance on the basis of a credit report, the consumer must be notified of that fact. The notice must include the name and address of the credit-reporting agency that issued the report. The same notice must be sent to consumers who are charged more than others ordinarily would be for credit or insurance because of their credit reports.

Under the FCRA, consumers may request the source of any information used by the credit agency, as well as the identity of anyone who has received an agency's report. Consumers are also permitted to access the information about them contained in a credit reporting agency's files.

If a consumer discovers that an agency's files contain inaccurate information, the consumer should report the problem to the agency. On the consumer's written (or electronic) request, the agency must conduct a systematic examination of its records. Any unverifiable or erroneous information must be deleted within a reasonable period of time.

Remedies for Violations A credit reporting agency that fails to comply with the act is liable for actual damages, plus additional damages not to exceed $1,000 and attorneys' fees.[29] Creditors and other companies that use information from credit reporting agencies may also be liable for violations of the FCRA. The United States Supreme Court has held that an insurance company's failure to notify new customers that they were paying higher insurance rates as a result of their credit scores was a willful violation of the FCRA.[30]

■ **Case in Point 24.13** After graduating from college, Richard Williams applied for a job with Rent-A-Center as an account representative. As part of the application process, he agreed to a criminal-background check. Rent-A-Center contracted with First Advantage LNS Screening Solutions, Inc., a credit-reporting agency that provides

background checks. First Advantage reported to Rent-A-Center that a Richard Williams had a sale-of-cocaine record in another part of the state. Williams disputed the report. When First Advantage investigated, it determined that the criminal record was for a different person with the same name. It removed that criminal record from Williams's report. By then, however, it was too late, as Rent-A-Center had hired someone else.

Williams continued applying for other jobs. Eventually, another prospective employer ran a background check through First Advantage. This time, First Advantage reported to the employer that Williams had been convicted of aggravated battery on a pregnant woman. Again, it turned out to be a different Richard Williams, but by then, the employer had rejected Williams and hired someone else. Williams sued First Advantage in a federal district court for willfully violating the FCRA. After a jury trial, he was awarded $250,000 in compensatory damages and $3.3 million in punitive damages. First Advantage filed a motion for a new trial, which the court denied. Evidence supported the jury's finding that First Advantage willfully violated the FCRA and that the damages awarded were appropriate and not unconstitutionally excessive.[31] ■

24–4c The Fair and Accurate Credit Transactions Act

Congress passed the Fair and Accurate Credit Transactions (FACT) Act in an effort to combat identity theft.[32] The act established a national fraud alert system. Consumers who suspect that they have been or may be victimized by identity theft can place an alert on their credit files. When a consumer establishes that identity theft has occurred, the credit reporting agency must stop reporting allegedly fraudulent account information.

The act also requires the major credit reporting agencies to provide consumers with free copies of their own credit reports every twelve months. Another provision requires account numbers on credit-card receipts to be

---

29. 15 U.S.C. Section 1681n.

30. *Safeco Insurance Co. of America v. Burr,* 551 U.S. 47, 127 S.Ct. 2201, 167 L.Ed.2d 1045 (2007). See also *Magallon v. Robert Half International Inc.,* 2023 WL 1796422 (D. OR 2023).

31. *Williams v. First Advantage LNS Screening Solutions, Inc.,* 238 F.Supp.3d 1333 (N.D. Fla. 2017). See also *Brooks v. Bank of America, N.A.,* 2021 WL 1541643 (S.D. CA 2021).

32. Pub. L. No. 108-159, 117 Stat. 1952 (2003).

truncated (shortened). Merchants, employees, or others who may have access to the receipts can no longer obtain the consumers' names and full credit-card numbers. Financial institutions must work with the FTC to identify "red flag" indicators of identity theft and to develop rules for the disposal of sensitive credit information.

24–4d The Fair Debt Collection Practices Act

The Fair Debt Collection Practices Act (FDCPA)[33] attempts to curb perceived abuses by collection agencies. The act applies only to specialized debt-collection agencies and attorneys who regularly attempt to collect debts on behalf of someone else, usually for a percentage of the amount owed. Creditors attempting to collect debts are not covered by the act unless, by misrepresenting themselves, they cause debtors to believe they are collection agencies.

Requirements of the Act Under the FDCPA, a collection agency may not do any of the following:

1. Contact the debtor at the debtor's place of employment if the debtor's employer objects.
2. Contact the debtor at inconvenient or unusual times (such as three o'clock in the morning), or at any time if the debtor is being represented by an attorney.

_____
33. 15 U.S.C. Sections 1692–1692p.

3. Contact third parties other than the debtor's parents, spouse, or financial adviser about payment of a debt unless a court authorizes such action.
4. Harass or intimidate the debtor (by using abusive language or threatening violence, for instance) or make false or misleading statements (such as posing as a police officer).
5. Communicate with the debtor at any time after receiving notice that the debtor is refusing to pay the debt, except to advise the debtor of further action to be taken by the collection agency.

The FDCPA also requires a collection agency to include a **validation notice** when it initially contacts a debtor for payment of a debt or within five days of that initial contact. The notice must state that the debtor has thirty days in which to dispute the debt and to request a written verification of the debt from the collection agency.

Enforcement of the Act The Federal Trade Commission is primarily responsible for enforcing the FDCPA. A debt collector who fails to comply with the act is liable for actual damages, plus additional damages not to exceed $1,000 and attorneys' fees.

Debt collectors who violate the act are exempt from liability if they can show that the violation was not intentional and resulted from a bona fide error. Furthermore, the error must have occurred in spite of procedures the company had already put in place to avoid such errors.

Practice and Review: Consumer Law

Leota Sage saw a local motorcycle dealer's newspaper advertisement offering a MetroRider EZ electric scooter for $1,699. When she went to the dealership, however, she learned that the EZ model had been sold out. The salesperson told Sage that he still had the higher-end MetroRider FX model in stock for $2,199 and would sell her one for $1,999. Sage was disappointed but decided to purchase the FX model.

When Sage said that she wished to purchase the scooter on credit, she was directed to the dealer's credit department. As she filled out the credit forms, the clerk told Sage, who is an Asian American, that she would need a cosigner to obtain a loan. Sage could not understand why she would need a cosigner and asked to speak to the store manager. The manager apologized, told her that the clerk was mistaken, and said that he would "speak to" the clerk. The manager completed Sage's credit application, and Sage then rode the scooter home. Seven months later, Sage received a letter from the manufacturer informing her that a flaw had been discovered in the scooter's braking system and that the model had been recalled. Using the information presented in the chapter, answer the following questions.

1. Did the dealer engage in deceptive advertising? Why or why not?
2. Suppose that Sage had ordered the scooter through the dealer's website but the dealer had been unable to deliver it by the date promised. What would the FTC have required the merchant to do in that situation?
3. Assuming that the clerk required a cosigner based on Sage's race or gender, what act prohibits such credit discrimination?
4. What organization has the authority to ban the sale of scooters based on safety concerns?

Debate This . . . Laws against bait-and-switch advertising should be abolished because no consumer is ever forced to buy anything.

Terms and Concepts

bait-and-switch advertising 511
cease-and-desist order 511
consumer law 508

"cooling-off" laws 514
counteradvertising 511
deceptive advertising 508

multiple product order 512
Regulation Z 518
validation notice 521

Issue Spotters

1. United Pharmaceuticals, Inc., believes that it has developed a new drug that will be effective in the treatment of patients with AIDS. The drug has had only limited testing, but United wants to make the drug widely available as soon as possible. To market the drug, what must United prove to the U.S. Food and Drug Administration? (See *Protection of Health and Safety.*)

2. Gert buys a notebook computer from EZ Electronics. She pays for it with her credit card. When the computer proves defective, she asks EZ to repair or replace it, but EZ refuses. What can Gert do? (See *Credit Protection.*)

- Check your answers to the Issue Spotters against the answers provided in Appendix B at the end of this text.

Business Scenarios and Case Problems

24–1. Credit-Card Rules. Maria Ochoa receives two new credit cards on May 1. She has solicited one of them from Midtown Department Store, and the other arrives unsolicited from High-Flying Airlines. During the month of May, Ochoa makes numerous credit-card purchases from Midtown Department Store, but she does not use the High-Flying Airlines card. On May 31, a burglar breaks into Ochoa's home and steals both credit cards, along with other items. Ochoa notifies the Midtown Department Store of the theft on June 2, but she fails to notify High-Flying Airlines. Using the Midtown credit card, the burglar makes a $500 purchase on June 1 and a $200 purchase on June 3. The burglar then charges a vacation flight on the High-Flying Airlines card for $1,000 on June 5. Ochoa receives the bills for these charges and refuses to pay them. Discuss Ochoa's liability for the charges. (See *Credit Protection.*)

24–2. Spotlight on McDonald's—Food Labeling. McDonald's Corp.'s Happy Meal® consists of an entrée, a small order of french fries, a small drink, and a toy. In the early 1990s, McDonald's began to aim its Happy Meal marketing at children aged one to three. In 1995, McDonald's began making nutritional information for its food products available in documents known as "McDonald's Nutrition Facts." Each document lists the food items that the restaurant serves and provides a nutritional breakdown, but the Happy Meal is not included.

Marc Cohen filed a suit against McDonald's in an Illinois state court. Among other things, Cohen alleged that McDonald's had violated a state law prohibiting consumer fraud and deceptive business practices by failing to adhere to the Nutrition Labeling and Education Act (NLEA). The NLEA sets out different requirements for products specifically intended for children under the age of four—for instance, the products' labels cannot declare the percent of daily value of nutritional components. Does it make sense to have different requirements for children of this age? Why or why not? Should a state court impose such regulations? Explain. [*Cohen v. McDonald's Corp.*, 347 Ill.App.3d 627, 808 N.E.2d 1 (1st Dist. 2004)] (See *Labeling and Packaging Laws.*)

24–3. Business Case Problem With Sample Answer— Fair Debt-Collection Practices. Bank of America hired Atlantic Resource Management, LLC, to collect a debt from Michael E. Engler. Atlantic called Engler's employer and asked his supervisor about the company's policy concerning the execution of warrants. The caller then told the supervisor that, to stop process of the warrant, Engler needed to call Atlantic about "Case Number 37291 NY0969" during the first three hours of his next shift. When Engler's supervisor told him about the call, Engler feared that he might be arrested, and he experienced discomfort, embarrassment, and emotional distress at work. Can Engler recover under the Fair Debt Collection Practices Act? Why or why not? [*Engler v. Atlantic Resource Management, LLC*, 2012 WL 464728 (W.D.N.Y. 2012)] (See *Credit Protection.*)

- For a sample answer to Problem 24–3, go to Appendix C at the end of this text.

24–4. Deceptive Advertising. Innovative Marketing, Inc. (IMI), sold "scareware"—computer security software. IMI's internet ads redirected consumers to sites where they were told that a scan of their computers had detected dangerous files—viruses, spyware, and "illegal" pornography. In fact, no scans were conducted. Kristy Ross, an IMI cofounder and vice president, reviewed and edited the ads, and was aware of the many complaints that consumers had made about them. An individual can be held liable under the Federal Trade Commission Act's prohibition of deceptive practices if the person (1) participated directly in the deceptive practices or had the authority to control them and (2) had or should have had knowledge of them. Were IMI's ads deceptive? If so, can Ross be held liable? Explain. [*Federal Trade Commission v. Ross*, 743 F.3d 886 (4th Cir. 2014)] (See *Advertising, Marketing, and Sales.*)

24–5. Debt Collection. Zakia Mashiri owns a home in San Diego, California. She is a member of the Westwood Club Homeowners' Association (HOA), which charges each member an annual fee. When Mashiri failed to pay the fee, the law firm of Epsten Grinnell & Howell sent her a letter demanding payment. The letter read, "Failure to pay your . . . account in full within thirty-five days from the date of this letter will result in a lien . . . against your property." Mashiri asked for validation of the debt. Within two weeks of receiving it, she sent the HOA a check for the fee. Meanwhile, the law firm filed a lien against her property. Mashiri filed a lawsuit in a federal district court against the law firm, alleging a violation of the Fair Debt Collection Practices Act. On what provision of the act did Mashiri likely base her allegation? Will she succeed in her lawsuit against the law firm? Explain your answer. [*Mashiri v. Epsten Grinnell & Howell*, 845 F.3d 984 (9th Cir. 2017)] (See *Credit Protection.*)

24–6. False Advertising. Rainbow School, Inc., has run a child-care facility in Fayetteville, North Carolina, for more than twenty years. In addition to using the word "rainbow" in its name, the school uses rainbow imagery on its logo. Rainbow Early Education Holding, LLC, operates child-care facilities in several states. Early Education opened a branch in Fayetteville near the Rainbow School under the name "Rainbow Child Care Center," which also used rainbow imagery on its logo. The school filed a suit in a federal district court against Early Education, alleging a violation of the Lanham Act. The parties entered into a settlement agreement that required Early Education to stop using the word "rainbow" in connection with its Fayetteville facility. The court issued an injunction to enforce the agreement. Nevertheless, Early Education continued to use the word "rainbow" in domain names, links, and meta tags associated with its Fayetteville facility's website. Rainbow School imagery was used in a mailer inviting residents to the "nearest Rainbow Child Care Center." Did Early Education violate the Lanham Act? Explain. [*Rainbow School, Inc. v. Rainbow Early Education Holding, LLC*, 887 F.3d 610 (4th Cir. 2018)] (See *Advertising, Marketing, and Sales.*)

24–7. Deceptive Advertising. Manuka honey is a variety of honey made from the flowers of the Manuka bush, which is native to New Zealand and Australia. Trader Joe's Company markets its Manuka Honey store brand as "100 percent New Zealand Manuka Honey" or "New Zealand's Manuka Honey." Lynn Moore and others filed a lawsuit against Trader Joe's claiming that the company was engaged in false, misleading, and deceptive marketing. The plaintiffs claimed that the honey consisted of only 57.3 percent to 62.6 percent honey derived from Manuka flower nectar. Trader Joe's countered that its labeling was consistent with all applicable Food and Drug Administration (FDA) guidelines. Those guidelines permit labeling honey by its "chief floral source," since "busy bees cannot be prevented from foraging on different types of flowers, despite their keepers' best efforts." Trader Joe's thus argued that the plaintiffs' complaint should be dismissed. What should the court decide? [*Moore v. Trader Joe's Company*, 4 F.4th 874, 21 Cal. Daily Op. Serv. 7088 (9th Cir., 2021)] (See *Advertising, Marketing, and Sales.*)

24–8. A Question of Ethics—The IDDR Approach and Consumer Protection. In Richland, Washington, Robert Ingersoll planned his wedding to include about a hundred guests, a photographer, a caterer, a wedding cake, and flowers. Ingersoll had been a customer of Arlene's Flowers and Gifts for more than nine years and had spent several thousand dollars at the shop. When he approached Arlene's owner, Baronelle Stutzman, to buy flowers for his wedding, she refused because Ingersoll and his fiancé, Curt Freed, were a same-sex couple. Deeply offended, Ingersoll and Freed dropped their wedding plans and married in a modest ceremony. [*State of Washington v. Arlene's Flowers, Inc.*, 193 Wash.2d 469, 441 P.3d 1203 (2019)] (See *Advertising, Marketing, and Sales.*)

(a) Federal and state laws attempt to protect consumers from unfair trade practices, including discriminatory requirements, related to consumer transactions. Using the Review step of the IDDR approach, consider whether it would be ethically fair to hold Stutzman personally liable for a violation of these laws.

(b) Using the Discussion step of the IDDR approach, consider actions that Ingersoll and Freed as consumers might take in response to Arlene's (Stutzman's) discriminatory rejection of their offer to do business.

Time-Limited Group Assignment

24–9. Consumer Protections. Many states have enacted laws that go even further than federal law to protect consumers. These laws vary tremendously from state to state. (See *Advertising, Marketing, and Sales.*)

(a) The first group will decide whether having different laws is fair to sellers who may be prohibited from engaging in a practice in one state that is legal in another.

(b) The second group will consider how these different laws might affect a business.

(c) A third group will determine whether it is fair that residents of one state have more protection than residents of another.

Chapter 25

Environmental Law

Concern over the degradation of the environment has increased over time in response to the environmental effects of population growth, urbanization, and industrialization. Environmental protection is not without a price, however. For many businesses, the costs of complying with environmental regulations are high, and for some they may seem too high. A constant tension exists between the desire to increase profits and productivity and the desire to protect the environment. This same tension exists in foreign nations. China, for instance, has traditionally focused on the growth of its industries. Today, the air in many Chinese cities is so polluted that it causes many premature deaths each year.

After the Chinese government discovered that many of its companies were violating environmental rules, it started a campaign against environmental violations that has penalized more than thirty thousand companies. In addition, legislation was enacted to strengthen the nation's environmental protections and to give government inspectors broader authority. China's wave of enforcement affects not only Chinese corporations but also foreign corporations doing business there.

In the United States, environmental law consists primarily of statutes passed by federal, state, or local governments and regulations issued by administrative agencies. Before examining statutory and regulatory environmental laws, however, we look at the remedies against environmental pollution that are available under the common law.

25–1 Common Law Actions

Common law remedies against environmental pollution originated centuries ago in England. Those responsible for operations that created dirt, smoke, noxious odors, noise, or toxic substances were sometimes held liable under common law theories of nuisance or negligence. Today, individuals who have suffered a harm from pollution continue to rely on the common law to obtain damages and injunctions against business polluters.

25–1a Nuisance

Under the common law doctrine of **nuisance,** persons may be held liable if they use their property in a manner that unreasonably interferes with others' rights to use or enjoy their own property. Courts typically balance the harm caused by the pollution against the costs of stopping it.

Courts have often denied injunctive relief on the ground that the hardships that would be imposed on the polluter and on the community are greater than the hardships suffered by the plaintiff. ■ **Example 25.1** Hewitt's factory causes neighboring landowners to suffer from smoke, soot, and vibrations. But if the factory is the core of the local economy, a court may leave it in operation and award monetary damages to the injured parties. Damages can include compensation for any decline in the value of their property caused by Hewitt's operation. ■

To obtain relief from pollution under the nuisance doctrine, a property owner may have to identify a distinct harm separate from that affecting the general public. This harm is referred to as a "private" nuisance. Under the common law, individuals were denied standing (access to the courts) unless they suffered a harm distinct from that suffered by the public at large. Some states still require this. A public authority (such as a state's attorney general), however, can sue to stop a "public" nuisance.

Authority to Regulate Greenhouse Gases

Many scientists and others around the world maintain that greenhouse gases, such as carbon dioxide (CO_2), contribute to climate change. The Clean Air Act, as amended, however, does not specifically mention CO_2 emissions. Therefore, the EPA did not regulate CO_2 emissions from motor vehicles until after the Supreme Court ruled that it had the authority to do so.

■ **Case in Point 25.3** Environmental groups and several states, including Massachusetts, sued the EPA in an effort to force the agency to regulate CO_2 emissions from motor vehicles. The case eventually reached the United States Supreme Court. The EPA argued that the plaintiffs lacked standing because global climate change has widespread effects, so the individual plaintiffs could not show particularized harm. Furthermore, the agency claimed that it did not have authority under the Clean Air Act to address global climate change and regulate CO_2 emissions.

The Court, however, ruled that Massachusetts had standing because its coastline, including state-owned lands, faced an imminent threat from rising sea levels purportedly caused by climate change. The Court also held that the Clean Air Act's broad definition of "air pollutant" gives the EPA authority to regulate CO_2. The Clean Air Act requires the EPA to regulate any air pollutants that might "endanger public health or welfare." Accordingly, the Court ordered the EPA to determine whether CO_2 was a pollutant that endangered public health.[4] ■

The EPA later concluded that greenhouse gases, including CO_2 emissions, do constitute a public danger.

In fact, the EPA now also regulates greenhouse gas emissions from airplanes.

Controlling Climate Change In 2016, a federal district court in Oregon allowed an unprecedented lawsuit to go forward against the U.S. government for doing too little to control climate change. ■ **Case in Point 25.4** A group of young people (aged eight to nineteen) filed a suit against the federal government, as well as the fossil fuel industry. The plaintiffs argued that the government has known for years that excessive CO_2 emissions cause climate change and threaten catastrophic consequences. They claimed that the government had violated their constitutional rights by failing to address the causes of the CO_2 emissions.

The court found that the plaintiffs had alleged particular, concrete harms to young people and future generations sufficient to give them standing to pursue their claims in court. Of course, this ruling means only that the plaintiffs have met their threshold burden of establishing standing. The court simply denied the government's motion to dismiss.[5] ■

Can the EPA regulate power plants' emissions of greenhouse gases by gradually eliminating the use of coal for energy generation? The Supreme Court examined this issue when state and municipal governments, power utilities, renewable energy trade associations, and coal miners petitioned for review of the EPA's Affordable Clean Energy (ACE) rule, which had been promulgated under the Clean Air Act.

4. *Commonwealth of Massachusetts v. Environmental Protection Agency,* 549 U.S. 497, 127 S.Ct. 1438, 167 L.Ed.2d 248 (2007). You will read in Case 25.2 that the Supreme Court ruled in 2022 that such "major questions" had to be specifically addressed by Congress.

5. *Juliana v. United States,* 217 F.Supp.3d 1224 (D. OR 2016), and 339 F.Supp.3d 1062 (D. OR 2018).

Case 25.2

West Virginia, et al., v. Environmental Protection Agency

Supreme Court of the United States, __ U.S. __ , 142 S.Ct. 2587, 213 L.Ed.2nd 896 (2022).

Background and Facts In 2015, the Environmental Protection Agency (EPA) promulgated regulations called the Clean Power Plan (CPP). At that time, the Obama administration was attempting to combat climate change by reducing carbon dioxide pollution from new and existing power plants. In particular, the EPA wanted the nation's overall mix of electricity generation to change from 38 percent coal to 27 percent coal by 2030. As part of the plan, the CPP would set goals for each state to cut power plant emissions by 2030.

The CPP never went into effect because of litigation. Then, in 2019, the Trump administration rescinded the CPP and replaced it with the more lenient Affordable Clean Energy (ACE) rule. That rule applied to coal-fired steam plants on an individual basis—state-wide change was no longer required. Further litigation followed.

In the Language of the Court

ROBERTS, C. J.

The Clean Air Act authorizes the Environmental Protection Agency to regulate power plants by setting a "standard of performance" for their emission of certain pollutants into the air. That standard

Case 25.2 Continued

may be different for new and existing plants, but in each case, it must reflect the "best system of emission reduction" that the Agency has determined to be "adequately demonstrated" for the particular category. For existing plants, the States then implement that requirement by issuing rules restricting emissions from sources within their borders.

Since passage of the Act 50 years ago, EPA has exercised this authority by setting performance standards based on measures that would reduce pollution by causing plants to operate more cleanly. In 2015, however, EPA issued a new rule concluding that the "best system of emission reduction" [BSER] for existing coal-fired power plants included a requirement that such facilities reduce their own production of electricity, or subsidize increased generation by natural gas, wind, or solar sources.

The question before us is whether this broader conception of EPA's authority is within the power granted to it by the Clean Air Act.
* * * *

Although the States set the actual rules governing existing power plants, EPA itself still retains the primary regulatory role in Section 111(d). The Agency, not the States, decides the amount of pollution reduction that must ultimately be achieved. It does so by again determining, as when setting the new source rules, "the best system of emission reduction . . . that has been adequately demonstrated for [existing covered] facilities." * * *
* * * *

B

Things changed in October 2015, when EPA promulgated two rules addressing carbon dioxide pollution from power plants—one for new plants under Section 111(b), the other for existing plants under Section 111(d). Both were premised on the Agency's earlier finding that carbon dioxide is an "air pollutant" that "may reasonably be anticipated to endanger public health or welfare" by causing climate change. * * *

The first rule announced by EPA established federal carbon emissions limits for new power plants of two varieties: fossil-fuel-fired electric steam generating units (mostly coal fired) and natural-gas-fired stationary combustion turbines. Following the statutory process set out above, the Agency determined the BSER for the two categories of sources. For steam generating units, for instance, EPA determined that the BSER was a combination of high-efficiency production processes and carbon capture technology. EPA then set the emissions limit based on the amount of carbon dioxide that a plant would emit with these technologies in place.

The second rule was triggered by the first: Because EPA was now regulating carbon dioxide from *new* coal and gas plants, Section 111(d) required EPA to also address carbon emissions from *existing* coal and gas plants. It did so through what it called the Clean Power Plan rule.

In that rule, EPA established "final emission guidelines for states to follow in developing plans" to regulate existing power plants within their borders. To arrive at the guideline limits, EPA did the same thing it does when imposing federal regulations on new sources: It identified the BSER.

The BSER that the Agency selected for existing coal-fired power plants, however, was quite different from the BSER it had chosen for new sources. The BSER for existing plants included three types of measures, which the Agency called "building blocks." The first building block was "heat rate improvements" at coal-fired plants—essentially practices such plants could undertake to burn coal more efficiently. But such improvements, EPA stated, would "lead to only small emission reductions," because coal-fired power plants were already operating near optimum efficiency. On the Agency's view, "much larger emission reductions [were] needed from [coal-fired plants] to address climate change."

So, the Agency included two additional building blocks in its BSER, both of which involve what it called "generation shifting from higher-emitting to lower-emitting" producers of electricity. Building block two was a shift in electricity production from existing coal-fired power plants to natural-gas-fired plants. Because natural gas plants produce "typically less than half as much" carbon dioxide per unit of electricity created as coal-fired plants, the Agency explained, "this generation shift [would] reduce[] CO_2 emissions." Building block three worked the same way, except that the shift was from both coal- and gas-fired plants to "new low- or zero-carbon generating capacity," mainly wind and solar. "Most of the CO_2 controls" in the rule came from the application of building blocks two and three.

The Agency identified three ways in which a regulated plant operator could implement a shift in generation to cleaner sources. First, an operator could simply reduce the regulated plant's own production of electricity. Second, it could build a new natural gas plant, wind farm, or solar installation, or invest in someone else's existing facility and then increase generation there. Finally, operators could purchase emission allowances or credits as part of a cap-and-trade regime. Under such a scheme, sources that achieve a reduction in their emissions can sell a credit representing the value of that reduction to others, who are able to count it toward their own applicable emissions caps.

* * * *

The point, after all, was to compel the transfer of power generating capacity from existing sources to wind and solar. The White House stated that the Clean Power Plan would "drive a[n] . . . aggressive transformation in the domestic energy industry." * * *

C

These projections were never tested, because the Clean Power Plan never went into effect. The same day that EPA promulgated the rule, dozens of parties (including 27 States) petitioned for review in the D.C. Circuit. After that court declined to enter a stay of the rule, the challengers sought the same relief from this Court. We granted a stay, preventing the rule from taking effect. * * *

EPA eventually repealed the rule in 2019, concluding that the Clean Power Plan had been "in excess of its statutory authority" under Section 111(d). * * *

* * * *

EPA argued that under the major questions doctrine, a clear statement was necessary to conclude that Congress intended to delegate authority "of this breadth to regulate a fundamental sector of the economy." It found none. "Indeed," it concluded, given the text and structure of the statute, "Congress has directly spoken to this precise question and precluded" the use of measures such as generation shifting.

* * * *

* * * The agency [EPA] instead must point to "clear congressional authorization" for the power it claims.

* * * *

As for the major questions doctrine "label[]," it took hold because it refers to an identifiable body of law that has developed over a series of significant cases all addressing a particular and recurring problem: agencies asserting highly consequential power beyond what Congress could reasonably be understood to have granted. * * *

* * * *

D

Under our precedents, this is a major questions case. In arguing that Section 111(d) empowers it to substantially restructure the American energy market, EPA "claim[ed] to discover in a long-extant statute an unheralded power" representing a "transformative expansion in [its] regulatory authority." It located that newfound power in the vague language of an "ancillary provision[]" of the Act, one that was designed to function as a gap filler and had rarely been used in the preceding decades. And the Agency's discovery allowed it to adopt a regulatory program that Congress had conspicuously and repeatedly declined to enact itself. Given these circumstances, there is every reason to "hesitate before concluding that Congress" meant to confer on EPA the authority it claims under Section 111(d).

* * * *

We also find it "highly unlikely that Congress would leave" to "agency discretion" the decision of how much coal-based generation there should be over the coming decades. * * * ("We are confident that Congress could not have intended to delegate a decision of such economic and political significance to an agency in so cryptic a fashion.") The basic and consequential tradeoffs involved in such a choice are ones that Congress would likely have intended for itself. * * * Congress certainly has not conferred a like authority upon EPA anywhere else in the Clean Air Act. The last place one would expect to find it is in the previously little-used backwater of Section 111(d).

* * * *

Capping carbon dioxide emissions at a level that will force a nationwide transition away from the use of coal to generate electricity may be a sensible "solution to the crisis of the day." But it is not plausible that Congress gave EPA the authority to adopt on its own such a regulatory scheme in Section 111(d). A decision of such magnitude and consequence rests with Congress itself, or an agency acting pursuant to a clear delegation from that representative body. The judgment of the Court of Appeals for the District of Columbia Circuit is reversed, and the cases are remanded for further proceedings consistent with this opinion.

It is so ordered.

Case 25.2 Continues

Case 25.2 Continued

Decision and Remedy The Supreme Court of the United States reversed the judgment of the court of appeals for the District of Columbia circuit. The case was remanded for further proceedings consistent with this opinion. The Court agreed that transitioning away from the use of coal to generate electricity might be a sensible "solution to the crisis of the day." Nonetheless, "it is not plausible that Congress gave the EPA the authority to adopt on its own such a regulatory scheme. . . . A decision of such magnitude and consequence rests with Congress itself, or an agency acting pursuant to a clear delegation from that representative body."

Critical Thinking

- **What If the Facts Were Different** Assume that the EPA had only planned to apply its regulations to the five states that generated the most carbon dioxide while generating power. Would the Supreme Court ruling have been the same? Why or why not?

25–3b Stationary Sources

The Clean Air Act also authorizes the EPA to establish air-quality standards for stationary sources (such as manufacturing plants). But the act recognizes that the primary responsibility for implementing these standards rests with state and local governments. The EPA sets primary and secondary levels of ambient standards—that is, maximum permissible levels of certain pollutants—and the states formulate plans to achieve those standards. Different standards apply depending on whether the sources of pollution are located in clean areas or polluted areas and whether they are existing sources or major new sources.

Hazardous Air Pollutants The Clean Air Act focuses on controlling hazardous air pollutants (HAPs)—those likely to cause death or a serious irreversible or incapacitating condition, such as cancer or neurological or reproductive damage. The act requires the EPA to list all HAPs on a prioritized schedule. In all, nearly two hundred substances—including asbestos, benzene, beryllium, cadmium, mercury, and vinyl chloride—have been classified as hazardous. They are emitted from stationary sources by a variety of business activities, including smelting (melting ore to produce metal), dry cleaning, house painting, and commercial baking.

Maximum Achievable Control Technology Instead of establishing specific emissions standards for each hazardous air pollutant, the Clean Air Act requires major new sources[6] to use pollution-control equipment that represents the maximum achievable control technology, or MACT, to reduce emissions. The EPA issues guidelines as to what equipment meets this standard.[7]

25–3c Violations of the Clean Air Act

For violations of emission limits under the Clean Air Act, the EPA can assess civil penalties of up to $25,000 per day. Additional fines of up to $5,000 per day can be assessed for other violations, such as failure to maintain the required records. To penalize those who find it more cost-effective to violate the act than to comply with it, the EPA is authorized to impose a penalty equal to the violator's economic benefits from noncompliance. Persons who provide information about violators may be paid up to $10,000. Private citizens can also sue violators.

Those who knowingly violate the act, including corporate officers, may be subject to criminal penalties. For instance, knowingly making false statements or failing to report violations may be punishable by fines of up to $1 million and imprisonment for up to two years.

25–4 Water Pollution

Water pollution stems mostly from industrial, municipal, and agricultural sources. Pollutants entering streams, lakes, and oceans include organic wastes, heated water, sediments from soil runoff, nutrients (including fertilizers and human and animal wastes), and toxic chemicals and other hazardous substances.

Federal regulations governing water pollution can be traced back to the 1899 Rivers and Harbors Appropriations Act.[8] These regulations prohibited ships and manufacturers from discharging or depositing refuse in navigable waterways without a permit. (The term "navigable waters" is interpreted today as including intrastate lakes and streams used by interstate travelers and industries, as well as coastal and freshwater wetlands.) In 1948, Congress passed the Federal Water Pollution Control Act (FWPCA),[9] but its regulatory system and enforcement powers proved to be inadequate.

---

6. The term "major new sources" includes existing sources modified by a change in a method of operation that increases emissions.

7. The EPA has also issued rules to regulate hazardous air pollutants emitted by landfills. See 40 C.F.R. Part 60.

8. 33 U.S.C. Sections 401 *et seq.*

9. 33 U.S.C. Sections 1251–1387.

25–4a The Clean Water Act

In 1972, Congress passed amendments to the FWPCA, and the amended act became known as the Clean Water Act (CWA). The CWA established the following goals: (1) make waters safe for swimming, (2) protect fish and wildlife, and (3) eliminate the discharge of pollutants into the water. The CWA also set specific schedules, which were later extended by amendment and by the Water Quality Act.[10] Under these schedules, the EPA limits the discharge of various types of pollutants based on the technology available for controlling them.

Permit System for Point-Source Emissions

The CWA established a permit system for regulating discharges from "point sources" of pollution, which include industrial, municipal, and agricultural facilities.[11] Under this system, called the National Pollutant Discharge Elimination System (NPDES), any point source emitting pollutants into water must have a permit. Pollution not from point sources, such as runoff from small farms, is not subject to much regulation.

NPDES permits can be issued by the EPA and authorized state agencies and Indian tribes, but only if the discharge will not violate water-quality standards. Permits must be reissued every five years. Although initially the NPDES system focused mainly on industrial wastewater, it was later expanded to cover stormwater discharges.

In practice, the NPDES system under the CWA includes the following elements:

1. National effluent (pollution) standards set by the EPA for each industry.
2. Water-quality standards set by the states under EPA supervision.

---

10. This act amended 33 U.S.C. Section 1251.
11. 33 U.S.C. Section 1342.

3. A discharge permit program that sets water-quality standards to limit pollution.
4. Special provisions for toxic chemicals and for oil spills.
5. Construction grants and loans from the federal government for publicly owned treatment works, primarily sewage treatment plants.

Standards for Equipment

Regulations generally specify that the best available control technology, or BACT, be installed. The EPA issues guidelines as to what equipment meets this standard. Essentially, the guidelines require the most effective pollution-control equipment available.

New sources must install BACT equipment before beginning operations. Existing sources are subject to timetables for the installation of BACT equipment and must immediately install equipment that utilizes the best practical control technology, or BPCT. The EPA also issues guidelines as to what equipment meets this standard.

Exhibit 25–3 reviews the pollution-control equipment standards required under the Clean Air Act and the Clean Water Act.

Wetlands

The CWA prohibits the filling or dredging of **wetlands** unless a permit is obtained from the Army Corps of Engineers. The EPA defines wetlands as "those areas that are inundated or saturated by surface or ground water at a frequency and duration sufficient to support . . . vegetation typically adapted for life in saturated soil conditions." Wetlands are thought to be vital to the ecosystem because they filter streams and rivers and provide habitat for wildlife.

■ **Case in Point 25.5** To build a home in Idaho, Michael and Chantell Sackett filled part of their residential lot with dirt and rock. A few months later, they received a compliance order from the EPA that required them to restore their property immediately or face fines of

---

Exhibit 25–3 Pollution-Control Equipment Standards Under the Clean Air Act and the Clean Water Act

The Clean Air Act

- Major sources of pollution must use pollution-control equipment that represents the *maximum achievable control technology*, or MACT, to reduce emissions.

The Clean Water Act

- New sources of pollution must install the *best available control technology*, or BACT, before beginning operations.
- Existing sources must immediately install equipment that utilizes the *best practical control technology*, or BPCT, and meet a timetable for installing BACT equipment.

$75,000 a day. The EPA order claimed that, because their property was near a major lake, the Sacketts had polluted wetlands in violation of the Clean Water Act.

The Sacketts requested a hearing with the EPA, but it was denied. They then sued the EPA in federal district court, asserting, among other things, that the compliance order was "arbitrary and capricious" under the Administrative Procedure Act. The district court held that it could not review the EPA's compliance order because it was not a final agency action. An appellate court affirmed, but the United States Supreme Court reversed. The Court held that the Sacketts could challenge the EPA's compliance order in federal court. The government could not force them to comply with the EPA order without providing an opportunity for judicial review.[12] ■

Violations of the Clean Water Act Because point-source water pollution control is based on a permit system, the permits are the key to enforcement. States have primary responsibility for enforcing the permit system, subject to EPA monitoring.

Discharging emissions into navigable waters without a permit, or in violation of pollution limits under a permit, violates the CWA. Violators are subject to a variety of civil and criminal penalties. Depending on the violation, civil penalties range from $10,000 to $25,000 per day, but not more than $25,000 per violation. Lying about a violation is more serious than admitting the truth about improper discharges.

Criminal penalties apply only if a violation was intentional. Criminal penalties range from a fine of $2,500 per day and imprisonment for up to one year to a fine of $1 million and fifteen years' imprisonment. Injunctive relief and damages can also be imposed. The polluting party can be required to clean up the pollution or pay for the cost of doing so.

25–4b Drinking Water

The Safe Drinking Water Act[13] requires the EPA to set maximum levels for pollutants in public water systems. The operators of public water systems must come as close as possible to meeting the EPA's standards by using the best available technology that is economically and technologically feasible.

Under the act, each supplier of drinking water is required to send an annual statement describing the source of its water to every household it supplies. The statement must also disclose the level of any contaminants in the water and any possible health concerns associated with the contaminants.

■ **Example 25.6** The city of Flint, Michigan, changed its source of drinking water from the Detroit water system to the Flint River. Detroit's water was treated to prevent lead from leaching into the water from aging lead pipes. The Flint River water was not treated, allowing lead to leach into the water from the aging pipes. Flint's drinking water became contaminated with lead—a serious public health hazard. By the time Flint sent out the required EPA notices, thousands of children had been exposed to drinking water with high lead levels. Numerous civil and criminal actions were filed as a result of the incident. In addition, fixing the water system cost the city millions of dollars. ■

25–4c Ocean Dumping

The Marine Protection, Research, and Sanctuaries Act[14] (popularly known as the Ocean Dumping Act) regulates the transportation and dumping of pollutants into ocean waters. It prohibits the ocean dumping of any radiological, chemical, and biological warfare agents and high-level radioactive waste.

The act also established a permit program for transporting and dumping other materials, and designated certain areas as marine sanctuaries. Each violation of any provision or permit requirement in the Ocean Dumping Act may result in a civil penalty of up to $50,000. A knowing violation is a criminal offense that may result in a $50,000 fine, imprisonment for not more than a year, or both. A court may also grant an injunction to prevent an imminent or continuing violation.

25–4d Oil Pollution

When more than 10 million gallons of oil leaked into Alaska's Prince William Sound from the *Exxon Valdez* supertanker in 1989, Congress responded by passing the Oil Pollution Act.[15] (At that time, the *Exxon Valdez* disaster was the worst oil spill in U.S. history, but the British Petroleum oil spill in the Gulf of Mexico in 2010 surpassed it.)

12. *Sackett v. Environmental Protection Agency,* 566 U.S. 120, 132 S.Ct. 1367, 182 L.Ed.2d 367 (2012). See also *Center for Biological Diversity v. Haaland,* 58 F.4th 412 (9th Cir. 2023).
13. 42 U.S.C. Sections 300f to 300j-27.
14. 16 U.S.C. Sections 1401 *et seq.*
15. 33 U.S.C. Sections 2701 *et seq.*

Under the Oil Pollution Act, any oil facility, oil shipper, vessel owner, or vessel operator that discharges oil into navigable waters or onto an adjoining shore may be liable for clean-up costs and damages. The polluter can also be ordered to pay for damage to natural resources, private property, and the local economy, including the increased cost of providing public services.

25–5 Toxic Chemicals and Hazardous Waste

Control of toxic chemicals and hazardous waste has become increasingly important. If not properly disposed of, these substances may seriously endanger human health and the environment—for instance, by contaminating public drinking water.

25–5a Pesticides and Herbicides

The Federal Insecticide, Fungicide, and Rodenticide Act (FIFRA)[16] regulates the use of pesticides and herbicides. These substances must be (1) registered before they can be sold, (2) certified and used only for approved applications, and (3) used in limited quantities when applied to food crops.

EPA Actions The EPA can cancel or suspend registration of substances that it has identified as harmful and can inspect the factories where the chemicals are made. A substance is deemed harmful if human exposure to the substance, including exposure through eating food, results in a risk of one in a million (or higher) of developing cancer.[17]

Violations and Penalties It is a violation of FIFRA to sell a pesticide or herbicide that is either unregistered or has had its registration canceled or suspended. It is also a violation to sell a pesticide or herbicide with a false or misleading label. For instance, it is an offense to sell a substance that has a chemical strength that is different from the concentration described on the label. It is also a violation to destroy or deface any labeling required under the act.

Penalties for commercial dealers include imprisonment for up to one year and a fine of up to $25,000 (producers can be fined up to $50,000). Farmers and other private users of pesticides or herbicides who violate the act are subject to a $1,000 fine and incarceration for up to thirty days.

Note that a state can also regulate the sale and use of federally registered pesticides. ■ **Case in Point 25.7** The EPA conditionally registered Strongarm, a weed-killing pesticide made by Dow Agrosciences, LLC. When Texas peanut farmers applied Strongarm to their crops, it damaged the crops and failed to control the growth of weeds. The farmers sued Dow for violations of Texas law, but the lower courts ruled that FIFRA preempted their claims. The farmers appealed to the United States Supreme Court. The Court held that under a specific provision of FIFRA, a state can regulate the sale and use of federally registered pesticides so long as the regulation does not permit anything that FIFRA prohibits.[18] ■

25–5b Toxic Substances

The Toxic Substances Control Act[19] regulates chemicals and chemical compounds that are known to be toxic, such as asbestos and polychlorinated biphenyls. The act also controls the introduction of new chemical compounds by requiring investigation of any possible harmful effects from these substances.

Under the act, the EPA can require that manufacturers, processors, and other entities planning to use chemicals first determine their effects on human health and the environment. The EPA can regulate substances that could pose an imminent hazard or an unreasonable risk of injury to health or the environment. The EPA can also require special labeling, limit the use of a substance, set production quotas, or prohibit the use of a substance altogether.

25–5c The Resource Conservation and Recovery Act

The Resource Conservation and Recovery Act (RCRA)[20] was Congress's response to growing concerns about the effects of hazardous waste materials on the environment. The RCRA required the EPA to determine which forms of solid waste should be considered hazardous and to establish regulations to monitor and control hazardous waste disposal.

---

16. 7 U.S.C. Sections 136–136y.

17. 21 U.S.C. Section 346a.

18. *Bates v. Dow Agrosciences, LLC*, 544 U.S. 431, 125 S.Ct. 1788, 161 L.Ed.2d 687 (2005).

19. 15 U.S.C. Sections 2601–2692.

20. 42 U.S.C. Sections 6901 *et seq.*

Among other things, the act requires all producers of hazardous waste materials to properly label and package any hazardous waste to be transported. Amendments to the RCRA decrease the use of land containment in the disposal of hazardous waste and require smaller generators of hazardous waste to comply with the act.

Under the RCRA, a company may be assessed a civil penalty of up to $25,000 for each violation.[21] The penalty is based on the seriousness of the violation, the probability of harm, and the extent to which the violation deviates from RCRA requirements. Criminal penalties include fines of up to $50,000 for each day of violation, imprisonment for up to two years (in most instances), or both. Criminal fines and the time of imprisonment can be doubled for certain repeat offenders.

25–5d Superfund

The Comprehensive Environmental Response, Compensation, and Liability Act (CERCLA),[22] commonly known as Superfund, regulates the clean-up of disposal sites in which hazardous waste is leaking into the environment. CERCLA, as amended, has four primary elements.

1. It established an information-gathering and analysis system that enables the government to identify chemical dump sites and determine the appropriate action.
2. It authorized the EPA to respond to emergencies and to arrange for the clean-up of a leaking site directly if the persons responsible fail to clean up the site within a reasonable time.
3. It created a Hazardous Substance Response Trust Fund (also called Superfund) to pay for the clean-up of hazardous sites using funds obtained through taxes on certain businesses.
4. It allowed the government to recover the cost of clean-up from persons who were (even remotely) responsible for hazardous substance releases.

Potentially Responsible Parties Superfund provides that when a release or a potential release of hazardous chemicals from a site occurs, the following persons may be held responsible for cleaning up the site:

1. The person who generated the wastes disposed of at the site.

2. The person who transported the wastes to the site.
3. The person who owned or operated the site at the time of the disposal.
4. The current owner or operator.

A person falling within one of these categories is referred to as a **potentially responsible party (PRP).** If the PRPs do not clean up the site, the EPA can clean up the site and recover the clean-up costs from the PRPs.

Strict Liability of PRPs. Superfund imposes strict liability on PRPs, and that liability cannot be avoided through transfer of ownership. Thus, selling a site where hazardous wastes were disposed of does not relieve the seller of liability, and the buyer also becomes liable for the clean-up.

Liability also extends to businesses that merge with or buy corporations that have violated CERCLA. A parent corporation is not automatically liable for the violations of its subsidiary. It can be held liable, however, if the subsidiary was merely a shell company or if the parent corporation participated in or controlled the facility.[23]

Joint and Several Liability of PRPs. Liability under Superfund is usually joint and several. In other words, a PRP who generated only a fraction of the hazardous waste disposed of at a site may nevertheless be liable for all of the clean-up costs. CERCLA authorizes a party who has incurred clean-up costs to bring a "contribution action" against any other person who is liable or potentially liable for a percentage of the costs.

Minimizing Liability One way for a business to minimize its potential liability under Superfund is to conduct environmental compliance audits of its own operations regularly. That is, the business can investigate its own operations and property to determine whether any environmental hazards exist.

The EPA encourages companies to conduct self-audits and promptly detect, disclose, and correct wrongdoing. Companies that do so are subject to lighter penalties for violations of environmental laws. (Fines may be reduced as much as 75 percent.)

In addition, under EPA guidelines, the EPA will waive all fines if a small company corrects environmental

---

21. 42 U.S.C. Section 6928(a).
22. 42 U.S.C. Sections 9601–9675.

23. The landmark case establishing the liability of a parent corporation under CERCLA is *United States v. Bestfoods,* 524 U.S. 51, 118 S.Ct. 1876, 141 L.Ed.2d 43 (1998). See also *U.S. v. Union Oil Company of California,* 2022 WL 16731922 (9th Cir. 2022).

violations within 180 days after being notified of the violations (or 360 days if pollution-prevention techniques are involved). The policy does not apply to criminal violations of environmental laws or to violations that pose a significant threat to public health, safety, or the environment.

Defenses There are a few defenses to liability under CERCLA. The most important is the innocent landowner defense,[24] which may protect a landowner who acquired the property after it was used for hazardous waste disposal.

To succeed in this defense, landowners must show, among other things, that at the time the property was acquired, they had no reason to know that it had been used for hazardous waste disposal. They must also show that at the time of the purchase, they undertook "all appropriate inquiries." That is, they investigated the previous ownership and uses of the property to determine whether there was reason for concern about hazardous substances. In effect, then, this defense protects only property owners who took precautions and investigated the possibility of environmental hazards before buying the property.

25–6 Sustainability Issues

A growing body of regulation in both the United States and Europe has resulted from concerns about sustainability. There is no official definition of **sustainability,** but the term generally refers to actions aimed at maintaining the environment so that it will meet the needs of future generations. When world leaders meet, particularly at the World Economic Forum in Davos, Switzerland, they consistently identify the environment as one of the greatest problems facing business (and humanity).

The United Nations provides world forums for discussion of sustainability issues and creation of so-called *legal conventions* that limit each nation's perceived environmental degradation. The current attempts to limit global warming to 2 degrees Celsius (about 3.6 degrees Fahrenheit) by the end of this century fall within the category of maintaining a sustainable environment worldwide.

Energy Creation A key sustainability issue concerns how energy is generated. As mentioned, many believe that energy generation that creates greenhouse gases, such as carbon dioxide, adds to the possibility of global warming and hence to unsustainable economic activity. To address this issue, some governments have announced that they will move their nations toward "net zero"—a situation in which the amount of greenhouse gases produced is equal to the amount removed. To the extent that governments create regulations in an attempt to do so, businesses will be impacted, sometimes dramatically. In the United States, for example, if the Biden-Harris administration's plan for 100 percent carbon neutrality by 2050 was put into place, it would mean a dramatic change in manufacturing, transportation, and lifestyles.

Waste Management Almost all manufacturing generates waste. Many consumer activities generate waste as well. One of the goals of environmental sustainability is to encourage less waste creation during production and consumption. This aspect of sustainability regulation is probably the easiest with which to deal. Nonetheless, new regulations are bound to be created as the world attempts to reduce waste.

Destruction of Species and Ecosystems An obvious outcome of nonsustainable environmental actions is the loss of species. Much publicity has concerned the destruction of rain forests, for example. Some scientists have predicted that if we do nothing, up to 20 percent of the earth's animal and plant species may disappear in the next several decades.

Environmental, Social, and Corporate Governance (ESG) Most business issues involving sustainability have become part of a relatively new framework called **environment, social, and corporate governance (ESG).** ESG investing examines how a company deals with the following matters:

- Environmental—how a company safeguards the environment, including issues such as sustainability and climate change.
- Social—how companies manage their relationships with customers, suppliers, communities, and employees.
- Governance—how a company exercises leadership; more specifically, executive pay, audits, and shareholder rights.

Many brokerage firms and mutual funds offer investing that specifically relies on ESG principles.

24. 42 U.S.C. Section 9601(35)(B).

Practice and Review: Environmental Protection

Residents of Lake Caliopa, Minnesota, began noticing an unusually high number of lung ailments among the local population. Several concerned citizens pooled their resources and commissioned a study to compare the frequency of these health conditions in Lake Caliopa with national averages. The study concluded that residents of Lake Caliopa experienced four to seven times the rate of frequency of asthma, bronchitis, and emphysema as the population nationwide.

During the study period, citizens began expressing concerns about the large volume of smog emitted by the Cotton Design apparel manufacturing plant on the outskirts of town. The plant had a production facility two miles east of town beside the Tawakoni River and employed seventy full-time workers. Just downstream on the Tawakoni River, the city of Lake Caliopa operated a public water works facility, which supplied all city residents with water.

The Minnesota Pollution Control Agency required Cotton Design to install new equipment to control air and water pollution. Later, citizens sued Cotton Design for various respiratory ailments allegedly caused or compounded by smog from Cotton Design's factory. Using the information presented in the chapter, answer the following questions.

1. Under the common law, what would each plaintiff be required to identify in order to be given relief by the court?
2. What standard for limiting emissions into the air does Cotton Design's pollution-control equipment have to meet?
3. If Cotton Design's emissions violate the Clean Air Act, how much can the EPA assess in fines per day?
4. What information must the city send to every household that it supplies with water?

Debate This . . .   The courts should reject all cases in which the wetlands in question do not consist of bodies of water that exist during the entire year.

Terms and Concepts

environmental impact statement (EIS) 528
environmental, social, and corporate governance (ESG) 537

nuisance 524
potentially responsible party (PRP) 536
sustainability 537

toxic torts 525
wetlands 533

Issue Spotters

1. Resource Refining Company's plant emits smoke and fumes. Resource's operation includes a short railway system, and trucks enter and exit the grounds continuously. Constant vibrations from the trains and trucks rattle nearby residential neighborhoods. The residents sue Resource. Are there any reasons why the court might refuse to issue an injunction against Resource's operation? Explain. (See *Common Law Actions*.)

2. ChemCorp generates hazardous wastes from its operations. Disposal Trucking Company transports those wastes to Eliminators, Inc., which owns a site for hazardous waste disposal. Eliminators sells the property on which the disposal site is located to Fluid Properties, Inc. If the Environmental Protection Agency cleans up the site, from whom can it recover the cost? (See *Toxic Chemicals and Hazardous Waste*.)

• **Check your answers to the Issue Spotters against the answers provided in Appendix B at the end of this text.**

Business Scenarios and Case Problems

25–1. The Clean Water Act. Fruitade, Inc., is a processor of a soft drink called Freshen Up. Fruitade uses returnable bottles, which it cleans with a special acid to allow for further beverage processing. The acid is diluted with water and then allowed to pass into a navigable stream. Fruitade crushes its broken bottles and throws the crushed glass into the stream. Discuss fully any environmental laws that Fruitade has violated. (See *Water Pollution*.)

25–2. Environmental Protection. Moonbay is a home-building corporation that primarily develops retirement communities. Farmtex owns a number of feedlots in Sunny Valley. Moonbay purchases 20,000 acres of farmland in the same area and begins building and selling homes on this acreage. In the meantime, Farmtex continues to expand its feedlot business, and eventually only 500 feet separate the two operations. Because of the odor and flies from the feedlots, Moonbay finds it difficult to sell the homes in its development. Moonbay wants to enjoin (prevent) Farmtex from operating its feedlot in the vicinity of the retirement home development. Under what common law theory would Moonbay file this action? Has Farmtex violated any federal environmental laws? Discuss. (See *Common Law Actions*.)

25–3. Spotlight on the Grand Canyon—Environmental Impact Statement. The U.S. National Park Service (NPS) manages the Grand Canyon National Park in Arizona under a management plan that is subject to periodic review. After nine years of background work and the completion of a comprehensive environmental impact statement, the NPS issued a new management plan for the park. The plan allowed for the continued use of rafts on the Colorado River, which runs through the Grand Canyon. The number of rafts was limited, however. Several environmental groups criticized the plan because they felt that it still allowed too many rafts on the river. The groups asked a federal appellate court to overturn the plan, claiming that it violated the wilderness status of the national park. When can a federal court overturn a determination by an agency such as the NPS? Explain. [*River Runners for Wilderness v. Martin*, 593 F.3d 1064 (9th Cir. 2010)] (See *Federal, State, and Local Regulations*.)

25–4. Business Case Problem With Sample Answer—Environmental Impact Statements. The U.S. Forest Service (USFS) proposed a travel management plan (TMP) for the Beartooth Ranger District in the Pryor and Absaroka Mountains in the Custer National Forest of southern Montana. The TMP would convert unauthorized user-created routes within the wilderness to routes authorized for motor vehicle use. It would also permit off-road "dispersed vehicle camping" within 300 feet of the routes, with some seasonal restrictions. The TMP would ban cross-country motorized travel outside the designated routes. Is an environmental impact statement required before the USFS implements the TMP? If so, what aspects of the environment should the USFS consider in preparing it? Discuss. [*Pryors Coalition v.*

Weldon, 551 Fed.Appx. 426 (9th Cir. 2014)] (See *Federal, State, and Local Regulations*.)

- For a sample answer to Problem 25–4, go to Appendix C at the end of this text.

25–5. The Clean Water Act. ICG Hazard, LLC, operates the Thunder Ridge surface coal mine in Leslie County, Kentucky, under a National Pollutant Discharge Elimination System permit issued by the Kentucky Division of Water (KDOW). As part of the operation, ICG discharges selenium into the surrounding water. Selenium is a naturally occurring element that endangers aquatic life once it reaches a certain concentration. KDOW knew when it issued the permit that mines in the area could produce selenium but did not specify discharge limits for the element in ICG's permit. Instead, the agency imposed a one-time monitoring requirement, which ICG met. Does ICG's discharge of selenium violate the Clean Water Act? Explain. [*Sierra Club v. ICG Hazard, LLC*, 781 F.3d 281 (6th Cir. 2015)] (See *Water Pollution*.)

25–6. State Regulations. Olivia Chernaik and other Oregon residents filed a suit in an Oregon state court against Governor Kate Brown and other state officials. According to the plaintiffs, the state holds "vital natural resources," including water, air, land, and wildlife, in trust for the benefit of its citizens. "Oregon has the ability to curtail greenhouse gas emissions, increase carbon sequestration, and take the steps necessary to protect the [state's resources] from the adverse effects of climate change." The plaintiffs claimed, however, that the state had failed to uphold its "fiduciary obligation to protect and preserve those resources." The plaintiffs asked the court to order the defendants to "develop and implement a carbon reduction plan that will protect [resources] by the best available science." The plaintiffs rooted their claim in the common law public-trust doctrine. Under this doctrine, a state holds certain resources in trust for the public's use and cannot convey or otherwise dispose of them in a manner that would interfere with this right. Is the court likely to grant the plaintiffs' request? Explain. [*Chernaik v. Brown*, 295 Or.App. 584, 436 P.3d 26 (2019)] (See *Federal, State, and Local Regulations*.)

25–7. Wetlands and Environmental Impact Statements. Preparation of an environmental impact statement is required under Minnesota law when a proposed project might eliminate a public waters wetland. Huber Engineered Woods, LLC, wanted to construct a manufacturing facility west of the city of Cohasset. The facility would occupy almost 160 acres of agricultural and undeveloped lands. The construction would involve filling or evacuating twenty-six of thirty-one wetlands. Nonetheless, the city decided that it was not necessary to prepare a detailed environmental impact statement (EIS). A realtor challenged the city's decision not to prepare an EIS. Should the Court of Appeals of Minnesota rule in favor of the city or the realtor? Explain. [*In re City of Cohasset's Decision on Need for an Environmental Impact Statement for*

Proposed Frontier Project, __ N.W.2d __, 2023 WL 1770149 (Ct. App. MN 2023)] (See *Water Pollution.*)

25–8. A Question of Ethics—The IDDR Approach and Superfund. Sevenson Environmental Services was hired to clean up a Superfund site in Manville, New Jersey, where the soil was contaminated with creosote. (Creosote is a flammable, oily mixture of chemical compounds often used for preserving wood or as a pesticide.) The Environmental Protection Agency (EPA) funded the effort. Sevenson's project manager was Gordon McDonald, whose responsibilities included hiring subcontractors through a bidding process. McDonald made the contamination look as severe as possible to pressure rival bidders to bid higher. He showed the bids to one of the competitors, John Bennett, and permitted him to submit a new "lowest" bid in exchange for a kickback of $13.50 per ton

of cleaned soil. Bennett won the contract, which (because of McDonald's manipulation of the bidding process) covered the amount of the kickback. The scheme was eventually discovered, and Bennett was charged with criminal fraud. [*United States v. Bennett,* 688 Fed.Appx. 169 (3d Cir. 2017)] (See *Toxic Chemicals and Hazardous Waste.*)

(a) What was Bennett's ethical dilemma in this case? Using the IDDR approach, discuss and evaluate the actions he chose to resolve it.

(b) Suppose that Bennett had refused the kickback scheme, had won the contract with an honest low bid, and had been paid for the work, but had not actually performed his part of the work. Would this situation have been ethically distinct from the true facts? Explain.

Time-Limited Group Activity

25–9. Clean-Up Costs. It has been estimated that for every dollar spent cleaning up hazardous waste sites, administrative agencies spend seven dollars in overhead. (See *Toxic Chemicals and Hazardous Waste.*)

(a) The first group will list and explain possible ways to trim these administrative costs.

(b) The second group will evaluate whether the laws pertaining to hazardous waste clean-up can or should be changed to reduce the costs to government.

Chapter 26

Real Property and Land-Use Control

From the earliest times, property has provided a means for survival. Primitive peoples lived off the fruits of the land, eating the vegetation and wildlife. Later, as the wildlife was domesticated and the vegetation cultivated, property provided pastures and farmland. Throughout history, property has continued to be an indicator of family wealth and social position. Today, in much of the world, individuals' right to property has become one of their most important rights.

In this chapter, we look at the nature of real property and the ways in which it can be owned. We examine the legal requirements involved in the transfer of real property. We even consider, in this chapter's Spotlight Case, whether the buyer of a "haunted house" can rescind the sale.

Realize that real property rights are never absolute. There is a higher right—that of the government to take, for compensation, private land for public use. Later in the chapter, we discuss this right, as well as other restrictions on the ownership or use of property, including zoning laws.

26–1 The Nature of Real Property

Real property (or realty) consists of land and everything permanently attached to it, including structures and other fixtures. Real property encompasses airspace and subsurface rights, as well as rights to plants and vegetation. In essence, real property is immovable.

26–1a Land and Structures

Land includes the soil on the surface of the earth and the natural products or artificial structures that are attached to it. Land further includes all the waters contained on or under its surface and much, but not necessarily all, of the airspace above it. The exterior boundaries of land extend down to the center of the earth and up to the farthest reaches of the atmosphere (subject to certain qualifications).

26–1b Airspace and Subsurface Rights

The owner of real property has rights to both the airspace above the land and the soil and minerals underneath it. Any limitations, or encumbrances, on either airspace rights or subsurface rights normally must be indicated on the document that transfers title at the time of purchase.

The ways in which ownership rights in real property can be limited will be examined later in this chapter.

Airspace Rights Disputes concerning airspace rights may involve the right of commercial and private planes to fly over property and the right of individuals and governments to seed clouds and produce artificial rain. Flights over private land normally do not violate property rights unless the flights are so low and so frequent that they directly interfere with the owner's enjoyment and use of the land. Leaning walls or projecting eave spouts or roofs may also violate the airspace rights of an adjoining property owner.

Subsurface Rights In many states, ownership of land can be separated from ownership of its subsurface. In other words, the owner of the surface may sell subsurface rights to another person. When ownership is separated into surface and subsurface rights, each owner can pass title to that owner's property without the consent of the other owner.

Subsurface rights can be extremely valuable, as these rights include the ownership of minerals, oil, or natural gas. But these rights would be of little value if the owner could not use the surface to exercise them. Hence, a subsurface owner has a right (called a "profit," discussed later in this chapter) to go onto the surface of the land to, for instance, find and remove minerals.

Of course, conflicts can arise between the surface owner's use of the property and the subsurface owner's need to extract minerals, oil, or natural gas. In that situation, one party's interest may become subservient (secondary) to the other party's interest either by statute or by case law.

If the owners of the subsurface rights excavate, they are absolutely (strictly) liable if their excavation causes the surface to collapse. Many states have statutes that also make the excavators liable for any damage to structures on the land. Typically, these statutes set out precise requirements for excavations of various depths.

26–1c Plant Life and Vegetation

Plant life, both natural and cultivated, is also considered to be real property. In many instances, natural vegetation, such as trees, adds greatly to the value of realty. When a parcel of land is sold and the land has growing crops on it, the sale includes the crops, unless otherwise specified in the sales contract. When crops are sold by themselves, however, they are considered to be personal property, or goods. Consequently, the sale of crops is a sale of goods and is governed by the Uniform Commercial Code (UCC) rather than by real property law.

26–1d Fixtures

Certain personal property can become so closely associated with the real property to which it is attached that the law views it as real property. Such property is known as a **fixture**—an item affixed to realty, meaning that it is attached to the real property in a permanent way. The item may be embedded in the land or permanently attached to the property or to another fixture on the property by means of cement, plaster, bolts, nails, or screws. An item, such as a statue, may even sit on the land without being attached, as long as the owner intends it to be a fixture.

Fixtures are included in the sale of land unless the sales contract specifies otherwise. The issue of whether an item is a fixture (and thus real estate) or not a fixture (and thus personal property) often arises with respect to land sales, real property taxation, insurance coverage, and divorces. How the issue is resolved can have important consequences for the parties involved.

Typical Fixtures Some items can only be attached to property permanently—such as tile floors, cabinets, and carpeting. Because such items are attached permanently, it is assumed that the owner intended them to be fixtures. Also, when an item of property is custom-made for

installation on real property, as storm windows are, the item usually is classified as a fixture.

In addition, an item that is firmly attached to the land and integral to its use may be deemed a fixture. For instance, a mobile home or a complex irrigation system bolted to a cement slab on a farm can be a fixture. The courts assume that owners, in making such installations, intend the objects to become part of their real property.

The Role of Intent Generally, when the courts need to determine whether a certain item is a fixture, they examine the intention of the party who placed the object on the real property. When the intent of that party is in dispute, the courts usually will deem that the item is a fixture if either or both of the following are true:

- The property attached cannot be removed without causing substantial damage to the remaining realty.
- The property attached is so adapted to the rest of the realty as to have become a part of it.

Trade Fixtures Are Personal Property Trade fixtures are an exception to the rule that fixtures are a part of the real property to which they are attached. A **trade fixture** is personal property that is installed for a commercial purpose by a tenant (one who rents real property from the owner, or landlord).

Trade fixtures remain the property of the tenant unless removal would irreparably damage the building or realty. A walk-in cooler, for instance, purchased and installed by a tenant who uses the premises for a restaurant, is a trade fixture. The tenant can remove the cooler from the premises when the lease terminates but ordinarily must repair any damage that the removal causes or compensate the landlord for the damage.

■ **Case in Point 26.1** EBC Properties, LLC, owned a strip mall in Maryland. It leased commercial retail space to Urge Food Corporation. The lease permitted Urge to freely make improvements and alterations to the premises. Such improvements, including trade fixtures not permanently affixed to the building, would remain Urge's property unless "abandoned" in the event of default or the termination of the lease. Because the property had served as a used clothing store when Urge took possession, Urge had to undertake extensive efforts to ready the location for its intended use as a grocery store. It installed heating and cooling systems, interior freezer cases, and four walk-in coolers connected to the outside of the building. When Urge vacated the premises at the end of its lease agreement, it removed these items. EBC brought suit for certain unpaid lease payments as well as for removal of the fixtures.

At issue was the classification of the fixtures that Urge removed. Were they simply fixtures, in which case Urge could not remove them, or were they trade fixtures that could be removed by Urge? The trial court ruled that they were trade fixtures. The appellate court of Maryland affirmed. "Sufficient evidence was presented to demonstrate that the various pieces of equipment Urge installed were both associated with running a grocery business and were not permanently affixed to the realty. We, therefore, hold that the circuit court was factually and legally correct in finding that the property installed by Urge constituted "trade fixtures because of their moveable status, coupled with Urge's clear intention to make such investitures as a means to benefit the use of the Premises to carry out its grocery business trade."[1] ■

26–2 Ownership and Other Interests in Real Property

Ownership of property is an abstract concept that cannot exist independently of the legal system. No one can actually possess, or hold, a piece of land, the air above it, the earth below it, and all the water contained on it. One can only possess rights in real property.

Numerous rights are involved in real property ownership, which is why property ownership is often viewed as a bundle of rights. One who possesses the entire bundle of rights is said to hold the property in *fee simple*, which is the most complete form of ownership. When only some of the rights in the bundle are transferred to another person, the effect is to limit the ownership rights of both the transferor of the rights and the recipient.

Ownership interests in real property have traditionally been referred to as *estates in land*, which include *fee simple estates, life estates*, and *leasehold estates*. We examine these types of estates in this section, and we also discuss several forms of *concurrent ownership of property*. Finally, we describe certain interests in real property that is owned by others.

26–2a Ownership in Fee Simple

In a **fee simple absolute,** the owner has the greatest aggregation of rights, privileges, and power possible. The owner can give the property away or dispose of the property by deed or by will. When there is no will, the fee

simple passes to the owner's legal heirs on the owner's death. A fee simple absolute is potentially infinite in duration and is assigned forever to owners and their heirs without limitation or condition.[2] The owner has the rights of exclusive possession and use of the property.

The rights that accompany a fee simple absolute include the right to use the land for whatever purpose the owner sees fit. Of course, other laws, including applicable zoning, noise, and environmental laws, may limit the owner's ability to use the property in certain ways. Persons who use their property in a manner that unreasonably interferes with others' right to use or enjoy their own property can be liable for the tort of nuisance.

■ **Case in Point 26.2** Nancy and James Biglane owned and lived in a building next door to the Under the Hill Saloon, a popular bar that featured live music. During the summer, the Saloon, which had no air-conditioning, opened its windows and doors, and live music echoed up and down the street.

The Biglanes installed extra insulation, thicker windows, and air-conditioning units in their building. Nevertheless, the noise from the Saloon kept the Biglanes awake at night. Eventually, they sued the owners of the Saloon for nuisance. The court held that the noise from the bar unreasonably interfered with the Biglanes' right to enjoy their property and prohibited the Saloon from opening its windows and doors while playing music.[3] ■

26–2b Life Estates

A **life estate** is an estate that lasts for the life of some specified individual. A **conveyance,** or transfer of real property, "to A for his life" creates a life estate.[4] The life tenant's ownership rights cease to exist on the life tenant's death.

Life tenants have the right to use the land, provided that they commit no **waste** (injury to the land). In other words, a life tenant cannot use the land in a manner that would adversely affect its value. The life tenant can use

---

1. *EBC Properties, LLC v. Urge Food Corporation,* 2023 WL 1453034 (App.Ct. MD, 2023).

2. In another type of estate, the *fee simple defeasible*, ownership in fee simple automatically terminates if a stated event occurs. For instance, property might be *conveyed* (transferred) to a school only as long as it is used for school purposes. In addition, the fee simple may be subject to a *condition subsequent*. This means that if a stated event occurs, the prior owner of the property can bring an action to regain possession of the property.

3. *Biglane v. Under the Hill Corp.,* 949 So.2d 9 (Miss. 2007). See, in contrast, *LaCroix v. Newson,* 324 So.3d 802 (Ct.App. MS 2021).

4. A less common type of life estate is created by the conveyance "to A for the life of B." This is known as an estate *pur autre vie*—that is, an estate for the duration of the life of another.

the land to harvest crops or, if mines and oil wells are already on the land, can extract minerals and oil from it, but the life tenant cannot establish new wells or mines. The life tenant can also create liens, *easements* (discussed shortly), and leases, but none can extend beyond the life of the tenant. In addition, with few exceptions, the life tenant has an exclusive right to possession during the life tenancy.

Along with these rights, the life tenant also has some duties—to keep the property in repair and to pay property taxes. In short, the owner of the life estate has the same rights as a fee simple owner except that the life tenant must maintain the value of the property during the period of tenancy.

The distinction between a life estate and a fee simple determined the result in the following case.

Case 26.1

In the Matter of the Estate of Nelson

Supreme Court of North Dakota, 2018 ND 118, 910 N.W.2d 856 (2018).

Background and Facts When Sidney Solberg died, 100 mineral acres—that is, the right to all of the minerals under a certain 100 acres—and other real property in his estate were distributed to his widow, Lillian, for her life. The remainder interest (the right of ownership after Lillian's interest ended) was conveyed to their four children, including Glenn Solberg.

Later, Lillian married Lyle Nelson. When Lillian passed away, a codicil (addition) to her will allegedly gave the 100 mineral acres to Glenn. The codicil also purported to create for Glenn an option to buy the other real property she had inherited from Sidney. When Nelson died, Glenn filed a claim in a North Dakota state court against Nelson's estate. Glenn asserted that under the terms of the codicil to Lillian's will, he was entitled to the ownership of the 100 mineral acres and the right to buy the other property. The court dismissed Glenn's claim. He appealed to the state supreme court.

In the Language of the Court
JENSEN, Justice.
 * * * *

Our law regarding the rights of someone who holds a life interest in property is * * * well established. It is well-settled [that] a life estate holder is entitled to both the possession and the use of the property, * * * including the right to rents, issues, and profits generated by the parcel * * *. A life tenant is entitled to possession and enjoyment of the property as long as the estate endures; he or she may convey or lease his or her interest, but may not disregard the rights of those who take when the life estate ends. * * * No future interest can be defeated or barred by any alienation [voluntary transfer of real property] or other act of the owner of the [life] interest.

In this case, Lillian Nelson obtained a life estate interest in the 100 mineral acres and in the option property * * * from Sidney Solberg's estate. The codicil relied upon by Glenn Solberg itself identifies Lillian Nelson's interest as being limited to a life estate. As a life tenant she was limited to conveying an interest in her property only to the extent of her life and she could not make any transfers that would disregard the rights of those who would take the property when her life ended. As such, Lillian Nelson's attempt to provide an interest in the 100 mineral acres to Glenn Solberg in her * * * will is invalid because it disregards the rights of those who would take the property when her life ended. Similarly, her attempt to convey a right of first refusal to the option property * * * is also invalid because it disregards the rights of those who would take the property when her life ended.

Upon Lillian Nelson's death * * * her life interest ended and the 100 mineral acres and the option property became the property of her four children as the holders of the remainder interest. * * * The Lyle Nelson Estate did not hold, and Lyle Nelson never held, an interest in the 100 mineral acres or the option property. * * * Glenn Solberg could not recover property from the Lyle Nelson Estate if Lyle Nelson never held an interest in the property.

Decision and Remedy The Supreme Court of North Dakota affirmed the dismissal of Glenn's claim. "The [lower] court properly concluded that, with certainty, it would be impossible for Glenn Solberg to obtain the relief he requested from the Lyle Nelson Estate."

Critical Thinking

- **Legal Environment** Lillian could not divest her children of their remainder interest in the property of her life estate. Are there any actions that the owner of a life estate could take legitimately that would divest the holder of a remainder interest in the property of this interest?
- **What If the Facts Were Different?** Suppose that Sidney Solberg had disposed of his entire estate in fee simple before his death. Would the result have been different? Discuss.

26–2c Concurrent Ownership

Persons who share ownership rights simultaneously in particular property (including real property and personal property) are said to have **concurrent ownership.** There are two principal types of concurrent ownership: *tenancy in common* and *joint tenancy.* Concurrent ownership rights can also be held in a *tenancy by the entirety* or as *community property*, but these types of concurrent ownership are less common.

Tenancy in Common The term **tenancy in common** refers to a form of co-ownership in which each of two or more persons owns an undivided interest in the property. The interest is undivided because each tenant shares rights in the whole property. On the death of a tenant in common, that tenant's interest in the property passes to the tenant's heirs.

■ **Example 26.3** Four friends purchase a condominium unit in Hawaii together as tenants in common. This means that each of them has a one-fourth ownership interest in the whole. If one of the four owners dies a year after the purchase, his ownership interest passes to his heirs (his wife and children, for instance) rather than to the other tenants in common. ■

Unless the co-tenants have agreed otherwise, a tenant in common can transfer that tenant's interest in the property to another person without the consent of the remaining co-owners. In most states, it is presumed that a co-tenancy is a tenancy in common unless there is specific language indicating the intent to establish a joint tenancy.

Joint Tenancy In a **joint tenancy,** each of two or more persons owns an undivided interest in the property, but a deceased joint tenant's interest passes to the surviving joint tenant or tenants.

Right of Survivorship. The right of a surviving joint tenant to inherit a deceased joint tenant's ownership interest—referred to as a *right of survivorship*—distinguishes a joint tenancy from a tenancy in common. ■ **Example 26.4** Varney and Eva are married

and purchase a house as joint tenants. The title to the house clearly expresses the intent to create a joint tenancy because it refers to Varney and Eva as "joint tenants with right of survivorship." Varney has three children from a prior marriage. If Varney dies, his interest in the house automatically passes to Eva rather than to his children from the prior marriage. ■

Termination of a Joint Tenancy. Joint tenants can transfer their rights by sale or gift to another without the consent of the other joint tenant. Doing so terminates the joint tenancy, however. The person who purchases the property or receives it as a gift becomes a tenant in common, not a joint tenant. ■ **Example 26.5** Two brothers, Kwame and Louis, own a parcel of land as joint tenants. Kwame is experiencing financial difficulties and sells his interest in the real property to Beth. The sale terminates the joint tenancy, and now Beth and Louis hold the property as tenants in common. ■

A joint tenant's interest can also be levied against (seized by court order) to satisfy the tenant's *judgment creditors*. If this occurs, the joint tenancy terminates, and the remaining owners hold the property as tenants in common. (Judgment creditors can also seize the interests of tenants in a tenancy in common.)

Tenancy by the Entirety A less common form of shared ownership of real property by married persons is a **tenancy by the entirety.** It differs from a joint tenancy in that neither spouse may separately transfer that spouse's interest unless the other spouse consents. In some states in which statutes give the wife the right to convey her property, this form of concurrent ownership has effectively been abolished. A divorce, either spouse's death, or mutual agreement will terminate a tenancy by the entirety.

Community Property A limited number of states[5] allow married couples to own property as **community**

---

5. These states include Alaska, Arizona, California, Idaho, Louisiana, Nevada, New Mexico, Texas, Washington, and Wisconsin. Puerto Rico allows property to be owned as community property as well.

property. If property is held as community property, each spouse technically owns an undivided one-half interest in the property. This type of ownership applies to most property acquired by the husband or the wife during the course of the marriage. It generally does not apply to property acquired prior to the marriage or to property acquired by gift or inheritance as separate property during the marriage. After a divorce, community property is divided equally in some states and according to the discretion of the court in other states.

26–2d Leasehold Estates

A **leasehold estate** is created when a real property owner or lessor (landlord) agrees to convey the right to possess and use the property to a lessee (tenant) for a certain period of time. The tenant's right to possession is temporary, which is what distinguishes a tenant from a purchaser, who acquires title to the property.

In every leasehold estate, the tenant has a qualified right to exclusive possession. It is qualified because the landlord has a right to enter onto the premises to ensure that no waste is being committed. In addition, the tenant can use the land—for instance, by harvesting crops—but cannot injure it by such activities as cutting down timber to sell or extracting oil.

Fixed-Term Tenancy A **fixed-term tenancy,** also called a "tenancy for years," is created by an express contract stating that the property is leased for a specified period of time, such as a month, a year, or a period of years. Signing a one-year lease to occupy an apartment, for instance, creates a fixed-term tenancy. Note that the term need not be specified by date and can be conditioned on the occurrence of an event, such as leasing a cabin for the summer or an apartment during Mardi Gras.

At the end of the period specified in the lease, the lease ends (without notice), and possession of the property returns to the lessor. If the tenant dies during the period of the lease, the lease interest passes to the tenant's heirs as personal property. Often, leases include renewal or extension provisions.

Periodic Tenancy A **periodic tenancy** is created by a lease that does not specify a term but does specify that rent is to be paid at certain intervals, such as weekly, monthly, or yearly. The tenancy is automatically renewed for another rental period unless properly terminated. ■ **Example 26.6** Jewel, LLC, enters into a lease with Capital Properties. The lease states, "Rent is due on the tenth day of every month." This provision creates a periodic tenancy from month to month. ■ A periodic tenancy sometimes arises after a fixed-term tenancy ends when the landlord allows the tenant to retain possession and continue paying monthly or weekly rent.

Under the common law, to terminate a periodic tenancy, the landlord or tenant must give at least one period's notice to the other party. If the tenancy is month to month, for instance, one month's notice must be given prior to the last month's rent payment. Today, however, state statutes often require a different period of notice before the termination of a tenancy.

Tenancy at Will With a **tenancy at will,** either party can terminate the tenancy without notice. This type of tenancy can arise if a landlord rents property to a tenant "for as long as both agree" or allows a person to live on the premises without paying rent. Tenancy at will is rare today because most state statutes require a landlord to provide some period of notice to terminate a tenancy. States may also require a landowner to have sufficient cause (a legitimate reason) to end a residential tenancy.

Tenancy at Sufferance The mere possession of land without a right is called a **tenancy at sufferance.** A tenancy at sufferance is not a true tenancy because it is created when a tenant wrongfully retains possession of property. Whenever a tenancy for years or a periodic tenancy ends and the tenant continues to retain possession of the premises without the owner's permission, a tenancy at sufferance is created.

26–2e Nonpossessory Interests

In contrast to the types of property interests just described, some interests in land do not include any rights to possess the property. These interests are therefore known as **nonpossessory interests.** They include *easements, profits,* and *licenses.*

An **easement** is the right of a person to make limited use of another person's real property without taking anything from the property. The right to walk across another's property, for instance, is an easement. In contrast, a **profit** is the right to go onto land owned by another and take away some part of the land itself or some product of the land. ■ **Example 26.7** Kaiden owns real property known as the Dunes. Kaiden gives Carmen the right to go there and remove all of the sand and gravel that she needs for her cement business. Carmen has a profit. ■

Easements and profits can be classified as either *appurtenant* or *in gross.* Because easements and profits are similar and the same rules apply to both, we discuss them together.

Easement or Profit Appurtenant An easement (or profit) appurtenant arises when the owner of one piece of land has a right to go onto (or remove something from) an adjacent piece of land owned by another. The land that is benefited by the easement is called the *dominant estate,* and the land that is burdened is called the *servient estate.*

Because easements appurtenant are intended to benefit the land, they run (are conveyed) with the land when it is transferred. ■ **Example 26.8** Owen has a right to drive his car across Green's land, which is adjacent to Owen's property. This right-of-way over Green's property is an easement appurtenant to Owen's land. If Owen sells his land, the easement runs with the land to benefit the new owner. ■

Easement or Profit in Gross In an easement or profit in gross, the right to use or take things from another's land is given to one who does not own an adjacent tract of land. These easements are intended to benefit a particular person or business, not a particular piece of land, and cannot be transferred.

■ **Example 26.9** Fatima owns a parcel of land with a marble quarry. Fatima conveys to Classic Stone Corporation the right to come onto her land and remove up to five hundred pounds of marble per day. Classic Stone owns a profit in gross and cannot transfer this right to another. ■ Similarly, when a utility company is granted an easement to run its power lines across another's property, it obtains an easement in gross.

Creation of an Easement or Profit Most easements and profits are created by an express grant in a contract, deed, or will. This allows the parties to include terms defining the extent and length of time of use. In some situations, however, an easement or profit can be created without an express agreement.

An easement or profit may arise by **implication** when the circumstances surrounding the division of a parcel of property imply its creation. ■ **Example 26.10** Barrow divides a parcel of land that has only one well for drinking water. If Barrow conveys the half without a well to Dean, a profit by implication arises because Dean needs drinking water. ■

An easement may also be created by **necessity.** An easement by necessity does not require division of property for its existence. A person who rents an apartment, for instance, has an easement by necessity in the private road leading up to it.

An easement arises by **prescription** when one person exercises an easement, such as a right-of-way, on another person's land without the landowner's consent. The use must be apparent and continue for the length of time

required by the applicable statute of limitations. (In much the same way, title to property may be obtained by "adverse possession," as will be discussed later in this chapter.)

■ **Case in Point 26.11** From 1993 to 2016, Charles and Mary Fee used a roadway located on the property of their neighbors, Richard and Gail Cheatham, to haul livestock to and from a nearby highway and for deliveries of products such as feed, fertilizer, and lime. In July 2016, Richard told the Fees that the road was now off-limits and erected a gate to block their passage. The Fees filed a lawsuit claiming that they had a right to access the roadway by prescriptive easement. A Kentucky statute holds that such an easement is created if the use is "unobstructed, open, peaceable, [and] continuous" without express permission of the landowner for at least fifteen years.

The trial court ruled in favor of the Cheathams based on its mistaken view that the relevant time period started when the gate was erected in July 2016. A state appeals court corrected this error, noting that the Fees had used the roadway for more than twenty years before being obstructed by the gate. Given Richard's testimony that he had seen the Fees' vehicles on the roadway "every now and then" at least once a year during that entire time, the appeals court found that the Fees had met the statutory requirements for easement by prescription.[6] ■

Termination of an Easement or Profit An easement or profit can be terminated or extinguished in several ways. The simplest way is to deed it back to the owner of the land that is burdened by it. Similarly, if the owner of an easement or profit acquires the property burdened by it, then it is merged into the property.

Another way to terminate an easement or profit is to abandon it and provide evidence of the intent to relinquish the right to use it. Mere nonuse will not extinguish an easement or profit, however, unless the nonuse is accompanied by an overt act showing the intent to abandon. An overt act might be, for instance, installing and using a different access road to one's property and discontinuing using an easement across the neighboring property. In any case, a court must be convinced that there was an intent to abandon the easement or profit.

License In the context of real property, a **license** is the revocable right of a person to come onto another person's land. It is a personal privilege that arises from the consent

---

6. *Fee v. Cheatham,* 2019 WL 2712604 (Ky. Ct. App. 2019).

of the owner of the land and can be revoked by the owner. A ticket to attend a movie at a theater or a concert is an example of a license.

In essence, a license grants a person the authority to enter the land of another and perform a specified act or series of acts without obtaining any permanent interest in the land. When a person with a license exceeds the authority granted and undertakes some action on the property that is not permitted, the property owner can sue that person for the tort of trespass.

■ **Case in Point 26.12** Richard and Mary Orman purchased real property owned at one time by Sandra Curtis. Part of the garage extended nine feet onto Curtis's neighboring property. In an agreement on file with the deed, Curtis had given the Ormans permission to use the garage as long as it continued to be used as a garage. After the Ormans moved in, they converted the garage's workshop into guest quarters but continued to use the garage as a garage.

A dispute arose over the driveway shared by Curtis and the Ormans, which straddled the property line. The Ormans filed a suit claiming that Curtis left "junk objects" near the driveway that impeded their access. Curtis countered that the permission she had given the buyers to use the garage was a license. She claimed that the Ormans, by converting the workshop into living quarters, had exceeded their authority under the license, which she could therefore revoke. The court looked at the agreement's wording, which clearly gave the Ormans the right to use the garage but did not mention the workshop. The court concluded that because the Ormans were continuing to use the garage as a garage, Curtis could not revoke their right to do so.[7] ■

Exhibit 26–1 illustrates the various interests in real property discussed in this chapter.

26–3 Transfer of Ownership

Ownership interests in real property are frequently transferred by sale, and the terms of the transfer are specified in a real estate sales contract. When real property is sold, the type of interest being transferred and the conditions of the transfer normally are set forth in a deed executed by the person who is conveying the property. Real property ownership can also be transferred by gift, by will or inheritance, by adverse possession, or by eminent domain.

26–3a Real Estate Sales Contracts

In some ways, a sale of real estate is similar to a sale of goods because it involves a transfer of ownership, often with specific warranties. A sale of real estate, however,

---

7. *Orman v. Curtis,* 54 Misc.3d 1206(A), 50 N.Y.S.3d 27 (2017).

Exhibit 26–1 Interests in Real Property

Type of Interest	Description
Ownership Interests	1. *Fee simple*—The most complete form of ownership. 2. *Life estate*—An estate that lasts for the life of a specified individual. 3. *Concurrent ownership*—When two or more persons hold title to property together, concurrent ownership exists. Examples of concurrent ownership include: a. Tenancy in common b. Joint tenancy c. Tenancy by the entirety d. Community property
Leasehold Estates	1. Fixed-term tenancy (tenancy for years) 2. Periodic tenancy 3. Tenancy at will 4. Tenancy at sufferance
Nonpossessory Interests	1. Easements 2. Profits 3. Licenses

is a more complicated transaction that involves certain formalities that are not required in a sale of goods. In part because of these complications, real estate brokers or agents who are licensed by the state assist the buyers and sellers during the sales transaction.

Usually, after some negotiation (offers, counteroffers, and responses), the parties enter into a detailed contract setting forth their agreement. A contract for a sale of land includes such terms as the purchase price, the type of deed the buyer will receive, the condition of the premises, and any items that will be included.

Unless the buyer pays cash for the property, the buyer must obtain financing through a mortgage loan. Real estate sales contracts are often contingent on the buyer's ability to obtain financing at or below a specified rate of interest. The contract may also be contingent on certain events, such as the completion of a land survey or the property's passing one or more inspections. Normally, the buyer is responsible for having the premises inspected for physical or mechanical defects and for insect infestation.

Closing Date and Escrow The contract usually fixes a date for performance, or **closing,** that frequently is four to twelve weeks after the contract is signed. On this day, the seller conveys the property to the buyer by delivering the deed to the buyer in exchange for payment of the purchase price.

Deposits toward the purchase price normally are held in a special account, called an **escrow account,** until all of the conditions of sale have been met. Once the closing takes place, the funds in the escrow account are transferred to the seller.

Marketable Title The title to the property is especially important to the buyer. A grantor (seller) is obligated to transfer **marketable title,** or good title, to the grantee (buyer). Marketable title means that the grantor's ownership is free from encumbrances (except those disclosed by the grantor) and free of defects.

If the buyer signs a purchase contract and then discovers that the seller does not have a marketable title, the buyer can withdraw from the contract. ■ **Example 26.13** Chan enters into an agreement to buy Fortuna Ranch from Hal. Chan then discovers that Hal has given Pearl an option to purchase the ranch and the option has not expired. In this situation, the title is not marketable, because Pearl could exercise the option and Hal would be compelled to sell the ranch to her. Therefore, Chan can withdraw from the contract to buy the property. ■

The most common way of ensuring title is through **title insurance,** which insures the buyer against loss from defects in title to real property. When financing the purchase of real property, almost all lenders require title insurance to protect their interests in the collateral for the loan.

Implied Warranties in the Sale of New Homes The common law rule of *caveat emptor* ("let the buyer beware") held that the seller of a home made no warranty as to its soundness or fitness (unless the contract or deed stated otherwise). Today, however, most states recognize a warranty—the **implied warranty of habitability**—in the sale of new homes.

Under this warranty, the seller of a new house warrants that it will be fit for human habitation even if the deed or contract of sale does not include such a warranty. Essentially, the seller is warranting that the house is in reasonable working order and is of reasonably sound construction. The seller can be liable if the home is defective. In some states, the warranty protects not only the first purchaser but any subsequent purchaser as well.

Seller's Duty to Disclose Hidden Defects In most jurisdictions, courts impose on sellers a duty to disclose any known defect that materially affects the value of the property and that the buyer could not reasonably discover. Failure to disclose such a defect gives the buyer a right to rescind the contract and to sue for damages based on fraud or misrepresentation.

There is normally a limit to the time within which the buyer can bring a suit against the seller based on the defect. Time limits run from either the date of the sale or the date that the buyer discovered (or should have discovered) the defect. ■ **Example 26.14** Ian Newson partially renovates a house in Louisiana and sells it to Jerry and Tabitha Moreland for $270,000. Two months after the Morelands move in, they discover rotten wood behind the tile in the bathroom and experience problems with the plumbing. The state statute specifies that the Morelands have one year from the date of the sale or the discovery of the defect to file a lawsuit. Therefore, the Morelands must file a suit within twelve months of discovering the defects (which would be fourteen months from the date of the sale). ■

In the following Spotlight Case, the court had to decide whether the buyer of a house had the right to rescind the sales contract because he was not told that the house was allegedly haunted.

Spotlight on Sales of Haunted Houses

Case 26.2 Stambovsky v. Ackley

Supreme Court, Appellate Division, New York, 169 A.D.2d 254, 572 N.Y.S.2d 672 (1991).

Background and Facts Jeffrey Stambovsky signed a contract to buy Helen Ackley's home in Nyack, New York. After the contract was signed, Stambovsky discovered that the house was widely reputed to be haunted. The Ackley family claimed to have seen poltergeists on numerous occasions over the prior nine years. The Ackleys had been interviewed and quoted in both a national publication (*Reader's Digest*) and the local newspaper. The house was described as "a riverfront Victorian (with ghost)" when it was part of a walking tour of Nyack. When Stambovsky discovered the house's reputation, he sued to rescind the contract and recover his down payment. He alleged that Ackley and her real estate agent made material misrepresentations when they failed to disclose Ackley's belief that the home was haunted. Ackley argued that, under the doctrine of *caveat emptor,* she was under no duty to disclose to the buyer the home's haunted reputation. The trial court dismissed Stambovsky's case. Stambovsky appealed.

In the Language of the Court

Justice RUBIN delivered the opinion of the court.
　　* * * *

　　While I agree with [the trial court] that the real estate broker, as agent for the seller, is under no duty to disclose to a potential buyer the phantasmal reputation of the premises and that, in his pursuit of a legal remedy for fraudulent misrepresentation against the seller, plaintiff hasn't a ghost of a chance, I am nevertheless moved by the spirit of equity to allow the buyer to seek rescission of the contract of sale and recovery of his down payment. New York law fails to recognize any remedy for damages incurred as a result of the seller's mere silence, applying instead the strict rule of *caveat emptor.* Therefore, the theoretical basis for granting relief, even under the extraordinary facts of this case, is elusive if not ephemeral [short-lived].
　　* * * *

　　The doctrine of *caveat emptor* requires that a buyer act prudently to assess the fitness and value of his purchase and operates to bar the purchaser who fails to exercise due care from seeking the equitable remedy of rescission. * * * Applying the strict rule of *caveat emptor* to a contract involving a house possessed by poltergeists conjures up visions of a psychic or medium routinely accompanying the structural engineer and Terminix man on an inspection of every home subject to a contract of sale. It portends [foretells] that the prudent attorney will establish an escrow account lest the subject of the transaction come back to haunt him and his client—or pray that his malpractice insurance coverage extends to supernatural disasters. In the interest of avoiding such untenable consequences, the notion that a haunting is a condition which can and should be ascertained upon reasonable inspection of the premises is a hobgoblin which should be exorcised from the body of legal precedent and laid quietly to rest.
　　* * * *

　　In the case at bar [under consideration], defendant seller deliberately fostered the public belief that her home was possessed. Having undertaken to inform the public at large, to whom she has no legal relationship, about the supernatural occurrences on her property, she may be said to owe no less a duty to her contract vendee. It has been remarked that the occasional modern cases, which permit a seller to take unfair advantage of a buyer's ignorance so long as he is not actively misled are "singularly unappetizing." Where, as here, the seller not only takes unfair advantage of the buyer's ignorance but has created and perpetuated a condition about which he is unlikely to even inquire, enforcement of the contract (in whole or in part) is offensive to the court's sense of equity. Application of the remedy of rescission, within the bounds of the narrow exception to the doctrine of *caveat emptor* set forth herein, is entirely appropriate to relieve the unwitting purchaser from the consequences of a most unnatural bargain.

Decision and Remedy The New York appellate court found that the doctrine of *caveat emptor* did not apply in this case. The court allowed Stambovsky to rescind the purchase contract and recover the down payment.

Critical Thinking

- **Ethical** In not disclosing the house's reputation to Stambovsky, was Ackley's behavior unethical? If so, was it unethical because she knew something he did not, or was it unethical because of the nature of the information she omitted? What if Ackley had failed to mention that the roof leaked or that the well was dry—conditions that a buyer would normally investigate? Explain your answer.
- **Legal Environment** Why did the court decide that applying the strict rule of *caveat emptor* was inappropriate in this case? How would applying this doctrine increase costs for the purchaser?

26–3b Deeds

Possession and title to land are passed from person to person by means of a **deed**—the instrument used to transfer real property. Deeds must meet certain requirements, but unlike a contract, a deed does not have to be supported by legally sufficient consideration. Gifts of real property are common, and they require deeds even though there is no consideration for the gift.

To be valid, a deed must include the following:

1. The names of the grantor (the giver or seller) and the grantee (the donee or buyer).
2. Words evidencing the intent to convey (for instance, "I hereby bargain, sell, grant, or give"). No specific words are necessary. If the deed does not specify the type of estate being transferred, it presumptively transfers the property in fee simple absolute.
3. A legally sufficient description of the land. The description must include enough detail to distinguish the property being conveyed from every other parcel of land. The property can be identified by reference to an official survey or recorded plat map, or each boundary can be described by metes and bounds. A **metes and bounds** system measures boundary lines by the distance between two points, often using physical features of the local geography. A property description might say, for instance, "beginning at the southwesterly intersection of Court and Main Streets, then West 40 feet to the fence, then South 100 feet, then Northeast approximately 120 feet back to the beginning."
4. The grantor's (and frequently the spouse's) signature.
5. Delivery of the deed.

Different types of deeds provide different degrees of protection against *defects of title*. A defect of title exists, for instance, if an undisclosed third person has an ownership interest in the property.

Warranty Deeds A **warranty deed** contains the greatest number of warranties and thus provides the most extensive protection against defects of title. In most states, special language is required to create a general warranty deed. Warranty deeds commonly include the following covenants:

1. A covenant that the grantor has the title to, and the power to convey, the property.
2. A covenant of quiet enjoyment (a warranty that the buyer's possession of the land will not be disturbed).
3. A covenant that transfer of the property is made without knowledge of adverse claims of third parties.

Generally, the warranty deed makes the grantor liable for all defects of title during the time that the property was held by the grantor and previous titleholders. ■ **Example 26.15** Sanchez sells a two-acre lot and office building by warranty deed to Fast Tech, LLC. Subsequently, Amy shows that she has better title than Sanchez had and evicts Fast Tech. Here, Fast Tech can sue Sanchez for breaching the covenant of quiet enjoyment. Fast Tech can recover the purchase price of the land, plus any other damages incurred as a result. ■

Special Warranty Deed A **special warranty deed**, or limited warranty deed, in contrast, warrants only that the grantor, or seller, held good title during the grantor's ownership of the property. In other words, the seller does not guarantee that there are no adverse claims by third parties against any previous owners of the property.

If the special warranty deed discloses all liens or other encumbrances, the seller will not be liable to the buyer if a third person subsequently interferes with the buyer's ownership. If the third person's claim arises out of, or is related to, some act of the seller, however, the seller will be liable to the buyer for damages.

Quitclaim Deed A **quitclaim deed** offers the least protection against defects in the title. Basically, a quitclaim deed conveys to the grantee whatever interest the grantor had. If the grantor had no interest, then the grantee receives no interest. (Naturally, if the grantor had a defective title or no title at all, a conveyance by warranty deed or special warranty deed would not cure the defect. Such a deed, however, would give the buyer a cause of action to sue the seller.)

Quitclaim deeds are often used when sellers are uncertain as to the extent of their rights in the property. They may also be used to release a party's interest in a particular parcel of property. This may be necessary, for instance, in divorce settlements or business dissolutions when the grantors are dividing up their interests in real property.

Grant Deed With a **grant deed,** the grantor simply states, "I grant the property to you" or "I convey, or bargain and sell, the property to you." By state statute, grant deeds carry with them an implied warranty that the grantor owns the property and has not previously transferred it to someone else or encumbered it, except as set out in the deed.

26–3c Recording Statutes

Once the seller delivers the deed to the buyer (at closing), legal title to the property is conveyed. Nevertheless, the buyer should promptly record the deed with the state records office. Every state has a **recording statute,** which allows deeds to be recorded in the public record for a fee. Deeds generally are recorded in the county in which the property is located. Many state statutes require that the grantor sign the deed in the presence of two witnesses before it can be recorded.

Recording a deed gives notice to the public that a certain person is now the owner of a particular parcel of real estate. By putting everyone on notice as to the true owner, recording a deed prevents the previous owners from fraudulently conveying the land to other purchasers.

26–3d Adverse Possession

A person who wrongfully possesses the real property of another (by occupying or using the property) may eventually acquire title to it through adverse possession. **Adverse possession** is a means of obtaining title to land without delivery of a deed and without the consent of—or payment to—the true owner. Thus, adverse possession is a method of involuntarily transferring title to the property from the true owner to the adverse possessor.

Essentially, when one person possesses the real property of another for a certain statutory period of time, that person acquires title to the land. The statutory period varies from three to thirty years, depending on the state, with ten years being most common.

Requirements for Adverse Possession For property to be held adversely, four elements must be satisfied.

1. **Possession must be actual and exclusive.** The possessor must physically occupy the property. This requirement is clearly met if the possessor lives on the property, but it may also be met if the possessor builds fences, erects structures, plants crops, or even grazes animals on the land.
2. **Possession must be open, visible, and notorious, not secret or clandestine.** The possessor must occupy the land for all the world to see. This requirement ensures that the true owner is on notice that someone is possessing the owner's property wrongfully.
3. **Possession must be continuous and peaceable for the required period of time.** This requirement means that the possessor must not be interrupted in the occupancy by the true owner or by the courts. Continuous does not mean constant. It simply means that the possessor has continuously occupied the property in some fashion for the statutory time. Peaceable means that no force was used to possess the land.
4. **Possession must be hostile and adverse.** In other words, the possessor cannot be living on the property with the owner's permission and must claim the property as against the whole world.

■ **Case in Point 26.16** Leslie and Ethel Cline owned a 141-acre property to the south of State Route 316 in Ohio. Rogers Farm Enterprises, LLC, owned 399 acres to the north of State Route 316. When the Clines originally bought their farm, they believed that State Route 316 was the dividing line between their property and Rogers Farm. Later, a survey showed that a 3.95-acre strip of land on the Clines' side of the road, which the Clines had been farming, actually belonged to Rogers Farm.

After twenty-one years, the Clines filed a suit claiming that they had acquired title to the property through adverse possession. The court granted title to the Clines. Rogers Farm appealed. An Ohio state appellate court affirmed. The Clines had been openly and continuously farming on the disputed strip of land for the requisite period of time under Ohio's statute (twenty-one years) and legally owned it.[8] ■

The following case involved adverse possession of property that its true owner did not know about for years.

8. *Cline v. Rogers Farm Enterprises, LLC,* 2017-Ohio-1379, 87 N.E.3d 637 (Ohio Ct.App., 4th Dist. 2017). See also *Szuber C, Ltd. v. Petrash,* 2022-Ohio-2694, 2022 WL 3106662 (Ct.App. OH, 5th Dist. 2022).

A2 Creative Group, LLC v. Anderson

Missouri Court of Appeals, Western District, 596 S.W.3d 214 (2020).

Background and Facts   Gary and Cristina Worden owned the Main Street Inn, a bed and breakfast, in Parkville, Missouri. A stone wall ran the length of the property behind the inn. A driveway and walkway along the wall were used to access the service entrance to the inn for the delivery of supplies and equipment. The Wordens also maintained the landscaping up to the wall—for example, they cut the grass, planted flowers, laid down a weed tarp and mulch, put down paver and edging stones, and removed dying trees.

After owning the inn for eleven years, the Wordens sold the business to A2 Creative Group, LLC, whose principals, Jason and Kathy Ayers, lived in the inn and had been operating it for the sellers. At about the same time, Soheil Anderson, owner of the property on the other side of the stone wall, obtained a survey of her property. The survey revealed that a 400-square foot tract on the inn's side of the wall was actually Anderson's property.

A2 filed a petition in a Missouri state court against Anderson to establish title to the tract based on a claim of adverse possession. The trial court concluded that A2's possession of the disputed property had been "(1) hostile; (2) actual; (3) open and notorious; (4) exclusive; and (5) continuous for at least 10 years," the requisite period for adverse possession under Missouri's statute. Anderson appealed, claiming that A2 had not proved that its possession was exclusive and continuous.

In the Language of the Court

MARK D. PFEIFFER, Judge

* * * *

Exclusive Possession   To show its possession was "exclusive," A2 was required to show that it (and its predecessors in interest) possessed the land for itself, and not for others, and that it wholly excluded the true owner from possession of the property. * * * Maintenance of a residential yard such that it appears to be part of the property on which the residence is situated is evidence from which a trier of fact can infer that the possession of the property was exclusive.

Here, there was evidence that during the requisite time period, A2 and its predecessors maintained and utilized the disputed tract of land for themselves, and never maintained the property for their neighbors, and exclusively used and maintained the disputed strip for the required ten-year time period.

* * * *

This * * * evidence supports the trial court's finding that A2 and the Wordens demonstrated visible acts of ownership over the premises.

* * * *

Continuous Possession for Ten Years   The ten years of possession must be consecutive years and need not be the ten years just prior to the filing of the lawsuit, but once the period has run, the possessor is vested with title and the record owner is divested. An adverse possession claimant may tack his possession to that of his predecessors in title to establish the requisite ten-year period.

* * * Here, there was evidence of occupancy, upkeep, and no intent to abandon the disputed property.

* * * *

[This] evidence supported the trial court's conclusion that A2 showed the "continuous" element of adverse possession.

Decision and Remedy   A state intermediate appellate court affirmed the trial court's judgment in favor of A2.

Case 26.3 Continues

Case 26.3 Continued   **Critical Thinking**

- **Legal Environment** Would an adverse possessor satisfy the element of "exclusive" on showing only that disputed property was not jointly possessed with the previous owner? Explain.
- **What If the Facts Were Different?** Suppose that for a year during the Wordens' ownership of the inn, they closed it for remodeling. Would the result in this case have been different? Discuss.

Purpose of the Doctrine There are a number of public-policy reasons for the adverse possession doctrine. These include society's interest in resolving boundary disputes, determining title when title is in question, and assuring that real property remains in the stream of commerce. More fundamentally, the doctrine punishes owners who do not take action when they see adverse possession and rewards possessors for putting land to productive use.

26–4 Limitations on the Rights of Property Owners

No ownership rights in real property can ever really be absolute—that is, owners of real property cannot always do whatever they wish on or with the property. Nuisance and environmental laws, for instance, restrict certain types of activities. Property ownership is also conditional on the payment of property taxes. Zoning laws and building permits frequently restrict the use of realty. In addition, if a property owner fails to pay debts, the property may be seized to satisfy judgment creditors. In short, the rights of every property owner are subject to certain conditions and limitations.

26–4a Eminent Domain

Even ownership in fee simple absolute is limited by a superior ownership. Just as the king was the ultimate landowner in medieval England, today the government has an ultimate ownership right in all land in the United States. This right, known as **eminent domain,** is sometimes referred to as the *condemnation power* of government or as a **taking.** It gives the government the right to acquire possession of real property in the manner directed by the takings clause of the U.S. Constitution and the laws of the state whenever the public interest requires it.

The power of eminent domain generally is invoked through **condemnation** proceedings. ■ **Example 26.17**

When a new public highway is to be built, the government decides where to build it and how much land to condemn. After the government determines that a particular parcel of land is necessary for the highway, it will first offer to buy the property. If the owner refuses the offer, the government brings a judicial (condemnation) proceeding to obtain title to the land. ■

Condemnation proceedings usually involve two distinct phases. The first seeks to establish the government's right to take the property, and the second determines the fair value of the property.

Right to Take the Property In the first phase of condemnation proceedings, the government must prove that it needs to acquire privately owned property for a public use. ■ **Example 26.18** Franklin County, Iowa, engages Bosque Systems to build a liquefied natural gas pipeline that crosses the property of more than two hundred landowners. Some property owners consent to this use and accept Bosque's offer of compensation. Others refuse the offer. A court will likely deem the pipeline to be a public use. Therefore, the government can exert its eminent domain power to "take" the land, provided that it pays just compensation to the property owners. ■

Just Compensation The U.S. Constitution and state constitutions require that the government pay just compensation to the landowner when invoking its condemnation power. Just compensation means fair value. In the second phase of the condemnation proceeding, the court determines the fair value of the land, which usually is approximately equal to its market value.

26–4b Taking for Economic Development

Property may be taken by the government for public use, not for private benefit. But can eminent domain be used to promote private development when the development is deemed to be in the public interest?

The United States Supreme Court has ruled that the power of eminent domain may be used to further "economic development."[9] This ruling would apply in cases where, for instance, a city government decides that it is in the public interest to have a larger parking lot for a local, privately owned sports stadium or to have a manufacturing plant locate in the city to create more jobs. The government may condemn certain tracts of existing housing or business property and then convey the land to the privately owned stadium or manufacturing plant.

Such actions may bring in private developers and businesses that provide jobs and increase tax revenues, thus revitalizing communities. Opponents of the practice continue to dispute, however, that the land is really being taken for "public use," as required by the Fifth Amendment.

The Supreme Court recognizes the right of individual states to pass laws that prohibit takings for economic development, and most have done so. Still, some states do allow takings for the redevelopment of economically stressed neighborhoods and, controversially, to promote recreational activities. See this chapter's Ethics Today feature for further discussion of this issue.

---

9. *Kelo v. City of New London, Connecticut,* 545 U.S. 469, 125 S.Ct. 2655, 162 L.Ed.2d 439 (2005).

26–4c Restrictive Covenants

A private restriction on the use of land is known as a **restrictive covenant.** If the restriction is binding on the party who initially purchases the property and on subsequent purchasers as well, it is said to "run with the land." A covenant running with the land must be in writing (usually it is in the deed), and subsequent purchasers must have reason to know about it.

■ **Example 26.19** In the course of developing a fifty-lot suburban subdivision, Levitt records a declaration of restrictions effectively limiting construction on each lot to one single-family house. Each lot's deed includes a reference to the declaration with a provision that the purchaser and the purchaser's successors are bound by those restrictions. Thus, each purchaser assumes ownership with notice of the restrictions. If an owner attempts to build a duplex (or any noncompliant structure) on a lot, the other owners may obtain a court order to prevent the construction.

Alternatively, Levitt might simply have included the restrictions on the subdivision's map, filed the map in the appropriate public office, and included a reference to the map in each deed. Under these circumstances, each owner would still have been held to have constructive notice of the restrictions. ■

Ethics Today

Should eminent domain be used to take private land for recreational uses?

Across the country, state and local governments are showing a willingness to take land for hiking paths, bike trails, and other recreational purposes. Public officials and nature enthusiasts argue that this use of eminent domain is justified because of the many benefits these projects bestow on the community. Bike trails, for instance, reduce automobile traffic and provide transportation options for residents with low incomes. Supporters also point to the general physical and emotional rewards of recreational activities for those who are able to take part.

Others—particularly those who own the land in question—have a different view of the situation. Farmers in Mahoning County, Ohio, went to court to fight a park service's efforts to take control of an abandoned railway that runs through their property.

The farmers argued that the proposed recreational bike path would cut their farm in half, making it difficult for livestock and heavy machinery to move freely. They also worried about liability if trail users wandered onto the farm and were injured.

Plaintiffs in Iowa and Massachusetts have taken similar legal action to keep recreational trails off private land. A Wisconsin legislator, defending his state's ban on the use of eminent domain for such purposes, says, "Somebody else's recreational opportunity should not be forced on my property."

Critical Thinking At what point might the predicted benefits of a new private commercial endeavor outweigh the constitutional requirement of a taking only for public use?

26–5 Land-Use Control and Zoning

The rules and regulations that collectively manage the development and use of land are known as **zoning laws.** Zoning laws were first used in the United States to segregate slaughterhouses, distilleries, kilns, and other businesses that might pose a nuisance to nearby residences. The growth of modern urban areas led to an increased need to organize uses of land. Today, zoning laws enable municipalities to control the speed and type of development within their borders by creating different zones and regulating the use of property in each zone.

The United States Supreme Court has held that zoning is a constitutional exercise of a government's police powers.[10] Therefore, as long as zoning ordinances are rationally related to the health, safety, or welfare of the community, a municipal government has broad discretion to carry out zoning as it sees fit.

26–5a Purpose and Scope of Zoning Laws

The purpose of zoning laws is to manage the land within a community in a way that encourages sustainable and organized development while controlling growth in a manner that serves the interests of the community. One of the basic elements of zoning is the classification of land by permissible use, but zoning extends to other aspects of land use as well.

Permissible Uses of Land Municipalities generally divide their available land into districts according to the land's present and potential future uses. Typically, land is classified into the following types of permissible uses.

1. **Residential.** In areas dedicated for **residential use,** landowners can construct buildings for human habitation.
2. **Commercial.** Land assigned for business activities is designated as being for **commercial use,** sometimes called *business use.* An area with a number of retail stores, offices, supermarkets, and hotels might be designated as a commercial or business district. Land used for entertainment purposes, such as movie theaters and sports stadiums, also falls into this category, as does land used for government activities.

3. **Industrial.** Areas designated for **industrial use** typically encompass light and heavy manufacturing, shipping, and heavy transportation. For instance, undeveloped land with easy access to highways and railroads might be classified as suitable for future use by industry. Although industrial uses can be profitable for a city seeking to raise tax revenue, such uses can also result in noise, smoke, or vibrations that interfere with others' enjoyment of their property. Consequently, areas zoned for industrial use generally are kept as far as possible from residential districts and some commercial districts.
4. **Conservation districts.** Some municipalities also establish certain areas that are dedicated to carrying out local soil and water conservation efforts. For instance, wetlands might be designated as a conservation district.

A city's residential, commercial, and industrial districts may be divided, in turn, into subdistricts. For instance, zoning ordinances may regulate the type, density, size, and approved uses of structures within a given district. Thus, a residential district may be divided into low-density (single-family homes with large lots), high-density (single- and multiple-family homes with small lots), and planned-unit (condominiums or apartments) subdistricts.

Other Zoning Restrictions Zoning rules extend to much more than the permissible use of land. In residential districts, for instance, an ordinance may require a house or garage to be set back a specific number of feet from a neighbor's property line.

In commercial districts, zoning rules may attempt to maintain a certain visual aesthetic. Therefore, businesses may be required to construct buildings of a certain height and width so that they conform to the style of other commercial buildings in the area.

Businesses may also be required to provide parking for patrons or take other measures to manage traffic. Sometimes, municipalities limit construction of new businesses to prevent traffic congestion.

Zoning laws may even attempt to regulate the public morals of the community. For instance, cities commonly impose severe restrictions on the location and operation of adult businesses and medical and recreational marijuana dispensaries.

26–5b Exceptions to Zoning Laws

Zoning restrictions are not absolute. It is impossible for zoning laws to account for every contingency. The purpose of zoning is to control development, not to prevent it altogether or to limit the government's ability to adapt to

---

10. *Village of Euclid, Ohio v. Ambler Realty Co.,* 272 U.S. 365, 47 S.Ct. 114, 71 L.Ed. 303 (1926). See also *Tingley v. Ferguson,* 57 F.4th 1072 (9th Cir. 2023).

changing circumstances or unforeseen needs. Hence, legal processes have been developed to allow for exceptions to zoning laws, such as variances and special-use permits.

Variances Property owners who want to use their land in a manner not permitted by zoning rules can request a **variance,** which allows an exception to the rules. The property owner making the request must demonstrate that the requested variance:

1. Is necessary for reasonable development.
2. Is the least intrusive solution to the problem.
3. Will not alter the essential character of the neighborhood.

Hardship Situations. Property owners normally request variances in hardship situations—that is, when complying with the zoning rules would be too difficult or costly due to existing property conditions. ■ **Example 26.20** Lin, a homeowner, wants to replace her single-car garage with a two-car garage. If she does so, however, the garage will be closer to her neighbor's property than is permitted by the zoning rules. In this situation, she may ask for a variance. She can claim that the configuration of her property would make it difficult and costly to comply with the zoning code, so compliance would create a hardship for her. ■

Similarly, a church might request a variance from height restrictions in order to erect a new steeple. Or a furniture store might ask for a variance from footprint limitations so that it can expand its showroom. (A building's *footprint* is the area of ground that it covers.)

Note that the hardship may not be self-created. In other words, buyers who purchase property with zoning restrictions in effect cannot usually then argue that they need variances in order to use the property as they intended.

Special-Use Permits Sometimes, zoning laws permit a certain use only if the property owner complies with specific requirements to ensure that the proposed use does not harm the immediate neighborhood. In such instances, the zoning board can issue **special-use permits,** also called *conditional-use permits.*

■ **Example 26.21** An area is designated as a residential district, but small businesses are permitted to operate there so long as they do not affect the characteristics of the neighborhood. A bank asks the zoning board for a special-use permit to open a branch in the area. At the public hearing, the bank demonstrates that the branch will be housed in a building that conforms to the style of other structures in the area. The bank also shows that adequate parking will be available and that landscaping will shield the parking lot from public view. Unless there are strong objections from the branch's prospective neighbors, the board will likely grant the permit. ■

Special Incentives In addition to granting exceptions to zoning regulations, municipalities may also wish to encourage certain kinds of development. To do so, they offer incentives, often in the form of lower tax rates or tax credits. For instance, to attract new businesses that will provide jobs and increase the tax base, a city may offer lower property tax rates for a period of years. Similarly, homeowners may receive tax credits for historic preservation if they renovate and maintain older homes.

Practice and Review: Real Property and Land-Use Control

Vern Shoepke purchased a two-story home from Walter and Eliza Bruster in the town of Roche, Maine. The warranty deed did not specify what covenants would be included in the conveyance. The property was adjacent to a public park that included a popular Frisbee golf course. (Frisbee golf is a sport similar to golf but using Frisbees.) Wayakichi Creek ran along the north end of the park and along Shoepke's property. The deed allowed Roche citizens the right to walk across a five-foot-wide section of the lot beside Wayakichi Creek as part of a two-mile public trail system. Teenagers regularly threw Frisbee golf discs from the walking path behind Shoepke's property over his yard to the adjacent park. Shoepke habitually shouted and cursed at the teenagers, demanding that they not throw objects over his yard. Two months after moving into his Roche home, Shoepke leased the second floor to Lauren Slater for nine months. After three months of tenancy, Slater sublet the second floor to a local artist, Javier Indalecio. (The lease agreement did not specify that Shoepke's consent would be required to sublease the second floor.) Over the remaining six months,

Indalecio's use of oil paints damaged the carpeting in Shoepke's home. Using the information presented in the chapter, answer the following questions.

1. What is the term for the right of Roche citizens to walk across Shoepke's land on the trail?
2. What covenants would most courts infer were included in the warranty deed that was used in the property transfer from the Brusters to Shoepke?
3. Suppose that Shoepke wants to file a trespass lawsuit against some teenagers who continually throw Frisbees over his land. Shoepke discovers, however, that when the city put in the Frisbee golf course, the neighborhood homeowners signed an agreement that limited their right to complain about errant Frisbees. What is this type of promise or agreement called in real property law?
4. Can Shoepke hold Slater financially responsible for the damage to the carpeting caused by Indalecio? Why or why not?

Debate This . . .   Under no circumstances should a local government be able to condemn property in order to sell it later to real estate developers for private use.

Terms and Concepts

adverse possession 552	implied warranty of habitability 549	residential use 556
closing 549	industrial use 556	restrictive covenant 555
commercial use 556	joint tenancy 545	special-use permits 557
community property 545	leasehold estate 546	special warranty deed 551
concurrent ownership 545	license 547	taking 554
condemnation 554	life estate 543	tenancy at sufferance 546
conveyance 543	marketable title 549	tenancy at will 546
deed 551	metes and bounds 551	tenancy by the entirety 545
easement 546	necessity 547	tenancy in common 545
eminent domain 554	nonpossessory interests 546	title insurance 549
escrow account 549	periodic tenancy 546	trade fixture 542
fee simple absolute 543	prescription 547	variance 557
fixed-term tenancy 546	profit 546	warranty deed 551
fixture 542	quitclaim deed 552	waste 543
grant deed 552	recording statute 552	zoning laws 556
implication 547		

Issue Spotters

1. Bernie sells his house to Consuela under a warranty deed. Later, Delmira appears, holding a better title to the house than Consuela has. Delmira wants to have Consuela evicted from the property. What can Consuela do? (See *Transfer of Ownership.*)
2. Grey owns a commercial building in fee simple. Grey transfers temporary possession of the building to Haven Corporation. Can Haven transfer possession for even less time to Idyll Company? Explain. (See *Ownership and Other Interests in Real Property.*)

• Check your answers to the Issue Spotters against the answers provided in Appendix B at the end of this text.

Business Scenarios and Case Problems

26–1. Property Ownership. Madison owned a tract of land, but he was not sure that he had full title to the property. When Rafael expressed an interest in buying the land, Madison sold it to Rafael and executed a quitclaim deed. Rafael properly recorded the deed immediately. Several months later, Madison learned that he had had full title to the tract of land. He then sold the land to Linda by warranty deed. Linda knew of the earlier purchase by Rafael but took the deed anyway and later sued to have Rafael evicted from the land. Linda claimed that because she had a warranty deed, her title to the land was better than that conferred by Rafael's quitclaim deed. Will Linda succeed in claiming title to the land? Explain. (See *Transfer of Ownership.*)

26–2. Zoning. The county intends to rezone an area from industrial use to residential use. Land within the affected area is largely undeveloped, but nonetheless it is expected that the proposed action will reduce the market value of the affected land by as much as 50 percent. Will the landowners be successful in suing to have the action declared a taking of their property, entitling them to just compensation? Why or why not? (See *Land-Use Control and Zoning.*)

26–3. Zoning and Variances. Joseph and Lois Ryan hired a contractor to build a home in Weston, Connecticut. The contractor submitted plans to the town that included a roof height of thirty-eight feet for the proposed dwelling. This exceeded the town's roof-height restriction of thirty-five feet. The contractor and the architect revised the plans to meet the restriction, and the town approved the plans and issued a zoning permit and a building permit. After the roof was constructed, a code enforcement officer discovered that it measured thirty-seven feet, seven inches high.

The officer issued a cease-and-desist order requiring the Ryans to "remove the height violation and bring the structure into compliance." The Ryans appealed to the zoning board, claiming that the error was not theirs but that of their general contractor and architect. The zoning board upheld the cease-and-desist order but later granted the Ryans a variance because "the roof height was out of compliance by approximately two feet, . . . the home [was] perched high on the land and [was] not a detriment to the neighborhood, and . . . the hardship was created by the contractor's error."

Neighbors (including Curtis Morikawa) appealed to a court. They argued that the hardship claimed was solely economic. In addition, they argued that even though it was unintended, the hardship was self-created. The trial court ruled in favor of the neighbors, and the Ryans appealed. How should the reviewing court rule? Were there legitimate grounds for granting a variance? Discuss. [*Morikawa v. Zoning Board of Appeals of Town of Weston*, 126 Conn. App. 400, 11 A.3d 735 (2011)] (See *Land-Use Control and Zoning.*)

26–4. Adverse Possession. The McKeag family operated a marina on their lakefront property in Bolton, New York.

For more than forty years, the McKeags used a section of property belonging to their neighbors, the Finleys, as a beach for the marina's customers. The McKeags also stored a large float on the beach during the winter months, built their own retaining wall, and planted bushes and flowers there. The McKeags prevented others from using the property, including the Finleys. Nevertheless, the families always had a friendly relationship, and at one point a member of the Finley family gave the McKeags permission to continue using the beach. He also reminded them of his ownership several times, to which they said nothing. The McKeags also asked for permission to mow grass on the property and once apologized for leaving a jet ski there. Can the McKeags establish adverse possession over the statutory period of ten years? Why or why not? [*McKeag v. Finley*, 93 A.D.3d 925, 939 N.Y.S.2d 644 (3 Dept. 2012)] (See *Transfer of Ownership.*)

26–5. Real Estate Sales Contracts. A California state statute requires sellers to provide a real estate "Transfer Disclosure Statement" (TDS) to buyers of residential property consisting of one to four dwelling units. Required disclosures include information about significant defects, including hazardous materials, encroachments, easements, fill, settling, flooding, drainage problems, neighborhood noise, damage from natural disasters, and lawsuits. Mark Hartley contracted with Randall Richman to buy Richman's property in Ventura, California. The property included a commercial building and a residential duplex with two dwelling units. Richman did not provide a TDS, claiming that it was not required because the property was "mixed use"—that is, it included both a commercial building and a residential building. Hartley refused to go through with the deal. Did Hartley breach their contract, or did Richman's failure to provide a TDS excuse Hartley's nonperformance? Discuss. [*Richman v. Hartley*, 224 Cal.App.4th 1182, 169 Cal. Rptr.3d 475 (2 Dist. 2014)] (See *Transfer of Ownership.*)

26–6. Business Case Problem With Sample Answer—Joint Tenancies. Arthur and Diana Ebanks owned three properties in the Cayman Islands in joint tenancy. With respect to joint tenancies, Cayman law is the same as U.S. law. When the Ebankses divorced, the decree did not change the tenancy in which the properties were held. On the same day as the divorce filing, Arthur executed a will providing that "any property in my name and that of another as joint tenants . . . will pass to the survivor, and I instruct my Personal Representative to make no claim thereto." Four years later, Arthur died. His brother Curtis, the personal representative of his estate, asserted that Arthur's interest in the Cayman properties was part of the estate. Diana said that the sole interest in the properties was hers. To whom do the Cayman properties belong? Why? [*Ebanks v. Ebanks*, 41 Fla.L.Weekly D291, 198 So.3d 712 (2 Dist. 2016)] (See *Ownership and Other Interests in Real Property.*)

• For a sample answer to Problem 26–6, go to Appendix C at the end of this text.

26–7. Eminent Domain. In the city of Tarrytown, New York, Citibank operated a branch that included a building and a parking lot with thirty-six spaces. Tarrytown leased twenty-one of the spaces from Citibank for use as public parking. When Citibank closed the branch and decided to sell the building, the public was denied access to the parking lot. After a public hearing, the city concluded that it should exercise its power of eminent domain to acquire the twenty-one spaces to provide public parking. Is this an appropriate use of the power of eminent domain? Suppose that Citibank opposes the plan and alternative sites are available. Should Tarrytown be required to acquire those sites instead of Citibank's property? In any event, what is Tarrytown's next step? Explain. [*Matter of Citibank, N.A. v. Village of Tarrytown*, 149 A.D.3d 931, 52 N.Y.S.3d 398 (2 Dept. 2017)] (See *Transfer of Ownership.*)

26–8. Transfer of Ownership. Craig and Sue Shaffer divided their real property into two lots. They enclosed one lot with a fence and sold it to the Murdocks. The other lot was sold to the Cromwells. All of the parties orally agreed that the fence marked the property line. Over the next three decades, each lot was sold three more times. Houses were built, and the lots were landscaped, including lilac bushes planted against the fence. Later, one of the owners removed the fence, and another built a shed next to where it had been. On the lot with the shed, the Talbots erected a carport abutting the lilac bushes, which all previous owners believed was planted on the property line. Then, the Nielsons bought the adjacent lot and measured it according to the legal description in the deed. The Nielsons discovered that the Talbots' carport encroached on their property by about thirteen feet. Are the Nielsons entitled to damages for their "lost" property from any party? Explain. [*Nielson v. Talbot*, 163 Idaho 480, 415 P.3d 348 (2018)] (See *Transfer of Ownership.*)

26–9. A Question of Ethics—The IDDR Approach and Easements. Two organizations, Class A Investors Post Oak, LP, and Cosmopolitan Condominium VP, LP, owned adjacent pieces of property in Houston, Texas. Each owner-organization planned to build a high-rise tower on its lot. The organizations signed an agreement that granted each of them an easement in the other's property to "facilitate the development." Cosmopolitan built its residential high-rise first. Later, Class A began moving forward with its plan for a mixed-use high-rise. Cosmopolitan objected that the proposed tower would "be vastly oversized for its proposed location; situated perilously close to [Cosmopolitan's] building; create extraordinary traffic hazards; impede fire protection and other emergency vehicles in the area; and substantially interfere with the use and enjoyment of [Cosmopolitan's] property." [*Cosmopolitan Condominium Owners Association v. Class A Investors Post Oak, LP,* 2017 WL 1520448 (Tex.App.—Houston 2017)] (See *Ownership and Other Interests in Real Property.*)

(a) On what basis can Class A proceed with its plan? Explain, using the IDDR approach.

(b) On what ethical ground might Cosmopolitan continue to oppose its neighbor's project? Discuss.

Time-Limited Group Assignment

26–10. Adverse Possession. The Wallen family owned a cabin on Lummi Island in the state of Washington. A driveway ran from the cabin across their property to South Nugent Road. Floyd Massey bought the adjacent lot and built a cabin on it in 1980. To gain access to his property, Massey used a bulldozer to extend the driveway, without the Wallens' permission but also without their objection. Twenty-five years later, the Wallens sold their property to Wright Fish Company. Massey continued to use and maintain the driveway without permission or objection. Later, Massey sold his property to Robert Drake. Drake and his employees continued to use and maintain the driveway without permission or objection, although Drake knew it was located largely on Wright's property. Still later, Wright sold its lot to Robert Smersh. The next year, Smersh told Drake to stop using the driveway. Drake filed a suit against Smersh, claiming adverse possession. (See *Transfer of Ownership.*)

(a) The first group will decide whether Drake's use of the driveway meets all of the requirements for adverse possession.

(b) The second group will determine how the court should rule in this case and why. Does it matter that Drake knew the driveway was located largely on Wright's (and then Smersh's) property? Should it matter? Why or why not?

(c) The third group will evaluate the underlying policy and fairness of adverse possession laws. Should the law reward persons who take possession of someone else's land for their own use? Does it make sense to punish owners who allow someone else to use their land without complaint? Explain.

(d) The fourth group will consider how the laws governing adverse possession vary from state to state. To acquire title through adverse possession, a person might be required to possess the property for five years in one state, for instance, and for twenty years in another. Are there any legitimate reasons for such regional differences? Would it be better if all states had the same requirements? Explain your answers.

Chapter 27

Antitrust Law

After the Civil War (1861–1865), the American public became increasingly concerned about declining competition in the marketplace. Large corporate enterprises at that time were attempting to reduce or eliminate competition by legally tying themselves together in business trusts.

The most famous trust was the Standard Oil trust of the late 1800s. Participants in the trust transferred their stock to a trustee. The trustee then fixed prices, controlled production, and established exclusive geographic markets for all of the oil companies that were members of the trust. Some observers began to argue that the trust wielded so much economic power that corporations outside the trust could not compete effectively.

Eventually, legislators at both the state and the federal level began to enact laws to rein in the trusts. Hence, the laws regulating economic competition in the United States today are referred to as **antitrust laws.** At the national level, important antitrust legislation includes the Sherman Antitrust Act,[1] passed in 1890, and the Clayton Act[2] and the Federal Trade Commission Act,[3] passed in 1914. We examine these major federal antitrust statutes in this chapter.

The purpose of antitrust legislation was—and still is—to foster competition. Behind these laws lies our society's belief that competition leads to lower prices, better products, a wider selection of goods, and more product information.

---

1. 15 U.S.C. Sections 1–7.
2. 15 U.S.C. Sections 12–27.
3. 15 U.S.C. Sections 41–58a.

27–1 The Sherman Antitrust Act

The author of the Sherman Antitrust Act, Senator John Sherman, was the brother of the famed Civil War general William Tecumseh Sherman. He was also a recognized financial authority. He had been concerned for years about what he saw as diminishing competition within U.S. industry and the emergence of monopolies. He told Congress that the Sherman Act "does not announce a new principle of law, but applies old and well-recognized principles of the common law."[4]

Indeed, today's antitrust laws are the direct descendants of common law actions intended to limit **restraints of trade** (agreements between or among firms that have the effect of reducing competition in the marketplace). Such actions date to the fifteenth century in England. The common law was not always consistent, however, and had not been effective in curbing the trusts. That is why Sherman proposed the Sherman Antitrust Act, often simply called the Sherman Act.

27–1a Major Provisions of the Sherman Act

Sections 1 and 2 contain the main provisions of the Sherman Act:

1. Every contract, combination in the form of trust or otherwise, or conspiracy, in restraint of trade or commerce among the several States, or with foreign nations, is hereby declared to be illegal [and is a felony punishable by fine and/or imprisonment].
2. Every person who shall monopolize, or attempt to monopolize, or combine or conspire with any other person or persons, to monopolize any part of the trade or commerce among the several States, or with foreign nations, shall be deemed guilty of a felony [and is similarly punishable].

27–1b Differences Between Section 1 and Section 2

The two sections of the Sherman Act are quite different. Section 1 requires two or more persons, because a person cannot contract, combine, or conspire alone. Thus, the essence of the illegal activity is the act of joining together. Section 2, though, can apply either to one person or to two

---

4. 21 *Congressional Record* 2456 (1890).

or more persons because it refers to "every person." Thus, unilateral conduct can result in a violation of Section 2.

It follows that the cases brought to the courts under Section 1 of the Sherman Act differ from those brought under Section 2. Section 1 cases are often concerned with whether an agreement (written or oral) leads to a restraint of trade. Section 2 cases deal with the structure of a monopoly that exists in the marketplace.

The term **monopoly** generally is used to describe a market in which there is a single seller or a very limited number of sellers. Whereas Section 1 focuses on agreements that are restrictive—that is, agreements that have a wrongful purpose—Section 2 looks at the so-called misuse of **monopoly power** in the marketplace. Monopoly power exists when a firm has an extreme amount of **market power**—the power to affect the market price of its product.

Both Section 1 and Section 2 seek to curtail market practices that result in undesired monopoly pricing and output behavior. For a case to be brought under Section 2, however, the "threshold" or "necessary" amount of

monopoly power must already exist. We illustrate the different requirements for violating these two sections of the Sherman Act in Exhibit 27–1.

27–1c Jurisdictional Requirements

The Sherman Act applies only to restraints that have a significant impact on interstate commerce. Courts have generally held that any activity that substantially affects interstate commerce falls within the scope of the Sherman Act. As will be discussed later in this chapter, the Sherman Act also extends to U.S. nationals abroad who are engaged in activities that affect U.S. foreign commerce.

Federal courts have exclusive jurisdiction over antitrust cases brought under the Sherman Act. State laws regulate local restraints on competition, and state courts decide claims brought under those laws.

In the following case, the defendants argued that their bid-rigging scheme did not fall under the Sherman Act because the proof of a connection between the scheme and interstate commerce fell short.

Case 27.1

United States v. Vega-Martínez

United States Court of Appeals, First Circuit, 949 F.3d 43 (2020).

Background and Facts Private bus companies owned by Luciano Vega-Martínez and others provided busing for students to public schools in Caguas, Puerto Rico. The municipality announced that it would hold an auction for four-year school bus transportation contracts. Instead of submitting competing bids, the bus company owners met and agreed to divide up the routes among themselves. For each route, they designated a "winner" whose noncompetitive "low" bid would not be outbid by the others.

Unaware of the lack of fair competition, the municipality awarded the routes to the "low bidders." When the scheme was revealed two years into the four-year term of the contracts, the federal government charged the owners of the bus companies with conspiracy to restrain trade in violation of the Sherman Act. A jury convicted the defendants, and a federal district court sentenced them to prison terms and ordered restitution.

Vega-Martínez appealed, contending that the bid rigging did not fall under the Sherman Act because there was insufficient proof of a connection between the scheme and interstate commerce.

In the Language of the Court
KAYATTA, Circuit Judge.
＊ ＊ ＊ ＊

The Sherman Act reaches only activities in the flow of interstate commerce or that, while wholly local in nature, would substantially affect interstate commerce if successful. [Bid rigging is a form of price fixing.] When confronted with horizontal agreements to fix prices within a single state, [federal] jurisdiction [is based] on a general conclusion that the defendants' agreement almost surely had a market-wide impact and therefore an effect on interstate commerce.
＊ ＊ ＊ ＊

At trial, the government ＊ ＊ ＊ had to submit evidence sufficient to establish an interstate nexus beyond a reasonable doubt. The government carried this burden. It proved, for example, that the funds used to pay the defendants were provided by the federal government * * *. Caguas used $436,566.32 in federal funds * * * to pay for school transportation [during the first two years of the four-year contracts with the defendants]. The [defendants'] grab of those federal funds is likely sufficient by itself to establish an interstate nexus, given that the funds flowed in interstate commerce.

Here we have more than the federal funds alone. The defendants' bid packages identified by vehicle identification number the specific buses that they planned to use for each route. Those buses were all purchased in Florida, meaning that they flowed in interstate commerce. As the government points out, if prices increased substantially, demand would likely fall. For example, Caguas might have responded by merging bus routes or reducing the bus services it used in other ways, resulting in fewer buses purchased by local companies from the continental United States.

Given the evidence that the contracts were funded in at least substantial part by federal funding that had flowed through interstate commerce and that the contracts were carried out by use of goods that flowed through interstate commerce, as well as the resulting inference that the effect of the [defendants' scheme] could have been to reduce demand for those goods, the evidence in total was sufficient to establish a nexus with interstate commerce.

Decision and Remedy The U.S. Court of Appeals for the First Circuit affirmed the trial court's determination that the defendants' activities were within the flow of, and substantially affected, interstate commerce. The appellate court also upheld the defendants' convictions, their prison sentences, and the trial court's order for restitution.

Critical Thinking

- **Legal Environment** Could the defendants have successfully argued that their agreement to rig bids and allocate the market for public school bus transportation was reasonable, or that it could be justified on an economic or business basis? Explain.

- **Economic** Following the discovery of the bid-rigging scheme, Caguas held a presumably fair auction to award new school bus transportation contracts. Could the bids in the second auction provide a benchmark for the restitution amounts? Discuss.

27–2 Section 1 of the Sherman Act

The underlying assumption of Section 1 of the Sherman Act is that society's welfare is harmed if rival firms are permitted to join in an agreement that consolidates their market power or otherwise restrains competition. The types of trade restraints that Section 1 of the Sherman Act prohibits generally fall into two broad categories: horizontal restraints and vertical restraints, both of which will be discussed shortly. First, we look at the rules that the courts may apply when assessing the anticompetitive impact of alleged restraints of trade.

Exhibit 27–1 Required Elements of a Sherman Act Violation

Section 1 Violation Requirements

1. An agreement between two or more parties,
2. That unreasonably restrains competition, and
3. Affects interstate commerce.

Section 2 Violation Requirements

1. The possession of monopoly power in the relevant market, and
2. The willful acquisition or maintenance of that power as distinguished from its growth or development as a consequence of a superior product, business acumen, or historic accident.

27–2a *Per Se* Violations Versus the Rule of Reason

Some restraints are so substantially anticompetitive that they are deemed *per se* **violations**—illegal *per se* (inherently)—under Section 1. Other agreements, even though they result in enhanced market power, do not unreasonably restrain trade and are therefore lawful. Using the **rule of reason,** the courts analyze anticompetitive agreements that allegedly violate Section 1 of the Sherman Act to determine whether they actually constitute reasonable restraints of trade.

Rationale for the Rule of Reason The need for a rule-of-reason analysis of some agreements in restraint of trade is obvious. If the rule of reason had not been developed, almost any business agreement could conceivably be held to violate the Sherman Act. United States Supreme Court Justice Louis Brandeis effectively phrased this sentiment in *Chicago Board of Trade v. United States,* a case decided in 1918:

> Every agreement concerning trade, every regulation of trade, restrains. To bind, to restrain, is of their very essence. The true test of legality is whether the restraint imposed is such as merely regulates and perhaps thereby promotes competition or whether it is such as may suppress or even destroy competition.[5]

Factors That Courts Consider When analyzing an alleged Section 1 violation under the rule of reason, a court will consider the following factors:

1. The purpose of the agreement.
2. The parties' ability to implement the agreement to achieve that purpose.
3. The effect or potential effect of the agreement on competition.
4. Whether the parties could have relied on less restrictive means to achieve their purpose.

---

5. 246 U.S. 231, 38 S.Ct. 242, 62 L.Ed. 683 (1918).

■ **Case in Point 27.1** A group of consumers sued NBC Universal, the Walt Disney Company, and other broadcasters, as well as cable and satellite distributors, claiming that the bundling of high-demand and low-demand television channels in cable and satellite programming packages violates the Sherman Act. Bundling forces consumers to pay for channels they do not watch to have access to channels they watch regularly.

The consumers argued that the defendants, through their control of high-demand programming, exercised market power that made it impossible for any distributor to offer unbundled programs. A federal appellate court ruled in favor of the defendants and dismissed the case. The court reasoned that the Sherman Act applies to actions that diminish competition and that the bundling of channels does not injure competition.[6] ■

27–2b Horizontal Restraints

The term **horizontal restraint** is encountered frequently in antitrust law. A horizontal restraint is any agreement that in some way restrains competition between rival firms competing in the same market. Horizontal restraints may include price-fixing agreements, group boycotts, market divisions, trade associations, and joint ventures.

Price Fixing Any **price-fixing agreement**—an agreement among competitors to fix prices—constitutes a *per se* violation of Section 1. The agreement on price need not be explicit. As long as it restricts output or artificially fixes price, it violates the law.

In the following case, several well-known packaged-tuna suppliers engaged in a price-fixing conspiracy in violation of Washington State's Consumer Protection Act. The question before the appellate court was whether the trial court had abused its discretion in its judgment against one of the suppliers.

---

6. *Brantley v. NBC Universal, Inc.,* 675 F.3d 1192 (9th Cir. 2012).

Case Analysis 27.2

StarKist Company v. State of Washington
Court of Appeals of Washington, Div. 1, 522 P.3d 594 (2023).

In the Language of the Court
ANDRUS, C.J.

StarKist Company appeals a summary judgment order holding it jointly and severally liable for the harm it and its competitors, Chicken of the Sea and Bumble Bee Foods, caused consumers when they conspired to fix the prices of packaged tuna * * *.

We reverse the summary judgment order—not because, as StarKist contends, it can be liable only for its own profits gained through the conspiracy, but because [Washington State law] does not mandate joint and several liability. The statute instead confers discretion on the trial court to determine what judgment "may be necessary" to restore to consumers the money acquired by an unlawful conspiracy. The trial court may impute to one conspirator the actions of all coconspirators and, as a result, may order StarKist to pay an amount equal to the conspiracy's gains if the court deems it necessary to do so.

But the State of Washington settled with coconspirators Chicken of the Sea, and Bumble Bee's chief executive officer, Christopher Lischewski, for a fraction of these alleged consumer losses. And StarKist contends it was an insignificant player in the overall price-fixing scheme. We therefore reverse the summary judgment order imposing joint and several liability on StarKist "for the harm caused by its co-conspirators Bumble Bee and Chicken of the Sea" and remand for the trial court to enter findings of fact to justify any restitution it orders StarKist to pay * * *.

FACTS

In 2016, Chicken of the Sea International (COSI) disclosed to federal investigators that it had conspired with competitors, including StarKist and Bumble Bee, to fix prices on packaged-tuna products. Following these disclosures, Bumble Bee and StarKist were charged with and pleaded guilty in federal court to conspiring to fix prices with competitors in violation of the Sherman Antitrust Act. Both companies admitted that from November 2011 until December 2013, they "participated in a conspiracy among major packaged-seafood-producing firms, the primary purpose of which was to fix, raise, and maintain the prices of packaged seafood sold in the United States."

In March 2020, the State of Washington, through the Attorney General, brought an antitrust lawsuit against Chicken of the Sea, seeking an injunction, damages, restitution, and other relief under the Consumer Protection Act (CPA) for this price-fixing conspiracy. Soon thereafter, Chicken of the Sea entered into a consent decree in which it agreed to pay $500,000 to the State of Washington in exchange for a release of liability.

On June 2, 2020, the State of Washington brought a similar antitrust lawsuit against StarKist, StarKist's parent company, Dongwon Industries Co. Ltd., and Bumble Bee Foods LLC's former chief executive officer, Christopher Lischewski, alleging these defendants had engaged in a conspiracy in restraint of trade with Chicken of the Sea.

In October 2020, the State entered into a consent decree with Lischewski in which he agreed to pay $100,000 to the State of Washington to compensate consumers allegedly harmed by the conspiracy.

In February 2021, the trial court held StarKist liable as a matter of law * * * for engaging in a price-fixing conspiracy during the period specified in its federal guilty plea.

On March 9, 2021, the State disclosed the report of its expert economist, Dr. David Sunding, who opined that the price-fixing scheme between StarKist, Chicken of the Sea, and Bumble Bee caused Washington consumers to overpay for packaged tuna by a total of $11,981,526. Sunding attributed $1,074,589 of the total losses to StarKist's sales.

The State then moved for partial summary judgment, seeking to hold StarKist "jointly and severally liable for the actions of its co-conspirators." The trial court granted the motion, concluding that StarKist "is jointly and severally liable for the harm caused by its co-conspirators Bumble Bee and Chicken of the Sea * * *." StarKist sought and we granted discretionary review of this order.

ANALYSIS

StarKist contends the trial court erred in imposing joint and several liability as a matter of law, arguing that the tort principle of joint and several liability cannot apply to an equitable action for restitution under [state law]. * * * [W]e reverse the trial court's summary judgment order because [Washington law] does not mandate joint and several liability, as the trial court's order implies.

* * * *

When the attorney general seeks a restitution award under [Washington law], it is not required to prove causation or injury. And the court may calculate restitution based on the amount of illegal gains rather than net damages sustained by consumers.

Scope of Restitution Under [Washington Law]

In this appeal, StarKist argues that any restitution award must be limited to the illegal gains StarKist itself enjoyed and cannot extend to the illegal gains realized by its coconspirators. * * *

Based on * * * principles of statutory construction, we reject StarKist's argument that it cannot be held liable for unlawful gains realized by the conspiracy under [Washington law] for three reasons. First, the plain language of [the law] does not limit restitution to monies acquired by a single coconspirator. Second, although [Washington law] does not explicitly refer to the common law principles of joint and several liability, these statutory provisions must be read together with [Washington law], the provision outlawing conspiracies in restraint of trade. Under well-established Washington common law, a conspiracy is a single enterprise for which all coconspirators are responsible. Finally, federal antitrust case law does not require a different result.

1. Plain Text of [the Washington Statute]
* * * *

[Washington law] states that "[t]he court may make such additional orders or judgments as may be necessary to restore to any person in interest any moneys or property, real or personal, which may have been acquired by means of any act herein prohibited or declared to be unlawful." The "prohibited" or "unlawful" acts referred to in this paragraph are the acts explicitly outlawed by other provisions of the CPA, including [Washington law] prohibiting conspiracies in restraint of trade. The court may thus order a party

Case 27.2 Continues

Case 27.2 Continued

participating in an unlawful conspiracy to pay "any moneys . . . which may have been acquired" by the conspiracy. * * *
* * * *

2. Common Law of Conspiracy

StarKist's interpretation is also unpersuasive because it fails to address the common law of conspiracy. The word "conspiracy" in [Washington law] is not defined in the CPA [Consumer Protection Act]. But this legal term has a well-understood legal meaning, and we assign a familiar legal term in a statute its familiar legal meaning.

A conspiracy is "a combination of two or more persons to commit a criminal or unlawful act, or to commit a lawful act by criminal or unlawful means." Under Washington common law, "[e]very person who enters into a conspiracy, no matter whether at

its beginning or at a later stage of its progress, is in law a party to every act of the conspirators, and is liable for all of the acts done in pursuance of the conspiracy in the same manner that they would be had they been a party to all of the wrongful acts." We presume the legislature enacted the CPA "with full knowledge of existing laws." * * *
* * * *

* * * We have no such expression of legislative intent here. We therefore conclude that when the legislature made conspiracies in restraint of trade unlawful and gave courts the authority to restore monies acquired through such a conspiracy, that authority included the pre-existing power under common law to hold one conspirator liable for all of the acts done in pursuance of the conspiracy, even

if they were not a party to all of the wrongful acts.
* * * *

Summary Judgment Order

The summary judgment order, however, did not represent an exercise of the trial court's discretion under [Washington law]. Instead, the trial court held StarKist liable for the conspiracy's profits without explaining its rationale for exercising its discretion in this manner and appears to have rendered this ruling as a matter of law. The failure to exercise discretion is itself an abuse of discretion. We therefore reverse the summary judgment order and remand to the trial court to allow it to determine, in the exercise of discretion, the amount of restitution it deems necessary under [Washington law].

Reversed.

Legal Reasoning Questions

1. What does the term "jointly and severally liable" mean?

2. What is at least one of the reasons why the reviewing court reversed the summary judgment order that imposed joint and severally liability on StarKist?

3. Why do you think that one of the co-conspirators, Chicken of the Sea International, voluntarily disclosed to federal investigators that it had conspired with competitors to fix prices on packaged-tuna products?

The Reason Behind the Agreement Is Not a Defense. A price-fixing agreement is always a violation of Section 1, even if there are good reasons behind it. ■ **Case in Point 27.2** In a classic price-fixing case, independent oil producers in Texas and Louisiana were caught between falling demand due to the Great Depression of the 1930s and increasing supply from newly discovered oil fields. A group of the major refining companies agreed to buy "distress" gasoline (excess supplies) from the independents so as to dispose of it in an "orderly manner." Although there was no explicit agreement as to price, it was clear that the purpose of the agreement was to limit the supply of gasoline on the market and thereby raise prices.

There may have been good reasons for the agreement. Nonetheless, the United States Supreme Court recognized the potentially adverse effects that such an agreement could have on open and free competition. The Court held that the reasonableness of a price-fixing agreement is

never a defense. Any agreement that restricts output or artificially fixes price is a *per se* violation of Section 1.[7] ■

Price-Fixing Cartels Today. Price-fixing cartels (groups) are still commonplace in today's business world, particularly among global companies. International price-fixing cartels have been alleged in numerous industries, including air freight, auto parts, computer monitors, digital commerce, and drug manufacturing.

■ **Case in Point 27.3** After Amazon.com released the Kindle e-book reader, it began selling e-book downloads at $9.99 (lower than the actual cost) and made up the difference by selling more Kindles. When the iPad entered the e-book scene, Apple and some book publishers agreed to use Apple's "agency" model, which Apple was already

---

7. *United States v. Socony-Vacuum Oil Co.,* 310 U.S. 150, 60 S.Ct. 811, 84 L.Ed. 1129 (1940).

using for games and apps. The agency model allowed the book publishers to set their own prices while Apple kept 30 percent as a commission.

The U.S. government sued Apple and the publishers for price fixing. Because the publishers involved in the arrangement chose prices that were relatively similar, the government argued that price fixing was evident and "would not have occurred without the conspiracy among the defendants." Ultimately, a federal appellate court held that Apple's agreement with publishers to raise e-book prices was a *per se* illegal price-fixing conspiracy. As a result, Apple was ordered to pay $400 million to consumers and $50 million in attorneys' fees.[8] ■

Group Boycotts A **group boycott** is an agreement by two or more sellers to refuse to deal with (that is, to boycott) a particular person or firm. Because they involve concerted action, group boycotts have been held to constitute *per se* violations of Section 1 of the Sherman Act.

To prove a violation of Section 1, the plaintiff must demonstrate that the boycott or joint refusal to deal was undertaken with the intention of eliminating competition or preventing entry into a given market. Although most boycotts are illegal, a few, such as group boycotts against a supplier for political reasons, may be protected under the First Amendment right to freedom of expression.

Horizontal Market Division It is a *per se* violation of Section 1 of the Sherman Act for competitors to divide up territories or customers. ■ **Example 27.4** AXM Electronics Basics, Halprin Servo Supplies, and Aicarus Prime Electronics compete against each other in the states of Kansas, Nebraska, and Oklahoma. The three firms agree that AXM will sell products only in Kansas, Halprin will sell only in Nebraska, and Aicarus will sell only in Oklahoma.

This concerted action violates Section 1 of the Sherman Act. It reduces marketing costs and allows all three firms (assuming there is no other competition) to raise the price of the goods sold in their respective states. The same violation would take place if the three firms divided up their customers by class rather than region. They might agree that AXM would sell only to institutional purchasers (such as governments and schools) in all three states, Halprin only to wholesalers, and Aicarus only to retailers. The result would be the same. ■

Trade Associations Businesses in the same general industry or profession frequently organize trade associations to pursue common interests. A trade association may engage in various joint activities, such as exchanging information, representing the members' business interests before governmental bodies, and conducting advertising campaigns. Trade associations also frequently are involved in setting regulatory standards to govern the industry or profession.

Generally, the rule of reason is applied to these horizontal actions. If a court finds that a trade association practice or agreement that restrains trade is sufficiently beneficial both to the association and to the public, it may deem the restraint reasonable.

In concentrated industries, however, trade associations can be, and have been, used as a means to facilitate anticompetitive actions, such as fixing prices or allocating markets. A **concentrated industry** is one in which either a single firm or a small number of firms control a large percentage of market sales. When trade association agreements have substantially anticompetitive effects, a court will consider them to be violations of Section 1 of the Sherman Act.

Joint Ventures Joint ventures undertaken by competitors are also subject to antitrust laws. If a joint venture does not involve price fixing or market divisions, the agreement will be analyzed under the rule of reason. Whether the joint undertaking violates Section 1 will then depend on the factors stated earlier in this chapter. A court will look at the venture's purpose, the potential benefits relative to the likely harms, and whether there are less restrictive alternatives for achieving the same goals.

27-2c Vertical Restraints

A **vertical restraint** of trade results from an agreement between firms at different levels in the manufacturing and distribution process. In contrast to horizontal relationships, which occur at the same level of operation, vertical relationships encompass the entire chain of production.

The chain of production normally includes the purchase of inventory, basic manufacturing, distribution to wholesalers, and eventual sale of a product at the retail level. For some products, these distinct phases are carried on by different firms. In other instances, a single firm carries out two or more of the separate functional phases. Such enterprises are said to be **vertically integrated firms.**

---

8. *United States v. Apple, Inc.,* 791 F.3d 290 (2d Cir. 2015). Apple had previously agreed to settle the case for these amounts if its appeal was unsuccessful.

Even though firms operating at different functional levels are not in direct competition with one another, they are in competition with other firms. Thus, agreements between firms standing in a vertical relationship may affect competition. Some vertical restraints are *per se* violations of Section 1. Others are judged under the rule of reason.

Territorial or Customer Restrictions In arranging for the distribution of its products, a manufacturing firm often wishes to insulate dealers from direct competition with other dealers selling its products. To do so, the manufacturer may institute territorial restrictions or attempt to prohibit wholesalers or retailers from reselling the products to certain classes of buyers, such as competing retailers.

May Have Legitimate Purpose. A firm may have legitimate reasons for imposing territorial or customer restrictions. For instance, an electronics manufacturer may wish to prevent a dealer from reducing costs and undercutting rivals by offering its products without promotion or customer service. In this situation, the cost-cutting dealer reaps the benefits (sales of the product) paid for by other dealers who undertake promotion and arrange for customer service. By not providing customer service (and relying on a nearby dealer to provide these services), the cost-cutting dealer may also harm the manufacturer's reputation.

Judged Under the Rule of Reason. Territorial and customer restrictions were once considered *per se* violations of Section 1.[9] In 1977, the United States Supreme Court held that they should be judged under the rule of reason. ■ **Case in Point 27.5** The Supreme Court case involved GTE Sylvania, Inc., a manufacturer of television sets. Sylvania limited the number of retail franchises that it granted in any given geographic area. It also required each franchisee to sell only Sylvania products from the location at which it was franchised. Sylvania retained sole discretion to increase the number of retailers in an area.

When Sylvania decided to open a new franchise, it terminated the franchise of Continental T.V., Inc., an existing franchisee in the area that would have been in competition with the new franchise. Continental filed a lawsuit claiming that Sylvania's vertically restrictive franchise system violated Section 1 of the Sherman Act. The Supreme Court found that "vertical restrictions promote interbrand competition by allowing the manufacturer to achieve certain efficiencies in the distribution of his products." Therefore, Sylvania's vertical system, which was not price restrictive, did not constitute a *per se* violation of Section 1 of the Sherman Act.[10] ■

The decision in the *Continental* case marked a definite shift from rigid characterization of territorial and customer restrictions to a more flexible, economic analysis of these vertical restraints under the rule of reason. This rule is still applied in most vertical restraint cases.

Resale Price Maintenance Agreements An agreement between a manufacturer and a distributor or retailer in which the manufacturer specifies what the retail prices of its products must be is known as a **resale price maintenance agreement.** Such agreements were once considered to be *per se* violations of Section 1 of the Sherman Act.

Today, however, both maximum resale price maintenance agreements and minimum resale price maintenance agreements are judged under the rule of reason.[11] The setting of a maximum price that retailers and distributors can charge for a manufacturer's products may sometimes increase competition and benefit consumers.

27–3 Section 2 of the Sherman Act

Section 1 of the Sherman Act proscribes certain concerted, or joint, activities that restrain trade. In contrast, Section 2 condemns "every person who shall monopolize, or attempt to monopolize." Thus, two distinct types of behavior are subject to sanction under Section 2: monopolization and attempts to monopolize.

One tactic that may be involved in either offense is predatory pricing. **Predatory pricing** occurs when one

---

9. See *United States v. Arnold, Schwinn & Co.,* 388 U.S. 365, 87 S.Ct. 1856, 18 L.Ed.2d 1249 (1967).

10. *Continental T.V., Inc. v. GTE Sylvania, Inc.,* 433 U.S. 36, 97 S.Ct. 2549, 53 L.Ed.2d 568 (1977).

11. The United States Supreme Court ruled that maximum resale price agreements should be judged under the rule of reason in *State Oil Co. v. Khan,* 522 U.S. 3, 118 S.Ct. 275, 139 L.Ed.2d 199 (1997). In *Leegin Creative Leather Products, Inc. v. PSKS, Inc.,* 551 U.S. 877, 127 S.Ct. 2705, 168 L.Ed.2d 623 (2007), the Supreme Court found that the rule of reason also applies to minimum resale price agreements.

As for profit maximization, we have no quarrel with the trial court's conclusion that it can be an acceptable business objective and can be advanced by price discrimination. As anyone who has attended an auction can attest, individuals may and often do value goods and services differently. Some are willing and able to pay a higher price than others for the same product. And, as any student of elementary microeconomics knows, sellers of goods and services could (at least theoretically) maximize profits if they could engage in price discrimination by charging higher prices to those consumers willing to pay them, and lower prices to the rest. For example, a seller might offer several versions of its product, with different features, trim, branding, etc., each at a different price, in an effort to increase overall profits. Or a seller might seek to attract bargain hunters by offering temporary price reductions during a sale or other promotion. But the quest for profit maximization can never serve as an excuse for prohibited discrimination among potential customers.

* * * *

As alleged, Tinder's pricing model discriminates against users age thirty and over * * *. While we make no judgment about the true character of Tinder's pricing model, or whether evidence exists to establish a sufficient justification for charging older users more than younger users, we conclude the complaint's allegations are sufficient to state a claim for age discrimination in violation of the [state's civil rights statute].

* * * *

The UCL prohibits, and provides civil remedies for, unfair competition, which includes any unlawful, unfair or fraudulent business act or practice. Its purpose is to protect both consumers and competitors by promoting fair competition in commercial markets for goods and services.

* * * Any law or regulation—federal or state, statutory or common law—can serve as a predicate [ground] for a * * * violation. Because we conclude the complaint adequately states a claim for violation of the [civil rights statute], we also conclude the allegations are sufficient to state a claim under * * * the UCL.

Decision and Remedy   A state intermediate appellate court reversed the judgment of the lower court. "Tinder's alleged discriminatory pricing model violates the public policy embodied in the [civil rights statute, and] the UCL . . . provides an independent basis for relief on the facts alleged."

Critical Thinking

- **Legal Environment**   A California statute provides for the waiver of fees at state university campuses for senior citizens. What distinguishes this differential treatment from the discriminatory practice at issue in the *Candelore* case?

- **Economic**   Instead of personal characteristics such as age, could a business such as Tinder use economic distinctions to broaden its user base and increase profits? Discuss.

27–4b Section 3—Exclusionary Practices

Under Section 3 of the Clayton Act, sellers or lessors cannot condition the sale or lease of goods on the buyer's or lessee's promise not to use or deal in the goods of the seller's competitor. In effect, this section prohibits two types of vertical agreements involving exclusionary practices—exclusive-dealing contracts and tying arrangements.

Exclusive-Dealing Contracts   A contract under which a seller forbids a buyer to purchase products from the seller's competitors is called an **exclusive-dealing contract.** A seller is prohibited from making an exclusive-dealing contract under Section 3 if the effect of the contract is "to substantially lessen competition or tend to create a monopoly."

In the past, courts were more inclined to find that exclusive-dealing contracts substantially lessened competition. ■ **Case in Point 27.11**   In one classic case, Standard Oil Company, the largest gasoline seller in the nation in the late 1940s, made exclusive-dealing contracts with independent stations in seven western states. The contracts involved 16 percent of all retail outlets, whose sales were approximately 7 percent of all retail sales in that market. The United States Supreme Court ruled that the market was substantially concentrated because the seven largest gasoline suppliers all used exclusive-dealing contracts with their independent retailers and together controlled 65 percent of the market.

Looking at market conditions after the arrangements were instituted, the Court found that market shares were extremely stable and that entry into the market was apparently restricted. Thus, the Court held that the Clayton Act had been violated because competition was "foreclosed in a substantial share" of the relevant market.[16] ■

---

16. *Standard Oil Co. of California v. United States,* 337 U.S. 293, 69 S.Ct. 1051, 93 L.Ed. 1371 (1949).

Note that since the Supreme Court's decision in this case, a number of subsequent decisions have called the holding into question.[17]

Today, it is clear that to violate antitrust law, an exclusive-dealing agreement (or a tying arrangement, discussed next) must qualitatively and substantially harm competition. To prevail, a plaintiff must present affirmative evidence that the performance of the agreement will foreclose competition and harm consumers.

Tying Arrangements When a seller conditions the sale of a product (the tying product) on the buyer's agreement to purchase another product (the tied product) produced or distributed by the same seller, a **tying arrangement** results. The legality of a tying arrangement (or tie-in sales agreement) depends on several factors, such as the purpose of the agreement. Courts also focus on the agreement's likely effect on competition in the relevant markets (the market for the tying product and the market for the tied product).

Section 3 of the Clayton Act has been held to apply only to commodities, not to services. Tying arrangements, however, can also be considered agreements that restrain trade in violation of Section 1 of the Sherman Act. Thus, cases involving tying arrangements of services have been brought under Section 1 of the Sherman Act. Although earlier cases condemned tying arrangements as illegal *per se,* courts now evaluate tying agreements under the rule of reason.[18]

■ **Case in Point 27.12** The City of LaGrange, Georgia, was the only provider of water and natural gas services to much of unincorporated Troup County. LaGrange passed an ordinance requiring that all new construction in this area be fitted with natural gas outlets. Failure to do so meant a denial of access to city water. In response, Diverse Power, a local, private electric company, filed suit against LaGrange, alleging that the ordinance constituted an unlawful tying arrangement. That is, Troup County residents who needed water (the tying product) were forced to use natural gas (the tied product) instead of electricity offered by Diverse Power.

LaGrange did not deny that it had created a tying arrangement. Rather, the city argued that, as a government entity, it was exempt from federal antitrust law. Disagreeing, a federal appeals court noted that, by this logic, LaGrange could pass anti-competitive ordinances

covering *any* product—from natural gas service to the "purchase of Goodyear tires"—as long as it was tied to the city's legal water-services monopoly. Not wishing to grant LaGrange "powers so unlimited," the court allowed Diverse Power's lawsuit to proceed.[19] ■

27–4c Section 7—Mergers

Under Section 7 of the Clayton Act, a person or business organization cannot hold stock or assets in more than one business when "the effect . . . may be to substantially lessen competition." Section 7 is the statutory authority for preventing mergers or acquisitions that could result in monopoly power or a substantial lessening of competition in the marketplace. Section 7 applies to both horizontal and vertical mergers, as discussed shortly.

A crucial consideration in most merger cases is **market concentration.** Determining market concentration involves allocating percentage market shares among the various companies in the relevant market. When a small number of companies share a large part of the market, the market is concentrated. ■ **Example 27.13** If the four largest grocery stores in Chicago account for 80 percent of all retail food sales, the market is concentrated in those four firms. If one of these stores absorbs the assets and liabilities of another, so that the other ceases to exist, the result is a merger that further concentrates the market and possibly diminishes competition. ■

Competition is not necessarily diminished solely as a result of market concentration. Courts will consider other factors in determining if a merger violates Section 7. One factor of particular importance is whether the merger will make it more difficult for potential competitors to enter the relevant market.

Horizontal Mergers A merger between firms that compete with each other in the same market is called a **horizontal merger.** If a horizontal merger creates an entity with a significant market share, the merger may be considered illegal because it increases market concentration. The Federal Trade Commission (FTC) and the U.S. Department of Justice (DOJ) have established guidelines for determining which mergers will be challenged.[20]

17. See, for example, *Illinois Tool Works, Inc. v. Independent Ink, Inc.,* 547 U.S. 28, 126 S.Ct. 1281, 164 L.Ed.2d 26 (2006); and *Stop & Shop Supermarket Co. v. Blue Cross & Blue Shield of Rhode Island,* 373 F.3d 57 (1st Cir. 2004).

18. *Illinois Tool Works, Inc. v. Independent Ink, Inc.,* 547 U.S. 28, 126 S.Ct. 1281, 164 L.Ed.2d 26 (2006). This decision was the first time the United States Supreme Court recognized that tying arrangements can have legitimate business justifications.

19. *Diverse Power, Inc. v. City of LaGrange, Georgia,* 934 F.3d 1270 (11th Cir. 2019).

20. These guidelines include a formula for assessing the degree of concentration in the relevant market called the Herfindahl-Hirschman Index (HHI), which is available at www.justice.gov/atr/herfindahl-hirschman-index. The HHI is calculated by squaring the market share of each firm competing in the market and then summing the resulting numbers.

When analyzing the legality of a horizontal merger, the courts consider three additional factors. The first factor is the overall concentration of the relevant market. The second is the relevant market's history of tending toward concentration. The final factor is whether the merger is apparently designed to establish market power or restrict competition.

Vertical Mergers A **vertical merger** occurs when a company at one stage of production acquires a company at a higher or lower stage of production. An example of a vertical merger is a company merging with one of its suppliers or retailers.

Whether a vertical merger will be deemed illegal generally depends on several factors, such as whether the merger creates a single firm that controls an undue percentage share of the relevant market. The courts also analyze the concentration of firms in the market, barriers to entry into the market, and the apparent intent of the merging parties. If a merger does not prevent competitors of either of the merging firms from competing in a segment of the market, the merger will not be condemned as foreclosing competition and thus will be deemed legal.

27–4d Section 8—Interlocking Directorates

Section 8 of the Clayton Act deals with interlocking directorates—that is, the practice whereby individuals serve as directors on the boards of two or more competing companies simultaneously. Specifically, no person may be a director for two or more competing corporations at the same time if either of the corporations has capital, surplus, undivided profits, or competitive sales that exceed a specified threshold amount. The Federal Trade Commission adjusts the threshold amounts each year.

27–5 Enforcement and Exemptions

The federal agencies that enforce the federal antitrust laws are the U.S. Department of Justice (DOJ) and the Federal Trade Commission (FTC), which was established by the Federal Trade Commission Act. Section 5 of that act condemns all forms of anticompetitive behavior that are not covered under other federal antitrust laws.

27–5a Agency Actions

Only the DOJ can prosecute violations of the Sherman Act, which can be either criminal or civil offenses. Violations of the Clayton Act are not crimes, but the act can be enforced by either the DOJ or the FTC through civil proceedings.

The DOJ or the FTC may ask the courts to impose various remedies, including dissolution or **divestiture** (making a company give up one or more of its operations). A meatpacking firm, for instance, might be forced to divest itself of control or ownership of butcher shops.

The FTC has sole authority to enforce violations of Section 5 of the Federal Trade Commission Act. FTC actions are effected through administrative orders, but if a firm violates an FTC order, the FTC can seek court sanctions for the violation.

27–5b Private Actions

A private party who has been injured as a result of a violation of the Sherman Act or the Clayton Act can sue for **treble damages** (three times the actual damages suffered) and attorneys' fees. In some instances, private parties may also seek injunctive relief to prevent antitrust violations. A party wishing to sue under the Sherman Act must prove that:

1. The antitrust violation either caused or was a substantial factor in causing the injury that was suffered.
2. The unlawful actions of the accused party affected business activities of the plaintiff that were protected by the antitrust laws.

Additionally, the United States Supreme Court has held that to pursue antitrust lawsuits, private parties must present some evidence suggesting that an illegal agreement was made.[21]

A private party can bring an action under Section 2 of the Sherman Act based on the attempted enforcement of a fraudulently obtained patent. This is called a *Walker Process* claim.[22] To prevail, the plaintiff must first show that the defendant obtained the patent by fraud on the U.S. Patent and Trademark Office and enforced the patent with knowledge of the fraud. The plaintiff must then establish all the other elements of a Sherman Act monopolization claim—anticompetitive conduct, an intent to monopolize, and a dangerous probability of achieving monopoly power.

27–5c Exemptions from Antitrust Laws

There are many legislative and constitutional limitations on antitrust enforcement. Most of the statutory and judicially created exemptions to the antitrust laws

---

21. *Bell Atlantic Corp. v. Twombly,* 550 U.S. 544, 127 S.Ct. 1955, 167 L.Ed.2d 929 (2007).

22. The name of the claim comes from the title of the case in which the claim originated—*Walker Process Equipment v. Food Machine and Chemical Corp.,* 382 U.S. 172, 86 S.Ct. 347, 15 L.Ed.2d 247 (1965).

Exhibit 27–2 Exemptions to Antitrust Enforcement

Exemption	Source and Scope
Labor	The Clayton Act—Permits unions to organize and bargain without violating antitrust laws and specifies that strikes and other labor activities normally do not violate any federal law.
Agricultural Associations	The Clayton Act and the Capper-Volstead Act—Allow agricultural cooperatives to set prices.
Fisheries	The Fisheries Cooperative Marketing Act—Allows the fishing industry to set prices.
Insurance Companies	The McCarran-Ferguson Act—Exempts the insurance business in states in which the industry is regulated.
Exporters	The Webb-Pomerene Act—Allows U.S. exporters to engage in cooperative activity to compete with similar foreign associations. The Export Trading Company Act—Permits the U.S. Department of Justice to exempt certain exporters.
Professional Baseball	The United States Supreme Court—Has held that professional baseball is exempt because it is not "interstate commerce."[a]
Oil Marketing	The Interstate Oil Compact—Allows states to set quotas on oil to be marketed in interstate commerce.
Defense Activities	The Defense Production Act—Allows the president to approve, and thereby exempt, certain activities to further the military defense of the United States.
Small Businesses' Cooperative Research	The Small Business Administration Act—Allows small firms to undertake cooperative research.
State Actions	The United States Supreme Court—Has held that actions by a state are exempt if the state clearly articulates and actively supervises the policy behind its action.[b]
Regulated Industries	Federal Agencies—Industries (such as airlines) are exempt when a federal administrative agency (such as the Federal Aviation Administration) has primary regulatory authority.
Businesspersons' Joint Efforts to Seek Government Action	The United States Supreme Court—Cooperative efforts by businesspersons to obtain legislative, judicial, or executive action are exempt unless it is clear that an effort is "objectively baseless" and is an attempt to make anticompetitive use of government processes.[c]

a. *Federal Baseball Club of Baltimore, Inc. v. National League of Professional Baseball Clubs,* 259 U.S. 200, 42 S.Ct. 465, 66 L.Ed. 898 (1922). See also *City of San Jose v. Office of the Commissioner of Baseball,* 776 F.3d 686 (9th Cir. 2015).
b. See *Parker v. Brown,* 317 U.S. 341, 63 S.Ct. 307, 87 L.Ed. 315 (1943).
c. *Eastern Railroad Presidents Conference v. Noerr Motor Freight, Inc.,* 365 U.S. 127, 81 S.Ct. 523, 5 L.Ed.2d 464 (1961); and *United Mine Workers of America v. Pennington,* 381 U.S. 657, 89 S.Ct. 1585, 14 L.Ed.2d 626 (1965). These two cases established the exception often referred to as the *Noerr-Pennington doctrine.*

apply only in certain areas (see Exhibit 27–2). One of the most significant exemptions covers joint efforts by businesspersons to obtain legislative, judicial, or executive action. Under this exemption, for example, movie producers can jointly lobby Congress to change the copyright laws without being held liable for attempting to restrain trade. Another exemption covers professional baseball teams.

27–6 U.S. Antitrust Laws in the Global Context

U.S. antitrust laws have a broad application. Not only may persons in foreign nations be subject to their provisions, but the laws may also be applied to protect foreign consumers and competitors from violations committed by U.S. business firms. Consequently, "foreign persons," a term that by definition includes foreign governments, may sue under U.S. antitrust laws in U.S. courts.

27–6a The Extraterritorial Application of U.S. Antitrust Laws

Section 1 of the Sherman Act provides for the extraterritorial effect of the U.S. antitrust laws. Any conspiracy that has a substantial effect on U.S. commerce is within the reach of the Sherman Act. The violation may even occur outside the United States, and foreign governments as well as individuals can be sued for violation of U.S. antitrust laws.

Before U.S. courts will exercise jurisdiction and apply antitrust laws, it must be shown that the alleged violation had a substantial effect on U.S. commerce. U.S. jurisdiction is automatically invoked, however, when a *per se* violation occurs. If a domestic firm, for instance, joins a foreign cartel to control the production, price, or distribution of goods, and this cartel has a substantial effect on U.S. commerce, a *per se* violation may arise. Hence, both the domestic firm and the foreign cartel can be sued for violation of the U.S. antitrust laws.

Likewise, if a foreign firm doing business in the United States enters into a price-fixing or other anticompetitive agreement to control a portion of U.S. markets, a *per se* violation may exist. This may be true even if foreign law directly conflicts with U.S. antitrust law. ■ **Case in Point 27.14** Science Products, Inc., and The Ranis Company, Inc., were U.S. companies that imported large amounts of vitamin C. These companies filed a lawsuit against four Chinese manufacturers that collectively controlled over 60 percent of the world's vitamin C market, alleging a conspiracy to fix prices and manipulate output in the United States in violation of the Sherman Act.

The defendants did not dispute these allegations. Instead, they offered proof that their actions were compelled by the Chinese government, and therefore were beyond the reach of the American legal system. An appeals court agreed and overturned the decision of the district court, which had ruled in favor of the plaintiffs and awarded them approximately $147 million in damages. The United States Supreme Court, in turn, reversed the appeals court, instructing American judges to "carefully consider" a foreign country's laws and views without allowing those factors to fully decide the matter. In this case, the Court found that evidence of the defendants' price fixing was persuasive, regardless of the policy goals of the Chinese government.[23] ■

27–6b The Application of Foreign Antitrust Laws

Large U.S. companies increasingly must be concerned about the application of foreign antitrust laws. The European Union (EU), in particular, has stepped up its enforcement actions against antitrust violators. Microsoft, Apple, and Amazon have each been investigated and/or fined by the EU's Competitive Commission, but the main target of European antitrust efforts has been Google.

After years of investigations, the EU found that Google had (1) abused its dominant position in the search engine market by promoting its own services over those of its rivals, (2) used its ownership of the Android operating system to illegally keep other smartphone manufacturers out of the market, and (3) forced websites that want to use Google's search bar to favor ads run by Google advertising clients. The EU imposed a combined $9.5 billion in antitrust fines against Google because of these infractions.

Along with Facebook, Google has also been the focus of billions of dollars in lawsuits under a set of European privacy rules called the General Data Protection Regulation (GDPR). These rules are designed to limit the amount of personal data that large technology companies can collect without the consent of users. One of the goals of the GDPR is to lessen the ability of Facebook (Meta), Google (Alphabet), and other tech companies to monopolize these data, to which they have greater access because of their large market shares. Once faulted for unfairly victimizing technology companies from the United States, the EU's efforts are now viewed as potential models for American antitrust efforts in this field, discussed earlier in the chapter.

---

23. *Animal Science Products, Inc. v. Hebei Welcome Pharmaceutical Co., Ltd.*, 585 U.S. __, 138 S.Ct. 1865, 201 L.Ed.2d 225 (2018).

Practice and Review: Antitrust Law

The Internet Corporation for Assigned Names and Numbers (ICANN) is a nonprofit entity that organizes internet domain names. It is governed by a board of directors elected by various groups with commercial interests in the internet. One of ICANN's functions is to authorize an entity to serve as a registry for certain "top-level domains" (TLDs). ICANN and VeriSign entered into an agreement that authorized VeriSign to serve as a registry for the ".com" TLD and provide registry services in accordance with ICANN's specifications. VeriSign complained that ICANN was restricting the services that it could make available as a registrar, blocking new services, imposing unnecessary conditions on those services, and setting the prices at which the services were offered. VeriSign claimed that ICANN's control of the registry services for domain names violated Section 1 of the Sherman Act. Using the information presented in the chapter, answer the following questions.

1. Should ICANN's actions be judged under the rule of reason or be deemed *per se* violations of Section 1 of the Sherman Act? Why?
2. Should ICANN's actions be viewed as a horizontal or a vertical restraint of trade? Why?
3. Does it matter that ICANN's directors are chosen by groups with a commercial interest in the internet? Explain.
4. If the dispute is judged under the rule of reason, what might be ICANN's defense for having a standardized set of registry services that must be used?

Debate This . . .   The internet and the rise of e-commerce have rendered our current antitrust concepts and laws obsolete.

Terms and Concepts

antitrust laws 561
attempted monopolization 570
concentrated industry 567
divestiture 575
exclusive-dealing
   contract 573
group boycott 567
horizontal merger 574
horizontal restraint 564

market concentration 574
market power 562
monopolization 569
monopoly 562
monopoly power 562
per se violations 564
predatory pricing 568
price discrimination 571
price-fixing agreement 564

resale price maintenance agreement
   568
restraints of trade 561
rule of reason 564
treble damages 575
tying arrangement 574
vertical merger 575
vertical restraint 567
vertically integrated firms 567

Issue Spotters

1. Under what circumstances would Pop's Market, a small store in a small, isolated town, be considered a monopolist? If Pop's is a monopolist, is it in violation of Section 2 of the Sherman Act? Why or why not? (See *Section 2 of the Sherman Act*.)
2. Maple Corporation conditions the sale of its syrup on the buyer's agreement to buy Maple's pancake mix. What factors would a court consider in deciding whether this arrangement violates the Clayton Act? (See *The Clayton Act*.)

- **Check your answers to the Issue Spotters against the answers provided in Appendix B at the end of this text.**

Business Scenarios and Case Problems

27–1. Group Boycott. Jorge's Appliance Corp. was a new retail seller of appliances in Sunrise City. Because of its innovative sales techniques and financing, Jorge's attracted many customers. As a result, the appliance department of No-Glow Department Store, a large chain store with a great deal of buying power, lost a substantial number of sales. No-Glow told a number of appliance manufacturers from whom it made large-volume purchases that if they continued to sell to Jorge's, No-Glow would stop buying from them. The manufacturers immediately stopped selling appliances to Jorge's. Jorge's filed a suit against No-Glow and the manufacturers, claiming that their actions constituted an antitrust violation. No-Glow and the manufacturers were able to prove that Jorge's was a small retailer with a small market share. They claimed that because the relevant market was not substantially affected, they were not guilty of restraint of trade. Discuss fully whether there was an antitrust violation. (See *Section 1 of the Sherman Act*.)

27–2. Antitrust Laws. Allitron, Inc., and Donovan, Ltd., are interstate competitors selling similar appliances, principally in the states of Illinois, Indiana, Kentucky, and Ohio. Allitron and Donovan agree that Allitron will no longer sell in Indiana and Ohio and that Donovan will no longer sell in Illinois and Kentucky. Have Allitron and Donovan violated any antitrust laws? If so, which law? Explain. (See *Section 1 of the Sherman Act*.)

27–3. Business Case Problem With Sample Answer— Price Discrimination. Dayton Superior Corporation sells its products in interstate commerce to several companies, including Spa Steel Products, Inc. The purchasers often compete directly with each other for customers. For three years, one of Spa Steel's customers purchased Dayton Superior's products from two of Spa Steel's competitors. According to the customer, Spa Steel's prices were always 10 to 15 percent higher for the same products. As a result, Spa Steel lost sales to at least that customer and perhaps others. Spa Steel wants to sue Dayton Superior for price discrimination. Which requirements for such a claim under Section 2 of the Clayton Act does Spa Steel satisfy? What additional facts will it need to prove? [*Dayton Superior Corp. v. Spa Steel Products, Inc.,* 2012 WL 113663 (N.D.N.Y. 2012)] (See *The Clayton Act*.)

- For a sample answer to Problem 27–3, go to Appendix C at the end of this text.

27–4. Section 1 of the Sherman Act. The National Collegiate Athletic Association (NCAA) and the National Federation of State High School Associations (NFHS) set a new standard for non-wood baseball bats. Their goal was to ensure that aluminum and composite bats performed like wood bats in order to enhance player safety and reduce technology-driven home runs and other big hits. Marucci Sports, LLC, makes non-wood bats. Under the new standard, four of Marucci's eleven products were decertified for use in high school and collegiate games. Marucci filed suit against the NCAA and the NFHS under Section 1 of the Sherman Act.

At trial, Marucci's evidence focused on injury to its own business. Did the NCAA and NFHS's standard restrain trade in violation of the Sherman Act? Explain. [*Marucci Sports, LLC v. National Collegiate Athletic Association,* 751 F.3d 368 (5th Cir. 2014)] (See *Section 1 of the Sherman Act*.)

27–5. Mergers. St. Luke's Health Systems, Ltd., operated an emergency clinic in Nampa, Idaho. Saltzer Medical Group, P.A., had thirty-four physicians practicing at its offices in Nampa. Saint Alphonsus Medical Center operated the only hospital in Nampa. St. Luke's acquired Saltzer's assets and entered into a five-year professional service agreement with the Saltzer physicians. This affiliation resulted in a combined share of two-thirds of the Nampa adult primary care provider market. Together, the two entities could impose a significant increase in the prices charged to patients and insurers, and correspondence between the parties indicated that they would. Saint Alphonsus filed a suit against St. Luke's to block the merger. Did this affiliation violate antitrust law? Explain. [*Saint Alphonsus Medical Center–Nampa, Inc. v. St. Luke's Health System, Ltd.,* 778 F.3d 775 (9th Cir. 2015)] (See *The Clayton Act*.)

27–6. Section 1 of the Sherman Act. Manitou North America, Inc., makes and distributes telehandlers (forklifts with extendable telescopic booms) to dealers throughout the United States. Manitou agreed to make McCormick International, LLC, its exclusive dealer in the state of Michigan. Later, Manitou entered into an agreement with Gehi Company, which also makes and sells telehandlers. The companies agreed to allocate territories within Michigan among certain dealers for each manufacturer, limiting the dealers' selection of competitive products to certain models. Under this agreement, McCormick was precluded from buying or selling Gehi telehandlers. What type of trade restraint did the agreement between Manitou and Gehi represent? Is this a violation of antitrust law? If so, who was injured, and how were they injured? Explain. [*Manitou North America, Inc. v. McCormick International, LLC,* 2016 WL 439354 (Mich.Ct.App. 2016)] (See *Section 1 of the Sherman Act*.)

27–7. Tying Arrangements. PRC-Desoto International, Inc., makes and distributes more than 90 percent of the aerospace sealant used in military and commercial aircraft. Packaging Systems, Inc., buys the sealant in wholesale quantities, repackages it into special injection kits, and sells the kits on the retail market to aircraft maintenance companies. PRC-Desoto bought one of the two main manufacturing companies of injection kits and announced a new policy to prohibit the repackaging of its sealant for resale. Packaging Systems was forced to buy both the sealant and the kits from PRC-Desoto. Due to the anti-repackaging constraint, the reseller could no longer meet its buyers' needs for pre-filled injection kits. Does this policy represent an unlawful tying arrangement? Explain. [*Packaging Systems, Inc. v. PRC-Desoto International, Inc.,* 2018 WL 735978 (C.D. CA 2018)] (See *The Clayton Act*.)

27–8. Exclusive Dealing Arrangements. The Commonwealth of Puerto Rico privatized most healthcare facilities. It also created a new government-run healthcare plan, the Puerto Rico Health Insurance Administration (ASES). ASES divided Puerto Rico into eight geographical regions and assigned a single private healthcare insurer to each region. It then entered into contracts with insurers to deliver the required services in the insurers' respective regions. When one region chose a group of urologists to become the exclusive provider of urology services in the area, a group of urologists who were "frozen out" brought an antitrust suit. The plaintiffs claimed that the exclusive-dealing agreement excluded them from specific markets. At trial, the defendants prevailed in their motion to dismiss the case because the plaintiffs lacked standing to bring an antitrust action. On appeal, should the United States Court of Appeals for the First Circuit affirm the district court's decision? Why or why not? [*Vasquez-Ramos v. Triple-S Salud, Inc.,* 55 F.4th 286 (1st Cir. 2022)] (See *The Sherman Antitrust Act.*)

27–9. A Question of Ethics—The IDDR Approach and Section 2 of the Sherman Act. Apple, Inc., controls which apps can run on its iPhone software. Apple's App Store is a website where iPhone users can find, buy, and download the apps. Apple prohibits third-party developers from selling iPhone apps through channels other than the App Store, threatening to cut off sales by any developer who violates this prohibition. Apple also discourages iPhone owners from downloading unapproved apps, threatening to void iPhone warranties if they do. Seven iPhone app buyers filed a complaint in a federal district court against Apple. The plaintiffs alleged that the firm monopolized the market for iPhone apps. [*In re Apple iPhone Antitrust Litigation,* 846 F.3d 313 (9th Cir. 2017)] (See *Section 2 of the Sherman Act.*)

(a) Using the Decision step of the IDDR approach, provide reasons why Apple might attempt to protect iPhone software by setting narrow boundaries on the sales of related apps and aggressively enforcing them.

(b) Explain why Apple's actions in this case might be considered unethical.

Time-Limited Group Assignment

27–10. Antitrust Violations. Residents of the city of Madison, Wisconsin, became concerned about overconsumption of liquor near the campus of the University of Wisconsin (UW). The city initiated a new policy, imposing conditions on area bars to discourage reduced-price "specials" that were believed to encourage high-volume and dangerous drinking. Later, the city began to draft an ordinance to ban all drink specials. Bar owners responded by announcing that they had "voluntarily" agreed to discontinue drink specials on Friday and Saturday nights after 8:00 P.M. The city put its ordinance on hold. Several UW students filed a lawsuit against the local bar owners' association, alleging violations of antitrust law. (See *Section 1 of the Sherman Act.*)

(a) The first group will identify the grounds on which the plaintiffs might base their claim for relief and formulate an argument on behalf of the plaintiffs.

(b) The second group will determine whether the defendants are exempt from the antitrust laws.

(c) The third group will decide how the court should rule in this dispute and provide reasons for the ruling.

Chapter 28

Investor Protection, Insider Trading, and Corporate Governance

After the stock market crash of October 29, 1929, and the ensuing economic depression, Congress enacted legislation to regulate securities markets. The result was the Securities Act of 1933[1] and the Securities Exchange Act of 1934.[2] Both acts were designed to provide investors with more information to help them make buying and selling decisions about securities and to prohibit deceptive, unfair, and manipulative practices.

Today, the sale and transfer of securities are heavily regulated by federal and state statutes and by government agencies. The Securities and Exchange Commission (SEC) is the main independent regulatory agency that administers the 1933 and 1934 securities acts. The SEC also plays a key role in interpreting the provisions of these acts (and their amendments) and in creating regulations governing the purchase and sale of securities. The agency continually updates regulations in response to legislation, such as the Dodd-Frank Wall Street Reform and Consumer Protection Act[3] and the Economic Growth, Regulatory Relief, and Consumer Protection Act.[4]

1. 15 U.S.C. Sections 77a-77aa.
2. 15 U.S.C. Sections 78a-78mm.
3. Pub. L. No. 111-203, 124 Stat. 1376 (2010), codified at 12 U.S.C. Sections 5301 *et seq.*
4. Pub. L. No. 115-174, 132 Stat. 1296 (2018).

28–1 The Securities Act of 1933

The Securities Act of 1933 governs initial sales of stock by businesses. The act was designed to prohibit various forms of fraud and to stabilize the securities industry by requiring that investors receive financial and other significant information concerning the securities being offered for public sale. Basically, the purpose of this act is to require disclosure. The 1933 act provides that all securities transactions must be registered with the SEC unless they are specifically exempt from the registration requirements.

28–1a What Is a Security?

Section 2(1) of the Securities Act contains a broad definition of **securities**, which generally include the following:[5]

1. Instruments and interests commonly known as securities, such as preferred and common stocks, bonds, debentures, and stock warrants.

2. Interests commonly known as securities, such as stock options, puts, and calls, that involve the right to purchase a security or a group of securities on a national security exchange.

3. Notes, instruments, or other evidence of indebtedness, including certificates of interest in a profit-sharing agreement and certificates of deposit.

4. Any fractional undivided interest in oil, gas, or other mineral rights.

5. Investment contracts, which include interests in limited partnerships and other investment schemes.

The Howey Test In interpreting the act, the United States Supreme Court has held that an **investment contract** is any transaction in which a person (1) invests (2) in a common enterprise (3) reasonably expecting profits (4) derived primarily or substantially from others' managerial or entrepreneurial efforts. Known as the *Howey test*, this definition continues to guide the determination of what types of contracts can be considered securities.[6]

5. 15 U.S.C. Section 77b(1). Amendments in 1982 added stock options.

6. *Securities and Exchange Commission v. W. J. Howey Co.,* 328 U.S. 293, 66 S.Ct. 1100, 90 L.Ed. 1244 (1946).

■ **Case in Point 28.1** JN Properties Solutions, owned by Koye Jemisin, is in the business of buying properties, renovating them, and then selling or renting out the properties. Brandi Hooker is a licensed real estate agent. Hooker introduced Jemisin to a group of investors, and Jemisin negotiated several projects with this group and with Hooker over a period of several years. Jemisin's role was to provide financing, and the others were to carry out the renovation and sale of the properties. Some of the projects involved so-called joint venture agreements. When several of the property deals yielded much lower returns than anticipated, Jemisin, through JN Properties, filed a multi-count complaint against Hooker and others.

At trial, Hooker and the other defendants were accused, among other things, of violating the Maryland Securities Act (MSA). Hooker argued that JN's real estate investments did not constitute a security under the MSA. JN Properties prevailed at trial. On appeal, the Court of Special Appeals of Maryland concurred with the trial court's ruling. The MSA regulates the offer and sale of securities in Maryland, as well as the individuals who advise about and effect such transactions. The *Howey* test applied in this case. The various agreements among the parties ultimately were declared investment contracts (even if they were labeled joint venture agreements) and thus were subject to securities laws.[7] ■

Are Cryptocurrencies Subject to the Howey Test?

Some contracts involve a future payment in cryptocurrency. Clearly, being paid in cryptocurrency involves some uncertainty about how much the actual payment, when made, will be worth in dollars. If there is a contract dispute about nonpayment in cryptocurrency, how does the court estimate what the damages are? In the case of *Diamond Fortress Technologies, Inc. v. EverID, Inc.,* the answer involved determining whether the cryptocurrency was an asset or a security. The Superior Court of Delaware, based in part on the Howey test, ruled that the cryptocurrency involved in the case represented a security rather than an asset.[8]

The court did provide some discussion of the future value of cryptocurrencies. If a cryptocurrency grows and reaches widespread adoption, it may transition from a security to an asset. That will occur when a cryptocurrency is accepted by some vendors and serves as a unit of exchange with widely adopted blockchain platforms. This analysis would argue that the popular cryptocurrencies Bitcoin and Ethereum may be assets rather than securities. For the moment, the ruling in this case acknowledges that cryptocurrencies are novel and evolving, and that there are no categorical classifications of them.

In the following case, the court applied the Howey test to determine whether an agreement to buy certain internet advertising services met the definition of an investment contract and was, therefore, a security.

---

7. *Hooker v. JN Property Solutions, LLC,* 2021 WL 4306899 (Ct. Special Appeals MD 2021).

8. 274 A.3d 287 (Del. Sup. Ct. 2022).

Case 28.1

Securities and Exchange Commission v. Scoville

United States Court of Appeals, Tenth Circuit, 913 F.3d 1204 (2019).

Background and Facts Internet traffic exchange businesses sell visits to a customer's website to make it look more popular than it really is and enable it to rank higher in search results displayed by Google and other search engines. Charles Scoville operated an exchange through his company Traffic Monsoon, LLC, selling Adpacks—bundled internet ad services that supposedly allowed a buyer to share in Traffic Monsoon's revenue. Buyers were offered the possibility of high rates of return on the amounts they paid for the Adpacks. The company represented that the revenue came from the sales of its advertising services, but in fact the returns on the purchases of Adpacks were paid with money from later Adpack sales.

The Securities and Exchange Commission filed an action in a federal district court against Scoville, alleging that he had violated federal securities laws by operating Traffic Monsoon as a fraudulent scheme in which the business paid returns to its investors financed not by the success of the business but with funds acquired from later investors. Before the trial, the court enjoined the defendant from continuing to operate his business. Scoville appealed, arguing in part that Adpacks were not securities.

In the Language of the Court

EBEL, Circuit Judge.

* * * *

* * * Congress enacted the Securities Acts in response to serious abuses in a largely unregulated securities market, and for the purpose of regulating investments, in whatever form they are made and by whatever name they are called. Congress painted with a broad brush in defining a security in recognition of the virtually limitless scope of human ingenuity, especially in the creation of countless and variable schemes devised by those who seek the use of the money of others on the promise of profits.

The [Securities] Act [of 1933] defines security to include an investment contract * * *. In *Howey* [the United States Supreme Court] defined [an investment contract] as a contract, transaction or scheme whereby a person invests his money in a common enterprise and is led to expect profits solely from the efforts of the promoter or a third party.

To distinguish an investment contract from other commercial dealings, the *Howey* test has subsequently been broken down into three requirements: (1) an investment, (2) in a common enterprise, (3) with a reasonable expectation of profits to be derived from the entrepreneurial or managerial efforts of others.

* * * *

An Adpack is an investment. * * * Traffic Monsoon was offering its Adpack purchasers something more than just advertising services. Adpacks also offered the purchaser an opportunity to share in Traffic Monsoon's revenue.

* * * *

An Adpack is an investment in a common enterprise. * * * The revenue in which Adpack purchasers could share * * * was generated from a common enterprise, Traffic Monsoon's sale of Internet advertising services.

An Adpack provides members with a reasonable expectation of profit derived from the entrepreneurial or management efforts of others.

* * * *

* * * Adpack purchasers expected Traffic Monsoon's success to turn significantly on the company's efforts to sell its advertising services.

* * * *

* * * The district court did not err in concluding that Adpacks meet *Howey*'s three-part test and, therefore, qualify as investment contracts and, thus, as securities subject to regulation under the federal securities laws.

Decision and Remedy The U.S. Court of Appeals for the Tenth Circuit affirmed the district court's decision to enjoin Scoville from continuing to operate his business.

Critical Thinking

- **Legal Environment** Scoville argued that Adpacks were not investment contracts because there was no guarantee that buyers would receive a return on their investment. Should the court have ruled in Scoville's favor based on this argument? Explain.

- **Economic** The return on an investment in an Adpack was not based on any underlying business activity. Instead, money from new investors was used to pay earlier investors. Is this a legitimate business model? Discuss.

Many Types of Securities For our purposes, it is convenient to think of securities in their most common form—stocks and bonds issued by corporations. Bear in mind, though, that securities can take many forms, including interests in whiskey, cosmetics, worms, beavers, boats, vacuum cleaners, muskrats, and cemetery lots. Almost any stake in the ownership or debt of a company can be considered a security. Investment contracts in condominiums, franchises, limited partnerships in real estate, and oil or gas or other mineral rights have qualified as securities.

28–1b Registration Statement

Section 5 of the Securities Act broadly provides that if a security does not qualify for an exemption, that security must be registered before it is offered to the public. Issuing corporations must file a registration statement with the SEC and must provide all investors with a prospectus.

A **prospectus** is a disclosure document that describes the security being sold, the financial operations of the issuing corporation, and the investment or risk attaching to the security. The prospectus also serves as a selling tool for the issuing corporation. The SEC allows an issuer to deliver its prospectus to investors electronically via the internet.[9]

In principle, the registration statement and the prospectus supply sufficient information to enable unsophisticated investors to evaluate the financial risk involved. The following case involved a suit alleging violations of the Securities Act of 1933 based on material misstatements or omissions in connection with investment offerings.

9. Basically, an electronic prospectus must meet the same requirements as a printed prospectus. 17 C.F.R. Section 232.304.

Case Analysis 28.2

Pino v. Cardone Capital, LLC

United States Court of Appeals, Ninth Circuit, 55 F.4th 1253, 2022 *Daily Journal* D.A.R. 12,778 (2022).

In the Language of the Court
LYNN, D.J.

Memorandum
* * * *

Pino filed suit alleging violations of the Securities Act of 1933, based on material misstatements or omissions in connection with real estate investment offerings. Specifically, Pino brought claims under [Section] 12(a)(2) of the Act against all Defendants, and a claim pursuant to [Section] 15 of the Act against Cardone and Cardone Capital. In the First Amended Complaint ("FAC"), Pino alleged that when soliciting investments in Funds V and VI, Defendants made untrue statements of material fact or concealed or failed to disclose material facts in Instagram posts and a YouTube video, and in the Fund V and VI offering circulars, during the period between February 5, 2019, and December 24, 2019, and that none of Defendants' "test the waters" communications—*i.e.*, statements not contained within the offering circulars—contained sufficient cautionary language.
* * * *

Discussion

Section 12(a)(2) of the Securities Act of 1933 ("Securities Act") imposes liability on "any person who . . . offers or sells a security . . . by means of a prospectus or oral communication, which includes an untrue statement of a material fact or omits to state a material

fact . . . to the person purchasing such security from him." To state a claim under Section 12(a)(2), a plaintiff must allege that (1) the defendant is a statutory seller; (2) the sale was effected by means of a prospectus or oral communication; and (3) the communication contains an "'untrue statement of a material fact or omits to state a material fact necessary in order to make the statements . . . not misleading.'"

The parties briefed the case with respect to our decision in [another case] which provides that a projection or statement of belief may be actionable under the federal securities laws if (1) the speaker does not actually believe the statement, (2) there is no reasonable basis for the statement, or (3) the speaker is aware of undisclosed facts tending seriously to undermine the statement's accuracy. * * *

The district court erred in holding that the FAC [first amended complaint] did not state an actionable claim based on alleged misstatements relating to [the] internal rate of return ("IRR") and distributions, which are not protected by the bespeaks [implied] caution doctrine [described later]. The FAC includes allegations that Cardone told investors they would realize a 15% IRR, while omitting that the SEC had previously requested that Defendants remove from the proposed Fund V offering circular references to their "strategy to pay a

monthly distribution to investors that will result in a return of approximately 15% annualized return on investment," because the Fund had commenced only limited operations, had not paid any distributions to date, and did not appear to have a basis for such a projected return.

The statements recited in the FAC relating to IRR and distributions are actionable. Pino plausibly alleges that by omitting mention of the SEC's communication to Cardone Capital that there was no basis to represent that investors would receive monthly distributions resulting in a 15% annualized return on their investments, the alleged misstatements relating to IRR and distributions were misleading to a reasonable person reading the statements fairly and in context. ("[I]f the issuer made the statement . . . with knowledge that the Federal Government was taking the opposite view, the investor again has cause to complain: He expects not just that the issuer believes the opinion . . . but that it fairly aligns with the information in the issuer's possession at the time.") Such facts likewise "call into question [Cardone's] basis for offering" his projections of a 15% IRR and promises of large monthly distributions or that investors would double or triple their investments.

The district court failed to interpret the FAC's allegations regarding debt obligations in the light most favorable to Pino, by disregarding defendants' statements about "who is responsible for the debt? The answer is, Grant [Cardone]!" and statements that the properties acquired by the Funds were assets, rather than liabilities. The FAC plausibly alleged that these statements were "untrue statements of fact," because they suggest investors are not responsible for the "significant monthly debt service payments."

* * * *

* * * [E]ven if we assume, without deciding, that cautionary language need not necessarily appear in the same document as the alleged misstatement, the warnings in the offering circulars do not insulate misstatements made in Instagram posts and YouTube videos under the bespeaks caution doctrine. "[T]he bespeaks caution doctrine applies only to precise cautionary

language which directly addresses itself to future projections, estimates or forecasts in a prospectus." Here, the offering circulars contain only generalized cautionary language that is too broad to immunize the otherwise actionable alleged misstatements about IRR and distributions, rendering the bespeaks caution doctrine inapplicable. In addition, the offering circulars for Funds V and VI were finalized and publicly filed in December 2018 and September 2019, respectively, while the alleged misstatements in the Instagram posts and YouTube video were primarily made later, from February through December 2019, and thus many of the misstatements are too attenuated from the release of the offering circulars to be insulated by the warnings contained therein. [The bespeaks caution doctrine holds that forward-looking statements are not misleading if they

are accompanied by adequate risk disclosure to warn readers about specific risks that may materially impact the forecast.]

* * * *

For the foregoing reasons, we reverse the district court's dismissal of Pino's [Sections] 12(a)(2) and 15 claims as to Defendants' alleged statements regarding a 15% IRR and distributions, as well as the Funds' debt obligations. Because Pino did not plead these claims under the standard in [another case], the district court shall grant Pino leave to amend the FAC to replead these claims consistent with this memorandum disposition and opinion. We affirm the district court on Pino's Securities Act claims on the remainder of the alleged misstatements.

AFFIRMED IN PART, REVERSED IN PART, AND REMANDED.

Legal Reasoning Questions

1. What did the defendants' "test the waters" communications involve?

2. When may statements made about projections be actionable under federal security laws?

3. What if the defendants had projected a 2 percent internal rate of return (IRR)? Would this lawsuit have proceeded?

Contents of the Registration Statement The registration statement must be written in plain English and fully describe the following:

1. The securities being offered for sale, including their relationship to the registrant's other securities.
2. The corporation's properties and business (including a financial statement certified by an independent public accounting firm).
3. The management of the corporation, including managerial compensation, stock options, pensions, and other benefits. Any interests of directors or officers in any material transactions with the corporation must also be disclosed.
4. How the corporation intends to use the proceeds of the sale.
5. Any pending lawsuits or special risk factors.

All companies, both domestic and foreign, must file their registration statements electronically so that they can be posted on the SEC's online EDGAR (Electronic Data Gathering, Analysis, and Retrieval) database. Investors can then access the statements via the internet. The EDGAR database includes material on initial public offerings (IPOs), proxy statements (concerning voting authority), annual reports, registration statements, and other documents that have been filed with the SEC.

Registration Process The registration statement does not become effective until it has been reviewed and approved by the SEC (unless it is filed by a well-known seasoned issuer, as discussed shortly). The 1933 act restricts the types of activities that an issuer can engage in at each stage of the registration process. If an issuer violates these restrictions, investors can rescind their contracts to purchase the securities.

Prefiling Period. During the prefiling period (before the registration statement is filed), the issuer normally cannot sell or offer to sell the securities. Once the registration statement has been filed, a waiting period begins while the SEC reviews the registration statement for completeness.[10]

Waiting Period. During the waiting period, the securities can be offered for sale but cannot be sold by the issuing corporation. Only certain types of offers are allowed at this time. All issuers can distribute a preliminary prospectus,[11] which contains most of the information that will be included in the final prospectus but often does not include a price.

Most issuers can distribute a free-writing prospectus during this period (although some inexperienced issuers will need to file a preliminary prospectus first).[12] A **free-writing prospectus** is any type of written, electronic, or graphic offer that describes the issuer or its securities and includes a legend indicating that the investor may obtain the prospectus at the SEC's website.

Posteffective Period. Once the SEC has reviewed and approved the registration statement and the waiting period is over, the registration is effective, and the posteffective period begins. The issuer can now offer and sell the securities without restrictions.

If the company issued a preliminary or free-writing prospectus to investors, it must provide those investors with a final prospectus either before or at the time they purchase the securities. The issuer can make the final prospectus available to investors to download from a website if it notifies them of the appropriate internet address.

28–1c Well-Known Seasoned Issuers

A well-known seasoned issuer (WKSI) is a firm that has issued at least $1 billion in securities in the last three years or has outstanding stock valued at $700 million or more in the hands of the public. WKSIs have greater flexibility than other issuers. They can file registration

---

10. The waiting period must last at least twenty days but always extends much longer because the SEC inevitably requires numerous changes and additions to the registration statement.
11. A preliminary prospectus may also be called a *red herring prospectus*. The name comes from the legend printed in red across the prospectus stating that the registration has been filed but has not become effective.
12. See SEC Rules 164 and 433.

statements the day they announce a new offering and are not required to wait for SEC review and approval. They can also use a free-writing prospectus at any time, even during the prefiling period.

28–1d Exempt Securities

Certain types of securities are exempt from the registration requirements of the Securities Act because they are low-risk investments or are regulated by other statutes. Exempt securities maintain their exempt status forever and can also be resold without being registered. Exempt securities include the following:

- Government-issued securities.
- Bank and financial institution securities.
- Short-term notes and drafts (negotiable instruments that have a maturity date that does not extend beyond nine months).
- Securities of nonprofit, educational, and charitable organizations.
- Securities issued by common carriers (railroads and trucking companies).
- Insurance policies, endowments, and annuity contracts.
- Securities issued in a corporate reorganization in which one security is exchanged for another or in a bankruptcy proceeding.
- Securities issued in stock dividends and stock splits.

28–1e Exempt Transactions

The Securities Act also exempts certain transactions from registration requirements (see Exhibit 28–1 for a summary of these exemptions). The transaction exemptions are very broad and can enable an issuer to avoid the high cost and complicated procedures associated with registration. For instance, private (nonpublic) offerings that involve a small number of investors generally are exempt. Securities offered and sold only to residents of the state in which the issuing firm is incorporated and does business are also exempt. In addition, crowdfunding is allowed without SEC registration, as discussed in this chapter's Digital Update feature. Note, however, that even when a transaction is exempt from registration requirements, the offering is still subject to the antifraud provisions of the 1933 act (and the 1934 act).

Regulation A Offerings An exemption from registration is available for an issuer's security offerings that

Exhibit 28–1   Exempt Transactions Under the 1933 Securities Act

Exempt Transactions

Regulation A

Securities issued by an issuer that has offered less than $50 million in securities during any twelve-month period if the issuer meets specific requirements:

• Tier 1—For offerings of up to $20 million in a twelve-month period. (Unlimited number of investors, both accredited and unaccredited.)

• Tier 2—For offerings of up to $50 million with additional review requirements in a twelve-month period. (Unlimited number of investors, but unaccredited investors may not invest more than 10 percent of their annual income or net worth.)

Regulation D

• **Rule 504:** Noninvestment company offerings up to $5 million in any twelve-month period.

• **Rule 506:** Private noninvestment company offerings in unlimited amounts that are not generally advertised or solicited. Unlimited number of accredited investors and thirty-five unaccredited investors.

• **Rule 147:** Offerings restricted to residents of the state in which the issuing company is organized and doing business.

Unregistered Restricted Securities

Restricted securities must be registered before a resale *unless* they qualify for a safe harbor under Rule 144 or 144A.

do not exceed a specified amount during any twelve-month period.[13] Under Regulation A,[14] the issuer must file with the

---

13. 15 U.S.C. Section 77c(b).
14. 17 C.F.R. Sections 230.251–230.263.

SEC a notice of the issue and an offering circular, which must also be provided to investors before the sale. Regulation A, as amended by rule changes commonly known as Regulation A+, provides a much less expensive process than full registration. In essence, a Regulation A offering functions like a lower-cost initial public offering (IPO). Companies can also advertise their newly issued stock to the general public. (This is not possible with transactions exempted under Regulation D, discussed shortly.)

There are two types of public offerings under Regulation A as amended:

• Tier 1, for securities offerings of up to $20 million in a twelve-month period.
• Tier 2, for securities offerings of up to $75 million in a twelve-month period.

An issuer of $20 million or less of securities can elect to proceed under either Tier 1 or Tier 2. Both tiers are subject to certain basic requirements, and Tier 2 offerings are subject to additional requirements. Purchasers under Tier 2 who are not accredited investors are limited in the amount they can invest in Tier 2 offerings. (An **accredited investor** is a sophisticated investor, such as a bank, an insurance company, or a person whose income or net worth exceeds a certain amount.)

Amendments to Regulation A (often called Reg A+) changed who can invest in such offerings. Now, anyone in the world can invest in Reg A+ offerings, not just accredited investors, although some restrictions apply to certain offerings. Companies can advertise their newly issued stock to the general public.

■ **Example 28.2** Myomo, Inc., is a company based in Massachusetts that makes robotic medical devices for people with upper-body paralysis. The company relied on venture capital funding for a number of years but decided to take advantage of the amended Regulation A when it became available. Seeking to raise $15 million, Myomo became the first company to issue an initial public offering under Regulation A+. ■

Small Offerings—Regulation D

The SEC's Regulation D contains several exemptions from registration requirements (Rules 504 and 506) for offers that either involve a small dollar amount or are made in a limited manner.

Rule 504. Rule 504 is an exemption formerly used by many small businesses. It provides that noninvestment company offerings up to $5 million in any twelve-month

Digital Update

Investment Crowdfunding—Regulations and Restrictions

Today, small entrepreneurs can gain access to public funds through crowdfunding without filing a registration statement with the Securities and Exchange Commission (SEC). Generally, *crowdfunding* refers to raising small sums of money from a large number of individuals via the internet. Crowdfunding as a way for businesses to raise equity capital was made possible by the Jumpstart Our Business Startups Act, or JOBS Act—specifically, by Title III, also known as the "Crowdfund Act."[a]

Restrictions on Those Who Invest

The Crowdfund Act imposes certain restrictions on investors. The aggregate amount sold to any investor cannot exceed the greater of $2,200 or 5 percent of the investor's annual income or net worth if that net worth is less than $107,000. For investors with higher incomes or net worth, the limit is 10 percent.

Other Restrictions

Companies seeking investment funds through crowdfunding cannot offer shares directly to investors. They must go through an online intermediary fundraising platform registered with the SEC. Some companies that provide such platforms take an active role in the crowdfunding process, drafting paperwork

and soliciting investors. Others take a more hands-off approach. An increasing number of approved crowdfunding portals are available. They usually impose a fee of 5 to 10 percent of the funds raised.

Of course, a potential start-up entrepreneur does not simply create a video and ask people to send money via the internet. Paperwork must be filed prior to the start of a crowdfunding campaign, and detailed financial statements must be available for potential investors. At the beginning of the COVID-19 outbreak, the SEC made it easier for small businesses that might not ordinarily be eligible for crowdfunding to take advantage of these procedures for much-needed infusions of capital.

State Regulation of Crowdfunding

In general, if a company's offering qualifies for a federal exemption, that offering need not be registered or qualified by state securities regulators. The states still have the authority to investigate and initiate enforcement actions for fraud.

Critical Thinking What alternatives are there to crowdfunding for a start-up business?

a. 17 C.F.R. Parts 200, 227, 232, 239, 240, and 249 (2016).

period are exempt.[15] Noninvestment companies are firms that are not engaged primarily in the business of investing or trading in securities. (In contrast, an **investment company** is a firm that buys a large portfolio of securities and professionally manages it on behalf of many smaller shareholders/owners. A **mutual fund** is a well-known type of investment company.)

■ **Example 28.3** Zeta Enterprises is a limited partnership that develops commercial property. Zeta intends to offer $600,000 of its limited partnership interests for sale between June 1 and next May 31. The buyers will become limited partners in Zeta. Because an interest in a limited partnership meets the definition of a security (discussed earlier), this offering would be subject to the registration and prospectus requirements of the Securities Act of 1933.

Under Rule 504, however, the sales of Zeta's interests are exempt from these requirements because Zeta is a

noninvestment company making an offering of less than $5 million in a given twelve-month period. Therefore, Zeta can sell its interests without filing a registration statement with the SEC or issuing a prospectus to any investor. ■

Rule 506—Private Placement Exemption. Rule 506 exempts private, noninvestment company offerings that are not generally solicited or advertised. This exemption is often referred to as the *private placement exemption* because it exempts "transactions not involving any public offering."[16] There are no limits on the amounts offered. In addition, there can be an unlimited number of accredited investors and up to thirty-five unaccredited investors. To qualify for the exemption, the issuer must believe that each unaccredited investor has sufficient knowledge or experience in financial matters to be capable of evaluating the investment's merits and risks.[17]

The private placement exemption has been an important exemption for firms that want to raise funds through the

15. 17 C.F.R. Section 230.504. Small businesses in California may also be exempt under 17 C.F.R. Section 230.1001 and Cal. Corporations Code Section 25102(n).1001. California's rule permits limited offerings of up to $5 million per transaction, if they satisfy certain conditions.

16. 15 U.S.C. Section 77d(2).
17. 17 C.F.R. Section 230.506.

sale of securities without registering them. ■ **Example 28.4** Citco Corporation needs to raise capital to expand its operations. Citco decides to make a private $10 million offering of its common stock directly to two hundred accredited investors and a group of thirty highly sophisticated, but unaccredited, investors. Citco provides all of these investors with a prospectus and material information about the firm, including its most recent financial statements.

As long as Citco notifies the SEC of the sale, this offering will likely qualify as an exempt transaction under Rule 506. The offering is nonpublic and generally not advertised. There are fewer than thirty-five unaccredited investors, and each of them possesses sufficient knowledge and experience to evaluate the risks involved. The issuer has provided all purchasers with the material information. Thus, Citco likely will not be required to comply with the registration requirements of the Securities Act of 1933. ■

Intrastate Offerings—Rule 147

Also exempt are intrastate transactions involving purely local offerings.[18] This exemption applies to most offerings that are restricted to residents of the state in which the issuing company is organized and doing business. For nine months after the last sale, virtually no resales may be made to nonresidents, and precautions must be taken against this possibility. These offerings remain subject to applicable laws in the state of issue.

Resales and Safe Harbor Rules

Most securities can be resold without registration. The Securities Act provides exemptions for resales by most persons other than issuers or underwriters. The average investor who sells shares of stock need not file a registration statement with the SEC.

Resales of restricted securities acquired under Rule 506, however, trigger the registration requirements unless the party selling them complies with Rule 144 or Rule 144A. These rules are sometimes referred to as *safe harbors*.

Rule 144. Rule 144 exempts restricted securities from registration on resale if all of the following conditions are met.

1. There is adequate current public information about the issuer. ("Adequate current public information" refers to the reports that certain companies are required to file under the 1934 Securities Exchange Act.)
2. The person selling the securities has owned them for at least six months if the issuer is subject to the reporting requirements of the 1934 act. If the issuer is not subject to the 1934 act's reporting requirements, the seller must have owned the securities for at least one year.

3. The securities are sold in certain limited amounts in unsolicited brokers' transactions.
4. The SEC is notified of the resale.[19]

Rule 144A. Securities that at the time of issue were not of the same class as securities listed on a national securities exchange or quoted in a U.S. automated interdealer quotation system may be resold under Rule 144A.[20] They may be sold only to a qualified institutional buyer (an institution, such as an insurance company or a bank, that owns and invests at least $100 million in securities). The seller must take reasonable steps to ensure that the buyer knows that the seller is relying on the exemption under Rule 144A.

Direct Listing We have already seen how Regulation A can make it possible for smaller companies to issue securities while avoiding the expense of an IPO. Another option is a direct listing, sometimes called a **direct public offering (DPO)**. A DPO allows a company's shares to be publicly traded without going through a formal IPO. A company engaging in a DPO does not hire an investment bank to underwrite or promote the sale of shares. Rather, the company sells only existing shares.

The benefit of a DPO is that the process reduces the regulatory requirements and saves funds for the company, which does not have to hire investment bankers. The DPO lists the existing private shares directly on an exchange, allowing the market rather than the underwriter to set the price. Note, though, that the company engaging in a DPO still must meet the requirements of both the intended exchange and the SEC.

Ben and Jerry's Ice Cream Company was the first company to use the direct listing method. In 1984, it successfully raised $750,000 through a DPO. Spotify, a music streaming company, went public by direct listing on the New York Stock Exchange in 2018. At the time, it was valued at over $20 billion.

Special Purpose Acquisition Companies (SPACs) In recent years, so-called blank-check investment companies have become popular. These companies—formally known as **special purpose acquisition companies (SPACs)**—are publicly traded companies created for the single purpose of acquiring or merging with an existing company. This means the acquired or merged company need not go through the traditional IPO process and the expense and regulations it involves.

---

18. 15 U.S.C. Section 77c(a)(11); 17 C.F.R. Section 230.147.

19. 17 C.F.R. Section 230.144.
20. 17 C.F.R. Section 230.144A.

SPACs have raised billions of dollars. Some of their most famous public spokespersons have been Shaquille O'Neal (former basketball superstar), Serena Williams (tennis player), and Gary Cohn (former banker at the investment banking firm Goldman Sachs). Early investors appear to have earned generous returns on their investments in SPACs. Later investors were not so fortunate. Investors who were not successful have occasionally filed lawsuits against the directors of the SPACs, claiming that those directors did not undertake any meaningful attempt to identify favorable acquisition or merger targets.[21]

28–1f Violations of the 1933 Act

It is a violation of the Securities Act to intentionally defraud investors by misrepresenting or omitting facts in a registration statement or prospectus. Liability may also be imposed on those who are negligent with respect to the preparation of these publications. Selling securities before the effective date of the registration statement or under an exemption for which the securities do not qualify also results in liability.

Remedies Criminal violations of the 1933 act are prosecuted by the U.S. Department of Justice. Violators may be fined up to $10,000, imprisoned for up to five years, or both. The SEC is authorized to impose civil sanctions against those who willfully violate the act. It can request an injunction to prevent further sales of the securities involved or ask a court to grant other relief, such as ordering a violator to refund profits. Private parties who purchase securities and suffer harm as a result of false or omitted statements or other violations may bring a suit in a federal court to recover their losses and additional damages.

Defenses There are three basic defenses to charges of violations under the 1933 act. A defendant can avoid liability by proving any of the following.

1. The statement or omission was not material.
2. The plaintiff knew about the misrepresentation at the time the stock was purchased.
3. The defendant exercised due diligence in preparing or reviewing the registration and reasonably believed at the time that the statements were true. This important defense is available to an underwriter or subsequent seller but not to the issuer.

In most instances, a defendant cannot escape liability for another party's false or misleading statements if the defendant knowingly passes those statements along to an investor or fails to correct them when given the chance. ■ **Case in Point 28.5**   Dennis Malouf worked for UASNM, Inc., an investment advice firm. Malouf steered his clients to purchase securities from a branch office of the financial service company Raymond James. The owner of this Raymond James branch earned commissions from these trades, making it easier for him to pay a large sum of money he owed Malouf. UASNM compliance procedures required Malouf to disclose this conflict of interest, but he failed to do so.

The SEC found that Malouf had engaged in a deceptive scheme under the 1933 act and banned him from the securities industry for life. Malouf countered that it was not his duty to warn UASNM's clients of the conflict of interest. Rather, that responsibility lay with UASNM's compliance officer. An appeals court rejected this attempt to shift the blame, holding that—clearly—Malouf knew he was required to report his conflict of interest to the compliance officer and failed to do so.[22] ■

28–2 The Securities Exchange Act of 1934

The 1934 Securities Exchange Act provides for the regulation and registration of securities exchanges, brokers, dealers, and national securities associations, such as the National Association of Securities Dealers (NASD). Unlike the 1933 act, which is a one-time disclosure law, the 1934 act provides for continuous periodic disclosures by publicly held corporations to enable the SEC to regulate subsequent trading.

The Securities Exchange Act applies to companies that have assets in excess of $10 million and five hundred or more shareholders. These corporations are referred to as Section 12 companies because they are required to register their securities under Section 12 of the 1934 act. Section 12 companies must file reports with the SEC annually and quarterly, and sometimes even monthly if specified events occur (such as a merger).

The act also authorizes the SEC to engage in market surveillance to deter undesirable market practices such as fraud, market manipulation, and misrepresentation. In addition, the act provides for the SEC's regulation of proxy solicitations for voting.

21. See, for example, *Delman v. GigAcquisitions3, LLC,* 288 A.3d 692, 2023 WL 29325 (Ct. of Chancery DE 2023).

22. *Malouf v. Securities & Exchange Commission,* 933 F.3d 1248 (10th Cir. 2019), applying the United States Supreme Court's ruling in *Lorenzo v. Securities & Exchange Commission,* 587 U.S. __, 139 S.Ct. 1094, 203 L.Ed.2d 484 (2019), which contemplated similar issues involving a violation of SEC Rule 10b-5.

28–2a Section 10(b), SEC Rule 10b-5, and Insider Trading

Section 10(b) is one of the more important sections of the Securities Exchange Act. This section prohibits the use of any manipulative or deceptive mechanism in violation of SEC rules and regulations. Among the rules that the SEC has promulgated pursuant to the 1934 act is **SEC Rule 10b-5,** which prohibits the commission of fraud in connection with the purchase or sale of any security.

SEC Rule 10b-5 applies to almost all cases concerning the trading of securities, whether on organized exchanges, in over-the-counter markets, or in private transactions. Generally, the rule covers just about any form of security. The securities need not be registered under the 1933 act for the 1934 act to apply.

Private parties can sue for securities fraud under Rule 10b-5. The basic elements of a securities fraud action are as follows:

1. A material misrepresentation (or omission) in connection with the purchase and sale of securities.
2. *Scienter* (a wrongful state of mind).
3. Reliance by the plaintiff on the material misrepresentation.
4. An economic loss.
5. Causation, meaning that there is a causal connection between the misrepresentation and the loss.

Insider Trading   One of the major goals of Section 10(b) and SEC Rule 10b-5 is to prevent **insider trading,** which occurs when persons buy or sell securities on the basis of information that is not available to the public. Corporate directors, officers, and majority shareholders, among others, often have advance inside information that can affect the future market value of the corporate stock. Obviously, if they act on this information, their positions give them a trading advantage over the general public and other shareholders.

The 1934 act defines inside information. It also extends liability to those who take advantage of such information in their personal transactions when they know that the information is unavailable to those with whom they are dealing. Section 10(b) of the 1934 act and SEC Rule 10b-5 apply to anyone who has access to or receives information of a nonpublic nature on which trading is based—not just to corporate "insiders."

Disclosure Under SEC Rule 10b-5   Any material omission or misrepresentation of material facts in connection with the purchase or sale of a security may violate Section 10(b) of the 1934 act and SEC Rule 10b-5. The key to liability (which can be civil or criminal) is whether the information omitted or misrepresented is material.

The following are some examples of material facts calling for disclosure under SEC Rule 10b-5:

1. Fraudulent trading in the company stock by a broker-dealer.
2. A dividend change (whether up or down).
3. A contract for the sale of corporate assets.
4. A new discovery, a new process, or a new product.
5. A significant change in the firm's financial condition.
6. Potential litigation against the company.

Note that any one of these facts, by itself, is not automatically considered material. It will be regarded as a material fact only if it is significant enough that it would likely affect an investor's decision as to whether to purchase or sell the company's securities.

■ **Example 28.6**   Zilotek, Inc., is the defendant in a class-action product liability suit that its attorney, Paula Frasier, believes the company will lose. Frasier has advised Zilotek's directors, officers, and accountants that the company will likely have to pay a substantial damages award. Zilotek plans to make a $5 million offering of newly issued stock before the date when the trial is expected to end. Zilotek's potential liability and the financial consequences to the firm are material facts that must be disclosed, because they are significant enough to affect an investor's decision to purchase the stock. ■

The case that follows is a Classic Case interpreting materiality under SEC Rule 10b-5.

Classic Case 28.3

SEC v. Texas Gulf Sulphur Co.

United States Court of Appeals, Second Circuit, 401 F.2d 833 (1968).

Background and Facts   Texas Gulf Sulphur Company (TGS) conducted aerial geophysical surveys over more than 15,000 square miles of eastern Canada. The operations indicated concentrations of commercially exploitable minerals. At one site near Timmins, Ontario, TGS drilled a hole that appeared to yield a core with an exceedingly high mineral content. The company did not disclose the results of the core sample to the public.

Case 28.3 Continues

Case 28.3 Continued

After learning of the sample, TGS officers and employees made substantial purchases of TGS's stock or accepted stock options (rights to purchase stock). On April 11, 1964, an unauthorized report of the mineral find appeared in the newspapers. On the following day, TGS issued a press release that played down the discovery and stated that it was too early to tell whether the ore find would be significant.

Several months later, TGS announced that the strike was expected to yield at least 25 million tons of ore. Subsequently, the price of TGS stock rose substantially. The Securities and Exchange Commission (SEC) brought a suit against the officers and employees of TGS for violating SEC Rule 10b-5. The officers and employees argued that the information on which they had traded had not been material at the time of their trades because the mine had not then been commercially proved. The trial court held that most of the defendants had not violated SEC Rule 10b-5, and the SEC appealed.

In the Language of the Court

WATERMAN, Circuit Judge.

* * * *

* * * Whether facts are material within Rule 10b-5 when the facts relate to a particular event and are undisclosed by those persons who are knowledgeable thereof will depend at any given time upon a balancing of both the indicated probability that the event will occur and the anticipated magnitude of the event in light of the totality of the company activity. Here, * * * knowledge of the possibility, which surely was more than marginal, of the existence of a mine of the vast magnitude indicated by the remarkably rich drill core located rather close to the surface (suggesting mineability by the less expensive open pit method) within the confines of a large anomaly (suggesting an extensive region of mineralization) might well have affected the price of TGS stock and would certainly have been an important fact to a reasonable, if speculative, investor in deciding whether he should buy, sell, or hold.

* * * *

* * * A major factor in determining whether the * * * discovery was a material fact is the importance attached to the drilling results by those who knew about it. * * * The timing by those who knew of it of their stock purchases * * *—purchases in some cases by individuals who had never before purchased * * * TGS stock—virtually compels the inference that the insiders were influenced by the drilling results.

Decision and Remedy The appellate court ruled in favor of the SEC. All of the trading by insiders who knew of the mineral find before its true extent had been publicly announced had violated SEC Rule 10b-5.

Critical Thinking

- **Impact of This Case on Today's Law** This landmark case affirmed the principle that the test of whether information is "material," for SEC Rule 10b-5 purposes, is whether it would affect the judgment of reasonable investors. The corporate insiders' purchases of stock and stock options indicated that they were influenced by the drilling results and that the information about the drilling results was material. The courts continue to cite this case when applying SEC Rule 10b-5 to cases of alleged insider trading.

- **What If the Facts Were Different?** Suppose that further drilling had revealed that there was not enough ore at this site for it to be mined commercially. Would the defendants still have been liable for violating SEC Rule 10b-5? Why or why not?

Outsiders and SEC Rule 10b-5 The traditional insider-trading case involves true insiders—corporate officers, directors, and majority shareholders who have access to (and trade on) inside information. Increasingly, however, liability under Section 10(b) of the 1934 act and SEC Rule 10b-5 has been extended to include certain "outsiders"— those who trade on inside information acquired indirectly. Two theories have been developed under which outsiders may be held liable for insider trading: the tipper/tippee theory and the misappropriation theory.

Tipper/Tippee Theory. Anyone who acquires inside information as a result of a corporate insider's breach of a fiduciary duty can be liable under SEC Rule 10b-5. This liability extends to **tippees** (those who receive "tips" from insiders) and even remote tippees (tippees of tippees).

The key to liability under this theory is that the inside information must have been obtained as a result of someone's breach of a fiduciary duty to the corporation whose shares were traded. The tippee is liable only if the following requirements are met:

1. There is a breach of a duty not to disclose inside information.
2. The disclosure is made in exchange for personal benefit.
3. The tippee knows (or should know) of this breach and benefits from it.

■ **Example 28.7** Eric McPhail was a member of the same country club as an executive at American Superconductor. While they were golfing, the executive shared information with McPhail about the company's expected earnings, contracts, and other major developments, trusting that McPhail would keep the information confidential. Instead, McPhail tipped six of his other golfing buddies at the country club, and they all used the nonpublic information to their advantage in trading. In this situation, the executive breached his duty not to disclose the information, which McPhail knew. McPhail (the tippee) is liable under SEC Rule 10b-5, and so are his other golfing buddies (remote tippees). All of the tippees traded on inside information to their benefit.[23] ■

Misappropriation Theory. Liability for insider trading may also be established under the misappropriation theory. This theory holds liable an individual who wrongfully obtains (misappropriates) inside information and trades on it for personal gain. Basically, this individual has stolen information rightfully belonging to another.

The misappropriation theory has been controversial because it significantly extends the reach of SEC Rule 10b-5 to outsiders who ordinarily would not be deemed fiduciaries of the corporations in whose stock they trade. It is not always wrong to disclose material, nonpublic information about a company to a person who would not otherwise be privy to it. Nevertheless, a person who obtains the information and trades securities on it can be held liable.

■ **Case in Point 28.8** Robert Bray, a real estate developer, first met Patrick O'Neill, an executive at Eastern Bank, at the Oakley Country Club, and the two men became good friends. One day, Bray told O'Neill that he needed cash to fund a project and asked O'Neill if he had any "bank stock tips" for him. O'Neill rattled off a few names of local banks. Then Bray wrote the word "Wainwright" on a napkin and slid it across the bar to O'Neill.

O'Neill, who knew that Eastern Bank was in the process of buying Wainwright Bank, told Bray, "this could be a good one." The next day, Bray bought 25,000 shares of Wainwright stock, and he bought another 31,000 shares a few weeks later. Eastern then publicly announced that it was buying Wainwright, and the stock price doubled. Bray eventually sold the stock at a profit of $300,000.

The SEC prosecuted Bray for insider trading using the misappropriation theory. He was convicted after a jury trial. On appeal, the conviction was affirmed. Bray and O'Neill had been good friends for years. The jury could reasonably have concluded that Bray not only knew that he had traded on material, nonpublic information, but also knew that O'Neill owed Eastern a duty of loyalty and confidentiality.[24] ■

The Personal-Benefits Test Courts have usually held that, under Section 10(b) and SEC Rule 10b-5, tippers/insiders are not guilty of securities fraud unless they disclosed the material information in exchange for a personal benefit. Examples of personal benefits are reputational benefits that lead to future profits and provision of inside information as a gift to a relative or friend.

The importance of the personal-benefits test was lessened for several years by a decision in a case in which the tippers were convicted on federal wire fraud charges. The United States Court of Appeals for the Second Circuit ruled that, under federal criminal law, prosecutors were not required to prove that tippers received any personal benefit in exchange for sharing material information with tippees. Without the need to prove a personal benefit to defendants, the federal government had a strong incentive to treat insider trading broadly as a white-collar crime rather than specifically as a violation of the 1934 Act. That case was appealed, though, and ultimately many of the government's charges against the defendants were dismissed.[25]

Insider Reporting and Trading—Section 16(b) Section 16(b) of the 1934 act provides for the recapture by the corporation of all profits realized by an

23. Three of the defendants in this case agreed to settle with the SEC and return the trading profits. See SEC press release 2014-134 "SEC Charges Group of Amateur Golfers in Insider Trading Ring."

24. *United States v. Bray,* 853 F.3d 18 (1st Cir. 2017). See also *United States v. Chan,* 981 F.3d 39 (1st Cir. 2020).

25. *United States v. Blaszczak,* 947 F.3d 19 (2nd Cir. 2019). For partial reversal on appeal, see *United States v. Blaszczak,* 56 F.4th 230 (2nd Cir. 2022). For an extensive analysis of these cases, see Curtis A. French, "Friends Without Benefits: Criminal Insider Trading Liability and the 'Personal Benefit' Test After *Blaszczak,*" 112 *J. Crim. L. & Criminology Online* 135 (2022).

insider on a purchase and sale, or sale and purchase, of the corporation's stock within any six-month period. The idea is to prevent insiders from taking advantage of their inside information about whether the company's stock price is likely to go up or down in the short term. It is irrelevant whether the insider actually uses the inside information—all such **short-swing profits** must be returned to the corporation.

In the context of Section 16(b), "insiders" means officers, directors, and large stockholders of Section 12 corporations. (Large stockholders are those owning 10 percent of the class of equity securities registered under Section 12 of the 1934 act.) To discourage such insiders from using nonpublic information about their companies to their personal benefit in the stock market, the SEC requires them to file reports concerning their ownership and trading of the corporation's securities.

Section 16(b) applies not only to stock but also to warrants, options, and securities convertible into stock. In addition, the courts have fashioned complex rules for determining profits. Note, though, that the SEC exempts a number of transactions under Rule 16b-3.

Exhibit 28–2 compares the effects of SEC Rule 10b-5 and Section 16(b). Because of the various ways in which

insiders can incur liability under these provisions, corporate insiders should seek the advice of competent counsel before trading in the corporation's stock.

The Private Securities Litigation Reform Act The disclosure requirements of SEC Rule 10b-5 had the unintended effect of deterring the disclosure of forward-looking information, such as financial forecasts. To understand why, consider the following situation. ■ **Example 28.9** XT Company announces that its projected earnings for a future time period will be a certain amount, but its forecast turns out to be wrong. The earnings are, in fact, much lower, and the price of XT's stock is affected negatively. The shareholders bring a class-action suit against XT, alleging that its directors violated SEC Rule 10b-5 by disclosing misleading financial information. ■

In an attempt to solve the problem and promote full disclosure, Congress passed the Private Securities Litigation Reform Act (PSLRA).[26] The PSLRA provides a "safe harbor" for publicly held companies that make

---

26. Pub. L. No. 104-67, 109 Stat. 737 (1995), codified in various sections of Title 15 of the *United States Code*.

Exhibit 28–2 Comparison of Coverage, Application, and Liability Under SEC Rule 10b-5 and Section 16(b)

Area of Comparison	SEC Rule 10b-5	Section 16(b)
What is the subject matter of the transaction?	Any security (does not have to be registered).	Any security (does not have to be registered).
What transactions are covered?	Purchase or sale.	Short-swing purchase and sale or short-swing sale and purchase.
Who is subject to liability?	Almost anyone with inside information—including officers, directors, controlling shareholders, and tippees.	Officers, directors, and certain shareholders who own 10 percent or more of the relevant securities.
Is omission or misrepresentation necessary for liability?	Yes.	No.
Are there any exempt transactions?	No.	Yes, there are a number of exemptions.
Who may bring an action?	A person transacting with an insider, the SEC, or a purchaser or seller damaged by a wrongful act.	A corporation or a shareholder by derivative action.

forward-looking statements. Those who make such statements are protected against liability for securities fraud if they include "meaningful cautionary statements identifying important factors that could cause actual results to differ materially from those in the forward-looking statement."[27]

The PSLRA also affects the level of detail required in securities fraud complaints. Plaintiffs must specify each misleading statement and say how it led them to a mistaken belief.

28–2b Regulation of Proxy Statements

Section 14(a) of the Securities Exchange Act regulates the solicitation of proxies from shareholders of Section 12 companies. The SEC regulates the content of proxy statements. Whoever solicits a proxy must fully and accurately disclose in the proxy statement all facts that are pertinent to the matter on which the shareholders are to vote. SEC Rule 14a-9 is similar to the antifraud provisions of SEC Rule 10b-5. Remedies for violations range from injunctions to prevent a vote from being taken to monetary damages.

28–2c Violations of the 1934 Act

As mentioned earlier, violations of Section 10(b) of the Securities Exchange Act and SEC Rule 10b-5, including insider trading, may lead to both criminal and civil liability.

Scienter Requirement For either criminal or civil sanctions to be imposed, *scienter* must exist—that is, violators must have had an intent to defraud or knowledge of their misconduct. *Scienter* can be proved by showing that defendants made false statements or wrongfully failed to disclose material facts. In some situations, it can even be proved by showing that defendants were consciously reckless as to the truth or falsity of their statements.

■ **Case in Point 28.10** Etsy, Inc., a Brooklyn-based company, operates a website that connects buyers and sellers of handmade and vintage goods. When Etsy went public, it filed a prospectus and registration statement that set forth its commitment to working solely with "responsible, small-batch manufacturing partners" that adhere to Etsy's ethical expectations. Further, it described the company as "a mindful, transparent, and humane business." The statement also explained the company's methods for safeguarding against counterfeit goods and goods that infringe on another's copyright or trademark rights.

Saleh Altayyar and several other investors sued Etsy, alleging that it had misrepresented or omitted material facts in its registration statement. The plaintiffs claimed that Etsy had made false and misleading statements about its values and that nearly 5 percent of its goods were counterfeit or infringing. Etsy argued that it had exercised due diligence and reasonably believed that the statements were true and contained no omissions of material facts. A federal district court in New York ruled in Etsy's favor and dismissed the case. The court found that the plaintiffs had not established *scienter*. "The plaintiffs may disagree with the defendants' opinions [statements about the company], but disagreement does not render the opinions false."[28] ■

Scienter Not Required for Section 16(b) Violations Violations of Section 16(b) include the sale by insiders of stock acquired less than six months before the sale. Selling securities that one does not yet own in the hope of purchasing them at a lower price before the delivery date is called a "short sale." It is a violation of Section 16(b) for insiders involved in a short sale to sell the acquired stock less than six months after the sale. These violations are subject to civil sanctions. Liability under Section 16(b) is strict liability. Neither *scienter* nor negligence is required.

Criminal Penalties For violations of Section 10(b) and Rule 10b-5, an individual may be fined up to $5 million, imprisoned for up to twenty years, or both. A partnership or a corporation may be fined up to $25 million. Under Section 807 of the Sarbanes-Oxley Act, for a willful violation of the 1934 act the violator can be imprisoned for up to twenty-five years (in addition to being subject to a fine).

For a defendant to be convicted in a criminal prosecution under the securities laws, there can be no reasonable doubt that the defendant was aware of acting wrongfully. In other words, a jury is not allowed merely to speculate that the defendant may have acted willfully.

■ **Case in Point 28.11** Kim Hannan had several clients that he had acquired from his former employment as a financial advisor. He also owned several small businesses. Hannan's lavish lifestyle and his method of raising funds from clients aroused the suspicion his girlfriend, Pamala Crawford, who lodged an anonymous complaint about Hannan with the SEC. State investigators determined that Hannan had deceived his clients into providing him with $1.6 million to fund not only a string of failed

---

27. 15 U.S.C. Sections 77z-2, 78u-5.

28. *Altayyar v. Etsy, Inc.*, 242 F.Supp.3d 161 (E.D. NY 2017). See also *Africa v. Jianpu Technology Inc., et al.*, Fed Sec. L. Rep P 101,472 (S.D. NY 2022).

businesses, but also gambling sprees, ex-spousal support, and other personal expenses. An Ohio jury found Hannan guilty on fifty-one counts of securities fraud, and he was sentenced to twenty years in prison.

Hannan appealed, arguing that prosecutors had never proved his intent to deceive his clients and that "misfortune does not constitute fraud." Evidence from his trial, however, showed that Hannan solicited funds from his clients by telling them that his businesses were flourishing, when in fact the opposite was true. The "returns" that he did provide clients invariably came from the pockets of other investors. Furthermore, he never informed clients that he was using their investments for personal expenses. An appeals court found that Hannan "intentionally made false representations" that misled his clients and affirmed his conviction accordingly.[29] ■

Civil Sanctions The SEC can also bring a civil action against anyone who purchases or sells a security while in possession of material nonpublic information in violation of the 1934 act or SEC rules.[30] The violation must occur through the use of a national securities exchange or a broker or dealer.[31] A court can assess a penalty amounting to as much as triple the profits gained or the loss avoided by the guilty party.[32]

The Insider Trading and Securities Fraud Enforcement Act enlarged the class of persons who may be subject to civil liability for insider trading. In addition, this act gave the SEC authority to offer monetary rewards to informants.[33]

Private parties may also sue violators of Section 10(b) and Rule 10b-5. A private party can obtain rescission (cancellation) of a contract to buy securities or damages to the extent of the violator's illegal profits. Those found liable have a right to seek contribution from those who share responsibility for the violations, including accountants, attorneys, and corporations. For violations of Section 16(b), a corporation can bring an action to recover the short-swing profits.

28–2d Securities Fraud Online

A problem that the SEC faces is how to enforce the antifraud provisions of the securities laws in the online environment. Internet-related forms of securities fraud

include many types of investment scams. Spam, online newsletters and bulletin boards, chat rooms, blogs, social media, and tweets can all be used to spread false information and perpetrate fraud. For a relatively small cost, fraudsters can even build sophisticated Web pages to facilitate their investment scams.

Investment Newsletters Hundreds of online investment newsletters provide information on stocks. Legitimate online newsletters can help investors gather valuable information, but some e-newsletters are used for fraud. The law allows companies to pay these newsletters to tout their securities. The newsletters are required to disclose who paid for the advertising, but many newsletters do not follow that law. Thus, an investor reading an online newsletter may believe that the information is unbiased, when in fact the fraudsters will directly profit by convincing investors to buy or sell particular stocks.

Social Media Social media sites have presented a particularly difficult problem for the SEC. Using sites such as Twitter and Facebook, anonymous fraudsters can quickly disseminate information to millions of people at little or no cost. Again, their aim is to convince others to trade in specific stocks. It can be difficult for the SEC to access social media accounts to investigate potential violations. The government must subpoena the sites to determine the users behind particular messages. In addition, social media sites are constantly being updated and changed, which adds another wrinkle for enforcement.

Still, the SEC can take steps to protect investors against deceptive behavior in this arena. For instance, the agency temporarily suspended the ability of twenty-three companies to sell shares in the wake of the COVID-19 outbreak of 2020. These companies had used social media to make false and misleading claims about their products' ability to "prevent, detect, or cure coronavirus." SEC officials worried that such claims were being used to "pump up" the value of a stock, which would then be "dumped" by the fraudulent promoters before the inevitable reality-based market correction.

28–3 State Securities Laws

Today, every state has its own corporate securities laws, or **blue sky laws,** that regulate the offer and sale of securities within its borders. (The phrase "blue sky laws" comes from a 1917 United States Supreme Court decision. The Court stated that the purpose of such laws was to prevent "speculative schemes which have no more basis than so

29. *State of Ohio v. Hannan,* 2020-Ohio-755, 2020 WL 1028925, Blue Sky L. Rep. P 75,284 (Ohio Ct. App. 5th Cir., Stark County 2020).

30. 15 U.S.C. Section 78u(d)(3)(A).

31. Transactions pursuant to a public offering by an issuer of securities are exempted.

32. 15 U.S.C. Section 78u(d)(3)(B).

33. 15 U.S.C. Section 78u-1.

many feet of 'blue sky.'")[34] Article 8 of the Uniform Commercial Code, which has been adopted by all of the states, also imposes various requirements relating to the purchase and sale of securities.

28–3a Requirements Under State Securities Laws

State securities laws apply mainly to intrastate transactions (transactions within one state). Typically, state laws have disclosure requirements and antifraud provisions, many of which are patterned after Section 10(b) of the Securities Exchange Act of 1934 and SEC Rule 10b-5. State laws also provide for the registration of securities offered or issued for sale within the state and impose disclosure requirements.

■ **Case in Point 28.12** Randall Fincke was a founder, director, and officer of Access Cardiosystems, Inc., a small start-up company that sold portable automated external heart defibrillators. Fincke prepared a business plan stating that Access's "patent counsel" had advised the firm that "its product does not infringe any patents." This statement was false—patent counsel never offered Access any opinion on the question of infringement.

Fincke gave this plan to potential investors, including Joseph Zimmel, who bought $1.5 million in Access shares. When the company later filed for Chapter 11 bankruptcy protection, Zimmel filed a complaint with the federal bankruptcy court, alleging that Fincke had violated the Massachusetts blue sky law. The court awarded Zimmel $1.5 million in damages, and the award was affirmed on appeal. Fincke had solicited investors "by means of" a false statement of material fact, in violation of the fraud provisions in the state's securities laws.[35] ■

Methods of registration, required disclosures, and exemptions from registration vary among states. Unless an exemption from registration is applicable, issuers must register or qualify their stock with the appropriate state official, often called a *corporations commissioner*. Additionally, most state securities laws regulate securities brokers and dealers.

28–3b Concurrent Regulation

Since the adoption of the 1933 and 1934 federal securities acts, the state and federal governments have regulated securities concurrently. Issuers must comply with

both federal and state securities laws, and exemptions from federal law are not exemptions from state laws.

The dual federal and state system has not always worked well. Today, many of the duplicate regulations have been eliminated, and the SEC has exclusive power to regulate most national securities activities.

The National Conference of Commissioners on Uniform State Laws substantially revised the Uniform Securities Act to coordinate state and federal securities regulation and enforcement efforts. Nearly half of the states have adopted the most recent version of the Uniform Securities Act.

28–4 Corporate Governance

Corporate governance can be narrowly defined as the relationship between a corporation and its shareholders. Some argue for a broader definition—that corporate governance specifies the rights and responsibilities among different participants in the corporation, such as the board of directors, managers, shareholders, and other stakeholders, and spells out the rules and procedures for making decisions on corporate affairs. Regardless of the way it is defined, effective corporate governance requires more than just compliance with laws and regulations.

Effective corporate governance is essential in large corporations because corporate ownership (by shareholders) is separated from corporate control (by officers and managers). Under these circumstances, officers and managers may attempt to advance their own interests at the expense of the shareholders. Well-publicized corporate scandals have clearly illustrated how the misconduct of corporate managers can cause harm to companies and to society. Indeed, with the globalization of business, corporate governance has become even more important because a corporation's bad acts (or lack of control systems) can have far-reaching consequences.

28–4a Aligning the Interests of Officers and Shareholders

Some corporations have sought to align the financial interests of their officers with those of the company's shareholders by providing the officers with **stock options.** These options enable holders to purchase shares of the corporation's stock at a set price. When the market price rises above that level, the officers can sell their shares for a profit. Because a stock's market price generally increases as the corporation prospers, the options give the officers

---

34. *Hall v. Geiger-Jones Co.,* 242 U.S. 539, 37 S.Ct. 217, 61 L.Ed. 480 (1917).

35. *In re Access Cardiosystems, Inc.,* 776 F.3d 30 (1st Cir. 2015). See also *Giul, LLC v. Shenghuo Medical, LLC,* 2020 WL 5993067 (Sup. Ct.Mass., Suffolk, Bus.Litigation Session 2020).

a financial stake in the corporation's well-being and supposedly encourage them to work hard for the benefit of the shareholders.

Problems With Stock Options Options have turned out to be an imperfect device for encouraging effective governance. Executives in some companies have been tempted to "cook" the company's books to keep share prices higher so that they can sell their stock for a profit. Executives in other corporations have experienced no losses when share prices dropped because their options were "repriced" so that they did not suffer from the price decline. Thus, although stock options theoretically can motivate officers to protect shareholder interests, stock option plans have sometimes become a way for officers to take advantage of shareholders.

Outside Directors With stock options generally failing to work as planned, there has been an outcry for more outside directors (those with no formal employment affiliation with the company). The theory is that independent directors will more closely monitor the actions of corporate officers. Hence, today we see more boards with outside directors. Note, though, that outside directors may not be truly independent of corporate officers. They may be friends or business associates of the leading officers.

28–4b Promoting Accountability

Effective corporate governance standards are designed to address problems such as those mentioned earlier and to motivate officers to make decisions that promote the financial interests of the company's shareholders. Generally, corporate governance entails corporate decision-making structures that monitor employees (particularly officers) to ensure that they are acting for the benefit of the shareholders. Thus, corporate governance involves, at a minimum:

1. The audited reporting of financial conditions at the corporation so that managers can be evaluated.
2. Legal protections for shareholders so that violators of the law who attempt to take advantage of shareholders can be punished for misbehavior and victims can recover damages for any associated losses.

Governance and Corporate Law State corporation statutes set up the legal framework for corporate governance. Under the corporate law of Delaware, where most major companies incorporate, all corporations must have certain structures of corporate governance in place. The most important structure, of course, is the board of directors, because the board makes the major decisions about the future of the corporation.

The Board of Directors Under corporate law, a corporation must have a board of directors elected by the shareholders. Directors are responsible for ensuring that the corporation's officers are operating wisely and in the exclusive interest of shareholders. Directors receive reports from the officers and give them managerial direction. In reality, though, corporate directors devote a relatively small amount of time to monitoring officers.

Ideally, shareholders would monitor the directors' supervision of the officers. In practice, however, it can be difficult for shareholders to monitor directors and hold them responsible for corporate failings. Although the directors can be sued if they fail to do their jobs effectively, directors are rarely held personally liable.

In relatively recent years, there have been controversies over how diverse corporate boards really are. At least with respect to gender diversity, some states have codified the proportion of board members that must be female. See this chapter's Ethics Today feature.

Ethics Today

Does corporate America need gender quotas for boards of directors?

Driven by pressure from institutional investors—as well as changes in the society at large—the nation's 500 largest companies increased the number of women on their boards of directors by 37 percent during the last half of the 2010s. At the same time, California became the first state to legally require the presence of women on corporate boards. Under California law, every publicly traded company based in the state must have at least one female director or be fined $100,000. Companies with five board members must have at least two female directors and those with six board members must have at least three female directors. Larger corporations face fines of $300,000 for every seat that should be filled by a woman but is not.

Given that the average director salary in California is about $180,000, complying with this law might be a financial hardship for some smaller firms. Still, the legislator who sponsored the law lauded its twin goals of "advancing gender equality" and enhancing "the economic well-being of the state." Opponents of the law counter that it is not only "patronizing" to women, but also violates the equal protection clause of the U.S. Constitution by perpetuating sex-based discrimination.

Critics also point out that a number of European countries have had board gender quotas in place for years, with no measurable impact on corporate financial performance or the expected "trickle-down" effect of increased hiring of female executives.

Critical Thinking The most pressure concerning the composition of boards of directors has come from large institutional investors, such as mutual funds. Why might this be so?

The Audit Committee. A crucial committee of the board of directors is the audit committee, which oversees the corporation's accounting and financial reporting processes, including both internal and outside auditors. Unless the committee members have sufficient expertise and are willing to spend the time to carefully examine the corporation's bookkeeping methods, however, the audit committee may be ineffective.

The audit committee also oversees the corporation's "internal controls." These controls, carried out largely by the company's internal auditing staff, are measures taken to ensure that reported results are accurate. For instance, internal controls help to determine whether a corporation's debts are collectible. If the debts are not collectible, it is up to the audit committee to make sure that the corporation's financial officers do not simply pretend that payment will eventually be made.

The Compensation Committee. Another important committee of the board of directors is the compensation committee, which determines the compensation of the company's officers. As part of this process, the committee must assess the officers' performance and attempt to design a compensation system that will align the officers' interests with those of the shareholders.

28–4c The Sarbanes-Oxley Act

In 2002, following a series of corporate scandals, Congress passed the Sarbanes-Oxley Act,[36] which addresses certain issues relating to corporate governance. Generally, the act attempts to increase corporate accountability by imposing strict disclosure requirements and harsh penalties for violations of securities laws. Among other things, the act requires chief corporate executives to take personal responsibility for the accuracy of financial statements and reports that are filed with the SEC.

Additionally, the act requires that certain financial and stock-transaction reports be filed with the SEC earlier than was required under the previous rules. The act also created a new entity, called the Public Company Accounting Oversight Board, to regulate and oversee public accounting firms. Other provisions of the act established private civil actions and expanded the SEC's remedies in administrative and civil actions.

Because of the importance of this act for corporate leaders and for those dealing with securities transactions, we highlight some of its key provisions relating to corporate accountability in Exhibit 28–3.

More Internal Controls and Accountability The Sarbanes-Oxley Act introduced direct federal corporate governance requirements for publicly traded companies. The law addressed many of the corporate governance procedures just discussed and created new requirements in an attempt to make the system work more effectively. The requirements deal with independent monitoring of company officers by both the board of directors and auditors.

Sections 302 and 404 of the Sarbanes-Oxley Act require high-level managers (the most senior officers) to establish and maintain an effective system of internal controls. The system must include "disclosure controls and procedures" to ensure that company financial reports are accurate and timely and to document financial results prior to reporting.

Senior management must reassess the system's effectiveness annually. Some companies have had to take expensive steps to bring their internal controls up to the federal standards. Hundreds of companies have reported that they identified and corrected shortcomings in their internal control systems as a result.

---

36. 15 U.S.C. Sections 7201 *et seq.*

Exhibit 28–3 Some Key Provisions of the Sarbanes-Oxley Act Relating to Corporate Accountability

Certification Requirements

Under *Section 906* of the Sarbanes-Oxley Act, the chief executive officers (CEOs) and chief financial officers (CFOs) of most major companies listed on public stock exchanges must certify financial statements that are filed with the SEC. CEOs and CFOs have to certify that filed financial reports "fully comply" with SEC requirements and that all of the information reported "fairly represents in all material respects, the financial conditions and results of operations of the issuer."

Under *Section 302* of the act, CEOs and CFOs of reporting companies are required to certify that a signing officer reviewed each quarterly and annual filing with the SEC and that none contained untrue statements of material fact. Also, the signing officer or officers must certify that they have established an internal control system to identify all material information and that any deficiencies in the system were disclosed to the auditors.

Internal Controls

Financial Controls—*Section 404(a)* requires all public companies to assess the effectiveness of their internal controls over financial reporting. *Section 404(b)* requires independent auditors to report on management's assessment of internal controls, but certain companies are exempted.

Loans to Directors and Officers—*Section 402* prohibits any reporting company—as well as any private company that is filing an initial public offering—from making personal loans to directors and executive officers.

Protection for Whistleblowers—*Section 806* protects "whistleblowers"—employees who "blow the whistle" on securities violations by their employers—from being fired or in any way discriminated against by their employers.

Blackout Periods—*Section 306* prohibits certain types of securities transactions during "blackout periods"—periods during which the issuer's ability to purchase, sell, or otherwise transfer funds in individual account plans (such as pension funds) is suspended.

Enhanced Penalties

- *Violations of Section 906 Certification Requirements*—A CEO or CFO who certifies a financial report or statement filed with the SEC knowing that the report or statement does not fulfill all of the requirements of *Section 906* will be subject to criminal penalties of up to $1 million in fines, ten years in prison, or both. *Willful* violators of the certification requirements may be subject to $5 million in fines, twenty years in prison, or both.

- *Violations of the Securities Exchange Act of 1934*—Penalties for securities fraud under the 1934 act were also increased. Individual violators may be fined up to $5 million, imprisoned for up to twenty years, or both. *Willful* violators may be imprisoned for up to twenty-five years in addition to being fined.

- *Destruction or Alteration of Documents*—Anyone who alters, destroys, or conceals documents or otherwise obstructs any official proceeding will be subject to fines, imprisonment for up to twenty years, or both.

- *Other Forms of White-Collar Crime*—The act stiffened the penalties for certain criminal violations, such as federal mail and wire fraud, and ordered the U.S. Sentencing Commission to revise the sentencing guidelines for white-collar crimes.

Statute of Limitations for Securities Fraud

Section 804 provides that a private right of action for securities fraud may be brought no later than two years after the discovery of the violation or five years after the violation, whichever is earlier.

Exemptions for Smaller Companies The act initially required all public companies to have an independent auditor file a report with the SEC on management's assessment of internal controls. Congress, however, later enacted an exemption for smaller companies in an effort to reduce compliance costs. Public companies with a market capitalization, or public float, of less than $75 million no longer need to have an auditor report on management's assessment of internal controls.

Certification and Monitoring Requirements Section 906 of the Sarbanes-Oxley Act requires that chief executive officers and chief financial officers certify the accuracy of the information in the corporate financial statements. The statements must "fairly represent in all material respects, the financial conditions and results of operations of the issuer." This requirement makes the officers directly accountable for the accuracy of their financial reporting and precludes any "ignorance defense" if shortcomings are later discovered.

The act also includes requirements to improve directors' monitoring of officers' activities. All members of a publicly traded corporation's audit committee, which oversees the corporation's accounting and financial reporting processes, must be outside directors. The audit committee must have a written charter that sets out its duties and provides for performance appraisal. At least one "financial expert" must serve on the audit committee, which must hold executive meetings without company officers present. In addition to reviewing the internal controls, the committee also monitors the actions of the outside auditor.

Practice and Review: Investor Protection, Insider Trading, and Corporate Governance

Dale Emerson served as the chief financial officer for Reliant Electric Company, a distributor of electricity serving portions of Montana and North Dakota. Reliant was in the final stages of planning a takeover of Dakota Gasworks, Inc., a natural gas distributor that operated solely within North Dakota. Emerson went on a weekend fishing trip with his uncle, Ernest Wallace. Emerson mentioned to Wallace that he had been putting in a lot of extra hours at the office planning a takeover of Dakota Gasworks. When he returned from the fishing trip, Wallace purchased $20,000 worth of Reliant stock. Three weeks later, Reliant made a tender offer to Dakota Gasworks stockholders and purchased 57 percent of Dakota Gasworks stock. Over the next two weeks, the price of Reliant stock rose 72 percent before leveling out. Wallace then sold his Reliant stock for a gross profit of $14,400. Using the information presented in the chapter, answer the following questions.

1. Would registration with the SEC be required for Dakota Gasworks securities? Why or why not?
2. Did Emerson violate Section 10(b) of the Securities Exchange Act of 1934 and SEC Rule 10b-5? Why or why not?
3. What theory or theories might a court use to hold Wallace liable for insider trading?
4. Under the Sarbanes-Oxley Act, who would be required to certify the accuracy of the financial statements Reliant filed with the SEC?

Debate This ... Insider trading should be legalized.

Terms and Concepts

accredited investor 587	investment company 588	short-swing profits 594
blue sky laws 596	investment contract 581	special purpose acquisition
corporate governance 597	mutual fund 588	companies (SPACs) 589
direct public offering (DPO) 589	prospectus 584	stock options 597
free-writing prospectus 586	SEC Rule 10b-5 591	tippees 592
insider trading 591	securities 581	

Issue Spotters

1. When a corporation wishes to issue certain securities, it must provide sufficient information for an unsophisticated investor to evaluate the financial risk involved. Specifically, the law imposes liability for making a false statement or omission that is "material." What sort of information would an investor consider material? (See *The Securities Exchange Act of 1934*.)

2. Lee is an officer of Magma Oil, Inc. Lee knows that a Magma geologist has just discovered a new deposit of oil. Can Lee take advantage of this information to buy and sell Magma stock? Why or why not? (See *The Securities Exchange Act of 1934*.)

● **Check your answers to the Issue Spotters against the answers provided in Appendix B at the end of this text.**

Business Scenarios and Case Problems

28–1. Registration Requirements. Estrada Hermanos, Inc., a corporation incorporated and doing business in Florida, decides to sell $1 million worth of its common stock to the public. The stock will be sold only within the state of Florida. José Estrada, the chair of the board, says the offering need not be registered with the Securities and Exchange Commission. His brother, Gustavo, disagrees. Who is right? Explain. (See *The Securities Act of 1933*.)

28–2. Registration Requirements. Huron Corp. has 300,000 common shares outstanding. The owners of these outstanding shares live in several different states. Huron has decided to split the 300,000 shares two for one. Will Huron Corp. have to file a registration statement and prospectus on the 300,000 new shares to be issued as a result of the split? Explain. (See *The Securities Act of 1933*.)

28–3. Insider Trading. David Gain was the chief executive officer (CEO) of Forest Media Corp., which became interested in acquiring RS Communications, Inc. To initiate negotiations, Gain met with RS's CEO, Gill Raz, on Friday, July 12. Two days later, Gain phoned his brother Mark, who bought 3,800 shares of RS stock on the following Monday. Mark discussed the deal with their father, Jordan, who bought 20,000 RS shares on Thursday. On July 25, the day before the RS bid was due, Gain phoned his parents' home, and Mark bought another 3,200 RS shares. The same routine was followed over the next few days, with Gain periodically phoning Mark or Jordan, both of whom continued to buy RS shares. Forest's bid was refused, but on August 5, RS announced its merger with another company. The price of RS stock rose 30 percent, increasing the value of Mark's and Jordan's shares by $664,024 and $412,875, respectively. Did Gain engage in insider trading? What is required to impose sanctions for this offense? Could a court hold Gain liable? Why or why not? (See *The Securities Exchange Act of 1934*.)

28–4. Business Case Problem With Sample Answer— Violations of the 1934 Act. Matrixx Initiatives, Inc., makes and sells over-the-counter pharmaceutical products. Its core brand is Zicam, which accounts for 70 percent of its sales. Matrixx received reports that some consumers had lost their sense of smell (a condition called *anosmia*) after using Zicam. Four product liability suits were filed against Matrixx, seeking damages for anosmia. In public statements relating to

revenues and product safety, however, Matrixx did not reveal this information.

James Siracusano and other Matrixx investors filed a suit in a federal district court against the company and its executives under Section 10(b) of the Securities Exchange Act of 1934 and SEC Rule 10b-5, claiming that the statements were misleading because they did not disclose information regarding the product liability suits. Matrixx argued that to be material, information must consist of a statistically significant number of adverse events that require disclosure. Because Siracusano's claim did not allege that Matrixx knew of a statistically significant number of adverse events, the company contended that the claim should be dismissed. What is the standard for materiality in this context? Should Siracusano's claim be dismissed? Explain. [*Matrixx Initiatives, Inc. v. Siracusano*, 563 U.S. 27, 131 S.Ct. 1309, 179 L.Ed.2d 398 (2011)] (See *The Securities Exchange Act of 1934*.)

● **For a sample answer to Problem 28–4, go to Appendix C at the end of this text.**

28–5. Violations of the 1933 Act. Three shareholders of iStorage sought to sell their stock through World Trade Financial Corporation. The shares were restricted securities—that is, securities acquired in an unregistered, private sale. Restricted securities typically bear a "restrictive" legend clearly stating that they cannot be resold in the public marketplace. This legend had been wrongly removed from the iStorage shares, however. Information about the company that was publicly available included the fact that, despite a ten-year life, it had no operating history or earnings. In addition, it had net losses of about $200,000, and its stock was thinly traded. Without investigating the company or the status of its stock, World Trade sold more than 2.3 million shares to the public on behalf of the three customers. Did World Trade violate the Securities Act of 1933? Discuss. [*World Trade Financial Corp. v. U.S. Securities and Exchange Commission*, 739 F.3d 1243 (9th Cir. 2014)] (See *The Securities Act of 1933*.)

28–6. Securities Act of 1933. Big Apple Consulting USA, Inc., provided small publicly traded companies with a variety of services, including marketing, business planning, and website development and maintenance. CyberKey Corp. sold customizable USB drives. CyberKey falsely informed Big Apple that CyberKey had been awarded a $25 million contract with the Department of Homeland Security. Big Apple used this information in aggressively promoting CyberKey's stock and was compensated for the effort in the form of CyberKey shares. When the Securities and Exchange Commission (SEC) began to investigate, Big Apple sold its shares for $7.8 million. The SEC filed an action in a federal district court against Big Apple, alleging a violation of the Securities Act of 1933. Can liability be imposed on a seller for a false statement that was made by someone else? Explain. [*U.S. Securities and Exchange Commission v. Big Apple Consulting USA, Inc.,* 783 F.3d 786 (11th Cir. 2015)] (See *The Securities Act of 1933.*)

28–7. The Securities Exchange Act of 1934. Dilean Reyes-Rivera was the president of Global Reach Trading (GRT), a corporation registered in Puerto Rico. His brother, Jeffrey, was the firm's accountant. Along with GRT sales agents and other promoters, the brothers solicited funds from individuals by promising to invest the funds in low-risk, short-term, high-yield securities. The investors were guaranteed a rate of return of up to 20 percent. Through this arrangement, more than 230 persons provided the brothers with about $22 million. This money was not actually invested. Instead, the funds received from later investors were used to pay "returns" to earlier investors. The Reyes-Riveras spent $4.6 million of the proceeds to buy luxury vehicles, houses, furniture, jewelry, and trips for themselves. What is this type of scheme called? What are the potential consequences? Discuss. [*United States v. Reyes-Rivera,* 812 F.3d 79 (1st Cir. 2016)] (See *The Securities Exchange Act of 1934.*)

28–8. Securities Fraud. First Solar, Inc., is one of the world's largest producers of photovoltaic solar panel modules. When First Solar revealed to the market that the company had discovered defects in its products, the price of the company's stock fell, causing the shareholders to suffer an economic loss. Mineworkers' Pension Scheme and other First Solar shareholders filed a suit in a federal district court against the firm and its officers, alleging a violation of Section 10(b). The plaintiffs contended that for more than two years, First Solar had wrongfully concealed its discovery, misrepresented the cost and scope of the defects, and reported false information on financial statements. On these facts, can the plaintiffs successfully plead the causation element of a securities fraud action under Section 10(b)? Explain. [*Mineworkers' Pension Scheme v. First Solar, Inc.,* 881 F.3d 750 (9th Cir. 2018)] (See *The Securities Exchange Act of 1934.*)

28–9. A Question of Ethics—The IDDR Approach and Insider Trading. Nan Huang was a senior data analyst for Capital One Financial Corporation. In violation of the company's confidentiality policies, Huang downloaded and analyzed confidential information regarding purchases made with Capital One credit cards at more than 200 consumer retail companies and used that information to conduct more than 2,000 trades in the securities of those companies. Capital One terminated Huang due to his violation of the company's policies. The next day, Huang boarded a flight to his home country of China. Four days later, the Securities and Exchange Commission filed a complaint against Huang, alleging violations of Section 10(b) and Rule 10b-5. [*Securities and Exchange Commission v. Bonan Huang,* 684 Fed.Appx. 167 (3d Cir. 2017)] (See *The Securities Exchange Act of 1934.*)

(a) Evaluate the ethics of Huang's actions, as an employee of Capital One, using the IDDR approach.

(b) When Capital One learned what Huang had done, was the company ethically obligated to terminate him? Explain.

Time-Limited Group Assignment

28–10. Securities Fraud. Karel Svoboda, a credit officer for Rogue Bank, evaluated and approved his employer's extensions of credit to clients. These responsibilities gave Svoboda access to nonpublic information about the clients' earnings, performance, acquisitions, and business plans from confidential memos, e-mail, and other sources. Svoboda devised a scheme with Alena Robles, an independent accountant, to use this information to trade securities. Pursuant to their scheme, Robles traded in the securities of more than twenty different companies and profited by more than $2 million. Svoboda also executed trades for his own profit of more than $800,000, despite their agreement that Robles would do all of the trading. Aware that their scheme violated Rogue Bank's policy, they attempted to conduct their trades in such a way as to avoid suspicion. When the bank questioned Svoboda about his actions, he lied, refused to cooperate, and was fired. (See *The Securities Exchange Act of 1934.*)

(a) The first group will determine whether Svoboda or Robles committed any crimes.

(b) The second group will decide whether Svoboda or Robles is subject to civil liability. If so, who could file a suit, and on what ground? What are the possible sanctions?

(c) A third group will identify any defenses that Svoboda or Robles could raise and determine their likelihood of success.

Unit Five: Task-Based Simulation

Alpha Software, Inc., and Beta Products Corporation—both small firms—are competitors in the business of software research, development, and production.

1. **Consumer Law.** To market its products profitably, Beta considers a number of advertising and labeling proposals. One proposal is that Beta suggest in its advertising that one of its software products has a certain function, even though the product does not actually have that capability. Another suggestion is that Beta sell half of a certain program in packaging that misleads the buyer into believing the entire program is included. To obtain the entire program, customers would need to buy a second product. Can Beta implement these suggestions or otherwise market its products in any way it likes? If not, why not?

2. **Environmental Law.** The production part of Beta's operations generates hazardous waste. Gamma Transport Company transports the waste to Omega Waste Corporation, which owns and operates a hazardous waste disposal site. At the site, some containers leak hazardous waste, and the Environmental Protection Agency (EPA) cleans it up. From whom can the EPA recover the cost of the cleanup?

3. **Antitrust Law.** Alpha and Beta form a joint venture to research, develop, and produce new software for a particular line of computers. Does this business combination violate the anti-trust laws? If so, is it a *per se* violation, or is it subject to the rule of reason?

Appendix A

How to Brief Cases and Analyze Case Problems

How to Brief Cases

To fully understand the law with respect to business, you need to be able to read and understand court decisions. To make this task easier, you can use a method of case analysis that is called *briefing*. There is a fairly standard procedure to follow when you "brief" any court case. You must first read the case opinion carefully. When you feel you understand the case, you can prepare a brief of it.

Although the format of the brief may vary, typically it will present the essentials of the case under headings such as the following:

1. **Citation.** Give the full citation for the case, including the name of the case, the date it was decided, and the court that decided it.
2. **Facts.** Briefly indicate (a) the reasons for the lawsuit; (b) the identity and arguments of the plaintiff(s) and defendant(s), respectively; and (c) the lower court's decision—if appropriate.
3. **Issue.** Concisely phrase, in the form of a question, the essential issue before the court. (If more than one issue is involved, you may have two—or even more—questions here.)
4. **Decision.** Indicate here—with a "yes" or "no," if possible— the court's answer to the question (or questions) in the *Issue* section.
5. **Reason.** Summarize as briefly as possible the reasons given by the court for its decision (or decisions) and the case or statutory law relied on by the court in arriving at its decision.

An Example of a Briefed Sample Court Case

As an example of the format used in briefing cases, we present next a briefed version of the sample court case that was presented in Chapter 1 in Exhibit 1–6.

Doe v. Knox Board of Education
United States Court of Appeals, Sixth Circuit,
56 F.4th 1076 (2023).

Facts A ninth-grade student using the placeholder name Jane Doe (to protect her privacy) suffers from a medical condition that makes her overly sensitive to sounds such as others chewing gum and eating food. Doe's parents asked the administration of her Knox County, Tennessee, high school to accommodate their daughter's condition by banning other students from engaging in these activities in her classes. School administrators refused, explaining that the "unique" nature of this particular college-like high school made it impractical to prohibit students from eating in

class. On their daughter's behalf, Doe's parents then sued the Knox County Board of Education in a federal district court, alleging— among other claims—that the county had violated the Americans with Disabilities Act (ADA). This federal law forbids public entities such as schools from discriminating against the disabled. The court dismissed the case on procedural grounds. Doe's parents appealed to the U.S. Court of Appeals for the Sixth Circuit, requesting that Knox County ban other students from eating and chewing gum in their daughter's classes during legal proceedings.

Issue Does the ADA compel the appeals court to grant a preliminary injunction overturning the high school's policy of allowing eating and chewing gum in class?

Decision No. The U.S. Court of Appeals for the Sixth Circuit denied Jane Doe's request for a preliminary injunction. The appeals court did, however, reverse the district court's motion to dismiss, allowing Doe's lawsuit to proceed.

Reason A federal regulation relating to the ADA holds that "A public entity shall make reasonable modifications in policies, practices, or procedures when the modifications are necessary to avoid discrimination on the basis of disability, *unless* the public entity can demonstrate that making the modifications would fundamentally alter the nature of the service, program, or activity." The appeals court interpreted this regulation as requiring Jane Doe to show that her requested temporary ban on chewing gum and, particularly, eating in class would be a "moderate" rather than a "significant" change. Given the unique character of the school, the court decided, such a ban would indeed be "significant" and was therefore not warranted under the ADA. As questions remained over whether the high school's overall treatment of Doe was reasonable, the appeals court did allow the lawsuit to go forward, with the high school's eating and gum chewing policies to remain in place during the proceedings.

A Review of Sample Court Case

Here, we provide a review of the briefed version that indicates the kind of information contained in each section.

Citation The name of the case is *Doe v. Knox County Board of Education*. Jane Doe is the plaintiff. The Knox County Board of Education is the defendant. The U.S. Court of Appeals for the Sixth Circuit issued its opinion in this case in 2023. The citation states that the case can be found in Volume 56 of the *Federal Reporter, Fourth Edition*, on page 1076.

Facts The *Facts* section identifies the plaintiff and the defendant, describes the events leading up to the suit, and states the allegations made by the plaintiff in the suit. Because this case is a decision of one of the U.S. Courts of Appeals, the lower court's ruling, the *appellant* (the party appealing), and the appellant's contention on appeal are also included.

Issue The *Issue* section presents the central issue (or issues) decided by the court. In this case, the federal appellate court considers whether the Americans with Disabilities Act compels Jane Doe's high school to change its policies in her favor while her lawsuit against the school plays out.

Decision The *Decision* section includes the court's decision on the issues before it. The decision reflects the opinion of the judge or justice hearing the case. Here, the appeals court rejected the appellant's request for a preliminary injunction that would have required Jane Doe's high school to ban chewing gum and eating food in class while her legal issues with the school were resolved. The appeals court did, however, "reverse" the lower court's outright dismissal of Doe's lawsuit and "remand" the case back to the lower court for further proceedings. (If the appeals court had agreed with the lower court's decision, it would have "affirmed" the motion to dismiss and Doe's legal action would have ended.)

Reason The *Reason* section includes references to the relevant laws and legal principles that were applied or distinguished in coming to the conclusion arrived at in the case before the court. Here, the appeals court rejected the appellant's request for a preliminary injunction that would have required Jane Doe's high school to ban chewing gum and eating food in class while her legal issues with the school were resolved. The appeals court did, however, "reverse" the lower court's outright dismissal of Doe's lawsuit and "remand" the case back to the lower court for further proceedings. (If the appeals court had agreed with the lower court's decision, it would have "affirmed" the motion to dismiss and Doe's legal action would have ended.)

Analyzing Case Problems

In addition to learning how to brief cases, students also find it helpful to know how to analyze case problems. Part of the study of business law and the legal environment usually involves analyzing case problems, such as those included in this text at the end of each chapter.

For each case problem in this book, we provide the relevant background and facts of the lawsuit and the issue before the court. When you are assigned one of these problems, your job will be to determine how the court should decide the issue, and why. In other words, you will need to engage in legal analysis and reasoning. Here, we offer some suggestions on how to make this task less daunting. We begin by presenting the following SAMPLE PROBLEM:

While Janet Lawson, a famous pianist, was shopping in Quality Market, she slipped and fell on a wet floor in one of the aisles. The floor had recently been mopped by one of the store's employees, but there were no signs warning customers that the floor in that area was wet. As a result of the fall, Lawson injured her right arm and was unable to perform piano concerts for the next six months. Had she been able to perform the scheduled concerts, she would have earned approximately $60,000 over that period of time. Lawson sued Quality Market for this amount, plus another $10,000 in medical expenses. She claimed that the store's failure to warn customers of the wet floor constituted negligence and therefore the market was liable for her injuries. Will the court agree with Lawson? Discuss.

Understand the Facts

This may sound obvious, but before you can analyze or apply the relevant law to a specific set of facts, you must clearly understand those facts. In other words, you should read through the case problem carefully—more than once, if necessary—to make sure you understand the identity of the plaintiff(s) and defendant(s) in the case and the progression of events that led to the lawsuit.

In the sample case problem just given, the identity of the parties is fairly clear. Janet Lawson is the one bringing the suit; therefore, she is the plaintiff. Quality Market, against whom she is bringing the suit, is the defendant. Some of the case problems you may work on have multiple plaintiffs or defendants. Often, it is helpful to use abbreviations for the parties. To indicate a reference to a plaintiff, for example, the *pi* symbol—π—is often used, and a defendant is denoted by a *delta*—Δ.

The events leading to the lawsuit are also fairly straightforward. Lawson slipped and fell on a wet floor, and she contends that Quality Market should be liable for her injuries because it was negligent in not posting a sign warning customers of the wet floor.

When you are working on case problems, realize that the facts should be accepted as they are given. For example, in our sample problem, it should be accepted that the floor was wet and that there was no sign. In other words, avoid making conjectures, such as "Maybe the floor wasn't too wet," or "Maybe an employee was getting a sign to put up," or "Maybe someone stole the sign." Questioning the facts as they are presented only adds confusion to your analysis.

Legal Analysis and Reasoning

Once you understand the facts given in the case problem, you can begin to analyze the case. The IRAC method is a helpful tool to use in the legal analysis and reasoning process. **IRAC** is an acronym for **Issue, Rule, Application, Conclusion.** Applying this method to our sample problem would involve the following steps:

1. First, you need to decide what legal **issue** is involved in the case. In our sample case, the basic issue is whether Quality Market's failure to warn customers of the wet floor constituted negligence. As discussed in the text, negligence is a *tort*—a civil wrong. In a tort lawsuit, the plaintiff seeks to be compensated for another's wrongful act. A defendant will be deemed negligent if they breached a duty of care owed to the plaintiff and the breach of that duty caused the plaintiff to suffer harm.

2. Once you have identified the issue, the next step is to determine what **rule of law** applies to the issue. To make this determination, you will want to review carefully the text of the chapter in which the relevant rule of law for the problem appears. Our sample case problem involves the tort of negligence. The applicable rule of law is the tort law principle that business owners owe a duty to exercise reasonable care to protect their customers ("business invitees"). Reasonable care, in this context, includes either removing—or warning customers of—*foreseeable* risks about which the owner *knew* or *should have known*. (Business owners need not warn customers of "open and obvious" risks.) If a business owner breaches this duty of care (fails to exercise the appropriate degree of care toward customers), and the breach of duty causes a customer to be injured, the business owner will be liable to the customer for the customer's injuries.

3. The next—and usually the most difficult—step in analyzing case problems is the **application** of the relevant rule of law to the specific facts of the case you are studying. In the sample problem, applying the tort law principle just discussed presents few difficulties. An employee of the store had mopped the floor in the aisle where Lawson slipped and fell, but no sign was present indicating that the floor was wet. That a customer might fall on a wet floor is clearly a foreseeable risk. Therefore, the failure to warn customers about the wet floor was a breach of the duty of care owed by the business owner to the store's customers.

4. Once you have completed Step 3, you should be ready to draw your **conclusion.** In our sample problem, Quality Market is liable to Lawson for her injuries, because the market's breach of its duty of care caused Lawson's injuries.

The fact patterns in the business scenarios and case problems presented in this text are not always as simple as those presented in our sample problem. Often, for example, a case has more than one plaintiff or defendant. A case may also involve more than one issue and have more than one applicable rule of law. Furthermore, in some case problems the facts may indicate that the general rule of law should not apply.

For example, suppose that a store employee advised Lawson not to walk on the floor in the aisle because it was wet, but Lawson decided to walk on it anyway. This fact could alter the outcome of the case because the store could then raise the defense of assumption of risk. Nonetheless, a careful review of the chapter text should always provide you with the knowledge you need to analyze the problem thoroughly and arrive at accurate conclusions.

Appendix B

Answers to the *Issue Spotters*

Chapter 1

1. Under what circumstances might a judge rely on case law to determine the intent and purpose of a statute? Case law includes courts' interpretations of statutes, as well as constitutional provisions and administrative rules. Statutes often codify common law rules. For these reasons, a judge might rely on the common law as a guide to the intent and purpose of a statute.

2. Assuming that these convicted war criminals had not disobeyed any law of their country and had merely been following their government's orders, what law had they violated? Explain. At the time of the Nuremberg trials, "crimes against humanity" were new international crimes. The laws criminalized such acts as murder, extermination, enslavement, deportation, and other inhumane acts committed against any civilian population. These international laws derived their legitimacy from "natural law."

Natural law, which is the oldest and one of the most significant schools of jurisprudence, holds that governments and legal systems should reflect the moral and ethical ideals that are inherent in human nature. Because natural law is universal and discoverable by reason, its adherents believe that all other law is derived from natural law. Natural law therefore supersedes laws created by humans (national, or "positive," law), and in a conflict between the two, national or positive law loses its legitimacy.

The Nuremberg defendants asserted that they had been acting in accordance with German law. The judges dismissed these claims, reasoning that the defendants' acts were commonly regarded as crimes and that the accused must have known that the acts would be considered criminal. The judges clearly believed the tenets of natural law and expected that the defendants, too, should have been able to realize that their acts ran afoul of it. The fact that the "positivist law" of Germany at the time required them to commit these acts was irrelevant. Under natural law theory, the international court was justified in finding the defendants guilty of crimes against humanity.

Chapter 2

1. What argument could the power utilities use as a defense to the enforcement of this state law? Even if commercial speech is neither related to illegal activities nor misleading, it may be restricted if a state has a substantial interest that cannot be achieved by less restrictive means. In this situation, the state's interest in energy conservation is substantial, but it could be achieved by less restrictive means. That would be the utilities' defense against the enforcement of this state law.

2. Is this a violation of equal protection if the only reason for the tax is to protect the local firms from out-of-state competition? Explain. Yes. The tax would limit the liberty of some persons (out-of-state businesses), so it is subject to a review under the equal protection clause. Protecting local businesses from out-of-state competition is not a legitimate government objective. Thus, such a tax would violate the equal protection clause.

Chapter 3

1. Does this raise an ethical conflict between Acme and its employees? Between Acme and its shareholders? Explain your answers. When a corporation decides to respond to what it sees as a moral obligation to correct for past discrimination by adjusting pay differences among its employees, an ethical conflict is raised between the firm and its employees and between the firm and its shareholders. This dilemma arises directly out of the effect such a decision has on the firm's profits. If satisfying this obligation increases profitability, then the dilemma is easily resolved in favor of "doing the right thing."

2. Does Delta have an ethical duty to remove this product from the market, even if the injuries result only from misuse? Why or why not? Maybe. On the one hand, it is not the company's "fault" when a product is misused. Also, keeping the product on the market is not a violation of the law, and stopping sales would hurt profits. On the other hand, suspending sales could reduce suffering and could stop potential negative publicity.

Chapter 4

1. Does the court in Fatima's state have jurisdiction over Tipton? What factors will the court consider in determining jurisdiction? Yes. The court in Fatima's state has jurisdiction over Tipton on the basis of the company's minimum contacts with the state.

Courts look at the following factors in determining whether minimum contacts exist: (1) the quantity of the contacts, (2) the nature and quality of the contacts, (3) the source and connection of the cause of action to the contacts, (4) the interest of the forum state, and (5) the convenience of the parties. Attempting to exercise jurisdiction without sufficient minimum contacts would violate the due process clause. Generally, courts have found that jurisdiction is proper when there is substantial business conducted online (with contracts, sales, and so on). Even when there is only some interactivity through a website, courts have sometimes held that jurisdiction is proper. Jurisdiction is not proper when there is merely passive advertising.

Here, all of these factors suggest that the defendant had sufficient minimum contacts with the state to justify the exercise of jurisdiction over the defendant. Two especially important factors were that the plaintiff sold the security system to a resident of the state and that litigating in the defendant's state would be relatively inconvenient for the plaintiff.

2. If the dispute is not resolved, or if either party disagrees with the decision of the mediator or arbitrator, will a court hear the case? Explain. Yes. If the dispute is not resolved, or if either party disagrees with the decision of the mediator or arbitrator, a court will hear the case. It is required that the dispute be submitted to mediation or arbitration, but this outcome is not binding.

Chapter 5

1. Tom can call his first witness. What else might he do? Tom could file a motion for a directed verdict. This motion asks the judge to direct a verdict for Tom on the ground that Sue presented no evidence that would justify granting her relief. The judge grants the motion if there is insufficient evidence to raise an issue of fact.

2. Who can appeal to a higher court? Either a plaintiff or a defendant, or both, can appeal a judgment to a higher court. An appellate court can affirm, reverse, or remand a case, or take any of these actions in combination. To appeal successfully, it is best to appeal on the basis of an error of law, because appellate courts do not usually reverse on findings of fact.

Chapter 6

1. Can Raphael recover from Jana? Why or why not? Probably. To recover on the basis of negligence, the injured party as a plaintiff must show that the truck's owner owed the plaintiff a duty of care, that the owner breached that duty, that the plaintiff was injured, and that the breach caused the injury.

In this situation, the owner's actions breached the duty of reasonable care. The billboard falling on the plaintiff was the direct cause of the injury, not the plaintiff's own negligence. Thus, liability turns on whether the plaintiff can connect the breach of duty to the injury. This involves the test of proximate cause—the question of foreseeability. The consequences to the injured party must have been a foreseeable result of the owner's carelessness.

2. What might the firm successfully claim in defense? The company might defend against the electrician's wife's claim by asserting that the electrician should have known of the risk and, therefore, the company had no duty to warn. According to the problem, the danger is common knowledge in the electrician's field and should have been apparent to this electrician, given his years of training and experience. In other words, the company most likely had no need to warn the electrician of the risk.

The firm could also raise comparative negligence. Both parties' negligence, if any, could be weighed and the liability distributed proportionately. The defendant could also assert assumption of risk, claiming that the electrician voluntarily entered into a dangerous situation, knowing the risk involved.

Chapter 7

1. Is Superior Vehicles liable? Explain your answer. Yes. Those who make, sell, or lease goods are liable for the harm or damages caused by those goods to a consumer, user, or bystander. Thus, Superior Vehicles, which installed defective rims on the vehicle, is liable for the injuries proximately caused to the buyer (Uri). A manufacturer is liable for its failure to exercise due care to any person who sustains an injury proximately caused by a negligently made (defective) product. By not inspecting and testing the rims and tires it had installed, Superior Vehicles failed to exercise due care.

2. What defense might Bensing assert to avoid liability under state law? Bensing can assert the defense of preemption. An injured party may not be able to sue the manufacturer of defective products that are subject to comprehensive federal regulatory schemes. If the federal government has a comprehensive regulatory scheme (such as it does with medical devices and vaccines), then it is assumed that the rules were designed to ensure a product's safety, and the federal rules will preempt any state regulations. Therefore, Bensing could not be held liable to Rothfus under state law if it complied with the federal drug-labeling requirements.

Chapter 8

1. Has Roslyn violated any of the intellectual property rights discussed in this chapter? Explain. Yes. Roslyn has committed theft of trade secrets. Lists of suppliers and customers cannot be patented, copyrighted, or trademarked, but the information they contain is protected against appropriation by others as trade secrets. Most likely, Roslyn signed a contract agreeing not to use this information outside her employment by Organic. But even without such a contract, Organic could make a convincing case against its ex-employee for a theft of trade secrets.

2. Is this patent infringement? If so, how might Global save the cost of suing World for infringement and at the same time profit from World's sales? Yes. This is patent infringement. A software maker in this situation might best protect its product, save litigation costs, and profit from its patent by the use of a license. In the context of this problem, a license would grant permission to sell a patented item. (A license can be limited to certain purposes and to the licensee only.)

Chapter 9

1. Has Karl done anything wrong? Explain. Karl may have committed trademark infringement. A website that appropriates the key words of other sites with more frequent hits will appear in the same search engine results as the more popular sites. But using another's trademark as a key word without the owner's permission normally constitutes trademark infringement. Of course, some uses of another's trademark as a meta tag may be permissible if the use is reasonably necessary and does not suggest that the owner authorized or sponsored the use.

2. Can Eagle Corporation stop this use of eagle? If so, what must the company show? Explain. Yes. This may be an instance of trademark dilution. Dilution occurs when a trademark is used, without permission, in a way that diminishes the distinctive quality of the mark. Dilution does not require proof that consumers are likely to be confused by the use of the unauthorized mark. The products involved do not have to be similar. Dilution does require, however, that a mark be famous when the dilution occurs.

Chapter 10

1. With respect to the gas station, has she committed a crime? If so, what is it? Yes. With respect to the gas station, she has obtained goods by false pretenses. She might also be charged with larceny and forgery, and most states have special statutes covering illegal use of credit cards.

2. Has Jaxon committed a crime? If so, what is it? Yes. The Counterfeit Access Device and Computer Fraud and Abuse Act provides that a person who accesses a computer online, without permission, to obtain classified data—such as consumer credit files in a credit agency's database—is subject to criminal prosecution. The crime has two elements: accessing the computer without permission and taking data. It is a felony if done for private financial gain. Penalties include fines and imprisonment for up to twenty years. The victim of the theft can also bring a civil suit against the criminal to obtain damages and other relief.

Chapter 11

1. Under what circumstances would a U.S. court enforce the judgment of the Ecuadoran court? Under the principle of comity, a U.S. court would defer and give effect to foreign laws and judicial decrees that are consistent with U.S. law and public policy.

2. How can this attempt to undersell U.S. businesses be defeated? The practice described in this problem is known as dumping, which is regarded as an unfair international trade practice. Dumping is the sale of imported goods at "less than fair value." Based on the price of those goods in the exporting country, an extra tariff—known as an antidumping duty—can be imposed on the imports.

Chapter 12

1. Under the Uniform Electronic Transactions Act, what determines the effect of the electronic documents evidencing the parties' deal? Is a party's "signature" necessary? Explain. First, it might be noted that the Uniform Electronic Transactions Act (UETA) does not apply unless the parties to a contract

agree to use e-commerce in their transaction. In this deal, of course, the parties used e-commerce. The UETA removes barriers to e-commerce by giving the same legal effect to e-records and e-signatures as to paper documents and signatures. The UETA does not include rules for those transactions, however.

2. Is Fred's promise binding? Explain. Yes. Under the doctrine of detrimental reliance, or promissory estoppel, the promisee is entitled to payment of $5,000 from the promisor on graduation. There was a promise on which the promisee relied, the reliance was substantial and definite (the promisee went to college for the full term, incurring considerable expenses, and will likely graduate). It would only be fair to enforce the promise.

Chapter 13

1. Before Ready or Stealth starts performing, can the parties call off the deal? What if Stealth has already shipped the pizzas? Explain your answers. Contracts that are executory on both sides—that is, contracts on which neither party has performed—can be rescinded solely by agreement of the parties. Contracts that are executed on one side—contracts on which one party has performed—can be rescinded only if the party who has performed receives consideration for the promise to call off the deal.

2. If Haney sues Greg, what will be the measure of recovery? A nonbreaching party is entitled to his or her benefit of the bargain under the contract. Here, the innocent party is entitled to be put in the position she would have been in if the contract had been fully performed. The measure of the benefit is the cost to complete the work ($500). These are compensatory damages.

Chapter 14

1. Is this an acceptance of the offer or a counteroffer? If it is an acceptance, is it a breach of the contract? Why or why not? What if Fav-O-Rite told E-Design it was sending the printer stands as "an accommodation"? A shipment of nonconforming goods constitutes an acceptance of the offer and a breach, unless the seller seasonably notifies the buyer that the nonconforming shipment does not constitute an acceptance and is offered only as an accommodation. Thus, since there was no notification here, the shipment was both an acceptance and a breach. If, however, Fav-O-Rite had notified E-Design that it was sending the printer stands as an accommodation, the shipment would not constitute an acceptance, and Fav-O-Rite would not be in breach.

2. Does Country have the right to reject the shipment? Explain. Yes. A seller is obligated to deliver goods that conform to a contract in every detail. This is the perfect tender rule. The exception of the seller's right to cure does not apply here, because the seller delivered too little too late to take advantage of this exception.

Chapter 15

1. If the employer complies with the order and Alyssa stays on the job, is one order enough to garnish all of Alyssa's wages for each pay period until the debt is paid? Explain. No. In some states, a creditor must go back to court for a separate order of garnishment for each pay period. Also, federal and state laws limit the amount of money that can be garnished from a debtor's pay.

2. Are these debts dischargeable in bankruptcy? Explain. No. Besides the claims listed in this problem, the debts that cannot be discharged in bankruptcy include amounts borrowed to pay back taxes, goods obtained by fraud, debts that were not listed in the petition, domestic-support obligations, certain cash advances, and others.

Chapter 16

1. When Darnell dies, his widow claims that as Darnell's heir, she is entitled to take his place as Eliana's partner or to receive a share of the firm's assets. Is she right? Why or why not? No. A widow (or widower) has no right to take a dead partner's place. A partner's death causes dissociation, after which the partnership must purchase the dissociated partner's partnership interest. Therefore, the surviving partners must pay Darnell's widow the value of his interest in the partnership.

2. Does this constitute "cause" for termination? Why or why not? Yes. Failing to meet a specified sales quota can constitute a breach of a franchise agreement. If the franchisor is acting in good faith, "cause" may also include the death or disability of the franchisee, the insolvency of the franchisee, and a breach of another term of the franchise agreement.

Chapter 17

1. What are their options with respect to the management of their firm? The members of a limited liability company (LLC) may designate a group to run their firm, in which situation the firm would be considered a manager-managed LLC. The group may include only members, only nonmembers, or members and nonmembers. If, instead, all members participate in management, the firm would be a member-managed LLC. In fact, unless the members agree otherwise, all members are considered to participate in the management of the firm.

2. If Elizabeth is petitioned into involuntary bankruptcy, will that cause a dissolution of the limited partnership? Bankruptcy of the limited partnership itself causes dissolution, but bankruptcy of one of the limited partners does not dissolve the partnership unless it causes the bankruptcy of the firm.

Chapter 18

1. Is there a way for Northwest Brands to avoid this double taxation? Explain your answer. Yes. Small businesses that meet certain requirements can qualify as S corporations, created specifically to permit small businesses to avoid double taxation. The six requirements of an S corporation are (1) the firm must be a domestic corporation, (2) the firm must not be a member of an affiliated group of corporations, (3) the firm must have fewer than a certain number of shareholders, (4) the shareholders must be individuals, estates, or qualified trusts (or corporations in some cases), (5) there can be only one class of stock, and (6) no shareholder can be a nonresident alien.

2. Yvon, a Wonder shareholder, learns of the purchase and wants to sue the directors on Wonder's behalf. Can she do it? Explain. Yes. A shareholder can bring a derivative suit on behalf of a corporation if some wrong is done to the corporation. Normally, any damages recovered go into the corporate treasury.

Chapter 19

1. Was Winona an independent contractor? Yes. An independent contractor is a person who contracts with another—the principal—to do something but who is neither controlled by the other nor subject to the principal's right to control with respect to the performance. Independent contractors are not employees, because those who hire them have no control over the details of their performance.

2. Can Davis hold Estee liable for whatever damages he has to pay? Why or why not? Yes. A principal has a duty to indemnify (reimburse) an agent for liabilities incurred because of authorized and lawful acts and transactions, and for losses suffered because of the principal's failure to perform his or her duties.

Chapter 20

1. Can AMC be held liable for breach of contract? If so, why? If not, why not? Yes. Some courts have held that an implied employment contract exists between employer and employee under an employee handbook that states employees will be dismissed only for good cause. An employer who fires a worker contrary to this promise can be held liable for breach of contract.

2. For Erin to obtain workers' compensation, must her injury have been caused by Fine Print's negligence? Does it matter whether the action causing the injury was intentional? Explain. Workers' compensation laws establish a procedure for compensating workers who are injured on the job. Instead of suing to collect benefits, an injured worker notifies the employer of an injury and files a claim with the appropriate state agency. The right to recover normally is determined without regard to negligence or fault, but intentionally inflicted injuries are not covered. Unlike the potential for recovery in a lawsuit based on negligence or fault, recovery under a workers' compensation statute is limited to the specific amount designated in the statute for the employee's injury.

Chapter 21

1. Is this sexual harassment? Why or why not? Yes. One type of sexual harassment occurs when a request for sexual favors is a condition of employment, and the person making the request is a supervisor or acts with the authority of the employer. A tangible employment action, such as threatening to fire an employee who rejects sexual advances, may also lead to the employer's liability for the supervisor's conduct. That the injured employee is a male and the supervisor a female, instead of the other way around, does not affect the outcome. Same-gender harassment is also actionable.

2. Could Koko succeed in a suit against Lively for discrimination? Explain. Yes, if she can show that Lively failed to hire her solely because of her disability. The other elements for a discrimination suit based on a disability are that the plaintiff (1) has a disability and (2) is otherwise qualified for the job. Both of these elements appear to be satisfied in this situation.

Chapter 22

1. What must Gara do under the Immigration Act to hire foreign employees for Skytech? To hire a foreign individual to work in the United States, an employer must submit a petition to the U.S. Citizenship and Immigration Services, which determines whether the job candidate meets the legal standards. Each visa is for a specific job. In this situation, because Gara is looking for persons with specialized skills, he needs to show the individual qualifies for an H-1B visa. To qualify, the person must have highly specialized knowledge and a bachelor's degree or higher. Because only sixty-five thousand H-1B visas are set aside each year for immigrants, Gara must be prepared and file the application within the first few weeks of the year.

2. Are these conditions legal? Why or why not? No. A *closed shop*—a company that requires union membership as a condition of employment—is illegal. A *union shop*—a company that does not require union membership as a condition of employment but requires workers to join the union after a certain time on the job—is illegal in a state with a right-to-work law, which makes it illegal to require union membership for continued employment.

Chapter 23

1. What safeguards promote the ALJ's fairness? Under the Administrative Procedure Act (APA), the administrative law judge (ALJ) must be separate from the agency's investigative and prosecutorial staff. *Ex parte* (private) communications between the ALJ and a party to a proceeding are prohibited. Under the APA, an ALJ is exempt from agency discipline except on a showing of good cause.

2. Does the firm have any opportunity to express its opinion about the pending rule? Explain. Yes. Administrative rulemaking starts with the publication of a notice of the rulemaking in the *Federal Register*. A public hearing is held at which proponents and opponents can offer evidence and question witnesses. After the hearing, the agency considers what was presented at the hearing and drafts the final rule.

Chapter 24

1. To market the drug, what must United prove to the U.S. Food and Drug Administration? Under an extensive set of procedures established by the U.S. Food and Drug Administration, which administers the Federal Food, Drug, and Cosmetic Act, drugs must be shown to be effective as well as safe before they may be marketed to the public. In general, manufacturers are responsible for ensuring that the drugs they offer for sale are free of any substances that could injure consumers.

2. What can Gert do? Under the Truth-in-Lending Act, a buyer who wishes to withhold payment for a faulty product purchased with a credit card must follow specific procedures to settle the dispute. The credit-card issuer then must intervene and attempt to settle the dispute.

Chapter 25

1. Are there any reasons why the court might refuse to issue an injunction against Resource's operation? Explain. Yes. On the ground that the hardships that would be imposed on the polluter and on the community are greater than the hardships suffered by the residents, the court might deny an injunction. If the plant is the core of the local economy, for instance, the residents may be awarded only damages.

2. If the Environmental Protection Agency cleans up the site, from whom can it recover the cost? The Comprehensive Environmental Response, Compensation, and Liability Act regulates the clean-up of hazardous-waste disposal sites. Any potentially responsible party can be charged with the entire cost of cleaning up a site. Potentially responsible parties include the party that generated the waste (ChemCorp), the party that transported the waste to the site (Disposal), the party that owned or operated the site at the time of the disposal (Eliminators), and the current owner or operator of the site (Fluid). A party held responsible for the entire cost may be able to recoup some of it in a lawsuit against other potentially responsible parties.

Chapter 26

1. What can Consuela do? This is a breach of the warranty deed's covenant of quiet enjoyment. The buyer (Consuela) can sue the seller (Bernie) and recover the purchase price of the house, plus any damages.

2. Can Haven transfer possession for even less time to Idyll Company? Explain. Yes. An owner of a fee simple has the most rights possible—he or she can give the property away, sell it, transfer it by will, use it for almost any purpose, possess it to the exclusion of all the world, or as in this situation, transfer possession for any period of time. The party to whom possession is transferred can also transfer his or her interest (usually only with the owner's permission) for any lesser period of time.

Chapter 27

1. Under what circumstances would Pop's Market, a small store in a small, isolated town, be considered a monopolist? If Pop's is a monopolist, is it in violation of Section 2 of the Sherman Act? Why or why not? Size alone does not determine whether a firm is a monopoly—size in relation to the market is what matters. A small store in a small, isolated town is a monopolist if it is the only store serving that market. Monopoly involves the power to affect prices and output. If a firm has sufficient market power to control prices and exclude competition, that firm has monopoly power. Monopoly power in itself is not a violation of Section 2 of the Sherman Act. The offense also requires that the defendant intended to acquire or maintain that power through anticompetitive means.

2. What factors would a court consider to decide whether this arrangement violates the Clayton Act? This agreement is a tying arrangement. The legality of a tying arrangement depends on the purpose of the agreement, the agreement's likely effect on competition in the relevant markets (the market for the tying product and the market for the tied product), and other factors. Tying arrangements for commodities are subject to Section 3 of the Clayton Act. Tying arrangements for services can be agreements in restraint of trade in violation of Section 1 of the Sherman Act.

Chapter 28

1. What sort of information would an investor consider material? Under the 1934 Securities Exchange Act and SEC Rule 10b-5, a corporation can be held liable for any material omissions or misrepresentations of material facts to investors. Minor omissions and inaccuracies do not lead to liability. A fact will be considered material to an investor only if it is significant enough that it would likely affect the investor's decision to purchase or sell the company's securities. This would include facts that have an important bearing on the condition of the issuer and its business—liabilities, loans to officers and directors, customer delinquencies, contracts for the sale of corporate assets, new discoveries or products, and pending lawsuits.

2. Can Lee take advantage of this information to buy and sell Magma stock? Why or why not? No. The Securities Exchange Act of 1934 extends liability to officers and directors in their personal transactions for taking advantage of inside information when they know it is unavailable to the persons with whom they are dealing.

Appendix C

Sample Answers for
Business Case Problems with Sample Answer

Problem 1–5. Reading Citations. The court's opinion in this case—*Ryan Data Exchange, Ltd. v. Graco, Inc.*, 913 F.3d 726 (8th Cir. 2019)—can be found in Volume 913 of the *Federal Reporter, Third Series*, on page 726. The U.S. Court of Appeals for the Eighth Circuit issued this opinion in 2019.

Problem 2–3. Freedom of Speech. No. Wooden's conviction was not unconstitutional. Certain speech is not protected under the First Amendment. Speech that violates criminal laws—threatening speech, for example—is not constitutionally protected. Other unprotected speech includes fighting words, or words that are likely to incite others to respond violently. Speech that harms the good reputation of another, or defamatory speech, is also unprotected.

In his e-mail and audio notes to the alderwoman, Wooden referred to a sawed-off shotgun, domestic terrorism, and the assassination and murder of various politicians. He compared the alderwoman to the biblical character Jezebel, referring to her as a "bitch in the Sixth Ward." These references caused the alderwoman to feel threatened. The First Amendment does not protect such threats, which in this case violated a state criminal statute. There was nothing unconstitutional about punishing Wooden for this unprotected speech.

In the actual case on which this problem is based, Wooden appealed his conviction, arguing that it violated his right to freedom of speech. Under the principles set out above, the Missouri Supreme Court affirmed the conviction.

Problem 3–6. Business Ethics. It seems obvious from the facts stated in this problem that Hratch Ilanjian behaved unethically. Ethics, of course, involves questions relating to the fairness, justness, rightness, or wrongness of an action. Business ethics focuses on how businesspersons apply moral and ethical principles in making their decisions and whether those decisions are right or wrong.

In this problem, Ilanjian misrepresented himself to Vicken Setrakian, the president of Kenset Corporation, leading Setrakian to believe that Ilanjian was an international businessman who could help turn around Kenset's business in the Middle East. Ilanjian insisted that Setrakian provide him with confidential business documents. Then, claiming that they had an agreement, Ilanjian demanded full and immediate payment. He threatened to disclose the confidential information to a Kenset supplier if payment was not forthcoming. Kenset denied that they had a contract. In the ensuing litigation, during discovery, Ilanjian was uncooperative. Each of these acts was unethical.

In the actual case on which this problem is based, a trial court concluded that there was no contract, ordered the return of the confidential documents, and enjoined (prevented) Ilanjian from using the information. The U.S. Court of Appeals for the Third Circuit affirmed.

Problem 4–6. Corporate Contacts. No. The defendants' motion to dismiss the suit for lack of personal jurisdiction should not be granted. A corporation normally is subject to jurisdiction in a state in which it is doing business. A court applies the minimum-contacts test to determine whether it can exercise jurisdiction over an out-of-state corporation. This requirement is met if the corporation sells its products within the state or places its goods in the "stream of commerce" with the intent that the goods be sold in the state.

In this problem, the state of Washington filed a suit in a Washington state court against LG Electronics, Inc., and nineteen other foreign companies that participated in the global market for cathode ray tube (CRT) products. The state alleged a conspiracy to raise prices and set production levels in the market for CRTs in violation of a state consumer protection statute. The defendants filed a motion to dismiss the suit for lack of personal jurisdiction. These goods were sold for many years in high volume in the United States, including the state of Washington. In other words, the corporations purposefully established minimum contacts in the state of Washington. This is a sufficient basis for a Washington state court to assert personal jurisdiction over the defendants.

In the actual case on which this problem is based, the court dismissed the suit for lack of personal jurisdiction. On appeal, a state intermediate appellate court reversed on the reasoning stated above.

Problem 5–5. Discovery. Yes. The items that were deleted from a Facebook page can be recovered. Normally, a party must hire an expert to recover material in an electronic format, and this can be time consuming and expensive.

Electronic evidence, or e-evidence, consists of all computer-generated or electronically recorded information, such as posts on Facebook and other social media sites. The effect that e-evidence can have in a case depends on its relevance and what it reveals. In the facts presented in this problem, Isaiah should be sanctioned for deleting items that were subject to a discovery request. He should be required to cover Allied's cost to hire the recovery expert and attorneys' fees to confront the misconduct. In a jury trial, the court might also instruct the jury to presume that any missing items are harmful to Isaiah's case. If all of the material is retrieved and presented at the trial, any prejudice to Allied's case might thereby be mitigated. If not, the court might go so far as to order a new trial.

In the actual case on which this problem is based, Allied hired an expert, who determined that Isaiah had in fact removed some photos and other items from his Facebook page. After the expert testified about the missing material, Isaiah provided Allied with all of it, including the photos that he had deleted. Allied sought a retrial, but the court instead reduced the amount of Isaiah's damages by the amount that it cost Allied to address his "misconduct."

Problem 6–3. Negligence.

Negligence requires proof that (1) the defendant owed a duty of care to the plaintiff, (2) the defendant breached that duty, (3) the defendant's breach caused the plaintiff's injury, and (4) the plaintiff suffered a legally recognizable injury. With respect to the duty of care, a business owner has a duty to use reasonable care to protect business invitees. This duty includes an obligation to discover and correct or warn of unreasonably dangerous conditions that the owner of the premises should reasonably foresee might endanger an invitee. Some risks are so obvious that an owner need not warn of them. But even if a risk is obvious, a business owner may not be excused from the duty to protect its customers from foreseeable harm.

Because Lucario was the Weatherford's business invitee, the hotel owed her a duty of reasonable care to make its premises safe for her use. The balcony ran nearly the entire width of the window in Lucario's room. She could have reasonably believed that the window was a means of access to the balcony. The window/balcony configuration was dangerous, however, because the window opened wide enough for an adult to climb out, but the twelve-inch gap between one side of the window and the balcony was unprotected. This unprotected gap opened to a drop of more than three stories to a concrete surface below.

Should the hotel have anticipated the potential harm to a guest who opened the window in Room 59 and attempted to access the balcony? The hotel encouraged guests to "step out onto the balcony" to smoke. The dangerous condition of the window/balcony configuration could have been remedied at a minimal cost. These circumstances could be perceived as creating an "unreasonably dangerous" condition. And it could be concluded that the hotel created or knew of the condition and failed to take reasonable steps to warn of it or correct it. Of course, the Weatherford might argue that the window/balcony configuration was so obvious that the hotel was not liable for Lucario's fall.

In the actual case on which this problem is based, the court concluded that the Weatherford did not breach its duty of care to Lucario. On McMurtry's appeal—Lucario's estate's personal representative—a state intermediate appellate court held that this conclusion was in error, vacated the lower court's judgment in favor of the hotel on this issue, and remanded the case.

Problem 7–4. Product Liability.

Here, the accident was caused by Jett's inattention, not by the texting device in the cab of his truck. In a product liability case based on a design defect, the plaintiff has to prove that the product was defective at the time it left the hands of the seller or lessor. The plaintiff must also show that this defective condition made it "unreasonably dangerous" to the user or consumer. If the product was delivered in a safe condition and subsequent mishandling made it harmful to the user, the seller or lessor normally is not liable. To successfully assert a design defect, a plaintiff has to show that a reasonable alternative design was available and that the defendant failed to use it.

The plaintiffs could contend that the defendant manufacturer of the texting device owed them a duty of care because injuries to vehicle drivers and passengers, and others on the roads, were reasonably foreseeable due to the product's design, which (1) required the driver to divert his eyes from the road to view an incoming text from the dispatcher, and (2) permitted the receipt of texts while the vehicle was moving. But manufacturers are not required to design a product incapable of distracting a driver. The duty owed by a manufacturer to the user or consumer of a product does not require guarding against hazards that are commonly known or obvious or protecting against injuries that result from a user's careless conduct. That is what happened here.

In the actual case on which this problem is based, the court reached the same conclusion, based on the reasoning stated above, and an intermediate appellate court affirmed the judgment.

Problem 8–5. Patents.

One ground on which the denial of the patent application in this problem could be reversed on appeal is that the design of Raymond Gianelli's "Rowing Machine" is *not obvious* in light of the design of the "Chest Press Apparatus for Exercising Regions of the Upper Body."

To obtain a patent, an applicant must demonstrate to the satisfaction of the U.S. Patent and Trademark Office (PTO) that the invention, discovery, process, or design is novel, useful, and not obvious in light of current technology. In this problem, the PTO denied Gianelli's application for a patent for his "Rowing Machine"—an exercise machine on which a user *pulls* on handles to perform a rowing motion against a selected resistance. The PTO considered the device obvious in light of a patented "Chest Press Apparatus for Exercising Regions of the Upper Body"—a chest press exercise machine on which a user *pushes* on handles to overcome a selected resistance. But it can be easily argued that it is not obvious to modify a machine with handles designed to be *pushed* into one with handles designed to be *pulled*. In fact, anyone who has used exercise machines knows that a way to cause injury is to use a machine in a manner not intended by the manufacturer.

In the actual case on which this problem is based, the U.S. Court of Appeals for the Federal Circuit reversed the PTO's denial of Gianelli's application for a patent, based on the reasoning stated above.

Problem 9–4. Social Media.

Law enforcement can use social media to detect and prosecute suspected criminals. But there must be an authenticated connection between the suspects and the posts. To make this connection, law enforcement officials can present the testimony or certification of authoritative representatives of the social media site or other experts. The posts can be traced through Internet Protocol (IP) addresses. An IP address can reveal the e-mail address, and even the mailing address, of an otherwise anonymous poster. The custodians of Facebook, for example, can verify Facebook pages and posts because they maintain those items as business records in the course of regularly conducted business activities. From those sources, the prosecution in Hassan's case could have tracked the IP address to discover his identity.

In the actual case on which this problem is based, on Hassan's appeal of his conviction, the U.S. Court of Appeals for the Fourth Circuit affirmed.

Problem 10–3. White-Collar Crime. Yes. The acts committed by Matthew Simpson and the others constituted wire and mail fraud. Federal law makes it a crime to devise any scheme that uses the U.S. mail, commercial carriers (such as FedEx or UPS), or wire (such as telegraph, telephone, television, the Internet, or e-mail) with the intent to defraud the public.

Here, as stated in the facts, Simpson and his cohorts created and operated a series of corporate entities to defraud telecommunications companies, creditors, credit reporting agencies, and others. Through these entities, Simpson and the others used routing codes and spoofing services to make long-distance calls appear to be local. They stole other firms' network capacity and diverted payments to themselves. They leased goods and services without paying for them. In addition, they assumed false identities, addresses, and credit histories, and they issued false bills, invoices, financial statements, and credit references, in order to hide their association with their entities and with each other. Through the use of this "scheme," the perpetrators defrauded telecommunications companies and other members of the public in order to gain goods and services for themselves. They used wire services—the Internet and, presumably, phones and other qualifying services—to further the scheme.

In the actual case on which this problem is based, a federal district court convicted Simpson of participating in a wire and mail fraud conspiracy (and other crimes). On appeal, the U.S. Court of Appeals for the Fifth Circuit affirmed the conviction.

Problem 11–4. Import Controls. Yes. An antidumping duty can be assessed retrospectively (retroactively). But it does not seem likely that such a duty should be assessed here.

In this problem, the Wind Tower Trade Coalition (an association of domestic manufacturers of utility-scale wind towers) filed a suit in the U.S. Court of International Trade against the U.S. Department of Commerce, challenging its decision to impose only *prospective* antidumping duties on imports of utility-scale wind towers from China and Vietnam. The Commerce Department had found that the domestic industry had not suffered any "material injury" or "threat of material injury," and that it would be protected by a prospective assessment. Without a previously cognizable injury—and given the fact that any retrospective duties collected would not be payable to the members of the domestic industry in any event—it does not seem likely that retroactive duties should be imposed.

In the actual case on which this problem is based, the court denied the plaintiff's request for an injunction. On appeal, the

U.S. Court of Appeals for the Federal Circuit affirmed the denial, holding that the lower court had acted within its discretion in determining that retrospective duties were not appropriate.

Problem 12–3. Requirements of the Offer. No. TCP is not correct—the bonus plan was not too indefinite to be an offer. One of the requirements for an effective offer is that its terms must be reasonably definite. This enables a court to determine whether a breach has occurred and award an appropriate remedy. Generally, the offer's terms include an identification of the parties and the object or subject of the contract, the consideration to be paid, and the time of performance.

In this problem, TCP provided its employees, including Bahr, with the details of a bonus plan. A district sales manager such as Bahr who achieved 100 percent year-over-year sales growth and a 42 percent gross margin would earn 200 percent of his or her base salary. TCP added that it retained absolute discretion to modify the plan. Bahr exceeded the goal and expected a bonus commensurate with her performance. TCP paid her less than half what its plan promised, however. In the ensuing litigation, TCP claimed that the bonus plan was too indefinite to constitute an offer, but this was not, in fact, the case. The plan provided clear criteria to determine an employee's eligibility for a certain amount within a specific time. A court asked to apply the plan would have little or no doubt as to the amount an employee would be entitled to. The term that reserved discretion to TCP to modify the plan did not sufficiently undercut the clarity of the offer to prevent the formation of a contract.

In the actual case on which this problem is based, the trial court concluded that the reservation of discretion to revoke a plan makes an offer too indefinite and issued a judgment in TCP's favor. A state intermediate appellate court reversed this judgment, holding that TCP's plan was a sufficiently definite offer.

Problem 13–5. Limitation-of-Liability Clauses. Yes. The limitation-of-liability agreement that Eriksson signed is likely to be enforced in her parents' suit against Nunnink, their daughter's riding coach. This will likely result in a judgment against them unless they can establish "direct, willful and wanton negligence" on Nunnink's part. A limitation-of-liability clause affects the availability of certain remedies. Under basic contract principles, to be enforceable, these clauses must be clear and unambiguous.

In this problem, Eriksson, a young horseback-riding competitor, signed an agreement that released Nunnink from all liability except for damages caused by Nunnink's "direct, willful and wanton negligence." During an event, Eriksson's horse struck a hurdle, causing her to fall from the horse. The horse fell on her, resulting in her death. Her parents filed a suit against Nunnink for wrongful death. The limitation-of-liability clause signed by Eriksson, however, was straightforward, clear, and unambiguous, and therefore enforceable. Nunnink would be liable only if Eriksson's death was caused by Nunnink's gross negligence. The facts do not state that Eriksson's parents proved that Nunnink was grossly negligent.

In the actual case on which this problem is based, the trial court issued a judgment in Nunnink's favor. A state intermediate appellate court affirmed the judgment on the basis explained here.

Problem 14–6. Remedies of the Buyer or Lessee. No. At this point, the Morrises are not entitled to revoke their acceptance of the cabinets that IO delivered. Under the Uniform Commercial Code, acceptance of a lot or a commercial unit can be revoked if a nonconformity substantially impairs the value of the lot or unit and acceptance was based on the reasonable assumption that the nonconformity would be cured, and it has not been cured within a reasonable period of time. One of the corollaries to this rule is, of course, that the seller must be given a reasonable time within which to effect a cure.

Here, the Morrises contracted with IO to rebuild the kitchen in their home on the Gulf Coast of Mississippi after it was extensively damaged in a hurricane. As part of the deal, IO delivered new cabinets. Some defects were apparent, and as installation progressed, others emerged. IO ordered replacement parts to cure the defects and later offered to remove the cabinets and refund the price. The Morrises asked to be reimbursed for the installation fee as well. IO refused this request, but at all times, the seller emphasized that it was willing to fulfill its contractual obligations. The buyers then attempted to revoke their acceptance of the cabinets—before the replacement parts arrived and without attempting to negotiate any other accommodation.

In the actual case on which this problem is based, the Morrises filed a suit in a Mississippi state court against IO. The court dismissed the complaint and entered a judgment in the defendant's favor. A state intermediate appellate court affirmed. "The Morrises were not entitled to recovery because they revoked acceptance of the cabinets before giving IO a reasonable opportunity to cure the defects."

Problem 15–3. Discharge in Bankruptcy. No. Educational Credit Management Corporation (ECMC) cannot resume its effort to collect on Hann's loans. After the debtor has completed all payments, the court grants a discharge of all debts provided for by the repayment plan. All debts generally are dischargeable, especially those for which the court either declared that there was no obligation or disallowed on the ground that the underlying debt was satisfied.

In this problem, Hann financed her education partially through loans. When she filed a Chapter 13 petition, ECMC filed an unsecured proof of claim based on the loans. Hann believed that she had repaid the loans in full and objected. The court held a hearing at which ECMC failed to appear, and Hann submitted correspondence from the lender indicating the loans had been paid. The court then entered an order sustaining Hann's objection to ECMC's claim, in effect declaring that there was no obligation and the underlying debt was satisfied. By later attempting to renew efforts to collect on the loans, ECMC would violate the court's order.

In the actual case on which this problem is based, ECMC resumed collection efforts after the bankruptcy. Hann reopened her case and filed a complaint against ECMC, alleging that it

had violated the order sustaining her objection. The court ruled in Hann's favor and sanctioned ECMC for attempting to collect on the debt. On ECMC's appeal, the U.S. Court of Appeals for the First Circuit affirmed.

Problem 16–7. Franchise Termination. No. Executive Care is not entitled to an injunction against the Marshals and their new company. An injunction is an extraordinary remedy. To obtain an injunction before a suit is resolved, or arbitration or other alternative dispute resolution procedure is undertaken and completed, a party must establish that he or she will suffer irreparable harm if the injunction is denied.

In the facts of this problem, the Marshalls entered into a franchise agreement with Executive Care to operate a home health-care franchise. The agreement provided that the franchisees' failure to comply with the terms would likely cause irreparable harm to the franchisor, thereby entitling it to an injunction. When the Marshalls gave up their franchise, presumably before the end of its term under the franchise agreement, they returned everything in their possession with Executive Care trademarks. They quit operating out of the franchised location. They transferred the phone number back to Executive Care and informed their clients that they were no longer associated with that firm. Although the Marshalls continued to operate a home health-care business, they did so under the name "Well-Being Home Care Corp." There is nothing in these facts to establish that Executive Care is entitled to a preliminary injunction on the basis of irreparable harm. There appears to be little else the Marshalls might have done to prevent such harm to the franchisor.

In the actual case on which this problem is based, Executive Care filed a suit in a federal district court against the Marshalls and asked the court to issue a preliminary injunction. The court denied the request. On the reasoning stated here, the U.S. Court of Appeals for the Third Circuit affirmed.

Problem 17–4. LLC Operation. Part of the attractiveness of a limited liability company (LLC) as a form of business enterprise is its flexibility. The members can decide how to operate the business through an operating agreement. For example, the agreement can set forth procedures for choosing or removing members or managers.

Here, the Bluewater operating agreement provided for a "super majority" vote to remove a member who has committed a felony or under other circumstances that would jeopardize the firm's contractor status. Thus, Smith could not unilaterally "fire" another member without providing a reason. In fact, even a super majority of the members (Smith, Mosser, and Floyd) could not terminate Williford's interest in the firm without providing an acceptable reason—a felony conviction or a circumstance that undercut the firm's status as a contractor. Therefore, Smith, Mosser, and Floyd breached their operating agreement by attempting to remove Williford as a member. They may also have violated their fiduciary duties to Williford (depending on whether Mississippi has adopted the ULLCA), but it is not clear from the facts provided whether they violated the state LLC statute.

In the actual case on which this problem is based, Smith attempted to "fire" Williford without providing a reason. In Williford's suit, the court issued a judgment in his favor. On appeal, the court of appeals reversed, but the Supreme Court of Mississippi reversed the appellate court's decision and reinstated the lower court's holding in favor of Williford. The evidence was sufficient to find that the defendants had breached the LLC's operating agreement.

Problem 18–6. Rights of Shareholders. Clifford can pursue his action on the companies' behalf against Frederick. When a corporation is harmed by the actions of a director or officer, the other directors can bring a suit in the name of the company against that party. If the directors do not bring a suit, the shareholders can do so filing what is known as a shareholder's derivative suit. When shareholders bring a derivative suit, they are not pursuing rights or benefits for themselves personally but are acting as guardians of the corporate entity. Thus, if the suit is successful, any damages recovered go into the corporate treasury, not to the shareholders personally.

Here, two firms—one a limited liability company (LLC) and the other a corporation—are owned by three brothers, including Frederick and Clifford. Frederick is a controlling shareholder, and the president, of the corporation. Clifford believed that Frederick had been misusing the companies' funds to pay nonexistent debts, divert LLC assets to the corporation, and disburse about $1.8 million in corporate funds to his separate business. Clifford hired an attorney and filed an action on behalf of the two companies against Frederick. This action qualifies as a shareholder's derivative suit. Under these facts, any damages recovered should be paid to the companies.

Frederick's contention that a shareholder who lacks the knowledge necessary to adequately represent a corporation's interest because he or she does not understand financial statements may be a factor that helps defeat a frivolous suit or an action driven by an outside party. But in this case, Clifford demonstrated the requisite knowledge required to represent the firms' interests even if he did not know the details of the companies' financial documents—the action was filed on his instigation, he clearly understood the allegations, and he hired an attorney on whom he could rely to represent the companies' interests.

In the actual case on which this problem is based, Frederick filed a motion to dismiss based on the argument that Clifford lacked standing to bring the suit because he was the wrong party to represent the companies. The court denied the motion, in part, on the reasoning stated above.

Problem 19–4. Determining Employee Status. No. Cox is not liable to Cayer for any injuries or damage that she sustained in the accident with Ovalles. Generally, an employer is not liable for physical harm caused to a third person by the negligent act of an independent contractor in the performance of a contract. This is because the employer does not have the right to control the details of the performance. In determining whether a worker has the status of an independent contractor, how much control the employer can exercise over the details of the work is the most important factor weighed by the courts.

In this problem, Ovalles worked as a cable installer for Cox under an agreement with M&M. The agreement disavowed any employer-employee relationship between Cox and M&M's installers. Ovalles was required to designate his affiliation with Cox on his van, clothing, and an ID badge. But Cox had minimal contact with Ovalles and limited power to control the manner in which he performed his work. Cox supplied cable wire and other equipment, but these items were delivered to M&M, not Ovalles. These facts indicate that Ovalles was an independent contractor, not an employee. Thus, Cox was not liable to Cayer for the harm caused to her by Ovalles when his van rear-ended Cayer's car.

In the actual case on which this problem is based, the court issued a judgment in Cox's favor. The Rhode Island Supreme Court affirmed, applying the principles stated above to arrive at the same conclusion.

Problem 20–5. Unemployment Compensation. Yes. Ramirez qualifies for unemployment compensation. Generally, to be eligible for unemployment compensation, a worker must be willing and able to work. Workers who have been fired for misconduct or who have voluntarily left their jobs are not eligible for benefits. In the facts of this problem, the applicable state statute disqualifies an employee from receiving benefits if he or she voluntarily leaves work without "good cause."

The issue is whether Ramirez left her job for "good cause." When her father in the Dominican Republic had a stroke, she asked her employer for time off to be with him. Her employer refused the request. But Ramirez left to be with her father and called to inform her employer. It seems likely that this family emergency would constitute "good cause," and Ramirez's call and return to work after her father's death indicated that she did not disregard her employer's interests.

In the actual case on which this problem is based, the state of Florida denied Ramirez unemployment compensation. On Ramirez's appeal, a state intermediate appellate court reversed, on the reasoning stated above.

Problem 21–5. Sexual Harassment. Newton's best defense to Blanton's assertion of liability against the employer for its general manager's actions is the "*Ellerth/Faragher* affirmative defense." To establish this defense, an employer must show that it has taken reasonable care to prevent and promptly correct any sexually harassing behavior and that the plaintiff unreasonably failed to take advantage of any opportunity provided by the employer to avoid the harm.

In this problem, Blanton was subjected to sexual harassment by the general manager at their place of employment, a Pizza Hut restaurant operated by Newton. Blanton alerted low-level supervisors about the harassment, but they, like Blanton, were subordinate to the general manager and had no authority over her. Newton had a clear, straightforward antidiscrimination policy and complaint procedure under which an employee was to complain to the harasser's supervisor in such a situation. Once

Blanton finally complained to a manager with authority over the general manager, Newton promptly and effectively responded to Blanton's complaint. His delay in reporting the harassment to the appropriate authority can be construed as an unreasonable failure to take advantage of the opportunity provided by the employer to avoid the harm.

In the actual case on which this problem is based, in Blanton's suit against Newton, a jury found that the plaintiff was harassed as he claimed, but also that the defendant proved the *Ellerth/Faragher* affirmative defense, and the court issued a judgment in the employer's favor. The U.S. Court of Appeals for the Fifth Circuit affirmed.

Problem 22–5. Unfair Labor Practices. Before invoking a union-security clause against an employee, the union has an obligation, under the National Labor Relations Act (NLRA), to deal fairly with the employee. The NLRA requires the union to (1) provide the employee with actual notice of the precise amount due, including the months for which dues are owed, (2) explain how it computed the amount due, (3) give the employee a reasonable deadline for payment, and (4) explain to the employee that failure to pay will result in discharge.

Here, substantial evidence supported the NLRB's decision that the union's conduct in arranging to have the employee fired because of outstanding union dues under a union-security agreement—without first having discharged its fiduciary duties—violated the NLRA's prohibition against coercing employees. Such action also violated the prohibition against causing an employer to fire an employee, because the record indicated that the union had not explained to the employee how it had calculated his dues or provided him a reasonable time period in which to make payment. In fact, there was evidence suggesting that the union did just the opposite, first agreeing to a payment schedule with the employee and then having him fired the next day, before he could complete the agreed schedule and while he was on track to do so.

Problem 23–3. Agency Powers. The United States Supreme Court held that greenhouse gases fit within the Clean Air Act's (CAA's) definition of *air pollutant*. Thus, the Environmental Protection Agency (EPA) has the authority under that statute to regulate the emissions of such gases from new motor vehicles. According to the Court, the definition, which includes "any" air pollutant, embraces all airborne compounds "of whatever stripe." The EPA's focus on congressional amendments to the act did not address the original intent behind the statute. Nothing in the statute suggests that Congress meant to curtail the agency's power to treat greenhouse gases as air pollutants. In other words, the agency has a preexisting mandate to regulate "any air pollutant" that may endanger the public welfare.

The EPA also argued that, even if it had the authority to regulate greenhouse gas emissions, the agency would not exercise that authority because any regulation would conflict with other administration priorities. The Court acknowledged that the CAA conditions EPA action on the agency's formation of a "judgment" but explained that judgment must relate to whether a pollutant "cause[s], or contribute[s] to, air pollution which

may reasonably be anticipated to endanger public health or welfare." Thus, the EPA can avoid issuing regulations only if the agency determines that greenhouse gases do not contribute to climate change (or if the agency reasonably explains why it cannot or will not determine whether they do). The EPA's refusal to regulate was thus "arbitrary, capricious, or otherwise not in accordance with law." The Court remanded the case for the EPA to "ground its reasons for action or inaction in the statute."

Problem 24–3. Fair Debt-Collection Practices. Engler may recover under the Fair Debt Collection Practices Act (FDCPA). Atlantic is subject to the FDCPA because it is a debt-collection agency and was attempting to collect a debt on behalf of Bank of America. Atlantic used offensive collection tactics when it gave Engler's employer the false impression that Engler was a criminal, had a pending case, and was about to be arrested. Engler suffered harm because he experienced discomfort, embarrassment, and distress as a result of Atlantic's abusive conduct. Engler may recover actual damages, statutory damages, and attorneys' fees from Atlantic.

Problem 25–4. Environmental Impact Statements. Yes. An environmental impact statement (EIS) is required before the U.S. Forest Service (USFS) implements its proposed travel management plan (TMP). An EIS must be prepared for every major federal action that significantly affects the quality of the environment. An action is "major" if it involves a substantial commitment of resources. An action is "federal" if a federal agency has the power to control it. An EIS must analyze (1) the impact on the environment that the action will have, (2) any adverse effects on the environment and alternative actions that might be taken, and (3) irreversible effects that the action might generate.

Here, the resources committed to the implementation of the USFS's TMP could include the resources within the wilderness and the time and effort dedicated by the agency. The wilderness resources would include the soil, the vegetation, the wildlife, the wildlife habitat, any threatened or endangered species, and other natural assets impacted by the TMP. The agency's resources would include the funds and staff necessary to design, map, maintain, and enforce the TMP. These resources seem substantial. Of course, the implementation of the TMP is federal because the USFS has the power to control it.

As for the aspects of the environment that the agency might consider in preparing the EIS, some of the important factors were just listed—the soil, vegetation, wildlife, wildlife habitat, and threatened or endangered species. Other aspects of the environment impacted by the TMP might include cultural resources, historical resources, wilderness suitability, and other authorized uses of the wilderness. There is a potential for impact by every route that is designed to be part of the system, as well as the "dispersed vehicle camping" to be permitted on the terrain.

In the actual case on which this problem is based, the USFS considered all of the factors listed above. The agency then issued an EIS and a decision implementing the TMP. On a challenge to the EIS, a federal district court issued a judgment in the USFS's favor. The U.S. Court of Appeals for the Ninth Circuit affirmed, stating, "The Forest Service took the requisite hard look at the environmental impacts."

Problem 26–6. Joint Tenancies.

Under the law of the Cayman Islands, and according to Arthur's will, the disputed property became Diana's sole property when Arthur died. In a joint tenancy, each of two or more persons owns an undivided interest in the property. A deceased joint tenant's interest passes to the surviving joint tenant or tenants. The right of a surviving joint tenant to inherit a deceased joint tenant's ownership interest is referred to as a right of survivorship.

In this problem, Arthur and Diana owned three properties in the Cayman Islands in joint tenancy. (For this purpose, Cayman law is the same as U.S. law.) When the couple divorced, the decree did not change the tenancy. Later, Arthur died. His will provided that any property he held in joint tenancy "will pass to the survivor, and I instruct my Personal Representative to make no claim thereto." Despite this provision, the personal representative of Arthur's estate (his brother, Curtis) asserted that Arthur's interest in the properties was part of the estate. Diana said that the properties were entirely hers. Clearly, Diana is correct. Under the applicable principles of ownership of property by joint tenancy, as the sole surviving joint tenant, Arthur's interest in the properties passed to her. And under the terms of Arthur's will, his interest passed to her (and Curtis was "to make no claim thereto").

In the actual case on which this problem is based, Curtis asked the Florida state court that issued the couple's divorce to declare that Arthur's interest in the Cayman properties was part of his estate. The court ruled in the estate's favor and ordered Diana to sell the properties or buy Arthur's interest in them. A state intermediate appellate court reversed the order.

Problem 27–3. Price Discrimination.

Spa Steel satisfies most of the requirements for a price discrimination claim under Section 2 of the Clayton Act. Dayton Superior is engaged in interstate commerce, and it sells goods of like grade and quality to several purchasers. Moreover, Spa Steel can show that, because it sells Dayton Superior's products at a higher price than competitors, it lost business and thus suffered an injury. To recover, however, Spa Steel will also need to prove that Dayton Superior charged Spa Steel's competitors a lower price for the same product. Spa Steel cannot recover if its prices were higher for reasons related to its own business, such as having higher overhead expenses or seeking a larger profit.

Problem 28–4. Violations of the 1934 Act.

An omission or misrepresentation of a material fact in connection with the purchase or sale of a security may violate Section 10(b) of the Securities Exchange Act of 1934 and SEC Rule 10b-5. The key question is whether the omitted or misrepresented information is material. A fact, by itself, is not automatically material. A fact will be regarded as material only if it is significant enough that it would likely affect an investor's decision as to whether to buy or sell the company's securities. For example, a company's potential liability in a product liability suit and the financial consequences to the firm are material facts that must be disclosed because they are significant enough to affect an investor's decision as to whether to buy stock in the company.

In this case, the plaintiffs' claim should not be dismissed. To prevail on their claim that the defendants made material omissions in violation of Section 10(b) and SEC Rule 10b-5, the plaintiffs must prove that the omission was material. Their complaint alleged the omission of information linking Zicam and anosmia (a loss of the sense of smell) and plausibly suggested that reasonable investors would have viewed this information as material. After all, Zicam products account for 70 percent of Matrixx's sales.

Matrixx received reports of consumers who suffered anosmia after using Zicam Cold Remedy. In public statements discussing revenues and product safety, Matrixx did not disclose this information. But the information was significant enough to likely affect a consumer's decision to use the product, and this would affect revenue and ultimately the commercial viability of the product. The information was therefore significant enough to likely affect an investor's decision whether to buy or sell Matrixx's stock, and this would affect the stock price. Thus, the plaintiffs' allegations were sufficient. Contrary to the defendants' assertion, statistical sampling is not required to show materiality—reasonable investors could view reports of adverse events as material even if the reports did not provide statistically significant evidence.

Glossary

A

acceptance In contract law, the offeree's indication to the offeror that the offeree agrees to be bound by the terms of the offeror's proposal.

accord and satisfaction An agreement for payment (or other performance) between two parties, one of whom has a right of action against the other. After the payment has been accepted or other performance has been made, the "accord and satisfaction" is complete, and the obligation is discharged.

accredited investor In the context of securities offerings, sophisticated investors, such as banks, insurance companies, investment companies, the issuer's executive officers and directors, and persons whose income or net worth exceeds certain limits.

actionable Capable of serving as the basis of a lawsuit.

act of state doctrine A doctrine that provides that the judicial branch of one country will not examine the validity of public acts committed by a recognized foreign government within its own territory.

actual malice A condition that exists when a person makes a statement with either knowledge of its falsity or reckless disregard for the truth. In a defamation suit, a statement made about a public figure normally must be made with actual malice for liability to be incurred.

actus reus (pronounced *ak*-tus *ray*-uhs) A guilty (prohibited) act. The commission of a prohibited act and the intent to commit a crime are the two essential elements required for criminal liability.

adequate protection doctrine In bankruptcy law, a doctrine that protects secured creditors from losing their security as a result of an automatic stay. In certain circumstances, the bankruptcy court may provide adequate protection by requiring the debtor or trustee to pay the creditor or provide additional guaranties to protect the creditor against the losses suffered by the creditor as a result of the stay.

adjudication The process of resolving a dispute by presenting evidence and arguments before a neutral third party decision maker in a court or an administrative law proceeding.

administrative agency A federal or state government agency created by the legislature to perform a specific function, such as to make and enforce rules pertaining to the environment.

administrative law judge (ALJ) One who presides over an administrative agency hearing and has the power to administer oaths, take testimony, rule on questions of evidence, and make determinations of fact.

administrative process The procedure used by administrative agencies in fulfilling their three basic functions: rulemaking, enforcement, and adjudication.

adverse possession The acquisition of title to real property through open occupation, without the consent of the owner, for a period of time specified by a state statute. The occupation must be actual, exclusive, open, continuous, and in opposition to all others, including the owner.

affidavit A written voluntary statement of facts, confirmed by the oath or affirmation of the party making it and made before a person having the authority to administer the oath or affirmation.

affirmative action Job-hiring (and school admission) policies that give special consideration to members of protected classes in an effort to overcome present effects of past discrimination.

affirmative defense A response to a plaintiff's claim that does not deny the plaintiff's facts but attacks the plaintiff's legal right to bring an action. An example is the running of the statute of limitations.

agency A relationship between two parties in which one party (the agent) agrees to represent or act for the other (the principal).

agreement A meeting of two or more minds in regard to the terms of a contract; usually broken down into two events—an offer by one party to form a contract, and an acceptance of the offer by the person to whom the offer is made.

alien corporation A corporation formed in another country but doing business in the United States.

allege To state, recite, assert, or charge.

alternative dispute resolution (ADR) The resolution of disputes in ways other than those involved in the traditional judicial process. Negotiation, mediation, and arbitration are forms of ADR.

answer Procedurally, a defendant's response to the plaintiff's complaint.

anticipatory repudiation An assertion or action by a party indicating that he or she will not perform an obligation that he or she is contractually obligated to perform at a future time.

antitrust law Laws protecting commerce from unlawful restraints and anticompetitive practices.

apparent authority Authority that is only apparent, not real. An agent's apparent authority arises when the principal causes a third party to believe that the agent has authority, even though she or he does not.

appellant   The party who takes an appeal from one court to another.

appellee   The party against whom an appeal is taken—that is, the party who opposes setting aside or reversing the judgment.

arbitration   The settling of a dispute by submitting it to a disinterested third party (other than a court), who renders a decision. The decision may or may not be legally binding.

arbitration clause   A clause in a contract that provides that, in the event of a dispute, the parties will submit the dispute to arbitration rather than litigate the dispute in court.

arson   The malicious burning of another's dwelling. Some statutes have expanded arson to include any real property, regardless of ownership, and the destruction of property by other means—for example, by explosion.

articles of incorporation   The document that is filed with the appropriate state official, usually the secretary of state, when a business is incorporated and that contains basic information about the corporation.

articles of organization   The document that is filed with the appropriate state official, usually the secretary of state, when a limited liability company is formed.

articles of partnership   A written agreement that sets forth each partner's rights and obligations with respect to the partnership.

artisan's lien   A possessory lien given to a person who has made improvements and added value to another person's personal property as security for payment for services performed.

assault   Any word or action intended to make another person fearful of immediate physical harm; a reasonably believable threat.

assignment   The act of transferring to another all or part of one's rights arising under a contract.

assumption of risk   A defense against negligence that can be used when the plaintiff was aware of a danger and voluntarily assumed the risk of injury from that danger.

attachment   In the context of judicial liens, a court-ordered seizure and taking into custody of property prior to the securing of a judgment for a past-due debt.

attempted monopolization   An action by a firm that involves anticompetitive conduct, the intent to gain monopoly power, and a "dangerous probability" of success in achieving monopoly power.

authorization card   A card signed by an employee that gives a union permission to act on his or her behalf in negotiations with management.

automatic stay   In bankruptcy proceedings, the suspension of almost all litigation and other action by creditors against the debtor or the debtor's property. The stay is effective the moment the debtor files a petition in bankruptcy.

award   In the context of litigation, the amount of money awarded to a plaintiff in a civil lawsuit as damages. In the context of arbitration, the arbitrator's decision.

B

bailment   A situation in which the personal property of one person (a bailor) is entrusted to another (a bailee), who is obligated to return the bailed property to the bailor or dispose of it as directed.

bait-and-switch advertising   Advertising a product at an attractive price and then telling the consumer that the advertised product is not available or is of poor quality and encouraging her or him to purchase a more expensive item.

bankruptcy court   A federal court of limited jurisdiction that handles only bankruptcy proceedings.

bankruptcy trustee   A person appointed by the court to manage the debtor's funds in a bankruptcy proceeding.

battery   The unprivileged, intentional touching of another.

benefit corporation   A type of for-profit corporation, available by statute in a number of states, that seeks to have a material positive impact on society and the environment.

beyond a reasonable doubt   The standard used to determine the guilt or innocence of a person criminally charged. To be guilty of a crime, one must be proved guilty "beyond and to the exclusion of every reasonable doubt." A reasonable doubt is one that would cause a prudent person to hesitate before acting in matters important to him or her.

bilateral contract   A type of contract that arises when a promise is given in exchange for a promise.

bilateral mistake   A mistake that occurs when both parties to a contract are mistaken about the same material fact.

Bill of Rights   The first ten amendments to the U.S. Constitution.

binding authority   Any source of law that a court must follow when deciding a case.

blue sky laws   State laws that regulate the offer and sale of securities.

bona fide occupational qualification (BFOQ)   An identifiable characteristic reasonably necessary to the normal operation of a particular business. Such characteristics can include gender, national origin, and religion, but not race.

bond   A security that evidences a corporate (or government) debt.

botnet   Short for robot network—a group of computers that run an application controlled and manipulated only by the software source. Usually, the term is reserved for computers that have been infected by malicious robot software.

breach   To violate a law, by an act or an omission, or to break a legal obligation that one owes to another person or to society.

breach of contract   The failure, without legal excuse, of a promisor to perform the obligations of a contract.

brief   A formal legal document submitted to an appellate court when a case is appealed. The appellant's brief outlines the facts and issues of the case, the judge's rulings or jury's findings that should be reversed or modified, the applicable law, and the arguments on the client's behalf. The appellee usually files an answering brief.

browse-wrap terms   Terms and conditions of use that are presented to an Internet user at the time a product, such as software, is downloaded but that need not be agreed to before the product is installed or used.

bureaucracy   A large organization that is structured hierarchically to carry out specific functions.

burglary   The unlawful entry into a building with the intent to commit a felony. Some state statutes have expanded burglary to include the intent to commit any crime.

business ethics   Ethics in a business context; a consensus of what constitutes right or wrong behavior in the world of business and the application of moral principles to situations that arise in a business setting.

business invitees   Those people, such as customers or clients, who are invited onto business premises by the owner of those premises for business purposes.

business judgment rule   A rule under which courts will not hold corporate officers and directors liable for honest mistakes of judgment and bad business decisions that were made in good faith.

business necessity   A defense to an allegation of employment discrimination in which the employer demonstrates that an employment practice that discriminates against members of a protected class is related to job performance.

buyout price   The amount payable to a partner on his or her dissociation from a partnership, based on the amount distributable to that partner if the firm were wound up on that date, and offset by any damages for wrongful dissociation.

buy-sell agreement   In the context of partnerships, an express agreement made at the time of partnership formation for one or more of the partners to buy out the other or others should the situation warrant.

bylaws   The internal rules of management adopted by a corporation at its first organizational meeting.

C

case law   The rules of law announced in court decisions. Case law interprets statutes, regulations, constitutional provisions, and other case law.

case on point   A previous case involving factual circumstances and issues that are similar to those in the case before the court.

categorical imperative   A concept developed by the philosopher Immanuel Kant as an ethical guideline for behavior. In deciding whether an action is right or wrong, or desirable or undesirable, a person should evaluate the action in terms of what would happen if everybody else in the same situation, or category, acted the same way.

causation in fact   An act or omission without ("but for") which an event would not have occurred.

cease-and-desist order   An administrative or judicial order prohibiting a person or business firm from conducting activities that an agency or court has deemed illegal.

certificate of limited partnership   The document that must be filed with a designated state official to form a limited partnership.

certification mark   A mark used by one or more persons, other than the owner, to certify the region, materials, mode of manufacture, quality, or accuracy of the owner's goods or services. Examples of certification marks include the "Good Housekeeping Seal of Approval" and "UL Tested."

charging order   In partnership law, an order granted by a court to a judgment creditor that entitles the creditor to attach a partner's interest in the partnership.

checks and balances   The system by which each of the three branches of the U.S. national government (executive, legislative, and judicial) exercises checks on the powers of the other branches.

citation   A reference to a publication in which a legal authority—such as a statute or a court decision—or other source can be found.

civil law   The branch of law dealing with the definition and enforcement of all private or public rights, as opposed to criminal matters.

civil law system   A system of law derived from that of the Roman Empire and based on a code rather than case law; the predominant system of law in the nations of continental Europe and the nations that were once their colonies. In the United States, Louisiana is the only state that has a civil law system.

click-on agreement   An agreement that arises when a buyer, engaging in a transaction on a computer, indicates his or her assent to be bound by the terms of an offer by clicking on a button that says, for example, "I agree"; sometimes referred to as a *click-on license* or a *click-wrap agreement*.

close corporation   A corporation whose shareholders are limited to a small group of persons, often family members.

closed shop   A firm that requires union membership on the part of its workers as a condition of employment.

closing The final step in the sale of real estate, in which ownership is transferred to the buyer in exchange for payment of the purchase price.

closing argument An argument made at a trial after the plaintiff and defendant have finished presenting their cases. Closing arguments are made prior to the jury charges.

cloud computing The delivery to users of on-demand services from third party servers over a network.

collective bargaining The process by which labor and management negotiate the terms and conditions of employment, including working hours and workplace conditions.

collective mark A mark used by members of a cooperative, association, or other organization to certify the region, materials, mode of manufacture, quality, or accuracy of the specific goods or services. Examples of collective marks include the labor union marks found on tags of certain products and the credits of movies, which indicate the various associations and organizations that participated in the making of the movies.

comity A deference by which one nation gives effect to the laws and judicial decrees of another nation.

commerce clause The provision in Article I, Section 8, of the U.S. Constitution that gives Congress the power to regulate interstate commerce.

commercial impracticability A doctrine under which a seller may be excused from performing a contract when (1) a contingency occurs, (2) the contingency's occurrence makes performance impracticable, and (3) the nonoccurrence of the contingency was a basic assumption on which the contract was made.

commercial use Use of land for business activities only; sometimes called *business use.*

commingle To put funds or goods together into one mass so that they are mixed to such a degree that they no longer have separate identities.

common law The body of law developed from custom or judicial decisions in English and U.S. courts, not attributable to a legislature.

common stock A security that evidences ownership in a corporation. A share of common stock gives the owner a proportionate interest in the corporation with regard to control, earnings, and net assets. Common stock is lowest in priority with respect to payment of dividends and distribution of the corporation's assets on dissolution.

community property A form of concurrent property ownership in which each spouse owns an undivided one-half interest in property acquired during the marriage.

comparative negligence A theory in tort law under which the liability for injuries resulting from negligent acts is shared by all parties who were negligent (including the injured party) on the basis of each person's proportionate negligence.

compelling government interest A test of constitutionality that requires the government to have compelling reasons for passing any law that restricts fundamental rights, such as free speech, or distinguishes between people based on a suspect trait.

compensatory damages A money award equivalent to the actual value of injuries or damages sustained by the aggrieved party.

complaint The pleading made by a plaintiff alleging wrongdoing on the part of the defendant; the document that, when filed with a court, initiates a lawsuit.

computer crime Any violation of criminal law that involves knowledge of computer technology for its perpetration, investigation, or prosecution.

concentrated industry An industry in which a single firm or a small number of firms control a large percentage of market sales.

concurrent jurisdiction Jurisdiction that exists when two different courts have the power to hear a case. For example, some cases can be heard in either a federal or a state court.

concurrent ownership Joint ownership of property (including tenancies in common and joint tenancies).

concurring opinion A court opinion by one or more judges or justices who agree with the majority but want to make or emphasize a point that was not made or emphasized in the majority's opinion.

condemnation The judicial procedure by which the government exercises its power of eminent domain. It generally involves two phases: a taking and a determination of fair value.

condition A possible future event, the occurrence or nonoccurrence of which will trigger the performance of a legal obligation or terminate an existing obligation under a contract.

condition precedent A condition in a contract that must be met before a party's promise becomes absolute.

confiscation A government's taking of a privately owned business or personal property without a proper public purpose or an award of just compensation.

conforming goods Goods that conform to contract specifications.

consequential damages Special damages that compensate for a loss that is not direct or immediate (for example, lost profits). The special damages must have been reasonably foreseeable at the time the breach or injury occurred in order for the plaintiff to collect them.

consideration Generally, the value given in return for a promise or a performance. The consideration, which must be present to make the contract legally binding, must be something of legally sufficient value and must be bargained for.

constitutional law Law that is based on the U.S. Constitution and the constitutions of the various states.

constructive discharge A termination of employment brought about by making the employee's working conditions so intolerable that the employee reasonably feels compelled to leave.

consumer-debtor One whose debts result primarily from the purchase of goods for personal, family, or household use.

consumer law The body of statutes, agency rules, and judicial decisions protecting consumers of goods and services from dangerous manufacturing techniques, mislabeling, unfair credit practices, deceptive advertising, and other such practices.

contract An agreement that can be enforced in court, formed by two or more parties, each of whom agrees to perform or to refrain from performing some act now or in the future.

contractual capacity The legal ability to enter into contracts; the threshold mental capacity required by law for a party who enters into a contract to be bound by that contract.

contributory negligence A theory in tort law under which a complaining party's own negligence contributed to or caused his or her injuries. Contributory negligence is an absolute bar to recovery in a minority of jurisdictions.

conversion The wrongful taking, using, or retaining possession of personal property that belongs to another.

conveyance The transfer of title to real property from one person to another by deed or other document.

cookie A small file sent from a website and stored in a user's Web browser to track the user's Web-browsing activities.

"cooling-off" laws Laws that allow buyers of goods sold in certain transactions to cancel their contracts within three business days.

copyright The exclusive right of authors to publish, print, or sell an intellectual production for a statutory period of time. A copyright has the same monopolistic nature as a patent or trademark, but it differs in that it applies exclusively to works of art, literature, and other works of authorship, including computer programs.

corporate governance A set of policies specifying the rights and responsibilities of the various participants in a corporation and spelling out the rules and procedures for making corporate decisions.

corporate social responsibility The concept that corporations can and should act ethically and be accountable to society for their actions.

corporation A corporation is a firm that is authorized by statute to act as legal entity separate and distinct from its owners (shareholders).

cost-benefit analysis A decision-making technique that involves weighing the costs of a given action against the benefits of the action.

co-surety A joint surety; one who assumes liability jointly with another surety for the payment of an obligation.

counteradvertising New advertising that is undertaken to correct earlier false claims that were made about a product.

counterclaim A claim made by a defendant in a civil lawsuit that, in effect, sues the plaintiff.

counteroffer An offeree's response to an offer in which the offeree rejects the original offer and at the same time makes a new offer.

court of equity A court that decides controversies and administers justice according to the rules, principles, and precedents of equity.

court of law A court in which the only remedies that can be granted are things of value, such as money damages. In the early English king's courts, courts of law were distinct from courts of equity.

covenant not to compete A contractual promise to refrain from competing with another party for a certain period of time and within a certain geographic area. Although covenants not to compete restrain trade, they are commonly found in partnership agreements, business sale agreements, and employment contracts. If they are ancillary to such agreements, covenants not to compete will normally be enforced by the courts unless the time period or geographic area is deemed unreasonable.

covenant not to sue An agreement to substitute a contractual obligation for some other type of legal action based on a valid claim.

cover A buyer's or lessee's purchase on the open market of goods to substitute for those promised but never delivered by the seller or lessor. Under the Uniform Commercial Code, if the cost of cover exceeds the cost of the contract goods, the buyer or lessee can recover the difference, plus incidental and consequential damages.

cram-down provision A provision of the Bankruptcy Code that allows a court to confirm a debtor's Chapter 11 reorganization plan even though only one class of creditors has accepted it.

creditors' composition agreement An agreement formed between a debtor and his or her creditors in which the creditors agree to accept a lesser sum than that owed by the debtor in full satisfaction of the debt.

crime A wrong against society proclaimed in a statute and punishable by society through fines and/or imprisonment—or, in some cases, death.

criminal law The branch of law that defines and punishes wrongful actions committed against the public.

cross-examination The questioning of an opposing witness during a trial.

crowdfunding A cooperative activity in which people network and pool funds and other resources via the Internet to assist a cause (such as disaster relief) or invest in a business venture (such as a startup).

cure Under the Uniform Commercial Code, the right of a party who tenders nonconforming performance to correct his or her performance within the contract period.

cyber crime A crime that occurs online, in the virtual community of the Internet, as opposed to the physical world.

cyber fraud Fraud that involves the online theft of credit-card information, banking details, and other information for criminal use.

cyberlaw An informal term used to refer to all laws governing electronic communications and transactions, particularly those conducted via the Internet.

cybersquatting Registering a domain name that is the same as, or confusingly similar to, the trademark of another and then offering to sell that domain name back to the trademark owner.

cyber tort A tort committed via the Internet.

D

damages A monetary award sought as a remedy for a breach of contract or a tortious act.

debtor in possession (DIP) In Chapter 11 bankruptcy proceedings, a debtor who is allowed to continue in possession of the estate in property (the business) and to continue business operations.

deceptive advertising Advertising that misleads consumers, either by making unjustified claims about a product's performance or by omitting a material fact concerning the product's composition or performance.

deed A document by which title to real property is passed.

defamation Any published or publicly spoken false statement that causes injury to another's good name, reputation, or character.

default Failure to pay a debt when it is due.

default judgment A judgment entered by a court against a defendant who has failed to appear in court to answer or defend against the plaintiff's claim.

defendant One against whom a lawsuit is brought, or the accused person in a criminal proceeding.

defense Reasons that a defendant offers in an action or suit as to why the plaintiff should not obtain what he or she is seeking.

delegation The transfer of a contractual duty to a third party. The party delegating the duty (the delegator) to the third party (the delegatee) is still obliged to perform on the contract should the delegatee fail to perform.

delegation doctrine A doctrine based on Article I, Section 8, of the U.S. Constitution, which has been construed to allow Congress to delegate some of its power to make and implement laws to administrative agencies. The delegation is considered to be proper as long as Congress sets standards outlining the scope of the agency's authority.

deposition The testimony of a party to a lawsuit or of a witness taken under oath before a trial.

destination contract A contract in which the seller is required to ship the goods by carrier and deliver them at a particular destination. The seller assumes liability for any losses or damage to the goods until they are tendered at the destination specified in the contract.

dilution With respect to trademarks, a doctrine under which distinctive or famous trademarks are protected from certain unauthorized uses regardless of a showing of competition or a likelihood of confusion. Congress created a federal cause of action for dilution in 1995 with the passage of the Federal Trademark Dilution Act.

direct examination The examination of a witness by the attorney who calls the witness to the stand at trial to testify on behalf of the attorney's client.

Direct Public Offering (DPO) The sale of a private company's shares directly to the public without going through an investment banking firm. In other words, no new shares of stock are created. Also called a direct listing.

disaffirmance The legal avoidance, or setting aside, of a contractual obligation.

discharge (1) The termination of an obligation, such as occurs when the parties to a contract have fully performed their contractual obligations. (2) The termination of a bankruptcy debtor's obligation to pay debts.

discharge in bankruptcy The release of a debtor from all debts that are provable, except those specifically excepted from discharge by statute.

disclosed principal A principal whose identity is known to a third party at the time the agent makes a contract with the third party.

discovery A phase in the litigation process during which the opposing parties may obtain information from each other and from third parties prior to trial.

disparagement of property An economically injurious false statement made about another's product or property. A general term for torts that are more specifically referred to as *slander of quality* or *slander of title*.

disparate-impact discrimination Discrimination that results from certain employer practices or procedures that, although not discriminatory on their face, have a discriminatory effect.

disparate-treatment discrimination A form of employment discrimination that results when an employer intentionally discriminates against employees who are members of protected classes.

dissenting opinion A court opinion that presents the views of one or more judges or justices who disagree with the majority's decision.

dissociation The severance of the relationship between a partner and a partnership or between a member and a limited liability company.

dissolution The formal disbanding of a partnership, corporation, or other business entity. For instance, partnerships can be dissolved by acts of the partners, by operation of law, or by judicial decree.

distributed network A network that can be used by persons located (distributed) around the country or the globe to share computer files.

distribution agreement A contract between a seller and a distributor of the seller's products setting out the terms and conditions of the distributorship.

diversity of citizenship Under Article III, Section 2, of the Constitution, a basis for federal court jurisdiction over a lawsuit between (1) citizens of different states, (2) a foreign country and citizens of a state or of different states, or (3) citizens of a state and citizens or subjects of a foreign country. The amount in controversy must be more than $75,000 before a federal court can take jurisdiction in such cases.

divestiture A company's sale of one or more of its divisions' operating functions under court order as part of the enforcement of antitrust laws.

dividend A distribution of corporate profits to the corporation's shareholders in proportion to the number of shares held.

document of title A writing exchanged in the regular course of business that evidences the right to possession of goods (for example, a bill of lading or a warehouse receipt).

domain name The series of letters and symbols used to identify a site operator on the Internet; part of an Internet "address."

domestic corporation In a given state, a corporation that is organized under the law of that state.

double jeopardy A situation occurring when a person is tried twice for the same criminal offense; prohibited by the Fifth Amendment to the Constitution.

down payment The part of the purchase price of real property that is paid in cash up front, reducing the amount of the loan or mortgage.

dram shop act A state statute that imposes liability on the owners of bars and taverns, as well as those who serve alcoholic drinks to the public, for injuries resulting from accidents caused by intoxicated persons when the sellers or servers of alcoholic drinks contributed to the intoxication.

due process clause The provisions of the Fifth and Fourteenth Amendments to the U.S. Constitution that guarantee that no person shall be deprived of life, liberty, or property without due process of law. Similar clauses are found in most state constitutions.

dumping The selling of goods in a foreign country at a price below the price charged for the same goods in the domestic market.

duress Unlawful pressure brought to bear on a person, causing the person to perform an act that he or she would not otherwise perform (or refrain from doing something that he or she would otherwise do).

duty-based ethics An ethical philosophy rooted in the idea that every person has certain duties to others, including both humans and the planet. Those duties may be derived from religious principles or from other philosophical reasoning.

duty of care The duty of all persons, as established by tort law, to exercise a reasonable amount of care in their dealings with others. Failure to exercise due care, which is normally determined by the "reasonable person standard," constitutes the tort of negligence.

E

e-agent A semiautonomous computer program that is capable of executing specific tasks.

early neutral case evaluation A form of alternative dispute resolution in which a neutral third party evaluates the strengths and weakness of the disputing parties' positions. The evaluator's opinion forms the basis for negotiating a settlement.

easement A nonpossessory right, established by express or implied agreement, to make limited use of another's property without removing anything from the property.

e-contract A contract that is entered into in cyberspace and is evidenced only by electronic impulses (such as those that make up a computer's memory), rather than, for example, a typewritten form.

e-evidence A type of evidence that consists of computer-generated or electronically recorded information, including e-mail, voice mail, spreadsheets, word-processing documents, and other data.

Electronic Notarization The use of webcams or audio-video teleconference technologies with which a signer can be located anywhere in the world and still lawfully "appear" online before a notary public who is physically located in the state of commissioning.

embezzlement   The fraudulent appropriation of money or other property by a person to whom the money or property has been entrusted.

eminent domain   The power of a government to take land from private citizens for public use on the payment of just compensation.

employment at will   A common law doctrine under which either party may terminate an employment relationship at any time for any reason, unless a contract specifies otherwise.

employment discrimination   Unequal treatment of employees or job applicants on the basis of race, color, national origin, religion, gender, age, or disability; prohibited by federal statutes.

enabling legislation   A statute enacted by Congress that authorizes the creation of an administrative agency and specifies the name, composition, purpose, and powers of the agency.

entrapment   In criminal law, a defense in which the defendant claims that he or she was induced by a public official—usually an undercover agent or police officer—to commit a crime that he or she would otherwise not have committed.

entrepreneur   One who initiates and assumes the financial risk of a new business enterprise and undertakes to provide or control its management.

environmental impact statement (EIS)   A formal analysis required for any major federal action that will significantly affect the quality of the environment to determine the action's impact and explore alternatives.

Environmental Social and Corporate Governance (ESG)   Relates to a set of standards for a company's behavior used by socially conscious investors to screen potential investments.

equal dignity rule   A rule requiring that an agent's authority be in writing if the contract to be made on behalf of the principal must be in writing.

equal protection clause   The provision in the Fourteenth Amendment to the U.S. Constitution that guarantees that no state will "deny to any person within its jurisdiction the equal protection of the laws." This clause mandates that state governments treat similarly situated individuals in a similar manner.

equitable maxims   General propositions or principles of law that have to do with fairness (equity).

escrow account   An account generally held in the name of the depositor and the escrow agent. The funds in the account are paid to a third person on fulfillment of the escrow condition.

e-signature   As defined by the Uniform Electronic Transactions Act, "an electronic sound, symbol, or process attached to or logically associated with a record and executed or adopted by a person with the intent to sign the record."

establishment clause   The provision in the First Amendment to the U.S. Constitution that prohibits Congress from establishing a state-sponsored religion, as well as from passing laws that promote religion or show a preference for one religion over another.

estopped   Barred, impeded, or precluded.

ethical reasoning   A reasoning process in which an individual links his or her moral convictions or ethical standards to the particular situation at hand.

ethics   Moral principles and values applied to social behavior.

exclusionary rule   In criminal procedure, a rule under which any evidence that is obtained in violation of the accused's constitutional rights guaranteed by the Fourth, Fifth, and Sixth Amendments, as well as any evidence derived from illegally obtained evidence, will not be admissible in court.

exclusive agency   An agency in which a principal grants an agent an exclusive territory and does not allow another agent to compete in that territory.

exclusive-dealing contract   An agreement under which a seller forbids a buyer to purchase products from the seller's competitors.

exclusive jurisdiction   Jurisdiction that exists when a case can be heard only in a particular court or type of court, such as a federal court or a state court.

exculpatory clause   A clause that releases a contractual party from liability in the event of monetary or physical injury, no matter who is at fault.

executed contract   A contract that has been completely performed by both parties.

executive agency   An administrative agency within the executive branch of government. At the federal level, executive agencies are those within the cabinet departments.

executory contract   A contract that has not yet been fully performed.

exhaustion doctrine   In administrative law, the principle that a complaining party normally must have exhausted all available administrative remedies before seeking judicial review.

export   To sell products to buyers located in other countries.

express authority   Authority expressly given by one party to another. In agency law, an agent has express authority to act for a principal if both parties agree, orally or in writing, that an agency relationship exists in which the agent has the power (authority) to act in the place of, and on behalf of, the principal.

express contract   A contract in which the terms of the agreement are fully and explicitly stated in words, oral or written.

express warranty A seller's or lessor's oral or written promise, ancillary to an underlying sales or lease agreement, as to the quality, description, or performance of the goods being sold or leased.

expropriation The seizure by a government of privately owned business or personal property for a proper public purpose and with just compensation.

F

family limited liability partnership (FLLP) A limited liability partnership (LLP) in which the majority of the partners are members of a family.

federal form of government A system of government in which the states form a union and the sovereign power is divided between a central government and the member states.

federal question A question that pertains to the U.S. Constitution, acts of Congress, or treaties. A federal question provides a basis for federal jurisdiction.

Federal Rules of Civil Procedure (FRCP) The rules controlling procedural matters in civil trials brought before the federal district courts.

fee simple absolute An ownership interest in land in which the owner has the greatest possible aggregation of rights, privileges, and power. The owner can use, possess, or dispose of the property as he or she chooses during his or her lifetime. On death, the interest in the property passes to the owner's heirs.

felony A crime—such as arson, murder, rape, or robbery—that carries the most severe sanctions, usually ranging from one year in a state or federal prison to the forfeiture of one's life.

fiduciary As a noun, a person having a duty created by his or her undertaking to act primarily for another's benefit in matters connected with the undertaking. As an adjective, a relationship founded on trust and confidence.

filtering software A computer program that screens incoming data according to rules built into the software and controls access to websites with content not consistent with these rules.

final order The final decision of an administrative agency on an issue. If no appeal is taken, or if the case is not reviewed or considered anew by the agency commission, the administrative law judge's initial order becomes the final order of the agency.

firm offer An offer (by a merchant) that is irrevocable without consideration for a period of time (not longer than three months). A firm offer by a merchant must be in writing and must be signed by the offeror.

fixed-term tenancy A type of tenancy under which property is leased for a specified period of time, such as a month, a year, or a period of years; also called a *tenancy for years*.

fixture An item of personal property that has become so closely associated with real property that it is legally regarded as part of that real property.

forbearance (1) The act of refraining from exercising a legal right. (2) An agreement between a lender and a borrower in which the lender agrees to temporarily cease requiring mortgage payments, to delay foreclosure, or to accept smaller payments than previously scheduled.

foreclosure A proceeding in which a mortgagee either takes title to or forces the sale of the mortgagor's property in satisfaction of a debt.

foreign corporation In a given state, a corporation that does business in that state but is not incorporated there.

forgery The fraudulent making or altering of any writing in a way that changes the legal rights and liabilities of another.

formal contract A contract that by law requires a specific form, such as being executed under seal, to be valid.

franchise Any arrangement in which the owner of a trademark, trade name, or copyright licenses another to use that trademark, trade name, or copyright in the selling of goods or services.

franchisee One receiving a license to use another's (the franchisor's) trademark, trade name, or copyright in the sale of goods and services.

franchisor One licensing another (the franchisee) to use the owner's trademark, trade name, or copyright in the selling of goods or services.

fraudulent misrepresentation (fraud) Any misrepresentation, either by misstatement or by omission of a material fact, knowingly made with the intention of deceiving another and on which a reasonable person would and does rely to his or her detriment.

free exercise clause The provision in the First Amendment to the U.S. Constitution that prohibits Congress from making any law "prohibiting the free exercise" of religion.

free-writing prospectus A written, electronic, or graphic communication associated with the offer to sell a security and used during the waiting period to supplement other information about the security.

frustration of purpose A court-created doctrine under which a party to a contract will be relieved of his or her duty to perform when the objective purpose for performance no longer exists (due to reasons beyond that party's control).

full faith and credit clause A clause in Article IV, Section 1, of the U.S. Constitution that provides that "Full Faith and Credit shall be given in each State to the public Acts, Records, and Judicial Proceedings of every other State." The clause ensures that rights established under deeds, wills, contracts, and the like in one state will be honored by the other states and that any judicial decision with respect to such property rights will be honored and enforced in all states.

fungible goods Goods that are alike by physical nature, by agreement, or by trade usage. Examples are wheat, oil, and wine that are identical in type and quality.

G

garnishment A legal process used by a creditor to collect a debt by seizing property of the debtor (such as wages) that is being held by a third party (such as the debtor's employer).

general damages In a tort case, an amount awarded to compensate individuals for the nonmonetary aspects of the harm suffered, such as pain and suffering; not available to companies.

general partner In a limited partnership, a partner who assumes responsibility for the management of the partnership and has full liability for all partnership debts.

Good Samaritan statute A state statute that provides that persons who rescue or provide emergency services to others in peril—unless they do so recklessly, thus causing further harm—cannot be sued for negligence.

goodwill In the business context, the valuable reputation of a business viewed as an intangible asset.

grand jury A group of citizens called to decide, after hearing the state's evidence, whether a reasonable basis (probable cause) exists for believing that a crime has been committed and whether a trial ought to be held.

grant deed A deed that simply states that property is being conveyed from the grantor to another. Under statute, a grant deed may impliedly warrant that the grantor has at least not conveyed the property's title to someone else.

group boycott An agreement by two or more sellers to refuse to deal with a particular person or firm.

guarantor A person who agrees to satisfy the debt of another (the debtor) only after the principal debtor defaults. A guarantor's liability is thus secondary.

H

hacker A person who uses one computer to break into another.

hearsay An oral or written statement made out of court that is later offered in court by a witness (not the person who made the statement) to prove the truth of the matter asserted in the statement. Hearsay is generally inadmissible as evidence.

historical school A school of legal thought that looks to the past to determine what the principles of contemporary law should be.

holding company A company whose business activity is holding shares in another company.

homeowner's insurance A form of property insurance that protects the home of the insured person and its contents against losses.

homestead exemption A law permitting a debtor to retain the family home, either in its entirety or up to a specified dollar amount, free from the claims of unsecured creditors or trustees in bankruptcy.

horizontal merger A merger between two firms that are competing in the same market.

horizontal restraint Any agreement that restrains competition between rival firms competing in the same market.

hot-cargo agreement An illegal agreement in which employers voluntarily agree with unions not to handle, use, or deal in the nonunion-produced goods of other employers.

I

I-551 Alien Registration Receipt A document, known as a "green card," that shows that a foreign-born individual can legally work in the United States.

I-9 verification The process of verifying the employment eligibility and identity of a new immigrant worker. It must be completed within three days after the worker commences employment.

identification In a sale of goods, the express designation of the specific goods provided for in the contract.

identity theft The act of stealing another's identifying information—such as a name, date of birth, or Social Security number—and using that information to access the victim's financial resources.

impeach To challenge the credibility of a person's testimony or attempt to discredit a party or witness.

implication A way of creating an easement or profit in real property when it is reasonable to imply its existence from the circumstances surrounding the division of the property.

implied authority Authority that is created not by an explicit oral or written agreement but by implication or inference. In agency law, implied authority of the agent can arise from custom, from the position the agent occupies, or from being reasonably necessary to carry out express authority.

implied contract A contract formed in whole or in part from the conduct of the parties (as opposed to an express contract).

implied warranty A warranty that the law derives by implication or inference from the nature of the transaction or the relative situation or circumstances of the parties.

implied warranty of fitness for a particular purpose A warranty that goods sold or leased are fit for a particular purpose. The warranty arises when any seller or lessor knows the particular purpose for which a buyer or lessee will use the goods and knows that the buyer or lessee is relying on the skill and judgment of the seller or lessor to select suitable goods.

implied warranty of habitability An implied promise by a seller of a new house that the house is fit for human habitation. Also, the implied promise by a landlord that rented residential premises are habitable.

implied warranty of merchantability A warranty that goods being sold or leased are reasonably fit for the ordinary purpose for which they are sold or leased, are properly packaged and labeled, and are of fair quality. The warranty automatically arises in every sale or lease of goods made by a merchant who deals in goods of the kind sold or leased.

impossibility of performance A doctrine under which a party to a contract is relieved of his or her duty to perform when performance becomes impossible or totally impracticable (through no fault of either party).

incidental damages Damages that compensate for expenses directly incurred because of a breach of contract, such as those incurred to obtain performance from another source.

independent contractor One who works for, and receives payment from, an employer but whose working conditions and methods are not controlled by the employer. An independent contractor is not an employee but may be an agent.

independent regulatory agency An administrative agency that is not considered part of the government's executive branch and is not subject to the authority of the president. Independent agency officials cannot be removed without cause.

indictment (pronounced in-*dyte*-ment) A charge by a grand jury that a reasonable basis (probable cause) exists for believing that a crime has been committed and that a trial should be held.

industrial use Land use for light or heavy manufacturing, shipping, or heavy transportation.

informal contract A contract that does not require a specified form or formality in order to be valid.

information A formal accusation or complaint (without an indictment) issued in certain types of actions (usually criminal actions involving lesser crimes) by a law officer, such as a magistrate.

information return A tax return submitted by a partnership that reports the business's income and losses. The partnership itself does not pay taxes on the income, but each partner's share of the profit (whether distributed or not) is taxed as individual income to that partner.

initial order In the context of administrative law, an agency's disposition in a matter other than a rulemaking. An administrative law judge's initial order becomes final unless it is appealed.

***in personam* jurisdiction** Court jurisdiction over the "person" involved in a legal action; personal jurisdiction.

***in rem* jurisdiction** Court jurisdiction over a defendant's property.

inside director A person on a corporation's board of directors who is also an officer of the corporation.

insider (1) A corporate director or officer, or other employee or agent, with access to confidential information and a duty not to disclose that information in violation of insider-trading laws. (2) In bankruptcy proceedings, an individual, partner, partnership, corporation, or officer or director of a corporation (or a relative of one of these) who has a close relationship with the debtor.

insider trading The purchase or sale of securities on the basis of information that has not been made available to the public.

insurable interest A property interest in goods being sold or leased that is sufficiently substantial to permit a party to insure against damage to the goods.

intangible property Property that is incapable of being apprehended by the senses (such as by sight or touch). Intellectual property is an example of intangible property.

intellectual property Property resulting from intellectual, creative processes. Patents, trademarks, and copyrights are examples of intellectual property.

intended beneficiary A third party for whose benefit a contract is formed; an intended beneficiary can sue the promisor if such a contract is breached.

intentional tort A wrongful act knowingly committed.

international law The law that governs relations among nations. International customs and treaties are generally considered to be two of the most important sources of international law.

international organization In international law, a term that generally refers to an organization composed mainly of nations and usually established by treaty. The United States is a member of more than one hundred multilateral and bilateral organizations, including at least twenty through the United Nations.

Internet service provider (ISP) A business or organization that offers users access to the Internet and related services.

interpretive rule A nonbinding rule or policy statement issued by an administrative agency that explains how it interprets and intends to apply the statutes it enforces.

interrogatories A series of written questions for which written answers are prepared and then signed under oath by a party to a lawsuit, usually with the assistance of the party's attorney.

inverse condemnation The taking of private property by the government without payment of just compensation as required by the U.S. Constitution. The owner must sue the government to recover just compensation.

investment company A company that acts on the behalf of many smaller shareholders/owners by buying a large portfolio of securities and professionally managing that portfolio.

investment contract In securities law, a transaction in which a person invests in a common enterprise reasonably expecting profits that are derived primarily from the efforts of others.

J

joint and several liability In partnership law, a doctrine under which a plaintiff may sue all of the partners together (jointly) or one or more of the partners separately (severally, or individually).

joint liability In partnership law, a doctrine under which a plaintiff must sue all of the partners as a group, but each partner can be held liable for the full amount.

joint tenancy Joint ownership of property by two or more co-owners in which each co-owner owns an undivided portion of the property. On the death of one of the joint tenants, his or her interest automatically passes to the surviving joint tenant(s).

judicial review The process by which courts decide on the constitutionality of legislative enactments and actions of the executive branch.

jurisdiction The authority of a court to hear a case and decide a specific action.

jurisprudence The science or philosophy of law.

L

laches The equitable doctrine that bars a party's right to legal action if the party has neglected for an unreasonable length of time to act on his or her rights.

larceny The wrongful taking and carrying away of another person's personal property with the intent to permanently deprive the owner of the property. Some states classify larceny as either grand or petit, depending on the property's value.

law A body of enforceable rules governing relationships among individuals and between individuals and their society.

leasehold estate An interest in real property that gives a tenant a qualified right to possess and/or use the property for a limited time under a lease.

legal positivism A school of legal thought centered on the assumption that there is no law higher than the laws created by a national government. Laws must be obeyed, even if they are unjust, to prevent anarchy.

legal realism A school of legal thought that holds that the law is only one factor to be considered when deciding cases and that social and economic circumstances should also be taken into account.

legal reasoning (1) The process of evaluating how various laws apply to a given situation. (2) The process by which a judge harmonizes his or her opinion with the judicial decisions in previous cases.

legislative rule An administrative agency rule that carries the same weight as a congressionally enacted statute.

liability The state of being legally responsible (liable) for something, such as a debt or obligation.

libel Defamation in writing or in some other form (such as a digital recording) having the quality of permanence.

license (1) In the context of intellectual property, a contract permitting the use of a trademark, copyright, patent, or trade secret for certain purposes. (2) In the context of real property, a revocable right or privilege of a person to come on another person's land.

licensee One who receives a license to use, or enter onto, another's property.

lien (pronounced *leen*) A claim against specific property to satisfy a debt.

life estate An interest in land that exists only for the duration of the life of a specified individual, usually the holder of the estate.

limited liability company (LLC) A hybrid form of business enterprise that offers the limited liability of a corporation and the tax advantages of a partnership.

limited liability limited partnership (LLLP) A type of limited partnership in which the liability of the general partner is the same as the liability of the limited partners—that is, the liability of all partners is limited to the amount of their investments in the firm.

limited liability partnership (LLP) A hybrid form of business organization that is used mainly by professionals who normally do business in a partnership. An LLP is a pass-through entity for tax purposes, but a partner's personal liability for the malpractice of other partners is limited.

limited partner In a limited partnership, a partner who contributes capital to the partnership but has no right to participate in its management and has no liability for partnership debts beyond the amount of her or his investment.

limited partnership (LP) A partnership consisting of one or more general partners and one or more limited partners.

liquidated damages An amount, stipulated in the contract, that the parties to a contract believe to be a reasonable estimation of the damages that will occur in the event of a breach.

liquidated debt A debt that is due and certain in amount.

liquidation The sale of the nonexempt assets of a debtor and the distribution of the funds received to creditors.

litigation The process of resolving a dispute through the court system.

probate court A state court of limited jurisdiction that conducts proceedings relating to the settlement of a deceased person's estate.

procedural law Law that establishes the methods of enforcing the rights established by substantive law.

product liability The legal liability of manufacturers, sellers, and lessors of goods to consumers, users, and bystanders for injuries or damages that are caused by the goods.

product misuse A defense against product liability that may be raised when the plaintiff used a product in a manner not intended by the manufacturer. If the misuse is reasonably foreseeable, the seller will not escape liability unless measures were taken to guard against the harm that could result from the misuse.

profit In the context of real property, the right to enter onto another's property and remove something of value from that property.

promise A person's assurance that he or she will or will not do something.

promissory estoppel A doctrine that applies when a promisor makes a clear and definite promise on which the promisee justifiably relies. Such a promise is binding if justice will be better served by the enforcement of the promise.

prospectus A written document required by securities laws when a security is being sold. The prospectus describes the security, the financial operations of the issuing corporation, and the risk attaching to the security.

protected class A group of persons protected by specific laws because of the group's defining characteristics, including race, color, religion, national origin, gender, age, and disability.

proximate cause Legal cause; exists when the connection between an act and an injury is strong enough to justify imposing liability.

proxy Authorization to represent a corporate shareholder to serve as his or her agent and vote his or her shares in a certain manner.

public corporation A corporation owned by a federal, state, or municipal government—not to be confused with a publicly held corporation.

public figure An individual in the public limelight. Public figures include government officials and politicians, movie stars, well-known businesspersons, and generally anybody who becomes known to the public because of his or her position or activities.

publicly held corporation A corporation whose shares are publicly traded in securities markets, such as the New York Stock Exchange or the NASDAQ.

puffery A salesperson's exaggerated claims concerning the quality of goods offered for sale. Such claims involve opinions rather than facts and are not considered to be legally binding promises or warranties.

punitive damages Money damages that may be awarded to a plaintiff to punish the defendant and deter future similar conduct.

Q

question of fact In a lawsuit, an issue involving a factual dispute. A question of fact can be decided by a judge or a jury.

question of law In a lawsuit, an issue involving the application or interpretation of a law. Only a judge, and not a jury, can decide a question of law.

quitclaim deed A deed that conveys only whatever interest the grantor had in the property and therefore offers the least amount of protection against defects of title.

quorum The number of members of a decision-making body that must be present before business may be transacted.

quota A government-imposed trade restriction that limits the number, or sometimes the value, of goods and services that can be imported or exported during a particular time period.

R

Ransomware Malicious software created by cybercriminals to block access to a computer system until a ransom is paid. Often, these ransoms must be paid in cryptocurrency such as Bitcoin

ratification The act of accepting and giving legal force to an obligation that previously was not enforceable.

reaffirmation agreement An agreement between a debtor and a creditor in which the debtor voluntarily agrees to pay a debt dischargeable in bankruptcy.

reasonable person standard The standard of behavior expected of a hypothetical "reasonable person." The standard against which negligence is measured and that must be observed to avoid liability for negligence.

rebuttal The refutation of evidence introduced by an adverse party's attorney.

record According to the Uniform Electronic Transactions Act, information that is either inscribed on a tangible medium or stored in an electronic or other medium, and that is retrievable.

recording statute A statute that allow deeds, mortgages, and other real property transactions to be recorded so as to provide notice to future purchasers or creditors of an existing claim on the property.

reformation A court-ordered correction of a written contract so that it reflects the true intentions of the parties.

Regulation Z A set of rules issued by the Federal Reserve Board of Governors to implement the provisions of the Truth-in-Lending Act.

rejoinder   The defendant's answer to the plaintiff's rebuttal.

release   A contract in which one party forfeits the right to pursue a legal claim against the other party.

relevant evidence   Evidence tending to make a fact at issue in the case more or less probable than it would be without the evidence. Only relevant evidence is admissible in court.

remedy   The relief given to an innocent party to enforce a right or compensate for the violation of a right.

remedy at law   A remedy available in a court of law. Money damages are awarded as a remedy at law.

remedy in equity   A remedy allowed by courts in situations where remedies at law are not appropriate. Remedies in equity include injunction, specific performance, rescission and restitution, and reformation.

replevin   (pronounced rih-*pleh*-vin) An action to recover specific goods in the hands of a party who is wrongfully withholding them from the other party.

reporter   A publication in which court cases are published, or reported.

requirements contract   An agreement in which a buyer agrees to purchase and the seller agrees to sell all or up to a stated amount of what the buyer needs or requires.

resale price maintenance agreement   An agreement between a manufacturer and a retailer in which the manufacturer specifies what the retail prices of its products must be.

rescission   (pronounced rih-*sih*-zhen) A remedy whereby a contract is canceled and the parties are returned to the positions they occupied before the contract was made; may be effected through the mutual consent of the parties, by their conduct, or by court decree.

residential use   Use of land for construction of buildings for human habitation only.

respondeat superior   A doctrine under which a principal-employer is liable for any harm caused to a third party by an agent-employee in the course or scope of employment.

respondent   In equity practice, the party who answers a complaint or other proceeding.

restitution   An equitable remedy under which a person is restored to his or her original position prior to loss or injury, or placed in the position he or she would have been in had the breach not occurred.

restraint of trade   Any contract or combination that tends to eliminate or reduce competition, effect a monopoly, artificially maintain prices, or otherwise hamper the course of trade and commerce as it would be carried on if left to the control of natural economic forces.

restrictive covenant   A private restriction on the use of land. If its benefit or obligation passes with the land's ownership, it is said to "run with the land."

retained earnings   The portion of a corporation's profits that has not been paid out as dividends to shareholders.

revocation   In contract law, the withdrawal of an offer by an offeror. Unless an offer is irrevocable, it can be revoked at any time prior to acceptance without liability.

right of contribution   The right of a co-surety who pays more than his or her proportionate share on a debtor's default to recover the excess paid from other co-sureties.

right of reimbursement   The legal right of a person to be restored, repaid, or indemnified for costs, expenses, or losses incurred or expended on behalf of another.

right of subrogation   The right of a person to stand in the place of (be substituted for) another, giving the substituted party the same legal rights that the original party had.

right-to-work law   A state law providing that employees may not be required to join a union as a condition of retaining employment.

robbery   The act of forcefully and unlawfully taking personal property of any value from another; force or intimidation is usually necessary for an act of theft to be considered a robbery.

Royalties   Payments made from the licensee to the licensor as part of an agreement for the ongoing use of the licensor's trademarked asset.

rulemaking   The process by which an administrative agency formally adopts a new regulation or amends an old one.

rule of four   A rule of the United States Supreme Court under which the Court will not issue a writ of *certiorari* unless at least four justices agree to do so.

rule of reason   A test used to determine whether an anticompetitive agreement constitutes a reasonable restraint on trade. Courts consider such factors as the purpose of the agreement, its effect on competition, and whether less restrictive means could have been used.

rules of evidence   Rules governing the admissibility of evidence in trial courts.

S

sale   The passing of title (evidence of ownership rights) from a seller to a buyer for a price.

sales contract   A contract for the sale of goods under which the ownership of goods is transferred from a seller to a buyer for a price.

scienter   (pronounced sy-*en*-ter) Knowledge by the misrepresenting party that material facts have been falsely represented or omitted with an intent to deceive.

S corporation   A close business corporation that has most of the attributes of a corporation, including limited liability, but qualifies under the Internal Revenue Code to be taxed as a partnership.

search warrant An order granted by a public authority, such as a judge, that authorizes law enforcement personnel to search particular premises or property.

seasonably Within a specified time period. If no period is specified, within a reasonable time.

secondary boycott A union's refusal to work for, purchase from, or handle the products of a secondary employer, with whom the union has no dispute, for the purpose of forcing that employer to stop doing business with the primary employer, with whom the union has a labor dispute.

SEC Rule 10b-5 A rule of the Securities and Exchange Commission that prohibits the commission of fraud in connection with the purchase or sale of any security.

securities Generally, stocks, bonds, or other items that represent an ownership interest in a corporation or a promise of repayment of debt by a corporation.

self-defense The legally recognized privilege to protect one's self or property against injury by another. The privilege of self-defense protects only acts that are reasonably necessary to protect one's self or property.

self-incrimination Giving testimony in a trial or other legal proceeding that could expose the person testifying to criminal prosecution.

seniority system A system in which those who have worked longest for an employer are first in line for promotions, salary increases, and other benefits, and are last to be laid off if the workforce must be reduced.

service mark A mark used in the sale or the advertising of services, such as to distinguish the services of one person from the services of others. Titles, character names, and other distinctive features of radio and television programs may be registered as service marks.

service of process The delivery of the complaint and summons to a defendant.

sexual harassment The demanding of sexual favors in return for job promotions or other benefits, or language or conduct that is so sexually offensive that it creates a hostile working environment.

shareholder agreement An agreement between shareholders that restricts the transferability of shares, often entered into for the purpose of maintaining proportionate control of a close corporation.

shareholder's derivative suit A suit brought by a shareholder to enforce a corporate cause of action against a third person.

shipment contract A contract in which the seller is required to ship the goods by carrier. The buyer assumes liability for any losses or damage to the goods after they are delivered to the carrier. Generally, a contract is assumed to be a shipment contract if nothing to the contrary is stated in the contract.

short sale A sale of real property for an amount that is less than the balance owed on the mortgage loan, usually due to financial hardship.

short-swing profits Profits earned by a purchase and sale, or sale and purchase, of the same security within a six-month period.

shrink-wrap agreement An agreement whose terms are expressed in a document located inside a box in which goods (usually software) are packaged; sometimes called a *shrinkwrap license.*

slander Defamation in oral form.

slander of quality The publication of false information about another's product, alleging that it is not what its seller claims; also called *trade libel.*

slander of title The publication of a statement that falsely denies or casts doubt on another's legal ownership of property, causing financial loss to that property's owner.

small claims court Special courts in which parties may litigate small claims (usually, claims involving $2,500 or less). Attorneys are not required in small claims courts and in many states are not allowed to represent the parties.

social media Forms of communication through which users create and share information, ideas, messages, and other content via the Internet.

sociological school A school of legal thought that views the law as a tool for promoting justice in society.

sole proprietorship The simplest form of business organization, in which the owner is the business. The owner reports business income on his or her personal income tax return and is legally responsible for all debts and obligations incurred by the business.

sovereign immunity A doctrine that immunizes foreign nations from the jurisdiction of U.S. courts when certain conditions are satisfied.

sovereignty The quality of having independent authority over a geographic area. For instance, state governments have the authority to regulate affairs within their borders.

space law Law consisting of the international and national laws that govern activities in outer space.

spam Bulk, unsolicited (junk) e-mail.

special damages In a tort case, an amount awarded to compensate the plaintiff for quantifiable monetary losses, such as medical expenses, property damage, and lost wages and benefits (now and in the future).

Special Purpose Acquisition Companies (SPACs) Blank-check investment vehicles that raise capital through initial public offerings for as yet unspecified investments in private firms at a later date.

special-use permit A permit granted by local zoning authorities that allows for a specific exemption to zoning regulations for a particular piece of land.

special warranty deed A deed that warrants only that the grantor held good title during his or her ownership of the property and does not warrant that there were no defects of title when the property was held by previous owners.

specific performance An equitable remedy requiring the breaching party to perform as promised under the contract; usually granted only when money damages would be an inadequate remedy and the subject matter of the contract is unique (for example, real property).

stakeholders Groups, other than the company's shareholders, that are affected by corporate decisions. Stakeholders include employees, customers, creditors, suppliers, and the community in which the corporation operates.

standing to sue The requirement that an individual must have a sufficient stake in a controversy before he or she can bring a lawsuit. The plaintiff must demonstrate that he or she has been either injured or threatened with injury.

stare decisis (pronounced *stahr*-ee dih-*si*-sis) A common law doctrine under which judges are obligated to follow the precedents established in prior decisions within their jurisdictions.

Statute of Frauds A state statute under which certain types of contracts must be in writing to be enforceable.

statute of limitations A federal or state statute setting the maximum time period during which a certain action can be brought or certain rights enforced.

statute of repose Basically, a statute of limitations that is not dependent on the happening of a cause of action. Statutes of repose generally begin to run at an earlier date and run for a longer period of time than statutes of limitations.

statutory law The body of law enacted by legislative bodies (as opposed to constitutional law, administrative law, or case law).

stock An ownership (equity) interest in a corporation, measured in units of shares.

stock certificate A certificate issued by a corporation evidencing the ownership of a specified number of shares in the corporation.

stock option A right to buy a given number of shares of stock at a set price, usually within a specified time period.

stock warrant A certificate that grants the owner the option to buy a given number of shares of stock, usually within a set time period.

strict liability Liability regardless of fault. In tort law, strict liability may be imposed on defendants in cases involving abnormally dangerous activities, dangerous animals, or defective products.

strike An action undertaken by unionized workers when collective bargaining fails. The workers leave their jobs, refuse to work, and (typically) picket the employer's workplace.

substantive law Law that defines, describes, regulates, and creates legal rights and obligations.

summary jury trial A method of settling disputes in which a trial is held, but the jury's verdict is not binding. The verdict acts only as a guide to both sides in reaching an agreement during the mandatory negotiations that immediately follow.

summons A document informing a defendant that a legal action has been commenced against him or her and that the defendant must appear in court on a certain date to answer the plaintiff's complaint. The document is delivered by a sheriff or any other person so authorized.

superseding cause An intervening force or event that breaks the connection between a wrongful act and an injury to another; in negligence law, a defense to liability.

supremacy clause The provision in Article VI of the U.S. Constitution that provides that the Constitution, laws, and treaties of the United States are "the supreme Law of the Land." Under this clause, state and local laws that directly conflict with federal law will be rendered invalid.

surety A person, such as a cosigner on a note, who agrees to be primarily responsible for the debt of another.

suretyship An express contract in which a third party to a debtor-creditor relationship (the surety) promises to be primarily responsible for the debtor's obligation.

Sustainability Maintaining the environment such that it will adequately satisfy the needs of not only this generation but, more importantly, future generations.

symbolic speech Nonverbal conduct that expresses opinions or thoughts about a subject. Symbolic speech is protected under the First Amendment's guarantee of freedom of speech.

T

taking The government's taking of private property for public use through the power of eminent domain.

tangible employment action A significant change in employment status or benefits, such as occurs when an employee is fired, refused a promotion, or reassigned to a lesser position.

tangible property Property that has physical existence and can be distinguished by the senses of touch, sight, and so on. A car is tangible property.

tariff A tax on imported goods.

tenancy at sufferance A tenancy that arises when a tenant wrongfully continues to occupy leased property after the lease has terminated.

tenancy at will A type of tenancy that either the landlord or the tenant can terminate without notice.

tenancy by the entirety Joint ownership of property by a married couple in which neither spouse can transfer his or her interest in the property without the consent of the other.

tenancy in common Joint ownership of property in which each party owns an undivided interest that passes to his or her heirs at death.

tender An unconditional offer to perform an obligation by a person who is ready, willing, and able to do so.

tender of delivery Under the Uniform Commercial Code, a seller's or lessor's act of placing conforming goods at the disposal of the buyer or lessee and giving the buyer or lessee whatever notification is reasonably necessary to enable the buyer or lessee to take delivery.

third party beneficiary One for whose benefit a promise is made in a contract but who is not a party to the contract.

tippee A person who receives inside information.

title insurance Insurance commonly purchased by a purchaser of real property to protect against loss in the event that the title to the property is not free from liens or superior ownership claims.

tolled The temporary suspension of the running of a prescribed period (such as a statute of limitations). For instance, a statute of limitations may be tolled until the party suffering an injury has discovered it or should have discovered it.

tort A civil wrong not arising from a breach of contract. A breach of a legal duty that proximately causes harm or injury to another.

tortfeasor One who commits a tort.

toxic tort A civil wrong arising from exposure to a toxic substance, such as asbestos, radiation, or hazardous waste.

trade dress The image and overall appearance of a product—for example, the distinctive decor, menu, layout, and style of service of a particular restaurant. Basically, trade dress is subject to the same protection as trademarks.

trade fixture The personal property of a commercial tenant that has been installed or affixed to real property for a business purpose. When the lease ends, the tenant can remove the fixture but must repair any damage to the real property caused by the fixture's removal.

trade libel The publication of false information about another's product, alleging that it is not what its seller claims; also referred to as *slander of quality*.

trademark A distinctive mark, motto, device, or implement that a manufacturer stamps, prints, or otherwise affixes to the goods it produces so that they may be identified on the market and their origins made known. Once a trademark is established (under the common law or through registration), the owner is entitled to its exclusive use.

trade name A term that is used to indicate part or all of a business's name and that is directly related to the business's reputation and goodwill. Trade names are protected under the common law (and under trademark law, if the name is the same as the firm's trademark).

trade secret Information or a process that gives a business an advantage over competitors who do not know the information or process.

transferred intent A legal principle under which a person who intends to harm one individual, but unintentionally harms a different individual, can be liable to the second victim for an intentional tort.

treaty An agreement formed between two or more independent nations.

treble damages Damages that, by statute, are three times the amount of actual damages suffered.

trespass to land The entry onto, above, or below the surface of land owned by another without the owner's permission or legal authorization.

trespass to personal property The unlawful taking or harming of another's personal property; interference with another's right to the exclusive possession of his or her personal property.

triple bottom line The idea that investors and others should consider not only corporate profits, but also the corporation's impact on people and on the planet when assessing the firm. (The triple bottom line is people, planet, and profits.)

tying arrangement A seller's act of conditioning the sale of a product or service on the buyer's agreement to purchase another product or service from the seller.

typosquatting A form of cybersquatting that relies on mistakes, such as typographical errors, made by Internet users when inputting information into a Web browser.

U

unconscionable (pronounced un-*kon*-shun-uh-bul) Describes a contract or clause that is void on the basis of public policy because one party is forced to accept terms that are unfairly burdensome and that unfairly benefit the dominating party.

undisclosed principal A principal whose identity is unknown by a third party, and that party has no knowledge that the agent is acting for a principal at the time the agent and the third party form a contract.

undue influence Persuasion that is less than actual force but more than advice and that induces a person to act according to the will or purposes of the dominating party.

unenforceable contract A valid contract rendered unenforceable by some statute or law.

uniform law A model law created by the National Conference of Commissioners on Uniform State Laws and/or the American Law Institute for the states to consider adopting. If a state adopts the law, it becomes statutory law in that state. Each state has the option of adopting or rejecting all or part of a uniform law.

unilateral contract A contract that results when an offer can be accepted only by the offeree's performance.

unilateral mistake A mistake that occurs when one party to a contract is mistaken as to a material fact.

union shop A firm that requires all workers, once employed, to become union members within a specified period of time as a condition of their continued employment.

unliquidated debt A debt that is uncertain in amount.

unreasonably dangerous product In product liability, a product that is defective to the point of threatening a consumer's health and safety. A product will be considered unreasonably dangerous if it is dangerous beyond the expectation of the ordinary consumer or if a less dangerous alternative was economically feasible for the manufacturer, but the manufacturer failed to produce it.

U.S. trustee A government official who performs certain administrative tasks that a bankruptcy judge would otherwise have to perform.

usury Charging an illegal rate of interest.

utilitarianism An approach to ethical reasoning in which ethically correct behavior is related to an evaluation of the consequences of a given action on those who will be affected by it. In utilitarian reasoning, a "good" decision is one that results in the greatest good for the greatest number of people affected by the decision.

V

validation notice An initial notice to a debtor from a collection agency informing the debtor that he or she has thirty days to challenge the debt and request verification.

valid contract A contract that results when the elements necessary for contract formation (agreement, consideration, contractual capacity, and legality) are present.

variance An exception from zoning rules granted to a property owner by local zoning authorities.

venture capital Financing provided to new business ventures by professional, outside investors—that is, *venture capitalists*, usually groups of wealthy investors and securities firms.

venue (pronounced *ven*-yoo) The geographical district in which an action is tried and from which the jury is selected.

verdict A formal decision made by a jury.

vertically integrated firm A firm that carries out two or more functional phases (manufacturing, distribution, and retailing, for example) of the chain of production.

vertical merger The acquisition by a company at one stage of production of a company at a higher or lower stage of production (as when a company merges with one of its suppliers or retailers).

vertical restraint A restraint of trade created by an agreement between firms at different levels in the manufacturing and distribution process.

vesting The creation of an absolute or unconditional right or power.

vicarious liability Indirect liability imposed on a supervisory party (such as an employer) for the actions of a subordinate (such as an employee) because of the relationship between the two parties.

virus A type of malware that is transmitted between computers and attempts to do deliberate damage to systems and data.

voidable contract A contract that may be legally avoided (canceled) at the option of one of the parties.

void contract A contract having no legal force or binding effect.

voir dire (pronounced *vwahr deehr*) A French phrase meaning, literally, "to see, to speak" that refers to the jury-selection process. In *voir dire*, the attorneys question prospective jurors to determine whether they are biased or have any connection with a party to the action or with a prospective witness.

voluntary consent Knowing and voluntary agreement to the terms of a contract. If voluntary consent is lacking, the contract will be voidable.

voting trust An agreement (trust contract) under which legal title to shares of corporate stock is transferred to a trustee who is authorized by the shareholders to vote the shares on their behalf.

W

waiver An intentional, knowing relinquishment of a legal right.

warranty deed A deed in which the grantor promises that she or he has title to the property conveyed in the deed, that there are no undisclosed encumbrances on the property, and that the grantee will enjoy quiet possession of the property; provides the greatest amount of protection for the grantee.

waste The use of real property in a manner that damages or destroys its value.

watered stock Shares of stock issued by a corporation for which the corporation receives, as payment, less than the fair market value of the shares.

wetlands Areas of land designated by government agencies as protected areas that support wildlife and that therefore cannot be filled in or dredged by private parties.

whistleblowing An employee's disclosure to government authorities, upper-level managers, or the media that the employer is engaged in unsafe or illegal activities.

white-collar crime Nonviolent crime committed by individuals or corporations to obtain a personal or business advantage.

winding up The second of two stages in the termination of a partnership or corporation, in which the firm's assets are collected, liquidated, and distributed, and liabilities are discharged.

workers' compensation law A state statute establishing an administrative procedure for compensating workers for injuries that arise out of, or in the course of, their employment, regardless of fault. Instead of suing the employer, an injured worker files a claim with the state agency or board that administers local workers' compensation claims.

workout agreement A formal contract between a debtor and his or her creditors in which the parties agree to negotiate a payment plan for the amount due on the loan instead of proceeding to foreclosure.

worm A type of malware that is designed to copy itself from one computer to another without human interaction. A worm can copy itself automatically and can replicate in great volume and with great speed.

writ of attachment A court's order, prior to a trial to collect a debt, directing the sheriff or other officer to seize nonexempt property of the debtor. If the creditor prevails at trial, the seized property can be sold to satisfy the judgment.

writ of *certiorari* (pronounced sur-shee-uh-*rah*-ree) A writ from a higher court asking the lower court for the record of the case for review.

writ of execution A court's order, after a judgment has been entered against the debtor, directing the sheriff to seize (levy) and sell any of the debtor's nonexempt real or personal property. The proceeds of the sale are used to pay off the judgment, accrued interest, and costs of the sale. Any surplus is paid to the debtor.

wrongful discharge An employer's termination of an employee's employment in violation of the law or an employment contract.

Z

zoning laws Rules and regulations that collectively manage the development and use of land.

Subject Index

Associations. *See* specific associations and
    types
Assumption of risk, 128
    product liability and, 143
Assurance, right of, 302
Astronauts, agreements on, 227–228
At common law. *See* Common law
At sufferance, tenancy, 546
Attachment
    defined, 317
    writ of, 317
Attempted monopolization, 569, 570
Attorney
    client relationship and, 88–89
    duty of, 126
    fees of, 89
    power of, 425–426
Attorney general (AG), 188
Attractive nuisance doctrine, 122
At will, tenancy, 546
Auctions
    live and online, 239
    offers, intent, and, 239
    online fraud in, 204
Audit committee, of board of directors,
    398
Authority
    of agent, 425–430, 432
    apparent, 425–428, 430, 432
    binding, 8
    certificate of, 386
    implied, 365, 426
    implied warranty of, 429
    of partner, 362
    persuasive, 8
Authorization card, 475
Authorized actions, contract liability and,
    428–429
Author, of online defamation, 180
Automatic stay, 327–329
Automobiles, emissions standards for,
    528–529
Award, 102. *See also* Damages
    in arbitration, 81

B

Bad faith
    in arbitration, 81
    in bankruptcy, 329
    in labor bargaining, 479
Bailee
    defined, 299
    goods held by, 299
Bailment, 134, 299
Bait-and-switch advertising, 511
Bankruptcy, 316, 322. *See also*
    Bankruptcy Code
    creditors' committees and, 337
    creditors' meeting and claims, 332
    as defense, 320

discharge in, 272, 332–334
dismissal of petition, 327
estate in, 325
exemptions in, 331–332
fraud in, 198, 331
involuntary, 327
LP and partner's, 381
petition in, 325
property distribution in, 332
reaffirmation agreements in, 335
relief in, 325–340
reorganization in, 325–326
sole proprietorship and, 351
tax returns during, 326
termination of agency relationship by,
    433
voluntary, 325–326
Bankruptcy Code, 324–325. *See also*
    Bankruptcy
    Chapter 7 of (liquidation proceedings),
        326
    Chapter 11 of (reorganization), 325,
        336–337
    Chapter 12 of (adjustment of debts
        by family farmers and family
        fisherman), 325, 339
    Chapter 13 of (adjustment of debts by
        individuals), 325, 338
    exemptions in, 331–332
Bankruptcy courts, 68, 324–325
Bankruptcy Reform Act. *See also*
    Bankruptcy
    of 1978 (*See* Bankruptcy Code)
    of 2005 (Bankruptcy Abuse Prevention
        and Consumer Protection Act),
        324
Bankruptcy Reporter, 18
Bankruptcy trustee, 325. *See also* Debtor,
    in possession
    duties and power of, 325
Bargained-for exchange, 247
Bargaining, labor union, 476, 479
Basis of the bargain, 309
Battery, assault and, tort law and, 112,
    194
Beneficiary
    intended, 258
    third party, 258
Benefit corporation, 390–391
Benefits, for FMLA leave, 442
Berne Convention (1886), 166, 167
Best available control technology
    (BACT), 533
Best practical control technology
    (BPCT), 533
Beyond a reasonable doubt, 102, 188, 202
BFOQ. *See* Bona fide occupational
    qualification
Big tech's monopoly problem, 571
Bilateral agreement, 213

Bilateral contracts, 235
    consideration in, 247
Bilateral mistakes of fact, 263
Bill of lading, 297
Bill of Rights. *See also* Constitution
    (U.S.); individual amendments
    business and, 30–38
    protections in, 30, 182
Binding authority, 8
Biometrics, 184
Bitcoin, 190–191
BitTorrent, 176
Blue sky laws, 596
Board of directors. *See* Directors,
    corporate
Bona fide occupational qualification
    (BFOQ), 467
Bond(s), 396
    posting of, 317
    as securities, 583
Books. *See* Accounting
Border searches, under ACTA, 167
Botnets, 207
Boycotts
    group, 567
    secondary, 480
Branches of government, 493
Breach of contract. *See also* Damages;
    Lease contracts; Sales contracts
    anticipatory repudiation and, 270–271
    by buyer or lessee, 304–305
    compensatory damages for, 275–277
    damages for
        compensatory, 275–277
        consequential, 277
        nominal, 277
        punitive, 277
    defined, 6, 270
    equitable remedies for, 279–282
    forced online classes, 276
    material *vs.* minor, 270
    remedies for, 274–280, 304–308
    risk of loss and, 298–299
    sale of land, by owner, 276
    sales contract, 304–308
    by seller or lessor, 299, 305–308
Breach of duty
    of care, 124
    fiduciary, 592–593
    by partner, 363–364
    by principal, 425
Breach of loyalty. *See* Duty of loyalty
Breach of warranty, 370
Bribery, 197
    Foreign Corrupt Practices Act and, 61
Brief, 19, 104
Britain. *See* England (Britain)
Broker, regulation of state securities, 597
Browse-wrap terms, 246
Bubble policy, 500–501

European Patent Office, website of, 159
European Union (EU), 223
  foods banned in, 516
  intellectual property protection and, 167
Event, occurrence of
  agency termination and, 432
  dissociation and, 363, 381
Evidence. *See also* Discovery
  admissible, 95
  hearsay, 101
  preponderance of the, 102, 188
  relevant, 101
  rules of, 101
  spoliation of, 98
Examination
  request for, 98
  in trial, 101–102
Exceptions
  to automatic stay, 329
  to bankruptcy discharge, 333–334
  fair use, 164
  to Government in the Sunshine Act, 503
  to perfect tender rule, 301–302
Exchange, bargained-for, 247
Exclusionary practices, under Clayton Act, 573–574
Exclusionary rule, 202
Exclusions, from Copyright Act, 162
Exclusive agency, 423
Exclusive-dealing contract, 573–574
Exclusive jurisdiction, 69
Exclusive possession and control, 543
Exculpatory clauses, 255, 282
Executed contract, 236–237
Execution, writ of, 105, 317
Executive(s). *See* Chief executive officer (CEO); Officers, corporate
Executive agencies, 5, 491
Executive branch, control over agencies by, 493
Executive committee, of board of directors, 398–399
Executory contract, 236–237, 271, 336–337
Exemptions
  from antitrust laws, 575–576
  federal, 331–332
  homestead, 329
  private placement, 588
  requirements, 586–589
  under Rule 504, 588
  under Rule 506, 589
  for smaller companies, 601
  state, 331–332
Exhaustion doctrine, 493
Existing goods, 296
Ex parte (private) communications, 499
Expert testimony, 138

Expert witnesses, 101–102
Exploration and exploitation of outer space, laws governing, 227
Export(s), 218–219
  controls of, 221
  of space technology, 229
Export Administration Act, 221
Export Trading Company Act, 576
Express authority, of agent, 425
Express authorization, 244
Express contracts, 236
Expressions of ideas, copyright exclusions and, 162
Expressions of opinion, 239
Express powers, corporate, 393
Express terms, in contracts, 236
Express warranty, 309–311
Expropriation, of private property, 215, 221
Extraterritorial application, of antitrust laws, 577
Exxon Valdez disaster, 534

F

Facebook
  investigations and, 178
  legal challenges to, 171
  revenge porn, 118
Facial recognition technology, 184
Fact(s)
  causation in, 126–127
  claims appearing to be based on, 510–511
  compilation of, copyright and, 162
  material, 262
  mistakes of, 200, 262–263
  public disclosure of private, 119
  statement of, 116, 120, 309
Fair and Accurate Credit Transactions Act (FACT Act, 2003), 520–521
Fair Credit Reporting Act (FCRA, 1970), 519–521
Fair dealing, franchises and, 357
Fair Debt Collection Practices Act (FDCPA), 520–521
Fair Labor Standards Act (FLSA), 439, 440, 462, 503
Fair notice, 495
Fair Packaging and Labeling Act (1966), 515
Fair trial, Americans, 9
"Fair use" exception, 164, 176
Fair value
  dissociation, 376
  of land, 554
False advertising, claims under Lanham Act, 512
False imprisonment, 113
False light, 119
Family and medical leave, 441–442

Family and Medical Leave Act (FMLA, 1993), 441–442
Family farmers and fishermen, Chapter 12 bankruptcy and, 325
Family limited liability partnerships (FLLP), 379
Fanciful trademarks, 155
Farmers. *See* Family farmers and fishermen
Fault. *See* Comparative negligence (fault); Strict liability
FCC. *See* Federal Communications Commission
FCPA. *See* Foreign Corrupt Practices Act
FCRA. *See* Fair Credit Reporting Act
FDCPA. *See* Fair Debt Collection Practices Act
Featherbedding, 475
Federal agencies. *See* Agencies (government); specific agencies
Federal Appendix, 18
Federal Arbitration Act (FAA), 82
Federal Aviation Administration (FAA)
  arbitration clauses, 82
  commercial spaceflight regulation by, 228–229
Federal Communications Commission (FCC), 5
  TCPA enforcement by, 513
  telephone solicitation, 513
Federal court system, 66, 68, 75–80, 87. *See also* Court(s); Supreme Court
  appellate courts of, 79
  boundaries of appellate and district courts, 78
  decisions of, 18
  district (trial) courts in, 18, 68
  jurisdiction of, 68–69
  reading citations for, 16–17
  right to jury trial in, 99–100
Federal crimes. *See also* Crime
  criminal negligence, 192–193
  sentencing guidelines for, 202
  statute of, 198
Federal Food, Drug and Cosmetic Act (FDCA, 1938), 516
Federal form of government, 25
Federal government
  courts of (*See* Federal court system)
  powers of, 25
  spam regulation by, 171–172
Federal Insecticide, Fungicide, and Rodenticide Act (FIFRA, 1947), 526, 535
Federal Insurance Contributions Act (FICA), 445–446
Federal law, 12, 13. *See also* specific laws
  franchising regulation by, 352–353
  labor, 474–475
  on privacy rights, 40–41
  on trade secrets, 165

Nutritional content, labeling of, 515
Nutrition Labeling and Education Act, 515

O

Obamacare. *See* Affordable Care Act (ACA, Obamacare, 2010)
Obedience, agent's duty of, 422
Objection, to discharge in bankruptcy, 334
Objective impossibility of performance, 272
Objective theory of contracts, 234–235
Obligations
    of buyer or lessee, 302–304
    of seller or lessor, 300–302
Obligee, 258
    performance by third party varies materially from that expected by, 257
Obligor, 258
Obscenity, 34
Obvious risks, 141–142
Occupational Safety and Health Act (1970), 442–445
Occupational Safety and Health Administration (OSHA), 491
    manufacturing and, 490
    rulemaking by, 495–496
Ocean Dumping Act (1972), 526, 534
ODR. *See* Online dispute resolution
Offenses against society, crimes as, 188
Offer
    acceptance of, 238, 243–244
    of bribe, 197
    communication of, 240–241
    for contract, 238–241
    counteroffers and, 241
    defined, 238
    definiteness of terms in, 240
    display for e-contract, 244
    irrevocable, 241, 312
    for mutual rescission, 271
    online, 245
    open term, 290–291
    rejection of, 241
    requirements of, 240–243
    revocation of, 241
    statements not offers, 239
    termination of, 241–242
    under UCC, 293
Offeror, offeree, of contract, 235, 292
Office of the National Ombudsman, at Small Business Administration, 504
Officers, corporate. *See also* Chief executive officer (CEO)
    duties of, 399–402
    implied powers of, 393
    liability of, 193, 402

Oil Pollution Act (1990), 534–535
Ombudsman, at Small Business Administration, 504
One-year rule, 257
Ongoing business, sale of, and covenant not to compete, 253–254
Online classes, forced, 276
Online dispute resolution (ODR), 84
Online environment. *See also* Internet
    acceptances, 245–246
    advertising, 511
    auction fraud, 204
    contracts (*See* E-contract)
    defamation, 116, 180
    harassment, 461
    Internet law and, 171–184
    privacy rights in, 182–184
Online fraud, for securities, 596
Online offers, 244–245
Online video game Counter Strike: Global Offensive (CS:GO), 206
Opening statements, 101
Open meeting law. *See* Government in the Sunshine Act
Open quantity terms
    output contracts and, 291
    requirements contracts and, 291
Open terms, UCC approach to, 290–291
Operating agreement, for LLC, 373–374
Operation of law
    agency by, 420
    contract discharge by, 272–274
    termination by, 242, 433
Opinion
    decisions and, 7
    expressions of, 239
    statement of, 116, 120, 266, 309–310
    types of, 19
Oppressive conduct, 408
Option contract, 241
Options, stock, 597
Oral contracts
    Statute of Frauds and, 261
    written contract incorrectly states, 280
Order(s)
    cease-and-desist, 474
    FTC, 511–512
    for relief, 327
Ordinances, 4
Ordinary (straight) bankruptcy, 325
Organization(s). *See also* specific organizations
    international, 213
Organizational form(s), 347
    of franchise, 353
Organized crime, 198–199
Original jurisdiction, 68
OSHA. *See* Occupational Safety and Health Administration

Outcome-based ethics, 51
    utilitarianism as, 52–53
Outer space. *See* Space entries
Outer Space Treaty, 227–229
Output contract, 291
Outrageous conduct, 115
Outside director, 398, 598
Outsiders, SEC Rule 10b-5 and, 592–593
Overtime, 50, 439–441
Owners
    breach of contract by, 276
    stock transfer, 407
Ownership. *See also* Landowner; Personal property; Property; Real property
    concurrent, 545–546
    by partners, 357–358
    of real property, 543–548
    of sole proprietorship, 348
    transfer of, 548–554

P

Packaging laws, 514–515
Parallel citation, 14
Parent company, 386
Paris Convention (1883), 166
Partial acceptance, 303
Partially disclosed principal, 428
Partial performance, commercial impracticability and, 302
Participation, right to, 398
Parties. *See* Third party
Partner
    authority of, 362
    buyout of, 364
    dissociation of, 363–364
    duties of, 360–363
    general, 379
    liability of, 364, 378
    limited, 378
    rights of, 359–360
    sharing LLP liability, 379
Partnership. *See also* Limited liability partnership; Limited partnership; specific forms
    agreement, 358
    articles of, 358
    buy-sell (buyout) agreements, 365, 381–382
    comparison of, with other forms of business, 410–411
    compensation and, 359
    creditors of, 364
    defined, 357
    duration of, 359
    duties of, 360–363
    elements of, 357–358
    by estoppel, 359
    formation of, 358–360
    interest in, 359
    law, 357

federal executive departments and, 491
liability under
   Section 10b-5 of, 591–595
   Section 10(b) of, 591–595
on offering and selling securities
   through crowdfunding, 397
on proxies and shareholder proposals,
   403
Regulation A of, 506–507
Regulation D of, 587
Rule 10b-5 of, 591–595
   outsiders and, 592–593
Rule 14a-9, 595
securities markets regulation by, 581
Securities Exchange Act (1934), 581,
   590–596
   Section 10b-5 of, 591–595
   Section 10(b) of, 591–595
   Section 12 of, 594
   Section 16(b) of, 593–594
   state securities laws and, 596–597
   violations of, 595–596
Security, 581
Security interest(s), 300
   warranty of title and, 309
Selection rates, of employer, 453
Self-defense, as defense to criminal
   liability, 199–200
Self-incrimination, 38, 201
Seller
   contract breached by, 299
   delivery of nonconforming goods by,
      307–308
   goods in possession of, 299, 305–306
   insolvency of, 305
   insurable interest of, 299–300
   obligations of, 300–302
   passage of title and, 297–298
   remedies of, 304–305
   withholding goods by, 306
Seller's talk, 119
Seniority systems, 468–469
Seniors, health-care protection for, 517
Sentencing, federal guidelines for, 202
Separation of powers, in national
   government, 26
Serious-and-objective-intent test, 238
Service(s). See also Personal services
   ADR, 83
   goods combined with, 288
Service-based hacking, 207
Service mark, 156, 347
Service members. See Military status
Service of process, 90
   waiver of, 90–91
Servient estate, 547
Settlement
   of claims, 89, 248–250
   negotiated, 498

Settlement agreements
   discharge by, 177, 271
   social media posts and, 177
Seventh Amendment, 99
Sexual harassment, 458–461
   for sexual orientation, 460–461
Sexual orientation, discrimination based
   on, 460–461
Shadow-Docket cases, 80
Share(s)
   transfer in close corporations, 389
   transfer of, 407
Shareholder agreements
   for close corporation, 389
   voting agreement, 405
Shareholders. See also Directors, corporate
   in benefit corporation, 390–391
   of close corporation, 389
   corporate, 369, 385
   derivative suit, 402, 407–408
   duties and liabilities of, 408
   limited liability of, 385
   majority, 409
   meetings of, 402–403
   minority, 409
   powers of, 402
   in professional corporation, 390
   rights of, 405–409
   role of, 402–409
   of S corporation, 390
   in ultra vires acts and, 393–394
   voting by, 403–405
Sharia, 213–214
Sherman Antitrust Act (1890), 561–570
   conspiracy with substantial effect
      under, 562
   private actions under, 575
   provisions of, 561
   Section 1 of, 561–568
   Section 2 of, 561–562, 568–570
   violations of, 563–564, 575
Shipment
   contract for, 297, 298, 301
   of nonconforming goods, 307–308
Short-run profit maximization, 54
Short sale, 322
Short-swing profits, 594
Shrink-wrap agreement (shrink-wrap
   license), 245–246
   enforceable contract terms and, 245–246
   terms that may not be enforced,
      245–246
Signature, on firm offer, 291
Silence, as acceptance, 243
Similar mark, as trademark dilution, 154
Simple contracts, 236
Sit-down strikes, 480
Sixth Amendment, criminal protections
   in, 201, 202

Slander, 116
   damages for, 116
   per se, 116–117
   of quality (trade libel), 123
   of title, 123
Sliding-scale standard, for Internet-based
   jurisdiction, 69–73
Small business
   bankruptcy choices for, 338
   "fast-track" Chapter 11 for, 336
   forms of, 347–351
   regulatory burden on, 504
Small Business Administration Act, 576
Small Business Administration (SBA),
   loans from, 348
Small Business Regulatory Enforcement
   Fairness Act (SBREFA, 1996),
   504
Small claims courts, state, 76
Small offerings, Regulation D, 587
Social hosts, 128
Social media
   company-wide networks, 179–180
   as constitutional right, 32
   Electronic Communications Privacy
      Act, 178–179
   employer policies for, 56, 178
   internal, in workplace, 179
   legal issues, 177–178
   password protection and, 179
   reasonable expectation of privacy, 182
   securities fraud online, 596
   threatening speech, 34
   work-related issues discussed on, 56
Social responsibility, corporate, 53
Social responsibility, corporations, 54
Social Security, 445
Social Security Act (OASDI, 1935), 445
Sociological school, 12
Software
   copyright protection for, 164–165
   e-agent, 429
   filtering, 34
   password theft and, 206
   trade secret protection and, 165
Sole proprietorships, 347
   advantages of, 348
   compared with other forms of business,
      410
   disadvantages of, 350–351
   LLC taxed as, 372
Solicitation, telephone, 513
Sovereign immunity, 215–218
Sovereignty, state, 25
Spaceflight, commercial, 229
Space law
   defined, 227
   international, 227–228
   U.S., 228–229